ECONOMICS

to Betty

ECONOMICS

A TEXT
WITH READINGS

RICHARD T. GILL

SECOND EDITION

GOODYEAR PUBLISHING COMPANY, INC.
PACIFIC PALISADES, CALIFORNIA

Library of Congress Cataloging in Publication Data

Gill, Richard T.,
  Economics.

  Includes bibliographies.
  1. Economics.   2. Economics—Addresses, essays,
lectures.
HB171.5.G459 1975   330   74-11739
ISBN 0-87620-255-5

© Copyright 1975 by
GOODYEAR PUBLISHING COMPANY, INC.
Pacific Palisades, California

Y-255-4
ISBN: 0-87620-255-5
Library of Congress Catalog Card Number: 74-11739
Current printing (last digit):
10 9 8 7 6 5 4 3 2

Type set by Computer Typesetting Services
Glendale, California
Manufactured by R.R. Donnelley & Sons, Company
Crawfordsville, Indiana
Einar Vinje: Art Direction
Doug Armstrong: Illustrations
Sally Kostal: Project Editor

Printed in the United States of America

CONTENTS

PREFACE

This book is the product of two decades of thought about how to present the basics of economics to college students and other interested readers. Its fundamental premise is that economics is controversial, and never more so than at the present time. Controversy in itself would pose no special problem were it not for the fact that economics also has a detailed theoretical structure, the mastery of which is required even by those who sharply disagree. (Indeed, the structure lets opponents know *how* they disagree!) The problem of teaching and learning the fundamentals of economics is the problem of reconciling these contrary aspects of the field.

One way of tackling this problem is to employ a standard text and then to assign outside readings to give a balanced point of view. This was the approach I myself used for many years as the director of Economics I at Harvard. Its advantages are clear, but so are its disadvantages. The text, behaving rather like bad money under Gresham's Law, tended to drive the readings out of circulation. Learn the textbook, it was said, and you can forget the rest. The readings also suffered from the disabilities that they were often written in different terminology from the text, were of widely unequal levels of difficulty, were in no way integrated with the rest of the course, and—depending on the libraries—were often inaccessible.

A major alternative approach—the one used here—is to include the readings within the text itself. The following volume contains over 500 pages of double-column text by the author, and nearly 300 pages of readings. In this second edition, as in the first, my objectives are:

First, to convey, in the initial introduction to the field, that economics is not a technical discipline only, but that differences of opinion exist and are important. This is a matter of degree and emphasis. My objection to the standard approach is that while disagreements are *mentioned* in the text, they are then dropped while the author develops either the standard position, or his own special point of view. The mechanism I have used in this connection is the *Great Debate*. There are six of these debates (Marxism, monetarism, the new industrial state, inflation and controls, ecology and growth, the energy crisis) and, in each case, the debate is basic and the participants are outstanding economists past and present.

Second, to integrate the readings into the text so that the reader is prepared to handle them without overwhelming difficulties. This objective greatly influenced the selection of readings and the way they have been handled in the text. I should say that at one point I thought of attempting to adapt, or even re-write the articles (with permission, of course), but eventually decided against it. For one thing, I found a surprisingly deep inner resistance to tampering with the words of, say, Adam Smith or John Maynard Keynes. Instead, I have edited ruthlessly, trying to get around concepts that had not been previously introduced or that were expressed in different terminology from the text itself. Where this was impossible, I have tried in the surrounding text to make reasonably clear what the basic point of the readings is. In one case—monetarism—I have written a whole chapter, the main purpose of which is to serve as a guide to the issues involved in the conflicting readings.

Third, and finally, to use the readings to enrich the text. One of the great advantages of having the readings right in the text is that one can *use* them, i.e., employ them as materials for economic analysis. In one case, it may be the *Economic Report of the President* that one uses to show the applicability of economic concepts; in another case, it may be Malthus on population or Ricardo on trade; in still another case, it may be an economist's analysis of the implications of multinational corporations. The advantage, quite simply, is that instead of being tacked on as an afterthought, the readings have influenced the shape, scope, and approach of the text proper—and much to its benefit.

This second edition, while continuing the basic philosophy of the first, is, in other respects, a major revision of the book. This was necessitated by the extraordinary economic events of the past two years. Double-digit inflation, food shortages, the energy crisis, the rise to prominence of the multinational corporation—events and changes (and failed forecasts) have come so rapidly that a new edition was required simply to include these developments.

But the second edition has also given me an opportunity to benefit from the experience of the thousands of students and teachers who have been using the book. This experience has been particularly valuable in that this text has so many features that had not, to my knowledge, ever before been tried in the field of economics. Some of these features worked very well; others not so well—all could be, and I believe, have been, improved. Also, it was pointed out to me by countless users that the microeconomic section of the book was more difficult than the macroeconomic section, and needlessly so. In response, I have eliminated the three-dimensional production and consumer preference analysis. The whole book is now much more of a piece and should be easily understood by any willing reader.

A few technical points about the use of this book: Part One (Basic Economic Systems) should ordinarily be studied first and Part Four (Contemporary Economic Problems) should ordinarily be studied last, but Parts Two and Three (Macroeconomics and Microeconomics, respectively) can be studied in either order. Roughly speaking, a one-semester course could be either a macroeconomically oriented course (Part One and Part Two), or a microeconomically oriented course (Part One and Part Three). Detailed course outlines are included as suggestions in our *Instructor's Manual*.

The Great Debates are not rivetted to a particular logical point in the argument of the text, but are located after the chapters of the book that provide the essential background for them. One could, in theory, read through the whole book except for the Great Debates and then come back and read them all at the end. My own view is that this would be an unfortunate approach, but it does suggest that there is some flexibility as to when each debate may be studied.

As far as the readings in general are concerned, I have not rewritten the words of any author, but, as already mentioned, I have done substantial cutting and pasting together again. No reading in this book should be considered the equivalent of the original article. These are excerpts only, shaped for our particular purposes. This caution is important because in most cases, to prevent the articles from looking like the Morse code, I have left out the dots and dashes that customarily show omissions. When in doubt, always consult the original piece.

A project of this size could not be accomplished without help from others. I owe a very great debt to my publisher, Al Goodyear, who was helpful from the inception of this book on, as he has been with most of my other books. I am also grateful to Professor John E. Elliott of the University of Southern California, who has made numerous helpful suggestions and who has prepared the extraordinary Student Resource Book, to Professor James A. Phillips of Cypress College, who wrote the imaginative Study Guide, to Professor Everett M. Kassalow of the University of Wisconsin, to Professor C. A. Berry of the University of Cincinnati, and to Professor Francis Shieh, of Prince George's Community College, who has sent me useful comments on this book in its various stages of development. My research could not have been completed without the help of Dr. Roger S. Nelson of the World Bank, Mrs. Myrtle G. Nelson of the Bureau of Labor Statistics, and David G. Gill, who was most helpful in assembling materials on the energy crisis. Gail Weingart, Sally Kostal, and Einar Vinje have similarly been invaluable in bringing this work to light.

In the background of all this is my debt to the literally thousands of students whose task it was to listen to my lectures at Harvard over these past many years. They convinced me that there was a com-munications problem and that the communications problem could be solved.

More than anyone else, my wife deserves credit, not only for her extensive help in the preparation of the manuscript, but above all for her encouragement when above all encouragement was needed. It is one of the pleasures of writing books to be able to acknowledge debts as deep as these.

Richard T. Gill

PART 1

BASIC
ECONOMIC
SYSTEMS

CHAPTER 1

THE ECONOMIC PROBLEM

We all know something about economics because we are everyday participants in the economic life of our society. "Getting and spending, we lay waste our powers," complained Wordsworth, and the complaint has decided relevance for a modern industrial economy. We do pass a great many of our waking hours "getting and spending." If we are clever, we even try to economize during the process. We try to economize on the things we buy; we try to economize on the time and effort we put into producing the products or services we are offering for sale.

In these respects, we are taking part in the economic system of the country, and we daily gain certain insights into how that system functions.

At other times, however, economics seems to be dealing with matters that are far removed from our personal knowledge and experience and, indeed, that seem far outside our personal control. The stock market rises or falls. Millions of people in Asia or Africa are suffering from malnutrition. The cost of living is going up. At such moments we feel we are being managed by external forces and we are inclined to say, as Mark Twain did about the weather: "Everybody talks about it, but nobody does anything about it." At such moments, the study of economics seems interesting, but also obscure and difficult.

ECONOMIC BREAKDOWNS—PAST AND PRESENT

The remarkable thing about a modern industrial economy is that it functions so smoothly. We become aware of this remarkable fact, however, mainly when the system breaks down. And let no one mistake the fact: Economic systems do break down, and when they do, the costs and consequences are incalculable.

The following four examples show us some of the ways in which economic systems can malfunction. They will also help us understand the nature of the economic problem in a more general sense.

Example I: Wild Inflation in Germany

Prices rose in all European countries after World War I. In Britain and France, the price level rose 3 or 4 times compared to prewar. In Austria, the rise was much more rapid—about 14,000 times the prewar level. Other countries suffered still more rapid inflation. In Hungary, prices rose 23,000 times their prewar level; in Poland, 2.5 million times; in Russia, 4 billion times.

But even these extraordinary increases pale beside those of Germany, where the forces of inflation went so wild that they virtually destroyed the fabric of society. Figure 1–1 shows what happened to the wholesale price level in Germany in the 1920s, but only up to a point. By 1922, the numbers would push the curve off the top of the page of this book and, indeed, up through the ceiling of any ordinary-sized room. By 1923, the curve would be out of sight in the clouds. In September 1923, German wholesale prices, in terms of marks, had risen 24 million times above the level of a decade earlier; two months later, the figure was close to a *trillion!*

Figures on a graph are one thing, human costs another—witness the following commentary:

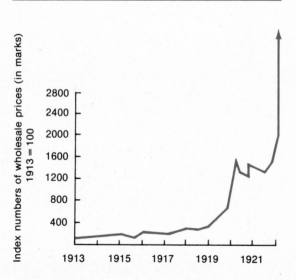

Figure 1–1. The German Hyperinflation of the 1920s.

This is an example of an inflation that got completely out of hand. By November 1923 in Germany, the index of wholesale prices that had stood at 100 in 1913 reached the level of 73 trillion!

Social Influences of the Inflation

Constantino Bresciani-Turroni

The period of most acute and widespread poverty was 1923, that year in which the dollar exchange rate rose from 10,000 to 4,200 milliard paper marks! From personal observation it appears that the poverty of the German people was certainly not general, but it was limited to certain classes, in fact to those which had been most severely hit by the inflation. The poverty was revealed by many symptoms, some of which are measurable by statistics: the condition of children (underweight, spread of tuberculosis and rickets); lack of clothing; the lowered feeding standards (fall in the consumption of cereals, meat, butter, milk, eggs, etc., and the substitution of poorer foods, as, e.g., the substitution of rye for wheat, margarine and other inferior fats for butter, and all sorts of substitutes for coffee); the very poor condition of houses; the excessive work of women; the appearance of certain maladies formerly almost unknown in Germany, such as acne and scurvy; the rise in the number of suicides due to the lack of means of subsistence; deaths through malnutrition (which were very rare before the war); and the rise in the number of pauper funerals because relatives could not pay the expenses, although a decree by the Minister of the Interior permitted the substitution of pasteboard shells for wooden coffins, which were too dear!

Excerpted from "Social Influences of the Inflation" from Constantino Bresciani-Turroni, *The Economics of Inflation: A Study of Currency Depreciation in Post-War Germany* (London: George Allen and Unwin. 1937). Reprinted by permission of the publisher.

UPI, ED YOTKA

The depreciation of currency was so extreme during the period of German hyperinflation that German marks were virtually worthless. Here, a German housewife uses marks to start the fire in her wood-burning stove, because marks are cheaper than kindling.

The statistics of meat consumption reveal some curious details which throw an interesting light on social conditions in Germany in 1922 and 1923. While the consumption of the better quality meats (bullocks, calves, pigs, and sheep) declined, the consumption of horseflesh and, still more, of dogs increased: obvious proof, as *Wirtschaft und Statistik* wrote, of the increasing poverty of the German people. From the last quarter of 1921 to the last quarter of 1922 the number of pigs killed fell from 1,416,051 to 1,131,148, while the number of horses increased from 30,967 to 47,652. During 1923 the fall in the consumption of pork continued, and at the same time the conditions of some classes became so bad that they were eventually obliged to reduce their consumption of horse-flesh. But consumption of dog-flesh increased. Statistics show that 1,090 dogs were slaughtered in the third quarter of 1921; 3,678 in the third quarter of 1922, and 6,430 in the third quarter of 1923.

Another direct index of the worsening of the economic conditions of many classes was the increase in both open and clandestine prostitution. A typical symptom of the sad condition of the old middle classes was also given by the very great number of little shops which sold furniture, *objets d'art,* jewellery, carpets, etc., belonging to very many families who, once well-to-do, were now living on the proceeds of the sale of their personal property.

Among the old middle classes, ruined by the inflation, extreme nationalist propaganda was started and made rapid headway, and among the workers communist ideas spread. The paper inflation, by reinforcing the economic position of those classes which formed the backbone of the "Right" parties, i.e., the great industrialists and the great financiers, encouraged the political reaction against democracy.

The great industrialists and landowners were enabled, by the profits obtained from the monetary depreciation, to finance generously the propaganda and the campaign against the Republic. It was carried on chiefly through the Press. The depreciation of the currency had created very serious difficulties for many papers, because of the enormous rise in the price of paper, of telegraph rates, and of the expense of maintaining their foreign correspondents, etc. Many papers were bought up by the controllers of the heavy industries. Besides this, they were astute enough to become masters of the most important news agencies which, by supplying news even to independent papers, were an effective instrument for influencing public opinion.

Large amounts of money were also used for the formation and maintenance of numerous national institutions of a military character which openly opposed the Republican-Liberal régime. Thus the currency inflation was responsible for the Liberal régime always showing a weak front to the new industrial and agrarian feudalism which was constantly threatening the basis of the new Republic.   □

Thus, the consequences of the German inflation were not only the hardships of the moment but also a grave weakening of the political institutions of the nation. No wonder that it is often listed as a major contributing cause to the rise of Nazism!

Example II: The Great Depression of the 1930s

An even greater economic catastrophe hit the Western world in the 1930s—the Great Depression, deeply familiar to anyone living in the United States at that time. In the case of this country, the depression lasted basically from 1929 until our entry into World War II in 1941. In 1933, the worst year of the depression, there were 13 or 14 million Americans out of work—25 percent or more of our entire labor force. It has been estimated that over the whole of the period unemployment cost us the waste of 104 million man-years of labor.[1]

Again, personal observation often conveys an experience more forcefully than cold statistics. Following are some comments by the then-mayor of Youngstown, Ohio.

---

1. Lester V. Chandler, *America's Greatest Depression, 1929–1941* (New York: Harper & Row, 1970) p. 6.

The Hungry City
A Mayor's Experience with Unemployment
Joseph L. Heffernan

Throughout this period the distress of the people continued without abatement. The great industries had displaced thousands of men, and business conditions showed no signs of improving. Many of the unemployed who had had small reserves to fall back upon in the beginning had now exhausted their resources. One began to see destitute women walking the streets begging for food, and often small children trudged after them. In one week the chief of police reported to me that four women with nursing infants in their arms had sought shelter at police stations.

By the early summer of 1931, demands for relief had become so heavy that the charity organizations were overwhelmed. Federal and state officials now admitted that they had sadly underestimated the gravity of the situation. By this time the city had come into possession of money from the first bonds that had been sold under the special bill passed by the legislature. We had planned a relief programme of our own to supplement that of the charities, with disbursements apportioned throughout the year. The head of the Community Chest pleaded with us, however, to take over immediately a number of his most urgent cases, and we could not refuse. Consequently we had to spend our money as rapidly as it came in, and the last half of the year was left to take care of itself, with the hope that other funds could be raised at that time.

In the autumn of 1931 a final blow laid the city of Youngstown prostrate. The atmosphere was poisoned with a new fever of apprehension, with rumors that began no one knew where and ended in panic. 'Have you heard?' everybody whispered excitedly. 'The banks . . . buzz, buzz, buzz . . . the banks!' People who were fortunate enough to have money deposited hurried to withdraw it. Day after day the

Excerpted from Joseph L. Heffernan, "The Hungry City: A Mayor's Experience with Unemployment," *The Atlantic Monthly*, May 1932, pp. 543–44, 546. Reprinted by permission of the publisher.

BROWN BROTHERS

In the 1930s, massive unemployment reduced many people to a state of poverty. Free-food lines, such as this one, often contained people from all walks of life.

drain continued, and the bankers had to stand by helplessly while their reserves melted away. Then three of the banks closed their doors, and fear ran riot.

At once concerted efforts were made to protect the other banks. Depositors were besought not to withdraw their savings and were urged to bring back what they had carried away to hide. Statements calling upon the people to have confidence were issued by everyone of supposed influence. The ministers joined the campaign with sermons on civic faith and hope. But confidence was shattered. Had not everybody in authority, from the President down, been making optimistic statements for two years, and had not subsequent events disproved all predictions? Could anybody be trusted to tell the truth? Did any-

body really know? People stood on the street corners asking each other anxious questions. Never before had all the old landmarks of security been so shattered. Never had Youngstown suffered such a shock to the spirit which had made it one of the great industrial centres of the world. Nobody could now deny that America was in the throes of a panic.

Another winter was approaching. The numbers of the unemployed had increased, and suffering had grown acute. Many heads of families had not earned a penny in two years. There is a world of difference between mere poverty and pauperism. The honest poor will struggle for years to keep themselves above the pauper class. With quiet desperation they will bear hunger and mental anguish until every resource is exhausted. Then comes the ultimate struggle when, with heartache and an overwhelming sense of disgrace, they have to make the shamefaced journey "spiritless despondency"

to the door of public charity. This is the last straw. Their self-respect is destroyed; they undergo an insidious metamorphosis, and sink down to spiritless despondency.

This descent from respectability, frequent enough in the best of times, has been hastened immeasurably by two years of business paralysis, and the people who have been affected in this manner must be numbered in millions. This is what we have accomplished with our bread lines and soup kitchens. I know, because I have seen thousands of these defeated, discouraged, hopeless men and women, cringing and fawning as they come to ask for public aid. It is a spectacle of national degeneration. That is the fundamental tragedy for America. If every mill and factory in the land should begin to hum with prosperity to-morrow morning, the destructive effect of our haphazard relief measures would not work itself out of the nation's blood until the sons of our sons had expiated the sins of our neglect.

Even now there are signs of rebellion against a system so out of joint that it can only offer charity to honest men who want to work. Sometimes it takes the form of social agitation, but again it may show itself in a revolt that is absolute and final. Such an instance was reported in a Youngstown newspaper on the day I wrote these lines:

FATHER OF TEN DROWNS SELF
JUMPS FROM BRIDGE, STARTS TO SWIM, GIVES UP, OUT OF WORK TWO YEARS

Out of work two years, Charles Wayne, aged fifty-seven, father of ten children, stood on the Spring Common bridge this morning, watching hundreds of other persons moving by on their way to work. Then he took off his coat, folded it carefully, and jumped into the swirling Mahoning River. Wayne was born in Youngstown and was employed by the Republic Iron and Steel Company for twenty-seven years as a hot mill worker.

"We were about to lose our home," sobbed Mrs. Wayne. "And the gas and electric companies had threatened to shut off the service."   □

Example III: Famine in Ethiopia

Our first two examples have been historical. Our third example is both contemporary and ancient. The events described are happening today, but the causes are similar to those that have been operating throughout most of human history. For the incredible fact in the 1970s is that the majority of the world's population still lives in conditions that most of us would describe as extreme want. Ethiopia is a particularly poor country but its economic conditions do not differ substantially from numerous other countries in Asia, Africa, and Latin America. These countries still face enormous hazards from natural disasters—witness the 1971 tidal wave and floods in East Bengal that took the lives of perhaps half a million people—and must struggle vigorously simply to achieve a margin above economic subsistence.

Ethiopian Famine Hits Millions

By Charles Mohr
Special to The New York Times

ADDIS ABABA, Ethiopia, Feb. 6—Almost unnoticed by a distant world, a cataclysm struck Ethiopia last year as famine swept at least two million farmers and herdsmen, killing uncounted thousands.

The famine, centered north of Addis Ababa in the provinces of Wallo and Tigre, was caused primarily by a prolonged and withering drought.

The deaths have diminished dramatically, but officials of the Government and of foreign relief agencies estimate that at least 1.7 million people in the original famine area will have to be fed for much of 1974 to prevent renewed starvation.

Important obstacles to this vast effort have yet to be overcome.

It has become increasingly clear in the last few weeks that the famine is certain to take a heavy toll this year in eastern and southern Ethiopia, areas where the December harvest failed badly or where the livestock that sustain life for nomadic peoples are dead or dying.

While it is not yet known how many new drought victims might need assistance, some estimates are that the total will be more than a million—perhaps as many as 1.7 million. This would double an already monumental national problem.

The problem seemed to materialize with frightening speed in Wallo and Tigre Provinces last year. What actually happened was that people who had always existed precariously near hunger were gradually pushed by natural and social misfortunes toward—and then over—the edge of disaster.

In the worst-affected areas the drought began early in 1971, and even before in some regions. Although some rain came and some food was harvested as time passed, the trend was downward.

Among the hardest-hit groups, slender foodstocks were gradually exhausted. Draft oxen needed to plow died for lack of grazing. Goats and other possessions were sold to buy grain. Then even seed grain, needed for future existence, was eaten. Finally, peasants who owned land sold it, some for as little as $2.50.

Among the great social consequences of the famine, such land sales were of particular importance, for they tended to increase the concentration of land ownership that was already the greatest single political and social problem in this northeast African country's population of 26 million.

Many people began to trek to the distant roads that have never touched their remote and mountainous homelands. Others stayed in the interior. Increasingly helpless and immobile.

For nomadic tribes in lowland areas—Danakils, Adals, Afars and Issas—the road to destitution was different but no shorter. First cattle died, then goats and camels. Weakened animals were driven long distances in hopeless quests for grass.

In September a report of the United Nations Children's Fund estimated that 50,000 to 100,000 had died; many more perished later in the fall. The Gov-

ernment insists the death toll is much smaller, but the argument seems political as well as statistical. In this semifeudal society in which the populations of districts and subdistricts are not even known, an accurate tally may never be possible.

Densely Populated Land

A drought in the sub-Sahara region of six West African nations covers a much larger area and has received more international attention. Ethiopia is much more densely populated, and even relatively small pockets of drought affect great numbers. Some experts in international disaster operations say the suffering rivals that in Biafra during the Nigerian civil war in 1967–70.

The Government of Emperor Haile Selassie says it was essentially unaware of the famine until mid-April because it was not informed by provincial officials. The Acting Governor of Wallo Province was dismissed and replaced in July.

The famine was clearly more than a simple crop failure. A Government report circulated in November entitled "The Drought Problem in Ethiopia" said that one alarming aspect was not merely the magnitude of the food shortage but signs that the underlying cause went beyond the failure of the rains.

"Throughout Tigre and good parts of Wallo and elsewhere, the ecological balance has been seriously disturbed," the report added, saying that while population had grown, the capacity to sustain existence "has been severely curtailed."

Even if farm consolidation and other increases in efficiency can be achieved, the report said, "it would still not be possible for all of the rural population to be gainfully employed in these regions." It suggested resettlement elsewhere in Ethiopia, but many informed sources believe this will be an awesomely difficult problem.

A report of the United Nations Development Program said of the nomads' habitat: "Over wide areas the grass is gone and it will take many years to re-establish. Indeed, there are places where a grass cover may never revive under natural conditions."

The famine has been a tragedy; it has also been

an example—at times instructive and at times baf-fling—of how Ethiopia works and of the difficulties of international disaster relief.

There seems little question that relief operations were slow to get an effective start; one concerned foreigner speaks of "hideous delays."

Charges have been made that Ethiopia has spent too little of her own money and resources on relief. Although grain exports are suspended, the country has exported large amounts of such specialized food as beans while requesting 164,000 metric tons of food from international donors.

A Cabinet minister said privately that total Govern-ment expenditure was about $1.5 million, a figure that may do little to assuage international opinion. From April to August, the most critical period, the Government distributed only about 1,400 metric tons of grain, according to one embassy; the total may now have reached 9,000 tons of Ethiopian grain. A foreign source said, "We don't know what Ethiopia has provided."

While the visible scale of suffering has been re-duced since the December harvest, severe problems could ensue if obstacles to carrying out the 1974 feeding program are not overcome quickly.

Some Improvement Found

A trip to the north seemed to indicate that condi-tions of the relief centers had dramatically improved and that severe malnourishment and disease had markedly decreased there.

The new crisis areas include much of Harar Prov-ince, with a population of perhaps 3 million, in the southeast, and Bale, Sidamo-Borana and Gamu-Gofa Provinces in the south.

A visit to some of the newly affected areas indicated that people were not yet dying or in extreme hunger, but at least some had exhausted their reserves and were selling possessions to buy food.

"We no longer can afford to buy grain by the bag," said a tattered cattle herder in a small town in eastern Ethiopia. "Now we must buy by the cup."   □

Example IV: The Energy Crisis

In the mid-1970s, the American people faced a psychological watershed in their awareness of eco-nomic problems. The "affluent" society of the 1960s seemed suddenly to have developed feet of clay. Not only was full employment proving remarkably difficult to achieve, not only was urban and rural poverty still a serious fact of life, not only was inflation rising to "double-digit" levels—a fate we had thought reserved for Latin America and possibly Japan—but real short-ages seemed to be developing in our productive capacities. Although the American economic system has been faulted for many reasons in the past, one of its greatest strengths seemed to be its ability to produce remarkable quantities of the goods we and the world needed and, in the case of foods and fibers, surpluses beyond what we and the world could readily absorb. Could this be the economy in which, in 1973, shortages could cause the price of meat to soar? Could this be the economy where, in 1974, bakers could warn that limited supplies might cause the price of bread to double?

But it was in the area of fuel and energy that the greatest shocks came during this period. Long lines at gas stations in metropolitan regions throughout the country produced many amusing stories. Stu-dents sometimes gave up baby-sitting for the more lucrative "car-sitting" in the gas lines. Motorists would buy the "Last Car" sign from the car just ahead of them. Not so amusing were occasional fist-fights and out-of-control arguments. And behind it all was an ominous phrase that was repeated hundreds of times a day in the papers and on the air waves: "energy crisis."

Is There an Energy Crisis?

S. David Freeman

The Chinese ideograph for crisis combines the characters for two other words: danger and opportunity. I believe this is a useful way for us to think about our country's energy crisis.

A genuine doomsday energy crisis is by no means inevitable. Yet, we have been drifting into "crisis country," and shortages will worsen if the nation does not face the fact that its energy budget is very much out of balance. The energy shortages are sending us the message that the era of carefree abundance is over; they warn of the danger of a breakdown if we continue our thoughtless habits of energy gluttony in the face of tighter supplies, pollution problems, rising prices and foreign policy concerns.

However, the public sense of unease over scarcities also offers an excellent opportunity. The so-called energy crisis can be used as a basis for education, information, debate and change in our seriously outmoded policies and in the wasteful manner in which society uses its very lifeblood.

MORE IS BETTER

We do have energy policies. They are not entirely coherent or consistent, but the general thrust is clear: for decades, our national policy has been geared towards promotion, growth and ever increasing use of energy. For decades, the government, public power, private power and fuel companies have agreed on the goals of fullest exploitation of resources and maximum consumption.

The acts which created our great public power systems made encouraging the use of energy the law of the land. Utility pricing patterns, which give sharp discounts with increased consumption, promoted lavish energy use. Our tax laws, with their

Excerpted from "Is There An Energy Crisis?" by S. David Freeman in volume no. 410 of THE ANNALS of The American Academy of Political and Social Science. © November 1973 by The American Academy of Political and Social Science. Reprinted by permission.

depletion allowances and other incentives, rewarded rapid exploitation and furthered the policy of promotion.

This policy has achieved extraordinary success. In the century or so since the age of energy began, our consumption of fuels and electric power has risen eighteenfold—nearly four times faster than population. Within the past decade, while general economic growth decelerated, growth rates for energy took a sharp turn upwards. The average yearly increase in energy demand has been nearly 5 percent since the mid-sixties—that is, a doubling of energy consumption in fourteen to fifteen years. An important feature of this growth is that, until very recently, energy prices held stable or actually declined, relative to other prices.

Until recently, no one seriously questioned our growth policies. Energy, which does most of our hard labor and gives us leisure, comfort and mobility, was seen as an unmixed blessing. The premise that more is better went unchallenged. Faith in science and technology—in man's ability to manipulate the material world for his own ends—was so great that we looked on our energy resources as endless and assumed the earth could absorb without limit the damage inherent in all energy use.

WHAT WENT WRONG? ROOT CAUSES OF THE ENERGY GAP

Why, all of a sudden, is energy a problem child? Brownouts, scarcities of fuel oil and dry gasoline pumps do not yet add up to a full-fledged energy crisis. However, they are certainly symptoms of something gone very wrong and indications of more trouble ahead. We are not running out of energy in a simple physical sense. Energy supplies are determined at least as much by general social goals, economics, science and technology, government actions and business decisions, as they are by what is beneath the earth's surface.

The wasteful and insatiable character of our energy demand, which is in conflict with our limited ability to expand supplies in a manner acceptable to society, is a fundamental cause of our trouble. The energy companies and the people who sell us cars, air-conditioners and other consumer goods have persuaded us to use more, and to waste more, energy. Yet, domestic production of energy companies is not keeping up with their sales. For a while we ate off the shelf, so to speak. Now, reserves are used up and production is at full capacity.

In recent years, we have at last become environment-conscious. We have learned that all of the current ways of getting and burning energy result, to some degree, in pollution of the earth and that our most abundant fuels are the dirtiest offenders. Coal is plentiful, but underground mining endangers human beings while strip mining, as it is usually practiced, ravages the earth. Burning coal is dirty. Technology to clean up sulphur and other noxious wastes from coal has not caught up with clean air standards; thus, power plants and industrial users seek out low sulphur oil and natural gas, instead. Yet, clearly, both the energy industry and the government have failed to give the development of clean energy a very high priority. As cheaper, more accessible domestic reserves of oil and gas run low, what is left will be costlier to drill out; we will do well to develop what remains as fast as we deplete the reservoirs on which we are now drawing.

In truth, there is an inherent conflict between the goal of low-priced, plentiful, ever-expanding energy consumption and the need to safeguard the biosphere which sustains life on our planet. This conflict is not, by any means, the whole story of the energy problem. Another major factor is the collective failure of industry and government to develop technology for cleaner, more abundant energy. We are paying a terrific price for a decade of shameful neglect in energy research and development: the price is not enough energy and too much pollution.

For fourteen years, before their overdue retirement in April of 1973, the federal government's oil import quotas compounded our energy problems. The restrictions on bringing in foreign oil were the chief, direct cause of last winter's heating oil shortage. In recent years, one of the many reasons for the oil companies' failure to enlarge refinery capacity to convert crude oil into gasoline and heating oil was the uncertainty about importing the necessary crude. Strained refinery capacity was the major cause of last summer's gasoline shortage.

The winter-summer seesaw of heating oil and gasoline shortages has brought the energy problem home to the consumer. Soaring prices will also attract the consumer's attention, and ire, in the years to come. Energy prices will go up, because costs are going up. Whether the price increases will be limited to cost increases or whether they will also include windfall profits is a multi-billion-dollar question. It could be that the consumer's response to the energy crisis will be one of save energy, save money.

Political and business leaders have yet to lead the nation away from the energy growth ethic. Many constraints put a brake on growth in supplies; meanwhile, demand continues to rise relentlessly. The inevitable result is that energy problems can merely worsen if the nation fails to face disagreeable facts, abandon old habits and make the difficult choices involved in shaping new energy policies.   □

The energy crisis has not caused a total breakdown of the world economy, nor even of one so prodigal in energy consumption as our own. Nor have we been destroyed by such problems as rapid inflation, continuing unemployment, urban rot, air and water pollution, and numerous other ills.

Still, these difficulties prove to us that even the most successful national economies have their flaws, and this fact causes us to wonder why such flaws should occur. Or—what comes to the same thing—it causes us to wonder how the modern economic system functions in the first place.

CHARACTER OF ECONOMIC PROBLEMS

If we were to try to link together the various problems we have been discussing, we should find, I believe, that they had certain common characteristics.

One such characteristic is that they usually have a *quantitative* side to them. If we look deeply enough at almost any economic problem we will sooner or later find some quantities—numbers—involved. We spoke of "getting and spending," and what we get and spend is, among other things, money; and money is measured numerically: so many dollars, so many marks, so many pesos. Furthermore, we typically get money by producing certain goods that we sell for certain prices. How much money we get depends on what quantities of goods we produce and how many dollars per unit the goods will sell for—both numbers.

Indeed, whenever we consider what we loosely think of as "economic" problems, we invariably seem to meet with these numbers. We may be concerned about the price level (a number); or the percentage of the labor force unemployed (a number); or the average yearly increase in U.S. energy demand (5 percent over the past decade); or the average real per capita income in Ethiopia (currently, $80 per year); and so on. Some of these numbers are hard to come by. Some are even philosophically complicated. But there is hardly any major economic problem into which a number does not enter somewhere.

And this fact is important because it helps explain certain aspects of the approach of modern economists to their subject. This approach is slightly different from that of the historian or of many other students of society. It is more statistical, more mathematical, more like the approach one might find in the natural sciences. Economists actually like to think of their subject as a science; and if one takes a look at a typical professional economics journal of today, its pages covered with differential equations and matrix algebra, one might think that he had wandered into physics or biochemistry by mistake!

But if this quantitative side is the first common characteristic of economic problems, the second—their *institutional* side—is almost the reverse.

Economic problems are not generally reducible to simple scientific formulae. They deal with society, they deal with people, they deal with institutions, history, culture, ideology. The field may be a science, but it is a social rather than a natural science. Behind the numbers, behind the hard facts of resources and technological capabilities, we ultimately come face to face with human beings and the psychology of their behavior, whether individual or collective. Since this behavior is, in turn, conditioned by the past history of their society and its relationships to other societies, there is really no aspect of history, political science, or sociology that does not have some relevance to most major economic problems. Without knowing the history of twentieth-century wars, who could follow the movements of price levels in our century? Without knowing the differences of history and culture that separate the continents, who could explain why people eat well in Europe and North America and starve in Africa or Asia? Without knowing the whole complex sociology of urban-rural life in the country, who could explain what is happening to American cities in the 1970s? Suburbia, exurbia, megalopolis—how complex these terms are, and yet they clearly have deep economic implications that the economist must try to comprehend.

Furthermore, and largely in consequence of the above, there is a third and final characteristic of most economic problems: They are usually *controversial*. This, by the way, is not unfortunate. Indeed, most economists have been drawn to the field at one time or another because of its controversial aspects. Economic problems are full of zest and spice, and economic discussions are quite capable of turning friends into distant acquaintances and vice versa. The "Great Debates" appearing throughout this book are testimony to the importance of controversy in this field.

Still, the controversial aspect of our subject does demand a special kind of self-awareness when one is pursuing the analysis of an economic problem. We have to know whether what we are saying is true because we have carefully and objectively verified it, or whether we are mainly expressing our own opinions—our own value judgments—which may conflict sharply with someone else's. Is my friend (or former friend) John wrong about the national debt because of logical error, empirical misinformation (he simply doesn't know the facts), or flaws in his moral character? Since John may also be asking the same questions about me, it is worthwhile to try to get the matter straight. Because economic problems characteristically weave these different threads together, it takes a particular effort of mental discipline to disentangle them.

SCARCITY AND THE CIRCULAR FLOW

So much for general characteristics. Now let us probe a bit more deeply. Can we define the nature of economic problems in a more fundamental way?

The answer will vary somewhat from economist to economist, but a fairly central definition would go something like this:

Economic problems in general arise because the means that society has for satisfying the material wants of its citizens are relatively limited. Human desires for material goods—for survival, for luxury, for ostentation, whatever—generally exceed the volume of goods that can be made available for satisfying these desires.

Another way of putting this is to say that, in most economic matters, a fundamental problem of *scarcity* is involved. Our desires are relatively unlimited. Our resources are relatively limited. The tension between desire and means of satisfying that desire is a reflection of the degree of scarcity involved.

Now this way of looking at the matter immediately brings out some important points about most economic problems. For one thing, it helps explain why many people when they talk about economics sometimes say, "It's all a matter of supply and demand!" Actually, this is one of those interesting statements that is true in some interpretations and quite false in others. In the technical sense in which economists use the terms *supply* and *demand*,[2] the statement isn't true at all. In fact, there is relatively little in real-world economics that can be analyzed unqualifiedly in these terms. In the very general sense of our present discussion, however, the statement does have some validity. What it says is that there is a fundamentally two-sided nature of economic problems—human desires and scarce resources—and that economics is deeply concerned with the relationship of these two different sides.

The two-sided aspect of economic problems leads us fairly directly to a simple and rather general representation of economic life, as shown in Figure 1–2. This representation may be called the *circular flow of economic life*. It shows the basic economic process as involving a relationship between human desires for goods—here located in the *Home*—and society's productive capacities—here symbolized by the *Factory*.

There are really two flows in this diagram: a money flow in the inner circle, and a goods-and-services flow in the outer. In money terms, what happens is that people at Home, wanting to buy goods, send money to the Factory to pay for these goods. The Factory, in turn, has to pay out money for labor and other productive services in order to be able to produce these goods. This money comes back to the Home, since consumers are also owners of labor and other productive services.

In goods-and-services terms, what happens is that the Factory takes the services of labor and other productive resources and combines these in such a way as to produce a stream of goods flowing out to the consumers in the Home. The goods-and-services flow goes clockwise in this diagram, the money flow counterclockwise. We could, of course, have shown it the other way around; whichever way we depicted it, however, the two flows would have had to be in *opposite* directions.

Now this diagram can be varied in a number of ways to bring out different aspects of the economic

---

2. See chapter 2, pp. 36–43, where the applicability of the technical terms *supply* and *demand* is discussed.

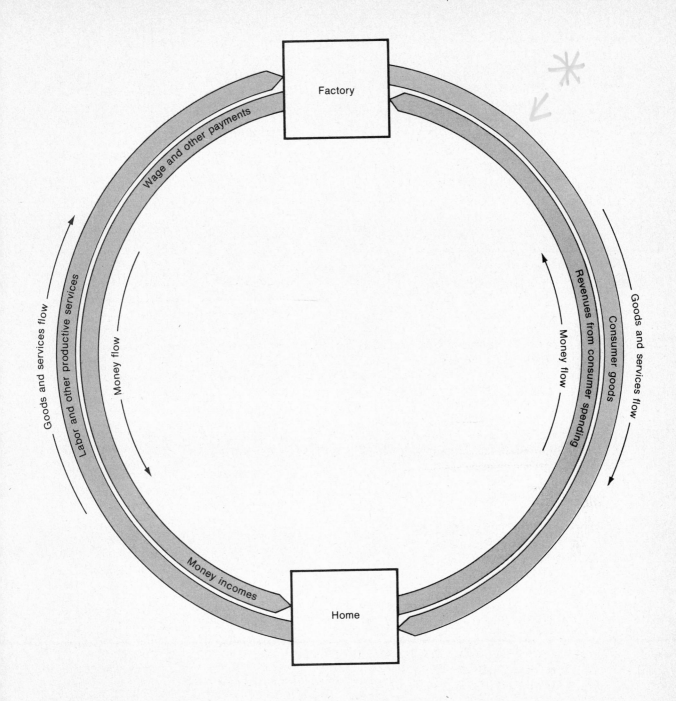

Figure 1-2. The Circular Flow of Economic Life.

problem. For example, in socialist societies many productive resources may be owned by the State and not by the Home. Or we might want to alter the diagram to show that many goods produced in the Factory go not to consumers directly but to building up productive capacity—that is, to expanding the Factory.

We shall be taking up many of these complications in later chapters of the book. For the moment we are using this drawing simply to illustrate some of the implications of *scarcity* in economics. Because of scarcity, economics is frequently concerned with a two-sided relationship between human desires and scarce resources, between demand and supply, between Home and Factory. An important way of capturing this relationship vividly is through a circular flow diagram like Figure 1–2.

ECONOMIC CHOICE— THE PRODUCTION-POSSIBILITY CURVE

Another point that comes out quite clearly when we think about the notion of scarcity is that economic problems frequently involve *choice*. We want all these various goods, but we cannot produce them all at once. We must therefore choose—either this or that, but not both. Scarcity forces choice on us, and a great many economic problems are concerned with the choices a society must make: What particular goods shall we produce? What scarce resources should we use in producing this or that good? And so on. Scarcity forces choice upon society, and the mechanisms employed in making economic choices are quite as significant facts about a society as are its political system or the way it organizes its family life. Indeed, as is obvious, these economic, political, and social matters are usually very much interrelated.

The problem of choice can also be illustrated by means of a simple diagram. We should probably pause here to point out that economists often find graphs and diagrams useful in explaining their subject to others and in understanding it themselves. Indeed,

TABLE 1–1

WHEN FOOD PRODUCTION IS (million bushels)	THEN THE MAXIMUM POSSIBLE STEEL PRODUCTION IS (thousand tons)
0	1,050
20	1,035
40	990
60	930
80	840
100	720
120	595
140	410
160	190
175	0

it will be worthwhile lingering a moment on Figure 1–3. It not only illustrates the choice problem very conveniently but also shows how graphs can be used to organize and expand our thinking about economic problems.

The diagram is called a *production-possibility curve,* or a *transformation curve.*[3] In order to draw it, let us imagine a hypothetical society that is capable of producing only two products: food and steel. The technologists in the society have given us the information contained in Table 1–1. They have told us the maximum amount of steel we can produce for each possible amount of food that is produced. We begin by producing zero units of food; i.e., all our resources are going into steel production. We then begin diverting our resources from steel to food production, until finally, when we are producing 175 million bushels of food, there are no resources left, and steel production is zero. The table, in theory, describes all the possible combinations of food and

---

3. The word *transformation* is sometimes used because the diagram is designed to show how a society, using all its resources, can produce different combinations of goods—i.e., how it can transform (by different resource use) one good into another.

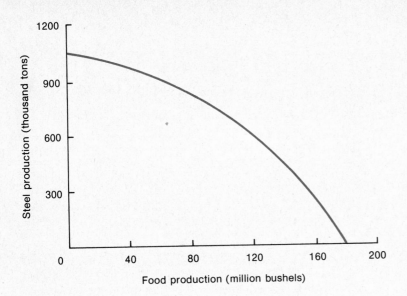

Figure 1–3. Production-Possibility or Transformation Curve.

This curve graphically presents the hypothetical data from the table to the left. It shows the characteristic bowed-out shape of the production-possibility curve.

steel that the society can produce—its *production possibilities*—when all its resources of land, labor, and machines are fully employed.

The figures from Table 1–1 have been displayed graphically in Figure 1–3. First, the data were plotted as points on the graph, and then the points were joined together with a continuous line, forming the curve shown in Figure 1–3.

Now this diagram is nothing but a representation of the material presented in Table 1–1. Basically it gives us no new information—but it does show us something that is not obviously read from the table: the *shape* of the production-possibility curve. We notice, in particular, that the curve is bowed-out or, technically, "concave to the origin"; it is not simply a straight line from the X (vertical) axis to the Y (horizontal) axis.

What does this bowed-out shape mean? And why is it a fairly characteristic shape for the production-possibility curve?

The *meaning* of the shape of the curve is fairly easy to see. It states that as we increase our production of one commodity it will be harder and harder to get still further units of that commodity. Harder in what sense? Harder in the sense that we will have to give up more units of the other commodity to add another unit of the first commodity. In other words, as we increase food production, we shall have to give up more and more units of steel to increase our food production by one unit.

The meaning of this last statement is illustrated in Figure 1–4. In the portion of the curve indicated by the Roman numeral I, we are producing relatively little food and a great deal of steel. To increase food production by a given amount a is relatively easy—we have to give up only b_I steel to do so. Now contrast this with the situation in area II. Food production is much higher here. To increase food production by the same amount as before (a), we must now give up much more steel; i.e., b_{II} is much greater than b_I. And the same would, of course, be true if steel production instead of food production were to be increased.

This, then, is what the shape of the curve *means*, but now we ask: *Why* does it have this particular shape? The fundamental answer to this question derives from the fact that not all productive agents and resources—*factors of production*, economists

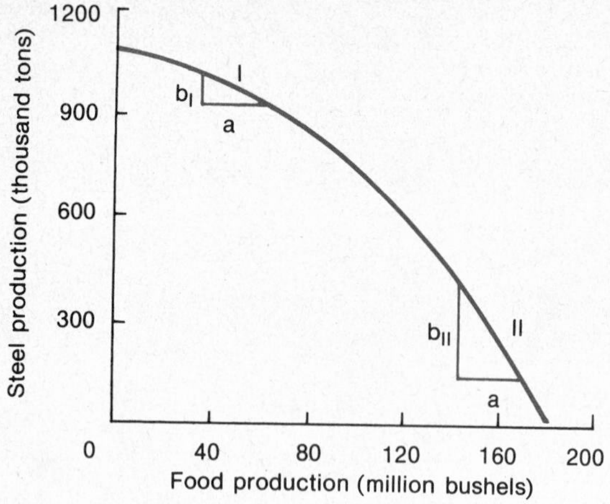

Figure 1–4.

The shape of the production-possibility curve illustrates this important generalization: As we produce more of one good, we must usually give up more of other commodities, to increase production of that good still further.

usually call them—are equally well suited to the production of different commodities. If *all* commodities were the product of *one* factor of production—say, homogeneous labor—then there would be no need for the curve to bow out as it does. But this is obviously not so. In our particular case, steel production requires iron ore while food production requires fertile, cultivable soils. Now there is no reason to expect that the best farming land will also be the land containing the richest iron deposits—quite the contrary, in fact. What happens then as we keep increasing our food production?

In the beginning, when we are producing a great deal of steel and almost no food, we are using excellent cultivable soil in our search for whatever bit of iron ore it may yield. By giving up just a bit of steel

production, we release this rich land to the farmer and consequently gain a great deal of food production for a relatively small loss (b_I) of steel. As we keep increasing our food production, however, the situation changes. Now all the really good farming lands have been used. If we wish to increase food production any more, we must take over the land rich in iron ore but relatively poor for crops. This means that to get the same increase in food production we must make major sacrifices (to the amount of b_{II}) in our steel production.

Thus, it is empirically (though not universally or necessarily) true that it usually costs us more to produce more of a particular good, the more of it we have. The *opportunity cost*—the steel we have to give up to get more food—generally goes up as we proceed further and further in any one line of production.

APPLICATION TO MAJOR ECONOMIC PROBLEMS

We can now use this diagram to illustrate specifically and meaningfully some of the fundamental economic problems all societies face.

Figure 1–5 illustrates the choice problem that we have emphasized so much in our earlier discussion. Should the society locate itself at point *A* (lots of steel; little food) or at point *B* (little steel; lots of food) on its production-possibility curve? This is not the only kind of choice a society must make, but since economic problems tend to be interrelated, this choice is reflective of the solutions to many other choice problems as well.

How can or should this choice be made between *A* and *B?* Clearly, the choice the society will want to make will depend on a whole host of different factors. For example, if it has a very large population, then presumably it will need a fairly large production of food. If it is a very rich country, then it will presumably consume a higher proportion of industrial products (steel) as opposed to agricultural products (food). Even if it is a poor country, it may decide to sacrifice food production today, to make machines (steel), so that it can produce *both* more food and more steel in the future.

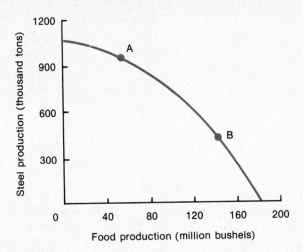

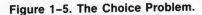

Figure 1–5. The Choice Problem.

Among the fundamental choices a society must make is the choice of the composition of its output (*A* or *B* or some other point). This choice will reflect not only the stage of development of the economy, but also its economic *system*. Is choice decentralized, centralized, mixed, or what?

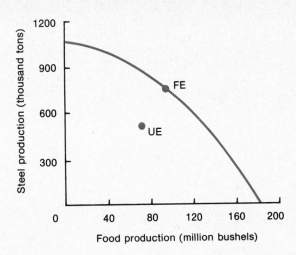

Figure 1–6. The Unemployment Problem.

Will total output be at its full-employment potential level (on the production-possibility curve) or will it be at a point *inside* the curve, signifying unemployment? Note that at *UE* we can have more of both food and steel, if we can only get our laborers and machinery back into full operation.

These are simply a few of the many considerations that will influence a society's choice between *A* and *B* on its production-possibility curve. *How* these factors influence that choice, moreover, is dependent upon a still further variable: the kind of economic *system* operating in that particular society. Does it have a traditional economy? A market economy? A planned or command economy? A mixed economy? The way in which these different economic *systems* work to influence economic choices will be a major concern for us in our remaining chapters of Part One.

Before carrying these matters further, however, let us use our diagram to illustrate two additional major economic problems. These two problems have received great attention among economists since the 1930s, and we will devote many later chapters to them.

The first of these problems lies in the field of what we might call *short-run aggregative* economics. It asks: What factors determine the state of health of the economy as a whole in the short run? One of the most important aspects of this question has to do with the employment problem. Are we utilizing all our available labor and other resources in production, or do we have men and factories standing idle and, consequently, a national income that is less than it might be? In terms of Figure 1–6, the two situations are contrasted at points *FE* (full-employment production) and *UE* (unemployment or undercapacity production). The production-possibility curve does not tell us where the society *will* be, but where technologically, it *can* be. It will take a good bit of analysis to show the forces that determine where the economy in the aggregate will, in fact, be located at any given moment of time.

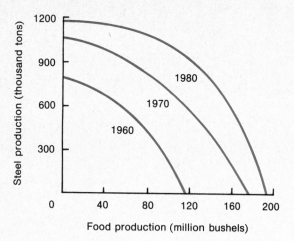

Figure 1–7. The Growth Problem.

A modern economy does not remain static but grows, as suggested by these outward shifts of the production-possibility curve.

The other problem that can be illustrated by our diagram is that of *long-run economic growth*. Here, as Figure 1–7 indicates, we are concerned with the shifting outward of the production-possibility curve over time. What these curves tell us is that in 1970 we were able to produce *both* more food and more steel than in 1960 and that, by 1980, we had hypothetically advanced still further.

Now this growth process—this shifting out of the production-possibility curve—does not happen automatically with the passage of time. Indeed, it is not too much of an exaggeration to say that economic growth, in its modern sense, was really unknown to the world until the British Industrial Revolution of the late eighteenth and early nineteenth centuries. Even today there are vast areas of the world, especially in Asia and Africa, where this process has not yet fully taken root. In the advanced industrial countries, however, growth has been a characteristic feature of economic life for a century or more. Through a

continuing process that involves population growth, the accumulation of machines and other capital goods, and—above all—a constant attention to invention and innovation (new products, new discoveries, new technologies of production), these modern economies have shifted their production possibilities outward at a rate unknown in the early history of mankind.

OUR ECONOMIC FUTURE: AFFLUENCE OR INCREASING SCARCITY?

The rapidity of modern growth led some observers in the 1960s to wonder if we had not reached a stage where our basic economic problems had been solved, or at least would be solved in the near future. People spoke freely of the "affluent society." They reasoned that if affluence is the opposite of scarcity, and if scarcity is central to the economic problem, then perhaps that problem is now a thing of the past—or will be after just a few more decades of rapid growth.

The energy crisis and other material shortages in the early 1970s deflated this line of reasoning. At a minimum, most observers became acutely aware of three points:

First, the concept of freedom from scarcity has never had much relevance for the majority of the world's population, which lives in the underdeveloped world. To speak of the "affluent society" in Ethiopia would be not only inappropriate but cruel. There are more hungry people in the world today than there were a century ago, because of the enormous growth of population in the poor countries of the world.

Second, there is evidence that the shoe still pinches in the United States, even among economic classes well above the poverty level. The worries about unemployment, the fear of inflation, the anxieties about taxes, pensions, old age, and health seem hardly less severe today than they were a decade ago. We are still very well off compared to the Great Depression, but the high cost of food and fuel has caused genuine concern.

Finally—and this is a point that has become more and more apparent in the last few years—economic growth has costs as well as benefits. Some argue that by now the costs exceed the benefits by a substantial margin. Some would go so far as to argue that economic growth is taking us down the path to disaster, perhaps irreversibly. A listing of these costs, both direct and indirect, is like a catalog of the ills of modern industrial—or, perhaps better, *post*industrial—society. Growth has been held responsible for the population explosion; urban overcrowding and congestion; air and water pollution; the despoliation of our landscapes; and the squandering of our resources; the alienation of the worker, of the young, of the old; and the creation of false values and a meaningless pattern of life.

These criticisms of modern industrial growth are all doubtless valid to some degree. Their net effect, moreover, is likely to *increase* rather than to decrease the importance of economics in the years ahead. For what is being suggested by many critics of modern growth is that this growth has been purchased too cheaply, by a cavalier and profligate use of our natural and social environment. If we are to husband our resources more carefully, if we are to secure the comforts of an affluent society but *without* pollution and waste, and with a proper attention to the less fortunate members of society, then even modest economic growth may be very hard to come by. We may find, in short, that beneficial, socially desirable economic advance is very expensive.

This does not mean that technology's advance will cease and that ever deepening energy crises and shortages—perhaps ultimate collapse—are our future. It does mean, however, that fundamental scarcity, the basis of all economic problems, seems likely to be with us for a very long time to come.

SUMMARY

We become aware of the workings of our economic system when there is some dramatic malfunction in one of its parts. Such malfunctions have occurred historically, as in the German hyperinflation of the 1920s and the worldwide Great Depression of the 1930s. However, deep economic problems still exist today, particularly in the underdeveloped countries of Asia, Africa, and Latin America—and also in the United States, where poverty, unemployment, inflation, and the energy crisis still pose serious difficulties.

The character of these various economic problems is similar in that (1) they usually involve a *quantitative* element—numbers appear in most economic problems; (2) they also involve an *institutional* element—they require a knowledge of the institutions, culture, and ideology of a particular society; and (3) they are often *controversial* problems—one must be careful to isolate value judgments from questions of fact or logic.

More deeply, these various economic problems ultimately arise from the problem of *scarcity*—the fact that human desires for material goods and services generally exceed the volume of goods and services the economy is capable of providing. The fact of scarcity suggests that many economic problems involve a two-sided relationship between human wants and a society's productive capabilities. The *circular flow* of economic life illustrates the process by which Home and Factory may be related in a simple economy.

The fact of scarcity also forces choice upon a society. Problems of choice are conveniently illustrated in a *production-possibility* or *transformation* curve, which enables us to show hypothetically how a society might choose between different combinations of goods.

The production-possibility diagram is also useful in allowing us to illustrate important aggregative problems such as (1) short-run unemployment and undercapacity production, and (2) modern long-run economic growth.

IMPORTANT TERMS TO REMEMBER

Economic Choice
Scarcity
Inflation
Depression
Unemployment
Underdevelopment
Energy Crisis
Circular Flow
Production-Possibility (Transformation) Curve
Opportunity Cost
Economic Growth

QUESTIONS FOR DISCUSSION

1. List a few of the major economic problems facing the United States at the present time. What features of these problems lead you to characterize them as *economic* problems?

2. Economists of a century or two ago worried about the so-called *paradox of value:* Water is very useful but cheap, while diamonds are much less useful but expensive. How does the fundamental role of scarcity in economic problems help you understand this paradox?

3. In a *barter* economy (an economy in which goods and services are exchanged directly rather than for money), could economic life still be pictured in terms of a "circular flow"? Discuss.

4. Under what special circumstances might the production-possibility curve have a shape such as the following:

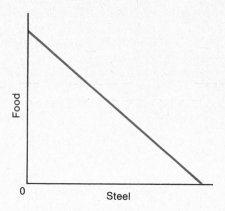

Could you imagine any circumstances in which it might have a shape such as this:

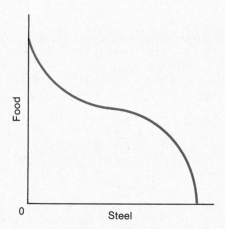

5. At the height of World War II, the United States was devoting some 50 percent of its total production to the war effort, yet private consumption, except for a few commodities, remained high. Use the production-possibility analysis to illustrate how these facts might be reconciled.

SUGGESTED READING

Heilbroner, Robert L. *The Making of Economic Society.* 2nd ed. Englewood Cliffs, N.J.: Prentice-Hall, 1968.

Kindleberger, Charles E. *The World in Depression, 1929–39.* Berkeley, Calif.: University of California Press, 1973.

Mulcahy, Richard E. *Readings in Economics from Fortune.* 3rd ed. New York: Holt, Rinehart & Winston, 1967, chaps. 1–5, 16–17.

Shannon, David. *The Great Depression.* Englewood Cliffs, N.J.: Prentice-Hall, 1960.

Slesinger, Reuben E., Perlman, Mark, and Isaacs, Asher, eds. *Contemporary Economics.* 2nd ed. Boston: Allyn & Bacon, 1967, pp. 1–51.

The hard fact of scarcity can force many choices upon a society, and these choices, as we have indicated, will be deeply influenced by the kind of economic *system* operating in that society. In the next five chapters we shall be examining some of the different systems by which fundamental economic choices can be made. In this chapter, we shall focus on what economists sometimes call a *market economy.* We shall try to show how, through the operation of prices and markets, without any central planning or guidance, a society can solve its economic problems in a coherent way.

THE SPECIAL ASSUMPTIONS OF A MARKET ECONOMY

Since everyone brought up in the United States is familiar with the workings of prices and markets of various kinds, the subject of a market economy may seem one of the easier topics in economics.

However, this view is misleading for three reasons. The first is that the successful functioning of a market economy is intrinsically complicated. Indeed, it is something of a social miracle. For the essence of such an economy is that nobody guides or even thinks about the economy as a whole. Everything is decentralized into the thousands and, indeed, millions of private, individual decisions being made by consumers, producers, and laborers—here, there, and everywhere. That such apparently haphazard means should produce anything like an orderly result is not something to be taken for granted—in fact, it should be regarded as rather astonishing.

The second reason for caution is that a pure market economy does not really exist in the modern world. Although we have all seen various markets—from the supermarket to the stock market—operating in the United States, it would be quite wrong to believe that this country makes all its crucial choices through the market mechanism. The government plays a considerable role in the present-day American economy, as, indeed, it does in all economies in the modern world. Furthermore, even in the private sector, as we shall see later on, the roles of business and labor in real life are often quite different from those described by standard economic theory.

Finally, we should be aware that even from an historical point of view, a pure market economy is something of a rarity and that the conditions making it possible are of fairly recent origin. It is quite incorrect to view markets as the normal or "natural" way to organize economic life or as organizations that have been modified by government intervention only in modern times. In recent centuries, the reverse is almost closer to the truth. The modern age was ushered into Europe under the auspices of mercantilist thought, which emphasized the need for detailed government regulation of every aspect of economic life. Mercantilist thought in its turn was derived in part from the highly regulated and tradition-bound approach of the medieval towns, with their numerous local ordinances and guild restrictions. The self-regulating market is a concept dating from the eighteenth and nineteenth centuries only, a product in part of the English Industrial Revolution.

That this concept does involve quite special assumptions is a major theme of the writings of Karl Polanyi, whose *The Great Transformation* is a significant analysis of the historical origins and effects of the market economy. In the following reading, Polanyi makes these basic points: (1) a market economy was not characteristic in Europe under either feudalism or mercantilism: (2) the coming of such an economy required the assumptions (a) that economic life is separable from political and social life; and (b) that labor, land, and money can be treated as commodities; and (3) that these are not normal but indeed "fictitious" assumptions. Although all economists will not agree with every detail of his analysis, most find Polanyi's work highly stimulating.

The Self-Regulating Market

Karl Polanyi

A market economy is an economic system controlled, regulated, and directed by markets alone; order in the production and distribution of goods is entrusted to this self-regulating mechanism. An economy of this kind derives from the expectation that human beings behave in such a way as to achieve maximum money gains. Self-regulation implies that all production is for sale on the market and that all incomes derive from such sales. Accordingly, there are markets for all elements of industry, not only for goods (always including services) but also for labor, land, and money.

To realize fully what this means, let us return for a moment to the mercantile system and the national markets which it did so much to develop. Under feudalism and the gild system land and labor formed part of the social organization itself (money had yet hardly developed into a major element of industry). Land, the pivotal element in the feudal order, was the basis of the military, judicial, administrative, and political system; its status and function were determined by legal and customary rules. Whether its possession was transferable or not, and if so, to whom and under what restrictions; what the rights of property entailed; to what uses some types of land might be put—all these questions were removed from the organization of buying and selling, and subjected to an entirely different set of institutional regulations.

The same was true of the organization of labor. Under the gild system, as under every other economic system in previous history, the motives and circumstances of productive activities were embedded in the general organization of society. The relations of master, journeyman, and apprentice; the terms of the craft; the number of apprentices; the wages of the workers were all regulated by the custom and rule of the gild and the town. What the mercantile system did was merely to unify these conditions either through statute as in England, or through the "nationalization" of the gilds as in France. As to land, its feudal status was abolished only in so far as it was linked with provincial privileges: for the rest, land remained *extra commercium*, in England as in France. Up to the time of the Great Revolution of 1789, landed estate remained the source of social privilege in France, and even after that time in England Common Law on land was essentially medieval. Mercantilism, with all its tendency towards commercialization, never attacked the safeguards which protected these two basic elements of production—labor and land—from becoming the objects of commerce. In England the "nationalization" of labor legislation through the Statute of Artificers (1563) and the Poor Law (1601), removed labor from the danger zone, and the anti-enclosure policy of the Tudors and early Stuarts was one consistent protest against the principle of the gainful use of landed property.

That mercantilism, however, emphatically it insisted on commercialization as a national policy, thought of markets in a way exactly contrary to market economy, is best shown by its vast extension of state intervention in industry. On this point there was no difference between mercantilists and feudalists, between crowned planners and vested interests, between centralizing bureaucrats and conservative particularists. They disagreed only on the methods of regulation: gilds, towns, and provinces appealed to the force of custom and tradition, while the new state authority favored statute and ordinance. But they were all equally averse to the idea of commercializing labor and land—the precondition of market economy. Craft gilds and feudal privileges were abolished in France only in 1790; in England the Statute of Artificers was repealed only in 1813–14, the Elizabethan Poor Law in 1834. Not before the last decade of the eighteenth century was, in either country, the establishment of a free labor market even discussed;

and the idea of the self-regulation of economic life was utterly beyond the horizon of the age. The mercantilist was concerned with the development of the resources of the country, including full employment, through trade and commerce; the traditional organization of land and labor he took for granted. He was in this respect as far removed from modern concepts as he was in the realm of politics, where his belief in the absolute powers of an enlightened despot was tempered by no intimations of democracy. And just as the transition to a democratic system and representative politics involved a complete reversal of the trend of the age, the change from regulated to self-regulating markets at the end of the eighteenth century represented a complete transformation in the structure of society.

A self-regulating market demands nothing less than the institutional separation of society into an economic and political sphere. Such a dichotomy is, in effect, merely the restatement, from the point of view of society as a whole, of the existence of a self-regulating market. It might be argued that the separateness of the two spheres obtains in every type of society at all times. Such an inference, however, would be based on a fallacy. True, no society can exist without a system of some kind which ensures order in the production and distribution of goods. But that does not imply the existence of separate economic institutions; normally, the economic order is merely a function of the social, in which it is contained. Neither under tribal, nor feudal, nor mercantile conditions was there, as we have shown, a separate economic system in society. Nineteenth century society, in which economic activity was isolated and imputed to a distinctive economic motive, was, indeed, a singular departure.

Such an institutional pattern could not function unless society was somehow subordinated to its requirements. A market economy can exist only in a market society. We reached this conclusion on general grounds in our analysis of the market pattern. We can now specify the reasons for this assertion. A market economy must comprise all elements of industry, including labor, land, and money. But labor and land are no other than the human beings themselves of which every society consists and the natural surroundings in which it exists. To include them in the market mechanism means to subordinate the substance of society itself to the laws of the market.

The crucial point is this: labor, land, and money are essential elements of industry; they also must be organized in markets; in fact, these markets form an absolutely vital part of the economic system. But labor, land, and money are obviously *not* commodities. Labor is only another name for a human activity which goes with life itself, which in its turn is not produced for sale but for entirely different reasons, nor can that activity be detached from the rest of life, be stored or mobilized; land is only another name for nature, which is not produced by man; actual money, finally, is merely a token of purchasing power which, as a rule, is not produced at all, but comes into being through the mechanism of banking or state finance. None of them is produced for sale. The commodity description of labor, land, and money is entirely fictitious.

Nevertheless, it is with the help of this fiction that the actual markets for labor, land, and money are organized; they are being actually bought and sold on the market; their demand and supply are real magnitudes; and any measures or policies that would inhibit the formation of such markets would *ipso facto* endanger the self-regulation of the system. The commodity fiction, therefore, supplies a vital organizing principle in regard to the whole of society affecting almost all its institutions in the most varied way, namely the principle according to which no arrangement or behavior should be allowed to exist that might prevent the actual functioning of the market mechanism on the lines of the commodity fiction.   □

ADAM SMITH AND THE CLASSICAL ECONOMISTS

In *The Great Transformation* and other writings, Polanyi stressed the inhumanities and hardships that were attendant upon the historical birth of the market economy. The leading economists of that historical period were, however, of a rather different mind. In the eighteenth century, the notion was born that the price-and-market mechanism was a quite good way for a society to handle its basic economic problems —in fact, the *best* way. Around the 1750s and 1760s, a number of French economists (sometimes called *physiocrats)* began to stress the view that there was a natural harmony between the decisions individuals made privately and the general social welfare. *Physiocracy* means "rule of Nature." Private self-interest and the social welfare were seen not as in conflict but as in a fundamental union, more or less as a matter of "natural law."

The most important development of this concept, however, came in Great Britain. Early British economists were interested in analyzing the implications of a market economy and in trying to demonstrate that if the government stayed in the background, the price-and-market mechanism could handle things quite satisfactorily. Since these early British economists did much to establish the field of economics as we know it today, it is worthwhile to say a word about them.

The key date is probably 1776. This year saw not only the beginning of the American Revolution—it saw also the publication of one of the most important economic treatises of all times: *The Wealth of Nations,* by Adam Smith. Smith was quite a remarkable man, although his life was notably without incident. He never married. Except for a Grand Tour of the Continent—where, incidentally, he met some of the leading French physiocrats—he never traveled extensively. But he was a philosopher, a historian of science, and, above all, the greatest economist of his day. *The Wealth of Nations* is a spacious book that can be read for pleasure even now. It is filled with rolling eighteenth-century sentences but also with sharp phrases that catch whole pages of argumentation in a word or two. When Smith speaks

Adam Smith (1723–1790). Often considered the founder of modern economics, Adam Smith influenced both economists and governments for many decades after he wrote. His central idea: that there is a basic harmony between private self-interest and social welfare and, consequently, that the State should (with some important exceptions) leave the economy to the workings of market competition.

of an "invisible hand" that brings private and social interest into harmony, he is not simply writing vividly; he is pinpointing an entire philosophy of economic life.

Smith is important not only because of his work but because of the influence of that work on others. *The Wealth of Nations* became the rock on which a whole school of economists based their theories. They are usually called the *classical economists,* and they included, in the decades following Adam Smith, some of the most important writers in the history of the subject. There was Thomas Robert Malthus, the English parson whose ideas on population cast a pessimistic pall over nineteenth-century thought and greatly influenced the evolutionist Charles Darwin. There was David Ricardo, who published his *Principles of Political Economy and Taxation* in 1817 after a highly successful career in business. Ricardo was one of a small number of economists who really have done well on the stock market. His work in economic theory was rigorous and systematic. Although not well known to the general public, he had an enormous impact on the development of technical economics.

Even in the middle of the nineteenth century, Smith's influence was still strong, and John Stuart Mill, who once had Ricardo for a tutor, is often regarded as a classical economist. Mill, of course, was a many-sided genius whose works in philosophy and political science easily match his very substantial contributions to economics.

Smith's message carried beyond his fellow economists to the world at large. And this message was, in essence, that except for certain unavoidable responsibilities,[1] the State ought to stay fairly well out of the economic sphere. *Laissez-faire* was the motto: Leave the economy alone; have the State keep a hands-off policy. Or in terms of our discussion in this chapter, let the society solve its economic problems largely through the functioning of a market economy.

But what reasons did Smith offer in support of this view? In the first reading that follows—containing the famous "invisible hand" quotation—Smith is arguing against the policy of mercantilism and especially against the view that it is nationally advantageous to restrict imports from abroad. In the course of this argument, he brings out a number of principles that underlie the laissez-faire philosophy. The reader should note that Smith does *not* argue that private individuals are philanthropic or in any way devoted to promoting the public welfare. He is quite skeptical about those individuals who "affected to trade for the public good." The public benefits occur when the individual is seeking his own *self*-interest through the market mechanism. Why these benefits to society? Smith points out that the individual, in seeking his own advantage, will be more efficient; that he knows his own local situation much better than any statesman can; that in trying to produce the most value for himself he will be effectively producing the greatest value for society. By contrast, state interference with private markets tends to be hurtful—in the case of trade restrictions, forcing us to buy more expensively at home what we could get more cheaply from abroad.

---

1. Smith acknowledged that the State had certain duties that would bring it actively into the economy: (1) national defense; (2) the administration of justice; and (3) the provision of certain socially necessary institutions—for example educational institutions—that private interests might neglect. Thus, neither he nor any of the classical economists advocated a truly *pure* market economy. The question was how much (or little) intervention was needed.

Restraints upon Imports

Adam Smith

No regulation of commerce can increase the quantity of industry in any society beyond what its capital can maintain. It can only divert a part of it into a direction into which it might not otherwise have gone; and it is by no means certain that this artificial direction is likely to be more advantageous to the society than that into which it would have gone of its own accord.

Every individual is continually exerting himself to find out the most advantageous employment for whatever capital he can command. It is his own advantage, indeed, and not that of the society, which he has in view. But the study of his own advantage naturally, or rather necessarily leads him to prefer that employment which is most advantageous to the society.

First, every individual endeavours to employ his capital as near home as he can, and consequently as much as he can in the support of domestic industry; provided always that he can thereby obtain the ordinary, or not a great deal less than the ordinary profits.

* * *

Secondly, every individual who employs his capital in the support of domestic industry, necessarily endeavours so to direct that industry, that its produce may be of the greatest possible value.

The produce of industry is what it adds to the subject or materials upon which it is employed. In proportion as the value of this produce is great or small, so will likewise be the profits of the employer. But it is only for the sake of profit that any man employs a capital in the support of industry; and he will always, therefore, endeavour to employ it in the support of that industry of which the produce is likely

Excerpted from Adam Smith, "Restraints upon Imports" from *The Wealth of Nations* (New York: Modern Library, Random House, 1937), pp. 421–24. Reprinted by permission of Random House, Inc.

to be of the greatest value, or to exchange for the greatest quantity either of money or of other goods.

* * *

As every individual, therefore, endeavours as much as he can both to employ his capital in the support of domestic industry, and so to direct that industry that its produce may be of the greatest value; every individual necessarily labours to render the annual revenue of the society as great as he can. He generally, indeed, neither intends to promote the public interest, nor knows how much he is promoting it. By preferring the support of domestic to that of foreign industry, he intends only his own security; and by directing that industry in such a manner as its produce may be of the greatest value, he intends only his own gain, and he is in this, as in many other cases, led by an invisible hand to promote an end which was no part of his intention. Nor is it always the worse for the society that it was no part of it. By pursuing his own interest he frequently promotes that of the society more effectually than when he really intends to promote it. I have never known much good done by those who affected to trade for the public good. It is an affectation, indeed, not very common among merchants, and very few words need be employed in dissuading them from it.

What is the species of domestic industry which his capital can employ, and of which the produce is likely to be of the greatest value, every individual, it is evident, can, in his local situation, judge much better than any statesman or lawgiver can do for him. The statesman, who should attempt to direct private people in what manner they ought to employ their capitals, would not only load himself with a most unnecessary attention, but assume an authority which could safely be trusted, not only to no single person, but to no council or senate whatever, and which would nowhere be so dangerous as in the hands of a man who had folly and presumption enough to fancy himself fit to exercise it.

To give the monopoly of the home-market to the produce of domestic industry, in any particular art or manufacture, is in some measure to direct private people in what manner they ought to employ their capitals, and must, in almost all cases, be either a useless or a hurtful regulation. If the produce of domestic can be brought there as cheap as that of foreign industry, the regulation is evidently useless. If it cannot, it must generally be hurtful. It is the maxim of every prudent master of a family, never to attempt to make at home what it will cost him more to make than to buy. The taylor does not attempt to make his own shoes, but buys them of the shoemaker. The shoemaker does not attempt to make his own clothes, but employs a taylor. The farmer attempts to make neither the one nor the other, but employs those different artificers. All of them find it for their interest to employ their whole industry in a way in which they have some advantage over their neighbours, and to purchase with a part of its produce, or what is the same thing, with the price of a part of it, whatever else they have occasion for.

What is prudence in the conduct of every private family, can scarce be folly in that of a great kingdom. If a foreign country can supply us with a commodity cheaper than we ourselves can make it, better buy it of them with some part of the produce of our own industry, employed in a way in which we have some advantage. The general industry of the country, being always in proportion to the capital which employs it, will not thereby be diminished, no more than that of the above-mentioned artificers; but only left to find out the way in which it can be employed with the greatest advantage. It is certainly not employed to the greatest advantage, when it is thus directed towards an object which it can buy cheaper than it can make. The value of its annual produce is certainly more or less diminished, when it is thus turned away from producing commodities evidently of more value than the commodity which it is directed to produce. According to the supposition, that commodity could be purchased from foreign countries cheaper than it can be made at home. It could, therefore, have been purchased with a part only of the commodities, or, what is the same thing, with a part only of the price of the commodities, which the industry em-

ployed by an equal capital would have produced at home, had it been left to follow its natural course. The industry of the country, therefore, is thus turned away from a more, to a less advantageous employment, and the exchangeable value of its annual produce, instead of being increased, according to the intention of the lawgiver, must necessarily be diminished by every such regulation.   □

In addition to the ''invisible hand'' theme, there was another main line in Adam Smith's defense of private initiative and the market. This second line had to do with the growth of the economy over time. Smith believed that economic advance depended on the accumulation of capital[2] and that the accumulation of capital depended on saving and ''parsimony.'' The following reading brings out his view that private individuals, motivated by the desire to better their own conditions, would be far more likely to save and add to society's productive capital than would governments, which have a tendency toward ''extravagance'' and ''errors of administration.''

2.   Modern economists also believe that economic growth depends in part on the accumulation of capital, although modern notions of capital are somewhat different from those of Adam Smith. We tend to think of capital as machines, tools, equipment and so on. Smith tended to emphasize how labor was employed—whether ''productively'' (producing goods that could be stored up and saved) or ''unproductively'' (like household servants who worked but left nothing that could be accumulated). Smith also emphasized the division of labor as a major element in economic growth. Indeed, he thought capital accumulation would stimulate a continually greater division of labor over time. We shall be taking up a number of these points about economic growth later on. (See chapter 16.)

The Accumulation of Capital

Adam Smith

Capitals are increased by parsimony, and diminished by prodigality and misconduct.

Whatever a person saves from his revenue he adds to his capital, and either employs it himself in maintaining an additional number of productive hands, or enables some other person to do so, by lending it to him for an interest, that is, for a share of the profits. As the capital of an individual can be increased only by what he saves from his annual revenue or his annual gains, so the capital of a society, which is the same with that of all the individuals who compose it, can be increased only in the same manner.

Great nations are never impoverished by private, though they sometimes are by public prodigality and misconduct. The whole, or almost the whole public revenue, is in most countries employed in maintaining unproductive hands. Such are the people who compose a numerous and splendid court, a great ecclesiastical establishment, great fleets and armies, who in time of peace produce nothing, and in time of war acquire nothing which can compensate the expence of maintaining them, even while the war lasts. Such people, as they themselves produce nothing, are all maintained by the produce of other men's labour. When multiplied, therefore, to an unnecessary number, they may in a particular year consume so great a share of this produce, as not to leave a sufficiency for maintaining the productive labourers, who should reproduce it next year. The next year's produce, therefore, will be less than that of the foregoing, and if the same disorder should continue, that of the third year will be still less than that of the second. Those unproductive hands, who should be

Excerpted from Adam Smith, "The Accumulation of Capital," from *The Wealth of Nations* (New York: Modern Library, Random House, 1937), pp. 321, 325–26. Reprinted by permission of Random House.

maintained by a part only of the spare revenue of the people, may consume so great a share of their whole revenue, and therefore oblige so great a number to encroach upon their capitals, upon the funds destined for the maintenance of productive labour, that all the frugality and good conduct of individuals may not be able to compensate the waste and degradation of produce occasioned by this violent and forced encroachment.

This frugality and good conduct, however, is upon most occasions, it appears from experience, sufficient to compensate, not only the private prodigality and misconduct of individuals, but the public extravagance of government. The uniform, constant, and uninterrupted effort of every man to better his condition, the principle from which public and national, as well as private opulence is originally derived, is frequently powerful enough to maintain the natural progress of things toward improvement, in spite both of the extravagance of government, and of the greatest errors of administration. Like the unknown principle of animal life, it frequently restores health and vigour to the constitution, in spite, not only of the disease, but of the absurd prescriptions of the doctor.□

Thus, Adam Smith combined a belief in the frugality and industry of private individuals with a conviction that the market would work in such a fashion that the profit-seeking self-interest of those same individuals would tend towards the public good. The corollary was: If the private sector can handle things so well, then the State need not intervene except for rather special and limited functions.

CHOICE THROUGH THE MARKET

Today we are aware of many qualifications to the "classical" economists' view of the world, but we can also state their own arguments more precisely than they could, because we have developed certain analytic tools that were not at their disposal. Let us now approach this matter a bit more systematically.

The Problem

The tasks that a market economy must perform are numerous. For one thing, it must determine in one way or another how the income of society is distributed. One man earns $10,000 a year, another $2,000, another $75,000. Whether one applauds or objects to any particular arrangement, it is clear that every economic system must have *some* determinate way of distributing goods and services among its members. Anything less would bring social chaos.

Similarly, every economic system must provide some determinate way of deciding how the goods and services of the society are to be produced. One might think that the question of how to produce potatoes or automobiles or table lamps is purely technological rather than economic. But this is not so, for there are many different ways of producing any given product; all may be feasible in a physical or engineering sense, but some may be better than others in an *economic* sense. Automation may be excellent for a society with a great deal of machinery and a shortage of labor, but it would hardly make sense for a society that is overflowing with unskilled labor and can barely afford the most rudimentary tools and machines. The question of how to produce different goods is vitally affected by the relative scarcities of the different factors of production. Thus, it falls squarely in the province of the economist, and like the question of the distribution of income, it is another problem for the market economy to solve.

Finally, there is the problem we have already spent some time on: What goods to produce? In terms of our earlier diagram (repeated here in Figure 2–1), shall we produce at point *A* (lots of steel; little food) or at point *B* (little steel; lots of food)? In the remainder of this chapter, we shall put particular emphasis on this aspect of the choice problem, for it will allow us to bring out quite clearly the essential features of the market economy in its overall operations.

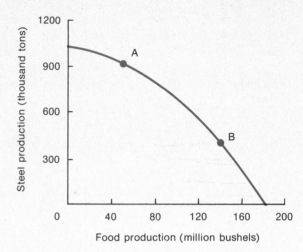

Figure 2–1. The Familiar Choice Problem.

In this chapter, we shall try to show how a decentralized market economy can make the choice between points *A* and *B* through the supply-and-demand mechanism.

Bird's-Eye Solution—The Circular Flow

Now, in the very broadest sense, the way in which a market economy solves its various choice problems can be illustrated by a circular flow diagram (Figure 2–2) similar to the one used in chapter 1. We have made a few changes in this diagram, to bring out the fact that we are now dealing specifically with a private market economy. Thus, instead of the very general term *Factory,* we have introduced the term *Private Business Firms;* similarly, *Home* has been replaced with *Private Households.*

But the most important change is that two boxes labelled *Product Markets* and *Factor Markets* have been added to the sides of the diagram. It is by the operation of these markets that our market economy will solve the various choice problems we have put to it. In the Product Market, the households operate as the buyers, the business firms as the sellers. Prices will have to be determined for the various consumer

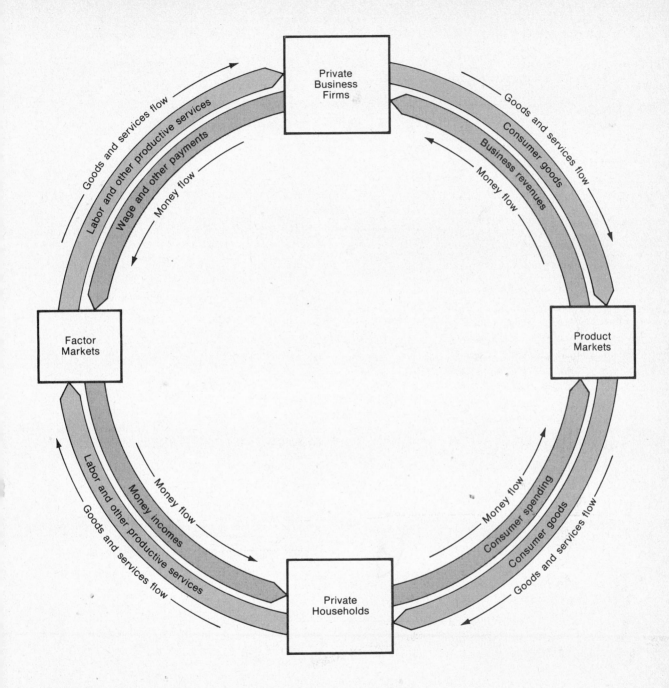

**Figure 2–2. The Circular Flow
of a Market Economy.**

goods brought to the market by industry. The quantities of these goods bought and sold will also have to be determined.

In the Factor Market, the buying and selling relationship is reversed—the business firms are now the *buyers*. They are trying to buy the services of laborers and the other factors of production that are, in this economy, privately owned. The sellers, in other words, are the households. In this market, prices will have to be determined for labor, land, and capital; these prices will, of course, affect the *money incomes* going to the households. In a private market economy, one of the most interesting (and controversial) features is that a society's distribution of income is determined by the way prices get set in the Factor Market. A high price of labor is just another name for a high wage—and, unfortunately, a low price of labor means low wages.

In this chapter we are focusing primarily on the Product Market. For it is through the determination of the prices and the quantities produced and sold in this market that we can suggest how a market economy makes its steel-versus-food decision (*A* versus *B* in Figure 2–1).

THE DEMAND CURVE

It is at this point that we must introduce one of the most important and famous tools of economics, the *demand curve*. Together with the *supply curve,* this tool will enable us to explain some of the essential features of a market economy. A demand curve may be defined as follows:

A demand curve is a hypothetical construction that tells us how many units of a particular commodity consumers would be willing to buy over a period of time at all possible prices, assuming that the prices of other commodities and the money incomes of the consumers are unchanged.

The last phrase in this definition is of some importance. It is usually called a *ceteris paribus* or "all

TABLE 2–1

AT PRICE (per dozen apples)	CONSUMERS WISH TO BUY PER MONTH (thousand dozens)
$1.00	20
.90	90
.80	150
.70	212
.60	278
.50	340
.46	365
.40	402
.30	465
.20	530
.10	590
.01	650

other things equal" phrase. It brings out the fact that we are isolating a particular part of economic life for close inspection and holding other areas in abeyance. This is clearly necessary here. How can we tell how many units of beefsteak a consumer will buy at one dollar a pound if we do not know what his income is or what the price of lamb or chicken is? Hence the need to proceed in this one-step-at-a-time fashion.

In Table 2–1 we have set out the raw data for a demand curve for a commodity: apples. (This will be our "food" when we come back to the food-steel choice problem later in this chapter.) We have asked consumers to tell us how many dozens of apples they would be willing to buy in a given month at prices ranging from $1.00 to 1¢ per dozen. Notice that we must specify the period of time involved; presumably the number of apples purchased at a given price will be 12 times as much in a year as in a month, and so on.

Figure 2–3 represents the material in Table 2–1 in a smooth curve. The procedure here is the same as in the production-possibility curve of chapter 1. The points from Table 2–1 are charted on graph paper and then joined together in a continuous line (as if, in fact, we actually had information on how

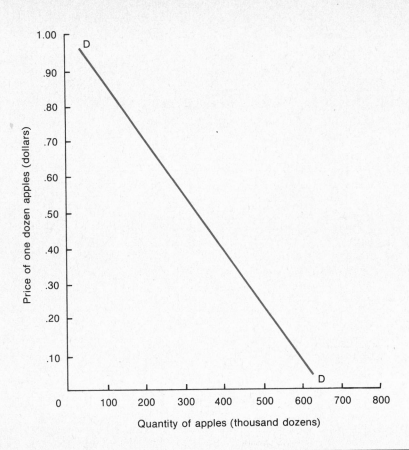

Figure 2–3. Consumer Demand Curve.

DD represents the consumer demand curve for apples. It is drawn on the assumption that money incomes of consumers are constant and that prices of other commodities (e.g., oranges) are constant.

many apples consumers would purchase at 31¢, 32¢, 33¢, and so on, per dozen). This curve is the consumer demand curve for apples.

Notice that the curve slopes downward from left to right. Why this particular shape? Actually, this is not too difficult to understand. At high prices for apples, the consumer will find that buying too many apples makes too big a dent in his budget; he will have to cut down his purchases. Furthermore, when apple prices are high, even the dedicated fruit lover will be tempted to substitute pears or peaches or oranges. This too, will mean fewer apple purchases. Thus, although we could imagine a few very curious

exceptions if we wished to,[3] the customary shape of a consumer demand curve will be as we have drawn it: sloping downward toward the lower right.

ELASTICITY OF DEMAND

Sometimes economists wish to go beyond the general shape of a demand curve and measure the responsiveness of the quantity of the commodity con-

---

3. A famous (among economists) exception to the rule of a downward-sloping demand curve is the so-called "Giffen paradox," named after a nineteenth-century British economist, Sir Robert Giffen. He noticed that when the price of potatoes goes up, very poor families may buy *more* potatoes. Why? Because the rise in the price of potatoes makes them poorer; and when they are poorer, they substitute potatoes for meat. This very exceptional case implies, among other things, that the commodity looms very large in the budgets of the consumers involved.

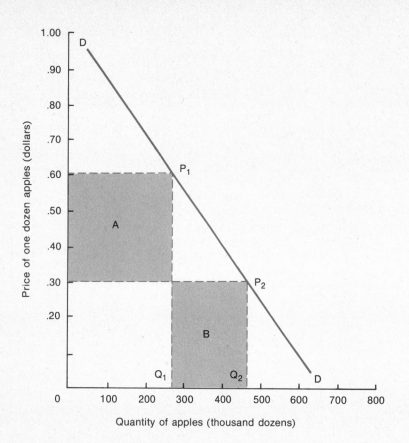

Figure 2–4. Elasticity of Demand and Total Revenue.

When demand is *inelastic,* an increase in quantity and decrease in price will lead to lowered total revenue for apple producers.

sumers wish to purchase to changes in its price. If the price of apples goes up by 10 percent, will the quantity demanded fall by 10 percent, 5 percent, 30 percent? Depending on the answer, we can determine numerically the _price elasticity_ of demand for a particular good. More specifically:

> *Price-elasticity of demand is defined as the percentage change in the quantity of a commodity demanded, divided by the percentage change in its price.*

If, when the price of apples goes up 10 percent, the quantity demanded falls by 10 percent, then we say that the price-elasticity of demand for apples is 1. If, under these same circumstances, the quantity demanded fell by 30 percent, we would say that the

price-elasticity is 3 and that the demand curve is relatively *elastic* at that point. If the quantity demanded fell by only 5 percent, the price-elasticity is .5 and the demand curve is said to be relatively *inelastic* at that point.

Another way of describing elasticity is in terms of the total sales revenues that come to an industry from selling its product. For example, if a demand curve is inelastic at a certain point, a decrease in price would cause only a small increase in quantity demanded—hence, on balance, total sales revenues (price times quantity) would decrease with a decrease in price. Conversely, if demand is relatively elastic, total revenues would *in*crease with a decrease in price. Try to figure out for yourself what will happen to total revenues if there is a price decrease when elasticity is precisely 1.

These concepts, as illustrated in Figure 2–4, add another perspective to the demand curve for apples. What happens to the quantity of apples demanded when the price falls from 60¢ to 30¢ a dozen? We know from Table 2–1 that the quantity demanded at 60¢ is 278 thousand dozens and at 30¢ is 465 thousand dozens. A halving of price leads to less than a doubling of quantity. Hence, we know that the demand curve is relatively inelastic when the price is 30¢. This, in turn, means that a fall in price should be associated with a decline in total sales revenues to apple-producers. And it is. At the higher price, total sales revenues were $166,800 (= .60 × 278,000); at the lower price they had fallen to $139,500 (= .30 × 465,000).

Note that a rough assessment of elasticity can be made by the use of various rectangles in Figure 2–4. When the price falls, apple producers will lose revenue equal to the area of rectangle A and will gain revenue equal to the area of rectangle B. If area A is bigger than area B, demand is inelastic. If area A is smaller than area B, demand would be elastic. If area A and area B are exactly equal, elasticity equals 1. In this last case, of course, a rise or fall in price or quantity will generally have no effect on the total sales revenues of the producers.[4]

Although price-elasticity of demand is not always easy to measure in practice, it often has important implications for practical problems. Thus, in 1974, the United States government wanted to know how much of a price rise would be needed to get consumers to cut back their consumption of gasoline by 20 percent. Since studies suggested that consumer demand for gasoline had a low elasticity—was relatively inelastic (see pp. 428–29)—this meant that a large price rise would be required to produce the desired cutback in consumption. This was obviously rather discouraging news for a nation already deeply concerned by price inflation.

We shall be returning to the demand curve frequently in the course of this book, but, before leaving it now, the reader should test his understanding of the concept by asking himself what will happen if some of the "other things equal" (*ceteris paribus*) items happen to change. Suppose all consumers have a 50 percent rise in their money incomes? Suppose the price of bananas goes up? Suppose the price

---

inelastic curves as fairly "steep," this is not fully accurate. Elasticity depends both on the slope of the curve and on its position. Thus, a straight-line demand curve will have different elasticities in different segments, depending upon whether we are considering the high-price–low-quantity range or the low-price–high-quantity range. A simple way of seeing this is given in the accompanying figure. Note

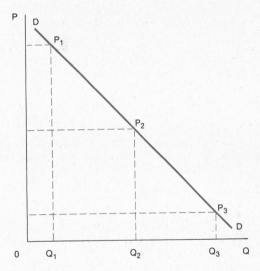

that the total revenue as measured by the various rectangles in this diagram increases from P_1 to P_2 but *decreases* from P_2 to P_3. This implies that the curve is relatively elastic in the P_1 to P_2 area and relatively *inelastic* in the P_2 to P_3 area. Ideally, then, elasticity should be measured at each particular point on a curve, though economists sometimes use the concept of *arc* elasticity to measure average elasticity over a certain range of a curve.

One other small point: Since price and quantity vary inversely on a demand curve, price-elasticity of demand would normally be a negative number. If we prefer positive elasticity, we can simply multiply these negative numbers by −1, calling that positive number *elasticity* as a matter of definition.

---

4. There is sometimes confusion between the elasticity of a demand curve and its slope. Although one may tend to think of relatively elastic curves as fairly "flat" and relatively

of oranges goes down? In each case, the answer is that the whole demand curve will *shift* its position. Can you determine the direction of and the reasons for the shifts?   *Related to production possibility curve*

THE SUPPLY CURVE

The second tool we need for our analysis of the market economy is the *supply curve.*

This curve tells us not about the consumers of apples, but about the *producers* of them. Instead of going around to consumers and asking, "How many apples would you buy this month at such-and-such a price?" we now ask producers, "How many apples would you produce and sell this month at such-and-such a price?"

A supply curve is a hypothetical construction that tells us how many units of a particular commodity producers would be willing to sell over a period of time at all possible prices, ceteris paribus.

This curve is derived by graphing Table 2–2, which is similar to Table 2–1 except that this time we are questioning producers rather than consumers. "If the market establishes a price of 70¢ a dozen, how many thousand dozens of apples will you bring to market?" we ask the apple-producers. Their answer, according to Table 2–2, is 631 thousand dozens. If this and the other points are plotted on a graph, we get a curve like *SS* in Figure 2–5: a supply curve for apples.

In some respects the supply curve is a bit more complicated to grasp than the demand curve, or at least it seems so at first glance. Two problems arise: Under what assumptions can a determinate supply curve be drawn? What explains the upward slope of the supply curve?

TABLE 2–2

AT PRICE (per dozen apples)	PRODUCERS ARE WILLING TO SUPPLY PER MONTH (thousand dozens)
$.20	76
.30	187
.40	298
.46	365
.50	410
.60	521
.70	631
.80	743
.90	854

ASSUMPTIONS BEHIND THE SUPPLY CURVE

One critical assumption is that apple producers take the prices of apples as given *by the market* and not as subject in any significant way to their personal control. They are price-takers, not price-setters. In technical economics terminology, they are *pure competitors.* We shall see in later chapters that *pure competition* is by no means the only form of real-life market structure, and this is one of the reasons our analysis of the market economy in the present chapter is necessarily only a beginning. By the term *pure competition,* we mean:

A market structure is purely competitive when the business firms comprising the industry in question are selling a homogeneous product and are so small in relation to the industry as a whole that they take the price of their product as given.

The implications of this definition will be developed later in great detail (especially in Part Three): for the moment, however, it is important only to understand that this kind of assumption is, in fact, being made when we draw our supply curve. And this can be seen simply by reflecting a moment on the question we asked each apple producer: "How many apples

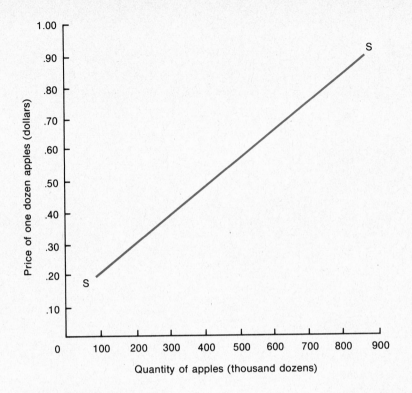

Figure 2–5. Supply Curve.

SS represents the producers' supply curve for apples. It tells us that producers are willing to supply more apples only if the price of apples goes up. A lower price, conversely, will lead to a smaller quantity supplied.

would you offer for sale at such-and-such a price per dozen?'' He is being asked to respond to a *given price*. If this were not the case, the only *relevant* question we could ask him would be: ''What price do you plan to *set* for apples this month?'' But that is not the question we asked. Our question—the question underlying the supply curve—does build in the assumption of price-taking or pure competition.

The curve is based on other assumptions as well, and we should not be surprised to find that each supply curve (like each demand curve) has the *ceteris paribus* clause attached. In the case of the supply curve, the meaning of this clause seems a bit more complicated, however, for it is so obviously affected by considerations of *time*. The British economist Alfred Marshall pointed out, late in the nineteenth century, the great importance of the time period in analyzing producer behavior and the supply curve. In the very short run, when we allow virtually nothing to vary except the price of apples, the apple producer really has nothing to offer but his given stock of apples. The supply curve in this case might be almost a straight, vertical line—i.e., he would offer his given supply of apples at any price. In a somewhat longer run, he will have time to adjust production to different prices. When the price of apples goes up and stays up for a few months, he may hire more laborers to pick apples, to pack them, and to fill orders. In the still longer run, his adjustment may be more flexible yet. He may plant more trees, buy more orchard land, acquire more farm machinery, and so on.

Thus, for any given supply curve, we must be careful to specify exactly what time period we are thinking of and, consequently, what factors we are holding constant and what factors we are allowing to change.

SHAPE OF THE SUPPLY CURVE

Considerations of the time period are also important with respect to our second problem—explaining the upward slope of the supply curve toward the right—for the shape of the supply curve will also be affected by what factors are being held constant and what time period is involved.

Now the main *general* reason that the supply curve rises toward the right is that costs tend to rise as the production of any particular commodity is increased. This is most easy to see in short-run situations. Each farmer can expand production to some degree by adding more laborers, but basically he will have fixed quantities of land, apple trees, buildings, and other capital at his disposal. Thus, it will become increasingly difficult to increase apple production—i.e., eventually costs will start to go up.

Actually, what we are describing here is a version of another famous tool of the economist: the *law of diminishing returns.*

The law of diminishing returns *states that, in the production of any commodity, as we add more units of one factor of production (the "variable" factor) to a given quantity of other factors of production (the "fixed" factors), the addition to total product with each subsequent unit of the variable factor will eventually begin to diminish.*

To put it in terms of short-run apple production: As we hire more labor to increase apple production from a fixed amount of orchard land, we will eventually find that the added number of apples we get from each extra laborer begins to diminish. If the laborers are hired at a fixed wage, this means, in turn, that the *added cost* of getting apples will rise higher and higher, the more apples we try to produce.[5]

What we have just said helps to explain why costs generally rise as a firm expands production in the short run. But how is this fact connected with the shape of the supply curve? The answer, essentially, is that if costs rise with output, business firms will be willing to expand output only at higher prices. If they did not get higher prices and still went ahead to expand output, they would find that the additional output cost them more than the revenues it brought in. Only at the higher price will the expansion of output prove to be profitable.

We have here an example of the workings of Adam Smith's principle of self-interest. The businessman will expand production at higher prices because it is in *his* interest to do so. When all businessmen in an industry behave this way, they will create an upward-sloping supply curve as shown in Figure 2–5.

These comments, of course, are about the short run. In the long run, the shape of the supply curve is somewhat more difficult to explain, though even in the long run the normal shape will still be upward-sloping toward the right. The main difference will be that the rise in costs will be less steep. This, in turn, reflects the fact that, in the long run, there are many different ways of expanding output—buying more land, planting more trees, purchasing new farm machinery and buildings. Generally, the long-run supply curve for a firm or an industry will usually rise less steeply than the short-run supply curve for that same firm or industry.

THE "LAW" OF SUPPLY AND DEMAND

We have explained the general meaning and shape of both the demand and the supply curves. Now we are in a position to combine them. In Figure 2–6, the demand curve and the supply curve for apples have been combined in one diagram. With the aid of this diagram, we shall now be able to determine the equilibrium market price of apples and the quantity of apples that will be bought and sold. This determination of the price and quantity of a particular product is what the so-called *law of supply and demand* is all about.

5.   We shall return to the law of diminishing returns in chapter 6 and to its relation to the supply curve in Part Three, especially chapters 19 and 20.

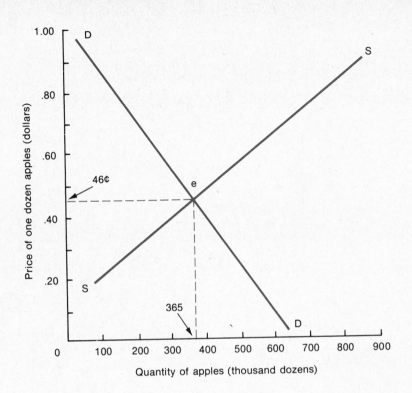

Figure 2–6.

Supply and demand are in equilibrium at point *e*, where the price of a dozen apples is 46¢ and the quantity bought and sold is 365 thousand dozens.

Needless to say, it seems likely that the key point will be where the two curves intersect. And, indeed, it is at this point that the equilibrium price and quantity are determined. In Figure 2–6, the market price will be 46¢ a dozen and the equilibrium quantity produced will be 365 thousand dozens.

The deeper question is: Why is this point of intersection significant? Why couldn't the price be somewhere else?

The answer to this, in essence, is that it is only at this particular price (46¢) that the quantity of apples consumers are demanding and the quantity of apples producers are willing to supply are exactly equal; i.e., supply = demand. At any other price, either the quantity supplied will be greater than the quantity demanded—and producers will accumulate large quantities of unwanted and unsold apples, *or* the quantity demanded will be greater than the quan-

tity supplied—and buyers will clamor for apples that producers simply do not have for sale. It is clear that neither of these alternatives could last long. If producers were accumulating unwanted apples, sooner or later they would decide to cut back on production. If, conversely, buyers kept asking for nonexistent apples, producers would sooner or later get the idea that it was time to raise prices and expand apple production.

It is only at the point of intersection that these problems cannot arise. Here, there is no accumulation of unsold apples; there are no queues of buyers trying to get apples that don't exist. We have then an equilibrium price—a price that will stay put unless some new fundamental change occurs—and this is the price at which supply and demand are equated.

CONSUMER SOVEREIGNTY— A SIMPLIFIED EXAMPLE

Our analysis so far has shown how the price and quantity of a particular commodity are determined in a market economy, all other things equal. This is an important step in understanding how a decentralized, private economy can function.

But these tools can also be used to go a step further. We want to show how a market economy makes some of the fundamental economic choices that all societies must face. One of those central choice problems, you will recall, was whether to locate at point *A* (lots of steel; little food) or at point *B* (little steel; lots of food) on our production-possibility curve.

Now in a market economy, as Adam Smith understood, the essence of the process is that producers will find it in their own self-interest to produce what is socially desirable. In particular, they will adjust their production of different commodities so that they are in accord with consumer desires. This is what is meant by the concept of *consumer sovereignty*. If the economy is at point *A*, and consumers prefer to be at *B*, the market will operate to shift production in the desired direction.

With our newly acquired supply and demand curves, we can give a bit more definition to this process. Let us imagine that we are dealing with two commodities. Apples will be our food commodity; our steel commodity will be, say, washing machines.

Now let us imagine that, for whatever reason, there is a shift in consumer desires from washing machines to apples. The example is a bit far-fetched, but the principle is clear enough: Consumer preferences have changed. How is this reflected through the market in changed production of these two commodities?

The general nature of the answer is given in the two diagrams in Figure 2–7. The increased demand for apples has resulted in an upward shift of the demand curve for apples. The decreased demand for washing machines has resulted in a downward shift in the demand curve for washing machines. The

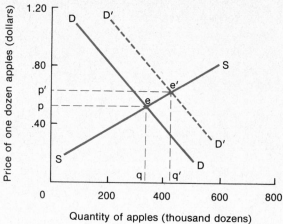

(a)

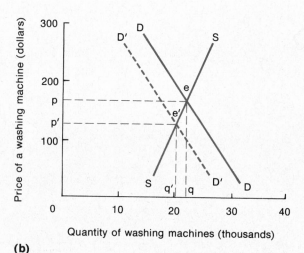

(b)

Figure 2–7.

These diagrams represent a simplified example of how consumer sovereignty operating through the supply-and-demand mechanism can alter the composition of output in a market economy. In particular, a shift in demand from washing machines to apples has led to an increased production of apples and a decreased production of washing machines. This new equilibrium would correspond to a new point on the society's production-possibility curve.

consequences of these shifts according to our diagrams are:

1. a greater production of apples at a higher price.

2. a lesser production of washing machines at a lower price.

Consumer preferences have shifted from washing machines to apples, and the result has been an increased production of apples and a decreased production of washing machines, and this without any planning or governmental intervention, but solely through the laws of supply and demand working in the marketplace.

Now this example is a first approximation, and it should be taken as suggestive rather than definitive. Actually, it wasn't until late in the nineteenth century, a hundred years after Adam Smith wrote, that economists began to pin down the full implications of a market economy. If we think about our circular flow diagrams of this chapter and chapter 1, we shall soon realize that it isn't possible to separate Product Markets (apples, washing machines, food, steel, etc.) from Factor Markets (labor, orchard land, steel mines, machinery, etc.). What happens anywhere in the flow is likely to have effects elsewhere in the system. To put it another way: In order to follow through any significant change in an economy—even a shift in tastes involving apples and washing machines—we ultimately have to inspect the whole system at once.

Though we shall have to wait until later chapters to achieve this larger objective, our present analysis already tells us a great deal about the workings of a market economy. In particular, we have suggested some key links between the producers on the one hand and the consumers on the other. Why is it that in a pure market economy, producers produce the goods that consumers want? Answer: Because the market, working through the supply-and-demand apparatus, will make it profitable—in their self-interest—for them to do so.

THE MARKET AND THE PUBLIC INTEREST

The market economy, then, is a possible system. Is it also, as Adam Smith was inclined to believe, the *best* possible system?

The answer, as one might expect, is very complicated and is subject to much disagreement among the experts. In a preliminary way, however, we can indicate at least two lines of argument that must affect all serious thinking about this theory.

The first line of argument really stems from the kind of analysis we have been presenting in this chapter. It emphasizes the essential viability of the market system. It says in effect: Consider how beautifully the supply and demand apparatus works, how remarkable it is that, without governmental intervention or planning or forethought, all these thousands of individual decisions nevertheless do lead to such desirable social results. This argument is in the full tradition of classical economic thought.

A second line of argument leads in quite a different direction. It stresses that there are important areas of economic life where competition and markets do not produce the results we want. To take one simple example: The analysis in this chapter has not even touched on the problem of unemployment. Essentially, in our washing machines-and-apples example we were assuming a full-employment economy. But we do know that unemployment does occur. Will the market economy be able to solve this problem? The critics would tend to be pessimistic. They would also be pessimistic about the way market economies deal with dozens of other problems: inflation, poverty, income distribution, pollution, and waste. They would point out that Adam Smith gravely underestimated the divergence between private and social interest.

History is partly on each side. We have already shown that the powerful Industrial Revolution of the early eighteenth and nineteenth centuries developed at a time when the market system was triumphing over earlier forms of economic organization. We shall also show in the next chapter how market elements keep intruding even in highly planned socialist economies. On the other hand, it is true historically—and it is true today—that a *pure* market economy has never been a reality. In one way or another, citizens of this and every country in the world have asked that governments step in to change this or that aspect of the functionings of a price-and-market mechanism. In the 1970s such requests are by no means abating.

Thus, the crucial question, as far as the public interest is concerned, is not whether there should be *any* intervention—that question has really been settled by history—but what *degree* of intervention should be permitted. This question cannot be answered easily.

SUMMARY

A *market economy* is one in which the crucial economic decisions and choices are made in a decentralized fashion by private individuals, operating through a price-and-market mechanism. Historically, the self-regulating market economy is a modern rather than an ancient invention, involving rather special assumptions such as the treatment of land and labor as commodities. This kind of economy—though never in a *pure* form—developed considerably at the time of the English Industrial Revolution. Most of the leading British economists of the day, especially Adam Smith, stressed the virtues of limiting government intervention in economic life so that the market, working through private self-interest, could bring benefits to society at large.

With modern analysis, we can give much sharper expression to Smith's views using such tools as *supply* and *demand curves.*

A demand curve for a product shows the quantities of the product that consumers are willing to buy over a given period of time at different prices. A supply curve shows the amounts of the commodity that producers are willing to sell over a given period of time at different prices. Both curves are drawn under certain important *ceteris paribus* or "other things equal" assumptions. In the case of the supply curve,

it is particularly important to notice the element of time, whether short run or long run, since, generally, costs will rise more steeply (and hence the supply curve will rise more steeply) in the short run than in the long run. The reason is that many of a firm's factors of production are fixed in the short run; thus, the *law of diminishing returns* comes into play.

Equilibrium price and quantity are determined in a market economy where supply and demand curves intersect. This is the so-called *law of supply and demand,* a law valid only under the special conditions of pure competition.

Using supply and demand curves, we can illustrate in a general way how consumer preferences are carried through the price system to affect the kinds of goods produced in the economy. If consumers want more apples and fewer washing machines in a market economy, supply and demand will work to produce this general result.

To prove that the market economy is a "possible" economy is one thing; to prove that it is the "best possible" economy is another. Economic analysis indicates points on both sides, as does historical experience. History does strongly suggest, however, that the issue is (and was) never one of a *pure* market economy, but rather one of what *degree* of government intervention should be allowed or encouraged.

IMPORTANT TERMS TO REMEMBER

Market Economy
Mercantilism
Classical Economics
Laissez Faire
"Invisible Hand"
Product Market
Factor Market
Demand Curve
Supply Curve
Ceteris Paribus
Elasticity of Demand
Law of Diminishing Returns
Law of Supply and Demand
Equilibrium
Consumer Sovereignty

QUESTIONS FOR DISCUSSION

1. In the thirteenth century St. Thomas Aquinas, the great Catholic philosopher, wrote: "To sell a thing for more than its worth, or to buy it for less than its worth, is in itself unjust and unlawful." Would you consider this point of view to be consistent or inconsistent with the assumptions of a "market economy"? Why?

2. Adam Smith was aware that businessmen, given the chance, might meet together and conspire against the consumer. In view of this danger, can you see why the "invisible hand," if it works at all, will only do so in an economy with substantial competition?

3. The choice of methods of producing different commodities is not only a technological but also an economic question. Discuss.

4. What does the phrase "other things equal" mean when applied to the ordinary consumer demand curve?

5. Suppose that there is an invention that substantially lowers the costs of producing a certain commodity. What general effect would this invention have on the supply curve of that commodity? What would be the resulting effect on the equilibrium price and quantity produced of the commodity in question?

6. Discuss the role of the time period of adjustment in analyzing producers' responses to changes in market prices. Might consumer responses to different prices (as shown by the demand curve) also be affected by the length of the time period under consideration?

7. "When some people are very rich and others are very poor, the whole notion of 'consumer sovereignty' in a market economy is misleading and prejudicial." Discuss some of the issues raised by this statement.

SUGGESTED READING

Dorfman, Robert. *Prices and Markets.* Englewood Cliffs, N.J.: Prentice-Hall, 1967, chaps. 1–5.

Heilbroner, Robert L. *The Worldly Philosophers.* New York: Simon & Schuster, 1953, chap. 3.

Marshall, Alfred. *Principles of Economics.* 8th ed. New York: Macmillan Co., 1948, Book V.

Samuelson, Paul A. *Readings in Economics.* 6th ed. New York: McGraw-Hill, 1970, readings 10, 11.

Smith, Adam. *The Wealth of Nations.* Modern Library Ed. New York: Random House, 1937.

Tax, Sol. "Penny Capitalism: A Guatemalan Indian Market," in Smithsonian Institution's *Institute of Social Anthropology,* Publication no. 16.

CHAPTER 3
THE COMMAND ECONOMY AND SOCIALISM

In the last chapter, we said that a *pure* market economy was something of an abstraction and is not to be encountered in its pristine form in the real world. Much the same can be said of its opposite: the *centrally planned economy,* sometimes called the *command economy*. Even in its closest approximation (the economy of the Soviet Union), important elements of a market system intrude—indeed, with increasing frequency in recent years.

It is clear, however, that the study of central planning is of great importance to the serious student of modern economics. For the mechanism of economic planning is in wide use in the present-day world. Elements of this mechanism appear in our own economy. In Western Europe, even in countries where the basic system is privately organized, planning is often an explicit part of public policy. Great Britain's Labour Party has limited aspirations to socialism; France has developed an interesting mix of the public and private sectors through what is called "indicative planning"; neutralist Yugoslavia is experimenting with "market socialism."

Furthermore, as everyone who follows the newspapers must be fully aware, a large fraction of the world's population regards private enterprise and the market system with suspicion and, indeed, outright hostility. Communism in all its varieties puts a considerable emphasis on governmental action, centralization of decision, high-level planning of fundamental economic choices. By referring to some of these systems as *command economies,* we emphasize the fact that the decision-making process often goes not from individual consumers to individual producers but from central planning boards or commissions to enterprises that are either State-owned or are highly regulated by the State. Consumer sovereignty largely gives way to the collective preferences of the central planners. It is this fundamentally different approach to economic problems that we shall consider in this chapter.

THE MARXIAN CRITICISMS

In discussing the market economy, we went back to Adam Smith. In discussing the great planned economies of the modern world, we must go back to another early economist, the controversial Karl Marx (1818–1883). In most of the countries that have planned economies, Marx is regarded as the true founder of scientific economic thought.

Actually, if we go to Marx in the hope of finding a detailed blueprint of how a planned economy should work, we shall be largely disappointed. Marx gave comparatively little attention to this important problem. He did, instead, two rather different things. First, he provided a massive critique of the workings of the capitalistic market economy. (The Marxian Critique of Capitalism is the subject of our first Great Debate, at the end of Part I, pp. 145–169). Second, he provided a revolutionary ideology that has proved very vigorous historically in leading to the overthrow of established economic systems and the installation of highly centralized economies.

Karl Marx, the man, was an activist and revolutionary. He took part in the Communist League of 1848 and summoned his followers to action with ringing phrases in his *Communist Manifesto*. But he was also a scholar—intense, very well read, sometimes even pedantic. He was born in Germany but spent the latter part of his life in England, working long hours each day in the British Museum in London. His major work, *Das Kapital* (*Capital*), is a vast document of literally thousands of pages, of which he was able to complete only the first volume (1867) in his lifetime. The remaining volumes were published posthumously under the editorship of various of his followers, especially Friedrich Engels. Engels played a very important role in Marx's life, sustaining him spiritually and, at times, financially. The *Communist Manifesto* was actually a joint product of Marx and Engels, though Marx was the guiding light in the collaboration and clearly had the superior mind of the two.

Marx's first achievement was of a negative kind: He presented a number of harsh criticisms of the capitalistic system. If he had perused the discussion of a market economy in our last chapter, he would have scoffed at its shortcomings as a description of historical reality. He certainly would have objected to the fact that there was no reference at all to the different classes of society and that, in particular, there was no reference to what he considered a fundamental feature of capitalism—the conflict between the capitalist class and the laboring class, between the owners of factories and machines and the dispossessed proletariat. For Marx, this *class conflict* was an absolutely central characteristic of capitalism; indeed, he tended to view all past history as evidence of one kind of class conflict or another. To write about the beauties of supply and demand and how they reflected consumer preferences, but to ignore the struggle between the wealthy capitalists and the downtrodden laborers—this, in Marx's eyes, would be to shut out the fundamental facts of the real world.

Another objection he would have made was that we failed to recognize the importance of *monopoly* elements in the price system. Our supply curve, for example, was drawn on the assumption that producers were pure competitors or price-takers; i.e., each firm was too small to have any appreciable direct effect on the price of its product. As far as Marx was concerned, however, the result of free markets in the modern industrial and commercial world would almost certainly be that big, monopolizing firms would swallow up the small, individual producers. In his view, it was not the small firm but the giant industrial corporation that was characteristic of capitalism, particularly in its advanced stages. Indeed, he believed that these large firms would come to control not only the economies but to a great degree the governments of capitalistic countries. In such a world, the notion of producers responding meekly to the will and wishes of consumers would be a mockery.

Finally, he would have objected, as we ourselves recognized, that our description of a market economy took no account of the *unemployment* problem. For Marx, this would have meant living in a fairy-tale world. In his theoretical structure, unemployment was not an accidental but an intrinsic feature of a capitalist

THE GRANGER COLLECTION

Karl Marx (1818–1883). Marx emphasized the dominating role of economic factors in social and political life. He produced the most massive critique of capitalism ever written.

economy. One reason for this was that, in a capitalistic economy, productive capacity regularly tended to outrun consumption: there was a constant tendency to overproduction and economic crisis. Another reason for unemployment was that capitalists had to find some way to keep wages down. The way they chose, according to Marx, was to introduce machinery in place of labor whenever wages started to rise. This machinery displaced the laborers; consequently, there was serious general unemployment. If any laborer asked for a raise, his employer simply took him to the factory window and showed him the line of workers who had no jobs at all—a crude but effective method of settling wage disputes! In terms

"labor saving technology"

of our production-possibility curve, Marx would have said that a market economy characteristically operated at some point, *UE,* inside the production frontier (see Figure 1–6, p. 19). Indeed, Marx argued that this problem would get worse and worse as time went on. Capitalism would be subject to great crises and depressions. These crises would, he believed, do much to make the Communist Revolution inevitable.

History has shown that most of these criticisms of a capitalistic market economy were seriously overstated. We would live in a fairy-tale world far more fanciful than the one that Marx condemned if we were to use Marxian analysis as a guide to what actually happens in countries where, as in the United States, heavy reliance is placed on the market mechanism. However, it would be just as misleading to think that there is no truth whatever in the Marxian criticisms. There clearly are numerous inequities in the distribution of wealth, income, and power in a completely unregulated market economy. The large industrial corporation with considerable influence over its markets is a substantial feature of modern life. And as far as the displacement of labor by machines is concerned, what workingman in an advanced industrial economy has not wondered at some time or other whether his job may not give way to automation and the computer? The point is that Marx did have a number of significant specific insights into the workings of the capitalistic system. Where he went wrong was in missing the possibilities of improvement and evolutionary change that such systems have proved capable of carrying forward. Indeed, it may well be that the most serious flaws of capitalism are due not to its capitalistic but to its *industrial* character. The ecological and environmental costs of capitalism *or* socialism are drawing deep criticisms in both the West and the Soviet Union in the 1970s.

The second major aspect of Marx's thought that concerns us is his role as revolutionary. Marx was (and still is) the spiritual leader of communism, and his writings have served as inspiration for the revolutions that have created the major planned economies of the modern world.

Now, in a sense, the most interesting and rather surprising point to be made in this connection is that the Marxist revolutions that have led to Communist governments have not been altogether in accord with Marx's own theory. Toward the end of his life, Marx once commented, ''I am not a Marxist''; and, indeed, if he had seen some of the interpretations his doctrines have since been subjected to, he might have made the point even more emphatically. The problem is essentially this—Marx argued that the weaknesses in capitalism we have just been describing would cause the eventual collapse of the system after capitalistic evolution had run its full course. In theory, the revolution comes at, or toward, the end of the capitalist phase. In practice, the revolutions have not come in the advanced capitalistic countries but rather in poor, relatively backward countries that have scarcely had time to go through the capitalistic stage. Although Russia had made some economic progress by 1917, she was economically still far behind the advanced capitalistic countries of Western Europe and North America. The Chinese claim to be orthodox Marxists, yet they had their revolution in the 1940s, before they could truly be said to have had any experience at all with modern industrial capitalism.

All this proves that Marx's theory was far from accurate in predicting when Marxian revolutions would occur. What happened, in effect, was that his doctrines were simply adjusted to the practical necessities of the situations at hand. In Russia, for example, there was Lenin, the great leader of the Communist Revolution. Lenin had little time to worry about whether or not Russia was in the appropriate stage of development for the collapse of capitalism to occur. He was much more interested in the strategy of the revolution itself. Another example is Stalin, who was fully aware that Russia in the 1920s was not an economically advanced country. On the contrary, he emphasized her need to catch up with the advanced countries and, therefore, proceeded to sacrifice everything to rapid industrialization. With him, communism became not the stage that follows modern development but rather an ideology for promoting forced-draft industrialization and growth.

And the reinterpretation goes on today. The post-Stalin leadership in Russia seems to have a somewhat more flexible view of economic organization than did its predecessors. The Chinese, however, seem to have embraced a particularly all-enveloping form of communism according to the precepts of Chairman Mao; to them, of course, the new breed of Russian leaders are crass revisionists.

The main common bond we can find in all these manifestations of Marxism is a built-in predilection for a much higher degree of centralization and economic planning than occurs in the major economies of the Western world. This takes us from the realm of ideology to the realm of economic organization and practice.

THE FUNCTIONING
OF A COMMAND ECONOMY

A centralized command economy must face the same fundamental problems as a decentralized market economy. Let us first say a few words about the general functioning of such an economy, and then make some specific comments about the actual experience of planning in the Soviet Union.

In the command economy, it is not the market but the central government (or some branch of the central government) that makes the basic decisions concerning the society's production targets, its allocation of resources, its distribution of income, and its desired rate of growth. In the pure command economy, the State would normally own all the means of production and most of the property. It would determine the incomes of different kinds of laborers and the salaries of production managers, doctors, artists, and bureaucrats. It would determine the planned outputs of all the different productive enterprises in the economy and the allocation of resources to each. In terms of our earlier examples, it would set, and attempt to secure fulfillment of, targets for food production and steel production, for the output of apples and the output of washing machines.

Now such a task, if carried through into every single corner of a modern economy, would be hopelessly complex and really beyond the capabilities of any group of planners, however sophisticated. Consequently, in most real-life command economies, at least some of these decisions are decentralized either to lower levels of authority or, in some cases, to what is a rough facsimile of a price-and-market mechanism. Frequently, a command economy will direct its main planning energies to certain broad areas of the economy or to certain particular targets that, for some reason, have special priority in the minds of the central planners.

Even when the task is limited in this fashion, it still involves a number of difficult and overlapping problems. These include problems of organization, coordination, efficiency, incentives and basic goals.

(1) Organization. The first and most obvious requirement of a command economy is a bureaucratic organization that makes it possible for anything like effective planning to proceed. It is one thing to make decisions about what the pattern of economic activity in the society should be and another to see that these are carried out.

There must be, first, an organizational chain of command that makes it possible to transmit the decisions, targets, and directives of the central body down *through the system to the level of the actual production units in the economy. There must be, also, an organizational structure that permits information and data from the production units to* rise up *through the system to furnish the ultimate decision-makers with the knowledge required for any kind of intelligent planning. It should be clear that many countries do not possess, or could build up only very slowly, the massive administrative mechanism necessary to carry out these vital functions. Even under the best of circumstances, the command economy carries a tremendous burden of bureaucracy, which is at least partially avoided in a more decentralized system.*

(2) Coordination. It is not enough that targets and directives be quickly communicated through the system; they must also be economically consistent. There is a serious problem of coordination in any command economy, arising from the interdependent nature of the modern industrial economy.

The problem may be put in terms of what economists refer to as input-output analysis.[1] *The outputs of one industry in the economy can be thought of as inputs into some other industry in the economy. Machines are necessary to produce steel, but steel is necessary to produce machines. Actually, steel output will be used as inputs into literally hundreds of other industries in the economy: machines, tractors, automobiles, typewriters, building construction, and so on. A modern economy is an infinitely complex network of interdependence, in which the production of one sector depends upon the inputs it can receive from a host of other sectors, while its own output will simultaneously be feeding back inputs into these and still other sectors. The point is that one cannot simply set a target for industry A and then, independently, set targets for industries B, C, and D. One must be sure that there is sufficient production of A, so that the input requirements of B, C, and D are met, and vice versa. With the large number of industries involved and their intricate interconnections, the coordination problem facing a command economy is necessarily extremely complex.*

(3) Efficiency. Even consistency is not sufficient, however; for it is necessary or at least desirable that a command economy be *efficient*—that is, that it employ its scarce resources in such a way that it gets as much output as possible from them.

---

1. For the standard reference on input-output analysis, see Wassily W. Leontief, *Structure of the American Economy, 1919–1939* (New York: Oxford University Press, 1951).

The subject of economic efficiency is a very large one that will be taken up in detail later on.[2] Suffice it to say here that a market economy is provided with some rough guidelines for efficient use of its resources, since the prices of the factors of production—land, labor, capital goods—will reflect their relative scarcities; hence, it will be profitable for firms to economize on the use of particularly scarce (therefore expensive) productive factors. In a command economy, difficulties may arise in this area, particularly if there is an aversion to using anything that may look like "capitalistic" market pricing. Historically, this has been a fairly serious problem for many actual command or near-command economies.

(4) Incentive. In the command economy—as in any economy—the workers, managers, and executives, not the central planners, produce the goods. Hence, sufficient *incentive* must be established, monetary or otherwise, to assure a vigorous labor force and intelligent managerial direction.

This problem is not necessarily as insurmountable as it may have seemed to some critics in the past. Many of these critics were doubtless going on the assumption that any form of socialism would characteristically involve a fairly equal distribution of income and, consequently, a denial of special rewards to those producers in the society who contributed most to the social product. However, there is nothing intrinsic in the nature of a command economy that requires an equal distribution of income; in fact, most command economies have set up fairly elaborate bonuses and other incentives to spur managers and workers to the fulfillment or, if possible, overfulfillment of their production targets.

(5) Basic Goals. We have left to the last in this brief list what in some senses should have come first: the question of basic goals. If the central planners do not rely on the wishes and preferences of the consumers to set the basic economic targets for which they are aiming, what then do they rely on?

This is a complex question, for ultimately its answer depends on the particular political organization of the command economy and the psychology of its effective leaders. A rough generalization on the basis of historical experience would go something like this: In general, command economies, while not ignoring the preferences of consumers (including their preference for at least some choice in the goods they buy), have nevertheless usually set goals that were different from what might have been expected had the market mechanism had somewhat fuller play. In particular, and probably because most of these economies tended to be somewhat economically backward at the outset, there has been a heavy emphasis on achieving economic growth at as rapid a rate as possible. The objective of catching up with the West has been paramount. If this has required sacrificing present standards of living to the demands of the future, then the sacrifice has been made, sometimes with a vengeance.

This last point can be illustrated by our familiar production-possibility curve. In Figure 3–1, we have drawn another such diagram, again with a choice between points A and B. This time, however, we have placed "consumers' goods" on the x-axis and "capital goods" (or "producers' goods") on the y-axis. One of the choices all societies face is how much of their output to devote to immediate consumption and how much to *invest* in machines, tools, equipment, and plant—what we call *capital goods*—which will make possible a larger productive capacity in the future. What we have been saying then is that most command or near-command economies have tended to locate nearer to A than to B.

In saying this, however, we are speaking less of the intrinsic features of a command economy than of actual historical experience, especially that of the major exemplar of this general approach, the Soviet

---

2. See chapters 17 and 22.

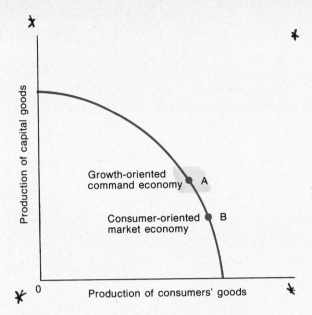

Figure 3–1.

In the determination of basic goals, most near-command economies in real life have put a heavy emphasis on investment and economic growth. They have moved in the direction of A (as opposed to B) on their production-possibility curve.

Union. Let us, therefore, now turn directly to the Soviet economy and make a few comments about its problems and accomplishments in the area of central planning.

THE SOVIET ECONOMY—PLANNING WITHOUT A FREE MARKET

The Soviet economy is not a pure command economy in every way. It is perhaps the closest approximation to such an economy that exists, however, and its durability (since the 1917 revolution) gives us an important opportunity to inspect both the strengths and weaknesses of this form of economic organization.

All the problems that we have mentioned in the previous section have troubled the Soviet government at one time or another. In the very early days of the

Communist regime, for example, organizational problems proved temporarily insurmountable. With the dislocation of the economy following World War I and the revolution, stringent economic controls had to be abandoned in the early 1920s, and a return to prices, markets, and capitalistic incentives had to be permitted in substantial areas of the economy. This was the period of the so-called New Economic Policy, a policy that, incidentally, was very successful in helping to restore the shattered Russian economy to its pre-World War I levels. Beginning in 1928, with the first Five-Year Plan, however, a near-command economy was established in most of the strategic sectors of the economy. Although this economy faced many difficulties, perhaps especially in the area of economic efficiency, and although modifications are now taking place, nevertheless the basic pattern of economic organization has remained fairly stable since 1928.

What conclusions, if any, can we draw from the Russian experience? Has it been basically successful or unsuccessful? One clear conclusion is that a command-type economy is capable of very rapid economic growth. Since we will be taking up Soviet growth in another connection later (chapter 28), this point will not be developed here, but it is important for the reader to keep it in the back of his mind.

What we are concerned with now is primarily how the Russians were able to handle the problems of organization, coordination, incentives, and especially economic efficiency. It is not sufficient to say, "Well, her economy *did* grow!" Its growth, however rapid, might have been better handled—it might have been still more rapid or might have involved less waste, fewer resources, less human suffering. Which, indeed, is what, on the whole, most Western commentators are inclined to say about the Soviet experience.

A balanced account of the Russian economic experience, directly relevant to our concerns, is given by Z. M. Fallenbuchl in the following reading. Of particular note is Fallenbuchl's explanation of how the Soviet planners preserved *some* consumer choice while reserving most major productive decisions for themselves.

How Does the Soviet Economy Function without a Free Market?

Z. M. Fallenbuchl

1

In a free enterprise economy the basic economic problems of what to produce, how to produce and for whom to produce are decided through the operation of a market. In the Soviet-type economy these problems are solved through a combination of administrative commands and market forces which are allowed to operate within certain limits in respect of some economic activities.

Administrative commands can effectively be applied because the state and the party exercise an enormous degree of control over the economy. This control is based on the three main institutional features of the system.

There is, first of all, the totalitarian political power and the state monopoly of information and education which give the leaders a considerably greater freedom of decision than that which would ever be possible under political democracy, at least in peace time.

Another feature is the state ownership of the great majority of the means of production. The state sector is responsible for about 92 percent of the gross value of industrial output. The whole land is owned by the state and 16 percent of the total area under cultivation belongs to state farms while over 80 percent of the area is allocated to collective farms over which the state has complete control. In addition, the government has at its disposal nationalized banking and finance, transportation, the monopoly of international trade, domestic wholesale trade, and over 90 percent of the retail outlets.

Excerpted from Z. M. Fallenbuchl, ''How Does the Soviet Economy Function Without a Free Market?'' *Queen's Quarterly* 70, no. 4 (Winter 1964); 559–74. Reprinted by permission of the author and publisher.

The third feature of the system is centralized planning with economic plans which are enacted as law and which are therefore backed by legal sanctions, supplemented by various kinds of administrative pressures and numerous economic and non-economic incentives.

This institutional framework enables the leaders to make some basic economic decisions in accordance with their own scales of preferences and to ignore, up to a certain point, the preferences of the consumers. It is impossible to understand the working of the Soviet economy without realizing that dictatorial objectives are the dominant force determining the direction of a great deal of economic activity.

However, not even the most autocratic leaders and the best planners can solve millions of detailed economic problems in a completely centralized way. Moreover, an excessive centralization and bureaucratization have serious drawbacks. The maintenance of an extensive bureaucratic machine is expensive, rigidity and inertia tend to develop and economic efficiency of the system declines. Hence the perennial dilemma of the Soviet economic organization: how to decentralize some economic activities without losing the control over the economy and the possibility of central planning.

2

The communists have rejected the consumers' sovereignty but they have left consumers with some degree of free choice in the market for consumption goods. Contrary to the early communist dreams, the consumers receive their incomes not in the form of allocation of various consumption goods but in the money form. They are free to decide what they want to buy within the limits imposed by the existing quantities of commodities which have been produced in accordance with the planners' decisions.

Two problems are involved here. The first is the maintenance of an overall balance between the effective demand of the population, i.e., the sum of personal incomes which are likely to be spent on consumption and the aggregate supply of consumption goods available. Any discrepancy between the two can be eliminated by adjustments in the general price level which can easily be effected by changes in the rates of the sales tax, in the total wage bill or in the aggregate supply of consumption goods, if the authorities are prepared to do it.

The second problem is that of maintaining balances between demand for and supply of particular commodities. If there are discrepancies, then adjustments in relative prices, changes in the production plans and, in the case of some serious shortages, rationing can be introduced.

Although the consumers are free to choose among the produced consumption goods, they have only a very limited opportunity to influence the production pattern, which is mainly determined by the planners. The planners decide whether or not the consumers should have more textile or electrical appliances, for example.

How is it possible for the Soviet planners to leave the freedom of choice to consumers and, at the same time, to deny them the power to decide the pattern of production?

The answer can be found in the maintenance of a permanent state of full employment on the one hand and the ability to control inflation on the other. In all communist countries the leaders try to achieve the fastest possible economic growth by directing a huge proportion of resources to investment while, at the same time, they tend to increase "communal consumption" (education, health, social welfare, entertainment, public administration) and to maintain a high level of defence expenditures. As a result of this policy, there is a chronic shortage of producers' goods in relation to the amounts which are needed. The producers' goods industries have permanently more than sufficient demand for their output.

A relatively small proportion of resources is left for consumption and this relative shortage creates the sellers' market conditions. The existence of the sellers' market makes it easy to sell anything which has been produced and the planners do not have to fear any serious over-production of individual commodities. Although cases of the overproduction of some particular commodities have occurred from time to time in the Soviet Union and other communist

countries, so far these cases have been relatively insignificant under the conditions of general scarcity.

The policy of over-committing the resources eliminates the danger of insufficiency of aggregate demand and reduces the importance of overproduction of particular commodities, but it also has its disadvantages.

First of all, it implies a relatively low standard of living. It creates inconvenience for the consumers who are faced with various shortages, delays and difficulties. In addition to these there are also some serious dangers involved. The danger of inflation is always present. There have been periods of open inflation in the Soviet Union and other communist countries, but as the planners have some effective means to fight inflation, it is a suppressed inflation rather than an open inflation which is more typical for the Soviet-type economy.

The existence of suppressed inflation is, however, responsible for a number of inefficiencies. It leads to hoarding of machines and raw materials by state enterprises, to a deterioration in the quality of both consumption and producers' goods, to bottlenecks and interruptions in the productive process, and to the "take it or leave it" mentality in the distribution process.

3

The communists have rejected not only consumers' sovereignty but also the maximization of consumers' satisfaction (at least the present consumers' satisfaction) as guiding principles for the planners, and they have rejected maximization of profits as a guiding principle for productive enterprises.

The method which is used in the preparation of the plans is the so-called "planning by material balances"—a crude input-output process expressed mainly in physical terms.

Because of the enormous practical difficulty of considering all interrelationships within the economy, the planners' approach has, until now, been to concentrate on certain key branches of material production which are selected by the Party leaders as the priority branches. The whole plan is built around output goals and investment projects in these key branches. The other branches of the economy are developed only to the extent which is required in order to achieve the main goals. This approach was recommended by Lenin who called it the principle of "decisive links." It simplifies planning and makes sure that the most important goals are achieved. Whenever their implementation requires more resources than have been planned for, the low-priority sectors are sacrificed. At the same time when plans were fulfilled, or even over-fulfilled in heavy industry, such branches of the economy as agriculture, housing and light industry were seldom able to fulfil their plans, although these plans were usually less ambitious than those for the high-priority branches of the economy.

tendency toward shortages

The Soviet economy is often referred to as "a war economy" because of this concentration on a few major goals, breaking of successive bottlenecks, general scarcity and the mobilization of all efforts and resources irrespective of costs. Just as it happens during a war in any country, decisions of central authorities in respect of major goals and corresponding resources allocation are decisive throughout the whole economy.

This type of economic system is well adapted to achieve the selected goals but it cannot usually secure economic efficiency. In other words, it can solve the problem of "what to produce" in accordance with the planners' scale of preferences but it is not completely successful in solving the problem of "how to produce" the required product mix.

4

As it is impossible for the central planning office to specify all details concerning the desired assortment and methods of production, a certain number of decisions have to be left to the management of the productive enterprises.

The manager's first duty is to maximize gross value of output and also to fulfil other tasks specified by the plan, such as, for example, reduction of costs,

increase in labour productivity and others There is a whole system of material incentives, the purpose of which is to induce enterprises to conform to the plan.

Piece rates and bonuses are used to induce greater efforts by workers. For the achievement of planned tasks and, above all, for the fulfillment of output plans, managers receive bonuses which form a considerable proportion of their total incomes. In addition to material incentives there are a number of non-economic incentives and administrative pressures.

Evaluating the effects of the existing system of incentives, [Professor J. S.] Berliner [in his study of informal organization of the Soviet firm] concludes that it "has created a corps of managers dedicated to their work and responsive to the production demands made upon them" by the planners, but that at the same time certain features of the system are "directly responsible for motivating management to make a variety of decisions contrary to the intent and the interest of the state."

Together with excessively high targets and general full employment conditions, the system induces some undesirable changes in the product mix (for example, when the target is expressed in tons there is a tendency to produce a heavier product), the concealment of the real productive capacity of enterprises (to make the fulfilment of high targets easier), and the falsification of reports and the deterioration of quality.

The system, as it exists now, tends to encourage the largest possible output but it does not provide a sufficient inducement to ensure the most efficient ways of producing this output.

The system also induces waste of raw materials. When, for example, the enterprises producing a variety of products have their plan targets expressed in value terms, the incentive system works in such a way as to induce the use of more expensive materials as the cost, plus a fixed margin of planned profit, will add up to a higher price in this case and will automatically increase the value of production thus helping fulfil the plan.

The communist leaders are now aware of the problem and economists are discussing the ways in which the system could be made more efficient. At least some economists are sceptical whether any solution other than introduction of the principle of profitability will give the required results.

Although some serious mistakes have been made in the field of investment planning, the importance of the inefficiency of the system should not be overestimated. The Soviet economy has not been fully efficient but it works and it has been able to produce very high rates of growth. One can only speculate that with improved efficiency these rates would have been even greater.

5

The problem of "for whom the economy produces" is again solved mainly by leaders' decisions in accordance with what they believe is in the interest of the nation and partly by market forces, operating within certain limits.

The distribution of income among the members of the industrial labour force depends on the wage scale, which is sharply differentiated in accordance with a relative scarcity of a particular skill, the importance of an industry (the high priority industries have higher wage scales than the low priority industries) and the geographical area (higher wages are paid in remote areas).

In agriculture, workers employed by the state farms receive wages based on the same principle as industrial wages, while members of collective farms receive their remuneration in accordance with the nature of the work, which determines the allocation of the "trudodni" (work days).

Although the general level of wages and the wage differentials are determined by the central authorities, a certain flexibility exists in practice.

Under the 1940 decrees unauthorized leaving of a job, as well as absenteeism or lateness were treated as criminal offences punishable by imprisonment, forced labour or fines. These decrees were not, however, applied in practice after 1953 and they were cancelled in 1956. At present the labour market is free in the sense that people can move to enterprises which offer higher wages. There is a penalty, however, if someone leaves his job and does not take another one within a month. Labour does not have the right to strike or to collective bargaining for wage increases.

The market forces operate in reality in a stronger way than it would appear on the basis of the study of existing regulations. In various ways managers are able to compete for better workers or scarce skills by offering higher wages than the official rates. This is often done by reclassifying upward a particular worker or by manipulation with bonuses and piece-work arrangements. There exists, therefore, a discrepancy between official and actual rates.

The labour market is, however, highly imperfect. There is usually only very limited knowledge of existing openings elsewhere. Geographical mobility is limited by housing shortages, the rigid system of housing allocation and by administrative restrictions imposed on moving to some areas. In addition, moving is complicated by the fact that usually more than one member of the family is working.

As a result of the imperfections of the market, workers with exactly the same skill have different wage rates in different industries, different geographical areas or even within the same industry and within the same area.

6

Summarizing, we may say that the decisions of the central authorities determine, to a considerable extent, the solution of what? how? and for whom? These decisions are mainly enforced by direct controls, but market forces are also utilized in some areas to strengthen these orders or, sometimes, to replace them. In some cases market forces act, however, against the wish of the planners and create undesirable results.

On the whole the Soviet-type economy can solve the problem of "what to produce" rather well in the sense that it secures the priority of the production of producers' goods and high rates of growth. It makes possible the concentration of huge resources on some selected goals and, in general, the required composition of output is produced, although some distortions of the product mix of both consumption and producers' goods tend to occur.

The solution of the problem of "how to produce" seems to be much less satisfactory. The system involves considerable waste and inefficiency, some of which will, no doubt, be eliminated in the future with a further improvement in planning methods, decentralization of economic administration and introduction of a better system of material incentives.

The problem of "for whom the system produces" is solved well in the sense that the state can secure for investment, communal consumption, public administration and defence a very high proportion of national income. It does not seem to secure to labour, however, that part of the value of the total product which labour contributes and it does not always secure equal pay for equal skill and equal effort. □

Fallenbuchl's article was written in the mid-1960s; since that time, there is evidence that Soviet concern for a more efficient economic organization has increased. As Russia's economy has matured, even her rapid rate of growth has become threatened by the kind of organizational difficulties we have been discussing.

An interesting consequence of this concern has been a willingness to experiment—still cautiously and incompletely—with what might heretofore have been considered capitalistic devices. A few years ago several Soviet economists, especially E. G. Liberman, began to recommend the greater use of prices and markets and the criterion of profitability in the management of Soviet industry. In July 1965, two clothing factories in Gorki and Moscow adopted a version of the Liberman system and soon reported substantial increases in both output and profits. In 1966 and 1967 the system was further extended, and by 1971, some 80 percent of industrial enterprises in Russia, producing over 90 percent of her industrial output, had been officially converted to the new system.

The degree of these changes, and their chances for success, should probably not be overstated. Profitability remains only one of several performance criteria for Russian managers. Furthermore, although the profit criterion can lead to efficiency when properly used, it can hardly do so when profits for enterprises are calculated on the basis of "prices" that are largely arbitrary and do not reflect underlying scarcities. In fact, under these circumstances, the profit criterion can actually do harm. Thus, it is by no means clear that a little decentralization plus a little "capitalism" will necessarily improve the functioning of a largely centralized command economy. It may cause problems of its own, providing strong arguments to the recentralizers who would like to take back even the limited reforms already introduced.[3]

Although the fate of the price mechanism in Russia cannot be fully foreseen, the above comments do raise interesting questions about how far an economy can go in introducing market elements into a system where the State owns the basic tools of production and wishes to influence important national objectives, as for example the distribution of income. To put it another way: Is it in fact possible to have *market socialism?*

MARKET SOCIALISM IN THEORY

In theory, the answer is yes, as was shown by the Polish economist Oskar Lange in an important essay written in the 1930s.[4] Indeed, market socialism is often called *Lange-type socialism.*

---

3.   George R. Feiwel makes this point (in *The Soviet Quest for Economic Efficiency, Issues, Controversies, and Reforms,* Expanded and Updated Edition, Praeger Publishers, New York, 1972), although his final conclusion is that "in the long run, the reform enthusiasts will be vindicated" (p. 555).

4.   Oskar Lange. "On the Economic Theory of Socialism," originally published in the *Review of Economic Studies* 4, nos. 1 and 2 (October 1936 and February 1937).

Lange objected to many features of a private enterprise system—its inequitable distribution of income, its tendency to monopoly and unemployment, its failure to deal with cases where private and social interest do not coincide—but he was also, unlike some doctrinaire Marxists, fully aware of the efficiency of Adam Smith's "invisible hand." Decentralized decision-making through the market does get many tough economic jobs done. Lange knew this and wanted to preserve as much of the market as he could.

What he worked out was a combination of command and market economies (or centralization and decentralization) along the following lines: The State will own the means of production of the society (land and capital), except that labor will continue to control its own services and will be free to offer these services on the market for wages. The wages of labor will not, however, constitute the full incomes of labor, because the State will be actively involved in subsidizing laborers in order to maintain a more equal (or otherwise more socially desirable) distribution of income. Consumers will be free to spend their incomes on consumer goods as they choose, but the State will largely determine the proportion of society's income devoted to the accumulation of capital. Business firms will produce and sell goods on the market, except that they will be instructed to behave as they would under conditions of pure competition. In effect, business managers are to *pretend* that they are in a market economy.[5] Finally, supply and demand will be equated in the labor market, so that there will be no problem of mass unemployment.

A simplified circular flow diagram showing how such a system of market socialism might work is depicted in Figure 3–2. In the inner flow, we have the ordinary market for labor and consumers' goods, except that labor is receiving a subsidy from the State

in order to bring about a more desirable income distribution. In the outer flow, on the left side, the State is providing the firms of the economy with the services of State-owned capital and land to use in the production process. On the right side, the State determines the rate of capital accumulation for the economy by its orders of new capital goods from the producing firms.

Since there is an ordinary market only for consumers' goods and labor services, how are the "prices" of land and capital to be determined? Essentially, the process is this: The Central Planning Board sets certain prices for the factors of production. These are simply accounting prices, since they need not result in an equivalent flow of income between the State-owned firms and the State as factor owner. The managers of the firms, however, are instructed to use these prices just as they would use ordinary market prices in a private economy. If the price of a factor is originally set too high, this will be reflected in an excess supply of the factor; in the next period, an adjustment would be made by a trial-and-error lowering of the price. Conversely, the price would be adjusted upward if demand exceeded supply in the previous period. These trial-and-error adjustments of prices would be analogous to similar adjustments in a private market, and the final equilibrium—as in a market economy—would be where supply equaled demand.

The virtue of the Lange scheme and of its numerous variants was that they demonstrated the possibility of combining the market and planning in a reasonably coherent way. But, as in the theory of the market economy, which also looks quite admirable in its ideal form, many difficult questions arise when we attempt to apply the Lange theory to economic reality. Will income subsidies from the State affect the laborers' incentives to work? Will management be as efficient in the absence of opportunities for building up fortunes and amassing wealth? Should the State or the households or business firms decide how much of

---

5.   In particular, they would be instructed to obey certain rules to guarantee efficient production. Such rules—for example, that the price of a product should equal the additional cost of producing a unit of that product—are developed on pp. 497–500.

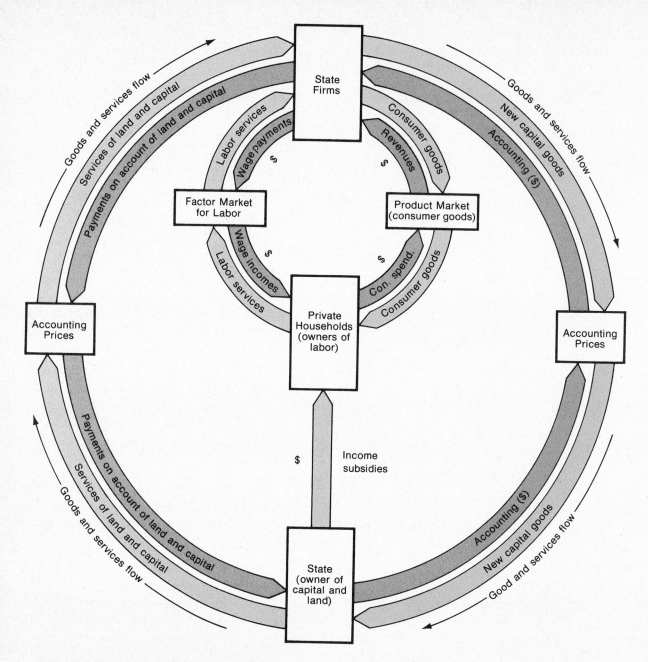

Figure 3–2. Simplified Circular Flow under "Market Socialism."

Under the Lange scheme, there would be an ordinary market for labor services and consumer goods, but the State would own the capital and land of the economy, would determine the rate of capital accumulation, and would pay subsidies to households to bring a "better" income distribution.

a society's income should be devoted to capital accumulation?

In short, has anyone ever actually tried to put market socialism into practice?

THE YUGOSLAV EXPERIMENT

The answer again is yes, although practice in economics never looks quite exactly like theory. Or, to put it another way, every example of economic practice has its own special features that are hard to disentangle from the general principles involved. Thus, it is often said that Yugoslavia is engaged in an experiment in market socialism, yet many elements in the Yugoslav economy are specific to her own situation.

Yugoslavia holds a particular interest for students of planning, because she began her postwar development with highly centralized planning along the lines of the Soviet model but then shifted to a decentralized socialism of the Lange variety. A relatively small country (population 18.5 million at the time of the 1961 census), Yugoslavia was basically underdeveloped before World War II, and she emerged from the conflict with considerable damage to such productive capacity as she possessed.[6] In 1947, she embarked on a Five-Year Plan aimed at fostering rapid development, especially industrial development. Planning was detailed, was weighted towards certain high-priority industries (electric power, steel, coal) and was complicated by an elaborate bureaucratic structure at the federal and regional levels. Prices and wages were arbitrarily fixed, "profitability" was largely irrelevant at the enterprise level, and efficiency considerations generally took a back seat.

This highly centralized approach was modified and then abandoned at the end of the first Five-Year Plan

in 1951. The political break with Stalin had already occurred in 1948. Moreover, although Soviet-style planning may have had its uses during the period of extreme economic difficulty immediately following the war, the defects of this approach soon became apparent. Plans drawn up for industrial enterprises were often unrealistic or inconsistent, necessary inputs were delivered late or not at all, consumer goods output fell far short of expectations, and agriculture "had a catalog of disasters all its own."[7]

Beginning in 1952, Yugoslavia embarked on a distinctive program of market socialism. This program involves considerable public ownership of industrial enterprises and some central planning—but also a heavy emphasis on the market as a means of relating the individual enterprise to the economy as a whole, with substantial worker participation in the actual management of the publicly owned enterprises. Briefly, there is private ownership in most of the agricultural sector (about 85 to 90 percent of arable land is in private hands) and in some small-scale trade outside of agriculture, but public ownership is dominant in the remainder of the Yugoslav economy. The publicly owned enterprises compete with each other in the marketplace, and their basic decisions about production techniques and output levels are guided by expected sales revenues in the market. Prices often vary according to supply and demand, although there have been periods of both increasing and decreasing price control since the dismantling of the centralized system in the early 1950s.

Although publicly owned, industrial enterprises in Yugoslavia have the rather unique feature of being subject to management by Workers' Councils. The Workers' Council is elected by the workers of an enterprise through direct and secret ballot. This council, in turn, elects a Managing Board that, together with a Director whose selection reflects both the workers' interests and those of the local government, is responsible for the management of the enterprise in question. Worker interest and participation

---

6.   Thus, in addition to a massive loss of human life (one person out of twelve of the population), Yugoslavia lost two-thirds of her prewar agricultural machinery and implements, 40 percent of her factories, and most of her transport capacity. See F. E. Ian Hamilton. *Yugoslavia* (New York: Frederick A. Praeger, 1968), p. 93.

7.   Thomas A. Marschak, "Centralized Versus Decentralized Resource Allocation: The Yugoslav 'Laboratory.' " *Quarterly Journal of Economics* 82, no. 4 (November 1968), 572.

are secured not only by this formal scheme but also by the fact that the incomes of the workers come from the net revenues or profits of the enterprise. The workers thus have a direct stake in the efficiency of the firm's operations, and they also have a say in determining what part of the firm's income shall be reinvested in the expansion of plant capacity.

This combination of market socialism and workers' management is evaluated in the following comments by Howard Wachtel, a sympathetic observer of participatory socialism.

Social Ownership and Markets in Yugoslavia

Howard M. Wachtel

The Yugoslav social system, a unique laboratory in which to study a functioning participatory socialist society, is dominated by two important general principles: *social ownership* and its accompanying workers' management, and *market socialism*.

SOCIAL OWNERSHIP AND WORKERS' MANAGEMENT

The Yugoslav system of social ownership and workers' management can be viewed as one in which labor employs capital, instead of a system in which capital employs labor, as is the case under capitalism. Property is *socially owned*, rather than privately owned or state-owned. Ownership rights are theoretically possessed by all the citizens, who delegate authority for managing the socially-owned property to autonomous enterprises and the representative

institutions of the employees of enterprises—the workers' councils and the management boards. From this system of enterprise management the term "workers' management" is derived.

A useful summary statement of the Yugoslav view of workers' management is provided by Branko Horvat:

"In an economy made up of self-governing bodies, the exercise of managerial functions is not the task of any social class of individuals, but of the collectivity of members of economic organizations. . . . Social evaluation and risk taking . . . are explicitly functions of the collective. Supervision is a two-directional process in which every member of the collective takes part. The remaining function, coordination, is purely technical and as such is left to technical experts, who are themselves members of the collective."*

Accompanying managerial decentralization are forms of political and social decentralization. Political decentralization is implemented by means of communal government, and social decentralization is accomplished via citizen participation and self-management in social institutions—schools, hospitals, and the like.

MARKET SOCIALISM

The second important principle guiding the Yugoslav social system is market socialism—the joining of social ownership of the means of production and markets to guide the allocation of resources in the economy. The use of markets to allocate resources at the micro level coexists with social ownership and the use of a planning mechanism to achieve macroeconomic objectives, making the Yugoslav economy the closest approximation extant to the classic model of a market-socialist economy developed by Oscar Lange in the 1930s.

The balance between the use of centralized controls and the use of markets to allocate resources

*Branko Horvat, *An Essay on Yugoslav Society* (White Plains: International Arts and Sciences Press, 1969), p. 97.

has gradually, but steadily, been tipped in the direction of markets. Since 1952, when workers' management was formally introduced into the economy, centralized controls have been gradually phased out as an important feature of the economy. Before 1952, Soviet-type central planning dominated economic affairs. The first five-year plan for the period 1947 to 1951 fixed detailed quantitative targets for about 600 groups of commodities. Even the quantity of goods and the number of passengers for each type of transportation was specified in the plan.

After 1952, Soviet-type central planning was replaced by a form of target planning. Annual plans were adopted affecting the rate of investment in the economy, a portion of the allocation of investment, the rate of development of different regions, and macro balance in the economy. No longer were detailed output targets given to enterprises; instead enterprises were given autonomy over most input and output decisions. For the most part, markets were used to allocate resources at the micro level. The reduced importance of planning was manifested in the size of the planning staff at the national level. The staff of the planning office in the early 1960s was one-third the size it had been when Soviet-type central planning was used. In addition to this general de-emphasis on national planning, there was also a strengthening of local and regional planning. Republics and local communities were permitted to write their own plans dealing with local and regional economic problems.

Since 1965, planning has played an even smaller role in the Yugoslav economy. Annual plans have been abolished and only medium-term and long-term plans are now adopted. These establish the broad lines of development for Yugoslav society—including long-run target rates of growth, major new investment projects, investment in social overhead, and so on. Increasingly, plans in Yugoslavia have taken on the character of forecasts.

SUMMARY COMMENTS

Societies embarking on radical social experiments invariably produce mixed results, with some of their objectives realized and others abrogated. Yugoslavia is no exception. In the tradition of participatory socialism, Yugoslavia sought to construct institutions of participatory socialism by granting workers substantial participation in enterprise decisions, and to create parallel institutions in the community by granting citizens substantial statutory power in the commune.

At the same time, faced with external military threat, with the traditional economic problems of growth and resource allocation, and with the problem of integrating the separate units of the economy, Yugoslavia first adopted central planning and then markets to organize the economy. Markets were introduced, replacing central planning, as the ideas of workers' management and the commune were introduced and strengthened. However, hierarchical divisions within society were not eliminated. Power is not shared equally within enterprises among different strata of labor. Those in the upper strata of the hierarchy have more influence over enterprise decisions. The fact that these distinctions flow from the division of labor inherent in industrial societies makes them only slightly more acceptable to a participatory socialist society than the class divisions based on ownership of a capitalist society or the status divisions within state capitalist societies of the Soviet type.

Commodity production with exchange on a market induces competition among enterprises and, most important for this experiment in participatory socialism, competition among workers employed in different enterprises. Experts and technicians ascend to power in the enterprise at the expense of blue-collar workers, and the studies of the distribution of power within Yugoslav enterprises confirm this. Enterprises begin to adopt familiar devices in their need to compete with other enterprises: advertising, product differentiation in form rather than substance, neglect of social costs, and the like. This does not mean that these negative consequences of commodity exchange are as intense in Yugoslavia as in Western capitalist societies; my observation is, they are not. However, we must not close our eyes to these consequences of markets and commodity production, while noting the accomplishments of Yugoslavia's brand of participatory socialism.

The evidence accumulated in this study is that markets have been "successfully" introduced into Yugoslavia. Whether one gloats over this finding or mourns it depends on the world view of the reader. The important point to note is that this development is not without its negative as well as positive consequences.

The principal contradiction faced by socialist societies is between the social character of ownership and production and the private individual character of rewards based on material incentives. As Wheelwright and McFarlane argue in their analysis of China, the principal contradiction is caused by the continued coexistence of motivation based on individual material advancement, operating within the framework of a collectivist ethos and institution. In such a contradiction something must eventually give way—either the motivation of individual advancement, or the collectivist ethos and institution.†

This is the basic challenge facing Yugoslavia and other societies attempting to build participatory socialist institutions.

This is not to deny the substantial accomplishments of Yugoslavia's form of participatory socialism. They have achieved a substantial rate of economic and social development and, at the same time, have strengthened the legal and institutional basis of workers' management. Although contradictions have been encountered between workers' management and commodity exchange on a market, the Yugoslavs have achieved more substantive industrial democracy than nearly all other countries in the world. Being the first country to embark on widespread workers'

participation, Yugoslavia could not avoid the growing pains associated with the erection of new institutions. Rome, as well as capitalism, was not built in a day, nor will workers' control be achieved in a day. Viewed in this light, Yugoslavia provides us with an important way-station along the road to the construction of participatory socialism. Partisans of participatory socialism can now study a living example and learn from its mistakes.
□

In the above article, Wachtel notes several potential contradictions in the Yugoslav experiment, most notably that between collective control of production and individual material incentives. There have been other difficulties as well: inflation, a tendency for the concentration of power in successful, large-scale enterprises (a socialist monopoly problem!), and imbalances and conflicts between the different regional and nationality groups in the country. Thus, despite the general success of her economic system, the future of market socialism in Yugoslavia, like the future of the Soviet reforms, remains quite unclear. A somewhat ominous sign in 1974 was a drift toward more emphasis on centralization and even orthodox communism in statements emanating from Yugoslavia. This has gone together with increasing Soviet closeness to Yugoslavia since 1971.[8]

In sum, we are dealing with an unfinished economic and social system in Yugoslavia. This is also true of Russia and, in fact, of the United States. Having seen the twists and turns of socialist experience, we shall examine in the next chapters some of the evolutionary features of our own *mixed* system.

---

†E. L. Wheelwright and Bruce McFarlane, *The Chinese Road to Socialism: Economics of the Cultural Revolution* (New York: Monthly Review Press, 1970), p. 149.

8. See, for example, Christopher S. Wren, "Soviet Hails Yugoslavia's Conservatism," *New York Times,* April 15, 1974.

SUMMARY

In analyzing the *centrally planned* or *command economy,* we naturally go back to Karl Marx, who gave the ideological backdrop for most of these economies in the modern world. Marx did not, however, provide a blueprint for economic planning; rather, he provided a detailed critique of capitalism—because of its class antagonisms between capital and labor, its monopolistic elements, and its inherent tendencies to depression and technological unemployment—and he developed an ideology that (when flexibly interpreted) could serve the purposes of Communist revolutions.

In practice, the pure command economy must make difficult economic decisions that often require elaborate institutional arrangements in the modern industrial world. The areas in which problems are likely to occur are: (1) organization of an adequate planning bureaucracy; (2) coordination of economic targets in a consistent manner; (3) making production efficient in the economic sense; (4) securing proper incentives for workers and managers; and ultimately (5) setting proper goals for the economy when consumer sovereignty no longer provides the guidelines.

A near-approximation to the command economy has been the Soviet Union, whose economic experience over the past half-century gives us our best case study of how the command mechanism works. Although the Soviet economy has demonstrated a high rate of growth (as we shall discuss later), her economy has shown many elements of inefficiency in the areas mentioned above. In recent years, Russia has, in fact, been experimenting with the introduction of certain market elements in her economic system. This raises the question of whether a mixture of centralization and decentralization along the lines of *market socialism* is a possible compromise approach.

Economic theory (as, for example, in the works of Oskar Lange) suggests that such a compromise is feasible, with the State owning the means of production and making certain decisions, but with many economic choices being left to the market. Practical experience in Yugoslavia in a specific version of market socialism (including, among other things, active Workers' Councils) tends to support the conclusion that such mixtures can work at least reasonably well.

IMPORTANT TERMS TO REMEMBER

Command Economy
Central Planning
Marxian Class Conflict
Monopoly Capitalism
Communism
Capital Goods/Consumer Goods
Problems of Planning:
   Organization, Coordination,
   Efficiency, Incentives,
   Basic Goals
Market Socialism
Accounting Prices
Workers' Councils (Yugoslavia)

QUESTIONS FOR DISCUSSION

1. Marx predicted an increasing class conflict between capitalists and the proletariat as the capitalistic system approached maturity. How well does this prediction stand up in the case of the United States, as judged by your general knowledge of American history? What economic factors may have moderated any tendency toward class conflict in this country?

2. Marxian economics, in a technical sense, is based on what is sometimes called the *labor theory of value.* This theory states that the prices of different commodities are proportional to the quantities of labor involved in producing those commodities. This theory is generally believed to be inadequate because it neglects the fact that there are different *qualities* of labor and also the fact that there are *other* factors of production besides labor (e.g., land and capital goods). Remembering your general supply-and-demand analysis from chapter 2, show how:

(a) a country with a shortage of cultivable land might generally expect higher food prices than a country where land was abundant.

(b) a sudden influx of highly skilled surgeons from abroad might lower the price of medical services.

3. In a pure command economy, what takes the place of a market economy's "consumer sovereignty"?

4. "The main problem with a command economy is that it has no way of providing incentives to its labor force and managers to work effectively and well." Discuss critically.

5. According to Fallenbuchl, the Soviet central planners have been able to allow some consumer choice while retaining control of many key production decisions. How has this been possible?

6. The Russian Revolution is often attributed in part to the fact that the Russian economy was relatively "backward" in the early twentieth century. Communism also has an appeal for a number of economically "backward" countries today. What factors do you imagine may have created this appeal for such countries? List what you would consider to be possible advantages and disadvantages of a highly centralized economic system for an economically backward nation.

7. Yugoslavia is a very different country from the United States in both size and stage of economic development. To what degree do you think her experience with market socialism is relevant to this country? (Incidentally, do you think that Workers' Councils might be a solution to the problem of "alienation"?)

SUGGESTED READING

Aboucher, Alan. "Transportation in Yugoslavia," *Challenge,* Vol. 16, No. 5 (November–December 1973).

Bergson, Abram. *Planning and Productivity under Soviet Socialism.* New York: Columbia University Press, 1968.

Campbell, Robert W. *Soviet Economic Power.* 2nd ed. Boston: Houghton-Mifflin Co., 1966.

Feiwel, George R. *The Soviet Quest for Economic Efficiency: Issues, Controversies and Reforms.* New York: Praeger, 1972.

Grossman, Gregory. *Economic Systems.* 3rd ed. Englewood Cliffs, N.J.: Prentice-Hall, 1974.

Marx, Karl. *Capital.* 3 vols. Chicago: Charles Kerr & Co., 1906–1909.

Schumpeter, Joseph A. *Capitalism, Socialism and Democracy.* 3rd ed. New York: Harper & Row, 1950, part I.

Sweezy, Paul M. *The Theory of Capitalist Development.* New York: Oxford University Press, 1942.

CHAPTER 4
THE MIXED AMERICAN ECONOMY: PUBLIC SECTOR

It should be clear from our discussion of socialism in the last chapter that the pure form of command economy does not exist. In the Soviet Union, market elements have always played some role and have done so increasingly in recent years. Furthermore, there has been a growing interest in market socialism, as the experience of Yugoslavia and other Eastern European economies suggests. Of course, we know that the pure market economy does not exist, either. These pure forms are simply the extremes on a scale that runs from highly centralized planning at one end to highly decentralized private decision-making at the other. Every planned economy uses the market mechanism to some degree; every market economy involves certain areas of government intervention and control.

All of which is to say that the *mixed economy* is the characteristic form of economic organization in the modern industrial world. This is an economy in which both public and private decision-making have a significant effect on the direction and well-being of the society, where economic planning is often practiced by the large private as well as by the public enterprise, where, in general, the interaction among government, business, and labor is constant and complex.

Of course, the proportions of the mix may vary considerably, and this is a matter of importance. Still, the old-fashioned view that put market economies on one side and planned economies on the other and said, "Choose one or the other, not both!" is simply inaccurate. Most modern countries *have* chosen both—but in different degrees.

For this reason, we shall devote the next two chapters to a study of the mixed economy. In this chapter we shall concentrate on the governmental or public part of the mix; in the next, on the private sector. We shall use the United States economy as our example throughout this discussion, because we are familiar with it and because of its enormous importance in the world economy generally.

GROWTH OF GOVERNMENT
IN THE UNITED STATES

It is often said that governmental activity has been growing rapidly in this country in recent years. Has it? If so, how rapidly, and in what ways?

One way of estimating the growth of the public sector in the American economy is to take all governmental expenditures—federal, state and local—lump them together, and see how they have expanded over time. In Table 4–1, we have done this for selected years since 1929, and these data have been plotted in Figure 4–1. In this graph, the top line represents the sum of all governmental expenditures in the United States from 1929 to 1973. This chart is drawn on a semilogarithmic scale, meaning that a straight line would represent a constant percentage increase. The strong upward drift of the curve makes it clear that the public sector has been expanding substantially in the United States—from about $10 billion total in 1929 to well over $400 billion at the present time.

To understand the extent of this expansion, however, it is necessary to inspect these figures a bit more closely. In the first place, they are in "current dollars," meaning that they reflect the upward drift of prices over this period as well as the increase in real or physical purchases by government. Both consumer and wholesale prices went up more than two-and-a-half times between 1929 and 1973.

Second, we should notice that recent years have seen a particularly rapid expansion of state and local expenditures. People often have a tendency to think of government intervention in the economy only in terms of "big government"—the federal government. But after a period of relative stagnation from 1929 until the end of World War II, state and local expenditures have been expanding very rapidly, from $9 billion in 1945 to $184 billion in 1970. One of the reasons (though not the only reason) for this expansion is the large role state and local governments play in education: More than one-third of all state and local expenditures go to schools and universities. An expansion of government of this sort is worth

TABLE 4–1

TOTAL, FEDERAL, STATE AND LOCAL
EXPENDITURES, SELECTED YEARS
(billions of current dollars)

YEAR	TOTAL GOVERNMENT EXPENDITURES	FEDERAL GOVERNMENT EXPENDITURES	STATE AND LOCAL GOVERNMENT EXPENDITURES
1929	10.3	2.6	7.8
1933	10.7	4.0	7.2
1939	17.6	8.9	9.6
1941	28.8	20.5	9.1
1945	92.7	84.6	9.0
1949	59.1	41.3	20.0
1953	101.2	77.0	27.0
1957	114.9	79.6	39.5
1961	149.0	102.1	54.1
1965	186.9	123.5	74.5
1969	287.9	189.2	119.0
1973	407.4	264.7	183.8

Total Government Expenditures increased 40 times between 1929 and 1973. Note that the sum of Federal and State and Local Expenditures is greater than Total Government Expenditures, the reason being that Federal grants-in-aid to State and Local governments ($41.2 billion in 1973) are reflected in both subcategories. The duplication is removed in the overall figures.

noticing, for it does not represent a new kind of government "interference" in the economy but is simply an expansion of an area long considered properly to be within the public sector.

A third point to make about these figures is that they include at least two fundamentally different kinds of governmental expenditures. In addition to ordinary government expenditures on goods and services,[1]

1. Sometimes called *exhaustive expenditures* by economists. It should be noted that these exhaustive expenditures include both direct governmental production (i.e., services of policemen and teachers) and also government purchases of goods (typewriters, buildings, etc.) from the private sector.

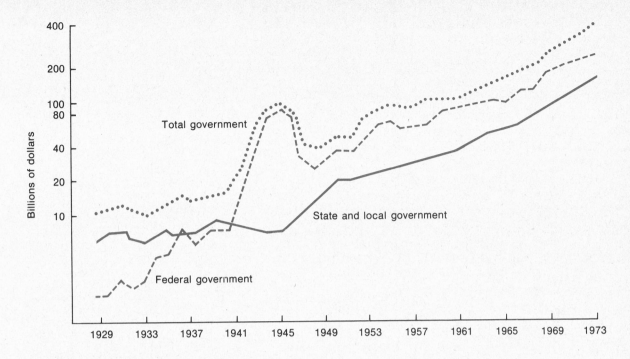

Figure 4–1. Total, Federal, and State and Local Government Expenditures.
Source: Economic Reports of the President, 1966, 1973.

they also include *transfer payments*. The difference is important. In the case of an ordinary government expenditure, the government pays a clerk for his services in the Defense Department or buys a truck or other commodity from a private firm; payment is for a service rendered or goods delivered. A *transfer payment*, however, involves neither a good delivered nor a service rendered. In a typical form it simply represents a transfer of purchasing power from a taxpayer to a recipient. Social security payments are transfer payments. So are payments for unemployment compensation. So also are some of the payments made to farmers under various agricultural programs. In each case, the key fact is that the

government does not produce goods itself nor does it direct private production into certain channels by its orders for goods. Elderly couples on social security do not have to provide any services to the government, and they are free to spend their money in such ways as they see fit.

In our present discussion, the relevance of this distinction derives from two considerations: (1) although transfer payments necessarily involve a degree of government intervention in the economy, the degree is somewhat less than that of ordinary government expenditures, which represent a claim of the government on the nation's output of goods and services; and (2) transfer payments have grown very rapidly in recent decades, increasing as a percentage of total governmental expenditures. Actually, this

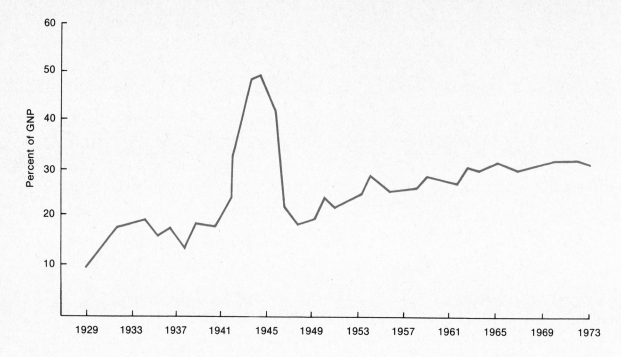

Figure 4–2. Total Government Expenditures as a Percentage of GNP, 1929–1973.

growth of transfer payments represents some important new functions of government in the American economy. But it also means that our figures on the expansion of government in Table 4–1 and Figure 4–1 may somewhat overstate the increasing impact of government on the economy during this period.

Finally, and perhaps most significantly, we should notice that while governmental activity has been growing over the past three or four decades, so also has the nation's economy as a whole. What we are interested in most directly is not governmental expenditures in isolation, but those expenditures in relation to the nation's total output of goods and services. Figure 4–2 represents the total of federal, state, and local expenditures expressed as a per-

centage of the U.S. gross national product.[2] Now this diagram makes it clear that in an all-important *relative* sense, the growth of government in the American economy is somewhat less dramatic than one might have expected. Indeed, the striking thing about the curve is not so much the growth of government in recent years—though the percentage has been increasing—but rather the extraordinary levels of expenditure reached during World War II. In 1943 and 1944, governmental expenditures were roughly *half* our total national output! There was a sharp

2. Gross national product is a common measure of a country's total output of goods and services. We shall discuss its precise definition in detail in chapter 8, pp. 190–95. The reader should note that transfer payments do not represent an addition of goods and services output and would not be included in gross national product.

cutback immediately after the war, then a gradual upward drift that has continued since that time. Overall, when transfer payments as well as ordinary expenditures are included, the general trend has definitely been upward—from 15 to 20 percent of GNP in the 1930s to about one-third of GNP at the present time—but it is less drastic in this relative sense than the absolute figures suggest.

Of course, governmental expenditures are only *one* of a number of possible indicators of the role of the government in the economy as a whole. Actually, many functions of government may affect the private sector very intimately and yet not show up in these particular figures. For example, the Justice Department attempts to enforce various antitrust laws with respect to American business. In terms of national output percentages, the expenditure side of antitrust enforcement is trivial, but antitrust policy is a very important sphere in which the government is engaged in giving shape to the market economy. A similar situation exists with the many other regulatory functions of government and with legislation such as the Wagner Act or the Taft-Hartley Act, which affect labor unions. Whether they are in the form of enforcing pure food and drug legislation or regulating airlines or requiring safety features on our automobiles, there are countless examples of government participation in the economy that do not show up in our expenditure graphs.

There is no way to quantify these manifold activities, although a rough generalization would be that they show very much the same picture that has emerged from our expenditure diagrams. That is, there has been a gradual expansion of regulatory and other activities from the 1930s to the 1970s. As with expenditures, these other activities reached a great height in World War II when there were price and rent controls, rationing of goods, and a general mobilization of the economy for war. After the war there was a relaxation of controls, and then, as with total governmental expenditures, there was a gradual, but still significant, increase from the prewar period.

CAUSES OF THE EXPANSION OF GOVERNMENT

Some of the forces behind the expansion of the public sector have quite clearly been of an economic nature; others derive more from political considerations, particularly those of international politics. An important example of a factor that seems to stem largely from political causes is the growth of defense expenditures in the American economy since the pre-World War I era. Defense, space, and foreign affairs currently account for more than $80 billion annually, or about a third of total federal budget expenditures.

Thus, the biggest single item of federal government expense is largely noneconomic in origin. Furthermore, it represents no new function of government. This last, as we have already noted, can also be said about most of our increasing expenditures on schools. In 1971–72 state and local expenditures for education were running at $65 billion a year, or nearly 40 percent of total state and local expenditures. A very great part of the modern expansion of government in America, therefore, has either resulted from noneconomic factors or has been in the traditional areas of governmental responsibility, or both. (Adam Smith, we recall, charged the State with the responsibility for defense and with certain duties with respect to public education.)

However, there has also been an expansion of government activity into relatively new areas of our common life, and for what are largely economic reasons. During recent years this expansion has been even more rapid than in education and far more than in defense (which has been declining percentage-wise.[3]) Through an increase in the role of the public sector, these activities attempt to correct deficiencies (or, more accurately, what the majority of Americans regard as deficiencies) in the workings of a market economy.

---

3. Although still huge by the standard of the 1930s, U.S. defense expenditures actually declined by 2.4 percent as a percent of GNP from 1955 to 1970.

A listing of these new programs would be very long. But certain general areas of concern stand out. One is the broad area of *income distribution*.

Private market forces operate efficiently with respect to many economic problems, but they often leave certain groups in the society without adequate protection. Elderly people, the disadvantaged, the uneducated, minority groups, the ill or the infirm—such individuals or groups will ordinarily receive a very small share of the nation's total output, and yet their economic needs may be as great as, or often greater than, their more fortunate neighbors. A great many of the government's welfare programs, ranging from the initial social security enactments of the 1930s to Medicare and Medicaid in the 1970s, have been designed to meet these needs. Not all transfer payments go from rich to poor, but many do, under these new welfare programs, and they consequently represent a redistribution of national income in favor of the needy.

Other broad areas of concern are unemployment and inflation, or, more generally still, the problem of stabilizing the economy in the aggregate and promoting its growth.

Ever since the 1930s, economists and, increasingly, public officials have recognized that an unregulated market mechanism does not ordinarily guarantee a full-employment economy with stable prices. We shall be studying this problem in much more detail in Part Two of this book, showing some of the underlying forces that bring about general unemployment and price inflation in a modern industrial economy. Suffice it to say here that many governmental actions in the past thirty years have been designed to cope with this problem. Part of the Social Security Act of 1937 set up a system of unemployment compensation. More recently, the government has been using its formidable fiscal and monetary policies to stabilize the economy in the aggregate. The tax cut of 1964 was aimed primarily at reducing unemployment and

speeding up economic growth. The stringent "tight money" policy of the Federal Reserve Board in 1966 was designed to combat inflation, as were the wage-price freeze of 1971 and the wage-price controls of 1972–73. Even with active governmental intervention, these problems are not easy to handle, but it is now widely agreed that they do form an appropriate area for governmental concern.

Another general field for government action has been in *providing certain goods or services that are valuable to society as a whole,* but are not likely to be produced by private market forces, or at least not in sufficient quantities.

Some goods are naturally collective as opposed to private, since it is difficult to withhold them from any citizen even if he doesn't pay for them. (For example, national defense shelters us all even if we do not pay a cent toward its cost.) But there are also many cases in which the marketplace will undervalue the actual social benefits to be derived from a particular act of production. A good example of this kind of problem is the construction of a dam. As a private party, I may build a dam on a river and find that a great many of the benefits of the dam go to other firms farther downstream. Now the dam may not be profitable for me to build, because although I must bear all the costs, I receive only part of the benefits. Yet if the government were to build the dam, the total benefits to society might be greater than the total costs. There are also important cases where there are significant social costs for which private parties are not charged—air pollution from private factories or private motorists is a notable example. Whenever there is a divergence between the private and social benefits or costs of an economic undertaking, there is a prima-facie case for governmental intervention.

We could list a number of other items that have influenced the expansion of the role of the American government in recent decades. Rather than going on, however, let us take three particular questions of government policy, trying to illustrate in this way the complexity of the interaction between the public and private sectors in our mixed economy.

ENVIRONMENTAL PROTECTION

A MACROECONOMIC EXAMPLE—
MONETARY POLICY

Our first example of government intervention has to do with stabilizing the economy as a whole. Economists often divide their field into two broad areas: *macroeconomics* (the study of the economy in the aggregate) and *microeconomics* (the study of the parts of the economy and their interrelationship). This breakdown will be discussed in detail later; for the moment, we simply note that our first example is in the area of macroeconomics, and it is a very important example: *monetary policy*.

Monetary policy is concerned with money, with credit and banks, and with how these features of the economy affect its tendency towards inflation or recession. It is a controversial field, for although the subject of money has been studied longer than any other aspect of economics, the mechanisms by which money affects our overall economic health are still not fully agreed upon.

What Is Money?

The first (but not necessarily the easiest) question is: What is money? Many different commodities have served in this capacity in different cultures and times, including paper, gold, other metals, cattle, shells, and beads. In an article written just after World War II, a British economist described the elaborate use of cigarettes as a currency in a prisoner of war camp.[4] Economists often distinguish a number of important functions that money serves: (1) a *measure of value* (prices are quoted in money); (2) a *medium of exchange* (money is acceptable for exchanges against all types of different commodities); and (3) a *store of value* (savings may be kept in the form of money for future purchases). In the POW camp, cigarettes

---

4. R. A. Radford, "The Economic Organization of a P.O.W. Camp," *Economica,* Vol. XII (1945), reprinted in Paul A. Samuelson, ed., *Readings in Economics,* 6th ed. (New York: McGraw-Hill, 1970), pp. 40–48.

served all these functions—prices, for example, were generally quoted in terms of cigarettes rather than in terms of particular commodities that might be bartered against each other. But cigarettes also suffered from some difficulties in serving as money. For one thing, like gold coins in the hands of a deceitful sovereign, they could be "clipped" or, more likely, "sweated by rolling them between the fingers so that tobacco fell out." More serious was the fact that they were a very desirable commodity in their own right. Radford notes that when Red Cross packages (the main source of the supply of cigarettes) failed to arrive, the smokers were likely to take over the nation's money supply:

Consequently our economy was repeatedly subject to deflation and to periods of monetary stringency. While the Red Cross issue of fifty or twenty-five cigarettes per man per week came in regularly, and while there were fair stocks held, the cigarette currency suited its purpose admirably. But when the issue was interrupted, stocks soon ran out, prices fell, trading declined in volume and became increasingly a matter of barter. This deflationary tendency was periodically offset by the sudden injection of new currency. Several hundred thousand cigarettes might arrive in the space of a fortnight. Prices soared, and then began to fall, slowly at first but with increasing rapidity as stocks ran out, until the next big delivery. Most of our economic troubles could be attributed to this fundamental instability.

The point of these comments about cigarettes is that, while almost any commodity *can* serve as money, not all commodities can serve money's functions equally well. In the old days, gold and other metals were valued as money because they had some useful value of their own and were also durable and relatively easily divisible. In the American economy of today, although the dollar retains a vague (but vanishing) connection to gold, we no longer use gold as a medium of exchange within our domestic economy, nor for that matter is currency in the form of coins *or* bills the main source of our "money." For this, we have to go to our banking system.

The Banking System

Most money in the American economy today is not in the form of currency but in the form of bank deposits. There are various kinds of bank deposits (and various definitions of money, which will be presented in chapter 11), but for our immediate purposes the most important are *demand deposits*. These are simply our ordinary checking accounts, which are subject to withdrawal on demand. They are regularly acceptable in exchange for goods and services and in payment of debts, and they fulfill the functions of money that we have just listed. These demand deposits are not only "money" but are, in fact, our most important form of money. In December 1973, of a total U.S. money supply of $270.4 billion, currency in the hands of the public accounted for only $61.6 billion, while demand deposits in commercial banks accounted for $208.8 billion, or 77 percent.

Students sometimes feel that their checking accounts are not really the equivalent of money, because occasionally personal checks (say, in a strange town) are not accepted as money, whereas cash would be. However, reflection should convince us that what is being doubted here is not the value of the demand deposit behind the check but whether such a demand deposit does, in fact, exist. Doubts about accepting a check disappear, once it is certain that "the money is in the bank to back it up"; i.e., that the person presenting the check had the necessary demand deposit in his name.

It is true that the bank must occasionally redeem demand deposits in currency. But the central fact about modern banking—and the fact that makes modern monetary policy possible—is that the bank does not need to back up its demand deposits with an equivalent amount of cash and currency (or gold or silver or whatever) but only with a fraction of that amount. We operate on a system of *fractional-reserve banking*. Withdrawals and deposits generally tend to cancel each other. Only a relatively small fraction of demand deposits needs to be kept on hand to meet excesses of withdrawals over deposits at any given time. In point of fact, the main reserves that commercial banks hold today are those that they are legally required to hold. (These are in addition to the so-called vault cash that is necessary to meet the ups and downs of withdrawals and deposits.)

And here we come to the crux of the issue as far as government intervention is concerned. For it is by influencing commercial bank reserves that the government—through the Federal Reserve System—operates its monetary policy. The main lines through which these governmental influences are exerted are outlined in the following reading.

Function of the Federal Reserve System

On December 23, 1913, President Woodrow Wilson signed the Federal Reserve Act establishing the Federal Reserve System. Its original purposes, as expressed by its founders, were to give the country an elastic currency, to provide facilities for discounting commercial paper, and to improve the supervision of banking.

From the outset, there was recognition that these original purposes were in fact parts of broader objectives, namely, to help counteract inflationary and deflationary movements, and to share in creating conditions favorable to a sustained, high level of employment, a stable dollar, growth of the country, and a rising level of consumption. Acceptance of the broader objectives has widened over the years.

Over the years, too, the public has come to recognize that these domestic objectives are related to the country's ability to keep its flow of payments with foreign countries in reasonable balance over time. Today it is generally understood that the primary

Excerpted from U.S. Board of Governors, Federal Reserve System, *Federal Reserve System—Purposes and Functions*, 5th ed., 5th printing, October 1969, Washington, D.C., pp. 1, 2, 8–13, 128, 129.

"fractional-reserve banking"

purpose of the System is to foster growth at high levels of employment, with a stable dollar in the domestic economy and with over-all balance in our international payments.

How is the Federal Reserve System related to production, employment, the standard of living, and our international payments position? The answer is that the Federal Reserve, through its influence on credit and money, affects indirectly every phase of American enterprise and commerce and every person in the United States.

HOW THE FEDERAL RESERVE INFLUENCES CREDIT AND MONEY

Practically all of the money that people use reaches them, directly or indirectly, through banks. They may receive their pay in cash, but the employer who pays them will have cashed a check at a bank or may have borrowed from a bank before making up his payroll. Therefore, the flow of money in the country depends greatly on the ability of commercial banks to make loans and investments.

The ability of commercial banks to extend credit and provide cash-balance and payment services to the people depends on the amount of reserve funds the banks have. This amount is directly affected by Federal Reserve operations. Banks can extend credit to customers or invest money in securities only in proportion to the reserves at their disposal. The reserve position of banks affects directly the willingness of banks to extend credit and the cost, or rate of interest, that borrowers from banks have to pay to obtain it.

As banks extend credit by exchanging bank deposits for the various assets they acquire—promissory notes of businesses and consumers, mortgages on real estate, and Government and other securities—they create demand deposits. These deposits can in turn be used to make payments by check or can be withdrawn for use in the form of currency. Ultimately, they may find their way into banks' time and savings deposits if the public prefers to save

in that form. In any event, by affecting the volume of reserves available to member banks, the Federal Reserve has the power to influence the country's over-all credit situation and its money supply.

While the Federal Reserve directly influences the availability and cost of bank credit and thereby affects the total flow of credit, a great variety of other forces also affect the flow of credit in the economy. These include, among others, governmental policies in regard to expenditures, taxes, and debt; the distribution of income among different groups of the population and the allocation of income between current consumption and saving; the bargaining strength and policies of management, labor, agriculture, and other sectors of the economy; the course of foreign trade and foreign investment; the prospects for peace or war; and the expectations of businesses and consumers as to future economic changes, including price changes.

Thus, the Federal Reserve alone cannot assure favorable economic conditions. Nor can it direct whether bank credit, or any other type of credit, shall flow into particular channels. But it can affect the general flow of bank credit and money as economic conditions change and thus help to counteract instability resulting from other forces. The crucial question for the Federal Reserve is how much expansion in bank credit and money it should encourage in view of current and prospective developments in the domestic economy and in our balance of payments.

HOW CHANGES IN CREDIT AND MONEY AFFECT PEOPLE

In a dynamic and growing economy, enough credit and money is that amount which will help to maintain high and steadily rising levels of production, employment, incomes, and consumption and to foster a stable value for the dollar. When credit, including bank credit, becomes excessively hard to get and costs too much, factories and stores may curtail operations and lay off employees. Smaller payrolls mean hardship for workers, who curtail their purchases; merchants feel the decline in trade and reduce their orders for goods. Manufacturers in turn find it necessary to lay off more workers. A serious depression, unemployment, and distress may follow.

Inflationary boom vs. depression & unemployment

When credit is excessively abundant and cheap, the reverse of these developments—an inflationary boom— may develop. An increase in the volume and flow of money resulting from an increase in the supply and availability of credit, coupled with a lowering of its cost, cannot in itself add to the country's output. If consumers have or can borrow so much money that they try to buy more goods than can be produced by plants running at capacity, this spending only bids up prices and makes the same amount of goods cost more. If merchants and others try to increase their stocks so as to profit by the rise in prices, they bid up prices further. Manufacturers may try to expand their plants in order to produce more. If so, they bid up interest rates, wages, and prices of materials. In the end they raise their own costs.

The nation as a whole does not profit from conditions of price inflation. At some point the upward spiral will break, perhaps because prices of finished goods get so high that ultimate consumers, even though many of them receive higher wages, can no longer buy the goods produced. Then a downward spiral will develop. The more values have risen because of inflation, the more abruptly and lower they are likely to fall and the greater will be the associated unemployment and distress.

FEDERAL RESERVE MONETARY POLICIES

The posture of Federal Reserve monetary policy at any moment—whether restrictive or expansive—is a reaction to prevailing economic conditions. Monetary policy functions restrictively when inflationary tendencies are present. In other circumstances it functions expansively or assumes a posture somewhere between stimulation and restraint. To help avoid the dangers of economic downturn, reserve banking works to prevent speculative or otherwise unsustainable expansion of bank credit.

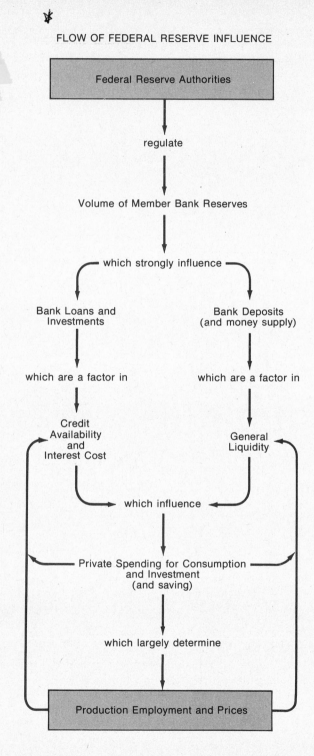

FLOW OF FEDERAL RESERVE INFLUENCE

Federal Reserve Authorities

regulate

Volume of Member Bank Reserves

which strongly influence

Bank Loans and Investments | Bank Deposits (and money supply)

which are a factor in | which are a factor in

Credit Availability and Interest Cost | General Liquidity

which influence

Private Spending for Consumption and Investment (and saving)

which largely determine

Production Employment and Prices

The diagram on the opposite page shows in a simplified way how actions taken by the Federal Reserve System influence total spending and thereby contribute to the ultimate objectives of high employment, maximum production, and stable prices.

The Federal Reserve carries out its responsibility for the public interest by influencing the reserves of member banks. As the diagram shows, that is where the initial impact of reserve banking policy falls. As banks respond to changes in the availability of reserve funds by altering their lending and investment policies, reserve banking comes to influence the supply of money, the availability of credit, and the cost of money in various credit markets.

Some observers stress the influence of reserve banking in terms of its effects on the money supply, others emphasize the impact of changes in the availability and cost of credit, and still others stress its effects on over-all liquidity. In the functioning of the economy each of these modes of influence has a role, and each must be taken into account. □

As the last paragraph of the above reading suggests, there is some disagreement about the way in which Federal Reserve actions on the money supply actually affect the economy. We shall be taking up this question in great detail later on,[5] as we shall also be taking up the specific mechanisms by which the Federal Reserve influences member-bank reserves.

What is not subject to much disagreement, however, is that the Federal Reserve does have important powers in the monetary field and, more significantly, that the government has an overall responsibility for stabilizing prices, production, and employment in the American economy. The full recognition of this responsibility, which has basically developed since World War II, is one of the many factors that have contributed to an expanded role of government in our economy in the past quarter-century.

---

5. See chapters 11 and 13, and especially Great Debate Two on Monetarism, pp. 311–38.

A MICROECONOMIC EXAMPLE— GOVERNMENT AND AGRICULTURE

Our second example of government intervention is more microeconomic in nature, dealing with a specific sector of the economy—agriculture. The main economic purpose of this public intervention has been to correct an income distribution that is felt to be unfair to the American farmer.

U.S. agriculture is a good example of some of the paradoxes of a mixed economy. In many respects, the agricultural sector is the closest approximation to a purely competitive market economy that our country has. Although farms have been decreasing in number and increasing in average size, in 1974 there was still a huge number of farms—2.8 million —and their average size was still small—385 acres. In general, the conditions for "responding" to an impersonal market seem to be met.

Yet for many decades the United States government has been active in this area of our economy. Until World War II, virtually all agricultural research was sponsored by the Department of Agriculture and other federal and state agencies.[6] Furthermore, the government has been involved in a whole series of programs—including price support, acreage limitation, crop storage, international disposal, and domestic food stamp distribution—that have crucially affected farm prices and farm incomes.

A brief review of the history of public agricultural programs as well as their state in 1974 is presented in the following reading.

---

6. In the past two decades, the leadership in agricultural research in the United States has passed to private parties and especially to the new "agribusiness corporations." This is an interesting reversal of what often seems the more usual trend from private to public enterprise.

Agricultural Policy: Different Now?

G. E. Brandow

On approximately the fortieth anniversary of the initiation of large-scale farm programs by Franklin Roosevelt's New Deal, Congress passed the Agriculture and Consumer Protection Act of 1973, to be effective through 1977. For decades, frequent revisions of farm legislation had been enacted against a backdrop of crop surpluses and farmer dissatisfaction with prices and incomes. But circumstances were different in 1973: surpluses were gone, prices were soaring, and net farm income had risen by half in two years.

A LITTLE HISTORY

Farm programs have been intended primarily to support farm income. The principal cause of the farm income problem since World War II has been rapid technological advance, which has created chronic surpluses and has displaced 50 to 60 percent of family and hired workers from agriculture in the past twenty-five years.

Current programs for rice, tobacco, and peanuts are the remnants of what was once standard policy. Prices were supported at high levels, acreage of individual crops was controlled to restrict production, and export subsidies of one kind or another often were used to find foreign markets. For feed grains, wheat, and cotton, which together occupy half the harvested cropland, the old policy proved unworkable, and was gradually replaced by a different set of devices.

Price supports for the three crops (counting the four feed grains—corn, barley, oats, and grain sorghums—as one) were reduced to the point where only a small subsidy was needed to export wheat and none was needed to export feed grains and cotton. Land diverted from production of the crops

was completely idled to prevent shifting surpluses to other crops. Farmers were much opposed to compulsory controls of this kind, so payments were offered to induce farmers to withdraw land. To get farmers to accede to lower price supports for wheat and cotton, payments on the crops were made higher than necessary to compensate for withdrawing acreage. Acreage controls tied to feed grains and cotton indirectly restrained production of soybeans, another leading crop.

This set of programs was first put together for the three crops by the Food and Agriculture Act of 1965, during a Democratic Administration. It had few unreserved admirers and many vocal critics. But it enabled production to be kept roughly in line with market outlets, it supported farm income, it promoted expansion of foreign markets, and prices were low enough to be more or less acceptable to consumers. Despite the high cost to the government—about $5 billion annually for all farm programs—the policy counteracted opposing pressures well enough to be politically workable.

The policy was continued without major alteration by the Agricultural Act of 1970, passed in a Republican Administration. One change was a response to criticism of large payments going to huge farms whose owners had little appeal as beneficiaries of public largesse: limits, though high ones, were put on payments one producer might receive.

Prices of meat animals, poultry, and eggs have been supported so little as hardly to count. Prices of these commodities, however, have been much affected by prices of feed grains, and thus by feed grain programs. Dairy prices have been supported by government purchases of manufactured dairy products and by marketing orders for fresh milk.

Food aid for less developed countries, initiated in 1954 under Public Law 480, was once an important outlet for farm surpluses, but was reduced in scope after 1966. The stamp program to give food aid to poor families in this country was much expanded at the beginning of the 1970s (ironically, virtually over the dead bodies of some farm-based politicians).

Excerpted from G. E. Brandow, "Agricultural Policy: Different Now?" *Challenge,* March–April 1974, pp. 54–55. Reprinted with permission from *Challenge* the Magazine of Economic Affairs.

THE 1973 ACT

The 1973 Act represents a further evolutionary step in which direct payments have a somewhat revised role. Three levels of prices must now be distinguished for feed grains, wheat, and cotton. First are support prices, which are floors the government is to maintain under markets. Support prices may be varied by the Secretary of Agriculture; the lower limits (which apply in 1974) are about where market prices were before inflation accelerated two years ago. Second are target prices, which for wheat and cotton are about 50 percent higher than the 1974 support prices, and for feed grains, about 25 percent higher. Target prices are used only to calculate payments to farmers. Third are actual market prices, which can vary upward from support levels. Market prices were well above target prices as 1973 ended.

Payments on the three crops are to be made to eligible farmers in any season when the market price is less than the target price. The payment rate per bushel or per pound is the difference between the two prices. The total payment on a farmer's crop is computed by multiplying the payment rate by the farmer's normal production on his acreage allotment. Eligible farmers are those who have allotments and who comply with certain requirements (principally, taking acreage out of production if requested).

Acreage allotments tie into the supply situation for each crop. The national allotment is the acreage determined by the Secretary to be necessary to produce enough for prospective domestic consumption and exports, adjusted for any needed changes in stocks. A farmer's acreage allotment is his historic share of the national allotment. The farm allotment is used to compute payments when payments are made and to determine how much land to withhold when production is to be restrained.

The maximum payment one farmer may receive has been much reduced from the amounts provided by the 1970 Act. Now no farmer may receive more than $20,000 for the three crops collectively.

How the new Act will operate will depend on circumstances and on decisions made by the Secretary of Agriculture. If the nation is so fortunate as to have significant excess farm capacity once again, presumably the Secretary will keep price supports near the lower limits, will avoid overproduction by requiring land withdrawal as a condition for payments, and will rely mainly on payments to support farm income.

If, in contrast, farm production capacity proves deficient and market prices are generally above target prices, no curbs on production will be in force (the situation in 1974). Target prices will be important mainly as insurance for farmers against large price declines in the future. Such insurance should encourage the investment required to increase output.

In the intermediate situation in which free market prices are below target prices but above minimum support prices, the Secretary will have a choice of several feasible combinations of price support, payments, and land withdrawal. Probably the limitation on payments to large producers will mildly but not critically impair the production control capability of the programs.

Rice, tobacco, and peanut programs are not included in the 1973 Act and remain about as they were except for a few administrative changes. Revisions of the dairy program are unlikely to be of much practical significance. P. L. 480 is extended, the food stamp plan is made more flexible and more obligatory upon localities, and a modest program for conservation of land for nonfarm purposes is provided.

THE ACT AS POLICY

The Act falls short of providing the true food and agriculture policy that the nation needs. Such a policy would be not a detailed blueprint for the future, but a coordinated set of strategies for dealing with circumstances that might develop. Latent inconsistencies such as those between farm and international trade policies would be resolved. The policy would not necessarily call for a substantial role for government, but would provide government action where it was the best way to achieve a desired objective.

The 1973 Act does supply many of the tools required for such a policy. The Act can stimulate production of farm products if needed or can be used to control surpluses and support farm income if excess capacity emerges. If supply conditions permit, prices can encourage exports, and food aid can be given to less developed countries. Food needs of the poorest families are at least partially met. □

The passage of the Agriculture and Consumer Protection Act of 1973, discussed in the above reading, makes it clear that government intervention in American agriculture will continue even though there have been some rather basic changes in the economic position of farmers in recent years. In 1972 and 1973 the United States found itself facing shortages rather than surpluses of many agricultural products, largely because of increased exports. Some of these exports were increased because of special factors—the low level of world grain harvests in 1972, the large grain sales to the Soviet Union in 1972–73, the growing China market. But in general, because of the growth of population and income in Europe, Japan, and the U.S.S.R., a higher level of agricultural exports may become a permanent feature of the American agricultural scene.

Whether the next few years bring shortages or surpluses, however, the government will continue to be involved in some form of price and quantity regulation in the agricultural sector. The supply and demand curves developed in chapter 2 can help us enormously in trying to understand how the various forms of possible government policy work. Take, for example, one of the simplest programs that has been used to raise farm incomes: reduction of crop acreage to restrict production. This is a policy that could be (and has been) used in a period of crop surpluses. There is too great a supply in relation to demand; therefore, farmers are told to cut back acreage and production, and the surplus is reduced or removed.

It might seem that supply and demand curves are unnecessary for understanding a policy as straightforward as crop restriction in a time of surplus. Remember, however, that the function of such a policy is not simply to reduce surpluses but also to raise farm incomes. How can we be sure that a reduction of output will raise the revenues going to farmers? The smaller crop will undoubtedly bring a higher price per unit, but the number of units sold will be less. Will the net effect raise or lower farmers' incomes?

This way of putting the question brings us to the concept of price-elasticity of demand, discussed on

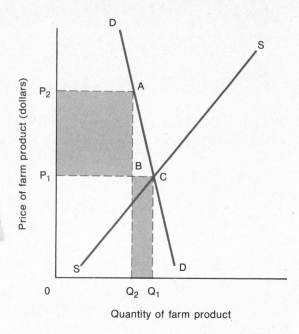

Figure 4–3. Crop Reduction and Farm Income.

This figure illustrates how a reduction of farm output (from OQ_1 to OQ_2) can raise total revenue for farmers. The reason is that the demand curve is inelastic, hence, rectangle $P_1 P_2$ AB is larger than rectangle $Q_1 Q_2$ BC.

pp. 37–40. Figure 4–3 makes it clear how a crop reduction program can raise farmers' incomes. Most farm products tend to have rather inelastic demand curves—i.e., people will be willing to pay fairly high prices rather than make major cuts in their consumption of these particular commodities. Thus, when a crop reduction program cuts farm production from OQ_1 to OQ_2, the result is a very substantial rise in price above the market-determined level (OP_1). Because the demand curve is inelastic, the gains in income (upper shaded rectangle), will be greater than the losses in income (lower shaded rectangle).

Supply and demand curves are even more necessary in analyzing complicated programs such as the

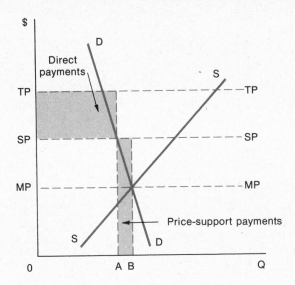

Figure 4–4. Two Components of the 1973 Act.

This figure illustrates two of the main features of the 1973 Agriculture and Consumers Protection Act: (1) price supports—if *MP* is below *SP,* the government supports the price by buying *AB* of the crop; and (2) direct-income payments—the government pays farmers the difference between *TP* and *SP* or *MP* (whichever is higher) in direct income payments.

Figure 4–4 is a simplified illustration of a situation where the market price (*MP*) is below both the support price (*SP*) and the target price (*TP*). The government raises the price to its support level by purchasing *AB* of the product from farmers and adding this quantity to government-held stocks of the commodity. However, the gap between the support price and the target price must be coped with. The upper shaded rectangle shows how much the government would pay in direct payments to farmers, and the lower shaded rectangle is what would be paid to them in price-support payments. The consumer, incidentally, will be buying the product at the support (*SP*) level, and not at the original market price (*MP*) level.

In 1973/74, a year of shortages rather than surpluses, the prices of most farm products were above the target price (*TP*) level; consequently, government intervention through price supports and direct payments declined. What the 1973 Act does make clear is that, in principle, American agriculture will continue to be a *mixed* public-private sector of the economy for many years to come. At a minimum, target prices are a government-sponsored insurance program for farmers; at a maximum, they could involve renewed and substantial government expenditures as in the past.

INTERGOVERNMENTAL RELATIONS— REVENUE-SHARING

In the two previous examples, we have been considering the role of government in relation to the private sector of our mixed economy. In our third and final example of public sector activities, we shall now mention a problem of relations among branches of government *within* that sector. In the early 1970s, intergovernmental relations have become one of the more controversial matters in the American political-economic arena.

We have already spoken of the great expansion of governmental expenditures at the state and local levels. An important part of these increased expenditures has been in education, as we know. In the first instance because of the postwar "baby boom," and continuing because of the desire for increased edu-

1973 Act described in the reading. Two of the components of this act are illustrated in Figure 4–4. The 1973 Act distinguishes three levels of prices: target prices, support prices, and actual market prices. When market prices are below the level of support prices, the government will raise prices by purchasing commodities from the farmers. This is the *price-support* feature of the act. But there is also a *direct-income-payment* component. The government, subject to various complications, will pay farmers the difference between the support price and the target price (when the market price is *below* the support price), or the difference between the market price and target price (when the market price is *above* the support price).

cation at all levels of our society, educational expenditures by state and local governments have increased ninefold in the past twenty years. But other expenses have also been increasing. In 1946, state and local governments were spending less than $1.5 billion on public welfare; twenty-five years later, the figure was over $20 billion. General expenses for health, hospitals, police, fire protection, and the dozens of other state and municipal services each citizen expects as a matter of natural right rose similarly during this same period. In the early 1970s, state and local governments were spending considerably more on nondefense expenditures than was the federal government.

At the same time, the federal government was becoming increasingly involved with state and local governments through various categorical grants. From 1950 to 1973, federal grants-in-aid to state and local governments rose from $2.3 billion to $41.2 billion. This increase caused serious questioning of the proper relationship of the federal government to the state and local governments in economic matters. How much centralization should there be? How much decentralization? Who should raise the money? Who should decide how it should be spent?

For a variety of reasons, *general revenue-sharing* seemed to many commentators to be an important part of the answer to the increasing tangle of intergovernmental relations. The idea behind general revenue-sharing is that the federal government should use its taxing powers to raise the revenues but that some part of these revenues is then fed back to state and local governments, more or less without strings, to spend on their own projects. In the following reading, authors from the Brookings Institute in Washington analyze a number of the rationales that have been used to justify revenue-sharing, concluding with a suggestion as to how this program might be designed to aid areas with heavy concentrations of poor families.

General Revenue Sharing

Edward R. Fried, Alice M. Rivlin, Charles L. Schultze, and Nancy H. Teeters

Few major domestic initiatives have received broader bipartisan support than the federal government's initial foray into the revenue sharing strategy—the State and Local Fiscal Assistance Act of 1972. Evidently the prospect of "less red tape" had great appeal. Furthermore, revenue sharing was seen as a way of getting at certain problems that lay beyond the established federal strategies. Various proponents hoped for various results. Some viewed revenue sharing as the solution for general fiscal problems confronting state and local governments. Others welcomed revenue sharing as a means of reducing the direct involvement of the federal government in domestic problems. Still others hoped that revenue sharing would redistribute resources among states and localities so as to enable the poorer ones to raise the level of public services they provided.

BROAD OBJECTIVES

During the years leading up to enactment, the major rationale given for pursuing a revenue sharing strategy was that it offered an all-purpose means of overcoming a number of very different general fiscal problems afflicting state and local governments. Although short-run economic conditions have changed considerably since the initial years, revenue sharing is still seen in part as a vehicle for fiscal reform.

Solving Fiscal Problems

A task force established by President Johnson in 1964 first proposed revenue sharing as a method of alleviating what was then seen as a growing fiscal imbalance in the federal system. In their judgment,

Excerpted with permission from Edward R. Fried et al., *Setting National Priorities: The 1974 Budget* (Washington, D. C.: The Brookings Institution), pp. 266–279, 287–298. © 1973 by the Brookings Institution, Washington, D. C. Reprinted by permission of the publisher.

the resources needed by states and localities to provide adequately the public services for which these units had traditionally been responsible were likely to grow more rapidly than the ability of these governments to raise revenues. At the same time, with continued economic prosperity, the progressive nature of the federal tax system would generate revenues at a pace far faster than that needed to maintain and even expand existing federal programs. A surplus, or ''fiscal dividend'' as it was called, would develop, which, unless disposed of, could become a drag on the nation's economy.

The fiscal dividend, however, was devoured first by the expanding war in Southeast Asia and then by a combination of federal tax cuts and growth in domestic federal spending.

By 1970 it became clear that the problem of fiscal drag had at least temporarily disappeared. But at about the same time the fiscal problem of state and local governments appeared to be getting worse. Many observers became convinced that the tax base on which state and local governments depended for their revenues was not expanding fast enough to furnish those governments with the revenue needed to meet their responsibilities. They were being asked not only to finance growth in their traditional programs but also to find funds to pay their share of the costs of new federal initiatives. Revenue sharing then attracted new attention as a potential means of providing the additional revenues. President Nixon expressed this view when first unveiling his general revenue sharing program in the 1971 State of the Union Message: ''All across America today, States and cities are confronted with a financial crisis. . . . Most are caught between the prospects of bankruptcy on the one hand and adding to an already crushing tax burden on the other.''

In retrospect, the fears of spreading municipal bankruptcy, chronic state budget deficits, and continuing program cutbacks were exaggerated. The fiscal tribulation of states and localities during the 1970 to 1972 period stemmed largely from the cyclical downturn in the economy. The recession increased the demand for state and local services.

Rising unemployment forced many onto the welfare rolls, and falling incomes caused more citizens to shun expensive private services in favor of their cheaper public counterparts, such as municipal hospitals and public colleges. While the demand for state and local services was increased by the recession, the downturn in the economy also undercut the revenues of these governments. During this three-year period, the revenues of state and local governments fell about $11 billion below what they would have been had the economy been running at full employment. To compensate for this increased demand and revenue shortfall, states and localities were forced to raise their tax rates and impose new taxes. Between 1969 and 1971 state sales taxes were enacted or raised twenty times, state personal income taxes were raised thirty times, and corporation income taxes went up thirty-six times.

As the economy began to pick up in 1972, the general fiscal crisis that many had predicted as the chronic condition of state and local governments began to abate. While the aggregate figures on state and local budgets published by the Department of Commerce are an inadequate measure of the fiscal health of these governments, the data for fiscal 1972, which revealed an aggregate general government surplus of $3.7 billion, made it clear that a dramatic change had taken place. By the year's end, almost one-third of the state governments expected to end their fiscal years with substantial surpluses—California $850 million, New York $75 million, Arkansas $100 million, Florida $300 million, and so on. A few large cities were rumored to have modest surpluses also.

Projections of the aggregate fiscal outlook for the next decade suggest that the cyclical crisis of the past three years did not foreshadow a long-run imbalance. Rather, the balance that appeared in 1972 should continue for some years. If the relative size of existing federal grant programs is maintained and an expanding economy leads to relatively full employment, states and localities *in the aggregate* should be able to maintain and improve the public services they now provide. On balance, the case for an expanded revenue sharing strategy cannot rest on a projected overall shortage of state and local revenues to meet the growth in existing programs.

An alternative fiscal rationale for general revenue sharing has recently emerged—to provide relief to state and local taxpayers. In his statement accompanying the signing of the general revenue sharing bill in Philadelphia in 1972, President Nixon put tax relief at the top of the list of possible effects of the new program: "In many States and localities, it will mean lower property taxes or lower sales taxes or lower income taxes than would otherwise have been the case. Revenue sharing can provide desperately needed tax relief for millions of Americans."

Compared with the growth of federal taxes, the increase in state and local revenues has been substantial: between 1960 and 1972 these receipts more than trebled. As a fraction of personal income, state and local taxes went up by a third. The political cost of this increase, however, was considerable. A widespread revolt against property tax increases manifested itself in the rejection of school budgets and bond issues; governors who had supported raising sales and income taxes were defeated in their bids for reelection almost without exception. Relieving the "crushing burden" of state and local taxes thus engendered a good deal of public support. The fiscal rationale for revenue sharing had not necessarily weakened, but it had shifted considerably since the mid-1960s—from a tool for providing increased public services to a method of providing tax relief at the state and local level.

Redistributing Income and Resources

In addition to its fiscal objectives, revenue sharing has been seen as a means of affecting the distribution of income and public services. Two different kinds of redistribution are involved: (1) a redistribution of income among individuals through a shift in the kind of taxes they pay and (2) a redistribution of public services so as to favor poorer states and local governments.

One kind of redistribution has to do with the tax system. Despite its numerous loopholes and special preferences, the federal tax system, which would raise the money needed for revenue sharing, is slightly progressive—the higher a taxpayer's income, the greater the share taken by federal taxes. State and local taxes, on the other hand, are generally regressive or at best proportional—the poor pay the same or possibly a higher share of their income in state and local taxes than do the rich. To the extent that revenue sharing substitutes federal for state and local taxes as a way of financing state and local services, the total tax system becomes somewhat more progressive, relieving some of the tax burden for lower-income groups and increasing it for upper-income groups. Redistribution would be greatest if the federal income tax were increased to pay for revenue sharing, balanced by an equal decrease in the less progressive of state and local taxes, especially sales levies.

Another possible redistributional objective involves the way in which shared funds are distributed among state and local units of government. States and localities differ tremendously both in their ability to raise revenues and in their needs for public services. Per capita income, which offers a crude measure of a jurisdiction's ability to raise revenues, varies widely among the states—the lowest (Mississippi) is about half the highest (New York). The disparities that exist within any one state are even greater; wealthy suburbs often have five or ten times the per capita tax base of poorer communities only a few miles away. Thus to generate an equivalent level of per capita spending on public services, poor jurisdictions would have to impose much higher tax rates than rich ones. This disparity is further complicated by the fact that equal spending may not guarantee equivalent levels of public services because the needs for and costs of such services vary tremendously from state to state or from community to community. Most often the areas with the greatest needs are those that are least able to raise necessary revenue.

Revenue sharing is intended to moderate the variation that now exists in state and local tax rates and public service levels. To the extent that revenue sharing displaces the federal grant-in-aid programs that now allot a disproportionate share of their funds to poorer or needier jurisdictions, its redistributive effect will be muted. It is worth noting that the redistributive goal of revenue sharing can be thwarted if states and localities use the receipts to reduce their most progressive taxes or spend their grants on programs and projects that disproportionately benefit their wealthiest citizens.

Decentralizing Power

A third broad objective that has been advocated for revenue sharing is decentralization. According to this view, revenue sharing is needed to restructure—or revitalize—the federal system. Supposedly the proliferation and expansion during the past decade of federal programs, particularly the categorical grants, has shifted too much of the decision making about public programs to Washington. There are three different, though related, aspects of this argument—the problem of power, the problem of effectiveness, and the problem of priorities.

In the view of the administration, federal bureaucrats and lawmakers make decisions that would best be left to state and local officials. Judgments about the details of local programs—where facilities are located, the specific kinds of services to be provided, who is eligible and who is not—are made in Washington rather than in the communities themselves and by the elected officials close to the problems. Though conceding that some programs must be national in scope and directed by the federal government, this view holds that the balance has shifted too far in that direction. Feeling that they have little say about their government, citizens have become frustrated, alienated, and cynical. A revenue sharing strategy, it is argued, will remedy the situation by shifting decision-making power and budgetary control back to states and localities, which are pictured as more attuned to local needs, more responsive to local pressure, and better able to deal with the actual problems of individual communities.

The second aspect of this rationale for revenue sharing deals with the related problem of program effectiveness and efficiency. No matter how capable the federal government is of administering any particular grant program effectively, the proliferation of categorical grants over the past ten years has enmeshed it so deeply in trying to control the delivery of hundreds of individual programs at the local level that it has become tied up in red tape and confusion.

Finally there is the problem of priorities. General revenue sharing is not simply an alternative means of accomplishing the same goals as other federal programs. It emphasizes different objectives. Depending on precisely how it is designed, it might result in some reduction of state and local taxes, some increase in the general level of services typically provided by state and local governments, and some narrowing of fiscal disparities among those governments, so that they can provide more nearly comparable services. Categorical grants and other federal domestic programs have different goals. They aim at delivering the kinds of public services that most states and localities, left to their own devices, would not provide at all or provide at a lower level, even with the additional revenues available. Hence, the emphasis given to revenue sharing over other strategies—particularly categorical grants—must depend not merely on judgments about the distribution of decision-making power in a federal system and the relative efficiency with which public services are delivered, but also on judgments about what combination of national goals it is important to pursue in a total federal budget that necessarily commands limited resources.

EXPANDING THE PROGRAM

In future federal budget strategies, revenue sharing is easily expandable. An expansion of general revenue sharing could be designed to focus on the peculiar problems of jurisdictions containing large concentrations of low-income families. In general, low-income families require more in the way of traditional public services as well as expensive, specialized services. For example, for equivalent levels of safety, cleanliness, and educational attainment, more would have to be spent in a slum than in a typical suburb for police protection, sanitation, and schools—not to

TABLE A

DISTRIBUTION OF $5 BILLION OF GENERAL REVENUE SHARING GRANTS UNDER A
COMPENSATORY PUBLIC SERVICE FORMULA, SELECTED STATES

STATE	TOTAL GRANT (millions of dollars)	GRANT PER CAPITA (dollars)	GRANT PER POOR PERSON (dollars)
States with largest per capita grants			
Mississippi	111.1	50	145
Louisiana	162.1	44	174
Alaska	12.9	43	363
New Mexico	42.3	42	186
District of Columbia	27.6	37	224
Median state			
Nevada	11.7	24	268
States with lowest per capita grants			
Indiana	85.7	17	174
New Jersey	114.1	16	199
Ohio	166.3	16	160
Connecticut	44.1	15	208
New Hampshire	10.3	14	158

Source: Authors' estimates, based on the formula described in the text.

mention the added resources needed for day care, welfare, drug treatment and health clinics, and public recreation facilities. The added burden that poor families place on public services is compounded by their inability to contribute appreciably to the support of these services through taxes. Middle- and upper-income residents of jurisdictions with large numbers of poor people, therefore, bear the cost of supporting the public services required by those who are unable to pay. Faced with the situation, middle- and upper-income families have tended to segregate themselves in exclusive suburban jurisdictions. Zoning and building requirements have been imposed to exclude those who would be a fiscal drain on the community.

A revenue sharing program that compensated states and localities for the cost of providing public services for their low-income residents would alleviate this problem. The amount any jurisdiction received would be equivalent to some fraction of that government's per capita expenditures (financed from its own resources) on public services, multiplied by its number of low-income residents. Such a program would concentrate money in central cities and rural areas. Wealthy suburbs would receive little if anything from such a grant, except as they began to admit low-income residents in larger numbers than they now do. Presumably a compensatory public service revenue sharing program would reduce the reluctance of suburbs to accept low-income housing and would thereby help break up the concentrations of persons with excessive public service needs in a few jurisdictions.

The cost of such a program and its precise distribution among various jurisdictions would depend on two characteristics: the definition of "low-income" residents and the fraction of per capita expenditures reimbursed under the grant formula. Table A shows the distribution of funds under a program making grants to any jurisdiction equal to one-third of its per capita expenditures times the number of residents whose incomes were below the poverty line (using 1970 census data for the calculation).* The total cost to the federal government would be $5 billion. The program could be made more or less generous by changing both the fraction of expenditures covered and the definition of low income. Each 10-percent-age-point change in the fraction of per capita expenditures covered would change program costs by about $1.5 billion.   □

---

*How such a program would distribute money within a state can be shown by what might happen, for instance, in New Jersey. The problem-ridden city of Newark would receive roughly $23 per capita, relatively wealthy neighboring Bergen County would receive only $5 per capita, and the relatively poor rural Cumberland County would receive about $10 per capita.

SUMMARY

The characteristic form of the modern economy is the *mixed economy* in which both government and the marketplace have important roles, though in different degrees in different countries.

In the United States, the public sector has grown substantially in the past three or four decades, though not so dramatically as is sometimes imagined. Total expenditures of governments at all levels have grown from about 15 to 20 percent of GNP in the 1930s to over 30 percent in the early 1970s. The growth in recent years has been particularly rapid in state and local expenditures, and in governmental transfer payments.

Much of this expansion is caused by political and other noneconomic forces, and it represents no particularly new areas of government responsibility (e.g.,

defense, schools, etc.), but there has also been a growth of the role of government in the economy for economic reasons as well. These reasons involve concern for (1) welfare of the needy and income redistribution; (2) stabilization and growth of the economy in the aggregate; and (3) provision of collective goods and other goods where private and social benefits or costs diverge.

The complicated role of the public sector in a mixed economy can be illustrated by several examples from the modern American economy. An example from the macroeconomic sphere is *monetary policy* as practiced in the United States by the Federal Reserve System. Most of the money in the present-day American economy is in the form of demand deposits, and Federal Reserve authorities can influence the volume of money and interest rates in the economy by actions affecting the reserves held by member banks. Such actions by the Fed are part of the government's responsibility to secure stability in the economy as a whole—of its trying (not always successfully) to achieve high employment and low inflation.

An example from the microeconomic sphere is United States *agricultural policy.* In the agricultural sector of the American economy many of the conditions of a market economy are fulfilled (many producers, much competition), yet the government has been highly active for many years in agricultural research and development as well as in acreage-restriction and price-support programs. These programs—continuing even in the period of shortages during the early 1970s—can usefully be analyzed in terms of the basic supply-and-demand apparatus.

Finally, the problem of *revenue-sharing* indicates that the complications of a mixed economy are not limited to the relations of the government to the private sector—they also occur in the relations among governments *within* the public sector. For fiscal reasons, but also to promote a redistribution of income and decentralization of power in the United States, the sharing of federal revenues with state and local governments is now an important feature of our economic system.

IMPORTANT TERMS TO REMEMBER

Mixed Economy
Public Sector
Transfer Payments
Money
Monetary Policy
Federal Reserve System
Demand Deposits
Agricultural Crop and Acreage Controls
Price Supports
Direct Income Payments
Revenue-Sharing
Decentralization of Government

QUESTIONS FOR DISCUSSION

1. Although government expenditure figures give an important indication of the degree of government intervention in the economy, they are not the only measure of government activity. What are some other forms that public intervention may take? Give some specific examples from the experience of the United States or of other modern mixed economies.

2. What are transfer payments? Why have governmental transfer payments been growing rapidly in recent years?

3. Show how in the case of industrial air and water pollution there may be a significant divergence between private interest and the social welfare. Does this have any relation to arguments for or against public intervention in these areas?

4. A government can, in principle, increase the money supply by printing more currency. Is this the way monetary policy is customarily handled in the United States? Explain your answer.

5. Suppose that we have a farm product with a relatively inelastic demand curve and a perfectly inelastic vertical supply curve as follows:

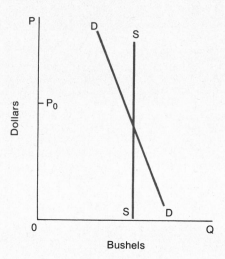

The government has two (politically feasible) alternatives:

(a) Support the price at P_0 by buying up all the product that consumers will not buy at that price.

(b) Guarantee the farmers the same total revenue as under the price support program, but do this by direct subsidy after the farmers have sold their entire crop to the public at the supply-and-demand-determined price.

Which program will cost the government more money?
Can you see any possible advantages to the more expensive program?

6. Considering the major economic problems facing the United States in the 1970s, do you consider it likely that there will be (a) further growth in federal government expenditures; (b) further growth in state and local expenditures; or (c) resurgence of private initiatives? Try to think of at least one example that might lead to expansion in each of these spheres.

SUGGESTED READING

Beckhart, Benjamin Haggott. *Federal Reserve System.* New York: Columbia University Press, 1972, chaps. 18–19.

Eckstein, Otto. *Public Finance,* 3rd ed. Englewood Cliffs, N.J.: Prentice-Hall, 1973, chaps. 1–3.

Hathaway, Dale E. *Government and Agriculture.* New York: Macmillan Co., 1963.

Levy, Michael, and DeTorres, Jean. *Federal Revenue-Sharing with the States: Problems and Promises.* Washington: National Industrial Conference Board, 1970.

Phelps, Edmund S. *Private Wants and Public Needs.* New York: W. W. Norton & Co., 1964.

Shonfield, Andrew. *Modern Capitalism.* New York: Oxford University Press, 1965, chaps. 5–10, 13–14.

CHAPTER 5

THE MIXED AMERICAN ECONOMY: PRIVATE SECTOR

Despite the growth of government in the American economy, described in the last chapter, our mixed economy remains heavily oriented to the private side. Although government expenditures amount to something over 30 percent of our gross national product, private expenditures amount to nearly 70 percent. Furthermore, many government expenditures are for the products of private industry. Thus, although government orders may determine the direction of certain areas of production, and although, as in the military-industrial complex, the distinction between government and industry becomes blurred, the organization of production in the United States nevertheless remains overwhelmingly in private hands. In this chapter, we shall look at some of the characteristic institutions of the private sector, attempting also to show some of the ways in which this and the public sector interact.

THE MIXED ECONOMY IN A SIMPLE CASE

A first approximation view of the private sector of the American economy can be given in terms of what we have earlier called a *pure market economy*. As a beginning, let us briefly reexamine our picture of the market economy and indicate the foundations it presupposes.

The main features of the market economy are that economic decisions are made individually, and that they are brought to bear on the economy as a whole through a price system operating in terms of a supply-and-demand mechanism. In this economy, we thought of every individual commodity—apples or washing machines—as having a demand curve drawn on the basis of consumer preferences and also a supply curve derived from producers' responses to various possible market prices. The equilibrium price and quantity for each commodity were then determined, where supply and demand curves intersected.

We also suggested that this same kind of mecha-

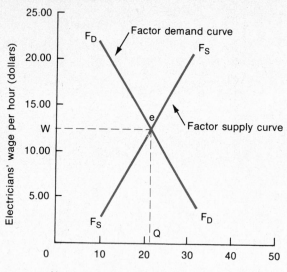

Figure 5–1. Supply and Demand for a Factor of Production.

In a market economy, we determine the price of the services of electricians (or welders or machinery) by supply and demand curves analogous to those determining prices of commodities. In the factor supply and demand curves, however, the business firms are the main demanders, and the suppliers are the owners of the factors of production (in the case of labor, the workingmen of the economy).

nism could be applied to the factors of production. Thus, let us suppose that we are dealing not with a commodity—washing machines—but with a kind of labor, that of electricians. In Figure 5–1, we have drawn supply and demand curves for electricians. In the market economy, the price of electricians (which we would normally call their wage) and the number of electrician-hours employed would be determined by the intersection of these two curves.

Of course, we should not imagine that these supply and demand curves for the services of a factor of production are the same curves that we would draw for a commodity. When we were talking about washing machines, the demanders were the consumers who wanted to buy washing machines for their homes. When we are talking about electricians—or about welders or truck drivers or machine tools or blast furnaces—the demanders are typically not consumers but business firms that will produce the products that we shall ultimately buy. The business firm, in other words, is characteristically a *supplier* of products to the consumer but a *demander* of the services of the factors of production.[1]

Now using this first approximation, we might picture a simplified mixed economy as in Figure 5–2. This is our familiar circular flow diagram except that we have drawn in suggestions of supply and demand curves in the Product and Factor Markets, and we have introduced the State as a provider of Public Goods and Services. This picture is simplified in many respects. For example, as we have shown it, the State provides public goods and services only to households and receives tax payments only from households. In the real world, as we know, business firms also receive public services and also pay taxes—corporate taxes, sales taxes, property taxes, and so on.

Our primary interest in this chapter, however, is with the private sector of the mixed economy and, in this connection, the main simplifying assumption we have made in Figure 5–2 is that the private sector can be treated as if it were a competitive market economy. Now this assumption would be completely satisfactory only if all firms in the economy were quite small, if they all responded to impersonal market conditions, if they had little direct power to influence the markets by their own actions—if, in short, they were *pure competitors* as defined in chapter 2.

Such a description is, however, inadequate to express both the variety of conditions in present-day American Product and Factor Markets and also the fact that there are many units in both markets—whether the giant modern corporation or the large

---

1.   For the derivation of factor supply and demand curves, see chapter 21.

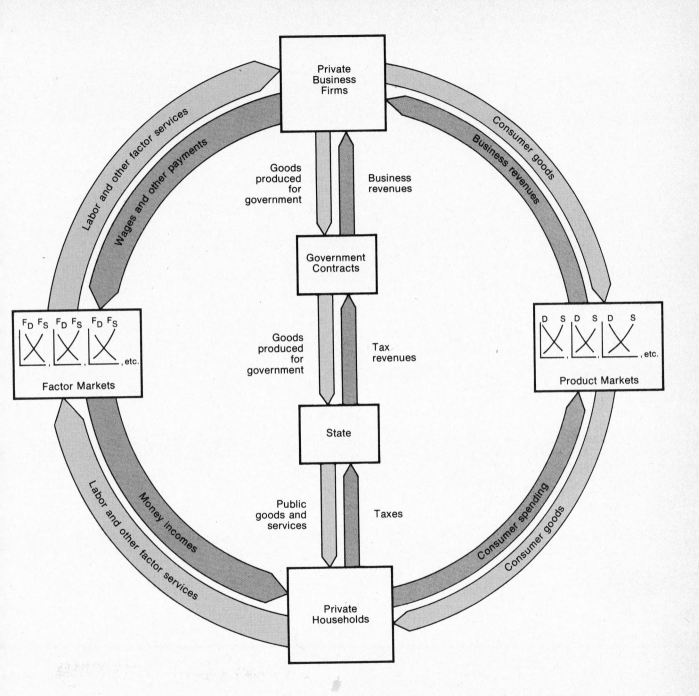

Figure 5–2. A Simplified Mixed Economy.

This is a simplified view of a mixed economy in which all public goods and services are provided to private households in exchange for tax payments, and where the private sector meets the assumptions of a competitive economy.

modern labor union—that clearly have power to shape and modify the market situations that they face. This fact does *not* mean that the study of purely competitive markets is a waste of time. As we shall show in Part Three of this book, the analysis of pure competition is vital to the student of economics because: (1) it provides the only truly coherent picture of the workings of a market economy we have; (2) it gives us tools that can be usefully applied to the analysis of other market structures (including, incidentally, the economic activities of governments); and (3) it provides a possible criterion for the social or "welfare" evaluation of other forms of market organization.

We must not make the opposite mistake, however —i.e., to confuse this simplified picture of the world with a realistic description of business operations and labor organization in a modern industrial economy. In the remainder of this chapter (and again in chapters 24–26 and elsewhere throughout the book), therefore, we shall try to give full attention to the actual complexity of the private sector of our mixed economy.

THE MODERN CORPORATION

Perhaps the most striking feature of industrial organization in the United States is its enormous variety. There are over 11 million business enterprises in the United States today. These may have vastly different economic impacts (American Telephone & Telegraph as compared to the corner grocery store), and they may also differ in legal form:

(1) **Single Proprietorship.** By number of firms (though not by economic impact), the overwhelming majority of American businesses are still single proprietorships where the individual businessman puts up his own capital and runs his own firm. This is the world of owner-employers that Adam Smith had in mind when he developed his concept of the "invisible hand."

(2) **Partnership.** A much smaller number (around one million) business enterprises in America today are of the partnership variety. Here a group of people get together to pool their capital and to share the profits and financial obligations of an enterprise. Since each partner is liable to an unlimited degree for the debts of other partners, this form is not particularly widespread nor significant in its impact.

(3) **Corporation.** In this form of business enterprise, the firm is a "legal person" that can own property, sell stocks, enter into contracts, etc. Furthermore, the corporation enjoys the privilege of limited liability. This is to say that the stockholders who own the corporation are *not* liable for the debts of the corporation beyond their original investment. By number of firms, the corporation is not much more common than the partnership—there are about 1.5 million corporations in the United States today (about one-sixth the number of single proprietorships)—but their economic impact is vast, as we shall see.

Because of the great size of some modern corporations, their activities are often characterized by what is termed a *divorce of ownership and control*. This concept was developed in the important study by Berle and Means, *The Modern Corporation and Private Property*. When corporations are owned by many hundreds of thousands of stockholders and when, as in many cases, no individual stockholder holds more than a tiny fraction of the corporation's common stock, then the actual operation of the firm tends to fall into the hands of the management. The managers may be owners as well, but they need not be, and their ownership in such cases will represent only an insignificant proportion of the total ownership of the corporation, and often, as compared to their salaries, a very small fraction of their own personal financial interest in the firm. This fact has many possible implications. If a manager is primarily a salaried employee rather than an owner of the firm, will it necessarily be in his own self-interest to maximize the profits of the firm? In Adam Smith's owner-proprietor world, the self-interest of the operator of the firm could be identified with making profits for the firm. When the connection between ownership and control is severed, may not the management run the corporation with other objectives in mind? Indeed, is the manager in this case very much different from the socialist bureaucrat? The latter runs a state-owned firm for the benefit of ''society''; the former runs a stockholder-owned firm for the benefit of the society of stockholders. In neither case is the making of *personal* profits considered appropriate.[2]

The complexity of the organization of the modern corporation is matched by the variety of its sizes and forms. Many corporations are quite small and have as little impact as a typical single proprietorship or partnership. Perhaps half the corporations in the United States have assets of less than $100,000. At the other extreme, however, we have the giant modern corporation with assets and annual sales running into the billions of dollars. The economic scale of these giants is obviously a social fact of great importance.

The accompanying Table 5–1, from the *Fortune Magazine* annual list of the nation's largest corporations, is worth studying for a few moments. There are many complications involved in gathering these numbers, but the general picture presented by the figures is quite clear. The largest American corporation by asset size (equipment, buildings, capital stock, etc.) in 1973 was American Telephone & Telegraph, which had $67 billion assets, or roughly $320 of assets for every man, woman and child in the United States. General Motors was the top employer, with over 800 thousand employees. General Motors also had the largest annual sales of any American corporation, $35.8 billion in 1973, and this despite the energy crunch. These sales represented a total income much larger than that of many *nations* in the world.

Overall, in 1973 there were 167 industrial corpora-

tions with sales of $1 billion or over. And if these sums are not large enough to stagger the mind, consider the life-insurance industry. In 1973, the top 17 American life-insurance firms had life insurance in force to the value of a *trillion* dollars. An appropriate sum, perhaps, since we now have more than a trillion dollar gross national product in the United States.

The leap from the world of Adam Smith to these corporate giants is clearly a large one!

CONCENTRATION IN AMERICAN INDUSTRY

Actually, the reference to our trillion-dollar gross national product in the previous section is a useful one because, however dazzling the figures on the size of corporations may be, those figures—like similar ones about the size of governmental expenditures discussed in the preceding chapter—must be placed in the context of an economy that has itself grown enormously in modern times. A single factory might be a dominant factor in the economy of a small underdeveloped country like, say, Upper Volta; a billion-dollar corporation might be one of the smaller corporations in a particular industry in the United States.[3]

There are various ways of measuring the size of our large corporations in relationship to the context in which they operate. One simple way is to ask what proportion of total industrial sales or assets is accounted for by the largest 50, 100, 500 (etc.) firms. *Fortune,* for example, estimates that the 500 largest industrial corporations accounted in 1973 for 65

---

2. We shall be returning to these issues again. See the reading by Edward Mason later in this chapter, pp. 105–108, and especially Great Debate Three: Galbraith and the New Industrial State, pp. 561–88.

3. For example, American Motors in 1970 was 110th on the *Fortune* list of industrial corporations, its sales being $1.1 billion. These sales were equal to only 3.5 percent of the sales of its three larger rivals, GM, Ford, and Chrysler. A clear case of a billion dollar corporation that hardly dominates its own industry. Incidentally—to stress the significance of context—American Motors sales in 1970 exceeded by a factor of three the ''measured'' national income of Upper Volta.

TABLE 5-1

AMERICA'S LARGEST CORPORATIONS, 1973 FORTUNE MAGAZINE

THE 100 LARGEST INDUSTRIAL CORPORATIONS (ranked by sales)

RANK '73	'72	COMPANY	HEADQUARTERS	SALES ($000)	ASSETS ($000)	EMPLOYEES
1	1	General Motors	Detroit	35,798,289	20,296,861	810,920
2	2	Exxon	New York	25,724,319	25,079,494	137,000
3	3	Ford Motor	Dearborn, Mich.	23,015,100	12,954,000	474,318
4	5	Chrysler	Detroit	11,774,372	6,104,898	273,254
5	4	General Electric	New York	11,575,300	8,324,200	388,000
6	8	Texaco	New York	11,406,876	13,595,413	74,918
7	7	Mobil Oil	New York	11,390,113	10,690,431	73,900
8	6	International Business Machines	Armonk, New York	10,993,242	12,289,489	274,108
9	9	International Tel. & Tel.	New York	10,183,035	10,132,571	438,000
10	11	Gulf Oil	Pittsburgh	8,417,000	10,074,000	51,600
11	12	Standard Oil of California	San Francisco	7,761,835	9,082,248	39,269
12	10	Western Electric	New York	7,037,290	4,828,143	206,608
13	13	U. S. Steel	New York	6,951,905	6,918,535	184,794
14	14	Westinghouse Electric	Pittsburgh	5,702,310	4,407,665	194,100
15	15	Standard Oil (Ind.)	Chicago	5,415,976	7,018,013	46,589
16	16	E. I. Du Pont de Nemours	Wilmington, Del.	5,275,600	4,832,200	118,423
17	•	General Telephone & Electronics	Stamford, Conn.	5,105,296	10,749,370	196,000
18	17	Shell Oil	Houston	4,883,808	5,381,164	32,080
19	18	Goodyear Tire & Rubber	Akron, Ohio	4,675,265	3,871,043	152,929
20	19	RCA	New York	4,246,800	3,300,800	126,000
21	24	Continental Oil	Stamford, Conn.	4,224,004	3,693,265	39,796
22	22	International Harvester	Chicago	4,192,544	2,812,667	107,890
23	21	LTV	Dallas	4,177,057	1,829,145	65,700
24	30	Bethlehem Steel	Bethlehem, Pa.	4,137,633	3,919,264	118,000
25	23	Eastman Kodak	Rochester, N.Y.	4,035,520	4,302,081	120,700
26	25	Atlantic Richfield	Los Angeles	3,982,585	5,108,756	26,284
27	28	Esmark	Chicago	3,951,018	1,088,134	33,000
28	27	Union Carbide	New York	3,938,754	4,162,449	109,417
29	26	Tenneco	Houston	3,910,472	5,427,261	83,500
30	20	Procter & Gamble	Cincinnati	3,906,744	2,686,876	47,000
31	29	Kraftco	Glenview, Ill.	3,601,535	1,390,897	48,909
32	31	Greyhound	Phoenix	3,408,725	1,309,159	54,538
33	43	Boeing	Seattle	3,335,189	1,683,059	68,200
34	34	Caterpillar Tractor	Peoria, Ill.	3,182,358	2,232,758	74,431
35	44	Rockwell International	Pittsburgh	3,179,049	2,014,181	100,341
36	37	Occidental Petroleum	Los Angeles	3,178,276	2,871,235	31,845
37	33	Firestone Tire & Rubber	Akron, Ohio	3,154,919	2,669,021	117,000
38	41	Dow Chemical	Midland, Mich.	3,067,888	3,896,193	49,800
39	32	McDonnell Douglas	St. Louis	3,002,626	2,503,340	78,799
40	36	Phillips Petroleum	Bartlesville, Okla.	2,989,952	3,606,773	33,429
41	40	Xerox	Stamford, Conn.	2,989,694	3,102,068	94,036
42	45	W. R. Grace	New York	2,807,830	2,003,834	74,500
43	42	Beatrice Foods	Chicago	2,786,970	1,087,514	62,000
44	38	Lockheed Aircraft	Burbank, Calif.	2,756,791	1,854,525	66,900
45	46	Monsanto	St. Louis	2,647,700	2,545,300	58,277

Fortune Magazine, America's Largest Corporations, 1973. Reprinted here from the 1974 Fortune Directory by permission. Footnotes and some table columns do not appear here.

RANK '73	'72	COMPANY	HEADQUARTERS	SALES ($000)	ASSETS ($000)	EMPLOYEES
46	39	General Foods	White Plains, N.Y.	2,632,264	1,728,708	48,000
47	35	Litton Industries	Beverly Hills	2,624,364	2,116,181	105,400
48	48	Borden	New York	2,553,994	1,448,408	46,500
49	52	Union Oil of California	Los Angeles	2,552,329	2,908,685	15,926
50	51	Minnesota Mining & Manufacturing	St. Paul	2,545,620	2,280,921	78,932
51	49	Continental Can	New York	2,539,701	1,753,076	64,801
52	47	Singer	New York	2,527,600	1,897,200	122,000
53	64	Ralston Purina	St. Louis	2,433,599	1,133,415	43,500
54	50	Honeywell	Minneapolis	2,390,592	2,583,114	98,122
55	60	Armco Steel	Middletown, Ohio	2,390,162	2,259,377	52,187
56	54	R. J. Reynolds Industries	Winston-Salem, N.C.	2,330,005	2,611,993	31,477
57	53	International Paper	New York	2,314,300	2,197,100	51,266
58	77	Weyerhaeuser	Tacoma, Wash.	2,301,731	2,327,354	47,477
59	56	United Aircraft	East Hartford, Conn.	2,288,947	1,266,113	64,942
60	59	Sun Oil	St. Davids, Pa.	2,286,021	3,381,647	24,979
61	71	Bendix	Southfield, Mich.	2,229,500	1,427,000	82,300
62	65	Sperry Rand	New York	2,229,253	1,840,635	91,345
63	58	Georgia-Pacific	Portland, Ore.	2,228,700	2,002,020	36,175
64	62	Champion International	New York	2,207,956	1,699,554	48,900
65	67	Colgate-Palmolive	New York	2,195,302	1,151,391	42,400
66	57	American Can	Greenwich, Conn.	2,181,576	1,544,395	47,500
67	75	TRW	Cleveland	2,164,632	1,446,047	93,011
68	72	Aluminum Co. of America	Pittsburgh	2,157,333	2,820,695	48,534
69	61	Coca-Cola	Atlanta	2,144,989	1,394,362	31,393
70	80	National Steel	Pittsburgh	2,103,279	2,024,378	37,330
71	66	Burlington Industries	Greensboro, N.C.	2,099,801	1,581,869	88,000
72	69	Uniroyal	New York	2,082,691	1,581,242	64,402
73	83	Republic Steel	Cleveland	2,068,605	1,862,011	43,803
74	79	United Brands	New York	2,066,165	1,237,908	51,000
75	70	Ashland Oil	Russell, Ky.	2,052,821	1,437,252	25,000
76	68	Consolidated Foods	Chicago	2,042,862	1,007,736	71,000
77	63	Cities Service	New York	2,034,600	2,659,600	13,000
78	90	Deere	Moline, Ill.	2,002,992	1,760,522	50,058
79	78	Gulf & Western Industries	New York	1,927,165	2,364,098	70,000
80	107	Amerada Hess	New York	1,896,362	1,921,992	4,867
81	82	CPC International	Englewood Cliffs, N.J.	1,874,302	1,200,821	43,451
82	73	American Brands	New York	1,864,938	2,160,756	50,000
83	76	Textron	Providence	1,858,402	1,310,368	66,000
84	81	Owens-Illinois	Toledo, Ohio	1,856,906	1,642,466	68,527
85	93	Inland Steel	Chicago	1,828,951	1,559,033	34,604
86	86	NCR	Dayton, Ohio	1,816,281	1,833,916	81,000
87	84	American Home Products	New York	1,784,376	1,125,974	45,457
88	101	American Motors	Detroit	1,739,025	712,955	28,259
89	88	B. F. Goodrich	Akron, Ohio	1,721,928	1,475,167	51,981
90	91	FMC	Chicago	1,719,282	1,380,398	49,546

RANK '73	'72	COMPANY	HEADQUARTERS	SALES ($000)	ASSETS ($000)	EMPLOYEES
91	96	Signal Companies	Beverly Hills	1,711,000	1,378,032	32,600
92	98	Philip Morris	New York	1,709,039	2,108,403	37,000
93	103	PepsiCo	Purchase, N.Y.	1,697,924	1,149,664	49,000
94	92	Warner-Lambert	Morris Plains, N.J.	1,670,427	1,388,820	59,000
95	89	Allied Chemical	Morristown, N.J.	1,664,551	1,762,536	33,627
96	87	General Dynamics	St. Louis	1,641,799	994,093	62,400
97	97	Whirlpool	Benton Harbor, Mich.	1,636,949	765,082	32,434
98	85	U. S. Industries	New York	1,636,756	1.033,460	46,000
99	109	Johnson & Johnson	New Brunswick, N.J.	1,611,811	1,189,092	49,100
100	105	Celanese	New York	1,609,000	1,747,000	37,400

THE 10 LARGEST COMMERCIAL BANKS (ranked by assets)

RANK '73	'72	COMPANY	ASSETS ($000)	DEPOSITS ($000)	LOANS ($000)	EMPLOYEES
1	1	BankAmerica Corp. (San Francisco)	49,404,764	41,453,816	27,408,397	56,250
2	2	First National City Corp. (New York)	44,019,218	34,942,367	27,971,300	41,800
3	3	Chase Manhattan Corp. (New York)	36,790,909	29,913,182	22,165,182	26,781
4	4	J. P. Morgan & Co. (New York)	20,374,529	15,366,811	10,567,585	9,050
5	5	Manufacturers Hanover Corp. (New York)	19,850,398	17,210,194	13,693,514	14,363
6	6	Chemical New York Corp.	18,592,219	14,373,956	10,574,782	12,444
7	8	Bankers Trust New York Corp.	18,514,550	14,705,908	10,014,742	12,585
8	7	Western Bancorp. (Los Angeles)	17,902,598	14,245,177	10,666,571	25,548
9	9	Continental Illinois Corp. (Chicago)	16,870,180	12,598,203	12,232,019	9,312
10	11	First Chicago Corp.	15,558,497	12,041,719	9,700,244	7,036

THE 10 LARGEST LIFE-INSURANCE COMPANIES (ranked by assets)

RANK '73	'72	COMPANY	ASSETS ($000)	LIFE INSURANCE IN FORCE ($000)	EMPLOYEES
1	1	Prudential (Newark)	34,963,969	197,428,389	58,554
2	2	Metropolitan (New York)	31,985,447	198,184,955	56,500
3	3	Equitable Life Assurance (New York)	17,152,473	97,508,226	20,367
4	4	New York Life	12,471,793	62,842,603	18,910
5	5	John Hancock Mutual (Boston)	11,447,249	75,056,201	20,676
6	6	Aetna Life (Hartford)	8,933,987	71,506,611	15,300
7	7	Northwestern Mutual (Milwaukee)	7,096,113	25,721,934	5,149
8	8	Connecticut General Life (Bloomfield)	6,622,110	41,428,713	7,825
9	9	Travelers Life (Hartford)	6,001,293	64,759,303	39,300
10	10	Massachusetts Mutual (Springfield)	5,129,051	24,280,822	7,473

THE 10 LARGEST RETAILING COMPANIES (ranked by sales)

RANK '73	'72	COMPANY	SALES ($000)	ASSETS ($000)	EMPLOYEES
1	1	Sears, Roebuck (Chicago)	12,306,229	10,427,431	401,000
2	3	Safeway Stores (Oakland)	6,773,687	1,341,220	117,221
3	2	Great Atlantic & Pacific Tea (Montvale, N.J.)	6,747,689	1,018,599	113,800
4	4	J.C. Penney (New York)	6,243,677	2,439,532	200,000
5	5	S.S. Kresge (Troy, Mich.)	4,702,504	1,652,773	125,000
6	6	Kroger (Cincinnati)	4,204,677	950,177	50,400
7	7	Marcor (Chicago)	4,077,415	2,847,485	142,184
8	8	F.W. Woolworth (New York)	3,722,107	1,973,940	213,414
9	9	Federated Department Stores (Cincinnati)	2,966,176	1,514,506	86,500
10	•	Rapid-American (New York)	2,341,028	1,755,535	90,000

THE 10 LARGEST TRANSPORTATION COMPANIES (ranked by operating revenues)

RANK '73	'72	COMPANY	OPERATING REVENUES ($000)	ASSETS ($000)	EMPLOYEES
1	1	UAL (Chicago)	2,060,268	2,417,196	56,008
2	2	Penn Central Transportation (Philadelphia)	1,963,673	4,262,609	78,258
3	4	Trans World Airlines (New York)	1,810,990	1,919,816	74,344
4	3	Southern Pacific (San Francisco)	1,551,265	3,414,630	50,100
5	5	American Airlines (New York)	1,481,987	1,687,264	37,612
6	6	Pan American World Airways (New York)	1,433,079	1,683,719	34,370
7	7	Burlington Northern (St. Paul)	1,331,524	3,082,112	48,436
8	8	Eastern Air Lines (New York)	1,259,808	1,432,623	34,800
9	9	Seaboard Coast Line Industries (Jacksonville)	1,230,055	2,441,312	40,867
10	10	Union Pacific (New York)	1,224,208	2,828,376	29,776

THE 10 LARGEST UTILITIES (ranked by assets)

RANK '73	'72	COMPANY	ASSETS ($000)	OPERATING REVENUES ($000)	EMPLOYEES
1	1	American Telephone & Telegraph (New York)	67,051,114	23,527,320	798,934
2	3	Consolidated Edison (New York)	5,968,175	1,736,239	24,541
3	4	Pacific Gas & Electric (San Francisco)	5,471,097	1,490,156	26,415
4	5	Southern Co. (Atlanta)	5,378,299	1,165,825	20,509
5	6	American Electric Power (New York)	5,071,320	966,493	16,303
6	7	Commonwealth Edison (Chicago)	4,649,169	1,266,154	15,080
7	8	Southern California Edison (Rosemead)	3,989,857	1,079,348	13,927
8	9	Public Service Electric & Gas (Newark, N.J.)	3,896,667	1,076,260	14,846
9	10	Philadelphia Electric	3,176,063	766,658	10,289
10	11	Detroit Edison	3,061,057	753,135	10,304

Relationship between company size, sales, and profit

percent of the sales, 76 percent of the employees, and 79 percent of the profits of all U.S. industrial corporations. A detailed estimate for 1962 is that, at that time, the largest 282 nonfinancial corporations owned 44.6 percent of all nonfinancial corporate assets in the United States and that the largest 627 nonfinancial corporations owned 53.8 percent of all nonfinancial corporate assets.[4] One can also look at it from the bottom up, but still considering size from the point of view of the economy as a whole. Thus, in the same study referred to above, it was estimated that the 96 percent of the nonfinancial corporations in the economy that are small account for only one-sixth of total nonfinancial corporate assets. The 4 percent of large corporations own all the rest.

The trouble with such estimates is that they are so broad that it is difficult to know what to conclude from them. Should we stress the fact that 500 or 600 firms control so much, or rather the fact that, under many circumstances, there might be a great deal of competition among several hundred firms?

Consequently, economists usually go beyond the "largest 100" type of statistic to ask (1) what is happening in particular industries, and (2) what is happening over time. With regard to specific industries, it is customary to speak of *concentration ratios*. These concentration ratios show how much of the sales of a particular industry are accounted for by the larger firms in the industry. Thus we might ask: What percentage of the sales of an industry are accounted for by the four largest firms, what percentage by the eight largest, and so on? One of the problems with this kind of measurement is that the degree of concentration will depend upon the way in which the industry classification is defined. If it is defined very broadly ("Food and Kindred Products"), concentration will tend to be less than if it is defined very narrowly ("Fresh Beef").

In Figure 5–3, an attempt is made to assess the importance of concentrated industries within larger "industrial groups." A *concentrated industry* is here defined as one in which the four largest firms account for 50 percent or more of the value of shipments of that industry. In the industry group "Tobacco Products," all the industries within that group in 1963 were concentrated in this sense. In the "Fabricated Metal Products" there were some concentrated industries within the group, but they accounted for only 12 percent of the value of shipments in this industry. In "Lumber and Wood Products" there were no concentrated industries so defined. The author of these estimates (John M. Blair, former chief economist of the Senate Subcommittee on Anti-Trust and Monopoly) calculates that, for American manufacturing as a whole in 1963, about a third of total output was produced by concentrated industries.

In a general sense, concentration tends to be highest in public utilities (including transportation) and manufacturing—these two sectors include the overwhelming majority of the giant nonfinancial corporations—and very low in the service industries, agriculture, and construction.

As far as trends are concerned, there is some disagreement as to whether concentration is increasing or staying roughly the same in the American economy, and some of this disagreement depends upon the period chosen for study. M. A. Adelman, professor of industrial relations at MIT, notes that most studies suggest that concentration overall tended to decrease from the early 1930s to the late 1940s, then to return to the 1930s level and perhaps increase beyond it in the 1960s.[5] He adds:

The trend can be embellished, for polemical purposes, by measuring from low to high, i.e., comparing 1948 with 1968, rather than from high to high (or at least the earliest to the latest). It is a bit like comparing department store sales, August with December, to show that sales are doing fine. Extrapolate the 1948–1968 "trend" by twenty or fifty years, and there is as much to view with alarm as there was decades ago; only a spoilsport would ask what happened to those earlier predictions of an imminent monopolistic economy.[6]

4. Joe S. Bain, *Industrial Organization,* 2nd ed. (New York: John Wiley & Sons, 1968), p. 86.

5. One (though not the only) reason for the increase in aggregate concentration in the 1960s was the conglomerate merger movement. See pp. 552–53.

6. M. A. Adelman. "The Two Faces of Economic Concentration," *The Public Interest,* Fall 1970, p. 123.

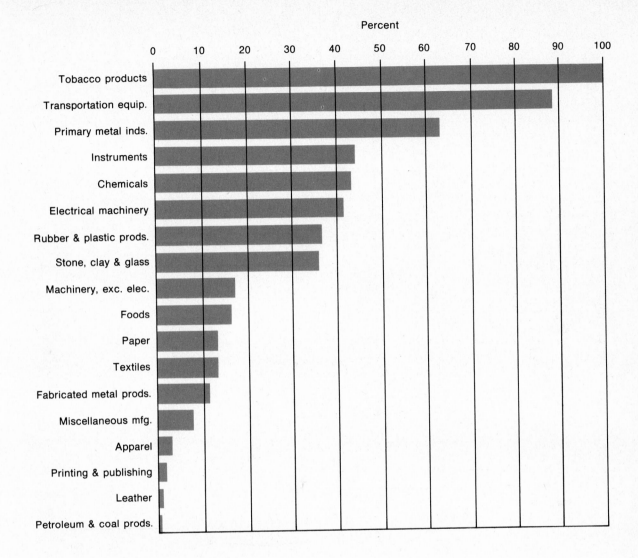

Figure 5-3. Percentage of Value of Shipments by Concentrated Industries within Industry Groups, 1963.

Concentrated industries are here defined as those in which the largest four firms account for over 50 percent of the value of the industry's shipments. The bars on the graph tell us the percentage of the industry group's shipments (an "industry group" includes several industries) accounted for by such concentrated industries.

Adapted from chart in *Economics Concentration: Structure, Behavior and Public Policy* by John M. Blair, © 1972 by Harcourt Brace Jovanovich, Inc. and reproduced with their permission.

A 1969 study by Nutter and Einhorn[7] has attempted to make an estimate of the amount of monopoly in the American economy in 1958 as compared to 1899. They divide industries in all sectors of the economy into three groups: (1) Effectively Monopolistic;[8] (2) Workably Competitive; and (3) Governmental or Governmentally Supervised. Their conclusion is that there is no clear evidence of an increase in the amount of monopoly in the economy over this period. In 1899, they found that 17.4 percent of national income was produced in effectively monopolistic industries, 76.1 percent in workably competitive industries, and 6.5 percent in governmental industries. In 1958, depending upon the specific measures used, monopolistic industries had either increased by four percentage points or decreased by one percentage point relative to total nongovernmental production; because of the growth of government, monopolistic industries had by each measure declined relative to the economy as a whole. In the specific sector of manufacturing, they found a "remarkable stability in the extent of monopoly."

These results, as the authors point out, must be used with great caution. And many economists reject them. John Blair, for example, finds a clear-cut increase in aggregate concentration over the past fifty years.[9] Still, the majority of economists would probably agree that the evidence is mixed. That there is a higher degree of concentration now than, say, at the beginning of our great industrialization surge in the early nineteenth century seems beyond doubt; but that this represents an irresistible trend towards ever-increasing monopolization of the private sector of the American economy is not conclusively borne out by experience.

---

7.   G. Warren Nutter and Henry Adler Einhorn, *Enterprise Monopoly in the United States* (New York: Columbia University Press, 1969).

8.   "Effectively Monopolistic" industries are not limited to those in which there is literally a single seller of the product, but would include, for example, industries, like "concentrated industries," in which the four largest firms account for over 50 percent of the output of the industry.

9.   Blair, John M., *op. cit.*, pp. 60–71.

BUREAUCRACIES—PRIVATE AND PUBLIC

Does this relative stability—or, at least, slow rate of increase—in the degree of concentration of American industry mean that the structure and organization of our business firms have been comparably stable over the past several decades? The answer is clearly no, for the growth in size of business corporations (even when they have not grown in relation to a rapidly expanding economy) is itself a significant fact and might be expected to have important consequences for the way in which these firms go about their business.

In particular, the *robber baron* of the nineteenth century has given way to the modern corporate bureaucracy. We no longer think of business firms in terms of particular individual leaders—who can name the presidents or chairmen of the boards of even half of the top ten industrial corporations on the *Fortune* list?—but in terms of committees, departments, memoranda, Xerox machines, and competent but faceless executives. We are in the world of the bureaucrat, a world strikingly similar whether it be in business, the university, the government, or, for that matter, the United Nations secretariat.

All of this raises deep questions about the meaning of *private* versus *public* sectors. Is this distinction any longer valid? The issue has come up in a number of specific ways during the past two decades. One instance is the concept of the *military-industrial complex*. This term, first used by President Eisenhower in 1961, denotes a large area of the economy in which public agencies (notably the Department of Defense) and private firms are inextricably linked by common problems and, to some degree, common interests. Many private defense contractors are, in effect, operating as submanagement units under a larger public management. Similarly, the relationship between public and private is very confused in the area of public regulatory agencies. Ralph Nader and others have argued that, in some cases at least, these governmental regulatory agencies tend to become captives of the industries they are allegedly regulating.

Is it possible, then, that the differences between public and private are now less significant than the similarities of bureaucracies, especially big bureaucracies, whether governmental or formally in the private sector? In the following reading, Edward S. Mason, former Harvard professor and dean of the Littauer School of Public Administration, a man who taught many of today's leading thinkers in the area of industrial organization, reflects on some dimensions of this question.

The Corporation in Modern Society

Edward S. Mason
＊ ＊ ＊

People who talk about a "managerial revolution" usually have in mind, on the one hand, the increasing importance of large corporations on the American scene and, on the other, changes in administrative techniques that have continually increased the size of the enterprise that can be effectively managed. Those who doubt the significance of this "revolution" point to figures on economic concentration, and indeed it is possible to show that, during the last fifty years, there has been no significant increase, however measured, in the share of economic activity controlled by the largest corporations. The largest corporations have grown mightily, but so has the economy. This, in my view, does not dispose of the matter. In the first place, conclusions on the trend of concentration depend heavily on the date from which one measures the trend. If the date chosen is before the great merger movement of 1897–1903, it can be shown that concentration has, in fact, increased. In the second place, the phenomena we are concerned with are more a product of absolute size than of relative share. And about absolute size, however measured, there is no shadow of doubt. In

the third place, there is probably a substantial lag between changes in the size of enterprises and changes in managerial techniques adapted to the new sizes. For these and other reasons, I conclude that, despite the lack of evidence of increased concentration during the last half century, there may well have occurred a profound change in the way industrial enterprises are managed. It goes without saying that in other broad sectors of the economy small-scale enterprise, managed in a traditional fashion, not only is holding its own but will continue to do so.

These changes in management are commonly grouped under the heading of bureaucracy. And bureaucracy, as the political scientists tell us, is characterized by a hierarchy of function and authority, professionalization of management, formal procedures for recruitment and promotion, and a proliferation of written rules, orders, and record keeping. All this is true of business administration in large corporations, but corporate bureaucracies also exhibit certain differences from typical government bureaucracies that are worth emphasizing. In the first place, corporate managements enjoy a much greater freedom from external influence than do the managements of government bureaucracies. As we have seen, management has pretty much escaped from ownership control, but though private ownership may no longer carry with it control, it does guarantee corporate management against most of the political, ministerial, and legislative interference that commonly besets public management. Perhaps in a corporate society this is becoming one of the primary contributions of private property. Needless to say, this independence of corporate management from any well-defined responsibility to anyone also carries with it the possibilities of abuse. . . .

In the second place, corporate managements have traditionally been considered to have as their single-minded objective, in contrast to most government bureaucracies, maximization of business profits. And traditionally the incentives connected with profit maximization have been thought to constitute an essential part of the justification of a private-enterprise system. Now managerial voices are raised to deny this exclusive preoccupation with profits and to assert that corporate managements are really concerned with equitable sharing of corporate gains among owners, workers, suppliers, and customers. If equity rather than profits is the corporate objective, one of the traditional distinctions between the private and public sectors disappears. If equity is the primary desideratum, it may well be asked why duly constituted public authority is not as good an instrument for dispensing equity as self-perpetuating corporate managements. . . .

Finally, since corporate managements work exclusively in the business area, which government bureaucracies ordinarily do not, it can be said that the possibility of monetary measurement in the former permits a closer adjustment of rewards to performance, and hence a closer observance of the causes of efficiency than is possible in the latter. This is true, and it is important, but the distinction is not between public and private efficiency but between the efficiency of operations susceptible to the measuring rod of money and the efficiency of those that are not. . . .

One of the leading characteristics of well-ordered bureaucracies both public and private—a characteristic justly extolled by the devotees of managerialism—is the increasing professionalization of management. This means, among other things, selection and promotion on the basis of merit rather than family connections or social status, the development of a "scientific" attitude towards the problems of the organization, and an expectation of reward in terms of relatively stable salary and professional prestige rather than in fluctuating profits. This professionalization of management has, of course, been characteristic of well-ordered public bureaucracies for a long time. It helps to explain why able young East Indians, for example, have in general preferred to cast their lot with a civil service selecting and promoting on the basis of merit rather than with the highly nepotistic business firms of the subcontinent. But it is a relatively new phenomenon in American business and one of increasing importance.

The degree of freedom enjoyed by corporate managements, in contrast to their governmental counterparts, has affected personnel as well as other policies. And no one who has observed at first hand the red-tape inefficiencies of the United States Civil Service can fail to be aware of the superiority of corporate practice. This relative freedom from hampering restrictions on selection plus a high level of monetary rewards has brought the cream of American professional management into business corporations. No one doubts the superiority of American business management. Unwitting testimony, if testimony is needed, is supplied by the care with which Soviet planners examine American management practices.

* * *

The economies of Western Europe and, increasingly, that of the United States are frequently described as "mixed" economies. This phrase is commonly interpreted to indicate a situation in which the role of government as owner and regulator has become sufficiently large to cast doubt on the validity of "capitalist" and "free enterprise" as appropriate adjectives but not sufficiently large to justify the appellation "socialist." Government ownership and regulation are important ingredients, but they inadequately characterize the "mixture" of public and private that the rise of the large corporation has produced. The growth of the modern corporation has been accompanied by an increasing similarity of public and private business with respect to forms of organization, techniques of management, and the motivations and attitudes of managers. Government has sought increasingly to use the private corporation for the performance of what are essentially public functions. Private corporations in turn, particularly in their foreign operations, continually make decisions which impinge on the public—particularly foreign—policy of government. And government, in pursuit of its current objectives in underdeveloped areas, seeks to use techniques and talents that only the business corporation can provide. . . . Under these circumstances the classic arguments of the socialism-versus-free-enterprise debate seem a bit sterile, to say the least.

The increasing similarity of public and private enterprise has impressed both liberals and conservatives, though the conclusions drawn therefrom have tended to differ. In an early recognition of this trend, Keynes described it as a "tendency of big enterprise to socialize itself." A point is reached in the growth of big enterprises, he says, at which "the stockholders are almost entirely dissociated from the management, with the result that the direct personal interest of the latter in the making of great profit becomes quite secondary." American managerial spokesmen supplement this thought by emphasizing management's responsibility to workers, customers, suppliers, and others, though they would hardly describe living up to this responsibility—as Keynes probably would—as behaving like Civil Servants. These and similar considerations have led elements in the British Labour Party to the conclusion that the form of ownership of large enterprise is irrelevant. "The basic fact is the large corporation, facing fundamental similar problems, acts in fundamentally the same way, whether publicly or privately owned."

While large private corporations have been forced by their sheer size, power, and "visibility" to behave with a circumspection unknown to the untrammeled nineteenth century, government, on the other hand, has attempted to give its "business-like" activities a sphere of independence approaching that of the private corporation. Experience with the public corporation in the United States has, it is true, somewhat dampened an earlier enthusiasm for this type of organization. And even Britain, which has sought much longer and harder than we for a workable compromise between independence and accountability in its publicly managed enterprises, has not yet found a satisfactory solution. Nevertheless, it remains true that managerial practices and attitudes in the public and private sectors of most Western economies tend to become more similar.

Private ownership in the United States, however, still confers an immunity from detailed government supervision that a public corporation does not enjoy. And government takes advantage of the independence and flexibility of the private corporation to contract out the performance of what are essentially public services. Private firms become official inspectors of aircraft; various types of military "operations analysis" are undertaken by Rand and other privately organized corporations, and substantially more than half of public research and development expenditures go to private rather than public organizations. In commenting on these phenomena, Don Price observes, "If the question (of public versus private) is seen in realistic terms, we shall have to devise some way of calculating whether a particular function can be performed best in the public interest as a completely governmental operation at the one extreme, or a completely private operation at the other extreme, or by some mixture of the nearly infinite possibilities of elements of ownership regulation and management that our variety of precedents suggests."

* * *

How really mixed—and perhaps mixed up—our economy is these days can be clearly seen by casting one's eye on United States policy and practices in the so-called underdeveloped areas of the world. Our announced policy is to give substantial assistance to the economic development of countries whose economies have long been stagnant. And our preferred means are the stimulation of private enterprise in the underdeveloped areas and the encouragement of United States private investment abroad. But in many of these areas, the opportunities for foreign private investment are negligible, and our grants and loans inevitably flow through local government channels. At the same time, in the provision of technical assistance we depend heavily on contracts with American private firms. And we actively encourage mixed enterprise, private and public and foreign and domestic, as a means of getting enterprise moving. The effort is sometimes described as an exercise in government-business cooperation in the promotion of foreign economic development, and perhaps that is as good a description as any. In any case, it is a good example of a mixed economy in motion.

This lack of a clear-cut separation of public and private authority and responsibility offends some people. And indeed, the eighteenth-century political philosophers and political economists provided for their epoch a much more satisfactory intellectual framework than any vouchsafed to us today. The fact seems to be that the rise of the large corporation and attending circumstances have confronted us with a long series of questions concerning rights and duties, privileges and immunities, responsibility and authority, that political and legal philosophy have not yet assimilated. What we need among other things is a twentieth-century Hobbes or Locke to bring some order into our thinking about the corporation and its role in society.   *   *   *

UNIONS AND THE AMERICAN LABOR MARKET

On the opposite side of the circular flow chart from the Product Markets are the Factor Markets. On this side of the flow are sold the services of the factors of production—labor, land, capital goods—that are then combined by business firms in production processes that ultimately lead to a stream of consumer and other goods.

Just as the existence of the large modern corporation affects the workings of the Product Markets, so also there are many institutions in the American economy that modify the pure "laws" of supply and demand in the markets for labor, land, and capital. Indeed, the existence of the large modern corporation also influences the Factor Markets, since business firms are, of course, the buyers or "demanders" on the Factor Markets. One theory of the growth of labor unions, for example, is that they represent a *countervailing power* to the concentrated buying power of large business enterprises on the other side of the labor market.[10] The individual workman could hardly be expected to bargain with U.S. Steel or Standard Oil of New Jersey—unionization of the labor force was the only possible answer.

Even apart from the influence of large corporations

and large unions, labor markets would probably not work as smoothly as we might, in theory, desire. There are all sorts of possible imperfections. Laborers may not generally know about jobs in other localities or occupations; there may be significant discrimination against minority groups, and, if women's organizations are correct, against the female majority of the population; there may be general unemployment in the economy (according to Marxists, this permits employers to "exploit" all laborers); furthermore, in local areas, even fairly small firms may have a degree of monopsony buying power.

We shall come back to many of these problems later; for the moment, let us just say a few words about labor unions, which represent a particularly important institution in the largest of American Factor Markets—the labor market.

Figure 5–4 shows the growth of labor union membership in the United States in the course of the twentieth century. The trend has clearly been upward during this period although there have been notable ups and downs, and, in recent years, union membership has been on the decline as a percentage of the labor force.[11] With the increase in the number of white-collar, as opposed to blue-collar, workers in the American economy, labor unions actually face some difficult organizational problems in the years ahead.

Difficult problems, however, are nothing new to the American labor movement. In one sense, as the diagram shows, their progress has been fairly continuous. In 1886, the American Federation of Labor (AFL) was founded under the leadership of Samuel Gompers. In 1935, the Congress of Industrial Organizations (CIO) joined the fray under the leadership of the controversial John L. Lewis. In 1955, under George Meany, the two large organizations joined together into the massive present-day AFL-CIO. In *another* sense, however, this progress has been

---

10.   This approach was advanced in an early book by John Kenneth Galbraith, *American Capitalism: The Concept of Countervailing Power* (Boston: Houghton Mifflin Co., 1952).

11.   Thus, while union membership increased absolutely between 1968 and 1972, it fell as a percentage of the labor force from 25.2 percent to 24.3 percent. Twenty years ago, this figure would have been closer to 35 percent. See James C. Hyatt, "A Sluggish Economy Complicates the Woes of Labor Organizers," *Wall Street Journal*, April 8, 1974.

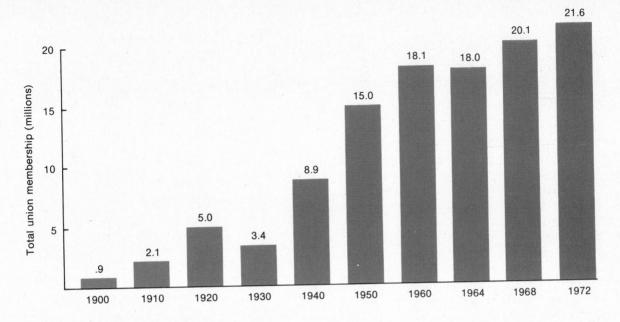

Figure 5–4. Labor Union Membership in the United States 1900–1972 (selected years).

pock-marked by problems and crises. This was especially true in the early days when American industry can hardly be said to have welcomed the new unions with open arms. Moreover, the attitude of the government was by no means friendly. The courts interpreted the Sherman Act of 1890 to restrict unions that were organizing in "restraint of trade"; and in the Danbury Hatters' case of 1908, the union was made to pay extensively for damages caused by a strike. It was not until 1914 that the Clayton Act stated explicitly that unions were not to be considered in "restraint of trade," and it was really not until the Wagner Act and other favorable legislation of the 1930s that the labor movement came strongly into its own.

Unions have an impact on many different aspects of the labor market. They have what we may think of as a primary objective—to raise wages for their members—but they bargain collectively about many more issues than this: seniority systems, hours and conditions of work, methods of production, job tenure, and so on. They are complicated institutions with their own meetings, elections, organizational structures, and often their own political views.

And, of course, when all else fails, they have the right to strike. It is probably this union action—especially when it seems to affect some vital public service—that most attracts general interest and attention.

THE STRIKE—BETTER THAN THE ALTERNATIVES?

Since strikes hurt all parties—employees (through wage losses), employers (through curtailed production and sales), and consumers (through interrupted service)—they might seem to be the worst method of settling labor disputes. Since they are the natural ultimate consequence of the whole system of collec-

POLITICAL STRIKES
IN EUROPE

tive bargaining, it might seem further that this system itself has outlived its usefulness.

Why do workers strike? There are many different possible reasons and, consequently, many different types of strikes. One classification distinguishes:[12]

Political strikes, where the hope is to influence governmental decisions. This is common in Europe but rare in the United States.

Organizational strikes, where the union is trying to force the employer to recognize it as the employees' representative.

Jurisdictional strikes, where unions disagree as to whose members should do a particular job, i.e., which union has jurisdiction.

Grievance strikes, where the union strikes because of the way management has handled some particular promotion, job assignment, or other day-to-day operation in the work of the firm. The great majority of labor contracts in the United States today use binding arbitration to settle such grievances; hence, this kind of strike is increasingly uncommon.

Indeed, in total, all the types of strikes mentioned so far account for less than 10 percent of man-days lost through strikes in this country. Thus, by far the most important category is the last:

Contract strikes, where labor and management cannot find mutually agreeable terms for the writing of a new labor contract. Here we have a recognized union, with no organizational or jurisdictional problems and no ulterior political motives, confronting management with a series of demands for higher wages or increased fringe benefits or better working conditions, which management rejects. The consequence: A shutdown of the firm or industry costly to all parties.

Whether the strike is a valid solution to this kind of problem, and how alternative methods stand up under examination, are subjects discussed in the following reading.

---

12. See Thomas Kennedy, "Freedom to Strike Is in the Public Interest," *Harvard Business Review*, July–August 1970.

Freedom To Strike Is in the Public Interest

Thomas Kennedy

HOW COSTLY ARE STRIKES?

Despite the fact that peaceful alternatives have replaced most organizational, jurisdictional, and grievance strikes, and despite the fact that strikes in utilities, oil refineries, and some chemical plants no longer create crises, strikes over new contract terms still do occur, and these can be quite costly to companies, employees, unions, suppliers, customers, and the general public. Also, of course, when the strike involves a critical material or service, the effect on the economy as a whole may be disastrous if the stoppage continues beyond a certain point.

Thus, while the strike performs a valuable function in our free collective bargaining system, it is legitimate to question whether the costs are too great in relation to the benefits. Might some alternative to the strike, such as compulsory arbitration, serve the interests of the parties and the public better? To answer this question, let us begin by examining the costs of strikes. We can next compare these with the costs of alternative procedures.

Because of the publicity which strikes get, it is easy for their extent and their impact on the economy to be overestimated. When one reads in the headlines that 147,000 GE employees have been on strike for over three months, one is likely to be greatly impressed. But when one realizes that the GE strikers represent only 0.2 percent of the 71,000,000 non-agricultural employees in the country, one sees it in a different light (although for the company, its dealers, and its employees, the strike is still very significant).

It is estimated that there are approximately 300,000 labor agreements in the United States. On the average, about 120,000 of these agreements terminate each year. Thus, across the country during an average year, 120,000 management bargaining teams sit across the table from 120,000 union bargaining teams and try to work out agreements on new contract terms. The issues which they deal with are wages, benefits, hours, and other important working conditions. These are matters which are extremely vital to the companies, the unions, and the employees. Despite the difficulties of these issues, the parties are successful in 96 percent or more of the negotiations. Only 4 percent or less of the negotiations result in strikes, and in most cases these strikes are short-lived. The problem is that a peaceful settlement is seldom front-page news, whereas a strike may be good for a number of headlines.

The Bureau of Labor Statistics estimates that the amount of working time in the total economy which was lost directly as a result of strikes in 1969 was only 0.23 percent. Moreover, the general trend has been down. As illustrated in Exhibit A, from 1945 to 1949 the average time lost per year was 0.47 percent, compared with 0.26 percent from 1950 to 1959, and only 0.17 percent from 1960 to 1969. We have been losing far more time in coffee breaks than in strikes!

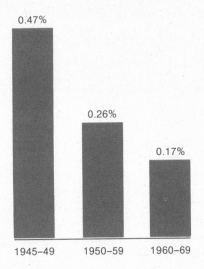

Exhibit A.

Working Time Lost in Strikes, as a Percent of Working Time in Total Economy.

Source: Data in Table 140, ''Work Stoppages in the U.S., 1881–1967,'' in *Handbook of Labor Statistics 1969* (Washington, Bureau of Labor Statistics, 1970). pp. 352–353, plus data for 1968 and 1969 reported currently by the Bureau of Labor Statistics.

Industrywide Bargaining

The effect of a strike on the economy depends, among other things, on the nature of the product or service and the structure of the bargaining. In the steel industry, where the product is essential to many other industries and where the bargaining is practically industrywide, one might expect that a strike of any sizable duration would have drastic effects on the overall economy. Such studies as are available, however, indicate that such is not the case.

Following the 116-day steel strike in 1959, E. Robert Livernash of the Harvard Business School made an extensive study for the Department of Labor of the impact of that and earlier steel work stoppages on the economy. Livernash concluded that:

The actual adverse effects of steel strikes on the economy have not been of serious magnitude. A major reason why steel strikes have had so little measurable impact is that when a strike approaches a critical state, pressure upon the parties to settle becomes substantially irresistible. It is significant that the public interest has not been seriously harmed by strikes in steel, or by steel collective bargaining agreements, despite common public opinion to the contrary.

In January 1970 the Department of Labor published an extensive study of the effect on the economy of the 1963, 1965, and 1969 longshore strikes. The study concluded that, although the companies and workers involved suffered losses, as did some workers and owners in collateral industries, "the strike had no visible impact on the economy as a whole." Many companies, according to the report, prepared for the strikes by stepping up their business before the stoppages and catching up again afterwards. "There appears to be no evidence," the report stated, "of a permanent loss of export markets because of the strikes." In talking to newsmen when he released the longshore strikes study, Secretary of Labor George P. Shultze stated that "despite warnings of catastrophic economic effects during some major strikes such results are kind of difficult to find afterwards."

HIGH PRICE OF COMPULSION

It has often been proposed that strikes in the private sector be made illegal. The managements of the railroads and the maritime industry openly advocate compulsory arbitration as a desirable alternative to free collective bargaining. There is reason to believe that unions in industries where automation has reduced the strike power will also move to that position. Suppliers and customers hurt by a strike are likely to mutter, "It should be outlawed."

Unfortunately, it is not a matter of eliminating strikes by devices which have no costs. The various compulsory settlement methods also are expensive, and it may be that managements, unions, and the public would find such costs more onerous than the costs of strikes. We should be fully aware of these costs before abandoning the present free collective bargaining system in the private sector.

Specter of More Failures

The costliness of a strike to management and labor is in itself a strong incentive for them to reach agreement. What happens if that incentive is removed? There is reason to believe that the number of failures to reach agreement would increase greatly. This was our experience during World War II, when the strike was replaced with compulsory settlement by a government agency. It was also our experience in the late 1940s, when a number of states replaced free collective bargaining in public utilities with compulsory arbitration.

There are two reasons that the companies and unions find it more difficult to reach agreement when the possibility of the strike has been removed:

1. The parties are not under so much pressure to work out a contract because, while the compulsory settlement may be less desirable than the contract that could have been negotiated, it does not carry a threat of immediate loss of production and wages.

2. If the compulsory settlement authority—whether it be a government board, a court, or an arbitrator—has the right to decide on what it thinks is a fair settlement, then the company and the union may well hesitate to make a move toward a settlement, fearing that the other party will hold at its old position and that the board, court, or arbitrator will split the difference. If for example, the company is offering a $.10-per-hour increase, and the union is asking for $.16 per hour, why should the company move to $.12 when there can be no strike anyhow and when the authority might then decide between $.12 and $.16 instead of between $.10 and $.16? For like reasons, the union hesitates to move down from $.16 to $.14. Thus, compulsory settlement interferes with the process of voluntary settlement.

In order to avoid the effect just described, the Nixon Administration now proposes that when strikes are threatened in the transportation industries, the President be permitted to order arbitration proceedings in which the arbitrator is required to decide only which of the two final offers of the parties is the more reasonable. It is believed that this method would remove one of the undesirable effects of the usual type of arbitration—that is, the hesitancy of the parties to improve their offers for fear that the arbitrator will split the difference. However, the new proposal has the disadvantage of forcing the arbitrator to choose between two proposals, both of which may seem unfair to him.

While the type of arbitration now proposed by the Administration would probably be less harmful than ordinary compulsory arbitration in terms of hampering efforts to reach a voluntary settlement, it would still have some such effect, for management and labor would not be prodded by fears of strike costs. I believe it is erroneous to expect that the number of disputes which would go to an arbitrator would be the same as the number of strikes which would occur without compulsory settlement. The removal of the strong incentive to settle would result in a great many more failures to reach agreement voluntarily. It would therefore be necessary to establish a sizable government bureaucracy to handle the increased volume of unsettled contract disputes.

More Federal Intervention

The size of the bureaucracy could be lessened by using private arbitrators (with the parties given an opportunity to choose the men they like) instead of a labor board or a labor court. However, the government would have to become involved when the parties were unable to agree on an arbitrator. Moreover, while the Federal Mediation and Conciliation Service has been free from political bias in placing arbitrators' names on its lists for selection by the parties in grievance arbitrations, there can be no guarantee that politics would not play a role in the selection process if the stakes were high enough—as they would be in the compulsory arbitration of new contract terms in the steel, coal, automobile, and other major industries.

If a board or labor court were used to settle disputes, it would have the possible advantage of being able to establish continuing policies. Nevertheless, appointment of at least some of the members would be made by the Administration. (A board could be tripartite, in which case some members would be appointed by labor and some by management.) One of the costs of compulsory settlement, therefore, would be to move management-labor disputes—to some degree at least—from the economic to the political arena.

Will Force Really Work?

Under the free collective bargaining system, the government has no problem of enforcement. For instance, while both the company and the employees suffered serious losses during the 14-week GE strike, once it was over both the management and the workers returned to their jobs voluntarily. This illustrates an important advantage of the present system which is often overlooked—that no use of force by the government is required. Moreover, since the agreement is one which the parties themselves have negotiated, the day-to-day operations under it are likely to be more cooperative. The company representatives sell it to management, and the union representatives sell it to the employees. Since the contract is the negotiators' own handiwork, they make a real effort to get it to work—a greater effort, I believe, than they would make if the agreement were the work of some authority appointed by the government.

This country's experience with legislation that has prohibited strikes on the part of public employees indicates that such legislation does not automatically put an end to the strikes. The Condon-Wadlin Act, which prohibited strikes by state and local government employees in New York State from 1947 to 1967, was violated often, but on only a few occasions were its penalties actually enforced. Since 1967 the Taylor Act, which also prohibits strikes by public employees in New York State, has been subject to numerous violations. Likewise, the illegality of strikes by federal employees has not prevented them from leaving the job.

What would happen, under compulsory settlement, if workers in the coal, steel, automobile, trucking, or some other major industry decided that they did not wish to accept the terms prescribed by the arbitrator or labor court and refused to work? How does a democratic government force 100,000 coal miners, 400,000 steel workers, 700,000 automobile workers, or 450,000 truckers to perform their tasks effectively when they elect not to do so? Perhaps it can be done—but I suggest that this is a question which it is well not to have to answer. It is unwise to run the risk of placing government in a position where the government may reveal its impotence unless it is absolutely necessary to do so.

Threat to Capitalism

Finally, if government becomes involved in the determination of labor contract terms in order to avoid
strikes, it may not be able to stop there. With our
democratic political structure it would be impossible,
I believe, to prevent compulsory settlement of wages
for union members from leading to compulsory determination of all wages; that, in turn, would lead to
government decisions concerning salaries, professional fees, and, finally, prices and profits.

So long as free collective bargaining is permitted,
it forms an outer perimeter of defense against government regulation in other areas. If it falls, the possibility of more regulation in the other areas becomes
much greater. It is worth noting that George Meany,
the president of the AFL-CIO, stated several months
ago that he would not be opposed to wage controls
if similar controls were placed on salaries, prices,
and profits. Meany's view of these relationships is
one that many people might share.

CONCLUSION

How do the costs of the right to strike compare with
the costs of the alternative, compulsory settlement?
Taking strike costs first, my analysis indicates that:

It is easy to overemphasize the costs of strikes.

*Much progress has already been made in replacing
organizational strikes, jurisdictional strikes, and
grievance strikes with peaceful alternatives.*

*Strikes—even the big industrywide ones—have a
minimal effect on the economy.*

*Some strikes, such as those in public utilities, which
once were very critical, are no longer so because
of automation.*

*The number of man-days lost because of strikes
is a very small part of the total (only 0.23 percent
in 1969), and the trend has been definitely downward.*

On the other hand, my analysis indicates that compulsory settlement involves major costs like these:

*The elimination from collective bargaining of the
strongest incentive to reach agreement which management and labor now have.*

*A great increase in the number of failures to reach
agreement.*

*The development of a large government bureau-
cracy to adjudicate the larger number of unsettled
disputes.*

*An increase in political aspects of collective bar-
gaining.*

*The difficulty of enforcement of compulsory orders,
with the attendant danger of divulging the impotence
of government.*

*The likely development of other wage, salary, price,
and profit controls by government.*

I conclude that the right to strike is preferable to
a compulsory settlement system. It does not follow
that the government should never move to protect
the public against strikes which create serious hardships, but it does follow that any move to prohibit
the use of the strike in the private sector should be
made cautiously and only to the extent which is
clearly required. Any broad prohibition of strike freedom would prove to be very costly in itself and also
lead to major government controls over other parts
of the economy. Free collective bargaining, which
includes the right to strike and the right to lockout,
constitutes the outer defense of the private enterprise
system.   □

UNION EFFECTS ON WAGES—A CAUTION

In 96 percent or more of labor negotiations, as Kennedy points out above, the result is not a strike but
a new contract. One of the most important objectives
of labor in the setting of this new contract will be
to raise the level of wages. Let us briefly indicate
how a union can cause a departure from the market-
determined wage and then suggest why caution must
be used in interpreting this piece of analysis.

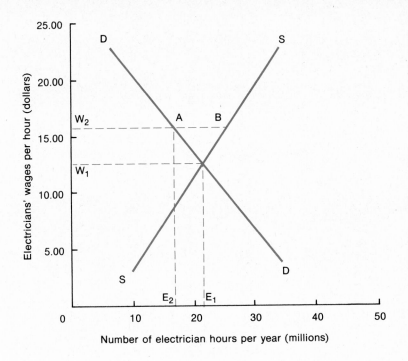

Figure 5–5. Effects of a Single Union on Wage Rates and Employment.

If one union in the economy succeeds in raising its wage (W_2) above the supply-and-demand determined wage (W_1), the consequences for those workers will be less employment but higher wages for those employed. One must not generalize this effect to the action of unions in the economy as a whole, however, since these curves are drawn on *ceteris paribus* assumptions that do not hold when all unions are acting together.

Figure 5–5 shows the effect of a wage increase for electricians above the supply-and-demand determined price. W_1 is the wage that would obtain if there were no external intervention in the market. The union's objective is to raise the wage to W_2. If it succeeds—and if everything else remains unchanged (our familiar *ceteris paribus* clause)—then, when the wage rate is raised to W_2, business firms will cut their employment from E_1 to E_2. Actually, the measure of unemployment among electricians would be greater than the difference between those formerly employed and those now employed. The reason is that at the new and higher wage rate, more electricians' services would be offered than before. (This is what the supply curve tells us.) Consequently, the amount of unemployment is measured by the horizontal distance between the demand and supply curves at the new wage (W_2), or the distance *AB*.

Now it would seem from this analysis that the main impact of unions in this area of bargaining would be to raise the wage rates of their members and to curtail the employment of their members. And, indeed, the objective of securing a wage that is high relative to other income receivers in the economy is an important one for most unions.

We must not conclude that this effort will be successful *in the aggregate,* however. And this is where we must exercise some caution in interpreting our results. For we cannot say that when one union does something alone, the same results will be achieved for that union as when *all unions together* attempt a similar thing. The relevance of the *ceteris paribus* phrase is particularly important here. When *all* unions are attempting to achieve wage increases, then this clause is no longer appropriate for any one labor market—other things *are* changing. In particular, if all wages go up, this will have an effect on the demand for most products in the economy; and when the demand for products goes up, this, in turn, will have an effect on the demand for labor. We could, in fact, imagine a case where everything more or less canceled out: There were higher wages in general, higher prices in general (so that the higher wages would purchase the same number of goods in the economy as before), and no change in the employment of workers throughout the economy.

This might seem like an argument against unions, since it would mean that they hadn't achieved much for all their pains. On the other hand, it can also be used to combat an argument frequently used in the past against labor unions—namely, that they are responsible for mass unemployment in the economy.

What we have actually done in these last two paragraphs has been to move on from a particular part of the economy (washing machines, electricians, and so on) to a consideration of the economy in the aggregate. Thus, we are foreshadowing matters that we shall be taking up in some detail in Part Two of this book, beginning with chapter 7.

THE COMPLICATED MIXTURE— GOVERNMENT, BUSINESS, LABOR

We cannot end these two chapters on the mixed American economy without stressing one basic point. The point is that not only is the economy "mixed" in the overall sense that there is a public and private sector, each of some significance, but also in the sense that each sector is itself increasingly "mixed." This was explicitly true of both Product and Factor Markets from 1971 to 1974. Through the Cost-of-Living Council and the Pay Board, the government was extensively involved in wage-price decisions throughout this period.

But, it is true in a more general sense as well. It can be argued (and has been argued, as we know), that corporate executives and corporate objectives are not all that different from the executives and objectives apparent in the public bureaucracy, whether it be the Department of Defense or the Department of Agriculture. Furthermore, the life-styles

of labor leaders are no longer much different from those of business executives (except, as someone once suggested, that they are better dressed). The antagonistic clash between labor and management, like the predicted antagonistic clash between the public and private sectors (between socialism and free enterprise), has not materialized in the way that Marx, or, for that matter, anyone else, anticipated.

This blurring of the traditional categories is an important notion to have in mind as we move forward to a more in-depth analysis of the workings of a modern economy. It will help free us to look at economic realities with a fresh and imaginative point of view.

SUMMARY

Despite the growth of government in the American economy in recent decades, our economy remains heavily oriented towards the private sector. This private sector is, however, not quite what one would expect from a simple supply-and-demand analysis appropriate to a market economy.

In the area of business, there are many different forms of business organization such as the *single proprietorship*, the *partnership*, and the *corporation*. The corporation, with its limited liability, its divorce of ownership from control, and its sometimes massive size is perhaps the most significant form of modern industrial organization. Many corporations are in the billion-dollar category, and these clearly will have some power to influence the markets in which they buy and sell. Because of the enormous size of the economy in which these giants operate, it is difficult to judge how powerful they are. Economists often try to measure *concentration ratios* (e.g., what percentage of shipments in an industry is accounted for by the four largest firms?) to determine the impact of firms relative to their particular industries. They also try to determine trends in concentration over time. Although the impact of large firms is certainly greater than it was, say, in the mid-nineteenth century, there is no universally accepted evidence of increasing concentration in the past several decades.

Even apart from concentration ratios, however, the simple bigness of the modern corporation probably has implications for the way in which it functions. Many observers have commented that public and private bureaucracies have increasingly come to share common features—the corporate manager and the public servant may not be so far apart as was once thought.

The Factor Markets of the American economy similarly function rather more complexly than simple supply-and-demand analysis might suggest. The labor union is a particularly important example of an institution that influences the functioning of our most important factor market. The effects of union action are not always what they seem. Strikes, for example, are probably much less costly to our society than is often imagined. Similarly, although one union may improve the position of its members relative to another's, it is not clear that, in the aggregate, labor unions can bring higher wages (i.e., in terms of real purchasing power) for all their members at once.

One general conclusion that emerges from a brief survey of the private sector of our economy is this: The American economy not only contains two sectors—public and private—but is in fact a thorough-going mixture of elements *within* each sector. There is very little black and white, but an astonishing range of greys.

IMPORTANT TERMS TO REMEMBER

Single Proprietorship
Partnership
Corporation
Limited Liability
Divorce of Ownership and Control
Concentration Ratios
Military/Industrial Complex
Factor Supply and Demand Curves.
Collective Bargaining
AFL-CIO
Strikes:
   Political, Organizational,
   Jurisdictional, Grievance,
   Contract
Compulsory Arbitration

QUESTIONS FOR DISCUSSION

1. Large modern corporations are clearly not *pure competitors* in the sense defined in chapter 2 (p. 40), but most businessmen would say that they definitely "compete" with each other and with foreign rivals, etc. What is your intuitive sense of what such "competing" involves? What forms of competition do you see most frequently in the present-day American economy?

2. John Kenneth Galbraith once said that when visitors from abroad come to study the efficiency of American industry, the firms they visit are the same ones most frequently visited by representatives of the Antitrust Division of the Justice Department. Why might this be?

3. How might the self-interest of a salaried manager differ from that of an owner-operator of a business firm? If you were the head of a large corporation (in which you owned little or no stock), what motives do you think would guide your conduct?

4. "The existence of large, even giant, corporations means that American business does not respond to the dictates of the market, but rather manages the market for its own purposes. For this very reason 'consumer sovereignty' is largely a myth in the modern industrial world." Discuss.

5. Write an essay on the pros and cons of strikes as a means of settling labor disputes.

6. The distinguished American economist Thorstein Veblen (1857–1929) once called the struggle between business and labor a mere game "played between two contending interests for private gain." How might the leader of a modern labor union respond to such a criticism?

7. Why is it impossible to generalize from the effects of one union, acting alone, to the effects of all unions, acting simultaneously, on real wages and employment in the national economy?

8. Enumerate some of the ways in which the U.S. government attempts to protect the public interest in the face of the growth of big business and big labor. What do you consider to be the major difficulties in defining an effective policy in this area?

SUGGESTED READING

Blair, John M. *Economic Concentration: Structure Behavior and Public Policy.* New York: Harcourt, Brace, Jovanovich, 1972.

Caves, Richard. *American Industry: Structure, Conduct, Performance.* 3rd ed. Englewood Cliffs, N.J.: Prentice-Hall, 1972.

Galbraith, John K. *American.Capitalism, the Concept of Countervailing Power.* Boston: Houghton Mifflin Co., 1952

Phelps, Edmund S., ed. *Problems of the Modern Economy.* New York: W. W. Norton & Co., 1966, pp. 7–106.

Taft, Philip. *Organized Labor in American History.* New York: Harper & Row, 1964.

Trebing, Harry M., ed. *The Corporation in the American Economy.* Chicago: Quadrangle Books, 1970.

Weiss, Leonard W. *Case Studies in American Industry.* New York: John Wiley & Sons, 1967.

Wilcox, Clair. *Public Policies Toward Business.* Rev. ed. Homewood, Ill.: Richard D. Irwin, 1960.

CHAPTER 6
THE UNDERDEVELOPED ECONOMY

In this chapter, the last in our discussion of basic economic systems, we move sharply from the affluent, industrial economy of the United States to the poor, *underdeveloped economy,* characteristic of much of Asia, Africa, and Latin America.

In discussing the underdeveloped economy, we are to some degree considering a set of economic conditions, rather than a kind of economic *system* (socialism, mixed economy, and so on). That is to say, the poor countries of the world at present operate under many different varieties of economic system, including specific national and local elements, some of which have no real analogue in the economically developed world. Still, the inclusion of this chapter in Part One is warranted on two grounds. First is the fact that the basic problems facing many of these countries are so overwhelming that they are likely to condition *any* economic system developed to meet them. And second is the fact (or at least the strong belief of most observers) that the characteristic underdeveloped country is likely to depart rather substantially from the kind of economic system under which much of the Western world industrialized. In

particular, it is widely believed that economic planning—specifically planning for growth—will loom larger in these countries than it did in many Western countries, certainly than it did in ''early developers'' like Britain and the United States when they were going through their industrial revolutions. In short, although there will still be variety, the economic systems of these countries are likely to show important similarities, if only because of the enormous problems they face.

MEANING OF ECONOMIC UNDERDEVELOPMENT

Many terms have been used to describe the underdeveloped economies of the world: ''economically backward,'' ''less developed,'' or ''developing,'' to cite a few. The common element is simply *poverty,* the depth of which can be attested by any traveler who has seen the conditions in which many of these peoples live.

Poverty can also be confirmed by a great variety of statistical measures. One might look at figures on life expectancy, calories in the diet, number of teach-

TABLE 6–1

ANNUAL PER CAPITA OUTPUT IN 1970*

GROUP A ANNUAL PER CAPITA OUTPUT OF $0–$100		GROUP B ANNUAL PER CAPITA OUTPUT OF $101–$300		GROUP C ANNUAL PER CAPITA OUTPUT OF $301–$600	

Africa
Burundi
Chad
Dahomey
Ethiopia
Lesotho
Malawi
Mali
Niger
Rwanda
Somalia
Tanzania
Upper Volta
Zaire
	**Asia and
	Middle East**
	Afghanistan
	Bhutan
	Burma
	Indonesia
	Maldive Islands
	Nepal
	North Vietnam
	Pakistan and
	  Bangladesh
	Sikkim
	Yemen
		Africa
		Algeria
		Angola
		Arab Republic
		  of Egypt
		Botswana
		Cameroon
		Cape Verde
		  Islands
		Central African
		  Republic
		Comoro Islands
		Congo
		  (Peoples' Rep.)
		Gambia
		Guinea
		Guinea
		  (Equatorial)
		Kenya
		Liberia
		Malagasy
		  Republic
		Mauritania
		Mauritius
		Morocco
		Mozambique
		Nigeria
		Portuguese
		  Guinea
		Senegal
		Sierra Leone
		Rhodesia
		Swaziland
		Togo
		Tunisia
			**Asia and
			Middle East**
			China
			  (Mainland)
			India
			Jordan
			Khmer Republic
			Korea (South)
			Laos
			Macao
			Philippines
			South Vietnam
			Sri Lanka
			Syria
			Thailand
			
			Latin America
			Bolivia
			Ecuador
			El Salvador
			Haiti
			Honduras
			Paraguay
			
			Oceania
			Papua New
			  Guinea
			Portuguese
			  Timor
				Africa
				Centa and
				  Melilla
				Ghana
				Ivory Coast
				Zambia
				
				Oceania
				Fiji Islands
				
				**Asia and
				Middle East**
				Bahrain
				China (Taiwan)
				Iran
				Iraq
				Korea (North)
				Lebanon
				Malaysia
				Mongolia
				Oman
				Saudi Arabia
					Latin America
					Barbados
					Brazil
					British
					  Honduras
					Colombia
					Costa Rica
					Dominican
					  Republic
					Guatemala
					Guyana
					Nicaragua
					Surinam
					
					Europe
					Albania
					Turkey

ers or doctors per head of population, steel output or electrical power output per capita, percentage of the population living in rural areas or working in the agricultural sector, number of automobiles, miles of road, movie theaters, household appliances, plumbing facilities, and so on. In each case, one would find a striking contrast between the material comforts of the industrialized world and the harsh facts of subsistence in their poorer neighbors.

Since economic "growth" is usually defined in terms of a rising output per capita, economists often use this index as a general measure of the degree of poverty or "underdevelopment" in any particular country. Actually, this measure is not a completely satisfactory one, for a number of reasons. One simple reason is that the necessary information is often lacking. Statistical collections in many poor countries are often either nonexistent or little better than not-so-educated guesswork. Another reason is that in many of these nations there is a great deal of production that never enters explicitly into the marketplace. A small village in India or in some African country may produce mainly for its own needs, with the result that only a small part of its total production would appear in formal statistics, even if we had them. There is also a fundamental difficulty involved in any attempt to make comparisons among societies that differ radically in their economic structure. If country A produces exactly the same goods as country B, and

GROUP D ANNUAL PER CAPITA OUTPUT OF $601–$1600	
Africa	**Latin America**
Gabon	Argentina
Malta	Chile
Reunion	Guadaloupe
South Africa	Jamaica
	Martinique
Asia and	Mexico
Middle East	Neth. Antilles
Brunei	Panama
Cyprus	Trinidad,
Hong Kong	Tobago
Ryukyu Islands	Uruguay
Singapore	Venezuela
Europe	
Bulgaria	
Greece	
Hungary	
Ireland	
Poland	
Portugal	
Romania	
Spain	
Yugoslavia	

GROUP E ANNUAL PER CAPITA OUTPUT OF $1600–$3000	
Africa	**Europe**
Libya	Austria
	Belgium
Asia and	Channel Islands
Middle East	Czechoslovakia
Israel	East Germany
Japan	Finland
Qatar	Iceland
United Arab	Italy
Emirates	Luxembourg
	Netherlands
North America	Norway
Puerto Rico	United Kingdom
	U.S.S.R.
Oceania	West Germany
Australia	
New Zealand	
West Indies	
Bahama Islands	

GROUP F ANNUAL PER CAPITA OUTPUT OF ABOVE $3000	
Asia and Middle East	**Average Per Capita Output**
Kuwait	$3,760
Europe	
Denmark	$3,190
France	$3,100
Sweden	$4,040
Switzerland	$3,320
North America	
Canada	$3,700
United States	$4,760

*These figures are Gross National Product at 1970 market prices, converted to U.S. dollars in most instances by means of foreign exchange rates, and divided by population.

Source: Taken from the *World Bank Atlas*, published by the International Bank for Reconstruction and Development 1973. Reprinted by permission.

in the same proportions, but has ten times more of each good, then we can say fairly unequivocally that country A has ten times the total output of country B. But if country A is a rich country and country B is a poor country, they will not in general be consuming the same goods and in the same proportions. Rice may be the most important product in country B, while in country A it may be automobiles, or washing machines, or vacuum cleaners. For that matter, what exactly would the significance of a vacuum cleaner be to country B if its villagers lived in huts with earthen floors? The point is that comparisons between countries with drastically different standards of living involve not only practical problems but also difficult philosophic problems. To a certain degree, these comparisons must be taken with a grain of salt.[1]

Still, the gap in levels of output per capita between the rich and the poor countries of the world is so great that even the very rough statistics we are able to gather tell a meaningful and dramatic story. Table 6–1 shows how great this gap is. Something like one-half the world's population has an annual per capita output of below $300. Even if we correct this

1. The same problems are also present when we try to measure the growth of a single country over very long periods of time. For a discussion of the meaning of a nation's output per capita and other "national income" concepts, see chapter 8. For the problems involved in measuring long-run growth, see chapter 16.

figure upward (as we probably should), we still have the fact that perhaps a majority of the people of the world live on little more than a tenth of the income we are accustomed to enjoying in the present-day United States.

Such a huge gap did not exist two centuries ago or even one century ago. There were differences, of course. Some countries were richer than others, as has been the case throughout history. But the salient fact of the past 100 or 200 years is that the gap has been widening, not just absolutely but in percentage terms, and not slowly but rapidly. The fundamental reason, of course, is that the nations of Europe and North America went through (and are continuing to go through) an industrial revolution during this period, while the poorer countries did not. Economically they stood still—in some cases, they may even have lost ground—while the advanced countries shot ahead at theretofore inconceivably rapid rates. Stagnation in one area of the world and rapid modern growth in the other brought about the great disparities in standards of living that are with us today.

HISTORICAL VERSUS MODERN DEVELOPMENT

The past twenty-five years have seen a sharp awakening, in both East and West, to the facts we have just been describing. Although the poor countries of the world are aware of some of the problems of industrialization, they want to have at least a fair share in the material progress that they have seen so bountifully distributed in the West.

Now to a certain degree the attempt to achieve this goal poses to the underdeveloped country of today the same problems faced by the economically advanced countries a century or two ago. One partial way of looking at the problem is to say that these countries are now trying to achieve the same kind of industrial revolution that Britain achieved in the late eighteenth century, the United States in the early nineteenth century, Russia and Japan in the late nineteenth century, and so on. To the degree that

this is true, one can look to past history for clues to steps that these underdeveloped countries must undertake today.

This, however, is only a partial and incomplete approach to the problem, because there are a number of important respects in which these countries face difficulties that are *different* from those of countries that achieved their industrial revolutions in the past. These differences, indeed, affect virtually every aspect of the development process, including, as we have already suggested, the form of economic system most appropriate for promoting rapid growth.

Let us spend the rest of this chapter taking up some of these differences with respect to the main factors behind economic development: (1) technological change, (2) capital accumulation, and (3) population growth.

TECHNOLOGICAL CHANGE IN POOR COUNTRIES

In chapter 1, when we were discussing how a country's production-possibility curve might shift outward over time, we suggested that technological change—the development of new products and new methods of production and distribution—would be an important element, perhaps the most important element, in the process. Interestingly, the one respect in which the modern underdeveloped country would appear to have a clear-cut advantage over its historical predecessors is in the area of technological change. Indeed, this constitutes the main single reason for some optimism about the ultimate prospects of the underdeveloped world.

The advantage derives from the fact that although these countries have been technologically stagnant during the past century, the world as a whole has not been. When England started her Industrial Revolution, the steam engine had not yet been invented, but for the underdeveloped country of today, the steam engine already exists. So also does electric power, the railroad, the telephone, the airplane, and even atomic energy and electronic computers. During the past century, there has been developed an enormous store of new technology that is potentially available even to the poorest and most backward

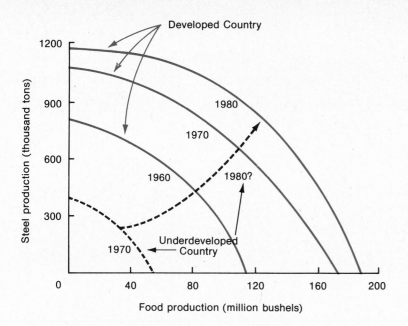

Developed Country

1980

1970

1960

1980?

1970

Underdeveloped Country

Steel production (thousand tons)

Food production (million bushels)

Figure 6–1. Rapid Techno-logical Advance.

Can a poor country, using available Western technology, leap forward in a few years to a much more developed state? There are, unfortunately, many difficulties in the way of such spectacular advances.

countries. Instead of having to start from scratch, they have open to them all the major scientific achievements of the industrial world, and this gives them a running start, compared to the "early developers."

The possibilities that this opens up are suggested in Figure 6–1. We have added to a similar diagram from chapter 1 a production-possibility curve for an underdeveloped country. The diagram conveys the possibility that, using advanced Western technology, the underdeveloped country (though starting down in the far left corner) might in a few years leap upwards to join its more economically favored neighbors.

The advantage conferred by the availability of Western technology is, however, qualified by a number of important drawbacks:

1. The advanced technology of the West is, in most cases, unsuited to the economic conditions prevalent in the less developed countries. Many of these countries are characterized by (a) an abundance of unskilled, semiliterate laborers, and (b) a shortage of

trained workers and managers, and also of machinery and other capital goods. The advanced technology of the West, however, requires both skilled labor and a great deal of machinery and other capital goods. The large-scale adoption of this technology in unmodified form would create enormous strains on an underdeveloped country and would also provide little employment for the vast numbers of unskilled laborers in the economy. Consequently, modification of Western technology (to make it more suitable to conditions in the underdeveloped country) is highly desirable. But such modification is difficult and, in many cases, is tantamount to the development of "new" technology.

2. Many less developed countries, particularly at an early stage of their efforts, do not have the productive capacity to produce the kinds of machinery, tools, and other equipment that the installation of Western technology requires. This means that they will often have to sustain large imports of industrial goods in the early stages of their development effort. But how are they to pay for these imports? In a country like

India, where exports have been sluggish and where there has been a need to import not only capital goods but also food, raw materials, and increasingly expensive fuel oil, the problem of a balance of payments crisis may be a serious one, severely limiting the country's development potentialities.

3. Not all Western technology is unequivocally helpful in promoting economic development. The clearest instance in this respect is public health and medical technology. As we shall see when we come to the problem of population growth, the importation of Western public health and medical technology has contributed to a sharp fall in the death rate in many underdeveloped countries. This is a desirable achievement in its own right, but it has contributed to the population explosion in these countries that may pose grave obstacles to successful development.

These qualifications do not mean that the technological advantage of the modern underdeveloped country is completely nullified. It is still a major asset to have the storehouse of the industrial world to draw upon. Still, it is clear that the advantage is somewhat less than might appear at first glance. Also, the qualifications make it clear that the effort simply to copy the latest and most advanced examples of Western technology may be an unwise and even foolhardy approach for many of these countries.

CAPITAL ACCUMULATION

Technological change is not the only factor making for an outward-shifting production-possibility curve. Another important element is the accumulation of capital goods. These goods include machines, tools, buildings, equipment, inventories of goods in stock, and any other *produced means of production* (in contrast, say, to natural resources that are not "produced" by man). Adam Smith, we recall, gave capital accumulation an important place in the growth process and attributed it largely to the frugality of private individuals, as opposed to the extravagance of governments. In the twentieth century, however, we have seen that governments often pursue capital accumulation more vigorously than private

individuals—witness the fact that most command or near-command economies in modern times have tended to give a preference to capital goods relative to consumer goods (see pp. 54–55).

Two important generalizations can be made about capital accumulation in the modern underdeveloped country. The first is that this accumulation may be particularly important for such a country's growth, for reasons we have just been discussing under the heading of technological change. If, as we have suggested, Western technology uses a high proportion of capital relative to other factors of production, then the ability of a poor country to apply this technology will depend in great part on its capacity for capital accumulation. In other words, the technological potentiality can be converted into an actual advantage only via an expanded accumulation of capital.

The second point is that, although the need for more capital may be great in these countries, the problem of supplying it may be even greater than it was in times past. There are several reasons for this, an important one being that these countries are very poor, even poorer than many of the industrialized nations were a century or two ago when they were embarking on *their* course of development. As Adam Smith correctly pointed out, capital accumulation requires saving. The process in its essence involves the setting aside of some of today's income, saving it, and investing it in more machines, tools, etc. If output per capita is very low, people may wish to consume all or nearly all of their very meager incomes. Indeed, some economists believe that there is a kind of vicious circle of poverty here:

Such a vicious circle will arise if saving depends upon output while output depends upon the rate of capital accumulation. Thus, in its simplest form, it would go: People are poor, therefore they do not save much. Since savings are small, capital accumulation will be slow. Since there is little capital accumulation, output will remain low. When output is low, people are poor. In other words, people remain poor because they are poor.

Other economists believe that these circles are not so vicious as might appear. They point out that historically even the poorest societies have been able to summon "surpluses" above consumption; for example, for waging wars. They also note that in many less developed countries there are extremely wealthy individuals—large landowners, merchants, the governing classes—who form a potential supply of savings and investment if the surplus can be tapped.

Still, no one would argue that general poverty is a condition that favors capital accumulation. Furthermore, there are other factors that may complicate the situation. The rapid development of communications in modern times has meant that poor nations are often keenly aware of the luxurious living standards present in the West. This increases their desire for growth, but it may also stimulate their desire for higher levels of consumption (and hence less saving and capital accumulation) in the immediate present. Also, the social structure of the underdeveloped country may not be favorable to the utilization of such economic surpluses as are potentially available. In the West, energetic private individuals developed the habit of frugality and thrift at an early stage, virtually as a matter of religious principle.[2] But the wealthy Latin-American landowner or the oil-rich potentate in the Middle East may prefer to live in luxury and ostentation and devote relatively little of the available surplus to growth-generating purposes.

All this is not to say that the modern underdeveloped country will be unable to summon the capital it so desperately needs. But it does mean that the effort to do so may impose a very great strain on the society and may possibly require a major reorganization of its structure.

The case of China is very interesting in this regard. After the end of the civil war in 1949, China took strong and immediate steps to raise her rate of capital accumulation. Although accurate figures are virtually impossible to come by, it would appear that gross investment,[3] which had been well below 10 percent of GNP in the 1930s, had risen to 19 percent by 1952 and to 25 percent or more in 1957. In 1958, moreover, China entered upon the period of her "Great Leap Forward." Through state action in industry (by 1957, over 96 percent of all industrial investment in China was undertaken by the government) and by collectivization of agriculture through the communes, which were to increase the available agricultural surplus, China made an effort to increase her total investment well above what was already an extremely high figure for such a relatively underdeveloped country. These facts prove (1) that a poor country *can* raise its investment level substantially even in a very short period of time, but also (2) that structural reorganizations of society of this magnitude can be very costly. There is little doubt that there was a general fall in the rate of investment in the early 1960s as China tried to recover from the extreme strains of the "Great Leap" period. Indeed, in the early 1960s, the economy was seriously depressed in both agricultural and industrial sectors. By 1970, China had recovered from this experience but she had also meanwhile gone through the strains of the "cultural revolution" (1966–69), and it seems fairly certain that her overall growth in the 1960s was slower than it had been in the 1950s.[4]

The point, then, is that although capital accumulation problems are not insurmountable in today's less developed country, they are very severe, because of the combination of a large need and a relatively inadequate means of supplying that need. The great question—from the point of view of the public interest of the world as a whole—is whether this problem can be solved without steps that rend the fabric of society and cause great temporary hardships for the peoples involved.

---

2. Indeed, some economic historians have argued that it *was* a matter of religious principle. See, for example, the classic work: Max Weber, *The Protestant Ethic and the Spirit of Capitalism* (New York: Charles Scribner's Sons, 1952).

3. The term *gross investment* refers to the production of new capital goods, *including* those that simply *replace* old or obsolescent machines or buildings. See discussion pp. 193–94.

4. In the case of the "cultural revolution," it can be argued that Chairman Mao was prepared to sacrifice high investment and high economic growth in order "to create a society radically different from those that now exist in the industrialized world." (Dwight H. Perkins, "The Economic Performance of China and Japan, 1842–1969," Harvard Institute of Economic Research, Cambridge, Mass., Discussion Paper Number 177, February 1971, p. 34). The highest possible rate of growth need not be the *only* objective, even in an extremely poor economy.

THE POPULATION PROBLEM

We come now to the third of what we called the main factors in economic development: population growth. Because of its extreme importance for the underdeveloped countries (and for the world generally), we must spend a bit more time on this particular problem.

The problem in a nutshell is given in Figure 6–2. No one should attribute more accuracy to this diagram than it possesses—population statistics are historically unreliable and projections of curves into the future even more so. Still, the basic situation is quite clear. There has been an enormous acceleration of world population growth in modern times. The period of doubling of world population—historically measured in centuries or millennia—is now thirty or forty years. Another thing is also quite clear —it can't go on this way. Increases at this rate would soon bring not only a "standing room only" world but also an evidently impossible situation in which the physical weight of people would exceed the weight of the earth itself. Thus, these rates of population growth will stop; *how* they will stop is a matter of no small concern for anyone who has any feeling at all for the future of the human race.

THE MALTHUSIAN APPROACH

The analysis of this problem must begin with one of the British classical economists, Thomas Robert Malthus, who predicted population disaster for the world nearly two centuries ago. Malthus (1766–1834) was a wide-ranging thinker whose contributions to economics included, besides population theory, some very interesting speculations about the causes of depressions (what he called "universal gluts") that were taken up again in the 1930s. He can also be given some credit for being the *first* professional economist because, although he was Reverend Malthus, he was also a professor of political economy at the East India College in Haileybury.

Malthus's views on population were presented to the world in *An Essay on the Principle of Population as It Affects the Future Improvement of Society,* the first edition of which was published in 1798. The immediate cause of his writing the *Essay* was a dis-

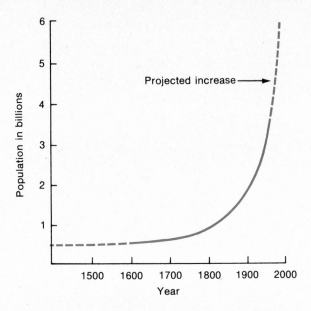

Figure 6–2. Acceleration of Population Growth.

The striking acceleration of population growth in modern times is made apparent in this curve. It should be noted that population figures for the world as a whole are only estimates, even today. For earlier centuries, they are very rough approximations.

cussion with his father about the perfectibility of man and society. Young Malthus wished to show that such eighteenth-century optimists as William Godwin and the Marquis de Condorcet were far too hopeful in their philosophies. The effect of the *Essay* was dramatic, both immediately and in the long run. It went through six editions and had a direct impact on the views of contemporary economists (also influencing Charles Darwin's evolutionary theory, as we have mentioned before). The essayist Thomas Carlyle was so disturbed by his reading of it that he labeled economics the "dismal science," a name that has persisted to this day. In the 1970s, it remains a basic starting place for any serious analysis of the problems of the underdeveloped economy.

Let us present Malthus's theory in his own words, and then, introducing some modern modifications, indicate its relevance for the present day.

An Essay on the Principle of Population

Thomas Robert Malthus

The subject will, perhaps, be seen in a clearer light, if we endeavour to ascertain what would be the natural increase of population, if left to exert itself with perfect freedom; and what might be expected to be the rate of increase in the productions of the earth, under the most favourable circumstances of human industry.

In the northern states of America, where the means of subsistence have been more ample, the manners of the people more pure, and the checks to early marriages fewer, than in any of the modern states of Europe, the population has been found to double itself, for above a century and half successively, in less than twenty-five years. Yet, even during these periods, in some of the towns, the deaths exceeded the births, a circumstance which clearly proves that, in those parts of the country which supplied this deficiency, the increase must have been much more rapid than the general average.

In the back settlements, where the sole employment is agriculture, and vicious customs and unwholesome occupations are little known, the population has been found to double itself in fifteen years. Even this extraordinary rate of increase is probably short of the utmost power of population. Very severe labour is requisite to clear a fresh country; such situations are not in general considered as particularly healthy; and the inhabitants, probably, are occasionally subject to the incursions of the Indians, which may destroy some lives, or at any rate diminish the fruits of industry.

But, to be perfectly sure that we are far within the truth, we will take the slowest of these rates of increase. It may safely be pronounced, therefore, that population, when unchecked, goes on doubling itself

Excerpted from Thomas Malthus, *An Essay on the Principle of Population*, 6th ed. (London, 1826), pp. 4–17.

every twenty-five years, or increases in a geometrical ratio.

The rate according to which the productions of the earth may be supposed to increase, it will not be so easy to determine. Of this, however, we may be perfectly certain, that the ratio of their increase in a limited territory must be of a totally different nature from the ratio of the increase of population. A thousand millions are just as easily doubled every twenty-five years by the power of population as a thousand. But the food to support the increase from the greater number will by no means be obtained with the same facility. Man is necessarily confined in room. When acre has been added to acre till all the fertile land is occupied, the yearly increase of food must depend upon the melioration of the land already in possession. This is a fund, which, from the nature of all soils, instead of increasing, must be gradually diminishing. But population, could it be supplied with food, would go on with unexhausted vigour.

Europe is by no means so fully peopled as it might be. In Europe there is the fairest chance that human industry may receive its best direction. The science of agriculture has been much studied in England and Scotland: and there is still a great portion of uncultivated land in these countries. Let us consider at what rate the produce of this island might be supposed to increase under circumstances the most favorable to improvement.

If it be allowed that by the best possible policy, and great encouragements to agriculture, the average produce of the island could be doubled in the first twenty-five years, it will be allowing, probably, a greater increase than could with reason be expected.

In the next twenty-five years, it is impossible to suppose that the produce could be quadrupled. It would be contrary to all our knowledge of the properties of land. The improvement of the barren parts would be a work of time and labour; and it must be evident to those who have the slightest acquaintance with agricultural subjects, that in proportion as cultivation extended, the additions that could yearly be made to the former average produce must be gradually and regularly diminishing. That we may be the better able to compare the increase of population and food, let us make a supposition, which, without pretending to accuracy, is clearly more favourable to the power of production in the earth, than any experience we have had of its qualities will warrant.

Let us suppose that the yearly additions which might be made to the former average produce, instead of decreasing, which they certainly would do, were to remain the same; and that the produce of this island might be increased every twenty-five years, by a quantity equal to what it at present produces. The most enthusiastic speculator cannot suppose a greater increase than this. In a few centuries it would make every acre of land in the island like a garden.

If this supposition be applied to the whole earth, and if it be allowed that the subsistence for man which the earth affords might be increased every twenty-five years by a quantity equal to what it at present produces, this will be supposing a rate of increase much greater than we can imagine that any possible exertions of mankind could make it.

It may be fairly pronounced, therefore, that, considering the present average state of the earth, the means of subsistence, under circumstances the most favourable to human industry, could not possibly be made to increase faster than in an arithmetical ratio.

The necessary effects of these two different rates of increase, when brought together, will be very striking. Let us call the population of this island 11 millions; and suppose the present produce equal to the easy support of such a number. In the first twenty-five years the population would be 22 millions, and the food being also doubled, the means of subsistence would be equal to this increase. In the next twenty-five years, the population would be 44 millions, and the means of subsistence only equal to the support of 33 millions. In the next period the population would be 88 millions, and the means of subsistence just equal to the support of half that number. And, at the conclusion of the first century, the population would be 176 millions, and the means of subsistence only equal to the support of 55 millions, leaving a population of 121 millions totally unprovided for.

Taking the whole earth, instead of this island, emi-

Thomas Robert Malthus (1766–1834). Known for his pessimistic views on population, Malthus has had a modern revival as over-population has become a global problem.

gration would of course be excluded; and, supposing the present population equal to a thousand millions, the human species would increase as the numbers, 1, 2, 4, 8, 16, 32, 64, 128, 256, and subsistence as 1, 2, 3, 4, 5, 6, 7, 8, 9. In two centuries the population would be to the means of subsistence as 256 to 9; in three centuries as 4096 to 13, and in two thousand years the difference would be almost incalculable.

In this supposition no limits whatever are placed to the produce of the earth. It may increase for ever and be greater than any assignable quantity; yet still the power of population being in every period so much superior, the increase of the human species can only be kept down to the level of the means of subsistence by the constant operation of the strong law of necessity, acting as a check upon the greater power.

OF THE GENERAL CHECKS TO POPULATION, AND THE MODE OF THEIR OPERATION

The ultimate check to population appears then to be a want of food, arising necessarily from the different ratios according to which population and food increase. But this ultimate check is never the immediate check, except in cases of actual famine.

The immediate check may be stated to consist in all those customs, and all those diseases, which seem to be generated by a scarcity of the means of subsistence; and all those causes, independent of this scarcity, whether of a moral or physical nature, which tend prematurely to weaken and destroy the human frame.

These checks to population, which are constantly operating with more or less force in every society, and keep down the number to the level of the means of subsistence, may be classed under two general heads—the preventive, and the positive checks.

The preventive check, as far as it is voluntary, is peculiar to man, and arises from that distinctive superiority in his reasoning faculties, which enables him to calculate distant consequences. The checks to the indefinite increase of plants and irrational animals are all either positive, or, if preventive, involuntary. But man cannot look around him, and see the distress which frequently presses upon those who have large families; he cannot contemplate his present possessions or earnings, which he now nearly consumes himself, and calculate the amount of each share, when with very little addition they must be divided, perhaps, among seven or eight, without feeling a doubt whether, if he follow the bent of his inclinations, he may be able to support the offspring which he will probably bring into the world.

These considerations are calculated to prevent, and certainly do prevent, a great number of persons in all civilized nations from pursuing the dictate of nature in an early attachment to one woman.

If this restraint does not produce vice, it is undoubtedly the least evil that can arise from the principle of population. Considered as a restraint on a strong natural inclination, it might be allowed to produce a certain degree of temporary unhappiness; but evidently slight, compared with the evils which result from any of the other checks to population; and merely of the same nature as many other sacrifices of temporary to permanent gratification, which it is the business of a moral agent continually to make.

The positive checks to population are extremely various, and include every cause, whether arising from vice or misery, which in any degree contributes to shorten the natural duration of human life. Under this head, therefore, may be enumerated all unwholesome occupations, severe labour and exposure to the seasons, extreme poverty, bad nursing of children, great towns, excesses of all kinds, the whole train of common diseases and epidemics, wars, plague, and famine.

On examining these obstacles to the increase of population which I have classed under the heads of preventive and positive checks, it will appear that they are all resolvable into moral restraint, vice, and misery.

Of the preventive checks, the restraint from marriage which is not followed by irregular gratifications may properly be termed moral restraint.

Promiscuous intercourse, unnatural passions, violations of the marriage bed, and improper arts to conceal the consequences of irregular connexions, are preventive checks that clearly come under the head of vice.

Of the positive checks, those which appear to arise unavoidably from the laws of nature, may be called exclusively misery; and those which we obviously bring upon ourselves, such as wars, excesses, and many others which it would be in our power to avoid, are of a mixed nature. They are brought upon us by vice, and their consequences are misery.

The sum of all these preventive and positive checks, taken together, forms the immediate check to population; and it is evident that, in every country where the whole of the procreative power cannot be called into action, the preventive and the positive checks must vary inversely as each other; that is, in countries either naturally unhealthy, or subject to a great mortality, from whatever cause it may arise, the preventive check will prevail very little. In those countries, on the contrary, which are naturally healthy, and where the preventive check is found to prevail with considerable force, the positive check will prevail very little, or the mortality be very small.

In every country some of these checks are, with more or less force, in constant operation; yet, notwithstanding their general prevalence, there are few states in which there is not a constant effort in the population to increase beyond the means of subsistence. This constant effort as constantly tends to subject the lower classes of society to distress, and to prevent any great permanent melioration of their condition.   ☐

The concluding sentence of this reading makes clear the pessimism of the Malthusian position. Despite man's moral capacity for looking ahead and hence preventing population growth, the basic biological power is so great that Malthus is clearly doubtful that general distress can be avoided for the mass of humanity.

Most British economists of the early nineteenth century tended to accept this view, although not all of them put it in terms of Malthus's "arithmetical" and "geometrical" ratios. Many of them stated the principle in terms of a generalized version of the law of diminishing returns. This law, we recall, states that as we add more and more of a variable factor to a stock of fixed factors, the added product with each extra unit of variable factor will eventually begin to diminish.[5] In this particular case, population—or, roughly, the labor force—is our variable factor; natural resources—the economist's "land"—are the fixed factors; and food is the product. Population growth is then seen as pressing against natural resources in the form of diminishing returns in the production of food and/or the other necessities of life.

Now the law of diminishing returns is not an *a priori* law, handed down from on high, and true in every conceivable circumstance. It is an empirical generalization, and could be wrong in any particular case.

More significant, perhaps, is the fact that there can be other factors that *offset* the operations of this law. Indeed, a fairly immediate and simple response to Malthusianism might be that his "principle" of population really holds only if there is no significant technological advance. If mankind can devise increasingly effective methods of producing food and other agricultural products, then, overall, natural resource limitations may not produce diminishing returns at all.

What Malthus and his followers would have said to this point is simply that such technological advance might help you temporarily but would certainly not in the long run. Think of it in terms of the supply and demand for labor. We might imagine the situation as in Figure 6–3. Suppose we started with a demand curve for labor such as $D_1 D_1$, a labor force of L_1 and a wage rate of W_s—this is the *subsistence wage*, or the wage just sufficient to keep a given population alive with neither increase nor decrease.

Now suppose we have an invention that increases labor productivity and gives rise, as we may imagine, to a greater demand for labor; i.e., a shift to $D_2 D_2$. What the Malthusians would say is this: in the *short* run, the wage would rise. Population and labor force are constant (L_1) for the moment. The increased demand would raise the wage to W_t; everybody would be better off, *But* this is temporary. Given the "constant effort in the population to increase beyond the means of subsistence," the labor force will now expand rapidly. In particular, it will expand all the way up to L_2. At L_2, the wage will be brought right back down again to W_s. And, indeed, this will clearly happen even if technological advance should manage to push the demand for labor way out to $D_n D_n$, or in fact as far out as can be imagined.

Temporary departures aside, the mass of mankind can never rise permanently above bare subsistence —this is the fundamental characteristic of the Malthusian world.

5. See chapter 2, p. 42.

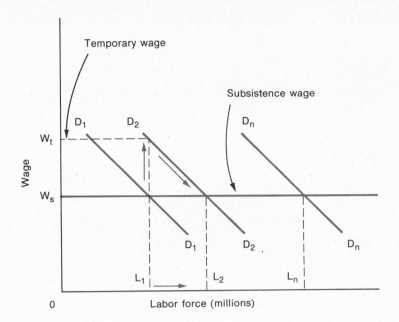

Figure 6-3. The Malthusian World.

Technological progress might push out the demand for labor (e.g., from D_1D_1 to D_2D_2) and raise the wage temporarily (from W_s to W_t), but, in the long run, population growth in the Malthusian world will bring the wage back down to the subsistence level once more.

THE DIFFERENT EXPERIENCE OF DEVELOPED AND UNDERDEVELOPED ECONOMIES

Still, the Malthusian answer does not seem quite satisfactory, if only for the obvious historical reason that some countries are clearly not operating at economic subsistence, and indeed are apparently concerned with problems of "affluence." For this reason, we must separate the population problems of the industrialized world from those facing the kind of economy we are studying in this chapter, the modern underdeveloped economy.

In the *developed* world, essentially two things happened historically. First of all, when the standard of living in these countries began to rise substantially above the subsistence level, population did *not* continue to expand at anything like its biologically maximum rate. The "preventive checks" proved to be far more active than Malthus would have thought.[6] People in the rich countries decided to have fewer children as a matter of choice, and it remains true today

that birthrates are far higher in poor countries than in rich countries. This development slowed the rate of population growth considerably.

Second, the rate of technological advance and capital accumulation was far more rapid than Malthus had anticipated. It was not just that there were occasional outward shifts of the demand curve for labor; shifts occurred all the time and at a rate far exceeding the (slower than expected) rate of population increase.

For the rapidly advancing industrial countries, the flaw in the kind of logic suggested by Figure 6-3 was that the Malthusians *over*estimated how rapidly the labor force would grow from L_1 to L_2, and seriously *under*estimated how rapidly the *DD* curves would shift outward. Instead of the temporary wage sinking back to the subsistence level, there was always another big shift of the demand curve outward (owing to capital accumulation and technological change), and a new temporary wage, even *further* above W_s, was established. This kind of process could go on indefinitely, and in fact has been going on in these countries ever since the industrial revolution.

---

6. For further discussion of why this was so, see pp. 403–404.

But this process did *not* take place in the underdeveloped economies. In these economies, the population problem has turned out in some respects to be even worse than Malthus anticipated. Many factors have played a role in this phenomenon, though the main single fact is that it has been possible to apply even in very poor countries many of the techniques of modern medicine, disease prevention, malaria control, public health, sanitation, and the like. This aspect of Western technological progress has been fairly easily transferable even to quite backward societies. The result has been very sharp declines in death rates in these countries. In some extreme cases, like Ceylon, the death rate fell to *one-third* its previous level in a matter of thirty-odd years. At the same time, birthrates have remained high—often twice the level of birthrates in the more developed countries.

Now this process is not exactly what Malthus had foreseen (he could hardly have anticipated the explosive advances in the medical sciences in the past century-and-a-half), but the effects are similar to what he feared. Characteristic rates of population increase in today's underdeveloped economies are extremely high, ranging from 2 percent, to 2½ percent, to even 3 percent or above per year. These figures are much higher than those for the developed countries today and they are also higher than the rates of increase for most of the developed countries when *they* were beginning to industrialize.[7] A reasonable projection of future trends suggests that the share of the poor countries of Asia, Africa, and Latin America in world population will go up from 70 percent to 80 percent over the next thirty years (Figure 6–4). There *is* a population explosion today and it is squarely located in the still poverty-stricken nations of the underdeveloped world.

---

7.   There were, of course, some advanced countries that had high rates of population growth in the nineteenth century (the United States was one), but these countries were in the so-called regions of recent settlement, where there was a superabundance of land and other natural resources. Population growth in this particular context may even have been advantageous.

1970

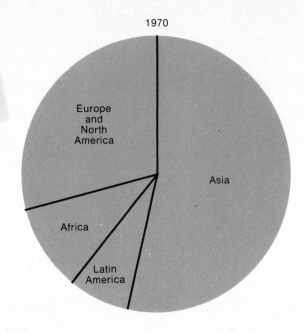

2000 (projected)

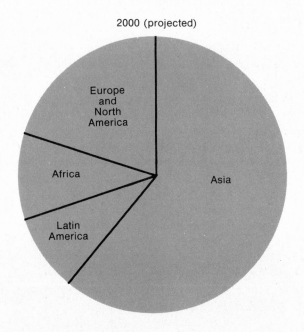

Figure 6–4. Percentage Distribution of World's Population.

CONSEQUENCES OF POPULATION GROWTH FOR THE UNDERDEVELOPED ECONOMY

The consequences of these very rapid rates of population growth are many. The general problem is that, with rapid population growth, a much higher rate of growth of output must be sustained if output per capita is to be raised at all significantly. With an annual 3 percent rate of growth of population, a country must maintain a 3 percent rate of growth of total output just to stay even. With a 4 percent growth rate, output per capita will rise only at roughly 1 percent per year. At such a rate of increase, a country that today has an output per capita of, say, $100 per year would still be well below $200 a year at the end of the twentieth century.

The problem is intensified, moreover, when we consider certain other aspects of population growth. For one thing, there is the structure of the population to consider. Countries with high birth rates will typically have a large proportion of children in their populations. Figure 6–5 contrasts the population structures of rapid-population-growth underdeveloped regions with those of slow-population-growth developed regions. A large proportion of children in the population means that there are more dependents and fewer productive workers in the society, creating a drain on the productive capabilities of the economy. Even more serious, perhaps, is the pressure that population growth creates in already densely populated areas.

Not all underdeveloped countries are overpopulated. There are regions in Africa, Latin America, and even in a few small countries in Asia that are relatively underpopulated. But the bulk of the world's poor live in countries where overpopulation is already a serious problem. (India with 600 million people and China with 850 million people comprise half or more of the underdeveloped world.) And in these countries additional numbers pose at least two extremely serious problems:

(1) Pressure on the land in agriculture. Population growth in these countries where arable land is already scarce means that the law of diminishing returns really does make further increases in agricultural output, and especially food supplies, very hard to come by. Some economists think that certain of these nations have already reached the stage of "absolutely diminishing returns"—i.e., where the further application of labor to the land brings no increase in agricultural output at all. If overcrowding on the land leads to less efficient methods of production, then food production might actually decrease as population increases. This does *not* mean that these countries will not be able to expand their food production in the future. The law of diminishing returns states what happens when only one element in the picture changes. But other elements may change, especially the technology of production, as we have noted before. The effects of overcrowding *do* mean, however, that favorable improvements will have to be that much stronger to offset the effects of rapid population growth.

(2) The unemployment problem. Perhaps even more serious is the unemployment problem to which rapid population growth in densely populated areas may give rise. There is no further room for employment in agriculture, because of the heavy rural overpopulation that already exists. On the other hand, the ability of the industrial sector to employ more workers is seriously limited by the nature of the technology employed. We have already mentioned that modern technology makes great demands on capital goods and on skilled labor but relatively smaller demands on massive infusions of unskilled labor. But if the agricultural sector cannot take them and if the rate of expansion of the industrial sector is insufficient to take them, where will these increasing numbers of unskilled laborers find employment? To understand just how serious a problem this is, one has to have some idea of the magnitudes involved. India, for example, in the course of a fifteen-year period adds

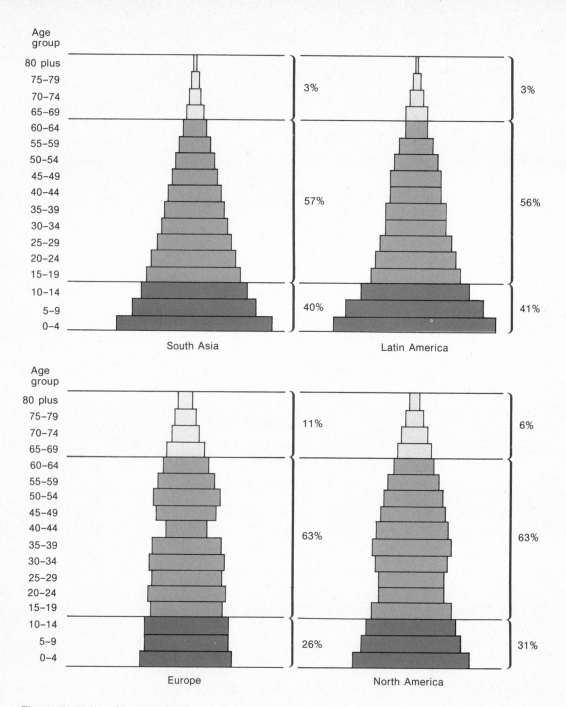

Figure 6-5. Age Structure of Population in Selected Regions.

(Width of bars indicates proportion of total population in age group.)

Adapted from *Seeds of Change* by Lester R. Brown. © 1970 by Praeger Publishers, Inc. Reprinted by permission.

to her labor force about 70 million workers, or, roughly, the equivalent of the total labor force of the present-day United States. Moreover, India adds this extraordinary number of workers to an economy that is already suffering from serious unemployment. As early as a decade ago, at the end of India's second Five-Year Plan (1962), it was estimated that there were 9 million unemployed Indian workers and another 15 to 18 million partially unemployed or underemployed workers. The problem of finding jobs for such huge numbers of laborers is one of the great costs of rapid population growth in densely populated areas.

When we add together all the various difficulties that rapid population growth entails for these poor countries, when we remember, further, the problems of capital accumulation and the difficulties of adapting Western technology to the drastically different conditions of the modern underdeveloped country—when we put all this together, we may begin to understand why many economists feel that the poor countries today face much greater obstacles to successful development than did their historical predecessors.

REPORT OF THE COMMISSION ON INTERNATIONAL DEVELOPMENT

Later in this book, we shall come back to the problems of the underdeveloped economy, hopefully to apply some of the tools of economic analysis developed in the course of the ensuing chapters.

For the moment, let us simply try to summarize where these economies stand now. In trying to do this, we are fortunate in having a report of the Commission on International Development, under the chairmanship of the late Lester B. Pearson of Canada. This report is the work of a distinguished group of economists and statesmen whose mission was to "meet together, study the consequences of twenty years of development assistance, assess the results, clarify the errors and propose the policies which will work better in the future."

The following reading is excerpted from chapter 3 of this report in which the commission takes a large overview of the problems ahead for the underdeveloped economy in the 1970s.

The Problems Ahead

Commission on International Development
Lester B. Pearson, *Chairman*

Despite the achievements of the past two decades, we are still far from a situation in which the developing countries, relying solely on their own resources, can assure effective and early modernization of their economies. We are, at best, in midstream, with many obstacles and problems ahead. This chapter attempts to summarize some of the more important of these problems.

THE POLITICAL PROBLEM

The present form of the aspiration to development is relatively new. The drive toward modernization has inevitably created conflicts between guardians of tradition and those who seek change. The controversies take on different complexions in different parts of the world but underlying all is the demand for a more equitable sharing among individuals and nations of the benefits of progress. Pressures to this end put a premium on the adaptability of political and social structures. Resulting conflicts have been difficult but, on the whole, surprisingly manageable as political structures in developing countries have improved in flexibility and responsiveness.

The balance between social and political objectives and economic growth is always a delicate one and involves difficult choices. Sometimes, as a matter of national survival, economic growth must be subordinated to the maintenance or creation of national identity and national sovereignty. In other cases, the objective of rapid growth and equitable distribution of income appear in conflict. Stable development

Excerpted from Lester B. Pearson, "The Problems Ahead," from *Partners in Development,* Commission on International Development, pp. 64, 66–73, 76–79. Published by permission of Praeger Publishers, Inc., New York and The Pall Mall Press, London, 1969.

would seem to require a more equitable distribution of wealth and a greater degree of participation in political and economic life than has so far been characteristic of many developing countries. Without popular commitment and participation, the sacrifices that will be necessary for development will not be easily borne.

THE POPULATION DILEMMA

No other phenomenon casts a darker shadow over the prospects for international development than the staggering growth of population. It is evident that it is a major cause of the large discrepancy between rates of economic improvement in rich and poor countries. On the other hand, the likelihood of a rapid slowing down of population growth is not great, although some countries are in a far more favorable position than others in this respect.

Twenty years ago, it was not expected that population growth would become such a major problem in low-income countries. As late as 1951, a U.N. projection assumed that between 1950 and 1980 the populations of Africa and Asia would grow at an annual rate of 0.7–1.3 percent. The remarkable and largely unexpected success in reducing mortality brought a sharp change. The rate of population growth in developing countries increased steadily in the 1950s. By the mid-1960s, it settled down at an average level of 2.5 percent.

Mortality is continuing its decline, but over-all fertility rates are only now beginning to drop. While in a number of developing countries, fertility has been declining for some time, in others it is increasing as a result of improvement in health and medical services. Even if fertility should be considerably reduced in coming decades, the population of the less developed world will double before the end of this century.

All the burdens from large families and high growth rates are not borne by parents alone. When the population doubles in twenty-five years, the task of development and modernization is compounded. It may even be impossible to attain significant improvement in living conditions and independence of foreign aid. Some of the direct difficulties created by very rapid population growth are the following:

1. Expenditures for education, health, housing, water supply, and so forth, increase sharply and create severe budgetary strains.

2. The quality of the next generation, on which the prospects for development crucially rest, is jeopardized. There is a strong inverse correlation between child health and family size. Rapid growth of the child population also delays educational improvement.

3. Considerable resources are devoted to the support of a large dependent population which would otherwise be available to raise living standards and increase capital formation.

4. Aid requirements are larger when population rises fast, and the possibility of future financial independence smaller than if fertility is declining.

5. The distribution of income is unequal, and population growth tends to make it more so by raising land values and rents while depressing wages. As ownership, too, is usually very unequally distributed, the bulk of the population may fail to participate in whatever improvement occurs.

6. Severe urban problems arise, partly from natural increase and partly from migration from the country into the cities. Urban populations tend to double in fifteen to eighteen years. Housing already presents almost insoluble problems in many developing countries.

Whether or not a deliberate policy on population should be adopted is a decision which each individual country itself must face. We are well aware of the controversial nature of the matter which, until very recently, placed family planning behind a wall of silence in the industrialized countries themselves. But it is clear that there can be no serious social and economic planning unless the ominous implications of uncontrolled population growth are understood and acted upon.

WIDE WORLD PHOTO

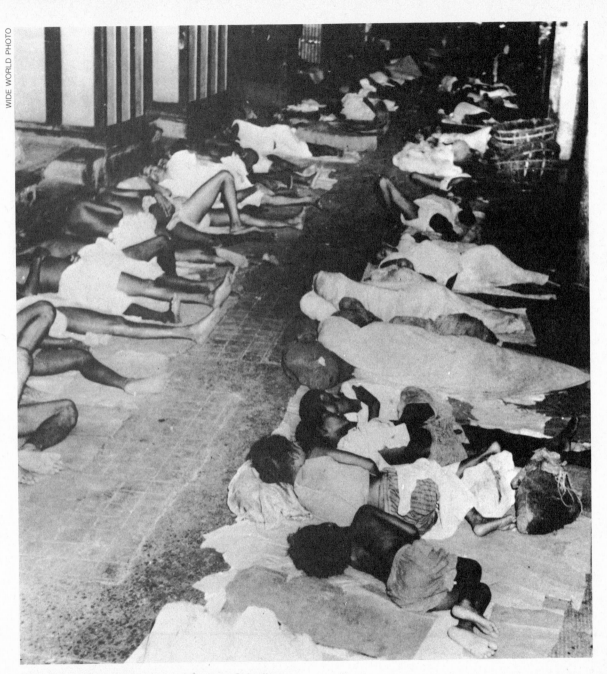

Homeless people sleep on the sidewalk in Calcutta during a heat wave. In 1974, with a still rising population, with poor harvests because of drought, with fertilizer and oil imports becoming ever more expensive, India faced one of her gravest economic crises since her independence.

UNEMPLOYMENT AND URBANIZATION

The rapid growth of population adds to the already severe unemployment problem in developing countries. In many, if not most of them, unemployment is turning into a major social problem and obstacle to development. The failure to create meaningful employment is the most tragic failure of development. All indications are that unemployment and under-utilization of human resources have increased in the 1960s, and that the problem will grow even more serious.

Although there is much evidence of the appalling magnitude of the unemployment problem, there is little specific information about it. The International Labor Organization is trying to muster the resources for a large employment survey in the developing countries, and this deserves all support. A great difficulty, especially in traditional societies, is that there is no hard and fast distinction between unemployment and underemployment. Underemployment describes a situation in which individual capacity to work is not fully engaged, as when highly trained personnel are forced to work at menial labor for lack of demand, or when agriculture does not begin to absorb the labor available. Although there are no firm estimates of underemployment, it is clear that recorded *une*mployment in the developing countries understates the problem.

Both unemployment and underemployment are results of the failure to absorb the large increase of the labor force which has followed the acceleration of population growth. Population policies can greatly affect this problem but only in the long term. Those who will constitute the labor force over the next fifteen years are already born.

Progress must be made in solving the unemployment problem if social and political turmoil is not to arrest the development process. For it is in the volatile cities of the developing world that agricultural stagnation and industrial unemployment combine to produce their gravest consequences. Urban growth is almost universally twice as rapid as the growth of the population in general, and some of the largest cities have even higher rates of expansion. Rural stagnation stimulates a flow of migrants from the land, and urban death rates are often lower than those in the countryside while fertility generally remains high.

It must be asked whether urban trends can be left to be the by-product of other forces in society. If present trends continued, the largest city in India would have over 35 million inhabitants by the year 2000. Planning strategy in developing countries must emphasize the growth of small and intermediate regional centers, to offer market, service and storage facilities, and light labor-intensive industries processing local materials. The construction of such new centers could offer a considerable measure of employment for unskilled labor.

AGRICULTURE

If the Green Revolution* signals a major breakthrough in food grain production, it also brings with it an array of new problems.

For one thing, continued heavy expenditures on agricultural research are necessary, as one seed variety is likely to last only for a few years and must be replaced by new varieties as new diseases evolve. Moreover, accelerated agricultural extension and massive investments in irrigation and fertilizer production are needed. Increasing production also raises the demand for better marketing and distribution facilities and for more farm credit. It will also be difficult to maintain a set of incentives for farmers which is adequate to elicit the necessary production, stimulate the continued adoption of new technology, and support diversification into other crops.

Increased tax revenue will be needed, but to tax agricultural income directly is difficult in most developing countries for the good reasons that most farmers are very poor, that such a tax would be politically explosive, and that the cost of collecting the tax might well exceed the yield. However, the new technology

---

*See our discussion of the Green Revolution, pp. 755–61.

is raising some rural incomes sharply. If large increases in income are to arise in agriculture, some of the increased revenue must come from these incomes. Agricultural taxation and the general division of the fruits of increased agricultural productivity among urban consumers, rural producers, and landowners will present thorny policy issues which have grave political implications and will also affect future development.

Areas untouched by the Green Revolution, such as most of Africa and Latin America, face a more difficult task in stimulating technological change in the countryside. Many of them still seriously neglect rural development. For all countries it is important to achieve new technical breakthroughs in crops other than foodgrains, especially in exportable ones, not only to increase the food supply but also to improve its quality.

Land reform and consolidation of fragmented holdings will be needed in many developing countries not only to accelerate technological change and stimulate production in the long run, but also to generate rural employment. History teaches us that land reform is seldom a tidy affair and is always time-consuming. However, most governments now have at their disposal the means to minimize the short-run disruptions and conflicts arising from a program of structural change in land ownership.

NUTRITION

Pervasive poverty and consequent low effective demand for food are among the causes of widespread hunger and nutritional deficiency, but fixed dietary habits also contribute to the nutritional deficiencies in many areas. The increases in food-grain production which have been achieved by some of the less developed countries in the past few years are by no means the complete answer to the problem of providing adequate diets in the developing countries.

Malnutrition, which is a more serious scourge to mankind even than hunger, is to a larger extent a matter of ignorance and inappropriate food habits.

Thus even when the commercial demand for food is met, this does not mean that nutritional needs are satisfied. In fact, nutritional deficiencies, especially in protein, are likely to persist for a long time to come. However, in order to raise general standards of health, the productivity of labor, and the general quality of life, improved nutrition is indispensable. It is especially important to child health.

Childhood malnutrition tends to retard both physical and mental development, often irreparably. In countries with a per capita income of less than $100 there are over 500 million children under the age of fifteen, and in the developing world as a whole this group represents over 40 percent of the population. The physical and mental development of this generation is not only a matter of immediate humanitarian concern. It is also of central importance to the whole process of development. In only a few decades this generation will have taken the place of their elders.

INDUSTRY

During the last two decades, many developing countries favored industry while neglecting agriculture. Just as rural policy is now being reconsidered, so is industrial policy. Policy-makers have generally become aware that further advances in import substitution will be difficult. In many countries, import substitution has taken place almost regardless of price or quality, and many industries now find themselves with a highly distorted price structure which makes them noncompetitive in export markets.

Continued growth may require continued protection for new industries, but the point has been reached for many established industries where the system of protection should be restructured and absolute prohibitions turned into reasonable tariff protection. Infant industry support should be limited to activities showing promise of long-run competitiveness. There should be greater reliance on exchange rate policy to handle payment difficulties. Such liberalization, however, need not be sudden and traumatic, and in some cases it may take place within the context of gradual regional integration.

THE PRIVATE SECTOR

There are a great many impediments to the creation of a dynamic private sector. Some are institutional and others reflect ingrained attitudes. Too often the attitude of many of the less developed countries toward their domestic private sector remains negative, though it is improving in many cases. It is still unusual for them to regard private enterprise as a suitable instrument of economic growth, or to create conditions which actively favor the emergence of new firms, particularly the establishment of financial institutions to assure adequate credit for the private sector. This is regrettable since experience shows that a strong and vigorous private sector is an important element in the achievement of rapid growth. A strong domestic private sector also serves to attract direct investment from abroad which can greatly stimulate the development process.

RESEARCH AND DEVELOPMENT

For many reasons, research and development in low-income countries has been extremely limited. Based on uncertain data, it is estimated that expenditure for research and development in Latin America amounts to only some 0.2 percent of GNP, while in Asia such expenditures fall between 0.1 percent and 0.5 percent of GNP. In Africa, except for some programs sponsored by industrialized countries, public and private outlay for research and development is negligible. Comparable figures for the Soviet Union and the United States are 4.2 percent and 3.2 percent of GNP respectively, and for most European countries between 1 and 2 percent.

Many changes will be required for more effective use of research and development. This is particularly true in industry, where lack of information, shortage of managerial ability and, perhaps most often, over-protection, result in little incentive to improve products and reduce costs. The situation in agriculture is somewhat more encouraging because of progress in developing extension services which are of such importance in bringing the results of the research station to the farmer. It is clear, however, that innovation and dissemination of technical knowledge remain immense problems in both sectors.

EDUCATION

Impressive quantitative improvements in education should not be allowed to conceal the very serious problems of quality which plague the educational systems of so many developing countries.

Of one hundred children entering primary school in developing countries, no more than thirty finish. Indeed, in most African and Latin American countries, more than 50 percent of primary school pupils do not return to school after the second grade. Secondary schools are generally oriented toward academic study; vocational training represents less than 10 percent of total secondary enrollment. Moreover, only one of about ten graduates from academic courses actually enters a university. Few of the graduates from vocational schools become active in fields for which they have been trained. At universities, most students attend courses in law or political science, or in the traditional fields of engineering and only a small fraction ever graduate. Facilities are inadequate, textbooks are lacking or antiquated, teachers are poorly trained.

Education is a basic human right and the low-income societies need literate and active citizens as well as citizens with skills appropriate to the changing economic structure. Yet, their educational systems fail to provide a satisfactory general education or a level of skill in the labor force appropriate to the needs of the country.

In too many instances, children who finish primary school in rural areas seem rather *less* fit to become creative and constructive members of their own community than if they had never been to school. The measure of achievement is the ability to enter secondary school, which is again oriented toward academic study. Educational systems are not generally designed to produce intermediate skills or proficiencies that correspond to the needs of industry, agriculture, or government in the less developed countries. One special need is for post-secondary technological or professional institutions offering training related to the needs of the labor market.

THE EXTERNAL CONSTRAINT

Most of the serious issues which we have enumerated in this chapter depend for their solutions on the action taken by the developing countries themselves. But their policies must be pursued within an international framework over which they have little or no control.

The major external constraint may be summed up as the availability of foreign exchange. Foreign exchange is a crucial resource in development planning. All developing countries are forced to rely on imported equipment and, to a large extent, on imported raw materials and spare parts without which their own resources cannot be pressed into service. The developing countries face problems both in increasing their earnings of foreign exchange and in the increasing claims on available foreign exchange of rising debt payments and other essential commitments.

India's foreign exchange situation exemplifies these difficulties. India earns about $1.8 billion per year from exports, of which about $300 million is received in barter or inconvertible currencies. This leaves about $1.5 billion in convertible foreign exchange. Debt service obligations of all kinds are about $450 million, leaving some $1 billion for other purposes. This must finance the import of essential commodities and services which cannot be financed by aid (petroleum, long staple cotton, some food, and the freight costs on 480 food shipments), as well as raw materials and spare parts for export industries which have earned the right to use free foreign exchange and which must have access to the lowest-cost source of supply. It must also cover the needs of small-scale industry, special requirements in the agricultural sectors and the needs of public departments. This means that most of the imports of industrial raw materials, as well as vital machinery and equipment, fertilizer, and pesticides must be financed by aid. In case of a poor export year, India could not meet even the minimal import requirements which must be met with free foreign exchange. Even in a normal year, there is little flexibility to search for the lowest-cost supplier, to relax import restrictions, or to provide reserves against the risks of new policies. This scarcity of foreign exchange is, of course, partly a reflection of India's pre-1968 export performance and could be somewhat eased over time if that per-

formance were improved. Nevertheless, this constraint has been and will continue to be a major obstacle to development.

Foreign exchange is available from three sources in addition to private investment: the country's own accumulated reserves, its export earnings, and aid.

The following paragraphs discuss prospects and problems for the developing countries in these areas, beginning with the critical shortage of reserves.

FOREIGN EXCHANGE RESERVES

After World War II and the Korean War boom, some developing countries were able to use their reserves to maintain high import levels, but they were soon depleted. Reserves of 15 percent in the table below are enough to finance no more than two months' imports. This is barely enough for prudent financial management and makes reserves generally irrelevant to meet emergencies or to provide risk capital for new policies. For many developing countries an increase in reserves would be an important asset permitting greater policy flexibility and better allocation of resources.

FOREIGN EXCHANGE RESERVES AS A PERCENT OF IMPORTS

	1955–57 AVERAGE	1965–67 AVERAGE
Brazil	39.2	26.1
Colombia	22.8	15.8
Mexico	37.7	25.5
Morocco	39.4	15.7
Tunisia	43.7	13.6
U.A.R.	99.6	19.5
Ghana	123.1	36.4
Taiwan	94.2	56.9
Korea	127.8	42.1
Philippines	19.3	16.7
India	79.6	26.0
Pakistan	80.5	19.3
Turkey	53.8	19.6

Source: IMF.

Export Earnings

The importance of export earnings for the development of the poorer countries can hardly be overestimated. They are by far the most important source of foreign exchange. In recent years, they have been nearly four times as large as the flow of aid and private investment. But trade is also, in a deeper sense, an "engine of growth," especially for smaller countries which are particularly dependent on the international division of labor.

Import requirements in the developing countries grow at about the same rate as over-all production, or slightly faster. If the rate of economic growth is to be accelerated to at least 6 percent, which seems both feasible and necessary, imports have to grow at 7 to 8 percent a year while the investment ratios accelerate. If foreign aid requirements are not going to get out of hand, exports too will have to grow at this rate. Great instability in export earnings has proved disruptive to growth in the past, so growth of exports must not only be rapid but also steady.

There are three prerequisites to assure rapid growth in exports. World trade must continue to expand vigorously, sustained by steady growth in the industrialized world. Perhaps the greatest threat to international development is the risk that major industrial powers will constantly be faced with serious balance-of-payments problems which impair their possibilities of expansion.

Second, the growth of world trade must be accompanied by liberalization. This in its turn implies a willingness on the part of industrialized countries to make the structural adjustments which will enable them to absorb an increasing range of manufactures and semi-manufactures from developing countries.

Third, the less developed countries themselves must make great efforts to diversify their exports, to seize the opportunities of expanding world markets. The developing countries could, and should, also reduce their dependence on imports from the industrialized countries and rely more on trade among themselves. At present, they take about 70 percent of their imports from developed countries and only 20 percent from one another.

The Debt Problem

The indebtedness of the developing countries imposes a large burden of debt service. There has already been a sequence of debt crises in the late 1950s and throughout the 1960s, and even a cursory inspection of the situation suggests that the debt servicing problems of the low-income countries will become even more serious in the years immediately ahead.

The external public debt of the developing countries rose by about 14 percent per annum in the 1960s. In June, 1968, the recorded debt stood at $47.5 billion. The reverse flow of debt service payments on official account amounted to $4.7 billion in 1967. In the last ten years, these payments have increased by as much as 17 percent per year.

In several countries (Brazil, Argentina, Uruguay, Mexico, Indonesia, India, Pakistan, U.A.R., Tunisia, and Yugoslavia), the ratio of public debt service to export earnings exceeds 15 percent.

Technical defaults on contractual obligations have not been common, but the repayment burdens have caused many debtor governments to deplete their reserves and suffer liquidity crises which have forced them to adopt stringent exchange controls. Most of these countries have sought and obtained a rearrangement of their debt. In some cases, a whole series of rescue operations have taken place in rapid succession.

The Crisis in Aid

Official development assistance increased rapidly between 1956 and 1961, increased very slowly through 1967, and began to decline in 1968. On the basis of aid commitments, a further decline can be expected in 1969.

The decline in official aid, its increased cost, and the growing complexity of the regulations by which it is provided come at a time when development expenditures in the low-income countries are rising rapidly. Despite major efforts at import substitution and export promotion, these accelerated development programs require additional external resources. The interests of both rich and poor require that devel-

OFFICIAL DEVELOPMENT ASSISTANCE
(billions of dollars)

1956	3.3
1961	5.2
1962	5.5
1963	5.9
1964	6.0
1965	6.1
1966	6.3
1967	6.6
1968	6.4

oping countries advance at the most rapid feasible rate, but, in fact, many of them face the prospect of cutting back on their planned rates of growth because they must now assume significant reductions in aid.

It is precisely because the developing countries see their forward momentum threatened by bleak aid prospects that they feel a growing sense of frustration which tends to embitter relations between rich and poor. The developing countries feel that their problems are ignored and they see no sign of real commitment to help alleviate their tremendous problems of poverty, social change, and economic development.

The need goes deeper than a mere call for more aid. International development means a willingness to look to the total economic relationship between developing and industrialized countries.

The problems to be faced remain great, but they are now better understood. The achievements of the last ten years give hope that they can be solved. Equally, they underline the need for greater effort and more effective international cooperation.   □

SUMMARY

In this chapter, we have taken up the subject of the *underdeveloped economy,* focussing more on problems than on economic systems, although the tasks facing these economies are so great that they are all engaged in planning for economic growth to a certain degree.

The main economic characteristic of the underdeveloped country is its *poverty.* Although output per capita figures are somewhat suspect, the depth of poverty in these countries shows up clearly in any measure we might use. Their average family incomes are perhaps one-tenth or less of what we enjoy today in the United States. These countries are trying to achieve now what the economically advanced countries achieved a century or two ago—an industrial revolution that will put them on the path of modern economic growth—but the circumstances they face are quite different from those that faced the "early developers" of Europe and North America:

(1) **Technology.** The less developed countries have the entire storehouse of modern technology to draw upon. This is a clear advantage, but it is qualified by the fact that this technology is not well suited to conditions in these countries, that it may require costly imports from abroad, and that, in certain cases (notably public health and medical technology) it may raise certain new problems (the population explosion).

(2) **Capital accumulation.** The need for capital goods in these countries is great, especially in view of the capital-intensive nature of much modern technology, but the ability to raise domestic savings and investment is limited by the general poverty of the countries, by the desire for increased consumption now, and, in many cases, by the absence of a social structure that promotes the productive use of economic "surpluses" that may exist.

(3) **Population growth.** Falling death rates (largely a result of improved public health and medical technology) and very high birthrates have caused a population expansion that raises the specter of Malthu-

sian problems for many underdeveloped countries. The rates of population growth in these countries are, on the average, much higher than were those of the economically advanced countries when they were setting out on the path of modern growth. The consequences are: the difficulty of raising total output fast enough to achieve increases in output per capita; the heavy burden of large numbers of dependent children on the productive workers of the society; and, especially in heavily populated regions, the problem of increasing agricultural output rapidly enough to feed the growing population and the difficulty of finding employment for these massive additions to the labor force.

The 1969 report of the Commission on International Development, surveying these and other problems of the modern underdeveloped countries, concludes that their problems are great but, with appropriate international cooperation, not insoluble.

IMPORTANT TERMS TO REMEMBER

Economic Underdevelopment
Per Capita Output
Technological Change
Capital Accumulation
Malthusian Theory of Population
Preventive Checks
Positive Checks
Vicious Circles of Poverty
Absolutely Diminishing Returns
Unemployment and Underemployment
"External Constraints" on Development

QUESTIONS FOR DISCUSSION

1. Discuss the advantages and disadvantages for an underdeveloped country of borrowing the latest Western technological ideas and methods.

2. It is sometimes argued that the poor countries of today will be able to achieve modern growth only if they begin with rather drastic and rapid changes in their social and economic structures. This has given rise to what are sometimes called the "big push" theories of economic development. Do any of the factors discussed in this chapter seem to you to support such a view? What reasons might be offered for the hypothesis that slow, step-by-step growth is generally insufficient for today's underdeveloped countries?

3. "Population growth was not always a problem for the countries that developed economically in the nineteenth century, but it is public enemy number one for the less developed countries of today." Discuss.

4. Is the kind of unemployment or underemployment one finds in a country like India today the same as the kind of unemployment you might find in an industrial economy like that of the United States? What differences do you think there might be?

5. The Pearson Commission speaks of an "external constraint" facing poor countries that are trying to raise their living standards. What is meant by this term? What implications might this constraint have for the policies of economically developed countries?

SUGGESTED READING

Brown, Lester R. *Seeds of Change.* New York: Frederick A. Praeger, 1970.

Cochrane, Willard W. *The World Food Problem.* New York: Thomas Y. Crowell Co., 1969.

Hirschman, Albert O. *The Strategy of Economic Development.* New Haven: Yale University Press, 1958.

Lewis, W. Arthur. *Development Planning.* New York: Harper & Row, 1966.

Maddison, Angus. *Economic Progress and Policy in Developing Countries.* New York: Norton, 1970.

Nurkse, Ragnar. *Problems of Capital Formation in Underdeveloped Areas.* New York: Oxford University Press, 1953.

Pearson, Lester B. *Partners in Development: Report of the Commission on International Development.* New York: Frederick A. Praeger, 1969.

GREAT DEBATE 1:
THE MARXIAN CRITIQUE OF CAPITALISM

GREAT DEBATE 1:
THE MARXIAN CRITIQUE OF CAPITALISM

In June 1971, Paul A. Samuelson, Nobel-prize-winning economist from Massachusetts Institute of Technology, published a highly technical article on Marx in the Journal of Economic Literature. *Its complex title was, "Understanding the Marxian Notion of Exploitation: A Summary of the So-Called Transformation Problem Between Marxian Values and Competitive Prices." Not the kind of article, one would think, that would make people sound the alarums and man the battle-stations. But it did. Few articles in the history of that journal have stirred such controversy. A flood of comments and rebuttals poured forth. As late as March 1974, the journal was carrying these articles: a critique of Samuelson's views by William J. Baumol of Princeton, a reply by Samuelson to Baumol, a reply to Samuelson by Michio Morishima of the London School of Economics, a comment by Baumol on Samuelson's reply, and a rejoinder by Samuelson to both Baumol and Morishima. And it was doubtful, even then, that the end was in sight!*

This episode is important to us for two reasons. First, it shows that beneath its technical veneer, economics is a subject pulsing with potential and very lively disagreements even among the experts. This recent debate involved a great deal of highly mathematical theoretical apparatus, but the controversy was warm and, at times, even emotional. On many basic issues, there is still deep division in our subject, and that is likely to remain the case even in the future.

Second, this incident proves again the special controversiality of Karl Marx. No aspect of his theory is fully agreed upon. The issue at dispute in the journal was the "transformation problem"—essentially, how does Marx get to a proper theory of prices when he begins with a creaky vehicle like the "labor theory of value."[1] If economists are ready to flail at each other over such an issue as this, how

---

1. *The "labor theory of value" says that the prices of commodities are proportional to the quantities of labor embodied in producing them. The degree to which, and the sense in which, Marx actually believed this theory is part of the Samuelson-et-alii controversy.*

much more vigorous might be their arguments about such other Marxian notions as the decline of capitalism, the ultimate victory of communism, the necessity of revolution, and so on!

Both these reasons are involved in the selection of the following Great Debate. We witness disagreement here among outstanding thinkers and scholars. Ultimately, difficult as it sometimes is, the student of economics must learn how to grapple with such differences of opinion. This is something that, as a citizen, he will necessarily be facing throughout his life. Further, the debate over Marxism is a particularly natural one with which to conclude Part One, dealing as it does with ''Basic Economic Systems.'' For Marx, as we have already noted, not only provided a Bible for communism, but developed a massive critique of capitalism and is the source of many of the ideological currents in the underdeveloped countries of the world.

We are focusing below not on technical matters but on the basic tenets of Marx's thought. The following group of articles brings out most of these fundamental notions. Each of these articles is written by an outstanding economist and, although these are all Western economists, the Marxian viewpoint is fully represented.

Where great men differ, each of us has no alternative but to come to his own individual conclusions. Hopefully the following pages will give the reader a useful framework for reaching an informed opinion about a matter that is still of major economic and political importance.

1.
The Communist Manifesto

The following reading is excerpted from one of the most famous documents in the Marxian literature, The Communist Manifesto. This document was written jointly by Karl Marx and Friedrich Engels in 1848, though Engels in a later introduction points out that "the fundamental proposition which forms its nucleus belongs to Marx." Although no single writing of Marx could cover the full range of his thought, the following excerpts bring out a number of the most important points in the Marxian liturgy. The reader should notice these related themes: (1) the view that the social and political conditions of a society are largely determined by its economic basis of production; (2) the view that history is a long story of class struggles; (3) the prediction that, under capitalism, economic classes will become more and more polarized into two contending groups—the bourgeoisie and the proletariat; (4) the related prediction that while small businessmen and others in the middle class will drop into the proletariat, the bigger capitalists will carry out production in large-scale factories, in effect getting bigger and bigger; (5) the view that there will be a strong tendency for the immiserization of the working-class proletarians over time; and (6) the analysis of capitalism in terms of internal contradictions, such as its tendency to overproduce and thus to need constantly expanding markets.

Manifesto of the Communist Party

Karl Marx

The history of all hitherto existing society is the history of class struggles.

Freeman and slave, patrician and plebeian, lord and serf, guild-master and journeyman, in a word, oppressor and oppressed, stood in constant opposition to one another, carried on uninterrupted, now hidden, now open fight, a fight that each time ended, either in a revolutionary re-constitution of society at large, or in the common ruin of the contending classes.

In the earlier epochs of history we find almost everywhere a complicated arrangement of society into various orders, a manifold gradation of social rank. In ancient Rome we have patricians, knights, plebeians, slaves; in the middle ages, feudal lords, vassals, guild-masters, journeymen, apprentices, serfs; in almost all of these classes, again, subordinate gradations.

The modern bourgeois society that has sprouted from the ruins of feudal society, has not done away with class antagonisms. It has but established new classes, new conditions of oppression, new forms of struggle in place of the old ones.

Our epoch, the epoch of the bourgeoisie, possesses, however, this distinctive feature; it has simplified the class antagonisms. Society as a whole is more and more splitting up into two great hostile camps, into two great classes directly facing each other: Bourgeoisie and Proletariat.

The bourgeoisie, historically, has played a most revolutionary part.

The bourgeoisie, wherever it has got the upper hand, has put an end to all feudal, patriarchal, idyllic relations. It has pitilessly torn asunder the motley feudal ties that bound man to his "natural superiors," and has left no other nexus between man and man than naked self-interest, than callous "cash payment." It has drowned the most heavenly ecstasies of religious fervor, of chivalrous enthusiasm, of Philistine sentimentalism, in

Excerpted from Karl Marx, *"Manifesto of the Communist Party,"* reprinted in *Capital and Other Writings of Karl Marx,* edited by Max Eastman (New York: Modern Library, Random House, 1932), pp. 321–34.

the icy water of egotistical calculation. It has resolved personal worth into exchange value, and in place of the numberless indefeasible chartered freedoms has set up that single, unconscionable freedom—Free Trade. In one word, for exploitation, veiled by religious and political illusions, it has substituted naked, shameless, direct, brutal exploitation.

The bourgeoisie cannot exist without constantly revolutionizing the instruments of production, and thereby the relations of production, and with them the whole relations of society. Conservation of the old modes of production in unaltered form was, on the contrary, the first condition of existence for all earlier industrial classes. Constant revolutionizing of production, uninterrupted disturbance of all social conditions, everlasting uncertainty and agitation distinguish the bourgeois epoch from all earlier ones. All fixed, fast frozen relations, with their train of ancient and venerable prejudices and opinions, are swept away, all new formed ones become antiquated before they can ossify. All that is solid melts into the air, all that is holy is profaned, and man is at last compelled to face with sober senses his real conditions of life, and his relations with his kind.

The need of a constantly expanding market for its products chases the bourgeoisie over the whole surface of the globe. It must nestle everywhere, settle everywhere, establish connections everywhere.

The bourgeoisie has subjected the country to the rule of the towns. It has created enormous cities, has greatly increased the urban population as compared with the rural, and has thus rescued a considerable part of the population from the idiocy of rural life. Just as it has made the country dependent on the towns, so it has made barbarian and semibarbarian countries dependent on civilized ones, nations of peasants on nations of bourgeois, the East on the West.

The bourgeoisie keeps more and more doing away with the scattered state of the population, of the means of production, and of property. It has agglomerated population, centralized means of production, and has concentrated property in a few hands. The necessary consequence of this was political centralization. Independent, or but loosely connected provinces, with separate interests, laws, governments, and systems of taxation, became lumped together in one nation, with one government, one code of laws, one national class interest, one frontier, and one customs tariff.

The bourgeoisie, during its rule of scarce one hundred years, has created more massive and more colossal productive forces than have all preceding generations together. Subjection of Nature's forces to man, machinery, application of chemistry to industry and agriculture, steam-navigation, railways, electric telegraphs, clearing of whole continents for cultivation, canalization of rivers, whole populations conjured out of the ground—what earlier century had even a presentiment that such productive forces slumbered in the lap of social labor?

We see then: the means of production and of exchange on whose foundation the bourgeoisie built itself up, were generated in feudal society. At a certain stage in the development of these means of production and of exchange, the conditions under which feudal society produced and exchanged, the feudal organization of agriculture and manufacturing industry, in one word, the feudal relations of property became no longer compatible with the already developed productive forces; they became so many fetters. They had to burst asunder; they were burst asunder.

Into their places stepped free competition, accompanied by social and political constitution adapted to it, and by economical and political sway of the bourgeois class.

A similar movement is going on before our own eyes. Modern bourgeois society with its relations of production, of exchange and of property, a society that has conjured up such gigantic means of production and of exchange, is like the sorcerer, who is no longer able to control the powers of the nether world whom he has called up by his spells. For many a decade past, the history of industry and commerce is but the history of the revolt of modern productive forces against modern conditions of production, against the property relations that are the conditions for the existence of the bourgeoisie and of its rule. It is enough to mention the commercial crises that by their periodical return put on its trial, each time more threateningly, the existence of the entire bourgeois society. In these crises a great part not only of the existing products, but also of the previously created productive forces, are periodically destroyed. In these crises there breaks out an epidemic that, in all earlier epochs, would have seemed an absurdity—the epidemic of overproduction. Society suddenly finds itself put back into a state of momentary barbarism; it appears as if a famine, a universal war of devastation, had cut off the supply of every means of subsistence; industry and commerce seem to be destroyed; and why? Because there is too much civilization, too much means of subsistence, too much industry, too much commerce. The productive forces at the disposal of society no longer tend to further the development of the conditions of the bourgeois property; on the contrary, they have become too powerful for these conditions by which they are fettered, and as soon as they overcome these fetters they bring disorder into the whole of bourgeois society, endanger the existence of bourgeois property. The conditions of bourgeois society are too narrow to comprise the wealth created by them. And how does the bourgeoisie get over these crises? On the one hand by enforced destruction of a mass of productive forces; on the other, by the conquest of new markets, and by the more thorough exploitation of the old ones. That is to say, by paving the way for more extensive and more destructive crises, and by diminishing the means whereby crises are prevented.

The weapons with which the bourgeoisie felled feudalism to the ground are now turned against the bourgeoisie itself.

But not only has the bourgeoisie forged the weapons that bring death to itself; it has also called into existence the men who are to wield those weapons—the modern working class—the proletarians.

Modern industry has converted the little workshop of the patriarchal master into the great factory of the industrial capitalist. Masses of laborers, crowded into factories, are organized like soldiers. As privates of the industrial army they are placed under the command of a perfect hierarchy of officers and sergeants. Not only are they the slaves of the bourgeois class and of the bourgeois state, they are daily and hourly enslaved by the machine, by the overlooker, and, above all, by the individual bourgeois manufacturer himself. The more openly this despotism proclaims gain to be its end and aim, the more petty, the more hateful, and the more embittering it is.

The lower strata of the middle class—the small tradespeople, shopkeepers and retired tradesmen generally, the handicraftsmen and peasants—all these sink gradually into the proletariat, partly because their diminutive capital does not suffice for the scale on which Modern Industry is carried on, and is swamped in the competition with the large capitalists, partly because their specialized skill is rendered worthless by new methods of production. Thus the proletariat is recruited from all classes of the population.

The proletariat goes through various stages of development. With its birth begins its struggle with the bourgeoisie. At first the contest is carried on by individual laborers, then by the workpeople of a factory, then by the operatives of one trade, in one locality, against the individual bourgeois who directly exploits them. They direct their attacks not against the bourgeois conditions of production, but against the instruments of production themselves; they destroy imported wares that compete with their labor, they smash to pieces machinery, they set factories ablaze, they seek to restore by force the vanished status of the workman of the Middle Ages.

At this stage the laborers still form an incoherent mass scattered over the whole country, and broken up by their mutual competition. If anywhere they unite to form more compact bodies, this is not yet the consequence of their own active union, but of the union of the bourgeoisie, which class, in order to attain its own political ends, is compelled to set the whole proletariat in motion, and is moreover yet, for a time, able to do so. At this stage, therefore, the proletarians do not fight their enemies, but the enemies of their enemies, the remnants of absolute monarchy, the landowners, the non-industrial bourgeois, the petty bourgeoisie. Thus the whole historical movement is concentrated in the hands of the bourgeoisie, every victory so obtained is a victory for the bourgeoisie.

But with the development of industry the proletariat not only increases in number; it becomes concentrated in greater masses, its strength grows and it feels that strength more. The various interests and conditions of life within the ranks of the proletariat are more and more equalized, in proportion as machinery obliterates all distinctions of labor, and nearly everywhere reduces wages to the same low level. The growing competition among the bourgeois, and the resulting commercial crisis, make the wages of the workers even more fluctuating. The unceasing improvement of machinery, ever more rapidly developing, makes their livelihood more and more precarious; the collisions between individual workmen and individual bourgeois take more and more the character of collisions between two classes. Thereupon the workers begin to form combinations (Trades' Unions) against the bourgeois; they club together in order to keep up the rate of wages; they found permanent associations in order to make provision beforehand for these occasional revolts. Here and there the contest breaks out into riots.

Further, as we have already seen, entire sections of the ruling classes are, by the advance of industry, precipitated into the proletariat, or are at least threatened in their conditions of existence. These also supply the proletariat with fresh elements of enlightenment and progress.

Finally, in times when the class-struggle nears the decisive hour, the process of dissolution going on within the ruling class—in fact, within the whole range of an old society—assumes such a violent, glaring character that a small section of the ruling class cuts itself adrift and joins the revolutionary class, the class that holds the future in its hands. Just as, therefore, at an earlier period, a section of the nobility went over to the bourgeoisie, so now a portion of the bourgeoisie goes over to the proletariat, and in particular, a portion of the bourgeois ideologists, who have raised themselves to the level of comprehending theoretically the historical movements as a whole.

Of all the classes that stand face to face with the bourgeoisie today the proletariat alone is a really revolutionary class. The other classes decay and finally disappear in the face of modern industry; the proletariat is its special and essential product.

Hitherto every form of society has been based, as we have already seen, on the antagonism of oppressing and oppressed classes. But in order to oppress a class, certain conditions must be assured to it under which it can, at least, continue its slavish existence. The serf, in the period of serfdom, raised himself to membership in the commune, just as the petty bourgeois, under the yoke of feudal absolutism, managed to develop into a bourgeois. The modern laborer, on the contrary, instead of rising with the progress of industry, sinks deeper and deeper below the conditions of existence of his own class. He becomes a pauper, and pauperism develops more rapidly than population and wealth. And here it becomes evident that the bourgeoisie is unfit any longer to be the ruling class in society, and to impose its conditions of existence upon society as an over-riding law. It is unfit to rule, because it is incompetent to assure an existence to its slave within his slavery, because it cannot help letting him sink into such a state that it has to feed him, instead of being fed by him. Society

can no longer live under this bourgeoisie; in other words, its existence is no longer compatible with society.

The essential condition for the existence, and for the sway of the bourgeois class, is the formation and augmentation of capital; the condition for capital is wage labor. Wage labor rests exclusively on competition between the laborers. The advance of industry, whose involuntary promoter is the bourgeoisie, replaces the isolation of the laborers, due to competition, by their involuntary combination, due to association. The development of Modern Industry, therefore, cuts from under its feet the very foundation on which the bourgeoisie produces and appropriates products. What the bourgeoisie therefore produces, above all, are its own grave diggers. Its fall and the victory of the proletariat are equally inevitable.   □

2.
Marx versus Orthodox Economists

Joan Robinson, the author of the following reading, has been an outstanding contributor to economic theory for four decades. A Cambridge University economist, she wrote the classic Economics of Imperfect Competition *in 1933; a recent book is her* Freedom and Necessity: An introduction to the Study of Society *(1970). Her* Essay on Marxian Economics *was published in 1942. In the excerpt below, Robinson's main theme is that, although Marx's analysis was imperfect, he nevertheless raised a set of problems that orthodox economics, following in the British classical tradition, had failed to cope with adequately. In the essay, she mentions the theory of ''imperfect* competition'' (a theory to which she herself was a major contributor). This theory refers to the analysis of market structures that do not meet the test of pure competition: i.e., market structures where firms are either very large or in other ways influence the markets in which they sell their goods.

Essay on Marxian Economics

Joan Robinson

The fundamental differences between Marxian and traditional orthodox economics are, first, that the orthodox economists accept the capitalist system as part of the eternal order of Nature, while Marx regards it as a passing phase in the transition from the feudal economy of the past to the socialist economy of the future. And, second, that the orthodox economists argue in terms of a harmony of interests between the various sections of the community, while Marx conceives of economic life in terms of a conflict of interests between owners of property who do no work and workers who own no property. These two points of difference are not unconnected—for if the system is taken for granted and the shares of the various classes in the social product are determined by inexorable natural law, all interests unite in requiring an increase in the total to be divided. But if the possibility of changing the system is once admitted, those who hope to gain and those who fear to lose

Excerpted from Joan Robinson, *An Essay on Marxian Economics* (London: Macmillan & Co., 1942), pp. 1–6, 115. Reprinted by permission of the author, St. Martin's Press, Inc., and Macmillan, London and Basingstoke.

by the change are immediately ranged in opposite camps.

The orthodox economists, on the whole, identified themselves with the system and assumed the role of its apologists, while Marx set himself to understand the working of capitalism in order to hasten its overthrow. Marx was conscious of his purposes. The economists were in general unconscious. They wrote as they did because it seemed to them the only possible way to write, and they believed themselves to be endowed with scientific impartiality. Their preconceptions emerge rather in the problems which they chose to study and the assumptions on which they worked than in overt political doctrine.

Since they believed themselves to be in search of eternal principles they paid little attention to the special historical features of actual situations, and, in particular, they were apt to project the economics of a community of small equal proprietors into the analysis of advanced capitalism. Thus the orthodox conception of competition entails that each commodity in each market is supplied by a large number of producers, acting individualistically, bound together neither by open collusion nor by unconscious class loyalty; and entails that any individual is free to enter any line of activity he pleases. And the laws derived from such a society are applied to modern industry and finance.

Again, the orthodox conception of wages, which has its origin in the picture of a peasant farmer leaning on his hoe in the evening and deciding whether the extra product of another hour's work will repay the extra backache, is projected into the modern labour market, where the individual worker has no opportunity to decide anything except whether it is better to work or to starve.

The orthodox economists have been much preoccupied with elegant elaborations of minor problems, which distract the attention of their pupils from the uncongenial realities of the modern world, and the development of abstract argument has run far ahead of any possibility of empirical verification. Marx's intellectual tools are far cruder, but his sense of reality is far stronger, and his argument towers above their intricate constructions in rough and gloomy grandeur.

He sees the capitalist system as fulfilling a historic mission to draw out the productive power of combined and specialised labour. From its birthplace in Europe it stretches out tentacles over the world to find its nourishment. It forces the accumulation of capital, and develops productive technique, and by these means raises the wealth of mankind to heights undreamed of in the peasant, feudal or slave economies.

But the workers, who, under the compulsion of capitalism, produce the wealth, obtain no benefit from the increase in their productive power. All the benefit accrues to the class of capitalists, for the efficiency of large-scale enterprise breaks down the competition of the peasant and the craftsman, and reduces all who have not property enough to join the ranks of the capitalists to selling their labour for the mere means of existence. Any concession which the capitalist makes to the worker is the concession which the farmer makes to his beasts—to feed them better that they may work the more.

The struggle for life binds the workers together and sets them in opposition to the propertied class, while the concentration of capital in ever larger concerns, forced on by the development of technique, turns the capitalists towards the anti-social practices of monopoly.

But the condemnation of the system does not only depend upon its moral repugnance, and the inevitability of its final overthrow does not only depend upon the determination of the workers to secure their rightful share in the product of their labour. The system contains contradictions within itself which must lead to its disruption. Marx sees the periodic crises of the trade cycle as symptoms of a deep-seated and progressive malady in the vitals of the system.

Developments in economic analysis which have taken place since Marx's day enable us to detect three distinct strands of thought in Marx's treatment of crises. There is, first, the theory of the reserve army of unemployed labour, which shows how unemployment tends to fluctuate with the relationship between the stock of capital offering employment to labour and the supply of labour available to be employed. Second, there is the theory of the falling rate of profit, which shows how the capitalists' greed for accumulation stultifies itself by reducing the average rate of return on capital. And thirdly, there is the theory of the relationship of capital-good to consumption-good industries, which shows the ever-growing productive power of society knocking against the limitation upon the power to consume which is set by the poverty of the workers.

In Marx's mind these three theories are not distinct, and are fused together in a single picture of the system, racked by its own inherent contradictions, generating the conditions for its own disintegration.

Meanwhile, the academic economists, without paying much attention to Marx, have been forced by the experiences of modern times to question much of the orthodox apologetic, and recent developments in academic theory have led them to a position which in some respects resembles the position of Marx far more closely than the position of their own intellectual fore-bears. The modern theory of imperfect competition, though formally quite different from Marx's theory of exploitation, has a close affinity with it. The modern theory of crises has many points of contact with the third line of argument, distinguished above, in Marx's treatment of the subject, and allows room for something resembling the first. Only the second line of argument—the falling rate of profit—appears confused and redundant.

In general, the nightmare quality of Marx's thought gives it, in this bedevilled age, an air of greater reality than the gentle complacency of the orthodox academics. Yet he, at the same time, is more encouraging than they, for he releases hope as well as terror from Pandora's box, while they preach only the gloomy doctrine that all is for the best in the best of all *possible* worlds.

But though Marx is more sympathetic, in many ways, to a modern mind, than the orthodox economists, there is no need to turn him, as many seek to do, into an inspired prophet. He regarded himself as a serious thinker, and it is as a serious thinker that I have endeavoured to treat him.

Marx, however imperfectly he worked out the details, set himself the task of discovering the law of motion of capitalism, and if there is any hope of progress in economics at all, it must be in using academic methods to solve the problems posed by Marx.   □

3.
Marx Was Wrong

In the late 1950s, Khrushchev challenged the West with a promise to "bury" us—economically speaking. This challenge drew a response from Adolf A. Berle, Jr., who points out below that Marx was in error in his predictions about the two contending classes—capitalists and labor—under capitalism and also in his view of the role of government in an advanced capitalistic society. (Marx had argued that such a government would be nothing but a tool of the ruling economic class.) Adolf A. Berle, Jr. has made many contributions to economics, perhaps his outstanding contribution being his collaboration with Gardner C. Means in the pathbreaking study, The Modern Corporation and Private Property *(1934).*

Marx Was Wrong and So Is Khrushchev

Adolf A. Berle, Jr.

"Your grandchildren will live under socialism," says Khrushchev to us. "We will bury you [capitalists]," he predicted to an American visitor in Moscow. Both comments capsule a major ingredient of Communist propaganda the world over: capitalism is doomed. It is self-destructive. Fate and history make communism the inevitably victorious system. Clever men had best get on the bandwagon now.

The line is not new. Westwardbound empire builders from Eurasia have always used it. Attila, Genghis Khan, Tamerlane, all urged their opponents to collapse gracefully because fate had written them off. But they did not base their claim on economics, or attempt a reasoned argument, as do present-day Communists.

But, in Moscow, doubts are arising. The American system, classified by Marxians as monopoly-capitalist and therefore due for death, gives surprisingly few signs of dying, or even of illness. Subtly, the Communist line is emphasizing a quite different note: "We can overtake and out-produce you; we can do everything you can faster and better."

One outspoken Soviet economist, Eugene Varga, ten years ago risked his career by predicting that the American system would not then destroy itself by a post-war economic crisis. After a period of disgrace, he was restored to favor. True, Karl Marx had asserted nearly a century earlier that capitalist industrial societies would create the conditions for their own self-destruction. But something had happened to delay the calculation, and careful Communist analysts knew it.

What had happened, certainly in the American case, was an evolution within the capitalist frame, knocking out the basis of Marx's prophecy and, incidentally, of the current Communist propaganda line. Briefly, the United States, without revolution, changed from a nineteenth-century "property system" to a social system. It did this in a way no Communist could have forecast, and it created what is, in essence, a different system; so different that one French scholar, Jacques Maritain, insists that it is a new and fluid system, still in the making, "which renders both capitalism and socialism things of the past."

Another scholar, Father Bruckberger, has recently written a book to prove it. It may not be an accident that both are French; the clearest estimates of America have come from France—witness Alexis de Tocqueville in the nineteenth century and André Siegfried in the twentieth.

This American system has not yet received a distinctive name. It has been called "people's capitalism." A new book about to come out, by Dr. Paul Harbrecht, calls it "paraproprietal society" (a society beyond property). When Khrushchev and his associates talk about capitalism, they describe a system which perhaps did exist a century ago. But in America it stopped existing somewhere between 1920 and 1930. It is important both for the Soviet Union and for America to know this. Kremlin Communists are fighting a ghost, and their more sophisticated analysts know it. Americans are just coming to realize that they are operators of a system more advanced and, in its way, more revolutionary than the Marxian.

Predictions of a short life for capitalist society, as it functioned about 1900, had, I think, a reasonable basis at the time. Marx thought private ownership of factories, plants and industry inevitably would cause the rich to grow richer as their profits accumulated. Meanwhile the workers and the poor would stay at subsistence level. The small owner class, he insisted, would own and operate the government, the courts and all social organization. These would be used to defend the growing accumulations of this class. As the poor stayed poor (or grew poorer) markets for manufactured goods would not increase as fast as production—the masses would not have the buying power.

So, markets would have to be extended by military conquest and every capitalist state must become a built-in "imperialism," always seizing more territory to increase markets for its owner class. There would be recurrent crises of growing severity, as production outran markets and the going got harder. Eventually an insuperable crisis would blow up the whole system. Then the Communist dictatorship of the proletariat representing the masses would take over. So ran the argument.

If we had looked at Europe in 1870—or at America from 1890 to 1900—circumstances would have lent color to the idea. At that time, individual owners of private capitalist enterprise were in fact accumulating, high, wide and handsome. In America we were having the "age of the moguls"—proprietor-tycoons piling up fabulous fortunes from the profits of railroads and mines, steel, copper and oil. In England, Charles Dickens had described the plight of the masses in "Bleak House" and "Oliver Twist." In the United States, Upton Sinclair and his friends were telling a similar story, American-style.

Marx was right in one respect: it could not (and in fact, did not) last. But he was completely wrong in his guess as to how it would change.

In the United States three new elements (among other less powerful factors) emerged and changed both the direction and structure of affairs, though none of them involved or contemplated blowing up the system.

The first development was the American corporation. This operated surprisingly. In one generation it replaced the individual or family-owners. In a second period, it displaced the tycoons and moguls, substituting professional management. It did not behave at all like a personal fortune-builder.

The second was the rise of American labor unions. These refused to try to seize the ownership position or take over government. Instead, they insisted only on representing workmen.

The third, and probably the most important, was the position of the American democratic government. This simply declined to be owned and operated by and in the interest of the tycoon (or any other) class. It intervened from time to time to steer the economic system toward social goals. None of these possibilities had figured in Marx's calculation, and Russian commentators today find difficulty in explaining them.

First, the corporations. These organizations became and now are, the titular "owners" of American industry. But corporations are not individuals or families and do not behave like them. As productive organizations they can and do pile up huge aggregations of property. But simultaneously they must distribute much of their profit to a continuously growing proportion of the population of the United States. Corporations whose stock is listed on the New York Stock Exchange carry on at least three-fourths of all American industry; the 500 largest of them probably carry on about two-thirds of it. Were these 500 families, the results might have justified Marx's predictions and produced the foreseen catastrophe.

Actually, according to the New York Stock Exchange, they have about 12,500,000 direct stockholders. Even more important, a large and growing amount of their stock is held by institutions—notably pension trusts, mutual funds and, increasingly, life insurance companies. These in turn distribute the industrial profits. Probably 50 million Americans who do not even know they derive income from stocks receive a share of these profits through the holdings of such institutions. This number will grow. Their proportionate take of industrial profits will also grow—both factors are expanding just now with considerable rapidity.

Nor are the managers and groups controlling corporations owners. They are almost always salaried officials. They are becoming a kind of nonstatist civil service. The corporate system at present is thus in effect operating to "socialize" American industry but without intervention of the political state. No Marxist could ever have thought up that possibility.

Then there is the phenomenon of the American labor movement. For practical purposes, organized labor became a substantial economic factor after World War I. It gained full recognition through the Wagner Act. It has now become a vast, permanent and powerful element in the American economic system.

But it refused to behave like its European ancestors. It did not wish to own and manage the plants. In fact, it has steadily declined to enter management. Instead, it aimed only to represent the workers and to get for them, through wages, pensions and fringe benefits, the largest practicable share of national income.

In the past thirty years it has succeeded in steadily raising the "real" wage of workers about 3 percent annually, or 30 percent in each decade—though workers do not receive this only in cash but also in shorter working hours, vacations and more leisure. The net result has been that American labor now has the highest workers' standard of living in the world. The workman himself lives, thinks and feels not as an oppressed proletarian seeking to be saved by revolution but as a member of the middle class to whose children any position is possible. It is, in fact, increasingly hard to find a "proletariat" in the United States except in a few isolated areas.

Still less has the labor movement followed European patterns in forming a political party or seeking to assume government; still less to overturn the existing system. It does get into politics very effectively to defend its own interests, dealing more or less impartially with both political parties. But it declines to become a Socialist party itself and shows no desire whatever to attempt creation of a "labor" government.

Finally, and certainly most important, the American Government most obstinately refused to be merely an expression of the "ownership class." According to Marx, such refusal could not happen—but it did. Surprisingly to European thought, many of the "ownership" group were outspoken in opposing that conception of government. President Theodore Roosevelt intervened violently against one ownership sector in the Mogul Age when he forced regulation of railroads and set a conservative party to control "malefactors of great wealth."

President Woodrow Wilson moved effectively against the financial ownership class, proclaiming the doctrines of the "New Freedom" and compelling passage of the Federal Reserve Act of 1913. With even more effect, he sponsored income and inheritance tax legislation about the same time.

In 1933, President Franklin Roosevelt and the New Deal undertook the larger task of hauling the whole system toward a socially directed commonwealth. Social Security legislation was one great instrument. Systematic direction of a larger share of national income toward farmers and agriculture was another. Development of public works and state-directed production when unemployment threatens was a third. Use of the credit system to assure housing, electricity and land reclamation was a fourth. And there were many more.

Thus, in mid-century, Americans are operating a so-called "capitalist system" in which all the elements dominant in the nineteenth century have changed. What is left of the old system is its form of organization and, in general, its separation from the political government.

That organization has achieved a per capita level of production beyond older dreams—so much so that equaling it is the present expressed dream of the Soviet Union and of Communist China. In terms of distribution it has done better than Communist systems because it had more to distribute. And its methods of distribution have been on the whole less arbitrary and infinitely less oppressive. The results have been more satisfactory to 175 million Americans than those of Socialist distribution to the 210 million citizens of the Soviet Union.

This American system is miles from being perfect. All kinds of things turn up in it that should not be there. All kinds of inequities have to be dealt with. Our methods for keeping production and distribution in balance are still unsystematic and crude; better means still need to be worked out. Steering an adequate amount of the national income into necessary noncommercial activities, notably education and the arts, remains a problem.

But, by comparative standards, our system is far out ahead. As a single example, during forty years of the Soviet system, Russia at all times has had more political prisoners in concentration camps behind barbed wire than the United States has ever had unemployed men—though Khrushchev is credited with having reduced the number materially in the past few years.

The vitality and rapid evolution of the American system—and it has not stopped growing and has not stopped evolving—has worried the Russian theoreticians. At the Twentieth Communist Congress in Moscow, a then favorite Communist doctrinaire, Dmitri Shepilov (later Foreign Minister), was put up as a principal speaker to explain true doctrine to the comrades. He did not ignore the fact that the United States and its system had evolved and was going great guns, but he had to prove nevertheless that "capitalism is doomed."

Taking account of the newer studies of the American system, he singled out for attention (along with John Foster Dulles) the work of Prof. J. Kenneth Galbraith of Harvard ("American Capitalism: The Concept of Countervailing Power") and a current book of mine. He made no attempt to meet the modern American facts. "It can't happen," he proclaimed. Socially directed capitalism, freed from the vices Marx had observed, must be like hot ice: it couldn't exist.

Sophisticated Communist scholars know better. A more serious explanation was attempted this summer, again by Eugene Varga, ablest of the Soviet economists. In the official "Problems of Peace and Socialism" last August, he published an article. He renewed the statement that "under capitalism crises of overproduction are inevitable," but he said we were now in a system of "state monopoly capitalism" and this system made it easier for "monopolies" to weather these crises.

Specifically, the state moved to support the "monopolies" (he means the big corporations) through Government orders, chiefly military, and thus assure a minimum of production even during crises. Further, we slowly inflated the currency, reducing real wages without direct wage cuts.

The fact that the corporations are not monopolies and neither control, nor are controlled by, the state, he ignored, and he omitted the fact that they now distribute profits as well as wages to a huge sector of the United States. Nor had he discovered that the real wage of the American workman steadily rises.

Still less, of course, had he noted that "Government orders" include nonmilitary items such as huge road systems, municipal improvements, housing, power, scientific development and other activities whose amount exceeds military expenditures. (If the armament burden were lifted tomorrow, that same machinery could be used with general approval from the American public to increase production and markets alike.) But he continues hopefully to assert that "the cyclic movement inherent in the capitalist mode of production will, we believe, resume its normal course with a world economic crisis occurring every six years or so."

Well, his reasoning does not take account of facts. It ignores the structural change in the property system achieved during the past fifty years, and the astonishing capacity of the American system to make new adaptations.

Its crises (there will be some) can be handled on a humane basis. They will be infinitely less dangerous than the recurrent bloody crises inescapable in the political power monopoly built into the Soviet dictatorship. The American system continues to evolve successfully, and is keeping right on. □

4.
Marx Was Right but Should Have Gone Further

Two highly influential American Marxist economists are Paul M. Sweezy and the late Paul A. Baran. In their analysis, Marx is credited with having foreseen the development of monopoly power under capitalism, but is not believed to have developed its full implications. Their writing, in the Marxist tradition, may be viewed as an attempt to extend the conclusions of the master. They point out, among other things, the all-pervasive nature of overproduction under monopoly capitalism and the irrationality of capitalist thought under modern conditions. When they use the term "surplus," they mean "the difference between total output and the socially necessary costs of producing total output." This is roughly the same thing as profits, broadly conceived.

Monopoly Capital

**Paul A. Baran
and Paul M. Sweezy**

Like the classical economists before him, Marx treated monopolies not as essential elements of capitalism but rather as remnants of the feudal and mercantilist past which had to be abstracted from in order to attain the clearest possible view of the basic structure and tendencies of capitalism. It is true that, unlike the classicists, Marx fully recognized the powerful trend toward the concentration and centralization of capital inherent in a competitive economy: his vision of the

Excerpted from Paul A. Baran and Paul M. Sweezy, *Monopoly Capital*, pp. 3–5, 108–11, 336–41, Copyright © 1966 by Paul M. Sweezy; reprinted by permission of Monthly Review Press.

future of capitalism certainly included new and purely capitalist forms of monopoly. But he never attempted to investigate what would at the time have been a hypothetical system characterized by the prevalence of large-scale enterprise and monopoly. Partly the explanation is no doubt that the empirical material on which such an investigation would have had to be based was too scanty to permit reliable generalization. But perhaps even more important, Marx anticipated the overthrow of capitalism long before the unfolding of all its potentialities, well within the system's competitive phase.

Engels, in some of his own writings after Marx's death and in editorial additions to the second and third volumes of *Capital* which he prepared for the printer, commented on the rapid growth of monopolies during the 1880s and 1890s, but he did not try to incorporate monopoly into the body of Marxian economic theory. The first to do this was Rudolf Hilferding in his important work, *Das Finanzkapital,* published in 1910. But for all his emphasis on monopoly, Hilferding did not treat it as a qualitatively new element in the capitalist economy; rather he saw it as effecting essentially quantitative modifications of the basic Marxian laws of capitalism. Lenin, who was strongly influenced by Hilferding's analysis of the origins and diffusion of monopoly, based his theory of imperialism squarely on the predominance of monopoly in the developed capitalist countries. But neither he nor his followers pursued the matter into the fundamentals of Marxian economic theory. There, paradoxically enough, in what might have

been thought the area most immediately involved, the growth of monopoly made the least impression.

We believe that the time has come to remedy this situation and to do so in an explicit and indeed radical fashion.

MONOPOLY CAPITALISM IS SELF-CONTRADICTORY

Twist and turn as one will, there is no way to avoid the conclusion that monopoly capitalism is a self-contradictory system. It tends to generate ever more surplus, yet it fails to provide the consumption and investment outlets required for the absorption of a rising surplus and hence for the smooth working of the system. Since surplus which cannot be absorbed will not be produced, it follows that the normal state of the monopoly capitalist economy is stagnation. With a given stock of capital and a given cost and price structure, the system's operating rate cannot rise above the point at which the amount of surplus produced can find the necessary outlets. And this means chronic underutilization of available human and material resources. Or, to put the point in slightly different terms, the system must operate at a point low enough on its profitability schedule not to generate more surplus than can be absorbed. Since the profitability schedule is always moving upward, there is a corresponding downdrift of the "equilibrium" operating rate. Left to itself—that is to say, in the absence of counteracting forces which are no part of what may be called the "elementary logic" of the system—monopoly capitalism would sink deeper and deeper into a bog of chronic depression.

Counteracting forces do exist. If they did not, the system would indeed long since have fallen of its own weight. It therefore becomes a matter of the greatest importance to understand the nature and implications of these counteracting forces. Here we confine ourselves to a few preliminary remarks.

The self-contradictory character of monopoly capitalism—its chronic inability to absorb as much surplus as it is capable of producing—impresses itself on the ordinary citizen in a characteristic way. To him, the economic problem appears to be the very opposite of what the textbooks say it is: not how best to utilize scarce resources but how to dispose of the products of superabundant resources. And this holds regardless of his wealth or position in society. If he is a worker, the ubiquitous fact of unemployment teaches him that the supply of labor is always greater than the demand. If he is a farmer, he struggles to stay afloat in a sea of surpluses. If he is a businessman, his sales persistently fall short of what he could profitably produce. Always too much, never too little.

This condition of affairs is peculiar to monopoly capitalism. The very notion of "too much" would have been inconceivable to all pre-capitalist forms of society; and even in the competitive stage of capitalism, it described a temporary derangement, not a normal condition. In a rationally ordered socialist society, no matter how richly endowed it might be with natural resources and technology and human skills, "too much" could only be a welcome signal to shift attention to an area of "too little." Only under monopoly capitalism does "too much" appear as a pervasive problem affecting everyone at all times.

From this source stem a whole series of attitudes and interests of crucial importance for the character and functioning of monopoly capitalist society. On the one hand, there is a stubborn spirit of restrictionism which pervades the institutional structure. Union featherbedding and Henry Wallace's plowing under of little pigs are only the best publicized examples of practices which are all but universal in business and government: the most primitive reaction to an excess of supply is simply to cut back. During the 1930s, when "too much" took on the dimensions of a universal disaster, primitive restrictionism acquired, in the National Industrial Recovery Act and the National Recovery Administration, the dignity and sanction of official national policy.

But cutting back as a remedy for "too much," even if beneficial to particular groups or individuals, only aggravates the situation as a whole. A secondary and more sophisticated set of attitudes and policies therefore emerges, gropingly and slowly at first but with increasing purposefulness and momentum as monopoly capitalism develops. Their rationale derives from the simple fact that the obverse of "too much" on the supply side is "too little" on the demand side; instead of cutting back supply they aim at stimulating demand.

The stimulation of demand—the creation and expansion of markets—thus becomes to an ever greater degree the leitmotif of business and government policies under monopoly capitalism. But this statement, true as it is, can easily be misleading. There are many conceivable ways of stimulating demand. If a socialist society, for example, should find that through some planning error more consumer goods were being produced than could be sold, given the existing structure of prices and incomes, the simplest and most direct remedy would clearly be to cut prices. This would reduce the amount of surplus at the disposal of the planning authorities and correspondingly raise the purchasing power of consumers. The threatened glut could be quickly and painlessly averted: everyone would be better off, no one worse off. Such a course of action is obviously not open to a monopoly capitalist society, in which the determination of prices is the jealously guarded prerogative of the giant corporations. Each makes its own decisions with a view to maximizing its own private profit. Except for short periods of all-out war, when inflationary pressures threaten the entire economic and social fabric, there is no agency charged with controlling prices. Moreover, every attempt to maintain or establish such an agency in peacetime has resulted either in ignominious failure (witness the fiasco of price control after the Second World War) or in the thinly disguised legalization of monopoly pricing practices in ''regulated'' industries. The plain fact is that the pricing process is controlled by the most powerful vested interests in monopoly capitalist society. To imagine that it could possibly be regulated in the public interest would be to imagine away the very characteristics of that society which make it what it is.

If stimulation of demand through price reduction is impossible within the framework of monopoly capitalism, this cannot be said of other possible methods. Take, for example, advertising and related forms of salesmanship. Every giant corporation is driven by the logic of its situation to devote more and more attention and resources to the sales effort. And monopoly capitalist society as a whole has every interest in promoting rather than restricting and controlling this method of creating new markets and expanding old ones.

Just as with price cutting and salesmanship, other forms of stimulating demand either are or are not compatible with the pattern of interests, the structure of power, the web of ideology that constitute the essence of monopoly capitalist society. Those which are compatible will be fostered and promoted; those which are incompatible will be ignored or inhibited. The question for monopoly capitalism is not whether to stimulate demand. It must, on pain of death.

THE IRRATIONAL SYSTEM

It is of the essence of capitalism that both goods and labor power are typically bought and sold on the market. In such a society relations among individuals are dominated by the principle of the exchange of equivalents, of *quid pro quo*, not only in economic matters but in all other aspects of life as well.

Not that the principle of equivalent exchange is or ever has been universally practiced in capitalist society. As Marx showed so convincingly in the closing chapters of the first volume of *Capital*, the primary accumulation of capital was effected through violence and plunder, and the same methods continue in daily use throughout capitalism's dependent colonies and semi-colonies. Nevertheless the ideological sway of *quid pro quo* became all but absolute. In their relations with each other and in what they teach those over whom they rule, capitalists are fully committed to the principle of *quid pro quo*, both as a guide to action and as a standard of morality.

This commitment reflected an important step forward in the development of the forces of production and in the evolution of human consciousness. Only on the basis of equivalent exchange was it possible to realize the more rational utilization of human and material resources which has been the central achievement of capitalism. At the same time, it must never be forgotten that the rationality of *quid pro quo* is specifically capitalist rationality which at a certain stage of development becomes incompatible with the underlying forces and relations of production. To ignore this and to treat *quid pro quo* as a universal maxim of rational conduct is in itself an aspect of bourgeois ideology, just as the radical-sounding assertion that under socialism exchange of equivalents can be immediately dispensed with betrays a utopian view of the nature of the economic problems faced by a socialist society.*

But even during the life span of capitalism itself, *quid pro quo* breaks down as a rational principle of economic and social organization. The giant corporation withdraws from the sphere of the market large segments of economic activity and subjects them to scientifically designed administration. This change represents a continuous increase in the rationality of the parts of

---

*Marx emphasized in his *Critique of the Gotha Program* that the principle of equivalent exchange must survive in a socialist society for a considerable period as a guide to the efficient allocation and utilization of human and material resources. By the same token, however, the evolution of socialism into communism requires an unremitting struggle against the principle, with a view to its ultimate replacement by the ideal "From each according to his ability, to each according to his need." In a fully developed communist society, in which social production would be organized as in one vast economic enterprise and in which scarcity would be largely overcome, equivalent exchange would no more serve as the organizing principle of economic activity than at the present time the removal of a chair from one's bedroom to one's sitting room requires charging the sitting room and crediting the bedroom with the value of the furniture. This is obviously not to imply that the communist society of the future can dispense with rational calculation; what it does indicate is that the nature of the rationality involved in economic calculation undergoes a profound change. And this change in turn is but one manifestation of a thoroughgoing transformation of human needs and of the relations among men in society.

the system, but it is not accompanied by any rationalization of the whole. On the contrary, with commodities being priced not according to their costs of production but to yield the maximum possible profit, the principle of *quid pro quo* turns into the opposite of a promoter of rational economic organization and instead becomes a formula for maintaining scarcity in the midst of potential plenty. Human and material resources remain idle because there is in the market no *quid* to exchange against the *quo* of their potential output. And this is true even though the real cost of such output would be nil. In the most advanced capitalist country a large part of the population lives in abysmal poverty while in the underdeveloped countries hundreds of millions suffer from disease and starvation because there is no mechanism for effecting an exchange of what they could produce for what they so desperately need. Insistence on the inviolability of equivalent exchange when what is to be exchanged costs nothing, strict economizing of resources when a large proportion of them goes to waste—these are obviously the very denial of the rationality which the concept of value and the principle of *quid pro quo* originally expressed.

The obsolescence of such central categories of bourgeois thought is but one symptom of the profoundly contradictory nature of monopoly capitalism, of the ever sharpening conflict between the rapidly advancing rationalization of the actual processes of production and the undiminished *elementality* of the system as a whole. This conflict affects all aspects of society. While rationality has been conquering ever new areas of consciousness, the inability of bourgeois thought to comprehend the development of society as a whole has remained essentially unchanged, a faithful mirror of the continuing ele-mentality and irrationality of the capitalist order itself.

Social reality is therefore conceived in outlived, topsy-turvy and fetishistic terms. Powerless to justify an irrational and inhuman social order and unable to answer the increasingly urgent ques-tions which it poses, bourgeois ideology clings to concepts that are anachronistic and moribund. Its bankruptcy manifests itself not so much in the generation of new fetishes and half-truths as in the stubborn upholding of old fetishes and half-truths which now turn into blatant lies. And the more these old fetishes and half-truths lose whatever truth content they once possessed the more insistently they are hammered, like adver-tising slogans, into the popular consciousness.

The claim that the United States economy is a "free enterprise" system is a case in point. At no time was enterprise really free in the sense that anyone who wanted to could start a busi-ness of his own. Still the concept conveyed an important aspect of the truth by pointing up the difference between the relative freedom of competitive capitalism on the one hand and the restrictions imposed by the guild system and the mercantilist state on the other. Having long ago lost this limited claim to truthfulness and referring as it now does to the freedom of giant corporations to exercise undisturbed their vast monopoly powers, "free enterprise" has turned into a shibboleth devoid of all descriptive or explanatory validity.

Bourgeois ideology is no longer a world out-look, a *Weltanschauung*, which attempts to dis-cern order in the existing chaos and to discover a meaning in life. It has turned into a sort of box of assorted tools and gimmicks for attaining the central goal of bourgeois policies. And this goal—which in its younger days the bourgeoisie defined in terms of material progress and individ-ual freedom—is more and more explicitly limited to one thing only: preservation of the status quo, alias the "free world," with all its manifest evils, absurdities, and irrationalities.

It is of course impossible to advance a rea-soned defense of this status quo, and indeed the effort is seldom made any more. Instead of taking the form of a demonstration of the ra-tionality and desirability of monopoly capitalism, the defense increasingly focuses on the repudia-tion of socialism which is the only real alternative to monopoly capitalism, and on the denunciation of revolution which is the only possible means of achieving socialism. All striving for a better, more humane, more rational society is held to be unscientific, utopian, and subversive; by the same token the existing order of society is made to appear not only as the only possible one but as the only conceivable one.

The contradiction between the increasing ratio-nality of society's methods of production and the organizations which embody them on the one hand and the undiminished elementality and irrationality in the functioning and perception of the whole creates that ideological wasteland which is the hallmark of monopoly capitalism. But we must insist that this is not, as some apologists of the status quo would have us be-lieve, "the end of ideology"; it is the dis-placement of the ideology of rising capitalism by the ideology of the general crisis and decline of the world capitalist order. That its main pillar is anti-Communism is neither accidental nor due to a transient conjunction of political forces, any more than is the fact that the main content of the political and economic policies of modern capitalism is armaments and Cold War. These policies can only be *anti;* there is nothing left for them to be *pro.*   □

5.
Conflict Yes, but Not of the Marxian Kind

Former president of the University of California, Clark Kerr, is also a distinguished economist specializing in labor and industrial relations problems. His view is that Marx was wrong in anticipating an intensification of class conflict under capitalism. What has happened instead is that conflict has become diffused over the whole society, and instead of being between those who do and those who don't own property, it is over the issue of who sets the rules and the life-style of the society.

Class Conflict and Class Collaboration

Clark Kerr

As seen from a more modern viewpoint than that of Marx, the conflict over class has largely dissolved. Instead of six classes or five or two, there are said to be none at all in the Communist world—all men are equal and some are more equal than others; and, in the capitalist world, there are such infinite variations and gradations that it is better to speak of interest groups or status positions rather than class at all in the sense of a class set apart by its common attachment to grievances or to privileges or to a common ideology—all men are unequal and some are more unequal than others.

Excerpted from Clark Kerr, "Class Conflict and Class Collaboration" from *Marshall, Marx and Modern Times: The Multi-Dimensional Society* (London: Cambridge University Press, 1969), pp. 37–41, 122, 129–30. Reprinted by permission of the publisher.

Morality attaches more to individual men than to classes, although there are now those who would urge a special moral position for the intellectuals. Evolution is leading towards an all-pervasive middle class—a middle class that expands its coverage so widely that it is no longer a class at all. There are few hard and fast lines in this middle group but, rather, many minor grades that shade off into one another; except that an "under-class" may be clearly distinguished and is in some places more visible where it has a special racial composition, as in the United States. The under-class stands outside the embrace of the great productive "middle" segment.

Conflict is not concentrated at one place and at one time—at the barricades that separate the proletariat and the bourgeoisie. Friction is spread around in the ball-bearing society that has evolved. Protest is fractionalized. It is not over property but over countless prices and rules. It is not against the capitalist alone, but also against the merchant and bureaucrat and politician. The evolution of industrial society has helped this. There are fewer isolated masses in the lumber camp or textile town or mining village with common grievances against a single source of authority. The one-industry community is less frequent, and employer paternalism gradually passes away. Workers are concentrated into larger communities but these communities are so heterogeneous that the individual and the group are absorbed and contained and subdued. Conflict is everywhere and this saves it from being anywhere to a degree that causes revolution—it is too scattered over time and place.

Marx saw a process that went on stage by stage until its ultimate conclusion—but the process stopped at about the stage he saw and went little further. Workers coalesced into trade unions and in some capitalist countries into political parties, but the trade unions remained bread-and-butter trade unions and the political parties remained cooperating political parties, and neither became revolutionary instruments. In England, at the time of the General Strike, and in the United States, with the I.W.W.s, it looked for a time as though the process might go on as Marx saw it, but the process was arrested. The process of developing increasing group consciousness stopped at the stage of economic trade unions and participating political parties.

Relations of workers and employees became less violent, not more. Real wages rose. Trade unions developed power and influence in the work place—enough to get better rules and to settle grievances; and in individual industries —enough to be concerned with the profitability and growth of "their" industry. As Bendix has noted, "the willingness of entrepreneurial classes to compromise may increase along with the capitalist development"*—not hold steady or decrease. Political parties with worker support came to rule governments. Marx never thought that the capitalists would yield so easily the authority he believed they had over the state—for this, to him, was "suicide." The state turned to welfare. The law was, to a degree, impartial and was not just a tool of the dominant class. Many buffers were created between contending parties. The "new economics" of Cambridge replaced the old. Slichter once wrote of the crucial race between the engineer and the union leader, the one pushing greater productivity and the other higher money wages. A far more important race was between Cambridge economists and the great depressions, and Cambridge won.† The hard and intricate problem of counter-cyclical policy was solved.

---

*Reinhard Bendix, *Work and Authority in Industry* (New York: John Wiley, 1956), p. 438.

†[Kerr is referring here to the work of John Maynard Keynes. See chapter 7.]

Marx was wrong about the evolution of class in maturing capitalist nations. He expected revolution from the workers during an industrial crisis as the standard case. Communist revolutions have come instead more from the peasants and from war. Peasants to Marx represented "barbarians" rather than civilized men. That they should have been important in Russia and particularly China and Cuba would have surprised him. Through foresight or by chance, however, he envisioned a war between Germany and Russia which "will act as the midwife to the inevitable social revolution in Russia." But Russia was not an advanced capitalist nation and thus fell outside his central theory.

Communism has appealed less to the stage of late capitalism and more to early development than Marx had thought it would. It has had a special appeal to people undergoing the transition from a traditional to a modern society. It speaks to their sense of revulsion against the old dynastic elite or against foreign domination. It speaks to their sense of exploitation. It speaks to their increasing sense of misery as they face the psychological impact of the "revolution of rising expectations." Communism, also, has some answers to the problems of the transition—control by the state, a social plan, fast capital accumulation. It is less well adapted to the complexities of an advanced industrial society where many small decisions must be made, and where individuals and groups achieve a degree of independence. Thus, in a world marked by many countries in the early transitional stages into industrialization, Marxism has come to have substantial influence even though it has little appeal in more advanced societies.

THE NEW STRUGGLE

The old struggle was seen by Marx as being over the ownership of property since property determined power. The new struggle is directly over power, almost regardless of the ownership of property: power to set the rules, fix the rewards, influence the style of life. It takes place in modern industrial societies between the several forms of pluralism as against the monolithic society of Stalinism on the one extreme and anarchism without any central coercive authority at the other, and within and among the several forms of pluralism themselves. The old struggle pitted the workers under the banners of socialism against the capitalists with control of the state as the major prize. The new struggle pits the managed under the banners of freedom and participation against the managers with the control and the conduct of a myriad of organizations involved. Instead of trying to concentrate power in the state, the new effort is to fractionalize it everywhere—the old salvation is the new tyranny; and general revolution gives way to piece-meal evolution. Communism, not capitalism, now faces the greatest challenge, for power there is most centrally held—the old radicalism is the new conservatism.

The new problems of modern industrial society call for more flexibility, for more individuality. The new imperative is to "humanize" the communities of work, adapt them to individual preferences. Rather than the unfolding of class relations or the perfecting of market mechanisms, the new force at work is further adaptation to individual preferences in many situations and for many reasons. The challenge once was to absorb and adjust to the factory, the worker and the capitalist; now it is to adjust to the more aggressive individual. Instead of socialism challenging the old capitalism, it is now anarchistic and individualistic and syndicalistic tendencies challenging the new communism and the new capitalistic pluralism. A new synthesis is in process.

Industrial pluralism has developed as the realistic alternative to both the monolithic and the atomistic society. Pluralism now struggles with some of the ultimate issues that go beyond class *versus* class and monopoly *versus* the market: (1) the role of the managed as against the managers, of the semi-managed as against the semi-managers, of the individual against the group; (2) the pressure of the ever newer technology to change the lives of men as against the desire of men to rule technology, to exercise their options in relation to it; (3) the interests of those inside the productive process as against those standing outside; and (4) the contrast between the imperfectibility of man and the hope for a more perfect society. No revolution, no alchemy of morality and knowledge can rid man of all his chains, can make all men into gentlemen; or so it seems one century later.   □

PART 2

MACROECONOMICS: ANALYSIS AND PROBLEMS

Having discussed economic systems in a broad, overarching way in Part One, we must now dig more deeply into the problems that this survey has uncovered. This will require us to develop new tools of economic analysis and to test out these tools in applications to important real-life economic situations.

In taking these further steps, we shall divide the field of economics into the two related subdivisions that we have mentioned earlier: (1) *Macroeconomics,* the study of the economy as a whole, or "in the aggregate," as it is sometimes put; and (2) *Microeconomics,* the study of the particular units (consumers, business firms, laborers, factor owners, etc.) that make up the economy and how their decisions and actions are interrelated.

These fields clearly are not wholly separable either in logic or practice. In Part Four of this book, we shall find that many of our most urgent contemporary economic problems require both microeconomic and macroeconomic tools.

Nevertheless, the division is a useful one, each of these fields having a certain history and logic of its own. In terms of the "circular flow of economic life," discussed frequently in Part One, we might say that while microeconomics analyzes the component elements of the flow, macroeconomics is concerned with the overall dimensions of the flow. Thus, in microeconomics, we want to know how price, output, the employment of labor, and other factors of production are determined for industry A or industry B. By contrast, in macroeconomics we want to know what determines the price-level *in general,* and the levels of *national* output and employment. These problems in turn will involve us with other social "totals": total consumption, total business investment, the total money supply, and so on.

In Part Two, immediately following, we shall take up macroeconomics: in Part Two A, presenting the basic analysis, and in Part Two B, extending and applying this analysis to various economic problems.

Part Three will do the same thing for microeconomics; it can, if preferred, be studied before Part Two.

PART 2A

THE BASICS OF NATIONAL INCOME DETERMINATION

CHAPTER 7
KEYNES AND THE NEW ECONOMICS

In 1947, the well-known American economist, Seymour Harris, edited a book called the *New Economics*. This book was dedicated to an analysis and evaluation of an economist whose main work had been completed a decade earlier. The "new economics" referred to the theory contained in *The General Theory of Employment, Interest and Money* (1936), written by perhaps the most famous economist of the twentieth century, the late John Maynard Keynes.

Like Adam Smith and Karl Marx, Keynes was one of a half-dozen economists whose work profoundly influenced large numbers of other economists and, indeed, the actions of statesmen and nations. Although the adjective "new" may seem a bit out of place for economics written so many years ago, the fact is that orthodoxies die hard. Conservative, and even middle-of-the-road public figures have, until quite recently, been distrustful of Keynesian thinking. Indeed, important scholars still are.[1]

From our point of view, the significance of Keynesian analysis is that it provided one of the major threads, and from the theoretical point of view, *the* major thread, that leads to modern macroeconomic analysis. Much of our discussion in Part Two A will consist of explaining and developing the Keynesian contribution. Before going in this direction, however, let us be clearer in our minds about what sort of problems macroeconomics involves.

PROBLEMS OF THE ECONOMY IN THE AGGREGATE

The first step is to alter somewhat the point of view we gain almost automatically from our daily participation in economic matters: a view of particular jobs, particular firms, and particular industries. We know that it is sometimes hard to find a job, or that some particular business firm may be having troubles; but now we ask: Might the nation sometimes face conditions when businesses *in general* were failing, when

---

1. See p. 183–84.

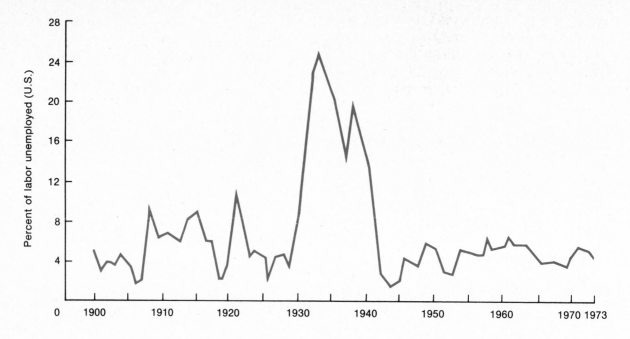

Figure 7–1. Unemployment in the United States (percent of the labor force, 1900–1973).

people *in general* could not locate work? Actually, the question need not be put pessimistically. We could also ask: Are there times when everyone has work, when labor is in great demand, when prices, profits, and wages are all high? The point, of course, is that these questions are about the performance of the economy as a whole.

Now if we look at the past in our own country or in other industrial countries, we can find many instances to prove that national economics do indeed suffer ups and downs in their general economic well-being. All of us know from our reading of American history of the great number of "panics" that have seized our country at one point or another. There were panics in the United States in 1819, 1837, 1857,

1893, 1907, 1914, 1920–1921, and, of course, the "great crash" in 1929. Various statistical measures of these ups and downs are also common. In Figures 7–1, 7–2, and 7–3, we present some diagrams of unemployment in the United States and the United Kingdom at various times in the past. These diagrams measure unemployment as a percentage of the labor force, and they indicate how variable this factor has been historically. The great leap in the unemployment percentage in the United States in the 1930s is a less picturesque but still telling way of describing the Great Depression, which we discussed in chapter 1. Figure 7–2 shows that the problem of unemployment in industrial societies goes back well before the twentieth century. Figure 7–3 indicates that unemployment is still a serious problem in the 1970s, particularly in certain states.

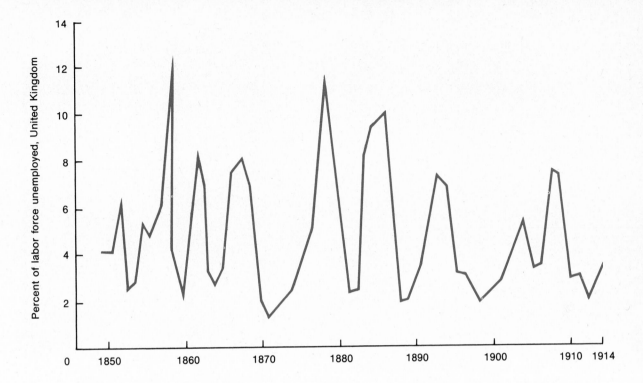

Figure 7–2. Unemployment in the United Kingdom (percent unemployed, 1850–1914).

But economies can get out of gear in other ways besides unemployment. In the first chapter we also talked of the German hyperinflation of the 1920s, when the price level soared to the trillions. This was truly an exceptional incident, but no more exceptional than completely stable prices would be. Almost all industrial countries have had some experience with inflation in the twentieth century and, in many under-developed countries, rapid inflation is a week-to-week phenomenon. Figure 7–4 shows the general course of consumer prices in the United States from 1929 to the present. Notable is the acceleration of price increases in the early 1970s. From December 1972 to December 1973 the U.S. consumer price index rose by 11.2 points (from 127.3 to 138.5). By 1974, many polls showed that the American public considered inflation our number one national problem.

We must remember that when we talk about the price *level,* we are talking about something slightly different from the price of apples or the price of washing machines. When the price of apples alone goes up, our demand curve tells us that we will buy fewer apples because, among other reasons, it will be cheaper for us to satisfy our desire for fruit with peaches and pears. When we talk about the price *level* rising, however, we are referring to a rise not

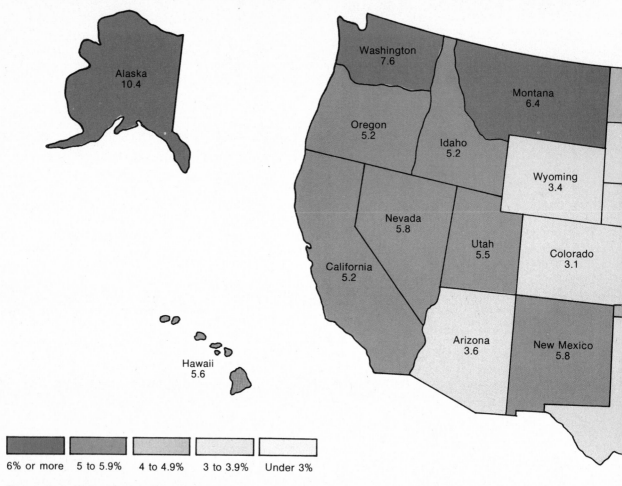

6% or more   5 to 5.9%   4 to 4.9%   3 to 3.9%   Under 3%

Figure 7–3. United States Unemployment Rates by State, 1973.
Source: Department of Labor

only in apple prices but in the prices of peaches and pears and washing machines as well.

Similarly, in the case of unemployment: If the wage of electricians goes down, people will turn toward other occupations, and fewer will offer their services as electricians. But suppose there is unemployment in all industries at once? What happens to the wage then? Where do people turn?

These are the heartland questions of macro-economics. What determines the general level of employment? What determines the general level

of national income?[2] What determines the overall level of prices? These are the problems of the economy in the aggregate.

2. The analysis of national income (or total production) that we shall consider in Part Two will be largely concerned with the short-run aspects of the problem; i.e., with the degree of utilization of a *given* labor force and productive capacity. In the short run (one or two years), this is a permissible assumption. In the long run, the labor force, the productive capacity, and the economy in general *grow;* and the problem changes. This problem of long-run economic growth will be taken up at the end of Part Two (chapter 16) and again in Part Four (especially chapter 28).

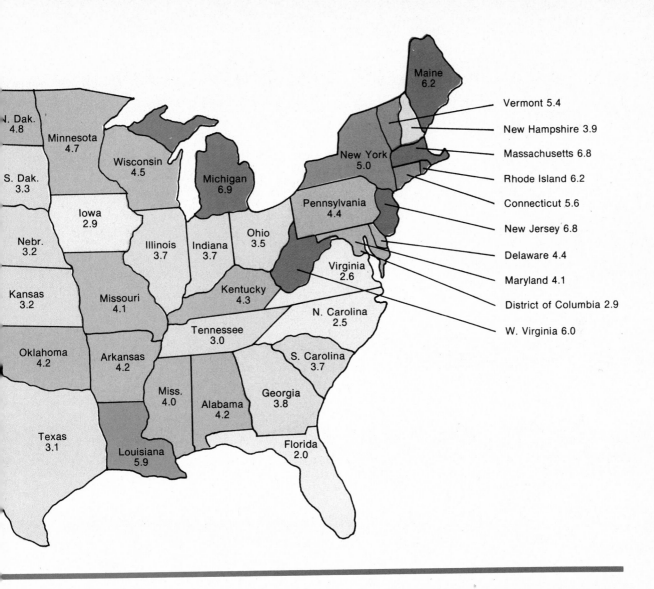

Vermont 5.4

New Hampshire 3.9

Massachusetts 6.8

Rhode Island 6.2

Connecticut 5.6

New Jersey 6.8

Delaware 4.4

Maryland 4.1

District of Columbia 2.9

W. Virginia 6.0

EARLY VIEWS

We have already indicated (Figure 7–2) that macro-economic problems were around long before the 1930s. What then did earlier economists have to say about them? What kind of analysis did they offer?

Now the truth is that until fairly modern times the economics profession did not do very well in this particular department, especially when it came to the problem of unemployment. There are some excep-

tions, but, for the most part, prevailing economic theory in the nineteenth century tended either to ignore the problem—i.e., to proceed on the *assumption* of a full employment economy and then to go on to analyze other problems—or to argue that theoretically there could not be a general unemployment problem except in a temporary or "frictional" sense.

This argument was not simply a personal whim on the part of these early economists; rather, they had certain systematic reasons for believing that an unfettered market economy would automatically solve

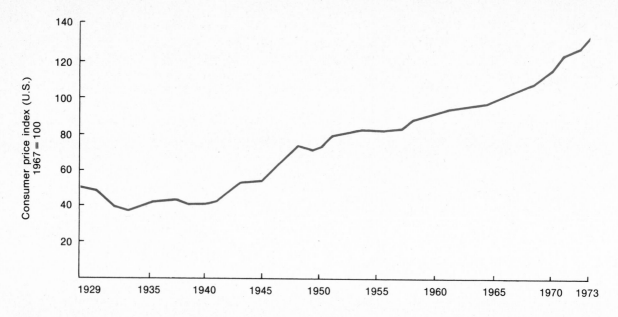

Figure 7–4. Inflation in the United States, 1929 through 1973.

The United States has experienced nothing like the German hyperinflation in the 1920s; nevertheless, like most countries, we have had a general rise in prices during the twentieth century, and this was accelerating in the early 1970's.

any short-run aggregative problems. Hence they could direct their attention to other areas, either to microeconomics or, in the case of the early classical economists, to population growth and food supplies, as discussed in chapter 6.

These systematic reasons are sometimes summarized in what is called *Say's law,* after a French economist, Jean Baptiste Say (1767–1832). Say's writings were well known to the eminent British economists of the period such as David Ricardo and Thomas Robert Malthus, whom we have mentioned earlier. Ricardo fully subscribed to Say's law, though Malthus, as we shall see, had serious reservations about it.

Say's law states that, in the economy as a whole, supply creates its own demand. When we produce goods, according to this law, we create a demand for other goods; consequently, there can be no over-production of goods in general. Since there can be no overproduction of goods in general, there can be no unemployment problem in general. To put it in different words: Since there is always a market for the goods we produce, there is no overall limit on the number of jobs the society can sustain. If people are unemployed, then it can be only because they make unreasonable wage demands or prefer leisure or are simply in transit between one job and another.

This is simply a statement of the law, not a defense. But Say and Ricardo, and in fact most nineteenth-century economists, also felt that they had a good defense for the law. The defense really had two parts. The first part consisted of relegating "money" to a minor role in the economy.

They said, in effect: "Money is just a veil that covers the realities of economic life. Money is simply a medium of exchange. In order to understand what really goes on, let us look at potatoes, steel, wheat, shoes, and so on. Then we will not be deceived by mere monetary changes and we will reach the fundamental phenomena involved."

If the first step was to underplay the role of money, the second step was more positive.

They argued: "Now look at this real, non-money economy. In this economy, when I put a laborer to work producing, say, more potatoes, I am increasing the supply of potatoes, but I am also increasing the demand for other goods. What will I use the potatoes for? Either I will consume them myself (my demand is increased), or I will offer them in exchange for some other commodity, say, clothing, and this will mean that the demand for clothing has increased. Either way, the added supply has created an added demand; thus, in general, supply creates its own demand. Hence, there can be no such thing as general overproduction or general unemployment. Q.E.D."

These arguments are not nonsense. In fact, they are rather persuasive and, for most of a century, they did persuade most economists that aggregative economic problems could be set to one side. Not all economists, however—Malthus worried about the problem and remained unconvinced. He saw the possibility that there might be a "universal glut" of commodities in the economy as a whole and that this might lead to widespread unemployment. He tried to argue the point with his friend, Ricardo; but Malthus's own arguments were far from airtight, and Ricardo won out on debating points fairly easily. Marx was another economist who remained unconvinced. As we have already seen, Marx made in-

creasing unemployment an intrinsic part of his analysis of capitalism. This unemployment arose from the technological displacement of labor by machines, but Marx also spoke generally about an overall inadequacy of markets. The capitalistic system, he thought, might produce more goods than it was constituted to absorb. This could also contribute to crises and depressions.

Neither Malthus nor Marx, however, made much of a dent on this part of the main body of economic analysis, and it wasn't until the very end of the nineteenth century that really serious thought began to be given to these problems. Here special credit should be given to the Swedish economist Knut Wicksell (1851–1926), who anticipated many of the elements in the "revolution" in economic analysis that was soon to take place. The economists of Sweden were, indeed, generally in the vanguard of this particular development, although the great breakthrough must be attributed to the man we shall turn to now. It was his theory that really did the trick. That man was John Maynard Keynes.

KEYNESIAN ANALYSIS

Keynes (1883–1946), the man, was a most remarkable and versatile figure. He was at one time or another a businessman, teacher, college administrator, high government official, patron of the arts, and, of course, the foremost economist of his age. His wife was Lydia Lopokova, a prima ballerina, and she and Keynes were members of the famous Bloomsbury group that included renowned artists such as E. M. Forster and Virginia Woolf. Even in his academic work he was versatile. His first book was on the theory of probability. His economic writings included controversial comment on current issues—like his *Economic Consequences of the Peace,* which made such a stir after World War I—and also highly abstract theoretical works that are quite incomprehensible to the general public. His *General Theory of Employment, Interest and Money* is in the latter group. It has to be studied hard, and a background in technical economics is required if the reader is to make much headway with it.

From the Preface to John Maynard Keynes'

General Theory of Employment, Interest and Money

This book is chiefly addressed to my fellow economists. I hope that it will be intelligible to others. But its main purpose is to deal with difficult questions of theory, and only in the second place with the applications of this theory to practice. For if orthodox economics is at fault, the error is to be found not in the superstructure, which has been erected with great care for logical consistency, but in a lack of clearness and of generality in the premises. Thus I cannot achieve my object of persuading economists to re-examine critically certain of their basic assumptions except by a highly abstract argument and also by much controversy. I wish there could have been less of the latter. But I have thought it important, not only to explain my own point of view, but also to show in what respects it departs from the prevailing theory. Those, who are strongly wedded to what I shall call "the classical theory," will fluctuate, I expect, between a belief that I am quite wrong and a belief that I am saying nothing new. It is for others to determine if either of these or the third alternative is right. My controversial passages are aimed at providing some material for an answer; and I must ask forgiveness if, in the pursuit of sharp distinctions, my controversy is itself too keen. I myself held with conviction for many years the theories which I now attack, and I am not, I think, ignorant of their strong points.

The matters at issue are of an importance which cannot be exaggerated. But, if my explanations are right, it is my fellow economists, not the general public, whom I must first convince. At this stage of the argument the general public, though welcome at the debate, are only eavesdroppers at an attempt by an economist to bring to an issue the deep divergences of opinion between fellow economists which have for the time being almost destroyed the practical influence of economic theory, and will, until they are resolved, continue to do so.

The composition of this book has been for the author a long struggle of escape, and so must the reading of it be for most readers if the author's assault upon them is to be successful—a struggle of escape from habitual modes of thought and expression. The ideas which are here expressed so laboriously are extremely simple and should be obvious. The difficulty lies, not in the new ideas, but in escaping from the old ones, which ramify, for those brought up as most of us have been, into every corner of our minds. □

Excerpted from the preface to *The General Theory of Employment, Interest and Money* by John Maynard Keynes. Reprinted by permission of Harcourt Brace Jovanovich, Inc., and Macmillan, London.

During the next few chapters, we shall be developing much of the essence of the analysis from this book and also bringing in some modern modifications of that analysis. In the remainder of this chapter, we shall simply suggest a few of the central features of Keynesian thought and comment about some of the controversy surrounding his work.[3]

What, then, in essence, was it that Keynes tried to do that sets his work off from that of most preced-

3. For a somewhat more extensive discussion of Keynesian theory along the lines suggested here, see my *Evolution of Modern Economics* (Englewood Cliffs, N.J.: Prentice-Hall, 1967), chap. 6.

John Maynard Keynes (1883–1946). Keynes was the most influential Western economist in the first half of the twentieth century. He brought economic analysis, which in the late nineteenth century had often been far removed from real problems, to bear on matters of urgent public interest—especially the problem of depression. Keynes' work on the theory of national income determination, combined with increased sophistication in the collection of national income data, caused an intense new interest in *macroeconomics*. Since his theories led to an argument for increased government intervention in the economy, Keynes was sometimes attacked for being close to Marxism in his thinking. It is now widely recognized that Keynes provided a major *alternative* to Marx; indeed, his basic approach has been adopted in one form or another by virtually every nation in the world outside the Communist bloc.

ing economic theorists? Let us mention five characteristics of his work and make a brief comment on each:

1. Keynes put his emphasis very clearly on the kind of problems we have just been discussing, problems dealing with the *economy as a whole.* His work was fundamentally macroeconomic in approach; meaning that his key variables were total national output, the general level of employment, the price level, and the like. Insofar as most preceding economic theory had had a strong weighting towards microanalysis, this represented something of a break with the past.

2. Keynes emphasized the key role of *aggregate demand* in determining the level of national income and employment in the economy as a whole. In chapter 2, when discussing a market economy, we spoke of supply and demand in particular industries. Keynes spoke of supply and demand in the aggregate. He felt that aggregate demand in a given economy might be high or low in relation to aggregate supply. In other words, he rejected the theory behind Say's law that suggested that supply invariably created its own demand in the economy as a whole.

3. He believed that the economy might come to rest at a position of *unemployment equilibrium;* that is, a position where there would be no natural forces operating to restore full employment to the economy. Suppose, he said, that aggregate demand falls short of aggregate supply at the full-employment level. What will happen? According to Keynes, the shortage of demand would mean that businessmen in general would cut back on production and jobs. He believed this cutting back process would go on until an equilibrium of supply and demand had been achieved. But this equilibrium might involve a great deal of unemployment in the economy as a whole. Indeed Keynes felt that this analysis helped explain why such a phenomenon as the Great Depression, in full sway while he was writing, could occur in a modern industrial economy.

These last two points indicate that Keynes rejected not only the conclusions of Say's law but, necessarily, the argument that lay behind it. One of these arguments, as we know, was that it was permissible to relegate "money" to a minor role in the workings of an economy. And this brings us to a fourth characteristic of Keynesian analysis.

4. Keynes tried to bring "money" back into economic analysis in a rather pivotal role. He attempted to perform a *synthesis of real and monetary analysis.*[4] More particularly, he argued that "money" was not simply a convenient medium of exchange. He called particular attention to a characteristic of money named *liquidity.* By *liquidity,* he meant "command over goods in general." If I have money, I can exchange it for goods or services or bonds or securities in any direction I choose. It is a perfectly generalized way of holding purchasing power. Now all commodities have some elements of liquidity. When I own a house, I can exchange it for some other goods if I so desire; however, I can never be quite sure what the house will sell for. Similarly, with securities (stocks and bonds): I can quickly turn them into money with which to buy other goods and services; still, it is never quite certain at what price I shall be able to sell them. They are nearly perfectly liquid, but not quite. In short, Keynes said that "money" had certain special properties that gave it an important role in the functioning of the economy. By recognizing this role, he argued, one could explain the possibility of a discrepancy between aggregate demand and aggregate supply in the economy, and hence the possibility of general unemployment.

5. Finally, Keynes argued that since a market economy could not guarantee full employment by its own devices, it might be necessary to have a somewhat greater degree of *government intervention* than had been thought desirable in the past. The government

---

4.   We use the term *real* here, as is customary in economics, to refer to the goods and services (potatoes, automobiles, etc.) that underlie their customary representation in money terms. The role of money, or *monetary* phenomena, is a complex one both in measuring and in analyzing this "real" goods-and-services world, as we shall see in succeeding chapters.

could remedy the problem directly, in the Keynesian view, by affecting aggregate demand by its own purchases of goods and services. On the other hand, it could also influence aggregate demand indirectly by lowering taxes (or raising them if the problem was too much demand) and thus stimulating private consumer and business demand. Still more indirectly, the government could affect the level of aggregate demand by altering the supply of money available to the economy. In general, however, the point was that since the market alone could not be counted on to do the job, the government might have to take a more active participating role.

This leads us directly to the more controversial aspect of Keynesian analysis: namely, the *degree* of government intervention thought necessary to make a mixed economy work.

CONTROVERSIES SURROUNDING KEYNESIAN THEORY

There are really two quite different kinds of controversy that surround the work of John Maynard Keynes. The first is based on a failure to read or at least to understand what Keynes actually wrote and said. The second is based on differing judgments about the actual and important limitations of the Keynesian theory.

The most extreme form of the first type of criticism (fortunately heard less frequently these days) is the charge that Keynes was attacking the capitalistic system in more or less the same manner as Karl Marx had attacked it seventy-five years earlier. Actually, it is closer to the truth to say that Keynes provided the main alternative *to* Marxism. For the fact is that the approaches of these two economists to the capitalistic system were radically different. Marx argued that the diseases of capitalism were intrinsic, inevitable, and fatal; they could be removed only by the overthrow of the entire system. By contrast, Keynes argued that the basic features of the capitalistic system could be preserved and its problems eliminated

by modifications of that system. The mixed economy—which we actually have in the United States and Western Europe—is the natural heir to Keynesian analysis; but it is anathema to the good Marxist. For if, through modification of the system, one can forestall serious problems from arising and can make the economy "work," then one has completely undercut the ground from the Marxist who believes that things *must* get worse and that "revolution" is the *only* cure.

No one would argue that the *General Theory* is a "conservative" book in the usual sense of the term; but it is not a "radical" book—certainly not in the Marxist sense—and, indeed, it does hope to "conserve" certain features of a private enterprise system. Keynes deeply prized individual liberty and also the economic efficiency of the market economy; he hoped that when one had solved the problem of depressions, these virtues might be preserved.

If this first line of criticism is of little interest to the serious student, the second line of criticism is quite a different matter. For the fact is that there *are* important limitations on the Keynesian analysis (it could hardly be otherwise, given the vast amount of economic research done in the past forty years) and, consequently, there are good grounds for debating both his arguments and his conclusions. A list of these limitations would be very long, but even a short list would include obviously important matters:

Keynesian theory is basically static; it is very much concerned with short-run problems, and it leaves to one side the whole matter of growth and changes in fundamental conditions.

Keynesian theory dwells in a purely competitive world where the real-life market structures of the modern corporation or labor union hardly figure at all. It is based on rough "psychological" generalizations that are inadequate for the complexities of economic behavior revealed by subsequent research.

Keynesian theory does not recognize some of the complications and difficulties of applying governmental expenditure, tax, and monetary policies to the solution of unemployment, inflation, and other problems of the modern economy in the aggregate. Some have argued further that it does not give a proper account of the powerful role of money in the economy.

Keynesian theory does not deal adequately with kinds of unemployment and kinds of inflation not caused by deficient or excessive aggregate demand.

It is apparent, just from this short list, that there is much ground for disagreement and debate even among serious students of Keynesian analysis.

KEYNESIAN AND NON-KEYNESIAN UNEMPLOYMENT AND INFLATION

Because these limitations exist, it is important to recognize that the next few chapters—while an indispensable starting point for macroeconomic analysis—do not offer final solutions to the problems considered. Indeed, the last point mentioned above (the existence of different *kinds* of unemployment and inflation) should be kept in the back of our minds throughout. Keynesian analysis is strongest where the heart of the problem is a deficiency or excess of aggregate demand. But this is not always the case. In fact, one of the central difficulties of the late 1960s and early 1970s has been the existence of situations where the manipulation of aggregate demand is insufficient. Suppose, for example, you have both unemployment *and* inflation. Keynesian analysis would suggest that we should both increase and decrease aggregate demand at the same time. Obviously, an impossible solution.

How could unemployment and inflation come to coexist simultaneously? There are many possible reasons, but a fairly obvious one occurred in 1973 and 1974 with the familiar energy crisis. A relative shortage drove up the price of fuel at very rapid rates, helping to cause a much sharper rise in consumer and other price indices than previously anticipated. At the same time, the fuel shortage caused at least some negative effects on employment in certain sectors of the economy, most notably in the automotive industry. Had the shortage been even sharper, both the inflation and unemployment effects would also have been sharper.

Now it is fairly clear that the stimulus for these particular difficulties came from the supply side, rather than from the demand side. And many other such cases may be imagined. The development of major shortages in any industrial raw material might at the same time curtail jobs and cause inflationary pressures. Also, pressure from labor unions or big business might cause price rises even where there was already unemployment, and where no particular natural shortages existed. In sum, after we have gone through the Keynesian analysis, we shall still have the job of amending it to include the many facets of economic reality that escaped the master's hand.

A PERMANENT CONTRIBUTION

Having acknowledged such difficulties, we ought, however, to end this chapter with something of a tribute to Keynes. There is no doubt that Keynesian theory has had an enormous impact on the development of the subject of economics in the past four decades. Even his harshest critics have been stimulated enormously by the challenge to new research that his work provided. It is also clear that a majority of economists (including those aware of the limitations of this theory) accept his general contention that there are serious problems in keeping an economy at or near the full-employment level and that there are times when only government intervention (of one sort or another) will have sufficient impact to turn the trick.

Finally, there is the important fact that most governments in the Western world now tend to accept: (1) the fact that governmental actions do have a substantial effect on the health of the economy as a whole, and (2) a governmental responsibility for maintaining at least a reasonably close approximation to a full-employment economy.

Thus, despite its critics, the "new economics" is very much in business in the modern mixed economy. And it is essentially because of this economics and its modern additions that one can predict with a high degree of certainty that such a thing as the Great Depression of the 1930s could not happen again in the United States or in Western Europe. Considering the hardship and despair that that Depression caused, this is no small tribute to the legacy of the late Lord Keynes.

SUMMARY

We shall be concerned in Part Two with the economy in the aggregate. Our interest will focus on broad questions concerning the level of national income, the general level of employment and unemployment, and the overall level of prices.

The history of modern industrial economies makes it quite clear that there have been fluctuations in the levels of employment and prices in various countries over the past century or two. Early economists (with some exceptions such as Malthus and Marx) tended on the whole to set aggregative problems, and especially the unemployment problem, to one side. They were confident that they could rely on *Say's law* to guarantee no major problems. Say's law depicted a "moneyless" economy in which supply always created its own demand, thus preventing any problems of general overproduction or general unemployment.

In the twentieth century, many economists began to criticize this point of view, and the great theoretical breakthrough was made by John Maynard Keynes. *Keynesian theory* departed from its predecessors by (1) its heavy emphasis on macroeconomics, (2) its stress on the role of aggregate demand, (3) its acknowledgment of the possibility of underemployment equilibrium, (4) its synthesis of real and monetary analysis, and (5) its recognition of the important role of government in curing unemployment and other aggregative problems.

Keynesian theory has been subject to many valid criticisms and also to some not so valid (e.g., the false identification of Keynes and Marx). Despite the critics, however, there is general agreement about his impact on the development of economics as a field and about the influence his work has had on the actual policies of governments in the Western mixed economies. The "new economics," in one form or another, is widely accepted and utilized by modern nations to avoid such harrowing disasters as the Great Depression of the 1930s.

IMPORTANT TERMS TO REMEMBER

The "New Economics"
Economy in the Aggregate
Macroeconomics/microeconomics
Say's Law: Supply Creates Its Own Demand
Money as a "Veil"
Aggregate Demand and Supply
Unemployment Equilibrium
Synthesis of Real and Monetary Analysis
Liquidity
Non-Keynesian Unemployment and Inflation

QUESTIONS FOR DISCUSSION

1. "The Great Depression of the 1930s made forever obsolete the view that an unregulated market economy could guarantee, save for a few minor frictions, full employment of the nation's labor force." Discuss.

2. What are the assumptions behind Say's law? Show how, given these assumptions, an economy would be able to find markets for an expansion of its total output caused, say, by a sudden immigration of labor from abroad.

3. What is meant by macroeconomics? By microeconomics?

4. We quoted Keynes (p. 180) from his *General Theory of Employment, Interest, and Money* as saying that the critics would fluctuate "between a belief that I am quite wrong and a belief that I am saying nothing new. It is for others to determine if either of these or the third alternative is right." What grounds might be offered today to support the third alternative?

5. Compare the views of John Maynard Keynes and Karl Marx on the problems facing capitalism and their prospective cures.

6. What evidence do you find today of the influence of Keynesian economics on actual governmental policies in the United States and in other modern industrial economies? Give as many specific examples as you can.

CHAPTER 8
THE CONCEPT OF GNP

Having outlined the general area of macro-economics, we shall now turn to a concept that is central to this field: the concept of *gross national product,* or GNP. The term GNP is widely used in our daily press, but the concept is somewhat complicated, and it is worth spending some time with it.

TOTAL OUTPUT AND ITS FLUCTUATIONS

The basic idea behind the gross national product is simple enough. This is one of the important measures economists use when they try to estimate the total output of goods and services produced in the nation over a given period, say a year.

Furthermore, it is apparent that some such concept of total output is indispensable to the field of macro-economics. For example, we have talked about the Great Depression of the 1930s, but mainly in terms of unemployment. We could just as readily have spoken about a fall in the nation's total output, its

GNP, during that period. Indeed, we should generally expect that when there is heavy unemployment in an economy, its total output of goods and services would fall, or at least would not rise as rapidly as might otherwise be the case.

In Figure 8–1, we have charted the changes in the United States' GNP since 1910. Two things about this diagram should strike us immediately. The first is the pronounced upward trend in our GNP over this period of time—our annual total output of goods and services has increased some 5 or 6 times in sixty years. The second striking feature is the irregularity of the upward movement. The curve does not move upward continuously, but with spurts and pauses, with occasional downward movements followed by rapid accelerations, and so on.

Now the first feature of this diagram, the long-run growth of our total output, we shall postpone until later in Part Two and again in Part Four (see especially chapters 16, 28, and 31). There we will take up various factors, such as population growth, capital accumulation, and technological change, that bring

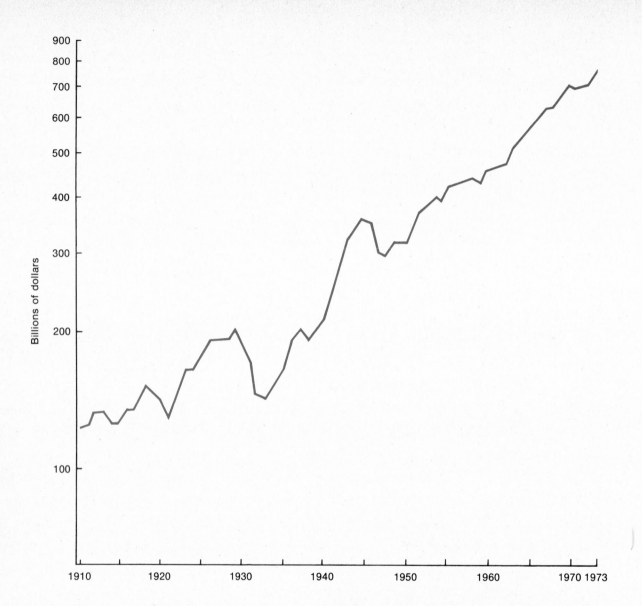

Figure 8–1. U.S. Gross National Product, 1910–1973 (in "constant" 1958 prices).

Growth and fluctuation of total output in the United States are brought out sharply in this diagram, which covers more than sixty years.

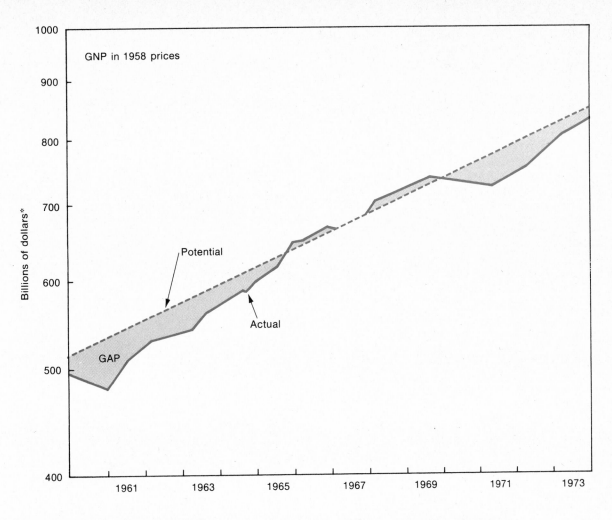

Figure 8-2. Gross National Product, Actual and Potential.

*Seasonally adjusted annual rates
Sources: Department of Commerce, Council of Economic Advisers, and the author.

about long-run gains in a country's productive capacity. We shall also discuss the important *costs* of economic growth.

The second feature, however, is of central interest to us now. It tells us that there has been, in addition to long-run growth, a considerable *short-run fluctuation* in the level of GNP in our country. Another way to put this is to say that there has been a changing gap between the total output our nation was actually producing in any given year and what it had the capacity for producing.

In Figure 8-2, we show the gap between actual and potential gross national product in the United States, as estimated for 1960–69 by the President's Council of Economic Advisers and for 1970–1973 by the author. This gap, when below the potential output line, reflects underutilization of our productive capacity. Since potential output is defined by the Council as "the output in the economy would be producing when operating at a 3.8 percent unemployment rate,'' it is possible for actual output to exceed potential output when unemployment is very low. The gap is, in general, highly correlated with the rate of unemployment. Similarly, two questions are very closely related: What determines our level of GNP in the short run? What determines our level of employment in the short run?

MEASURING TOTAL OUTPUT

Having observed that GNP is an important concept, we now have to ask the more difficult question: Is it a meaningful concept? What is this thing, ''total output,'' and how would we go about measuring it? The difficulty is an obvious one; in fact, it takes us back to elementary school days. We were told then that we cannot add oranges and apples and pears. But the total output of our economy includes oranges, apples, and pears, *plus* lathes, tractors, toy balloons, soft drinks, and several thousand other commodities. How can these different commodities be added together to form a single numerical total?

What is needed is a common denominator, and the common denominator in our particular economy is dollars. Oranges have a price; apples and pears have prices; so do tractors, lathes, and toy balloons. What we do is to give a money valuation to the production of each particular commodity, then add up the total of these money values, and this will give us a number in dollars for our total output during the given year.

Say that 600 million oranges are produced in the country in a certain year and that the price of oranges is 5¢ each. Then the value of orange output will be determined:

$$5¢ \times 600 \text{ million} = \$30 \text{ million}$$

We can then do the same thing for apples, pears, and lathes, and come up with money figures for each. We would then add these money figures together to

form an estimate of aggregate output. To be specific: Suppose there is, in addition to oranges, only one other commodity in our economy: toy balloons. Toy balloon production is 50 million units a year at a price of 10¢ apiece.

Total output in this fictitious economy might then be defined as equal to

$$P_o \times Q_o + P_b \times Q_b$$

where P_o, Q_o and P_b, Q_b are price and quantity produced of oranges and balloons, respectively. In numerical terms, we should have:

$$
\begin{aligned}
\text{Total output} &= 5¢ \times 600 \text{ million} + 10¢ \\
&\quad \times 50 \text{ million} \\
&= \$30 \text{ million} + \$5 \text{ million} \\
&= \$35 \text{ million}
\end{aligned}
$$

It is fairly obvious that what we have done for these two commodities, we could do for the remainder of the commodities in a real-life economy: shirts, missiles, secretarial services. They all have prices and can all be added together in this fashion.

COMPONENTS OF TOTAL OUTPUT

Now there are some serious problems in the kind of measurements we have just performed, and we must go into these rather carefully. First, however, let us mention in passing the basic component parts into which the total output of the economy can be divided. The most common breakdown, and one we shall be referring to often in the future, is in terms of three main categories of goods and services:

1. **Consumption.** There are first of all the goods bought by ordinary consumers like ourselves: clothing, food, automobiles, tennis racquets. These include consumer expenditures for services as well as commodities, and for durable as well as nondurable consumers' goods. The category of durable consumers' goods has grown very rapidly in recent dec-

ades as we have expanded our purchases of automobiles, television sets, washing machines, and the like. In total, consumption expenditures in the United States currently average between 60 to 65 percent of our GNP.

2. Investment. Part of the goods produced in the economy each year is funneled back into the productive process, either to replace worn-out buildings, machines, and so on, or to add to our general stock of capital goods. Gross investment in our economy includes these replacement items and the net additions to our capital stock.[1] Investment expenditures in the United States may run in the neighborhood of 15 or 16 percent of GNP, though this percentage is subject to a fairly high degree of variability. The term *investment* in the sense we are now using it is, of course, different from the kind of investing we do when we buy a stock or a bond. It is better to regard the latter as *financial investment,* and to think of *investment* (unmodified) as indicating those goods devoted to building up the real productive capacity of the economy. The main categories of investment expenditure are fixed business investment (machinery, factories, etc.), residential construction (apartments and also private homes), and additions to inventories (stocks of products kept on hand to meet orders from other producers or consumers).

3. Government. The third main category is governmental expenditures. If we exclude transfer payments—which, as we recall, do not represent governmental purchases of goods and services—then government expenditures currently run at something above 20 percent of GNP. We have already indicated (chapter 4) that a great part of these government expenditures at the federal level are related in one way or another to defense. Educational expenditures are the most important single category at the state and local level. For our present purposes, the important point to note is that when the government buys goods and services, the destination it pro-

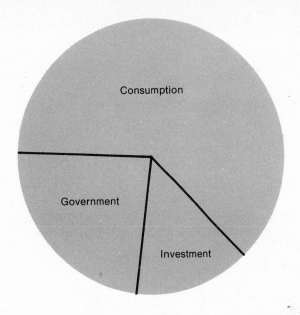

Figure 8–3. Major Components of United States' GNP.

These are average proportions of GNP. Remember that they change from year to year, investment being a particularly variable item.

vides for the total output is exactly analogous to that provided by private investment or consumption purchases.

These then are the three main categories by which the total output of the society can be classified: consumption, private investment, and government expenditures.[2] We shall be mentioning each of these categories often in the pages that follow.

---

1.   We shall come to the distinction between ''gross investment'' and ''net investment'' in a moment (p. 194).

2.   A further category would be *net* exports of American goods abroad. We will mention this category again later; it is a very small category, however, perhaps 1 percent or so of GNP. See chapter 15.

PROBLEM OF CONSTANT PRICES

But now it is time to return once again to the basic concept of total output. We said that our procedure of simply adding together the dollar values of different outputs involved a number of problems. Let us now mention three specific and major problems. The first is that of *constant prices;* the second is the problem of *double-counting;* the third concerns the relationship of measured GNP to *economic well-being.*

The first problem, the problem of what is happening to the price level in our economy as we try to measure total output is a complicated one. The difficulty arises when we try to compare total output or GNP in two different years. To return to our simplified world of oranges and toy balloons:

In our earlier example (p. 190), we determined that the total output of oranges and toy balloons in our economy was worth $35 million. Let us suppose this was for the year 1960. Suppose someone now comes along and tells us that the combined money-value of orange and toy balloon production in 1975 had risen to $70 million. The question is: What can we conclude from this fact? Can we conclude that both orange production and toy balloon production had doubled from 1960 to 1975? Or that if one product less than doubled in quantity, the other more than doubled? Or does the given information actually enable us to conclude nothing at all about the production of oranges and toy balloons in this period?

The correct answer, unfortunately, is the last. We can conclude nothing whatever about orange and toy balloon production in 1975 as compared to 1960 unless, and until, we know what has happened to the prices of these goods during that period. To take an obvious case: Suppose the prices of both goods had *quadrupled* in this fifteen-year period. A rise in total output from $35 million to $70 million would, in this case, represent not an increase in real GNP, but a *halving* of GNP from 1960 to 1975. If, on the other hand, prices had remained absolutely constant, then it would be clear that real GNP was expanding; indeed, if prices are constant, then the changes in the money value of GNP would reflect changes in the real output value of GNP.

The problem thus becomes one of finding some rough equivalent to constant prices when prices are, in fact, changing all the time. The way economists do this is by taking prices for some given year and using these prices throughout the series of measurements of GNP in different years. Thus, you will notice that in the charts of United States' GNP (Figures 8–1 and 8–2), prices are described as "1958 prices." More generally, we should have to amend our formula for calculating total output to indicate a specific date for the prices involved. Using 1960 prices throughout, our comparison of the total output of oranges and toy balloons in 1960 and 1975 would look as follows:

(1) Total Output $(GNP)_{(1960)} =$
$$P_{o(1960)} \times Q_{o(1960)} + P_{b(1960)} \times Q_{b(1960)}$$

(2) Total Output $(GNP)_{(1975)} =$
$$P_{o(1960)} \times Q_{o(1975)} + P_{b(1960)} \times Q_{b(1975)}$$

In this way, by using 1960 prices throughout, the problem of fictitious changes in total output caused by mere changes in the price level is removed, and the focus is put on changes in the actual outputs of the goods involved.

The reader should notice that the prices and quantities in equation (2) are differently dated; from what we have said, he should be able to explain this fact fully.[3]

PROBLEM OF DOUBLE-COUNTING

A second major problem arises in measuring GNP because many of the goods we produce in a given year are actually already included in the value of other goods being produced.

---

3.   Before leaving the "constant prices" problem, it should at least be noted that when we are making comparisons of GNP over long periods of time, it is by no means easy to handle this problem. Prices are changing not only absolutely, but *relatively* (i.e., the price of oranges relative to the price of toy balloons), and when this happens, changes in "total output" do not have an unambiguous meaning. In general, using "earlier" prices will suggest a higher rate of growth than using "later" prices. This is sometimes called "the index-number problem."

Suppose we are using all the oranges to produce frozen orange juice. Then we have:

Stage 1   **Value of oranges** $30 million
             produced (as sold
             by the grower)

Stage 2   **Value of canned** $40 million
             orange juice (as sold
             by the canner)

Stage 3   **Value of canned** $48 million
             orange juice
             (as bought by
             the consumer from
             the retailer)

The double-counting problem arises here because the $48 million of final output produced includes the value of the oranges and canned orange juice at the earlier stages of production. If we were to add them all together, we would get a fictitiously large total because of *double-counting.*

How does one avoid this problem, given the great number of different industries and different uses for their products in an economy like ours? One way (and the simplest conceptually) is to be careful to avoid all kinds of "intermediate" products when adding up GNP, and to concentrate wholly on "final" products in the various lines of production (i.e., to count only Stage 3 orange juice at $48 million and to exclude Stage 1 and Stage 2 orange products).

An equivalent, though more roundabout, way of achieving the same result is through what is known as the *value-added* method of calculating GNP. A firm's or an industry's *value added* to total output is the value of its sales minus its purchases of products from other firms or industries. If we assume for simplicity that the orange growers in our example purchased no inputs from other firms, then we could represent value added at each stage of orange production as follows:

The reader should notice that the sum of the values added equals the value of the final products ($48 million). He should prove to himself that this is not an accident but will necessarily be the case. The ultimate reason, of course, is that in both methods we have scrupulously avoided counting intermediate products.[4]

Before we leave the double-counting problem, however, we should remark on one aspect of measuring GNP where double-counting is in fact countenanced. The reader by now must have wondered why the "G" (Gross) is always prefixed to this measure of national production. The answer has to do with the way we evaluate the *investment* category mentioned earlier.

It should be clear that the proper way to evaluate the total output of machines, say, in a given year, would be to take the number of machines produced in that year and to subtract from it the number of machines that have become worn out, obsolete, and have been discarded during the year. Put it this way—we have been using machines throughout the year; when we produce a quantity of new machines, at least some of those machines are necessary to replace those that have become worn out through use; they do not all constitute a net addition to our stock of machines.

This is a problem that all businessmen are familiar with—the problem of depreciation and replacement. The difficulty, however, is that really accurate and

---

4. In the early 1970s, there has been much discussion of a so-called "value-added tax." The reader should be able to understand from what we have just said that this is in many ways equivalent to a "sales tax" on the final values of commodities.

Stage	Value of sales	minus	Purchases from other firms	equals	Value added
1	$30 million		$ 0		+$30 million
2	$40 million		$30 million		+$10 million
3	$48 million		$40 million		+$ 8 million
	Sum of *values added*			=	$48 million

meaningful depreciation figures are hard to come by, and even hard to define. Hence, economists and government statisticians often include *all* the machines produced in a given year without making the depreciation adjustment. This figure is called *gross investment*. When gross investment is added to consumption and government expenditures, we call the total *gross* national product. If the depreciation of the country's capital stock is estimated and deducted, we would get *net* investment and, correspondingly, *net* national product (NNP).

PROBLEM OF ECONOMIC WELFARE

The distinction between "gross" and "net" that we have just drawn involves a consideration of the costs involved in producing a year's output in terms of the wear and tear on the society's capital stock. But what of other costs of producing that output—costs in terms of the depletion of our natural resources or in terms of adverse effects on the quality of our lives? Such questions involve the relationship between measured GNP and economic welfare.

This relationship is a very large matter, which, for those interested, is discussed in more detail in the appendix to this chapter. The point to be made now is that this relationship is involved in the very definition of GNP. Since we have mentioned toy balloons, let us imagine a rather odd society in which one man's product is inflated balloons (he spends all day blowing up balloons and tying them) and another's is deflated balloons (he spends *his* day untying them and letting the air out). Common sense tells us that, however GNP is measured, there should be no addition to the total here, since from an economic welfare point of view we end up exactly where we started. But is this farfetched example very different from, say, a society whose industrial activities pollute the air and whose GNP also includes the expenditures (on air conditioners, antipollution devices for automobiles, etc.) needed to restore the air more nearly to

its original condition? Or consider this example of A. A. Berle, Jr.:

Cigarettes (to which I am addicted) satisfy a widespread want. They also, we are learning, engender a great deal of cancer. Now it is true that at some later time the service rendered in attempting to care for cancer (generated by cigarettes manufactured five years ago) will show up as "product"; so the work of attempted cure or caretaking will later appear as a positive product item. But that item will not be known until later. What we do know without benefit of figures is that against this year's output of tobacco products whose cash value is recorded we have also brought more cancer into being—an unrecorded "disproduct." [5]

The more one considers the relationship of measured GNP to society's welfare, the more complex it becomes. Is it appropriate to separate "economic welfare" from political or other social considerations? Whose judgment of welfare is to be considered decisive when opinions differ? If the pile of goods and services produced each year does not have any relationship to economic welfare, just what *does* it signify?

Some people feel, for example, that we have been accumulating far too many material goods during the past century. Such a person might be well within his rights in considering as additions to GNP during the next few years all the elaborate efforts and services of labor and machines that would be required to dismantle and dispose of our material possessions and restore the "simple life." We are getting very close to our (perhaps not so far-fetched) toy balloon example again!

In short, although it is easy enough to give a definition of "total output" with respect to some agreed upon method of eliminating double-counting, inflationary price increases, etc., it is by no means easy

5.   A. A. Berle, Jr., "What GNP Doesn't Tell Us," *Saturday Review*, August 31, 1968.

to determine what that final index means. Numerically measurable, GNP, in terms of economic welfare, remains somewhat shrouded in mystery.[6]

PRODUCT AND INCOME CONCEPTS

The discussion so far, although mainly definitional, allows us to move fairly quickly into the heart of modern macroeconomic analysis. Much of this modern analysis proceeds from the recognition of a fact that we should be able to understand easily now, though it might have been obscure before. This fact is that there is a *basic equivalence between the national product or output of a society and the real national income of that society.* "Annual total output" is really another name for "annual total income." The latter, in turn, is the sum of all incomes earned in the production of this "total output"; i.e., wages, profits, interest, and rents. These are basically two different ways of looking at the same thing.

The simplest way to convince ourselves on this point is to recall our value-added method of measuring GNP. At each stage of production, we subtracted, from the value of the products a firm sells, the value that it has paid out to other firms for their products. Now the sum of these values added is our total "product," but it is also clearly our total "income." For to what uses are these values added put? Since, by definition, they do not represent sales to other

firms, they must represent either payments to the factors of production—wages to labor, rent on property, interest on borrowed funds—or profits to the firm. Indeed, profits can be thought of as being precisely the surplus of value added after payments are made to other factors of production. If we subtract all other incomes from our national product, we get profits as the residual, and profits, of course, are income. Hence the point is established: National product and national income are essentially equivalent concepts.

In present-day practice in the United States, we actually have a great number of related but still distinct "product" and "income" concepts for use in different connections. If we start with GNP and work downward, we get the following definitions:

   Gross national product
— **Depreciation**
= **Net national product**

We have discussed this relationship earlier. "Depreciation" is sometimes replaced by the term "capital consumption allowances." NNP represents in a theoretical sense the basic *product* concept, all double-counting having been removed. In order to translate this into an *income* concept, we have to recognize that not all of the final values of commodities are reducible to factor incomes since these values include sales taxes and other *indirect business taxes.* When this deduction (and a number of much smaller deductions and additions) has been made, we get the national income concept:

   Net national product
— **Indirect business taxes**
= **National income**

Although *national income,* so defined, is a basic income concept, it is not the same thing as the *personal income* paid out to the factor owners. There

6. Some rather heroic economists (notably William Nordhaus and James Tobin) have actually attempted to devise a *measure of economic welfare* as distinct from gross national product (i.e. MEW instead of GNP). Starting from GNP figures they adjust for leisure, household work, the costs of urban living, etc. As the article by Simon Kuznets in the appendix (pp. 204–208) makes clear, any such effort must involve tremendous practical and philosophic difficulties. For what it is worth, MEW is found to grow more slowly in the United States than GNP from 1929–1965, particularly in the period from shortly after World War II on. (See W. Nordhaus and J. Tobin, "Is Growth Obsolete?" 50th Anniversary Colloquium, V, National Bureau of Economic Research, New York, Columbia University Press, 1972.)

are two main reasons for this: (1) *Corporate income* —Corporations receive income, not all of which is paid out to individuals. Some of the income is retained by the firm (undistributed profits), some is paid to the government (corporate profit taxes), and some is set aside for contributions for social insurance; and (2) *Government transfer payments—* Transfer payments, as we know (p. 71) are not a part of the product accounts but they do contribute to personal income. Thus, we have the following:

National Income
— { **Retained profits**[7]
    Corporate profit taxes
    Contribution for social insurance
+   **Transfer payments**

=   **Personal Income**

In terms of actually having money in our pockets, however, even personal income does not get us all the way. For, at this point, the government steps in and taxes us *directly* on our incomes; it is here that the personal income tax comes into play. Thus, we have finally:

Personal income
— **Personal taxes**

= **Disposable personal income**

---

7. There is another way of handling these deductions, which is equivalent to that used above. Instead of subtracting retained profits and corporate profit taxes, we could subtract the *whole* of corporate profits and then *add* the dividends that are paid out to corporate owners (stockholders) and that *are* a part of personal income. This equivalent method is shown in Table 8–1.

In Table 8–1, we present figures for these various concepts for the United States in 1973. We have also included some of the smaller deductions and additions beyond the major ones discussed above.

Incidentally, in the pages to come, we shall use the term *national income* in a less technical sense than in the above definition, as a symbol of the whole family of *total output* concepts. Where a more specific definition is called for, we shall note it explicitly in the course of the analysis.

NATIONAL INCOME AND THE CIRCULAR FLOW

Quite apart from definitions, the basic equivalence of income and output in the aggregate is not difficult to understand if we will reflect upon it for a moment. For what determines how much income you and I and our neighbors will have to share amongst ourselves? Ultimately, it has to be what all of us together have produced. Barring special cases where there is a net inflow of aid from abroad, there is simply no other source from which our collective incomes can emanate.

This equivalence is also illustrated by the diagram we have used in various forms in Part One—the *circular flow* diagram. In Figure 8–4, we show a very simple form of such a diagram for an economy producing and consuming $100 billion of output (or income) per year. In ordinary parlance, we might think of the "income flow" in this diagram as the inner arrow on the left-hand side and the "output flow" as the outer arrow on the right-hand side: They are both equal to $100 billion. Since (in this hypothetical economy) there is no problem of capital consumption, corporate earnings, government taxes or transfer payments, etc., all the income and output concepts would amount to the same thing.

A circular flow diagram can also be used, however, to give us a first approximation view of how macroeconomic problems can arise. This begins to move us away from questions of definition to matters of actual economic behavior.

TABLE 8–1

U.S. NATIONAL INCOME ACCOUNTS, 1973 (in billions of dollars)

Gross National Product		**1,288.2**
Less:		
Capital consumption allowances	109.6	
Net National Product		**1,178.6**
Plus:		
Subsidies less current surplus of government enterprises	.7	
Less:		
Indirect business tax and nontax liability	117.8	
Business transfer payments	4.9	
Statistical discrepancy	2.3	
National Income		**1,054.2**
Less:		
Corporate profits and inventory valuation adjustment	109.2	
Contributions for social insurance	92.1	
Plus:		
Government transfer payments to persons	112.5	
Interest paid by government (net) and by consumers	37.1	
Dividends	27.8	
Business transfer payments	4.9	
Personal Income		**1,035.5**
Less:		
Personal tax and nontax payments	152.9	
Disposable Personal Income		**882.6**

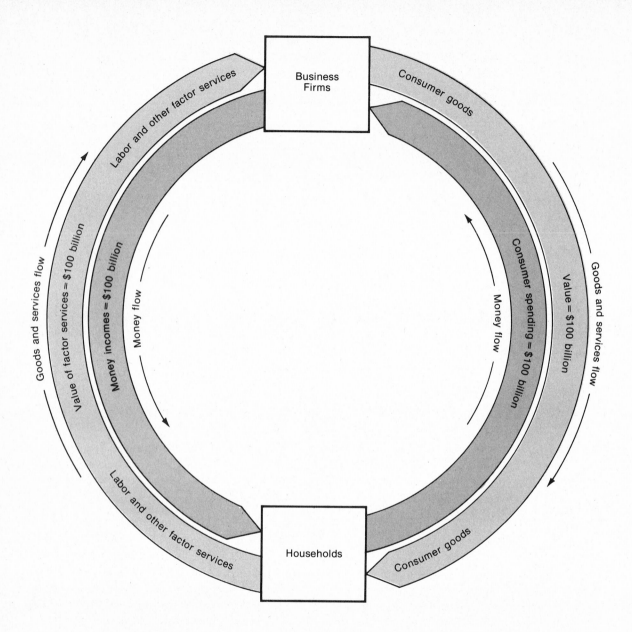

Figure 8–4. Circular Flow Diagram.

In this simplified economy, there is no saving or investment. Problems of too much or too little aggregate demand do not arise.

To illustrate what we mean, let us work with a slightly more complicated version of the circular flow, as shown in Figure 8–5. We may now imagine two changes occurring. Consumers have decided not to spend all their money incomes on consumers' goods, but to save $10 billion out of their annual income of $100 billion. In our primitive example, they have decided to do this by putting the money under their mattresses. Thus $10 billion goes under the mattress and $90 billion is left over to buy consumers' goods.

Business behavior has also changed. Businessmen have decided to build up their inventories of goods in stock by $10 billion. Thus, although they have produced $100 billion worth of consumers' goods as before, they now wish to invest $10 billion in added inventory and to sell $90 billion worth to the consumer. How did the businessmen get the money to make this $10 billion investment? Let's suppose they got it from a friendly banker. (Of course, they might also have got it from some of the consumers who have money under the matresses. Or the consumers might have taken their money from under the mattresses and given it to the bankers who *then* lent it out to the businessmen, etc. Clearly, all sorts of complications can quickly arise, but for the moment, we will concentrate on the bare essentials.)

Now notice that the flows in Figure 8–5 are still basically all right. That is to say, consumers come to the market wanting to buy $90 billion of goods and producers are there offering to sell $90 billion of goods. Thus, not only is national income ($90 billion consumption and $10 billion saving) equal to national output ($90 billion consumers' goods and $10 billion inventory investment), but the aggregate demand for the goods the economy is producing is equal to the aggregate supply of goods the economy has produced.

But we can easily imagine a case in which this is not so. Let us suppose that households still wish to save $10 billion but that business firms do *not* wish to add $10 billion in inventories. They want to sell the whole $100 billion to consumers as consumer

goods. The first question that may occur to us is: Is this really possible? Can we have $100 billion going out in the income loop and only $90 billion coming back in the spending loop? The answer, essentially, is no, because incomes are created by customers buying the products of businesses. This, in a sense, is the whole point of the circular flow representation of economic life.

The second question becomes, then, how are the flows equated in the case we have described? One way this might happen is through inventory accumulation. Businessmen might find that they themselves were spending the missing $10 billion. They would do this by not selling $10 billion of the goods they had produced and thus automatically accumulating $10 billion of added inventories. This accumulation of added inventories would make the flows come out all right arithmetically, but it would hardly make sense *economically*. For, in contrast to our previous example, these added inventories are unwanted and unsought. What they tell the businessman is that he has produced more of his products than the market will bear. His natural reaction is to cut back output and employment until he finds himself producing just the amounts that his customers want.

The reader should recognize that what we have just done has been to describe what is nothing more nor less than a deficiency in aggregate demand. We recall from the last chapter that Lord Keynes attributed the major causes of depressions to precisely such deficiencies. What we have shown is that one reason why aggregate demand may be too low is that consumer spending may be too low (or, equivalently, consumer saving may be too high).

Still in this preliminary way, we might ask: Can we also describe a situation where aggregate demand is too high? The answer is yes. Let us suppose this time that consumers want to spend all of their incomes on consumption goods (i.e., to save nothing). Let us suppose that at the same time businessmen, realizing that markets are good, want to divert part

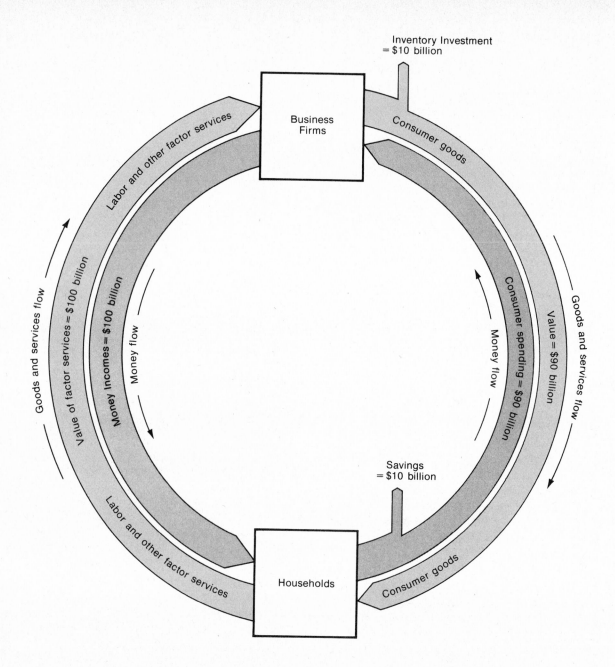

Figure 8–5. Circular Flow with Saving and Investment.

If businessmen want to invest as much ($10 billion) as consumers want to save, everything works out fine. If not, serious macroeconomic problems can arise.

of the national product to investment, either in buildings and machinery or in added inventories. The consumers, then, want to spend the whole $100 billion on consumption goods. But businessmen want to spend some sum—say $20 billion—on investment.

Again, we ask: Is this possible, and if it is possible in some mechanical way, is it economically possible? That is, what will the economic repercussions be?

The answer is that consumer and business behavior in this instance will create a situation in which "something has to give," and that the economic consequences of this behavior would normally be an *expansion* of national output and employment. Essentially, we have $120 billion of spending trying to buy $100 billion worth of goods. If we assume that prices are constant (actually, they would probably rise), the only way businessmen could meet the demand would be by selling off some of their inventories of goods in stock. Now this is a good thing from the point of view of the businessman—he has all these customers clamoring for his goods—but it is not something he will simply sit back and watch without doing anything. In particular, he will try to increase his employment and output to the point where he can not only meet consumer demands but also maintain (or add to) his stock of inventories. An excess of aggregate demand, then, will generally lead to a business expansion.

We have moved now from definitions into the very core of the modern theory of national income determination. We have seen that consumer decisions on consumption and saving may be crucial; we have also just seen how business investment decisions can influence the macroeconomic outcome. In short, we are now in a position to move ahead in a systematic way into this very important area of modern economics, and this will be our central task in the next chapter.

SUMMARY

In studying the modern economy in the aggregate and its short-run fluctuations, we need some measure of annual total output. *Gross national product* (GNP) is such a measure. Its major components are (1) consumption, (2) gross investment, and (3) government expenditures on goods and services.

The common denominator used to make possible the adding together of the various outputs in the economy is the price of each of these goods expressed in money terms. In performing this aggregation of outputs, however, three significant problems arise. The first is the problem of constant prices, or ruling out changes in GNP that derive simply from inflationary (or deflationary) changes in the price level and do not reflect changes in the real output value of GNP. To accomplish this end, prices in some one base year are used; e.g., "constant 1958 prices." The second problem is that of avoiding double-counting in adding up the outputs of different industries in the economy. This may be done by rigorously excluding intermediate products and concentrating on final goods and services only. Or, equivalently, it may be done by the *value-added* method of calculating national income. The third problem concerns the relationship of measured GNP to economic welfare. Particularly difficult to assess are the many economic costs that may accompany (and cancel part of) the production of a given level of GNP.

The value-added approach to measuring national income has the virtue of bringing out quite clearly the fundamental equivalence of national product and national income. In our society, our real income in the aggregate (wages, salaries, rents, etc.) is nothing but our total production in the aggregate. From this basic consideration a number of more specific measures are derived for national accounting purposes: gross national product, net national product, national income, personal income, and disposable personal income.

This equivalence of product and income leads, in turn, to a circular flow representation of a modern economy. A money-income-and-spending flow, representing households as they sell their services (labor, land, etc.) to business firms and then buy the products of the business firms with their incomes, is matched by an opposite national-product-and-factor-services flow, showing the business getting the services of the factors of production and transforming these into useful commodities. With the circular flow diagram in mind, we can begin to understand how deficiencies or excesses of aggregate demand may make their presence felt in the modern economy. Thus, excessive consumer saving or deficient business investment might lead to a contraction of the flow, while too much investment and too little saving might lead to expansion. These matters will occupy our attention in detail in the next chapters.

IMPORTANT TERMS TO REMEMBER

Gross National Product (GNP)
Potential Output
Actual Output
Constant Prices
Index-Number Problem
Double-Counting
Value-Added Method
GNP and Economic Welfare
Savings and Investment
Gross vs. Net Investment
Net National Product
National Income
Personal Income
Personal Disposable Income
Inventories

QUESTIONS FOR DISCUSSION

1. Show the equivalence of the final-product and the value-added methods of measuring GNP.

2. Explain the basic relationships among the following terms: gross national product, net national product, national income, personal income, disposable personal income.

3. An increase in real GNP can be defined unambiguously only when the prices of all goods or the quantities of all goods change in the same proportions. If relative prices change and the relative quantities of goods produced change, then the change in GNP will be different depending upon what set of prices is used to make the measurement. This is known as the *index number problem* (see footnote, p. 192).

In the following example, determine the percentage change in GNP from 1960 to 1975 as measured (a) in 1960 prices and (b) in 1975 prices:

1960

	Oranges	Toy balloons
Price	$.10	$.05
Quantity	1,000	2,000

1975

	Oranges	Toy balloons
Price	$.15	$.10
Quantity	3,000	2,500

Which measure—in 1960 prices or 1975 prices—gives the larger percentage change in total output? Can you see why this problem might pose some difficulties for measuring changes in GNP over long periods of time?

4. Distinguish *financial investment* from *investment* as a component of GNP. What is the difference between *gross investment* and *net investment?*

5. In a private economy, total output consists of consumption and investment while total real income consists of consumption and saving. Since total output and total income are equivalent, saving and investment must always be equal. However, *decisions* to invest and *decisions* to save are not the same. Is there any inconsistency in saying that saving must always equal investment but that decisions about saving and decisions about investment are often made by different people for different reasons? (Hint: Remember the supply and demand diagrams of chapter 2. The quantity of a good bought and the quantity of a good sold must always be equal. However, the decisions of buyers, reflected in the demand curve, are quite different from the decisions of sellers, reflected in the supply curve.)

6. Using the circular flow diagram as a guide, show how a decision of consumers to save more than, businessmen want to invest can lead to a deficiency of aggregate demand. Show, conversely, how a decision of businessmen to invest more than consumers wish to save can lead to an excess of aggregate demand.

APPENDIX 8:
NATIONAL INCOME
AND WELFARE

National Income and Welfare

Simon Kuznets

Over the past several decades, the world's leading authority on the measurement of national income has been Simon Kuznets. Indeed, the empirical work done by Kuznets and his associates in the period before World War II is regarded by many economists as a foundation for modern macroeconomic analysis very nearly as significant as the theoretical contribution of Lord Keynes. Since the 1940s, Dr. Kuznets' work has branched out into many different fields and has been especially valuable in the study of growth in both developed and less developed economies. In recognition of his many contributions, he was awarded the Nobel Prize in Economics in 1971, the second American so honored.

The following reading, although published in 1946, is still relevant to a judgment of the relationship between measured national income and economic welfare.

Do estimates of national income measure the net contribution of economic activity to its primary goal—provision of goods to individuals—without errors of commission and omission? Do all commodities and services ordinarily included contribute to the satisfaction of consumers' wants, present or future? Are all the goods, i.e., all the sources of satisfying consumers' wants, made available in any year included in national income as estimated in this country today? We consider first the possible errors of commission, then those of omission.

Things desirable in the eyes of one individual may be matters of indifference to the group of which he is a member, or even considered deleterious by many; and things wanted by the majority may be frowned upon by the minority. In determining what are goods from the viewpoint of satisfying consumers' wants, we cannot assign both positive and negative signs to those wanted by some but deemed pernicious by

Excerpted from Simon Kuznets, *National Income, A Summary of Findings*, National Bureau of Economic Research, Inc. New York, 1946, pp. 121–28. Reprinted by permission of the publisher.

others, then strike algebraic balances. Rather we must decide what, on the whole, are goods and should be included. In the statistical measurement of national income the question reduces itself to what commodities and services should be excluded because, by and large, they do not contribute to the goal of economic activity—satisfaction of consumers' wants. Specific examples may range from services, such as are rendered Mr. Smith by a professional gang of killers in disposing of his rival Mr. Jones, to commodities, such as harmful drugs or useless patent medicines.

If in such a classification needs and relevance to needs were defined in terms of an imagined application of scientific knowledge and broad principles of ethics, we would exclude from national income many commodities and services now included. Many foods and drugs are worthless by scientific standards of nutrition and medication; many household appurtenances are irrelevant to any scientifically established needs for shelter and comfort; many service activities as well as commodities are desired for the sake of impressing foreigners or our fellow countrymen and could hardly measure up to ethical principles of behavior in relation to the rest of mankind. National income, as estimated here, is subject to errors of commission in that it includes commodities and services that are not goods, i.e., do not contribute to the satisfaction of needs, *if* the criteria are scientific standards and broad canons of ethics.

It would be instructive to estimate national income as the sum of products that are unequivocally sources of satisfying needs objectively determined from the viewpoint of mankind as a whole. The estimate could be described as a given nation's share in the world's current new supply of "approved" goods. Such estimates would aid national groups in appraising their social activities in general and their economic performance in particular. But they would not be what national income estimates as customarily prepared are designed to be—measures of the contribution of the nation's economy to satisfying the wants society recognizes as legitimate.

We exclude all illegal commodities or services, e.g., hired murder and the manufacture and sale of illegal

Simon Kuznets. By his research on the quantitative dimensions of national income, Kuznets has done more than any other modern economist to provide an empirical foundation for the investigation of Keynesian-type questions. Winner of the Nobel prize, he has also conducted vast researches on the subject of economic growth.

drugs, as far as we can with the inadequate statistical data at hand. We include commodities and services not prohibited as long as they find a buyer (presumably they would not exist without one), though they may not be useful from any objective standpoint. In short, in the absence of society's explicit declaration to the contrary, the wants of the individual buyer are the criterion. Erratic the test of legality may be (consider the prohibition years) and difficult of application to certain activities (consider a shady business deal that has not as yet been prosecuted in courts and may never be), but it is the only one at the disposal of a national income estimator unless he sets himself up as a social philosopher and decides to ignore the consensus of society as to what are not goods, i.e., not positive contributions to the approved ends of economic activity.

There are of course numerous payments and transactions that do not represent a commodity produced or a service rendered: and whenever national income is estimated from payments (rather than from the value of commodities and services), such transfers also are omitted; e.g., gambling gains, net gains on sales of capital assets without any preceding input of resources to account for the gain, and gifts. All these transfers among individuals may greatly affect the eventual shares various members of society receive of the current net product; but they do not directly determine its size, if it is defined as the net value of commodities and services produced during the year. The distinction between transfer payments and payments that are evidence of real production is scarcely so simple, but this is another of those problems we can no more than mention.

Judged in the light of all possible ways of satisfying consumers' wants, national income as customarily measured is subject to larger errors of omission than of commission. Errors of omission arise, first, from the deliberate restriction of national income to the net product of *economic* activity proper, and hence the deliberate exclusion of activities that may satisfy wants but are not economic. Even within the area of economic activities proper, especially if broadly defined, national income estimates omit some types of product. Finally, by definition, they neglect completely any consideration of such costs of economic activity as impinge directly upon consumers' satisfaction or the welfare of the community.

Life is full of activities that lead to the satisfaction of consumers' needs and hence their welfare, only some of which can be classified as economic. In extreme cases the distinction is easy. Taking a pleas-

ant walk or playing a game of chess with a friend satisfies certain wants, but is not an economic activity; working in a factory or an office is. But what about the household services performed by the housewife and other members of the family? What about cultivating one's own vegetable garden?

It has become customary to base the distinction between economic and noneconomic activities on the closeness of ties with the market. Every pursuit whose products are either sold on the market or are largely directed toward it is treated as economic; no others are, though their yield in the way of satisfying wants may be substantial. This solution has a great advantage in that it segregates the sector of life concerned largely with economic activities, and in which measurement is feasible because the yardstick (no matter how it may have to be adjusted) is the market price. In a highly developed economy the disadvantages are reduced by the fact that the majority of the activities intended to produce goods for consumers are marketbound. Even so, the magnitudes omitted are far from minor. For example, the value of housewives' services are roughly estimated at some $23 billion in 1929, or more than one-fourth of national income. And in countries where the market is less developed than in the United States, the limitation of economic activities to those marketbound leads to a major undercount.

The national income estimator must choose between comprehensive definition—with the consequence that large sectors of the economy either cannot be measured on a continuous basis or cannot be included with more precisely measurable sectors because the errors are so enormous—and a narrower definition that confines economic activities to those marketbound—for which tolerably reliable estimates can be made. In current national income measurement in this country, the decision is usually in favor of the second alternative. And it finds support in the argument that the activities so segregated for measurement are the ones subject primarily to economic criteria and rationale; whereas those that are not directed at the market are much more a part of life in general. One may and does discharge a housekeeper for inefficiency in managing a household, but by itself this is rarely a ground for divorce.

However justified, this limitation results in omitting a substantial group of activities important in satisfying the needs and wants of the members of society. Moreover, some marketbound activities are omitted largely because they cannot be measured on a continuous basis—taking boarders or lodgers, spare-time jobs, and the like. In coverage, a continuous national income series is thus always on the short side even in terms of marketbound activities, which it tends to omit if they are casual and hence elusive of measurement.

The national income estimator cannot do much about such omissions, since scarcity or lack of data is inherent in the nature of the omitted areas. But in interpreting national income movements in terms of satisfying consumers' wants, the limitation of national income largely to noncasual marketbound activities must be stressed. In this country as in many others where the market is always being extended, the relative importance of the household as a source of consumer goods is declining. Many activities formerly performed by the housewife or other members of the family and not measured (baking, sewing, canning, etc.) have progressively been taken over by business enterprises and gone into marketbound activities; other household functions have vanished without leaving a direct substitute in business activity. Hence, national income totals tend to exaggerate the upward movement in the supply of goods to consumers, if such supply is comprehensively defined as coming from both marketbound and family activities. Likewise, a comparison of the national income of two countries at different stages of the commercialization of family production must take into account the differing importance of the market sphere in the total provision of goods to consumers. The omission of casual activities also imparts an upward bias to the secular trend of national income, since their importance relative to those covered diminishes as more people move to cities and engage in regular, full time pursuits.

The effect on the interpretation of short term changes in national income is at least as great. During any expansion, whether associated with business cycles or with wars, people move from nonmarket to market areas and from occasional to full time jobs; and in the larger net product the proportion of measurable marketbound activities increases at the expense of nonmarket activities or occasional jobs. As many of us are all too aware, during recent years, when the pressure of war needs for the expansion of marketbound production was especially intense, the number of persons available for family household work decreased materially. *Total* net production, including production within the household, increased much less than production on farms, in factories, shops, and offices. During short term contractions, on the contrary, the shrinkage of the market sphere swells the number of persons available for services both within the household and for casual jobs. Being confined to noncasual marketbound activities, national income is thus a more cyclically sensitive index than a more comprehensive total that would include the large productive sector of the household as well as occasional jobs and pursuits. Variations in it therefore exaggerate short term changes in the more comprehensive total.

We come finally to what some may consider the gravest omission—the deliberate exclusion of the human cost of turning out the net product; i.e., such disadvantages as are concomitants of acquiring an income and cramp the recipients' (and others') style as a consumer. One example would be long working hours. If to turn out a net product of a given size requires a work week that leaves little time for leisure, the producers cannot derive much satisfaction as consumers, i.e., as individuals who have certain wants and preferences. Another example would be the strain some jobs impose. If by and large a task is disagreeable, exhausting, dull, monotonous, or nerve wracking, the cost to the producer as a consumer is higher than when the task is light, instructive, diversified, or amusing. The range of illustrations is wide—from these obvious ones to more tenuous allegations concerning the costs of unpleasant features of the business-urban civilization such as blatant advertising and the ruthless despoiling and defacing of the countryside.

National income is not intended to measure such costs. It gauges the net positive contribution to consumers' satisfaction in the form of commodities and services; the burden of work and discomfort are ignored. And it may well be questioned whether such costs are measurable; or if measurable, could be estimated in terms comparable to those in which net product is estimated. Nor is it easy to say whether the long term trends or short term fluctuations in these costs parallel those in net product or are in opposite directions. Some of these trends are clear. Working hours have been progressively shortened, and many of the heavier jobs, demanding stamina and endurance, are now performed by machinery. On the other hand, it is claimed that the monotony and dissatisfaction to the individual as an individual due to greater specialization and the repetition of a few motions have increased, and that so has the nervous tension. The balance of such claims and counterclaims cannot be struck.

The reason for calling attention to this aspect of economic activity, completely neglected in national income measurement, is its possible contribution toward understanding some of the longer term trends. It warns us against too easy an acceptance of the thesis that a high national income is the sole desideratum in theory or the dominant motive in fact in a nation's economy. The reduction in working hours, the decisions made by countries that discourage as rapid a growth of population and of national product as could be attained (consider immigration restrictions); the willingness of some businessmen to adopt a policy of live and let live when they might expect a greater net return from vigorous and aggressive competition; the emphasis some individuals put on the importance of other than economic incentives proper—are all indications that both in society at large and among the groups and individuals it comprises definite limits are set upon a maximum net product as measured in national income. Both recently and in the past a potentially larger net national product has been forfeited for the sake of mitigating some intangible costs of the type illustrated above. Though unable to measure them, we must recognize that their omission renders national income merely one element in the evaluation of the net welfare assignable to the nation's economic activity.   □

CHAPTER 9

THE THEORY OF NATIONAL INCOME DETERMINATION

We have been setting the stage for the analysis we shall undertake now. It has to do with what economists usually call "the theory of national income determination," but a somewhat more vivid description might be: An analysis of some of the root causes of depressions and inflations in the modern industrial economy.

THE PROBLEM AND SOME CLUES

What we have done so far has been to state the problem and to provide a few clues to its solution.

The problem, briefly, is this: Given the basic productive capacity of the nation, how can we determine where the actual level of GNP will be? We know historically that there have been gaps between actual and potential GNP in our own and in other industrial economies. What determines the size of these gaps?

To assist in the approach to this problem, we have developed a number of important clues to the nature of the solution.

We noticed that John Maynard Keynes, in his theorizing about these matters, placed great stress on the role of aggregate demand. If aggregate demand fell short, Keynes argued, actual GNP would be below potential GNP and there would be substantial unemployment in the economy.

We showed that national income and national product are basically two different views of the same object. This was illustrated by the familiar circular flow approach to economic life. Businesses pay incomes to the owners of labor, land, etc., who then use these incomes to buy the goods and services that businesses have produced.

We observed that the three main categories of GNP are: (1) consumption expenditures, (2) investment expenditures, and (3) government expenditures.

We showed how a deficiency in one of the spending categories (say, consumer spending) might lead through the circular flow to business troubles and thus to a contraction of output and employment. Such a deficiency in the spending flow, we said, was really what Keynes meant when he talked about inadequate aggregate demand. We also suggested how aggregate demand might be "too high," as it would be when businessmen want to invest more than consumers wish to save.

These clues give us the basic structure for analyzing the problem of national income determination. We must first determine the factors that influence the three main categories of spending: consumer spending, private business investment, and government expenditure. Then we must "add up" these expenditure items and see whether they will provide us with sufficient aggregate demand to sustain GNP at its full employment potential level. If they will not sustain full employment GNP, then we must ask: What *is* the level of national income that can be sustained? When we have answered these questions, our theory of national income determination will be basically complete.

We shall follow this suggested structure except for one point. In this chapter, we shall consider the theory of national income determination in a purely private economy—i.e., we shall assume that there are no government expenditures or taxes and that our only sources of aggregate demand are consumer spending and business investment spending. Having presented the theory in this simplified case, we shall introduce government once again in the following chapter. This procedure, besides being easier to follow, also has the advantage that it enables us to show very clearly and explicitly what the impact of various government policies on the economy will be.

CONSUMPTION DEMAND

The level of national income that can be sustained in a private economy will be determined by the strength of (1) consumer demand for the various categories of consumption goods the nation can produce, and (2) business demand for goods to invest, i.e., to add to the stock of machines, buildings, inventories, and other capital goods in the economy. We shall consider these two components of aggregate demand in order.

What are the factors that influence consumption demand in a modern industrial economy? Can we generalize about them in any way?

Of course, the truth of the matter is that there are countless elements that may influence our demand for consumer goods to at least some degree. An advertising campaign may affect our buying habits and preferences. So may a medical report on the virtues or harmfulness of certain products. There may be consumer fads that sweep the nation, changes in ladies' fashions, new sports that interest either spectators or participants. In some societies, there may develop a general philosophy of "eat, drink, and be merry"—spend as much of your income on consumption today as possible! In other societies, there may be a puritanical and thrifty code: "A penny saved is a penny earned."

It is worth mentioning the great variety of factors influencing consumer demand because this makes it clear that if we single out any one factor as all-important, we are doing a certain injustice to the facts. Any generalization we get will be only in the nature of an approximation.

Still, even rough generalizations can be important—indeed, we seldom do much better than that in the social sciences—and many economists feel that such is the case in the area of consumer demand. The basic generalization, in this instance, states that consumer spending can be usefully related to consumer income. If you wish to know how much a family will spend on consumption, find out what their family income is. If you want to know how much the nation will spend on consumption in general, find out what the national income is. It is this *income-consumption* relationship that has played a pivotal role in the modern theory of national income determination.

The roots of this, as we would expect, were in Keynes' *General Theory*. In this book Keynes expressed his belief in a "psychological law" that as an individual's (or society's) income rises, that individual (or society) will spend part, but not the whole, of the increase in income on added consumption. Another way of putting this is to say that individuals or society will divide any increase in income into (1) added consumption, and (2) added saving. Since

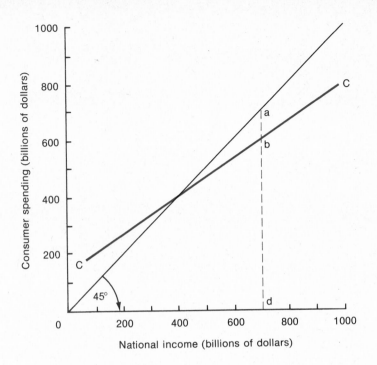

Figure 9–1. The Consumption Function.

This diagram shows a fairly typical consumption function. The line *CC* shows how much consumers will want to spend on goods and services at various levels of national income. The reader should understand that any line (e.g., *ad*) drawn from the 45° line to the horizontal axis will be equal to national income as measured at its point of intersection with the horizontal axis (in this case $700 billion). He should also understand that the distance *ab* will represent anticipated consumer saving.

saving is defined as that part of income that is not consumed, (1) + (2) will necessarily equal the given increase in income.

Today we can go somewhat further than this and suggest that, in the short run, saving will tend to increase absolutely and, to a lesser degree, as a percentage of national income as national income increases. A typical shape for the curve relating consumption to national income is shown in Figure 9–1. In this diagram, you will notice that we have drawn a 45° line from the origin. On this 45° line, vertical and horizontal distances from the axes are equal, meaning that the vertical distance is equal to national income. Since, in our simplified economy, consumption plus saving equals national income, we can calculate saving by measuring the distance between the consumption function and the 45° line.

What does the shape of this so-called *consumption function* mean? And on what kind of empirical evidence is it based?

The shape, as we have said, indicates a slightly rising percentage of income devoted to saving and a declining percentage devoted to consumption as income increases. At a rather low level of national income ($400 billion), consumption expenditures equal the whole of national income. At still lower levels—and here we must imagine the nation in a condition of general poverty—people would, in the aggregate, spend more than their entire incomes on consumption. In the economist's phraseology, at very low levels of income, people will *dissave*. They will go to their past savings; they will live on their capital assets, their homes and personal property, without replacing them; they will be consuming on the average more than they have actually produced that year. This is a pathological case (though not an unknown case, since there *was* net dissaving in the depths of the Great Depression in 1932 and 1933), and hence the more interesting part of the curve lies to the right of $400 billion. In this range, we can see that consumption is continually rising with income but that saving is increasing as a percentage of income.

The evidence for this general shape of the consumption function is both macro- and microeconomic in nature. In Table 9–1 and Figure 9–2, we have presented data on personal consumption expenditures in relationship to disposable personal income in the United States from 1929 to 1973. The shape of the line we have fitted to this data is roughly what we should expect, although there are years that obviously need special explanation—for example, the years during World War II when voluntary saving was quite high even after large income taxes. Since the end of the war, savings have been a fairly constant fraction of personal disposable income.

Another quite different kind of information is provided by microeconomic studies of family spending at different income levels. Thus, we should expect that families with higher incomes will generally save more than families with lower incomes, not only absolutely, but also in percentage terms, and various studies have confirmed this general tendency. Thus, in 1950, a family with a disposable income of $4,000 a year probably saved little if anything on the average, while a family with $10,000 a year might save close to 20 percent of its larger income. In 1970, as everyone's incomes had risen, the percentages changed —at $4,000 a year, families were *dis*saving on the average; at $10,000, they were saving not 20 percent but closer to 10 percent—but the general relationship of higher percentage savings with higher levels of family income still remained valid.

It must be stressed that none of this evidence is absolutely conclusive. One problem that makes this whole area so difficult is that of distinguishing between long-run and short-run effects and causes. We

TABLE 9–1

TOTAL U.S. DISPOSABLE PERSONAL INCOME AND PERSONAL CONSUMPTION EXPENDITURES 1929–73 (billions of dollars)

YEAR	DISPOSABLE PERSONAL INCOME	PERSONAL CONSUMPTION EXPENDITURES
1929	83.3	77.2
1933	45.5	45.8
1939	70.3	66.8
1940	75.7	70.8
1941	92.7	80.6
1942	116.9	88.5
1943	113.5	99.3
1944	146.3	108.3
1945	150.2	119.7
1946	160.0	143.4
1947	169.8	160.7
1948	189.1	173.6
1949	188.6	176.8
1950	206.9	191.0
1951	226.6	206.3
1952	238.3	216.7
1953	252.6	230.0
1954	257.4	236.5
1955	275.3	254.4
1956	293.2	266.7
1957	308.5	281.4
1958	318.8	290.1
1959	337.3	311.2
1960	350.0	325.2
1961	364.4	335.2
1962	385.3	355.1
1963	404.6	375.0
1964	438.1	401.2
1965	473.2	432.8
1966	511.9	466.3
1967	546.3	492.1
1968	591.0	536.2
1969	634.4	579.5
1970	691.7	617.6
1971	746.0	667.2
1972	797.0	726.5
1973	882.6	805.0

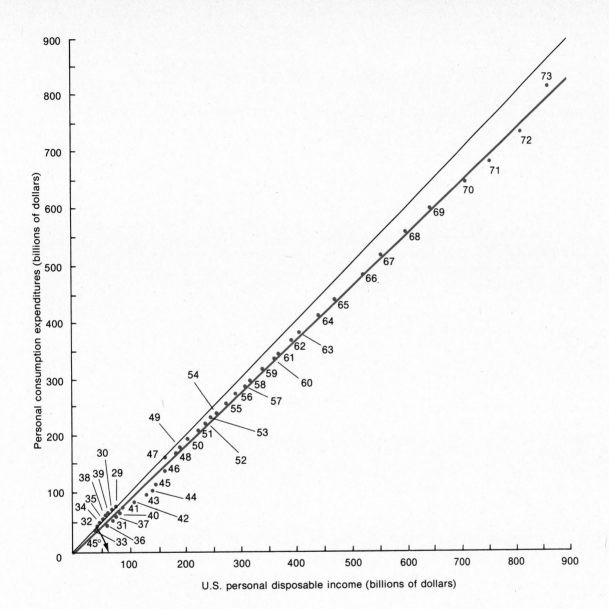

Figure 9–2. U.S. Consumption in Relation to Disposable Income, 1929–1973.

In this diagram, we have fitted a line to actual data on consumption in relation to income in the U.S. for each year, 1929–1973. In general, the data show the same pattern exemplified in our hypothetical consumption function, Figure 9–1.

do know that in the long run, a consumption function such as we have drawn in Figure 9–1 will shift upward. At a given level of income, as we have shown, families spent more in 1970 than in 1950, and they will presumably spend still more at that same level of income in 1980. Why? Because there were many new products in 1970 that hardly existed in 1950, and we can expect still more product changes by 1980. Even more significant, perhaps, is the fact that we are in a society in which everyone's family income (on the average) is rising. Insofar as our consumption expenditures reflect our relative position in the income distribution, then, if we stay at the same absolute level while other families around us are improving their positions, we may feel relatively poorer, and this may lower our willingness to cut consumption and save for the future.[1] To complicate matters still more, some economists, like Milton Friedman of the University of Chicago, have argued that our income is really of two sorts: "permanent income" and "transitory (or windfall gain or loss) income." Saving and consumption patterns will generally be different depending on which sort of income we are talking about.

There are, in short, many complications in this area, and no one should take any statements about the income-consumption relationship as though they were established beyond possibility of doubt. Still, the view that makes consumption demand depend substantially on the level of national income has proved quite a durable one.

Our first question, then, is answered as follows: consumer spending in a private economy will be largely determined by the level of national income in the general manner described by the consumption function of Figure 9–1.[2]

INVESTMENT DEMAND

We now turn to our second question: What factors will determine the level of investment spending in our hypothetical economy?

Now the determinants of investment demand are, if anything, even more complicated than those that influence consumer demand. Indeed, while economists often stress the relative dependability of consumer spending at a given level of national income, they usually point out the great variability of business investment spending. For this reason, changes in investment spending are often seen to be pivotal in causing upswings or downswings in a modern economy.

To appreciate the problem, put yourself in the place of a businessman and ask what factors are likely to influence you in a decision to expand the size of your factory, to add new machines, equipment, and so on. There are a host of obvious factors that you would have to take into account at the outset. Basically, you would be trying to judge the future profitability of the investment. This would involve an assessment of your present position. Are sales good? Is demand for your product high? Is the extra machinery needed to produce more output? But it also requires an assessment of the future. Are sales likely to expand or contract over the life of the new machinery? Demand may be buoyant today, but does

---

1. The dependence of our consumption habits on our relations to other consumers was stressed forcefully by Thorstein Veblen over seventy years ago. In his *Theory of the Leisure Class* (1899), Veblen emphasized the concept of "conspicuous consumption"—i.e., consumption to prove our superior status to our neighbors. More recently, another American economist, James S. Duesenberry added the notion that our consumption may be a function not of our absolute level of income but of our relative position in the income distribution of the society.

2. This discussion of consumption and saving has been limited to household consumption and saving out of personal disposable income. In a fuller discussion, we should have to take into account the fact that business corporations also save and that their savings form an important source for business investment in the modern American economy. These corporate savings arise when businesses pay out less in dividends than their after-tax profits. These retained profits are part of national income but do not go to the consumers as personal income. The reader who wishes to follow through in this matter should consult the excellent treatment of the subject in Charles L. Schultze, *National Income Analysis*, 3rd ed. (Englewood Cliffs, N.J.: Prentice-Hall, 1971), especially chap. 3.

Joseph A. Schumpeter (1883–1950). Schumpeter, the Austrian-born Harvard economist, emphasized the role of entrepreneurship and innovation in explaining business investment and economic growth.

the future look bright or gloomy? In other words, the first thing one would have to do would be to formulate some general opinion about the future market for one's particular product. *Business expectations* are a crucial factor influencing investment spending.

But it is not just the state of the market that one has to estimate. As a businessman, you would also have to investigate whether there are new productive methods and processes available to you that will make the investment profitable in terms of reducing costs of production or producing an improved product. The kinds of plant, tools, and machinery we have in the economy today are vastly different from what

they were fifty years ago, and this is a consequence of the fact that businessmen invest not only in more of the "old" machines, but also in replacing "old" machines with "new" machines.

Here we enter the whole area of *technological progress*. If there is an important new invention, for example, this may create a wide range of opportunities for profitable business investment. The great Austrian-American economist, Joseph A. Schumpeter (1883–1950) emphasized the pivotal role of new products and new productive methods as stimuli to business investment. He considered the introduction and absorption of innovational advances to be the mainspring of the major fluctuations of a modern economy. The judgment on whether investments in a new line of business or new productive process will work is not a mechanical one; it involves considerable uncertainty and, indeed, Schumpeter felt that those who took the lead in innovations had to have certain special qualities of character and leadership ability. Once these creative *entrepreneurs* had shown the way, other businessmen would follow in a swarm, introducing their new methods and business combinations. Schumpeter found herein the whole secret of the business cycle:

The swarm-like appearance of new combinations easily and necessarily explains the fundamental features of periods of boom. It explains why increasing capital investment is the very first symptom of the coming boom, why industries producing means of production are the first to show supernormal stimulation, above all why the consumption of iron increases. It explains the appearance of new purchasing power in bulk, thereby the characteristic rise in prices during booms, which obviously no reference to increased need or increased costs alone can explain. Further, it explains the decline of unemployment and the rise of wages, the rise in the interest rate, the increase in freight, the increasing strain on bank balances and bank reserves, and . . . the release of secondary waves—the spread of prosperity over the whole economic system.[3]

3. Joseph A. Schumpeter, *The Theory of Economic Development* (Cambridge: Harvard University Press, 1949), p. 230.

Thus, technological progress in one area of the economy may lead to increased investment and expansion throughout the system as a whole.

There is still more to the matter of investment, however. Even if you were aware of the future state of demand and also the full range of technological possibilities open to you, you would not have solved the problem of whether or not to invest in a particular factory or piece of machinery. For you would now come up against the problem of financing the new investment. Does your firm have a great sum in the form of retained profits that can be used to purchase the added capital equipment? Or will you have to go to the money markets to raise funds from the outside? In either case, the cost of borrowing money—the *interest rate*—will have to be a factor in your decision.[4] If interest rates are high, this will mean that you will have to pay more to borrow money and, consequently, that you will be more reluctant to undertake any vast expansion schemes. High interest rates are often associated with "tight money." It is difficult to get loans from the bank, and when one does get a loan, the interest charge is very stiff. In such circumstances, business investment is likely to be considerably curtailed.

In short, we have a whole series of factors that are likely to lead to more or less investment spending in the economy. Current demand for our product, pressure on our plant capacity, future expectations, technological progress, our profit position, the rate of interest—all these are factors that may significantly affect this second great component of aggregate demand, business investment expenditure.

We shall return to some of these factors later, especially when we come to our discussion of the economic effects of changes in the rate of interest (chapter 11).[5] For the moment, however, so that we can get on with our argument, let us simply assume that business investment spending has been determined. Let us suppose that all these various factors have done their work and that the net result has been to give us a level of investment of, say, $100 billion. This is a short cut, but it will help us get the overall picture in the clearest possible terms.

Very well, then. We have (1) a consumption-function (Figure 9–1) relating consumer spending to national income, and (2) a given $100 billion of investment demand. How then is the level of national income determined?

DETERMINATION OF THE LEVEL OF NATIONAL INCOME

The determination of the equilibrium level of national income takes place basically in the following way:

We add up the sum of planned consumer spending and planned business investment spending at each level of national income and determine whether this sum exceeds the level of national income or falls short of it. If there is an excess, it will mean that aggregate demand exceeds aggregate supply. In this case, forces will be set in motion to produce an expansion of national income. If, however, there is a deficiency, this will mean that aggregate demand is less than aggregate supply and this will bring about a fall in national income and, with it, of course, a fall in employment.

In short, the root cause of depressions, at least as far as our simplified economy is concerned, is a sum of consumption and investment spending that falls short of national income at the full-employment level.

---

4. It might seem that the interest rate would affect our decision only if we had to borrow money from outside, say, take a bank loan, and not if we already had the funds ourselves. However, this is not so. If the machine promises us a return of 7 percent a year, and we can get 10 percent in a savings account, are we likely to purchase the machine? What will we do with our money?

5. We shall also consider investment in a microeconomic context in Part Three. There we shall show that in a simple world, the interest rate is a means of adjusting the technological possibilities of capital accumulation to the society's preferences with respect to present versus future income. (See pp. 482–83.)

It is one thing to state the conclusion, another thing to demonstrate it in a convincing way. Actually, there are several approaches, all of which we have already suggested in our various clues along the way. One approach, for example, would be to return to our *circular flow* diagram of the last chapter and to show that consumers and businessmen will be content with what they are doing only when the sum of planned consumer spending and planned business investment in the spending flow is equal to the national product flow. In Figure 9–3, for example, we show an economy in which the sum of planned consumer spending and planned business investment spending is *less* than the national income of the economy, and hence we have an economy that is in macroeconomic *dis*-equilibrium. This economy is due for a contraction of national output and employment.

Notice that we have used the term "planned" while talking about consumer and investment spending. Figure 9–3 makes clear why this is the case. In this particular example, *planned* investment is $100 billion but *actual* investment is $150 billion. What has happened is that consumers have divided their national income of $900 billion into $150 billion of planned savings and $750 billion of planned consumption. Thus, the sum of planned consumption ($750 billion) and planned investment ($100 billion) is $850 billion. This is below the level of national income ($900 billion). Now the sum of *actual* consumption and investment must equal national income since there is no other place in a private economy for national product to go. The discrepancy is made up by unplanned, unwanted accumulation of $50 billion of added inventory. The consequence of actual investment exceeding planned investment is that businessmen will now want to cut back on their total production and employment. This will lead to a fall in national income from $900 billion to, say, $870 billion or $790 billion.

To determine exactly how far national income would have to fall to bring about equilibrium, we would have to examine how savings and consumption spending responded to changes in national income. The circular flow approach is rather awkward for doing this, however, since it would require drawing a new diagram for each new level of income. An equivalent, but much clearer, approach is to build on the basis of our consumption function diagram (Figure 9–1).

In Figure 9–4, we have taken this earlier diagram and made two additions to it. The first addition is the vertical line *FE* drawn at the level of national income of $910 billion. This line tells us what national income (or product) would be if all the factors of production in the economy were fully employed. Actually, full-employment national income is not quite so definite a concept as this single line would suggest. The size of the labor force seeking jobs in the labor market is itself a function of economic conditions to some degree. Hence, we could, if we wished, think of *FE* not as a line but as a band of a certain width suggesting the range of possible full-employment outputs.

The second addition is the line *C + I*, which has been drawn above our *C* curve. The vertical distance between the two lines is $100 billion. This represents the amount of planned business investment that we are taking as determined by the host of factors influencing such investment. The vertical distance from the *x*-axis to the *C + I* line at each level of national income represents the sum of investment and consumption demand at that level of national income.

How then will the equilibrium level of national income be determined? To see the process involved, let us start out at the full-employment level, or at the national income of $910 billion. We now ask: What is the level of aggregate demand when the economy is fully employed? The answer can be read from the diagram. Consumption demand is equal to the distance *FB,* or about $740 billion. Investment demand, of course, is $100 billion. The sum of the two, there-

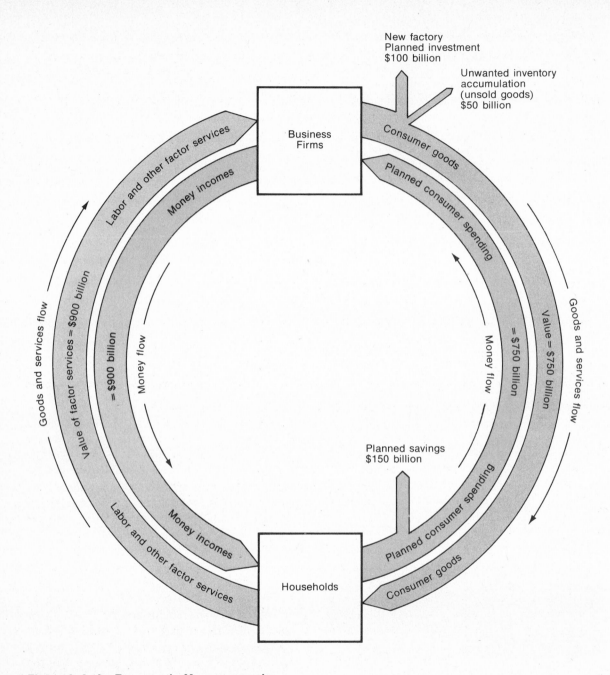

Figure 9–3. An Economy in Macroeconomic Disequilibrium.

In this economy, planned consumer savings exceed planned business investment. This would lead to an unwanted investment in inventory ($50 billion). But businessmen would not long put up with this situation. What would they do? Answer: Cut back on total production and employment.

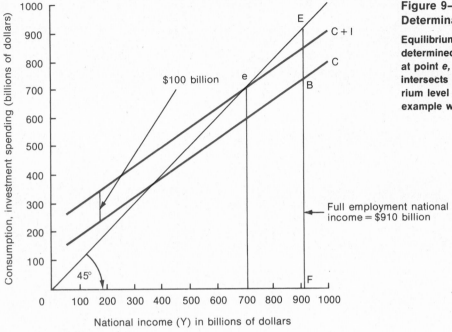

Figure 9-4. National Income Determination.

Equilibrium national income will be determined in this private economy at point *e*, where the *C + I* curve intersects the 45° line. The equilibrium level of national income in this example will be $700 billion.

fore, is about $840 billion. This is $70 billion less than the value of full employment national income.

Now it does not take any very sophisticated analysis to show that this is an untenable situation. Businessmen are paying out into the income stream far more than consumers (through their consumption expenditures) and businessmen (through their own investment expenditures) are willing to pay back to them. The effects of this will be direct and compelling. If we assume that prices remain unchanged (they might actually start to fall somewhat under these circumstances), businessmen in general will find that they are accumulating unwanted inventories of goods in stock. This is investment, but it is unplanned and unwanted investment. Furthermore, it is a kind of investment that the businessman knows how to re-

spond to directly: He will start cutting production and employment. This will be true of businessmen throughout the economy. There will be general cutbacks in national output and employment. Full-employment national income, in short, has proved unsustainable; employment and income will have to fall.

But how far? Where will the equilibrium level of national income in our economy be?

The answer is that equilibrium national income will be at the level determined by the intersection of the *C + I* line with the 45° line (point *e*). At this level of national income, aggregate demand will equal aggregate supply. Since the distance between the *C* curve and the 45° line equals the amount of their incomes consumers wish to save, this equilibrium level of national income is also one at which planned business investment and anticipated consumer savings are equal. In this instance, the amount businessmen want to invest and the amount consumers want to save are both equal to $100 billion.[6]

To prove that the point e has significance, we must show that levels of national income either higher or lower will not work. We must also show that higher levels will set in motion forces bringing national income *down,* whereas lower levels will set in motion forces bringing national income *up.*

Actually, we have already done half of this by showing the unsustainability of full-employment income and the way in which businessmen would react to unwanted inventories of their goods in stock. This logic can be applied to all points to the right of e in our diagram. In each case, there will be some accumulation of unwanted inventories and consequently a further reduction of production and employment.

Similarly, we can show that points to the left of e will not work either, though for an opposite reason.

Here the sum of C + I *exceeds* the level of national income (Y). This fact would manifest itself to producers in the form of clamoring buyers who would be trying to purchase more of the firms' products than had been produced in the given period. If, again, we assume that prices remain unchanged (in this case they would have a tendency to rise), the consequence would be depleted inventories, empty store shelves, unfulfilled orders, and the like. The effect of this, in turn, would be to suggest to businessmen that they ought to expand production and employment. In short, at all levels of national income lower than e, we would have forces working for an expansion of national income.

Thus, at lower levels, national income will expand; at higher levels, national income will contract; at point e, aggregate demand will be just sufficient to match the output the economy is producing and thus there will be no forces effecting any change in the level of national income. Q.E.D.

At point e, do we have an equilibrium level of national income? Yes. No consumer, businessman, or laborer can improve his situation by an indicated change in his pattern of actions. Do we have general contentment in the economy? Definitely no! Our equilibrium level of national income is short of full-employment income by $210 billion. Translated into employment figures, this amount means that our economy is suffering from massive unemployment. We are, indeed, precisely at the kind of "underemployment equilibrium" mentioned in our discussion of Keynes. There are people who want work, but there are no jobs. There is, to use a phrase current in the 1930s, "poverty in the midst of plenty."

---

6.   Still another way of showing equilibrium national income is precisely by showing the interaction of the planned savings and investment schedules. This method is given in the following figure. The reader should test his understanding of this subject matter by (1) showing for himself exactly how the figure is derived from Figure 9–4, and (2) analyzing the process of national income (Y) determination (which we have done largely in terms of C + I = Y) in terms of savings and investment decisions (or I = S).

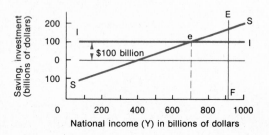

Determination of Equilibrium National Income by Saving and Investment Schedules.

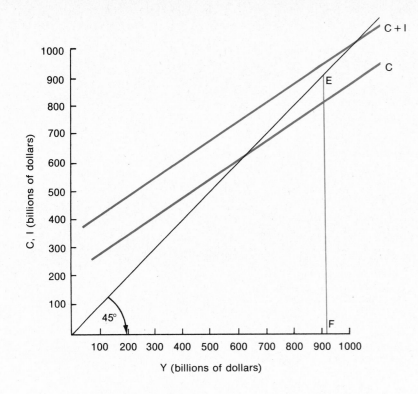

Figure 9–5. A Keynesian Demand-Pull Inflation.

When the sum of *C + I* exceeds full employment income at *FE* in our private economy, there will be heavy pressures on prices to rise, because of excess aggregate demand.

EXCESS DEMAND AND INFLATION

But there is a further possibility to be discussed. Suppose that we have a situation where the *C + I* curve intersects the 45° line at a point *beyond* the full employment level? Such a case is shown in Figure 9–5.

Now it is clear that we would not be able to produce at the indicated level of income since, by hypothesis, it exceeds full-employment income. What this diagram tells us, therefore, is that when we reach full employment, we still will be faced with a condition of considerable excess demand. The forces for expansion in the economy will still be strong, but, in the short run, where will be no way in which these forces can be expressed in further expansions of real output. How will they be expressed, then? The an-

swer: in inflation. The situation depicted in Figure 9–5 is a perfect example of a Keynesian, *demand-pull* inflation. Barring any change in basic conditions, the economy depicted here will have persistent pressures on its price level. Businesses will be trying to expand; they will be competing against each other for labor and other factors of production; wages and incomes will rise; consumer demands will rise in money terms with the higher money incomes; prices will rise again; and so on.

This is not the only type of inflation, as we have mentioned before. However, it is an important type of inflation. Also, it should be said that demand-pull *elements* are frequently present in the mix of factors that produce the more complicated kinds of inflation we see in the real world. Hence, an understanding of Figure 9–5 is an important step in the analysis of this crucial twentieth century phenomenon.

WORK TO BE DONE

This, then, is the basic theory of national income determination in a purely private economy. Our next steps consist in developing and modifying this analysis in a number of ways. We are interested not only in depressions and prosperities, but in the fact that our economy seems to fluctuate back and forth from one to the other, a fluctuation that is sometimes called the *business cycle*. We must introduce government expenditures and taxes into our analysis. Further, we must introduce "money" into the picture. We recall from chapter 4 that the Federal Reserve System, by influencing the money supply and interest rates, ultimately affects "production, employment and prices" (p. 78). How do these influences come to bear in relation to the analysis we have presented above? Finally, of course, we must deepen our understanding of the inflation process and extend our analysis to an "open" economy—taking up the macroeconomics of international trade.

The enumeration of what remains to be done is in itself a clear indication that the analysis of this chapter is only a first step along the way. It is, however, a major step. What we have done here is to equip ourselves with an important and flexible set of tools that can be used in many different connections. Whether the problem is inflation, the balance of payments, unemployment, or what have you, modern macroeconomic analysis essentially begins with the instruments we have provided in this chapter. Thus if careful attention is necessary here, that attention will have its reward in the numerous applications of the analysis we shall be able to make in the chapters ahead.

SUMMARY

In this chapter, we have presented the essentials of the theory of national income determination in a simplified private economy.

In such a private economy, the main components of aggregate demand will be consumer spending and business investment spending. Consumer spending is related to national income through the *consumption function*. This function tells us that consumers will consume more as their income increases, but that they will also save more. The evidence is that, in the short run, saving increases slightly as a percentage of income as income rises.

Investment spending is a function of many different factors including such important elements as business expectations, technological progress, the amount of profits available for investment purposes, and the cost of borrowing funds, or the rate of interest. Investment spending is, on the whole, a more variable and unpredictable factor than consumer spending. In our simplified analysis, we take a certain amount of planned investment as already determined by the workings of these various factors.

The equilibrium level of national income is determined at the level where aggregate supply equals aggregate demand or, equivalently, where the sum of planned consumption and investment spending equals national income (or output) or, equivalently still, where savings and investment decisions are equated. At levels of national income higher than this equilibrium level, forces will be set in motion to bring about a contraction in output and employment. At levels of national income below the equilibrium level, forces will be set in motion to bring about an expansion in output and employment.

The equilibrium level of national income is not necessarily a "full-employment" level and, indeed, is compatible with major mass unemployment in the economy. In the case where aggregate demand exceeds national income at the full-employment level, we will have persistent upward pressures on the price level. This is Keynesian or *demand-pull* inflation.

Although simplified at this stage, the present analysis is fundamental to modern thinking about macroeconomic problems and has a wide range of reference to everything from the monetary and fiscal policies of the government to the problems of inflation, employment, and trade.

IMPORTANT TERMS TO REMEMBER

Income-Consumption Relation
Consumption Function
Saving and Dissaving
Investment Demand
Technological Progress: Innovations
Interest Rate
Planned Saving and Planned Investment
$Y = C + I$
Equilibrium National Income
Underemployment Equilibrium
Demand-Pull Inflation

QUESTIONS FOR DISCUSSION

1. State in your own words the basic theory of national income determination as you have understood it from this chapter.

2. Define the *consumption function*. What cautions should be kept in mind in employing this important tool?

3. In our analysis in this chapter, we have assumed that all saving is done by households and that all investing is done by businesses. In reality, however, households also invest (e.g., building homes) and businesses save (corporate saving now provides a substantial percentage of the funds for business investment in the United States). How might these facts modify the general analysis of national income determination as we have presented it?

4. In the pre-Keynesian era, it was sometimes argued that the main reason for unemployment in the economy was that labor was making unreasonable wage demands. If wages were lower, it was argued, employers would find that they could afford to hire more workers and the unemployment problem would be solved. Do you find this argument satisfactory? If not, why not? (Hint: Think back to the supply-and-demand curve for electricians of chapter 5. If electricians and all other workers accepted lower wages, would this be likely to affect the demand curves for electricians and for other workers? In what direction?)

5. If you were going to use the analysis of this chapter to help gain an understanding of the depression of the 1930s, what are some of the facts that you would look for in your research?

6. Explain the basics of demand-pull inflation as presented in this chapter. Suggest some reasons why price increases might start occurring even before full employment was reached.

CHAPTER 10

THE MULTIPLIER, BUSINESS CYCLES, AND FISCAL POLICY

In chapter 9, we presented the basic tools of the modern theory of national income determination. In this chapter, we shall sharpen those tools and begin their application to important new topics. We shall consider the repetitive ups and downs of a modern industrial economy, usually known as the *business cycle*. We shall also introduce a topic that will be with us frequently in the future: government expenditure and tax policies—collectively referred to as a nation's *fiscal policy*.

But first we must develop a most important general tool of macroeconomic analysis.

THE MULTIPLIER

In the last chapter, we indicated that an increase in consumer or business investment spending would raise the level of national income. What we did not specify was how much the rise would be. This is what the *multiplier* tells us.

The multiplier tells us by how much an increase in spending will raise the equilibrium level of national income. If a $1 billion increase in spending leads to a $5 billion increase in national income, the multiplier = 5; if the increase is $2 billion, the multiplier = 2.

It is important to stress at the outset that the multiplier is a *general* tool applying to all categories of spending. So that there will be no mistake about the matter, we will first discuss the multiplier with respect to a change in private investment demand. Later in the chapter we will illustrate it again with respect to government expenditures and taxes.

In Figure 10–1, we are in a purely private economy and we wish to show the effects of a change in investment demand on equilibrium national income. Investment demand was originally $100 billion. But

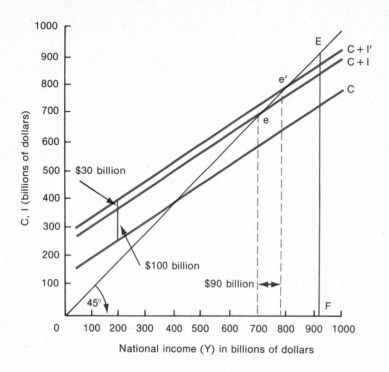

Figure 10–1. The Multiplier.

The principle of the multiplier is here illustrated in increased investment spending. A $30 billion increase in *I* leads to a $90 billion increase in *Y*.

now we imagine that some change has taken place (perhaps there has been an improvement in business confidence, owing to some international development, or perhaps there has been a new technological breakthrough, or perhaps the Federal Reserve System has lowered the interest rate), and planned investment spending has risen to $130 billion. The increase in investment is $30 billion, measured by the vertical distance between *C* + *I* and *C* + *I'*. The effect of this change has been to raise equilibrium national income from $700 billion to $790 billion, or by $90 billion. A $30 billion increase in investment spending has brought about a $90 billion increase in national income. The *multiplier,* then, is 3.

Why 3? The geometrically-minded reader will see that the size of this number depends very much on how steep the consumption function (*C* curve) is. Indeed, everyone can see this in a general way. Imagine that the *C* curve in our diagram were per-

fectly horizontal, i.e., running parallel to the *x*-axis. In this case, a rise in investment of $30 billion would raise the intersection with the 45° line by $30 billion only and, consequently, would raise the national income level by only $30 billion. Here the multiplier = 1. If we imagined the *C* curve as very steep, however, we would get the opposite effect. Suppose the curve ran almost parallel to the 45° line; then one can see that even slight changes in investment spending would raise national income by great multiples.

Thus, we can see that the size of the multiplier in general depends on the steepness of the *C* curve. But we can be more precise than this. Let us first state our conclusion and then offer two different demonstrations of its validity.

The conclusion is that the multiplier (m) will in ordinary circumstances obey the following rule:

$$m = \frac{1}{1 - MPC}$$

where MPC refers to the *marginal propensity to consume* or, geometrically, the *slope* of the consumption function.

The meaning of this conclusion can be elaborated with reference to Figure 10–2, where we have blown up a small fragment of the CC curve. The marginal propensity to consume is defined as that part of an extra dollar of income that consumers will wish to spend on consumption. In Figure 10–2 we give an example in which a $1 increase in income increases consumption demand by 67¢, roughly 2/3. The same result would be obtained if the numbers were not written in, but we simply measured distance BC and divided it by distance AC. This term BC/AC is the slope of the CC line, meaning that the marginal propensity to consume is the slope of the consumption function. The multiplier in this example can be worked out as follows:

$$m = \frac{1}{1 - MPC} = \frac{1}{1 - \dfrac{BC}{AC}} = \frac{1}{1 - \dfrac{2}{3}} = 3$$

Another way of stating the same conclusion would be in terms of the *marginal propensity to save* (MPS). The MPS is defined as the part of an extra dollar of income that consumers wish to save. Since the extra dollar of income will be either saved or spent on consumption,

$$MPS = 1 - MPC \text{ (by definition)}$$

This means that we could, if we wished, rewrite the multiplier very simply as:

$$m = \frac{1}{MPS}$$

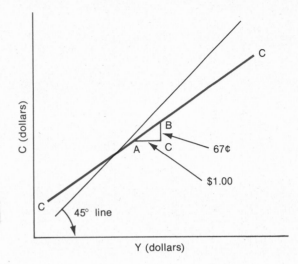

Figure 10–2. The Marginal Propensity to Consume.

The marginal propensity to consume (MPC) is equal to the slope of the consumption function or *BC/AC*. In this case, MPC = 67/100 or 2/3.

What we have stated here (but have yet not proved) is that the multiplier in our simplified private economy will be equal to the reciprocal of the marginal propensity to save, or, equivalently,

$$\frac{1}{1 - MPC}.$$

When we ask *why* this is so, we come to the matter of proof. Let us show in two different ways why the multiplier will follow this rule.

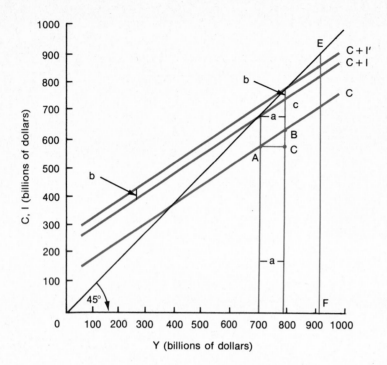

Figure 10–3.

The first is a geometrical demonstration:

Figure 10–3 is simply Figure 10–1 with some additional notation. Say that we have an increase in investment of the amount b. *The diagram tells us that this leads to an increase in national income of the amount* a. *By definition, then, the multiplier is:*

$$(1) \qquad m = \frac{a}{b}$$

Our 45° line tells us that a = b + c; *hence equation (1) can be rewritten:*

$$(2) \qquad m = \frac{a}{a - c} = \frac{1}{1 - \dfrac{c}{a}}$$

The marginal propensity to consume (MPC), we know, is measured by the slope of the C curve, or, MPC = BC/AC. Since the investment curves are drawn parallel to the C curve, we can also say that MPC = c/a. Substituting for c/a in equation (2), we get:

$$(3) \qquad m = \frac{1}{1 - MPC}$$

And this was what we set out to show.

This geometrical demonstration is useful enough, but it gives us little insight into the economic logic of what is going on. The second demonstration, which we shall take up now, will make this clearer. For it is based on observing what happens at each stage of the game as the increase in investment or other expenditure makes its way through the economy. The *economics* of what happens is essentially this: When businessmen decide to invest in a new factory, they buy products (iron, steel, machinery, etc.) from other people, thus creating *income* for these people. This is in the first stage. But now these people have more income than before, and *they* will want to spend more on consumption. So in the second stage, consumption spending increases. *But not by the whole amount of the increase in income.* That is to say, they will spend part, but will also save part. In particular, the marginal propensity to consume tells us what fraction of this extra income they will want to spend. But then we go on to a third stage. The additional consumer spending (on food, shoes, etc.) creates more income for the producers of food, shoes, and other consumers' goods. This income, in turn, will also be spent in part (determined by the MPC) on consumption. The process repeats itself indefinitely and, at each new stage, further income (though in increasingly smaller amounts) is added to national income.

Our second demonstration of the theory of the multiplier simply involves adding together all these successive rounds of additionally created income:

Let us suppose that there is a $100 increase in investment spending, and that the MPC = 2/3. The amount of income created at each stage will be as follows (to the nearest dollar):

Stage 1: $100 (the original added investment)
Stage 2:   2/3 ($100) = $67   (MPC × $100)
Stage 3:   2/3 ($67) = $44   [(MPC)^2 × $100]
Stage 4:   2/3 ($44) = $30   [(MPC)^3 × $100]
Stage 5:   2/3 ($30) = $20   [(MPC)^4 × $100]
. . . .
Stage n+1:   (2/3)^n($100)   [(MPC)^n × $100]

The total of all these stages of added income will be the increase in the equilibrium level of national income. If we use the term ΔY to signify the total increase in national income, then:

(1) $\Delta Y = \$100 + \$67 + \$44 + \$30 + \$20 + \ldots$
or
(2) $\Delta Y = \$100 [1 + 2/3 + (2/3)^2 + (2/3)^3 + (2/3)^4 + \ldots + (2/3)^n + \ldots]$

or, most generally, where ΔI is the added investment.

(3) $\Delta Y = \Delta I (1 + MPC + MPC^2 + MPC^3 + MPC^4 + \ldots + MPC^n + \ldots)$

Since the multiplier is equal to ΔY/ΔI, we get:

(4) $m = (1 + MPC + MPC^2 + MPC^3 + MPC^4 \ldots + MPC^n + \ldots)$

Knowing that MPC is less than 1, we can conclude from algebra that[1]

(5) $$m = \frac{1}{1 - MPC}$$

Which again is what we set out to prove.[2]

Both these demonstrations prove the same point about the multiplier, but the second is perhaps more vivid in bringing out the economic aspect of what is going on. We must always imagine the successive rounds of expenditures and incomes created by any new act of spending. A businessman invests in an additional typewriter. This creates income for a seller of typewriters, who spends part of his increased income in buying a pair of shoes. This creates income for the producer of shoes, who now buys himself an umbrella. And on and on and on, the amounts getting smaller and smaller each time, as part of the added income leaks into added savings. Indeed, it will be precisely when savings in total have increased by the same amount as business investment that the process finally ends. This the reader can verify by looking at Figure 10–1 again. Notice that, at the new equilibrium level of national income, saving, like investment, has increased by $30 billion.

---

1.   The general formula, where $a < 1$, is:

$$1 + a + a^2 + a^3 + \ldots + a^n + \ldots = \frac{1}{1 - a}$$

2.   We are dealing here with what is sometimes called the *instantaneous multiplier.* As every reader will recognize, it would normally take a considerable amount of time for all these successive stages of spending and income creation to occur. In more advanced treatments, the multiplier is often worked out over time in what is sometimes called *period analysis.*

BUSINESS CYCLES: PAST AND PRESENT

As we shall see in a moment, the multiplier concept can help us to understand an important feature of industrial society: the *business cycle*. First, a few descriptive comments.

In the previous chapter, we discussed ups and downs of business activity (national income, employment, investment, etc.) without, however, trying to relate these movements to each other in any kind of pattern. The concept of a business cycle implies certain recurrent features in these ups and downs. There are common phases in these cycles that repeat themselves over time. There is a cumulative expansion process rising up to a "peak" that, shortly thereafter, gives way to a cumulative contraction process. This contraction process in due course reaches bottom—the "trough" of the cycle—after which forces for recovery, and renewed expansion, assert themselves. These expansions and contractions (or recessions) are exhibited in a whole host of different statistical series. There are similar swings in employment, money and credit, investment and output, and stock market and commodity price data. In some cases, these statistical series tend to "lead" (turn down just before the peak and turn up just before the trough) the cycle; in other cases, they "lag" behind; in still other cases they are "coincident."[3]

Historically speaking, the concept of a business cycle in the United States and most other industrial nations has won wide support among economists. Figure 10–4 suggests that these recurrent ups and downs of business activity go back to the pre-Civil War period. Similar charts could be prepared for other

---

3.   In the appendix to this chapter, we present a reading by Arthur Burns describing the phases of the cycle in more detail. Figure 1 (p. 246) indicates some important *leading indicators*.

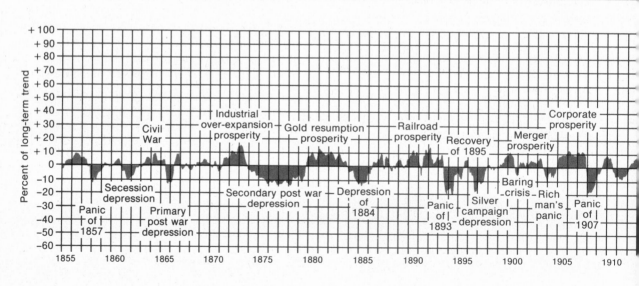

Figure 10–4. A Century of U.S. Business Cycles.

Adapted from "American Business Activity From 1790 To Today," by The Cleveland Trust Company. Reprinted by permission.

economically advanced countries—England, Germany, Canada, Japan, etc.

Still, this chart, with the wide amplitude it suggests in our historic prosperities and depressions, raises a number of important questions about the business cycle phenomenon.[4]

1. Just how regular are business cycles? Obviously, they are not completely regular. Some expansions are longer than others. Some contractions are

---

4. Even the drawing of a chart like Figure 10–4 raises a number of questions. One of the most important of these is the validity of abstracting from the long-run trend in presenting business cycle fluctuations. Business activity in Figure 10–4 is presented as occurring around a horizontal line. In fact, of course, GNP, employment, investment, etc. were all expanding over this century. If, like Schumpeter, you believe that the cycle is an incident of the growth-process—i.e. that cycles are the *form* that industrial growth takes—then you will object strenuously to this procedure.

shorter. Some peaks are higher, some troughs deeper, etc. How, after all, are we to compare the Great Depression of the 1930s with the Panic of 1907? These may be of one family but the sibling differences are clearly enormous. The difficulty of timing cycles is, in turn, a reflection of the fact that very probably more than one kind of cycle is involved. If we have a number of overlapping cycles of different lengths, this would account for a certain amount of apparent irregularity in the data and also might explain why certain recessions are, say, milder than others. (For example, if a downturn of one cycle overlaps with the expansion of another cycle, this might lead to a gentle recession as opposed to a major depression).

Various economists have suggested that three and perhaps four cycles may be involved: (a) a minor cycle of forty months or so largely reflective of increases and decreases of business inventories; (b) the major, or ordinary business cycle, reflecting a whole series of different indices and lasting histori-

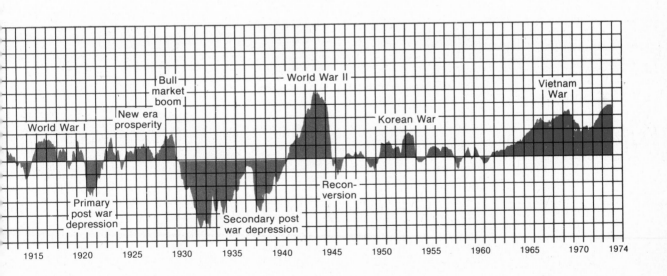

cally an average of eight or nine years; (c) a construction or Kuznets cycle of perhaps double or more the length of the major business cycle, being particularly apparent in the building construction trades; and, finally, and more dubiously, (d) long waves of 50 years or more whose upswings—so Schumpeter thought—were associated with periods of major innovations (e.g., the Industrial Revolution, the advent of the railroads, the coming of electricity and the automobile, etc.).

2. How much of the business cycle is caused by external shocks and how much by internal mechanisms?

The degree of regularity (or periodicity) of the cycle is further complicated by the fact that external events—especially wars—are so obviously capable of throwing off the rhythm of a regular cycle, even if we clearly had one. Indeed, the question invariably arises of the relation of external (sometimes called *exogenous*) factors to internal (*endogenous*) factors in the causation of the cycle. Possible views could range from a belief that the ups and downs of Figure 10–4 are simply reflections of wars, gold rushes, good and bad weather (totally exogenous) to an opinion that the whole mechanism is built into industrial society, making, for example, wars and gold rushes themselves a function of the cyclical behavior of the economy (a completely endogenous theory). An intermediate theory might be that shocks to the system do often come from the outside and that they affect the economy, but that the economy itself is so constructed that it *reacts to* these shocks in a cyclical way.

We cannot settle these complicated issues here. Suffice it to say that most economists tend to agree that, historically, the structure of the economy has tended to reinforce cyclical behavior in a number of ways. Without denying the importance of huge phenomena like World Wars I and II, these economists would say that there are also certain built-in tendencies for expansions to be cumulative, for prosperities to create conditions which tend to lead to down-turns, for cumulative downward forces to develop, and for these situations, in turn, to lead to their own correc-

tives. External factors greatly intensified, most observers would say, but did not create the historical business cycle.

3. Is the concept of the business cycle obsolete?

At the same time that the majority of economists were agreeing on the existence of important internal mechanisms in the historic business cycle, they would also very probably agree that those mechanisms have changed considerably in the post-World War II period. At least one important new "external" factor has made its appearance in this period: the existence of governments that are (a) committed to ironing out the worst features of the business cycle, and (b) armed with important new—if not perfect—knowledge of the macroeconomic functioning of a modern economy. This raises the question of whether we really *have* a business cycle in the United States at the present time. Is the whole idea an anachronism?

Most economists would probably shy away from this strong a conclusion, although again, there is difference of opinion. Figure 10–5 suggests that the various indicators of economic activity still show fluctuations in a reasonably coherent pattern. There have been five recessions in the period covered by this diagram. However, the pattern is somewhat different from our historical experience. The general degree of prosperity in the post-World War II world took many economists rather by surprise (especially since many of them were raised in the period of the Great Depression). An idea that has developed in recent years is that, while a form of the cycle is still with us, this form has altered. In particular, we should think of the cycle not in the classical sense of ups and downs of economic activity but rather in terms of "alternations of periods of fast growth with periods of slow growth."[5] This remains a tentative notion (it could be shot down by a serious recession), but it does at least reaffirm the importance economists still attach to the cyclic concept.

---

5. See Ilse Mintz, "Dating American Growth Cycles," in Victor Zarnowitz, ed. *The Business Cycle Today*, 50th Anniversary Colloquium, I, National Bureau of Economic Research, Columbia University Press, 1972, p. 39.

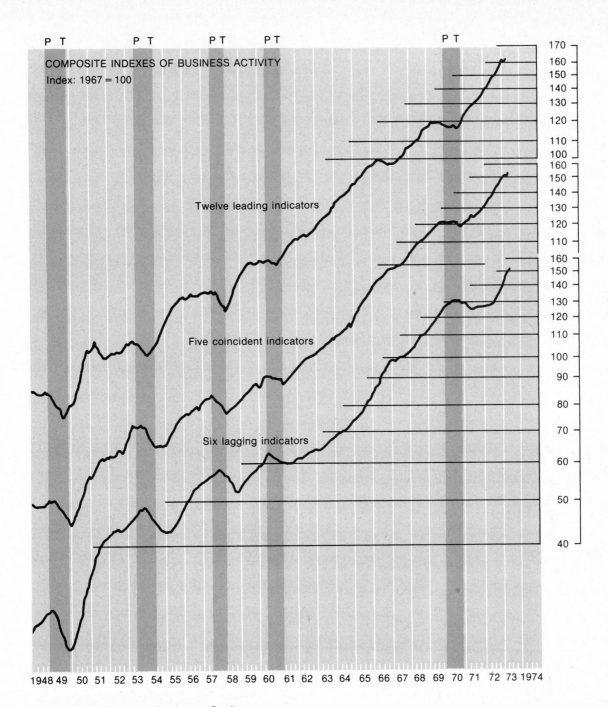

Figure 10–5. Postwar Business Cycles.

A number of indicators, some of which lead, some of
which lag behind, and some of which coincide with
business peaks (P) and troughs (T) suggest continued fluctuation in the postwar American economy.

But the pattern may be different: note, for example,
the long expansion from 1961 to 1969.

Adapted from *Business Conditions Digest.* June 1973. U.S.
Department of Commerce, Bureau of Economic Analysis.
Reprinted by permission.

THE MULTIPLIER AND
THE BUSINESS CYCLE

Our special interest in the business cycle in this chapter is that it enables us to apply our new tool of macroeconomic analysis. A great majority of theories of the business cycle involve the use of the multiplier principle.

The fundamental reason for this is that the multiplier helps explain cumulative movements of the economy either upward or downward; it does so because, as its name implies, movements in any direction tend to have a *multiplied* impact. An increase of $1 billion in investment spending tends to give rise not to a $1 billion increase but to a $3 or $4 or $5 billion increase in national income.

The multiplier itself, of course, is not sufficient to explain so complicated a phenomenon as the business cycle. But even at this stage of our knowledge of national income determination, we can see how it might be combined with other economic hypotheses to give us real clues as to how cyclical behavior originates. Let us, for example, take a fairly simple idea about investment spending, often referred to in business cycle analyses. The idea is that since investment (whether in machines, buildings, or inventories of goods in stock) represents an *increase* in our capital stock, it will be undertaken by businessmen primarily in response to an *increase* in the level of GNP. Business firms, in this view, will try to keep their stock of capital and their output in some kind of relatively fixed relationship.[6]

Now this principle—sometimes called the *acceleration principle* because, as we shall see below, it can speed up a change in any particular direction—can be combined with our multiplier to provide a first

approximation view of how an "ideal" business cycle might work. Briefly:

Suppose that, for whatever reason (it could be one of Schumpeter's innovations), business investment increases just slightly. What will happen? The multiplier guarantees us that this increase in investment will lead to a substantial increase in GNP. But an increase in GNP is precisely what will lead to a further increase in investment. A cumulative process of expansion is now under way. Multiplied increases in national income give rise to further increases in investment, which in turn give rise to still further multiplied increases in national income.

And the same logic applies to contractions or recessions. Let investment fall, and this will cause a multiplied decrease in national income. But when total output is decreasing, businessmen will be reducing their investment and indeed disinvesting; i.e., they will reduce their inventories (remember the minor cycle) and/or let machines and buildings wear out without proper replacement. Thus, we have forces making for cumulative downturns as well as cumulative expansions.

But what of "peaks" and "troughs"? Why don't these cumulative expansions and contractions go on forever? Why do they turn around? Several explanations are possible, but one might go like this:

The upward expansion can't go on indefinitely, because we run out of labor and other factors of production to keep output growing so rapidly. As we near full employment, the rate of increase of GNP has to slow down. But a slowing down of the increase in total output is enough (by the acceleration principle) to bring an actual decline in investment. This decline then leads, through the multiplier, to a decline in GNP, and we start downward. In other words, a slowdown of the expansion may be enough to turn it into an actual decline. This would explain why the expansion peaks, and then turns into a recession.

By the same logic, a slowing down of the contraction might lead to an upward turnabout. This would explain the trough of the cycle and the subsequent

---

6.   The notion here is one of at least short-run constancy in what is called the *capital/output ratio*. We shall return to this matter toward the end of Part Two, especially p. 408.

recovery. Why might the contraction begin to slow down after a while? There are many possible reasons. Consumers, after a point, might resist any further decreases in their consumption levels (this would reduce the MPC and the multiplier). Similarly, businessmen might find it harder to disinvest after a time. For example, after inventories are reduced to virtually nothing, there is no further way one can disinvest in inventories. Such factors might explain a slowdown in the rate of decline of GNP. And, with the powerful multiplier and accelerator behind us, that would be sufficient to get an actual expansion going again.

Thus we see how our new tool of national income analysis can be combined with other economic insights to explain so complicated a matter as the business cycle. The multiplier has a very wide range of reference over the whole area of modern macroeconomics.

INTRODUCING GOVERNMENTAL EXPENDITURES: *G*

And this range includes the actions of government. To show that the multiplier applies not only to investment (*I*) and consumption (*C*), we must now bring a third major component into our previously private economy: government (*G*). This will be simply an introduction to a topic that will engage our attention again and again.[7] To make the analysis as straightforward as possible, we shall deal separately with government expenditures and government taxation, and then combine them.

We begin, then, with government expenditures. In a mixed economy, the government, along with households and private business investors, is purchasing goods and services. What will the effect of this government demand be?

---

7. See especially chapter 12 for the development of various concepts introduced in the remainder of this chapter.

The fundamental answer is that this demand will have precisely the same effect as any other demand. To the business firm producing, say, automobiles and trucks, it makes no essential difference whether the buyers are consumers, other business firms, or the United States government. In each case, the added demand means added sales and added profits.

Since this government demand is to be treated in the same general way as any other demand, we can represent it in our diagram by simply adding it on to our *C* + *I* curve, just as, earlier, we added investment spending to our consumption function. Let us pull a number out of the hat. Suppose that in our hypothetical economy, government expenditures for goods and services are running at $50 billion a year. Neglecting the tax side, what will happen?

The answer is given in Figure 10–6, where $50 billion of *G* has been added vertically to the *C* + *I* curves. The consequence is that the equilibrium level of national income has been changed. Before, the equilibrium was at $700 billion; now it is where the *C* + *I* + *G* curve intersects the 45° line, or at $850 billion. As a result of governmental expenditures, this particular economy is much closer to full-employment national income than before.

In its most primitive and fundamental form, this is the justification for those who argue that the government ought to act to bring the economy as near as possible to the full-employment level.

We can also see that the multiplier has come into play exactly as in our earlier case of investment spending. $50 billion of *G* has led to a $150 billion increase in national income; with an MPC of 2/3, the multiplier is again 3. Since we are adding *G* to our *C* + *I* curve in precisely the same way we added *I* to the *C* curve, this is very much what we would expect.

The multiplier also allows us to say a further word about the effect of government expenditures. Suppose our economy is not yet at full employment and we wish to know by how much governmental expenditures would have to be increased (assuming no change in tax revenues) to bring us to the full-

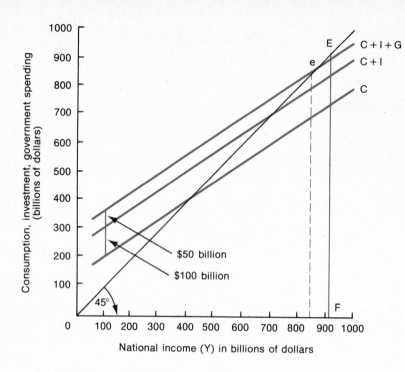

Figure 10–6. Adding Government Expenditures.

In this diagram, we add government expenditures of $50 billion and get an expansion of national income from $700 billion (without *G*) to $850 billion (with *G*). We have not, however, taken taxes into account at this point in the argument.

employment level. The needed change in *G* can easily be shown graphically. Figure 10–7 is identical to Figure 10–6, except that we have added *G'* to represent the increased government expenditures necessary to bring us to full-employment national income.

What the multiplier tells us in this case is how much the increase in governmental expenditures will have to be in numerical terms. Before *G'* was added, equilibrium national income was $850 billion. We wish to raise national income to the full-employment level, which is $910 billion. The MPC in this figure, as before, is 2/3 and the multiplier is 3.

We can find our answer, then, simply by dividing the desired increase in national income, $60 billion, by 3. This gives us $20 billion, the amount by which we shall have to increase government expenditures if we wish to bring national income to the full-employment level.

GENERAL EFFECTS OF TAXATION—*T*

The preceding discussion has necessarily had an air of incompleteness. We have been discussing government expenditures without discussing government revenues. But we all know that the government taxes as well as spends. What can we say in a general way about the effects of tax policy on aggregate demand and equilibrium national income?

There are many different kinds of taxes, direct or indirect, taxes falling mainly on consumers or mainly on corporations, progressive or regressive taxes, taxes emanating from the federal, state, or local governments, and so on. In future chapters, we shall consider some of the consequences of this variety of forms of taxation. But for the moment, to keep the argument clearly in mind, we must simplify as much as possible. Let us suppose that the particular taxes that are levied fall entirely on the incomes of consumers. The government levies a tax of $30 billion

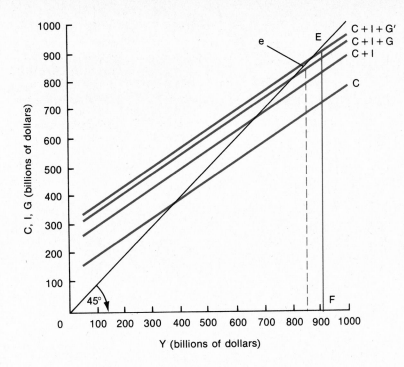

Figure 10–7.

In this diagram we have sufficiently raised government expenditures *(G)* to bring us to an equilibrium level of national income at full employment. (Again, assuming no change in tax revenues.)

on consumers in the economy. What effect will this have?

What we must do now is to reverse our field—or almost reverse it. *G* added demand, but *T* takes away income that might have added to demand. The effect of *T*, considered in isolation, then, is to reduce aggregate demand and hence to put a downward pressure on the economy.

The introduction of a $30 billion tax will lower equilibrium national income. Like government expenditures, taxation will have its effect magnified by the multiplier, but not in quite the same way. This is why we must "almost reverse" our field. There is a certain asymmetry in the effects of *G* and *T*. In particular, the multiplied downward effect of $1 of taxes is somewhat less than the multiplied upward effect of $1 of government expenditures.

To see why this is so, let us show how taxes affect the position of the consumption function in our case of a $30 billion levy. Figure 10–8 indicates, as we would expect, that the consumption schedule is shifted downward by the impact of taxes. At a national income of $600 billion, consumers now have at their disposal only the same amount of income that they previously had at a national income of $570 billion, the difference being the amount of the tax. Hence, their consumption demand at $600 billion will now be the same as it was previously at $570, or $513 billion. This is reflected graphically by moving horizontally to the right by the amount of *T* ($30 billion). (The reader should repeat this argument for other points on the consumption function; for example, the shift between $430 billion and $400 billion national incomes.) The after-tax consumption function (*C'C'*), then, is simply the original consumption function, (*CC*) shifted horizontally to the right by $30 billion.

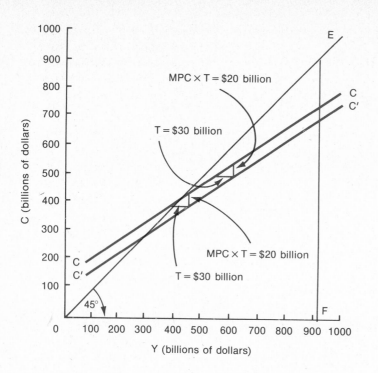

Figure 10–8. Effect of Taxes on Consumption.

A tax on consumers lowers the consumption function, but not by the full amount of the tax. If the MPC=2/3 and the tax is $30 billion, the CC curve will shift downward by 2/3×$30 billion (=$20 billion).

The effect of this shift on equilibrium national income is determined, however, not by rightward movements but by the *downward* shift of the schedule. It is the height of the C + I + G line that ultimately determines where our equilibrium will be. Now this downward shift is not $30 billion, but $20 billion. More generally, it is equal to the MPC × T. This is easily seen in graphical terms, since the little triangles we have drawn at $600 and $430 billion represent the slope of the consumption function—the MPC—and if the horizontal side of the triangle is $30 billion, the vertical side must be $20 billion. The vertical side, of course, tells us how much the function has shifted downward.

To determine the effect of T on national income, we take this $20 billion and then multiply it by the same factor we used in the case of G; i.e., 3. The downward effect of $30 billion of T, therefore, will be $60 billion. This would be in contrast to the upward effect of an equal $30 billion of G, which would lead to a $90 billion increase in national income. We use the same factor (3) in each case, but we use a different starting point: $20 billion in the case of taxes, $30 billion in the case of an equivalent increase in government expenditures.

Why this asymmetry? The economic logic behind these differential effects can best be seen at the very first point of impact of G or T. When the government spends $1 to purchase some stationery for one of its offices, it has created in that very first step an added output (or income) of $1. This income then goes the rounds of consumption and saving, according to the multiplier principle. Now when the government taxes $1, it lowers consumption demand and income immediately, but not by the full $1. The consumer, had he not been taxed, would have *saved* part of this $1; in our case, he would have saved 33¢. This means that the initial impact of $1 taxes is to cut consumption demand not by $1 but by 67¢. And this explains why the total effect of a $30 billion tax increase is only 2/3 as great as an equivalent increase in government expenditures ($60 billion as opposed to $90 billion).[8]

G AND *T* COMBINED—DIFFERENT ROUTES TO MACROSTABILITY

We are now in a position to combine the effects of government expenditures and taxes and, even more important, to make some significant general comments about different kinds of fiscal policies.

Figure 10–9 represents a capsule summary of the points we have been making about the effects of government on the equilibrium level of national income. In Figure 10–9, (a) shows the purely private economy of the previous chapter; (b) introduces $30 billion of *G* without taxes; (c) includes $30 billion of *G* and $30 billion of *T*. This third picture shows us the effects of government when there is a balanced budget.

---

8. When *G* and *T* are equal, we have a balanced budget in the government. The principle according to which national income will expand when there are equal increases of *G* and *T* is sometimes called the *balanced budget multiplier*. The size of this multiplier will depend very much on the kinds of taxes levied and expenditures undertaken. In our simplified case, however, the *balanced budget multiplier* will be 1. That is, an equal increase of *G* and *T* (in our case $30 billion) will lead to an increase of national income of $30 billion. This is essentially because the effects of *G* and *T* are the same, except that *G* has one extra round of impact—the very first—and in this first round the full amount of the government expenditures ($30 billion) is added to national income. Afterwards, the process cancels out as the effects of *G* and *T* match each other exactly.

Now there are four main fiscal approaches an economy can use when it faces problems of unemployment and below potential national income. We can now state some of the advantages and disadvantages of these different approaches.

1. **Laissez-faire or modified laissez-faire.** The most ancient approach is for the government to do nothing (always assuming, of course, some modest—or not-so-modest—role of government in defense, education, and the like). The disadvantages of this approach are quite obvious; and after the Great Depression of the 1930s, these disadvantages seem decisive to most economists. For the laissez-faire approach runs the risk of leaving the economy, as in Figure 10–9 (a), with substantial mass unemployment and unutilized productive capacity. The few economists who still support this view in anything like its pure form might argue either (a) that private recuperative forces are much stronger than might be imagined and that, consequently, recoveries will proceed fairly quickly along natural lines; or (b) that unemployment is not too high a price to pay to avoid the encroachments of government on the private sector, or to fight inflationary price increases; or (c) that government policies, either because of political pressures or lack of information or bad timing, will not be as effective as pure theory supposes them and, indeed, may often make things worse, rather than better; or (d) that fiscal policy is basically ineffective, since it is the supply of money that crucially determines the health of the economy,[9] or, finally, (e) that no *discretionary* fiscal policy be used but that the job be left to the *automatic stabilizers* that already exist in the economy.

This last point, (e), explains why we called this first approach laissez-faire or *modified* laissez-faire. For some economists (though not many, even with this qualification) might say that although the government has a role to play in stabilizing the economy, it can fulfill this role without taking any direct or conscious action towards this end. The reason: so

---

9. For this last position, the position taken by some "monetarists," see p. 305.

many government programs automatically achieve these stabilizing effects. When national income and employment go down, individual and corporate income tax receipts go down, unemployment compensation payments go up, farm subsidies go up, and so on. A recession automatically restores purchasing power to the private economy; hence, it moderates the fall in income and brings the economy closer to full employment than otherwise would have been the case.

The disadvantage of the modified laissez-faire approach is suggested by the word "closer" in the last sentence. For although there is no doubt that automatic stabilizers *help* in alleviating depressed conditions, there is no evidence that they can solve them completely, or even in great part.

2. Increase government expenditures. The main macroeconomic advantage of an unmatched increase in government expenditures as a way of raising national income in a time of slump is that a dollar's worth of effort, so to speak, gives the maximum possible effect. In Fig. 10–9 (b), $30 billion of G alone raises national income by $90 billion. This is a greater impact than will result from any other policy. The disadvantages of this approach will be judged differently by different economists. The policy will ordinarily mean an expansion of the governmental national debt and will involve a greater impact of the government on the allocation of the resources of the economy. Some economists disapprove in varying degrees of both features. Other economists argue that the effects of an increased national debt may not be so harmful as generally supposed and that

Figure 10–9. Various Approaches to a Below-Capacity National Income.

(a)

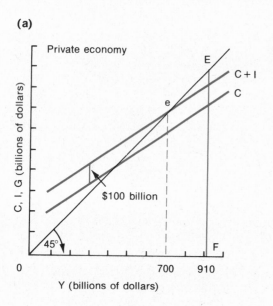

(b)

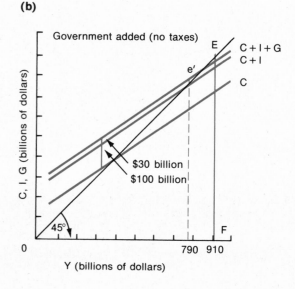

In (a), the problem is that, without government intervention, the private economy may not generate enough demand to produce full employment income.

In (b), added *G* has increased national income by $90 billion.

there are advantages in a greater public, as opposed to private, allocation of resources in an economy such as ours.

3. Reduce taxes. This policy also increases the national debt (assuming that the government continues its spending unchanged), and it has the disadvantage that for a given increase in the debt, it has slightly less impact on national income than an equivalent expansion of government spending. This is because of the asymmetrical effect of T and G that we have already discussed. A reduction of taxes of $30 billion in our hypothetical economy will raise national income by $60 billion instead of by $90 billion. Another way of putting this is to say that the size of the increase in the national public debt necessary to raise national income to the full-employment level will be greater by this method than by the route of increased government spending. On the other hand, this method restores purchasing power to the private sector and therefore gives relatively greater private, as opposed to public, control over the allocation of resources in the economy.

4. Increase G and T equally. The final basic method of using fiscal policy to cure macroeconomic ills in a depression is to expand government expenditures and taxes by the same amount. Such an expansion will lead to some expansion in the economy, although each step forward (increased government demand) is partially offset by a step backward (decreased private demand because of higher taxes). Figure 10–9 (c) shows that a combined increase of $30

(c)

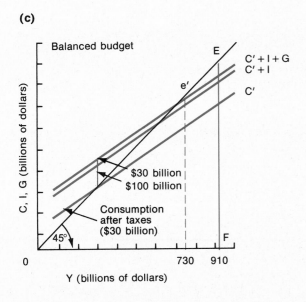

The fourth alternative—reducing taxes—can be assessed by comparing figures (b) and (c). If $30 billion in taxes from (c) are removed, then we get (b). This $30 billion tax reduction would raise national income from $730 to $790 billion, or $60 billion. (We use an MPC=2/3, throughout.)

In (c), the same amount of *G, but now matched by equal taxes,* has raised national income by a lesser amount, $30 billion.

billion in both *G* and *T* will lead to an increase of $30 billion in national income. If we assume that the government has definitely been given the responsibility of maintaining full employment in the economy, then this approach maximizes the degree of public intervention in the economy. If the total required increase in national income is $180 billion, then the increase in governmental expenditures on this approach will have to be equal to that gap, or $180 billion. This would contrast with an increase in *G* unmatched by taxes, which would have to be only 1/3 of the gap, or $60 billion. Thus, a balanced budget approach involves, almost paradoxically, the highest level of governmental expenditure to achieve a given rise in national income. But then, of course, it involves no increase in the public debt.

These four approaches by no means exhaust all the steps the government might take (or not take) to deal with a problem of unemployment in the economy as a whole. There are any number of variants of tax and expenditure policies that could be used to reduce unemployment, or to achieve other objectives—say, a more equitable income distribution or a higher rate of growth—simultaneously. We must also consider the implications of increases or decreases in the national debt. These matters will be subjects for chapters later in this book.

There is one topic we must attend to now, however. This is the subject of *monetary policy*. For the government clearly can influence the national economy not only through the fiscal measures we have been discussing but also by measures designed to affect the supply of money and the interest rate in the economy. Indeed, quite apart from the issue of governmental policy, we have reached the point in our argument where we must show explicitly how ''money'' fits into the workings of the economy in the aggregate. When we do this, in the next chapter, we will have completed the basic structure of the theory of national income determination.

SUMMARY

In this chapter we have considerably expanded our treatment of national income determination. We have introduced an important general tool of macroeconomics: the *multiplier*. The multiplier tells us by how much an increase in any kind of spending (consumption, investment, government) will raise the equilibrium level of national income. The size of the multiplier in a simplified economy is determined by the *marginal propensity to consume,* or the fraction of an extra dollar of income that consumers will spend on consumption. (The *marginal propensity to save,* by contrast, is the fraction of that extra dollar that consumers will be willing to save, or MPS = 1 − MPC.) The formula for the multiplier is:

$$m = \frac{1}{1 - MPC}$$

or, alternatively,

$$m = \frac{1}{MPS}$$

The economic logic behind multiple expansions of national income as spending expands centers on the fact that each stage of spending creates further incomes that, in their turn, lead to further spending, further income creation, further spending, and so on. Each time, however, the amounts added to income are less because part of the income is leaked into extra savings.

With the multiplier concept we are much better able to understand an important phenomenon, the *business cycle*. Historically, there have been recurrent ups and downs of business conditions in the United States and other industrial nations that seem to show some common features, particularly periods of cumulative expansion leading to ''peaks,'' which are followed by cumulative contractions leading to ''troughs'' and then recovery. Because of the existence of several different kinds of cycle, because of important external effects like wars, and because of government stabilization efforts in the post-war world, the business cycle is not a perfectly regular phenomenon. However, most economists do believe that certain internal (endogenous) mechanisms in our economy tend to give business conditions a cyclical character. The multiplier, along with other principles such as the *accelerator,* helps us to understand not only the cumulative nature of such expansions and contractions, but also possible reasons for the turning-points at the peak and trough.

The multiplier concept also enables us to show what the effects of government expenditure and tax policies (collectively, *fiscal policy*) may be under certain simple circumstances:

1. An expansion of government expenditures (*G*) unmatched by an expansion of taxes would lead to a fully multiplied increase in national income.

2. An increase of taxes (*T*) unmatched by *G* would lead to a multiplied decrease in national income, though the total effect would be somewhat less than under (1) because, in the first round, taxes cut down spending by less than the full amount of the tax. This, in turn, derives from the fact that part of the income taxed away would have been saved anyway.

3. An equal increase of *G* and *T* will lead to some expansion of national income, but less than under an equivalent expansion of *G* or reduction of *T* taken singly. Under certain simplified conditions, an equal expansion of *G* and *T* would lead to an expansion of national income by the same amount (i.e., the multiplier in this case is 1).

In approaching the problem of underemployment, or below potential GNP, in an economy, the government may decide on many different courses; e.g., doing nothing, raising expenditures, cutting taxes, or raising both expenditures and taxes. The judgment about which policy is best to pursue in any given circumstance will be influenced by a host of considerations including confidence in the recuperative power of the private sector, desire to expand or contract the area of public intervention in the allocation of resources, one's views on the dangers of the public "national debt," one's faith in automatic stabilizers, and/or one's opinions as to the relative merits of fiscal versus monetary policy (to be discussed in chapter 11).

IMPORTANT TERMS TO REMEMBER

The Multiplier
Marginal Propensity to Consume (MPC)
Marginal Propensity to Save (MPS)
$$m = \frac{1}{1 - \text{MPC}} = \frac{1}{\text{MPS}}$$
Business Cycle
Exogenous/Endogenous Factors
Acceleration Principle
Disinvestment
Fiscal Policy
Multiplier Effects of Government Expenditures
Multiplier Effects of Taxes
Balanced Budget Multiplier
Discretionary Fiscal Policy
Automatic Stabilizers

QUESTIONS FOR DISCUSSION

1. Imagine that there is a change in tastes resulting in an upward shift of the consumption function by $20 billion at each level of national income. Show how this could lead to an increase of $60 billion in national income if the MPC is 2/3. How much would the increase in national income be if the MPC were 4/5? 1/2? 9/10?

2. Our analysis in this chapter involved a number of simplifying assumptions. Some of the complications that may arise in reality are:

(a) The MPC falls as the level of national income rises.

(b) Investment is not a fixed amount but increases as the level of national income increases.

(c) Tax revenues of the federal government increase automatically (in the absence of any change in the tax structure) with any increase in national income.

In each case, explain why these complications may arise. Then show what the general effect of each complication would be on the graphs we have been using in this chapter. Finally, indicate the ways in which we would have to modify our multiplier analysis to take these effects into account.

3. Marx predicted crises of ever increasing magnitude in capitalist countries. How does this prediction jibe with our experience with the business cycle over the twentieth century? Would your answer possibly have been different if you were responding in 1939?

4. What is the accelerator principle? Explain how it might combine with the multiplier to account for cyclical activity in an industrial economy.

5. *Discretionary fiscal policy* occurs when the government alters its tax and expenditure patterns to affect the overall stability of the economy. But we have said that there are also certain *automatic stabilizers* that work in the right direction even in the absence of any discretionary policy moves. The fact that federal income tax receipts automatically rise and fall with rises and falls in national income (see question 2c) is one such stabilizer. Name a number of other government programs that would be likely to have the effect of stabilizing the economy in this automatic way.

6. Government fiscal policy to combat the business cycle might require deficits $(G>T)$ during contractions and surpluses $(T>G)$ during expansions. Might it possibly require deficits (though of different magnitudes) in *both* periods? Surpluses in both periods? Explain your answers.

APPENDIX 10:
PHASES OF
THE BUSINESS CYCLE

Some students may want a more detailed description of the course of a characteristic business cycle than has been conveyed in our brief survey in the foregoing chapter. The amount of detail possible is enormous, because the business cycle affects so many different kinds of economic activities. In Figure 1, for example, we have selected just a few of the many possible "leading indicators" that often anticipate business cycle activity. Note that these indicators include such diverse data as employment, investment orders, consumer credit, stock market figures, and so on. In short, virtually all areas of economic activity—"real" or "monetary"—are affected.

Under these circumstances, understanding involves careful selectivity, which, in turn, requires long familiarity with business cycle data. Such experience is notably displayed by Arthur F. Burns, who has been a major contributor to the analysis of cycles for over forty years. In the following excerpts, he gives an account of some of the salient features of the different phases of the business cycle.

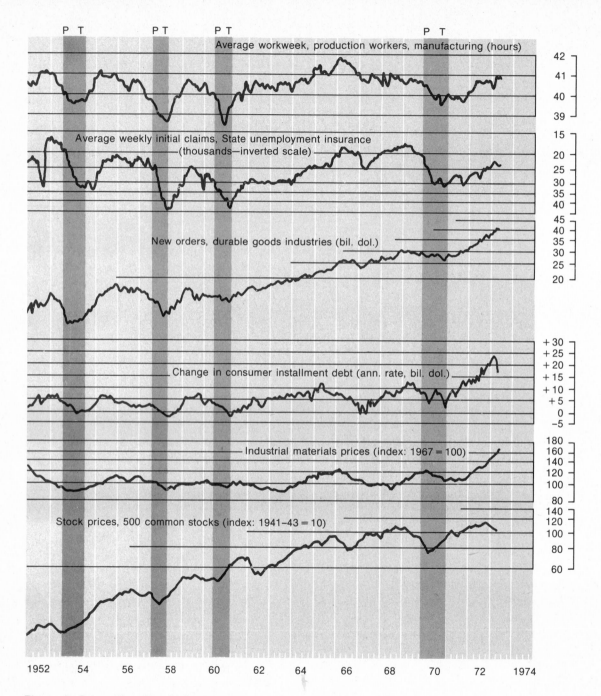

**Figure 1. Some "Leading Indicators,"
1952–1973.**

Adapted from *Business Conditions Digest*, June 1973, U.S.
Department of Commerce, Bureau of Economic Analysis.
Reprinted by permission.

Phases of the Business Cycle

Arthur F. Burns

Diversity and individuality are no less characteristic of business cycles than the family resemblance among them, and this fact inevitably complicates the task of understanding the nature and causes of business cycles. Fortunately, there is less uncertainty about the broad processes that typically generate business cycles than about the specific causes of this or that cyclical episode.

THE CUMULATIVE PROCESS OF EXPANSION

The continual transformation of the economy during a business cycle indicates that once the forces of recovery have taken hold, they will cumulate in strength. In other words, the expansion will spread out over the economic system, gather momentum, and for a time become a self-reinforcing process.

The proximate impulse to expansion may come from an increase of spending by business firms, consumers, or the government, or it may originate outside the domestic economy. A chain of familiar consequences will then be set in motion. Contractors will hire additional labor, disburse larger sums in wages, place larger orders for materials, supplies, and equipment with dealers or manufacturers, and finance at least a part of their rising outlays from new bank loans. The employment of labor on construction sites will at first increase only a little but after a few weeks or months—as the sequence of technical operations permits—more rapidly. Sales by retail shops and service establishments that cater to consumers will follow suit; for most construction workers will soon spend all or part of their larger income, and some will even feel encouraged to buy on the installment plan. The impact of the additional

Excerpted from Arthur F. Burns, *The Business Cycle in a Changing World* (New York: National Bureau of Economic Research, 1969), pp. 25–42. Reprinted by permission.

spending by contractors and their workmen will be spotty and uneven, but the effects will gradually spread out. Although some dealers or manufacturers will be content to meet the enlarged demand by drawing down their inventories, others will want to maintain inventories at their current level, and still others will seek to expand them in order better to accommodate a rising volume of sales. Here and there, therefore, not only will production of services and of goods made to specification be stimulated but also of staples that are normally carried in stock.

In response to larger construction spending, the rough balance between expanding and contracting enterprises that had previously ruled in the economy will thus be tipped, albeit irregularly, toward expansion. As firms revise their production schedules upward, they also will often increase their purchases from other firms, give fuller work to their present employees, perhaps recall some former employees or hire new ones, but in any event disburse larger sums in wages. Thus, each expanding center of production will stimulate activity elsewhere, including lending by the banks, in ever-widening circles. The spread of expansion from these centers will serve to check or counteract spirals of contraction that meanwhile are being generated at other points. With the scope of the expansion gradually becoming wider, retailers will be more prone to place orders with their suppliers in quantities that exceed their current sales, wholesalers and manufacturers will behave similarly, working hours will lengthen here and there, the work force will grow in an increasing number of firms and in the aggregate, and so too will income disbursements and sales to consumers.

We have supposed thus far that the higher volume of newly initiated construction will merely be maintained. In fact, construction work will tend to grow and so too will the activity of those making all sorts of machinery and equipment. Business firms, viewed in the mass, will still be operating well below capacity; but some firms—and their number is now increasing—will be operating at or close to full capacity. Moreover, as production rises, the profits of these firms, and indeed of business generally, will tend to improve. With business profits and consumer incomes improving on a wide front, with shortages of capacity looming more frequently, with delivery periods lengthening, and with interest rates, machinery and equipment prices, and construction costs still relatively favorable, it is only natural that contracts and orders for investment goods should rise briskly. Investment expenditures will follow suit, though with an irregular lag and diminished amplitude.

Moreover, as the expansion spreads, it generates in more people a feeling of confidence about the economic future—a mood that may gradually change from optimism to exuberance. Even an adverse development, such as a strike in a major industry or a deliberate effort to reduce inventories of some major product, may now be taken in stride. At an early stage of the expansion, any such reversal of fortune could have sufficed to terminate it. Now, in view of the high level of business and consumer optimism and the large backlog of outstanding commitments for capital goods, a brief inventory adjustment is merely apt to bring a pause to the growth of aggregate economic activity; once this adjustment is completed the economy can resume its advance in spirited fashion.

GATHERING FORCES OF RECESSION

And yet, as history so plainly teaches, a general expansion of economic activity sometimes lasts only a year and rarely lasts more than three or four years. Why does not the process of expansion continue indefinitely? And if the expansion must end, why is it not followed by a high plateau of economic activity instead of a decline? A partial answer to these questions can sometimes be found in disturbances that originate outside the mainstream of the domestic economy—such as political developments that threaten radical changes in property rights, or a drastic cut of military expenditures at the end of a war, or a major crisis abroad. Developments of this nature are entirely capable of cutting short an expansion that otherwise would have continued. However, experience strongly suggests that even in the absence of serious external disturbances the course of aggregate activity will in time be reversed by restrictive forces that gradually but insistently come into play as a result of the expansion process itself.

First, as the expansion continues, the slack in the economy is taken up and reduced. Although improvements of technology and new installations keep adding to the capacity of the nation's workshops, production generally rises still faster; hence, idle or excess capacity diminishes in a growing majority of the nation's businesses. Although the nation's labor force keeps growing, jobs increase faster; hence, unemployment declines. Although the reserves of the banking system may be expanding, bank loans and investments generate deposits at a faster rate; hence, the ratio of reserves to deposits keeps falling. Although producers of metals and other materials and supplies respond to the brisk demand by raising production schedules, they are frequently unable to move quickly enough; hence, deliveries stretch out or become less dependable. The pecuniary expression of the mounting shortages is a general rise of prices—of labor, credit, raw materials, intermediate products, and finished goods; but that is not all. The shortages are real and their physical expression is a narrower scope of the expansion itself. Rising sales by a particular firm or industry still release forces of physical expansion elsewhere, but their effects are blunted since more and more businessmen must now contend with bottlenecks. Once labor is in short supply in a community, an increase of employment by one firm must often result in some reduction of employment elsewhere in the same community. Once this or that material is in short supply, some firms must get along with less than they need or wait longer for deliveries. Once the banking system stops expanding credit or materially reduces its rate of expansion, any new loans to some firms will affect adversely the ability of other firms to get the credit they need. Instances of this sort multiply as the economy moves toward full employment. At some point, therefore, the scope of the expansion stops widening

WIDE WORLD PHOTO

Arthur F. Burns, Chairman of the Federal Reserve Board, testifies before the Joint Economic Committee. Burns has been a major contributor to the analysis of business cycles for over forty years.

and begins to narrow. Although aggregate activity is still growing, it can no longer maintain its initial rapid pace.

Second, the advance of prosperity tends to raise unit costs of production and therefore threatens profit margins—unless selling prices rise sufficiently. Taking the business system as a whole, much the largest item in costs and one which businessmen watch with the greatest care is labor—more precisely, the cost of labor per unit of output. This cost depends, first, on the hourly wage of labor and, second, on output per man-hour. Both tend to rise as the expansion

progresses, but at unequal rates. The price of labor moves sluggishly in the early part of the expansion, but advances of wages tend to become more frequent and larger as competition for labor increases and trade unions take advantage of improved market conditions. Increasing resort to overtime work at premium rates of pay accentuates the rise in the average price of labor, and so too does the faster upgrading of workers. On the other hand, output per man-hour, which improved sharply early in the expansion, tends to increase more gradually as the expansion lengthens, and it may also decline before the expansion is over. To be sure, improvements in organization and technology continue to be made at a thousand points at this as at every stage of the business cycle. However, their effectiveness in raising productivity is offset by developments that increasingly grow out of prosperity—such as a decline in the average quality of newly hired labor, fatigue of both workers and their managers, restlessness among workers and rapid turnover of labor, the need to put some obsolete plants or equipment back into use, the need to operate some highly efficient plants beyond their optimum capacity, and the need or wish to add liberally—once substantial increases of business have occurred—to indirect or overhead types of labor. Thus, as the expansion of aggregate activity continues, increases of productivity tend to diminish or even vanish, while the price of labor not only rises but tends to rise faster than productivity. The result is that unit labor costs of production tend to move up persistently.

Third, the increases of construction costs, equipment prices, and interest rates that are generated by the expansion process gradually become of more serious concern to the investing community. After all, a rise in long-term interest rates tends to reduce the value of existing capital goods at the very time that it raises the carrying charges on new investments. Higher costs of new capital goods likewise serve to raise fixed charges. Investors know that they will have the new plant or equipment on their hands for a long time and that their annual carrying charges will depend on the cost of the new capital goods, if not also on the rate of interest. They have got along thus far without the desired investment, and they will have to manage in any event without it for some months or years. If, therefore, they expect costs to be appreciably lower a year or so from now, they may well bide their time. Such postponements in placing orders and contracts become more frequent even as business decisions to invest continue to accumulate.

The rise in construction, equipment, and financing costs during an expansion impinges so broadly on the investing class that it would eventually check the investment boom even if prosperity were diffused uniformly over the economic community. However, this is not the case, and the uneven spread of profits is still another major development that impedes the continuance of expansion. In some industries, sales have recently been pushed with such vigor that the markets for their products are approaching saturation at existing prices. In other industries, exaggerated notions concerning the volume of sales that could be made at a good profit have led to overstocking or overbuilding, so that prices come under pressure. Errors of this type occur at all times, but they are likely to be bunched when enthusiasm has infected a large and widening circle of businessmen. In still other cases, business custom, long-term contracts, or governmental regulation make it difficult or inexpedient to raise selling prices. Of course, firms that cannot advance selling prices will try all the harder to resist increases in costs, but such efforts meet with limited success at a time of extensive shortages. With the rise in unit costs of production continuing across the business front, more and more firms therefore find that their profit margins are becoming narrower, thus offsetting the influence on profits of rising sales or reinforcing the influence of declining sales—instances of which now become more numerous. We thus find in experience, as we should expect, that after a business expansion has run for

some time, the proportion of firms enjoying rising profits begins to shrink, although profits of business in the aggregate still continue to advance.

These developments—the narrowing scope of expansion as full employment is approached, the rise of unit labor costs, the rise of financing costs, the rising cost of new capital goods, the spread of these cost increases across the economy, and the shrinkage in the proportion of business firms experiencing rising profits—tend gradually to undermine the expansion of investment. Public expenditures may still rise, but they are unlikely to do so on a sufficient scale to offset the declines of private investment. The growth of consumer spending, therefore, is retarded, if it does not actually stop. As these adjustments proceed, the balance between expanding and contracting economic activities tips steadily toward contraction. The need for overtime is much reduced, unemployment begins to rise, aggregate production soon turns down—in short, a business recession gets under way.

THE PROCESS OF CONTRACTION

The course of a typical recession is well known. A decline of production is accompanied by a reduction in the number of jobs, besides a reduced work week for many. The flow of incomes to individuals, therefore, tends to decline, and consumer spending—at least for expensive durable goods—follows suit. Retailers and wholesalers are now more apt to place orders for merchandise that are below the level of their respective sales. Many manufacturers, in their turn, also attempt to reduce their inventories. Taking the economy as a whole, the broad result of these efforts is that production declines more than sales, and that inventory investment not only declines but is soon succeeded by liquidation. Meanwhile, quoted prices of many commodities, especially of raw materials, tend to soften, and discounts or concessions from list prices become more numerous and larger. Wage rates, however, are generally maintained and actually rise here and there. Even when they decline somewhat, unit costs of production still tend to rise, perhaps sharply, because it takes time before overhead costs, including the employment of indirect types of labor, can be adjusted to the lower volume of business. Many firms that are already experiencing lower profit margins therefore find that they must put up with still lower margins, while others first begin to feel the profit squeeze. With sales more often than not also declining, an increasing majority of businesses now experience falling profits, bankruptcies become more frequent, business profits in the aggregate—which probably began shrinking before sales did—decline further, and stock exchange prices extend their fall as well. In view of these developments, many businessmen and consumers, even if they are not actually poorer, become more concerned about the future. New business commitments for investment in fixed capital therefore tend to become less numerous, and—unless forces of recovery soon come into play—investment expenditures of this type as well as outlays on consumer durables will extend their decline, which is as yet modest, and reinforce the contraction process.

As a decline in one sector reacts on another, the economy may begin spiraling downward on a scale that outruns the magnitudes that we ordinarily associate with recession. The likelihood that a depression will develop depends on numerous factors—among them, the scale of speculation during the preceding phase of prosperity, the extent to which credit was permitted to grow, whether or not the quality of credit suffered significant deterioration, whether any major markets became temporarily saturated, how much excess capacity had been created before the recession started, whether and in what degree the balance of international payments has become adverse, the organization of the financial system and its ability to withstand shocks, the shape of political developments, and the aptness and scale of monetary actions and other governmental efforts, if any, to stem the economic decline. If the onset of the contraction is marked by a financial crisis or if one develops

somewhat later, there is a substantial probability that the decline of aggregate activity will prove severe and perhaps abnormally long as well. For when businessmen and their bankers begin to scramble for liquidity, both trade credit and bank credit will decline and so too will the money supply; commodity prices at wholesale and retail will slump and wage rates decline, while interest rates for a time rise sharply; confidence will become impaired and many investment projects will be abandoned instead of merely being postponed; business losses and bankruptcies will multiply; more workers will earn less or become totally unemployed; and, since spells of unemployment also lengthen, more and more families will deplete their savings and be forced to reduce their spending drastically. Even if the shift from expansion to contraction is made gradually, untoward disturbances originating outside the economy may still strike with great force and transform a mild contraction into a depression.

FORCES OF PROGRESS AND RECOVERY

Normally, however, a contraction in aggregate activity does not lead to depression. A contraction is not a mirror image of expansion, as it might well be if the business cycle were merely an oscillation. A contraction does not usually cumulate and feed on itself in the manner of an expansion. Normally, many progressive developments continue, and some even become stronger, during the contraction phase of the business cycle; in other words, the forces making for contraction are powerfully counteracted by forces of growth that limit the degree to which it can cumulate.

What are these forces of growth? First, businessmen and consumers in a modern nation are accustomed to seeking and to expecting economic improvement. This optimistic state of mind generally continues during a contraction, provided its dimensions remain moderate. Investment opportunities, connected with new technology or market strategy, always keep arising in the minds of imaginative and resourceful men. Not a few of these opportunities are acted on promptly in spite of the recession. Second, most people are extremely reluctant to give up the standard of living that they have managed to attain, and in any event they cannot quickly readjust family expenditures. Hence, consumer spending is well maintained in the face of declines of income that are judged to be temporary. Third, the pitch of both interfirm and interindustry competition becomes more intense during a recession. Unlike investment commitments, which are at their highest level before aggregate activity turns down, the bunching of installations of new plant and equipment is likely to be heaviest when the recession is well under way. The newer facilities typically serve new products or permit lower costs of production of old products. Many progressive enterprises are therefore able to extend their markets even when business as a whole is falling off. Firms that suffer from shifts of demand or from an outworn technology may have managed to limp along or even do reasonably well when activity was brisk. Now, finding that competitors are penetrating their markets on a scale that threatens survival, the hard-pressed firms are more likely to move with energy to modernize their plant, acquire new equipment, improve their products, try out new marketing strategies, and eliminate waste. Meanwhile, vigorous businesses whose plants are operating at or close to optimum capacity do not stand still. Not a few of them anticipate a large expansion of sales when the dull season is over, and therefore undertake additions or improvements to their plant and equipment. Fourth, a nation's resources normally continue to grow even during a recession. Since the population is still growing, the stabilizing force of consumption is reinforced. Since the number of business firms is still increasing, the formation of new businesses contributes, although at a reduced rate, to the demand for capital goods. Since the stock of housing, consumer durables, and industrial facilities is still expanding, a large market is assured for repairs, improvements, and replacements, although there is undoubtedly some postponing of this type of expenditure. Fifth, public efforts to promote economic growth and the general welfare are customary in a well-governed nation. These efforts may not always be wise or geared closely to the business cycle, but neither are they confined to times of prosperity. On the contrary, they are more likely to come during recessions—especially in recent times when full employment has become an increasingly firm objective of the public policy of nations.

The progressive forces that operate during recessions serve as a brake on the cumulative process of contraction. True, aggregate activity falls below the level reached at the peak of prosperity. The decline, however, is usually of moderate proportions. Not only that, but sales decline much less in the aggregate than production and the level of sales soon becomes higher than that of production. For a while, the liquidation of inventories proceeds at an increasing rate, but this cannot continue. To handle the volume of business on hand, especially if sales stabilize or decline very gradually, manufacturers and distributors must soon slow down, if not halt, the decline of their inventories. Taking the economic system as a whole, once inventory disinvestment declines more rapidly than the decline of sales, production must begin rising. Of course, a recovery of production will be preceded by an increase of orders, and an early upturn of orders is precisely what occurs when dealers and manufacturers take steps to slow down appreciably the decline of their inventories.

While business firms keep bringing inventories into better alignment with their sales, other developments that grow out of the recession also favor an early recovery. Since the reserves of commercial banks tend to pile up again, reserve ratios improve. Hence, interest rates decline and credit becomes more readily available. Meanwhile, numerous readjustments in the nation's workshops serve to lower unit costs of production. In view of the decline of aggregate demand, wage rates often stop rising and sometimes decline a little, overtime operations become less frequent, not a few of the less efficient enterprises go out of business, production is increasingly concentrated in the most modern plants and on the best equipment, many of the less efficient workers are let go, the ranks of the overhead types of labor are thinned here and there, and workers generally become more attentive to their duties. These changes reinforce the improvements of organization and technology which always occur in a progressive economy and which are often speeded up during a recession, in response to the keener competition that develops at such a time.

Thus, corrective forces released by the recession combine with the more persistent forces of growth to bring the contraction of aggregate activity to a halt. Typically, the process works fairly speedily and the contraction is over in about a year or a year and a half. However, as previously noted, a contraction sometimes develops into a spiraling depression. When that happens, declining investment in fixed capital supplants inventory disinvestment as the principal drag on the economy. Worse still, the stubborn human trait of optimism begins to give way, so that a mere readjustment of inventories may bring only an abortive recovery. Once many men begin to lose faith in themselves or in the institutions of their society, full recovery may need to wait on substantial innovations or an actual reduction in the stock of fixed capital, unless powerful external influences come into play—such as a reorganization of the monetary system, massive governmental expenditures, or a sudden increase of exports on account of foreign developments. Fortunately, no industrial country has suffered a spiraling depression since World War II, and the likelihood of such a development has been greatly reduced.   □

CHAPTER 11
MONEY AND MONETARY POLICY

In the preceding four chapters, we have been setting out the basic structure of national income analysis and the relationship of this analysis to public policy. Our presentation so far has a basic limitation: It has omitted any explicit discussion of the role of "money" in the national economy. This omission of money in our analysis is a particularly serious one. As early as chapter 4, we indicated that Federal Reserve Bank influence on the money supply could affect national income and production in our economy. Furthermore, the development of the modern theory of national income determination is specifically related to certain developments in the theory of money. We mentioned when we were discussing the work of John Maynard Keynes that one of the main things he did was to try to provide a synthesis of *real* and *monetary* analysis—attempting to show the impact of financial mechanisms and institutions on *real* things like output and employment. And, finally, we know from reading the newspapers that the management of our country's money supply is considered of vital importance to our overall economic health. *Monetary policy* is concerned with action designed to affect both the level of the interest rate and the size and availability of the money supply in the national economy. Monetary policy must be put next to *fiscal policy* (the government tax and expenditure programs we have just been discussing) as one of the main avenues by which the government can moderate the business cycle and influence the overall level of employment, output, and prices in the nation.

Despite the importance of money and its economic impact, however, it cannot be said that economists are agreed on the extent of that impact or even the avenues by which it is felt. The discussion to be presented in this chapter would be accepted in broad outline by many economists, but certainly not by all. The controversy over money and monetary policy—which has been called the most highly contested issue in modern macroeconomics—will be taken up in chapter 13 and in Great Debate Two on Monetarism (pp. 311–38). So as not to interrupt the flow of the argument, we shall postpone qualifications to this chapter's analysis until then.

TABLE 11–1

MEASURES OF U.S. MONEY STOCK

NOVEMBER 1973	(in billions of dollars)
Components of Money Stock	
Currency	60.9
Demand deposits	207.9
Time and savings deposits at commercial banks	359.9
Deposits at mutual savings banks and savings and loan associations	320.2
Overall Measures of Money Stock	
M_1 (currency plus demand deposits)	268.8
M_2 (M_1 plus certain time deposits at commercial banks)	566.7
M_3 (M_2 plus deposits at mutual savings banks and savings and loan associations)	886.9

Various measures of money (M_1, M_2, etc.) tend to merge with each other near the margins. There are also near-monies (e.g., U.S. government bonds) that are for some purposes (though not for all purposes) similar to money. In this text, we shall think of money as M_1, unless otherwise specified.

Adapted from Board of Governors of the Federal Reserve System (April 1974), p. A, 9. Reprinted by permission.

MONEY AND THE BANKING SYSTEM

In our discussion of money in Part One, we noted that currency was a relatively small proportion of the American money supply at the present time, a larger item by far being demand deposits in commercial banks. We also noted that there were various definitions of money. Table 11–1 makes these points explicit.

The components of three definitions of the money stock are described in this table. Currency and de-

mand deposits have been discussed before. The other two categories involve various kinds of time and savings deposits. These deposits, whether held at ordinary commercial banks or in special savings institutions, are not usually cashable "on demand." Often, however, it is possible to cash them on quite short notice. For this reason, many people treat time and savings deposits as not much different from their demand deposit accounts.

Various definitions of "money" can be built by combining these components in different ways, as suggested by the M_1, M_2, and M_3 headings. Indeed, it is possible to go further than this, extending the concept of money to what most economists would call near-money, particularly various forms of U.S. government bonds. The fact is that we are on a spectrum here in which one category shades into another, very much complicating not only our definitions but also the analysis of what happens as we move from one form of asset to another.

In this book, we shall still adhere primarily to the currency-plus-demand-deposits (M_1) definition of money. This is partly for simplicity, but also partly because this definition covers the only form of money that can be directly spent. If you want to spend your savings account, you have to convert it into M_1 money before it will be accepted in payment for goods or services. Whatever definition is most useful in a particular situation, one thing we must never forget is that money cannot be identified as *folding green* or by pictures of the presidents. The banking system is crucial to our money supply and *deposit-creation* is at the heart of the banking system's role.

BALANCE SHEET OF AN INDIVIDUAL BANK

Deposit *creation?* That may sound rather illegal, or at least questionable. Are not demand deposits created by our depositing "money" in the commercial bank? Surely, a commercial bank cannot simply create these deposits out of thin air?

The answer to this kind of question requires us to look at the balance sheet of a typical commercial

SIMPLIFIED BALANCE SHEET
OF A COMMERCIAL BANK

JANUARY 1, 1974

Assets		Liabilities	
Cash	$200,000	Demand deposits	$1,000,000
Loans, investments, bonds	$800,000		

bank, simplified for the purposes of our analysis.[1] We include three items:

1. A cash item of $200,000. We can think of this as currency held by the bank to meet occasional excesses of withdrawals over deposits. As indicated in chapter 4, we operate with a fractional reserve banking system. A bank does not need to hold in the form of cash (or in the form of reserves with the Federal Reserve Bank, as we shall develop the analysis in a moment) the full amount of its deposit liabilities. Not all depositors come rushing in for their funds at once. While some come in demanding cash, others are depositing cash. This particular bank has $200,000 set aside for such contingencies.

---

1. A more detailed balance sheet would include many other items. For example, among the bank's assets we would clearly want to include the buildings and equipment it owns. The liability side would include time and saving deposits as well as demand deposits. Also, on the credit side of the ledger would be the item *net worth.* This is essentially the value of the bank's assets after the claims of creditors are allowed for. The bank *owes* some part of its assets to its depositors—i.e., they can come and claim these assets under specified conditions. What is left, the net worth, is what the bank itself *owns:* i.e., the original capital paid in by stockholders plus surplus and undivided profits.

2. The second asset item represents loans, investments, and government bonds. Here the bank is engaged in lending out money or buying bonds or other securities in order to make money in the form of interest. These are the interest-earning assets of the bank, and they are, of course, an essential feature of the commercial banking system.

3. On the liability side, we have $1 million worth of demand deposits. These deposits are called liabilities because they are owed by the bank to its depositors. It would be through the creation of more of these demand deposits, that this commercial bank would be able to "create money," if it in fact could accomplish such a miracle. But can it do so?

Let us first imagine circumstances in which the bank clearly could create more demand deposits—without any miracle or even any risk to its shareholders or other depositors. Suppose that it were the only bank on an isolated island, or that for some other reason it had a monopoly on all the banking business in a particular area. Suppose further that everyone in this area used the banking system for all their money-payments. It might be very awkward to use literally *no* cash (e.g., to write out a check for a bus ride or the evening newspaper), but assume that the need for coin and currency is trivial. Basically, all payments of any size are made by check, and all these checks are drawn on one monopoly bank.

We imagine, now, that a businessman comes to the bank and wants to borrow $50,000. A vice-president of the bank, forgetting that the bank already has demand deposit liabilities of $1 million and cash assets of only $200,000, agrees to the loan. He adds to the bank's assets the $50,000 loan and to the bank's liabilities $50,000 of demand deposits in the name of this particular businessman. There is now $50,000 more money in this economy than before.

Does this mean that the vice-president has been reckless? On the contrary, he has been all too conservative. For, on our assumptions, not only is the new position tenable, but the bank is making more

**BANK'S BALANCE SHEET
AFTER NEW $50,000 LOAN**

Assets		Liabilities	
Cash	$200,000	Demand deposits	$1,050,000
Loans, investments, bonds	$850,000		

money (through the interest on the added $50,000 loan), and the reserve cash of $200,000 hasn't even been touched. Nor will it be touched under our special assumptions. When the businessman wants to use this money to hire workmen to build, say, an addition to his factory, he will pay these workmen by a check drawn on his account with our bank. The bank, receiving these checks for deposit, will simply deduct the total amount from the businessman's account and add it to the workers' accounts. Eventually, when the loan is due, the businessman will have sold additional products to consumers who will pay him by their checks, thus building up his demand deposit account again. When he actually pays off the loan, the bank will simply cancel the $50,000 on the asset side and his $50,000 of demand deposits.

We can now see why this bank vice-president has been conservative. He should have loaned out not $50,000 but $100,000 or $500,000. Or $10 *million*, if he could find a sufficient number of creditworthy customers. Under our assumptions, there is no limit whatsoever to the amount of new demand deposits —and hence additional money—this bank could, in principle, create.

Now this situation is unrealistic as a description of a modern American commercial bank for three reasons: (a) there are *some* demands for currency in our system—no bank could operate on the assumption that the public would never want to increase its holdings of cash in the least amount; (b) commercial banks that are members of the Federal Reserve are required to hold certain percentages of their demand deposits in the form of reserves with the

Federal Reserve System—i.e., there is a *legal reserve requirement;* and (c) no bank in this country, however big, is so isolated or as much a monopoly as the bank in our example—funds can be withdrawn from one bank and put into some *other* bank. This means that all the checks won't come back to one bank; hence, there can be a *net* withdrawal of funds instead of everything just "canceling out."

This last point is rather crucial. Indeed, it is clear that a small bank, operating in a big system, simply could not hope to "create money" in the way our isolated, monopoly bank did. When it created the $50,000 demand deposit for the businessman, it would have to recognize that when he drew checks on this account, the chances are that they would be deposited in other banks (or, at least, that only a small fraction would come back to this bank). Deposits in other banks would create claims on the bank that it would meet by transferring cash to these other banks. Hence, its $200,000 cash *would* come under assault. An undue expansion of loans and investments by this bank alone would mean that its vice-president was indeed reckless (as perhaps some of us have believed all along).

MULTIPLE CREDIT CREATION THROUGH THE SYSTEM

What a small, single commercial bank cannot accomplish by itself, a system of such banks can. In fact, the banking system can operate very much as our earlier "monopoly" bank did. The first bank that creates the $50,000 loan (and $50,000 demand deposits for the borrower) is subject to a net withdrawal of cash as the businessman starts using his loan. But this cash goes to another bank that now finds its deposit-creating ability enhanced. It, too, is subject to a net withdrawal when it increases its loans; but this, in turn, means more cash for a third bank, and so on.

This process has to be followed through with some care if we are to understand it properly. To make our example a bit more realistic, let us at this time formally introduce a legal reserve requirement of 20 percent. Suppose that the actual demands for increased cash and currency by the public are trivial, but that to guard against possible dangers, the federal authority (in the United States, it would be the Federal Reserve System) requires that every bank in the system keep a cash holding of $20 for every $100 of demand deposits it creates. We shall follow through the following case:

All banks in the system are "fully loaned up" at the outset; i.e., their cash reserves are equal to exactly 20 percent of their demand deposit liabilities. Then, suddenly, a widow withdraws $100,000 of cash from under her mattress and deposits it in her neighborhood bank.

To show: that the banking system can now create substantial additional money beyond this $100,000. In particular, that it can create an additional $400,000. In total, there will be $500,000 of demand deposits created in response to the $100,000 cash deposit—or a 5-to-1 ratio.

By following the balance sheets below, the reader will see exactly how this happens.

THE PROCESS OF MULTIPLE CREDIT EXPANSION

1.

Bank A	Assets	Liabilities
Before $100,000 is deposited)	$200,000 Cash $800,000 Loans and investments	$1,000,000 Demand deposits
(*After* $100,000 is deposited)	$300,000 Cash $800,000 Loans and investments	$1,100,000 Demand deposits

Bank A now lends out $80,000 and its balance sheet becomes:

	Assets	Liabilities
	$220,000 Cash $880,000 Loans and investments	$1,100,000 Demand deposits

Addition to demand deposits in first round = $100,000

2. The $80,000 loaned out by Bank A is now deposited in Bank B.

Bank B	Assets	Liabilities
(*Before* $80,000 deposit)	$200,000 Cash $800,000 Loans and investments	$1,000,000 Demand deposits
(*After* $80,000 deposit)	$280,000 Cash $800,000 Loans and investments	$1,080,000 Demand deposits

Bank B now lends out $64,000 and its balance sheet becomes:

	Assets	Liabilities
	$216,000 Cash $864,000 Loans and investments	$1,080,000 Demand deposits

Addition to demand deposits in second round = $80,000

3. The $64,000 loaned by Bank B is now deposited in Bank C.

Bank C	Assets	Liabilities
(*Before* $64,000 deposit)	$200,000 Cash $800,000 Loans and investments	$1,000,000 Demand deposits
(*After* $64,000 deposit)	$264,000 Cash $800,000 Loans and investments	$1,064,000 Demand deposits

Bank C now lends out $51,200 and its balance sheet becomes:

	Assets	Liabilities
	$212,800 Cash $851,200 Loans and investments	$1,064,000 Demand deposits

Addition to demand deposits in third round = $64,000

In the next round, Bank D will be able to lend out 80 percent of $51,200 or $40,960 in the next round, Bank E will be able to lend out 80 percent of $40,960 or $32,770; and so on.

The *total* addition to demand deposits (ΔDD) when all the rounds are completed will be:

$$\Delta DD = \$100,000 + \$80,000 + \$64,000 + \$51,200 + \$40,960 + \$32,770 + \dots$$

$$\Delta DD = \$100,000 (1 + .80 + (.80)^2 + (.80)^3 + (.80)^4 + \dots + (.80)^n + \dots)$$

$$\Delta DD = \$100,000 \left(\frac{1}{1 - .80} \right)$$

$$\Delta DD = \$100,000 (5) = \$500,000$$

Notice that this process resembles the action of the national income multiplier of the last chapter. We increase C, I, or G by $1 and get a $3 or $4 increase in national income. In the case of multiple credit creation, we get $1 more in cash reserves and $5 more in demand deposits, or money. Actually, in formal terms the processes are very similar, the role of the MPS in the multiplier (remember that m = 1/MPS) being played in the case of credit expansion by the legal reserve requirement. Thus, assuming that all banks lend out all their funds up to the legal requirements, we would get, where ΔM equals the addition to the money supply, ΔR equals the new reserves, and LR, the legal reserve requirement:

$$\Delta M = (1/LR) \, \Delta R$$

The term, $1/LR$, can be thought of as the *money creation multiplier* or the *credit creation multiplier*. In this case, it would be 1/.20, or 5.

If we consolidated all these balance sheets and looked at the process before, during, and after the expansion had taken place, it would look like the

CONSOLIDATED COMMERCIAL BANK BALANCE SHEETS

If we assume that there are ten banks in the system, each with a balance sheet identical to those we have been describing, then we have:

1. Consolidated balance sheet before $100,000 cash deposit:

Assets	Liabilities
$2,000,000 Cash	$10,000,000 Demand deposits
$8,000,000 Loans and investments	

2. Consolidated balance sheet immediately after $100,000 Cash deposit:

Assets	Liabilities
$2,100,000 Cash	$10,100,000 Demand deposits
$8,000,000 Loans and investments	

3. Consolidated balance sheet after multiple expansion of credit has taken place:

Assets	Liabilities
$2,100,000 Cash	$10,500,000 Demand deposits
$8,400,000 Loans and investments	

situation shown in the table above. The total cash reserves of the member banks have gone up from $2,000,000 to $2,100,000. As a consequence, and on the assumption that each bank at each stage of the game lends out any excess reserves that come its way, the demand deposits in the system have gone up from $10,000,000 to $10,500,000—i.e., in total, there has been a $500,000 expansion of the money supply.

THE ROLE OF MONEY—A SYNOPSIS

With the above analysis of multiple credit creation in mind, and remembering our earlier discussion of the Federal Reserve System in chapter 4, we are now ready to show how money fits into our overall theory of national income determination. The best approach is to sketch out very quickly the picture as a whole and then look at each part in somewhat greater detail.

Let us put the issue in the way it would actually appear to a policy-maker with the Federal Reserve System:

How is the monetary policy of a government like that of the United States supposed to affect in theory the level of prices, output, and employment in the economy as a whole? By what chain of logic does government action affecting the money supply reach down into the economy and influence such important variables as the number of jobs available or the number of tons of steel produced or the cost-of-living index?

The chain of logic connecting these different variables can then be set out in four basic propositions. These are:

1. An increase in the quantity of money, *cet. par.*, will generally cause a fall in the interest rate.

2. A fall in the interest rate, *cet. par.*, will generally cause an expansion of business investment.

3. An expansion of business investment, *cet. par.,* will generally cause an expansion of GNP and employment.

These first three points indicate that the basic direction of monetary policy in a depression or recession should be expansionary. According to these points, an expanded money supply will lead through changes in the interest rate and business investment to a higher level of GNP and employment in a previously depressed economy. A fourth point deals with the opposite problem of inflation—i.e., when there is not too little but too much aggregate demand.

4. When the quantity of money is decreased, the opposite effects will generally occur; that is, a decrease in the money supply will cause a rise in the rate of interest, which will cause a fall in business investment, which, in turn, will cause a fall in GNP and employment or, if the problem is inflation, a reduction of inflationary pressures.

Since one would normally follow a contractionary monetary policy in an inflation and because the problem of inflation will be the subject of chapter 14, we shall concentrate for the moment solely on the first three points.

Each of these points represents one important link in the chain of logic connecting the money supply with national income and employment. As far as our understanding is concerned, these links are of very different degrees of difficulty, particularly in view of what we have already accomplished in earlier chapters. To make things as clear as possible, let us take up these links in the order of less to greater difficulty of understanding; this will mean proceeding in the reverse order, beginning with point (3) and ending with point (1).

THE INVESTMENT-GNP LINK

The easiest link for us to understand is clearly that expressed in point (3):

An expansion of business investment, cet. par., *will generally cause an expansion of GNP and employment.*

This is nothing but our theory of national income determination again. Figure 11–1 is similar to diagrams we have used many times before, the difference being that we have put investment on the top to show more clearly the effects of an increase of investment. If investment goes up by whatever amount, national income will rise by a multiplied amount, the multiplier being determined in the simplest case by the formula:

$$m = \frac{1}{1 - MPC}$$

In this particular diagram, MPC = 2/3, and m = 3; the increase in investment is $25 billion and the resulting increase of equilibrium national income is $75 billion. This should be completely familiar to us from our previous work.

THE INTEREST RATE-INVESTMENT LINK

The next easiest link, though one we shall want to say a few words about, is that expressed in point (2):

A fall in the interest rate, cet. par., *will generally cause an expansion of business investment.*

Point (3) was about the *effects* of an increase in investment; this point is about the *causes* of an increase in investment. What is the logic behind the interest rate-investment link?

We have already discussed this matter briefly (chapter 9), but there are two further comments, one a clarification, the other a qualification, that we should add here.

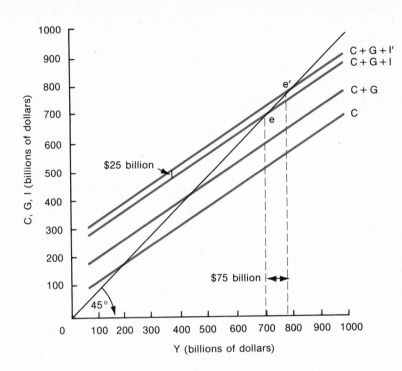

Figure 11–1. Effects of an Increase in Investment on National Income.

The clarification has to do with ascertaining the *direction* in which changing interest rates move the level of investment. There is a potential possibility of misunderstanding here, largely because of the different ways we use the term "investment" in everyday discourse. Nowhere is it more important than now to remember our earlier distinction between "financial" investment (buying a stock or a bond) and ordinary business investment (building a new factory, adding to one's inventories of goods in stock, etc.). The reason for this special caution is that the effect of changes in the rate of interest will be very different—in fact, ordinarily in opposite directions—depending on which kind of investment one has in mind.

To make this point clear, let us consider "financial" investment first. Now from the point of view of the "financial investor" a high rate of interest is a good

thing. The issue before him is not whether or not to build a factory, but whether or not to buy a bond. If the interest rate is high, this will not discourage him from buying the bond; on the contrary, it will ordinarily make him eager to do so. At 6 percent interest, he gets $6 a year by putting $100 into a bond. At 10 percent, he gets $10 a year from the same $100. In certain circumstances, this difference may induce him to buy an extra bond or two. The point is that for the "financial investor," the interest rate appears as a *payment* for the use of the money he has lent.

It is just the reverse when we come to investment in the ordinary sense in which we have been using the term—i.e., the actual adding of new productive capacity to our economy. For when we talk about this kind of investment we are approaching everything from the point of view not of the lender but of the borrower. The businessman wishes to borrow money to expand his productive capacity. To say that the interest rate has gone up is nothing but to say that the *costs* of borrowing have gone up. As a businessman, you wish, say, to invest in a new machine that costs $1,000. You go to the bank to finance this purchase with a loan. If the bank charges you 6 percent on the loan, then you have to pay out interest charges of $60 per year on the machine. If the rate is 10 percent, you have to pay out $100 a year. It may be that the machine will be just profitable to you at 6 percent, but not profitable at 10 percent and decidedly unprofitable at 11 or 12 percent. A high interest rate then is not an encouragement but a definite *dis*couragement as far as ordinary business investment is concerned.

This clarification should make it apparent that the direction of changes in investment in this second sense will be in the opposite direction from changes in the rate of interest. A high interest rate will tend to discourage investment. A low interest rate—meaning that the costs of borrowing are low—will tend to foster higher levels of investment. And this, in fact, is precisely what our point (2) states.

We now ask: How *great* an effect on investment will these changes in the interest rate have? And this leads us to a certain qualification that should be made in connection with point (2). For although the *direction* of this effect is now perfectly clear, it is much less certain how *large* that effect will be.

The problem, essentially, is that many different factors influence business investment, and the interest rate is only one—in many circumstances not the most important one. We have mentioned some of these factors before: business expectations, technological progress, amount of retained profits, and, of course, the interest rate. If, say, business expectations are sufficiently pessimistic, then it may be that investment will stay small no matter how enticingly low the interest rate may be. Conversely, if certain remarkable new products or processes are available for investment, businessmen may be difficult to discourage, no matter what the costs (within limits) of borrowing.

A technical way of describing this is to say that investment demand may, for wide ranges of different interest rates, be *interest-inelastic;* i.e., the percent-

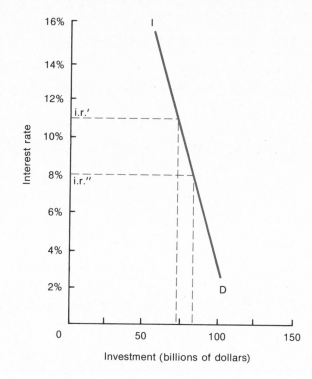

Figure 11–2. The investment Demand Schedule.

age change in investment for a given percentage change in the interest rate may be quite small.[2]

An *investment demand schedule* displaying this feature is shown in Figure 11–2. The amount of investment businessmen are willing to undertake does increase with lower interest rates as we would expect; however, the percentage increase is rather slight. Thus, a substantial percentage reduction in the interest rate (from 11 to 8 percent) brings only a few billion dollars increase in investment.[3]

2. For a discussion of the concept of *elasticity,* see pp. 37–40.

3. The effect of interest changes will often be different, depending upon the type of investment involved. Thus, while business spending on plant and equipment may be relatively insensitive to the interest rate, construction investment may be quite sensitive. See p. 348.

This does not mean that our point (2) is incorrect. It simply means that the strength of this link may not be great. If under particular circumstances a fall in the rate of interest produces only a modest increase in investment, then clearly this will limit the results we can hope for when we are trying to cure unemployment by interest rate changes.

The reader should notice that points (3) and (2), combined, suggest that—other things equal—different levels of the interest rate will lead to different levels of national income. High interest rates will produce low levels of investment that, via the multiplier, will produce low levels of national income;[4] low interest rates will have the converse result. However, this is only *half* the picture. For now we must turn to the crucial factor of the money supply itself.

MONEY SUPPLY-INTEREST RATE LINK

We are now ready to discuss point (1), the money supply-interest rate link. It is at this juncture that the role of money at last enters explicitly into our picture. Point (1) states:

An increase in the quantity of money, cet. par., will generally cause a fall in the interest rate.

If we can establish this point in a general way, then we shall have succeeded in building our logical chain from money, on the one side, to national income, employment, and prices, on the other.

Let us begin by considering the way in which the quantity of money might actually increase in the present-day American economy. Essentially, the Federal Reserve Board can bring about an expansion of the money supply either by making more reserves available to the commercial banks or by changing the legal reserve requirement. The Fed has numerous means at its disposal for doing this, but the three main tools are the following:

1. Altering the legal reserve requirement. As we have mentioned before, the basic reserves of banks

---

4. This relationship is treated graphically in the appendix to this chapter. See pp. 274–75.

TABLE 11-2

RESERVE REQUIREMENTS
ON DEPOSITS OF MEMBER BANKS

| | MARCH 31, 1974 |
TYPE AND SIZE OF BANK'S DEPOSITS	REQUIRED RATIO OF RESERVES (PERCENT)
Demand deposits	
0–$2 million	8
$2–$10 million	10½
$10–$100 million	12½
$100–$400 million	13½
Over $400 million	18
Time deposits	
Savings deposits	3
Other time deposits	
0–$5 million	3
Over $5 million	5

Adapted from *Federal Reserve Bulletin*, April 1974 (Washington, D.C.: U.S. Board of Governors, Federal Reserve System), p. A. 9. Reprinted by permission.

that are members of the Federal Reserve system are not in cash but in reserves held by the Federal Reserve Banks. The Federal Reserve Banks are sometimes called "banker's banks." In the case of our example of a widow with $100,000 in cash to deposit, the bank that received this deposit would not hold most of it in cash but would deposit it with the Federal Reserve Bank in its region. The money would then become part of the reserves that the bank is legally required to hold against its demand deposits. Now it is clear that one way the Fed can influence the money supply in the economy is by changing the legal reserve requirement. Table 11-2 shows the various legal reserve requirements in effect on March 31, 1974. If the Fed were to *reduce* these requirements, it would suddenly create excess reserves for its member banks. These banks could then increase their loans and investments, with a consequent possibility of multiple expansion in the money supply.

2. Altering the discount rate. As the Fed is a banker's bank, it can also lend money to member banks to augment or replenish their reserves if they are running short. The rate of interest it charges member banks for such loans is called the *discount rate*. By lowering the discount rate, the Fed would, in effect, be making reserves available to its member banks on easier terms than heretofore. This action could also, in principle, lead to a multiple expansion of the money supply.

3. Open-market operations in Government securities. Although the above two methods are important, the most significant way in which the Fed has historically influenced the money supply in this country has been by open-market purchases and sales of government securities. Essentially, if the Fed wishes to *increase* the money supply, it will *purchase* government bonds on the open market. If it wishes to *reduce* the money supply, it will sell government bonds on the open market. The way this works is, as we should expect, through the effect of these actions on member bank reserves. In the particular case of a purchase of $100,000 in government bonds, we may imagine that the Fed buys these bonds directly from a member bank.[5] In this case, the member bank's balance sheet will be affected as follows:

The key change here is the increase in reserves to $300,000. Assuming a 20 percent legal reserve requirement, this means the member bank now has excess reserves of $100,000 that it can lend to businessmen and other investors. This $100,000 will now go the rounds of the other banks in the system, each

---

5. It need not necessarily do so. If, for example, it bought the bonds from a private individual who was a depositor at the member bank, that individual would receive a check from the Fed, which he would deposit in the member bank. The effect would be the same as in the example shown in the text. The member bank's reserves with the Fed would be increased by $100,000 in either case.

MEMBER BANK BALANCE SHEET BEFORE OPEN-MARKET OPERATION

Assets		Liabilities	
Reserves in Federal Reserve Bank	$200,000	Demand deposits	$1,000,000
Loans, investments, bonds	$800,000		

MEMBER BANK BALANCE SHEET AFTER FEDERAL RESERVE BANK PURCHASES OF $100,000 GOVERNMENT BOND

Assets		Liabilities	
Reserves in Federal Reserve Bank	$300,000	Demand deposits	$1,000,000
Loans, investments, bonds	$700,000		

---

of which will in turn increase its loans and investments. The net effect will be an increase of the money supply by—in a "fully loaned up" system—$500,000.

As we are understanding how these open-market operations work, we are also learning to understand why an expansion of the money supply tends to bring the interest rate down—and this, of course, is the main point we are trying to demonstrate here.

To see this, all one needs to do is to visualize what is happening in each of the banks in the system as it receives its share of excess reserves. Each bank, being a commercial institution, is now eager to make money by lending out this excess; there is a generally increased willingness on the part of lenders in the economy to lend. This is really analogous to the kind of supply-and-demand analysis for goods and services that we described in chapter 2. In this case, the good is "loans" and the "price" is the interest rate. There has been no change in the position of the borrowers (i.e., business investors), but the banking system's willingness to supply more loans has increased. The consequence, as we would expect, is that the price—i.e., the interest rate—will fall.

This is the essence of the process by which Federal Reserve open-market purchases of government securities can lead both to an expansion in the money supply and to an easing of the terms on which banks are ready to lend to businesses, and especially to a decline in the interest rate. (To test his understanding of the process, the reader should follow through the opposite policy, showing how Federal Reserve sales of government bonds to the member banks can lead to a contraction of reserves, a multiplied contraction of demand deposits, and a raising of the interest rate.) The banks find themselves with excess reserves. Whereas previously they would lend to businesses—or, for that matter, to home builders, or state and local governments—only at 10 percent interest, now they are willing to lend at 9 percent or 8 percent.

Thus, our point (1)—the link between the money supply and the rate of interest—has been demonstrated, and the chain connecting the money supply with the level of national income and employment is now complete.

A RECAPITULATION AND FURTHER DEVELOPMENT

Rather, the chain is "complete" but subject to a number of additions and amendments. Let us first go over the whole process from beginning to end, and then make some further comments.

To recapitulate: The Federal Reserve Board finds the economy suffering from unemployment and below-potential national income. It can use *monetary policy* to combat this situation in many ways; e.g., changing the reserve requirement, lowering the discount rate, or engaging in open-market operations. Let us suppose it decides to combat the recession by open-market purchases of government securities.

Let us suppose further that it purchases these securities directly from its member banks:

As a consequence of these open-market purchases, the member banks will find their reserves in excess of the legal requirements. They will be ready and eager to lend more to businesses. In this process of lending more, the money supply will be increased, and the banks will find themselves offering better terms—lower interest rates—to businessmen. Businessmen, in their turn, will find the lower interest rates attractive, an inducement to expand their investments. They will now be willing to undertake expansions of their plant and equipment and machinery that heretofore would not have been profitable. The same willingness to borrow will also be true of people who wish to build homes, or of state and local governments that may need to float loans for new schools. In general, then, the lowered interest rates and the increased availability of money will cause an expansion of investment and other spending in the economy. This expansion will, by virtue of the national income multiplier, lead to an expansion of national income and employment in the economy as a whole. Thus, monetary policy, like fiscal policy, is shown to be a tool by which the government can influence the level of spending and, consequently, the level of national income and employment in the economy.

This, in capsule form, is the fundamental way by which the nation's monetary policy reaches down into the economy to affect the major economic aggregates of output, employment, and prices.

One factor we have not mentioned—though in all logic it should have been part of the chain that we have been attempting to construct—is sometimes called the *transactions demand for money.* One of the reasons we hold any of our wealth in the form of money (as opposed, say, to stocks or bonds or other assets) is quite simply that we need money to carry on the ordinary business of life. We need a certain amount of money to handle our normal day-to-day or month-to-month financial transactions. Now the *amount* of money we need for these transactions purposes will, on the whole, be determined by the amount of business we do or, for the national economy, by the level of national income in money terms. At a national income of $400 billion annually, we need considerably less transaction money than at a national income of, say, $1 trillion. The point is this: in our capsule summary we spoke of the end product of monetary policy as being a certain expansion of national income. What we did *not* do was to take account of the extra transaction demand for money that such an expansion brings. What this factor means, in essence, is that only *part* of the expanded money supply can, so to speak, go into financing a lower rate of interest; another part of it must be made available to finance the expanded transactions required by the increased national income.

Another matter we did not investigate fully was *how much* of an effect an expansion of the money supply might have in lowering the rate of interest. Some of that added money supply, as we have just said, may be needed to finance a higher level of transactions if national money income expands in response to Federal Reserve action. But what of the impact of the added money beyond this? We have already suggested that Federal Reserve action affecting bank reserves will bring about a fully multiplied expansion of the money supply only if the member banks desire to remain "fully loaned up." But if interest rates are already low and business conditions look poor, then the member banks may not lend out all their excess reserves, as assumed in our bank balance sheets above. They may decide to hold excess reserves, thus frustrating the multiple credit expansion that the Fed is attempting to promote.

More generally, when interest rates are low, people in the economy as a whole may find that their desire to hold money as opposed to other assets is quite strong. For businesses and individuals want money not simply for the transaction purposes just mentioned but also for what are sometimes called *liquidity*

purposes. If you are holding a stock or a bond, its price may fall (say from $80 a share to $60 a share), and you will have sustained a monetary loss. In the case of money, the price of a dollar remains forever a dollar. If interest rates are low (in which case the opportunity cost of holding money is low), you may decide to hold *perfectly liquid* money rather than take a risk that your stocks or bonds may fall in money value.[6] What this means is that even when the money supply is substantially increased, it may not have a very great effect on bringing down interest rates. As these rates fall lower and lower, people may simply decide to hold all the additional money *as money*, for these liquidity reasons. After a certain point is reached, people may refuse to buy bonds and other securities, with the consequence that even if more money is pumped into the economy, it will not bring a lowered interest rate and hence will have little or no effect on business investment.

This last point not only suggests some potential weaknesses of monetary policy in curing a depression (Keynesians often call this phenomenon the "liquidity trap"), but also leads us to a deeper understanding of the role of money in the total economy. We might say that people want to hold wealth in the form of money for two main reasons: (1) *transactions* demand, and (2) *liquidity* or, as it is also called, the *precautionary motive*. When the quantity of money

---

6. A *liquid* asset is one readily turned into money. Since money *is* money, it is *perfectly liquid*. When interest rates are low, this is the same thing as saying that bond prices are high: $5 a year on a bond that sells for $100 is an interest rate of 5 percent; $5 a year on a bond that sells for $50 is 10 percent. When bond prices are high, people generally may fear that they are due for a fall. This is an important reason for preferring money to bonds when interest rates are low.

The reader should understand that perfect liquidity does not imply a constant purchasing power. Although a dollar is always worth a dollar, it may be worth less in terms of real goods when there is a general inflation. Indeed, when prices in general are rising, the costs of holding perfectly liquid money are increased, because that money will be worth less (in real terms) in the future.

in the economy is "too small" to sustain full employment income, we have the following situation in mind:

A high, full-employment national income will naturally create a great demand for the use of money for transactions purposes. This will leave only a small amount of the stock of money in the economy for liquidity or precautionary purposes. If the interest rate is low, people will feel that they want to exchange securities (say, bonds) for money to assuage their precautionary concerns. When everybody tries to sell his bonds, however, the price of bonds will fall, and this is equivalent to a rise in the interest rate. This rise in the interest rate, in turn, will cause some fall in investment and hence in national income. At equilibrium, when it is finally achieved, the fall in national income will have reduced the demand for money for transactions purposes and provided more for liquidity or precautionary purposes. The "cost" of a "too small" money supply, therefore, will be reduced national income and employment.[7]

With this general picture in mind, it can be said that we have completed the "basics of national income determination" that was the object of Part Two A of this book. There are many further points to be made and many applications of these basic tools that must be considered, and we will now turn directly to these matters. The reader should recognize, however, that if he has mastered the materials in Part Two A he already has at his disposal a powerful theoretical apparatus that will enable him to achieve a deeper insight into the important macroeconomic problems of our time. And this is no small achievement.

---

7.   Just as the "cost" of a "too big" money supply would be inflationary pressures. See chapter 14, pp. 347–48. For the graphically minded reader, the points covered in this brief paragraph in the text are discussed in terms of diagrams in the appendix to this chapter.

SUMMARY

In this chapter, we have brought the role of money explicitly into our analysis of national income, attempting to show how the monetary policy of the government may affect the levels of national income and employment in the economy.

The basic links in the logical chain connecting money with national income, employment, and prices are as follows:

1. An increase in the money supply will generally lower the interest rate. The agency responsible for handling the money supply of the United States is the Federal Reserve Board. The Fed has various instruments available for increasing the money supply, including: changing the reserve requirements of its member banks, lowering the interest rate *(discount rate)* at which the member banks may borrow from the Federal Reserve Bank in their district, and making open-market purchases of government securities.

The analysis of this chapter enables us to follow through a Federal Reserve purchase of government bonds from one of its member banks. We now understand that this purchase would (a) increase the reserves of the member banks; (b) lead to a multiple expansion of demand deposits in the economy; and (c) bring about generally lowered interest rates and easier availability of credit to business investors. In understanding this process, it is necessary to remember that demand deposits are the most common form of money in the United States.

2. A fall in the interest rate will generally lead to an increase in business investment. To understand this point, we should recall that we are talking about "investment" in the sense of adding machinery and plant to the productive capacity of the economy (not "financial investment," i.e., buying a stock or a bond). To the businessman who is thinking of buying a new machine or expanding his factory, a low interest rate will mean lowered costs of borrowing money. Hence, it will generally encourage *investment,* in our sense of the word.

3. An increase in business investment will generally lead to an expansion of national income and employment. This is simply our old friend the national income multiplier from earlier chapters.

(Point (4)—which relates decreases in the money supply to higher interest rates, lowered investment, and a contraction of aggregate demand—is being postponed until chapter 14, which deals with inflation.)

In evaluating this logical chain, one has to remember some important qualifications:

(a) A certain proportion of our money supply is used for *transactions* purposes. If national income expands, there will generally be an increased demand for money for transactions, with the consequence that not all of any given increase in the money supply will go into bringing lowered interest rates.

(b) A low interest rate may have fairly little impact on raising the level of investment if other factors affecting investment are strongly negative; e.g., the existence of excess capacity, pessimistic business expectations, and so on.

(c) If the banks are cautious about lending out their excess reserves and if there is a strong *liquidity* or *precautionary* demand for money in the economy as a whole, then the Fed may be largely frustrated in its efforts to bring interest rates down.

IMPORTANT TERMS TO REMEMBER

Money Stock (M_1, M_2, M_3)
Near-Money
Bank Balance Sheet
Assets
Liabilities
Deposit Creation
Legal Reserve Requirements
Fractional Reserve Banking
Discount Rate
Investment-GNP Link
Interest Rate-Investment Link
Money Supply-Interest Rate Link
Open-Market Operations in Government Securities
Excess Reserves
Multiple Credit Creation
Transactions Demand for Money
Precautionary or Liquidity Demand for Money

QUESTIONS FOR DISCUSSION

1. Define *money*. What are some other forms, besides money, in which people might hold their wealth? Rank the various assets you have listed according to their degree of liquidity.

2. What is meant by the phrase "a synthesis of real and monetary economics"? Is this synthesis achieved in the analysis presented in this chapter? If so, explain how.

3. Suppose an individual, having come to distrust the banking system, withdraws his $1,000 demand deposit from a commercial bank and buries the $1,000 in his backyard. Will this have any effect on the money supply of the economy? Follow through the steps involved.

4. It sometimes happens that the Treasury, unable to market government securities to the public on acceptable terms, sells them to the Federal Reserve System. The balance sheet of the Federal Reserve Bank is thereby altered as follows for a $1 million sale:

Stage I: The Treasury is credited with a $1 million deposit at the Federal Reserve Bank:

FEDERAL RESERVE BANK BALANCE SHEET

ASSETS	LIABILITIES
+ $1 million government bonds	+ $1 million U.S. Treasury deposits

Stage II: The Treasury spends the money, and the individuals who receive it deposit it in their commercial banks. The commercial banks thereby increase their reserves at the Federal Reserve Bank:

FEDERAL RESERVE BANK BALANCE SHEET

ASSETS	LIABILITIES
+ $1 million government bonds	+ $1 million Member bank reserves

What effect will this transaction be likely to have on the money supply of the country?

It has been said that this way of financing the federal debt is very much like "printing money." Do you agree?

Suppose the Treasury, instead of selling its bonds to the Federal Reserve System, sells them to private individuals who pay for them by check on their demand deposit accounts at their commercial banks. Will this have a similar or different effect on the money supply of the country? Explain.

5. Explain (a) the money supply-interest rate link; (b) the interest rate-investment link; (c) the investment-GNP link. Indicate the main weaknesses in these links if our objective happens to be to "cure" a depression by monetary policy.

APPENDIX 11: MONEY AND NATIONAL INCOME DETERMINATION

In this appendix, we shall gather together a number of points made in chapter 11 and earlier chapters, showing graphically how money fits into our general analysis of national income determination.

We begin with the two different kinds of demand for money that were mentioned toward the end of chapter 11: (1) the *transactions* demand (depending mainly on the level of national money income), and (2) the *liquidity* or precautionary demand (depending mainly on the rate of interest). When national money income is high, the transactions demand for money will be high. When the rate of interest is high, the liquidity demand for money will be low. The reason is that, at high interest rates, people will prefer to hold their wealth in the form of interest-earning assets, rather than in the form of money. Also, we recall, a high interest rate on bonds implies a low price of bonds; hence, people may wish to hold bonds rather than money, anticipating that the price of bonds may rise. The converse of these reasons will explain the opposite proposition, namely, that at low

interest rates, the liquidity demand for money will be high.

These two demands for money are summed horizontally in Figure 1 for a given level of national income (Y_0).* The transactions demand for money is represented by the vertical line (T_0), indicating that we are assuming a given level of national income (and hence of transactions). As we move further to the right, we add on the amounts of money that people wish to hold for liquidity purposes. These amounts will become greater as the interest rate becomes lower. The diagram suggests the possibility of a "liquidity trap" at very low levels of the interest rate. That is to say, the curve becomes very nearly horizontal at low levels of the interest rate, meaning that

---

*The transactions demand for money will, of course, depend on the level of *money* national income, not *real* national income. In this appendix, however, we will assume that the price level is unchanged and, therefore, that changes in money income reflect changes in real income (i.e., income at constant prices). In this somewhat simplified world, we can say that the transactions demand for money will depend mainly on the level of real national income.

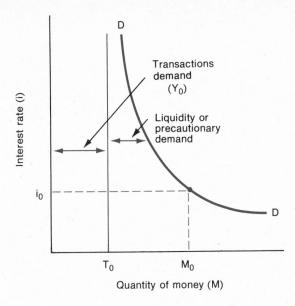

Figure 1. Demand for Money at a Given Level of National Income (Y_0).

Curve *DD* represents the demand for money in an economy at different interest rates, given a certain level of national income (Y_0). If the quantity of money in the economy is given (M_0), then the rate of interest compatible with this level of national income is i_0.

even substantial additions to the money supply will not bring much further reduction in the interest rate.

In this diagram, if we assume that the Federal Reserve Banks have determined a given stock of money for the nation (M_0), then we can say that, *with the assumed level of national income, Y_0,* the equilibrium rate of interest will be determined at i_0. Why an equilibrium rate? Because this is the rate of interest at which the amount of their wealth that people are willing to hold in the form of money is exactly equal to the stock of money (as determined by the Fed) in existence. At a *higher* rate of interest, people want to hold (for both transactions *and* liquidity purposes) less money than was actually in existence. What would they then do? They would start

trying to get rid of their money by buying securities, say, bonds. This attempt by everyone to buy bonds would raise the price of bonds, which, in turn, is equivalent to a *fall* in the interest rate. Hence, a higher interest rate than i_0 would lead to forces tending to bring the interest rate down. (The reader should show for himself that, by exactly analogous logic, an interest rate *below* i_0 would set in motion forces tending to *raise* the interest rate.)

But we have just begun the story in Figure 1, because we are there assuming a given level of national income. However, it is the level of national income that we are precisely trying to determine.

To do this, we need to proceed further, the next step being to observe what happens to the demand for money at some different level of national income. In Figure 2, we again have a given level of national income but this time a higher level of national income ($Y_1 > Y_0$). The effect of this change is to push the transactions demand for money further out to the right. This, in turn, pushes the whole *DD* curve out to the right (to $D'D'$). The net result is that, for our given stock of money (M_0), the equilibrium rate of interest will be higher at the higher level of national income ($i_1 > i_0$).

This is an important point to note, because it suggests that we can use this logic to find a systematic relationship between the level of national income and the interest rate (always assuming a given stock of money). In particular, the higher the level of national income, the higher the equilibrium rate of interest will be. This relationship is depicted in Figure 3 in what economists usually call the *LM* curve (standing for liquidity-money). Notice that we have changed the quantity on the horizontal or *x*-axis. It no longer represents the quantity of money, but the level of national income (Y). *LM* generally slopes upward from left to right, the basic reason being that a higher level of income raises the transactions demand for money; thus, a higher interest rate is necessary to make people content to hold only the smaller amount of money left over for liquidity or precautionary purposes.

We have now gone exactly *half* the way to the solution of our overall problem—which remains, as always, to determine the equilibrium level of national

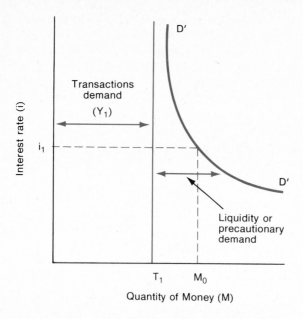

Quantity of Money (M)

Figure 2. Demand for Money at a Higher Level of National Income (Y_1).

With a higher level of national income ($Y_1 > Y_0$), and the same quantity of money (M_0), the rate of interest will have to be higher ($i_1 > i_0$).

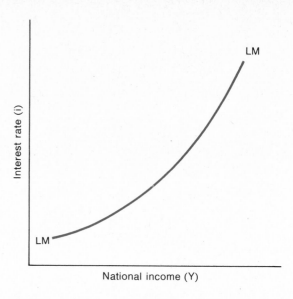

National income (Y)

Figure 3. The *LM* (Liquidity-Money) Curve.

This curve shows that, for a given quantity of money (M_0), the equilibrium rate of interest will have to rise with national income. Notice that we now have national income (Y), not the money supply, measured on the horizontal axis.

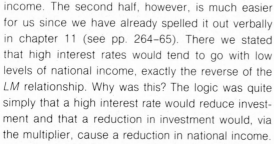

income. The second half, however, is much easier for us since we have already spelled it out verbally in chapter 11 (see pp. 264–65). There we stated that high interest rates would tend to go with low levels of national income, exactly the reverse of the *LM* relationship. Why was this? The logic was quite simply that a high interest rate would reduce investment and that a reduction in investment would, via the multiplier, cause a reduction in national income.

Of course, there is nothing contradictory between these two relationships. Indeed, if we did not have another relationship between national income and the interest rate beyond that shown in Figure 3, we would be unable to determine the equilibrium level of national income. We would simply be able to say that, for this or that level of national income, we will have this or that interest rate.

Figure 4 pulls all this material together in one diagram. We have added what economists usually call an *IS* curve (investment-savings curve), which shows that the lower the level of the interest rate, the higher will be the equilibrium level of national income. The reason is, as we have stated, that lower interest rates will lead to high investment, which, via the multiplier (which guarantees us that planned investment and planned savings will be equated), will produce higher levels of national income.

In this diagram, we finally *do* determine the equilibrium level of national income. It is Y_e. We also determine the equilibrium rate of interest, i_e. At this overall equilibrium, planned investment and saving are equal, and also the amount of their wealth that people want to hold in the form of money (for both transactions and liquidity purposes) is exactly equal to the assumed stock of money (M_0).

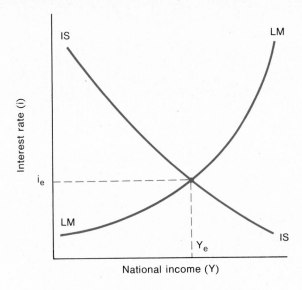

Figure 4. Overall Equilibrium Achieved.

Although subject to many qualifications, this is a very useful diagram for showing equilibrium where I = S and also where the demand for money equals the given supply (M₀).

Now this diagram, properly understood, is remarkably helpful as an aid to coping with many of the different problems we have mentioned from time to time in this and preceding chapters. How, for example, would a change in the money supply—from M_0 to M_1—affect the equilibrium levels of national income and interest rate? The effect would be manifested through the LM curve. If, say, M_1 is greater than M_0, the general effect will be to push the LM curve to the right. You can see this by going back to Figure 1 and showing how an increase in the stock of money will mean a lower equilibrium rate of interest for any given level of national income. Knowing that LM is shifted to the right, we can see that the general effect of the increase in the money supply will be a rise in the equilibrium level of national income and a fall in the equilibrium rate of interest.

The diagram can be used even more specifically than this, however. The reader should follow through the exercise below, which involves the analysis of both the shapes of these LM and IS curves and also shifts in these curves. If he works these problems out, he will hopefully agree that, despite a number of qualifications that we shall be taking up later on, these tools are really quite remarkable for organizing one's thoughts about the complexities of modern macroeconomics.

EXERCISE

Many economists believe that the following statements are wholly or partly true and that they have a significant bearing on many macroeconomic issues. Your task is to show how to represent these statements in terms of the shapes and/or positions of the IS and LM curves:

1. At very low levels of the interest rate, further increases in the quantity of money will not lead to any further reductions in the interest rate. (This is what we referred to in the text as the "liquidity trap.")

2. Technological progress, if it stimulates businessmen to increase investment, may raise both the equilibrium level of national income and the equilibrium rate of interest.

3. An increased desire to save (shift in the consumption function) can lead to lower equilibrium levels of national income and interest rate.

4. It is sometimes argued that while very high levels of interest rates may choke off investment, very low levels of interest rates may have little effect in increasing investment after a certain point. If true, how would this be reflected in our diagram?

5. Suppose we live in an economy in which both points (1) and (4) above are true. It can be argued that in such an economy, monetary policy may be effective in restraining an over-exuberant economy but that it will be of little use in curing a depression. (This is sometimes put in terms of the maxim: "You can pull on a string, but you can't push a string.") Explain your answer in terms of our diagrams.

PART 2B   MACROECONOMICS: PROBLEMS AND APPLICATIONS

CHAPTER 12
TAXES AND THE NATIONAL DEBT

In Part Two A, we presented the basics of national income determination in a roughly logical sequence, including as well the underlying theory of fiscal and monetary policy. Now, in Part Two B, we shall try to extend and apply this analysis to some of the problems facing a modern industrialized economy. In doing this, we necessarily touch on many issues on which economists differ among themselves. Whereas in the preceding chapters on macroeconomics we largely avoided controversy in order to present the argument in a reasonably uninterrupted way, we must now give full weight to these differences of opinion—some of which, indeed, are about the basic theory itself.

The topics under consideration—the national debt, monetarism, inflation, balance of payments problems, growth—are among the most fascinating in all of economics. At the end of Part Two B, the reader should have a sense (1) that economists do not have fully agreed upon answers to these problems, and yet (2) that modern economic analysis provides an indispensable starting point for approaching such issues—for the citizen quite as much as for the professional economist.

In this chapter we shall consider some of the issues involved in financing government expenditures, whether by taxation, or, more controversially, by increasing the national debt.

VARIOUS KINDS OF TAXES

In chapter 10, we talked of various combinations of government expenditure and tax policies, and their effects on the level of national income. In this discussion, however, we considered only one kind of tax—a rather special lump-sum tax on consumers. It is obvious, of course, that in reality there are many different kinds of taxes and that they have very different loci of economic impact. In the United States at the present time, the major sources of tax revenue are the following:

Individual income tax. This is the most important single tax and a tax with which most of us are familiar. It accounts for nearly 45 percent of all federal tax revenues, about a sixth of state revenues, and a very small proportion of local revenues. Overall, it accounts for about a third of tax revenues at all governmental levels. Because of its special importance, we will return to this tax in the next section of this chapter.

Payroll taxes. These are of importance at the federal level only, but they are now the second largest source of federal revenue—about 30 percent of all federal revenue in 1974—and they are growing very rapidly (ten years ago they were only 20 percent of federal revenue). The purpose of these taxes is to finance the social security program and certain other unemployment insurance programs. This tax tends to be regressive and to weigh particularly heavily on lower income groups.

Corporation income taxes. Taxes are levied directly on corporations as well as on individuals. These taxes are collected by both state governments and the federal government, although the latter is by far the larger collector. In 1973, corporate income taxes overall ran to about $55 billion in the United States.

Sales and excise taxes. This is by far the largest single category of revenue at the state level, accounting for nearly half of state tax revenues; it is much smaller, though not insignificant (between 5 and 10 percent of tax revenues), at both the local and federal levels. These sales and excise taxes are important examples of *indirect taxes*.. An indirect tax is one that is levied on goods and services, as opposed to direct taxes that fall "directly" on persons (e.g., the individual income tax). Thus, it can be said

that while the U.S. federal government relies heavily on direct taxes, the states tend to rely much more on indirect taxes. In comparison to *other countries,* with a few exceptions, the United States depends more on income and other direct taxes in total and less on indirect taxes than do other national governments.

Property tax. The property tax, the most important tax at the local level, brought in about $42 billion in revenue in 1973. This tax is a mainstay of local school systems, though it has come under attack in some instances from the courts as leading to unequal schools in different localities. Long considered a regressive tax, recent studies have suggested that it may be on the progressive side on balance.[1]

There are a number of other taxes of lesser impact (for example, estate and gift taxes), but the above listing is enough to bring out the obvious point that the *way* in which taxes are raised will clearly have a significant impact on the avenues by which taxation influences aggregate demand and equilibrium national income. Take, for example, sales taxes as opposed to the individual income tax. We can easily understand the multiplier analysis in the case of the latter, but how about the former? The answer quickly gets quite complicated. *Part* of a sales tax will usually be borne by consumers in the form of higher prices for the goods they buy. This will reduce their real income and thus, like an individual income tax, will result in a lowering of the consumption (C) schedule of our earlier chapters. Another part of the sales tax, however, will fall on the producers of the goods, both the wage-earners and the employers. In the case of the wage-earners, we could probably again treat this effect in terms of a fall in real income and thus a further downward shift of the C schedule. But the other part will fall on profits and the main effect here

---

1.   See Henry Aaron, "A New View of Property Tax Incidence," and Richard A. Musgrave, "Is a Property Tax on Housing Regressive?" in *The American Economic Review,* Papers and Proceedings, May 1974.

may be on the level of investment in that particular industry. Thus, both *C* and *I* may be affected, but in ways that can be analyzed only in terms of the detailed structure of supply-and-demand conditions in the industries affected.

Much the same is the case with corporate profits taxes. The main impact there might seem to be on profits, hence on the employers, and hence on business investment (*I*). However, it is not clear in general where the strongest effect of the corporate profits tax is—on the firm, the workers, or the consumers. If these taxes can be passed along to the consumer then, of course, they affect *C* as well as *I*.

Thus, our general analysis of the effects of taxation on equilibrium national income of chapter 10 must be modified to recognize that (1) taxes may affect *I* as well as *C*; and (2) the strength of the effect on *C* will depend on who exactly pays the tax—matters that often have to be analyzed in great detail for particular taxes and circumstances.

IMPACT OF THE FEDERAL INCOME TAX

What about the effects of the federal individual income tax in particular? This is our most important single tax. What can be said in a general way about its performance in relation to *Y, C* and *I?* The following reading by the noted tax authority, Joseph A. Pechman, touches on some of these issues, bringing out among other points the role of the income tax as an *automatic stabilizer* of national income.

Economic Effects of the Individual Income Tax

Joseph A. Pechman

Three issues are of particular importance in appraising the economic effects of the individual income tax: its role as a stabilizer of consumption expenditures, its effect on saving, and its impact on work and investment incentives.

ROLE AS STABILIZER

Stability of yield was once regarded as a major criterion of a good tax. Today there is general agreement that properly timed changes in tax yields can help increase demand during recessions and restrain the growth of demand during periods of expansion. The progressive individual income tax has the virtue that its yield automatically rises and falls more than in proportion to changes in personal income. Moreover, the system of paying taxes currently has greatly accelerated the reaction of income tax revenues to changes in income. An important by-product of current payment is that changes in tax rates have an almost immediate effect on the disposable income of most taxpayers. These features have made the personal income tax extremely useful for promoting economic stabilization and growth.

The automatic response of the individual income tax—its *built-in flexibility*—can be explained by the following example. Suppose a taxpayer with a wife and two children earns $10,000 a year when he is employed and uses the standard deduction. His taxable income is $5,500 ($10,000 less $1,500 for the standard deduction and $3,000 for the personal exemptions), and the tax under 1973 rates and exemp-

Excerpted from Joseph A. Pechman, *Federal Tax Policy*, rev. ed. pp. 62–67, Brookings Institution. © 1971 by the Brookings Institution, Washington, D.C. Reprinted by permission of the publisher.

tions is $905. The following table shows what the effect on his taxable income and tax would be if his income dropped to $8,000:

Adjusted gross income	$10,000	$8,000
Less exemptions	3,000	3,000
Less standard deduction	1,500	1,200
Taxable income	5,500	3,800
Tax	905	586
Disposable income	9,095	7,414

Whereas adjusted gross income declined by only 20 percent, taxable income declined 31 percent (from $5,500 to $3,800), and the tax declined 35 percent.

Such examples are multiplied millions of times during a recession, while the opposite occurs during boom periods. Those with lower or higher incomes find that their tax is reduced or increased proportionately more than their income. As a result, disposable income is more stable than it would be in the absence of the tax. (In the above example, disposable income declined only $1,681 while income before tax declined $2,000.) Since disposable income is the major determinant of consumption, expenditures by consumers are also more stable than they would be in the absence of the tax.

Individual income tax rate changes are also used to restrain or stimulate the economy. The Revenue Act of 1964 reduced tax receipts by $11.4 billion, of which the individual income tax reduction accounted for $9.2 billion. The Vietnam war surtax, which was enacted in 1968 to reduce inflationary pressures, increased tax receipts by a total of $10.2 billion, including $6.8 billion of individual income tax. The tax cut was designed to raise the level of expenditures by consumers and businessmen and thus to stimulate a higher rate of economic growth. Consumer expenditures had already increased in anticipation of the tax cut when it went into effect for withholding purposes early in March 1964; in the succeeding year, they rose $28 billion. While the increase in consumption cannot be attributed wholly to the tax cut, this was undoubtedly the most important factor. However, the Vietnam war surtax did not have a major effect on spending, because monetary policy was relaxed prematurely and because expectations of inflation were more pervasive than had been anticipated. Those who believe that consumption is determined largely by what individuals regard as their "permanent" income argue that the surtax was not effective because it was a temporary tax change. Nevertheless, most people are persuaded that income tax changes can have a significant effect in helping to regulate the rate of growth of private demand, but that the effect is greater for permanent than for temporary changes.

Countercyclical changes in tax rates seem to be rare in most countries, partly because there are long delays in recognizing significant changes in economic conditions and partly because the legislative process is too slow. However, it should be possible to devise procedures for varying tax rates quickly in response to changes in the level of economic activity.

EFFECT ON SAVING AND CONSUMPTION

The individual income tax applies to the entire income of an individual whether it is spent or saved. Some have argued that the income tax is unfair to those who save because it applies both to the income that gives rise to the saving and to the income produced by the saving. But almost all economists now agree that, on equity grounds, this double taxation argument does not have much merit. At any particular point in time, an individual has the option to make a new decision to spend or save from the income that is left to him after tax. If he decides to save the income, he does not necessarily incur a new tax. It is only if the saving is invested in an income-producing asset that new income is generated, and this new income is subject to additional tax.

The individual income tax is often contrasted with a general consumption or expenditure tax, which is an alternative method of taxing individuals in accordance with "ability to pay." In the case of the income tax, the measure of ability to pay is income; in the case of the expenditure tax, the measure is consumption. The tax on consumption may also be levied at progressive rates (but the rates must be greater than 100 percent to equal the impact of the progressive income tax in the higher brackets).

Consumption taxes can be avoided simply by reducing one's consumption. This means that an expenditure tax encourages saving more than does an equal-yield income tax that is distributed in the same proportions by income classes. In practice, where the income tax is paid by the large mass of the people, much of the tax yield comes from income classes where there is little room in family budgets for increasing saving in response to tax incentives. As a consequence, the differential effect on total consumption and saving between an income tax and an equal-yield expenditure tax is likely to be small in this country.

Economics alone does not provide a basis for deciding whether the income tax is more or less "equitable" than an expenditure tax. The income tax reduces the gain made when an individual saves rather than consumes part of his income, while an expenditure tax makes future consumption relatively as attractive as present consumption. Under the income tax, the interest reward for saving and investing is reduced by the tax; under the expenditure tax, the net reward is always equal to the market rate of interest regardless of the tax rate.

While this subject has not been widely discussed in the United States, the continued heavy reliance on the income tax suggests that it is probably more acceptable on equity grounds than an expenditure tax. An expenditure tax was recommended by the Treasury during World War II, but it was rejected by the Congress primarily because of its novelty and complexity.

Graduated expenditure taxes are often proposed as a method of avoiding or correcting the defects of the income tax base, particularly in the top brackets, where the preferential treatment of capital gains, tax-exempt interest, depletion allowances, and other favorable provisions permit the accumulation of large fortunes with little or no payment of income tax. An expenditure tax would reach such incomes when they are spent without resort to regressive taxation. Despite this advantage, the expenditure tax has not been widely used. It is more difficult to administer and also raises more serious problems of compliance for the taxpayer. Although it is difficult to imagine total replacement of the income tax by an expenditure tax, the latter might be a useful supplement if and when it became necessary to discourage consumption. . . .

WORK AND INVESTMENT INCENTIVES

The individual income tax affects economic incentives in two different directions. On the one hand, it reduces the financial rewards of greater effort and risk-taking and thus tends to discourage these activities. On the other hand, it may provide a greater incentive to obtain more income because it cuts down on the income left over for spending. There is no basis for deciding which effect is more important on an a priori basis.

Taxation is only one of many factors affecting work and investment incentives. This makes it extremely difficult to interpret the available statistical evidence or the results of direct interviews with taxpayers. The evidence suggests that income taxation does not significantly reduce the amount of labor supplied by workers and managers. Work habits are not easily changed, and there is little scope in a modern industrial society for most people to vary their hours of work or the intensity of their efforts in response to changes in tax rates. Nearly all people who are asked about income taxation grumble about it, but relatively few say that they work fewer hours or exert less than their best efforts to avoid tax.

As for risk-taking, the problem is much more complicated. In the first place, the tax rates on capital gains are much lower than those on ordinary incomes. Numerous studies have demonstrated that the opportunity to earn income in the form of capital gains stimulates investment and risk-taking. Second, taxpayers may offset business losses against ordinary income not only for the current year but also for three prior years and five succeeding years; capital losses may similarly be offset against capital gains, and half of these losses (up to $1,000 a year) may be offset against ordinary income for an indefinite period. Such offsets greatly diminish the consequences of loss by the investor. Third, much of the nation's investment is undertaken by large corporations. These firms are generally permitted to retain earnings after payment of tax at the corporation rate, which is more moderate than the rates applying to investors in the top personal income tax brackets. Finally, the law provides incentives to invest through generous depreciation allowances. In any case, experience suggests that the major stimulus to investment comes from a healthy and prosperous economy.

Much can be done to improve the structure of the income tax. But there is little basis for the assertions made from time to time that the income tax has had an adverse effect on the economy. ☐

FINANCING *G* THROUGH THE NATIONAL DEBT

So far, we have been discussing financing government expenditures (*G*) through various forms of taxes. But we know that governments—including certainly our own—often finance expenditures by borrowing. They sell bonds and add to the national debt. One of the important ways in which government can affect aggregate demand, we know, is by increasing expenditures without equivalent increases in taxes (or, similarly though not quite exactly the same, decreasing taxes without cutting expenditures). Such actions lead inevitably to a growth in the national debt.

But is it legal to do this? Or, if it is legal, is it moral? Or, if it is both legal and moral, is it *wise*? Here we come to one of the age-old controversies in the field of macroeconomics, where there is no way to proceed but to spell out some of the different points of view on the public debt and then try to sort through the issues as objectively as we can.

View I: The Importance of a Balanced Budget

The traditional view, to which many political figures still pay tribute to this day, is that governmental budgets ought simply to be kept in balance. An often-quoted statement of this position was made by Senator Harry Flood Byrd of Virginia in a 1955 speech that was later recorded in the *Congressional Record*. The following is an excerpt from that speech:

The Importance of a Balanced Budget

Senator Harry F. Byrd

I am pleased to have this opportunity to speak on the subject: Is it important to balance the budget?

As I see it, balancing the budget without resorting to legerdemain or unsound bookkeeping methods is certainly in the category of our No. 1 problems.

Beginning with 1792, the first fiscal year of our Federal Government, and through 1916, Federal deficits were casual and usually paid off in succeeding years. In this 124-year period there were 43 deficit years and 81 surplus years. As late as July 1, 1914, the interest-bearing debt was less than $1 billion.

In Andrew Jackson's administration the public debt was paid off in toto, an achievement in which President Jackson expressed great pride.

It can be said for this first 124 years in the life of our Republic we were on a pay-as-you-go basis. In that period I think it can be accurately said that we laid the foundation for our strength today as the greatest nation in all the world.

Excerpted from "The Importance of a Balanced Budget," a speech by Senator Harry F. Byrd. Reprinted in *Congressional Record, 84th Cong., 1st sess., 1955, 101, pt. 4: 5693–95.*

Then, in 1917, 1918, and 1919, World War 1 deficits aggregated $13 billion. Heavy current taxation in those years paid much of the war cost.

The next eleven years, from 1919 to 1931, were surplus years and the war debt was reduced.

In 1932 Mr. Roosevelt came into office, and the most outstanding plank in his platform was to reduce Federal expenditures by 25 percent and to keep the budget in balance. He accused Mr. Hoover of "throwing discretion to the winds and indulging in an orgy of waste and extravagance." Mr. Hoover spent $4 billion in his last year, and the record shows that this spendthrift Hoover was the only President to leave office with fewer Federal employees than when he came in.

Mr. Roosevelt added more than $200 billion to the public debt during his administrations.

I took my oath as a Senator the same day Mr. Roosevelt took his as President—March 4, 1933. The first bill I voted on was the legislation recommended by President Roosevelt to redeem his economy pledge by reducing all expenditures 15 percent—a difference of 10 percent less than his original promise, it is true—but I thought this was a substantial redemption of a campaign pledge, as such things go, and I enthusiastically supported him.

The title of the bill was "A bill to preserve the credit of the United States Government." Our debt was then about $16 billion. This economy program was short-lived—about six months—and the spending then began to steadily and rapidly increase.

Mr. Roosevelt presented thirteen budgets and in every peacetime budget he promised a balance between income and outgo for the next year, but it turned out that next year never came. He was in the red all the way, and in every year of his administration a substantial deficit was added to the public debt.

There were eight Truman budgets. Three were in the black—those for fiscal years 1947, 1948, and 1951. Two resulted from war contract cancellations following the end of World War II and the third resulted from increased taxes for the Korean war before the war bills started coming due. Five Truman budgets were in the red.

Mr. Eisenhower has presented two budgets—both in the red but on a declining ratio. The Eisenhower deficit estimates for fiscal years 1955 and 1956 aggregate $7 billion as compared to the last Truman budget which alone contemplated a $9 billion deficit.

The cold facts are that for twenty-one years out of the last twenty-four years we have spent more than we have collected. In these twenty-four years we have balanced the budget in only three; and these were more by accident than by design.

We must recognize that we have abandoned the sound fiscal policies strictly adhered to by all political parties and all Presidents for considerably more than a century of our existence. It is true that during these twenty-one deficit years we were engaged in World War II for four years and in the Korean war for two years. Yet, in the years when the pay-as-you-go system prevailed we also had quite a few wars.

It is the quarter of a century of deficit spending which now makes balancing the budget so imperative. Young men and women, born in 1930, have lived in the red virtually all their lives. Our acceptance of deficit spending for so long a period has weakened public resistance to the evils of this practice. Bad habits are hard to change.

Will the deficits become permanent and continue to pile debt upon debt until real disaster comes? If we cannot balance the budget in this day of our greatest dollar income, when taxes are near their peak, and when we are at peace. I ask, when can we?

It is disturbing these days to hear some economists argue the budget should not be balanced and that we should not begin to pay on the debt because, they allege, it will adversely affect business conditions. Have we yielded so far to the blandishments of Federal subsidies and Government support that we have forgotten our Nation is great because of individual effort as contrasted to state paternalism?

EVILS OF DEFICIT SPENDING

Here are some of the evils of deficit spending:

The debt today is the debt incurred by this generation, but tomorrow it will be debt on our children and grandchildren, and it will be for them to pay, both the interest and the principal.

It is possible and in fact probable that before this astronomical debt is paid off, if it ever is, the interest charge will exceed the principal.

Protracted deficit spending means cheapening the dollar. Secretary Humphrey testified before the Finance Committee that the greatest single factor in cheapening the American dollar has been deficit spending.

Since I have been in the Senate, interest alone on the Federal debt has cost the taxpayers of this country more than $75 billion. At present rates, on the Federal debt at its present level, interest on it in the next twenty years will cost taxpayers upwards of $150 billion.

Since 1940 the Federal Government has borrowed and spent a quarter of a trillion dollars more than we have collected in taxes.

Year by year, nearly in direct ratio to deficit spending, the purchasing value of the dollar has declined. Beginning with a 100-cent dollar in 1940, the value of the dollar had declined to 52 cents in 1954.

As proof of the fact that deficit spending is directly responsible for cheapening the dollar, let me mention that in 1942, when we spent $19 billion in excess of revenue, the dollar in that one year declined ten cents in value.

In 1943, another big deficit year, the dollar lost five cents more in value, and another nine cents in 1946. From 1940 through 1952, an era of heavy deficit spending, the dollar lost forty-eight cents in value, or nearly four cents each year, and it is still slipping but in much lesser degree.

Some may regard these facts and figures lightly, but the loss of half the purchasing power of its money in thirteen years should be a serious warning to any nation.

Cheapened money is inflation. Inflation is a dangerous game. It robs creditors, it steals pensions, wages, and fixed income. Once started, it is exceedingly difficult to control. This inflation has been partially checked but the value of the dollar dropped slightly again in the past year. It would not take much to start up this dangerous inflation again.

Public debt is not like private debt. If private debt is not paid off, it can be ended by liquidation, but if public debt is not paid off with taxes, liquidation takes the form of disastrous inflation or national repudiation. Either is destructive of our form of government.

Today the interest on the Federal debt takes more than 10 percent of our total Federal tax revenue. Without the tremendous cost of this debt our annual tax bill could be reduced 10 percent across the board.

The interest charge would be greater if much of the debt was not short-termed with lower interest rates. Should this debt be long-termed at the 3¼ percent paid on recent thirty-year bonds, the interest would be nearly 15 percent of the Federal income. No business enterprise could survive such heavy interest out of its gross income.

I am an old-fashioned person who believes that a debt is a debt just as much in the atomic age as it was in the horse and buggy days.

A balanced budget could be in sight if (a) we do not increase spending, and (b) we do not reduce taxes. Assuming no further cut in taxes, only a 4 percent reduction in spending, in terms of the President's budget, would bring us to that highly desirable goal.   □

View II: We Owe the National Debt to Ourselves

A view diametrically opposed to that just presented is that the size of the national debt is really a matter of total irrelevance. There are few citizens—whether economists or laymen—who would take quite such an extreme position. Indeed, the author of the following excerpt, Abba Lerner, a distinguished economist, is well aware of the many complications of the debt issue. However, the tone of the following remarks is so different from the Byrd speech that it helps put the question of the debt in a dramatically different perspective. For, in the preceding analysis by the senator, there is the unmistakable implication that the national debt is a debt to someone else. Or, to put it in different words, there is no apparent awareness of the fact that as we are national "debtors," we are also national "creditors." For after all, we do in many instances hold government bonds and count them as part of our wealth. The full recognition of this fact is likely to lead to a much more sanguine view of the national debt than that suggested in View I.

The National Debt— Do We Owe It to Ourselves?

Abba Lerner

When an editor of a newspaper or a cartoonist runs out of ideas, he can always call attention to the "national debt." The cartoonist can show the citizen being crushed by an enormous burden. The editorial writer will express himself arithmetically. Since nobody knows what is meant by a million dollars, let alone two hundred and ninety billions of dollars, the arithmetic can be very impressive. For example, he might ask how long you thought it would take you to pay off the national debt if you were given a full-time job of repaying it at the rate of one dollar every second. Years? Maybe hundreds of years? Not so easy. To pay out two hundred and ninety billion dollars at one dollar per second for seven hours a day working 300 days a year would take about 40,000 years. And at the end of the 40,000 years would the national debt have disappeared? On the contrary, all this repayment would not even have begun to make a dent on the compounding of the debt into really astronomic trillions of trillions of dollars. It would take a *thousand* people each paying out a dollar a second just to pay off the interest so as to stop the debt from growing any bigger than the accumulated unpaid interest.

On Mondays, Wednesdays and Fridays the editorials frighten us with these unimaginably large numbers and tell us that the country is being destroyed by the tremendous national debt. But on Tuesdays, Thursdays and Saturdays the same editorial page will remind us that we are enjoying a higher standard of living and greater prosperity than ever before. If

Excerpted from Abba Lerner, "The National Debt—Do We Owe It to Ourselves?" in *Everybody's Business* (East Lansing, Mich.: Michigan State University Press, 1961), pp. 104–14. Reprinted by permission of the publisher.

we remembered Monday's editorial on Tuesday we might wonder how we are able to manage so well in spite of the national debt and whether this could possibly be because we owe it only to ourselves.

Editorials dismiss the notion that we owe the national debt to ourselves as too ridiculous to deserve further analysis, and continue their arithmetical exercises. But when the scoffing and the arithmetic are over, the question still remains, "If we do not owe the national debt to ourselves, to whom *do* we owe it?" To this there is no answer. There is *nobody else* to whom we owe the debt. The national debt is a debt which the people in the United States owe, through the government, to the holders of the government bonds who, with some insignificant exceptions, happen to be the people in the U.S. No matter how funny it may seem to some, we don't owe it to Germany or Japan or Russia or any other country. We do, as a nation, owe the national debt to ourselves.

Our owing it to ourselves has important consequences. For every dollar which you and I as residents of the United States owe, through our government, to the owners of the national debt, there is a corresponding creditor who owns a United States debt certificate of one kind or another. When we total the debt, it is our duty, if we do not want to mislead, to total the credit too. And if we count both, they cancel out.

While it is common for only the debit side of the national debt to be counted, I don't know of anybody who has counted only the credit side. But it could be said with equal logic, or rather illogic, that the United States is *richer* because among the things which Americans own are two hundred and ninety billions of national debt—in the form of first-class, gilt-edged securities guaranteed by the United States government. You can repeat the arithmetical exercises of the editorialist and see how long it would take to count this part of our *wealth*. This, of course, would be just as silly as doing the opposite. The United States is not any richer on account of the national debt than it is poorer because of it. Against

the credit there is a debit, just as against the debit there is a credit.

Our conclusion is that we *do* owe the national debt to ourselves, that it is not a terrible danger to our society as imagined by those who think it is the same kind of thing as personal or inter-personal debt, and that there are some real problems, but that these problems are due to the existence and growth of *any* private claims to national wealth rather than of that part of private claims to wealth that are the counterpart of the national debt.   □

View III: A Balanced Budget but at Full Employment

An intermediate (though not necessarily correct) view, between the two suggested so far, is one that has attracted special attention in the early 1970s: balance the federal budget, argues this approach, but only as that budget would emerge in a *full employment economy*. The *President's Economic Report* of 1971 took this position:

We need to abide by a principle of budget policy which permits flexibility in the budget and yet limits the inevitable tendency to waste and inflationary action. The useful and realistic principle of the full-employment budget is that, except in emergencies, expenditures should not exceed the revenues that the tax system would yield when the economy is operating at full employment.

This principle implies a criticism of the strict, year-by-year, balance-the-budget approach. It is based on the view that adherence to such a target when there is unemployment would mean effectively that the government was exercising an *inhibiting* effect on the expansion of the economy. Why? Because if the economy were at full employment, its tax revenues would automatically be higher than when the economy was producing at below its full-employment potential. Thus, for example, we know that the U.S. personal income tax automatically increases federal revenues when national income rises.[2] For a given level of federal spending, this increased tax revenue would imply a *full-employment surplus* in the federal budget. Thus, a balanced budget when the economy was suffering unemployment would imply that the effective policy with respect to full employment tended to be contractionary.

Although the full-employment balanced budget principle does depart considerably from the more narrow balanced budget view (and is consistent with the possibility of the national debt regularly increasing over time), it is still quite far from the notion implicit in View II that the public debt should be regarded primarily as a useful instrument in the operation of a flexible fiscal policy. For those who accept this flexible approach, the question remains: Why limit yourself to the basically arbitrary principle of full-employment balance? Suppose that conditions in the economy are so depressed that the deficits implied by this principle are insufficient to cure a serious unemployment condition. Why should the government bind itself not to act in such grave circumstances?

ARGUMENTS AND FACTS

Given the divergent viewpoints suggested above, we clearly must sort out the opposing arguments with some care. Let us do this now, first dispelling some alarmist notions, and then analyzing the actual costs and benefits of the public debt.

One common concern about the expansion of the national debt may be put this way:

The federal government is no different from any private individual. Everyone knows that a private individual cannot keep accumulating indebtedness all the time. Consequently, the federal government should (or must) reduce the size of the public debt.

---

2. This tendency of tax revenues to rise with every expansion of national income has been called *fiscal drag,* a term coined by Walter Heller, former Chairman of the Council of Economic Advisers.

Now this argument is, in part, a throwback to the view that Adam Smith expressed in his famous declaration: "What is prudence in the conduct of every private family can scarce be folly in that of a great Kingdom." And, indeed, this is part of the problem with the argument, because Smith's statement is clearly untrue in a number of important circumstances. To take a couple of obvious examples: It is clearly prudent for a private individual to refrain from printing money, but does this mean that it is folly for the national government to print money? It is prudent for a private individual not to take the law into his own hands, but are we then to conclude that it is folly for the state to maintain a police force and legal system? And so on. The point is that the actions of the state and the actions of private individuals are often regulated by different principles, and argument by analogy from one to the other is filled with pitfalls.

In the particular case of the public debt, moreover, there is at least one feature that distinguishes it from the debt of private individuals. This is the feature brought out in the Abba Lerner reading. When I owe a debt to you, I owe it to an external party. The proper analogy in the case of the nation as a whole would be a debt owed to some foreign country, or an *external debt.* However, the public debt is not external but internal, and, indeed, we could imagine hypothetical circumstances in which the holders of government bonds and the payers of taxes were identical individuals, in which case it would be literally true that we owe the debt to ourselves.

But even if the analogy were completely correct, there is another major flaw in this particular argument. And this is the incorrect assumption that private parties—individuals or business firms—do not increase their indebtedness in the aggregate over time. Figure 12–1 shows what has been happening to the public debt of the federal, state, and local governments in recent decades, compared to the debt of individuals and private corporations. Although the federal debt was growing substantially relative to private indebtedness in the period from the 1930s

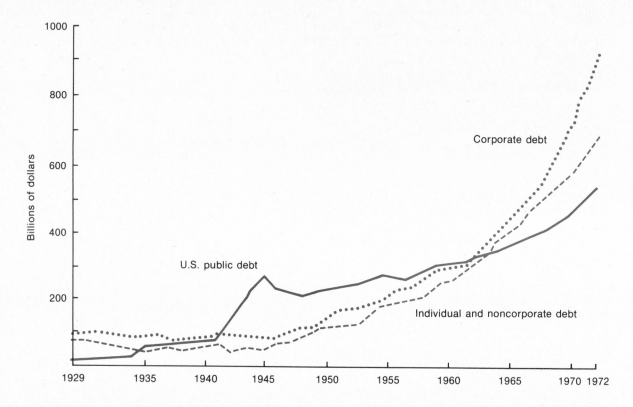

Figure 12–1. Public versus Private Debt in the U.S.

to the end of World War II, the last twenty-five years have seen a complete reversal of form. Private debt has been growing much more rapidly during this period and, at the present time, it is almost three times as great in total as the whole public debt. Nor is this surprising. We all know that businesses regularly issue bonds to finance new ventures and expansions; in a growing economy, we should expect this kind of indebtedness to increase over time. This is also true of households. We do pay back each debt as it comes due; but in the meanwhile, we incur new debts. While we are buying a car on credit, we are also taking out a mortgage on a new house and

buying a washing machine and dryer on the installment plan. As the population grows and the average real income per capita rises, we should naturally expect a continuing expansion in outstanding mortgage loans and consumer credit. And this is exactly what we do have.

These facts should bring home the danger of loose analogies between the government and private parties. For if we were to take the analogy literally, then this would come perilously close to saying, "It's perfectly all right to expand the public debt indefinitely. After all, look at what consumers and businessmen are doing!" In short, this first argument is fallacious on two fundamental counts and would not be worth spending time on, except that it is heard so frequently in everyday discussion.

Much the same can be said for a second common worry about the public debt, which might be put this way:

All debts must ultimately be repaid, and so it is with the public debt. The U.S. federal debt is now between $300 and $400 billion. This sum is so enormous that any attempt to repay it will cause huge burdens on the economy. Under these circumstances, any further increases in the public debt will ultimately lead us to national bankruptcy.

Like the earlier argument, this one also involves at least two major problems. The first is the assumption (very evident in the Byrd speech) that all debts, including the federal debt, must in the aggregate be repaid. This assumption involves difficulties similar to those we have already noticed. In the case of private debt, each particular loan does get paid back (unless someone goes bankrupt), but, in the aggregate, private indebtedness increases over time, as indicated by Figure 12–1. Similarly, the government is regularly engaged in paying back its indebtedness to particular individuals as various government bonds come to maturity. But it then engages in issuing new bonds, with the result that although every individual can count on getting his money back at the proper time, the total of indebtedness can remain the same or increase for the government over time. In fact, it is inconceivable that the debt of the United States government ever will be repaid. It may be (and has been) reduced from time to time by surpluses in the federal budget, but the notion that we will ever get rid of the debt in total is ultimately fanciful. Nor is there any need to do so.

Moving away from these incomplete analogies between the private and public sectors, we run into another and more specific criticism of this alarmist argument. The real question of how "huge" the federal debt is cannot be decided by absolute figures in isolation. Is $400 billion or $500 billion "huge"? How can we say, unless we indicate the standard that we are using for comparisons? There are different standards that one might choose, but a fairly

obvious one is the size of the public debt (federal, state, and local government debt) in relation to the size of the economy as a whole, or roughly our annual GNP. Figure 12–2 shows this relationship in percentage terms over the past few decades. Notice that there has been a very substantial decline in the *relative* importance of the public debt since World War II. This is significant when people start worrying about national bankruptcy. If we managed to survive the great expansion of debt that took place during World War II, it seems highly unlikely that we are seriously threatened by anything that has happened since. This is particularly true if we are thinking of the *federal* debt, which has increased in absolute terms much more slowly than state and local government debt during the past two decades;[3] its decline relative to GNP has been even more rapid than suggested by Figure 12–2. This is simply to say that although the absolute debt has grown, the economy as a whole has grown much more rapidly, reducing the weight of the debt in relation to our capacity for sustaining it.

Still another common concern is this:

By increasing the public debt, we are putting the burdens of the present generation off onto the shoulders of the future generations. In Senator Byrd's words: "The debt today is the debt incurred by this generation, but tomorrow it will be debt on our children and grandchildren." In effect, we are saddling them with financial responsibilities that really ought to be borne by ourselves now.

Whether we *could* manage the shifting of burdens implied in this statement of concern is an interesting question. Admittedly, there are some future burdens to the public debt—we shall come to these in a moment—but in the sense in which this worry is usually conceived, the possible shifting is very limited. We know from Figures 12–1 and 12–2 that our great modern increase in the national debt came during World War II. We ask, then: Does this mean that the

---

3. Thus from 1950 to 1970, while state and local government debt was increasing more than *sixfold*, federal government debt was increasing only by about one third, GNP during this same period more than tripled.

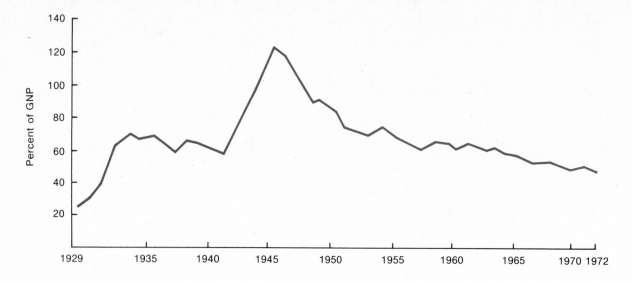

Figure 12–2. U.S. Public Debt as a Percentage of GNP.

fundamental burdens of fighting World War II were passed on to later generations? Are we in fact "paying for" the war now?

Had the war been financed by external debt to other countries, so that the resources to produce the tanks and planes and ships had come from abroad, and had we in the 1970s been sending equivalent resources back to these foreign countries, then we would be "paying for" the war now in an economic sense. But we did not borrow from abroad; consequently, the resources required had to be our own, and they had to be put up *then,* not now. We are certainly not producing tanks, planes, and ships for World War II at the present time. Subject to a qualification we shall mention presently, the resources had to be used and were in fact used in the 1940s. Imagine a full employment economy operating on its

transformation or production-possibility curve.[4] If it wants to produce more of one commodity (armaments), it must give up some of the other commodity (private production). When a war effort of the magni-

---

4. See chapter 1, p. 19. Of course, it may be said that when we entered World War II, we were far from a full-employment economy. This, of course, is true, and it is also true that the economic sacrifices (not speaking, of course, of the tremendous human sacrifices involved) of the war in terms of actually "giving up things" were minimal. In a fundamental sense, we financed the war by taking up the tremendous slack in our economy—i.e., moving out to the production-possibility frontier—and also by pushing the curve outward. This, however, is not an argument against debt financing as opposed to the major alternative: total reliance on increased taxation. Indeed, it seems highly doubtful that without some debt financing we could have moved out so quickly to the production-possibility frontier. The huge burdens of taxation would have made mobilization on this scale very difficult. Hence, while it is not right to say that the debt postponed the fundamental burdens of the war, it is fair to give debt financing some credit for easing the pains of the war effort at the time it occurred.

tude of our own in the 1940s is involved—50 percent of our national income was given to defense purposes—then the basic costs must be sustained when they occur (by the current generation) and not in the future.

In sum, this source of alarm has little more fundamental foundation than the others we have discussed.

COSTS AND BENEFITS OF THE NATIONAL DEBT

Still, we must not go to the other extreme and assume that the size of the national debt is a complete irrelevance to our economic life. It clearly does involve certain burdens for the nation. It also may involve certain possible benefits. Without attempting to be all-inclusive, let us list a few features of the debt that may have real economic impact, primarily to get a sense of the scale of the problems involved.

Interest Charges on the National Debt

An important burden of the federal debt arises from the fact that we have to pay interest on it. Generally, as Senator Byrd's speech pointed out, these interest payments will have to be met by increased taxation, and taxes are not only personally unpleasant but may involve certain disincentive effects on effort and productivity in the economy.

This particular burden of the debt is somewhat offset by the fact that American citizens are both (1) the taxpayers who finance the interest payments on the debt, and (2) the bondholders who receive the interest payments. Even in the unlikely case that precisely the same individuals were involved, however, the net economic effect would still be some lessening of incentives, because the interest comes to us for doing nothing, but the taxes come out of personal incomes produced by our hard efforts. If taxes rise high enough, then we may ask: Why put

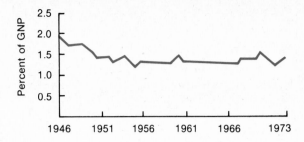

Figure 12–3. Interest Payments on the Federal Debt as a Percentage of GNP.

Interest payments on the federal debt have fallen slightly as a percentage of GNP in the postwar period, but they have been a relatively constant percentage since the 1950s because of the rise in interest rates.

in the extra hour or two of effort if it will mostly go to the government anyway? The magnitude of this disincentive effect, however, must be judged in any given case by the magnitude of the interest charges in relation to our capacity to sustain them, or basically our GNP. Figure 12–3 shows that federal interest payments have declined somewhat as a percentage of GNP since the end of World War II. The relative constancy of this percentage since the 1950s reflects the twin facts that the federal debt has been declining as a percentage of GNP but that interest rates have been rising during this period. Since state and local government debt has also been rising substantially in these years, it should be clear that the interest burden of the total public debt is a real phenomenon.

It should be noted, however, that these interest payments are to some degree simply payments for benefits being currently received. A portion of government expenditure goes into what in the private sector we would call capital formation, as it does when highways, schools, dams, etc., are built by the federal, state, and local governments. Insofar as these capital projects are financed by increases in the public debt, they bring to us not only increased interest payments and taxes but also increased economic benefits.[5]

Postponing Burdens: The Problem of Investment

We mentioned in our discussion of World War II that there was a qualification to the basic truth that the costs of the war were borne at the time of the war. This qualification arises from the fact that it is possible to postpone present burdens to the future to the degree that one "lives off" one's capital stock today and consequently bequeaths a smaller capital stock to the future generation. And, in fact, during World War II, we did limit the replacement and repair of a certain portion of our capital stock in order to achieve a maximum war effort.

To what degree debt financing was responsible for this postponement of burdens is, however, a different question. Even had the war been financed completely by current taxes, the same problem would have occurred, and it is doubtful that the solution would have been different in any fundamental way. Furthermore, it is possible to argue that an expansion of the national debt may in many circumstances effectively *increase* the capital stock available to a future generation. If an expansion of the debt is part of a successful fiscal policy that brings the economy closer to its full employment potential, then it has stimulated greater production today, part of which will go into greater consumption today. But *part* of this production will probably go into greater investment today and hence a greater capital stock tomorrow.

This is not to say that the debt may not have an unfavorable effect on investment or that it may not involve postponement to later generations. For example, insofar as the government, faced with the need to market large quantities of bonds, comes into competition with private investors for sources of financial capital, it may contribute to "tighter" money, and hence to some lowering of private investment.[6] But the picture is quite mixed. Some effects of the debt may be in the direction of increasing future burdens, while others—as in the case of a successful fiscal policy—may benefit our children's children.

National Debt in Relation to Government Activities

Taxes are considered politically unpopular. If the government does not have to balance the budget, it may, some people fear, engage in "reckless" spending projects, thus spurring inflation, increasing the sphere of government in our mixed economy, and appropriating resources that might be more effectively used in the private sector. This notion was apparent in the *President's Economic Report*, which defended the principle of a full-employment balanced budget that "limits the inevitable tendency to waste and inflationary action."

One's judgment on the importance of this point depends upon one's general opinion about the desirability or undesirability of governmental spending in the economy, as well as on the more specific question of the degree to which the pressure for balancing the budget is an effective means of limiting government spending. Insofar as one is committed to reducing government expenditures at all costs, it is probably true that by insisting on some form of a balanced budget, one is at least creating a further argument

---

5.   Some countries, in fact, distinguish between the *current* expenditures of government (paying the mailman to deliver the mail) and *capital* expenditures (building a post office). Although one could argue that debt financing is especially appropriate for governmental capital expenditures, this in effect would imply a much too limited and inflexible role for a country's fiscal policy, which ultimately must be guided by the macroeconomic needs of the economy as a whole.

---

6.   It is also possible to argue that the debt involves some redistribution of income between generations, on the grounds that the "younger generation" of today has to work to pay the taxes to pay the interest payments to the bondholding "older generation." Actually, it is doubtful that this qualification is of much practical importance.

against additional public spending. The opposite point of view might be expressed as follows: (1) There are a great many public needs having to do with our cities, our environment, minorities, the aged, the poor, and the ill, which must not be neglected because of an arbitrary budget-balancing principle; and (2) the question of balancing or not balancing the budget should be determined on the general grounds of its effect on employment and price stability in the economy as a whole.

Ultimately, this third feature of the debt comes down to the question of whether or not this country needs the kind of financial discipline that a balance-the-budget principle requires. This, in turn, is really a question not about the burden of the debt but rather about the burden of "reckless" spending. It is undoubtedly true historically and even today that some governments need every possible constraint imaginable to keep them from spending themselves into financial insolvency. Whether this is true of the United States in the 1970s, however, is a different question.

The Debt and Money Creation

Finally, the costs and benefits of the national debt may be significantly affected by the way in which increases in the debt occur. We have been speaking in this chapter of financing government expenditures either through taxation or through increases in the public debt. But there is another question involved as well: How do we finance the increase in the debt itself? The Treasury has to sell its bonds somewhere. Does it make any difference where, or to whom, it sells them?

The answer is very definitely yes. Imagine two cases: In one, the Treasury goes on a bond drive and gets the public to withdraw its deposits from banks and pay these to the Treasury in exchange for bonds. In due course, the Treasury spends the money and it comes back to individuals in the form of replenished demand deposit accounts. In this transaction, other things equal, no addition has been made to the nation's stock of money.

But suppose, by contrast, the Treasury sells some of these bonds to the Federal Reserve System. What this does is add to the previous operation an increase by that amount of Fed purchases of government bonds in the open market. We already know what such purchases mean: an increase in member bank reserves, with the potential multiplied increase in demand deposit money throughout the economy. In this case, the financing of the debt has brought about an increase in the money supply.

Thus, we have to add to our other potential costs and/or benefits of the national debt, those that stem from its monetary consequences. To take an obvious case: If we were in an inflationary situation, an increase in the national debt would be doubly bad if it were financed by Fed purchases of Treasury bonds, leading to a flood of "printing press" money in the economy.

But this last point cuts even deeper. For some economists believe that the macroeconomic effects (i.e., in terms of stabilizing the business cycle) of the debt, and of fiscal policy in general, are virtually limited to the kinds of monetary effects we are just now talking about. It has been argued that the whole, or almost the whole, expansionary effect of fiscal policy is a result of the way in which debt is financed rather than through the $C + I + G$ mechanism we have been discussing. This is a central tenet of the doctrine known as *monetarism,* which is based on a different analysis of the role of money in the economy than we have given so far.

It is time now, therefore, to turn to this very important issue. And this we do in the next chapter and in Great Debate Two that follows thereafter.

SUMMARY

Government expenditures may be financed either by taxes or by increases in the public debt. The impact of taxes on the macroeconomic health of the economy depends very much on the kind of tax employed. The most important taxes in the United States at the present time are: the individual income tax (which is an important *automatic stabilizer* of the economy), payroll taxes (which are used to finance the social security program and are regressive), corporation income tax (whose burden—on business, worker, consumer?—has to be analyzed carefully in each case), sales and excise taxes (*indirect taxes* that can partly affect C and partly affect I), and the property tax (the mainstay of local governments, and perhaps not so regressive a tax as once thought). The multiplier analysis of these taxes has to be carefully tailored to each specific case.

When we leave balanced budgets and begin financing G through the national debt, we run into some unduly alarmist fears. The argument that the government is just like a private party and that private parties cannot keep going into debt is refuted by the facts that (1) the government is not identical to a private party in many instances, and (2) individual and corporate debt in the United States has been growing more rapidly than the public debt in recent years. The argument that the federal debt is so "huge" that its repayment will cause the country to go bankrupt is refuted by the facts that (1) the national debt will almost certainly never be repaid in total, and (2) as far as size is concerned, the federal debt has been declining as a percentage of GNP ever since World War II. Finally, the argument that the debt is a way of foisting our burdens upon our grandchildren is seen, in its simplistic form, to ignore the fundamental facts about the way resources are mobilized and used in an economy such as ours, as exemplified by our experience in World War II.

The actual costs and benefits of the public debt are much more subtle than these alarmists' arguments would imply. The costs of the debt include substantial interest payments that are financed by taxation, possible diminution of business investment under certain circumstances, a possible loss of financial discipline if "reckless" government spending is encouraged by the absence of a balance-the-budget constraint, and certain monetary effects (considered in the next chapter) if the debt is accompanied by an increased money supply.

All these points have comebacks; e.g., interest charges have not risen as a percentage of GNP, investment may be increased if an increase in the debt results in higher general employment and output, government spending and deficits may be needed in many circumstances to promote the health of the economy.

Although no one would deny the importance of keeping an eye on the size of the national debt, it seems fairly safe to conclude that the burdens of the debt in the present circumstances of the United States do not in themselves constitute a major obstacle to the application of a flexible modern fiscal policy.

IMPORTANT TERMS TO REMEMBER

Individual Income Tax
Payroll Taxes
Corporation Income Taxes
Sales and Excise Taxes
Property Taxes
Direct vs. Indirect Taxes
National Debt
Balanced Budget
Full Employment Balanced Budget
Deficit Spending and Money Creation

QUESTIONS FOR DISCUSSION

1. Comment on the theoretical and factual issues involved in the following statements:

(a) "The trouble with modern economics is that it does not play by its own rules. In theory, budget deficits in bad times should be balanced by budget surpluses in good times. But the proponents of deficit spending always seem to forget the latter. And this, of course, is the road to national bankruptcy."

(b) "When there is a balanced budget, the government is acting in a completely neutral way as far as the overall health of the economy is concerned."

(c) "When there is a full-employment balanced budget, the government is acting in a completely neutral way as far as the overall health of the economy is concerned."

(d) "A good general rule for modern fiscal policy is that the public debt should grow at the same overall rate as national income."

(e) "The government should follow the following maxims in regulating its tax and expenditure policies: (1) pay for all current expenditures out of taxation; and (2) finance the construction of all capital assets (highways, school buildings, etc.) by bond issues."

2. Argue the pros and cons of having a specific, congressionally determined limitation on the size of the federal debt.

3. Since private indebtedness has been growing more rapidly than public indebtedness in recent decades, should there be some attempt to limit the increase of private indebtedness in the economy? What might be some of the issues involved?

4. In the late 1930s and 1940s, a group of American economists called the "stagnationists" predicted that there would be a tendency for saving to outrun investment in the American economy and, consequently, that there would be increasing unemployment unless the government stepped up its intervention. Considering what has been said so far in this book about the performance of the American economy and the changing role of the government since World War II, do you feel that these predictions have been verified or refuted by our experience? Explain your answer.

SUGGESTED READING

Bowen, W. G.; Davis, R. G.; and Kopf, D. H. "The Public Debt," *American Economic Review* 50 (September 1960).

Buchanan, J. M. *Public Principles of Public Debt.* Homewood, Ill.: Richard D. Irwin, 1958.

Eckstein, Otto. *Public Finance.* 3rd ed. Englewood Cliffs, N.J.: Prentice-Hall, 1973, chapter 7.

Fried, Edward R.; Rivlin, Alice M.; Schultze, Charles; Teeters, Nancy H. *Setting National Priorities: The 1974 Budget.* Washington, D.C.: The Brookings Institution, 1973.

Okun, Arthur M. *The Political Economy of Prosperity.* New York: W. W. Norton & Co., 1970, pp. 109–15.

Pechman, Joseph A. *Federal Tax Policy.* Rev. ed. New York: W. W. Norton & Co., 1971, chapter 2.

CHAPTER 13
CONTROVERSIES OVER MONEY AND MONETARY POLICY

In our discussion of the role of money in the economic system (chapter 11), we tried to avoid controversy so as to keep the overall theory of national income determination clearly in mind. This objective required us to go over certain aspects of the functioning of monetary mechanisms rather more quickly than we might have wanted. It also made us skim over the fact that there is disagreement not only on details but also on the basic way in which money is related to our important macroeconomic variables—GNP, total employment and unemployment, and the price level.

This disagreement is centered on a debate over what is called *monetarism*. This debate has attracted the energies and abilities of some of the nation's leading economists. The father of monetarist thought in the United States is Milton Friedman, a University of Chicago economist whose incisive arguments and often provocatively conservative opinions have made him well known to the general public as well as to the economics profession. One of Friedman's opponents has been Paul A. Samuelson of Massachusetts Institute of Technology, who probably vies with John Kenneth Galbraith for being the most famous economist in the world in recent decades. Samuelson, besides being active in public policy debates, is an outstanding theoretician who was the first American to be honored with a Nobel Prize in economics.

However, the debate is not between two men or even two groups of men. It concerns the correct analysis of the impact of money on a modern economy and, consequently, the appropriate role of public policy, fiscal policy quite as much as monetary policy.

These questions are the subject of Great Debate Two: The Issue of Monetarism. In order to understand that debate, however, the reader must go somewhat more deeply into the complexities of money than we have done so far. This chapter can, therefore, be considered both a guide to Great Debate Two and an opportunity to deepen our comprehension of monetary phenomena.

Paul A. Samuelson. Samuelson is America's first Nobel laureate in economics. Although known to the general public for his widely read books and articles, he is best known to economists as a brilliant theoretician, especially in mathematical economics.

Milton Friedman. By all odds the most articulate spokesman for the conservative point of view in economics, Professor Friedman has brought original thinking to many fundamental economic problems, including particularly the role of money in the economic system.

INCOME ANALYSIS IN A SIMPLIFIED "REAL" WORLD

If we think back to Part Two A, when we were first discussing the theory of national income determination, we can recall that we did the original analysis in *real* terms. Not only was there no explicit discussion of money in the economy, but we dealt with national income as expressed in unchanging prices (constant dollars). In this world, Keynesian analysis told us that real national income would be determined by the sum of consumption, investment, and government spending, all expressed in given prices. Thus, in Figure 10–6 (p. 236), we used our 45-degree line

diagram to determine real national income (and hence the level of employment) without mentioning money or possible changes in the levels of prices and money wages in our economy.

An interesting question arises: If these are the forces that determine where the level of real national income will be, what will determine where the level of *money* national income will be? To answer this, we would have to know how to determine the general price level (P) as well as the real level of GNP (let us call this Q, to signify that we are talking about real quantities). If consumption, investment and government spending determine real national income (Q), what determines money national income ($P \times Q$)?

Now a true Keynesian would have brought in the money supply at an earlier stage of the analysis, but a more sloppy disciple might largely avoid it even now. He might say something like the following:

In order to determine prices, what we really have to know is the general level of money wages (W). Let's suppose that these money wages have been set by union-management agreements throughout our fictitious economy. Basically, once this is done, P will be pretty well set, too. The reason for this is that once we have settled where real national income is, we have also settled where the level of employment is. This will roughly determine what labor's productivity is and this, in turn, will tell us what labor's real wage (W/P) will be. Knowing both the money wage and real wage, we more or less automatically know where the price level will be. Admittedly, the money supply has to be consistent with this overall solution, but this is not difficult, or particularly important to achieve.[1]

In other words, this sloppy ultra-Keynesian might say that real national income (Q) is effectively determined by consumption, investment, and government spending, and that prices (P) for a given level of real national income are effectively determined by the level of money wages (W), and hence that $P \times Q$ can be determined with only the most minimal discussion of the money supply.

Now this kind of logic is associated with an extreme position that, in Great Debate Two, says: "Money doesn't matter." No one, living or dead, has taken this position in quite such an uncompromising form, yet in the period just after World War II many economists left money seriously underrepresented in their analyses. They would talk of W and P and Q and then, almost as an afterthought, they would say that, of course, the quantity of money (M) had to be mentioned as a factor, too. The truth is that many of these economists, unlike Keynes himself, felt that changes in the quantity of money had so little impact that, for practical purposes, they could be ignored.

QUANTITY THEORY OF MONEY

This emphasis on the real side of things contrasted in many (though not all) ways with the prevailing theory of the role of money prior to Keynesian analysis. In general, that previous theory, while it did not give money much of a role in affecting real national income or employment, nevertheless gave money an absolutely central role in determining the general price level. The basic hypothesis here is usually referred to as the *quantity theory of money*. The quantity theory of money can be expressed in terms of the following equation:

$$M \times V = P \times Q$$

M is the stock of money in the economy—for the moment, currency plus demand deposits—*V* represents the *income velocity of money, P* is the price level, and *Q* is the level of real national income.[2]

The key concept here is that of the income velocity of money. It is meant to measure the number of times the average dollar bill or demand deposit circulates through the economy during a given period in exchange for final output. In particular, it is defined as:

$$V = \frac{P \times Q}{M}$$

In words, money national income in a given year is divided by the total of currency and demand deposits available on the average during the course of that year.

This definition raises a possible source of confusion about our quantity theory equation; namely, the equation appears to be true by virtue of the meaning of income velocity. $MV = PQ$ becomes a truism that

---

1. This argument assumes, among other things, that labor will be paid according to its productivity. More specifically, it assumes that labor will be paid according to its *marginal productivity*. The reasoning behind this aspect of the argument is developed extensively in chapter 21, pp. 472–73.

2. This equation has many different forms, with approximately similar meanings. Thus it is often written: $MV = PT$, where T stands for transactions, including, for example, purchases and sales of intermediate goods not included in national income. In this case, of course, we would have to speak of the transactions velocity of money, rather than its income velocity.

tells us nothing whatever about the real world. This is quite correct, and what it means is that in order to get a proper theory about the role of money in the economy from this equation we have to make some further statements about its terms. And this the quantity theorists did.

They said, first, that on the whole, national income in real terms (Q) was determined by real factors—size of the labor force, amount of capital, technology, etc. These factors would alter over time but very slowly, and in any event they would not be affected by the quantity of money in any serious or enduring way. This was full-employment economics in the tradition of Say's Law.[3]

Second, they argued that V was largely determined by institutional factors and could be regarded as also independent of changes in M. V would be influenced by such factors as the state of banking practice and the ways in which wage payments and other disbursements of funds were made in the economy. Consider, for example, the differences in the velocity of money when a man gets his salary on a weekly basis and when he gets it on a monthly basis. If the man gets $250 in a weekly paycheck and spends it all each week, he will, at any given moment of time, be holding on the average $125 in money. (If all payments are by check, this will be his average bank balance.) If, however, he is paid by the month (something over $1,000 per month), his bank balance will on the average be over $500. The income velocity of money will be four or more times as great if his paychecks are on a weekly as opposed to a monthly basis.

What the quantity theorists said was that these and other such institutional factors largely determined V. At the same time, Q was largely determined by tech-

nology and the available quantities of factors of production. What then happened when you altered M? Clearly, the only variable left to be affected is P. And this was the main contention of the quantity theory; namely, that changes in the quantity of money produced roughly proportional changes in P (and presumably also in W) throughout the economy.

In a sense, this theory embodied a combination of two views of money: (1) "Money doesn't matter," and (2) "Money alone matters." In terms of real national income and employment, money mattered very little according to this theory. In terms of prices and wages, by contrast, the quantity of money more or less completely called the tune.

KEYNES WITH MONEY

Keynes was concerned about bridging the gap between real and monetary analysis. He did not deny that institutional factors could affect the velocity of money, nor even that, under certain special circumstances (particularly when full employment had been achieved), the quantity theory might be a fair approximation to reality. But he did deny that full-employment national income could be taken as the natural state of affairs, and he also stressed the effects of M on the interest rate (r).

As we have already indicated at the end of chapter 11, Keynes spoke of a transactions demand for money and also a liquidity demand for money. As far as the transactions demand for money is concerned, we are essentially in the world of the quantity theorists; i.e., given the prevailing institutional arrangements, the amount of money we will need to carry out our day-do-day transactions will depend on the size of money income in the economy (P × Q). This is tantamount to saying that the V for transactions money is effectively given.

But in the liquidity sphere, this is not so. The amount of money that people wish to hold for precautionary purposes is, we recall, dependent on the rate of interest. The higher r, the less money people hold for liquidity purposes, and vice versa. Translated into quantity theory terms, what this means is that

---

3. Recall that we said earlier (p. 179) that the classical economists had regarded money as a "veil" as far as real phenomena were concerned. Another way of putting this is to say that changes in M have no effect on Q.

the velocity of this liquidity money will depend on the rate of interest. At low rates of interest, people will be willing to hold large amounts of currency and deposit balances; at high interest rates, they will try to put this money to use in interest-bearing assets and they will be willing to hold only much smaller average bank balances. Thus, V, in terms of all kinds of money, will depend in the Keynesian theory on the interest rate—it is not simply given by institutional factors.

The problem that this kind of analysis causes for the quantity theory can be shown with reference to what we earlier called the "liquidity trap" (p. 268). In a serious depression, it may happen that the interest rate is so low and expectations are so pessimistic that when the Fed keeps pumping M into the system everyone simply holds this money as money and does not try to invest it in bonds or other securities. Hence, there is no effect on the interest rate, investment, national income, or prices. In effect, an increase in M is being offset by a decrease in V with the consequence that $P \times Q$ is left unaffected.

But if the quantity theory is amended in this way—if, for example, the connection between M and P can be severed by the liquidity trap—then how exactly is P determined in the Keynesian system? If the quantity of money doesn't determine the level of prices and wages, what does?

This question is of some importance because a major objection to the Keynesian system (referred to by Friedman as the system's dependence on "rigidities or imperfections," p. 314) has been that it works properly only if money wages are held up artificially, say by union-management wage contracts that prevent wages from falling. In the absence of such rigidities, will not the existence of unemployment cause a progressive bidding-down of money wages in the economy as the unemployed workers try to secure jobs? If wages and prices are falling, will this not lead to an increase in total employment and output? To put it in terms of the quantity theory

equation: If P is falling, and if M and V remain constant, won't this mean a rise in Q?

Of course, the key phrase in that last question is "if M and V remain constant." In a sense that is the whole issue. To see why this is so, and to show how wages and prices fit into the Keynesian system, let us follow through on the suggestion that unemployed workers will bid down wages in order to get work. Let us imagine an economy with high unemployment, and wages flexible downward. W is going down and P along with it. What effects will this have, according to Keynes?

The interesting thing is that these declines in money wages and prices would theoretically have much the same net effect as an *increase* in the money supply:

As wages and prices fall, the value of money national income falls ($P \times Q$ falls). This means that, for a given quantity of money (M), less money is needed in the transactions sphere and more is available for the liquidity sphere. The effect of more money in the liquidity sphere, under favorable circumstances, will be a lower interest rate. This lower interest rate, according to our familiar chain of logic, should raise investment and, by the multiplier, national income (Q). Thus, the potentially favorable effects of a general fall in wages and prices on total output and employment will come through a similar route—via the interest rate—as the effects of an increase in the money supply.

And, by the same token, such favorable effects can be nullified by the liquidity trap (a falling V) in a seriously depressed economy. In other words, in the Keynesian theory, the route to full employment via either monetary policy *or* general wage cuts is a highly uncertain one.[4]

---

4. Another possible difficulty is that although *low* wages and prices might be favorable to higher employment (through these interest rate effects), *falling* wages and prices might be very discouraging to business investment. The reader should notice that there is a distinction between a *high* or *low* variable and a *rising* or *falling* variable. This distinction is frequently of considerable importance in this area of economics.

PIGOU EFFECT

There is, however, another effect of such wage-price cuts, often referred to as the *Pigou effect.*[5] It was, in part, this particular effect that led to the "rediscovery" of money and the spread of monetarism in the postwar period.

What Pigou said was that as wages and prices fall systematically throughout the economy, the *real* (as opposed to *nominal*) value of the money supply increases in the same proportion. Suppose we have an economy with unemployment (because of too low $C + I + G$) and a given stock of money, M. Wages and prices are completely flexible downward, we assume, and this means that unemployed workers will bid down wages, which will have the further consequence of lowering prices throughout our economy. Let us suppose that P falls to half its previous value. What Pigou said was that this means a doubling of the real value of the money wealth held in this economy. My individual share of the money supply (my average bank balance) is, say, $1,000. Before the fall in P this was equivalent to a certain amount of purchasing power. *After* the halving of P, this same $1,000 is equivalent to twice as much purchasing power—$2,000 at the original P. My *real wealth* has thus been increased by the fall in W and P and there is every likelihood that I will spend more. Thus, we would expect consumption to rise and this would have a favorable effect on the real national income and employment.

It might be objected that this increase in my real wealth from $1,000 to effectively $2,000 is too small to have any major effect on my consumption, which would still depend mainly on my income. However, notice that, in our assumed economy, this process of raising the real value of M can go on indefinitely. If halving P isn't sufficient, then it can be lowered to a tenth or a thousandth of its original value. In this last case, my $1,000 becomes the equivalent of $1 million in terms of purchasing power at the original prices. Surely this will have substantial effects on my C.

Now the Pigou effects we have been discussing are not so easily applicable to the real world as it might seem from this discussion. In our modern economy, where the problem tends to be inflation even with considerable unemployment (see the next chapter), the notion of W and P falling to one-half their previous levels is rather fanciful. To expect them to fall to a tenth or a thousandth of their previous levels is simply delusionary. Furthermore, it is not so clear that the M in our equation would remain constant as this massive fall in W and P took place. To some extent, the supply of money in the economy depends, for any given level of bank reserves, on the demands for money in the system. Such a large contraction in the transactions demand for money might be expected to be accompanied by at least some contraction in M. And, finally, of course, the problem of *low* versus *falling* wages and prices arises again. The process of reducing W and P by half in the present-day American economy might be so fraught with hazard that it would nullify the goal for which the process was launched.

Nevertheless, the Pigou effect does suggest that money can enter into the macroeconomic picture in more ways than the original Keynesian model allowed for. Consideration of such effects had something to do with the desire of some economists to upgrade the role of money well beyond what the master himself had prescribed.

MONETARIST DOCTRINE

All that we have said so far represents a development and extension of the basic Keynesian or post-Keynesian position that, with innumerable variations, is accepted by most modern economists. But the monetarists go much further than this. As a guide to Great Debate Two, let us now summarize briefly the main doctrines, empirical issues, and policy questions raised by Professor Friedman and his monetarist colleagues.

---

5.   After the British economist A. C. Pigou. Friedman notes that Haberler (Gottfried von Haberler, then of Harvard University) also made an important contribution on this matter.

Basically, monetarism involves a complicated re-statement of the quantity theory of money and a return to the idea that "money matters much" or, as Professor Samuelson says critically, that "money alone matters." Once we know what *M* is in the monetarist world we can fairly well determine what money national income (*P* × *Q*) is. The whole income-expenditure approach to national income determination, including the basic macroeconomic role of fiscal policy, is abandoned in this doctrine.

This major difference is, in turn, premised on a variety of more specific differences. In an introductory essay to a book on the quantity theory,[6] Professor Friedman suggested three areas of difference between quantity theorists and Keynesians. The first concerns the "stability and importance of the demand for money." This has to do ultimately with the amount of variability of the velocity of money, *V*. While Friedman does not argue that *V* is a numerical constant, nevertheless the monetarist position is dependent on reasonably modest fluctuations in *V* and on a limit to the number of variables that affect *V*. Second, the monetarist doctrine depends on the view that the demand and supply for money are to a large degree independent. If the banking system simply adjusts the supply of money to the demands for it, then changes in the quantity of money will be a reflection of, not a cause of, changes in economic conditions. Finally, a good quantity-theorist will reject the notion that there is a "liquidity trap" and/or that the "only role of the stock of money and the demand for money is to determine the interest rate."

Given the monetarist approach to these issues —and especially the notion of a reasonably stable *V*—we can understand that *M* will largely determine *P* × *Q*. But what will its specific effects on *Q* be? In the old-fashioned quantity theory, *M* merely af-

fected *P*, while real national income remained happily pegged at something close to the full-employment level.

On this important point the monetarist position does not seem wholly clear. It is beyond doubt that the monetarists believe that changes in the money supply can have massive and disastrous effects on real national income and employment. Thus, the depression of the 1930s (called the "Great Contraction" in Friedman's article) is attributed by monetarists largely to the fact that the Federal Reserve System followed a deflationary policy, reducing the amount of money in the economy by one-third. This implies an extremely potent role of money in its effects on real variables and, if the analysis is accepted, it would indeed be "tragic testimony to the power of monetary policy."

On the other hand, as Friedman makes clear in his article on "The Role of Monetary Policy" (Great Debate Two), he does not feel that monetary policy can determine the long-run rate of employment in the economy. The role of *M* is to affect nominal quantities (like the price level) and not real quantities (like employment or real national income). This is because the initial effects of actions to alter *M* will be different from long-run effects. Thus, suppose the monetary authority increases the supply of money to raise the rate of employment above its "natural" level. *Initially* this will affect *Q* more than *P*, but in the long run, wages and prices will rise in money terms that—with a largely constant *V*—will mean a reverse in the increase of employment back to its original level.

Thus, the monetarist position would seem to be something like this: In the long run, real national output and employment are determined by real factors, not by *M*. However, *M* can substantially affect these factors in the short run and, indeed, when *M* gets out of whack, it can cause major dislocations in real, as well as in money, or nominal, values in the system.

6. Milton Friedman, ed., *Studies in the Quantity Theory of Money* (Chicago: University of Chicago Press, 1956).

EMPIRICAL ISSUES

At this point, the reader might wish to ask the simple question: Well, which theory is right? The impulse behind this question is sound, in that we are dealing with (or should be dealing with) questions of fact, not of ideology or normative values. However, as Great Debate Two and the Appendix to this chapter make clear, there is very considerable disagreement on how to interpret the facts.

The difficulties here are characteristic of many economic problems and not just of the monetarist issue alone. They reflect the fact that the economic system is highly complex, that it is characterized by great interdependence among all the variables in the system, and that it is not subject—as, say, a chemistry problem might be—to carefully controlled experiments. In the particular case of monetarism, these general difficulties are reflected in a number of problems.

What are the key variables we are talking about? Thus, for example, it is not perfectly clear what concept of money (*M*) the monetarists wish to emphasize. We have usually interpreted money in this book as currency plus demand deposits. As we know, economists often use the term M_1 for this definition. But we also know that there are other definitions (e.g., M_2, M_3, etc.) that include time and savings deposits as well. Furthermore, it is not certain that it is the size of the money stock (whether M_1, M_2, etc.) but its *rate of change* that may be crucial. Thus, one of the differences between monetarists and their critics concerns the question of whether monetarists have played fair, or whether they change their key variables (and hence their theories) as the evidence alters.

What are the relevant leads and lags? Since economic effects are produced by causes that precede them in time, we might expect there would be various leads and lags when we come to examine the empirical relationships between variables. Thus, in the simplest case it might seem that if variable A is exerting a causal influence on variable B, this would be reflected in changes in A preceding changes in B by some fairly regular period of time. This problem causes difficulties (1) because it is hard to determine what the appropriate "lead" or "lag" is, and (2) because economic systems are so complex that precedence in time may have no connection with causality at all. Thus, James Tobin has constructed a theory in which the quantity of money has no influence on money income, yet this quantity is regularly predicted to change in advance of changes in money income.[7]

How to distinguish cause and effect? The lag problem is one aspect of the more general problem of distinguishing cause and effect. How do we decide, when the money supply and money national income expand simultaneously, how much of this represents a response of the money supply to the expanded requirements of national income and how much represents the causal impact of an expanded money supply *on* national income? How do we decide whether money is an *exogenously* determined variable (determined by forces outside the system—e.g., by a policy decision of the Federal Reserve Board) or an *endogenously* determined variable (a function of other variables in the system)?

How to weigh "mountains" and/or "hills" of evidence? Professor Friedman has done massive empirical research on the influences of money in the economy, as have a number of his colleagues. Because of the general difficulties we have cited, however, there is still more work to be done. Also, despite sophisticated modern statistical techniques, questions of judgment keep arising. Thus, the monetarist position heavily depends on some reasonable degree of stability in *V*. But how much? For example, income velocity of money (M_1) in the United States varied between 1.93 in the first quarter of 1946 to 3.87 in

---

7. In addition to Tobin's article in Great Debate Two, see James Tobin, "Money and Income: Post Hoc Ergo Propter Hoc?" *Quarterly Journal of Economics,* May 1970.

the fourth quarter of 1962—exactly doubling in this period. Furthermore, V went down in recessions and rose in prosperities during this period.[8] Should this be regarded as part of the "mountains of evidence" (to use Samuelson's terms) *for* Friedman's position or part of the "hills of evidence" Samuelson adduces *against* the Friedman position?

At the present time, most economists believe that the verdict comes down slightly against the monetarists, but there are many exceptions in the universities, business, and government (the Federal Reserve Board of St. Louis is a notable example), and it is clear that the excavation of further mounds of evidence will be required.

THE POLICY ISSUES

It is also clearly of great importance that this further evidence be accumulated. The reason is that the monetarist versus Keynesian (or post-Keynesian) debate has enormous consequences for the policies that the government should follow in the whole area of macroeconomic stability.

We have already mentioned the increased potency attributed to monetary policy by the monetarists. Even more striking, however, is the *impotence* attributed by them to fiscal policy. This is the nub of the discussion between Friedman and Walter Heller. Heller's views on the impact of fiscal policy are in the Keynesian tradition as expressed in our own analysis (chapter 10). Friedman's position is that fiscal policy influences the *division* of national income between the public and private sector but not the overall *level* of national income, employment, prices, etc. This is a direct consequence of the theory that M basically determines $P \times Q$. All that increasing government expenditures do is increase public Q as opposed to private Q. Being generally against increasing the

public as opposed to the private sector, Professor Friedman is, of course, opposed to such a reallocation of resources.

Related to this view of the impotence of fiscal policy is the theory that the way in which fiscal actions are financed is all-important. Suppose there is a tax cut leading to an increased national debt that is financed by the Treasury selling bonds to the Federal Reserve System. We know from the last chapter that this action will cause an increase in the money supply. While the Keynesians would attribute direct economic impacts to the tax cut itself (by raising the C schedule), the monetarists argue that the really important effect is the continuing increase in the money supply that this deficit would entail. Indeed, if the deficit were financed by selling bonds to the public (with no increase in the money supply), it would, according to the monetarists, have minimal macroeconomic effects.[9]

These are dramatic differences of opinion, and they are matched by another that is in some respects still more basic. This is the issue of whether or not the government should employ *any discretionary policy at all* in the area of macroeconomic stability. Friedman's general conclusion is that both logic and historical experience suggest that discretion produces far more errors (and serious errors) than it produces triumphs. Hence he favors the establishment of a fixed rule of conduct that the government should observe, increasing the money supply by a certain percentage every year—say, 3 to 5 percent a year—and then letting the market do the rest. This rule is perhaps even more restrictive, in that it would focus the Federal Reserve Board's attention exclusively on a single monetary aggregate—the quantity of money—as opposed to interest rates, tightness of credit, general market conditions, and the like.

Thus the issues at stake are of great magnitude. Are the monetarists gaining ground or losing? In a paper presented to the annual meeting of the American Economic Association in December 1971, An-

---

8. Lawrence S. Ritter, "The Role of Money in Keynesian Theory," reprinted in *Readings in Macroeconomics,* ed. M. G. Mueller (New York: Holt, Rinehart & Winston, 1966), p. 171.

9. Contrasting views on the effects of a tax cut are taken up graphically in the appendix to this chapter.

drew F. Brimmer, then a member of the Board of Governors of the Federal Reserve System, spoke of the "highwater mark of monetarism in 1970," and concluded:

Taking the Federal Reserve as it is today, I would conclude that all elements in the system (with the exception of the Federal Reserve Bank of St. Louis) remain highly eclectic and pragmatic in their conception of the tasks of monetary management. They show no signs of being led astray by simple prescriptions offered by the monetarists as to how they should perform their jobs.[10]

Thus, the majority remains in the mainstream tradition, in government as well as in the academic world. However, almost everyone who has participated in this debate (including Brimmer) believes that the monetarists have both produced and stimulated important research that will definitely continue into the future.

---

10.   Andrew F. Brimmer, "The Political Economy of Money: Evolution and Impact of Monetarism in the Federal Reserve System." *The American Economic Review,* Papers and Proceedings, 62, no. 2 (May 1972): 351.

SUMMARY

The debate over *monetarism* is a central issue in macroeconomics, both in terms of analysis and of public policy. In the Keynesian world, money fits into the analysis via a transactions demand (dependent on the level of money income) and a liquidity demand (dependent on the interest rate). Monetary policy may run into a "liquidity trap" when it tries to cure a depression and unemployment.

The monetarist position is a restatement of an older view known as the *quantity theory of money.* In this older theory, the tautology—$MV = PQ$—takes on meaning when it is hypothesized that Q is determined by technological and production factors and V is institutionally determined. In this case, changes in M are reflected in proportional changes in the price level.

The monetarists, under Professor Milton Friedman, have taken off from this starting point to develop an approach that differs from the Keynesian in terms of the analysis of monetary mechanisms and also in terms of the appropriate range of governmental actions. Among the questions that are taken up in this chapter and Great Debate Two are: Does money matter—not at all, very much, or supremely? Does fiscal policy work or does M alone effectively determine long-run $P \times Q$? Should the government regulate its monetary policy in terms of the money supply alone, or in terms of interest rates and other credit conditions? Should the Fed use *any* discretion or should it bind itself to a fixed increase in the money supply rule?

The empirical issues are difficult to settle because of the interdependence of economic phenomena, the problems of sorting out leads and lags, and the difficulty of determining cause and effect. So far, most economists would give the edge to the eclectic post-Keynesians, although everyone gives credit to the monetarists both for their own intensive researches and for their stimulation of research by others.

IMPORTANT TERMS TO REMEMBER

M X V = P X Q
Quantity Theory of Money
Income Velocity of Money
Role of Money in Keynesian Theory
Liquidity Trap
Pigou Effect
Monetarism
Nominal vs. Real Quantities
Fiscal vs. Monetary Policy
Rules vs. Discretionary Authority

QUESTIONS FOR DISCUSSION

1. Theories of the role of money in the economy have been ranked according to the following spectrum of possibilities:

(a) Money doesn't matter.

(b) Money matters.

(c) Money matters much.

(d) Money alone matters.

On this spectrum, rank the following theories: quantity theory of money, Keynesian and post-Keynesian theories, and monetarism.

2. It has been claimed that Keynesian theory does not, contrary to common opinion, provide for the possibility of a genuine below-full-employment equilibrium, the reason being that unemployed workers will have a motive for bidding down the money wage, which, in turn, will bring a general fall in prices. To this the Keynesians have usually replied that although W and P might fall under these circumstances, their fall might have little or no effect on the rate of unemployment in the economy. Show how falling W and P could, in the Keynesian theory, affect the level of real national income and employment. What factors might keep this effect small? Why have we said that, in the Keynesian theory, a general fall in W and P is rather similar in effect to an increase in the money supply, M?

3. What is the Pigou effect? Would this effect apply to government bonds in the hands of the public? Discuss the issues involved.

4. When the government runs a budget deficit, it might sell its bonds to the public or to the Federal Reserve System. If it sells them to the Federal Reserve System, this will lead to a general increase in bank reserves and an expansion in M. Explain why, according to the monetarists, an increase in government expenditures, G, unmatched by any change in taxes may have either *(a)* no effect or *(b)* a substantial effect on money national income, depending completely on how the deficit is financed.

5. Explain what you see as the advantages and disadvantages of an automatic versus discretionary monetary and fiscal policy.

SUGGESTED READING

Friedman, Milton. *Program for Monetary Stability.* New York: Fordham University, 1959.

_____. ''A Monetary Theory of Nominal Income,'' *Journal of Political Economy,* 79, no. 2 (January–June 1971).

_____. ''Have Fiscal and/or Monetary Policies Failed?'' *The American Economic Review* 62, no. 2 (May 1972).

Kaldor, Nicholas. ''The New Monetarism,'' *Lloyds Bank Review,* July 1970.

Samuelson, Paul A. ''Monetarism Objectively Evaluated.'' In *Readings in Economics,* 6th ed., ed. Paul A. Samuelson. New York: McGraw-Hill, 1970.

The Federal Reserve Bank of Boston. *Controlling Monetary Aggregates.* Boston: Proceedings of the Monetary Conference, Federal Reserve Bank of Boston, June 1969.

Tobin, James. ''Friedman's Theoretical Framework,'' *Journal of Political Economy,* 80, no. 5 (September–October 1972).

APPENDIX 13:
TAX CUT: KEYNES VERSUS THE MONETARISTS

For readers who have completed the appendix to chapter 11, we can illustrate some of the issues involved in the monetarist debate by means of *IS* and *LM* curves. The complexities of the matter are brought home by the facts that (1) there are different interpretations of what the monetarists are saying; (2) the monetarists stress certain distinctions more than non-monetarists; and (3) there is throughout a need to distinguish between short-term and long-term effects. We shall illustrate these matters by analyzing the macroeconomic effects of a general tax cut.

Let us assume that the government, starting from a balanced budget, decides to cut taxes across the board, thus engaging in deficit spending and an increase each year in the national debt. Let us suppose further that this policy is persisted in for at least a few consecutive years.

Initial Effect in the Keynesian System. The initial impact in the Keynesian world of chapter 11 will be an upward shift of the *IS* curve. This occurs because the tax cut increases disposable income, which should increase consumption. Assuming the investment schedule is unaffected, the level of national income that equates *I* and *S* will be higher for each interest rate than before the tax cut. In short, *IS* in Figure 1 moves to *IS'*. This leads to an increase in equilibrium national income (from Y to Y') and the equilibrium interest rate (from i to i').

Monetarism According to Tobin. Professor James Tobin, a critic of monetarism, interprets Friedman's position to involve primarily a different view of the *LM* curve from that of the Keynesians.[1] In particular, he believes that monetarism advances the theory that *LM* is basically vertical. According to monetarism, *M* largely determines money national income ($P \times Q$, or, if *Y* stands for *real* income, $P \times Y$). The income velocity of money (*V*) is insensitive to changes in the interest rate. Now, if we assume for the moment

---

1. See James Tobin, "Friedman's Theoretical Framework," *Journal of Political Economy*, 80 (5), September–October 1972.

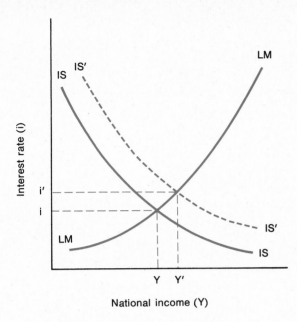

Figure 1. Tax Cut in Keynesian System.

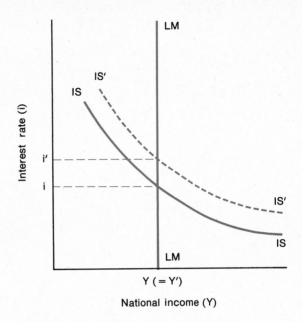

Figure 2. Tax Cut in Monetarist System, According to Tobin.

that the price level is given, then *M* will pretty well determine *Y*. Or to put it in other words, in the absence of changes in *M* which will cause shifts in the *LM* curve, *Y* stays where it is.

In particular, there is no direct effect of a tax cut such as we are discussing. This tax cut will shift *IS* as in the Keynesian world, but all this will do is increase the rate of interest—assuming no change in *M* to finance the new Treasury bonds. *Y* will remain at its original level. (See Figure 2).

Monetarism According to Friedman (Case I). Friedman disagrees with Tobin's interpretation of his (Friedman's) theory.[2] He distinguishes two cases in the short run. The first is where the tax cut and ensuing increase in the national debt is financed by the Treasury selling bonds to the general public. In this case, there is no increase in *M*. The impact of this fiscal policy action, according to Friedman, would be "minor" but not zero. He does not claim, in con-

trast to Tobin's assertion, that the *LM* curve is vertical. He does say that the *LM* curve "is very far from being horizontal"; however, this is only part of the reason why the direct effects of the tax cut are so limited. The other part is that he believes that the *IS* curve shift will be only very "minor." Putting these two propositions together, we have Figure 3, which leads to an increase in *Y* in response to a tax cut, but only a very small increase compared with the Keynesian system. However, this is only the beginning of the monetarist position according to Friedman.

Monetarism According to Friedman (Case II). Friedman now goes on to contrast this very minor impact of fiscal policy of Figure 3 with the dominating impact of monetary policy if the debt is financed with an increasing *M*. Suppose the Treasury in the first year finances its new deficit by selling bonds to the Fed. This will cause an increase in the money supply in the first year of the new policy. However, notice that this increase is not limited to the first year; the

---

2.   Milton Friedman, "Comments on the Critics," *Journal of Political Economy*, 80 (5), September–October 1972.

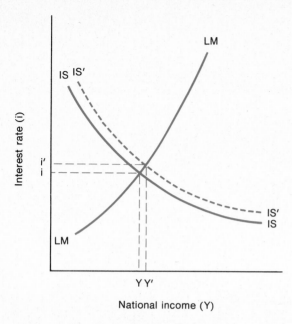

Figure 3. Tax Cut in Monetarist System, According to Friedman (Case I).

Case I involves no increase in the money supply to finance the increased deficit resulting from the tax cut.

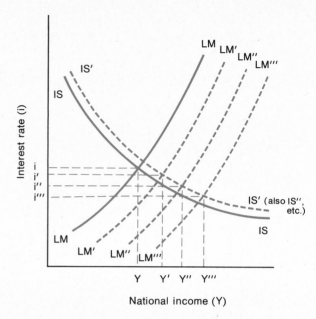

Figure 4. Tax Cut in Monetarist System, According to Friedman (Case II).

Case II involves financing the new deficit each year by increasing *M* (selling bonds to the Fed).

next year will involve a further increase in the money supply. In fact, we will get a constantly increasing *M* every year that the policy is in effect.

In terms of our diagrams, this means that while *IS* shifts only once—and a very "minor" shift at that, according to Friedman—the *LM* curve will be shifting outward constantly. Whatever the effect of the initial shift in *IS* (measuring the impact of Keynesian style fiscal policy), it will soon be dwarfed by these constant increases in the quantity of money. Figure 4 shows *Y* constantly rising and *i* constantly falling as this flood of new money keeps pouring into the system.

Longer-run Effects under Monetarism. But even Figure 4 does not tell the full story. It cannot, because it is framed in terms of *real* income, whereas, according to the monetarists, the long-run effects of an increased stock of money are not on real but on *money* income. What this means is that, in the long run, the basic effects of the tax cut and the financing of it through increased *M* will be on prices (*P*). This tax cut will in the long run be inflationary because of its associated monetary effects; the favorable effects on real national income will be only temporary.

The reader should now go on to Great Debate Two and then, at the end, return to this appendix and interpret some of the arguments he will have read in terms of the material presented here.

GREAT DEBATE 2:
THE ISSUE
OF MONETARISM

GREAT DEBATE 2:
THE ISSUE
OF MONETARISM

The following readings take up that large cluster of analytic and policy issues that center on the matter of monetarism. As the reader knows from chapter 13, this doctrine is one of the most hotly contested subjects in the whole area of macroeconomics.

The first reading is excerpted from the Presidential Address to the Eightieth Annual Meeting of the American Economic Association in 1967 by its (then) president, Milton Friedman. It is followed by an exchange between Friedman and Walter Heller, an outstanding neo-Keynesian economist and the chairman of the Council of Economic Advisers under President John F. Kennedy. This exchange has been excerpted from a discussion between these two economists at the Graduate School of Business Administration of New York University in November, 1968.

The final three readings are taken from another discussion about monetarism held under the auspices of the Federal Reserve Bank of Boston in 1969. The participants in this discussion, besides Paul Samuelson, are James Tobin, Sterling Professor of Economics at Yale University, and Allan H. Meltzer, professor of Economics and Industrial Administration, Carnegie-Mellon University in Pittsburgh.

The Role of Monetary Policy

Milton Friedman

There is wide agreement about the major goals of economic policy: high employment, stable prices, and rapid growth. There is less agreement that these goals are mutually compatible or, among those who regard them as incompatible, about the terms at which they can and should be substituted for one another. There is least agreement about the role that various instruments of policy can and should play in achieving the several goals.

My topic for tonight is the role of one such instrument—monetary policy. What can it contribute? And how should it be conducted to contribute the most? Opinion on these questions has fluctuated widely. In the first flush of enthusiasm about the newly created Federal Reserve System, many observers attributed the relative stability of the 1920s to the System's capacity for fine tuning—to apply an apt modern term. It came to be widely believed that a new era had arrived in which business cycles had been

rendered obsolete by advances in monetary technology. This opinion was shared by economist and layman alike, though, of course, there were some dissonant voices. The Great Contraction destroyed this naive attitude. Opinion swung to the other extreme. Monetary policy was a string. You could pull on it to stop inflation but you could not push on it to halt recession. You could lead a horse to water but you could not make him drink. Such theory by aphorism was soon replaced by Keynes' rigorous and sophisticated analysis.

Keynes offered simultaneously an explanation for the presumed impotence of monetary policy to stem the depression, a nonmonetary interpretation of the depression, and an alternative to monetary policy for meeting the depression and his offering was avidly accepted. If liquidity preference is absolute or nearly so—as Keynes believed likely in times of heavy unemployment—interest rates cannot be lowered by monetary measures. If investment and consumption are

Excerpted from Milton Friedman, "The Role of Monetary Policy," *American Economic Review* 58, no. 1 (March 1968): 1–17. Reprinted by permission of the author and the publisher.

little affected by interest rates—as Hansen and many of Keynes' other American disciples came to believe—lower interest rates, even if they could be achieved, would do little good. Monetary policy is twice damned. The contraction, set in train, on this view, by a collapse of investment or by a shortage of investment opportunities or by stubborn thriftiness, could not, it was argued, have been stopped by monetary measures. But there was available an alternative—fiscal policy. Government spending could make up for insufficient private investment. Tax reductions could undermine stubborn thriftiness.

The wide acceptance of these views in the economics profession meant that for some two decades monetary policy was believed by all but a few reactionary souls to have been rendered obsolete by new economic knowledge. Money did not matter. Its only role was the minor one of keeping interest rates low, in order to hold down interest payments in the government budget, contribute to the "euthanasia of the rentier," and maybe, stimulate investment a bit to assist government spending in maintaining a high level of aggregate demand.

These views produced a widespread adoption of cheap money policies after the war. And they received a rude shock when these policies failed in country after country, when central bank after central bank was forced to give up the pretense that it could indefinitely keep "the" rate of interest at a low level. In this country, the public denouement came with the Federal Reserve-Treasury Accord in 1951, although the policy of pegging government bond prices was not formally abandoned until 1953. Inflation, stimulated by cheap money policies, not the widely heralded postwar depression, turned out to be the order of the day. The result was the beginning of a revival of belief in the potency of monetary policy.

This revival was strongly fostered among economists by the theoretical developments initiated by Haberler but named for Pigou that pointed out a channel—namely, changes in wealth—whereby changes in the real quantity of money can affect aggregate demand even if they do not alter interest rates. These theoretical developments did not undermine Keynes' argument against the potency of orthodox monetary measures when liquidity preference is absolute since under such circumstances the usual monetary operations involve simply substituting money for other assets without changing total wealth. But they did show how changes in the quantity of money produced in other ways could affect total spending even under such circumstances. And, more fundamentally, they did undermine Keynes' key theoretical proposition, namely, that even in a world of flexible prices, a position of equilibrium at full employment might not exist. Henceforth, unemployment had again to be explained by rigidities or imperfections, not as the natural outcome of a fully operative market process.

The revival of belief in the potency of monetary policy was fostered also by a re-evaluation of the role money played from 1929 to 1933. Keynes and most other economists of the time believed that the Great Contraction in the United States occurred despite aggressive expansionary policies by the monetary authorities—that they did their best but their best was not good enough. Recent studies have demonstrated that the facts are precisely the reverse: the U.S. monetary authorities followed highly deflationary policies. The quantity of money in the United States fell by one-third in the course of the contraction. And it fell not because there were no willing borrowers—not because the horse would not drink. It fell because the Federal Reserve System forced or permitted a sharp reduction in the monetary base, because it failed to exercise the responsibilities assigned to it in the Federal Reserve Act to provide liquidity to the banking system. The Great Contraction is tragic testimony to the power of monetary policy—not, as Keynes and so many of his contemporaries believed, evidence of its impotence.

In the United States the revival of belief in the potency of monetary policy was strengthened also by increasing disillusionment with fiscal policy, not so much with its potential to affect aggregate demand as with the practical and political feasibility of so using it. Expenditures turned out to respond sluggishly and with long lags to attempts to adjust them to the course of economic activity, so emphasis shifted to taxes. But here political factors entered with a vengeance to prevent prompt adjustment to presumed need, as has been so graphically illustrated in the months since I wrote the first draft of this talk. "Fine tuning" is a marvelously evocative phrase in this electronic age, but it has little resemblance to what is possible in practice—not, I might add, an unmixed evil.

It is hard to realize how radical has been the change in professional opinion on the role of money. Hardly an economist today accepts views that were the common coin some two decades ago. The pendulum has swung far since then, if not all the way to the position of the late 1920s, at least much closer to that position than to the position of 1945. There are of course many differences between then and now, less in the potency attributed to monetary policy than in the roles assigned to it and the criteria by which the profession believes monetary policy should be guided. I stress nonetheless the similarity between the views that prevailed in the late twenties and those that prevail today because I fear that, now as then, the pendulum may well have swung too far, that, now as then, we are in danger of assigning to monetary policy a larger role than it can perform, in danger of asking it to accomplish tasks that it cannot achieve, and, as a result, in danger of preventing it from making the contribution that it is capable of making.

Unaccustomed as I am to denigrating the importance of money, I therefore shall, as my first task, stress what monetary policy cannot do. I shall then try to outline what it can do and how it can best make its contribution, in the present state of our knowledge—or ignorance.

I. WHAT MONETARY POLICY CANNOT DO

From the infinite world of negation, I have selected two limitations of monetary policy to discuss: (1) It cannot peg interest rates for more than very limited periods; (2) It cannot peg the rate of unemployment for more than very limited periods. I select these because the contrary has been or is widely believed, because they correspond to the two main unattainable tasks that are at all likely to be assigned to monetary policy, and because essentially the same theoretical analysis covers both.

Pegging of Interest Rates

History has already persuaded many of you about the first limitation. As noted earlier, the failure of cheap money policies was a major source of the reaction against simple-minded Keynesianism. In the United States, this reaction involved widespread recognition that the wartime and postwar pegging of bond prices was a mistake, that the abandonment of this policy was a desirable and inevitable step, and that it had none of the disturbing and disastrous consequences that were so freely predicted at the time.

The limitation derives from a much misunderstood feature of the relation between money and interest rates. Let the Fed set out to keep interest rates down. How will it try to do so? By buying securities. This raises their prices and lowers their yields. In the process, it also increases the quantity of reserves available to banks, hence the amount of bank credit; and, ultimately the total quantity of money. That is why central bankers in particular, and the financial community more broadly, generally believe that an increase in the quantity of money tends to lower interest rates. Academic economists accept the same conclusion, but for different reasons. They see, in their mind's eye, a negatively sloping liquidity preference schedule. How can people be induced to hold a larger quantity of money? Only by bidding down interest rates.

Both are right, up to a point. The *initial* impact of increasing the quantity of money at a faster rate than it has been increasing is to make interest rates lower for a time than they would otherwise have been. But this is only the beginning of the process not the end. The more rapid rate of monetary growth will stimulate spending, both through the impact on investment of lower market interest rates and through the impact on other spending and thereby relative prices of higher cash balances than are desired. But one man's spending is another man's income. Rising income will raise the liquidity preference schedule and the demand for loans; it may also raise prices, which would reduce the real quantity of money. These three effects will reverse the initial downward pressure on interest rates fairly promptly, say, in something less than a year. Together they will tend, after a somewhat longer interval, say, a year or two, to return interest rates to the level they would otherwise have had. Indeed, given the tendency for the economy to overreact, they are highly likely to raise interest rates temporarily beyond that level, setting in motion a cyclical adjustment process.

A fourth effect, when and if it becomes operative, will go even farther, and definitely mean that a higher rate of monetary expansion will correspond to a higher, not lower, level of interest rates than would otherwise have prevailed. Let the higher rate of monetary growth produce rising prices, and let the public come to expect that prices will continue to rise. Borrowers will then be willing to pay and lenders will then demand higher interest rates—as Irving Fisher pointed out decades ago. This price expectation effect is slow to develop and also slow to disappear. Fisher estimated that it took several decades for a full adjustment and more recent work is consistent with his estimates.

These subsequent effects explain why every attempt to keep interest rates at a low level has forced the monetary authority to engage in successively larger and larger open market purchases. They explain why, historically, high and rising nominal interest rates have been associated with rapid growth in the quantity of money, as in Brazil or Chile or in the United States in recent years, and why low and falling interest rates have been associated with slow growth in the quantity of money, as in Switzerland now or in the United States from 1929 to 1933. As an empirical matter, low interest rates are a sign that monetary policy *has been* tight—in the sense that the quantity of money has grown slowly; high interest rates are a sign that monetary policy *has been* easy—in the sense that the quantity of money has grown rapidly. The broadest facts of experience run in precisely the opposite direction from that which the financial community and academic economists have all generally taken for granted.

Paradoxically, the monetary authority could assure low nominal rates of interest—but to do so it would have to start out in what seems like the opposite direction, by engaging in a deflationary monetary policy. Similarly, it could assure high nominal interest rates by engaging in an inflationary policy and accepting a temporary movement in interest rates in the opposite direction.

These considerations not only explain why monetary policy cannot peg interest rates; they also explain why interest rates are such a misleading indicator of whether monetary policy is "tight" or "easy." For that, it is far better to look at the rate of change of the quantity of money.

Employment as a Criterion of Policy

The second limitation I wish to discuss goes more against the grain of current thinking. Monetary growth, it is widely held, will tend to stimulate employment; monetary contraction, to retard employment. Why, then, cannot the monetary authority adopt a target for employment or unemployment—say, 3 percent unemployment; be

tight when unemployment is less than the target; be easy when unemployment is higher than the target; and in this way peg unemployment at, say, 3 percent? The reason it cannot is precisely the same as for interest rates—the difference between the immediate and the delayed consequences of such a policy.

At any moment of time, there is some level of unemployment which has the property that it is consistent with equilibrium in the structure of *real* wage rates. At that level of unemployment, real wage rates are tending on the average to rise at a "normal" secular rate, i.e., at a rate than can be indefinitely maintained so long as capital formation, technological improvements, etc., remain on their long-run trends. A lower level of unemployment is an indication that there is an excess demand for labor that will produce upward pressure on real wage rates. A higher level of unemployment is an indication that there is an excess supply of labor that will produce downward pressure on real wage rates.

Let us assume that the monetary authority tries to peg the "market" rate of unemployment at a level below the "natural" rate. For definiteness, suppose that it takes 3 percent as the target rate and that the "natural" rate is higher than 3 percent. Suppose also that we start out at a time when prices have been stable and when unemployment is higher than 3 percent. Accordingly, the authority increases the rate of monetary growth. This will be expansionary. By making nominal cash balances higher than people desire, it will tend initially to lower interest rates and in this and other ways to stimulate spending. Income and spending will start to rise.

To begin with, much or most of the rise in income will take the form of an increase in output and employment rather than in prices. People have been expecting prices to be stable, and prices and wages have been set for some time in the future on that basis. It takes time for people to adjust to a new state of demand. Producers will tend to react to the initial expansion in aggregate demand by increasing output, employees by working longer hours, and the unemployed by taking jobs now offered at former nominal wages. This much is pretty standard doctrine.

But it describes only the initial effects. Because selling prices of products typically respond to an unanticipated rise in nominal demand faster than prices of factors of production, real wages received have gone down—though real wages anticipated by employees went up, since employees implicitly evaluated the wages offered at the earlier price level. Indeed, the simultaneous fall *ex post* in real wages to employers and rise *ex ante* in real wages to employees is what enabled employment to increase. But the decline *ex post* in real wages will soon come to affect anticipations. Employees will start to reckon on rising prices of the things they buy and to demand higher nominal wages for the future. "Market" unemployment is below the "natural" level. There is an excess demand for labor, so real wages will tend to rise toward their initial level.

Even though the higher rate of monetary growth continues, the rise in real wages will reverse the decline in unemployment, and then lead to a rise, which will tend to return unemployment to its former level. In order to keep unemployment at its target level of 3 percent, the monetary authority would have to raise monetary growth still more. As in the interest rate case, the "market" rate can be kept below the "natural" rate only by inflation. And, as in the interest rate case, too, only by accelerating inflation. Conversely, let the monetary authority

choose a target rate of unemployment that is above the natural rate, and they will be led to produce a deflation, and an accelerating deflation at that.

To state the general conclusion still differently, the monetary authority controls nominal quantities—directly, the quantity of its own liabilities. In principle, it can use this control to peg a nominal quantity—an exchange rate, the price level, the nominal level of national income, the quantity of money by one or another definition—or to peg the rate of change in a nominal quantity—the rate of inflation or deflation, the rate of growth or decline in nominal national income, the rate of growth of the quantity of money. It cannot use its control over nominal quantities to peg a real quantity—the real rate of interest, the rate of unemployment, the level of real national income, the real quantity of money, the rate of growth of real national income, or the rate of growth of the real quantity of money.

II. WHAT MONETARY POLICY CAN DO

Monetary policy cannot peg these real magnitudes at predetermined levels. But monetary policy can and does have important effects on these real magnitudes. The one is in no way inconsistent with the other.

My own studies of monetary history have made me extremely sympathetic to the oft-quoted, much reviled, and as widely misunderstood, comment by John Stuart Mill. "There cannot . . . ," he wrote, "be intrinsically a more insignificant thing, in the economy of society, than money; except in the character of a contrivance for sparing time and labour. It is a machine for doing quickly and commodiously, what would be done, though less quickly and commodiously, without it: and like many other kinds of machinery, it only exerts a distinct and independent influence of its own when it gets out of order."*

True, money is only a machine, but it is an extraordinarily efficient machine. Without it, we could not have begun to attain the astounding growth in output and level of living we have experienced in the past two centuries—any more than we could have done so without those other marvelous machines that dot our countryside and enable us, for the most part, simply to do more efficiently what could be done without them at much greater cost in labor.

But money has one feature that these other machines do not share. Because it is so pervasive, when it gets out of order, it throws a monkey wrench into the operation of all the other machines. The Great Contraction is the most dramatic example but not the only one. Every other major contraction in this country has been either produced by monetary disorder or greatly exacerbated by monetary disorder. Every major inflation has been produced by monetary expansion—mostly to meet the overriding demands of war which have forced the creation of money to supplement explicit taxation.

The first and most important lesson that history teaches about what monetary policy can do—and it is a lesson of the most profound importance—is that monetary policy can prevent money itself from being a major source of economic disturbance. This sounds like a negative proposition: avoid major mistakes. In part it is. The Great

Contraction might not have occurred at all, and if it had, it would have been far less severe, if the monetary authority had avoided mistakes, or if the monetary arrangements had been those of an earlier time when there was no central authority with the power to make the kinds of mistakes that the Federal Reserve System made. The past few years, to come closer to home, would have been steadier and more productive of economic well-being if the Federal Reserve had avoided drastic and erratic changes of direction, first expanding the money supply at an unduly rapid pace, then, in early 1966, stepping on the brake too hard, then, at the end of 1966, reversing itself and resuming expansion until at least November 1967, at a more rapid pace than can long be maintained without appreciable inflation.

Even if the proposition that monetary policy can prevent money itself from being a major source of economic disturbance were a wholly negative proposition, it would be none the less important for that. As it happens, however, it is not a wholly negative proposition. The monetary machine has gotten out of order even when there has been no central authority with anything like the power now possessed by the Fed. In the United States, the 1907 episode and earlier banking panics are examples of how the monetary machine can get out of order largely on its own. There is therefore a positive and important task for the monetary authority—to suggest improvements in the machine that will reduce the chances that it will get out of order, and to use its own powers so as to keep the machine in good working order.

A second thing monetary policy can do is provide a stable background for the economy—keep the machine well oiled, to continue Mill's analogy. Accomplishing the first task will contribute to this objective, but there is more to it

---

*J. S. Mill, *Principles of Political Economy,* Bk. III, Ashley ed. New York, 1929, p. 488.

than that. Our economic system will work best when producers and consumers, employers and employees, can proceed with full confidence that the average level of prices will behave in a known way in the future—preferably that it will be highly stable. Under any conceivable institutional arrangements, and certainly under those that now prevail in the United States, there is only a limited amount of flexibility in prices and wages. We need to conserve this flexibility to achieve changes in relative prices and wages that are required to adjust to dynamic changes in tastes and technology. We should not dissipate it simply to achieve changes in the absolute level of prices that serve no economic function.

In today's world, if monetary policy is to provide a stable background for the economy it must do so by deliberately employing its powers to that end. I shall come later to how it can do so.

Finally, monetary policy can contribute to offsetting major disturbances in the economic system arising from other sources. If there is an independent secular exhilaration—as the postwar expansion was described by the proponents of secular stagnation—monetary policy can in principle help to hold it in check by a slower rate of monetary growth than would otherwise be desirable. If, as now, an explosive federal budget threatens unprecedented deficits, monetary policy can hold any inflationary dangers in check by a slower rate of monetary growth than would otherwise be desirable. This will temporarily mean higher interest rates than would otherwise prevail—to enable the government to borrow the sums needed to finance the deficit—but by preventing the speeding up of inflation, it may well mean both lower prices and lower nominal interest rates for the long pull. If the end of a substan-

tial war offers the country an opportunity to shift resources from wartime to peacetime production, monetary policy can ease the transition by a higher rate of monetary growth than would otherwise be desirable—though experience is not very encouraging that it can do so without going too far.

I have put this point last, and stated it in qualified terms—as referring to major disturbances—because I believe that the potentiality of monetary policy in offsetting other forces making for instability is far more limited than is commonly believed. We simply do not know enough to be able to recognize minor disturbances when they occur or to be able to predict either what their effects will be with any precision or what monetary policy is required to offset their effects. We do not know enough to be able to achieve stated objectives by delicate, or even fairly coarse, changes in the mix of monetary and fiscal policy. In this area particularly the best is likely to be the enemy of the good. Experience suggests that the path of wisdom is to use monetary policy explicitly to offset other disturbances only when they offer a "clear and present danger."

III. HOW SHOULD MONETARY POLICY BE CONDUCTED?

How should monetary policy be conducted to make the contribution to our goals that it is capable of making? I shall restrict myself here to two major requirements for monetary policy that follow fairly directly from the preceding discussion.

The first requirement is that the monetary authority should guide itself by magnitudes that it can control, not by ones that it cannot control. If, as the authority has often done, it takes interest rates or the current unemployment percentage as the immediate criterion of policy, it will be like a space vehicle that has taken a fix on the wrong star. No matter how sensitive and sophisticated its guiding apparatus, the space vehicle will go astray. And so will the monetary authority. Of the various alternative magnitudes that it can control, the most appealing guides for policy are exchange rates, the price level as defined by some index, and the quantity of a monetary total—currency plus adjusted demand deposits, or this total plus commercial bank time deposits, or a still broader total.

For the United States in particular, exchange rates are an undesirable guide. It might be worth requiring the bulk of the economy to adjust to the tiny percentage consisting of foreign trade if that would guarantee freedom from monetary irresponsibility—as it might under a real gold standard. But it is hardly worth doing so simply to adapt to the average of whatever policies monetary authorities in the rest of the world adopt. Far better to let the market, through floating exchange rates, adjust to world conditions the 5 percent or so of our resources devoted to international trade while reserving monetary policy to promote the effective use of the 95 percent.

Of the three guides listed, the price level is clearly the most important in its own right. Other things the same, it would be much the best of the alternatives—as so many distinguished economists have urged in the past. But other things are not the same. The link between the policy actions of the monetary authority and the price level, while unquestionably present, is more indirect than the link between the policy actions of the authority and any of the several monetary totals. Moreover, monetary action takes a longer time to affect the price level than to affect the monetary totals and both the time lag and the magnitude of effect vary with circumstances. As a result, we cannot predict at all accurately just what effect a particular monetary action will have on the price level and, equally important, just when it will have that effect. Attempting to control directly the price level is therefore likely to make monetary policy itself a source of economic disturbance because of false stops and starts. Perhaps, as our understanding of monetary phenomena advances, the situation will change. But at the present stage of our understanding, the long way around seems the surer way to our objective. Accordingly, I believe that a monetary total is the best currently available immediate guide or criterion for monetary policy—and I believe that it matters much less which particular total is chosen than that one be chosen.

A second requirement for monetary policy is that the monetary authority avoid sharp swings in policy. In the past, monetary authorities have on occasion moved in the wrong direction—as in the episode of the Great Contraction that I have stressed. More frequently, they have moved in the right direction, albeit often too late, but have erred by moving too far. Too late and too much has been the general practice. For example, in early 1966, it was the right policy for the Federal Reserve to move in a less expansionary direction—though it should have done so at least a year earlier. But when it moved, it went too far, producing the sharpest change in the rate of monetary growth of the postwar era. Again, having gone too far, it was the right policy for the Fed to reverse course at the end of 1966. But again it went too far, not only restoring but exceeding the earlier excessive rate of monetary growth. And this episode is no exception. Time and again this has been the course followed—as in 1919 and 1920, in 1937 and 1938, in 1953 and 1954, in 1959 and 1960.

The reason for the propensity to overreact seems clear: the failure of monetary authorities to allow for the delay between their actions and the subsequent effects on the economy. They tend to determine their actions by today's conditions—but their actions will affect the economy only six or nine or twelve or fifteen months later. Hence they feel impelled to step on the brake, or the accelerator, as the case may be, too hard.

My own prescription is still that the monetary authority go all the way in avoiding such swings by adopting publicly the policy of achieving a steady rate of growth in a specified monetary total. The precise rate of growth, like the precise monetary total, is less important than the adoption of some stated and known rate. I myself have argued for a rate that would on the average achieve rough stability in the level of prices of final products, which I have estimated would call for something like a 3 to 5 percent per year rate of growth in currency plus all commercial bank deposits or a slightly lower rate of growth in currency plus demand deposits only. But it would be better to have a fixed rate that would on the average produce moderate inflation or moderate deflation, provided it was steady, than to suffer the wide and erratic perturbations we have experienced.

Short of the adoption of such a publicly stated policy of a steady rate of monetary growth, it would constitute a major improvement if the monetary authority followed the self-denying ordinance of avoiding wide swings. It is a matter of record that periods of relative stability in the rate of monetary growth have also been periods of relative stability in economic activity, both in the United States and other countries. Periods of wide swings in the rate of monetary growth have also been periods of wide swings in economic activity.

By setting itself a steady course and keeping to it, the monetary authority could make a major contribution to promoting economic stability. By making that course one of steady but moderate growth in the quantity of money, it would make a major contribution to avoidance of either inflation or deflation of prices. Other forces would still affect the economy, require change and adjustment, and disturb the even tenor of our ways. But steady monetary growth would provide a monetary climate favorable to the effective operation of those basic forces of enterprise, ingenuity, invention, hard work, and thrift that are the true springs of economic growth. That is the most that we can ask from monetary policy at our present stage of knowledge. But that much—and it is a great deal—is clearly within our reach.   □

Is Monetary Policy Being Oversold?

Walter W. Heller

At the outset, let's clarify what is and what isn't at issue in today's discussion of fiscal-monetary policy. The issue is *not* whether money matters—we all grant that—but whether *only* money matters, as some Friedmanites, or perhaps I should say Friedmanics, would put it. Or really, whether only money matters *much,* which is what I understand Milton Friedman to say—he is more reasonable than many of the Friedmanites.

Again, in the fiscal field, the issue is not *whether* fiscal policy matters—even some monetarists, perhaps in unguarded moments, have urged budget cuts or tax changes for stabilization reasons. The issues are *how much* it matters, and how heavily we can lean on discretionary changes in taxes and budgets to maintain steady economic growth in a dynamic economy.

Summing up the key operational issues, they are: Should money be king? Is fiscal policy worth its salt? Should flexible man yield to rigid rules?

Let me review with you the factors that say "stop, look, and listen" before embracing the triple doctrine that only money matters much; that control of the money supply is the key to economic stability; and that a rigid fixed-throttle expansion of 4 or 5 percent a year is the only safe policy prescription in a world of alleged economic ignorance and human weakness and folly.

One should note in passing that Professor Friedman's findings and conclusions fit into a steady process of rescuing monetary policy from the limbo into which it was put by the interest-rate peg of World War II and the late forties—a rescue effected by the Monetary Accord of 1951 and by the subsequent steady expansion of its scope. This has been a healthy renaissance. But having been resurrected from the debilitating rate peg of the 1940s, does monetary policy now face the threat of a new peg, Milton's money-supply peg, in the years ahead? Is it doomed to go from cradle to grave in twenty years?

I exaggerate, of course, for emphasis. President Nixon, for example, has been reported as saying that he doesn't buy the fixed-throttle formula. At the same time, he has reportedly suggested that he intends to put more emphasis on money supply. So this is a particularly apt juncture for a close look at the monetarists' doctrine.

Now, turning to doubts, unresolved questions, and unconvincing evidence, I group these into eight conditions that must be satisfied—if not completely, at least more convincingly than they have been to date—before we can even consider giving money supply sovereignty, or dominance, or greater prominence in economic policy.

The first condition is this: the monetarists must make up their minds which money-supply variable they want us to accept as our guiding star—M_1, the narrow money supply, just currency and bank deposits; M_2, adding time deposits; or perhaps some other measure like the "monetary base?" And when will the monetarists decide? Perhaps Milton Friedman has decided; but if he has, his disciples do not seem to have gotten the word.

Reprinted from *Monetary vs. Fiscal Policy: A Dialogue* by Milton Friedman and Walter W. Heller. By permission of W. W. Norton & Company, Inc. Copyright © 1969 by the Graduate School of Business Administration, New York University. Excerpts from pp. 15–23, 25–28, 30–31.

It doesn't seem too much to ask that this confusion be resolved in some satisfactory way before putting great faith in money supply as our key policy variable.

Second, I would feel more sympathetic to the money-supply doctrine if it were not so one-track-minded about money stock—measured any way you wish—as the *only* financial variable with any informational content for policy purposes.

As Gramley has noted, for example, if we look at money stock alone for 1948, it would indicate the tightest money in the post-war period.* Yet, the rate on Treasury bills was 1 percent, and on high-grade corporates 2¾ percent. (That *does* sound like ancient history.) But isn't it curious that we had tight money by the money-supply standard side by side with 1, 2, and 3 percent interest rates? We were swamped with liquidity—so interest rates do seem to have been telling us something very important.

Or, if we look at 1967 *only* in terms of the money stock, it would appear as the easiest-money year since World War II. M_1 was up 6 percent, M_2 was up 12 percent. Yet there was a very sharp rise in interest rates. Why? Probably because of a big shift in liquidity preference as corporations strove to build up their protective liquidity cushions after their harrowing experience the previous year—their monetary dehydration in the credit crunch of 1966. Again, the behavior of interest rates is vital to proper interpretation of monetary developments and guidance of monetary policy. Interest rates are endogenous variables and cannot be used alone —but neither can money stock. Either interest

rates or money stock, used alone, could seriously mislead us.

I really don't understand how the scarcity of any commodity can be gauged without referring to its price—or, more specifically, how the scarcity of money can be gauged without referring to interest rates.

Third, given the fluctuations in money velocity, that supposedly inexorable link between money and economic activity has yet to be established. We should not forget this, however sweet the siren song of the monetarists may sound. Clearly, velocity has varied over time—some might say "greatly," others "moderately." Let me sidestep a bit and say, for purposes of this discussion, "significantly." For I would remind you that the income velocity of money rose roughly 28 percent during the 1960–68 period. Had velocity been the same in 1968 as it was in 1960, nominal GNP would have been not some $860 billion, but only $675 billion.

Fourth, it would help us if the monetarists could narrow the range on *when* money matters. How long are the lags that have to be taken into account in managing monetary policy?

Fifth, I'd be happier if only I knew which of the two Friedmans to believe. Should it be the Friedman we have had in focus here—the Friedman of the close causal relationship between money supply and income, who sees changes in money balances worked off gradually, with long lags before interest rates, prices of financial and physical assets, and, eventually, investment and consumption spending are affected? Or should it be the Friedman of the "permanent-income hypothesis," who sees the demand for money as quite unresponsive to changes in current income (since current income has only

*Lyle Gramley, "The Informational Content of Interest Rates as Indicators of Monetary Policy," in *Proceedings: 1968 Money and Banking Workshop*, Federal Reserve Bank of Minneapolis (May 1968), p. 23.

a fractional weight in permanent income), with the implied result that the monetary multiplier is very large in the short run, that there is an immediate and strong response to a change in the money stock? As Tobin has noted, he can't have it both ways. But which is it to be?

Sixth, if Milton's policy prescription were made in a frictionless Friedmanesque world without price, wage, and exchange rigidities—a world of his own making—it would be more admissible. But in the imperfect world in which we actually operate, beset by all sorts of rigidities, the introduction of his fixed-throttle money-supply rule might, in fact, be destabilizing. Or it could condemn us to long periods of economic slack or inflation as the slow adjustment processes in wages and prices, given strong market power, delayed the economy's reaction to the monetary rule while policy makers stood helplessly by.

A seventh and closely related concern is that locking the money supply into a rigid rule would jeopardize the U.S. international position. It's quite clear that capital flows are interest-rate sensitive. Indeed, capital flows induced by interest-rate changes can increase alarmingly when speculators take over. Under the Friedman rule, market interest rates would be whatever they turned out to be. It would be beyond the pale for the Fed to adjust interest rates for balance-of-payments adjustment purposes. Nor is it clear that by operating in the market for forward exchange (which in any event Milton would presumably oppose) the system could altogether neutralize changes in domestic market rates.

Milton has heard all of this before, and he always has an answer—flexible exchange rates. Yet, suffice it to note that however vital they are to the workings of his money-supply peg, floating exchange rates are not just around the corner.

Eighth, and finally, if the monetarists showed some small willingness to recognize the impact of fiscal policy—which has played such a large role in the policy thinking and action underlying the great expansion of the 1960s—one might be a little more sympathetic to their views. This point is, I must admit, not so much a condition as a plea for symmetry. The "new economists," having already given important and increasing weight to monetary factors in their policy models, are still waiting for signs that the monetarists will admit fiscal factors to theirs.

The 1964 tax cut pointedly illustrates what I mean. While the "new economists" fully recognize the important role monetary policy played in facilitating the success of the tax cut, the monetarists go to elaborate lengths to "prove" that the tax cut—which came close to removing a $13 billion full-employment surplus that was overburdening and retarding the economy—had nothing to do with the 1964–65 expansion. Money-supply growth did it all. Apparently, we were just playing fiscal tiddlywinks in Washington.

It seems to me that the cause of balanced analysis and rational policy would be served by redirecting some of the brilliance of Friedman and his followers from (a) single-minded devotion to the money-supply thesis and unceasing efforts to discredit fiscal policy and indeed all discretionary policy to (b) joint efforts to develop a more complete and satisfactory model of how the real world works; ascertain why it is working far better today than it did before active and conscious fiscal-monetary policy came into play; and determine how such policy can be improved to make it work even better in the future.

In a related asymmetry, as I've already suggested in passing, some Friedmanites fail to recognize that if fiscal policy actions like the 1964 tax cut can do no good, then fiscal policy actions like the big budget increases and deficits associated with Vietnam can also do no harm. Again, they should recognize that they can't have it both ways.

Now, one could lengthen and elaborate this list. But enough—let's just round it off this way: if Milton Friedman were saying that (as part of an active discretionary policy) we had better keep a closer eye on that important variable, money supply, in one or more of its several incarnations—I would say well and good, by all means. If the manifold doubts can be reasonably resolved, let's remedy any neglect or under-emphasis of money supply as a policy indicator relative to interest rates, free reserves, and the like. But let's not lock the steering gear into place, knowing full well of the twists and turns in the road ahead. That's an invitation to chaos.

Again, we need to stop, look, and listen lest we let simplistic or captious criticism operate to deny us the benefits of past experience and thwart the promise of future discretionary action on the monetary and fiscal fronts.

What has been the course of the American economy during the postwar period of an increasingly active and self-conscious fiscal-monetary policy for economic stabilization? Or, for that matter, let's broaden it: what has been the course of the world's advanced industrial economies during this period? The correlation is unmistakable: the more active, informed, and self-conscious fiscal and monetary policies have become, by and large, the more fully employed and stable the affected economies have become. Casual empiricism? Perhaps—yet a powerful and persuasive observation.

Witness the conclusion of the two-and-a-half-year study for the OECD by a group of fiscal experts from eight industrial countries:

The postwar economic performance of most Western countries in respect of employment, production and growth has been vastly superior to that of the pre-war years. This, in our view, has not been accidental. Governments have increasingly accepted responsibility for the promotion and maintenance of high employment and steady economic growth. The more conscious use of economic policies has undoubtedly played a crucial role in the better performance achieved—an achievement which, from the point of view of the ultimate social objectives of policy, is of paramount importance.

Perhaps an even more telling testament to the effectiveness of active modern stabilization-policy is the change in private investment thinking and planning not only in the financial sense of sustained confidence in the future of corporate earnings and stock market values, even in the face of temporary slowdowns in the economy—but more important, in the physical sense of sustained high levels of plant and equipment investment which seem to be replacing the sickening swings that used to be the order of the day.

Why? In good part, I take it to be the result of a constantly deepening conviction in the business and financial community that alert and active fiscal-monetary policy will keep the economy operating at a higher proportion of its potential in the future than in the past; that beyond short and temporary slowdowns, or perhaps even a recession—that's not ruled out in this vast and dynamic economy of ours—lies the prospect of sustained growth in that narrow band around full employment.   □

Reply

Milton Friedman

I want to comment on some of the points that Walter made initially and try to answer some of the questions he raised. I think that I might very well start with a point he made before and which he repeated now. He said that he would like us to stop being asymmetrical about tax increases or tax cuts on the one hand, and expenditure decreases on the other.

I want to make it clear that I have never favored expenditure decreases as a stabilization device. I agree with Walter that it would be inconsistent, completely inconsistent, for me to argue that tax increases and decreases are ineffective in stemming inflation or promoting expansion, but that spending decreases or increases are effective. That would be a silly position and, as far as I know, I have never taken it, though maybe I've been careless in what I have written and have given a misleading impression. I have been in favor of tax decreases and expenditure decreases in 1964, in 1966, and in 1968, but not for stabilization purposes. I am in favor of expenditure decreases from a long-range point of view because I think that the U.S. federal budget is too large compared to what we're getting for it. We're not getting our money's worth out of it. And, therefore, I would like to see government spending brought down. I have not argued—at least, if I have, I will immediately admit that I should not have and I don't know of any quotation in which I have (if Walter has any, I hope he will give them to me)—that expenditure de-

Reprinted from *Monetary vs. Fiscal Policy: A Dialogue* by Milton Friedman and Walter W. Heller. By permission of W. W. Norton & Company, Inc. Copyright © 1969 by the Graduate School of Business Administration, New York University. Excerpts from pp. 73–80.

creases are a way to achieve stabilization at a time of inflationary pressure.

I have said something different. I have said that, from the point of view of the fiscalists, a tax increase or expenditure decrease are equivalent. And, therefore, I have often said that if you are going to adopt the policy of the fiscalist, I would rather see you adopt it through expenditure decreases than through tax increases. But I personally have never argued that that is an effective stabilization device, and I don't believe that it is.

Let me turn to some of the specific issues that Walter raised in his first discussion and see if I can clarify a few points that came up.

First of all, the question is, Why do we look only at the money stock? Why don't we also look at interest rates? Don't you have to look at both quantity and price? The answer is yes, but the interest rate is not the price of money in the sense of the money stock. The interest rate is the price of credit. The price of money is how much goods and services you have to give up to get a dollar. You can have big changes in the quantity of money without any changes in credit. Consider for a moment the 1848–58 period in the United States. We had a big increase in the quantity of money because of the discovery of gold. This increase didn't, in the first instance, impinge on the credit markets at all.

You must sharply distinguish between money in the sense of the money or credit market, and money in the sense of the quantity of money. And the price of money in that second sense is the inverse of the price level—not the interest rate. The interest rate is the price of credit. As I mentioned earlier, the tax increase we had would tend to reduce the price of credit because it reduces the demand for credit, even though it didn't affect the money supply at all.

So I do think you have to look at both price and quantity. But the price you have to look at from this point of view is the price level, not the interest rate.

Next, he said that 1967 was the easiest money year since 1962. Yet there was a big rise in interest rates. In other connections, I have argued that our researches show that a rapid increase in the quantity of money tends to lower interest rates only for a brief period—about six months. After that, it tends to raise interest rates. Conversely, a slow rate of increase in the quantity of money tends to raise interest rates only for about six months, and after that, it tends to lower them.

If you ask where in the world interest rates are higher, the answer is in Brazil, Chile, places like that where the quantity of money has been going up like mad. Interest rates in the U.S. fell dramatically from 1929 to 1933. The quantity of money declined by a third. So it's not a surprise to us that you could have the quantity of money easy in the sense of quantity, and interest rates rise or fall or do almost anything else.

Next, he asks, "Which of the Friedmans do you believe—the one who stresses permanent-income relationships or the one who stresses the close causal connection?" Well, believe both of them if you take them at what they said. The permanent-income analysis has to do with the demand for real money balances, and it was an analysis that was based on annual data covering decades. There is no Friedman who has argued that there is an immediate, mechanical, causal connection between changes in the quantity of money and changes in income.

What I have always argued is that there is a connection which is, on the average, close but which may be quite variable in an individual episode. I have emphasized that the inability to pin down the lag means that there are lots of factors about which I'm ignorant. That doesn't mean that money doesn't have a systematic influence. But it does mean that there is a good deal of variability in the influence.

The data support the view that a 1 percent change in the rate of expansion of the quantity of money tends to produce, on the average, a 2 percent change in the rate of growth of nominal income. There is a big multiplier, as the permanent income analysis would lead you to expect. And there is a cyclical relation. I'm sorry, but I really don't see any inconsistency between the position I've taken on these two points.

Next, Walter Heller asks, Which of the money supplies do you want? M_1 or M_2? Which quantity of money do you want to use? A perfectly reasonable and appropriate and proper question and I'm glad to answer it. In almost all cases, it makes no difference. The only time it makes a difference is when our silly Regulation Q gets in the way. We have a Regulation Q that pegs the maximum rate that commercial banks can pay on time deposits. Whenever you either hit that Regulation-Q limit or you come through from the other side, the two monetary totals diverge and tell you different stories, and you cannot trust either one.

At all other times, you will very seldom find that the message told to you by M_1 is much different than the message told to you by M_2.

Then there was all this talk about being locked into a rigid rule. You know, I have always found it a good rule of thumb that when somebody starts resorting to metaphors, there is something wrong with his argument.

When you start talking about cars driving along a road, and whether you want to lock the steering wheel, well that's a good image; the automatic pilot, I agree, is a good one. But metaphors or similes are to remind you of arguments; they are not a substitute for an argument.

The reason I believe that you would do better with a fixed rule, with a constant rate of increase in the quantity of money, is because I have examined U.S. experience with discretionary monetary policy. I have gone back and have asked, as I reexamine this period, "Would the U.S. have been better off or worse off if we had had a fixed rule?" I challenge anybody to go back over the monetary history of the United States, and come out with any other conclusion than that for the great bulk of the time, you would have been better off with the fixed rule. You would clearly have avoided all the major mistakes.

The reason why that doesn't rigidly lock you in, in the sense in which Walter was speaking, is that I don't believe that money is all that matters. The automatic pilot is the price system. It isn't perfectly flexible, it isn't perfectly free, but it has a good deal of capacity to adjust. If you look at what happened to this country when we adjusted to post–World War II, to the enormous decline in our expenditures, and the shift in the direction of resources, you have to say that we did an extraordinarily effective job of adjusting, and that this is because there is an automatic pilot.

But if an automatic pilot is going to work, if you're going to have the market system work, it has to have some basic, stable framework. It has to have something it can count on. And the virtue of a fixed rule, of a constant rate of increase in the quantity of money, is that it would provide such a stable monetary framework. I

have discussed that many times in many different ways, and I really have nothing to add.

The final thing I want to talk about is the statement that Walter made at the end of his initial talk, when he said, Look at the world economy; hasn't it been far healthier during post–World War II than it was between the Wars? Of course. It certainly has been enormously healthier. Why? Well, again, I'm sorry to have to be consistent, but in 1953, I gave a talk in Stockholm, which is also reprinted in that collection of papers, under the title of "Why the American Economy is Depression Proof."

I think that I was right, that as of that time and as of today, the American economy is depression proof. The reasons I gave at that time did not include the fact that discretionary monetary and fiscal policy was going to keep things on an even keel. I believe that the reason why the world has done so much better, the reason why we haven't had any depressions in that period, is not because of the positive virtue of the fine tuning that has been followed, but because we have avoided the major mistakes of the interwar period. Those major mistakes were the occasionally severe deflations of the money stock.

We did learn something from the Great Depression. We learned that you do not have to cut the quantity of money by a third over three or four years. We learned that you ought to have numbers on the quantity of money. If the Federal Reserve System in 1929 to 1933 had been publishing statistics on the quantity of money, I don't believe that the Great Depression could have taken the course it did. There were no numbers. And we have not since then, and we will not in the foreseeable future, permit a monetary authority to make the kind of mistake that our monetary authorities made in the 30s.

That, in my opinion, is the major reason why we have had such a different experience in post–World War II.   □

The Role of Money in National Economic Policy

Paul Samuelson
James Tobin
Allan H. Meltzer

1
Paul Samuelson

The central issue that is debated these days in connection with macroeconomics is the doctrine of monetarism.

Let me define monetarism. It's not my particular title. Monetarism is the belief that the primary determinant of the state of macro-economic aggregate demand—whether there will be unemployment, whether there will be inflation—is money, M_1 or M_2, and more specifically, perhaps, its various rates of change.

I'm going to borrow a method of exposition that I understand Jim Tobin used at an American Bankers' Association meeting some years ago, when *A Monetary History of the United States* of Mrs. Schwartz and Mr. Friedman was being discussed. I wasn't present, but I was told that Jim wrote three sentences on the blackboard: "Money doesn't matter," "Money matters," and "Money alone matters." And he then said that Professor Friedman, having established to everybody's satisfaction the untruth of the first statement, went on as if it were a *sequitur* to think that he had established the third statement.

Excerpted from Paul A. Samuelson, "The Role of Money in National Economic Policy," in Federal Reserve Bank of Boston, *Controlling Monetary Aggregates* (Boston: Federal Reserve Bank, 1969), pp. 7–13. Reprinted by permission of the publisher.

Well now, I wasn't provided with a blackboard, and I can't lapse into my academic mannerisms, but I have written down a spectrum of remarks from "Money doesn't matter," to "Money matters," to "Money matters much," to "Money matters most," and to "Money alone matters." Now, monetarism is certainly at the right of this spectrum. There is nobody, I think, worth our notice on the American scene who is at the left end of that spectrum, although there still do exist in England men whose minds were formed in 1939, and who haven't changed a thought since that time, and who do belong at the left of that spectrum and say money doesn't matter. And so, monetarism, which is a correction to that extreme view—and, I think, an excess on the other side—is very much an item for export to the British Isles. For so many years they exported wisdom and knowledge to us, it's only proper that we requite that past with export. I would argue that the right view, the extreme view is not the most persuasive view, but monetarism is that.

Now, you may think that's a straw man that I'm setting up—that there is nobody who believes in monetarism as I've defined it. But I believe that I'm correct in saying that there is at least one person in this country who does believe in it, and that is Dr. Friedman.

I've an advantage probably not vouchsafed to all of you. Once a week I am privileged for 28½ minutes to listen to the voice of Dr. Friedman —and his view, as expressed repeatedly in those tapes, is this: that as far as macro-economic aggregate state of demand is concerned, money alone matters. Now, this doesn't mean that money alone determines everything. It will not cure flat feet, or dandruff, or marital fidelity. It is not true, for example, that fiscal policy has no role: For example, how big the Galbraithian public sector is is very much determined by fiscal policy; and what the composition of any state of aggregate demand is, in terms of consumption goods and capital formation, does depend upon a fiscal policy. But as for the general issues—of whether you are going to have more inflation or deflation, or whether you are going to have unemployment—we know a very little bit about it. About something like half of the squared variation in the state of aggregate demand can be explained by the monetary factor; the rest is noise. There are no systematic predictable elements.

Now, I think that that is an extreme view, and it is not a persuasive view if you look at all of the evidence. There was a great debate at NYU between Professor Friedman and Walter Heller. I wasn't privileged to be there. I talked to various people in New York who were there and, generally speaking, those who were in favor of one view when they came in, went out thinking that their man had won the debate. I talked to one Wall Street character who alleged to be neutral, and he said, "Well, Heller had the better wisecracks, but Friedman had mountains of evidence. He didn't have time to give those mountains of evidence there at that time, but, you can't laugh off the evidence."

I have reviewed these mountains of evidence, and I think that there is a great amount of evidence—much of it is due to the efforts of Professor Friedman at the National Bureau, much of it is due to workshop students working with him, and much of it to colleagues—but most of that evidence is not, in the sense of the statistician, a powerful test of monetarism as I've defined it.

TYPES OF EVIDENCE

Now, since other speakers have to speak, I can't review all these mountains of evidence, but let me just mention what some of the types of evidence are. First—and I've heard several tapes dealing with this—take particular incidents in American history. In 1919, for example, we came out of World War I; there was a much-underbalanced budget; the Federal Reserve was under the thumb of the Treasury; and then, on a certain day, it can be established, just as a diplomatic historian can establish facts, that the Federal Reserve was given its freedom from the Treasury. On that certain day, it took certain acts, so you have almost a controlled experiment in which something happened to the money supply and then—within six months or seven months or nine months, whatever the lag period is—something happened to the business conditions. Now, I think that is good evidence that money matters. That does not tell you what its role is with respect to the importance of fiscal policy or other matters. But we have a lot of evidence like that.

There is another kind of evidence. Namely, that people who use monetarism deliver the goods. Don't ask me why money matters; it's as if it matters, but we don't know what the exact connections are.

There's somebody in a Chicago bank who gets better forecasts using this method than anybody else in that part of the country; there's somebody in a New York bank which shall be nameless, who gets better estimates; and, in the academic community, there are a few people who are armed with this knowledge of monetarism and—why, we don't know—they deliver the goods.

We had a crucial experiment in 1966 in which the monetarists said certain things with which the other people—I'll call them neo-Keynesians or post-Keynesians, since nobody can quite stand to be called a Keynesian in this country—differed. There was a joust between these different forecasters, and who do you think won on that occasion? It was the monetarists.

The same thing happened again after the middle of last year.

Now, this is a very complicated story, but let me say that, if you are going to use that kind of evidence, you have to use all of it, and you have to be quantitative.

I keep a little black book, and I find there is a great overlap in estimates between different users, different methods, and at one time one of the groups seems, in its meaning, to differ from that of the other groups. Much of the time they, in fact, coincide . . . as, for example, I think right now the kind of forecasts I hear myself making on those tapes are not very different from that a monetarist makes. But occasionally you find a difference and, occasionally, the monetarist's view is the more accurate one. Occasionally the opposite happens.

Suffice it to say that since the middle of last year I have a collection of estimates from people of both schools that cross each other.

I have more pessimistic estimates for the first quarter of the year from monetarists, in some cases, than from the other method. In the middle of 1966, the monetarists tended to be right with respect to a slowing down ahead. By year's end they tended to be wrong in prophesying that recession of 1967.

MAGIC AND FORECASTING

And so I say, based upon this and much other evidence, that the people who call themselves monetarists do not have a magic way of making a better forecast. I simply assert that I have hills of evidence bearing upon that point. And I add something—namely, a man who believes he's a monetarist, who makes forecasts, does not himself know what his forecasts are based upon. Some of those whom I have observed most closely, who do make good forecasts, I find combine witchcraft and arsenic in killing their neighbors' sheep. If their flair for forecasting tells them *not* to follow monetarism to its logical conclusion, they don't; and they are amply rewarded.

I'm going to pass over the evidence of timing and turning points, which is a very mixed kind of evidence, is consistent with many different theories, and also is not a powerful test of where you are on this spectrum that I spoke of . . . at the extreme right or something less than the extreme right.

It's important to decide whether monetarism is true, because whether, for example, the tax bill goes through and the surcharge is extended—which is now something that is in doubt—to a monetarist doesn't matter. It really doesn't matter; the Fed just does its business and keeps that money supply growing in the proper range at the proper rate. It couldn't matter less as far as aggregate demand is concerned. And that's point number one.

Another example. We had a big surprise. The SEC survey showed 14 percent intentions of increase in plant and equipment. What's the effect of that to a monetarist? Nothing. It's of absolutely no importance and—you might think I'm making this up, but I heard it right from the tape, itself—it's of absolutely no importance that investment is stronger than people had thought, because there is no systematic relationship. If there is no systematic relationship between government expenditures in the income accounts, and taxes in the income accounts, when you bracket this with autonomous changes in private investment, there is also no systematic thing.

Now, you might say it takes a stern man to follow his logic down to that extreme. Well, we've got a hero in this country who follows his logic all the way, and this is his assertion.

I think that's very unpersuasive in terms of all we know about economic history, and I think it's wrong.

Now, I want to conclude on a more academic note. What is it that makes one who doesn't even follow the year-to-year and month-to-month business cycle situation skeptical about monetarism in the extreme—and I think hard to defend—form that I have defined?

If you actually examine the logic of economics—and I now am going into the neo-classical economics on which I was brought up in the pre-Keynesian period—there is no reason in the world why, in an equation like MV = PQ, the V should be thought to be independent of the rate of interest. There is every plausible reason in terms of experience, in terms of rarified neo-classical theory, for the velocity of circulation to be a systematic and increasing function of the rate of interest; and the minute you believe that, you have moved from the right of the spectrum—that of monetarism—to that noble eclectic position which I hold, the post-Keynesian position.

Now, if you will, examine, for example, the new *Encyclopedia of Social Sciences* article by

Professor Friedman on money—as I read that article which goes on for, I suppose, 100 paragraphs.

The first ninety-eight paragraphs of that, I could agree with completely. The demand for money is a complicated thing. It depends upon many things, including the rate of interest and all the plausible things, etc.

The last two paragraphs assert, quite strongly, the literary equivalent of the following equation: that the change in the level of money income with respect to government expenditures, or with respect to taxation, or with respect to the difference between them ($M = \overline{M}$, holding the supply of money constant) is zero. On the tapes, I hear the exact equivalent of that. That is a *non sequitur*. It does not follow from the previous analysis.

Finally—and this, again, is the important thing that interests me as an academic—if you actually analyze different wealth assets in the differing degrees of liquidity, there is no reason in the world, that I can see, why an ordinary open market operation, in which you swap one kind of used asset for another kind of used asset, should be expected, when it gives rise to the increase in what the Federal Reserve Bank of St. Louis reports to me every-hour-on-the-hour as a change in the supply of money, to have the same effect and be in the same invariant relationship to a different kind of increase in money, let's say an increase in money due to gold mining, where income is created along the way, or an increase in money due to deficit financing.

So I've tried to make a thought experiment—to redo the period from February 1961, to, let's say early 1965, leaving out the war, and taking that wonderful Camelot period when the GNP grew mightily. Let us redo the experiment in which the money supply grows exactly as it did in that period but the budget is kept at a balance—at a low balance level—such as the outgoing Eisenhower Administration had promised and had looked to.

I think that what would have happened was that if you had to create the same amount of money by that method with an entirely different kind of fiscal policy, you would have had, in the short run, to have depressed interest rates.

I forget, for example, about the international exchange problem, because of course the exchange rate can float; there is no restraint on domestic policy in a rational world. I don't, by the way, want to cast any scorn on that view. The biggest problem that we face in the world today is how to get from here to there. The "here" is rigid exchange rates and the "there" is exchange rates with some kind of flexibility.

But I think there is every theoretical reason for expecting there to have been a different effect and so, as I look over the evidence, I say, "Money, yes; but monetarism, no."

2
James Tobin

I will concentrate on the question of evidence, which is crucial to the great debate. One kind of evidence, which has been presented at some length, is timing evidence: namely, the leads of changes in stock of money, or of changes in the rate of change of the stock of money, or of other monetary aggregates over income, or over the rate of change of income or over other measures of economic activity. A large amount of the work of Friedman and Schwartz in their *Monetary History of the U.S. 1867–1960* and in their article, "Money and Business Cycles,"[*] is concerned precisely with pinning down these timing patterns. Now I think it is clear that timing evidence—leads, lags and so on—is no evidence about causation whatsoever.

I have engaged in a little irreverent exercise which constructs two models: on the one hand, one of these British models that Paul Samuelson was referring to, an ultra-Keynesian model where money has no causal relationship to anything, and on the other hand, a Friedman-like model in which money is the driving force of the business cycle. I have then compared the timing patterns of money and the change in money relative to money income and the change in income implied by these two different worlds. As it turns out, the ultra-Keynesian world produces a pattern of leads and lags in business

[*]Milton Friedman and Anna Jacobson Schwartz, *A Monetary History of the United States, 1867–1960* (Princeton, N.J.: Princeton University Press, 1963); Milton Friedman and Anna Jacobson Schwartz, "Money and Business Cycles," *Review of Economics and Statistics*, 65 (Supplement: February 1963), 32–78.

Excerpted from James Tobin, "The Role of Money in National Economic Policy," in Federal Reserve Bank of Boston, *Controlling Monetary Aggregates* (Boston: Federal Reserve Bank, 1969), pp. 21–24. Reprinted by permission of the publisher.

cycles that superficially looks much more like money causing income than the Friedman world in which money actually is causing income. Moreover, the ultra-Keynesian model produces patterns of leads and lags in business cycles which coincide precisely with the summary of empirical results about such timing that appears in the Friedman-Schwartz article, whereas the implications of Friedman's and Schwartz's own theory diverge considerably from their own empirical findings.

Milton Friedman has responded that he knows better than to think that timing evidence has anything to do with causation. If this is stipulated, we can regard as descriptive but irrelevant detail all those pages about timing that an unwary reader might think were there for the purpose of making some point about causation.

There is a related point about evidence, which has to do with the effects on the data of the sins of the Federal Reserve and other monetary authorities in the past. Now let me give you a ridiculous example to make the point. Don't take it too seriously. Suppose that some statistician observes that over a long period of time there is a high association, a very good fit, between gross national product and the sales of, let us say, shoes. And then suppose someone comes along and says, "That's a very good relationship. Therefore, if we want to control GNP, we ought to control production of shoes. So, henceforth, we'll make shoes grow in production precisely at 4 percent per year, and that will make GNP do the same." I don't think you would have much confidence in drawing this second conclusion and policy recommendations from the observed empirical association.

Over the years, according to the monetarists, the Federal Reserve has been acting like the producers and sellers of shoes. That is, the Fed has been supplying money on demand from the economy instead of using the money supply to control the economy. The Fed has looked at the wrong targets and the wrong indicators. As a result, the Fed has allowed the supply of money to creep up when the demand for money rose as a result of expansion in business activity, and to fall when business activity has slacked off. This criticism implies that the supply of money has, in fact, not been an exogenously controlled variable over the period of observation. It has been an endogenous variable, responding to changes in economic conditions and credit market indicators via whatever response mechanism was built into the men in this room and their predecessors.

The evidence of association between money and income reflects, to a very large degree, this response mechanism of the Federal Reserve and the monetary authorities. It cannot be used simultaneously to support the reverse conclusion: namely that what they have done is the *cause* of the changes in income and GNP. Perhaps the monetarists will be sufficiently persuasive of the Federal Reserve and of Congressional committees to bring about, in the future, a controlled experiment in which the stock of money is actually an exogenous variable.

Much evidence has been presented purporting to show the superior power of monetary variables over fiscal variables and private investment measures in explaining changes in GNP. This evidence comes in what I call pseudo-reduced-forms.

The meaning of the term *reduced-form* is this: If you think of the economy as really a complex set of equations—basic structural relationships describing business investment, demands for loans, demands for money, the consumption function and so on—conceivably you could solve such a system and relate the variables in which you are ultimately interested, such as GNP, to the truly exogenous variables including the instruments of the monetary and fiscal authorities. Such a solution of a big complicated model you would call a *reduced-form*. And then one possible way of estimating a model of the system would be not to estimate the structural equations, the building blocks of the system, but to estimate the condensed equations which relate the ultimate outputs like GNP to the ultimate causal factors. That would be reduced-form estimation.

There are a lot of difficulties in that procedure. Therefore, most builders of big and small models of the economy do not proceed in that way; but, instead, try to estimate the individual structural equations one by one. What I mean by a pseudo-reduced-form is an equation relating an ultimate variable of interest, like GNP, to the supposedly causal variables, but one which doesn't come out of any structure at all. Instead, the investigator just says, "Here are the effects and here are the causes, let's just throw them into an equation." The form and content of the equation—the list of variables and the lag structure—are not derived from any structural model. That is what we have had presented to us as the main evidence for the supposed superiority of monetary variables in explaining GNP.

When, in contrast, we try to take a *theory* of how money affects the economy, and test it in the form it is presented, we have to look at one of two things: either a demand for money equation, or some complicated set of linkage equations through which changes in the money stock affect investment demand, consumption de-

mand, etc. As far as the demand for money equation is concerned, as Paul Samuelson mentioned, the crucial assumption of some monetarists is that interest rate variables are of no importance, so that there is a tight linkage between the stock of money and GNP. If real GNP and prices, current and lagged, are the only important factors in the demand for money balances, then we know that control of money stock is uniquely decisive, and we don't have to look elsewhere in the system. However, all the tests that I know in which interest rates are allowed to enter demand for money equations, indicate that interest rates have important explanatory power.

If we do not really know that the demand for money is exclusively determined by income, then things other than income may absorb changes in money supply. There is no short cut. We have to look for the effects of changes in the stock of money, and it is hard work. We have to look through the system of structural equations to see how money enters directly and indirectly into investment demand and consumption demand and so on. We have to examine long chains of causation. In those chains there could be many slips, and there could be many structural changes, innovations in markets and institutions. That is the purpose, I suppose, of the hard work involved in large econometric models, work which these other attempts to find evidence try to short-circuit completely.

3
Allan H. Meltzer

TWO OPPOSING VIEWS

An understanding of monetary policy, of the role of money as an indicator, and of the difference between the effects of changes in credit and money can be obtained by contrasting two frameworks. In one view, monetary and fiscal policies are seen as the means by which the public sector offsets instability in the economy resulting from changes that occur in the private sector. Fluctuations in prices and output are seen as the result primarily of real forces and changes mainly in attitude or outlook that raise or lower investment, thereby raising or lowering the nominal value of income, market interest rates, and the demand for money. The task of monetary policy, in this framework, is to offset undesired changes in interest rates caused by the unforeseen changes in investment. The task of fiscal policy is to offset the unforeseen changes in the private expenditure and maintain expenditures at the full employment level. Monetary policy is called "restrictive" if market rates are permitted to rise; "permissive" if market rates are prevented from rising; and "coordinated" if the balance of payments is in deficit, and market rates are permitted to rise so as to attract an inflow of short-term capital from abroad. With this framework, it appears reasonable to accept interest rates as the main indicator of monetary policy. If the framework were correct, the decision might be more tenable—although still not correct.

Excerpted from Allan H. Meltzer, "The Role of Money in National Economic Policy," in Federal Reserve Bank of Boston, *Controlling Monetary Aggregates* (Boston: Federal Reserve Bank, 1969), pp. 27–29. Reprinted by permission of the publisher.

The alternative view—at least my view—does not deny that changes in market interest rates are partly the result of changes in attitude or changes in technology that shift private expenditures. The difference—and it is an important difference—is a difference of emphasis and interpretation. Not only are changes in private expenditure assigned a smaller role, but many of these so-called autonomous changes are viewed as a delayed response to past monetary and fiscal policies.

The effect of a monetary or fiscal policy is not limited to the initial change in interest rates. An expansive monetary policy raises the monetary base, stocks of money and bank credit, and initially lowers market interest rates. The expansion of money increases expenditure, increases the amount of borrowing, and reduces the amount of existing securities that individuals and bankers wish to hold at prevailing market interest rates. These changes in borrowing and in desired holdings of securities reverse the initial decline in interest rates; market rates rise until the stock of existing securities is reabsorbed into portfolios, and the banks offer the volume of loans that the public desires. If expansive operations continue, expenditures, borrowing, and interest rates rise to levels above those in the starting equilibrium. Later, prices rise under the impact of increases in the quantity of money, further reducing the desired holdings of bonds and other fixed coupon securities, and increasing desired borrowing. A rise in holdings of currency relative to demand deposits adds to the forces raising interest rates on the credit market.

In this interpretation, the effect of monetary (or fiscal policy) is not limited to the initial effect.

The response to a maintained change in policy includes the effects on the credit market, the acceleration and deceleration of prices, and ultimately, if policy makers persist, the changes in attitudes and particularly in anticipations of inflation or deflation. These changes, however, are regarded as reliable consequences of maintaining an expansive or contractive monetary policy, just as much to be expected as the initial effect.

It is the temporary changes in the level of interest rates observed on the credit market that frequently mislead monetary policy makers into believing their policy is restrictive when it is expansive. Large changes in the growth rate of money become a main source of instability precisely because the credit market and price effects dominate the initial effect of monetary policy in an economy close to full employment. Misled by the change in market interest rates—or their interpretation of the change—the Federal Reserve permits or forces the stock of money to grow at too high or too low a rate for too long a time. Excessive expansion and contraction of money becomes the main cause of the fluctuations in output and of inflation or deflation. Inappropriate public policies, not changes in private expenditures, become the main cause of instability.

A portion of the second interpretation has now been accepted by the principal spokesman of the Federal Reserve System. In his March 25th statement to the Senate Banking Committee, Chairman Martin said:

I do not mean to argue that the interest rate developments in recent years have had no relation to monetary policy. We know that, in the short run, expansive monetary policies tend to reduce interest rates and restrictive monetary policy to raise them. But in the long run, in a full employment economy, expansive monetary policies foster greater inflation and encourage borrowers to make even larger demands on the credit markets. Over the long run, therefore, expansive monetary policies may not lower interest rates; in fact, they may raise them appreciably. This is the clear lesson of history that has been reconfirmed by the experience of the past several years.

With that statement, Chairman Martin abandoned the framework that has guided Federal Reserve policy through most of its history and has been responsible for major errors in policy. Recognition that interest rates generally rise fastest under the impact of monetary expansion—that the credit market effects dominate short-term changes in interest rates—is probably the single most important step toward an understanding of the role of money that has been taken in the entire history of the Federal Reserve System.

If we develop our analysis and concentrate on improving our understanding of money and of the differences between money and credit, rather than on the issue of whether Milton Friedman is wholly right or wholly wrong, we will have more progress to report next time we meet. Thank you. □

Although we have made a number of references to inflation in the earlier chapters of Part Two, it is now time to face directly what, in 1974, has been described as America's number one economic problem.

It was not always so. It is seldom realized today (and, therefore, is worth stressing) that prices in the United States during the nineteenth century were on the whole on a *downward* trend. At one point in our history, things actually cost *more* in the "good old days." The very oddity of this earlier phenomenon suggests how strikingly things have changed. Prices in the United States have been rising ever since World War II, and, in recent years, the rise has been accelerating. In 1973, inflation by some measures was reaching "double-digit" (10 percent and above) levels. To make matters more complicated, substantial inflation and substantial unemployment have occurred simultaneously. This has made even more difficult the application of those fiscal and monetary tools whose merits and demerits we have just been discussing.

We shall devote this chapter to an analysis of inflation—its effects, causes, and possible cures.

INFLATION AND THE PUBLIC INTEREST

What exactly is inflation? And what is its impact on the public at large?

By *inflation,* we mean any general increase in the price level of the economy in the aggregate. This is a macroeconomic concept. While in microeconomics one may be concerned with a rise in the price of one commodity relative to other commodities, inflation involves a rise in the prices of all commodities, or of most commodities, or, most commonly, of some *index* that measures the average of various prices taken together.

This definition, however, is still too general. For one thing, we might wish to know exactly *what* prices are being included in any particular index of inflation. In the United States, for example, there are three main indices of inflation in common use: (1) the Index of Consumer Prices, (2) the Wholesale Price Index, and (3) the GNP Price Deflator. The third index, which reflects the distinction between changes in *real* GNP and changes merely in money GNP, is the most general of these indices. For particular purposes, we may be more interested in one of the other two. As consumers, we may have a special concern about the consumer price index, since this attempts to estimate the cost of living as it affects the average American family.[1]

Even more important, however, is the fact that this definition of inflation fails to distinguish between different *kinds* of inflation. In the very first chapter of this book, we mentioned the German hyperinflation of the 1920s, when the price index soared into the trillions. Now this kind of runaway inflation, with its enormously destructive effects on the whole fabric of the society, has to be distinguished from the serious but very different kind of inflation that the United States suffered from, say, 1960 to 1970, when the cost-of-living index rose overall by perhaps 35 percent in the course of the decade.

Indeed, when we look at the world today, we find quite striking differences in the degree of inflationary pressures in different countries. In the less developed countries, and especially in certain Latin-American countries, rapid year-to-year (or even month-to-month) inflation is a fairly common occurrence. Between 1950 and 1965, it is estimated that prices in Brazil were rising at a yearly rate of 31 percent; in Argentina, 25 percent; in Chile, 33 percent.[2] Brazil

reduced her rate of inflation in the early 1970s, but, in 1973, it was still double that of the United States.

The distinction between rapid or runaway inflation and a more moderate general rise in prices is important, when it comes to determining the impact of inflation on the well-being of the economy. Runaway inflation may have seriously destructive effects on a country's domestic economy and its economic relations with other nations. Moderate inflation—which will be our main concern here—is much more limited in its effects and, indeed, not all of these effects must be considered harmful. Most economists would consider stable prices to be ideal, but it is not unthinkable to take the position that a "little inflation" can be a "good thing." Take, for example, this well-known defense of moderate inflation written by the labor economist, Sumner Slichter, in the 1950s:

The obvious injustices of even a slow long-term rise in prices lead many people to insist that such a rise must be prevented—that nothing but a stable price level will be satisfactory. At the risk of being called an irresponsible and dangerous thinker, let me say that in the kind of economy possessed by the United States a slowly rising price level is actually preferable to a stable price level.

The reason for this conclusion is that the maintenance of a stable price level would conflict with other important interests of the country. For example, the maintenance of a stable price level in the long run would require that the country relax its efforts to keep business recessions as mild as possible. Furthermore, the maintenance of a stable price level would require the acceptance of chronic unemployment or drastic intervention by the government in the relations between employers and employees. Finally, the policies necessary to keep prices stable would severely handicap the United States in its efforts to contain communism by building up the economies of the free world.[3]

---

1. The choice of which index to use is no trivial matter, since they often give quite divergent results. Thus, between November 1972 and August 1973, the consumer price index rose 6.5 percent, the wholesale price index 18.2 percent, and the GNP deflated 5.0 percent. Part of these divergences are doubtless caused by defects in the indices used. See William Nordhaus and John Sloven, "Inflation 1973: The Year of Infamy," *Challenge* (May–June 1974), pp. 14–15.

2. Angus Maddison. *Economic Progress and Policy in Developing Countries* (New York: W. W. Norton & Co., 1970). p. 93.

---

3. On this last point, Slichter's argument was that we could build up our allies economically only by accepting imports from them and that American businessmen would be willing to do this (i.e., not press Congress for trade restrictions) only if there were also a rising demand for American products, reflected in a slow inflation of prices.

The champions of a stable price level do not seem to be aware of the conflicts between the goal which they advocate and other desirable goals. Indeed, they are so impressed by the injustices caused by inflation that they fail to see that serious injustices would have to be imposed in order to keep the price level stable —injustices even greater than those which would accompany a slowly rising price level. . . .

The net advantage to the country of a slowly rising price level over a stable one is the greater amount of employment, and hence the greater amount of production and the higher standard of consumption, that are made possible by a slowly advancing price level.[4]

But if it is possible to argue that a moderate inflation is not all that bad, and perhaps even desirable, why has there been such an outcry in the United States on this subject in recent years? Why do some people seem to consider inflation an evil to be ranked with, if not worse than, unemployment? Part of the answer, it seems, lies in a failure to look beyond immediate and apparent effects. Another part lies in the fact that inflation, even moderate inflation, does have certain clearly unfortunate consequences, particularly when it appears to be accelerating.

The misunderstanding stems from the fact that people often fail to connect the process that raises prices and the process that raises their earnings, with which they will meet these increased costs. They sometimes talk as if every rise in prices impoverishes them by exactly that amount, since they can buy that much less with a given income. Or they may speak disparagingly about how little a dollar is worth now, failing to ask at the same time how many more dollars per week or per year they and other people now earn. Such an approach is clearly inadequate. We know from our earlier discussion of the concept of gross national product that a rise in the money value of output will necessarily be a rise also in the money value of national income. They are two different ways

4. Sumner H. Slichter. "How Bad is Inflation?" *Harper's*, August 1952, pp. 53–54; 57.

TABLE 14–1

SHIFTS IN PERCENTAGE SHARES OF U.S. NATIONAL INCOME IN INFLATION, 1950–1971

	1950–71
Wages and salaries	+ 6.6
Income from unincorporated business	
Nonfarm	−3.8
Farm	−3.7
Rents	−1.0
Interest	+ 3.4
Corporate before-tax profits	−6.2

Adapted from G. L. Bach and James B. Stephenson, "Inflation and the Redistribution of Wealth," *The Review of Economics and Statistics,* 56, no. 1 (February 1974): 2. © The President and Fellows of Harvard College. Reprinted by permission.

of looking at the same thing. To speak of the harmful effects of a general rise in prices on the assumption that all money incomes in the society remain unchanged is very nearly a contradiction in terms. The interesting and much more relevant question is: What are the effects of inflation when prices and wages, salaries, and other incomes are all rising at the same time?

These effects might generally include the following:

1. Changes in the distribution of income. Although all incomes may be rising to some degree in an inflation, some income-receivers will be gaining much more rapidly than others. The people who will be hurt will be those who are living on fixed pensions or on the interest from government or other bonds; or salaried individuals employed by institutions like churches, which may find it difficult to adjust their pay scales to rapid increases in the cost of living. Although there are not many people in the economy whose incomes are strictly "fixed"—i.e., do not adjust at all to inflation—the rate of adjustment varies in different groups. It has often been thought that inflation tends to redistribute income from wage earners to profit receivers. This does not appear to be true in the United States in the postwar period, as Table 14–1 suggests.

2. Changes in the position of creditor, debtor, saver. Inflation undermines the value of past savings if these savings are held in a form that represents a fixed claim on money (i.e., savings accounts, government bonds, life insurance policies, etc.). More generally, it alters the creditor-debtor relationship. Creditors suffer because the real value of their credits falls while debtors benefit, since their debts are also falling in real value. Thus, inflation involves not only a redistribution of income but also a redistribution of the stock of wealth in the community. Bach and Stephenson estimate that this wealth-redistribution effect in the postwar American economy is quite large. The net beneficiaries tend to be the government (a large-scale debtor), and, within the private sector, young versus old families, and middle-income groups as opposed to the very rich or the very poor.[5]

3. Production and the use of resources. Inflation may cause productive resources to be devoted to speculative or other uneconomic uses. This problem is really serious only when the inflation is rapid, but it may exist to some degree even when prices are rising moderately. Inflation increases the general level of uncertainty in the economy. Especially if the inflation is fairly rapid, planning for the future may be more difficult if tomorrow's prices are substantially different from today's.

4. Effects on the international balance of payments. Most countries, as we shall see in the next chapter, are concerned about preventing their imports from exceeding their exports. Inflation at home may generally go with high demand for imports from abroad. At the same time, our high domestic prices may discourage foreign countries from buying our exports. This can lead to difficult balance of payments problems. It should be noted, however, that this is not so much an argument against inflation, per se, as it is an argument against inflation that is more rapid than that of the countries with which one trades.

5.   G. L. Bach and James B. Stephenson, *op. cit.,* pp. 2–13.

5. Forced savings, investment, and growth. Under certain circumstances, inflation can lead to a redistribution of output at the expense of consumption and in favor of investment and future growth. This is one of the reasons inflation is sometimes favored in less-developed countries where the desire for growth is particularly intense. Suppose that all consumers are wage earners and that all wage earners wish to spend all their income on consumption. If it happens that prices rise more rapidly than wages, then the *real* incomes, and hence total consumption of the wage earners, will be less than they would have been under stable prices. The gain in a private economy will accrue to business firms that will have higher profits and will be able to invest more than they would be able to otherwise. In a publicly oriented economy, the gain would accrue to the state which could undertake large-scale investment projects. The process is sometimes called *forced saving,* since the society as a whole is saving more, even though the wage earners themselves would have preferred to consume more.

It should be apparent from this list that inflation can and does have certain definitely harmful effects. The classic case of misfortune is represented by the widow or elderly couple living on a fixed pension with a small savings account and a few government bonds. This is no longer an exceptional case in our economy. Because of increasing life expectancies, the number of persons above the age of sixty-five in the American economy has increased from 4 percent in 1900 to 10 percent today. Furthermore, a fifth of these families have incomes below the poverty level. For such families, prolonged inflation even of the moderate sort means a continual reduction in the purchasing power of their already small incomes and the value of their past savings. For many elderly people, inflation can bring economic tragedy.[6]

On the other hand, it is also apparent that some of the harmful effects of inflation really become serious only when the inflation is either very rapid

6.   Though even this effect must be qualified somewhat, since social security and other transfer payments favorable to the elderly have generally increased more rapidly than has inflation in the post-war United States.

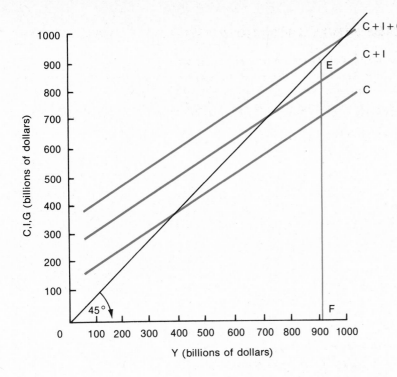

Figure 14–1. Keynesian Demand-Pull Inflation.

When the sum of *C + I + G* exceeds full employment income at *FE,* then there will be a natural tendency for prices to rise. Price rises, in turn, will be accompanied by wage increases, further price rises, further wage increases, and so on, in a continuing inflationary spiral.

or at least more rapid than that of other nations. Furthermore, it is apparent that there are some cases, at least, where a mild inflation may divert production away from consumption and into areas that are considered more important. This may be true in the case of investment and growth, especially in a less developed country.

In short, the picture is a mixed one. Stable prices remain the ideal. It is also clear that people often overstate the dire consequences of moderate inflation.

CAUSES OF INFLATION

We have been speaking of effects; now let us turn to the question of causes. Let us begin by reminding ourselves of the basic "Keynesian" or "demand-pull" case, where inflation is caused by an aggregate demand for goods and services that exceeds national income at the full-employment level.

Such a situation is depicted in Figure 14–1. This diagram is the same as Figure 9–5 in chapter 9 (p. 221) except that the earlier discussion of inflation was in terms of a private economy, whereas now we include *G* as well as *C + I.* In Figure 14–1 we are assuming that the total demand of consumers, businessmen, and the government exceeds the full employment limit. What happens in this case is that something has to give. And what is likely to give is the general price level.

We cannot actually picture this process in the terms used in Figure 14–1, because this diagram depicts national income in *real* terms; i.e., as measured in "constant prices." We can easily imagine the inflationary process, however. The situation at full employment is that not just one industry, but all industries in the economy, are faced with more demand for their products than they can supply.

When businessmen are confronted by a situation in which demand exceeds supply, we know from chapter 2 that there will be a rise in the prices of their products. This, however, is not the only effect. Businessmen in such circumstances will also be trying to expand production. To do this, they will try to hire more laborers. But the economy, as we know, is already at full employment. Consequently, the main effect of businesses bidding for laborers will be to raise the price of labor—i.e., the general level of wages throughout the economy. This rise in wages, however, will only *add fuel to the inflationary fire.* The rise in wages means that wage earners will have higher money incomes than before, and this will increase the money value of their demand for goods. This rise in demand will mean that aggregate demand still exceeds aggregate supply, even at the new and higher level of prices. Therefore, the whole process is likely to repeat itself. Businessmen will raise prices and attempt to expand production once again. Wages and consequently the money value of the wage earners' demand for goods and services will rise a second time. And again businessmen will find themselves with a situation in which the demand for their products exceeds the available supply. This will repeat for a third round, a fourth round, and so on. A continuing inflationary process is now under way, the rapidity of which will be determined in a very general way by how great the excess of aggregate demand is at the full-employment level.

A question arises immediately: What could lead to such an excess of demand? It is here that one would seek for the causes of this kind of inflation.

The general answer to the question is, of course, that any factors that tend to bring consumption, business investment, or government spending to unusually high levels will be likely to result in an excess of $C + I + G$ at full employment. Historically, the major factor in our own experience has been wartime circumstances that have led to extraordinary expansions of G not fully balanced by taxes. However, excess demand can also originate in the private sector. Schumpeter, we recall, emphasized the role of innovation and private investment in causing swings of economic activity. Suppose there is some major technological breakthrough like the develop-

ment of railroads in the mid-nineteenth century. The introduction of this new technology may require substantial investment, which may raise aggregate demand sufficiently to get the inflation started. But then the inflation itself may be a stimulus to further innovations. Prices are rising, profits are high; other innovators may come along wishing to invest in the railroads or in subsidiary industries or even in unrelated industries whose prospects have been improved by the generally buoyant state of demand in the economy as a whole. Sudden changes in private consumption demand could also in theory give rise to inflationary pressures, although this situation is probably somewhat less common in actual fact.

In short, all those circumstances that may affect government, investment, and consumption demand —war, technology, new products, tastes, future expectations, the past and predicted behavior of prices —would be the elements we would want to study to explain a possible excess of aggregate demand at full employment as depicted in Figure 14–1.

THE MONETARIST EXPLANATION

The above, however, is not the only possible analysis of inflation. (Nor is it the only kind of inflation that needs to be explained.) We need not dwell on this point, since we have explored the controversy over monetarism in detail in the last chapter and in Great Debate Two. Suffice it to say that, according to the monetarist doctrine, the basic cause of inflation would be a growth in the money supply that exceeded the growth of full employment national income. In the quantity theory of money, as expressed in its simplest terms: If the growth of real GNP (because of capital accumulation, technological progress, etc.) is 3 percent per year and the growth of the money supply is 3 percent per year, we will have stable prices. If, however, the growth of the money supply exceeds 3 percent, we will have inflation roughly in proportion to the excess of the growth of the money supply above the rate of growth of real income. To evaluate this alternative explanation of inflation, the reader should consult the earlier discussion, especially where the assumptions of the monetarist and Keynesian positions are contrasted (pp. 302–303).

INFLATION *AND* UNEMPLOYMENT

There is another point regarding our discussion of inflation so far—it is not the only kind of inflation that needs to be explained. Most economists would agree that, on three grounds, the kind of inflation analyzed above is inadequate as a rendering of present-day American experience. First, it assumes that inflationary pressures arise completely from the demand side. Second, it represents demand and supply conditions largely in domestic terms, without taking into account possible international repercussions on our domestic price level. And third, it describes inflation as occurring only when the economy is at full employment. But we know that prices in general often rise even when there is some unemployment in the economy.

Indeed, the characteristic situation in the 1970s in the United States is one in which inflation and unemployment occur simultaneously. We have said that consumer prices rose by perhaps a third during the decade 1960 to 1970; during this same period unemployment averaged nearly 5 percent of the labor force. It is widely believed that, had unemployment been less, inflation might have been at least somewhat higher; that is, that there is a ''trade-off'' between inflation and unemployment in a modern industrial economy.

An important element in the explanation of these facts lies in the structure of labor and business organization in the United States, which, as we know, is far from that implied by the theory of pure competition. If labor unions throughout the economy or in certain major industries are particularly strong, they may be able to get wage increases that are excessive even when aggregate demand is not pressing against the full-employment barrier. By ''excessive'' here we do not mean *any* general rise in wages, for labor productivity is increasing annually, and the laborers would ordinarily expect to share in that productivity increase even in the most purely competitive economy. But suppose the wage increase exceeds the productivity increase. Laborers, say, are producing 3 percent more output this year because of technological progress, but they demand and receive a wage increase of perhaps 10 percent. Such a wage increase is clearly inflationary. It will be sustainable by industry only if industry raises its prices. But a general rise in prices may stimulate further wage demands. The wage-price spiral is on. This upward movement of wages and prices would look very similar to that occurring in a demand-pull inflation (in fact, the two cases are not always easy to distinguish in practice), but it differs from it in that its origins have been inflationary wage increases, not the pressures of excess aggregate demand. And the main test of this fact is that such wage increases can and do take place when there is unemployment and other evidence of ''slack'' in the economy as a whole. This type of inflation is usually called *cost-push* inflation.

Such supply-originating inflations reflect the structure of American business as well as American labor. The ability of industry to absorb inflationary wage increases and to pass them on to the consumers through price increases is to some degree a testimony to the existence of substantial market power, such as we would expect in oligopolistic industries. More generally, there is a considerable resistance to downward changes in prices in much of American business. This means that a fall in demand for an industry's products may be reflected in lowered output, lowered employment, and excess capacity, rather than in lowered prices. An increase in demand, however, will ordinarily bring a rise in prices. When price changes take place only on a one-way street—rigid downward, but flexible upward—then inflationary situations can arise even when there is no excess of aggregate demand in total. A shift in demand from one industry to another may bring rising prices in one industry while leaving prices in another unchanged. The effect in total is inflationary, although there is no overall excess in demand.

Such institutional factors as these help explain why inflation may arise in a non-Keynesian situation. They also help explain why inflation may sometimes be more difficult to cure than it would be in a demand-pull situation. For if inflation can get started even when there is considerable slack in the economy, then it may be impossible to control except at the expense of considerable unemployment.

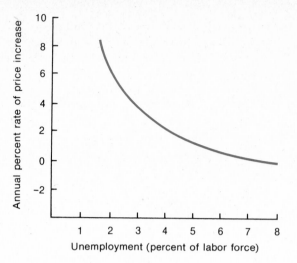

Figure 14–2. A Phillips Curve.

This curve shows the relationship between unemployment and inflation. At low levels of unemployment, the hypothetical economy shown here would suffer substantial inflation. The exact shape and position of the Phillips curve must be determined empirically for any particular country at any particular time.

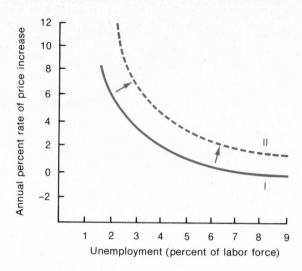

Figure 14–3. Shifting Phillips Curves.

Is it possible that persistent inflation may cause people to attempt to anticipate inflation, leading to an adverse shift of Phillips curves (from I to II)? Many economists think so.

THE PHILLIPS CURVE

The general relationship between inflation and unemployment is sometimes set out in terms of what is called a *Phillips curve,* after the economist A. W. Phillips, who originated it. The actual shape of this curve for a given country at a given time would have to be determined empirically, but its typical shape is shown in Figure 14–2. The economy represented in this figure would be able to get stable prices (zero rate of price increase) only if it were prepared to suffer 7 or 8 percent unemployment. At this level the institutional and other factors exerting inflationary pressures on the supply side are exactly counterbalanced by the downward pressures of inadequate aggregate demand. At lower levels of unemployment, however, price rises begin to occur, even though the economy is still short of full employment.

The degree to which this conflict between full employment and price stability is a problem will clearly depend on the actual shape and position of this curve. Even more important, perhaps, it depends on whether the curve will *shift* over time. Many economists believe that as inflation reaches a certain level, businessmen, wage-earners and consumers begin to anticipate further inflation. Having seen that a 4 percent wage increase last year was wiped out by a 6 percent price increase, unions may demand, say 8 percent next year. Thus, the level of inflation accompanying any given level of unemployment may tend to rise over time. This would lead to a Phillips curve shifting up and out as in Figure 14–3.

Nor is this the end of the possible complications. For, as we have already mentioned in passing, inflation takes place increasingly in an international setting. Rapid inflation abroad may affect inflation at home. And how about various specific shortages?

One year it may be wheat, the next it may be oil, then perhaps copper. May such events as these also affect the rate of inflation at home, and the good or bad positioning of our domestic Phillips curve?

The answer is: Yes, they can. And, indeed, they have.

THE INFLATION OF 1973–74

Perhaps the most striking aspect of the acceleration of U.S. inflation in 1973 and early 1974 was that it took place in a context in which many of the *cost-push* factors were relatively quiescent.[7] The strongest example here is the behavior of American labor. Whereas increases in wages may have caused half or more of the inflation we experienced in 1971, in 1973 they probably accounted for as little as 5 or 10 percent of the more rapid inflation that then occurred. Profit increases were somewhat more prominent in 1973 than in 1971, but even they probably were responsible for no more than a tenth of the later inflation.

What basically happened was a shift in a number of the international aspects of our economic position, some affecting the demand side and some affecting the supply side. These changing international factors include the following: (1) devaluation of the dollar, which, as we shall discuss in the next chapter, increased the demand for American products; (2) strong worldwide economic expansion that also added to this demand; (3) a poor crop year that caused a general shortage of agricultural products; (4) the sale (at subsidized low prices) of more than a billion bushels of U.S. wheat to Russia; and (5) the enormous increases in petroleum prices in 1973 and early 1974, because of numerous factors (see Great Debate Six, pp. 791–817) including the Arab oil embargo, the increased profit margins of the international oil companies, the attempted cartelization of producing countries, etc.

The consequence of such factors was an enormously rapid increase in the prices of certain agricul-

tural products (notably grain and livestock) in 1972–1973 and in the prices of petroleum products in 1973–1974. To the older categories of demand-pull and cost-push inflation, it appears that a new category—*commodity inflation*—may have to be added. As Nordhaus and Shoven put it: "It appears that the industrialized countries have caught a virulent strain of inflation flu, 'commodity inflation,' which had been successfully contained for at least two decades. Will the inflation flu die out or turn into an epidemic?" On the answer to that question will obviously hang much of the inflationary future of the Western world.

POLICIES TO COMBAT INFLATION

On that answer will also depend the nature of the policies designed to combat inflation. We have been talking about effects and causes. Now we turn to possible cures. And the effectiveness of any cure will clearly depend on the kind of inflation we are trying to control.

Insofar as there is a strong demand-pull element in any given inflation, the obvious remedies consist of using fiscal policy or monetary policy, or both, to restrain aggregate demand and hence to reduce the inflationary pressures.

In the case of fiscal policy, the measures to be taken would be some variant of increasing taxes or reducing government spending. An increase in taxes would lower the $C + I + G$ curve either by reducing personal consumption or, if the taxes were directed primarily at business corporations, by reducing business investment. A reduction of government spending would, of course, lower G directly. The choice between the reduced spending or the increased tax approach, and also the choice between different variants of these approaches, would reflect a number of other considerations. Are government spending programs essential or are they expendable? Is the allocation of output between consumption and investment too heavily weighted for the consumer or for the investor? And so on.

In the case of monetary policy, the approach would be the reverse of that used in the case of a depression. The Federal Reserve System could increase reserve requirements, raise the discount rate, or

---

7. The analysis of the following section draws on William Nordhaus and John Shoven, *op. cit.*, pp. 16–22.

engage in open-market sales of government securities. These open-market sales of securities would have the effect of lowering the reserves of the commercial member banks. If the banks in the system were fully "loaned up," there would be a curtailment of loans and investments to business. The money supply would fall, businesses would find it harder to obtain credit, the interest rate would rise. The effect would be to curtail areas of spending that are most sensitive to changes in the interest rate—certain kinds of business investment, construction, state and local government spending that is dependent on bond issues, and so on. This curtailment, in turn, would mean a reduction of aggregate demand and of the inflationary pressures arising from the demand side.

In earlier chapters, we have noticed that monetary policy had certain weaknesses when it came to curing problems of depression and unemployment. Used to combat inflation, it is undoubtedly a somewhat stronger tool. Indeed, it is difficult to imagine an inflation of any substantial magnitude continuing very long unless there is an increase in the money supply to feed it. As the money value of national income rises, the amount of money necessary to support the transactions demand for money increases. If there is a continuing inflation and *no* increase in the money supply, there will be very little money left over for liquidity purposes. Ultimately this leads to such a "tight money" situation and to such a rise in interest rates that investment, and other interest-dependent spending, is almost certain to fall.

In ordinary circumstances, then, monetary policy is likely to be more effective in inflationary than in depressed situations. However, if monetary policy alone is used—i.e., without accompanying fiscal restraint—it may have to be applied so strenuously that it causes serious problems in certain areas of the economy. The United States faced a situation rather like this in 1966. The price level, which had been fairly stable up to this point, began rising more rapidly in 1966. Many voices were raised advocating fiscal restraint, and especially a rise in taxes, but on the whole these voices were not heeded; except for one or two measures, government spending and tax policies were unchanged. Thus, monetary policy was given the whole burden of restraining the inflationary pressures. It was applied quite vigorously. The money supply that had heretofore been expanding with the general expansion of the economy at about 5 percent or 6 percent a year was actually reduced, falling, in the second half of 1966, from about $172 billion to $167 billion.

And costs in terms of certain specific activities were quite high. Tight credit hurt local governments, which had to put off plans for needed schools, parks, and highways. The residential home-buyer was hit particularly hard. As mortgage rates climbed, housing starts fell to a postwar low, and the construction industry was in tight straits. A similar fear has been expressed in 1973–74, as interest rates have soared to historic highs and, again, construction has been especially hard hit. The point is that the restrictive effects of monetary policy are felt keenly in certain areas of the economy; if general inflationary pressures are to be curbed by monetary measures alone, the result is likely to be very destructive to those specific areas.

Furthermore, monetary policy is unable to solve inflationary problems adequately when they originate from cost-push factors or particular commodity shortages. More carefully tailored instruments must be devised. This limitation applies also to fiscal policy and, indeed, to any set of measures that attempts to work through changes in the level of aggregate demand.

IMPROVING THE INFLATION-UNEMPLOYMENT TRADE-OFF

In the past ten or fifteen years, a number of different approaches have been used to cope with the differing varieties of inflation. In the 1960s, a great deal of "moral suasion" or *jawboning* on the part of the federal government was common. Business and labor were urged and cajoled to keep wage and price increases down. In some cases, not very clearly disguised threats were used—the most notable example being the confrontation between the government and the steel industry in the Kennedy years. Because of the great impact of this episode, we present a reading on the Kennedy-steel confrontation in the appendix to this chapter.

In the 1960s, the federal government also attempted a somewhat more systematic effort to restrain inflation through the use of wage-price *guideposts*. These guideposts were indicated each year by the President's Council of Economic Advisers and were based on the principle that wage increases should be no greater in general than the nation's increase in productivity and that industry's prices, on the average, should be stable. (Industries where productivity increase was lower than the national average might raise prices under this policy, but this should be counterbalanced by reduced prices in industries with higher than average productivity increase.)

From 1968 to early 1971, the President's Council of Economic Advisers shied away from guideposts and, instead, began issuing *inflation alerts,* which consisted of periodic reports designed to call attention to particularly disturbing features of inflationary price and wage behavior. The hope was that such reports would cause public opinion to focus on unacceptable business and labor settlements and that this public opinion might have some favorable effect on future settlements.

All the above approaches were basically voluntaristic (with occasional arm-twisting as in Kennedy vs. Big Steel), and on the whole they were disappointing in their effects. By 1971, inflation was more rapid than it had been before, and unemployment was still at an unacceptable level. In a televised address on Sunday, August 15, 1971, President Nixon announced a "new economic policy" that included, besides its international provisions, a ninety-day *wage-price freeze* and a package of measures designed to stimulate the domestic economy.

After the ninety-day period, the administration decided that controls would have to be maintained on a mandatory basis in what was called *Phase II*. To this end, a seven-member Price Commission and a fifteen-member Pay Board (five business, five labor, and five public members) were established. These agencies promulgated a general approach suggesting that pay increases should not exceed 5½ percent per year. Assuming a 3 percent annual increase in

labor productivity, this would mean a 2½ percent rate of inflation per year—clearly down from the much higher rate of 1970. Almost immediately, however, the Pay Board made certain exceptions to these guidelines; also the Board was subjected to attack from labor, including several of its labor members, who quickly resigned. Phase II controls were lifted on January 11, 1973, and this was followed by a period of very loose regulation (*Phase III*), which, in turn, led to another freeze and series of controls six months later (sometimes called *Phase III½*). These, in *their* turn, quickly gave way to the easing of controls in *Phase IV* and the final dismantling of the whole program in April 1974.

We shall take up later some of the pros and cons of using wage-price controls to achieve price stability in a modern economy.[8] It can be argued that the program did have at least some favorable effect on wage behavior, the restraint of which we have just noted. On the other hand, it can also be argued that the reintroduction of controls in the summer of 1973 was irrelevant at best, because these controls were aimed at unionized, oligopolistic industries when, in fact, the problem was in basic commodities.

The difficulty of curing inflation—or really the various *kinds* of inflation—is hard to overestimate. Still, there are certain things that can be done. One important area of approach is governmental manpower training programs. The effort here is to reduce frictional unemployment and thus make possible a closer approach to full employment before serious upward pressures on prices are induced. If various bottlenecks can be removed and shifting from job to job can be facilitated, then, in effect, the Phillips curve can be moved at least slightly to the left. Thus, after the 1971 downturn in the aerospace and other defense-related industries, the federal Technology Mobilization and Reemployment Program assisted many technicians, engineers, and scientists in their

---

8. See especially Great Debate Four: "Combating Inflation: Controls or Competition?" (pp. 631–53). Our reason for postponing this discussion until later is that the issue of direct controls involves central problems of both *macro-* and *microeconomics*. Thus, the debate can best be evaluated after the reader has done work in both Part Two and Part Three of this book.

efforts to seek new employment. This assistance included both searching for new job opportunities and training in the conversion of skills to industries and occupations where employment vacancies were more abundant[9].

Another approach involves the government in activities that stimulate production and productivity or, negatively, that stop practices designed to hold back production and keep prices up. Clearly, this is very important in the commodity inflation area. It is ironic that the sectors of the economy with the most rapid rates of price increases in 1973–74 (agriculture and petroleum) had both earlier been regulated to reduce the available supply (the various farm programs discussed in chapter 4 and the now defunct oil import quotas). Governmental fair-trade laws and certain medical care payment systems also tend to have the effect of keeping prices up. In an earlier age, the economic problem often seemed one of surpluses looking for markets. If, as some think, we are now entering a period of inflationary shortages, then clearly the mood must shift to increasing production and letting prices fall, or, at least, not purposely striving to keep them up.

In general, a greater number of different and hopefully vigorous policies should be tried to lick our new version of the "macroeconomic problem." We do not face the disastrous form of that problem—mass unemployment—that we did in the 1930s. But we do face a particularly stubborn and persistent challenge in our efforts to move forward simultaneously towards two goals—price stability *and* full employment.

---

9.   Professor Martin Feldstein believes that, in addition to these manpower programs, unemployment can be reduced by expediting the employment of young workers (e.g., by Youth Employment Scholarships for on-the-job training), and by altering the structure of the current unemployment compensation system (to make it less of an incentive to delay returning to work). He suggests that such measures in total could reduce our permanent rate of unemployment from its current 4 to 5 percent minimum to a 2 to 3 percent minimum. This, of course, would be an effective shifting of the Phillips curve to the left. See Martin Feldstein, "The Economics of the New Unemployment," *The Public Interest,* No. 33, Fall 1973.

SUMMARY

Inflation is the economist's term for a general rise in prices, though there are many different kinds of inflation, some very rapid, others—like that of the United States in recent years—more moderate, though recently accelerating.

The harmful effects of a moderate inflation are sometimes overstated by those who fail to realize that rising prices and rising incomes (wages, salaries, profits, etc.) are not wholly separable phenomena. In general, a moderate inflation will have the following effects (some harmful, some less so) on an economy: (1) redistribution of income at the expense of groups whose incomes rise less rapidly than prices; (2) improvement in the position of debtors relative to creditors; (3) possible uneconomic use of resources; (4) harmful effects on the international balance of payments when inflation is more rapid than that of other countries; (5) possible forced saving as investment or government spending increases at the expense of consumption. In a society with certain vulnerable groups—for example, the elderly, who have become a substantial portion of our population—the costs of inflation can be very real.

In the classic Keynesian case, inflation arises because of an excess of aggregate demand at the level of full-employment national income. However, inflation is not necessarily of the *demand-pull* type. It may result from structural features on the supply side, as in the case of *cost-push* inflation. Labor may succeed in reaching wage settlements that exceed the increase in labor productivity. Businesses may be resistant to downward adjustments of prices but may be able and willing to increase prices when there are shifts in demand or increases in wage costs. Because of these structural features, inflation may occur even when there is fairly substantial unemployment in the economy. The *Phillips curve* (to be derived empirically for any given country at any given time) shows the relationship between price changes and unemployment. Moreover, further complications can arise because the Phillips curve may shift unfavorably as people come to anticipate inflation and take action in attempts to forestall it. Also, as the

United States has learned, our domestic rate of inflation may be influenced substantially by international factors. *Commodity inflation* involving specific worldwide shortages (whether naturally or artificially induced) seems to have been a major factor in the acceleration of American inflation in 1973 and in early 1974.

When inflation is of the demand-pull variety, both fiscal and monetary policy can be used to curtail aggregate demand. On the whole, monetary policy is probably better suited to "curing" inflation than it is to halting recessions; but if used without fiscal restraint, it may lead to serious difficulties in certain areas of the economy. Both fiscal and monetary policy, moreover, are limited when the inflation originates from the supply side or is caused by specific shortages. These macroeconomic policies may be able to halt the rise in prices only by lowering aggregate demand to the point where there is serious unemployment in the economy.

The task of improving the inflation-unemployment trade-off is a central policy problem for today's industrial economy. In the past a variety of voluntary approaches such as wage-price *guideposts* and *inflation alerts* have been used, but without clear success. In 1971, President Nixon went to direct regulation with his ninety-day *wage-price freeze* followed by Phases II through IV; the impact of those actions is still being debated.

Many economists feel, however, that certain other steps can improve the situation. Specific measures to reduce government legislation that supports higher prices and to improve the allocation of labor through manpower training programs are examples of tools that may have to be used if the nation is to achieve its goal of price stability and full employment at the same time.

IMPORTANT TERMS TO REMEMBER

Double-Digit Inflation
Consumer Price Index
Wholesale Price Index
GNP Price Deflator
Demand-Pull Inflation
Cost-Push Inflation
Commodity Inflation
Unemployment-Inflation Trade Off
Phillips Curve
Wage-Price Guideposts
Wage-Price Controls
Manpower Programs

QUESTIONS FOR DISCUSSION

1. Distinguish between the harmful effects of a runaway inflation and those of a moderate inflation. Can you see any way in which inflation might be cumulative; i.e., moderate price increases might lead to behavior on the part of businesses or individuals that would lead to more rapid price increases? Why is it said that a runaway inflation can never occur unless it is fed by a fairly substantial increase in the money supply?

2. "Inflation is an even worse threat to our economic well-being than depression; for whereas depression impoverishes only some of us, inflation impoverishes us all." Discuss.

3. Distinguish between *demand-pull* and *cost-push* inflation. Why might this distinction be difficult to ascertain in an actual empirical situation? What structural features of American business and labor markets might contribute to inflationary pressures from the supply side?

4. Draw two possible Phillips' curves, one showing a severe, the other a less severe, conflict between full employment and price stability. How would your recommendations for governmental policy be different, depending upon which curve was descriptive of the situation the nation actually faced?

5. How may a country's international position affect its rate of inflation? Does the consideration of worldwide commodity prices help explain the phenomenon of *commodity inflation*?

SUGGESTED READING

Bach, G. L., and Stephenson, James B., ''Inflation and the Redistribution of Wealth,'' *The Review of Economics and Statistics,* LVI. no. 1 (February 1974).

Heller, Johnson, Schnittker, and Wallich. ''Current Economic Policies.'' *American Journal of Agricultural Economics* (May 1970).

Phelps, Edmund S., ed. *Problems of the Modern Economy.* New York: W. W. Norton & Co., 1966, pp. 63–105.

Schultze, Charles L. *National Income Analysis.* 3rd ed. Englewood Cliffs, N.J.: Prentice-Hall, 1971, chap. 5.

Wallich, Henry C., and Wallich, Mable I., ''What Have We Learned About Inflation?'' *Challenge* (March–April 1973).

APPENDIX 14: KENNEDY AND THE STEEL PRICE CONTROVERSY

Few incidents in the war against inflation in the American economy have attracted as much attention as the famous confrontation between President Kennedy and the large steel companies in 1962. This incident is important not only as indicating the problems of controlling inflation but also as confirming the complexities of the relationship between government and the private economy that we have stressed in earlier chapters on the "mixed" economy.

The background, briefly, was that a wage settlement in steel in 1959 had led to a rise in steel prices. As plans for the 1962 talks between labor and management were being made in 1961, speculations began to develop about the possibility of a rise in the price of steel by four to five dollars a ton. This led to a debate in Congress with liberal Democrats (like Senator Albert Gore of Tennessee) accusing the steel companies of "administering prices" above those dictated by the market, and conservative Republicans (like Senator Barry Goldwater of Arizona) rebutting these charges and accusing the Democrats of "laying the groundwork for controls." The following reading takes up the battle from the day of President Kennedy's first intervention.

The Steel Price Controversy

S. Prakash Sethi

THE PRESIDENT ACTS

On September 6, 1961, the day before the Republican rebuttal in the Senate, President Kennedy sent telegrams to the chief executive officers of the twelve* largest steel companies, saying: "I am taking this means of communicating to you, and to the chief executive officers of eleven other steel companies, my concern for stability of steel prices. . . ."

Using 1947 as the base period he contended that between 1947 and 1958 steel prices rose by 120 percent—during the same period industrial prices as a whole rose by 30 percent, and employment costs in the steel industry rose by 85 percent—providing much of the inflationary impetus in the American economy and adversely affecting steel exports and United States balance of payments. He went on to say that although since 1958 the general price level and steel prices had stabilized, this was accomplished at the cost of persistent unemployment and under-utilized productive capacity including that of the steel industry whose utilization rate during the preceding three years had averaged 65 percent. In consequence,

many persons have come to the conclusion that the United States can achieve price stability only by maintaining a substantial margin of unemployment and excess capacity and by accepting a slow rate of economic growth. This is a counsel of despair which we cannot accept.

For the last three years, we have not had to face the test of price behavior in a high-employment economy. This is the test which now lies ahead.

The amount of the increase in employment cost per man-hour [on October 1] will be difficult to measure in advance with precision. But it appears almost certain to be outweighed by the advance in productivity resulting from a combination of two factors—the steady long-term growth of output per man-hour, and the increasing rate of operations foreseen for the steel industry in the months ahead.

The Council of Economic Advisors has supplied me with estimates of steel industry profits after October 1. . . . and the steel industry, in short, can look forward to good profits without an increase in prices.

The owners of the iron and steel companies have fared well in recent years.

A steel price increase in the months ahead could shatter the price stability which the country has now enjoyed for some time. In a letter to me on the impact of steel prices on defense costs, Secretary of Defense McNamara states: "A steel price increase of the order of $4 to $5 a ton, once its effects fanned out through the economy, would probably raise the military procurement costs by $500 million per year or more. . . ."

In emphasizing the vital importance of steel prices to the strength of our economy, I do not wish to minimize the urgency of preventing inflationary movements in steel wages. I recognize, too, that the steel industry, by absorbing increases in employment costs since 1958, has demonstrated a will to halt the price-wage spiral in steel. If the industry were now to forego a price increase, it would enter collective bargaining negotiations next spring with a record of three and one-half years of price stability. The moral position of the steel industry next spring—and its claim to the support of public opinion—will be strengthened by the exercise of price restraint now.

---

*Armco Steel Corporation, Bethlehem Steel Corporation, Colorado Fuel & Iron Corporation, Inland Steel Company, Jones & Laughlin Steel Corporation, Kaiser Steel Corporation, McLouth Steel Corporation, National Steel Corporation, Republic Steel Corporation, United States Steel Corporation, Wheeling Steel Corporation, and Youngstown Sheet & Tube Company.

WIDE WORLD PHOTO

A Presidential Press Conference. President Kennedy reacted strongly when, in 1962, the big steel companies announced plans to raise steel prices. As a result of intense pressure from the government, the companies involved rescinded the price increases.

I have written you at length because I believe that price stability in steel is essential if we are to maintain the economic vitality necessary to face confidently the trials and crises of our perilous world. Our economy has flourished in freedom: let us now demonstrate again that the responsible exercise of economic freedom serves the national welfare.

I am sure that the owners and managers of our nation's major steel companies share my conviction that the clear call of national interest must be heeded.

Sincerely,
John F. Kennedy

RESPONSE TO THE PRESIDENT'S LETTER

According to *Iron Age*, Kennedy's letter stunned the industry. The steel executives thought that by refraining from a price rise for three years, despite employment cost boosts, they were already acting in the national interest and being competitive with foreign steel and domestic substitute materials.

Business Week said the response to the letter was "immediate anger and long-term alarm." The steel industry scorned Kennedy's reasoning, resented his motivation, and the list of United States presidents it did not trust now read: Harry Truman, Dwight Eisenhower, John Kennedy. Compounding the resentment was the widespread belief that Kennedy would not act against any excessive wage demands by the United Steelworkers. Where only selective price boosts were the most any "realist" could have expected from the industry, now even that was extremely unlikely. Where would the industry with such a rapidly advancing technology get the $1 billion a year needed to replace obsolete plants and implement new efficiencies?

The recipients of the president's letter—who were generally critical of the steel industry's being singled out while other causes of inflation were ignored—were largely noncommittal in regard to steel prices. The most publicized reply came from Roger Blough, chairman of U. S. Steel.

I am certain, Mr. President, that your concern regarding inflation is shared by every thinking American who has experienced its serious effects during the past twenty years. . . . First, let me assure you that if you seek the causes of inflation in the United States, present or future, you will not find them in the levels of steel prices or steel profits.

Blough then used 1940 as a base year and noted that although steel prices had risen 174 percent since that time, employment costs had risen 322 percent. Wage-earner costs had increased and "far exceeded any productivity gains that could be achieved," despite new investment. Blough continued:

So far as profits are concerned, your advisers have chosen to measure them in terms of the return on reported net worth; and again I am afraid that this does more to confuse than to clarify the issue in the light of the eroding effects of inflation on investments in steel-making facilities over the past twenty years. If we compare the 50-cent profit dollars of today to the 100-cent dollars that were invested in our business twenty years ago, the resulting profit ratio can hardly be said to have any validity.

The most useful measurement of the profit trend in a single industry, over an inflationary period, is, of course, profit as a percentage of sales. On this basis . . . profits in the steel industry have only once in the past twenty years equaled the 8 percent level at which they stood in 1940, and have averaged only 6½ percent in the past five years. . . . [Moreover] averages can be dangerously misleading. Some companies will earn more than the average, while some may be suffering losses which they cannot sustain indefinitely. So it was in 1960 that among the 30 largest steel companies the profit rate as a percentage of sales ranged from a plus 9.3 percent to a loss of 5.2 percent.

Whatever figures your advisers may elect to use, however, the simple fact is that the profit left in any company, after it pays all costs, is all that there is out of which to make up for the serious inadequacy in depreciation to repay borrowings, to pay dividends and to provide for added equipment. If the profit is not good enough to do these things, they cannot and will not be done; and that would not be in the national interest.

So reviewing the whole picture, I cannot quite see how steel profits could be responsible for inflation —especially when their portion of the sales dollar over the last twenty years has never exceeded 8 cents and is lower than that today.

As for the admittedly hazardous task which your economic advisers have undertaken in forecasting steel industry profits at varying rates of operation . . . it might reasonably appear to some—as frankly, it does to me—that they seem to be assuming the role of informal price-setters for steel—psychological or otherwise. But if for steel, what then for automobiles, or rubber, or machinery or electric products, or food, or paper, or chemicals—or a thousand other products? Do we thus head into unworkable, stifling peacetime controls of prices? Do we do this when the causes of inflation—in a highly competitive economy with ample industrial capacity such as ours—are clearly associated with the fiscal, monetary, labor and other policies of Government?

Blough noted that steel prices were at a level "slightly lower" than two years previously and that competitive factors such as foreign steel and domestic substitute materials provided effective competition for steel. He argued that no company, industry, or for that matter, country could disregard the inexorable pressure of the market if it wanted to maintain its position in a competitive world. Furthermore, he contended that as far as inflation was concerned the price of steel was a symptom and not the major cause of the problem.

THE ADMINISTRATION AND THE STEEL TALKS

That steel prices were not raised in October was attributed to economic forces and not to the president's letter. Kennedy's letter was not the final involvement of the government in the industry's affairs, however, for—although the United Steelworkers' contract was to expire on July 1, 1962—in November 1961, Labor Secretary Arthur Goldberg pointed out that the administration was willing to use its good offices to achieve an early settlement not only to prevent steel users from stockpiling but also to achieve a modest contract and thus prevent another wage-price spiral.

In January several union and industry officials met at the White House to discuss with the president the importance of an early settlement. Goldberg later contacted both union and industry and they began negotiating in early February—the first time since World War II that the two parties had met so early in the year. By discussing the new contract at the time, the union was setting aside its strongest weapon—the threat of a strike at the last minute if its demands were not met. The union also limited its demands to a seventeen-cents-per-hour job security package, foregoing a wage increase. The four industry representatives to the talks said that while the demands "cannot be considered moderate in any sense," they were more moderate than previously and were appropriate considering the problems the country faced.

Apparently, after pressuring the industry, the administration was now pressuring the union (even on national television). Goldberg said that large-scale labor management conflicts were intolerable because of the Soviet threat and the competition from the European Common Market. (George Meany, head of the AFL-CIO, was reported to have exploded with anger at Goldberg's statements and said that he was "infringing on the rights of a free people and a free society.")

During the talks, in an interview in *U.S. News and World Report,* Blough said that steel employment costs had risen 12 percent in three years:

And you're asking me how long can that continue to increase and how long it can be borne without some kind of remedy. I would give you the answer that it's not reasonable to think of it as continuing. In other words, even now there should be a remedy. If any additional cost occurs, the necessity for the remedy becomes even greater.

Renewed negotiations fell flat on March 2, industry saying the benefit package cost was too high. Secretary Goldberg then talked to Roger Blough, who said that the union proposal was inflationary but agreed to resume talks if the union would lower its proposals. Upon Goldberg's intervention, David J. McDonald, president of the United Steelworkers Union, agreed to lower the demands.

Toward the end of March agreement was reached for a contract which would add ten to eleven cents an hour in a job security package. The contract, signed on April 6, was to be effective at least until April 1963. President Kennedy said the settlement was "obviously noninflationary and should provide a solid base for continued price stability."

Even the business community praised the contract. Roy Hoopes said: "Of course, the steel industry had given no commitment that it would hold the price line, but many people, including most businessmen, assumed that labor's restraint would be followed by no increase in the steel prices for at least six months to a year. Obviously the White House assumed this, and the settlement was considered not only a major victory for the Administration, but a long stride toward a historic transformation in labor-management relations."

THE SHATTERED MASTERPIECE*

With the strike threat averted, most executives were optimistic about the near future. On April 9, 1962, the *Wall Street Journal* reported that most producers of steel doubted there would be a general rise in steel prices in 1962 (14). However on Friday, April 6, U.S. Steel's operations policy committee—the company's top ten executives—unanimously decided to raise base steel prices about 3.5 percent. On the following Tuesday the Executive Committee of the Board of Directors approved the decision. The Public Relations Department prepared a press release announcing the "catch-up" price as "adjustment."

The reason given for the price increase was the profit squeeze facing the company. The company had spent $1.2 billion for modernization and replacement of plant and equipment since 1958 of which the two sources of money for this investment—depreciation and reinvested profit—contributed only two-thirds. The rest of the money had to be borrowed and "must be repaid out of profits that have not yet been earned and will not be earned for some years to come." The release concluded that the new resources that would be generated by the price increase would improve the company's products and would be "vital not alone to the company and its employees, but to our international balance of payments, the value of our dollar, and to the strength and security of the nation as well" (293).

When the board meeting broke up at 3:00 P.M. Roger Blough phoned for an appointment with Kennedy and after flying to Washington was admitted to see the president at 5:45 P.M. on his as yet unannounced business (220). With a minimum of ameni-

---

*All statements in the ensuing discussion not otherwise specifically documented can be found in Roy Hoopes, *The Steel Crisis* (New York: The John Day Company, 1963). (Page references shown.)

ties, Blough handed Kennedy the company press release which was at that moment being sent to newspapers in Pittsburgh and New York, explaining that it was a matter of courtesy to inform the president personally. Kennedy is reported to have said, "I think you have made a terrible mistake." Forthwith he summoned Labor Secretary Arthur Goldberg who raced to the White House and angrily lectured Blough on the effect of the company's decision on the administration's economic policy, in which U.S. Steel also had an important stake, and the effect of the decision on Goldberg's, indeed the whole administration's, credibility in its pleas to unions to restrain their wage demands.

Blough quietly defended U.S. Steel's price increase and left the president's office in less than an hour. Neither Goldberg nor the president asked him to rescind the increase.

As soon as Blough left, Kennedy was reported to have "exploded" with anger and called together high level administration officials and the Council of Economic Advisers. During the meeting the president found that only a "gentlemen's agreement" and never a firm price commitment had been made during the negotiations. Indeed, a request for such a pledge might have violated antitrust laws. As the meeting progressed the president called his brother, Attorney General Robert F. Kennedy, who later released the announcement that "because of past price behavior in the steel industry, the Department of Justice will take an immediate and close look at the current situation and any future developments." The president also called Senator Kefauver who agreed to issue a statement of "dismay" at U.S. Steel's action and to say that "I have ordered the staff of [my] subcommittee to begin an immediate inquiry into the matter" (22–26). Thus ended the opening moves of the war to hold steel prices. The *Wall Street Journal* said of the day's events, "Wage-price stability in steel was intended as the graven image of a total program of stability: the Kennedy sculptors unveiled it as a finished masterpiece—and then suddenly it was shattered" (53).

REACTION TO THE PRICE HIKE

At the very least, U.S. Steel's timing was extremely poor and clearly embarrassed the White House for, as expected, the United Steel workers were later to say that they would have upped their demands if they had known prices would be raised. The business community was surprised at the move since the early settlement meant that steel users had not stock piled and that demand was expected to be low until fall. Even so, any price increases were expected to be selective—not across the board—and to occur *after* the union security package took effect on July 1.

The company's lack of understanding of the "gentlemen's agreement" angered administration officials because it had entered into labor management negotiations to keep the price of steel down. The *St. Louis Dispatch* was skeptical of U.S. Steel's motivations and said that "it looks very much as if the steel masters used the President and his Secretary of Labor, who happens to have been the steelworker's own agent in the 1960 settlement, for the purpose of beating down wage demands prior to a price decision they had in mind all along" (108).

The administration knew about Roger Blough's statement concerning the industry's poor profit situation but attributed it merely to the game of collective bargaining where each side attempts to justify its position. Regardless of Blough's actual reasons it appeared to the White House as either of two things: (1) a challenge to the administration on the broad issue of government intervention in labor-management disputes, or (2) a personal affront to Democratic President John F. Kennedy designed to demonstrate that American industry could be as tough as the much publicized toughness of the New Frontiersmen.

The president accepted the challenge. Rumors soon circulated in Washington that both the Justice Department and the FTC would be conducting antitrust investigations, that the Treasury Department would abandon plans to relax tax depreciation rules,

and that the IRS was checking up on U.S. Steel's stock option plan.

In the Congress the Democrats attacked U.S. Steel's action and Speaker John McCormack called it "shocking, arrogant, irresponsible." Most Republicans were cautiously silent as the price hike had taken them by surprise. Senator Gore prepared legislation that would begin government regulation of the steel industry and would establish a cooling-off period before the new prices would be allowed to go into effect.

THE FIRST DAY OF BATTLE

On Wednesday morning, April 11, the president met with members of his administration at a regular pre-press-conference breakfast which was devoted entirely to what to do about steel. The decision was to concentrate on persuading a select group of the large steel companies to hold the price line. Industry sources friendly to the administration had told the White House that if companies producing 16 percent of the industry's output were to hold the line, they would soon capture 25 percent of the market. In a market as competitive as steel, this action would force the other companies to lower their prices. Everyone in the administration who knew anyone in the business world—especially in the steel industry—was urged to telephone him to explain the president's point of view. These calls were "an organized, strategic, integral part of the Administration's campaign." In none of the calls was there an attempt to coax or to threaten—the approach was to explain the government's position, nothing more. The callers discovered that important segments of the business community were far more opposed to the increase than they had been willing to admit publicly.

Inland Steel was deemed to be the key company in the dispute because of its close ties with the government through its board chairman, Joseph L. Block, and because it was probably the most profitable of the large steel companies. But Block was vacationing in Japan at the time.

The purpose of the calls was to get the industry to delay price increases long enough for the administration to launch a counterattack that would make other companies hesitate before raising their prices. The administration learned that if Inland or Armco Steel were to raise prices they would wait at least one or two days, but Bethlehem Steel did not wait. By noon Wednesday Bethlehem announced a raise of six dollars a ton, although less than a day before —at its annual meeting and before U.S. Steel raised its prices—its president had told reporters that Bethlehem would *not* increase prices.

According to *Business Week*, after Bethlehem's announcement, ''it looked like a race against time for other producers to get themselves on record before Kennedy's press conference at 3:30 P.M. Most of them made it.'' These were Republic, Wheeling, Youngstown, and Jones & Laughlin—half of the twelve largest companies had announced higher prices. The president felt that the steel company actions had blatantly and openly challenged the anti-trust laws in the noon to 3:30 P.M. rush. Of the six large companies that had not yet raised prices, five had not reached a decision. The combined volume of these five was 14 percent of the market—close to the 16 percent the administration thought necessary to hold the price line.

That afternoon as Kennedy rode to the State Department where he usually held his weekly press conferences, he put the finishing touches on his statement.

Good afternoon. I have several announcements to make.

The simultaneous and identical actions of United States Steel and other leading steel corporations increasing steel prices by some six dollars a ton constitute a wholly unjustifiable and irresponsible defiance of the public interest.

In this serious hour in our nation's history when we are confronted with grave crises in Berlin and Southeast Asia, when we are devoting our energies to economic recovery and stability, when we are asking reservists to leave their homes and families . . . to risk their lives—and four were killed in the last two days in Vietnam—and asking union members to hold down their wage requests . . . the American people will find it hard, as I do, to accept a situation in which a tiny handful of steel executives whose pursuit of private power and profit exceeds their sense of public responsibility, can show such utter contempt for the interest of one hundred and eighty-five million Americans . . .

In short, at a time when they could be exploring how more efficiency and better prices could be obtained, reducing prices in this industry in recognition of lower costs, their unusually good labor contract, their foreign competition and their increase in production and profits which are coming this year, a few gigantic corporations have decided to increase prices in ruthless disregard of their public responsibility.

Kennedy then praised the steel workers' union for abiding by its responsibilities; announced that the FTC would conduct an ''informal inquiry'' into the possibility that its 1951 consent order with the steel industry had been violated; hinted that the Department of Defense might shift its contracts for steel to price-line holding companies, and mentioned that proposed tax benefits to the steel industry through liberalized depreciation schedules were being reviewed (77–86).

In response to the president's accusation that U.S. Steel had not acted in the public interest, Roger Blough declared: ''I feel that a lack of proper cost-price relationship is one of the most damaging things to the public interest.'' Blough announced that he would be giving his own news conference the next afternoon, Thursday, April 12.

THE SECOND DAY, APRIL 12

The Justice Department, considering a possible anti-trust suit against various members of the steel industry, was much interested in the reported Tuesday afternoon statement by Bethlehem's President Martin that his company would not raise prices. But when U.S. Steel raised its prices, Bethlehem was the first to follow suit. There were antitrust implications here—U.S. Steel, because of its immense size, might exercise undue influence over other steel producers—so at 6:00 P.M. Wednesday, Attorney General Kennedy ordered his department to proceed with all possible speed in gathering necessary information. Apparently the FBI overreacted to this order, and between 3:00 A.M. and 4:00 A.M. Thursday phoned several reporters who had been present at Martin's press conference and announced their intention to come calling immediately.

On Thursday morning, Kennedy asked every cabinet member to hold press conferences in the next few days to outline the effect the price increase would have on each department and on every citizen of the land. The Justice Department, instead of the FTC, was given the principal responsibility for investigating the steel industry. The investigation was to include possible price collusion and the extent to which U.S. Steel had monopoly powers dangerous to the national interest.

Also on Thursday two more steel companies, one in the top twelve, announced price increases. On Wall Street the stock market dropped to a new low for 1962, with steel leading the retreat. On Thursday morning Blough himself called Treasury Secretary Douglas Dillon for his assessment of the situation. At the same time, FBI agents showed up at eight steel companies with subpoenas requesting information and a look at their files—all but two of these (Inland and Armco) had already raised their prices. Talk from the Pentagon was that exceptions to the Buy America Act might allow the Pentagon to increase its purchases of foreign steel. Secretary Luther H. Hodges gave a noon speech denouncing price fixing and other unethical business tactics (109–10).

THURSDAY AFTERNOON—BLOUGH'S PRESS CONFERENCE

On Thursday afternoon Blough held his news conference:

. . . We have no wish to add to acrimony or to misunderstanding. We do not question the sincerity of anyone who disagrees with the action we have taken. Neither do we believe that anyone can properly assume that we are less deeply concerned with the welfare, the strength, and the vitality of this nation than are those who have criticized our action . . .

The President said, when questioned regarding any understanding not to increase prices, "We did not ask either side to give us any assurances, because there is a very proper limitation to the power of the Government in this free economy." Both aspects of this statement are quite right [118–120] . . .

Our problem in this country is not the problem with respect to prices, our problem is with respect to costs. If you can take care of the costs in this country, you will have no problem taking care of the prices. The prices will take care of themselves [133].

Blough also denied that U.S. Steel was in any way defying the president by its decision, which it had a right to make, and, on the White House role in labor negotiations said, "I have no criticism. I do believe that when the air clears a little bit, I think we will all realize that this type of, shall I say—assistance?—has some limitations."

Blough denied having an understanding with other companies about prices. That prices were raised in a Democratic administration but had been kept level during a Republican one was not significant: "You can readily see that I do not know anything about politics!" One reporter asked if the increase "coming as it did right on the heels of the labor pact—was timed to check expanded government influence in collective bargaining: in other words, that you acted politically as well as economically." Again Blough denied any political motivation. He did mention, though, that if other companies did not raise their prices, U.S. Steel would be obliged to reconsider. The administration interpreted this to mean that victory was possible and that U.S. Steel was seeking an escape route.

All in all, industry sources felt that Blough did not present the best possible case.

THE TURNING POINT

At seven o'clock Thursday evening Attorney General Kennedy announced that he had authorized the Grand Jury to investigate the steel price increases and to find out if U.S. Steel "so dominated the industry that it controls prices and should be broken up." At about the same time Walter Reuther, head of the United Auto Workers Union, proposed that a price board be created to hold hearings on important prices such as steel before they could be increased. Later in the evening Tyson (Chairman of the Finance Committee of U.S. Steel's board of directors) and several other U.S. Steel executives met in New York. According to Hoopes, "If there was any single turning point in the steel crisis, it probably came at this meeting." Previously the executives had thought all the uproar political in nature and probably short-lived but were now "convinced that the Administration men meant business." The executives had noticed that Inland had not gone along with the increase, and if it did not soon, Bethlehem would rescind its price and others would naturally follow (145).

THE THIRD DAY

Early in the morning of Friday the thirteenth, Kennedy talked to Roger Blough who suggested that communications should be maintained. Seeing this as a hopeful sign, Kennedy then moved to restrain members of his administration and to preserve a mood of conciliation. Also on Friday morning, Inland's late-Thursday decision not to raise prices was made public. The statement by Joseph Block was that although "profits are not adequate, we do not feel

that an advance in steel prices at this time would be in the national interest." Attention now turned to Armco Steel, which had led off the price increase in 1958 when U.S. Steel refused and had a reputation for unpredictability. The real maverick of the industry, Kaiser Steel, had also not yet raised its prices.

Meanwhile rumors circulated that Roger Blough would resign; Inland's stock prices rose; other steel stocks fell; Colorado Fuel and Iron intimated that any price increase would be selective; Youngstown and Reynolds Metals implied that they would wait and see before acting on price levels.

At 10:00 A.M. Defense Secretary Robert S. McNamara stated that "where possible, procurement of steel for defense production will be shifted to those companies which have not increased prices," but he put an end to speculation that the department might increase its purchases of foreign steel because of the resulting unemployment that it might cause in this country.

All during the battle between steel and the administration, public opinion was firmly behind the president as was shown by a number of newspaper polls and by telegrams received by the White House. According to Roy Hoopes, "the majority of the nation's most influential newspapers [were] critical of the steel companies' action, [and] the business community [was] only lukewarm in its support of the steel industry . . ."

THE FINAL BATTLE

The direct result of Blough's telephone conversation with Kennedy on Friday morning was a meeting the same afternoon of Clifford and Goldberg, and Blough, Tyson, and Worthington (president of U.S. Steel). According to reports, Clifford (a Washington attorney who was friendly to the Kennedy administration) explained that many continuing investigations of steel would be very uncomfortable, especially since Kennedy would be in office for a number of years and doing business in Washington might be difficult. Clifford and Goldberg also explored ways U.S. Steel could roll back its prices and still save face. During the meeting the various members were kept informed of events as they occurred outside: one in particular came at 3:25 P.M. announcing that Bethlehem had rescinded its price increase in order to remain competitive. This was the final blow to the company, and before the meeting was over, Blough and his fellow executives told Clifford and Goldberg that they too would later be announcing a rollback (164).

Within a few hours, in the words of *Time* magazine, there was a "precipitous rush to surrender" as the other steel producers rolled back their prices. The reason given for the rollbacks was "to remain competitive" in spite of poor profit conditions.

GRANT AT APPOMATTOX

Naturally the administration's plans for further attacks on the steel industry and proposed legislation were canceled or filed away and, for once, the administration was not crowing about its victory. As *Business Week* aptly said, "The President went out of his way to assure there will be no public recriminations now that the mistake has been retracted. Like Grant at Appomattox, he is letting the vanquished forces keep their horses and sidearms."

The relationship between the White House and U.S. Steel returned to normal, and Roger Blough agreed to stay on the president's business advisory committee. On other fronts, although the Grand Jury probe would continue, it was obvious that the administration would not press too hard for any indictments. (However, a New York Grand Jury did indict U.S. Steel, Bethlehem, Erie Forge and Steel, and Midvale-Heppenstall on price fixing charges from an investigation begun in March 1961.) The activities of the Justice Department and the FTC were effectively curtailed, and the House investigation of the steel industry was called off, but Kefauver's Senate subcommittee investigation did proceed as scheduled.

THE KENNEDY ANTIBUSINESS CRUSADE

Most of the steel companies held their annual meetings soon after the "price fiasco." All those that had originally raised prices and then backed down maintained that they were forced to do so because the competition did not follow. One element of agreement among all steel spokesmen was that the need for a price increase had not passed—even Joseph Block agreed on this point and said Inland had refused to raise its prices only as a concession to the national interest. One steel executive said, "No company of industry may now raise prices without harboring the fear, and justifiably so, that the Administration may decide to employ the crushing weapons so recently displayed." Despite the industry's unanimous cry for more profits, every company's profit picture for the first quarter of 1962 showed a substantial improvement over the recession-affected first quarter of 1961 (224–25).

Despite its campaign of conciliation, the administration persisted in its economic policies and announced that it might act to prevent a price hike in the aluminum industry. There then began to emerge a "growing hostility" by the business community toward Kennedy, and a stock market crash in the summer of 1962 was attributed by many businessmen to the "Kennedy crowd." According to Roy Hoopes, "By late June and early July, the 'hate Kennedy' mood in the business community had almost reached a state of hysteria" and even rated a cover story in *Newsweek*. Even the Kennedy jokes became bitter and personal.

The animosity collapsed, however, by mid-autumn, perhaps because the administration's attempts at dialogue eventually got through or because a number of business leaders (including Blough and Block) helped to restore the peace. During the summer the Congress passed an administration-backed investment tax credit law and the Treasury Department announced revised tax depreciation schedules.

KENNEDY'S LAST YEAR WITH STEEL

A year passed without steel's making any price increases, but in April 1963 Wheeling Steel Corporation, with less than 2 percent of the United States market, announced a selective price increase of $4.50–$10.00 per ton on six items. "It was as though an electric shock had hit the President and his aides. . . ."

The President's formal reply to the hike was a surprise:

I realize that price and wage controls in this one industry, while all others are unrestrained, would be unfair and inconsistent with our free competitive market . . . and that selective price adjustments up or down—as prompted by changes in supply and demand as opposed to across-the-board increases—are not incompatible within a framework of general stability and steel-price stability and are characteristic of any healthy economy.

In a free society both management and labor are free to do voluntarily what we are unwilling to enforce by law—and I urge the steel industry and the steel union to avoid any action which would lead to a general across-the-board increase.

Actually, throughout 1963 the government allowed increases on 75 percent of the industry's product mix—all without protest.   □

The sequel to the Kennedy-Steel experience involved further government-steel confrontations in the Johnson administration, though less dramatically than that described above. The steel companies raised their prices substantially in 1967 but in 1968 compromised a price increase under governmental pressure. Overall, between 1960 and early 1969, steel prices increased rather slowly, in part at least because of import competition from abroad. Interestingly, steel prices rose most rapidly between January 1969 and December 1972, when European and Japanese exporters accepted *voluntary* quotas on steel exports to the United States. Thus, in this later period, government policy was effectively contributing to steel price increases by limiting overseas competitors.

CHAPTER 15

INTERNATIONAL BALANCE OF PAYMENTS

No man is an island unto himself. Certainly no nation is. In this chapter we shall extend our macro-economic analysis to the area of international trade, considering both the modifications of the theory of national income determination that are required for an ''open'' economy and also some of the international problems facing the United States in the 1970s.

HISTORIC CONTROVERSIES

International trade is one of those areas of economics that has been of interest to economists since the birth of the field. It has also been a particularly controversial subject, perhaps because it involves national self-interest—and nationalism, for good or ill, has been a major force in shaping the modern world.

In the sixteenth and seventeenth centuries, much of the economic writing of Europe was dominated by the so-called mercantilists, who were passionately interested in trade, commerce, and other mercantile activities. These writers (who were a varied lot of public officials, merchants, and pamphleteers, and who gave only part of their time to economics) tended to see international trade as an instrument in the growing commercial and political rivalries among the then emerging nation-states. One of their characteristic doctrines was that each nation should strive to secure a *favorable balance of trade*—roughly an excess of exports over imports. This would bring precious metals into the country, providing revenues for the sovereign and also stimulating the domestic economy. They saw trade as competitive: My nation's gain is your nation's loss. And in this competition they wanted to see their own nation benefit at the expense of others.

The mercantilist view gathered strength in the seventeenth century, but in the eighteenth century it ran headlong into the opposition of ''classical'' economists. Adam Smith devoted a long section of *The Wealth of Nations* to an attack on the mercantile system. David Ricardo and also Robert Torrens, a lesser known classical writer, tried to show that trade was not necessarily a rivalry; i.e., that *all* countries could benefit from trade. The mercantilists had favored regulating trade, but the hallmark of classical thought was the cry for free trade, a battle climaxed by the repeal of the Corn Laws in 1846.[1]

Now many of these arguments about trade have to do with essentially microeconomic questions, and especially the problem of economic efficiency. These matters we shall take up in detail in Part Three and particularly in chapter 23. We shall be concerned there with the arguments for and against tariffs and other regulations of the flow of trade among nations.

A major part of the controversy about world trade does, however, have a macroeconomic focus, being concerned especially with what are called *balance of payments* problems. At no time has this been more true than in the United States in very recent years. In the immediate aftermath of World War II, everyone spoke of a dollar shortage in the world. Our European allies as well as former enemies were badly in need of our exports, yet they lacked the productive capacity to send us their own exports in sufficient quantity to pay for them. The dollar shortage produced the Marshall Plan and also a tendency for many Americans to assume that this country's balance of international payments was immune to any major difficulties. Thus, it was with something of a shock that economists and the general public awoke in the late 1950s and 1960s to realize that the United States was running a regular and substantial deficit in its balance of payments and, furthermore, that we were rapidly losing gold to other countries. Suddenly, old mercantilist fears began to arise again. We were losing gold. Would this bankrupt the nation? What would happen to our credit abroad? What would the effects on the domestic economy be?

---

1. The Corn Laws involved duties on imported wheat. The issues at stake in the Corn Laws involved not only free versus regulated trade in general, but also a specific conflict between the interests of the English landowner (who wanted to keep food and raw materials out, so that there would be a great demand and high price for land) and the English manufacturer (who needed cheap food, to keep wages low, and cheap raw materials for his factories). The repeal of the Corn Laws thus became a kind of symbol of Britain's full emergence as an industrial—as opposed to agrarian —economy.

BALANCE OF PAYMENTS ACCOUNTS

In order to answer such questions, our first task is to get a firm grasp on the concept of a balance of international payments. This is a fairly complicated subject, so let us begin by imagining the simplest possible situation.

Let us suppose that we have a hypothetical nation whose balance of payments can be represented by three items, as in Table 15–1: commodity exports, commodity imports, and gold exports or imports. Table 15–1 tells us that this nation has exported commodities to foreign countries to the value of $500 million, while importing $300 million worth of commodities from these countries. This leaves a $200 million excess of exports above imports. How are these paid for by the foreign countries? By shipping $200 million in gold to our hypothetical country. We have here, then, the simplest possible case of a nation with a favorable balance of trade *à la* the mercantilists. And the mercantilists would have been delighted with the country's position, since it is receiving "treasure" from abroad.

Table 15–1

A SIMPLIFIED HYPOTHETICAL
BALANCE OF PAYMENTS (in millions)

Debit	Credit
$300 Commodity imports	$500 Commodity exports
$200 Gold imports	

This hypothetical balance of payments table is simply a point of departure for studying trade problems. In reality, a country's balance of payments includes many different items. The classification of these items, however, is made easier if we remember the central principle that a *credit* item is any item that creates a demand for your currency, while a *debit* item is one that creates a supply of your currency demanding other currencies.

Now even this highly simplified situation can serve as a useful point of departure for understanding more complex matters. For one thing, we notice that we have listed two kinds of items—credits and debits. What makes one item a credit and another a debit in international trade accounting?

Perhaps the best way to look at this matter is to recognize the fact that every transaction in international trade is essentially two-sided. Every good that we import from abroad must be paid for in one way or another. If we import an automobile from a European country, we must pay for it either by exporting goods of equivalent value or by exporting gold abroad or by transferring dollars to a foreign account or by sending an IOU to the foreign country (in which case the foreign country is increasing its investment in the United States). Since every transaction is two-sided in this way, there is a certain accounting sense in which the balance of payments is always in "balance."

Now as far as the classification of items is concerned, the fundamental rule is that any transaction that creates a demand for your currency—say, dollars—is a credit item. By contrast, any transaction that creates a supply of your currency seeking other currencies—say, dollars being offered in exchange for francs or pounds—is a debit item. Our commodity exports create a demand for dollars in terms of other currencies. The German who wants to buy an American good must ultimately pay the American producer in dollars. Hence, he uses his marks to buy dollars to pay us for the export. This is a credit item in the U.S. balance of payments because it represents an increase in the demand for dollars. When Americans import commodities from abroad, however, they must pay the foreigner in *his* currency. In this case, we use the dollars we have to buy marks to pay for the import. The supply of dollars offered in exchange for other currencies has increased; consequently, our imports are a debit item. Gold imports are a bit more complicated to see, but, essentially, we can treat them as any other import. When a foreign country ships gold to us, it receives dollars in exchange, and thus the supply of dollars has been increased. (These dollars may then be used to pay for the extra exports

the country has taken from us.) Thus, gold imports are a debit item, and gold exports are a credit item.

Once these general principles are clear, it becomes possible to apply them to the many more complex items that make up a country's actual balance of payments; e.g., tourist expenditures of Americans abroad, our military expenditures abroad, interest and dividend payments to American owners of foreign securities, U.S. private business investment abroad, and so on. Take the last for example: A long-term investment by an American firm, say in a factory in France. Does this create a demand for dollars or a supply of dollars? The American puts up the dollars that are then exchanged for francs to pay workmen in France to build the factory. Hence, the answer is that the supply of dollars has been increased and that U.S. investment abroad is to be treated as a debit item.

In Table 15–2, we present an actual (but still somewhat simplified) balance of payments table for the United States in 1972. From what we have just said, the classification of most of the items in this table should be clear. Thus, for example, the plus (credit) item of $7,862 million for net investment income means that American investors were receiving that much more from their investments abroad than foreigners were receiving from their investments here. Similarly, the negative (debit) item of −$1,491 million on long-term capital flows means that Americans were investing that much more abroad in factories, firms, etc., than foreigners were investing here. (Note that investment *income*—which creates a supply of, say, yen or marks demanding dollars to pay off the American investor—is a *credit* item and thus exactly the opposite of the investment itself, which, as we have just said, creates a supply of dollars seeking to buy yen or marks and is thus a *debit* item.)

Some of these items we shall return to later in this chapter (especially the rather complex term, Special Drawing Rights, or "SDRs"). But for the moment, let us focus on the concept, or various concepts, of *balance* in the "balance of payments." In a certain accounting sense, as we have mentioned, a country's

TABLE 15–2

U.S. BALANCE OF PAYMENTS, 1972 (millions of dollars)

TYPE OF TRANSACTION	AMOUNT	BALANCES
Merchandise balance (net)	−6,912	
Exports (+)†	+ 48,769	
Imports (−)	−55,681	
Services		
Military transactions (net)	−3,558	
Investment income (net)	+ 7,862	
Travel and other services (net)	−2,002	
Balance on goods and services		**−4,610**
Remittances, pensions and other unilateral transfers	−3,619	
Balance on current account		**−8,353**
Long-term capital flows (net)	−1,491	
Balance on current account and long-term capital ("basic" balance)		**−9,843**
Nonliquid short-term private capital flows (net)	−1,637	
Allocation of Special Drawing Rights (from IMF)	+ 710	
Errors and omissions (net)	−3,112	
Net liquidity balance		**−13,882**
Liquid private capital flows (net)	+ 3,542	
Official reserve transactions balance		**−10,340**
Changes in liabilities to foreign official agencies (net)	+ 10,308	
Changes in U.S. official reserve assets (net)	+ 32	
Net gold and reserve assets movements	+ 10,340	
Formal accounting balance		**0**

†A plus (+) represents a credit item; a minus (−), a debit item.

Source: Economic Report of the President, 1974; adapted by the author.

balance of payments is always in balance. This the reader can verify by looking at the bottom of Table 15–2, where the deficit of −$10,340 in the Official Reserve Transactions Balance is exactly equalled by credit items of ''Net gold and reserve assets movements,'' leaving a total Formal Accounting Balance of $0.

What then do we mean when we speak of a *surplus* or *deficit* in a country's balance of payments? Actually, many specific definitions are involved, but a central characteristic is that the surplus or deficit is intended to measure pressure on the country's reserve assets. A deficit in the balance of payments means that the country in question is either losing gold (or other reserve assets, such as convertible foreign currencies) to other countries or that other countries are increasing their holdings of liquid claims against that country (claims that could ultimately be translated into a loss of gold or other reserve assets).

Now the different definitions of surpluses or deficits arise because there are many borderline cases to be classified. Thus, we have to decide whether our liquid liabilities abroad include only those held by official foreign agencies (e.g., central banks), or whether they also should include dollar-holdings of private businesses and individuals. Similarly, we have to decide the difference between a capital transaction and a current or cash transaction. If a foreigner buys up an American firm, that is a capital transaction, which would be listed under ''Long-term capital flows'' (and would, of course, be a credit in the U.S. balance). If the foreigner accumulates dollars, that is clearly a cash transaction. But suppose he holds his dollars in a short-term security—say, a three-month Treasury bill. Should this be considered an investment (capital) or a cash transaction (he considers the bill equivalent to cash except that he earns some interest on it)?

Usually, accountants include in the capital accounts only those claims having a maturity date of more than a year (or no maturity date). But this is fairly arbitrary and, in actual practice, the ''correct'' definition of surpluses and deficits will depend on the particular problem under consideration.

In Table 15–2, we would probably be interested in noting that the U.S. Balance on Current Account in 1972 was seriously in deficit (−$8,353 million). This was because our large credit on investment income was insufficient to balance the numerous current deficit items: Our imports exceeded our exports; we spent more on travel and other services than foreigners did in this country; our governmental military and foreign aid grant programs (the latter included under ''other unilateral transfers'') were substantially in deficit.

Furthermore, capital transactions tended only to darken the picture further. Our businessmen made more long-term investments abroad than foreigners did here, with the result that our Balance on Current Account and Long-Term Capital was an additional billion and a half in deficit (−$9,843 million). This particular balance is worth noting, since it is sometimes called the *basic balance*. It excludes short-term capital movements, which are often volatile, and, in some respects, it measures the *underlying* demand and supply conditions in the dollar and foreign exchange market.

The next balance down, the Net Liquidity Balance, includes nonliquid short-term capital flows and what may seem a surprisingly large item for ''Errors and omissions.'' Actually, this item is sometimes even larger (in 1971, for example, it was well over $10 billion), and it reflects the fact that many transactions, especially short-term capital movements, take place perfectly legally but leave no statistical record. When the remaining liquid short-term capital flows are added on, we get the Official Reserve Transactions Balance. This Balance was *unfavorable* in 1972 to the tune of −$10,340 million. How did we *pay* for this huge (but not unprecedented) deficit? In very small part, by the export of U.S. official reserve assets (e.g., gold, convertible currencies, etc.), but mainly by the increase in liabilities to foreign official agencies. Foreign central banks agreed, in effect, to increase substantially their holdings of dollar assets.

But is that a tenable long-term situation? Basically, no. And, as we shall see in a moment, the international position of the United States changed dramatically in 1973. But first let us try to get a deeper sense of the economic principles underlying the accounts that we have been discussing.

CLASSICAL GOLD STANDARD

Going back to our very simple case again (Table 15–1), we now ask: What is the economic significance of the fact that this hypothetical country is running a surplus in its balance of payments? Suppose the figures were reversed and the country was exporting gold in the amount of $200 million a year. Would its basic economic position be any different? Why all the fuss about these matters?

In effect, this is what the British classical economists said, in criticism of the mercantilists, about balance of payments problems. Say's law, you will recall, postulated that money didn't truly matter, that real phenomena (steel and potatoes) were what counted. If a country is getting more potatoes (imports) for less steel (exports), then what difference does a little loss of "treasure" make? Perhaps a deficit should be a cause for rejoicing.

Of course, the classical economists were not so foolish as to offer such a naïve argument, for it is clear on the face of the matter that, unless the country is a gold-producer (like Russia or South Africa), exports of gold cannot continue indefinitely. The country will run out, or run so low on gold that it will not have sufficient reserves to carry on trade on any substantial scale or without elaborate government currency restrictions.

To answer this problem, the classical economists, and especially the philosopher and friend of Adam Smith, David Hume (1711–76), developed the notion of a self-correcting mechanism by which surpluses and deficits in international trade would automatically solve themselves. Let us imagine that the following conditions are fulfilled:

1. The countries in question are on a pure *gold standard* under which the price of gold is fixed in terms of each of their currencies. This means that the exchange rates of the currencies are fixed or, more accurately, are fixed within the limits set by the cost of transferring gold from one country to another. If currency A became more expensive in terms of currency B, people would pay in gold rather than in currency A. In our simple case, let us assume that there is little or no cost of transferring gold; hence, currency exchange rates will be almost completely stable.

2. A gold flow into (or out of) a given country is matched by a roughly proportionate increase (or decrease) in the country's money supply (currency and demand deposits).

3. The *quantity theory of money*[2] holds true. That is, an increase (or decrease) in the supply of money will lead to a roughly proportionate increase (or decrease) in a country's price level.

Given such assumptions, the *price-specie-flow* mechanism might work as follows:

Two countries, A and B, are trading together. Country A has a surplus with country B as in hypothetical Table 15–1. Country B has an equal and opposite deficit with Country A. Gold flows will now take place between the two countries, gold going from country B to country A. As a result of the gold flows, the money supply in country A will rise and the money supply in country B will fall. Because of the quantity theory of money, these changes in the money supplies will result in a rise in the price-level in country A and a fall in the price-level in country B. These changes in the price levels, however, will lead to consequences for the trading positions of the two countries. Country A's exports are now more expensive, while exports from country B are less expensive.

2. For a discussion of the quantity theory, see pp. 299–300.

Citizens in country A will now want to purchase more goods from country B, while the citizens of country B are curtailing their purchases of the now more expensive goods from A. Under ideal circumstances, these changes will lead to (a) a correction of the original trade imbalance, and (b) a cessation of the gold flow. The net result will be a redistribution of the world's gold supply between country A and country B.

Indeed, we can put the classical case quite simply by saying that the original problem between country A and country B was a maldistribution of gold stocks. Country A had too little gold (hence, its prices were too low, and thus its exports were too high), while country B had too much (with consequent high prices and a poor export performance). The market mechanism, at one stroke, corrects the trade imbalance and the gold maldistribution, and brings overall equilibrium to both countries.

Any theory, unfortunately, is only as good as its assumptions.[3] In practice, few countries have been willing to stick with a pure gold standard (condition 1) when faced with massive gold losses. Furthermore, modern nations are seldom willing to allow their money supplies to be determined by gold flows (condition 2). In the United States, for example, the Federal Reserve Board *might* let an increase or decrease in the gold stock affect member bank reserves, or, on the other hand, it might *not*, i.e., it might "neutralize" the gold flows by open-market operations. If gold were coming in, and the Fed feared an inflationary increase in the money supply, it might engage in open-market sales of government securities, or other restrictive monetary actions, to offset the gold inflow. This happened in 1939–41, when the U.S. gold stock rose by over $5 billion and most of the increase was neutralized by open-market operations. The opposite happened in 1961–1963 when a loss of $4.4 billion in gold was completely offset by the Fed's actions.[4]

And, finally, of course, the quantity theory of money (condition 3) is not held in the uncritical classical form by any serious twentieth-century economist. Indeed, the overall weaknesses in the classical doctrine are so great that it should come as no surprise that the gold standard, in anything like a pure form, has long since disappeared from the modern world.

NATIONAL INCOME DETERMINATION IN AN OPEN ECONOMY

Still, we are left with the question of what effects a country's balance of payments actually does have on that country's domestic economy. What do we substitute for the unsatisfactory classical analysis?

Two main points should be made in this connection. The first concerns the monetary effects of a trade surplus or deficit such as we have been discussing. If a country's central bank is willing to allow a gold inflow or outflow to affect the nation's money supply, then we would analyze the monetary effects by the same kind of analysis we used in chapters 11 and 13. There is disagreement about this analysis, as we know, but mainstream economics would argue that effects would proceed from the money supply to the economy as a whole via the interest rate, according to our familiar chain of logic. The general effect of these changes would be in the *direction* of bringing equilibrium in international trade but (1) it is unlikely that the magnitudes of the effects would be sufficient to correct the payments imbalance, and (2) the mechanism would involve not only prices but also real phenomena, such as national income. In particu-

---

3. The reader should notice that the classical mechanism requires even further assumptions than those we have mentioned. For example, we have tacitly assumed that export and import prices directly reflect changes in a country's overall price level. Also, we have assumed that when, say, a country's export prices fall, this will lead to an improvement in its balance of payments position (and vice versa for a rise in its export prices). But the effect of such changes will depend on various *elasticities*. If, for example, the increase in sales caused by a fall in export prices is a smaller percentage than the fall in prices, then total receipts for the country will actually fall. Thus, the classical mechanism is even weaker than it might seem at first glance.

4. See Peter B. Kenen and Raymond Lubitz. *International Economics,* 3rd. ed. (Englewood Cliffs, N.J.: Prentice-Hall, 1971), pp. 63–72.

lar, a deficit country would suffer a fall in its money supply, which would lead to higher interest rates, which, in turn, would lead to some potential fall in national income (and hence to greater unemployment). The fall in national income would be in a corrective direction—that is to say, citizens of the country in question would have less income to purchase imports from abroad[5]—but the process is clearly more painful than when simple price decreases (without income and employment effects) are involved.

But this is not the only way in which trade affects national income. And here we come to our second main point, which concerns the direct influence of international trade on the level of aggregate demand in a given country.

Consider exports first. When we bring foreign nations into the picture, we have to recognize that the demand for the products of our country is no longer limited to domestic consumption, investment, and government expenditures. We also have a foreign demand for our products. When a foreign firm puts in an order for a certain number of our machines, the effects of this order on production are the same as if it came from a business firm in the United States or from the U.S. government. Aggregate demand, therefore, must include an allowance for demand originating from abroad.

But there is also the import side to look at. As a consumer, say I have an income of $10,000 a year. Of this total, I decide to save $1,000, to buy $8,000 worth of American goods, and to buy $1,000 of goods imported from abroad. Now as far as *American* industry is concerned, it is not my total of $9,000 consumer demand that is relevant, but only the $8,000 that I shall be spending on American goods. The $1,000 I spend on goods abroad has no more direct effect on American industry than does the $1,000 I decided to put in my savings account. This is to say, then, that our import spending must be *subtracted* from our total spending to give us the aggregate demand that will be effective in creating jobs and income in this country.

---

5. Also, higher interest rates would presumably attract some short-term capital from abroad.

If we use X to stand for exports, M for imports, and Y for national income we can contrast the equilibrium situation in a "closed" and in an "open" economy as follows:

Closed Economy

We have equilibrium when national income equals the sum of intended consumption, investment, and government spending:

$$Y = C + I + G$$

Open Economy

We have equilibrium when national income equals the sum of intended consumption, investment, and government spending, *plus* exports *minus* imports:

$$Y = C + I + G + (X - M)$$

In the case of our particular hypothetical economy of Table 15–1, we could conclude that its balance of payments was definitely having an expansionary effect on the economy, since its net exports $(X - M)$ was positive ($200 million).

This conclusion, incidentally, suggests why some modern writers have shown more tolerance for the mercantilist desire for a favorable balance of trade than did the classical economists. If a country's exports are buoyant and its imports are restrained, then the effect on a depressed economy will be just like a little dose of expansionary fiscal policy. The only problem with using the balance of payments as an instrument of domestic policy is that not every country can be doing it at once. If one country is exporting more than it imports, some other country will be importing more than it exports. A policy to curtail imports and expand exports is rather like trying to export one's depression abroad. And it is likely to be met by countervailing action by other countries, so that no one's position is improved (though all countries are likely to suffer the losses that occur when trade is subjected to detailed national regulation).

Even if trade policy is not to be used to correct domestic employment problems, however, the foregoing analysis suggests some rather deep flaws in a fixed exchange rate regime. If a country's balance of payments goes into deficit, the fall in aggregate demand would normally bring about a depressed domestic economy. Should a country allow this to happen? Should it permit the "international tail" to wag the "domestic dog"? Or should it try to find some way to insulate its domestic economy from these potentially harmful international effects?

Which brings us to the important possibility of allowing the main adjustments to be made not by the domestic economy, but by the exchange rates themselves. In the early 1970s, the floating of exchange rates became the dominant method of international adjustment.

FLEXIBLE INTERNATIONAL EXCHANGE RATES

The opposite of a completely fixed set of exchange rates among currencies (as implied by the pure gold standard) is a completely flexible set of exchange rates. The rate at which dollars could be exchanged for yen or marks or francs would be determined in the exchange markets of the world. One day the dollar might be up, another down, and this would also be true of pounds, pesos, and all other currencies.

Since most economists support exchange flexibility and because this is now very much an operative mechanism in the world at large, we must spend some time understanding its workings. Basically, flexible exchanges operate through supply and demand. If there is a great demand for, say, Japanese products in Italy and there is little Japanese demand for Italian products, this would be reflected in a large supply of Italian lire being offered in exchange for a small supply of Japanese yen. Ignoring possible reserves of yen in Italy, this demand for yen would tend to raise the price of yen in terms of the lira. The rise in the price of yen would be equivalent to a rise in the prices of all Japanese exports in terms of lire; conversely, Italian exports to Japan would now fall in price. In its effects on importers and exporters in

the two countries, the change in effective prices is similar to what might happen if the classical price-specie flow mechanism were functioning. The difference, of course, is that domestically, prices have remained unchanged. All the work is being done by the exchange rates.

Now the advantage of such a system is apparent from what we have already said. Instead of a painful adjustment of prices, wages, and very probably national income and employment to make our payments balance, the domestic economy is allowed to proceed along its own (presumably full-employment) course. Particularly in countries like our own, where trade is a fairly small proportion of national income, this seems a clearly correct ordering of priorities.

The case for fully flexible exchanges is made clearly in the following reading.

The Case for Flexible Exchange Rates

by Harry G. Johnson

By "flexible exchange rates" is meant rates of foreign exchange that are determined daily in the markets for foreign exchange by the forces of demand and supply, without restrictions imposed by governmental policy on the extent to which rates can move.

THE CASE FOR FLEXIBLE EXCHANGE RATES

The case for flexible exchange rates derives fundamentally from the laws of demand and supply—in particular, from the principle that, left to itself, the competitive market will establish the price that equates quantity demanded with quantity supplied and hence clears the market. If the price rises tempo-

Excerpted from Harry G. Johnson, "The Case for Flexible Exchange Rates," in *Federal Reserve Bank of St. Louis Review* (St. Louis: Federal Reserve Bank, 1969), pp. 12; 16–20. Reprinted by permission of the publisher.

rarily above the competitive level, an excess of quantity supplied over quantity demanded will drive it back downwards to the equilibrium level; conversely, if the price falls temporarily below the competitive level, an excess of quantity demanded over quantity supplied will force the price upwards towards the equilibrium level. Application of this principle to governmental efforts to control or to support particular prices indicates that, unless the price happens to be fixed at the equilibrium level—in which case governmental intervention is superfluous—such efforts will predictably generate economic problems. If the price is fixed above the equilibrium level, the government will be faced with the necessity of absorbing a surplus of production over consumption. To solve this problem, it will eventually have to either reduce its support price, or devise ways either of limiting production (through quotas, taxes, etc.) or of increasing consumption (through propaganda, or distribution of surpluses on concessionary terms). If the price is fixed below the equilibrium level, the government will be faced with the necessity of meeting the excess of consumption over production out of its own stocks. Since these must be limited in extent, it must eventually either raise its control price, or devise ways either to limit consumption by rationing, or reduce the costs of production (e.g., by producer subsidies, or by investments in increasing productivity).

Effects of Fixed-Rate Disequilibrium

Exactly the same problems arise when the government chooses to fix the price of foreign exchange in terms of the national currency, and for one reason or another that price ceases to correspond to the equilibrium price. If that price is too high, i.e., if the domestic currency is undervalued, a balance-of-payments surplus develops and the country is obliged to accumulate foreign exchange. If this accumulation is unwelcome, the government's alternatives are to restrict exports and encourage imports either by allowing or promoting domestic inflation (which in a sense subsidizes imports and taxes ex-

ports) or by imposing increased taxes or controls on exports and reducing taxes or controls on imports; or to appreciate its currency to the equilibrium level. If the price of foreign exchange is too low, the domestic currency being overvalued, a balance-of-payments deficit develops and the country is obliged to run down its stocks of foreign exchange and borrow from other countries. Since its ability to do this is necessarily limited, it ultimately has to choose among the following alternatives: imposing restrictions on imports and/or promoting exports (including imports and exports of assets, i.e., control of international capital movements); deflating the economy to reduce the demand for imports and increase the supply of exports; deflating the economy to restrain wages and prices and/or attempting to control wages and prices directly, in order to make exports more and imports less profitable, and devaluing the currency.

In either event, a deliberate choice is necessary among alternatives which are unpleasant for various reasons. Hence the choice is likely to be deferred until the disequilibrium has reached crisis proportions; and decisions taken under crisis conditions are both unlikely to be carefully thought out, and likely to have seriously disruptive economic effects.

All of this would be unnecessary if, instead of taking a view on what the value of the currency in terms of foreign exchange should be, and being therefore obliged to defend this view by its policies or in the last resort surrender it, the government were to allow the price of foreign exchange to be determined by the interplay of demand and supply in the foreign exchange market. A freely flexible exchange rate would tend to remain constant so long as underlying economic conditions (including governmental policies) remained constant; random deviations from the equilibrium level would be limited by the activities of private speculators, who would step in to buy foreign exchange when its price fell (the currency appreciated in terms of currencies) and to sell it when its price rose (the currency depreciated in terms of foreign currencies).

On the other hand, if economic changes or policy changes occurred that under a fixed exchange rate would produce a balance-of-payments surplus or deficit, and ultimately a need for policy changes, the flexible exchange rate would gradually either appreciate or depreciate as required to preserve equilibrium. The movement of the rate would be facilitated and smoothed by the actions of private speculators, on the basis of their reading of current and prospective economic and policy developments. If the government regarded the trend of the exchange rate as undesirable, it could take counter-active measures in the form of inflationary or deflationary policies. It would never be forced to take such measures by a balance-of-payments crisis and the pressure of foreign opinion, contrary to its own policy objectives. The balance-of-payments rationale for interventions in international trade and capital movements, and for such substitutes for exchange rate change as changes in border tax adjustments or the imposition of futile "incomes policies," would disappear.

Freeing Domestic Economic Management

The adoption of flexible exchange rates would have the great advantage of freeing governments to use their instruments of domestic policy for the pursuit of domestic objectives, while at the same time removing the pressures to intervene in international trade and payments for balance-of-payments reasons. Both of these advantages are important in contemporary circumstances. On the one hand, there exists a great rift between nations like the United Kingdom and the United States, which are anxious to maintain high levels of employment and are prepared to pay a price for it in terms of domestic inflation, and other nations, notably Western Germany, which are strongly adverse to inflation. Under the present fixed exchange rate system, these nations are pitched against each other in a battle over the rate of inflation which is to prevail in the world economy, since the fixed rate system diffuses that rate of inflation to all the countries involved in it. Flexible rates would allow each country to pursue the mixture of unemployment and price trend objectives it prefers,

consistent with international equilibrium, equilibrium being secured by appreciation of the currencies of "price stability" countries relative to the currencies of "full employment" countries.

The Mechanics of Flexible Exchange Rates

At this point, it is sufficient to make the following observations. First, under a flexible rate system most countries would probably peg their currencies to one or another major currency, so that much international trade and investment would in fact be conducted under fixed rate conditions, and uncertainty would attach only to changes in the exchange rates among a few major currencies or currency blocs (most probably, a U.S. dollar bloc, a European bloc, and sterling, though possibly sterling might be included in one of the other blocs). For the same reason—because few blocs would imply that their economic domains would be large and diversified—the exchange rates between the flexible currencies would be likely to change rather slowly and steadily. This would mean that traders and investors would be able normally to predict the domestic value of their foreign currency proceeds without much difficulty.

But, secondly, traders would be able to hedge foreign receipts or payments through the forward exchange markets, if they wished to avoid uncertainty; if there were a demand for more extensive forward market and hedging facilities than now exist, the competitive profit motive would bring them into existence.

THE CASE AGAINST FLEXIBLE EXCHANGE RATES

The case against flexible exchange rates, like the case for fixed exchange rates, is rarely if ever stated in a reasoned fashion. Instead, it typically consists of a series of unfounded assertions and allegations, which derive their plausibility from two fundamentally irrelevant facts. The first is that, in the modern European economic history with which most people are familiar, flexible exchange rates are associated either with the acute monetary disorders that followed the

First World War, or with the collapse of the international monetary system in the 1930's; instead of being credited with their capacity to function when the fixed exchange rate system could not, they are debited with the disorders of national economic policies that made the fixed exchange rate system unworkable or led to its collapse. The second, and more important at this historical distance from the disastrous experiences just mentioned, is that most people are accustomed to the fixed exchange rate system, and are prone to assume without thinking that a flexible rate system would simply display in an exaggerated fashion the worst features of the present fixed rate system, rather than remedy them.

The historical record is too large a topic to be discussed adequately in a brief essay. Suffice it to say that the interwar European experience was clouded by the strong belief, based on pre-First World War conditions, that fixed exchange rates at historical parity values constituted a natural order of things to which governments would seek eventually to return, and that scholarly interpretation of that experience leaned excessively and unjustifiably towards endorsement of the official view that any private speculation on the exchanges based on distrust of the ability of the authorities to hold an established parity under changing circumstances was necessarily "destabilizing" and anti-social. It should further be remarked that European interwar experience does not constitute the whole of the historical record, and that both previously (as in the case of the United States dollar from 1862 to 1879) and subsequently (as in the case of the Canadian dollar from 1950 to 1962) there have been cases of a major trading country maintaining a flexible exchange rate without any of the disastrous consequences commonly forecast by the opponents of flexible rates.

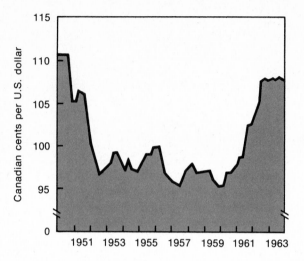

Canadian Foreign Exchange Rate

Note: Canada was on a floating exchange rate from late 1950 to mid-1962. The sharp movements at both ends of the period represent the transition from fixed rates to flexible rates. Once the free market equilibrium rate was established, it moved in a relatively narrow quarter-to-quarter range.
Source: Bank of Canada

Flexible Rates and Uncertainty

One of the common arguments under the heading of uncertainty is that flexible rates would be extremely unstable rates, jumping wildly about from day to day. This allegation ignores the crucial point that a rate that is free to move under the influence of changes in demand and supply is not forced to move erratically, but will instead move only in response to such changes in demand and supply—including changes induced by changes in governmental policies—and normally will move only slowly and fairly predictably. Abnormally rapid and erratic movements will occur only in response to sharp and unexpected changes in circumstances; and such changes in a fixed exchange rate system would produce equally or more uncertainty-creating policy changes in the form of devaluation, deflation, or the imposition of new controls on trade and payments. The fallacy of this argument lies in its assumption that exchange rate changes occur exogenously and without apparent economic reason; that assumption reflects the mentality of the fixed rate system, in which the exchange rate is held fixed by official intervention in the face of demand and supply pressures for change, and occasionally changed arbitrarily and at one stroke by governmental decisions whose timing and magnitude is a matter of severe uncertainty.

A further argument under the heading of uncertainty is that it will encourage "destabilizing speculation." The historical record provides no convincing supporting evidence for this claim, unless "destabilizing speculation" is erroneously defined to include any speculation against an officially pegged exchange rate, regardless of how unrealistic that rate was under the prevailing circumstances. A counter-consideration is that speculators who engage in genuinely destabilizing speculation—that is, whose speculations move the exchange rate away from rather than towards its equilibrium level—will consistently lose money, because they will consistently be buying when the rate is "high" and selling when it is "low" by comparison with its equilibrium value; this consideration does not however exclude the possibility that clever professional speculators may be able to profit by leading amateur speculators into destabilizing speculation, buying near the trough and selling near the peak, the amateurs' losses being borne out of their (or their shareholders') regular income. . . . The fixed exchange rate system courts "destabilizing speculation," in the economically incorrect sense of speculation against the permanence of the official parity . . . ; in so doing it places the monetary authorities in the position of speculating on their own ability to maintain the parity. It is obviously fallacious to assume that private speculators would speculate in the same way and on the same scale under the flexible rate system, which offers them no such easy mark to speculate against.   □

There are, of course, some further arguments against fully flexible exchanges in addition to those mentioned above. It has been argued, for example, that such flexibility would introduce great new uncertainties into the international trade picture that might, in turn, produce constant government intervention. If an unfavorable shift in exchange rates subjected a branch of a nation's industry to sharp foreign competition, there would doubtless be a great demand from that industry for protection by the government. This protection could, in turn, provoke retaliation from other countries. The net result, according to Yale professor Henry Wallich, might be the "increasing disintegration" of the international economy. Wallich has contended that if nations were willing to cooperate enough to make flexible exchanges work, they could also make fixed exchanges work, so why not have the better system in the first place!

Despite such arguments, however, flexible exchanges remain the favorites with most economists and—perhaps more significantly—the world has moved increasingly along this route under the press of actual events. Why has this happened? And what have the results been?

FLEXIBILITY IN PRACTICE: THE UNITED STATES IN 1973

The international balance of payments position of the United States in recent years has attracted such worldwide attention and involves so many important issues in international economics that it is worthwhile to use this experience to deepen our understanding of the trading relations among nations.

The Background. The basic facts are these: The United States had been running a deficit in its balance of payments since 1950. Figure 15–1 shows that, except for occasional moments, the annual deficit (liquidity basis) has been substantial, and in 1971 it became enormous (nearly $22 billion!). In most years (except 1971 and 1972), the deficit was accompanied by an actual surplus of U.S. commodity exports over commodity imports. This surplus item

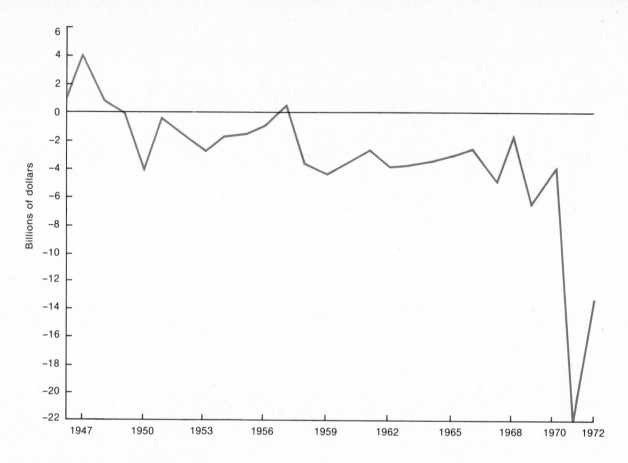

**Figure 15–1. U.S. Balance of Payments,
1946–1972 (liquidity basis).**
Source: Department of Commerce

was offset by a number of debit items, including military expenditures abroad (costs of the war in Vietnam, etc.), foreign aid programs, U.S. tourist expenditures in foreign countries, and U.S. private business investment abroad.

How had this large and persistent deficit been financed? Partly, as we would expect, by the export of gold. The U.S. gold stock in 1949 was running in the neighborhood of $25 billion; by 1971, it had fallen to a little over $10 billion.

Our accumulated deficit, however, was much larger than the decline in our gold stock, and the fact is that by far the greater part of the deficit was financed by the export of dollars. During the past twenty-odd years, the dollar served along with gold as a generally acceptable medium of exchange for the purposes of international transactions. In fact, the matter in its most favorable light could be put this way: The United States' balance of payments deficit was a significant means of expanding the total supply of international "liquidity" during the past two decades.

In the absence of vast new discoveries of gold, this expansion of dollars held by foreigners facilitated the enormous (and mutually beneficial) expansion of world trade that has been one of the most striking features of the postwar period.

The Crisis of 1971. But if this is so, what was the problem? Why did we have what has become known as the "dollar crisis of 1971"?

There are many reasons why this state of affairs occurred, not least those suggested by Table 15–3. As our deficit persisted, an increasing gap opened up between our liquid liabilities (dollars and dollar-convertible assets) held by foreigners and our reserves, especially our gold reserves, for meeting these liabilities. As long as the dollar is as good as gold, this gap need not be troublesome. But if it were widely believed that the dollar was *not* as good as gold—if, for example, it came to be believed that the dollar might be devalued in terms of gold (the dollar-price of gold raised) or that the dollar might be altogether cut free from the price of gold—then it could be in the interest of foreign holders of dollars to convert them into gold. Clearly, this would be an impossible solution. In 1971, the central bank of Germany alone held enough U.S. dollars to exhaust our entire gold stock at $35 an ounce. Clearly, also, the existence of this gap between the enormous potential demand for, and the limited supply of, our reserves could become a major factor that might lessen confidence in the dollar.

Thus, the system was essentially poised on a knife-edge. Already, in March 1968, the U.S. government had divorced gold prices on the private market from the then official parity price of $35 an ounce, leaving the private price to find its market level. Meanwhile, our creditors unhappily faced a vast supply of dollars, and found themselves in the position of either buying these dollars with their own currencies, thus leading to domestic inflationary pressures, or revaluing upward their own currencies in terms of dollars. Revaluation is always a painful process, because it raises the costs of a country's exports in foreign markets and thus is likely to hurt those industries that are heavily engaged in export trade.

TABLE 15–3

FOREIGN CLAIMS IN RELATION TO U.S. RESERVES

YEAR	U.S. GOLD STOCK AND OTHER RESERVE ASSETS (billions of dollars)	U.S. LIQUID LIABILITIES TO FOREIGNERS* (billions of dollars)
1960	19.4	21.0
1968	15.7	38.6
1970	14.5	47.0
1971	12.2	67.8

*Includes a small amount of nonliquid liabilities to foreign official agencies.

Source: *Economic Report of the President*, 1974, pp. 356, 357.

All these various elements began to come to a boil in early May 1971, when there was a flood of dollars seeking to buy German marks in anticipation of a possible change in the exchange rate between the mark and the dollar. At first, West Germany responded by a rapid increase in the supply of marks to meet the demand. Presently, however, the attempt to hold the dollar-mark exchange rate firm was abandoned; the mark was allowed to "float" upward to find a new and more viable exchange rate.

For a moment the crisis subsided, but only temporarily. The Netherlands had gone along with West Germany in allowing its currency to float upward, but the major U.S. creditor, Japan, had not. Moreover, evidence began coming in that the United States was facing its first deficit on its goods and services account since 1893. The stage was set for a dramatic development: and in August 1971, such a development did occur.

On the same August day he announced the wage-price freeze, President Nixon announced a package of international measures as part of his "new economic policy." These included a temporary 10 percent surtax on imports and, more significantly, the removal of the last remaining tie between the dollar and gold. The United States would no longer buy gold even from the governments and central banks of foreign countries—the dollar would float and find its natural level in relation to other foreign currencies.

For the next year-and-a-half, through a series of formal agreements (e.g., the Smithsonian agreement of December 18, 1971) and innumerable international consultations, an attempt was made to find a more viable set of international exchange rates than had existed up to August 15, 1971. This more viable set would obviously include a devalued dollar, since the persistence of our large (and increasing) deficits was now a subject of urgent concern.

The effects of the devaluation of the dollar during this period were dramatic. Devaluation, as we know, makes the prices of our exports less expensive abroad and the prices of foreign imports more expensive to us. In the case of the United States, devaluation helped change a $9.8 billion deficit in our "basic balance" in 1972 (see Table 15–2) into a $1.2 billion surplus in that same balance in 1973. Although the huge cost increases of imported oil were adversely affecting our balance of payments in early 1974, many commentators feel that our deficit may at least be ameliorated through the remainder of the decade.

Equally interesting from our point of view is that, in the first quarter of 1973, the attempt to operate with any form of fixed exchange rates was largely abandoned in the United States and abroad. We did not have perfectly flexible or floating exchanges during this next year—they have been described as "dirty or managed floating" rates, because of the continual intervention of governments[6]—but they came reasonably close to being an experiment in the kind of system economists have long advocated. The workings of this experiment are described in the *Economic Report of the President, 1974.*

---

6. H. S. Houthakker, "Policy Issues in the International Economy of the 1970's," *The American Economic Review,* Vol. LXIV, No. 2, May 1974, p. 138.

What Happened in 1973?

Economic Report of the President, 1974

In the area of international economic relations, the year 1973 may be characterized as one of continuing adjustment to past disequilibria as well as to new developments that entered the picture during the year. Early in the year the governments of most major countries abandoned attempts to fix exchange rates at negotiated levels. While central banks continued to intervene to some extent, foreign exchange markets played the major role in determining the exchange rates that would clear the market. This process was marked at times by unusually large fluctuations of market exchange rates. Nevertheless, the market performed its intermediating function well, and neither trade nor long-term capital flows were seriously disrupted at any time during the year.

The developments in the balance of payments accounts of individual countries reflected, in part, the developments in the foreign exchange markets. The appreciation and depreciation of individual currencies, achieved either through formal measures by the authorities or as a result of free movement of exchange rates, continued to influence the flows of international commerce and thus the deficits and surpluses of individual countries. Special developments, such as the shortages of food in certain parts of the world and, later in the year, the emerging world energy crisis, also affected the direction and magnitude of trade and capital flows among countries.

Excerpted from *Economic Report of the President, 1974,* pp. 182–188; 219–220.

WHAT HAPPENED TO EXCHANGE RATES?

Developments during 1973 in the foreign exchange market can be conveniently broken into four periods, coinciding with the four quarters of the year. These developments are described in detail below.

The first quarter of 1973: Fixed exchange rates are abandoned. Foreign exchange markets were stable in the beginning of 1973. In most foreign exchange markets the dollar was above the level where central banks were committed to buy dollars to keep its value within the agreed margins. The stability was so fragile, however, that any disturbance had a highly unsettling effect on the market. The first such disturbance was an acceleration of the capital flight from Italy into Switzerland. Confronted with massive outflows, the Italian authorities allowed the lira to float, first for financial transactions and later for all transactions. In Switzerland, the influx of funds from abroad intensified an already high rate of inflation. To gain greater control over its monetary policy, Switzerland decided on January 22 to allow the franc to float. By terminating their purchases of foreign currencies in support of a fixed value of the franc vis-a-vis other currencies, the Swiss monetary authorities were able to avoid further involuntary increases in the Swiss money supply.

The floating of the franc by Switzerland, a country viewed by many as the epitome of financial orthodoxy, strengthened expectations that other exchange rate adjustments were inevitable, particularly for currencies of countries with large payments imbalances such as Japan and Germany. These expectations led to increasingly large speculative purchases of marks and yen for dollars. Such sales reached a peak in the first week of February, forcing the closing of foreign exchange markets on February 10. Extensive consultations among the monetary officials of major countries followed and culminated in a number of coordinated exchange rate adjustments. On February 12 the Administration announced that it would ask Congress to approve a 10 percent devaluation of the dollar in terms of Special Drawing Rights (SDR's).*

At the same time, the Japanese authorities announced that the Japanese yen would be allowed to float upward. The resulting exchange rate structure was endorsed by the 14 major industrial nations.

The multilateral adjustment of exchange rate patterns in February, including the devaluation of the dollar, did not, however, restore market confidence in the entire pattern of rates—in particular, the rate for the German mark. Large-scale flows of speculative funds out of dollars into marks and some other currencies continued until exchange markets were officially closed on March 2.

The exchange markets remained officially closed until March 19, although private trading of currencies continued. On March 19, five of the European Community (EC) countries—Belgium, Denmark, France, Germany, and the Netherlands—allowed their currencies to float jointly vis-a-vis the dollar and other currencies. As before, these countries decided to keep the exchange rates between any two of their currencies within 2¼ percent of an agreed relationship. In addition, Norway and Sweden subsequently decided to peg their currencies to the jointly floating EC currencies.

The second quarter of 1973: The dollar drops further. Between the end of March and the end of June the markets were characterized by a substantial depreciation of the dollar against most European currencies. At the same time, the dollar remained relatively unchanged against the currencies of Japan, Canada, and a number of other countries. The dollar declined about 11 percent in terms of most EC currencies floating jointly and 5 percent in terms of the trade-weighted average of 14 currencies. The dollar declined by as much as 15 percent vis-a-vis the German mark, which was revalued by 5½ percent relative to the other EC currencies floating jointly. (See Chart A, p. 382.)

---

*[See p. 388.]

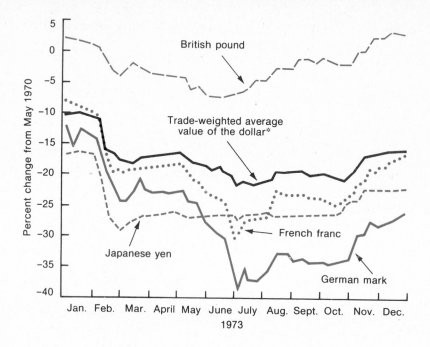

Chart A. Change in the Value of the U.S. Dollar Relative to Selected Foreign Currencies

*Relative to 14 major currencies; computed by Morgan Guaranty Trust Company.

Source: Morgan Guaranty Trust Company.

There were three sources of downward pressure on the dollar in European exchange markets during this period. First, the United States continued to have a deficit vis-a-vis Europe on basic balance transactions—which include trade, grants and other unilateral transfers, and long-term investment. This meant that the public was supplying more dollars through these transactions in exchange for European currencies than were being purchased with European currencies through these transactions. Second, many non-European countries besides the United States had deficits vis-a-vis Europe in basic transactions. Since most of these countries use the dollar as a reserve currency, they tended to finance their deficits vis-a-vis Europe with dollars. Dollars from non-American sources were thus competing with dollars from the United States in European exchange markets. Third, the dollar is widely held abroad not only by central banks but also by many private individuals, banks, and corporations. With the continuing decline of the dollar during the previous 2 years, many of these private foreign holders wanted to exchange their dollars for foreign currencies.

As long as markets clear, however, there can be no "additional" dollars remaining unsold. Exchange rates will change until enough sellers have been discouraged from selling or enough buyers have been encouraged to buy. Equilibrium in the market was established during this period by private foreigners on balance increasing their dollar holdings. Figures for dollars held by private foreigners in Europe are not available, but the changes in these holdings are reflected in the $2 billion increase of U.S. liquid liabilities to all private foreigners from the end of March to the end of June. Foreign central banks decreased their holdings of dollars over this period by $650 million.

The rapid drop of the dollar significantly below what many considered its longer-term value created widespread uncertainty regarding future exchange market trends; for a short period during the end of June and the beginning of July the spread between buying and selling rates widened, and it became increasingly difficult for traders to obtain forward coverage. Nevertheless foreign exchange markets remained open throughout this period, and normal international trade and investment transactions continued without major disruption. Fears by many that floating exchange rates would disrupt international trade proved to be without foundation.

The third quarter of 1973: The dollar begins to rise.

The decline of the dollar relative to European currencies was reversed in the third quarter as an increasing body of opinion in the market held that the dollar had become undervalued, a view that was strengthened by the emergence of a sizable surplus in U.S. trade of goods and services. In this favorable atmosphere, some further impetus to the turn in market opinion came from the announcement on July 18 of U.S. intervention in the foreign exchange market in order to maintain orderly market conditions.

This move discouraged speculation against the dollar by raising the possibility that the U.S. authorities would buy as many dollars (or sell as many foreign currencies) as would be necessary to prevent a further decline.

The fourth quarter of 1973: The dollar rises further.

During the fourth quarter the appreciation of the dollar continued, in part because it was thought that the United States was in a relatively better position than Western European countries and Japan to deal with the cutback of oil production in the Middle East and the simultaneous increase in world oil prices. At the same time, the surpluses in U.S. trade were becoming larger, and figures published for the long-term investment account began to show a surplus. Between September 28 and December 27 the dollar rose by about 11 percent against the jointly floating European currencies. By the end of the year the dollar was thus approximately back to its February post-devaluation level. The dollar was rising so fast, in fact, that some foreign central banks found it increasingly desirable to reduce their controls on capital inflows and to sell off some of the dollars which they had accumulated in the past. Foreign exchange reserves of the Bank of Japan and the Bundesbank declined by $1 billion each during the October to November period as a result of their dollar sales.

Increasingly in the fourth quarter the exchange markets became dominated by the energy crisis and the abrupt and massive additions to import costs of oil. Early in January 1974 both the yen and the European currencies floating jointly depreciated sharply, and in some cases reached levels lower than those prevailing immediately after the multilateral adjustment of February 1973. On January 21, the French franc was allowed to float freely, and immediately declined by 5 percent.

Over the year as a whole the functioning of the exchange market improved as traders gained experience with floating exchange rates. This can be seen, for instance, in the narrowing spread between the buying and selling rates of the major currencies traded and in the diminished day-to-day fluctuations of these currencies. In general, one has to conclude that despite the dramatic decline and the equally dramatic rise of the dollar against the major European currencies, foreign exchange markets functioned remarkably well, and only on a few days was it difficult to carry out foreign exchange transactions.

WHAT HAPPENED
TO ALL THOSE DOLLARS?

Over the years a large volume of dollars has been accumulated by foreigners, both governments and private individuals. To a large extent these dollars are held because the dollar is the most widely used currency for international transactions, and a stock of dollars was therefore useful for all the reasons that induce people to hold money. Dollars are thus held voluntarily by private banks, corporations, and individuals. They are also held voluntarily by foreign central banks, even though central banks to some extent hold these dollars not because they want to increase their dollar reserves, but because they want to avoid a rise in the value of their currencies relative to the dollar.

When they are sold in the foreign exchange market, dollars owned by foreigners become indistinguishable from dollars owned by Americans. That is, when they are sold they exert a downward pressure, and when they are purchased they exert an upward pressure on the market value of the dollar. Private American holders of dollars and private foreign holders of dollars, whether these are held in U.S. or in foreign banks, have similar economic motives in selling or buying dollars in the foreign exchange market. For instance, if the dollar is expected to fall relative to foreign currencies, holders of dollars will have an incentive to sell dollars and to buy foreign currencies. If the dollar is expected to rise relative to foreign currencies, holders of foreign currencies have an incentive to buy dollars and to sell their foreign currencies. While the average foreign holder of dollars is likely to be more sensitive to such changes in the foreign exchange value of the dollar than domestic holders of dollars, the experience of the last few years has shown that Americans will exchange large amounts of dollars for foreign currencies when they find it profitable to do so.

There is some reason to believe that during the first half of 1973 expectations of a future fall in the value of the dollar may have induced some dollar holders, both in the United States and abroad, to sell their dollars, thereby depressing the market value. Thus there were occasions when the value of the dollar was declining in the market, even though the United States was experiencing a rapid improvement in its underlying balance of payments. In the second half, expectations of a future rise of the dollar may have reinforced an upward trend by inducing both Americans and foreigners to shift from foreign currencies into dollars.

* * *

In the context of the postwar period, developments in the international economy during the past year appear rather turbulent. Massive capital flows led to fluctuations in exchange rates that were far in excess of any that attracted attention in the recent past. Inflation accelerated throughout much of the world, as demand for goods outgrew the productive capacity of the world economy. Shortfalls in farm output and cutbacks in oil production, combined with selective embargoes on oil exports, created intense international competition for food and energy. In all these different ways, the world received an effective demonstration of the extent to which economic interdependence has become a reality.

Despite the economic difficulties, most nations were able to record significant economic gains; and despite some stresses and strains in international economic relations, the postwar framework for economic cooperation among nations remained intact. This ability of the world economy to adjust to the new realities was in large part due to the willingness of most governments to accept greater flexibility in their economic relationships, while continuing to recognize the need for self-discipline in the pursuit of individual national goals. Certainly the introduction of more flexible exchange rate relationships facilitated the adjustment of economic relations among individual national economies experiencing widely different domestic circumstances. Equally important was the willingness of governments to negotiate pragmatic accommodations to politically difficult international monetary and trade issues.

In the coming year, the new arrangements for international cooperation that were evolving in the past year will be put to a strenuous test. The continuing constraints imposed on the production and export of oil by a number of countries in the Middle East will intensify the competition for energy supplies and chemicals. In addition, the recent large increase in world oil prices will require major adjustments in relative incomes both within and among nations, in relative prices of both domestic and internationally traded goods, in world patterns of production and trade, and in the worldwide flow of capital and the means of putting this capital to its most productive uses. These adjustments are likely to pose severe hardships for some countries, and some domestic economic difficulties for all nations. The pressures to take unilateral measures at the expense of one's neighbors could become quite intense in such an environment. Were just one nation, and then others, to pursue such a course, however, the resulting disruption of international trade would be likely to cause even more serious losses of economic welfare for everyone. International conferences such as the recently concluded meeting of finance ministers in Rome, and the coming conferences on the world oil and the world food situation, will be useful in the search for cooperative solutions. At the same time, the international monetary discussions and the multilateral trade negotiations will be indispensable to a broader effort to strengthen the international framework for managing the increasing number of economic problems that are of global significance.   □

TOWARD INTERNATIONAL MONETARY REFORM

Although the experiment with flexibility in 1973 seems to have been a reasonable success, many commentators feel that we have not yet developed an international monetary *system* that will stand the test of time. We have had some reliance on the market, but also a considerable amount of uncoordinated, ad hoc intervention, and much international disagreement about what the shape of the future world monetary structure should be. Is it possible to come to some overall agreement on the *degree* of flexibility that there should be in exchange rates? Also, can the countries of the world agree on how to provide the liquidity needed to finance an ever expanding world trade? What should be the future role of the dollar? Of gold? Of "paper gold"?

Flexibility through crawling pegs and wider bands. On the issue of exchange flexibility, economists and statesmen have been searching for some kind of compromise between the completely flexible (or floating) exchanges of pure theory and the narrow rigidity of the old-fashioned gold standard. One idea has been to widen the range around any given exchange rate in which market supply and demand forces can operate. Even under the gold standard, there would be some *slight* flexibility in the exchange rate between two currencies, caused by the expense of transporting and insuring gold in the settlement of balance of payments accounts. Suppose you were an American importer who owed a German exporter a certain number of marks for goods purchased in Germany. Should you buy marks with your dollars directly—or should you purchase gold with your dollars, ship the gold to Germany, and give the exporter gold? The answer is that you will buy the marks directly until the point (called the "gold point") where the mark rises in value—say, by ½ of 1 percent—and it becomes marginally cheaper to buy the gold. Thus, within these "gold points" on either side of the exchange rate, the price of marks in terms of dollars is freely floating even under a rigid gold standard.

A suggested compromise, then, would be to *widen* this band around the official exchange rate between two currencies within which supply and demand forces could operate. This already happened, to some degree, in the Smithsonian agreement of December 18, 1971, when the participating nations agreed to allow a band of 2.25 percent above or below the new "central rates" for the fluctuation of market rates. But this band could be widened still further, perhaps to 4, 5, or 6 percent. This solution represents one way in which the conflict between fixed and flexible rates might be resolved.

But how about the "central rates" themselves? Need these be negotiated afresh each time a country runs into serious balance of payments problems? Such was, in effect, the system that the trading nations of the world adopted after World War II. The agency that conducted these negotiations was theoretically the International Monetary Fund (IMF). If a country ran into continuing deficits, reflecting a basic international disequilibrium, the IMF, after orderly discussion and consultation, would permit the country to depreciate its currency by 10 percent, and later, to depreciate further if the disequilibrium persisted. It did not always work this way, but the principle of stable exchange rates, with changes occurring in an orderly, negotiated fashion, was central to the world monetary system until just recently.

A compromise on this matter would involve allowing some shifting even in the central rates of exchange without formal negotiation. Suppose you allowed these central rates to change by 1 or 2 percent a year. Then you would have what is known as a *crawling peg*. It might take you five or ten years to accomplish a 10 percent depreciation of your currency, but, taken together with a widened band *around* the crawling peg, perhaps this would be enough to make allowance for the various changes in economic conditions that might affect your balance of payments position during that period. The way the combination of crawling peg and wider bands might work is shown in Figure 15–2, where it is assumed hypothetically that West Germany is running into

balance of payments difficulties with the United States over the future. The mark "crawls" slowly downward over the years, although from time to time, as short-run changes occur, it may shoot up to the top of the band.

This rather fancy mechanism is not a sure-fire solution to the exchange-rate problem. We discovered how, in 1973 and 1974, massive changes in world trading positions can occur in a short period; e.g., because of the oil embargo and the sudden great increases in the price of oil. However, it might be a useful step in moving toward greater flexibility, yet within a basically orderly context.

Liquidity through dollars, gold, SDRs? The second major aspect of a new and reformed monetary system concerns the problem of liquidity and the financing of expanded world trade. As we have said earlier, the way this was done in the post-war period was basically through the export of dollars by the United States and the acceptance of dollars as, in effect, an international currency (a "key" currency, as it was often called). But what happens now, after the dollar crisis of 1971 and the cutting of the economic link between the dollar and gold?

One approach would be to say that these difficulties were only temporary and that we can return to the former system. After all, the dollar in 1973–1974 was in a much stronger state than it had been a year or two earlier. This solution seems unacceptable both politically and economically, however. The earlier system had, as an underpinning, the massive gold stock owned by the United States in the late 1940s. Trade is on a much larger scale now than it was then, and our gold stock is enormously reduced. And the dollar crisis of 1971 *did* happen. Although our great importance in the economic affairs of the world guarantees an important place for the dollar for the foreseeable future, its unique, postwar preeminence seems clearly a thing of the past.

Another approach would be to restore gold to its "rightful" place as the sole internationally accepted medium of exchange. It is not a decisive objection to say that the world does not have enough gold (world gold production increases much less rapidly than world trade), because we can get all we need

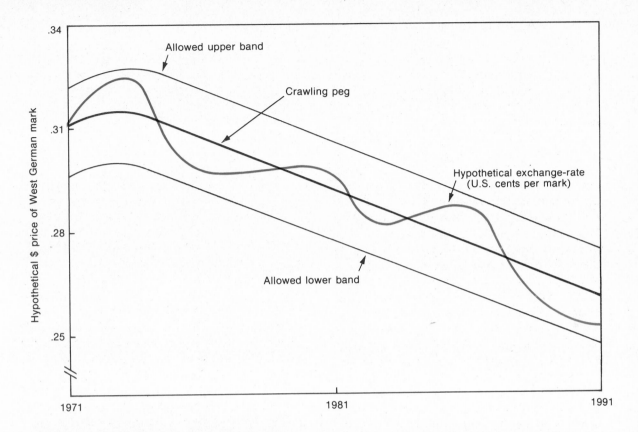

Figure 15–2. Combination of Wider Bands and a Crawling Central Exchange Rate.

In this hypothetical example, the West German mark, beginning with its Smithsonian exchange rate in 1971 ($.310316 to the mark), experiences a temporary ad-vantage and then a long-run decline against the dollar. Considerable short-run flexibility is permitted by the wider bands.

simply by allowing the price to rise sufficiently. In mid-1974, the official price of gold was $42.22 an ounce, but the free market price of gold was plus or minus $160 an ounce.[7] At its official price, gold is virtually meaningless for settling balance of payments deficits, but let it go to $100, $200, or whatever

an ounce and world markets can be as *liquid* as we want them.

The objections are many. Such an upward reevaluation of the price of gold would bring an enormous reward to gold-producing countries (for which, read Russia and South Africa), and for precisely those nations and individuals who have speculated against the survival of the present system by hoarding their liquid wealth in the form of gold. Even more significant, perhaps, is the simple question: Why gold?

7. In the so-called official tier, gold is exchanged only between governments and only at the official rate. In the private market—which includes, among others, many speculators on the future world monetary system and the role of gold therein—the price of gold is determined by supply and demand.

Many people object to this solution on the grounds that it makes sense *only if we are going to return to a full-fledged gold standard* (which is what the French Gaullists wanted all along), and such a return is regarded as courting potential international disaster yet once again.

Is a compromise possible here, too? Many have been offered, and one example is the increased use of "paper gold." We have mentioned in passing the IMF's Special Drawing Rights or "SDRs." The basic idea here is that the IMF (subject to certain veto provisions and to the determination of the Director General) can create new means of payment each year in the form of drawing rights on each country's account with the fund. These SDRs are allocated to each country in proportion to its original contribution to the IMF, although other principles of distribution could be imagined.[8] Surplus countries are required to accept SDRs in settlement of payment of claims (up to a limit of three times their own SDR allocations), and deficit countries are free to use them to meet payment deficits, subject to keeping a certain minimum balance of SDRs in their accounts. For most practical purposes, therefore, SDRs can be used like gold or, in happier days, U.S. dollars.

Up until now, the volume of SDRs is still rather small compared to quantities involved in many international settlements. Thus, in Table 15–2, the reader can see that with a basic deficit of nearly $10 billion in 1972, the U.S. allocation of SDRs was only $710 million. However, the potential long-run expansion of SDRs is very great. Combined with a crawling peg and wider band, which may, in total, reduce the pressures of liquidity on the system as a whole, the SDRs seem likely to be an important part of the compromise on international monetary reform that will take place in the years ahead. That such a reform will take place, and is much overdue, is one of the few things on which most commentators agree in this period of economic uncertainty.

---

8. It has been argued, for example, that poor countries ought to get more than their quota-determined shares. This would be a form of mutually agreed upon foreign aid from rich to poor countries.

SUMMARY

This chapter has been concerned with the macroeconomic aspects of international trade, and especially with balance of payments problems.

Balance of payments accounting is complex because of the many different kinds of items that appear in international exchanges. Basically, credit items are those that create a demand for a country's currency, while debit items are those that create a supply of your currency that is seeking to purchase other currencies. An overall surplus or deficit in the balance of payments measures the pressure on the country's reserve assets. Thus, a deficit in the balance of payments means that a country is either losing reserve assets (gold, convertible currencies) or that other countries are increasing their liquid claims against this country's reserve assets. Depending on the question at hand, many different balances may be used, e.g., balance on current account and long-term capital (the "basic" balance), liquidity balance, official reserve transactions balance, etc.

The classical economists (including the philosopher David Hume) argued that surpluses and deficits in the balance of payments would be self-correcting. According to the theory of the *price-specie-flow* mechanism, countries on the gold standard would lose gold if their balance of payments were in deficit and would gain gold if it were in surplus. These gold flows would, on the quantity theory of money, bring rises in price-levels in surplus countries and declines in price-levels in deficit countries. These price changes, assuming that they were reflected in export and import prices as well, would correct the balance of payments disequilibria and also, in due course, terminate the gold flow.

This classical mechanism depends on many special assumptions, few of which are accepted uncritically today. Mainstream economics at the present time would analyze the monetary effects of gold flows via the money supply–interest rate-investment-GNP logic we have discussed before. Modern analysis would also link international trade to the more general theory of national income determination. Foreign demand for our exports is similar in effect to domestic consumption, investment, or government demand. Conversely, our demand for imports from abroad must be subtracted from overall demand for goods and services. The total aggregate demand for an economy therefore will be represented by domestic consumption, investment, and government spending, plus an item representing *net exports* $(X - M)$.

Because trade can affect national income and employment—an unfavorable balance, for example, could cause a recession, other things equal—many economists favor flexible exchange rates over the fixed exchange rates implied by a pure gold standard. Under a regime of flexible exchanges, favorable or unfavorable trade trends would be reflected in the supply-and-demand conditions relative to the country's currency, the price of that currency (its exchange rate) going up or down as the market determined.

Turning to actual world trade problems, we discovered that the United States' balance of payments has been in substantial deficit for several years now. This deficit has caused a considerable outflow of monetary gold and a very large increase in the dollar holdings of foreigners. Although the increase in dollar holdings has helped finance the post-war expansion of world trade (dollars having been a reserve asset rather similar to gold), it also contributed directly to the Dollar Crisis of 1971 and the complete severing of the dollar from gold as part of the "new economic policy" of August 15, 1971.

Subsequently, intense consultations led to the revaluation of world currencies under the Smithsonian agreement of December 18, 1971; to a period of floating exchange rates beginning in 1973; to a new emphasis on alternatives to dollars as means of international payments—especially the Monetary Fund's new Special Drawing Rights (SDRs)—and finally, to an increased awareness of the need for a general reform of the international monetary system.

IMPORTANT TERMS TO REMEMBER

Balance of Payments
Credit/Debit Items
Mercantilist: Favorable Balance of Trade
"Basic" Balance of Payments
Classical Gold Standard
Price-Specie-Flow Mechanism
$Y = C + I + G + (X - M)$
Flexible Exchange Rates
Devaluation
Crawling Pegs and Wider Bands
International Liquidity
Special Drawing Rights (SDR's)

QUESTIONS FOR DISCUSSION

1. Classify the following items as credits or debits in the United States balance of payments and explain your reasoning: export of computer hardware to Italy; German tourist expenditures in the United States; United States renting of the services of Norwegian ships; U.S. foreign aid grant to Thailand; import of Japanese automobiles; U.S. investment in a factory in Brazil; income for U.S. investors from a factory in France.

2. Until very recently, the United States enjoyed a favorable balance of merchandise exports over imports and yet still suffered from an overall deficit in its balance of payments. Explain how this was possible.

3. Imagine a country that has the following situation:

(a) a constant level of commodity exports;

(b) a level of commodity imports that increases with the level of national income;

(c) commodity exports exceed commodity imports at all levels of national income.

How would you display this general information in the familiar diagrams with 45° lines that we have used in the theory of national income determination?

4. Discuss the advantages of flexible exchanges over fixed exchanges in protecting a country's domestic economy. One of the *dis*advantages of flexible exchanges is said to be that they would encourage widespread inflation. Explain why this might be true in general, and why it might be particularly true of countries that depend heavily on trade for the basic necessities of life. (Hint: an exchange rate depreciation will raise the domestic cost of imported items.)

5. Consider alternative means of providing more "liquidity" for an expanded world trade. What means do you prefer? Why?

SUGGESTED READING

Friedman, Milton. "The Advantages of Flexible Exchange-Rates," from U.S. Congress, Joint Economic Committee, *Hearings: The United States Balance of Payments*, 88th Cong., 1st sess., 1963.

Houthakker, H. S. "Policy Issues in the International Economy of the 1970's," *The American Economic Review*, 64, no. 2, May 1974.

Kenen, Peter and Lubitz, Raymond. *International Economics*, 3rd ed. Englewood Cliffs, N.J.: Prentice-Hall, 1971.

Mikesell, Raymond F. *Financing World Trade*. New York: Thomas Y. Crowell Co., 1969.

Wallich, Henry C. "A Defense of Fixed Exchange Rates," from U.S. Congress, Joint Economic Committee, *Hearings: The United States Balance of Payments*, 88th Cong., 1st sess., 1963.

CHAPTER 16
THE PROBLEM OF ECONOMIC GROWTH

In this chapter, we will complete our extensions and applications of macroeconomic analysis by introducing the problem of economic growth. Economic growth is such a large topic in our field that we shall be coming back to it many times again. In chapter 28, we shall consider growth in an international context. In chapter 30, we will be particularly concerned with the *costs* of economic growth. We have already talked about growth in the case of the underdeveloped nations (chapter 6), and we will return to this major twentieth-century problem in the next to the last chapter of the book.

For the moment, we have two main objectives: (1) to indicate the extent and character of modern economic growth, and (2) to relate the problem of growth to the body of macroeconomic analysis that we have been developing throughout Part Two.

SHORT- AND LONG-RUN MACROECONOMICS

Most of the analysis of Part Two to this point has been of a short-run nature. We have assumed that the nation's basic productive capacity was given, and we have asked: Where will a society's *actual* level of national income be in relation to this given productive *potential* in any particular period? In this analysis, we have put special emphasis on the factors that contribute to the aggregate demand for the nation's output—consumption, investment, government spending, and, in the preceding chapter, the net foreign demand for our exports.

Now when we shift our attention toward the long run, our emphasis has to change somewhat both in terms of analysis and in terms of policies. We can no longer take the productive capacity of the nation as given; its expansion over time is precisely what makes possible the growth phenomenon. And this fact is likely to influence the kind of policies we use to attack even our short-run problems. Thus, if we face a gap between actual and potential income and a substantial amount of unemployment, we may find that certain policies designed to correct this situation have an unfavorable effect on the expansion of productive capacity over time. Other policies may have a favorable effect. As in the case of balance of payments problems, the attempt to secure a higher rate of growth (if that is what the society wants) imposes certain restrictions on the kinds of policies we will want to employ.

These points can be made most clear by thinking of investment spending, a matter we have discussed frequently in the preceding chapters. In the *short run,* the main fact about investment spending is that it increases the level of aggregate demand and hence may help reduce the gap between potential and actual output. In the *long run,* however, the most significant fact about investment is that it means an increase in the society's stock of capital, or its productive capacity. A policy designed to reduce unemployment may work equally well in the short run whether it focuses on increasing consumer or investment spending; however, this question of focus may be a prime issue when we are concerned with long-run growth.

We shall return to these points again, but enough has been said in a preliminary way to indicate the relationship of the work we will take up now to the work completed in earlier chapters. Let us begin by getting some historical sense of what modern growth means.

BEGINNINGS OF MODERN GROWTH— THE INDUSTRIAL REVOLUTION

In discussing the emergence of the "market economy" (p. 26), we pointed out that this was basically a modern phenomenon, dating roughly from the eighteenth century. Very much the same thing can be said about modern economic growth.[1] The beginnings of the process are usually located in the English Industrial Revolution of the late eighteenth century. This dating is necessarily somewhat arbitrary. England had been making substantial economic progress for at least two centuries before the revolution occurred. Furthermore, even this earlier progress was dependent upon the general expansion of the European economy, which had its roots back at least as far as the tenth or eleventh century. Historians, eager to prove the essential continuity of the British experience, are easily able to find antecedents for virtually every change that took place in the economic structure of late eighteenth-century England.

Still, the concept of a genuine revolution is not altogether arbitrary. For it was only in late eighteenth-century Britain that certain distinctive features of what we think of as "modern growth" appeared unequivocally on the scene. For the first time in the history of mankind, a nation began to produce an output of goods and services that was regularly expanding at a rate far in excess of its rate of population growth. We can put this even more strongly. The Industrial Revolution in England was accompanied by a marked acceleration in the rate of population growth. To have *matched* this growth of population with an equal growth of production would have been achievement enough by any previous historical standard. To have *exceeded* it so that output *per capita* was also growing rapidly was something basically new in historical experience.

And this is what we mean by "modern economic growth":

Modern economic growth is a sustained, relatively regular and rapid increase in a nation's GNP, and especially in its GNP per capita.

---

1.   Indeed, some commentators have felt that these two phenomena—the emergence of a market-oriented economy and the beginnings of rapid modern growth—were intrinsically related. Although there may be some historical truth in this for the case of England, it is not a point that can be pressed very far, for it has become abundantly clear in the twentieth century that highly controlled and centralized economies can also produce rapid growth. See chapter 28, p. 659.

It is this kind of growth that was born in Britain in the late eighteenth century.

This birth process had many different aspects. Some of them were clearly favorable and were so regarded by the more perceptive observers of the time. This was particularly true of the rapid development of new technologies of production. Economically useful inventions were being developed and applied at what earlier would have been considered an astonishing rate. There were improvements in virtually all branches of industry—in cotton textile production, in iron and steel, in pottery making, even in agriculture. The greatest single invention of the period was probably James Watt's steam engine (1769). This invention came to affect many different branches of industry and was important in giving durability to the growth process as it continued into the nineteenth century. It was not, however, the "cause" of the Industrial Revolution, since the process of technological change was general and pervasive, and the revolution was well under way before the steam engine made its impact felt.

Some other aspects of the birth process were clearly unfavorable. This period saw the development and spread of the factory system and, in consequence, a substantial dislocation of the traditional British way of life. It was a period that witnessed great distress among certain groups in society—children employed in the new cotton mills, craftsmen displaced by new techniques of production, rural villagers and squatters dispossessed of their lands. Indeed, these unpleasant features of the transformation of English society were so pronounced that the leading economists of the early nineteenth century (recall Thomas Robert Malthus) took a very pessimistic view of the future. They were convinced that society was heading toward a dismal "stationary state" in which the great mass of people would be buried in poverty.

As a great watershed in human history, the English Industrial Revolution has received many analyses, but none more penetrating than the classic work of the great French economic historian Paul Mantoux. The following brief selection is the concluding summary of his masterpiece, *The Industrial Revolution in the Eighteenth Century:*

The Industrial Revolution in the Eighteenth Century

Paul Mantoux

CONCLUSION

In the first decade of the nineteenth century, which closes the period we set out to study, the industrial revolution was far from being completed. The use of machinery was still limited to certain industries, and in these industries to certain specialities or certain districts. Side by side with great metal works such as Soho and Coalbrookdale the small workshops of the Birmingham toyman and of the Sheffield cutlers continued to exist, and survived for many decades. Side by side with the Lancashire cotton mills and the West Riding woollen mills, thousands of weavers went on working at home on their old hand looms. Steam, which was to multiply and generalize the results of all other mechanical inventions, had hardly begun its triumphant progress. Nevertheless the modern industrial system did already exist with all its essential features, and it is possible to detect in the developments which had taken place at that time the main characteristics of the great change.

From the technical point of view the industrial revolution consists in the invention and use of processes which made it possible to speed up and constantly to increase production: some are mechanical processes, as in the textile industries, others chemical as in the metal-working industries: they help either to prepare the raw material or to determine the form of the finished product, and the phrase machine industry is inadequate to the variety and to the possibilities offered by such developments. The invention of such processes (at least in the beginning) owed little to conclusions drawn from purely scientific discoveries. It is an established fact that most of the first inventors were anything but scientists. They were technical men who, being faced with a practical problem, used their natural faculties and their expert knowledge of the habits and needs of the industry to solve it. Highs, Crompton, Hargreaves, Dudley, Darby and Cort were men of this type. A few others, such as Wyatt and Cartwright, undertook their researches instinctively and out of pure curiosity, without either scientific or professional training. Under the pressure of necessity and on purely concrete data they set to work without a definite plan, and only reached their goal after much groping in the dark. They represent economic necessity, silently and powerfully moulding men to its will, overcoming obstacles and forging its own instruments. Science came later and brought its immense reserves of power to bear on the development which had already begun, thus giving at once to partial developments in different industries a common direction and a common speed. This is specially noticeable in the case of Watt and the steam engine. Thus two streams from different sources met, and though it was to their combined power that the industrial revolution owed its actual size and strength, yet the change had already begun and its first results were conspicuous.

From the economic point of view the industrial revolution is characterized by the concentration of capital and the growth of large undertakings, the existence and working of which from being only exceptional came to be the normal conditions of industry. Though, not without reason, this concentration is often considered as the result of technical inventions, yet to a certain extent it preceded such inventions. It was essentially a commercial phenomenon and was connected with the gradual hold obtained by merchants over industry. Not only was it accompanied, but it was also prepared by the expansion of trade and credit. Its necessary conditions were internal security, the development of communications and of maritime trade. The historical transition between the master craftsman of the Middle Ages and

the modern industrialist was provided by the merchant manufacturer. We find him at first, so to speak, on the margin of industry, with the sole function of linking up producers with markets which were becoming too large and too distant for them. Later on, as his capital grew and the manufacturer came to rely on him more and more, he became the master of production and finally the owner of all raw material, buildings and equipment, while independent workmen were degraded to the rank of mere wage-earners. This concentration of the means of production in the hands of capitalists who were more concerned with trade than with industry is a fact of paramount importance. No doubt 'manufacture', with the great number of men it employed, the highly specialized division of its labour and its many likenesses to the factory system, was a more striking fact, but it played a much smaller part in the evolution of industry. It marked a stage on the road, but a stage no sooner reached than passed. Economists, studying this evolution, have conceived and described it as a simple development, one phase following another like the different parts of a geometrical curve. But to the eyes of the historian a movement of such complexity is more like a river, which does not always flow at the same pace but sometimes slackens its course, sometimes rushes on, now running through narrow gorges and now spreading out over the plain, now breaking up into many divergent branches and now winding about, so that it seems to curve back on itself. Merely to enumerate the different points it passes by is not to describe it. To do this we must follow, step by step, its varied winding course, which in spite of its changes of direction remains continuous like the slope which bears it to its end.

From the social point of view the industrial revolution had such extensive and profound results that it would be presumptuous for us to attempt to summarize them in a short formula. Even though, unlike political revolutions, it did not actually alter the legal form of society, yet it modified its very substance. It gave birth to social classes whose progress and mutual opposition fill the history of our times. It would be easy, by quoting some of the facts mentioned in this very book, to try and show that in this respect there has been no revolution, that the same social

Early industrial application of the steam engine: Coal-whimsey, or engine, drawing coal in the Staffordshire Collieries. Engraving, ca 1880.
Source: The Bettmann Archive

classes were already in existence, that their opposition had begun long before, its nature and cause always remaining the same. One of the objects we have always kept in mind was precisely to show the continuity of the historical process underlying even the most rapid changes. None of these changes took place suddenly, as by a miracle, but each of them had been expected, prepared and outlined before it actually took place. It would be an equal error either to undervalue those preliminaries or to take them for what they only foreshadowed. We know that there were machines before the era of machinery, 'manufacture' before factories, combinations and strikes before the formation of industrial capitalism and of the 'factory proletariat'. But in the slow-moving mass of society a new element does not make itself felt immediately. And we have not only to note its pres-

ence but its relation to its environment and, as it were, the space it occupies in history. The industrial revolution is precisely the expansion of undeveloped forces, the sudden growth and blossoming of seeds which had for many years lain hidden or asleep.

After the beginning of the nineteenth century the growth of the factory system was visible to all. It was already influencing the distribution as well as the material condition of the population. To the factory system were due the importance and sudden prosperity of districts such as Lancashire, South Wales and part of the Lowlands of Scotland, which until then had been considered as being among the least prosperous parts of the country. It was the factory system which, following on the redistribution of landed property, quickened the migration of the rural population towards the factories. When the census of 1811 was taken, 60 to 70 percent of the inhabitants in the counties of Middlesex, Warwickshire, Yorkshire and Lancashire were employed in trade or industry, and at least 50 percent of those of Cheshire, Leicestershire, Nottinghamshire and Staffordshire. In these new centres, full of such intense activity, with their contrasting extremes of wealth and poverty, the data of the social problem, much as we know them today, could already be descried. The moment was not far off when that problem was to be defined for the first time by Robert Owen in his *Letter to the Manufac-* *turers of England* and his *Observations on the Consequences of the Factory System.* And he spoke not for England alone but for all the nations of the West, for while the factory system continued to develop in the country of its birth it had already begun to spread to other countries. It had made its appearance on the Continent, and from that time onward its history was no longer English but European—until it extended to the whole world.   □

Figure 16–1. The Spread of Modern Economic Growth

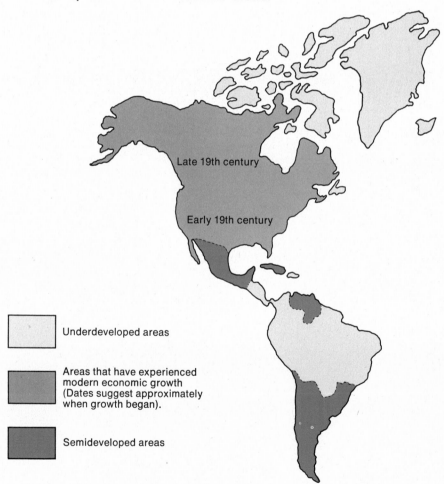

Late 19th century

Early 19th century

☐ Underdeveloped areas

☐ Areas that have experienced modern economic growth (Dates suggest approximately when growth began).

☐ Semideveloped areas

THE PROCESS SPREADS

By historical standards, the spread of the modern growth process of which Mantoux speaks was very rapid, although it is by no means universal even now. Figure 16–1 gives a rough sense of how the Industrial Revolution has reached across the map of the world. The United States was already very much embarked on the growth race before the Civil War. Germany began making major strides in the second half of the nineteenth century. Russia was a very "back-ward" economy through most of the nineteenth century but then, in the 1890s, she began to make her move. It is an interesting fact of history that the Russian Revolution of 1917 came not when the Russian economy was deteriorating, but after two decades of quite substantial economic progress under the Czars.

The process went beyond the boundaries of Europe and the United States—to Canada, Australia, and, rather remarkably, to Japan. The astonishing rate of

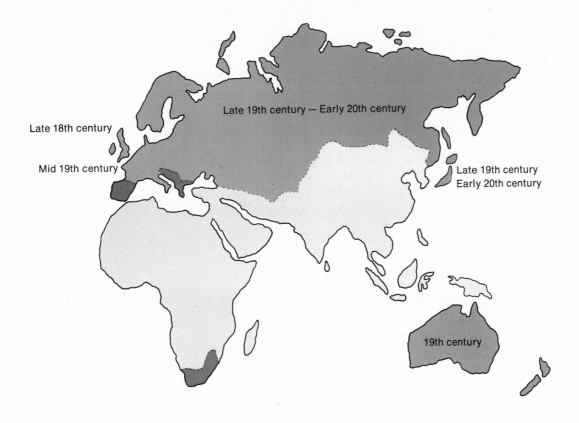

growth of the Japanese economy since World War II was made possible ultimately by the groundwork that Japan laid in the late nineteenth and early twentieth centuries. Indeed, this early achievement is really more astonishing than the later one. Japan had to face all kinds of obstacles—poor natural resources, dense population, a culture largely isolated from the industrial world of Europe, relatively meager assistance through foreign investment—and yet she still managed to have an industrial revolution of her own beginning in the 1870s and 1880s. The Japanese experience, to this day, remains a particularly fascinating one for those who wish to understand the underlying causes of modern growth.[2]

The variety of conditions under which industrial revolutions have occurred make it difficult to generalize about the essential nature of this process. One well-known attempt to do so, however, was that of W. W. Rostow, who described the process with the phrase, "take-off into self-sustaining growth," and then attempted to apply this concept to the beginnings of modern growth in many different countries.[3] The underlying idea here is that growth begins only after a certain minimum speed of change has been achieved. Slow, marginal changes are insufficient; the country simply sinks back to its former level of poverty. Only a spurt, a "big push" of some kind will do the trick.

Rostow then went on to analyze what he conceived to be the essential elements of this "take-off." Unfortunately, this proved to be an elusive goal. Some of the elements he described were too vague to be subjected to adequate historical tests. Other more specific elements—for example, the claim that a country engaged in take-off would experience a doubling of the percentage of its national income devoted to investment, from, say, 5 percent to 10 percent or more—have not convinced other economic historians.[4] What remains then is a sense that the beginnings of growth are in some sense "revolutionary." As to the specific form and content of the revolution, detailed studies of each individual country seem required.

The process spread, but not everywhere. Large areas of the map—most of Asia, Africa, Latin America—are either blank or ambiguously shaded. But wherever the process did spread—Europe, North America, Australasia, Japan—the countries involved began to experience a dramatic expansion of their GNP and GNP per capita, and also rather extraordinary consequences for their general way of life.

GROWTH TRENDS IN THE UNITED STATES

Later, in chapter 30, we shall examine some of the less fortunate consequences of the modern growth process. For the moment, let us simply sketch out a few of the statistical characteristics of this transformation, using the American economy as an example. The trends we will now describe, though differing in detail from one country to another, are fairly typical of the modern growth process in general.

1. **Population growth.** Figure 16–2 shows the massive increase in American population over the past 170 years, from 5 million or 6 million to 210 million in 1973 and still growing. Population increase was more rapid in the United States than in most of the industrial nations during this period (because of spe-

---

2.   See chapter 28, pp. 658–76, for a more extensive discussion of both the Japanese and Russian experiences.

3.   For Rostow's analysis, see W. W. Rostow, *The Stages of Economic Growth* (London: Cambridge University Press, 1960).

4.   For a major critique of Rostow's work, see Simon Kuznets, "Notes on the Take-off" (paper presented at the September 1960 meeting of the International Economic Association).

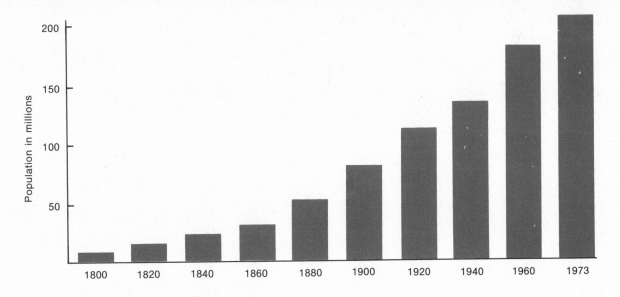

Figure 16–2. United States Population 1800–1973.
Source: Bureau of the Census, U.S. Dept. of Commerce.

cial circumstances, including, of course, heavy immigration from Europe), but an increasing population is a characteristic feature of a growing economy, especially in the earlier stages of growth.

2. Increase in life expectancy. One of the causes of our substantial population increase was a sharp increase in life expectancy during this period, as Table 16–1 shows. In the economically advanced countries, increases in life expectancies have been reflective of the overall growth process in the dual sense that growth brings higher standards of living and material comfort, and that growth has also been accompanied by considerable improvement in our medical technology.

3. Urbanization. The growth process has transformed the United States from a largely rural to a predominantly urban society. Increasing urbanization

TABLE 16–1

INCREASING LIFE EXPECTANCY IN THE UNITED STATES

YEAR	AVERAGE OF MALE AND FEMALE LIFE EXPECTANCIES AT BIRTH, YEARS*
1850	39.4
1878–1882	42.6
1890	43.5
1900–1902	49.24
1909–1911	51.49
1919–1921	56.40
1929–1931	59.20
1939–1941	63.62
1949–1951	68.07
1954	69.6
1967	70.5
1971	71.1

*For years 1850, 1878–1882, and 1890, life expectancies are for Massachusetts only.
Source: Gilboy and Hoover, *Statistical Abstract of the U.S.*, 1973.

TABLE 16–2

URBANIZATION IN THE UNITED STATES

YEAR	PERCENTAGE OF POPULATION IN URBAN AREAS
1800	6.7
1820	7.2
1840	10.8
1860	19.8
1880	28.2
1900	39.7
1920	51.2
1940	56.5
1950	61.0
1960	69.9
1970	73.5

Source: U.S. Statistical Abstract, 1970, 1973.

is a characteristic feature of modern economic growth.

4. Changing occupations. At the beginning of the nineteenth century, the characteristic American worker was a farmer. Over the course of the last century and a half, however, the occupational structure of the American labor force has changed drastically. There has been an enormous decline in the number of farm families and farm workers. This has been accompanied by a substantial rise in the percentage of the labor force in manufacturing and construction, and an even more dramatic increase in the percentage of the labor force in the professions, commerce and finance, government service, and other so-called service occupations. Within industry as a whole there has been a strong movement toward "white-collar" positions, as shown in Figure 16–3.

5. More leisure time. The standard workweek has been falling steadily over the past century. In the 1870s, the average was about sixty-seven hours per week. By 1920, it had fallen to forty-six hours; by 1973, to 37 hours. Individuals enter the work force later now and, with increasing life expectancies, they also have more leisure after retirement.

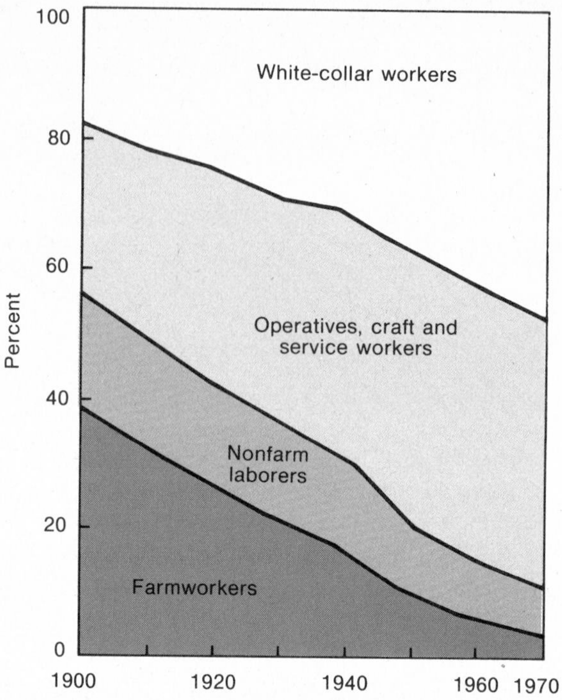

Figure 16–3. Changing Composition of the Labor Force, 1900–1970.
Source: U.S. Department of Labor and U.S. Department of Commerce.

TABLE 16–3

INCREASING EDUCATION IN THE UNITED STATES

PERCENTAGES OF AGE-GROUPS ENROLLED IN SCHOOL

AGE-GROUP	1950	1960	1972
16–17	71.3	82.5	88.9
18–19	29.4	38.4	46.3
20–24	9.0	13.1	21.6

Source: U.S. Statistical Abstract, 1970.

6. Increasing education. Today the average American—man or woman—has far more formal education than most people had in 1900. The number of years of schooling per member of the population over fourteen and per member of the labor force both increased by roughly 40 percent between 1900 and

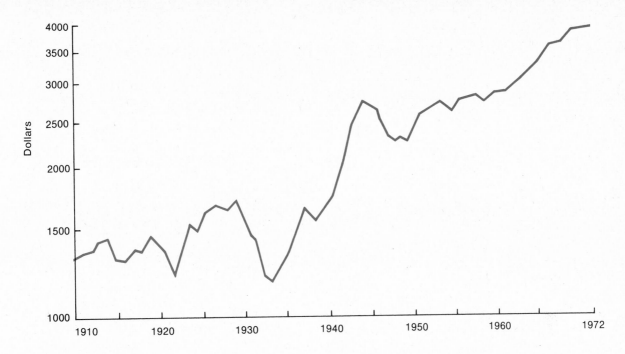

Figure 16–4. Growth in U.S. Per Capita GNP (in "constant" 1958 prices).

Over the past sixty-two years, per capita output in the United States has increased by over 190 percent.
Source: Department of Commerce.

the present time. Around 1900, only about 7 percent of all children attended college. By the late 1940s the figure had already risen to approximately 20 percent, and it has doubled since. Table 16–3 shows how rapidly the percentages of young men and women enrolled in school has increased in the past two decades.

7. Growth in output per capita. Finally, we come to the trend in output per capita itself. Professor Raymond Goldsmith has estimated the growth of U.S. GNP per capita from 1839 to 1959 as measured in "constant 1929 prices." His calculations show that, over this century and more, output per capita was increasing by the healthy rate of 1.64 percent per year. Figure 16–4, based on Department of Commerce estimates, tells the same general story in terms of 1958 prices. From 1910 to 1972 per capita GNP in the United States rose by 191 percent.

Are these rapid rates? By present-day American and European standards they are nothing very remarkable. But by any past historical standard—that is, prior to the industrial revolution—they are very extraordinary rates indeed. To see this, all one has to do is to get out a compound interest table and observe that a 1.64 percent annual increase implies a fivefold increase every 100 years. The present level of family income in the United States is more than $10,000 a year. If we actually succeed in continuing at a 1.64 percent annual expansion for the next century, then in 2070 the average family income in the United States would be $50,000, and this in terms of *today's prices and purchasing power*. It is this extraordinary multiplicative power of apparently modest annual increases in output per capita that makes it clear that modern economic growth is a fairly recent historical phenomenon. Had it been going on long at these rates, we would be far richer than we are now.

This, then, is the story of modern growth as exemplified in the American experience. We live longer now, we are a much bigger nation, we live in cities instead of on the farm, we work at manufacturing and the professions rather than agriculture, we are much better educated, we enjoy an increased productive power that dwarfs anything in past history, and at the same time our leisure has been significantly increased. And all this is directly attributable to, or is in large part a reflection of, the phenomenon of modern economic growth. This is not to say that we are happier now—the affluent society also has very deep problems—nor is it clear that this phenomenon can long continue, for the resource and ecological costs of modern growth are high. But, without question, it does mean that our entire way of life has been transformed in what, historically speaking, is a very short period of time.

MAJOR FACTORS IN MODERN GROWTH

As we know, the growth process technically involves a continual shifting outward of our production-possibility curve. In year one, we have to choose between various determinate amounts of, say, food and steel. In year two, we can have more of both commodities; in year three, still more. A possible path of choices is indicated in Figure 16–5, where our hypothetical society is seen to be choosing relatively more steel and relatively less food as it becomes richer. This reflects the relative shift toward industry and away from agriculture that we observe in all economically advancing societies.

But the matter is a bit more complicated than this, because some of the choices we make today may affect the rate at which the production-possibility curve shifts outward. If we consume all our income today in the form of luxuries and "riotous living," then we shall not be accumulating additional productive capacity for tomorrow. If instead of consuming

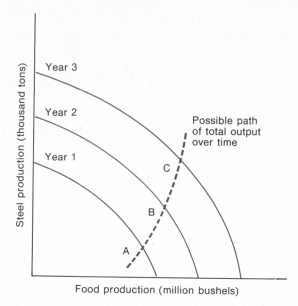

Figure 16–5.

Growth shifts the production-possibility curve outward. A society may follow the path indicated by line *ABC*. Food production is increasing absolutely, but steel production is increasing much more rapidly.

champagne and caviar we use part of our output to build a factory, we shall have a higher potential output next year. If instead of spending our nights dancing, we study how to become engineers, we shall be more productive workers next year. As a consequence of such choices, our production-possibility curve will shift outward more rapidly, meaning that we may have more consumption (champagne and caviar) and more leisure (for dancing) in the future.

This brings us then to the question of the *causes* of modern economic growth. This question is a very large one, because growth is such a pervasive phenomenon that virtually no aspect of our social organization is irrelevant to it. For example, one can readily see that a society's political structure may have a decided impact on its rate of growth. We have already noted (chapter 3) that command-type or near-command economics might accumulate capital at a more rapid rate than a more consumer-oriented market economy. Even in a pure market economy there is an underlying assumption that the State is strong enough to guarantee the rights of property and the orderly administration of justice. However, in many societies, past and present, such an assumption is unjustified: property is destroyed, lawlessness is unchecked, civil strife is the order of the day. In such a society, it may be necessary to build up the political preconditions for stability before modern economic growth can even begin.

Faced with such a wide range of influences, economists tend to be selective. Roughly speaking, they try to analyze growth in terms of increases in factor inputs (notably, the labor force and the stock of capital) and increases in output per unit of input (especially technological change). Now the relationship of factor inputs to production will be a major concern of Part Three of this book, and thus a more detailed analysis of growth must await the development of these theoretical tools. Even now, however, we can shed a good deal of light on the American growth record by making some comments about our specific historical experience in the areas of population growth, capital accumulation, and technological progress.[5]

ACCOUNTING FOR AMERICAN GROWTH

The American growth experience has been characterized by rapid increases both in factor inputs and in output per unit of input.

Population Growth

The main immediate cause of the growth of the American labor force, of course, has been our large growth in population, as charted in Figure 16–2. The deeper question might be put as follows: How did

5.   The following account draws partly on chapter 4 of my *Economic Development: Past and Present*, 3rd ed. (Englewood Cliffs, N.J.: Prentice-Hall, 1973).

a country that experienced such a very rapid rate of population growth manage to escape the Malthusian fate, as described in chapter 6? Why didn't the famous law of diminishing returns keep output per capita and wage rates at or near the level of subsistence?

The answer, as might be imagined, has several parts. In the first place, it is clear that population growth did not take place in the context of anything like "fixed" natural resources as the British classical writers usually hypothesized. The century following the American Revolution saw a vast expansion of United States territorial boundaries. The Louisiana Purchase in 1803 virtually doubled the country's land area—and at a cost of less than $12 million. Before the Civil War a further series of acquisitions, cessions, and purchases added well over a million square miles to the nation's land. Overall, between 1800 and 1860, the United States expanded more than three times geographically, with the consequence that, despite the rapid rate of population growth, the number of persons per square mile rose by the relatively slight margin of from 6.1 to 10.6 over a sixty-year span. Indeed, throughout the nineteenth century, we remained essentially a sparsely settled country.

Second, although our population growth was rapid, it by no means reached the rates that a thoroughgoing Malthusian would have anticipated. This was because, despite the fall in the death rate and substantial immigration, the birth rate in the United States did not react in Malthusian fashion. Very high in the early 1800s, the American birth rate was on the decline for the remainder of the century. Beginning long before the Civil War and continuing until the end of the nineteenth century, there was a trend in America both toward later marriages and smaller families.

Such a trend has in fact been characteristic of all the nations that have industrialized. Why would industrialization tend to lower a country's birth rate? Some of the reasons are: (1) urban living is less conducive to child-rearing than rural living; (2) industrial development means that women have job and career opportunities that they may prefer to their traditional roles as mothers and homemakers; (3) a rising standard of living may make parents want educational and other advantages for their children that can be better secured with smaller families; (4) the fact that economic development tends to bring lower infant mortality rates means that parents need have fewer children to achieve a family of any given size; and (5) an economically advanced and educationally sophisticated society is aware of the ecological costs of an ever-increasing population (hence the popularity of "zero population growth" in present-day America).

Now the experience of the United States in this regard has not been absolutely uniform. We all know, for example, that there was a sharp *rise* in the American birthrate in the 1940s, producing the much publicized "baby boom" of the postwar period. However, birthrates began declining again in the late 1950s and in the early 1970s the decline was quite sharp. It seems reasonable to regard this phenomenon as a fairly predictable response to the growth process.[6]

Thus, the United States was able to escape the effects of diminishing returns partly because of its large and increasing land resources and partly because of the less-than-maximum rate of population growth with which it had to cope.

This means that other favorable factors—those that would tend to *raise* the level of output per capita—had ample time to achieve their effects.

Capital Accumulation

One of the favorable factors, clearly, was capital accumulation. Since the early days of the republic, there have been vast additions to the American stock of capital. Raymond Goldsmith estimates that the stock of wealth as a whole rose from a little over $1 billion in 1805 to something over $400 billion in 1948.[7] This increase far exceeded the growth of American population and labor force. In the period from 1879 to 1944, for example, the capital-to-labor ratio in the United States nearly tripled.[8] The average American worker, whether in industry or on the farm, has had increasingly more machinery, tools, equipment, buildings, and power to work with. At the same time, the housewife has come to be assisted by an impressive array of devices and mechanical appliances. Over this period, "produced means of production" have been systematically taking over and amplifying the labors of man.

The sources of the great expansion of the American stock of capital have been many. Some of it, particularly in the early stages, was foreign capital. In the 1860s and 1870s, probably half the capital invested in American railroads was foreign. Overall, the United

---

6. A general theory of the response of population growth to economic development has been put forward under the title: "the theory of demographic transition." This theory predicts first an increase and then a decrease in the rate of population growth as a country's standard of living improves. At the beginning, when the country is very poor, population growth is slow because, although the birthrate is high, so also is the death rate. When development begins, the first effect is to lower the death rate. (The birthrate, being more influenced by social and cultural factors, tends to change more slowly.) Thus, with a high birthrate and a falling death rate, population growth increases. At this point, however, the effects of industrialization and urbanization on the birthrate come into play. Birthrates begin to fall. This brings a slowing-down of the rate of population increase. Finally, we have both low birthrates and low death rates. Under these circumstances population growth will be fairly slow again, and possibly even zero or less.

Does such a theory hold out hopes that today's underdeveloped countries may eventually escape the population problem? Yes, some hope, but not too much. The reason is that population growth in many of these countries is rapid even *in advance of* any substantial economic development. It is extremely difficult to get the whole process off the ground (see pp. 131–35 and pp. 752–55).

7. Real reproducible wealth, including consumers durables and government wealth, but excluding military capital (in constant 1929 dollars). Raymond Goldsmith, "The Growth of Reproducible Wealth in the U.S.A. from 1805 to 1950," *Income and Wealth,* series II (Cambridge, Bowes and Bowes, 1952).

8. Simon Kuznets, "Long Term Changes in the National Product of the United States of America Since 1870," *Income and Wealth,* series II.

States was an importer of capital throughout the nineteenth century.

Some of it was mobilized with the assistance of various agencies of the federal, state, and local governments. It was New York State that engineered the construction of the famous Erie Canal. The 9,000-mile southern railway network of 1860 cost $245 million to construct and, of this, more than 60 percent of the financial capital was furnished by public authorities. In countless instances, the government has stepped in either directly or indirectly to provide the means whereby capital could be accumulated for important public needs.

Nevertheless, over this historical span as a whole, it is clear that the primary sources of American capital accumulation were found within the domestic economy and were in the hands of private individuals and institutions. Through direct investment, or through the complex mechanisms of securities markets, banks, and financial intermediaries, individual savings have found their way to private businesses that could use them to expand their physical plants and equipment. Moreover, businesses, farms, and corporations have regularly set aside part of their profits for reinvestment purposes. Such a pattern of "internal financing" has, indeed, increasingly become the dominant form of industrial and capital formation in the United States. In the modern American corporation, internal funds—retained profits and depreciation allowances—now ordinarily provide more than half of corporate expenditures on gross investment.

These private, domestic sources of capital accumulation, in turn, can be looked on as largely a reflection of the growth of the American economy. Because this year's output has regularly been greater than last year's, it has been possible for Americans to increase their savings and investment without having thereby to cut into their previous levels of consumption. By the same token, businesses and corporations have found in their own expansion the source of surpluses that could be used for further expansion. Growing production, therefore, has made possible a growing absolute volume of investment over the course of American development.[9]

Technological Progress

Both population growth and capital accumulation involve increases in the supplies of our factors of production; by contrast, technological progress is concerned with the new and different ways in which we utilize our basic factors of production. Briefly,

We attribute to technological progress in the broadest sense those increases in output that cannot be accounted for by the increase in our inputs alone. Technological progress involves new knowledge and the application of this new knowledge to economically useful ends. It may occur through the development of new kinds of machinery, an increase in the skills of the labor force, a reorganization of the productive process, or through the development of products previously unknown. In any case, the emphasis is on doing things in new and different ways as compared to times past.

Technological progress, in this broad sense, has been a characteristic feature of the growth process since the British Industrial Revolution. From the spinning jenny and steam engine of the eighteenth century to electric power, synthetics, atomic energy, and computer technology in our own, there has been a virtually unbroken line of major innovations in our methods of production.

In recent years, economists have been attempting to separate the effects of technological progress on growth from the effects caused by the increases in

---

9. The adjective "absolute" is necessary here because it does not seem to be the case that the *percentage* of national output saved and invested has been rising over the years. In the past half-century, at least, this percentage has remained constant or possibly declined. See, for example: L. R. Klein and R. F. Kosobud, "Some Econometrics of Growth: Great Ratios of Economics," *Quarterly Journal of Economics,* vol. 75, no. 2 (May 1961). In short, American *consumption* of goods and services has been rising as rapidly (and possibly even more rapidly) during this period as the level of national output itself.

factor inputs (labor and capital). In practice, this is very difficult to do. For one thing, new techniques of production may become effective only when they are embodied in new productive capacity. To develop the technology of the railroad is one thing; to make railroads economically effective is something else again, requiring large investments of capital. In general, the expansion of our capital stock and the expansion of our technological knowledge have gone hand-in-hand, and difficult interpretive problems arise when one tries to separate them. For another thing, there are some "investments" that are intended precisely to expand the technological know-how of the society and the ability of the society to absorb technological advance. Consider education, for example. If individuals or firms devote time and money to education or research, they are making an investment that may lead to the development of new technology or to an increased ability to operate the new technologies as they come into being. This process is very similar to ordinary capital accumulation, except that we are dealing not with physical capital but with what we might call "intangible" capital. We are saving and investing not in new machines, but in new knowledge. Again, the borderline between capital accumulation and technological progress may become blurred.

These points are well worth keeping in mind, because they are important qualifications to a general conclusion of some significance that economists have developed in recent years. The conclusion is this: If we try to evaluate the relative effects of technological progress and capital accumulation on the rise in output per capita in the American economy, we find that over the past fifty years technological progress has been the more important factor. Some estimates are that technological progress may account for as much as 75 to 80 percent of the rise in our output per capita, leaving only 20 to 25 percent or so to be explained by the fact that each worker has more capital to work with.

Now this hypothesis—and it is no more than that because of the great difficulties of isolating and measuring "technological progress"—probably applies less well to American growth during the nineteenth century, when the expansion of factor inputs (labor, land, and capital) was doubtless more important in growth.[10] Even modified, however, the hypothesis still has interesting implications. In particular, it suggests that the growth process must be understood as a continuing development into new areas as well as a simple quantitative expansion of what we already have. And this makes sense intuitively. Consider the products we buy today. How many of them were in existence or even had equivalents a hundred years ago? Not the automobile, telephone, television, household appliances, electric lights, synthetics, or plastics. And this is quite apart from the technological progress involved in finding new methods for producing "old" products. Think of the agricultural revolution in this country over the past century. Today, 5 percent of our population not only feeds us but sustains exports to the outside world. Growth, in other words, is not just more tools or more people to use the tools; it is new products, new methods, new approaches—nothing less than a continuing refashioning of our day-to-day lives.[11]

GROWTH AND AGGREGATE DEMAND

The bulk of the discussion in this chapter so far has been concerned with growth in terms of *potential* output. We have looked at population growth, capital accumulation, and technological change from the "supply" side. But Part Two has been especially concerned with the relationship of aggregate demand to our productive capacity. In growth terms, this question appears as follows: How can we be sure that aggregate demand will *grow* in such a way as

---

10. See Abramovitz, M., and David, P. A., "Reinterpreting Economic Growth: Parables and Realities," *The American Economic Review*, LXIII, no. 2 (May 1973).

11. In this brief explanation of American growth, we have not mentioned one element that was probably quite important historically: *economies of scale.* The growth in size of the country and the development (especially with the aid of the railroads) of a large "national market" undoubtedly had favorable effects on per capita productivity, especially in the nineteenth century. We shall take up the concept of scale economies, pp. 461–62.

to balance aggregate supply at something like a full employment level?

We have, in other words, certain factors that make for a more or less rapid growth of potential output. How do we know whether aggregate demand will be able to keep pace with this growth on the supply side? Will we have approximately full employment over time, or occasional depressions, or—as Marx predicted—ever worsening crises? These are very complicated questions, and economists have often differed about the correct answers to them.

The Stagnationists

In the 1940s, for example, there developed a school of economists called the *stagnationists*. These economists, led by the distinguished Keynesian Alvin Hansen, argued that there might be a persistent tendency for aggregate supply to outgrow aggregate demand over time. They argued that the nineteenth-century experience of the United States—during which time fairly full employment was not uncommon—was actually caused by a set of special, favorable conditions. In particular, they noted such factors as the expansion of the country, the rapid growth in population with its needs for more building and construction, the exploitation of the Western frontier, and the introduction of capital-intensive innovations like the railroads—all these factors had conspired to keep investment demand very high. Thus, more often than not, economic conditions were buoyant and employment was reasonably good.

They then pointed out, however, that most of these conditions had ceased in the twentieth century. The frontier had been exhausted, population growth was slowing down, new innovations were less capital-intensive than the railroads, and so on. They feared a persistent tendency of investment demand to fall short of savings and hence a tendency to deepening depressions, or economic "stagnation."

As it turned out, the postwar economy of the United States was far more buoyant than the stagnationists had anticipated, and it is reasonable to say that these theorists had been unduly influenced by

the Great Depression of the 1930s. Still, their theory was important, because it suggested that Keynesian-type problems might occur not only in the short run but as persistent difficulties in the growth of an economy over time. The gap between actual and potential output might not narrow in the long run; it might get increasingly larger and more difficult to handle.

The Harrod-Domar Model

The problem of aggregate supply and demand in the long run is complicated by the dual role of investment that we have mentioned before. Investment is demand-creating—via the multiplier, but it is also supply-creating—by adding to our productive capacity. How do we know which aspect will be more important over the long run?

This problem led, in the period after Keynes' *General Theory,* to a number of attempts to make that theory dynamic; i.e., to enable us to predict not only national income in a particular period but also its path of change over time. An example of this kind of approach is what is usually called the Harrod-Domar model. This theory, with somewhat different features, was developed independently by Sir Roy Harrod of England and Evsey Domar of Johns Hopkins and later M.I.T.[12] In its simplest form, the theory involves the careful examination of the following equation, in which Y stands for annual national income (or output), ΔY for a year's increase in national income, I for annual investment, and S for annual savings:

$$\frac{\Delta Y}{Y} = \frac{\Delta Y}{I} \times \frac{S}{Y}$$

If we make certain assumptions, it is possible to use this equation to show some of the difficulties of keeping aggregate supply and demand in proper balance in a growing economy. Taking the terms in

12. See R. F. Harrod, *Towards a Dynamic Economics* (London: Macmillan & Co., 1949; and Evsey D. Domar, "A Theoretical Analysis of Economic Growth," in his *Essays in the Theory of Economic Growth* (New York: Oxford University Press, 1957).

reverse order, let us suppose that the fraction of income people wish to save is some fixed number, say, one-tenth. This is not too unreasonable an assumption. Although in the short run the marginal propensity to save might be expected to rise with income, this may not be the case at all in the long run, as people have time to adjust their living standards to higher levels of income.

Let us further suppose that the amount of machinery and other capital goods used to produce a given level of output is more or less fixed. This is clearly a questionable assumption and is one of the reasons why the Harrod-Domar type models can be regarded only as a beginning in this difficult area. If, however, we do make this simplifying assumption, then we can argue that the term $\Delta Y/I$, which represents the *increase in income* in a year divided by the *increase in the stock of capital* (i.e., investment) in a year, will be some determinate number—say, 1/3. Or to put it another way, businessmen who expand their plants and equipment by $3 will have the capacity for producing $1 a year more output than before. Like our figure for savings, 1/3 is an "in the ball park figure" for this *output/capital ratio* in a modern economy.[13]

Now from these first two ratios, we are able to determine a "rate of growth" for this economy. In equilibrium, the amount that households want to save will have to be equal to the amount that businessmen want to invest, or, $S = I$. Hence, it will be true that:

$$\frac{S}{Y} \cdot \frac{\Delta Y}{I} = \frac{\not{I}}{Y} \cdot \frac{\Delta Y}{\not{I}} = \frac{\Delta Y}{Y}$$

$\Delta Y/Y$, being the increase in output divided by the level of output, is the rate of growth of this economy. In our example, it will be equal to 1/30, or 3.3 percent:

$$\frac{\Delta Y}{Y} = \frac{\Delta Y}{I} \cdot \frac{S}{Y} = \left(\frac{1}{3}\right)\left(\frac{1}{10}\right) = \left(\frac{1}{30}\right) = 3.3\%$$

---

13. The reader may recognize the accelerator principle of chapter 10 (pp. 234–35) in this analysis. If the output-capital ratio is fixed, then investment (an increase in capital) will be required only to sustain increases in income (ΔY).

But this seems rather strange. We have apparently determined a rate of growth for our economy—3.3 percent annually—but we have said nothing about major factors that might influence the growth of productive potential; e.g., population growth or technological progress. Suppose that these factors on the supply side can generate a growth of output of only 2 percent per year? Or suppose they can generate a very high rate of growth of 6 or 7 percent per year? How do *these* numbers relate to the 3.3 percent rate of growth that we have just determined?

And, indeed, it is this problem that the Harrod-Domar and similar theories see as a major one for a growing economy. The growth rate that keeps investment and savings happily in balance (sometimes called the *equilibrium* or *warranted* rate of growth) may be quite different from the rate of growth that fundamental supply conditions permit (sometimes called the *natural* rate of growth). In this theory, there really is no guarantee at all that aggregate supply and aggregate demand will grow in harmony over time. On the contrary, the system is forever poised toward runaway inflations or depressions.

GROWTH AND PUBLIC POLICY

The trouble with both the stagnationist theory and the Harrod-Domar type of theories is that they paint a rather worse picture of things than actual American experience would justify. We have had depressions, but these have not been getting worse, as the stagnationists feared, nor is the system as wildly unstable as the Harrod-Domar theories might lead one to predict.

Consequently, economists have tried to develop somewhat more flexible theories than the examples we have cited.[14] And they have also inspected ways in which governmental fiscal, monetary, and other policies might profitably be adjusted when the growth of the economy is being taken explicitly into account. For the fact is that governmental policies—even those

---

14. See, for example, Robert M. Solow, "A Contribution to the Theory of Economic Growth," *Quarterly Journal of Economics,* 70 (February 1956).

with short-run objectives—may have substantial effects on the growth rate of the economy. If a high rate of growth is a major goal of the economy (and it may *not* be—see pp. 705–707), then the following generalizations offer at least some guidance to the policy-maker:

1. Full-employment policies will also usually be growth-promoting policies. Throughout Part Two, we have been discussing various ways in which the government can contribute to full employment in the economy. Insofar as these policies are successful in bringing the economy closer to its full-employment potential, they will have some favorable effect on growth. They will do this in the short run by speeding up the rate of growth as the economy moves from a below-full-employment to a near-full-employment level of output, and in the longer run by the presumably larger amount of investment that will occur at the higher levels of national output.

2. Fiscal and monetary policies to secure full employment can also be specifically adapted to growth promotion. The point is that there is not simply one, but a variety of different fiscal and monetary policies to raise the level of aggregate demand and that, among these various alternatives, the nation can try to select measures that will be most favorable to future growth. Fundamentally, there are two approaches that may be used to achieve this end:

(a) Follow a relatively expansionary monetary policy ("easy money"), to encourage as much business investment as possible, and if this threatens to create too much aggregate demand, follow a relatively contractionary fiscal policy.

(b) Select the instruments of fiscal policy so that the burdens fall more heavily on consumption while, simultaneously, attempts are being made to stimulate investment activity.

In other words, keep interest rates low, and if it is necessary to increase taxes (to prevent inflation from developing), make sure that the tax burdens fall as much as possible on the consumer and as little as possible on investment.

Now the real problem with these policies is that they may conflict with other economic objectives. The greatest single conflict, as we know, is that between full employment and price stability. Although the policies we have just discussed may harmonize full-employment and growth objectives, they do nothing in themselves to reduce the full-employment–price-stability conflict.

But there are other possible conflicts, too. We have suggested selecting taxes that fall heavily on consumption and lightly on investment. But such taxes are likely to increase rather than decrease the inequality of income distribution in our society. If growth and equality conflict, which will the average citizen choose? Who is to decide which is preferable?

Moreover, the balance of payments can be added complication. In the early 1970s, with the extensive deficits in the U.S. balance of payments, a policy-maker might have preferred relatively high interest rates that would attract international capital to this country. A good balance-of-payments-plus-full-employment policy would have consisted of high interest rates with a relatively expansive fiscal policy to counteract the contractionary impact of tight money.

What this means is that there are limits to the degree that we can use full-employment monetary and fiscal policies as a specific stimulant to economic growth. However, there is at least some flexibility in this area: and if a government continually has its eye on the goal of growth, in the long run it will doubtless produce a more rapidly growing economy than would otherwise be the case. This general conclusion is very much strengthened, moreover, when we come to our third point.

3. Technological progress can be strengthened by giving greater emphasis to education and research. We know from our earlier discussion that technological change has been a major factor in American economic growth, especially in recent decades. We also know that such change involves new methods of production, new products, new skills in the labor force, new managerial talents, and so on. The most direct ways of encouraging this process are through increased basic and applied scientific research (the wellspring of technological progress) and through the increased education and training of our citizens (contributing both to the creation of new knowledge and to the introduction of new techniques into actual practice).[15] That increased attention to education and allied fields is likely to promote a continuing high rate of growth (if that is our objective), there should be little doubt.

SUMMARY

In this chapter, we have presented our first extensive treatment of the subject of *modern economic growth*. We have given an historical and descriptive account of the growth process, and also shown how long-run and short-run macroeconomics are interrelated.

Modern economic growth can be said to have begun with the English Industrial Revolution of the late eighteenth century, the beginnings being characterized by rapid technological change, increased capital accumulation and the growth of the factory system, and profound consequences (by no means all favorable) on the status of different social and economic classes. The result was that output began to grow so rapidly that, even with an increased growth of population, output per capita in Britain began to rise significantly.

This growth process spread to many other countries in the following century and a half. In the United States, as in most other countries, the process involved rapid population growth, increased life expectancies, urbanization, changing occupational structures, more leisure time, increased education for all classes of society, and, above all, rapid rates of growth of GNP and GNP per capita. (The environmental and other costs of this process will be discussed in chapter 30.)

Economists account for this growth in terms of increased factor inputs (especially labor and capital)

and increased output per unit of input (especially technological progress). In the case of the United States, although our population growth was rapid, it did not reach Malthusian proportions, because of declining birthrates as industrialization proceeded. Also, abundant and newly acquired land enabled this country to escape the harsher effects of the law of diminishing returns. All of this meant that other factors that increased output per capita—massive capital accumulation and rapid technological change—had ample time to achieve their effects. In most studies, it appears that technological change has had a special importance in accounting for the sustained increase in American output per capita over the past fifty years.

The analysis of growth must include, beside these elements on the supply side, an indication of how aggregate demand can be expected to grow over time. It is here that the Keynesian-type analysis of the earlier chapters of Part Two has a bearing on economic growth. Will aggregate demand keep up with aggregate supply over time so that actual and potential output will be fairly close? Or will it grow too slowly or too rapidly?

Various theories have been presented to explain the growth of aggregate demand and supply over time, such as the *stagnationist* theory of the 1940s or the *Harrod-Domar* model. In this latter theory, we see some of the characteristic problems of relating long-run and short-run macroeconomics. Investment, in the short run, creates aggregate demand through the multiplier; in the long run, it adds to our productive capacity and hence to the growth of aggregate supply. Will the rate of growth that keeps investment and savings decisions in harmony also be the rate of growth that basic long-run factors such as population growth and technological change determine? Harrod and Domar were pessimistic on this point, though other models show somewhat more flexibility.

Also, of course, it is possible to influence the growth rate through governmental policies. If it is the objective of a government to increase the country's rate of growth, it will usually find (1) that full employ-

---

15. Professor Francis Shieh of Prince George's Community College has pointed out to me the importance of the recent great expansion of community colleges in this connection.

ment policies are also growth-promoting; (2) that, among the fiscal and monetary policies used to promote full employment, some will be more growth-promoting than others; and (3) that expenditures on education, training, and research are likely to yield important growth dividends.

IMPORTANT TERMS TO REMEMBER

English Industrial Revolution
Modern Economic Growth
Urbanization
Service Occupations
Life Expectancies
Population Growth: Birth Rates/Death Rates
Produced Means of Production
Internal Financing of Investment
Increases in Output per Unit of Input
Stagnationist Theory
Harrod/Domar Model
Output/Capital Ratio

QUESTIONS FOR DISCUSSION

1. Define *modern economic growth*. Indicate some of the changes in the structure of a society that usually accompany the growth process.

2. It has been said that because the English Industrial Revolution was largely self-generated, it was somewhat more gradual than similar industrial revolutions in other countries, where many of the changes were "imported" from abroad. Why might this be the case? What implications do you see in this for the modern underdeveloped country of today?

3. In the early twentieth century, the Austrian-American economist Joseph Schumpeter gave a central role to *innovation*—the introduction of new methods of production and new products into the economy—in the growth process. How has modern analysis tended to verify Schumpeter's basic intuition? Schumpeter also characterized the growth process as one of "creative destruction." Does this term seem apt to you?

4. "The problem with short-run national income analysis is that it focuses completely on the demand-creating side of investment and neglects the capacity-creating side." Discuss.

5. Suppose we are in an economy in which "natural" factors (e.g., population growth and technological progress) make for rather slow growth, but in which people want to save a very high proportion of their income. Why might this situation make for trouble in a Harrod-Domar type world? (Hint: Use the Harrod-Domar equation,

$$\frac{\Delta Y}{Y} = \left(\frac{\Delta Y}{I}\right)\left(\frac{S}{Y}\right)$$

and show that if $\Delta Y/Y$ is low and S/Y is high, then businessmen will tend to find that they have more additional capital (I) than the extra output they are producing (ΔY) justifies. Explain why this might lead to a general contraction of output and employment.)

6. Show how a government that wished to promote economic growth might select certain policies above others when it was attempting to achieve short-run full employment.

SUGGESTED READING

Deane, Phyllis. *The First Industrial Revolution.* London: Cambridge University Press, 1965.

Denison, Edward F. *Sources of Economic Growth in the United States.* Committee for Economic Development, Supplementary Paper No. 13, January 1962.

Mansfield, Edwin. *Technological Change.* New York: W. W. Norton & Co., 1971.

North, Douglass C. *Growth and Welfare in the American Past: A New Economic History.* Englewood Cliffs, N.J.: Prentice-Hall, 1966.

Rostow, W. W. *The Stages of Economic Growth.* London: Cambridge University Press, 1960.

PART 3

MICROECONOMICS: ANALYSIS AND PROBLEMS

In Part Three, we temporarily leave the world of macroeconomics and enter that of *micro*economics—that part of economics concerned with the interrelationship of the individual business firms, industries, consumers, laborers, and other factors of production that make up a modern economy. (In our final section, Part Four, we shall be taking up a number of problems that feature significant macro- *and* micro- elements.)

Part Three A is mostly analytical. In particular it is a detailed analysis of the workings of a purely competitive economy (or what, in chapter 2, we sometimes called a pure market economy). In this economy, it is assumed that business firms, households, and the owners of factors of production are all price-takers. That is to say, each unit is too small to have any significant effect on the price of the product or service it buys or sells. This analysis will be designed to bring out certain overarching economic concepts, particularly *interdependence* and *efficiency.*

Part Three B will involve an application and modification of these tools for various real-life industrial situations, especially including a consideration of the problems—both in terms of analysis and public policy—involved when there are other than purely competitive structures in business and labor markets.

PART 3A

ANALYSIS OF THE PURELY COMPETITIVE ECONOMY

CHAPTER 17

PRICES AND COMPETITION: AN OVERVIEW

Léon Walras, a great late nineteenth-century economic theorist, once wrote: ''Pure economics is, in essence, the theory of the determination of prices under a hypothetical regime of perfectly free competition.'' This statement indicates the absolutely central place that the analysis of the purely competitive economy has held in the history of our subject.

For the modern student, however, some further justification is needed. Why give a special place to the analysis of pure competition, when it is only one of a variety of possible market structures and when, in the age of the great corporation and big labor union, it is not necessarily the most typical or influential?

We have given our answer before—that the tools we develop in this field can be applied to other market structures, that the analysis of pure competition allows us to show the overall coherence of an economic system and to bring out certain social welfare criteria—but seeing (not simply hearing about) is believing. In this chapter, therefore, we shall underline two of the central concepts that derive from the analysis of competitive markets: the notions of economic *interdependence* and economic *efficiency*.

These concepts will be our guiding themes throughout Part Three A.

First, however, let us define the area of microeconomics in a more practical way.

MICROECONOMICS AND THE ENERGY CRISIS

In 1973 and 1974, the United States and most other industrial nations experienced a sharp example of microeconomics in action: the energy crisis. Although the crisis had (and still has) important *macro*economic dimensions[1], it also provided object lessons in the role of particular prices in a modern economy and in the interrelationship of the component parts of such an economy. These interrelationships are at the heart of microeconomic analysis.

---

1. Because oil plays such a large role in a modern economy, any basic change in conditions of oil supply would be bound to have large general—or *macro*—consequences. We have already noted the importance of the rising price of oil for our recent inflation (p. 347) and for our future balance of payments prospects. Later on, in Great Debate Six (pp. 791–817), we will consider both macro- and micro-aspects of the world energy situation.

Basically, the situation at the time of the Arab oil embargo in 1973 was an American demand for oil in excess of the supply then available at previously prevailing prices. Now this situation simultaneously created pressures and opportunities on a variety of fronts. Aside from the obvious political aspects of the case, we can say that this initial shortage could be expected to have an important impact on the role of oil in the economy in four different ways.

1. *The price of oil would tend to rise.* And, of course, it did, adding greatly to general inflationary pressures in the American economy. The *microeconomic* question is slightly different, however. Here we would stress that the *relative* price of oil would tend to rise. Gasoline would tend to become more expensive as compared to cotton textiles. Heating oil would become more expensive as compared to household furniture. Furthermore, products that require a great deal of petroleum in their manufacture, such as fertilizers, would also become relatively more expensive.

2. *The rise in price would tend, at least in the long run, to increase the quantity of oil being produced.* What effect the rise in price would have on incentives to produce more oil was much debated in the United States in 1973 and 1974; Senator Henry M. Jackson and the *Wall Street Journal* engaged in a running controversy on the matter. The *Journal's* position was that the market could determine the best price from the point of view of supply incentives. Senator Jackson's position was that higher oil prices did have some effect on future supplies but that "for the probable duration of the present acute shortage . . . supply is not very responsive to price, and prices higher than the long-term supply price play no useful economic function."[2] Jackson, in other words, accepted the general proposition that higher prices would bring forth more supply, but felt that this was true only up to a point. He believed that this point had already been passed and that a rollback in oil prices was thus desirable. The debate involved the *degree* of the impact of higher

prices on supply, not the existence and general direction of this impact.

3. *Higher oil prices would tend, at least in the short run, to increase the profits of oil producers (whether private companies or nations).* The great rise in oil company profits in late 1973 and early 1974 was, of course, an important reason for the Jackson-*Journal* debate. Indeed, the question of the effects of oil prices on supply was to a great degree a question of the impact of higher oil *profits* on supply. Would the companies use their increased revenues to expand exploration for oil, to undertake previously marginal methods of producing oil, and so on? The point here is that the distribution of income in our society was altered during the energy crunch: Producers of oil benefited more than other producers and consumers in the economy.

4. *The higher prices would tend to encourage businessmen to use less oil in their productive operations.* Actually, the society could economize on the use of higher-priced oil in two ways. First, it could substitute other fuels or machines or labor for oil products wherever substitution is technically feasible. Second, it could consume less of those products that require much oil in their making and more of those products that require little or no oil. The price system, in other words, reacts to the initial shortage not only by spurring efforts to produce more of the product in short supply (through higher prices and profits) but also by tending to curtail demand (through encouraging the use of substitutes in both the production and consumption of the product).

An indication of the way in which higher-priced oil can influence the economy is suggested by the following reading from *Fortune.* The interdependence of the various sectors of the economy is brought out very practically here. With higher oil prices, for example, the production of alcoholic beverages is likely to increase more rapidly over the next few years than was previously expected. In contrast, the production of farm machinery and knitted goods will increase much less rapidly than previously expected. The basic reason: Some commodities tend to consume more or less oil in their production.

---

2. Senator Henry M. Jackson, "Rolling Back Oil Prices," *The Wall Street Journal,* March 13, 1974, p. 12.

Impact of Oil Price Increases on Various Industries

Sanford Rose

INDUSTRIES THAT WILL BE HELPED

Assessing the impact of oil-price increases on the sales of various industries has become a favorite pastime of economists lately. The charts below, which are based on data prepared especially for *Fortune* by Chase Econometrics, Inc., a subsidiary of the

Chase Manhattan Bank, show a few of the "winners"—industries expected to benefit from the higher prices. The blue portion of the bars is proportional to the extent of the gain expected. (For a look at some losers, see the next page.)

Most of the winners win because they consume relatively small quantities of energy in the manufacturing process. In alcoholic beverages, for example, energy costs represent less than 1 cent per dollar of sales. Costs in the liquor business will rise less rapidly than costs in the more energy-intensive industries. With demand for alcoholic beverages acutely sensitive to price changes, consumers will presumably take advantage of the fall in the *relative* price of liquor and increase their purchases. Result: a gain in real spending that is 3 percent higher than what would be projected without the oil-price increase.

Excerpted from Sanford Rose, "The Far-Reaching Consequences of High-Priced Oil," *Fortune Magazine,* March 1974, pp. 107–108. Adapted with permission of *Fortune Magazine.*

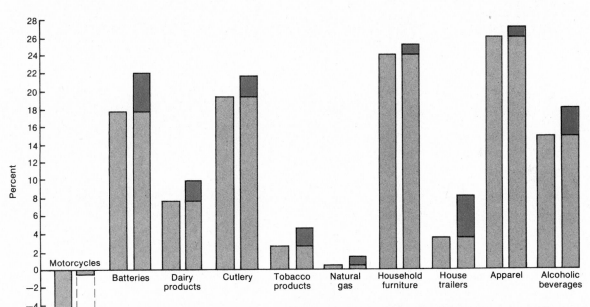

The bars represent percentage gains or losses in consumer spending for the products of various industries during 1971–75. All the expected spending changes have been calculated in constant 1971 dollars. For each industry the bars on the left assume no increase in the price of oil during the five years; those on the right are based on a price increase of 85 percent. Both projections assume adequate supplies of oil.

Source: Adapted from charts originally appearing in *Fortune Magazine*/Parios Studios.

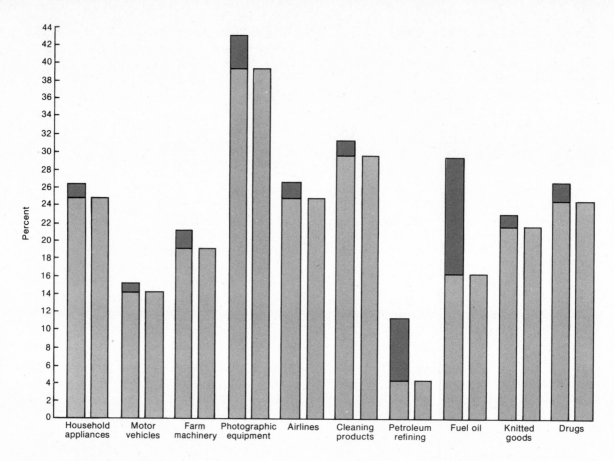

Source: Adapted from charts originally appearing in *Fortune Magazine*/Parios Studios.

INDUSTRIES THAT WILL BE HURT

Less fortunate than the industries on the preceding page are the ten shown above. Petroleum refining, which would have had whopping sales gains without the price hikes, now ends up with only a small gain. Note that the sales projections are in constant dollars. In current, or inflated, dollars, petroleum refining will do quite well: it will be able to raise prices enough to more than offset the expected losses in physical volume.

Makers of photographic equipment will lose sales, not because the industry is so energy-intensive, but because demand for photographic products is quite sensitive to change in personal income. Rising oil prices will clearly slow the pace of income gains. Most of the other losers are in energy-intensive industries: detergents, for example, are derived from petro-chemicals, as are some types of drugs and the packaging used to wrap them.   □

THE PRINCIPLE OF INTERDEPENDENCE

We shall be returning to various aspects of the energy crisis frequently in the pages to follow, but for the moment, we are using the subject mainly to bring out certain overarching principles that will guide our microeconomic investigations. One principle that emerges from the above discussion, and that we can now consider quite generally, is that of *interdependence.*

We have really met the notion of *interdependence* in Parts One and Two through our use of the circular flow diagram. In a market economy, for example, we showed a flow of goods and services going to the product markets from private business firms, moving through the households to the factor markets, where, in the form of the services of factors of production, it returned to the private firms. In a general way, we might say that interdependence means that what happens in one set of markets (say, the product markets) will influence what happens in the other (say, the factor markets), and vice versa.

More specifically, we can say that the supply-and-demand mechanism, working through prices and markets, is expected—when all the dust is settled—to have answered four basic economic questions. These four questions are nothing but generalizations of the four points we have just discussed in relation to higher-priced oil.

1. **Relative values of commodities.** With the determination of the prices of all products, the society can answer the fundamental question of which products are more or less valuable (economically) than others. Does coffee have a higher or lower value (price) than tea? Is a vacuum cleaner worth one, two, or three carpet sweepers? When prices have been established throughout the economy, we have definite answers to all such questions.

2. **Quantities of commodities produced.** How many tons of coffee are produced annually in the economy? How many tons of tea? How many vacuum cleaners? How many carpet sweepers? When the supply-and-demand mechanism has completed its work, we will know the equilibrium quantities of all the thousands of different commodities produced in our economy. In each case, the quantity produced will be that at which supply equals demand.

3. **Distribution of income.** By determining the prices of the factors of production in our economy, we are also determining the distribution of income in our economy. A high price for clerical workers' services means high *wages* for clerical workers; a low price, a low wage. Who gets more of the income of the society—the owner of land, the owner of capital, or the laborer? When supply-and-demand in the factor market has determined factor prices, all these questions about the distribution of income in the society can be answered.

4. **Methods of production.** Should the businessman economize on the use of labor or machinery or land? Will he choose, say, a labor-intensive method of producing wheat or will he choose a highly mechanized method of farming? Once the prices of the factors of production have been determined, the businessman will know what method of production is most economical. In some economies, a given commodity will be produced with vast quantities of labor using the simplest tools; in other economies, highly mechanized, capital-intensive methods will be used. The "answer" will be determined by the factor prices that have been set through supply and demand.

The principle of interdependence can now be expressed by saying that, in theory, the solution of each of these four basic questions is dependent upon the solutions of the others. Or, as suggested by Figure 17–1, there is mutual influence between product and factor markets. We determine, for example, what quantities of commodities are to be produced via supply and demand in the product market. *But* supply and demand in the product market will be influenced by factor prices that, in turn, affect methods of production, the distribution of income, and so on.

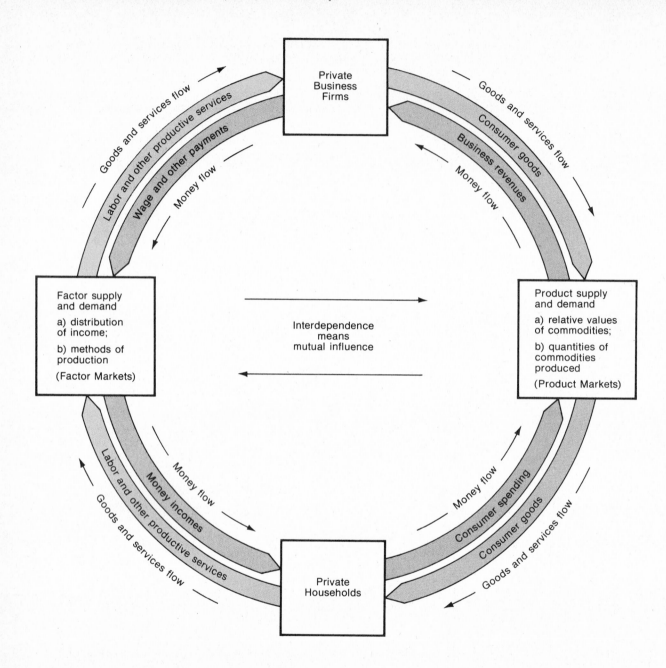

**Figure 17–1. The Circular Flow
of a Market Economy.**

It is important for us to note that the full working out of this principle of interdependence was first accomplished by economists who were considering the case of pure competition. Indeed, to this day there is no comparable theoretical apparatus that can be applied to areas of the economy where oligopolistic, monopolistic, and other imperfectly competitive forces are dominant.

This fact leaves the student of economics in something of a quandary. If he concentrates on pure competition, he can fully grasp the principle of interdependence, but there is a great loss in realism. (Who, for example, would describe the great multinational oil companies as price-taking pure competitors, totally governed by impersonal market forces?) On the other hand, to focus exclusively on more realistic market structures is to lose a sense of the overarching principles at stake. (Who, after all, can look at those same oil companies without taking into account the underlying impact of competition and supply and demand?) So we must compromise. We will first study the structure of supply and demand under pure competition, and then, in Part III B, we will try to modify our results to bring in greater realism. Not all economists agree with this approach (see Great Debate Three, pp. 561–88), but many do, and it is the approach that will govern the work that follows in this book.

WELFARE AND EFFICIENCY

Similar considerations are at stake when we come to a second overarching principle that runs through the whole of microeconomics: the principle of economic *efficiency*. This is a rather complicated principle, because it refers ultimately to economic welfare. It is one thing to know that an event in one part of the economy, *A*, will, through the principle of interdependence, affect parts *B, C, D,* and *E*. It is another to ask whether these effects will be "good," "bad," "satisfactory," or "unsatisfactory." Here we come to policy questions that pose an enormous challenge to the economist—and to other citizens—yet which must be answered in one way or another.

To go back to oil, we earlier mentioned the debate between Senator Jackson and the *Wall Street Journal*

over what should be done about the oil shortage. A number of possible actions (or inactions) might have been taken at the time:

Let the market determine the price. This was the *Journal's* position, as noted. In a condition of sudden shortage, the price presumably will go very high under a completely market-determined solution.

Roll back the price of oil. This was Senator Jackson's basic position: have Congress legislate that oil at $7 a barrel is acceptable but $10 a barrel is not allowed. A ceiling is set on prices by law.

Use supply and demand, but with heavy taxes either on oil company profits or on the prices paid for gasoline or home heating oil. This approach allows the price to rise without any particular ceiling, but the higher prices lead to increased taxes going to the government.

Roll back the price but institute rationing to prevent long lines at gas stations. Under this solution, it is recognized that a "low" price might lead to too many buyers for the available supply. Hence, to prevent endless queues, direct physical rationing is instituted.

Many variations on these possible actions can be imagined, but enough have been suggested to make the general point that there is no way to choose among these policies without making a decision that some are "better" than others. But "better" in what way? One fairly obvious aspect of the problem is the impact of a particular solution on the distribution of income in the society. Central to Senator Jackson's objections to allowing the market to determine the price of oil was clearly that soaring prices would enrich oil company profits at the expense of other groups in the society. The question of what is a "just" distribution of income has been a particularly vexing one for economists, because it seems to require them to weigh one person's welfare against that of another. Should citizen A get an extra dollar at the expense of citizen B? Economists do not agree among themselves as to what circumstances justify such redistributions of income. The subject is a highly important one (see chapter 29, where the issues are considered in some detail), but it is by no means one in which economists have any monopoly of wisdom. Each citizen must remain his own philosopher in this particular area of social life.

There is, however, another aspect of "better" among these possible policies that economists have studied in great detail. Is it possible that a policy could be "better" not just for citizen A as against citizen B, but for both citizen A and citizen B—i.e., for everybody? This is where the economist's concept of efficiency comes in.

Let us first indicate what the term *efficiency* means in the language of economics and then relate this concept to the workings of a competitive price system. A commonly accepted definition of the term would read as follows:

An economic system is operating efficiently *when it is impossible to make any individual better off without making some other individual worse off in terms of their economic situations. Conversely, an economic system is operating* inefficiently *when it is possible to make one or more individuals better off economically without making anybody else worse off.*

In other words, if we could improve the economic position of part of the society while not hurting the rest of society, it would be inefficient not to be doing so. An efficient economic system implies that there is no room for such maneuvering—when we try to help someone it is at the expense of someone else.

In the abstract, this definition may seem complicated, but it is easy to imagine examples that make it understandable. Suppose that we had two individuals—one with a large supply of clothing, the other with a large supply of food. It would be inefficient for the society to have a law saying that people could not trade clothing for food. Why? Because it is likely that such trading would make *both* individuals better off and would hurt no one else. The principle of efficiency would dictate that such trade be allowed.

Or take the question of how to apportion our factors of production among different employments, an apportioning that economists call the *allocation of resources.* Suppose the food-and-clothing society made a law that you could use machines only in food production, while all clothing had to be produced by hand labor alone. (This situation is not so unrealistic as it might seem. Many societies have, at one time or another, attempted to protect handicraft textile industries against factory competition!) It is likely that in such a society one could increase the total production of both food *and* clothing by secretly (and illegally) transferring a few laborers to food production in exchange for a few machines in clothing production. In other words, the law, if followed, would create an inefficient allocation of resources.

Now efficiency, as we have defined it, is not the *only* welfare objective of an economy, but it is an important goal. And the question arises: What is the relationship of economic efficiency to the workings of a competitive market economy?

The broad answer to this question is that under certain conditions and circumstances, a competitive market system guarantees an efficient allocation of resources in the economy as a whole. This is what Adam Smith, in more colorful language, was driving at when he spoke of the "invisible hand." This is why the study of the competitive economy remains important as providing a norm against which to measure other market structures and the activities of governmental agencies or, for that matter, socialist states.[3] This is also why, in terms of our oil price example, the *Wall Street Journal* wanted to rely as heavily as possible on market-determined prices. Essentially, its belief is that markets are more efficient allocators of resources than are governments and regulatory agencies.

Obviously, certain cautions are in order. Even if an economy were perfectly efficient, we might prefer another economy on other grounds—for example, on the grounds that it had a more equitable distribution

---

3. Recall the rediscovery of efficiency and markets in Russia and Eastern Europe in recent years (see p. 60).

of income.[4] As we have said, Senator Jackson objected to the market solution partly on the grounds that it meant excessive profits for the oil companies.

Furthermore, we cannot identify real world market results with what theoretical pure competition would give us. One might object to the *Journal's* position on the grounds that while we might be happy to turn over the establishment of oil prices to competitive markets, we would not willingly turn them over to a handful of billion-dollar corporations.

Finally, as we shall be discussing frequently in later chapters, there are many ways in which inefficiencies can crop up even in a purely competitive economy. Air and water pollution provide characteristic modern examples.

Thus, the objective of the next few chapters is an important but a limited one. In a world where scarcity exists, efficiency in the sense of getting the most out of our resources must be a central concern, and there is no doubt that in many cases competitive markets provide a quick route to that particular goal. We must not lose sight of this important point, nor of the fact that we shall have to qualify it significantly later on.

---

4. It is important that the reader notice that nothing whatever about the "market solution" suggests that it will lead to a "fair" distribution of income. Who, for example, will argue that an orphaned child ought to starve because his low productivity would not bring in a living wage in a competitive economy? The question in this area is not really whether to let the purely competitive solution stand, but rather how much to alter it, and what the consequences of this alteration will be for other areas of the economy. Again, the reader is referred to Chapter 29.

SUMMARY

The field of *microeconomics* is concerned with the ways in which the individual units that make up an economy—consumers, owners of factors of production, businessmen—interact and, through their interaction, meet many of society's needs. In this chapter, we used the economics of the energy crisis to illustrate certain underlying themes of microeconomic analysis.

Two basic principles have to be kept in mind. First, the principle of *interdependence.* In economic life, changes in one part of the system have complicated, roundabout effects on the system as a whole. Basically, the price system gives determinate answers to four central questions: (1) relative values of commodities; (2) quantities of commodities produced; (3) distribution of income; and (4) methods of production. In the circular flow, these questions are answered by the workings of supply and demand in the products markets and in the factor markets. The principle of interdependence tells us that these questions are answered simultaneously, or, to put it in other words, that there is mutual influence between the product and factor markets.

Second, the principle of economic *efficiency.* An economy is said to be efficient when it is impossible to make one person better off without making someone else worse off. It would be *inefficient,* for example, if it had two commodities and could reallocate its resources to produce more of *both* commodities. Efficiency is not the only welfare objective of a society—for example, a "just" distribution of income might be considered as, or even more, important—but it is a subject on which economists have lavished much careful study. In a world where scarcity is significant, efficiency considerations cannot wisely be ignored.

These two basic principles help explain why it is necessary to devote considerable time to the analysis of a purely competitive economy. Through the workings of this economy we can understand in detail how economic interdependence works. Furthermore, we can provide an important model of economic efficiency. For, under certain conditions and circumstances, a competitive market economy will guarantee us an efficient allocation of resources. Thus, such an economy provides a useful point of reference for considering the strengths and weaknesses of alternative real-life market structures.

For these reasons, Part III A of this book will be devoted to a full analysis of the competitive price system. In careful steps, it will build an understanding of the principles of interdependence and efficiency. In Part III B, we will fully consider the realistic qualifications one must make to this analysis.

IMPORTANT TERMS TO REMEMBER

Principle of Interdependence
Four Basic Questions:
    Relative Values of Commodities
    Quantities of Commodities Produced
    Distribution of Income
    Methods of Production
Energy-intensive Industries
Substitution of Factors of Production
Economic Efficiency
Allocation of Resources

QUESTIONS FOR DISCUSSION

1. Define *microeconomics*. Since microeconomics is deeply concerned with prices, why do we say that inflation is a *macro*economic problem?

2. In a purely competitive economy, individuals and business firms are assumed to be price-takers, not price-setters. As a consumer, do you ordinarily respond to market prices, or do you have a significant influence on the prices of the goods you buy? How would you answer the question if you were a businessman or a laborer, and the prices referred to were those of the goods or labor services you sold? What institutions in the present-day United States economy might you take into account in trying to answer these questions?

3. What is meant when it is said that in an interdependent economy there is mutual influence between product markets and factor markets? Show how a change in supply and demand in one of these markets might influence supply-and-demand conditions in the other. (For example, show how an increased consumer demand for food might affect the price of agricultural land and how this might influence the relative use of labor and land in methods of production throughout the economy. Or, alternatively, show how a sudden migration of labor to the economy might cheapen labor-intensive consumer goods in the product market.)

4. Explain in your own words what is meant by the concept of economic *efficiency.*

5. "Increased economic efficiency may seem a rather abstract notion, but it underlies every exchange of goods between every set of individuals, firms, and, indeed, nations—in short, it is at the very heart of economic life." Discuss.

Our task in this and the next few chapters will be to go behind the supply-and-demand mechanism that determines product and factor prices in a competitive economy, in order to relate that mechanism to the underlying data on which society's economic life is founded. These data concern (1) the basic technological facts of production and resources, and (2) the basic psychology of the human beings whose wishes, motives, and actions give the economy its purpose and direction.

In this chapter, we will go behind the demand curve of the product market, relating this curve to underlying consumer satisfactions.

DEMAND AND SUPPLY—A REMINDER

In Part One, we showed how equilibrium price and quantity were determined by supply and demand for a particular commodity, apples. Figure 18–1 shows the same thing for tea. Let us recall the logic by which we concluded that the price at which supply equals demand (in this case, $1.50) would be the equilibrium price.

Essentially, our conclusion was based on the demonstration that neither higher nor lower prices could prove tenable in a competitive market. Suppose, for example, that the price was mistakenly established at $1.00. What would the consequences be? The main consequence would be excess demand in the amount *ab*. Consumers are ready and willing to buy over 200,000 pounds of tea at this price, while businessmen have brought forth only 100,000 pounds. What will happen? Will businessmen refuse to sell tea to consumers? Hardly, since it is precisely their

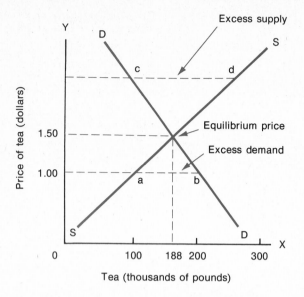

Figure 18–1. Price Determination by Supply and Demand.

Equilibrium price and quantity will be determined at the intersection of the demand and supply curves. At this equilibrium, quantity demanded and quantity supplied will be equal.

business in life to sell tea to willing consumers. Each businessman will begin selling tea from his shelves, his back room, his storehouse; he will begin reducing his inventory. But still the consumer demand remains strong. Consumers now occasionally find stores that have run out of tea; they indicate a willingness to pay higher prices. Businessmen, sensing this willingness, begin both to raise prices on their remaining (now scarce) tea and also to increase their orders for tea from the wholesalers. We have begun a gradual process of rising prices and increasing production that must continue until the condition of excess demand is removed.

Essentially the same process happens in reverse when the price of tea is mistakenly established above its equilibrium level. Now we have, not excess demand, but excess supply. There is over-production of tea in relation to demand, and this results in continuing, unwanted additions to the businessman's inventory of tea. He cannot sell each year's production; consequently, his tea supply begins to overflow his shelves, his back room, his storehouse. This time it is the producer who begins to make bargains with the consumer, offering lower prices while at the same time cutting his orders from the wholesaler. Again, there is a process of price and quantity adjustment until the equilibrium price and quantity are reached.

Now to say that these higher or lower prices are untenable in a competitive market is not to say that such prices could never exist nor be maintained under other market structures or circumstances. Indeed, every modern nation has at one time or another practiced price control with the precise objective of keeping the price of some or all commodities below their supply-and-demand determined equilibrium values. In 1971 the United States, for example, established a temporary wage-price freeze and then a rather elaborate method of controlling wages and prices below the levels it was thought the market would establish. In terms of tea, this might be the equivalent of setting a price of $1.00 and legislating into existence excess demand of amount *ab*.

Can such legislation work? Some people think not.[1] Others would answer, "it depends." It depends on the particular crisis involved, the length of time the controls are in operation, and the general attitudes of the people toward governmental authority. In the United States during World War II, for a limited period and with a limited number of commodities, price controls in combination with a certain amount of direct rationing worked fairly well. Even under these conditions, the operation was imperfect—that is, ille-

---

1. See Great Debate Four, Combating Inflation: Controls or Competition?

gal private or black markets developed. The wage-price controls of 1971–74 may have succeeded in part (some observers felt that Phase II was moderately useful), but by the end of their period of use, few people were unhappy to see them go.

It should be understood, however, that under the right circumstances such controls *could* succeed. That is, supply and demand *can* be interfered with —our earlier discussion of governmental agricultural programs showed this. At the same time, these curves do symbolize important forces. In a competitive economy, these forces will be strong enough to make violations of the "law" of supply and demand difficult to sustain, especially on any kind of permanent basis.

EARLY THEORIES OF VALUE

What are these "important forces"? Actually, for a long time economists could not really agree on what lay behind the supply and demand mechanism. In the late eighteenth and early nineteenth centuries this difference of opinion took the form of a disagreement about whether the value of tea, or any other commodity, should ultimately be related to the satisfaction or "utility" that the commodity brought to the consumers who used it or to the technological difficulty of procuring the commodity as reflected in its "cost of production."

In general, the British classical economists, including Adam Smith and his notable follower, David Ricardo (1792–1823), leaned toward a "cost of production" analysis. The main difficulties they found with "utility" were, first, the problem of measuring it (how could something as intangible as consumer satisfaction be given a numerical value that could then be related to the numerical price of a commodity?), and second, the problem of divergences between "utility," however measured, and observed market prices. The second problem found expression in the famous *paradox of value* noted by both Smith and Ricardo. By any conceivable standard, water gives greater satisfaction to consumers than gold or

diamonds, but gold and diamonds have the higher prices. How then can the "utility" of a commodity help explain its price?

The general solution of the classical school was to state that utility was essential to the value of a commodity—useless products would command no price at all—but that the particular values of coffee and tea (or water, diamonds, and gold) were to be explained from the cost side. Since the concept of "cost" itself involves prices—the prices of raw materials used and the prices of labor and other factors of production employed—Ricardo went further and tried to analyze costs in terms of the quantities of physical labor involved in the production of a commodity. Why does coffee cost more per pound than tea? Ultimately, Ricardo said, because it takes more labor to produce a pound of coffee than it takes to produce a pound of tea. Thus, the relative prices of coffee and tea and all other commodities were grounded in the basic technological facts of production.

There were clearly deep problems involved in this approach, and Ricardo was aware of most of them. For example, what about the obvious problem of different *qualities* of labor? Why, if labor is the source of all value, do the products of one kind of labor (say, surgeons) command a much higher price than the products of other kinds of labor (say, unskilled factory hands)? There seemed, however, to be no satisfactory alternative to this approach. Economists who sought the answer on the utility side (like the French economists J. B. Say and the Abbé Condillac) were forced into unsatisfactory contortions by the paradox of value. Say was forced to conclude, for example, that air and water are so useful that their value is infinite and, therefore, we cannot buy them. Not a very convincing argument, especially to a rigorous mind like that of Ricardo. He (and Karl Marx, who was very much influenced by Ricardo in terms of technical economics) stayed with a labor-cost approach.

What Price, Demand?

ECONOMISTS FIND 'GAS' COST RISES, UNLESS HUGE, WON'T TRIM USE BY TARGET LEVELS

By Soma Golden

The soaring price of gasoline may do little to drive consumers away from the pump this year. Instead, Americans seem inclined to pay more to fill up the car—and to spend less of their money on other things. This at least is the first finding of economists who have tried to estimate what higher prices will do to cut demand for gasoline by the targeted 20 percent for 1974.

Economic Analysis

The finding should disappoint the Nixon Administration, whose free-marketers, such as William E. Simon, director of the Federal Energy Office, had hoped to use rising prices to trim gasoline demand and avoid the necessity of rationing. It seems that price increases alone—unless they are very large—will not help Mr. Simon much, at least not for the next few months.

Soma Golden, "What Price, Demand?" *New York Times,* January 11, 1974. © 1974 by the New York Times Company. Reprinted with permission.

DEMAND CURVES IN PRACTICE

In this chapter, we are going behind the consumer-demand curve to the underlying consumer tastes on which it is based. Sometimes, however, it is desirable to try to estimate the demand curve for a product directly from the price and quantity data generated by the marketplace. This is difficult to do, because the *other things equal* phrase is constantly being violated in practice—i.e., other prices, consumer incomes, etc. are constantly changing. Both the difficulty and the importance of estimating demand—in this case, the price elasticity of the demand for gasoline—are suggested in the following news article.

THE MARGINAL UTILITY REVOLUTION

All this changed around 1870 when a number of major economists in several different countries simultaneously brought forth a quite different approach to the value problem. The leaders were Carl Menger (1840–1921) from Austria, William Stanley Jevons (1835–1882) and Alfred Marshall (1842–1924) from England, and Léon Walras (1834–1910) from Switzerland. These economists, in turn, were following leads developed by a number of earlier writers: Jules Dupuit of France, Hermann Heinrich Gossen of Germany, and several others. Many of these economists were convinced that their new approach would "revolutionize" the whole field of economics.

As far as our problem is concerned, this group of economists made two significant contributions —one of which has proved durable, the other more transitional. The durable contribution was nothing

Elasticity at Heart of Matter

At the heart of this policy matter is what economists call elasticity—a measure of how much demand falls for a product when its price is raised. The economics profession seems convinced that gasoline demand—like the demand for other critical consumer goods—is relatively inelastic to price changes.

Policymakers say they are relying primarily on elasticity estimates put together by Data Resources, Inc., a Cambridge, Mass., consulting concern working on contract for the Council on Environmental Quality.

The work at Data Resources, which is still under way, is based on historical relationships between price and demand for gasoline in the United States.

According to the study, gasoline prices, which rose by about 15 percent in 1973, would have to double from current highs to cut gasoline demand back by the Government's 20 percent goal.

Effect of Doubled Price

A 100 percent increase in price to generate a 20 percent cut in demand means a price elasticity of minus .2. And, according to Philip Verleger Jr., Dennis Sheehan and Hendrick Houthakker, analysts at Data Resources, consumers would take about two years and one-half years to cut back demand that much.

The problem with these elasticity estimates is that they are drawn from historical experience quite unlike the current period. From 1963 to 1972, the years studied by Data Resources, gasoline prices held fairly steady relative to the general price indexes. Now gasoline prices are charging ahead. In November alone, gasoline and motor oil measured by the Consumer Price Index rose by 3.5 percent, while the overall index rose only seven-tenths of 1 cent.

Kenneth Saulter, an economist with the Energy Policy Project in Washington, thinks history cannot be stretched far enough to predict consumer reactions to prices today. "In the short run," he said, "we are pretty much flying in the dark."

Alan Greenspan, president of Townsend-Greenspan, Inc., a New York consulting concern, also casts doubts on the use of old elasticity measures to predict future demand. He concedes that economists must turn to the past, but he warns that "elasticity of small changes in price is not the same as elasticity over a broad range."

Mr. Greenspan, like most analysts who have studied the gasoline problem, puts elasticity in the minus .2 to minus .5 range. But, he concedes, "we're only going to find out what the elasticity really was after the fact." □

less than the explicit recognition of the problem of interdependence. They showed the possibility of general equilibrium in all the markets of the economy simultaneously, a matter we shall return to later.

The more transitional but also highly significant contribution of this group was the development of a concept that permitted consumer satisfactions and preferences to be brought explicitly to bear on the analysis of price. This concept was *marginal utility*.

These economists argued that the reason earlier writers had difficulty with the paradox of value was that they were always thinking in terms of total utility. Once one focuses on the correct concept—*marginal utility*—the paradox immediately dissolves. The definition is:

The marginal utility *of a commodity is the addition to the total utility (or satisfaction) we receive from having one additional unit of the commodity.*

William Stanley Jevons (1835–1882). An exponent of marginal utility and an enthusiast for mathematics in economics, Jevons is also remembered for his theory (not absurd in the case of an agricultural economy) that sunspots cause the business cycle.

Alfred Marshall (1842–1924). Marshall was probably the most famous British economist in the late nineteenth and early twentieth centuries. Although a marginal utility theorist, he stressed links with the earlier "cost of production" theorists, like Ricardo.

Suppose, for the moment, that we do have some way of measuring utility. Then what we ask about a given commodity is not how much total utility or satisfaction it affords us, but rather how much *additional* utility we get from one more unit of the commodity. We are consuming say, 200 ounces of tea per year, and we add one more ounce, so that we are then consuming 201 ounces per year. How much has our total utility from tea consumption increased by virtue of having this one extra unit of tea? If we have a measuring unit for utility, say, "utils," then we can give a numerical answer to this question. If the total satisfaction of consuming 200 ounces of tea per year

is 4,000 utils and the total satisfaction of consuming 201 ounces is 4,010 utils, then the marginal utility of tea, at the annual consumption rate of 200 ounces, is 10 utils. At some other annual rate of tea consumption (e.g., 100 ounces, a year), the marginal utility of tea to this particular consumer would be different (perhaps 20 utils). Given the possibility of making such measurements, we could in principle determine the marginal utility of tea for each consumer at every rate of tea consumption.

Suppose that we have, in fact, made such a measurement for each different rate of tea consumption for an individual consumer. What would his *curve of marginal utility* from tea consumption look like? In answer to this question, the late nineteenth-century

TABLE 18–1

MARGINAL UTILITY OF TEA CONSUMPTION FOR
ONE INDIVIDUAL

AT AN ANNUAL RATE OF TEA CONSUMPTION OF: (ounces)	TOTAL UTILITY OF TEA IS: ("utils")	MARGINAL UTILITY OF TEA IS: ("utils")
100	2500	(2520—2500 =) 20
101	2520	
120	2880	(2898—2880 =) 18
121	2898	
140	3220	(3236—3220 =) 16
141	3236	
160	3520	(3534—3520 =) 14
161	3534	
180	3780	(3792—3780 =) 12
181	3792	
200	4000	(4010—4000 =) 10
201	4010	

This hypothetical table has been constructed to display
the law of diminishing marginal utility.

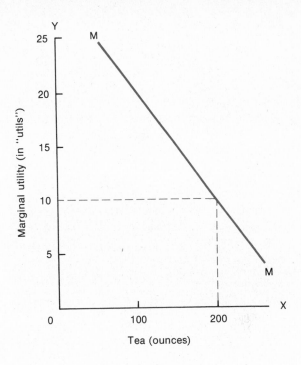

Figure 18–2. Marginal Utility Curve.

MM represents the marginal utility of tea to one consumer at different rates of tea consumption. The curve
slopes downward from left to right because of the
"law of diminishing marginal utility."

theorists brought forth a fundamental principle that
they called the *law of diminishing marginal utility*. This
law states:

*As a consumer increases his rate of consumption
of a particular commodity (say, from 100 to 200
ounces of tea per year), its marginal utility for him
will diminish.*

Psychologically, this seems to make sense under
ordinary circumstances. The first few units of tea
presumably will satisfy our most deep-seated cravings
for tea-drinking; by contrast, when we are having
several cups a day, the addition of still another cup
will add very little to our total satisfaction. At still
higher rates of consumption, additional tea may bring
no satisfaction whatever—indeed, you may have to
pay the consumer in order to get him to take still
another cup.

In Table 18–1, we have presented some selected
data for our hypothetical consumer of tea. Figure
18–2 represents this material in graph form. The
particular shape of the curve is of no great importance to us, but we do notice that it expresses the
law of diminishing marginal utility, sloping downward
from left to right. In fact, we notice that it has very
much the same general shape as the demand curve
for tea described earlier in this chapter.

Are we to conclude then that Figure 18–2 is, in
fact, the demand curve of a single consumer for tea?
No, clearly not. In Figure 18–2 we are measuring
marginal utility on the y-axis. In the case of a consumer demand curve for tea, we measure *price* on
the y-axis. In order to relate these two quite different
quantities, we must find some bridge between them.

FROM MARGINAL UTILITY
TO THE DEMAND CURVE

The bridge can be found if we will now do two things. The first and most important is to make the assumption that the consumer will act in such a way that he will *maximize* his utility or satisfaction when he is making his purchases. How will a consumer act if he is interested in maximizing his satisfactions?

He will be maximizing his utility if he spends his income on different commodities in such a way that the marginal utility he gets from spending a dollar on any one commodity will be equal to the marginal utility he gets from spending a dollar on any other commodity. Another way of putting this is to say that he will adjust his purchases of commodities so that the ratio of their marginal utilities (for him) will be equal to the ratios of their prices. The consumer, purchasing n commodities, then, will have achieved maximum satisfaction when he is obeying the following rule:

$$\frac{P_1}{P_2} = \frac{MU_1}{MU_2} \; ; \; \frac{P_2}{P_3} = \frac{MU_2}{MU_3} \; ; \ldots ;$$

$$\frac{P_{n-1}}{P_n} = \frac{MU_{n-1}}{MU_n} \; ; \ldots$$

where P_n is the price of commodity n, and where MU_n is the marginal utility of commodity n.

The common sense of this assumption is not difficult to understand. If the last dollar I spend on tea consumption adds five utils to my total satisfaction, and if by spending an additional dollar on butter I can add *ten* utils to my total satisfaction, then I can improve my overall situation by shifting my purchases from tea to butter. A one-dollar shift will mean a loss of five utils and a gain of ten utils, or a *net* gain of five utils. If I am interested in maximizing my satisfactions, I will certainly make the shift. How long will such shifting continue? Not indefinitely, because of the law of diminishing marginal utility. As I continue making butter purchases, its marginal utility to me will fall; as I consume less and less tea, its marginal

utility to me will rise. Eventually I reach the following situation:

$$\frac{\text{Price of butter}}{\text{Price of tea}} = \frac{\text{M. U. of butter}}{\text{M. U. of tea}}$$

At this point, I will no longer be able to improve my position further and a condition of consumer equilibrium will have been achieved.

Now this principle—sometimes called the *equimarginal principle*—gives us an important link between marginal utility, on the one hand, and price, on the other. Indeed, in order to complete the connection between the marginal utility curve and the consumer demand curve, the late nineteenth-century theorists needed only one further assumption—that the commodity in question is sufficiently unimportant in the consumer's total budget, so that if he buys more or less of the commodity, he will not significantly affect the marginal utility of his income. This assumption means that for a consumer with a given income, the marginal utility of one dollar to him (to be spent on housing, clothes, automobiles, or any other commodity) will not be much affected, whether he buys 100 or 200 ounces of tea per year.[2]

The individual consumer's demand curve for tea can now be derived as follows: A consumer with a given income and a given marginal utility curve for tea (Figure 18–2) is asked, "How many ounces of tea will you be willing to buy at various prices per ounce?" Since tea is, by assumption, a relatively small item in this consumer's budget, we can say that the marginal utility of a dollar is constant for him—at, say, 20 utils. Suppose the price of tea is set at 50¢ an ounce; how much will the consumer buy? By the equimarginal principle, we know that the consumer will be maximizing his satisfactions at

---

2. If the commodity in question is very important in the consumer's budget, this assumption clearly will not hold. Suppose that I now spend 20 percent of my income on housing and decide to increase that to 30 percent. From a given income, this will mean that I will be able to buy decidedly less of other commodities in general. Consequently, these marginal utilities would rise, and the marginal utility of each dollar spent on those other commodities would also rise.

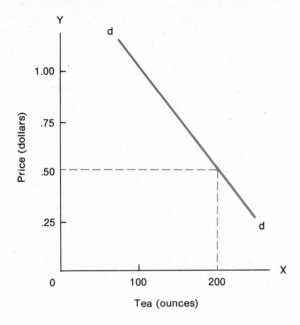
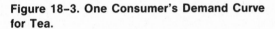

Figure 18–3. One Consumer's Demand Curve for Tea.

This demand curve is derived from Figure 18–2 on the assumption that the marginal utility of a dollar is constant at 20 utils.

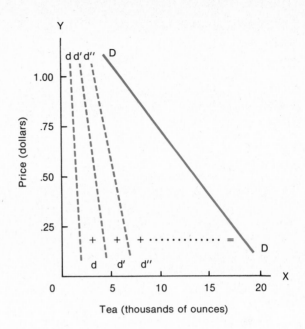

Figure 18–4. Economy-Wide Demand Curve for Tea.

The final step is to add horizontally all the individual consumer-demand curves for tea, to get the overall demand curve. (Note that each individual's curve will look much steeper because of the different measuring units on the horizontal axis.)

this price if he buys tea to the point where its marginal utility per ounce is 10 utils. According to Figure 18–2, tea will have a marginal utility of 10 utils per ounce at the quantity 200 ounces. Consequently, the answer is that this consumer will buy 200 ounces of tea at 50¢ per ounce. This gives us one point on his demand curve. We could repeat the procedure for other prices—60¢, 70¢, $1.00, and so on. For example, at 80¢ an ounce, the consumer will wish to purchase tea at the rate of 140 ounces, because its marginal utility at that rate is 16 utils.

If we continue in this fashion, we will have constructed this individual's demand curve for tea, as graphed in Figure 18–3. To get to the overall demand curve, we would repeat this procedure for the other tea-drinkers in the economy, adding the quantities that they would consume at each price—and we would get, finally, Figure 18–4, the economy-wide demand curve for tea.

Thus, the "marginal utility revolution" has enabled us to go behind the demand curve for tea and to show how the consumer's behavior in the marketplace is related to his fundamental tastes and preferences.

But what of the paradox of value that stirred up so much trouble in the prerevolutionary era? Actually, this particular problem is now quite easily resolved. Water is admittedly more useful than diamonds in total, but it is available in such large quantities that its marginal utility is far below that of naturally (or artificially) scarce diamonds. Since it is *marginal* and not total utility that counts, water is, therefore, much cheaper than diamonds. Q.E.D.

CONSUMER PREFERENCE ANALYSIS

The marginal utility revolution in economic theory was a profound one, if for no other reason than that it caused economists throughout the field to begin focusing attention on *marginal changes*.[3] Still, the revolution was not without its flaws. Indeed, the very central concept, on which everything else seemed to hang—marginal utility—was suspect from the beginning. How *do* you measure marginal utility? The answer is that you don't. You can't. Or, at least, no one as yet has found any acceptable way of registering consumer satisfactions on a ruler or thermometer. An old-fashioned classical economist could have looked at the whole so-called revolution and dismissed it as scientifically unacceptable.

Oddly enough, this difficulty, though fundamental, did not pose as much of a problem in the area of price theory as might have been expected. Early in the twentieth century, certain economists—especially the Italian scientist, sociologist, and economist Vilfredo Pareto (1848–1923)—discovered that you could develop much of the body of price theory without assuming a quantitatively measurable utility. If you could determine that a consumer "preferred" one

set of goods to another or was "indifferent" as between them, you did not have to get him to specify that one set of goods gave him, say, 3.5 times as many utils as another set.

In this modern theory,[4] we confront the consumer with two different combinations or "baskets" of commodities, basket A and basket B, and ask him these basic questions: Would you prefer to have basket A instead of B? Would you prefer to have basket B instead of A? Or are you "indifferent" to which basket you have? Thus, basket A may contain five pounds of butter and three pounds of tea, while basket B may contain four pounds of butter and six pounds of tea. If the consumer is particularly fond of butter, he may prefer basket A; if he is an avid tea-drinker, basket B; if he is somewhere in between, he may just as soon have one basket as the other; i.e., he is "indifferent" about the two.

A somewhat more orderly way of doing this would be to start with one particular basket of tea and butter, basket A, which contains five pounds of butter and three pounds of tea; then we could try to locate all other combinations of butter and tea that are equally satisfactory to this consumer. In Table 18–2, we have set out the possible results of this investigation. What the table tells us is that this particular consumer would be equally satisfied with thirteen pounds of butter and one pound of tea, or with one pound of butter and nine pounds of tea, or with five pounds of butter and three pounds of tea, or with any other combination listed. The consumer is "indifferent" about all the different choices represented on this table.

Now from a table like this—suitably expanded to cover all possible combinations of tea and butter, and, of course, other commodities as well—one can derive many of the results that the nineteenth-century economists founded on the uncertain principle of a cardinally measurable marginal utility.[5] Take, for example, the famous law of diminishing marginal utility.

---

3.   Much of economics, and especially microeconomics, is concerned with maximizing behavior of one sort or another. The consumer maximizes his satisfactions by purchasing this set of commodities instead of that. The businessman attempts to maximize profits for his firm. The laborer tries to find the maximally satisfying combination of work and leisure. Marginal analysis is well-suited to the logical (and also specifically mathematical) investigation of such problems. Many of the conclusions of the marginal analysts of the late nineteenth century can be accepted with little or no qualification even to this day.

---

4.   Sometimes called *indifference curve analysis*. If the reader used the data from Table 18–2, plotted the points on a graph with one axis *butter* and the other, *tea,* and joined the points, he would have a *consumer indifference curve.*

Table 18–2
A CONSUMER'S PREFERENCES

The following combinations of butter and tea are neither more nor less satisfactory to our consumer than the particular combination, five pounds of butter and three pounds of tea. That is, he is "indifferent" to which of the combinations we might offer him:

Combination	I	II	III	IV	V	VI
Butter (lb)	1	3.0	5	8	10.0	13
Tea (lb)	9	4.5	3	2	1.5	1

Modern analysis cannot use this law because it assumes a measurable utility, but it can derive a very similar law from these consumer preference tables. It is called, rather complicatedly, the *law of diminishing marginal rate of substitution in consumption*. The key term in this phrase may be defined as follows:

The marginal rate of substitution in consumption of commodity A for commodity B is the amount of commodity B the consumer will give up for one unit of commodity A while still remaining equally well off.

Thus, look back at Table 18–2 for a moment. Suppose the consumer is at combination *IV* (2 lb. of tea and 8 lb. of butter) and that tea is our commodity A and butter is commodity B. The marginal rate of substitution of tea for butter will then be the amount of butter the consumer will give up for one pound of tea while still remaining equally well off. We know that this

---

5. Economists often distinguish between *cardinal* and *ordinal* measurement. In the late nineteenth century, utility was assumed to be *cardinally* measurable, or measurable in definite amounts: 1000 utils, 1100 utils, etc. In the modern analysis, it is assumed simply that the consumer can order his choices. Given five different combinations of tea and butter, he can rank them by order of preference: first, second, third, fourth and fifth (in the case of ties, he is said to be indifferent). This ranking is what is meant by *ordinal* measurement.

consumer will be equally well off at combination IV as he is at combination III. This means that he can give up 3 lb. of butter (from 8 lb. to 5 lb.) for one lb. of tea (from 2 lb. to 3 lb.) and still remain equally well off. Or, in other words, the marginal rate of substitution of tea for butter in this particular area of tea/butter consumption is 3.

Now this marginal rate of substitution (*MRS*) can change as the consumer has more or less of one commodity or the other. That is, in terms of Table 18–2, the *MRS* of tea for butter is likely to be different in the area of combinations I and II from what it is in the areas V and VI. And this is what the law of diminishing *MRS* in consumption tells us: that as we have more and more of one commodity relative to the other, its *MRS* will decline. Thus, in Table 18–2, as we move from area VI in the direction of areas II and I—increasing our consumption of tea relative to that of butter—we will find that the *MRS* of tea for butter will constantly decline. The reader should compare the *MRS* between IV and III (where it equals 3) to the *MRS* between II and I. In this heavy tea-drinking range, a pound of tea is worth less than a pound of butter to this consumer (*MRS* < 1), whereas previously it was worth 3.

Now this "law" is no more irrevocable than was the "law" of diminishing marginal utility. Both are basically attempts at broad empirical generalization. Still, they are both reasonable, and it is fairly easy to see how they are related. *If* we had a measure of utility, we could easily see that the *MRS* of any two commodities is simply the ratio of their marginal utilities, or:

$$MRS_{(tea\ for\ butter)} = \frac{MU_{tea}}{MU_{butter}}$$

Thus, when we say that we will give up 3 units of butter for 1 unit of tea and remain equally well off (*MRS* = 3) we are saying that the marginal utility of a unit of tea is three times as great as the marginal utility of a pound of butter. If it were less (or more), we would not be equally well off when we made the exchange.

Seen in these terms, the law of diminishing *MRS* can be recognized as largely derivative from the law of diminishing marginal utility. As we get more and more tea and less and less butter (moving from area VI toward area I in Table 18–2), we would expect the marginal utility of tea to fall and the marginal utility of butter to rise. This, of course, would have the effect of lowering the ratio MU_{tea}/MU_{butter}, or, equivalently, lowering the $MRS_{tea\ for\ butter}$. The only reason for going this roundabout way to reach what seems to be a very similar conclusion is that we do not, in fact, have to use a cardinally measurable marginal utility to do so. The whole analysis can be drawn from consumer preference tables similar to those of Table 18–2.

FROM CONSUMER PREFERENCES TO DEMAND CURVES

Similar logic is involved in the construction of demand curves from consumer preference data as opposed to marginal utility data. We will not follow through this process in detail here, except to note some resemblances and one difference from the marginal utility route. As before, we assume that the consumer is attempting to maximize his satisfactions. In the older marginal utility theory this gave us the equimarginal principle (p. 432) or, in terms of tea and butter, that the consumer would be in equilibrium when:

$$\frac{P_{tea}}{P_{butter}} = \frac{MU_{tea}}{MU_{butter}}$$

Although the modern theory will not allow us to use these marginal utility terms, it will allow us to use their *ratio*. That ratio, as we know, is nothing other than the $MRS_{tea\ for\ butter}$. Hence, we can easily see that the new rule for a consumer bent on maximizing his satisfactions will be to purchase tea and butter to the point where:

$$\frac{P_{tea}}{P_{butter}} = MRS_{tea\ for\ butter}$$

The reader can easily show for himself that if the consumer does not follow this rule, he can

gain additional satisfaction by shifting either in the direction of more tea (and less butter) or more butter (and less tea), depending upon whether the $MRS_{tea\ for\ butter}$ is less than or greater than the tea/butter price ratio.

The other step that the marginal utility theorists used in going from marginal utility curves to demand curves was to assume that the commodity was fairly unimportant in the totality of consumer purchases, and hence that the marginal utility of a dollar to the consumer was given—i.e., was unaffected by his purchases of this commodity. In this respect, the modern analysis is clearly an improvement on its predecessor. For consumer preference theory does take into account what is usually called the *income effect* of price changes of a particular commodity. What this effect tells us is that when a commodity falls in price, we are slightly "richer" in general—i.e., we could buy the same quantity of this commodity as before and, at the same money income, have some money left over to purchase more of either this commodity or other commodities. Modern theory now explains the downward slope of a consumer demand curve in terms of two effects.

First, there is the *substitution effect*. As tea falls in price, we will substitute tea for butter (or other commodities), until the MRS's are once again equal to the new price ratios. Hence, one reason we buy more tea when its price falls is because we will substitute tea for other products that are now relatively more expensive.

But there is a second reason, the *income effect* that we have just mentioned. When tea falls in price, *ceteris paribus,* we are richer in general (even though it might be just a little bit richer in the case of a small item like tea), and we will want to purchase more of all commodities, including tea.

Because both effects tend to increase the quantity demanded at the lower price, they provide an explanation of why the consumer demand curve almost invariably slopes downward from left to right. Thus, this modern analysis not only allows us to get rid of the sticky problem of measuring marginal utilities, but it also gives us a somewhat more complete explanation of why demand curves look the way they usually do.

SUMMARY

In this chapter, we have begun the process of going behind the supply and demand curves for a commodity and rooting these curves in the basic psychological and technological data that are the underpinning of economic life.

In the early days of economics, British classical economists such as Smith and Ricardo sought the key to economic values on the "cost" side. Although they recognized that consumer utility or satisfaction was a necessary element in the value of a commodity, they saw no way of measuring utility, nor could they reconcile a utility approach with the obvious fact that water is both more useful and less expensive than diamonds (the *paradox of value*).

In the latter part of the nineteenth century, one of these problems was solved by the *marginal utility* theory. A number of economists pointed out that the paradox of value could be resolved if we concentrated not on the *total* utility a commodity gave consumers but upon the *marginal* (additional) utility consumers derived from the last unit of the commodity they purchased. The total utility of water is greater than that of diamonds; but because of the great abundance of water, the last unit of water *adds* less to our total utility than an additional diamond.

The marginal utility theory also provided a way of relating a consumer's demand curve for a commodity to the consumer's psychological preferences. Each consumer would maximize his satisfactions by purchasing goods to the point where their price ratio P_1/P_2 was equal to the ratio of their marginal utilities MU_1/MU_2. By arguing that the marginal utility of a commodity for the consumer would diminish as he consumed more and more of it (a reasonable empirical generalization) and by assuming that the marginal utility of money was constant (or, effectively, that the particular commodity in question was unimportant in the consumer's total budget), the marginal utility theorists could construct a consumer demand curve.

This analysis, however, still contained the objectionable notion of a numerically measurable utility.

Thus, in the late 1800s and early 1900s, economists turned to a different approach that requires simply that the consumer state whether he "prefers" one set of goods to another or is "indifferent" to a choice between them. In place of the law of diminishing marginal utility, the newer theory stated that there was a *diminishing marginal rate of substitution* as we increased the consumption of one commodity at the expense of the other. In place of the equality of price ratios and ratios of marginal utility, the newer theory said that the consumer would maximize his satisfactions when he obeyed the rule that:

$$\frac{P_n}{P_m} = MRS_{(n \text{ for } m)}$$

where *n* and *m* are any two commodities.

This newer consumer preference theory also demonstrated that the consumer demand curve will ordinarily slope downward from left to right for two reasons: (1) the "income effect" (as the price of any commodity goes down the consumer will be "richer" and hence will buy more of all commodities in general, including this one); and (2) the "substitution effect" (as the price of the commodity goes down the consumer will substitute this commodity for other commodities). This analysis, by bringing the income effect into play, also dispensed with the earlier assumption that the commodity in question had to be "unimportant" in the consumer's overall budget.

IMPORTANT TERMS TO REMEMBER

Excess Demand
Excess Supply
Inelastic Demand
Classical Theory of Value
Paradox of Value
Marginal utility
Law of Diminishing Marginal Utility
Equimarginal Principle
Consumer Preferences
Marginal Rate of Substitution in Consumption (MRS)
Diminishing MRS
Income Effect
Substitution Effect

QUESTIONS FOR DISCUSSION

1. "There is no need to have a marginal utility theory to explain the paradox of value. Water is less expensive than gold because water is cheaper to produce than gold and that is all that needs to be said about the matter." Discuss.

2. Show how the *law of diminishing marginal utility* might be exemplified in the different uses to which you would put water if you had at your disposal (a) one gallon a week, (b) one gallon a day, (c) one gallon an hour, or (d) one gallon a minute.

3. State the condition a consumer must fulfill in his purchases of commodities in order to achieve maximum satisfaction from a given income under (*a*) the marginal utility theory and (*b*) modern consumer preference analysis. How are these two conditions related?

4. Imagine a consumer with a given income buying two commodities, tea and butter. As the price of tea falls, the consumer will ordinarily purchase more tea. Will he also purchase more butter? Less butter? Can't say? Explain your answer.

5. A criticism sometimes made of modern consumer preference analysis is that it presents the consumer's tastes and preferences as independent of the actions of other consumers in the economy. Explain why this criticism must be taken seriously. From your own experience, cite cases in which consumers' tastes have clearly been altered by the behavior of surrounding consumers.

6. Show that, if two consumers have stocks of tea and butter but the $MRS_{tea\ for\ butter}$ of Consumer A is different from that of Consumer B, they can trade tea for butter in such a way that *both* will be better off. Does this have anything to do with economic *efficiency*?

CHAPTER 19
SUPPLY AND COST

In the preceding chapter, we located the roots of the demand curve in the basic tastes and preferences of consumers. Now we must look behind the supply curve and perform a similar analysis. We shall do this in two stages. In this chapter, we shall try to show how supply curves in a competitive economy are related to the costs of production expressed in money terms. In the following chapter, we shall relate these money costs to the underlying theory of production. In both chapters, we shall focus special attention on the behavior of the business firm; for in a competitive economy, just as the behavior of the private consumer is central to the operation of demand, so the behavior of the small, private business firm is central to the workings of the supply side.

TOTAL COST CURVE OF THE FIRM

Let us suppose that we have a small business firm producing bicycles, and that the businessman operating the firm is interested in maximizing profits.[1] He faces the consumer whose purchases of his products will provide him with his sales revenue, and on the other side he faces the costs of producing his particular commodity. The firm's total profits will be equal to the difference between its total revenues and its total costs. By hypothesis, the businessman will "supply" to the market that quantity of bicycles at which his total profit—excess of total revenues over total costs—is at a maximum.

---

1. Whether the managers of business firms in the real world are interested primarily or solely in "maximizing profits" is a question much debated by economists. See pp. 537–38.

What will his total costs include? Obviously, many different items. They will include the costs of the raw materials or the semifinished goods that he will be manufacturing into final products. They will include his payments to the laborers and professional workers who serve him in his factory. They will include the payments he must make for the rental of land or machinery that he is hiring from individuals or other firms. If the firm owns its buildings, plant, and equipment, its costs will include the interest charges on the money tied up in the firm's physical capital (whether it was the owner's money or borrowed money makes no real difference). Also, in principle, it will include a payment for the services of the businessman himself. Such payments are sometimes called the *wages of management* or *normal profits,* although *normal profits* may be a misleading term, because these payments do not constitute part of the "pure" profits that the businessman is trying to maximize. If a businessman is to stay in a particular line of production, he must be paid the equivalent of what he could earn elsewhere, and this payment is properly considered a cost.[2] This point, incidentally, will help explain the possibility—which we shall come to in a moment—that competitive firms will continue to operate indefinitely even at *zero* (pure) *profits.*

The nature of the firm's costs will also be influenced by the length of time over which the businessman adjusts to changing conditions. For the moment, let us concentrate completely on the short run. By the term *short run* we mean, in this connection, a period

sufficiently short that (*a*) the business firm has no time to alter its basic plant and equipment, its "capacity," and (*b*) there is insufficient time either for this firm to enter another industry or for firms in other industries to enter this one. Thus, we have firms with fixed plant capacity, and there is no exit from, or entry into, the industry. In the short run, so defined, total costs may be conveniently grouped into two main categories:

1. **Fixed costs.** These are costs that are incurred by the firm in the short run, *independent* of its level of output. They include, primarily, costs connected with the given "capacity" of the plant: rents paid for land, buildings, and equipment that are fixed by contract; depreciation of plant and machinery, which is independent of whether or not the equipment is being used; certain basic maintenance costs, and the like. Another commonly used term for such costs is *overhead costs.*

2. **Variable costs.** These are costs that *vary* with the level of output produced. They include the costs of raw materials and semifinished goods and also most labor costs.

In the long run, of course, *all* costs are variable costs: contractual agreements run out; buildings and machinery can wear out, be replaced or expanded; basic plant "capacity" can be allowed to vary. In the short run (our present concern), however, each firm will find itself faced with certain unavoidable expenses even at zero output; after that, total costs will expand with output as variable costs are incurred.

These two categories of cost are displayed in Table 19–1 and in Figure 19–1, which is derived from it. The fixed costs of this hypothetical firm in the bicycle industry are $6,000. This is shown in the figure by a horizontal line that intercepts the *y*-axis at *A*. When the firm is producing zero output, its fixed costs will be *OA,* or $6,000; and, by definition, they remain *OA* at all levels of bicycle output. Variable costs, as we would expect, increase as the level of output increases. They are measured by the distance between the total cost curve and the fixed cost line. At zero output, variable costs are zero (all costs are "fixed"); they rise to the northeast with increasing output, reaching $15,000 at 300 units of output.

---

2. This kind of cost is sometimes called an *opportunity cost.* Similarly, if a businessman has invested his own money in his firm (instead of borrowing it), he must charge the firm interest on his money, as a cost (even though there is no actual outpayment of interest money), because opportunity cost is involved. Indeed, the concept of opportunity cost—meaning that the cost of anything is the alternative one must forego to secure it—is really applicable to economic phenomena in a quite general sense. For example, it underlies our whole concept of the production-possibility curve (chapter 1, pp. 16–18).

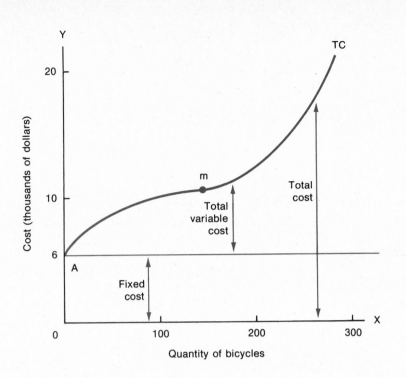

Figure 19-1. A Bicycle Firm's Total Cost Curve.

The firm producing bicycles or any other product is characteristically faced with a total cost curve like *TC*. It is composed of two main elements: (1) fixed costs and (2) total variable cost.

TABLE 19-1

MONTHLY COSTS OF PRODUCING BICYCLES FOR A FIRM

(1) QUANTITY OF BICYCLES	(2) FIXED COSTS	(3) TOTAL VARIABLE COSTS	(4) TOTAL COSTS [= (2) + (3)]
0	$6,000	$ 0	$ 6,000
25	6,000	1,250	7,250
50	6,000	2,150	8,150
75	6,000	2,960	8,960
100	6,000	3,700	9,700
125	6,000	4,375	10,375
150	6,000	5,000	11,000
175	6,000	5,650	11,650
200	6,000	6,512	12,512
225	6,000	7,575	13,575
250	6,000	8,797	14,797
275	6,000	10,401	16,401
300	6,000	15,000	21,000

The figures in Table 19-1 indicate that the total variable cost curve rises in a rather special way—it increases at a diminishing rate until point *m* and then begins to increase at an increasing rate. This particular shape ultimately reflects the law of diminishing returns, which we have defined before (p. 42) and which we will discuss in connection with the laws of production in the next chapter.

At the beginning we are adding very small quantities of variable inputs—labor and raw materials—to our given set of buildings, machinery, and equipment; as we add more of these variable inputs, we begin to approach the natural capacity of our plant; as we add still more variable inputs, we begin to reach and go beyond the natural capacity of the plant; and it becomes more and more difficult to expand output. These facts are naturally reflected in our variable costs: they increase less rapidly than output as we move toward the natural "capacity" of the plant and increase more rapidly thereafter.

With the total cost curve—and its components of fixed and variable cost—we have all the information on the cost side that we need to demonstrate the short run equilibrium of the purely competitive firm. However, it is convenient for some purposes to present this same data in an alternative form. The cost curves that we develop in the next section can all be derived from the total cost curve and its two components.

AVERAGE AND MARGINAL COSTS

The new curves are those of *average total cost (AC)*, *average variable cost (AVC)*, and *marginal cost (MC)*. These concepts are defined as follows:

1. **Average total cost** at a particular output (*Q*) is equal to total cost divided by output, or:

$$AC = \frac{TC}{Q}$$

In Table 19–1, at an output of 100 units, average total cost is:

$$AC = \frac{\$9,700}{100} = \$97$$

2. **Average variable cost** at a particular level of output is equal to total variable cost divided by output, or:

$$AVC = \frac{TVC}{Q}$$

In Table 19–1, at an output of 100 units, average variable cost is:

$$AVC = \frac{\$3,700}{100} = \$37$$

3. **Marginal cost** is the *addition* to total cost occasioned by the production of one more unit of output.[3] We can use the Greek symbol Δ, delta, to indicate a *small* change in any quantity. If a small increase in output (ΔQ) leads to a certain increase in total cost (ΔTC), then we can think of *marginal cost* as:

$$MC = \frac{\Delta TC}{\Delta Q}$$

Or, more specifically, where the small increase in output (ΔQ) is one more unit:

$$MC = \frac{\Delta TC}{1}$$

Viewed in this way, *MC* is actually the slope of the total cost curve, as suggested by the enlarged triangles in Figure 19–2. In order to calculate what *MC* would be numerically at 100 units of output, we would have to know what total cost was at both 100 units of output and 101 units of output (recall marginal utility, p. 431). If *TC* at 101 units of output is \$9,725, then we have:

Q	*TC*	*MC*
100 bicycles	\$9,700	\$25
101 bicycles	\$9,725	

3.   The reader should notice the similarity of this definition to that of the other "marginal" terms we have used, for example, *marginal utility* (p. 429). In each case, "marginal" refers to a small addition to a total—previously "total utility," now "total cost."

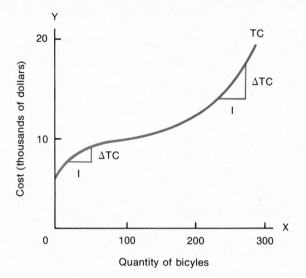

Figure 19–2. Marginal Cost.

Marginal cost is essentially measured by the slope of the total cost curve.

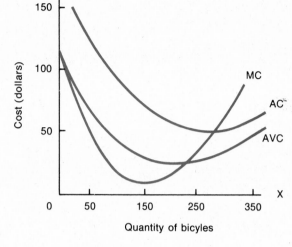

Figure 19–3. Average Total Cost, Average Variable Cost, and Marginal Cost Curves.

Relationships among the Curves

In Figure 19–3, we have brought the three cost curves together in a single diagram. Let us look at the important characteristics and relationships of these curves and give a brief word of explanation about each.

1. Average cost, average variable cost, and marginal cost curves are all characteristically U-shaped—i.e., they are high at the beginning, fall to a minimum as output is increased, and then begin to rise again as output is increased still further.

Reason: The basic *economic* reason is that, in the short run, with a fixed plant capacity, the cost per unit of output or the additional cost of units of output tend to be high at the beginning when we are underutilizing our plant. They fall to a minimum as we approach the more effective utilization of our plant,

and rise as we begin to press output beyond the normal plant capacity.

2. The average variable cost curve will always lie below the average total cost curve when there are any fixed costs.

Reason: Average total cost at any output includes the average variable cost at that output *plus* average fixed cost.

3. As output is increased, the average variable cost curve will approach closer and closer to the average total cost curve (though never reaching it, as explained in point 2).

Reason: The difference between average total cost and average variable cost at any output, as just explained, is *average fixed cost*. Average fixed cost is defined as total fixed cost divided by the number of units of output. Total fixed cost is, by definition, a constant, independent of the number of units of output produced. As output increases, average fixed cost decreases. If the total fixed cost is $6,000, at 100 units of output the average fixed cost is $60; at 200 units of output, it is $30; at 1,000 units, it is $6. Because average fixed cost is declining as output increases, the difference between average total cost and average variable cost is diminishing.

4. Average variable cost reaches a minimum at a lower level of output than average total cost does.

Reason: To say that average variable cost reaches a minimum before average total cost is to say, in effect, that when average variable cost is at a minimum, average total cost will *still be falling.* But this must be true, because the difference between these two curves is average fixed cost, and average fixed cost is *always* falling as output increases (point 3, above). It is only when average variable cost begins to rise, and when this rise just exactly counterbalances the fall in average fixed cost, that average total cost will be at a minimum. This, of course, will occur at a level of output higher than that of minimum *AVC.*

5. Marginal cost and average variable cost will be equal at the level of one unit of output.

Reason: Marginal cost is the addition to total cost of producing one more unit of output. The addition to total cost of producing the *first* unit of output is the *total* variable cost, and the total variable cost of *one* unit of output is the same as the *average* variable cost. The economic importance of this point is that it brings home the significant fact that fixed costs have *nothing to do with marginal costs.* Fixed costs, so to speak, are already "there"; marginal cost is concerned with *additions* to total cost as we produce more output.

6. The marginal cost curve will lie below *the average total cost curve when* AC *is falling and* above *it when* AC *is rising. It will intersect the* AC *curve at the* minimum *point of* AC. *The same can also be said of marginal cost in relation to average variable cost* (AVC).

Reason: This is a quite important point in terms of its economic consequences, as we shall presently, as we shall see presently. The logic involved applies to all *marginal* and *average* quantities and is essentially this: In order for an *additional* unit of anything to bring up an *average* it must itself be *above* average. Conversely, for an additional unit to *bring down* an average, it must be *below* average. Only when the additional unit is *equal* to the average will the average neither rise nor fall—i.e., be constant. Consider the following example: suppose an eleventh student walks into a class of ten students where the average I.Q. previously was 115. Suppose that with the eleventh student, the average I.Q. of the class now rises to 117. Is the I.Q. of the additional student above or below 115? Suppose the average I.Q. of the class falls to 112? Suppose it remains the same at exactly 115? An identical principle applies in the case of *marginal* (additional) cost and *average* (whether variable or total) cost. If average cost is rising, marginal cost must be above it to pull it up; if average cost is falling, marginal cost must be below it to pull it down; if average cost is neither rising nor falling (i.e., is exactly at its minimum), marginal cost must be equal to it.

Note carefully that what we have just said is *not* equivalent to the following statement: when marginal cost is *rising,* it must be above average cost. This is untrue. You should show that it is untrue in our diagram (Figure 19–3) and explain to yourself how this statement differs from our point 6.

REDEFINITION OF THE PURELY COMPETITIVE FIRM

To recapitulate our position: We are trying in this chapter to get behind the supply curve in a purely competitive market. We have focused on an individual business firm—a producer of bicycles—and we have said that this firm will operate on the principle of maximizing its profits. Profits were defined as the difference between the firm's total revenue and its total cost (including wages of management). We have now analyzed the different components and categories of cost, but we have so far said nothing about the revenue side.

In order to analyze the firm's revenue situation, we must now give a somewhat more formal definition of *pure competition* than we have used previously. The basic idea of pure competition—the idea that is implicit in the very notion of a supply curve—is that the firm does not control prices or markets but essentially *responds to* price conditions as determined *by the market.* The supply curve, we recall, asks the individual producer not what price he will *set* for his product, but what quantity of the commodity he will offer for sale at various *given* prices.

We could phrase this idea by saying, as we have before, that this kind of business firm is a price-*taker* rather than a price-*setter.* The firm is so small in relation to the overall market (it may be one out of 30,000 bicycle producers) that it has no control whatsoever over the price of its product. Such a producer simply has to take whatever price is set in the market and make the best of it.[4]

Let us express this notion graphically and then relate it to the overall consumer demand for the commodity in question.

We define a *purely competitive* firm as follows:

Pure competition will exist in a given market when the individual firms that make up the market are so small that each faces a horizontal (perfectly elastic)[5]

---

4. Of course, it could not be true that the producer has literally *no* control over the price of his product; he could always *lower* the price beneath the market price if he so chose. What this analysis says really is: (*a*) that he cannot raise the price above the market price without losing all his customers; and (*b*) he has no motive to lower the price, since he can sell all he is capable of producing at the going market price.

5. Our definition of price elasticity of demand (p. 38) was percentage change in quantity demanded divided by the percentage change in price. As the demand curve gets flatter and flatter, elasticity gets larger and larger until, with a horizontal demand curve, it becomes *infinitely* (or *perfectly*) elastic.

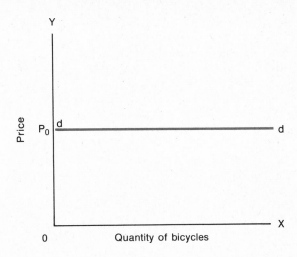

Figure 19–4. Demand Curve for Pure Competition.

In true pure competition, an individual producer has no control over the price of his product. This fact is expressed in the form of a horizontal (infinitely elastic) demand curve, which is the way the market appears to this small competitive firm.

demand curve for its output. Such a demand curve (as shown in Figure 19–4) means that the individual firm cannot raise its price above the market level and still sell any output at all. It also means that the firm is so small that even if it doubled or tripled its output (or conversely dropped out of the market altogether), its individual impact on the industry-wide price of the commodity would be negligible. Another way of saying this is that the individual firm can sell all it reasonably can produce without causing any fall in the market price. Consequently, it has no motive to lower its price below the market level.

In short, the purely competitive firm simply takes the price as *given.* When the owner of the firm tries to maximize his profits, he does so solely by adjusting the quantity he produces in the light of a price over which he has no control.

But how is this perfectly horizontal demand curve for the individual bicycle producer to be related to the overall consumer demand curve for bicycles in the economy as a whole? After all, we spent considerable time in the last chapter showing why the consumer demand curve for a given product will be downward-sloping from left to right.

The answer that a wise man might give to this question is that, in truth, the demand curve facing the individual purely competitive firm does slope downward, but so very slightly that, for practical purposes, the firm can and does ignore it. What we are, in effect, dealing with in the firm's demand curve is a tiny dot on the overall industry demand curve for bicycles. Our firm produces 300 bicycles. In the economy as a whole, 9 million bicycles are being produced. If this firm goes out of business (and produces zero bicycles), or if it trebles its output (to 900 bicycles), will this have any effect on the overall price of bicycles in the economy? Well, yes—a mini-minuscule effect. Will the owner calculate on that effect in making his decision as to whether to stop producing or to expand production threefold? Certainly not. The effect is so small that it would not be worth the time spent calculating it.

The preceding paragraph brings out what is in many ways the central paradox of the theory of pure competition. Individual firms believe and act as though they had no effect on prices; yet when all firms happen to act in a certain way, then the collective effect is to change and indeed to help determine what the price will be. Thus, the firms do affect prices but each feels that it is being governed by an external and impersonal market.

SHORT-RUN EQUILIBRIUM OF THE COMPETITIVE FIRM

We now need to take only one more step, and then we shall be in a position to show how an individual firm's supply curve in the short run is related to its costs. This step is to show how the firm determines the quantity of output at which its profits will be at a maximum. This is the problem of the short-run equilibrium of the competitive firm.

In Figure 19–5, we have brought together the whole of the analysis of this chapter, so far, in one diagram. We have set out our individual firm's average cost, average variable cost, and marginal cost curves. We have then superimposed on these cost curves the consumer demand curve for bicycles as it appears to this small firm; i.e., a horizontal line at the given price, P_0. The question is: At what output will this firm be maximizing its profits?

Let us give the answer first and then state the reasons behind it.

In pure competition, each individual firm will be maximizing its profits when it produces at that output where its marginal cost is equal to market price, or, in symbols, where $P = MC$.

In Figure 19–5, this particular bicycle producer will be maximizing profits when it is producing the output OQ_0.

Why? To understand this conclusion, let us look at the terms MC and P, separately. MC, we know, measures the additional cost of producing one more unit of output. Now if the firm is interested in maximizing profits, it will have to make sure as it produces more and more units of output that each unit brings in at least as much additional revenue as it does additional cost. If a firm is producing 1,000 bicycles, should it produce 1,001 bicycles? If the additional revenue brought in by the 1,001st bicycle is greater than MC, then it will be profitable to do so. If, by contrast, the additional revenue of the 1,001st unit is below MC, then the added production will reduce profits, and the firm will not undertake it. To say that a firm is maximizing its profits, then,

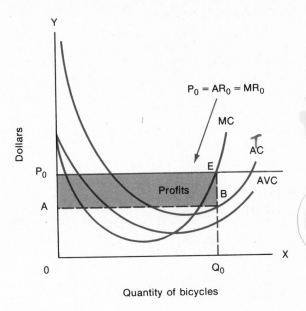

Quantity of bicycles

Figure 19–5. Short-Run Profit Maximization for the Competitive Firm.

The competitive firm will maximize profits at that output where price = marginal cost. In pure competition, this follows from the fact that price is taken as given by the individual producer. This means, in turn, that price = marginal revenue. And the general condition for profit maximization is MR = MC.

is equivalent to saying that it will produce all units of output as long as the added revenue of each is above *MC* and that it will forego the production of any units if the added revenue is below *MC.*

What happens when the additional revenue is just *equal* to *MC*? Actually, this particular point is the dividing line. It represents that point where the firm can no longer *add* to profits by expanding production and where any further expansion of production will *reduce* profits. But this is the same thing as saying that it is the point of *maximum* profits. When the

additional revenue is just equal to *MC*, the firm, under ordinary circumstances, will have squeezed out the last penny of profit possible.

The term economists use for this additional revenue is, as we might expect, *marginal revenue.*

Marginal revenue is the addition to total revenue the firm receives from selling one more unit of output.

Our conclusion about profit maximization, then, can be restated as follows:

The individual firm will be maximizing its profits when its marginal revenue is just equal to its marginal cost. Or, in symbols, when MR = MC.

Actually, this conclusion applies to imperfectly competitive as well as purely competitive firms, but our interest, for the time being, is solely with the latter.[6]

We now seem to have *two* conditions that our purely competitive firm must fulfill in order to maximize profits: the first, that $P = MC$; the second, that $MR = MC$. When we look more closely at the term P, however, these two conditions turn out to be the same for the competitive firm. Price is related to revenue in a competitive market by the simple rule that the total revenue received by a firm is equal to the price of its product times the number of units of output it sells: $TR = P \times Q$. This is equivalent to saying that price is the same thing as *average* revenue, or

$$P = AR = \frac{TR}{Q}$$

But what about *marginal* revenue? Now here we come to a special feature of the purely competitive

---

6. The condition $MR = MC$ is applied to the analysis of imperfectly competitive markets in chapter 24. It should be noted that this condition assures the firm maximum profits as long as *MC* is rising and *MR* is falling or constant as more units of output are produced. When *MC* is falling (as at the very beginning of the marginal cost curve), $MC = MR$ could actually mean *minimum* profits.

firm. Since its price is given (independent of the level of the firm's sales), its average revenue from sales is always equal to its marginal revenue, or $AR = MR$. This would not be the case if the price of the product fell as more units were sold, because then average revenue would be falling and marginal revenue would have to be below average revenue (remember point 6 from the previous section). But since in pure competition, price is taken by the firm as given, we have

$$P = \frac{TR}{Q} = AR = MR$$

Thus, in a purely competitive market, the condition that $MR = MC$ (the condition for maximizing profits) implies that $P = MC$. When the competitive firm produces up to the point where its marginal cost equals the given market price, it is, in fact, squeezing out the last penny of profit available to it.

To demonstrate to yourself that this conclusion applies in our diagram Figure 19–5, inspect what happens to the profits of this particular bicycle producer when he deviates from the maximum profit output of OQ_0. Total profits in this diagram can be read off by means of rectangles such as the rectangle P_0EBA. That is: Total profits = Total revenue — Total costs = $(P \times Q) - (AC \times Q)$. If you will examine what happens to such a rectangle at higher and lower outputs, you will find that, in each case, it is smaller in size than the rectangle at output OQ_0.

One final caution: notice that the short-run profit maximization position of the firm is not necessarily (or characteristically) at the point where the difference between AR (or P) and AC (average total cost) is the greatest. This point defines the output where profit *per unit* is greatest. But what the firm is interested in is not per unit profits but *total* profits. In Figure 19–5, the firm will be producing at an output greater than that where per unit profits are highest, the reason being that the expansion of sales more than makes up for the slightly lower profit per unit at the higher quantity.

THE SHORT-RUN SUPPLY CURVE FOR THE FIRM

In analyzing the equilibrium of the competitive firm, we have really solved our problem of the firm's short-run supply curve. In the preceding section, we asked, in effect: What quantity of output will the competitive firm produce at a given price (P_0)? This is nothing but the standard question we ask any producer when we want to construct a supply curve for him. If we repeat the same question for all possible prices, we shall have that curve laid out before us.

In doing so, moreover, we will notice an interesting thing—that we do not need to draw any *new* curve at all; i.e., that the supply curve is already present in our diagram. The reason for this is quite simply that when we ask the firm what output it will produce at any price it will characteristically answer: the output where price equals marginal cost.[7] The firm's supply curve is thus *nothing but a segment of its MC curve.*

This statement needs slight amplification, because the individual firm, even in the short run, always has the option of producing no output at all. In Figure 19–6, the heavy line represents the firm's supply curve. We notice that the line travels up the y-axis until the price P_1 is reached; then it jumps over to the marginal cost curve and follows the MC curve upward indefinitely. The point is that when the market price is below P_1, the firm is better off producing no output at all. This is because at these very low prices, it is not covering its *variable* costs. When the price is below minimum average variable cost (AVC), the firm does best simply to stand idle and suffer

---

7. In real life, some business firms might object to this statement, saying, in effect, that they do not use the term "marginal cost" and would not recognize it if they saw it. However, such a comment cannot be taken at face value. If you ask a competitive firm whether it could alter its output and make more money, and if the firm said "no," then that firm is producing at $P = MC$, whether the manager has heard of marginal cost or not.

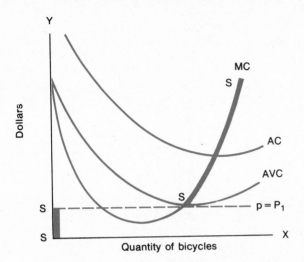

Figure 19–6. The Competitive Firm's Short-Run Supply Curve.

The competitive firm's short-run supply curve is nothing but a segment of its marginal cost curve (i.e., that segment lying above average variable costs). If the market-given price is below the minimum *AVC*, the firm will stop supplying output, even in the short run.

the losses due to fixed costs. If it produces any output, it will be losing money *additional* to its fixed costs. Once price rises above P_1 (is above average variable cost), however, the firm will do better to produce at the level where $P = MC$. Mind you, if the price is low—if it is above *AC*—but below *AC*—there will still be losses; however, because the price more than covers variable costs, losses will be smaller than if the firm stood idle. It will be making *something* toward covering its unavoidable (in the short run) fixed costs.

Summarizing, then,

In the short run, the supply curve of the purely competitive firm will be the segment of the firm's MC curve that lies above its AVC curve. At prices below AVC, the firm will supply zero output to the market.

When it is operating along such a supply curve, the competitive firm will be maximizing profits, or (when price is below average total cost but above average variable cost), minimizing losses. In either case, the producer is doing the best he can, economically, in the situation he faces.

INDUSTRY SUPPLY AND THE LONG RUN

So far, we have been considering the supply curve of the individual firm in the short run. But what happens when we consider the firm in the long run? And what are the consequences when we have not one firm, but a whole industry of firms expanding and contracting production simultaneously?

Fundamentally, the shift from short run to long run and from firm to industry involves three major alterations in our analysis: (1) the firm has more flexibility in its productive operations, and, therefore, its cost curves are altered; (2) since firms have time enough to enter and leave different industries, no firms will be able to enjoy "abnormal profits" in the long run; and (3) the expansion and contraction of production in the industry as a whole will cause changes in the prices of the basic factors of production, leading to upward or downward shifts in the cost curves of each individual firm.

Let us comment briefly on each of these important points.

1. Costs in the Long Run

Earlier, we defined the *short run* as a period of time so brief that each firm in the industry was saddled with a certain plant or productive capacity and that no firms could enter or leave the industry. Now when we move to the *long run,* one of the first things that changes is that the firm is no longer bound to any particular plant size. It can construct new factories, buy new machinery, enter into new contractual arrangements; or conversely, it can contract its operations, allow plant and machinery to depreciate without replacement, reduce its office staff, cut down on

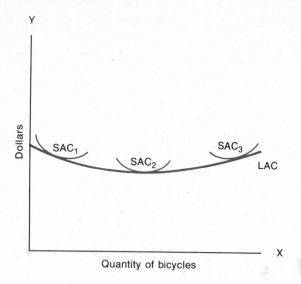

Figure 19–7. Relationship of Long-Run Average Cost (*LAC*) to Short-Run Average Cost Curves (*SAC*$_1$, *SAC*$_2$, etc.).

overhead, and so on. This added flexibility means that in the long run there is really no such thing as fixed costs. All costs are variable costs. It also means that there is no reason for average costs or marginal costs to rise so steeply when the firm tries to expand its output. In the short run, such expansions of output are operating against the constraint of a given productive capacity. In the long run, the firm is free to adjust its capacity to the higher level of output.

In the next chapter, when we relate costs to the underlying productive apparatus, we can be somewhat more specific about the behavior of a firm's costs in the long run. However, the general relationship of long-run and short-run costs can be shown, as in Figure 19–7. The added flexibility of varying plant capacity means that the long-run average cost curve (*LAC*) is much flatter than the vari-

ous short-run average cost curves (*SAC*$_1$, *SAC*$_2$, etc.), each of which represents a given plant capacity.

A similar alteration will affect the firm's *MC* curve. What this means is that the firm's supply curve in the long run will be more *elastic* than it is in the short run. Because firms can adjust their basic capacity, a change in market demand will produce a greater supply response in the long run than in the short run.

2. Entry of New Firms

Another important feature of the long run is the possibility that additional firms may enter (or leave) a particular industry. Free entry is an important component of the common-sense use of the term *competition,* and, indeed, it has a very significant long-run consequence.

If we look back at Figure 19–5, we can notice that we represented the firm as being in short-run equilibrium at OQ_0 and thus in a position to enjoy pure profits equal to the area of the shaded rectangle. These pure profits are *in addition to* what we earlier called *normal profits* or *wages of management,* or essentially what the owners of this firm could have made in some alternative employment. Now the moment we move to the long run and allow free entry (and exit) of firms, such abnormal profits must disappear. For the existence of such pure profits is a beacon signaling producers in other industries to enter bicycle production and share the wealth. If the firm were burdened with losses, they would be a signal for firms to leave the industry.

The consequence of large numbers of new firms entering the bicycle industry will be a great expansion of bicycle output and, in turn, because of the downward-sloping consumer demand curve, a reduction in the price of bicycles. Thus, the short-run equilibrium position described in Figure 19–5 could not maintain itself in the long run. If all firms in the bicycle industry are making profits comparable to those shown in Figure 19–5, then firms from other industries will quickly be attracted into bicycle production. As

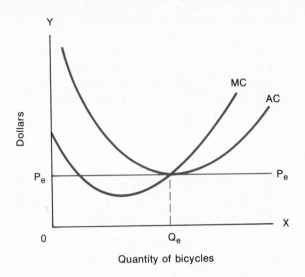

Figure 19–8. Long-Run Equilibrium of the Competitive Firm.

With free entry of other firms in the long run, abnormal profits disappear for the competitive firms, and long-run equilibrium is established where $P = AC$ ($= MC$). Note that *AC* is at a minimum at this equilibrium. This is one reason why economists speak of the *efficiency* of a purely competitive economy.

bicycle production expands with this influx of firms, the market price will begin to fall below the original level P_0. It will continue falling, indeed, until there are no longer abnormal profits in bicycle production, or to the point where price is equal to average total cost ($P = AC$).

This long-run equilibrium for the firm is shown in Figure 19–8. The price has been driven down by the entry of new firms until it is exactly equal to average total cost. The firm is enjoying normal profits but no pure profit. Long-run equilibrium price will be P_e and long-run equilibrium quantity will be OQ_e. At this output, $P = MC = AC$.

Now notice an interesting thing. The firm that in short-run equilibrium (Figure 19–5) was producing at rising average cost is now, in long-run equilibrium, producing at *minimum average cost*. It is operating at the very bottom of its U-shaped cost curve, and this will be true of all firms in the industry.

This is an important point, because *costs* in a market economy ultimately reflect the basic resources and factors of production required to produce the commodity. And what we have shown is that in pure competition, business firms will be producing at the lowest average cost—implicitly the least use of resources—per unit of the commodity in question. This is one of our first concrete examples of the meaning of *efficiency* in a competitive economy, and a rather striking illustration of what Adam Smith sensed intuitively when he spoke of the beneficent "invisible hand."

3. Industry Supply in the Long Run

With the foregoing consideration of the entry of new firms into an industry, we have entered the area of the supply curve for an industry as a whole. It is one thing for a particular firm to expand its output along its *MC* curve in response to different market prices. But what happens when all firms expand simultaneously and when, moreover, new firms are free to enter the industry at the least sign of higher profits? This raises the question of the shape of the long-run supply curve for the bicycle industry as a whole.

The question may be put this way: Is there really any reason to suppose that the long-run industry supply curve for bicycles will slope upward at all? May it not simply be a horizontal straight line? (Or, for that matter, may it not slope downward from left to right rather like a demand curve?)

These problems did not arise seriously in the short run because (a) the fixed plant and equipment of the firm guaranteed us a marginal cost curve that would rise as we pressed against capacity, and (b) we ruled out the possibility of other firms entering the industry. In the long run, average and marginal costs as we have seen tend to become "flatter" (Figure 19–7). But even if they do ultimately curve upward,[8] we still have the problem of free entry. If additional firms are free to enter the industry and if their cost curves are identical, or very similar, to those of the firms already in the industry, then why should the long-run supply curve slope upward? The industry will expand its output not by each firm moving up its *MC* curve but rather by the addition of new firms to the industry, each of which will be producing at the same *MC* = minimum *AC* as the firms already there. The marginal cost of industry expansion will be constant.

Now the truth is that this may, in fact, happen. We have already said that the supply curve will be more *elastic* in the long run than in the short run. The possibility exists that it may be *infinitely elastic*—i.e., a horizontal straight line.

Although this is a *possible* case, it is not the characteristic case. The general reason for expecting the long-run supply curve of an industry to rise as output expands is that this expansion of the industry will generally cause a rise in the average price of the factors of production employed by that industry. The main reason for this rise in the prices of factors of production, in turn, is that the production of bicycles (or of any other commodity) does not involve either the same kinds of factors or the same proportions of factors as do all other commodities. When production in the economy as a whole shifts from other commodities in the direction of producing more bicycles, this creates particular demand pressure on the factors peculiarly or heavily used in bicycle production. Thus, the costs of producing bicycles are likely to go up.

---

8.   In the next chapter, we shall discuss the conditions under which costs will or will not curve upward. It should be noted in advance that long-run average cost and marginal cost for a firm sometimes do *not* curve upward—i.e., they may continue to fall as output increases. When this happens, we cannot have a purely competitive market; we have a *natural monopoly.* See p. 464.

AN APPLICATION: A TAX ON BICYCLES

We can use the curves we have been developing in this chapter to show quite simply how to answer an important economic problem. Suppose the government decides to put a $20 per unit tax on bicycles. What effect will this tax have on the price at which bicycles are sold and on the quantity of bicycles brought to market?

In order to answer this question, we first consider the individual producer of bicycles. Assuming pure competition, we can say that each bicycle producer will produce bicycles to the point where $P = MC$. After the tax has been imposed, however, each time the producer sells one more bicycle he must pay the government $20. Consequently, his marginal cost is now equal to the old marginal cost (MC) plus the tax: $MC' = MC + \$20$. His new equilibrium position will be where the price (*including* tax) is equal to MC'.

This analysis is illustrated in Figure 19–9 (*a*) and (*b*), where we show first the shifting upward of the marginal cost curve for each individual firm and then the equivalent upward shift in the supply curve for the industry as a whole. The result is a reduction in the quantity of bicycles produced from *q* to *q'*. The price of a bicycle inclusive of tax rises from *p* to p'.

Incidentally, the reader will notice that the new equilibrium has resulted in a splitting of the $20 tax between the consumer and the producer. The consumer must pay more for bicycles now, but *not* the full $20 more. The producer receives (after tax) less per bicycle but *not* the full $20 less. This question of who actually pays the tax is sometimes referred to as the problem of the *incidence of taxation.* You should demonstrate to yourself how the incidence of the $20 tax will vary, depending on the specific supply and demand curves involved. (What happens if the supply curve is almost perfectly horizontal? If the demand curve is nearly vertical?)

Applications of supply and demand, as in the case of the incidence of taxes, should indicate the wide range of problems for which these powerful tools can be used. Sometimes diagrams can get at problems very directly, when it might be extremely difficult to do so by using words alone.

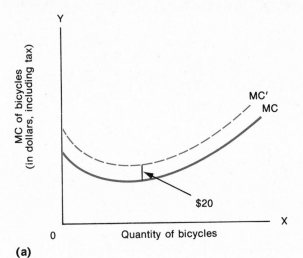

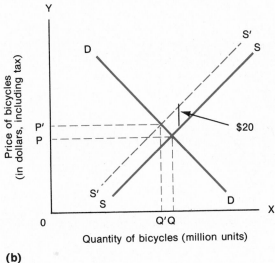

Figure 19–9. A Tax on Bicycles.

(a) Individual firm's marginal cost curve is shifted upward by the tax. (b) Industry shift in supply curve.

SUMMARY

The main purpose of this chapter was to take the first major step in going *behind* the competitive supply curve, by relating supply to cost in a money sense. In undertaking this task, we encountered the following cost and revenue concepts for the individual firm:

Total cost
Total fixed cost
Total variable cost

Average cost
Average variable cost
Marginal cost

Total revenue
Average revenue
Marginal revenue

Be certain that you can define each of these concepts exactly and that you understand the various inter-relationships among them.

Given these cost concepts, we focused our attention first on the supply curve for an individual purely competitive firm in the short run. A *purely competitive firm* is defined as a firm so small in relation to the overall market that it takes the price of the commodity as "given." In other words, its own contribution to total industry production of the commodity is so negligible that any conceivable expansion or contraction of its output would have a minimal effect on price, an effect the firm would be likely to ignore. Technically, this means that the purely competitive firm faces an infinitely (or perfectly) elastic demand curve for its product; i.e., a horizontal straight line at the going market price. *Short run* is defined as a period so brief that there is no time (1) for the firm in question to alter its basic plant capacity, nor (2) for firms to leave or enter the industry.

Our conclusion in this first case was that the purely competitive firm's supply curve in the short run would be a segment of its marginal cost curve; namely, that part of its marginal cost curve lying above its average variable cost curve (at lower prices, the firm "supplying" zero output). This conclusion followed from a previous conclusion that the purely competitive firm would ordinarily maximize its profits (or minimize its losses) by producing at an output where $P = MC$. *This* conclusion in turn derived from two considerations: (1) firms in general will maximize profits where $MR = MC$; and (2) in the specific case of pure competition, since $P (= AR)$ is given, it will be true that $MR = AR = P$.

We then turned to the questions of long run and industry supply. Three main points were established:

1. In the long run, the individual firm will be able to adjust its plant capacity to different levels of output; there are no "fixed costs" in the long run. This means that the individual firm's cost curves (average and marginal) will be "flatter" in the long run than in the short run. Accordingly, the firm's supply curve will tend to be more elastic in the long run.

2. In the long run, other firms will be free to enter the industry in response to any "pure" profits (i.e., profits above the "wages of management" included in the cost curves). What this means is that the individual firm will not be able to enjoy persistent "pure" profits in the long run in pure competition. The entry of other firms will drive the industry-wide price of the product down until a zero profit equilibrium has been achieved for each firm. Such an equilibrium in pure competition will be characterized by the fact that each firm will be producing where $P = MC = AC$. This will be at the minimum point of the AC curve. This conclusion suggests why pure competition is often described as an "efficient" market structure. Minimizing average costs per unit of output ultimately means (subject to later qualifications) minimizing the use of scarce resources to produce the commodity in question.

3. The possibility of firms entering and leaving the industry in the long run means that the industry-wide supply curve will be more elastic than if there were a fixed number of firms in the industry. The question is then raised: Is there any reason why the long-run industry supply curve should have any upward slope at all? The answer (to be elaborated further in the next chapter) is that it may not do so—it could, for example, be perfectly horizontal—but that ordinarily it will have at least a gentle upward slope because the expansion of the industry will normally cause some rise in the average price of the factors of production employed in that industry.

IMPORTANT TERMS TO REMEMBER

Normal Profits
Pure Profits
Opportunity Cost
Fixed vs. Variable Costs
Short Run vs. Long Run
Cost concepts: TC, AC, AVC, MC
Revenue Concepts: TR, AR, MR
Price-Taker vs. Price-Setter
Pure Competition: Infinitely Elastic Demand Curve
Profit Maximization: MR = MC
Short-Run Equilibrium of the Purely
    Competitive Firm: P = MC
Free Entry
Minimum Average Cost
Long-Run Equilibrium of the Purely
    Competitive Firm: P = MC = AC
Elasticity of Supply
Incidence of Taxation

QUESTIONS FOR DISCUSSION

1. "The theory of pure competition is completely bogus. It assumes that firms eager to maximize profits will cavalierly go about destroying each other's profits. Even worse, it ends up with a ridiculous equilibrium in which these profit maximizers are making no profits at all! Clearly, under these circumstances, any intelligent businessman would pull out of the industry altogether."

Give a critical analysis of the above statement.

2. Suppose that the cost curves of all firms in an industry and of all potential entrants into the industry are identical and that the prices of factors of production are unaffected by any expansion or contraction of this industry. Can you show why, under these circumstances, the long-run supply curve in this industry would be a horizontal straight line? Does it bother you that each firm in the industry also faces a horizontal demand curve? How would you determine where the price of the product and the quantity of the product supplied would settle in long-run equilibrium?

3. If there is a sudden increase in consumer demand for a product, usually the price of the product will rise higher and the quantity produced will increase less in the short run than in the long run. Explain the logic behind this statement, using diagrams to show how the process would work.

4. Now that you have a technical definition of pure competition, take a dozen or so consumer goods industries with which you are familiar in the real world and rank them according to the degree of closeness to the competitive model. What factors seem to you primarily responsible for the more extreme departures from the purely competitive market structure?

5. "I'm a businessman producing pencil sharpeners, and I do my best to make as much money for the firm as I can, but I certainly don't make marginal revenue equal marginal cost. In fact, I've never even heard of those terms."

Discuss this hypothetical (but not uncommon) expression of sentiment about the value of microeconomic theory.

CHAPTER 20

COST AND PRODUCTION

Having shown the relationship between supply and cost, we must now try to root the concept of cost in the basic facts of production and technology in our economy, much as we rooted the demand curve in the basic preferences of consumers (chapter 18). Ultimately, the concept of ''cost'' involves not just the laws of production but everything else in the system (including consumer preferences). For the moment, however, we shall hold these more distant relationships in abeyance and concentrate on the analysis of cost as it would appear to a single small business firm.

THE ECONOMICS OF PRODUCTION

When it comes to his costs, the basic problem facing the individual businessman is how to combine the factors of production into a working enterprise in the most economical way possible. What are these factors of production? Economists often divide them into three broad categories:

1. *labor,* including professional and white-collar as well as blue-collar workers;
2. *land,* which is the economist's term for all natural resources, including land in the narrower sense; and
3. *capital,* including machinery, buildings, tools, inventories of goods in stock, and, in general, all *produced* means of production.

Corresponding to these very general categories are three categories of payment, which we shall discuss in the next chapter; *wages* to labor, *rent* to land, and *interest* to capital. The problem for the individual businessman is to combine his land, labor, and capital in the cheapest possible ways in order to produce bicycles—continuing our earlier example—at the point where his marginal cost in terms of wages, rent, and interest is equal to the competitively determined market price (our $P = MC$ condition from the last chapter).

Let us begin, as before, with a short-run situation where the business firm has a certain fixed plant capacity, to which it is adding variable inputs to increase its production of bicycles. To simplify, let us suppose this firm is using two factors of production only: (1) a fixed amount of capital in the form of six bicycle-making machines; and (2) a variable amount of labor in the form of a greater or lesser number of man-hours used in conjunction with these machines in a given period, say a month.

Now the first thing our businessman will have to know is how many bicycles he can produce as he alters the quantities of labor employed in conjunction with his fixed quantity of machinery. This is his basic technological data in the short run. In the longer run, he will want to know more. He will want to know what happens when he changes the number of machines as well as the amount of labor. He will also want to know if there are *new* methods of producing bicycles—*technological innovations*—that will enable him to get more bicycles (or better bicycles) from various combinations of labor and machinery. But in the short run, these considerations can be set aside.

The basic kind of information this businessman will need is provided in Table 20–1. We have also sketched in the curve of bicycle production that would result from the data provided in Table 20–1; Figure 20–1 can be called a *total product curve*, to be distinguished from some other types of product curves that we shall come to in the next section. This total product curve underlies the total cost curve (Figure 19–1) of the last chapter.

TABLE 20–1

MONTHLY PRODUCTION OF BICYCLES BY LABOR WITH A FIXED QUANTITY OF MACHINES

(1) FIXED NO. OF MACHINES	(2) QUANTITY OF LABOR (man-hours)	(3) QUANTITY OF BICYCLES
6	0	0
6	250	25
6	500	60
6	750	102
6	1,000	150
6	1,250	190
6	1,500	223
6	1,750	249
6	2,000	269
6	2,250	283
6	2,500	292
6	2,750	297
6	3,000	300

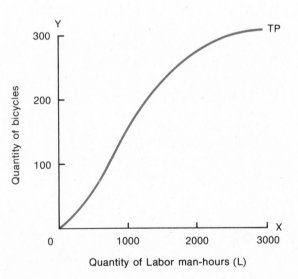

Figure 20–1. Total Product Curve.

This curve shows how many bicycles our hypothetical firm can produce in a month as it combines greater or lesser amounts of labor (man-hours) with a fixed quantity of capital (6 machines).

THE LAW OF DIMINISHING RETURNS

The reader will notice that our total product data in Table 20-1 and Figure 20-1 indicate a curve rising in a rather special way—rising rather rapidly at first and then increasing less and less until, at large units of bicycle production, it is almost flat.[1] This shape reflects a generalization we have met several times before, the law of diminishing returns. Let us now state this law a bit more accurately, using a new term, *marginal product,* which may be defined as follows:

The marginal product *of a factor of production is the addition to total product derived from the employment of one more unit of that factor, when all other factors of production are held constant.*

In this definition, it is important to keep in mind that marginal product is defined for an increase in one factor only (the *variable* factor) while holding the employment of all other factors (the *fixed* factors) constant. Our variable factor is the number of labor hours, and we have only one fixed factor—our six machines. To determine the marginal product of a labor hour (MP_L) at any level of labor employment, we must add one more hour and see how much increase there is in total bicycle production.

We have done this roughly (with the triangles enlarged to make them more visible) in Figure 20-2. In each case we move to the right by one additional labor hour and then observe how much total product has increased. This gives us a series of little triangles that also measure the slope of the total product curve. We can see, indeed, that the slope of the total product

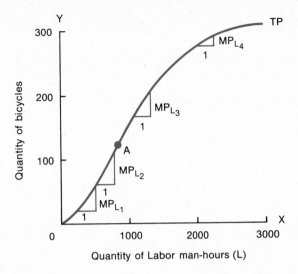

Figure 20-2. Relationship of Marginal to Total Product.

The marginal product of any factor (here labor) is really the slope of the total product curve. (Incidentally, the reader should understand that the same slope relationship holds for other marginal/total terms, e.g., marginal and total cost, marginal and total utility, etc.)

curve is at first increasing ($MP_{L_1} < MP_{L_2}$), but that from point *A* on, the slope is decreasing (though still positive). This decreasing slope is shown by the fact that $MP_{L_2} > MP_{L_3} > MP_{L_4}$.

If we now draw a marginal product curve by itself, we would have a curve that looked like Figure 20-3, with MP_L rising up to point *A* but then declining as production increases. This figure also gives us a means for expressing the law of diminishing returns. This law we now express as follows:

The law of diminishing returns *states that as we add more and more of a variable factor to a given quantity of fixed factors, the marginal product of the variable factor will eventually begin to diminish.*

---

1. The reader may also notice that this is rather the reverse of the way the total cost rises—the latter rising rather slowly at first and more rapidly at higher levels of output. Try, in anticipation, to think why these curves would behave in different ways.

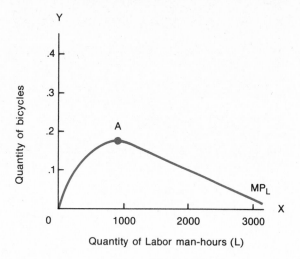

Figure 20–3. The Law of Diminishing Returns.

Returns are diminishing—that is, MP_L is diminishing —from point A on, as we increase our bicycle output.

The "eventually" in Figure 20–3 is from point A on to the right. From that point on, diminishing returns—meaning in our case the diminishing marginal productivity of labor man-hours in bicycle production—has set in.

PRODUCTION AND COST IN THE SHORT RUN

With this information behind us, we are now in a position to show how the basic facts of production underlie the short-run cost curves (and hence the short-run supply curves) used in our previous chapter.

To relate our total product curve (Figure 20–2) to the total cost curve of the last chapter, we need to have two further pieces of information: the price of a man-hour of labor, and the price of a machine. Let us set these prices at $5.00 and $1,000 respectively. Suppose now we wish to find a point on the total cost curve; say, the total cost of producing 150 bicycles. Table 20–1 tells us that to produce 150 bicycles, the firm will use 6 machines and 1,000 man-hours of labor. This means that fixed costs will be $6,000; total variable costs, $5,000; and total cost (*TC*), $11,000. This is the same total cost figure presented in Table 19–1 (p. 441). Indeed, except for the fact that we have not filled in all the possible numbers, Table 19–1 is simply derived from Table 20–1, with the added stipulation that a machine costs $1,000 and a man-hour of labor $5.00. (The reader should show for himself how this relationship works for bicycle outputs of 25 and 300. He should also show what total cost will be at other levels of output—60, 102, 190, etc.—by deriving them from Table 20–1.

Once this principle is understood we have really solved the question of the relationship between production, cost, and supply in the short run. Given a total product curve and the prices of the factors of production, we can in principle derive the firm's total cost curve. From this total cost curve, we can derive the firm's short-run marginal cost curve and from this curve, in turn, the firm's short-run supply curve.

We might wish to go further and show directly how the firm's short-run marginal cost is related to these production data. This can be done if we have the price of labor and, for any given output, the marginal product of labor. Suppose we add to our machines and labor force the services of one laborer for 20 man-hours. If the price of labor is $5.00, then the added cost of these 20 extra hours will be $100. Let us further suppose that the addition of this extra labor will result in the addition of two bicycles to our total productive output that month (i.e., that the marginal product of a man-hour of labor is approximately .1, which equals 2 bicycles ÷ 20 man-hours of labor).

What, then, is the *MC* of producing bicycles? Roughly, it is equal to $100 divided by 2, or $50. More generally, it is equal to the price of the factor labor divided by the marginal product of labor (P_L/MP_L). Or, stated as a formula:

$$MC = \$50 = \frac{\$100}{2} = \frac{(20)(\$5)}{(20)(.1)}$$

$$= \frac{(L)(P_L)}{(L)(MP_L)} = \frac{(P_L)}{(MP_L)}$$

where *L*, of course, is the number of man-hours of labor added (20).

Now this simple relationship—$MC = \dfrac{P_L}{MP_L}$—enables us to understand very clearly how the laws of production will affect the shape of a firm's short-run *MC* curve. Remember that this business firm is a purely competitive enterprise with no effect on the prices of its product or the factors it hires. In particular, it takes the price of labor, P_L, as given. This means that what happens to *MC* will depend solely on changes in MP_L. In particular, when MP_L goes up, *MC* will go down; when MP_L goes down, *MC* will go up.

Once this is clear, we can understand that *MC* will go down at low levels of output and rise as output increases. Why? Because, in the short run, the MP_L curve will rise and then, because of the law of diminishing returns, fall (as in Figure 20–3). Thus, we have now gone behind the firm's short-run supply curve not only to its *MC* curve, but to the basic production data behind the *MC* curve itself.

RETURNS TO SCALE

All that we have said so far has been concerned with the economic short run where our particular firm is operating with a given plant capacity (6 machines). In the long run, of course, the firm is free to hire more machines as well as more labor (and buildings, raw materials, etc.). All factors tend to become variable, just as all costs tend to become variable in the long run.

Thus, we have to ask what happens to bicycle output when not just labor, but all factors are increased. If we double both man-hours and machines, will output double? Less than double? More than double?

These questions refer to the overall *size* or *scale* of the production process. Economists use three categories to describe the possible responses of total output to changes in the scale of the production process:

1. **Constant returns to scale.** When the employment of all factors of production is doubled, total output is *double*.

2. **Increasing returns to scale (or economies of scale).** When the employment of all factors of production is doubled, total output is *more* than double.

3. **Decreasing returns to scale (or diseconomies of scale).** When the employment of all factors of production is doubled, total output is *less* than double.

Of course, the employment of the factors could be tripled or quadrupled as well as doubled. The general form of the question is: Given any proportionate increase in the employment of all factors, will total product increase in the same, a greater, or a lesser proportion? According to which result occurs, returns to scale will be defined as constant, increasing, or decreasing.

Which of these three different returns to scale is most common? The common-sense answer would seem to be constant returns. It appears reasonable to argue that if 6 machines and 500 man-hours of labor produce 60 bicycles, then 12 machines and 1,000 man-hours of labor will produce 120 bicycles.

However, this result does not necessarily occur. Economists since the days of Adam Smith have recognized that sheer size may make a great difference. In the discussion of Smith in chapter 2, we mentioned that he considered the "division of labor" a major factor in economic growth. Indeed, he favored capital accumulation in part because he felt that it would lead to increased division of labor. Smith argued that, as the size of the productive operation was increased, the producer would be able to increase the skill and specialization of his workers, to save time in moving from one part of the productive process to another, and to develop more effective and more specialized machinery to increase output. The consequence, according to Smith, was that an increase from one to ten men in a given factory might increase output not tenfold but much more, perhaps even a hundredfold. In terms of modern analysis, he predicted very substantial *economies of scale.*

Experience since Adam Smith's day has, of course, reinforced his prediction. By common consent, we live in the age of mass production and the age of specialization. Many of our major industrial producers use large-scale machinery that simply cannot be replicated on a smaller scale; similarly, a small number of men, each a jack-of-many-trades, could not possibly hope to duplicate on a small scale what a highly trained and specialized labor force can achieve on a large scale. Many modern industries are virtually inconceivable except on a mass production basis. Imagine trying to establish an automobile industry in Monaco or the Dominican Republic. Or imagine trying to produce steel with small "backyard blast furnaces." Actually, the Chinese *did* try to do this at the time of their "great leap forward" in the 1950s. The consequence: tremendous exertion, a great many melted-down pots and pans, and practically no usable steel.

However, we mustn't go to the extreme and assume that there are *no* factors limiting the economically effective size of business enterprises. There are types of industries—for example, the ever-growing service industries—where large-scale production is not always necessary or even desirable. Also, even in the manufacturing sector, decreasing returns to scale can set in after a time, largely because of the great organizational difficulties of managing a large and unwieldy corporate bureaucracy.

Thus, increasing returns to scale are an important possibility, but by no means the only possibility the careful student of economics will want to investigate.

SUBSTITUTION OF FACTORS OF PRODUCTION

Besides expanding or contracting its scale of production, the individual firm can, in the long run, *substitute* factors of production, one for another. For a given scale of enterprise, the firm may decide to produce bicycles by using relatively more labor and relatively fewer machines, or vice versa. What rules will govern the behavior of the competitive firm that is interested in making these substitutions in the most economically effective way?

Actually, the analysis here is very similar to the analysis in chapter 18 of the individual consumer who is trying to choose the proper quantities of tea and butter to buy. The consumer is trying to maximize his satisfactions by so allocating his expenditures between tea and butter that he cannot improve his position by shifting a dollar from one commodity to the other. But this is the same kind of logic that the businessman will use. He wants to allocate his expenditures between, say, labor and machines in such a way that, for a given expenditure, he cannot increase his production by shifting a dollar from labor to machines, or vice versa. Thus, for each possible output of bicycles he will want to find the least-cost combination of machines and labor to use. Both producer and consumer are, in effect, trying to get "the mostest" from "the leastest."

The reader will recall that in the case of the consumer (p. 432), the general condition guaranteeing that he was doing as well as he could was the equimarginal principle, or, to use consumer preference analysis:

$$\frac{P_{tea}}{P_{butter}} = MRS_{tea\ for\ butter}$$

In other words, the price ratios of any two commodities would be equal to their marginal rates of substitution.

The principle is extremely similar for the producer who is trying to allocate his resources between machines and labor (or land or any other factor). He will also try to hire machines and labor to the point where their marginal rate of substitution is equal to their price ratio. But what do we mean by "marginal rate of substitution" in this connection? We can define the *marginal rate of substitution in production* as follows:

The marginal rate of substitution in production of factor A for factor B is the amount of factor B that the producer can give up for one unit of factor A, while still leaving his total output unchanged.

If we replace 10 units of labor with one machine and bicycle output remains unchanged, then the marginal rate of substitution of machines for labor is 10. In this case, the producer would be operating with the "right" combination of machines and labor only if the price of machines is ten times the price of labor. Thus, the firm will be in equilibrium only when

$$\frac{P_{machines}}{P_{labor}} = MRS_{machines\ for\ labor} = 10$$

But why is this so? The way to convince oneself of the truth of this proposition is to imagine what would happen if the producer behaved differently. Suppose the price of machines is 10 times that of the price of labor, but that the businessman is operating at a point where 1 machine adds only as much to total output as 5 units of labor. What would such a businessman do? Clearly he would start replacing machines with labor (as he can do in the long run). Each time he gave up a machine, he could afford to hire 10 units of labor, and these 10 units would add twice as much to his production as he lost through giving up the machine. For the same outlay, he could get more bicycle output, and, ultimately, more profits. By the same logic, if, at the 10-to-1 price ratio, a machine added 15 times as much production as a unit of labor, the businessman would find it profitable to replace labor with machinery. Only when the ratio of the factor prices is equal to their

marginal rate of substitution in production will the businessman be doing the best he can.

One can also move a step beyond this analysis and show that *MRS* is really nothing but the ratio of the marginal products of the factors. Or, in terms of machines and labor:

$$MRS_{machines\ for\ labor} = \frac{MP_{machines}}{MP_{labor}}$$

When we say that the $MRS_{machines\ for\ labor}$ is 10, what we are saying is that 1 machine can produce at the margin as much output as 10 units of labor. How much output can one machine produce at the margin? The answer is: the marginal product of a machine, or MP_M.

How much output can 10 laborers produce at the margin? The answer is 10 times the marginal product of labor, or $10 \times MP_L$.

Because 1 machine can produce at the margin as much as 10 laborers, we have:

$$1 \times MP_M = 10 \times MP_L \text{ or,}$$

$$\frac{MP_M}{MP_L} = 10$$

or, in symbols,

$$\frac{MP_M}{MP_L} = MRS_{M\ for\ L}$$

This may seem a laborious sort of calculation, but it does lead to a highly interesting conclusion: Under pure competition, a business firm will be in equilibrium only when it is hiring factors of production in such a way that their price ratios are the same as the ratios of their marginal products. The condition that the price ratio of machines and labor must equal their marginal rate of substitution also means that:

$$\frac{P_{machines}}{P_{labor}} = \frac{MP_{machines}}{MP_{labor}}$$

This condition is a very important one. It tells us, first, that the business firm that obeys it is producing each given output in the least costly way. It provides us, second, with a potential link between the productivity of a factor of production and its price. (In the next chapter, as we follow our competitive economy a step further, we shall find that the production process is, indeed, interdependently linked to the distribution of income to factor owners.) And it gives us, finally, an important clue to the *efficiency* of the productive process. (This clue will be taken up in chapter 22.)

COST CURVES IN THE LONG RUN

Before going on to these other matters, however, we must complete the basic work of this chapter by showing the relationship of our analysis of production to the competitive firm's long-run cost curves. We know that in the long run the firm can increase or decrease its scale. We know that it can substitute factors of production one for another. We also know that firms that are losing money can leave the industry and that, if profits are good, firms can enter the industry. What will be the shape of the firm's cost curves under these more flexible long-run conditions?

Three important cases need to be distinguished:

1. Natural Monopoly

Suppose a bicycle-producing firm finds that it enjoys increasing returns (economies of scale) over the range of production relevant to the overall national market for bicycles. As this firm increases its employment of both labor and capital, the production of bicycles regularly increases in a greater proportion —or, equivalently, the average amount of labor and capital per unit of output declines.

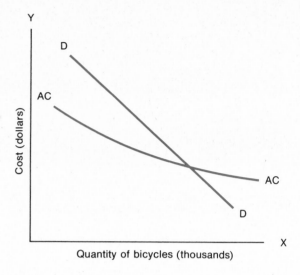

Figure 20-4. Natural Monopoly.

Increasing returns over a wide range of output mean a falling *AC* curve and a tendency for a single firm to monopolize the industry.

In cost terms, this productive condition will mean, at given factor prices, that the firm's average cost curve will be declining through the relevant market range. This is shown in Figure 20-4, where *DD* is the nationwide demand curve for bicycles.

Now, in these circumstances, pure competition could not survive, nor would there be a firm or industry supply curve in the sense that we have described them. For the fact is that the bigger the firm, the lower its costs and, consequently, the greater its ability to drive competitors out of the market. In the long run, the bicycle industry in these circumstances would come to be dominated by a single producer. Hence, the term *natural monopoly* is used to categorize industries in which the individual firm enjoys ever-continuing economies of scale.

2. Competition and U-Shaped Average Cost

Pure competition can exist, then, only when economies of scale do not persist over such large ranges of output that "big"[2] firms are required for efficient production or where there is some *fixed* factor that causes diminishing returns even in the long run. We suggested earlier that organizational difficulties in handling a large corporate bureaucracy might serve as a limiting factor in the expansion of individual firms. The "fixed" factor in this case would be the decision-making authority of the firm. Even decision-making can, of course, be decentralized and specialized within a single firm. Nevertheless, there are some overall policy decisions that must be made at the center; and as the firm grows bigger and more complex, there will be increasing problems of organization, communication, and execution that will complicate this central function. If such problems arise at output levels that are "small" relative to the overall market, then the firm's average cost curve will have the customary U-shape and the bicycle industry will be able to support the large number of small firms that the conditions of pure competition require.

3. Intermediate Cases

Between the extremes of natural monopoly and efficient small-sized firms, there are many intermediate possibilities. In many real-world industries, productive conditions are such that the market can support more than one but not an indefinite number of firms. Economies of scale are strong but are not so pervasive that they require a single giant firm. In such industries, it is typical to have a few large firms (often along with some smaller firms) that engage in "competition" with each other but not in "pure" competition. Such firms have *some* control over the markets for their products but do not have monopoly control. (These intermediate cases of *imperfect* or *monopolistic competition* will be discussed frequently later in Part Three, especially in chapters 24 and 25.)

---

2. "Big" in relation to the overall market for the commodity.

COMPETITIVE SUPPLY IN THE LONG RUN

Returning now to the competitive case, let us assume that productive conditions in our bicycle industry can support a large number of small firms. We now ask: What happens to "supply" in this industry when all firms together begin to expand or contract production, and when firms are free to enter the industry from the outside or to leave the industry?

Now when an industry as a whole expands or contracts, effects on the economy may be far different from the scarcely noticeable—perhaps nonexistent—results of the expansion or contraction of a single firm. This difference is certainly true when it comes to the prices of the factors of production.[3] The individual competitive firm takes the prices of the factors of production as fixed. When the whole industry expands or contracts, however, these prices are likely to be altered.

Suppose that bicycle production requires more capital and less labor (at the original factor prices) than the average industry in the economy. When bicycle production expands nationwide, what happens is that the economy as a whole is transferring resources from other industries to bicycle production. These other industries, however, are releasing relatively too many units of labor and relatively too few units of capital to meet the bicycle producers' demands at the going factor prices. This will create a general tendency for the price of labor to fall and the price of capital to rise in the economy as a whole.

These changing factor prices will produce an adjustment on the part of bicycle producers (and, in-

---

3.   The expansion of industries may, in fact, have a variety of different effects on the economic environment that will not fully be taken into account by firms within those industries. Later on, we shall take up a number of these *external effects*. Externalities are very important in modern economics (as, for example, in the case of pollution), because they significantly alter the conclusion that pure competition is "efficient." (See chapter 30.)

deed, all other industries). The firms had been operating before on the least-cost condition that

$$\frac{P_{machines}}{P_{labor}} = \frac{MP_{machines}}{MP_{labor}}$$

The changing factor prices will mean that this relationship no longer holds. Each bicycle firm will want to increase its hirings of the now relatively less expensive labor, as a substitute for the now relatively more expensive machines. This kind of substitution, throughout the economy, will to some degree offset the pressure on the prices of labor and machines to fall and rise respectively.

However, even when this adjustment is made, there will still be some net increase in the price of machines relative to labor. Because, by hypothesis, the bicycle industry tends to use more than its share of machines, the long-run cost curves of bicycle firms will rise somewhat. This, as we noted in the last chapter, is the main general reason for expecting that as industry output increases, the long-run supply curve of a competitive industry will rise upward (as opposed, say, to being perfectly horizontal).

Of course, this situation need not happen. If, for example, the bicycle industry and the economy as a whole use labor and machines in more or less the same proportions, then the expansion of the bicycle industry would not cause any particular change in relative factor prices. In this case, there would be no need to substitute labor for machines in bicycle production, there would be no reason for bicycle producers' cost curves to shift upward, and there would be a perfectly elastic long-run supply curve for bicycles. Because factor proportions do in fact vary rather widely among industries, however, the upward-sloping (at least gently) supply curve is the more general and important case.

AN APPLICATION: TECHNOLOGICAL CHANGE

To help provide an understanding of the relationships we have been discussing in this and the last chapter, let us follow through on how a change in the basic productive conditions of the bicycle industry affects the supply curve for bicycles and, ultimately, the price of bicycles.

Let us suppose that a technological change or innovation improves our methods of bicycle production. As a consequence of this new invention, we are able to produce a greater number of bicycles from the same quantities of labor and machines used previously. Going back to Table 20–1, we might imagine that the new innovation will enable us to produce 20 percent more bicycles for each combination of labor and machines in that table. Thus, with 6 machines and 1,000 man-hours of labor, we can now produce not 150, but 180 bicycles. Our new short-run total product curve would thus appear as in Figure 20–5(a).

Assuming that we still have factor prices of $1,000 per machine and $5.00 per man-hour of labor, we can see that now our firm's total cost curve will be shifted downward. For $11,000, we had previously been able to produce 150 bicycles; for $11,000, we are now able to produce 180, as shown in Figure 20–5(b).

This downward shift in the total cost curve means a downward shift in the average and marginal cost curves of our firm. Thus, average cost at 150 units of output was originally $11,000 ÷ 150, or $73.33. Now we can produce 150 units with the same quantity of men and machines that we had previously used to produce 125 units. According to Table 19–1 from the last chapter, the total cost of producing 125 units was originally $10,375. Now this same cost will give us 150 units, so our new average cost at 150 units is $10,375 ÷ 150, or $69.17.

The downward shift in the cost curves of this, and every other, bicycle firm will finally lead to a downward shift in the industry supply curve, as shown in Figure 20–5(d). This shift, in turn, will bring about

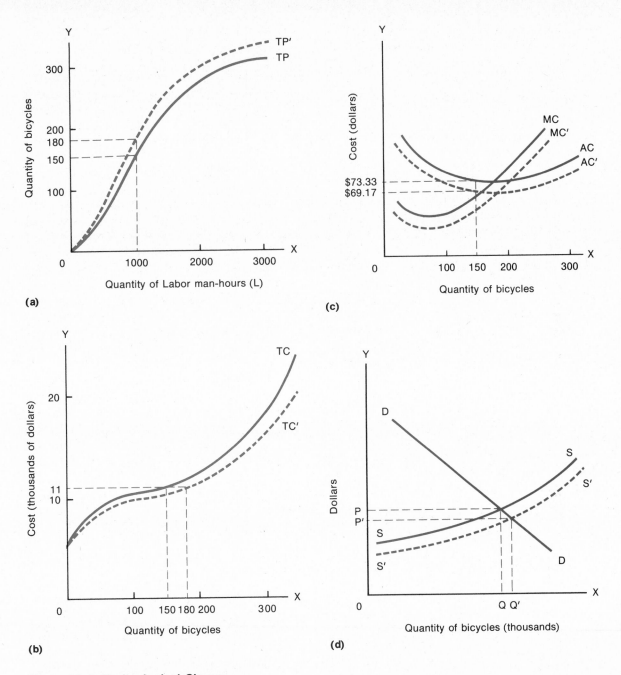

(a)

(b)

(c)

(d)

Figure 20–5. Technological Change.

A technological change brings about an upward shift in the firm's total product curve, leading to a downward shift in its cost curves, and leading ultimately to an industry-wide downward shift of the supply curve. Results: (1) an increased production of bicycles, and (2) a lower price for bicycles.

a lowered price for bicycles and an expanded production of bicycles in the country as a whole. Thus, we have traced through the basic directions of a change in the technology of bicycle production to its ultimate effects on consumer purchases of bicycles.[4]

---

4.   The last step, whereby we move from the firm's cost curves to the industry-wide supply curve (Figure 20–5d) is a bit more complicated than we have shown. The reason is that when the industry as a whole expands, the prices of the factors of production facing each individual firm are likely to change. This means that each firm is likely to alter its combinations of labor and machines (it will operate on a different total product curve) and that the relationship of the TP curve to the total cost (TC) curve will also change. In a more advanced treatment, one would want to follow all of these changes through; for our purposes, indicating the route and direction of the changes is sufficient.

SUMMARY

In this chapter, we have attempted to relate a firm's costs to its basic productive situation, and thus, ultimately, to root the industry supply curve in the underlying technology of production.

We began with a firm's short-run total product curve, adding labor to a fixed quantity of machines. This curve normally exhibits diminishing returns, by which we now mean the (eventually) diminishing *marginal productivity* of a variable factor of production as more and more units of that factor are added, other factors being held constant.

With the prices of the factors established, we can derive a firm's short-run total cost curve (and hence its short-run supply curve) directly from the total product curve. Alternatively, we can derive the firm's MC curve from its marginal product (*MP*) curve. The relationship between the firm's *MC* and the marginal product of a factor (say, *L* for labor) will be:

$$MC = \frac{P_L}{MP_L}$$

where P_L is the price of labor (or wage). As we add more units of labor and produce more units of output, the firm's MP_L will at first rise and then fall. This situation, with a given factor price (P_L), will explain the falling and then rising behavior of the *MC* curve.

In the long run, the firm can expand or contract its *scale,* with possibilities of increasing, decreasing, or constant returns to scale. It can also substitute machines for labor and vice versa. In substituting one factor for another, the firm will be guided by a maximizing rule similar to that of the consumer. It will hire factors to the point where

$$\frac{P_M}{P_L} = MRS_{\text{machines for labor}}$$

where P_M is the price of machines and *MRS* is the marginal rate of substitution in production of one factor for another. An important alternative way of phrasing this condition is

$$\frac{P_M}{P_L} = \frac{MP_M}{MP_L}$$

The conclusion that the competitive firm will hire factors to the point where their price ratios are equal to the ratios of their marginal products is an important one that we shall return to again.

What happens to competitive supply in the long run, where the scale and factor combinations in the firm are all variable and where, moreover, new firms can enter and old firms can leave the industry? Assuming constant or decreasing returns to scale (with significant increasing returns to scale we would have *natural monopoly* or some other form of *imperfect competition*), the competitive supply curve will generally tend to rise at least gently upward toward the right as industry output expands. The reason is that the expansion of output will increase the relative prices of those factors most heavily used in a particular industry. Firms will, of course, try to economize by shifting factor combinations (according to the price ratio/marginal product ratio rule), but this effort will not offset some tendency for costs, and hence long-run supply, to rise.

IMPORTANT TERMS TO REMEMBER

Factors of Production:
   Labor, Land, Capital
Factor Prices:
   Wages, Rent, Interest
Total product curve
Marginal Product
Law of Diminishing Returns
   (Diminishing Marginal Productivity)

$$MC = \frac{P_F}{MP_F}$$

Least Cost Combination of Factors:

$$\frac{P_{F_1}}{P_{F_2}} = \frac{MP_{F_1}}{MP_{F_2}}$$

Returns to Scale:
   Constant
   Increasing (Economies of Scale)
   Decreasing (Diseconomies of Scale)
Division of Labor
Marginal Rate of Substitution in Production
Natural Monopoly
Pure competition
Imperfect or Monopolistic Competition
Elasticity of Long-Run Supply Curve

QUESTIONS FOR DISCUSSION

1. Assuming that a machine costs $1,000 and a man-hour of labor costs $5.00, take the data from Table 20–1 (p. 458) and, with a piece of graph paper, plot all the points you are able to on this firm's total cost curve.

2. Now go to Table 19–1 and reverse the above procedure. That is, assuming these same factor prices, take the data from Table 19–1 and plot all the points you are able to on this firm's total product curve.

If you have followed the correct procedure, then the total cost curve of question 1 should resemble at least roughly Figure 19–1 on page 441; and the total product curve of question 2 should resemble Figure 20–1 on page 458. Do they?

3. Define the *marginal product* of a factor of production. What is the general relationship of the marginal product of labor to the total product curve you have drawn in question 2? Explain the relationship of the concept of marginal productivity to the law of diminishing returns and the relationship of the law of diminishing returns to the shape of a firm's short-run marginal cost curve.

4. Why would a competitive firm try to combine its factors in the long run so that their price ratios will be equal to the ratios of their marginal products? What analogy does this attempt have in consumer behavior?

5. Explain, in your own words, the route by which a useful invention in the cotton textile industry might be expected ultimately to lower the consumer price of cotton textiles.

CHAPTER 21
DEMAND AND
SUPPLY OF FACTORS
OF PRODUCTION

In the last few chapters we have been slowly working our way around the circular flow (p. 420) of a competitive economy. We began with consumer households and the consumer preferences that lie behind the demand curves of the product markets. Then we looked behind the supply side of the product markets to the business firms whose decisions about output and factor combinations determine the quantities of commodities that will flow forth in response to consumer demands. But business decisions about hiring factors of production take us immediately to the factor markets. In these factor markets, business firms are the "demanders," and the owners of the factors of production (in our simple hypothetical economy, private individuals) are the "suppliers." In taking up the demand and supply of factors of production in this chapter, therefore, we are essentially completing the circle. What will remain for the final chapter of Part Three A (chapter 22) will simply be to bring out the central features of what we have done, notably the concepts of interdependence and efficiency.

Now, however, let us focus directly on the problem of factor markets and how these markets function in a purely competitive economy.

DEMAND FOR THE FACTORS OF PRODUCTION

We have already laid the basic groundwork for our analysis of the *demand* side of a competitive factor market. In chapter 19, we said that the competitive firm would be maximizing its profits when it was producing at an output where

$$P = MC$$

In chapter 20, we analyzed the concept of cost further and discovered that, in the long run, the competitive firm would substitute factors to the point where, in terms of labor and machines:

$$\frac{P_{machines}}{P_{labor}} = \frac{MP_{machines}}{MP_{labor}}$$

or, in general, where the ratio of factor prices is equal to the ratio of their marginal products.

Now if we link these two conditions together we come to a rather interesting result. Our way of joining them together is to remember that marginal cost will equal the price of a factor over its marginal product (see p. 461). This principle, together with the rule about equating the ratios of factor prices and marginal products, enables us to say that a competitive firm will be in equilibrium only when

$$MC = \frac{P_{machines}}{MP_{machines}} = \frac{P_{labor}}{MP_{labor}} = \frac{P_F}{MP_F}$$

where *F* is any factor of production the firm may be hiring. This essentially tells us that the firm is producing each output at the *least cost*. If we now add that the *best output*—i.e., the one that maximizes the firm's profits—will be where the price of the product equals its marginal cost, we get:

$$P = MC = \frac{P_F}{MP_F}$$

where *P* is the price of the product (say, our bicycles).

It is at this point that a quite interesting conclusion about factor pricing emerges. If we drop out the *MC* from the last equation and rearrange the terms slightly, we can get:

$$P_F = P \times MP_F$$

This equation says that a competitive firm will be in equilibrium only when it is hiring any factor of production to the point where the price of the factor of production is equal to the price of the product times the marginal product of that factor. The expression on the right—$P \times MP_F$—might be called the marginal product of the factor in money terms, or, more customarily, the *value of the marginal product* of the factor.

Suppose that the particular factor of production is bicycle mechanics. Suppose further that adding one more bicycle mechanic to our staff results in an addition of eighty bicycles produced per year, with bicycles selling at $100 each. The value of the marginal product in this case is $100 \times 80 = \$8,000$. And what our equation tells us is that the bicycle producer will be maximizing his profits only if this term is equal to the price (wage) of a bicycle mechanic. If the wage of bicycle mechanics happens to be $8,000, the businessman will be doing exactly what a profit maximizer should. If the wage is different—if it is $6,000 or $10,000—then he will want to change his operations. In particular, he will want to hire either more or fewer bicycle mechanics.

What we have just stated is actually the crucial key to the understanding of a business firm's *demand for a factor of production*. To repeat:

In pure competition, a business firm will hire any factor of production up to the point where the value of its marginal product is equal to the price of the factor.

Why? What is the common sense of this statement? Why, for example, could a competitive firm not be in equilibrium when the value of the marginal product of bicycle mechanics was $10,000 and their wage $8,000? Wouldn't this, in fact, be a good thing for the businessman?

It might be a good thing, but the point is that he could do better—in particular, by hiring more bicycle mechanics. It is a simple matter of revenues and cost. Hiring another bicycle mechanic would bring $10,000 in additional revenue for the firm, and it would cost the firm only $8,000. This means $2,000 of additional "pure" profit. Any businessman in this position would therefore start hiring more bicycle mechanics. By similar logic, the reader can show that a value of marginal product *below* the given wage would cause the profit maximizing competitive businessman to lay off some of his bicycle mechanics.

The term *competitive* in the above sentence is essential, for the rule that a factor price must equal the value of its marginal product *holds true only under pure competition*. The rule is valid because the competitive firm has no control over the market price of its product or the market prices of the various factors of production. We shall consider in later chapters how the rule must be modified when these conditions are not fulfilled.[1]

How, then, can we generate a demand curve for a factor of production—bicycle mechanics—from this competitive rule that the value of the marginal product of bicycle mechanics must, in equilibrium, equal the wage of bicycle mechanics? We can best approach this problem in two steps: first, by showing the demand curve of an individual bicycle producer for bicycle mechanics when this is the only variable factor of production; and second, by showing how this analysis is altered when we allow other variable factors and also when we consider the demand for mechanics from the bicycle industry as a whole.

FACTOR DEMAND IN A SIMPLE CASE

We begin with the case in which bicycle mechanics are the only variable factor of production, because it is extremely easy in this case to relate the competitive rule—factor-price (P_F) equals value of marginal product (VMP)—to the individual firm's demand curve for bicycle mechanics.

We are dealing with a competitive firm that takes the price of bicycles as given by the market: $100. This firm also possesses, we assume, the technological information given in Figure 21–1 (a); i.e., the marginal product curve for bicycle mechanics as we add more and more bicycle mechanics to a fixed stock of other factors (e.g., machinery). This curve, as we have drawn it, exemplifies the law of diminishing returns throughout. To translate this marginal physical product curve into the value-of-marginal-product (VMP) curve in Figure 21–1 (b), all we need do is multiply the MP for any quantity of labor employed by the price of bicycles, or $100. Thus, when the firm is employing 100 bicycle mechanics, the MP of bicycle mechanics is 100 and the VMP will be 100 × $100 = $10,000. By similar calculations, we can derive the VMP curve for all levels of employment of bicycle mechanics.

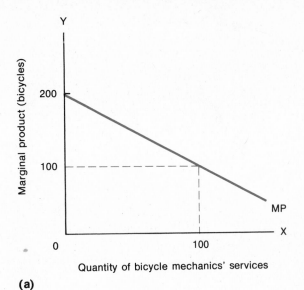

(a)

(b)

Figure 21–1. Relation Between *MP* and *VMP* Curves.

The ***VMP*** curve will represent the firm's demand curve for bicycle mechanics in the simple case presented here.

---

1. See especially pp. 590–93.

9

Now under our assumed conditions, this *VMP* curve *is* the firm's demand curve for bicycle mechanics. The competitive rule tells us that the firm will hire bicycle mechanics to the point where *VMP* equals their wage. Suppose the wage is set at w_0. How many bicycle mechanics will this firm be willing to hire? To get the answer, we simply keep adding bicycle mechanics until their $VMP = w_0$. This happens when the firm has hired q_0 bicycle mechanics. Thus, e_0 is one point on the firm's demand curve for bicycles. If we repeated the process for each and every possible wage, we would get the whole demand curve, and it would be identical with the *VMP* curve shown in Figure 21–1 (b).

OTHER VARIABLE FACTORS AND INDUSTRY-WIDE DEMAND

The factor demand curve we have just drawn is straightforward enough, but it does not take us as far as we need to go. For in the long run, bicycle producers can vary *all* factors of production, not just bicycle mechanics. Also, there is the problem that when all firms together expand or contract their employment of bicycle mechanics, this will alter the industry-wide production and hence the *price* of bicycles. And in the final analysis, it is this industry-wide demand curve for bicycle mechanics that we are interested in.

1. Other Variable Factors

When all factors are allowed to vary—when the bicycle firm can hire more machinery as well as more bicycle mechanics—the firm's demand curve for a particular factor becomes somewhat more complicated. The reason is basically this: when the wage of bicycle mechanics goes down, the bicycle producer will try to substitute bicycle mechanics for machinery. As we know from chapter 20, he will find it profitable to produce any level of output with machinery and mechanics in combinations different from those he used before. Consequently, we cannot draw

the marginal product curve for bicycle mechanics on the assumption of a fixed stock of machinery, as we did in Figure 21–1 (a).

The possibility of the firm's altering its combinations of machines and mechanics leads us to a principle of some importance. This principle is that the firm's demand for a particular factor of production will be influenced by the degree to which this factor is *substitutable* for other factors, and vice versa. If bicycle mechanics are easily substitutable for machinery, then even a slight fall in the wage of bicycle mechanics will cause a very substantial substitution of mechanics for machines. In this case, the demand curve for bicycle mechanics will tend to be relatively *elastic*—i.e., a small percentage change in price will tend to lead to a large percentage change in quantity of bicycle mechanics demanded. On the other hand, suppose that there is very little flexibility in productive methods. It is almost a one-mechanic-to-one-machine production process. In this case, a fall in the price of bicycle mechanics will not permit any great substitution of mechanics for machines; hence, the factor demand will be relatively *inelastic*. In general:

The demand for a factor of production will be influenced by the ease with which other factors can be substituted for it in the production process. If there is high substitutability, then—other things equal—factor demand will tend to be elastic. *If there is little substitutability, other things equal, factor demand will tend to be* inelastic.

We have thus uncovered one of the important principles governing factor demand.

2. Industry-Wide Factor Demand

However, this is not the only principle involved. Indeed, there is a very important omission in our analysis so far. In chapter 17, when discussing the principle of interdependence, we noted that we could talk about the scarcity of factors of production only in relation to the demand for the products they produced—that is, consumer demands. Economists often talk about the demand for factors of production as derived demand, meaning precisely this point: Business demand for factors is essentially "derived" from consumer demands for the products the businesses produce. But we have not yet brought the consumer into the picture at all. How, then, will the consumer demand for bicycles come to influence the producers' demand for bicycle mechanics?

In order to trace this particular influence, we must shift focus from the firm to the industry as a whole. The firm's factor demand curve (VMP curve) in Figure 21-1 (b) was drawn on the assumption of a given price of bicycles ($100). This was appropriate because in pure competition the price of the product is independent of the expansion or contraction of production of any individual firm's output. When all firms are expanding or contracting output and when new firms are entering or leaving the industry, however, this assumption no longer holds.

From this industry-wide point of view, let us follow through the consequences of a decrease in the wage of bicycle mechanics.

The first consequence of a fall in the wage of bicycle mechanics (other things equal) will be a lowering of all the cost curves of firms in the bicycle industry. These new cost curves will be drawn substituting, wherever profitable, the now less expensive mechanics for machines at each level of output.

The next consequence will be that firms in the bicycle industry will find it profitable to begin hiring more factors of production and expanding output. Furthermore, new firms will begin to be attracted into the bicycle industry. The lowering of costs means that there are now abnormal profits in this particular industry. Hence, we will begin to get an expansion of output both by the expansion of existing firms and by the entry of new firms.

The consequence of this expanding output, however, will be a *fall in the price of bicycles*. This is really the point where consumer demand enters crucially into the picture. The bicycle firms are hiring more bicycle mechanics both to substitute for machines and to expand output, but the consumers (having a downward sloping demand curve) will buy more bicycles only at a lower price.

What this means, in turn, is that in the industry as a whole, the value of the marginal product of bicycle mechanics is falling not only because of diminishing marginal productivity but also because the price of the product is falling. (Remember: VMP = Price of the product × Marginal product.)

When final equilibrium is reached, there will be a greater bicycle output in the industry as a whole at a lower price. Bicycle mechanics will have been hired to the point where their marginal product valued at the new (and lower) price is equal to the new wage. $P_F = VMP$ still holds for each and every firm in the industry, but the V has changed as well as the MP.

By understanding the process just outlined, you will be able to see the essence of the notion of *derived demand*. Suppose, for example, that the consumer demand for bicycles is highly inelastic. Consumers will expand or contract their purchases of bicycles only slightly in response to considerable changes in bicycle prices. Now in this case it can be shown that a fall in the wage of bicycle mechanics will produce only a slight increase in the quantity of mechanics demanded; for as firms in the industry begin expanding bicycle production as outlined above, the price of bicycles will immediately turn sharply downward. This will very quickly lower the VMP of bicycle mechanics to the new, lower wage level. There will be little expansion of bicycle output and consequently relatively little increase in the employment of bicycle mechanics. An inelastic consumer demand curve, in other words, has led to a relatively inelastic factor demand curve. You should satisfy yourself that the opposite is also true—i.e., the more elastic the consumer demand curve, the more elastic the factor demand will tend to be. In general,

The elasticity of the demand for a factor of production, other things being equal, will depend upon the elasticity of consumer demand for the products which that factor helps to produce. If consumer purchases of the products of the factor are highly responsive to price changes, then the business firms' demand for the factor will also be more responsive to changes in its price.

This important principle is illustrated in Figure 21-2. The point to note here is that when the consumer demand curve (DD) is relatively inelastic (Figure 21-2a) the factor demand curve (F_DF_D) will be more inelastic than when the consumer demand curve is relatively elastic (Figure 21-2b). Thus, we have shown that the demand for a factor of production is not simply a matter of technology; it also reflects, through the intermediary of the business firms, the tastes and preferences of the consumers of the economy.

SUPPLY OF A FACTOR OF PRODUCTION

To determine the price of a factor of production, we need to know not only the conditions that affect the demand for the factor, but also the conditions that will affect its *supply*. How many hours of bicycle mechanics' services will be offered for sale on the market at various different wages for those services?

In terms of our "circular flow," this question takes us back to the private individuals (households) who, in a competitive economy, own the factors of production. The prices of the services of labor, land, and capital, which appear as *costs* to the business firms, appear as incomes—*wages, rent,* or *interest*—to the households who provide those services. What circumstances will influence these factor supplies?

As we might expect, one important consideration will be the *time period* in view. As in the case of the supply curves for commodities, the supply curves for factors of production will generally tend to be more elastic in the long run than in the short run. This will not always be the case, but it often does apply. Since we have been dealing with bicycle mechanics, let us focus first on the supply of the factor, labor.

SHORT-RUN SUPPLY OF LABOR

In the very short run—a few weeks, perhaps—the quantity of any particular kind of labor available in the economy as a whole may be virtually fixed. There is too little time for our bicycle mechanics to retrain for other trades, and equally little time for other work-

men to learn the skills of the bicycle mechanic. In the very short run, then, we are drawing from an almost fixed pool of bicycle mechanics.

What will happen when the wage of bicycle mechanics goes up? Will the supply of their services be unaffected? That is, will the short-run supply curve be completely inelastic? Not necessarily. It is true that the supply curve will be less elastic than it would be in the longer run, but there is still some element of flexibility. This element derives from the fact that each bicycle mechanic is faced with a choice between working more or fewer hours per week, or more or fewer days per year. He has a choice, in other words, between work and leisure.[2]

This particular choice can be viewed in much the same way as we earlier thought of the consumer's choice between two commodities—tea and butter. When the hourly wage rises, this is really the same thing as saying that the price of an hour of leisure has risen in terms of other commodities. With each leisure hour more expensive than before, the worker will presumably rearrange his combination of working and leisure hours so that he has maximum satisfaction. Indeed, there is both a *substitution* and an *income* effect here (recall chapter 18, p. 436). A rising wage means a rising price for leisure relative to other commodities and, hence, a tendency to substitute other commodities for leisure—i.e., the laborer may work more hours. However, the income effect, particularly at high incomes, can work the other way. Because the rising wage makes him richer, the worker may want to have more of all commodities, *including the commodity, leisure.* This could cause him to work less.

The combination of these effects has suggested to economists that the short-run supply curve of labor

---

2.   In real life, such a choice may be considerably modified by the fact that the number of hours per week and the amount of vacation time per year may be institutionally fixed for any given job. When this occurs, the worker faces an all-or-nothing proposition, and, unless he has a private income, he will customarily choose "all" rather than "nothing." However, even where hours of work are institutionally set, there is usually some flexibility, either in terms of overtime work or, in many cases, in taking additional part-time work elsewhere (moonlighting). We will discuss the labor market further in chapter 26.

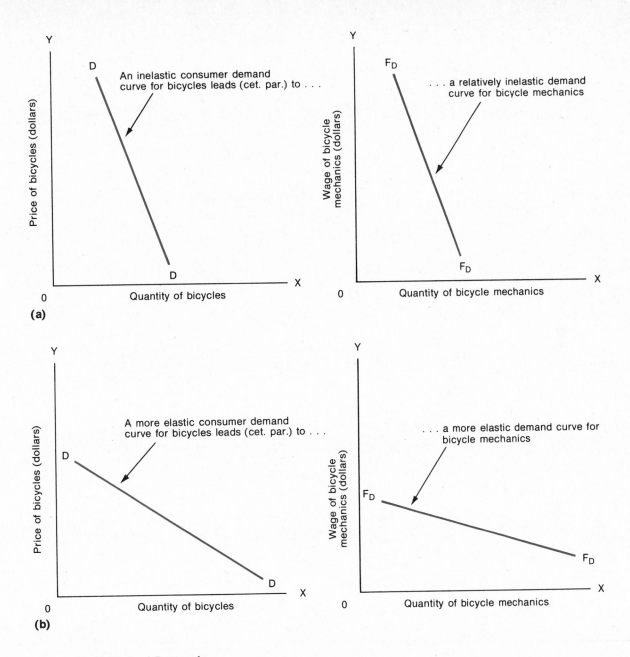

Figure 21–2. Derived Demand.

These diagrams point up the important fact that the demand for a factor of production is influenced by the consumer demand for that factor's products.

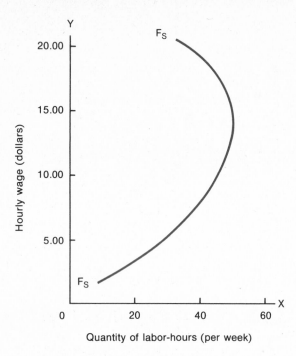

Figure 21–3. Backward-Bending Supply Curve.

This supply curve for the services of an individual laborer might bend backward at high hourly wages. At the higher income level, he might wish to purchase more leisure.

---

may, in fact, be *backward-bending,* as in Figure 21–3. We have put the choice here in terms of how many hours a week this particular laborer will offer on the labor market. At low wages, the substitution effect is dominant, and he increases his offering of hours as the wage rises. At higher wages, however, the income effect is dominant and he actually begins curtailing his offer of labor hours.

Thus, even in the very short run, there is likely to be some variation in hours of work offered and, hence, *some* elasticity of supply in response to wage changes.

LONG-RUN LABOR SUPPLY

As we move into the longer run, of course, this elasticity greatly increases. Consider, for example, a period of one or two years. During a period of this length, bicycle mechanics will be able to shift into related trades (e.g., auto mechanics), and workers in related trades will be able to learn the skills of the bicycle mechanic. If the price of bicycle mechanics rises above that of other mechanics generally, then there will be a substantial shifting of workers from these related fields into the bicycle field. Supply elasticity will be much increased.

In the very long run—say, a generation of thirty years—the elasticity of supply will increase even further. For now it will be possible for the entire supply of mechanics in the economy generally to expand. Young men and women who might have become welders or bricklayers or plumbers or secretaries may now decide to train for the more lucrative field of the mechanic. In the extremely long run—assuming, of course, a purely competitive economy—the wage of bicycle mechanics could not long sustain itself above the wage of any other employment of comparable skill and attraction. At this point, labor supply begins to be dominated by those long-run factors—some economic, some not—that affect the growth of the society's population (see pp. 131 and 403). Will higher incomes produce larger or smaller families? As we know, these issues are most complicated and may vary from society to society, perhaps especially in the less developed as compared to the developed.

DETERMINATION OF FACTOR PRICE

So that we can get on with the process of factor price determination, let us suppose that we are dealing with the supply of bicycle mechanics in the intermediate run. Figure 21–4 is neither perfectly elastic nor perfectly inelastic. It tells us that, as the wage of bicycle mechanics goes up, workers from related fields will be drawn into this particular trade. On the other hand, the period is not so long that it makes possible the redirection of a whole new generation of workers. Consequently, there is some limit to the

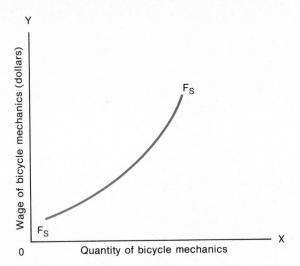

Figure 21-4. A Factor Supply Curve.

Curve $F_S F_S$ represents a reasonable shape for the supply curve of a factor (bicycle mechanics' services) in the intermediate run.

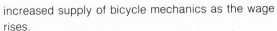

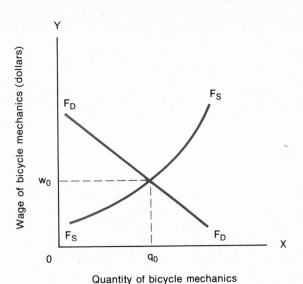

Figure 21-5. Supply and Demand in the Factor Market.

If $F_D F_D$ is the factor demand curve and $F_S F_S$ is the factor supply curve, equilibrium wage will be w_o, and equilibrium quantity of bicycle mechanics hired will be q_o.

increased supply of bicycle mechanics as the wage rises.

We have now both a demand curve and a supply curve for bicycle mechanics. The price or wage of bicycle mechanics will be determined by the intersection of these two curves. In particular, the equilibrium wage will be w_0 and the equilibrium quantity of bicycle mechanics hired will be equal to q_0 (Figure 21-5). At this particular equilibrium point, the bicycle firms will be satisfied that they are doing as well as they can, because they are hiring bicycle mechanics to the point where their *VMP* = w_0. At the same time, the supply curve assures us that the workers are also doing as well as they can under the circumstances, for the supply curve includes within it the adjustments that individual workmen have made between work and leisure at the various possible wage rates and also the shifting of labor in and out of the bicycle mechanic field in the intermediate run. Taking

all these elements into consideration, the workers at w_0 will offer q_0 units of bicycle mechanics' services for hire, and this is precisely the quantity that is being hired at the equilibrium point.

To test your understanding of this matter, explain to yourself why a wage higher than w_0 would leave labor unsatisfied (leading them to bid the wage down) and why a lower wage would leave the bicycle producers unsatisfied (leading them to bid the wage up).

Since we have already made some comments about labor markets, and since we will return to them again in chapter 26, let us now make some comments about the other major factors—land and capital. For the remainder of this chapter we shall say a few words about land and rent, capital and interest, and then add a very brief note about "profits."

LAND AND RENT

In the early nineteenth century, David Ricardo defined *land* as meaning "the original and indestructible" powers of the soil. The implied generalization was that land and natural resources are given to the economy once and for all, or in more technical terms, that the supply of land for the economy as a whole is perfectly inelastic even in the long run. (Indeed, land was treated by classical authors as the economic opposite of labor, which Malthus considered to be in perfectly elastic supply.[3])

Now this generalization about the fixity of land is obviously not completely accurate: Land and natural resources can be depleted by excessive or improper usage; mineral deposits can be exhausted; *new* land can be created by drainage, irrigation of desert areas; and so on. But on the whole, our natural resource base does tend to change relatively slowly compared with the other factors of production. Consequently, we might represent the supply curve for land as we do in Figure 21–6—a vertical straight line. No matter what the price of land is, the supply of land will be roughly the same.

The British classical economists called the payment to land *rent.* Even today the term *economic rent* is used to describe the payment to any factor that is offered in completely inelastic supply.[4] Such rent payments have two rather special and interesting characteristics.

The first is that, given the fixed supply of the factor, it is the demand for the factor that determines the

---

3. See pp. 130–31.

4. Economists today, however, recognize more clearly than their predecessors that other kinds of factors of production besides land may be in inelastic supply. Opera singers and professional football quarterbacks are cases in point. As you might say, there was only one Caruso—had the price of tenors increased, there still would have been only one. It is therefore perfectly proper and logical to say that opera singers and other inelastically supplied factors earn a "rent" in basically the same way that land earns rent.

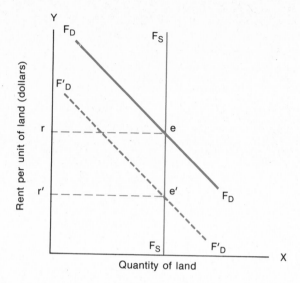

Figure 21–6. Land and Rent.

This diagram could be applied to land or to any other factor in completely inelastic supply.

price (rent). Thus, in Figure 21–6, any shift in the demand curve of the factor (from F_D to F'_D) will completely determine the change in rent going to the factor (from r to r'). Supply is given; demand does all the work. In cases like this we can see with special clarity why factor prices and consequently "costs" in a society cannot be determined without reference to consumer preferences. The demand curve for land will (as all factor demand curves do) reflect consumer demands for the products of land. If the consumers suddenly conceive a dislike of products with a high land factor component, their distaste will bring down the demand curve, bring down the rent of land, and change the "costs" facing each firm that uses land in its production process.

The other rather special characteristic of rent is that it is in some senses a surplus or unnecessary payment. By this we mean that although most economic payments serve as inducements to secure more work from the factors of production, rents do not function in this way. By definition, *economic rents* refer to payments made to a factor in inelastic supply—the amount of factor services offered in the market is the same, no matter what you pay for them. This has led many economists—especially the nineteenth century "single-tax" economist Henry George —to advocate concentrating taxation on land rent. In terms of our diagram, we can see that if the government took away from the landowner an amount equal to the rectangle *rr'e'e,* the supply of land offered on the market would be unaffected. (In theory, of course, the same principle could be applied to other inelastically supplied factors. You could heavily tax opera singers, and they would doubtless still continue to sing.) While this feature of rent taxation is a clear advantage, it does not necessarily mean that such taxes are best, for a *major* consideration in taxation must be its effects on *income distribution.* Do you want landowners (or opera singers for that matter) to be taxed much more heavily than factory owners, business managers, or government officials? Rent taxation does avoid some of the incentive distortions of other taxes, but it must also be evaluated in terms of its effects on the distribution of income in the society as a whole. We shall return to this large question of income distribution in chapter 29.

CAPITAL AND INTEREST

The other big category of factors of production, beside labor and land, is *capital.* It includes machinery, tools, plant, equipment, buildings, inventories, and all those means of production that are themselves a product of the economic system. If land is a gift of nature, capital is clearly one factor of production whose creation and continuing supply is determined by the workings of the economy as a whole. For capital, as we have said before, is a *produced* factor

of production, and the motives governing its production are almost wholly economic in nature.

Actually, this distinction between capital and land is more significant in the long run than in the short run. At any given moment of time, it makes little difference to a producer whether the factor of production he is using to make bicycles was wholly or partially "produced" by man. It is very doubtful that he could (or would want to) separate the "natural" from the "man-made" component of a steel wrench or a hammer. At any given moment of time, we have a stock of goods that can be used in production; these goods are the cooperative product of man and nature in times past, and they can be substituted for each other more or less easily as technology production permits. Indeed, in the short run, it can be said that man-made machines earn a payment that is very much like land-rent. If the demand for the products of machinery increases, then the prices of those machines will go up. Because in the short run it is impossible to increase the stock of machines substantially, they tend to be in rather inelastic supply and to earn what the great British economist, Alfred Marshall, called a *quasi-rent.*

In the longer run, however, quasi-rents will disappear because capital can be accumulated. In many societies, indeed, the rapid accumulation of capital is a major objective of national policy.

We have already discussed capital accumulation in two contexts. The first was in the analysis of economic growth and development (chapters 6 and 16) where we emphasized the role of capital in expanding production over time. The second was in Part Two A, where we were discussing the macroeconomic effects of investment. We noted the differences between saving and investment decisions and how these differences could lead to excessive or inadequate aggregate demand—inflation or below-full-employment national income.

In microeconomics it is customary not to forget, but to abstract from these macro-effects. Let us suppose we are operating in an economy in which there are no complications of a monetary nature that stand in the way of full employment. Given our stocks of factors of production—labor, land, capital—we can then determine what our full employment income will be. Having settled all this, we then ask: What will the process of capital accumulation look like in this society? What forces will determine how much income people in this society will set aside for capital accumulation—investment—as opposed to consumption?

One might think of the basic process this way: The economy has a choice between consuming all the goods it produces in a given year or *saving* some of its income and *investing* this income in new machines, tools, and other capital goods. We have produced a national income of $100 billion. Shall we consume all the $100 billion or shall we consume $80 billion and realize the remaining $20 billion in the form of machinery, plant, and equipment? The primary reason for a society's saving and investing $20 billion in this way is that with more capital, it will be able to produce a higher income in the future. The choice is between greater satisfaction *now* (consuming the whole $100 billion) and greater satisfaction *later* (saving and investing $20 billion and thus having the tools to produce a greater income in future years).

Now in a society free from short-run fluctuations of income and other macroeconomic problems, we can see that a rather key element in the supply and demand for capital will be the *rate of interest*. Look at it first from the consumer's point of view: Shall he consume all his income today or shall he save some of it for tomorrow? On the whole, he will be willing to save some of his income (say, $1,000) only if he can expect to get something rather larger tomorrow (say, $1,050). The rate of interest tells the consumer how much future income he may expect to get from a sacrifice of some of today's income.

Thus, on the saving side, within limits, a higher rate of interest may induce people to save more.[5]

From the producer's side, the interest rate represents the price he must pay for his capital. If a machine costs $1,000 and the interest rate is 9 percent a year, then, assuming no depreciation, the effective cost of that machine to that businessman is $90 per year. When the businessman hires a unit of capital, he must make sure that its net rate of return (the marginal productivity of capital) is above or equal to the interest rate. The businessman will add units of capital to his firm until, at the margin, the net productivity of capital is just equal to the interest rate. What this means is that the higher the interest rate, the lower will be the quantity of additional capital demanded.

Thus we have the two sides of our capital market. At very high interest rates, the consumers' desire

---

5.   We have to say ''within limits'' because the effect of the interest rate on savings is a bit complex. Essentially, the problem comes from our familiar friends, the *income* and *substitution effects* (see p. 436, where we discuss these effects in relation to labor supply). We can imagine the savings process in terms of a consumer buying some income for tomorrow with some of today's income. For $100 saved today, I can get $110 tomorrow (or more accurately, a year from today) if the rate of interest is 10 percent. Now suppose the rate of interest increases to, say, 15 percent. This is the equivalent to a *fall in the price of tomorrow's income.* I used to have to pay $100 to get $110 tomorrow. Now I can get $110 tomorrow for about $95.65 (i.e., $110 ÷ 1.15).

Now, according to the *substitution effect,* when the price of a commodity goes down, the consumer will substitute it for other more expensive commodities. This effect would tend to *increase* saving when the interest rate rose. Tomorrow's income is cheaper; hence, I will substitute more of tomorrow's income for today's—i.e., I will save more.

But the *income effect* works differently. When the interest rate goes up, I am richer in general since I can have more income tomorrow and no less today. But when I am richer in general, I want to buy more of all commodities in general. In particular I want to have more consumption today. But this would mean *less* saving today.

The net result of an increase in the interest rate on savings, therefore, is hard to gauge, because it will be the resolution of these two quite different effects.

This, of course, also abstracts from the *further* complications raised by money, liquidity preference, etc., which we discussed in Part Two.

to save will exceed the willingness of businessmen to invest; at very low interest rates, businessmen will want to accumulate more capital than consumers wish to save. Equilibrium will be achieved at that level of the interest rate where savings decisions are equated to investment decisions. What this means at a deeper level is that the consumer's evaluation of present income in relation to future income (sometimes called *consumer time-preference*) will have been equated to the technological possibilities of turning present into future income via the accumulation of capital (reflecting the marginal productivity of capital). At this deeper level, we can understand that a *higher* interest rate (i.e., above the equilibrium level) would, in effect, be an unkeepable promise to consumers to bring them future income at a rate beyond that which is technologically feasible. Conversely, a *lower* rate would represent a failure of the society to recognize and exploit the full possibilities of translating present into future income by a more capital-using technology.

In the real world, as we know, these issues are much complicated by the role of uncertainty, by the operation of "money," and by the complex financial, credit, and other institutions that influence the capital market. These complications, however, should not be allowed to obscure the element of fundamental truth in what we have just been saying. Societies *do* have basic choices to make between present and future, and what we have just indicated is that the most important way such choices are made economically is through the mechanism of capital accumulation.

A NOTE ON PROFITS

In discussing the basic factors of production—land, labor, and capital—we have also described three categories of payment: rent, wages, and interest. What we have said, in effect, is that in determining the prices of the factors of production, we are determining the distribution of income in the society. Very roughly, the owners of land will get rent, laborers

will get wages, and the owners of capital will get interest. This is "very roughly" the case because, as we have noticed, these categories are broad and sometimes overlapping. (Thus, if opera singers are in inelastic supply, they may earn a rent; moreover, machinery and buildings may be in inelastic supply in the short run, and they then earn a *quasi-rent;* and so on.)

There is, however, one omission that is a bit more worrisome: the category of *profits.* For as any national income accountant will tell you, the total income of our society includes rents, wages, interest, *and profits.* Indeed, in some sense, the pursuit of profits is what a private, competitive economy is supposed to be all about, so let us make a few brief comments about this problem of profits.

(1) Our rent, wages, and interest payments include *part* of what people often call profits. You will recall that our cost curves always include normal profits or what we have sometimes called *wages of management.*

(2) We know that in long-run equilibrium in a purely competitive economy, no "pure" profits would exist. Whenever pure or abnormal profits exist in any particular industry, firms will quickly enter in and compete them down to the normal wages-of-management level. Be sure to note that there is nothing contradictory in saying that (*a*) profits are the motive spur of the entire system and (*b*) in long-run equilibrium, no pure profits will exist. For it is precisely the attempt by firms to maximize profits that drives them in and out of various industries and leads to the elimination of abnormal profits where they exist. This may be a paradox, but it is not a contradiction; indeed, this paradox lies at the very core of a private market economy.

(3) The real world is, in fact, more complex than our purely competitive world. Some element of what are called profits represents the exercise of market control by individual firms in an *imperfectly* competitive way. This monopoly element in profits has no place in the present chapter but will be discussed in Part Three B.

(4) We should remember that in this analysis of pure competition we have largely skirted important questions having to do with uncertainty and change. One of the great sources of turbulence in our economic life is the fact that the products we consume and their methods of production are both *constantly being revolutionized.* There is, as the great Austro-American economist Joseph A. Schumpeter (1883–1950) used to say, a constant process of *innovation* in the modern economy. Schumpeter said that beside the laborer, landowner, and capitalist, there is another figure in modern industrial life that must be reckoned with: the *entrepreneur.* The precise role of the entrepreneur is to innovate, to introduce new products and new methods of production, to discover new markets and new sources of new materials, and so on. He is regarded as the agent of change, and his reward, according to Schumpeter, is *profits.* The process works as follows: The economy is in equilibrium with no abnormal profits for anyone. The entrepreneur bursts in with his new innovation. (Think of computers, automation, plastics, other synthetic materials.) The first men in the field enjoy tremendous advantages over their competitors. Presently, the competition sees what the situation is; hosts of firms swarm into the new field; the temporary advantages are lost. In the interim, however, there has been a once-over accrual of profits to the original entrepreneurs. Moreover, since there is always some innovation going on *somewhere* in the economy, there will always be someone earning profits at any given moment in time. Profits created by innovation are temporary in any one field; but in an economy where innovation is quite general, they become a permanent category of income.

Thus, the closer we approach real-world conditions, the more important it becomes for us to recognize that in addition to the standard factor payments—wages, rent, and interest—there exists a fourth category of income—profits—which is closely linked with the uncertainty, change, and imperfection of the modern industrial economy.

SUMMARY

Like product prices, factor prices in a competitive economy are also determined by supply and demand. The demanders, however, are now business firms and the suppliers are factor owners.

Under pure competition, each firm will hire a factor to the point where its price (or wage) is equal to the value of its marginal product, or $P_F = P \times MP_F$. This follows from the two conditions, developed in earlier chapters, that the firm will be producing where $P = MC$, and where $MC = P_F/MP_F$.

This rule enables us to determine a *demand curve for a factor* quite directly in a simple case. If we have an individual firm hiring one variable factor in the short run, then its demand curve for the factor will simply be the marginal product curve of that factor multiplied at each MP by P, or the *value-of-the-marginal-product* curve.

When several variable factors are taken into account, the demand for any factor will depend in part on the ease with which this factor can be substituted for other factors and vice versa. The easier it is to make these substitutions, the more *elastic* will be the factor demand.

When we move from the individual firm to the industry as a whole, we must now take into account the fact that as all firms expand hirings of a factor and increase the output of the commodity in question, the price of the commodity will fall. In general, the more elastic the consumer demand for the product the factor produces, the more elastic the factor demand will be. Because of this relationship between consumer demand and factor demand, the latter is often spoken of as a *derived demand*. In an ultimate sense, producers demand the services of factors only because consumers are demanding the products that those factors help produce.

The *supply curve of a factor* will depend on the nature of the particular factor involved and also, quite generally, on time. For the most part, the longer the period allowed for, the more *elastic* the factor supply. In the case of *labor,* the short-run supply curve may be *backward bending* due to the combination of income and substitution effects.

Given both factor demand and factor supply curves, the price of any factor will be determined by the intersection of these curves. At this factor price, quantity supplied and quantity demand will be equated.

Certain factors of production have rather special features:

Land. In the past, it was considered that the distinguishing feature of land was that it was in completely inelastic supply: the "original and indestructible" powers of the soil. Although this characterization is not accurate, nevertheless it is true that natural resource supplies tend to change relatively slowly in comparison to the other two factors of production—labor and capital. The payment to land is often called *rent* although the modern economist also uses *rent* to mean the payment to other factors besides land that may be in inelastic supply (e.g., pro football quarterbacks). Rent payments have the characteristic that they are a taxable surplus, in the sense that factor supply (being perfectly inelastic) will not be affected by a reduction in the payment to the factor in question.

Capital. In a simplified full-employment economy, we may imagine capital accumulation involving a choice between present and future consumption. In this simple world, the *rate of interest* will be such that supply and demand in the capital market are equated. A high interest rate, within limits, may encourage consumers to save more in order to enjoy greater income in the future. A high interest rate, by contrast, will discourage producers from investing in more capital, since they will undertake projects only to the point where the marginal productivity of capital is equal to the interest rate. Equilibrium will be achieved when the interest rate is such that the consumers' desires to save (reflecting their feelings about present versus future income) are equated to the businessmen's desires to invest (reflecting their judgments about the marginal productivity of capital).

Finally, besides rents, interest, and wages, there is a fourth category of income: *profits. Pure* profits do not exist in equilibrium under pure competition. However, *normal profits, or wages of management,* are included in the competitive cost curves. Also, profits may arise in the real world because of monopoly elements in the economy and because of uncertainty, change, and innovation.

IMPORTANT TERMS TO REMEMBER

Competitive equilibrium:

$$P = MC = \frac{P_F}{MP_F}$$

Value of the Marginal Product of a Factor (VMP)

$$P_F = P \times MP_F \neq VMP$$

Short Run Factor Demand Curve

Elasticity of Factor Demand

Substitutability of Factors

Derived Demand

Elasticity of Consumer
  Demand/Elasticity of Factor Demand

Backward-Bending Supply Curve for Labor

Perfectly Inelastic Factor Supply

Economic Rent

Interest and Capital

Consumer Time Preference

Profits

Entrepreneurs

QUESTIONS FOR DISCUSSION

1. Suppose that we have a marginal product curve for bicycle mechanics as drawn in Figure 21–1 (a). Suppose further that bicycle mechanics are necessary to producing bicycles in the sense that when no mechanics are employed, bicycle output will be zero.

(*a*) Define the term *average product* of bicycle mechanics.

(*b*) Draw in an approximate *average product curve* for bicycle mechanics, to go with your marginal product curve.

(*c*) Comment on the following statement: "It is unfair to pay labor its marginal product only; what labor should get is what it actually produces—namely, its average product."

2. Suppose that the consumer demand curve for a particular product were completely inelastic (consumers will buy the same amount of the product, no matter what the price). Do you think that this would lead to a completely inelastic demand for a factor of production engaged in producing that product? Explain your answer fully.

3. Another element affecting the elasticity of demand for a factor of production, besides those mentioned in this chapter, is the importance of the factor in relation to the total costs of the firms hiring the factor. It is claimed that if the factor is relatively *un*important, the demand for that factor will tend to be relatively more *in*elastic. Explain the reasoning that might produce this conclusion. Can you see any argument here that might lead a labor organizer to advocate a union with membership based on a particular craft rather than on the industry-wide labor force as a whole?

4. What would a modern ecologist be likely to say about the view that land (natural resources) is ''original and indestructible''?

5. Considering what you have learned about the determination of factor prices in this chapter, write an essay on the possible effects of capital accumulation and technological progress on the real wages of labor in a competitive economy.

APPENDIX 21:
A CASE STUDY OF FACTOR SUPPLY AND DEMAND

High-Priced Oil and the Labor and Capital Goods Markets

Sanford Rose

One interesting consequence of the energy shortage, and the resulting higher prices of oil products, is that it may affect the relative demand for labor services as compared to capital goods, and thus ultimately the income distribution between laborers and owners of property (recipients of interest, dividends, etc.). The following reading gives us a case analysis of factor supply and demand by suggesting how these differential effects on labor and capital might be produced.

Higher energy costs will have an across-the-board impact on the structure of demand. In turn, changes in the structure of demand, even marginal ones, will greatly influence the total demand for labor and capital goods for the rest of the decade.

A REPLACEMENT FOR LABOR

Logically, energy and labor are substitutes for one another. As every beginning-science student is taught, energy is simply the capacity to do work. The more complex an industrial society becomes, the more it learns how to organize electrical, mechanical, thermal, or nuclear means of doing the work that men once did with their hands. Those industries that have been most successful in harnessing energy to the productive process require the least labor. The five most energy-intensive industries account for

Excerpted from Sanford Rose, "The Far-Reaching Consequences of High-Priced Oil," *Fortune*, March, 1974, pp. 191–196.

about two-thirds of all the energy consumed by man-ufacturers—but provide only about a quarter of all manufacturing jobs.

According to Bruce Hannon,* an extra $100,000 worth of aluminum could be produced with about 38 billion more BTU's and five more people. By contrast, an extra $100,000 worth of tobacco requires only five billion more BTU's but creates thirty-two new jobs. In other words, a shift of $100,000 of final demand from aluminum to tobacco should reduce our energy consumption by 33 billion BTU's, while creating twenty-seven new jobs.

Thus higher energy prices would, in principle, favor tobacco consumption over aluminum consumption. It is admittedly not easy to think of situations in which the two are competitors. Yet consumers will ultimately find the trade-offs between them. For example, if the price of aluminum products increases because of a rise in the cost of energy needed to make them, consumers might spend less money to relax with soft drinks out of aluminum cans and more to relax with tobacco.

To forestall this process, soft-drink manufacturers might abandon aluminum in favor of steel cans. Steel is energy-intensive, but less so than aluminum. A shift from $100,000 of aluminum to $100,000 of steel reduces overall energy consumption by about 11 billion BTU's and creates two new jobs.

Costlier energy will not merely change the com-position of the demand for goods, it will also acceler-ate the shift from goods to services. Nearly all ser-vices consume more modest amounts of energy than do goods. As a result, the price of most services will be falling in relation to the price of most goods. Demand for, say, entertainment services can be ex-pected to benefit in any broad consumer shift from high-priced goods to lower-priced services.

Changes in public policy will presumably accom-modate a shift toward industries and activities that require less energy and more labor. As the demand

---

*Professor of engineering at the University of Illinois.

for motor-vehicle travel weakens because of rising gasoline prices, there will be increasing pressures to divert Highway Trust Fund revenues to mass-transit facilities. Hannon has studied the impact of rechan-neling an estimated $5 billion in trust-fund revenues in 1975. He calculates that shifting all $5 billion in the fund from highways to railroad construction would be immensely energy-saving and moderately job-creating.

Highway construction is one of our largest con-sumers of energy: asphalt is itself a petroleum prod-uct and cement manufacturing is highly energy-intensive. Thus, a $5-billion highway-building pro-gram uses 220 trillion BTU's, whereas a $5-billion railroad-building program would demand only 80 trillion BTU's. It would take 256,000 people, directly and indirectly, to build the highways, compared to 264,000 people for the railroads—a net gain of 8,000 jobs.

AN INVESTMENT IN HEALTH

Suppose that, as part of a massive reordering of priorities, Congress decided to invest highway funds in national health programs rather than in mass tran-sit. The energy savings would decrease in that case —but there would be even more new jobs. Medical services consume a fair amount of energy, e.g., in the form of electricity for lighting and for running small machines and air conditioners. But health care is also one of the most labor-intensive industries around. A $5-billion health program would provide 423,000 jobs: 167,000 more than the highways and 159,000 more than the railroads.

Congress might become even more venturesome and decide to link energy savings with the solid-waste problem, by imposing heavy taxes on throwaway cans and bottles. Throwaways, particularly those made of aluminum, require much more energy to manufacture than do glass returnables. If all beer and soft-drink manufacturers were to abandon throwaways entirely in favor of returnables, the nation would save about 30 billion kilowatt-hours of electricity a year, which is equal to about one-half of 1 percent of total energy consumption. At the same time, the demand for labor would rise, since it would require many more man-hours at the retail level to handle the returnables. On balance some 30,000 new jobs would be created.

In a much oversimplified fashion, these examples illustrate one long-term consequence of rising energy prices: the number of job opportunities will increase more rapidly than would otherwise have been the case. And as the demand for labor rises, so will wages. Other things being equal, labor's share of national income will rise. The share going to property holders, dividend recipients, and bondholders will fall.

Note that this process will reverse the short-term trend. The first effect of a rise in energy prices will be to shift income away from labor and toward the owners of capital and natural resources. But after companies and consumers have had a chance to adjust to higher energy prices, by altering their patterns of demand, the money will flow in a different direction.

BAD NEWS FOR CAPITAL GOODS

The impact of rising energy prices on the demand for capital goods could well be the exact opposite of the impact on labor. The greatest demand for capital goods obviously comes from industries that have the highest capital-output ratios—industries in which investments in plant and equipment have the highest payoffs in sales. But these industries, which include aluminum, chemical, and paper, are also among the biggest users of energy. The more machinery one needs, the more BTU's one consumes.

The relationship between energy use and the demand for capital goods has been studied in some detail by Ernst Berndt, a professor of economics at the University of British Columbia, and by David Wood of the Federal Energy Office. Analyzing unpublished data for the postwar years, the two found that capital and energy are indeed highly complementary—that

is, greater demand for one is invariably accompanied by a greater demand for the other. If the price of energy rises, energy consumption decreases and demand for capital goods falls. Berndt and Wood calculated that, from 1947 to 1971, every 1 percent increase in the price of energy reduced the demand for capital goods by .14 percent to .16 percent.

If the same relationship prevails in the future, a doubling of energy prices would cut off about 15 percent of all capital-goods demand. The key question is whether the same relationship would indeed prevail. Can the events of a period of stable or falling energy prices tell us very much about a period in which prices are rising rapidly?

There is no doubt that all the past relationships favored efforts to substitute energy for labor. From 1947 to 1971 the proportion of total manufacturing costs spent on energy was relatively stable, averaging around 5 percent. Thus it did not pay companies to allocate very much capital for the purpose of saving energy. Instead, it made sense to use capital, in conjunction with cheap energy, to economize on labor, whose share of total manufacturing costs was rising, from about 25 percent in 1947 to about 29 percent in 1971.

Now that relative prices are changing, managerial attitudes may also change. Capital and energy will become less complementary and more interchangeable.

Here again there will be a critical difference between the long run and the short run. In the short run, the demand for capital goods will probably increase despite—indeed, because of—higher energy prices. Energy producers will be buying more drilling and mining equipment. And industry in general will be buying a great deal of energy-saving capital equipment. Heat exchangers, temperature-control equipment, and more efficient kilns and furnaces will be very much in demand.

But, if energy prices continue rising, demand for the products of the energy-intensive industries will eventually weaken. This means that output will tend to increase at a slower rate in those areas of the economy that have traditionally bought the most capital goods. The increased demand for energy-saving equipment will only soften the blow.

THE THREAT TO EFFICIENCY

In the final analysis, rising energy prices will tend to lower the rate of productivity gain in the entire economy. This process will come about in two ways. First, changes in the structure of final demand will reduce the growth rate of the energy-intensive industries, which are the most capital-intensive and, typically, the most efficient. In addition, these industries will increasingly be forced to curb their demand for *productive* capital goods (those that boost output) and increase their demand for essentially *nonproductive* capital goods (those that save energy).

By the same token, final demand will shift to those goods-producing industries that use a higher proportion of labor per unit of output. These industries are generally among the less efficient in the economy. Demand will also shift from goods to services, where productivity has been lower than in most goods-producing industries.   □

CHAPTER 22
INTERDEPENDENCE AND EFFICIENCY

With the work of chapter 21, we have completed our analysis of the basic relationships that link together the determination of prices and quantities in a purely competitive economy. At the very beginning of this analysis, we said that its purpose was twofold. In the first place, the study of the purely competitive economy allows us to demonstrate the fundamental *interdependence* of the elements of an economic system. This principle of interdependence applies to all kinds of economic systems, but the variety and complexity of the real world often modify and obscure the principle to the point where it is almost impossible to discern. What the analysis of pure competition gives us is a useful starting point for making our way through this real-world maze. The general tendencies we have been describing *are* meaningful, although they may not fit without qualification in any particular case.

In the second place, we said that pure competition gives us a standard by which to judge the *efficiency* of an economic system. Adam Smith's "invisible hand" referred to a union of private and social interest. The analysis of pure competition enables us to indicate under what circumstances this is true and under what circumstances it is not true. By comparing the functioning of other systems, including socialist systems, with the purely competitive model, we are able to gain important clues for economic *policy*. Should the government intervene? If so, how? What are the consequences? Efficiency, as we shall stress, is not the only significant economic objective, but it is an important one that no citizen or state would wish to ignore for long.

In this final chapter on the competitive system, we shall pull together various strands from earlier discussions and attempt to demonstrate the meaning of *interdependence* and *efficiency* from an overall point of view.

FOUR INTERDEPENDENT QUESTIONS

Why does coffee cost more per pound than tea? In the early days of economics, writers like Ricardo or Marx tried to detach this question from the overall workings of the economic system, and they argued that the answer depended on the quantity of labor embodied in each commodity. Modern economics, by contrast, recognizes that this question is simply one of a series of interdependent questions and that, in principle, one can answer it only by addressing all these other questions simultaneously.

Ultimately, there are four basic sets of questions involved in the kind of economy we are dealing with. Two of these sets of questions deal with *prices;* the other two deal with *quantities.* The reader should be able to recognize the four sets of problems described below as simply rephrasings of the questions we raised in chapter 17.

1. Prices of all commodities. Our economic system must find some way of giving a determinate value to the prices of coffee, tea, bicycles, vacuum cleaners, and all other commodities.[1]

2. Quantities of commodities produced. How many units of tea, coffee, bicycles, vacuum cleaners, and all other commodities will be produced by our economy in equilibrium?

3. Prices of the factors of production. We must determine the prices of land, labor, and capital as their services are employed in the productive process. Since these factor payments are the incomes of the factors (rent, wages, and interest), we earlier referred to this question as that of the "distribution of income" in our economy.

---

1.   In chapter 17, we called this the question of the "relative values of commodities." In a more advanced treatment, it would be shown that one commodity (tea, if you will) is used as a measuring rod for the prices of other commodities. That is, price of tea = 1. Other prices are then determined *in relation to* the price of tea.

4. Quantities of the factors of production employed in producing each commodity. We have to determine what quantities of different kinds of labor, land, and capital will be used in the production of each commodity. This involves knowing how much labor, land, and capital will be supplied to the economy as a whole and how these supplies are divided up among all the different producers of commodities. The answer to this question will tell us the methods of production in use in our economy in equilibrium.

These, then, are the basic questions that, when the economy is in overall or *general equilibrium,* must all be answered.

Now if these questions were *not* interdependent, we could separate questions 1 and 2 in one group and questions 3 and 4 in another group. Questions 1 and 2 refer to the market for commodities, or the *product markets.* If we have a consumer demand curve for each and every product and an industry supply curve for each and every product, then we could simultaneously determine: (1) the prices of all commodities and (2) the quantities of all commodities produced. The intersection of each supply and demand curve, as we recall, determines both equilibrium price and equilibrium quantity produced.

Similarly, we can recognize that questions 3 and 4 refer to the markets for the services of the factors of production, or, briefly, the *factor markets.* If we had a business demand curve and a factor supply curve for each factor of production, we could determine the price of the factor of production and the quantity of that factor of production that would be employed in the economy as a whole. We would also have the information needed to show what quantity of that (and every other) factor of production would be used by each industry and business firm in the economy. As in the case of products, supply and demand would enable us to determine both (1) factor prices and (2) factor quantities.

Now what the principle of interdependence tells us is that these two markets are in fact *interrelated.* The results in one market will influence the results in the other market, and vice versa. Thus, in the final analysis, *both* markets must reach equilibrium simultaneously. To prove this point, let us show (*a*) how the results in the factor market can influence the product market and (*b*) how the results in the product market can influence the factor market.

Factor Market Influences Product Market

Suppose that there is some new invention that greatly economizes on labor and greatly increases the productivity of land. This invention is likely to cause an upward shift in the business demand curve for land. Suppose now that the supply and demand process has worked itself out and, in particular, that new factor prices have been determined in the factor market. Will these new prices of the factors influence consumer demands for commodities in the product market? The answer, in general, is yes.

Factor prices, in our example, have been altered in such a way that the price of land has risen in relation to the price of labor. This is the same thing as saying that there has been a redistribution of income in favor of the landowner compared to the laborer. How will this affect consumer demand? Suppose landowners as a group are richer than laborers (i.e., per individual). An increase in landowners' income relative to laborers' income should then have the effect of increasing consumer demand for "luxury" goods (yachts, trips to the Riviera) as opposed to "necessaries" (meat and potatoes). The new total *equilibrium situation, therefore, may be characterized by a relative increase in the quantity and price of "luxuries" compared to the quantity and price of "necessaries."*

In short, a change in factor prices has altered consumer incomes, and these incomes influence the patterns of consumer purchases in the product market.

Product Market Influences Factor Market

The influence of the product market on the factor market has been noted in earlier chapters, particularly in our consideration of derived demand. Suppose that there is a sudden shift in demand by consumers, away from handicraft products (mainly produced by labor) and toward various kinds of mechanical household appliances (produced, let us say, by highly capital-intensive methods). Now the final result in the product market of this shift in demand will be an increase in both the price and quantity of household appliances and a decrease in the price and quantity of handicraft products. Will this change in the product market influence the determination of prices and quantities in the factor market? Again, the general answer is yes.

The initial effect of the shift in consumer demand will be to raise the value of the marginal product of those factors (mainly certain kinds of capital) employed in the household appliance industries and to lower the value of the marginal product of those factors (mainly certain kinds of labor) employed in the handicraft industries. If these factors were specific to these industries and were in completely inelastic supply, the end result would be simply a shift upward in the demand curve and an increase in the price of the appliance-capital factors and a shift downward in the demand curve and the price of the handicraft-labor factors. This would be a direct impact of the shift in consumer demand on the factor market.

In the long run, however, it is more likely that labor and capital can be shifted between the two industries. As handicraft production falls, it will release labor and capital for the appliance industry. But it will release very little capital and a great deal of labor. Thus the supply of labor will exceed the demand for it in the appliance industry, whereas the supply of capital will be inadequate. The total long-run effect, then, will be a rise in the price of capital, compared to the original situation; a fall in the price of labor;

CHARLES PHELPS CUSHING

Léon Walras (1834–1910). A French-Swiss economist, Walras is known for his theory of general equilibrium and, in terms of economic methodology, his strong preference for the use of mathematics in economics.

and, depending upon the ease of factor substitution, a general tendency to use a higher proportion of the now cheaper labor in the production of both handicraft goods and household appliances. Thus, price-and-quantity determination in the factor market has been altered by the changed circumstances of the product market.

In sum, the principle of interdependence tells us that our four questions must all be solved at the same time. Prices and quantities in the factor market and prices and quantities in the product market are all component parts of one overarching, indivisible system of economic relationships.

INTERDEPENDENCE AND THE CIRCULAR FLOW

The discovery of the full implications of interdependence is usually credited to Léon Walras, the late nineteenth-century economist whom we have mentioned before, although many other economists, including England's Alfred Marshall, should be acknowledged as well. It is no accident that Walras' work—unlike that of the classical school of Smith, Ricardo, and Malthus—was presented in mathematical form. For what we have been describing reduces essentially to a set of simultaneous equations. Since Walras' day, economic theory at advanced levels has increasingly been formulated in mathematical terms, and we can now begin to appreciate the reasons why.

For our purposes, however, the essence of the relationships we have been describing can be set forth in our familiar circular flow diagram. Since this diagram (Figure 22–1) has now been expanded to include much of what we have been saying in the preceding chapters, it is necessarily a bit complex and requires some study and comment.

We start out by taking certain things as *given.* In the case of the business firms, we are assuming a given technology or *technological horizon,* as it is sometimes put. In particular, we are assuming that we have the necessary production information for each product in our economy. On the household side, we are given the basic tastes and preferences of consumers. As part of these tastes and preferences, we also take as given their preferences as between work and leisure. These preferences will determine how much labor supply will be offered on the factor market at various wage levels. Finally, we assume that the stock of land, population, and capital is given.

Over time, of course, all these *givens* will change. Innovations will alter business production technology, population will grow, capital will be accumulated, even consumer tastes will alter. When any of these changes occur, the whole system will be altered. Indeed, one of the purposes of this analysis is to provide a way of analyzing the full effects of any

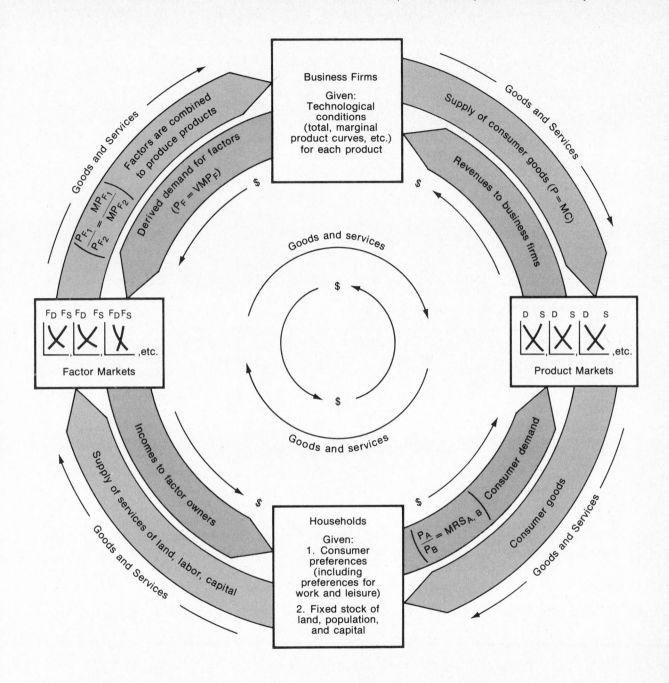

Figure 22–1. General Equilibrium in a Purely Competitive Economy.

change in basic conditions.[2] Our immediate question, however, is: Assuming these given conditions, how are our four interdependent questions of the previous section to be solved?

The next step is to represent our two basic units—business firms and households—as coming together in two markets: the product market and the factor market. As described previously, we have two flows. In the *goods-and-services* flow, the households dispatch the services of the factors they own to business firms, which combine these factors to produce products that they then can sell back to the households as consumer goods.[3] In the case of the *money ($)* flow: The households, demanding consumer goods, spend their money incomes, which provide business firms with the revenues to hire the factors of production whose payments, in turn, return to the households as their money incomes. After the fact, these flows must always match perfectly since it is tautologically true that "quantity bought" must always equal "quantity sold."

Now what we have done in the preceding chapters is to spell out a number of conditions that households and business firms will meet as they participate in this process under the assumption of pure competition. Within the arrows of Figure 22–1 we have in-

dicated some of these important conditions. Make certain that you understand what each of these conditions means and why it holds true in a purely competitive economy.

Finally, guided by these various principles of action, the flows meet in the product market and in the factor market. The overall equilibrium condition is that the price and quantity of each product and each factor is such that the quantity supplied equals the quantity demanded throughout the entire economy. When this happens, not only will the money and goods-and-services flows be equal (quantity bought always equals quantity sold), but more significantly, no participant in the economy—whether business firm or householder—will be able to improve his position by any indicated change in his actions. Overall equilibrium will have been achieved.

COMPETITIVE EQUILIBRIUM AND EFFICIENCY

But is it a good thing? The general equilibrium we have just described proves the interdependence of a competitive economy, but does it prove its efficiency? We turn now to our second main question, that of the relationship between a market economy and economic welfare.

The general proposition we wish to demonstrate is the following:

Under certain circumstances, a purely competitive economy will achieve a general equilibrium of prices and quantities such that we cannot improve the position of any participant in the economy without diminishing someone else's satisfactions. Under these circumstances, we say that the purely competitive economy has achieved an efficient allocation of resources.

---

2. The analysis of the effects of changing conditions in this manner is sometimes called *comparative statics*. We start with a set of *givens* and work out the equilibrium prices and quantities. Then we change the *givens* (introducing, say, a 20 percent increase in population) and work out the new overall equilibrium. Then we compare the two equilibrium situations to see what the total effect of the change has been. A somewhat different approach to the treatment of economic change concerns itself with the *path of change over time*. This is usually called *economic dynamics*.

3. We have purposefully neglected the fact that business firms also produce *capital goods* for *investment* purposes. When this happens, consumers cannot consume all the goods the factors of production have produced. Some of these goods are added to the society's capital stock or, equivalently, society is *saving* part of its income for future production. For the introduction of saving and investment into the circular flow, see Part Two, p. 200.

We shall be qualifying this statement many times in later chapters; for the moment, let us concentrate on its positive aspects.[4]

We have already given a number of illustrations of how pure competition may be efficient in this sense. In chapter 19 we noted that under pure competition, the business firm would be in long-run equilibrium only when it was producing at the minimum of its average cost curve—or at a minimum average cost per unit of the product. Since costs reflect the underlying scarcity of resources in the economy, we could see that purely competitive firms would be using the least possible quantities of scarce resources to produce their products. This is *efficient,* since if firms were using more than the minimally required resources to produce their outputs, it would generally be possible to produce more of all commodities (and hence make everyone better off) simply by reallocating resources throughout the economy.

We can now generalize from such examples by looking first at the problem of production, second at the problem of consumption, and third at the relationship between production and consumption.

1. Efficiency in Production.

We will have efficiency in production when it is impossible to shift our factors of production from one product to another in order to increase the production of both products (or to increase one without decreasing the other). This condition will be fulfilled when

---

4. Even while concentrating on the positive aspects, however, we must keep reminding ourselves that there are many objectives besides "efficiency" for which an economy will ordinarily strive; for example, a better distribution of income or a high rate of growth. In general, when we try to decide which objectives should have the highest priorities, we cannot escape making value judgments. Value judgments are ascientific in the sense that each person must ultimately make up his mind about what he considers desirable or undesirable. It is impossible to make statements about the goals or the welfare of an economy without making such personal value judgments. This is one reason why economists who share the same analytic framework can nevertheless differ sharply on many economic policy questions.

the ratio of the marginal products of the factors (say, labor and machines) is the same in the production of all commodities. Or to put it in symbolic terms: If we represent the marginal product of labor in the production of commodity A as MP_{L_A}, the marginal product of labor in the production of commodity B as MP_{L_B}, the marginal product of machines in the production of commodity A as MP_{M_A}, and the marginal product of machines in production of commodity B as MP_{M_B}, then the condition for efficiency in production is

$$\frac{MP_{L_A}}{MP_{M_A}} = \frac{MP_{L_B}}{MP_{M_B}}$$

To see why this is so, imagine that these ratios differed. Suppose (to take the simplest possible numbers) that

$$MP_{M_A} = 1; \quad MP_{L_A} = 1;$$
$$MP_{M_B} = 1; \quad \text{but } MP_{L_B} = 2$$

This would mean that the ratio of the marginal product of labor to machines in the production of commodity A was 1, while for commodity B, the ratio was 2. It can now be shown this would be inefficient.

Why? Because we can increase total production by transferring factors from one commodity to the other. In particular, let us transfer one unit of labor from commodity A to commodity B and one unit of machines from commodity B to commodity A. Now notice what the consequence is. Production of commodity A is unchanged. Since the marginal products of labor and machines in the production of A are both equal to one unit, the substitution of a unit of machines for a unit of labor makes no difference at the margin. But notice that the production of commodity B has increased! B producers lost one unit of output when they gave up a unit of machines, but they have gained *two* units of output when they added a unit of labor. This is because $MP_{L_B} = 2$.

The reallocation of resources has thus increased commodity B production by one unit and left commodity A unchanged.

If the ratios of the marginal products had been the same, no such overall improvement would have been possible—i.e., we would have had efficient production.

Now the significance of this point for the market economy is that when pure competition prevails, the condition of equal ratios of the marginal products of all factors in the production of all commodities will be guaranteed by the workings of the marketplace. In our general equilibrium diagram (Figure 22–1), we indicated in the upper left-hand corner that the ratio of the marginal products of the factors in producing any one commodity would have to be equal to the ratio of the factor prices. Assuming that the price of each factor is uniform throughout the economy, this condition will guarantee us that the ratios of the marginal products of the factors in all their uses will also be equal. In other words, pure competition working through decentralized markets will make certain that efficiency in production is achieved.

2. Efficiency in Consumption

In the case of the consuming households, we have a quite analogous problem. We will have efficiency in consumption when it is impossible to transfer commodities between any two consumers in such a way that we make both consumers better off (or make one better off without making the other worse off). This condition will be fulfilled when any two consumers are purchasing commodities A and B in such a way that the marginal rate of substitution (*MRS*) of A for B is the same for both consumers.

Again, a moment's reflection will show us why this is so. Suppose, for example, that I am purchasing bananas and apples and that, at the margin, one banana is worth four apples as far as my satisfaction is concerned. Suppose that you are also purchasing these two commodities but that at *your* margin, one banana brings you the same additional satisfaction as one apple. Bring us together and what will happen? Clearly, we can perform an exchange and *both* of us will be better off. For example, suppose I offer to give you four apples for two bananas. Will you accept the exchange? Yes, because apples and bananas are equally satisfying to you at the margin, and you get four of one in exchange for only two of the other. But my position is improved, too! Two bananas are actually worth eight apples to me, but I had to give up only four apples to get them.

If, on the other hand, our marginal rates of substitution had been equal to begin with, no such mutually profitable exchange would have been possible—i.e., there would have been efficiency in consumption.

As in the case of production, the interesting thing here is that pure competition will bring about the desired result without any conscious effort to promote this kind of efficiency. In the lower right-hand corner of our general equilibrium diagram, we notice that each consumer will purchase commodities to the point where their price ratios are equal to their marginal rates of substitution. That is, for any given consumer:

$$\frac{P_A}{P_B} = MRS_{A,B}$$

Since all consumers face the same market prices, we can conclude that $MRS_{A,B}$ for consumer 1 will be equal to the $MRS_{A,B}$ of consumer 2, and so on for all consumers in the economy. The competitive market has given us efficiency in consumption as well as efficiency in production.

3. Relationship of Consumption and Production

If we now bring these two sides together—production and consumption—we can perceive what efficiency means in terms of a competitive economy in full general equilibrium. In the upper right-hand corner of our general equilibrium diagram, we state the familiar condition that under pure competition, the price of any commodity will be equal to its marginal cost. Stated in terms of two commodities, this means

$$\frac{P_A}{P_B} = \frac{MC_A}{MC_B}$$

Now what this condition tells us is that given efficiency in both production and consumption, there is no way in which production can be altered to increase the satisfactions of any consumer without hurting some other consumer. We already know that consumers will so adjust their purchases of the two commodities that the ratio

$$\frac{P_A}{P_B}$$

will be equal to the marginal rate of substitution of A for B for each and every consumer. This new condition now tells us that this marginal rate of consumer substitution will be equal to the ratio of the marginal costs of producing the two commodities.

Think of it this way: The consumers in our economy substitute apples for bananas according to their preferences. The producers in our economy also perform such a substitution, in the sense that they can shift factors of production from banana to apple production. Now the MRS for consumers for apples in terms of bananas tells us under what terms consumers desire to make this first substitution. Similarly, the ratio of the marginal costs of the two commodities

tells us under what conditions the producers can make this second substitution. If the marginal cost of apples is twice that of bananas, then producers will be able to "transform" one unit of apples into two units of bananas through shifting of factors.

The equality of price ratios and marginal costs, then, signifies the following:

When P = MC throughout the economy, the marginal rate of consumer substitution of one commodity for another will be equal to the marginal rate of producer substitution of that commodity for the other. If we think of the producers as "transforming" one commodity into another by shifting factors of production, we can say that the P = MC condition means that the marginal rate of substitution (MRS) of consumers will be equal to the marginal rate of transformation (MRT) of producers. Or, simply, MRS = MRT for the economy as a whole.

The analysis here may seem complicated, but the common sense of this conclusion can be made clear. What we are saying broadly is that the economy will be "efficient" overall only if the consumer valuation of different products at the margin corresponds to their relative difficulties of production. Suppose that we have ended up in a curious kind of position in which all consumers consider apples to be twice as valuable as bananas at the margin. Suppose, however, it is equally easy (in terms of marginal cost) for the society to produce apples or bananas. Could this be a satisfactory position? Clearly not. We would want a system that would produce more apples and fewer bananas. And we know in principle that we could get this result, because we know that producers are economically able to transform a unit of bananas into a unit of apples simply by shifting the factors of production.

In short, for the economy to be efficient overall, we need not only efficiency in consumption and efficiency in production, but also the assurance that the marginal rates of consumer substitution for all commodities are everywhere equal to the marginal rates of producer transformation. When these conditions are fulfilled—and pure competition will (subject to later qualifications) fulfill them—then we will have achieved a truly "efficient" economy.[5]

A FOOTNOTE ON SOCIALISM

Is this analysis of the "efficiency" of pure competition really relevant? Interestingly, one of the strongest affirmative answers, historically, has been given not by the defenders of free enterprise but by the theoreticians of socialism!

In chapter 3, when we were discussing the Lange variety of market socialism, we suggested that the plant managers in such an economy would have to obey certain "rules"—in effect, they would be required to *pretend* that they were in a market economy. What we have just provided in this chapter is the basic structure of those rules. As a plant manager, I shall be required by law to combine factors of production so that their price ratios are equal to the ratios of their marginal products and to produce output up to the point where $P = MC$. A socialist society (like a free enterprise society) may not get the prices exactly right the first time—i.e., there is a certain amount of trial-and-error involved in any real-life economic operation—but the criteria for the price system will be strongly influenced by the example of pure competition.

Thus, far from being a defense of the *status quo,* the arguments in this chapter have sometimes been used to call for a socialist revolution. *Only* under socialism, it has been claimed, can we really get pure competition functioning properly. What Adam Smith would have made of this particular argument, we do not venture to guess.

---

5.   In the appendix to this chapter, we relate some of the themes of the above section to our familiar production-possibility (or transformation) curve.

SUMMARY

Two central questions about any economic system are those of *interdependence* and *efficiency.* In this chapter, the workings of a competitive economy are examined from these two points of view.

The four questions that the competitive price system must solve are: (1) prices of commodities; (2) quantities of commodities produced; (3) prices of the factors of production; and (4) quantities of the factors of production employed in producing each commodity. The first two questions refer to the product market; the second two—which we might alternatively call the questions of income distribution and methods of production—refer to the factor market.

The principle of *interdependence,* as exemplified in a competitive economy, shows that these two markets are interrelated. The operation of the factor market will influence the workings of the product market, since factor prices are the incomes of the factor owners and these incomes will influence the consumer demands for goods in the product market. Similarly, the operation of the product market will influence the workings of the factor market, since consumer demands will influence the demands for factors of production and, hence, factor prices, income distribution, and methods of production.

The final general equilibrium solutions to all these questions must, therefore, be reached simultaneously. The resulting situation can be conveyed in a circular flow diagram in which supply will be equal to demand for every product and every factor, and each participant in the economy will be maximizing his satisfactions subject to the conditions facing him.

This competitive general equilibrium also has (subject to later qualifications) certain *efficiency* attributes. Efficiency in production normally requires that the ratios of the *MP*'s of all factors be the same in the production of all commodities. Since every purely competitive firm will hire factors so that the ratios of their *MP*'s are equal to the ratios of their P_F's (and assuming that the price of every factor is uniform throughout the economy), this condition will be met.

Efficiency in consumption normally requires that the *MRS*'s of all commodities be the same for all consumers throughout the economy. In pure competition, each consumer will equate his *MRS* for any two commodities to their price ratios; hence, the *MRS*'s for all consumers will be equal. Finally, efficiency ordinarily requires that the *MRS* of consumers for any two goods be equal to the *MRT* (marginal rate of transformation) for the firms producing those goods. This condition means roughly that the relative satisfactions consumers derive from different goods at the margin should be equated to the relative difficulties of producing those goods in terms of the use of society's scarce resources. This requirement is met when the production of all firms is such that *P* = *MC*, and this is nothing but the condition for maximizing profits in pure competition.

There are all kinds of modifications and developments that must be made to render this analysis applicable to the real world. But a certain *fundamental* relevance is suggested by its use as a model by socialist thinkers and planners.

IMPORTANT TERMS TO REMEMBER

General Equilibrium
Four Basic Questions Restated:
   Commodity Prices and Quantities;
   Factor Prices and Quantities
Factor Market Influences Product Market
Product Market Influences Factor Market
Efficiency in Production
Efficiency in Consumption
P = MC
Purely Competitive Efficiency
Efficiency in Market Socialism

QUESTIONS FOR DISCUSSION

1. Return to the general equilibrium diagram (Figure 22-1) and explain carefully why each of the equations in the various arrows holds true under pure competition. In each case, try to imagine circumstances in which, competition not being "pure," the equation might not hold. (For example, suppose firms charged different prices to different consumers for the same services—say, doctors charging different prices to different patients. Would it then be true that the *MRS*'s for any two goods would be the same for all consumers?)

2. "The beauty of pure competition is that every individual is able to maximize his own satisfactions. This means that—subject to the overall limitations of resources in the economy—every individual is as well off as he could possibly be."

Set the author of this declaration straight by a careful critical analysis of his statement.

3. Using your full knowledge of the workings of a competitive economy as developed in Part Three A, but employing as little technical vocabulary as possible, explain to someone who knows no economics why a typewriter costs on the average five times as much as a pair of shoes.

4. Suppose that you have a purely competitive economy in which there is only one factor of production: labor of a standard, homogeneous quality. Would the labor theory of value (prices of goods are proportional to the quantities of labor employed in their production) hold true in this case? Explain your answer.

5. Would you like to live in a perfectly "efficient" society? For what economic objectives might you be willing to sacrifice some economic efficiency? For what non-economic objectives?

APPENDIX 22: ANALYSIS OF THE PRODUCTION-POSSIBILITY CURVE

In the first chapter of this book, we introduced a favorite tool of economists, the production-possibility or transformation curve. We have used it again in other chapters and will be using it still later on. Now we can say a bit more about what lies behind this curve.

In the foregoing chapter we have spoken of the marginal rate of transforming one commodity into another, indicating that it would be equal to the ratio of the marginal costs of the two commodities. If the marginal cost of one unit of food is \$3.00 and the marginal cost of one unit of steel is \$6.00, then the marginal rate of transformation of food into steel will be 2—i.e., it will require us to give up two units of food to produce an additional unit of steel at the margin.

EXPLAINING THE SHAPE OF THE PRODUCTION-POSSIBILITY CURVE

The above logic is, of course, identical with that used when we try to explain the meaning of the production possibility curve. In Figure A, the original production possibility curve from chapter 1 has been reproduced. We said at the time that, as we moved from one point on the curve to another, we were giving up, say, food and adding steel. The curve tells us under what conditions we can transform one commodity into another.

We can now phrase this, with our new understanding of cost curves, by saying that the slope of the production possibility curve will be equal to the ratio of the marginal costs of the two products. This is shown by the two little triangles in Figure B. Notice that the food and steel terms seem to be reversed in the triangles; i.e., one might think it should be MC_S/MC_F rather than the other way around. This

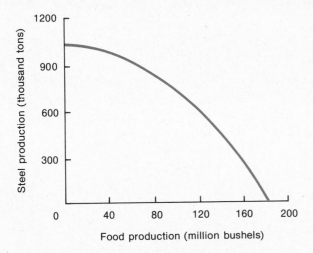

Figure A. Production-Possibility or Transformation Curve.

This is a reproduction of Figure 1–3 from chapter 1.

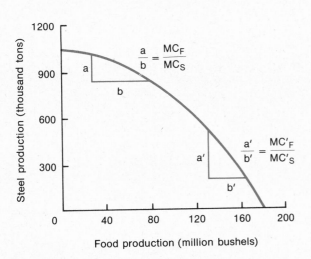

Figure B. Shape of the Production-Possibility Curve.

The shape of the curve will reflect the ratio of the MC's of the two products. Note that the slope is MC_F/MC_S, not the other way around.

is not a printer's error; it simply reflects the fact that there is another step in the argument. If a is the amount of steel we have to give up to add b food production, then a triangle on our curve would appear as:

What cost do we save by giving up a units of steel? Answer: $a \times MC_S$. What cost do we add by adding b units of food? Answer: $b \times MC_F$. Because these costs must be equal as we move from one point on the curve to a neighboring point, we have:

$$a \times MC_S = b \times MC_F, \quad \text{or}$$
$$\frac{a}{b} = \frac{MC_F}{MC_S}$$

Thus, the terms are in fact printed correctly in the diagram.

Now the shape of the production possibility curve will clearly reflect what happens to these marginal costs, as we move from the production of one commodity to the other. This really is what our whole discussion of long-run cost and supply curves in chapters 19 and 20 was all about. The main reason for MC's increasing as we expand the production of a commodity is that this commodity uses factors of production in different proportions than do other commodities. Food production, for example, may use more land but less labor and machines than steel production. As we expand food production, land will tend to become more expensive and labor and machines relatively cheaper. Because food is heavily dependent on the more expensive land, its MC will rise relative to that of steel. This explains the change in the ratio as we move down to the right along the curve, and also the bowed shape of the characteristic production possibility curve.

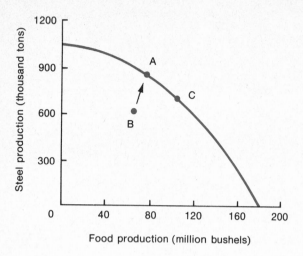

Figure C. Efficiency and the Transformation Curve.

Efficiency in production means that we produce at points like *A*, rather than *B*. To be efficient overall, however, we must also produce what consumers want—i.e., at *C* instead of *A*.

What *in*efficiency in production means is essentially that we are operating at some point *B* inside the curve as opposed to some point *A* on the curve (Figure C). Inefficiency, thus, is equivalent in its effects on output to unemployment (compare Figure 1–6, p. 19).

But this economy could also be inefficient if it were operating at *A* when consumers wanted to be at point *C*. In other words, it is not sufficient that the economy simply be producing goods efficiently. It must also be producing the combinations of goods that consumers *want*—the old idea of "consumer sovereignty."

Even then, point *C* may not represent the best of all possible worlds. Suppose, for example, that it is based on an economy with a grossly unequal distribution of income: *I* own all the capital and land in the economy, the rest of *you* own your own labor! As we have said often before, efficiency can never be the only important economic goal. However, it is *an* important goal and one that is not to be forgotten in an age of scarcities.

PRODUCTION-POSSIBILITY CURVE AND EFFICIENCY

This curve also allows us to say, in perhaps a somewhat clearer way, what economic *efficiency* involves. Each point on this curve shows the maximum of steel production we can get for each quantity of food production, and vice versa. Thus, the curve already exemplifies efficiency in production. This, in turn, means that we can only get to the edge of the curve, in the ordinary case, if the productive units (whether private business firms or state enterprises) are combining the factors of production in the proper way; i.e., if the ratio of the marginal products of any two factors is equal in the production of all commodities (p. 497).

PART 3B

MICROECONOMICS: PROBLEMS AND APPLICATIONS

CHAPTER 23
EFFICIENCY AND INTERNATIONAL TRADE

It is highly appropriate to begin our applications of the tools of microeconomics with the field of international trade since it was in this field, historically, that some of the most significant advances in microeconomic analysis first took place. We shall say a word about these early steps and then bring the theory of the benefits of trade up to date. In the second half of the chapter, we shall take up some of the varied arguments that have been used to support restrictions on trade, and then present a specific case of (almost) *free* trade between the United States and Canada.

RICARDO—ENGLAND AND PORTUGAL, CLOTH AND WINE

The question of efficiency in international trade is very much like the question of efficiency with respect to the domestic economy. Essentially, that question is: Can we reallocate our resources so as to make everybody better off, or at least somebody better off and nobody worse off?

A difference in the case of international trade, of course, may be political. We may not *want* to make everybody better off, or they us. In the extreme case of a war, a country may go to great lengths (including blockades) to prevent another nation from becoming "better off" even though this effort is at great cost to the originating country. We shall return to some of the political aspects of trade in a moment. Let us begin, however, with the assumption that the countries involved are concerned with economic efficiency only—i.e., that they wish to continue to trade as long as it can be shown that there are *mutual benefits* to be achieved that way.

Now it was one of the great triumphs of the British classical economists of the late eighteenth and early nineteenth centuries to have demonstrated that "efficient" trade (though they did not use that term) could best be secured by *free trade*. In earlier mercantilist thought, the tendency had been to regard international trade as a case of my (or your) gains versus your (or my) losses. "Whatsoever is somewhere gained is elsewhere lost" is a characteristic statement of mercantilist philosophy. The general question of economic efficiency, as we have been discussing it in the past few chapters, however, is precisely concerned with situations where *all* parties can gain. And this was precisely what the later British classical economists showed for international trade: remove tariffs, quotas, and restrictions, they said, and *all nations will benefit*.

Since the classical argument is largely convincing even to this day, let us quote directly from one of its first proponents, David Ricardo:

On Foreign Trade

David Ricardo

Under a system of perfectly free commerce, each country naturally devotes its capital and labour to such employments as are most beneficial to each. This pursuit of individual advantage is admirably connected with the universal good of the whole. By stimulating industry, by rewarding ingenuity, and by using most efficaciously the peculiar powers bestowed by nature, it distributes labour most effectively and most economically: while, by increasing the general mass of productions, it diffuses general benefit, and binds together by one common tie of interest and intercourse, the universal society of nations throughout the civilized world. It is this principle which determines that wine shall be made in France and Portugal, that corn shall be grown in America and Poland, and that hardware and other goods shall be manufactured in England.

If Portugal had no commercial connexion with other countries, instead of employing a great part of her capital and industry in the production of wines, with which she purchases for her own use the cloth and hardware of other countries, she would be obliged to devote a part of that capital to the manufacture of those commodities, which she would thus obtain probably inferior in quality as well as quantity.

The quantity of wine which she shall give in exchange for the cloth of England, is not determined by the respective quantities of labour devoted to the production of each, as it would be, if both commodities were manufactured in England, or both in Portugal.

England may be so circumstanced, that to produce the cloth may require the labour of 100 men for one year; and if she attempted to make the wine, it might require the labour of 120 men for the same time. England would therefore find it her interest to import wine, and to purchase it by the exportation of cloth.

To produce the wine in Portugal, might require only the labour of 80 men for one year, and to produce the cloth in the same country, might require the labour of 90 men for the same time. It would therefore be advantageous for her to export wine in exchange for cloth. This exchange might even take place, notwithstanding that the commodity imported by Portugal could be produced there with less labour then in England. Though she could make the cloth with the labour of 90 men, she would import it from a country where it required the labour of 100 men to produce it, because it would be advantageous to her rather to employ her capital in the production of wine, for which she would obtain more cloth from England, than she could produce by diverting a portion of her capital from the cultivation of vines to the manufacture of cloth.

□

Excerpted from David Ricardo, "On Foreign Trade," in *On the Principles of Political Economy and Taxation* (New York: Cambridge University Press, 1951), pp. 133–35. Reprinted by permission of the publisher.

David Ricardo (1782–1823). David Ricardo was a businessman before he became an economist, but his economic writings are very lean and abstract. Besides his contribution to international trade theory, he expounded Malthusian ideas on population, developed a version of the labor theory of value (which greatly influenced Karl Marx), and set an example of rigor in economics that influenced generations of economists who followed. Keynes said that Ricardo conquered England the way the "Holy Inquisition conquered Spain."

This rather sparse prose in presenting a major argument is typical of Ricardo, who was, in his way, one of the most rigorous economists of all time. Let us rephrase his argument, using tools we have developed earlier in this book.

What we really have here are two production-possibility curves for the products wine and cloth—one for England and one for Portugal. They are rather special production-possibility curves, however, in that they are not bowed (see our earlier discussion on pp. 17–18) but are straight lines. The basic reason for this is that Ricardo is talking about one factor of production only—labor. In his example, the amount of labor it takes to produce either commodity in either country does not *vary* as the production of that commodity increases or decreases. Since this is the hypothetical situation, England (or Portugal) could expand cloth production at the expense of wine production without running into the problem of increasing costs.[1]

The two production-possibility curves are shown in Figure 23–1. Notice, first, that each country's curve has a constant slope—meaning, as we have just said, that we can add more of one commodity at an unchanged cost in terms of the other commodity no matter what the level of production is. Also notice, however, that this constant slope is *different* for each country. In particular, England's slope is steeper.

Why? The answer is in the Ricardo reading. England uses relatively less labor to produce cloth, relatively more to produce wine; in Portugal, it is the reverse. With all her labor devoted to wine production, England would produce only 5/6 as many units of wine as she would produce units of cloth if all her labor were devoted to cloth production. In the case of Portugal, the comparable number would be 1⅛. The reader should make sure he understands these

---

1. In terms of the appendix to chapter 22, the ratio of marginal costs of cloth and wine production is constant (although different) in each country.

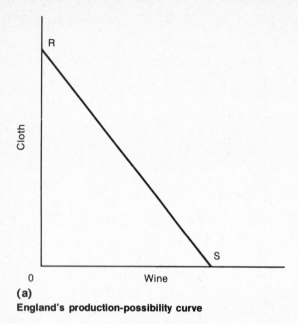

(a)
England's production-possibility curve

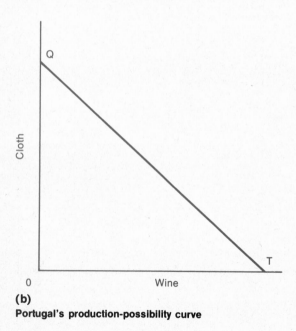

(b)
Portugal's production-possibility curve

**Figure 23–1. Production-Possibilities
in the Ricardian Example.**

two numbers and can relate them to the slopes of lines *RS* and *QT* in Figures 23–1(*a*) and (*b*).[2]

Now to show how both countries can benefit from trade, we bring these two production-possibility curves into one diagram, as in Figure 23–2. Ignoring the little triangles for a moment, let us suppose that England, initially, is at some point, E_1, on its production-possibility curve, and that Portugal, initially, is at P_1. How then can we show that trade can be mutually beneficial?

Ricardo says that England should specialize in cloth and import its wine; Portugal, the reverse. After this specialization has taken place, England's production position will be at *R* (producing *OR* units of cloth), but, by trading *a* units of cloth for *b* units of Portuguese wine, she will end up at E_2, having more of *both* commodities than originally. By the same logic Portugal will produce at *T,* but, by trade, will be able to reach P_2, *also* with more of both commodities.

In the Ricardian example, he speaks of one unit of cloth being traded for one unit of wine. In our drawing, this ‸exchange ratio would be given by the slope of the dotted lines RE_2 or P_2T. An exchange ratio of one would mean that $a/b = 1$, or that $a = b$. This specific exchange ratio is not required to demonstrate mutually beneficial trade in this case, however. What *is* necessary is that the slope of these lines be somewhere in between the slopes of the two production-possibility curves. The reader should figure out for himself what the range of possible slopes would be in this case and why any slope *outside* the range would not work. Of course, the determination of the finally effective exchange rate in a real situation would have to take into account additional information, e.g., how much people in England and Portugal liked wine, etc.

---

2. What we have said in the text will explain the fact that these two production-possibility curves have (1) a constant slope, and (2) a different slope. What we have not explained is the position of these two lines—i.e., how far out from the origin. This position, of course, would basically reflect the size of the two countries. In our hypothetical case, for convenience, we have made the countries about the same size.

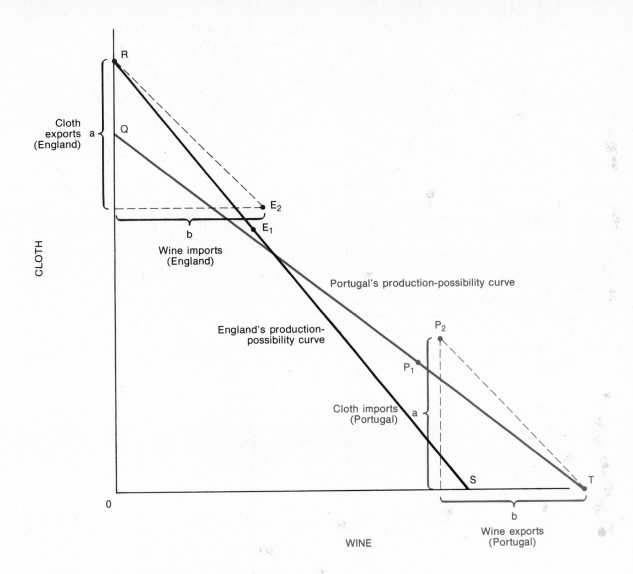

Figure 23–2. Hypothetical Gains from Trade.

Suppose hypothetically, that England and Portugal, without trade, are located at points E_1 and P_1, respectively. Ricardo showed that, *with* trade, both countries could be better off (e.g., moving to points E_2 and P_2, respectively). In this example, both countries specialize completely.

DOCTRINE OF COMPARATIVE ADVANTAGE

Without going any further into the Ricardian world, however, we can already note the impressive accomplishment of this piece of analysis. In particular, it has shown us that trade can be mutually beneficial between two countries even when one country—in this case, Portugal—has an absolute advantage in the production of *both* commodities. Portugal requires less labor to produce wine *and* cloth than England, in Ricardo's examples. The key is relative cost, or what economists call *comparative advantage*. Portugal has an absolute advantage in both wine and cloth, but England has a *comparative* advantage in cloth because she has to give up fewer units of wine to produce a unit of cloth than does Portugal. This is shown by the greater steepness of her production-possibility curve. By the same logic, Portugal has a comparative advantage in wine—shown by the greater flatness of *her* production-possibility curve.

The classical theory and philosophy of trade can now be summed up:

Countries can gain benefits from trade in almost every conceivable circumstance since it is not absolute *but* comparative advantage *that counts. Countries should specialize in those commodities in which they have comparative advantages and trade for those commodities in which they have disadvantages. Since restrictions on trade simply limit the degree to which mutual benefits can be enjoyed by all nations, free trade is the best way for everyone!*

A simple, clear and rather convincing statement!

MODERN TRADE ANALYSIS

As it basically remains to this day. Probably more economists agree on the desirability of free (or at least "freer") trade than on any other proposition in the field of economics.

Still, the case as presented so far is clearly based on rather special assumptions, and also there are a few plausible arguments against free trade that should be noted. Let us first modernize the Ricardian argument and then take up some of the reasons that are urged for placing tariffs or other restrictions on international trade.

The main limitations of the Ricardian argument derive from the fact that it uses only one factor of production, labor, and that it presents a final equilibrium in which one country produces all of one commodity and the other all of the other commodity. In real life, several factors of production cooperate in the production of any given commodity. Furthermore, the characteristic trading situation is for a country to produce part of the supply of a commodity domestically and to import the rest. It would be very rare for a country to import all its machinery, or all its food, or even all its wine.

We can avoid these limitations by presenting the analysis in terms of production-possibility curves of the same shapes as those developed earlier in this book. Two such curves are drawn in Figure 23–3, one for England and one for Portugal. The curves are bowed this time, because we are using more than one factor of production to produce these commodities. As either country tries to produce more of one commodity, she must pay a higher cost in terms of the other commodity (opportunity cost), because the factors of production suited to one commodity are not ideally suited to the production of the other and commodities ordinarily use different factors in different proportions. This point has been discussed before. The difference between England and Portugal that makes trade desirable in this case is that the two countries have different factor availabilities, or *factor endowments*, as they are sometimes called. England has large quantities of textile machinery, Portugal abundant vineyard land. Without trade, the two countries might be located at points E_1 and P_1, respectively. Notice that at these two points, England has a comparative advantage in cloth production and Portugal has a comparative advantage in wine production. How do we know this? Because the slope of England's production-possibility curve is steeper

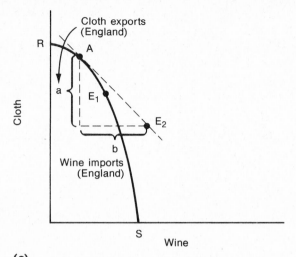

(a)
England's production-possibility curve (England has lots of textile machinery).

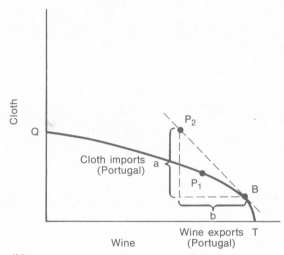

(b)
Portugal's production-possibility curve (Portugal has abundant vineyard land).

Figure 23–3. Trade Between England and Portugal.

at E_1 than is Portugal's at P_1. The spirit of the Ricardian argument now tells us that England will tend to specialize in cloth production and Portugal in wine production.

This is correct, but the specialization will no longer be complete. That is to say, both countries in this example will end up producing both commodities. In each case, trade will have the effect of increasing the country's production of the commodity in which she has a comparative advantage.

A possible equilibrium situation is shown by the triangles in Figure 23–3 (a) and (b). Portugal is now producing at point B (as opposed to P_1) and is consuming wine and cloth at P_2. This involves exchanging her b wine exports for a cloth imports from Britain. The fact that she is better off is indicated by her ability to move out beyond her original production-possibility curve. Trade in this sense is very much like an outward shift of the production-possibility curve such as we associate with economic growth.

The same sort of thing has happened to England, although she has moved from E_1 to A in terms of production (*increasing* cloth and *decreasing* wine production) and ends up consuming at point E_2.[3]

This analysis enables us to show in a more complicated case how trade benefits both parties, and it also gives us some insight into the underlying economic reasons that make this possible. Essentially, what our example tells us is that trade is a way of getting around shortages of various factors of production. Portugal is short of textile machinery, but she can, so to speak, "ease" this factor scarcity by letting British machinery produce some of her cloth

---

3. The reader may be interested to note that the dotted lines AE_2 and P_2B have a slope that is equal to the price ratio of wine to cloth. This is because $a \times P_C = b \times P_W$, or $a/b = P_W/P_C$. (We are assuming, in our simple world, that the value of imports and exports balances for both countries.) Those who have read the appendix to chapter 22 will know that the slope of the production possibility curve will be equal in each case to MC_W/MC_C. Since the dotted lines are tangent to the curves for each country, this means that $P_W/P_C = MC_W/MC_C$ in both countries. This, of course, is exactly the result we would expect in a purely competitive—$P = MC$—world.

for her. The same thing happens in reverse for the British, who, being short of vineyards, can happily enjoy Portugal's abundance of the same.[4] Thus, this modern analysis, far from contradicting the essential message of the classical economists, tends to strengthen and expand upon those early insights.

Furthermore, these benefits will be the greater to the degree that there are important economies of scale in the various industries involved in trade. It will often happen that a small country that tries to produce many different commodities for herself will have to produce them all inefficiently, because in no case can she take advantage of the natural scale economies that exist. Trade and specialization will, in this case, mean concentrating on a smaller number of products but producing them with fewer scarce resources in each case. Such logic was often used a few years ago when the European Common Market was being devised; these countries sought, by lessening trade barriers among themselves, to achieve some of the economies of scale that they believed had been important in the growth of the great United States domestic market.

Finally, trade can be a method of increasing overall efficiency by allowing the "fresh winds of competition" from abroad to stimulate the urge for improving productivity in domestic markets. This may be particularly true where domestic producers are not pure competitors but are the kind of oligopolistic, semi-monopolistic firms that will be our concern in the next few chapters. In these cases, the consumer may not only have the wider choice permitted him by being allowed to buy the foreign version of the domestic product, but he may also get a better and cheaper

domestic product as local industry tries to compete more effectively with its Japanese or German rivals.

These arguments in total all tend in the same general direction. They leave the classical case for free trade largely intact.

SOME ARGUMENTS FOR RESTRICTING TRADE

Still, there is a bit more to the story than this. For although economists as a group are fairly unanimous about the wisdom of freer trade, the fact is that tariffs, quotas, and other trade restrictions have been a central fact in the economic history of every modern nation, the United States very much included. Before Ricardo ever wrote his analysis, Alexander Hamilton was defending protection for infant industries in his famous *Report on Manufactures*. In the period between the War of 1812 and the Civil War there was great strife between the North and the South on the tariff question. When the so-called Tariff of Abominations was passed in 1828, South Carolina responded by proclaiming the doctrine of "nullification."

Actually, the tariff history of the United States is one of great upswings and downswings in tariff rates, as one or the other side of the controversy has held the upper hand. After World War I, there was a sharp rise in tariffs around the world, including the United States, but since the mid-1930s, the trend has been downward. Thus, while in 1930–31, duties collected on dutiable imports into the United States averaged over half the value of the imports, by 1970 the percentage had fallen below 10 percent. In the early 1970s, however, the United States began hearing renewed murmurings in favor of increased protection.

Clearly, statesmen and governments from time to time have felt compelling reasons for restricting trade. What are some of these reasons? And how do they stand up to modern analysis?

The truth is that some of them don't stand up very well at all. Many of them involve arguments that are incomplete. For example, it is often stated that United States industries need protection against low-wage foreign industries. This argument is incomplete be-

---

4.   In advanced theoretical treatments of trade, it is sometimes pointed out that trade will lead to a tendency toward the *equalization of factor prices*. We cannot develop this point here, but the reader can already see some of the basic logic involved. Before trade, textile machinery would tend to be relatively scarce (and expensive) in Portugal and vineyard land relatively scarce (and expensive) in Britain. Since the effect of trade is to "ease" these scarcities in each country, it will tend to bring the factor prices closer together.

cause it does not take into account the fact that wage rates in different countries will reflect to a significant degree the productivity of labor in those countries. The incompleteness of the argument can be seen by noting how easily the whole thing can be reversed. That is, low-wage foreign industries often demand protection on the grounds that their laborers, unskilled and without much machinery, cannot compete with the well-trained American labor force with its complement of high-speed computers and assembly-line techniques.

There are, however, some arguments for tariffs and other trade restrictions that cut a bit deeper than this. In most cases, these arguments involve a weighing of one objective against another. In particular, free trade is usually agreed to be the most "efficient" arrangement at any given moment of time; but it is then argued that other objectives can outweigh economic efficiency and that quotas or tariffs will help achieve these other objectives. Let us mention a few of these arguments:

1. Short-Run Macroeconomic Objectives

We know from chapter 15 that international trade can have significant effects on macroeconomic objectives, such as achieving full employment. Since imports are like savings in having a direct negative impact on aggregate demand, it has been argued that a country, suffering unemployment, should restrict trade through tariffs or import quotas (or conversely stimulate exports by various kinds of subsidies). These actions would increase aggregate demand for domestic products and cause a general expansion of employment in the country. Tariffs can also be used in a general macroeconomic way to "protect" the country's balance of payments. This was the stated purpose behind the President's 10 percent import surcharge of August 15, 1971.[5]

---

5.   However, this action was also clearly used as a bargaining weapon in the effort to get certain other countries, like Japan, to revalue their currencies.

Since we have discussed these macroeconomic problems before, let us simply note here that there are two main disadvantages of using tariff or other trade restrictions as a way of solving these problems. The first is the general point that these restrictions always impose *some* cost in terms of efficiency. The second is that retaliation is so easy. In our interdependent modern world, if one nation is suffering from severe unemployment problems it is not unlikely that others will face similar difficulties. The effort to improve one's own position by tariffs is essentially an effort to impose one's own problems on other nations. (After all, if it is good for us to cut imports, it is very likely to be harmful for them to have their exports reduced.) If retaliation does take place, then the nations involved may have achieved the worst of all possible worlds—trade has been inefficiently reduced, while no one's employment position has improved.

2. National Security

Tariffs, quotas, and other restrictions are sometimes justified as a necessary cost that must be paid by the nation for overall security reasons. Usually this involves some strategic goods, or, in the case of exports, certain classified processes. One is not allowed to export the plans and materials for building a hydrogen bomb factory! Where trade in strategic goods is limited, there are two possible arguments involved. One is that we should try to conserve our domestic supplies of the good; this would lead in theory to high imports of the good and restrictions on export of the good. The second line of argument is the reverse, namely, that we should keep our domestic producers vigorous by protecting them from foreign competition; this would lead to the imposition of tariffs or quotas on the import of the product from abroad. This second argument was regularly used in defense of oil import quotas in the United States. But the argument—and the quotas—were quickly abandoned when the oil shortages of the 1970s hit the nation.

3. Terms of Trade Arguments

If a country holds a significant position in trading relations with other countries, it may try to exert monopoly power through the use of trade restrictions in order to improve what economists call its *terms of trade*. There are various technical definitions of this phrase, but its simplest meaning is the ratio of the prices a country receives for its exports to the prices it pays out for its imports. Suppose that a country is aware that the price of a particular import will rise as it imports more of that commodity from abroad. It may be in the country's interest to restrict imports of that particular commodity so as to keep its price lower. Although the advocates of free trade are correct in saying that, under ordinary conditions, departures from free trade cannot benefit *both* parties, nevertheless it may be true that departures from free trade can benefit one party *at the expense of* the other. This "beggar-my-neighbor" policy is like the similar policy of improving a country's domestic employment situation by exporting its depression abroad. In both cases, the policy invites retaliation. Thus, a country seeking to improve its terms of trade by worsening the terms of trade of its neighbor runs the risk of gaining only a short-term advantage until the exploited country or countries retaliate, and then all parties together lose because of the inefficiency of heavily regulated trade.

4. Infant Industries and Development

Another category of arguments for protection has to do with young or "infant" industries that, if unprotected, might fall victim to disastrous competition from abroad. These arguments clearly have most relevance to underdeveloped countries where the necessary capital and skills have not yet been accumulated to make competitively viable modern industries possible. However, they could also be applied to particular industries in more developed countries where the country happens to take up this industry at a later date than a few leading countries and, in particular, where substantial economies of scale exist. In the long run, free trade is the natural ally of industries with large economies of scale, since it offers the largest possible market for the product, i.e., the world market. However, in the short run, it may take time before an industry can reach the stage where it is large enough to enjoy the potential economies of scale involved; in this interim, protection could be justified to keep the industry's head above water.

These arguments have wide appeal today in many of the less developed countries of the world, particularly among those who feel that they are suffering worsening terms of trade at the hands of the industrialized nations.[6] However, these arguments run some danger of being overused. It is certainly not clear in efficiency terms (though it may be defended on national security or other grounds) that every nation should have every large-scale modern industry represented within its borders. Nor is it clear that when infant industries "grow up" the clamor for their continued protection will cease. There *are* some valid cases for infant industry protection, but most economists suspect that they are rather fewer in number than their proponents might suggest.

5. Protection for Particular Industries

Finally, there are a number of arguments for trade restrictions that have to do with the well-being of particular sectors of the economy. These arguments are perhaps the ones most frequently heard when it comes, say, to removing any particular tariff or other trade barrier; indeed, some cynics believe that such arguments underlie most, if not all, of the other "defenses" of protection.

---

6.   The thesis that poor countries will face deterioration in their terms of trade over time is sometimes called the *Prebisch Thesis*, after Dr. Raoul Prebisch, a Latin American economist who argued that this would be the case. This thesis has been seriously challenged by the oil situation, however. Since many of the oil-producing nations are also less-developed nations, it is becoming evident that (*a*) some less-developed countries are experiencing radical improvement in their terms of trade, but (*b*) other countries, like India, may be experiencing worsening terms of trade, in part, at least, because of the actions of other under-developed (but oil-rich) nations.

Occasionally, protection for particular industries is supported on a merely transitional basis. It may be agreed, for example, that X-industry is less efficient than its foreign competitors, but it may be felt that it would be too harsh on both the employers who have sunk their capital in this industry and the workers whose livelihoods depend on this industry to subject them to the full force of foreign competition. This is, so to speak, the infant industry argument in reverse—protect a decaying industry so that it can decay with less hardship to the people currently working in that industry. This argument sometimes gains added force if a whole region is heavily dependent upon the particular industry, and, therefore, the problems of shifting capital and labor to other industries are more difficult.

One of the troubles here is that decaying industries, like infant industries, may stay that way for a very long time. When this happens, what we have is the pure form of the question—namely, do we want to use tariffs, quotas, and other trade restrictions as a way of redistributing income in our society? There are really two subquestions to this larger question: (1) does this kind of trade legislation usually benefit those people in society who are most needy; and (2) is this the most efficient way of benefiting those people?

In general, most economists would be inclined to answer no to both questions. It seems highly unlikely that the very crude instruments of tariff or quota legislation would be able to single out exactly those people in society who are most deserving of aid on welfare grounds. Nor is there any evidence that the comparative neediness of the recipients has, historically, been a determining factor in judging who is to be so helped. Furthermore, the efficiency argument applies here as elsewhere. Tariffs and quotas lead to departures from the norm of efficiency that we have developed in earlier chapters, and, although all attempts to redistribute income are likely to have some adverse effects on efficiency, those that operate directly on the prices and quantities of commodities bought and sold are likely to have the most serious effects.

Thus, the majority of economists tend to prefer to let the price system work as well as it can, and then to redistribute income through taxes and direct subsidies that have as few disincentive effects as possible. At a minimum, such programs make it perfectly clear what is being done by way of income distribution, and do not hide it in the enormous complexities of international trade transactions.

In short, the above qualifications suggest that while the case for free trade is by no means crystal clear, it is still no bad place to start in formulating actual government policies.

A CASE STUDY—U.S.-CANADIAN AUTOMOTIVE TRADE

And, in fact, this is the place where the governments of the United States and Canada decided to start in the case of the automotive trade in 1965. Or, rather, almost the place. For although the agreement signed between the two governments in that year provided for duty-free trade in autos, trucks, buses, and certain automotive parts between the United States and Canada, it included various conditions and restrictions that prevent it from being a pure example of "free trade in practice."

Nevertheless, this agreement provides a very interesting case study, for a number of reasons. First, it does show very clearly some of the benefits of freer trade between two countries. In this particular situation, Canadians have been able to enjoy new economies of scale that were not possible before in the much smaller, previously protected Canadian market. The enormous expansion of trade following the agreement is itself proof of the mutual benefits now being enjoyed by consumers in each country.

Second, the agreement also shows some of the possible objections to freer trade. In particular, the agreement through 1970 had changed U.S. automotive trade with Canada from a balance-of-payments surplus to a deficit. Considering the overall balance-of-payments problems this country has been facing in recent years, this is no small consideration.

Finally, the agreement exemplifies some of the complications involved in going from theory to practice. For, as we noted, trade is only partly liberalized by the agreement, and many special protections and devices are involved. In addition, the motives for which the agreement was instituted are much more complicated than a simple desire for greater economic "efficiency." Questions of dividing up the overall automotive market in a "fair" way arise, as does understandable Canadian sensitivity to American investment in Canadian business ventures.

These complications are important because, on the face of it, freer trade—if it ever has a chance of success in the world—certainly should have a good chance in the case of the United States and Canada. The automotive agreement, most economists would hope, is a portent of a bright future in this regard.

The U.S./Canada Automotive Agreement

William Diebold, Jr.

If some day there is free trade between the United States and Canada, the automotive agreement of 1965 may look like the great first step toward it. It was not designed that way, however, nor intended as a trial run. It did not rise out of an atmosphere of great good will and the desire on both sides to get rid of trade barriers. Instead the origin of the agreement was an effort to avoid an imminent worsening of trade relations between the two countries. It eliminated tariffs but only freed trade in a rather special sense on conditions quite foreign to the usual idea of liberalization. But it was a major innovation in Canadian-American relations.

Almost all the automobiles, trucks, and buses produced behind Canada's 17.5 percent tariff were

Excerpted from *The United States and the Industrial World: American Foreign Economic Policy in the 1970s,* by William Diebold, Jr. © 1972 Council of Foreign Relations, Inc. Excerpted and reprinted by permission of Praeger Publishers, Inc., New York.

manufactured by American-owned companies. Turning out a wide variety of vehicles for the limited Canadian market, these firms had higher costs than in the United States. They exported some cars and parts to the United States, but Canadian imports of these products, predominantly parts, were over nine times as great as exports in 1964. In that year Canadian exports had already risen in response to an incentive scheme which to American eyes looked like a subsidization of exports. Under American law it seemed certain that the imposition of countervailing duties was only a matter of time. Canada, worried about its trade deficit and wishing to expand automobile production, could be expected to retaliate.

The two governments set about finding a better solution. After difficult negotiations they emerged with an agreement signed in January 1965 which, subject to certain conditions, removed tariffs on trade between them in new cars, buses, trucks, and most original but not replacement parts and accessories. On the American side the limiting provisions are simple, requiring only a provision to be sure that products of other countries do not come indirectly through Canada and administrative agreements to be sure that parts were for original and not replacement use. The Canadian arrangements are more complex. The only ones who can take advantage of the duty-free entry are companies producing automobiles, buses, and trucks in Canada,* and they must satisfy two conditions. They must continue to produce in Canada enough vehicles to maintain the proportion to their sales of vehicles in Canada that existed just before the agreement came into effect. Moreover, this output must have "Canadian content" (i.e., value added by materials, parts, and labor) no lower in absolute value than the total amount in the base year. These provisions of the agreement were augmented by commitments the Canadian government elicited from Ford, General Motors, Chrysler, and the other producers. In "letters of undertaking" the companies

[*In 1974, the U.S. government was trying to alter this agreement so that individual Canadian consumers, as well as Canadian companies, could import American cars duty-free. As of July 1974, Ottawa was reported as being opposed to this alteration.   RTG.]

agreed that in each year they would increase the Canadian value added of their output by 60 percent of the increase in the value of their sales of passenger cars in Canada (50 percent in the case of commercial vehicles). They also promised that by mid-1968 they would increase their Canadian value added by another Canadian $260 million.

It is easy to satirize the result as an agreement to free trade with the assurance that the consequences of free trade will not follow. But there is more to it than that. Two basic ideas are embodied in the agreement. For years Canadians had been studying and debating the possibility of integrating the North American automobile market so that Canadian plants could get the economies of scale by producing larger numbers of fewer models while importing others from the United States at lower cost than if they were produced in smaller quantities in Canada. The elimination of tariffs points in that direction. At the same time, the Canadians wanted to be sure that their country continued to have a significant place in producing for the integrated market. Most analysts thought they had little to worry about, and some suspected that in the natural course of events the Canadian share of the continental output would rise. But there could be no certainty and it was understandable that the Canadian government should insist on safeguards. Those written into the agreement amounted to an assurance that the assembly of vehicles in Canada would keep pace with sales in Canada and that the companies would not cut their expenditures in Canada below the 1964 level (which gave some assurance to the Canadian parts makers as well). But the letters went further. They made it certain that the companies' expenditures in Canada would increase faster than their sales there, at least for the time being. This was a step toward another Canadian aspiration: a "fair share" of North American automobile production, usually thought of as a share equal to the Canadian market. Had permanent assurances of that sort been written into the agreement, real doubt would have been cast on whether it would in fact achieve its proclaimed objective of "the development of conditions in which market forces may operate effectively to attain the most economic pattern of investment, production, and trade." However, the letters focused on the three initial years, and, while they caused some resentment in the United States, they did not seem to vitiate the agreement for the long run. In the short run, there was certainly ample room for much rationalization of the industry within the limits set by the Canadian conditions.

The impact on trade was rapid and enormous. Exchange between the two countries of vehicles and parts tripled in two years and in 1969 came to over $6 billion, eight and one-half times the 1964 level of $731 million. The rise was not a balanced one. Though the export of American automobiles to Canada increased greatly, the movement in the opposite direction was much larger. By 1966, the United States was importing more cars (by value) from Canada than it was selling there and by 1969 the balance in favor of Canada was $800 million, even though American exports of cars amounted to sixteen times their 1964 levels.

The smaller trade in trucks and buses followed a similar pattern. Matters were different in parts and accessories, which made up 90 percent of American automotive sales to Canada in 1964. The great expansion of assembling in Canada led to more than a tripling of imports from the United States and in 1969 the trade balance on these items (including repair parts that were not tariff-free) came to $1.2 billion in favor of the United States, in spite of a relatively more rapid growth of Canadian exports. The result was to give the United States an export surplus in all automotive trade of $96.7 million in 1969—a sharp drop from the $588.9 million of 1964. (A deficit was predicted for 1970.)[†] No one had expected so large a shift or thought that the 1964 agreement would lead to a situation in which Canadian exports of automobile products "far exceeded the combined export values of wheat and newsprint."

[†The U.S. deficit in 1970 was about $200 million.   RTG.]

Behind these unexpected trade developments was just the kind of adaptation of production that was expected by proponents of the plan. The companies have been producing longer runs of models in Canadian plants, in some cases new ones, and exporting to the United States while importing other models that were formerly produced in smaller numbers in Canada. The commitments made in the "letters of undertaking" were overfulfilled and the Canadian share of the North American market has risen. Employment has not risen as fast as output, which suggests a rise in productivity. These changes in Canada are clearly largely attributable to the agreement; it is hard to judge the impact of the reorganization on the much higher level of production and employment in the United States market.

In 1969 popular car prices were still 4 or 5 percent higher in Canada than in the United States after allowing for differences in taxes. This was an improvement for the Canadian consumer over the 9 or 10 percent difference that had been usual in 1964, but suggested that he was still not getting all the benefits of an integrated market. The Canadian automobile worker, however, gained more. The automotive agreement was a signal for the United Automobile Workers, the principal union in both countries, to press for the wage parity to which it had long aspired. It seemed only natural that men doing the same work for the same companies should be paid the same in Windsor as in Detroit, especially if Canadian productivity was about to rise. An agreement reached in 1967 provided for nominal wage parity by 1970, i.e., the same dollar pay, but in national currencies. At the time, the Canadian dollar was worth 92.5 American cents, but when it was allowed to float in June 1970 it soon appreciated to the point at which nominal wage equality became actual wage equality. In the parts industry, however, some wage differences continued.

Not everything has gone smoothly. When the agreement came up for review in 1968, the Canadians resisted the American suggestion that the need had passed for special arrangements to insure that production in Canada would keep on growing. The targets set in the original letters of undertaking had been passed, but the American companies again gave assurances that they would increase output in Canada.

In 1969 the State Department initiated further discussions that had produced no visible results by mid-1971. The atmosphere was not one in which farsighted, broad-gauged thinking about the future of the agreement was likely to flourish. The American automobile industry was in a slump. Foreign cars were increasing their inroads in the North American market. Both Canada and the United States suffered from a combination of unemployment and inflation. Disputes about oil and the arctic probably spilled over into the automobile case. The large shift in the trade balance was attracting some unfavorable notice in the United States. An intensification of nationalist sentiment in Canada made it difficult for Ottawa to make any concessions to the United States without receiving clear benefits in return, while the main thing the Americans wanted was to make the agreement more equitable by modifying the Canadian safeguards. In Canada, equity was seen rather differently, as requiring some insurance that the weak would not lose out to the strong.

Official statements about the disagreement were restrained. The Americans argued that Canada had come through the three years' transitional period superbly and could now discard its special insurance policies. At best they were no longer necessary; at worst they were unfair and incompatible with the idea that trade and investment should be guided by the market. The Canadians thought that the adjustment was not complete. There was as yet no hard proof of the long-run competitiveness of Canadian automobile production; the speed with which production and trade had increased was a reminder of how fast change might go if it moved in the other direction. Cast in these terms, the argument seemed to be only about the timing of the removal of the safeguards. Some informed Canadians thought their government was taking a much tougher position. While free trade was important to permit rationalization, the real Canadian objective, according to this view, was the assurance that Canada would continue to have a "fair share" of the total North American output. It was hardly meaningful to speak of "the market" determining what was done when the decisions were in fact made by a handful of American companies in an industry noted for oligopoly and administered prices and not immune to pressure from Washington, or from the UAW. There was no reference in the agreement to a transitional period and Ottawa was, in effect, looking for permanent safeguards.

Pushed far enough, such positions could only lead to an impasse and raise questions about whether the two governments realized what they were doing when they negotiated the agreement in the first place. If a breakdown is avoided by compromise, a question would remain about the standards by which the agreement should be judged. By traditional measures of the benefits of reciprocal trade—and certainly any mercantilist-flavored concern with exports—the United States made a bad bargain. It was not as bad as it looked in the automotive trade figures alone; much of the equipment for the expanded operations in Canada probably came from the United States and an increase in Canadian incomes and employment creates a demand for American goods. Since the expansion of Canadian production was largely in the hands of American-owned companies, their increased earnings would help the balance of payments. So far as the American consumer was concerned, it was hard to argue that he reaped important benefits of the sort usually attributed to removing tariffs. But there were clearly gains in efficiency and productivity in the automobile industry as a whole, and, while a good bit of the advantage must have

gone to Canadians, it is to be presumed that in so integrated a pair of economies some of the gains would flow into American hands as well. Instead of a conventional trade analysis what is needed is an approach that looks at the agreement as a way of increasing the efficiency of a major industry and so improves the allocation of economic resources. In such terms there are no commonly accepted standards for saying how the national interest shall be defined, but it is increasingly in such terms that foreign economic policy issues may have to be judged in the future. To be sure the gain to the U.S. automotive industry might not be massive since Canada remains only a small part of its market and productive base. The gains to Canada are almost bound to be greater because it loses the disadvantages of its smallness and obtains the advantages of size. But this result flows from the relation of the two countries and will characterize most arrangements that move toward fuller integration of the two economies.

Americans should be able to accept this disparity, I believe, and refrain from the fruitless attempt to extract a neatly balanced, point-by-point set of advantages from every agreement, provided the direction in which it moves makes sense. What makes the automotive agreement hard to swallow is the belief that Canada has tilted the board by insisting on special conditions that seem to create a privileged position with few, if any, risks. Though political opposition to the agreement in the United States has not been very serious, a perpetuation of the appearance of one-sidedness in combination with a shift in trade that looks unfavorable to the United States could lead to difficulties.

Americans, for their part, should understand that the Canadian government also has a domestic problem. At a time when many Canadians complain about American investment and worry about the heavy weight of the United States in their lives, Ottawa, through the automobile agreement, is stimulating American investment and making Canada more dependent on the United States market. Though the agreement's short-run benefits to Canada are demonstrable, there can be no certainty that free trade with no other conditions will always work the same way. Consequently, the Canadian government must feel a real need to be able to show that the benefits will continue and that it has a way of influencing the actions of the American companies. Given the disparities in size of the two economies, the fact that the main companies are all American, and the natural nervousness of a small neighbor, Americans, who are not uncritical of the automobile industry, ought not to have too much trouble understanding the Canadian position.   □

SUMMARY

In this chapter, we have applied our microeconomic tools to the field of international trade, investigating especially the relationship of trade to economic efficiency.

The general result of this analysis is to suggest that free trade tends to produce the most efficient overall result. This was shown in the early nineteenth century by economists like Ricardo, who used a model in which labor is the only factor of production and in which the quantities of labor used to produce wine and cloth are constant no matter what the levels of production of either commodity. In this case, the two countries involved will each specialize completely in the commodity in which they have a *comparative advantage*. A country has a comparative advantage in the production of a particular commodity when the relative cost (in terms of other commodities) of producing a unit of that commodity is less than in the other country. According to Ricardo, this specialization will result in mutual benefits for both countries, i.e., everybody is better off with free trade.

Modern analysis generally confirms this point. Using a production-possibility curve where more than one factor of production is employed, we get increasing costs as we expand one commodity as compared to the other. In this world, countries will again specialize in the commodities in which they have a comparative advantage, but not fully. Again, free trade will bring increased benefits to *both* countries. These benefits, moreover, will be greater if there are important economies of scale in the industries involved and if free trade brings a stimulating competitiveness to domestic industry.

Although these general points enjoy wide acceptance, there are a number of specific arguments for restricting trade that help explain why countries throughout history have used tariffs, quotas, and other protective devices to at least some degree. These arguments generally involve weighing other objectives against the claims of economic efficiency. These other objectives may include short-run macroeconomic objectives, national security, improving the terms of trade ("beggar-my-neighbor" policy), protection of infant industries (mostly relevant to underdeveloped countries), and protecting particular domestic industries. In almost every case, these arguments are subject to the criticism that they would involve the nation in certain efficiency losses; in many cases, also, they lead to policies that invite retaliation. The U.S./Canadian Automotive Agreement of 1965 shows some of the advantages and complications of instituting free (almost) trade between two countries.

IMPORTANT TERMS TO REMEMBER

Free Trade
Absolute Advantage
Comparative Advantage
Factor Endowments
Mutual Benefits from Trade
Terms of Trade
Infant Industries
Tariffs
Beggar-My-Neighbor Policies
Retaliation
Decaying Industry Problem
U.S./Canada: Automotive Agreement of 1965

QUESTIONS FOR DISCUSSION

1. Suppose that we have country A and country B each capable of producing commodity X and commodity Y according to the following table:

COUNTRY	X	Y
	MAN-HOURS REQUIRED TO PRODUCE 1 UNIT	
A	5	50
B	12	40

(*a*) Which country has a comparative advantage in producing commodity X? Commodity Y?

What is the range of possible exchange rates of X for Y under which mutually beneficial trade between A and B could take place?

(*b*) Fill in the blank in the following table so that neither country has a comparative advantage in either commodity.

COUNTRY	X	Y
	MAN-HOURS REQUIRED TO PRODUCE 1 UNIT	
A	5	50
B	12	?

2. "The fairest tariff policy is that which puts our domestic producers on equal terms with their foreign competitors." Discuss.

3. Explain how Adam Smith's views on the division of labor (pp. 461–62) might be used to advance the cause of free trade. Can economies of scale ever be used to argue *against* free trade?

4. "Tariffs and trade restrictions are an expression of national interest; free trade is an expression of world interest." Discuss.

5. Write an essay giving an assessment of the 1965 Automotive Agreement from the point of view of (a) a Canadian, and (b) an American.

SUGGESTED READING

Kenen, Peter B., and Lubitz, Raymond. *International Economics.* 3rd ed. Englewood Cliffs, N.J.: Prentice-Hall, 1971.

Meier, Gerald M. *International Trade and Development.* New York: Harper & Row, 1963.

Miller, Roger LeRoy, and Williams, Raburn M. *The New Economics of Richard Nixon: Freezes, Floats & Fiscal Policy.* San Francisco: Canfield Press, 1972, chap. 10.

Ricardo, David. *Principles of Political Economy and Taxation.* Edited by P. Sraffa. Cambridge: Cambridge University Press, 1951, chaps. VII, XXII.

Stern, Robert M. "Tariffs and Other Measures of Trade Control: A Survey of Recent Developments," *Journal of Economic Literature,* September 1973, Vol. XI, No. 3.

CHAPTER 24
MONOPOLY AND IMPERFECT COMPETITION

In this chapter and the next, we shall take up a number of issues that arise because industrial markets in the real world are at best "imperfectly competitive." Pure competition, as we know, is efficient under certain circumstances: it leads producers in the society to produce the goods that consumers want at the least possible cost. It takes us out to the edge of our production-possibility curve and then locates us on that curve in accord with consumer preferences as expressed through their money demands.

But if competition is *not* pure, what then? Will the consumer get what he wants, or will he get a shoddy deal instead? Will large firms engage in "workable competition," or will they have to be regulated by governmental controls or prosecuted for antitrust violations? In this chapter, we shall present an analysis of the different kinds of market structure in a modern industrial economy, and in the following chapter we shall take up some of the public policy issues raised by our analysis.

THE REVOLUTION IN TRADITIONAL ECONOMICS

When we come to Great Debate Three: Galbraith and the New Industrial State (pp. 561–88), we shall see that there is a deep division among economists as to the best way to analyze modern industrial markets. Galbraith urges a radical change of approach. Robert Solow is somewhat more traditional.

Even among *traditional* economists, however, there has been a considerable change in outlook over the past few decades. Indeed, in the 1930s and 1940s, somewhat overshadowed by the Keynesian Revolution but important in its own right, there was another "revolution" in economic analysis, specifically concerned with imperfectly or "monopolistically" competitive markets.

One of the leaders of this intellectual break-through was the late Edward H. Chamberlin,[1] who not only

---

1. Another very important contributor to this field was Joan Robinson, whose *The Economics of Imperfect Competition* was published a few months after Chamberlin's book in 1933. For Mrs. Robinson's views on Marx, see pp. 154–56.

stressed the complexity of modern industrial life but, in at least one important case, showed how the theory of pure competition would have to be modified to make it applicable to real-world conditions. Chamberlin's book was called *The Theory of Monopolistic Competition,* and the title itself is intriguing. We think of competition as involving very large numbers of small firms. Monopoly, on the other hand, means a *single* seller. How can such polar opposites be combined, as by implication they are, in the phrase "monopolistic competition"?

Actually, the difficulty quickly disappears if we think of products with brand names. The makers of Ivory Soap have an absolute monopoly on the specific product "Ivory Soap," but not on soap products generally. The soap "monopolist" is, in fact, engaged in competition with other similar soap "monopolists," each of whom has his own particular variety of the product with its own particular brand name. The brand name problem, in turn, is simply one example of a general phenomenon that Chamberlin called *product differentiation.* The following reading is from his classic treatment of this subject.

The Differentiation of the Product

Edward H. Chamberlin

*   *   *

A general class of product is differentiated if any significant basis exists for distinguishing the goods (or services) of one seller from those of another. . . .

Differentiation may be based upon certain characteristics of the product itself, such as exclusive patented features; trade-marks; trade names; peculiarities of the package or container, if any; or singularity in quality, design, color, or style. It may also exist with respect to the conditions surrounding its

Reprinted by permission of the publishers from pp. 56–57, 68–70, of Edward H. Chamberlin, "The Differentiation of the Product," in *The Theory of Monopolistic Competition* (Cambridge, Mass.: Harvard University Press, 1962) 8th ed. Copyright 1933, '37, '38, '42, '48, '56, '62 by the President and Fellows of Harvard College.

sale. In retail trade, to take only one instance, these conditions include such factors as the convenience of the seller's location, the general tone or character of his establishment, his way of doing business, his reputation for fair dealing, courtesy, efficiency, and all the personal links which attach his customers either to himself or to those employed by him. In so far as these and other intangible factors vary from seller to seller, the "product" in each case is different, for buyers take them into account, more or less, and may be regarded as purchasing them along with the commodity itself. When these two aspects of differentiation are held in mind, it is evident that virtually all products are differentiated, at least slightly, and that over a wide range of economic activity differentiation is of considerable importance.

In explanation of the adjustment of economic forces over this field, economic theory has offered (*a*) a theory of competition, and (*b*) a theory of monopoly. If the product is fairly individual, as the services of an electric street railway, or if it has the legal stamp of a patent or a copyright, it is usually regarded as a monopoly. On the other hand, if it stands out less clearly from other "products" in a general class, it is grouped with them and regarded as part of an industry or field of economic activity which is essentially competitive.

*   *   *

Monopoly and competition are very generally regarded, not simply as antithetical, but as mutually exclusive. To demonstrate competition is to prove the absence of monopoly, and vice versa. Indeed, to many the very phrase "monopolistic competition" will seem self-contradictory—a juggling of words. This conception is most unfortunate. Neither force excludes the other, and more often than not both are requisite to an intelligible account of prices.

*   *   *

Monopolistic competition is evidently a different thing from either *pure* monopoly or *pure* competition. As for monopoly, *as ordinarily conceived and defined,* monopolistic competition embraces it and takes it as a starting point.

HARVARD NEWS BUREAU

Edward H. Chamberlin (1899–1967). Chamberlin helped bring an increasing realism to microeconomics by his study of monopolistic competition and other imperfectly competitive market structures.

The theory of monopoly, although the opening wedge, is very soon discovered to be inadequate. The reason is that it deals with the isolated monopolist, the demand curve for whose product is given. Although such a theory may be useful in cases where substitutes are fairly remote, in general the competitive interrelationships of groups of sellers preclude taking the demand schedule for the product of any

one of them as given. It depends upon the nature and prices of the substitutes with which it is in close competition. Within any group of closely related products (such as that ordinarily included in one imperfectly competitive market) the demand and cost conditions (and hence the price) of any one are defined only if the demand and cost conditions with respect to the others are taken as given. Partial solutions of this sort, yielded by the theory of monopoly, contribute nothing towards a solution of the whole problem, for each rests upon assumptions with respect to the others. Monopolistic competition, then, concerns itself not only with the problem of an *individual* equilibrium (the ordinary theory of monopoly), but also with that of a *group* equilibrium (the adjustment of economic forces within a group of competing monopolists, ordinarily regarded merely as a group of competitors). In this it differs both from the theory of competition and from the theory of monopoly.

The matter may be put in another way. It has already been observed that, when products are differentiated, buyers are given a basis for preference, and will therefore be paired with sellers, not in random fashion (as under pure competition), but according to these preferences. Under pure competition, the market of each seller is perfectly merged with those of his rivals; now it is to be recognized that each is in some measure isolated, so that the whole is not a single large market of many sellers, but a network of related markets, one for each seller. The theory brings into the foreground the monopoly elements arising from ubiquitous partial independence. These elements have received but fragmentary recognition in economic literature, and never have they been allowed as a part of the general explanation of prices, except under the heading of "imperfections" in a theory which specifically excludes them. It is now proposed to give due weight to whatever degree of isolation exists by focusing attention on the market of the individual seller. A study of "competition" from this point of view gives results which are out of harmony with accepted competitive theory. □

CLASSIFICATION OF MARKET STRUCTURES

Differentiation of the product is certainly one feature of modern industrial life that must cause us to modify the theory of pure competition developed in Part Three A. Perhaps an even more important modification is caused by the *size* of firms. In chapter 5, we spent some time describing the large modern corporation and its influence on certain sectors of the economy. This influence varies greatly from sector to sector of the economy. Large firms still have very little impact in construction, agriculture, forestry, certain types of mining, the service trades, and in much of wholesale and retail trading. But in public utilities, transportation, manufacturing, and in other branches of mining, they are very significant and, in many cases, dominating.

This variety makes it necessary for us to expand our analysis of pure competition by adding not just one "real-world" market structure, but a range of such structures. A useful and common classification is as follows:

1. **Pure competition.** We have already discussed this market structure at length. It involves large numbers of small firms, each producing a homogeneous product and each responding to impersonally given market prices. In the American economy, the most important industry approximating pure competition is agriculture. There are over 2 million farming units in the United States; and, although they are expanding somewhat in the 1970s, very large corporations are still of negligible importance in this sector. Although agriculture has a basically competitive structure, it must be remembered, of course, that government intervention in this sector has been frequent and significant for many decades. Other industries that approximate purely competitive conditions are lumbering and some forms of mining, notably bituminous coal mining.

2. **Pure monopoly.** We have "pure monopoly" where there is a single seller of a particular product for which no close substitutes are available. Since all products in an economy are to *some* degree substitutes for one another, even the pure monopolist is subject to a degree of competitive influence. However, where the substitutes are not close, the monopolist will have considerable freedom to vary the price of his product to achieve maximum profits. Pure monopoly, in an unregulated state, does not exist in the United States, being expressly forbidden by our antitrust laws. In a regulated state, it does exist in a number of important industries, notably in transportation and public utilities, especially at the local level.

3. **Monopolistic competition.** As we have suggested above, monopolistic competition involves a combination of elements from pure monopoly and pure competition. It is characterized by large numbers of sellers who sell not a homogeneous but a "differentiated" product. Many of the products we buy, from soap to automobiles, are surrounded by clusters of similar products—other brands of soap or makes of automobile—which, though distinguishable in the minds of consumers, nevertheless clearly belong to the same product classification. Products within the same industry can be differentiated in various ways: design, style, special features, attractive packaging, brand-name advertising, convenience of location of the retail outlet, even the manner of their sale (e.g., "service with a smile"). A hardheaded consumer might classify some product differentiation as "real" (one product actually gives better service than another) and some as "irrelevant" ("A rose is a rose is a rose."), but if these "irrelevant" differences actually influence consumer behavior in the sense that buyers will pay a higher price for one product than another, then they are important data for economists to analyze.

The element of "monopoly" in monopolistic competition derives from the fact that once products are "differentiated," each particular firm has an absolute monopoly on its own special brand. Only the Lorillard

Corporation can produce Kent cigarettes. There is thus literally a single seller of Kents. The element of "competition" arises because other firms can produce very close substitutes (Camel Filters, etc.). If a great number of firms produce close substitutes, then we have the market structure of monopolistic competition.[2] In the American economy, the best examples of this structure are to be found in the retail and service trades. There are thousands upon thousands of grocery stores, barber shops, beauty parlors, stationery stores, and shoe-repair shops, in which product differentiation is based on small variations in the products or, very often, on the location, attractiveness, and general atmosphere of the place of sale.

4. Oligopoly. Oligopoly means "few sellers." Since, as we have seen, large corporations play a dominant role in many industries in the manufacturing sector, much of that sector can be classified as oligopolistic. This classification is in many ways less precise and covers more ground than the others on our list. For one thing, an industry dominated by a few sellers may produce either a homogeneous or a differentiated product. Automobile production in the United States is highly oligopolistic (largely dominated by three firms), and the products are significantly differentiated. By contrast, copper production is relatively undifferentiated, though there is very high concentration of sellers of newly-mined copper.

Another problem is that "few sellers" may mean anything from more than one or two[3] to less than the vast numbers required for strict pure or monopolistic competition. There is no reason to expect the

same behavior patterns in an industry like automobile manufacturing, where one firm (General Motors) produces roughly half the national output and the top three firms 90 percent of output, and an industry like meat-packing, where the top three firms (Swift, Armour, Wilson) control only one-third of the market and the rest is serviced by over two thousand other firms.

A final problem with oligopoly—though not so much with the classification as with the difficulty of analyzing this market structure—is that it is likely to be characterized by mutually recognized interdependence among the larger firms in the industry. Where a few firms dominate a particular market, each is likely to realize that *its* actions will produce reactions from the other firms involved, and the whole strategy of decision making is made much more complex by that fact.

The above classification of market structures is only one of several that could be—and have been—made. It is useful, however, in bringing out two of the important dimensions along which the structures of different industries may vary. One dimension is that of numbers. Pure competition and monopolistic competition are alike in requiring very large numbers of small firms; monopoly involves one firm; oligopoly an intermediate number though, in reality, there are often a few rather large firms that play a significant role in a particular industry. The second dimension concerns degrees of product differentiation. Purely competitive, monopolistic, and some oligopolistic firms sell homogeneous products; monopolistically competitive and other oligopolistic firms sell differentiated products.

A summary of structures arranged along these two dimensions is presented in Table 24–1. This summary also brings out two other features of market structures that are of interest. One is the role of advertising in different market structures. There is no need for advertising in pure competition (the firm can sell all it can produce at the going price) and little need in pure monopoly or undifferentiated oligopoly. Ad-

---

2. This structure is sometimes specifically called "Chamberlinian monopolistic competition," because this was the case that the late Professor Chamberlin did so much to analyze. See the reading on pp. 526–27.

3. Economists have a specific name for a market in which there are precisely two sellers: *duopoly*. We shall not consider this particular structure in the analysis that follows.

TABLE 24-1

A CLASSIFICATION OF MARKET STRUCTURES

		NUMBER OF FIRMS IN THE INDUSTRY	
	MANY SMALL FIRMS	A "FEW" LARGE FIRMS	A SINGLE FIRM
HOMOGENEOUS PRODUCT	Pure Competition (many small firms; no product differentiation; no advertising; price is taken as *given;* U.S. agriculture closest approximation)	Undifferentiated Oligopoly (a few usually dominating firms; not much advertising; more or less identical products; firms' decisions tend to be interdependent)	Monopoly (a single seller of a product without close substitutes; "public interest" advertising; is rare in the U.S.; usually governmentally regulated as in public utilities)
DIFFERENTIATED PRODUCT	Monopolistic Competition (many small firms with slightly different products; local advertising; fairly common in retail markets)	Differentiated Oligopoly (a few big firms with much competition through product differentiation and advertising; interdependent decisions; *both* forms of oligopoly common throughout U.S. industry)	

Left axis label: DEGREE OF PRODUCT DIFFERENTIATION IN THE INDUSTRY

vertising is mainly significant, therefore, in monopolistic competition and in differentiated oligopoly.

The other important aspect of market structures suggested by the table has to do with the question of the recognition of interdependence among business firms. The taking into account of the reactions of other firms to *its* action is characteristically significant only for the oligopolistic firm. The absence of direct rivals in monopoly and the inability of a very small firm to *have* a significant effect on its rivals in pure and monopolistic competition mean that recognition of mutual interdependence is of little importance in these market structures.

These varying characteristics result in firm and industry behavior different from what might be expected if, as in Part Three A, we were dealing with a wholly competitive economy. Using this earlier analysis as our framework, let us now analyze briefly how these other market structures cause departures from the conclusions derived in the case of pure competition.

ANALYSIS OF MONOPOLY IN THE PRODUCT MARKET

Monopolies may be either "natural"—as, for example, when economies of scale produce a continuously failing average cost curve and thus make it inefficient to maintain more than one firm in a particular industry—or "contrived"—as when firms with rising average cost curves merge simply to enjoy the increased profits possible through the exploitation of monopoly. In most industrial nations, the growth of large firms has resulted at one time or another from either or both of these circumstances; where "natural" monopoly was unavoidable (as in telephone or postal service), governments have either regulated or, more usually, nationalized the services.

Whatever the original source of the monopoly, the main effect in the product market is that the individual firm (monopolist) will have as *its* demand curve the industry-wide consumer demand curve for the product in question. The contrast with pure competition is shown in Figure 24–1. In pure competition, the individual firm faces a horizontal (perfectly elastic) demand curve, signifying that its share of total industry output is so small that the overall price of the product will be virtually unaffected by any conceivable contraction or expansion of output by that firm. This horizontal demand curve represents little more than a dot on the industry-wide consumer demand curve (see our earlier discussion, p. 446). The monopolist, in contrast, faces the downward-sloping demand curve of the industry as a whole. He is, therefore, confronted by a set of decisions unknown to the pure competitor. He can *set* the price of his product as he chooses. Of course, he is not without constraints in doing this. If he sets a higher price, consumers will buy less; if he sets a lower price, they will buy more. However, the questions facing the pure competitor and the monopolist are different. The pure competitor must determine how he will maximize profits at the *given* price. The monopolist must determine how he should *set* the price, to maximize profits.

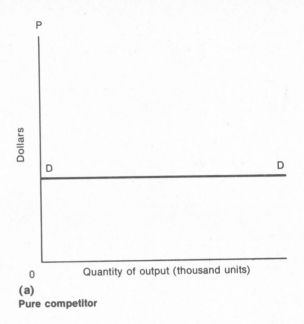

(a)
Pure competitor

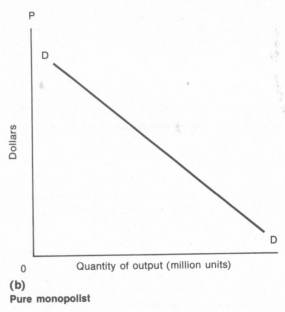

(b)
Pure monopolist

Figure 24–1. Firm Demand Curves for Pure Competitor and Pure Monopolist.

In pure monopoly, the firm has the industry-wide consumer demand curve for its firm demand curve. Notice the different units of measurement on the quantity axes in the two diagrams.

In one sense, since both firms are attempting to maximize profits, the answers given to these different questions will be the same. We learned in chapter 19 that the purely competitive firm will maximize profits by producing where its marginal revenue equals its marginal cost ($MR = MC$). The same logic applies to a profit-maximizing monopolist—he, too, will continue to expand output until that point where the additional cost of a unit of output is equated to the additional revenue from that unit of output. To produce at a lower output would mean foregone additional profits; to produce at a higher output would mean a diminution of profits, since added revenues are now below added costs.

The difference arises when we come to the further conclusion about the purely competitive firm: that it will produce at an output where price equals marginal cost. In the case of pure competition, where P (= Average Revenue) is given, MR is always equal to P. Hence the condition $MR = MC$ also implies the condition that $P = MC$. But this is not true of the monopolist. In his case, P (= AR) is falling as he produces more and more output for sale on the market. When an "average" of anything is falling, the "marginal" of that thing must be below it.[4] Since P (= AR) is falling for the monopolist as sales expand along the industry-wide consumer demand curve, MR must be below AR. When the monopolist produces at an output where $MR = MC$, therefore, he is producing at an output where P is greater than MC.

The equilibrium of the monopolist is shown in Figure 24-2. The MR curve starts at the intersection of the demand curve (DD) with the vertical axis ($MR = AR$ at one unit of output) and then falls more sharply down to the right as the "marginal" brings the "average" down. The monopolist will maximize profits by producing the output OQ_0 and setting a price of OP_0. Explain to yourself why the amount of "pure" profits in this case will be equal to the area of the shaded rectangle.

---

4. Cf. analysis of "average" and "marginal" cost, pp. 443–44.

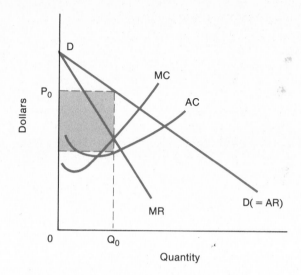

Figure 24–2. Equilibrium of the Pure Monopolist.

The monopolist, like the pure competitor, will maximize profits where $MR = MC$; but unlike the purely competitive case, this will *not* mean $P = MC$. In monopoly, equilibrium P will be greater than MC, and "pure" profits (equal to shaded rectangle) may persist over time.

Two points should be noticed about this equilibrium position. The first is that, as we have said, the monopolist's equilibrium price will not be equal to marginal cost; it will always be above it. The second point is that unlike the case of pure competition, where abnormal profits are always temporary (being competed away as other firms enter the industry), the profit rectangle in Figure 24–2 can persist indefinitely. By hypothesis, there are no close competitors. Unless there is some change in fundamental conditions (in the real world an antitrust suit or government regulation would be a strong possibility), abnormal profits may persist as a condition of *long*-run equilibrium in the case of a monopolist. We shall return to both of these points later in this chapter.

FIRM AND INDUSTRY EQUILIBRIUM IN MONOPOLISTIC COMPETITION

Until the third decade of this century, the two cases we have analyzed—pure competition and pure monopoly—were virtually the only market structures about which the economic theorist could say anything very definite. This situation was altered with Chamberlin's analysis of markets where there are large numbers of small firms competing with differentiated products.

One of the interesting aspects of Chamberlin's work was that it showed the possibility (though not the necessity) of a zero-profit equilibrium under monopolistic competition. We remember that in this particular market structure, each firm does have a "monopoly" of its own individual product, which may be *Movie Stars,* a picture magazine about Hollywood. At a given moment in time, there may be a number of other roughly similar magazines in the field, including such hypothetical competitors as *Flickland* and *Reel Romances.* Since *Movie Stars* is a differentiated product, it will be able to raise its subscription price within limits above those of the others in the field and still retain some subscribers; by lowering its price, it may hope to increase the volume of its sales. In short, it has a downward sloping demand curve as shown in Figure 24–3(a). Because it has a number of fairly close competitors, its demand curve may be relatively more elastic than that of a "pure" monopolist, and its profits may not be quite so high. However, in other respects, the firm's equilibrium is rather similar to that of the monopolist in that it will achieve maximum profits at a point where $MC = MR$; P will be above MC; and, for the moment at least, the firm will be making abnormal profits.

Now the position described in Figure 24–3(a) may be where the matter ends. Unlike pure competition, where the product is homogeneous and any competent businessman can presumably produce it, there is no certainty that the abnormal profits earned by *Movie Stars* (and the similar profits, let us assume, earned by its competitors) will give some businessmen the idea for still further differentiation in the

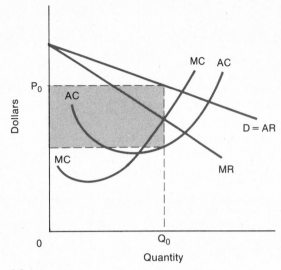

(a)
Monopolistic competitor in the short run (profits are shaded area).

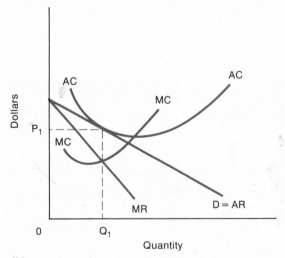

(b)
In the long run, other monopolistic competitors might enter in with new (but similar) products. In this case, pure profits will disappear; but unlike the pure competitor, this firm produces with (1) $P > MC$ and (2) "excess capacity."

Figure 24–3. Equilibrium under Monopolistic Competition.

movie magazine field. However, it *may* do so. *If* it does so, we can imagine the demand curve for *Movie Stars* (and that of each of the other magazines in the field) being pushed to the left until it reaches the position shown in Figure 24–3(b). What has happened is that a number of new competitors—*Stardust, Falling Stars,* and *Startled!,* among others—have been attracted by the profits in this field and have, so to speak, crowded into the not unlimited economic space of consumer demand for movie magazines.

Notice that in this new equilibrium position, *Movie Stars* is not making profits beyond the normal profits included in the cost curve itself. In this respect, monopolistic competition can lead to a long-run, zero-profit equilibrium similar to that of pure competition. Even in this case, however, the equilibrium position is different from that of pure competition in that (1) *P* is still above *MC,* and (2) the firm is not producing at the minimum point of its average cost curve. Because the firm's demand curve is downward-sloping, such a zero-profit condition, where the demand curve is tangent to the average cost curve, will always be to the left of the point of minimum average cost. As it is sometimes put, each firm will be operating under conditions of ''excess capacity.''

Two further departures of monopolistic competition from pure competition should be noticed. The first is that the possibility of advertising now makes a significant appearance on the economic scene. In pure competition, advertising does not occur, since the individual firm is able to sell all that it can reasonably produce at the going price, and (unless it joins in the activities of a noncompetitive trade association) it is too small by its own actions to affect the industry-wide demand for its product. Advertising could in theory occur under pure monopoly, since the firm might hope to alter favorably the overall consumer demand for its product. Still, its prospects would be somewhat limited by the fact that because the firm has no close rivals, their share of the market cannot be captured by advertising. When product differentiation occurs, however, advertising becomes a significant means for creating special preferences and attachments among consumers for one's own particular version of the product in question. Advertising expenditures, moreover, tend to be highest where product differentiation is relatively slight and where, therefore, the creation of buyer preferences rests most heavily on various kinds of promotional campaigns.

The other departure from pure competition lies in the fact that the firm must decide not only what output of its product to produce, but the nature of the product itself. Product differentiation is not a once-and-for-all phenomenon, but occurs continuously over time. *Movie Stars* may change its format, its mix of articles and photography, the slant of its stories. Television watchers have all observed the virtues of new brand-name detergents being touted at the expense of the old version of the same brands. Changes of style, design, chemical formula, color, shape, and gadgetry (some doubtless improvements, others less clearly so) in the product itself become an important form of *nonprice* competition in all industries where product differentiation has taken hold.

PATTERNS OF BEHAVIOR IN OLIGOPOLISTIC MARKETS

Many of the comments we have just made about nonprice competition under monopolistic competition could also be widely applied to oligopolistic firms. For constant changes in the style, design, and technical gadgetry of its products, no industry is a better exemplar than the American passenger car industry, which, as we know, is highly concentrated. Advertising may also be a significant factor in oligopolistic industries. Three American industries noted for their very high advertising expenditures are the makers of soap, cigarettes, and liquor, each of which spends over 10 percent of its revenues (excluding excise taxes) on advertising. All three are clearly oligopolistic industries. In soap, 80 percent of the market is held by the "Big Three": Procter & Gamble, Colgate, and Lever Brothers; in cigarettes, the top three firms account for over 70 percent, and the top six nearly 100 percent, of the national market; in liquor, the eight largest firms account for about three-quarters of the American market.

The special feature of oligopoly—whether the product is differentiated or not—is, as we have said, the problem of mutually recognized interdependence among the larger producers of the industry in question. When there are large numbers of competitors ("pure" or otherwise) in an industry or where there is only one (monopoly), the problem of estimating the actions and reactions of one's rivals is of relatively little significance. When there are a few mammoth firms in the industry, this problem is of the essence.

One important consequence of the problem is that the characteristic oligopoly firm does not have a firm-demand curve in the same sense in which we have drawn such curves for other market structures. Let us suppose that we have a fairly well-defined, industry-wide consumer demand curve for the product in question and that there are four firms in the industry producing slightly differentiated products, each with a roughly equal share of the market and a price more or less in line with the others.

For any one of the firms (say, Firm A) we would appear to have one point on its demand curve defined by its price and quantity of sales. However, the firm-demand curve should tell the businessman what will happen to his quantity of sales when he *alters* his price over a wide range of alternatives. But this we cannot do for Firm A, at least not in any simple sense. If Firm A were to cut its price by 10 percent *and* if there were no reaction from Firms B, C, and D, then the firm might be able to determine how its quantity of sales would increase. But the essence of the problem is that, in general, the other firms *will* react and, further, that Firm A is *aware* of that fact. In order to determine the impact on his sales of a given change in price, therefore, the busi-

nessman must know in advance exactly how the other firms will react, and whether their reaction will cause a further reaction on his part, and whether in that event there will be still further reactions from his rivals—matters that, in the absence of some form of collusion, are likely to be obscure.

One partial way of getting around this problem is to try to make certain generalizations about the *kind* of assumptions an oligopolistic firm will make about his rivals' reactions. Suppose we make the not unreasonable assumption that oligopolistic firms like to undersell their rivals but dislike being undersold. If a firm's price is just slightly below its rivals, it may gain appreciably at their expense in increasing its overall share of the market, but without much sacrifice in revenue per unit. Even more specifically, the owner of Firm A may conclude that if he raises his price, his rivals, now put in the preferred position of underselling him, will hold theirs constant; whereas if he lowers his price, his rivals, not wishing to be undersold, will lower their prices along with him.

Given these assumptions and Firm A's initial price and output position, we can now draw a form of demand curve—usually called a *kinked demand curve* —for Firm A, as shown in Figure 24–4. Firm A is originally located at point B, producing OQ_0 output and selling it at the price OP_0. If the businessman raises his price, other firms are assumed to hold theirs constant, meaning that he is now being undersold and that he can expect a sharp reduction in his sales. Thus the segment of the demand curve AB is quite elastic—a large percentage decrease in quantity following upon a small percentage increase in price. If he lowers price, the hypothesis states that other firms will lower with him to avoid being undersold. This means that he will make little or no gains with respect to his competitors, and the increase in quantity sold will reflect only consumer willingness to buy more of the commodity from all producers at the now industry-wide lower price. Hence, the segment of the demand curve BD is much less elastic—a given percentage decrease in price bringing only a small percentage increase in quantity. The MR curve, in this

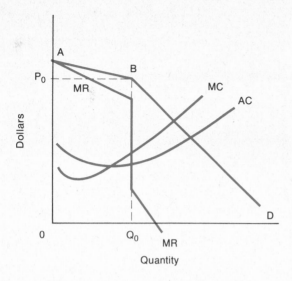

Figure 24–4. Kinked Demand Curve under Oligopoly.

If an oligopolist assumes that his rivals will react to an "I lower, they all lower; I raise, I raise alone" philosophy, then he will have a *kinked demand curve*. Explain why this might lead to rigid prices.

case, will have the rather peculiar shape shown in Figure 24-4, sloping gently downward at first and then breaking vertically downward when the "kink" in the demand curve occurs. It should be apparent that it will be in the interest of Firm A to maintain the original price and quantity even if there should be quite substantial shifts in its cost curves, since MC will equal MR at a different output only with a radical increase (or decrease) in costs.

The kinked demand curve is useful in explaining an element of rigidity in oligopolistic pricing and also the preference many of these firms seem to show for nonprice competition—advertising and product differentiation—as discussed earlier. However, it does not explain the setting of the original prices for the firms, and it makes those original prices seem a bit *too* stable. In the inflationary period that the American economy has experienced since World War II, it is obvious that all firms in the economy—definitely including those in oligopolistically organized industries—have found some way or other to raise prices without causing traumatic losses to those who have initiated the changes.

PRICE LEADERSHIP AND OTHER FORMULAS

Because of the intricacies caused by mutual interdependence and also the different historical experiences of various industries, there is no airtight "pure theory" of oligopolistic pricing. However, two useful comments can be made. The first is that there may be certain patterns or formulas for setting prices in a particular industry. When Firm A finds that conditions make it desirable to raise its price, such formulas can give it reasonable assurance that the other firms will come to similar conclusions. Firm A will not be left out on a limb.

A fairly common method of setting prices in oligopolistic industries is to add a certain percentage *markup* above average or, usually, average variable costs. At a certain level of output, this markup will cover fixed costs, and the firm will have hit its break-even point; further increases in output will lead to positive net profits. If firms in a particular industry behave in this way and there is a sudden change in cost conditions that affect all firms in the industry—perhaps a new higher-wage labor contract is negotiated in the industry—then each firm will be able to raise its prices with some confidence that its rivals will do the same. Each firm has acted independently, yet the net effect is as if they had acted in concert.

Such common formulas do not usually cover all relevant changes in conditions, however, and oligopolistic industries will often develop other means for initiating orderly price changes. This leads to our second comment, which is that a quite common mechanism for meeting this problem is *price leadership.* One of the firms in the industry—always a large firm but not necessarily the largest—undertakes to make an assessment of the relevant conditions in the market and to initiate a price change that, if the pattern is functioning effectively, other firms will follow. Of course, the price leader must be sure that its actions take into account the interests of other firms in the industry, as well as its own interest; also, it must be aware of the possibility of potential new entrants into the field who may threaten the profits of all existing firms including itself. If these factors are taken into account—if, in effect, the problem of mutual interdependence is wisely handled by the price leader—then this pattern of behavior can lead to orderly changes in prices with only tacit (and not illegally collusive) cooperation among the firms in the industry.

Even then, of course, formulas and patterns can always break down. And the history of American industry is filled with challenges for the role of price leadership (the struggle over price leadership in the tobacco industry in the 1930s is a good example) and defections by follower firms who feel that their interests are not being adequately served. It is also filled with numerous cases in which covert but explicit, direct agreements among oligopolistic firms have been made for setting prices. The complications and uncertainties of mutual interdependence make such agreements perhaps understandable, though it is also perhaps understandable that when they are detected, the courts take a dim view of them.

PROFIT MAXIMIZERS?

One final question about oligopolistic firms we have raised before: are these firms truly interested in the maximization of profits in the first place? This is a very basic question since it is an underlying presumption of a market economy that individuals are expected to pursue their own private interests and

that businessmen's private interest can be equated to profits. The motives of individuals, however, are usually more complicated than this—prestige, respectability, and standing in the community will ordinarily count for something with even the most hardheaded businessman—and for giant corporations that dominate many industries in the American manufacturing sector, there is the divorce of ownership and control to complicate matters further.

Where such a divorce of ownership and control occurs, the private interest of the stockholder in higher profits (and higher dividends) need not in theory correspond with the private interest of the management of the firm. To take a crass case, management might like higher managerial salaries and more time on the golf course in preference to maximum profits for the owner-stockholders. More generally, as some economists have argued, management may be primarily interested in the prestige, influence (and often higher salaries) associated with big firms, and managers may, therefore, make decisions conducive to the growth of the firm even when these decisions conflict with strict profit-maximization objectives.

In an even more philosophic vein, Professor Galbraith has suggested that the goals of management may be a reflection of the goals of the members of what he calls the "technostructure." Thus, for example, achieving rapid technological change may become an important management objective that is independent of the traditional pursuit of profits.[5]

Although these qualifications are important to keep in mind, it is not absolutely clear that they require us to abandon the profit-maximization hypothesis *in toto.* Profit-maximization may be a necessary condition for the achievement of other possible corporate objectives such as the growth of the firm over time. Also, what appears to be a failure to maximize profits in the short run may often be the result of trying to maximize them in the longer run. Thus, although some businessmen would doubtless be annoyed at being referred to as crude profit-maximizers, they

5. See Great Debate Three, pp. 566–70.

might be equally annoyed if different language were used and they were charged with having failed to cut costs or having missed some opportunity to increase revenues. And that, of course, is what profit maximization is all about.

IMPERFECT COMPETITION AND EFFICIENCY

Having analyzed the behavior of variously imperfectly competitive markets, let us conclude this chapter by briefly considering the significance of these departures from pure competition in relationship to economic efficiency. (In the following chapter, we shall comment on some of the public policy issues these departures raise.)

A layman's indictment of monopolies or monopolistic elements in an economy might go as follows:

Monopolistic power is bad, economically, for three reasons: (1) monopolists are rich and make high profits at the expense of laborers whom they exploit and of poor people in general; (2) monopolistic power enables firms to overcharge consumers—i.e., to set higher prices than the goods are "worth"; and (3) monopolistic power allows firms to "hold back" on production and thus to provide the economy with fewer of the monopolized goods than it would have had under pure competition.

To this, he might add the essentially political criticism that the concentration of economic power in the hands of very large firms may lead to the concentration of political power in a way that is inimical to the processes of a democratic society. President Eisenhower's concern about the military-industrial complex in the United States was focused on the potential effects of the concentration of economic power (in this case a linking of governmental and private power) on political decisions. (See chapter 5, p. 104.) The political question is important, as is the sociological question of the effects of working for large, impersonal, corporate bureaucracies—though, of course, the economist has no special qualifications to render final judgments on these matters.

Even the more narrowly "economic" points in the indictment are rather complicated. The first point has to do with the evils of monopoly profits. We have shown in the preceding analysis that many forms of imperfect competition can lead to persistent "pure" profits. We have also shown, however, that there can be monopoly elements without pure profits, as in the zero-profit case of monopolistic competition. Nor is the characteristic monopolistic competitor—say, the corner grocery store—necessarily a very rich firm. If large firms do make substantial profits, it is in theory possible to tax the profits of these firms without affecting their immediate price and output decisions. If Firm X is maximizing profits at a certain level of price and output, it will still be maximizing profits at that price and output if the government taxes away a given percentage of those profits. Whether it is desirable to have such taxes—and how large they should be—is likely to be determined by the effects of such action on growth (a large part of investment in the United States is financed by the reinvestment of retained earnings) and on income distribution (what *is* an equitable income distribution?). We shall return to the growth question in the next chapter and to the problem of income distribution in chapter 29.

The second and third points of the layman's indictment of monopoly power center on what we have come to call the problem of economic *efficiency.* Monopoly power, it is asserted, allows firms to charge too much and to produce too little. The implicit judgment is that there are "better" levels of price and output—i.e., those that will lead to a more efficient allocation of resources in the economy as a whole.

This implicit argument can easily be made explicit on the basis of our analysis of efficiency in chapter 22. Let us suppose that we have a very simple economy producing two goods, Good A and Good B, and that Good A is produced by a pure monopolist and Good B is produced by a large number of purely competitive firms. The price of Good A will be above its marginal cost, since it is produced by a monopolist. When the economy is in general equilibrium, let us suppose that P_A = $10 and that MC_A = $5. The price of competitive Good B, by contrast, will be equal to its marginal cost. For simplicity, let us suppose that both goods have the same marginal cost. Hence, MC_B = $5 and also P_B = $5. Why is this inefficient?

The answer is that this economy does not fulfill the condition that the rate of consumer substitution between these two goods be equal to the rate of producer transformation of these same goods. In equilibrium, consumers are paying twice as much for a unit of Good A ($10) as they are for a unit of Good B ($5). This means that the rate of substitution of Good A for Good B is 1/2. Give any consumer 1/2 unit of A and he will be willing to give up 1 unit of B and still remain equally well off. The rate of producer transformation between A and B, however, is not 1/2 but 1. If we transfer $5 of resources from the production of B to the production of A, we lose 1 unit of B and gain 1 unit of A. Since this is the case, it should be clear that the economy as a whole can gain from a reallocation of resources, specifically a transfer of resources from the production of Good B to Good A. Each time $5 of resources is so transferred, consumers lose 1 B and gain 1 A, but 1 A is worth twice as much to consumers as 1 B. Hence there is a net gain from the reallocation.

A few comments should be made about this analysis. The first is that as the process of reallocation goes on, the rates of substitution and transformation will, of course, change. As the consumers get more and more of Good A relative to Good B, the marginal rate of substitution of A for B will rise (i.e., it will take more than 1/2 unit of A to compensate the con-

sumer for the loss of 1 unit of B). Similarly, as resources are transferred from the production of B to the production of A, the ratio of the marginal costs is likely to alter; the marginal cost of A will rise relative to that of B. The final "efficient" equilibrium (occurring if industry A is reorganized along purely competitive lines) will ordinarily involve a price ratio between the two goods intermediate between the original price ratio (2:1) and the original ratio of marginal costs (1:1).

A second point is that this example should make clear what is meant by a monopolist's charging "too much" and producing "too little." Our reorganization of this economy toward greater efficiency has involved a relative lowering of the price of Good A and a greater production of Good A relative to Good B in the economy as a whole.

A final point about this analysis is that, although we have used a "pure monopolist" in our example, the same general kinds of conclusions could be reached for oligopoly and monopolistic competition as long as the firms involved charged a price that was above marginal cost. This is the case even when we are dealing with the zero-profit monopolistic competitor. For we recall that even in that case, the tangency of the firm's demand curve to its average cost curve will involve charging a price above marginal cost and producing under conditions of "excess capacity."

The conclusion of the above analysis seems—and is—a strong economic argument against monopoly elements in the private sector of the economy. Before we jump to the brave judgment that the American government should immediately start breaking up all large firms and instituting pure competition throughout our economy, however, we had best be aware that the making of public policy is always a very complicated matter, and perhaps particularly so in this area of industrial structure.

We will turn to these complications and to the fascinating general problem of devising a public policy toward business in our next chapter.

SUMMARY

The private sector of a modern industrial economy is far more complex than the theory of pure competition suggests. Industries in the present-day American economy vary along a number of different dimensions. In some industries, there are many firms, in others only a few. In some industries, there is vigorous product differentiation; in others, very little. Advertising is very intense in some industries; almost absent in others. In some markets, firms largely ignore their rivals; in others, they are intensely aware of every move (or potential move) the other firms make.

Such facts suggest the need for a fairly elaborate classification of market structures. One such classification is:

Pure competition: large numbers of small firms selling a homogeneous product.

Pure monopoly: a single seller of a product without close substitutes.

Monopolistic competition: large numbers of small firms selling differentiated products.

Oligopoly: a "few" firms selling either a homogeneous or a differentiated product.

Each of these imperfectly competitive market structures will lead to market behavior and conduct different from that predicted for pure competition.

Monopoly

The firm's demand curve will now be identical with the industry-wide consumer demand curve for its particular product. The firm will maximize profits where $MR = MC$; but since it has a downward-sloping demand curve, MR will be below price, and hence, $P \quad MC$. In the absence of competitors producing close substitutes, the monopolist will be able to enjoy persistent "pure" profits, although he is also likely to enjoy some form of government regulation.

Monopolistic Competition

(This was the case particularly stressed by Edward H. Chamberlin in the 1930s.) A monopolistic competitor will also face at least a slightly downward-sloping demand curve, since it has a "monopoly" of its own particular brand or other variant of the product in question. It will maximize profits where $MR = MC$, and it may enjoy persistent "pure" profits. However, since other monopolistic competitors can enter the field with their own version of the product, competition may reduce the monopolistic competitor to a zero-profit equilibrium. The absence of "pure" profits makes this equilibrium position similar to that of pure competition, but it differs from the latter in that $P > MC$, and the firm will be producing under conditions of "excess capacity." Other contrasts with pure competition are (1) the importance of advertising and (2) the continuing further differentiation of the product in a monopolistically competitive industry.

Oligopoly

Oligopoly, in one form or another, is particularly important in the American manufacturing industry. Oligopolists, with some product differentiation, are likely to engage in advertising and other nonprice competition, as do monopolistic competitors. The special feature of oligopoly is the recognition of mutual interdependence by the large firms in the industry. Such interdependence may lead to price rigidity (as explained by the *kinked demand curve*), to the adoption of commonly accepted procedures for setting prices, to a pattern of price leadership, or in extreme cases, to illegally collusive activity. In large oligopolistic firms, the divorce of ownership and control raises thorny questions for the theory of profit maximization. Perhaps management will pursue other objectives than profits—prestige, expansion of the size of the firm, rapid technological advance under the influence of Professor Galbraith's "technostructure." However, many observers believe that, in the long run at least, even oligopolistic firms are likely to give substantial attention to the profit-maximizing objective (but see Great Debate Three).

These different patterns of behavior raise important questions about the performance of imperfectly competitive firms in relation to significant economic objectives. Apart from possible political and social arguments, one of the main economic arguments against monopolistic elements in the economy is that they lead to "too high" profits and prices and to "too low" outputs. The question of prices and outputs is essentially one of economic efficiency. It is possible to show in a simple world, where one part of the economy is "monopolized" and the other is purely competitive, that resources will be misallocated. An efficient reallocation would require a lower price and a greater output for the previously monopolized product.

Although this argument is an important one, it is not sufficient to serve as an unqualified basis for public policy decisions in this complex area—as we shall show in chapter 25.

IMPORTANT TERMS TO REMEMBER

Market Structures
Pure Monopoly
MR = MC ($\neq$ P)
Monopoly Profits
Monopolistic Competition
Product Differentiation
Excess Capacity
Advertising and Nonprice Competition
Oligopoly (Differentiated and Undifferentiated)
Price Mark-Ups
Mutually Recognized Interdependence
Price Leadership
Kinked Demand Curve
Inefficiencies of Monopoly

QUESTIONS FOR DISCUSSION

1. Give specific examples, from your own experience or observation, of business firms that seem to you to fall approximately within the categories of pure competition, pure monopoly, monopolistic competition, and oligopoly. Explain in each case why you think the industries in question developed along the particular lines they did.

2. We mentioned in this chapter that it might be possible to tax the profits of a monopolist without altering the immediate price and output decisions of the firm. Suppose we have a monopolist whose before-tax equilibrium may be described as follows:

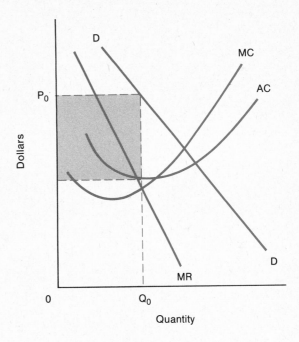

Analyze the effects, if any, that the following taxes would have on price and output:

(a) a lump-sum tax of $1 million on this firm (assume that the profit rectangle is larger than $1 million).

(b) a 50 percent corporate profits tax.

(c) a tax of $X on each unit of the product sold.

(d) a tax of y percent of the price of each unit of the product sold.

3. In the case of oligopoly, the problem of price setting is seriously complicated by the problem of mutually recognized interdependence. Might this problem also apply to nonprice competition? Discuss.

4. State the economist's case against monopoly elements in the economy on ''efficiency'' grounds. Might these arguments hold even in an industry where ''competition'' was quite fierce?

5. ''For all its faults, advertising *does* increase the competitiveness of the economy.'' Discuss critically.

SUGGESTED READING

Baumol, William. ''The Revenue Maximization Hypothesis.'' In *Economic Analysis and Policy: Background Readings for Current Issues,* 3rd ed., edited by Myron L. Joseph, Norton C. Seeber, and George Leland Bach. Englewood Cliffs, N.J.: Prentice-Hall, 1971.

Galbraith, John Kenneth. ''Economics in the Industrial State: Science and Sedative.'' *American Economic Review,* May 1970.

Kahn, Alfred. ''The Structure and Functioning of the U.S. Petroleum Industry.'' In *Microeconomics: Selected Readings,* edited by Edwin Mansfield. New York: W.W. Norton & Co., 1971.

''A Symposium'':

Peterson, Shorey. ''Corporate Control and Capitalism.''

Berle, Adolf A. ''The Impact of the Corporation on Classical Economic Theory.''

Kaysen, Carl. ''Another View of Corporate Capitalism.''

(The above three articles are in the *Quarterly Journal of Economics,* 79, No. 1, February 1965).

This chapter is basically a continuation of chapter 24, but with the focus now on the public policy issues that are raised by imperfectly competitive markets. If pure competition is often "efficient," does that mean that the United States government should immediately break up all but the very smallest of firms? Or should it regulate the behavior of these firms? Or is there some standard of workably competitive markets that would enable the beneficial effects of competition to be felt without a new set of inefficiencies (or worse) caused by the daily intervention of the State? These are the questions to which we now address ourselves.

WHY THE SIMPLE SOLUTION ISN'T SIMPLE

In the last chapter, we made the important theoretical point that, in a simple case, pure competition could be shown to be more efficient than monopoly. In an economy where there were two products, one pro-

duced by a purely competitive industry and the other by a monopoly, we proved that, under certain circumstances, the monopolist's output would be too low and his price too high to achieve an efficient outcome. We could apparently make everybody better off by making both industries purely competitive.

This raises the obvious question: why not do it? Why not dismantle all large firms and insist that their successors be reduced to a size where they would have little or no control over the markets they serve?

Although this approach is tempting, our common sense tells that, even apart from the nightmarish *administrative* task that dismantling all these firms would involve, there is something over-simple about this pat solution. Three major difficulties should be noted:

1. **Economies of scale.** One clear difficulty is that a regime of very small firms will *not* be efficient if there are significant economies of scale. These economies of scale need not be so extensive that they create a condition of "natural monopoly"—a single firm industry. Production techniques may be

such that an industry can support a number of firms, but not the number necessary to make pure competition effective. This is one of the reasons why we always have to qualify our statements about the efficiency of pure competition with phrases like "under certain circumstances." Insofar as important economies of scale exist, the dismemberment of large firms might lead not toward but *away from* productive efficiency.

2. The problem of growth. In addition to the question of productive efficiency, there is the question of growth over time. The late Joseph A. Schumpeter argued that whereas small-firm competition might lead to efficiency at a particular moment of time, it was large-scale industry that promoted growth. He visualized modern capitalism as involving a constant competition not between producers of the same product but between producers of new and producers of old products. The true competition for a stagecoach producer comes not from another stagecoach producer but from the new railroad entrepreneurs. They, in turn, find their competition not from other railroads but from the new aviation industry. And so on. In such a world, a case for the large firm with some fairly strong monopoly powers can be made along the following lines: (*a*) *negatively:* the consumer cannot be hurt too much by monopoly at any moment of time because it is transitory and subject to the constant competition of new products; (*b*) *positively:* monopoly profits are necessary in an uncertain, fluctuating state of affairs, to provide businessmen with incentives and to give them some minimum of security against the threat of change; (*c*) as progress becomes more and more a regular feature of economic enterprise, it will require expensive research and development operations that only larger firms can afford. To which can be added the point that profits are a very important source of investment or capital accumulation in the economy as a whole and, therefore, that monopoly profits may contribute to a strong overall growth performance.

Now none of these pro-large-firm arguments is decisive. In fact, they often rest upon highly controversial readings of the historical record. The advocate of pure competition can point to numerous large firms that have decentralized their productive operations, thus suggesting that economies of scale were not all-important, or to smaller firms that have engaged in more active research and produced proportionately more innovations than larger firms produced. However, these points about scale economies and growth do suggest caution in any draconic scheme of dismantling our larger firms, and this caution is reinforced by our third point.

3. The problem of "second best." Our analysis in the last chapter described a simple world in which there was monopoly in one industry and pure competition in the other. In the real world, as we know, the more accurate description is that of monopoly elements *pervading* the economy, though in varying degrees. What this fact means is that instituting pure competition in one or few selected industries may not be an "efficient" thing to do.

This is sometimes referred to as the problem of *second best.*[1] What the theory of second best tells us is that if anywhere in the economy there are departures from the efficiency conditions (say, the rule that price should equal marginal cost) then the fulfillment of those conditions in a particular sector (say, making marginal price equal marginal cost in the steel industry) will not necessarily lead to an optimal resource allocation for the economy. In general, some solution where price deviates from marginal cost in the steel industry will be more efficient.

Now this approach does not refute any of the arguments about efficiency made in the last chapter or anywhere in this book; it is concerned, as the name of the theory suggests, with second-best situations—i.e., with situations where complete efficiency is impossible to achieve. Nevertheless, the second-best logic has great practical bearing on an

---

1. For a rather technical discussion of this problem, see R. G. Lipsey and Kevin Lancaster, "The General Theory of Second Best," *Review of Economic Studies,* no. 63 (1956–1957).

economy where monopoly elements are rather pervasive, for it casts doubt on the wisdom of any selective or piecemeal approach to increasing the "competitiveness" of the economy. Since a total reconstruction of any modern economy along purely competitive lines is difficult to conceive (there are certainly *some* important economies of scale around, and Schumpeter's arguments cannot be completely dismissed). Because even state ownership and market socialism will not totally avoid the monopoly problem (remember Yugoslavia!), it should be clear that second-best considerations really do complicate the role of the public policy maker in this area. In practical situations, it is difficult to know not only exactly what to do but even in what direction to move.

THE RISE OF CONSUMERISM

Still, the opposite approach of leaving the business sector pretty much to its own devices is definitely unsatisfactory, too. This point needs no stressing in the 1970s, when we are witnessing a great ground swell of discontent about business malpractice in almost every sector of the economy. The general name for this new popular movement is *consumerism,* and it owes its origins and much of its continuing strength to one individual, Ralph Nader. Through his personal leadership and with vigorous teams of Nader's Raiders operating out of the Center for Responsive Law, a constant flow of comments, complaints, documents, reports, and books have brought to the attention of the American people areas in which the business sector has not provided consumers with the goods and services that they seek (or that they thought they were getting!).

The example of Ralph Nader proves that the modern world of communications makes possible not only the rise of the large corporation, but also the rise of the large individual. Nader's work has stimulated a critical approach to the claims of business advertising and public relations campaigns, but it has also pointed up the difficulties of correcting business behavior. For Nader-sponsored research has shown

WIDE WORLD PHOTO

Bess Myerson. Consumerism has given rise to a new group of individuals, consumer advocates, who, like Bess Myerson in New York City, attempt to protect consumers from business malpractice.

that the consumer is threatened not only by the concentration of economic power in small numbers of firms, but also by the failure in many cases of the so-called regulatory commissions to do anything to improve the situation. Who regulates the regulators? If—as we noted earlier in discussing the military-industrial complex—the business and public sectors tend to merge together in a union of common goals, then there is obviously great danger in relying upon an agency of the government to curb the possible abuses of power by vested industrial interests.

The following reading, written by Ralph Nader, conveys the flavor of consumerism and suggests the stage of development it has currently reached.

The Consumer Movement

Ralph Nader

In this age of big business, camouflaged services, pre-packaged goods, and impersonal distribution and billing systems, knowing what you buy and what you pay for is not easy. But that is not the only problem confronting the consumer. Many Congressional hearings, court cases, investigative reports, and industry whistleblowers have revealed to a dismayed public that hazardous products, monopolistic practices, endlessly clever frauds, overpricing, and swindles run rampant through the economy with very little law enforcement to deter them. The costs in diminished health, safety, and consumer income are massive. And too, unscrupulous business practices give an unfair economic advantage to the unethical businessman and make honest practices unprofitable.

After years of detailed hearings on corporate crime and other mistreatment of the consumer, Senator Philip Hart, Chairman of the Senate Subcommittee on Antitrust and Monopoly, estimated in 1969 that about 25 percent of the consumer dollar receives no value. That totals approximately $200 billion a year! When this waste and fraud are added to the preventable fatalities and injuries which occur because of dangerous automobiles, drugs, household products, flammable fabrics, medical malpractice, and a score of other consumer hazards, it becomes clear that a social and economic emergency prevails. We are not warned of this state of emergency because it is a profitable climate for its sponsors in the business community. When the polluting byproducts of producing goods and services—the lethal chemicals, gases and particulates—result, as they do, in massive compulsory consumption which leads to diseases such as cancer, emphysema, and other

Excerpted from Ralph Nader, ed., Introduction to *The Consumer and Corporate Accountability*, Harcourt, Brace, Jovanovich, New York, 1973, pp. viii–xii; 1–3. Copyright © 1973 by Harcourt, Brace, Jovanovich, Inc. and reprinted with their permission.

ailments, the situation becomes even more precarious. But all this, serious as it is and has been, pales before the prospect for the next generation as the risk levels of consumer and environmental technology (e.g., nuclear power plants and their wastes) threaten the very foundation of organized society. The tender balance between human beings and their environment can be destroyed by the chemical, radioactive, and biological devastations of a tunnel-visioned industrial juggernaut. And the gross national product of our economy can continue to grow without reducing or preventing many of our domestic problems such as unemployment, housing, hunger, poverty, discrimination, mass transit inadequacies, medical needs, crime, and waste.

CONSUMER EDUCATION

Consumer education can help to develop a variety of life skills and steadfast personal traits through a daily relating of knowing and doing. Many common experiences become relevant material for studies in consumer education; for example, watching television advertisements, purchasing auto insurance, having your automobile repaired, going to your dentist or doctor, buying books at the bookstore and food at the cafeteria, selecting clothes and cosmetics, dealing with your landlord, or obtaining a loan. How rare it is for most people to reflect on these incidents, and to perfect their critical capacities for evaluating any imperfections and consequences.

Take, for instance, a commonplace observation—the front bumper of an automobile. Nearly everyday most people casually or unconsciously look at car bumpers. Their view usually stops there. A few moments of consumer education would open the following sequence: Bumpers are supposed to protect automobiles from minor property damage in minor collisions. For many years, however, bumper design has been largely ornamental; bumpers have been recessed and of different heights for different models. Much needless property damage has resulted when cars bumped or crashed at two, three, five, or eight miles per hour. Such damage costs U.S.

Ralph Nader. The leader of the consumerist movement, Nader calls it "one of the most significant social movements in this century."

motorists over one billion dollars a year. Insurance premiums rise as a consequence. More replacement parts, such as fender sectors, grille segments, and headlights have to be produced. More coal, steel, glass, plastic, and other raw materials must be used, and more electricity and fuel expended. Prices of these commodities mount. Pollution of the air and water increases. What consumers spend on bumper repair, they do not spend on other goods and services which they might otherwise have purchased, and so reduce their standard of living as they would have it. Why did the auto companies design such bumpers? It is obvious that they knew how to do better, judging from the models of some fifty years ago, if not from the last generation's advances in technology. Could it be that the companies profited by faulty design and covered their actions by promoting the aesthetics of egg-shell bumpers? Why not write and ask these companies? Why did the auto insurance companies take so long to expose the facts and criticize the auto industry? Why not write and ask insurance companies, government auto safety agencies, university research institutes, and other sources for facts and viewpoints? Why do auto companies now promise to build more protective bumpers in future vehicles? How did this process of change get underway?

A sequential analysis of this kind can be made on literally hundreds of ordinary experiences and observations. Actual projects can be undertaken such as sampling different supermarkets to determine whether different prices are charged for exactly the same food items, as has been found to be the case. Watching television for a few evenings to record a variety of advertisements describing consumer products and service lines can be followed by an analysis of the emotional appeals, factual claims, and other devices employed to imprint the desirability of the products on the viewer's mind. Attempts at verification by writing to the presidents of the companies sponsoring the ads can provide additional information and increase your awareness about the nature of the economy, the quality of competition, and the susceptibilities of people. The breakfast cereal, soft drink, cosmetic, pain reliever, auto, tire, detergent, and insurance ads spring from a knowledge of applied social science that deserves study and evaluation from many sides.

Once the zest and skill for acquiring hard-to-get information is developed, the very process of seeking generates an understanding of citizen rights, remedies, and participation in decisions that affect everyone. Institutions, from government agencies to corporations, become household names—as indeed they and their leaders should be. Hearing the names of companies such as General Motors, Standard Oil, Dupont, Citibank, and Prudential should stimulate more than images of products and brand names; it should stimulate us to an awareness of the obligations these companies have to their customers, to their workers, and to the government agencies which regulate them. These obligations are part of the relationships of fairness and justice which we must understand if we are to understand the respective obligations of citizenship in a democratic society. The same should hold true for such agencies as the Department of Transportation, the Interstate Commerce Commission, the Federal Power Commission, state public utilities, insurance and banking agencies, and so forth. Their purpose is to serve the public interest. How they actually operate is a subject for consumer education involvement.

CHALLENGE TO POWER

Art Buchwald, syndicated newspaper columnist and well-known satirist, once put the problem precisely, if in exaggerated form. It was 1978 and, according to Buchwald's prescience, corporate power had become so concentrated in the United States that, after numerous mergers, only two corporations remained: Samson Securities west of the Mississippi and the Delilah Company east of the Mississippi. Still, in the "public interest," these two giants desired to merge, leaving but a single corporation in the entire country. After lengthy discussions the Antitrust Division in the Department of Justice approved the merger. Buchwald's piece ends with this announcement from the attorney general:

While we find drawbacks to only one company being left in the United States, we feel the advantages to the public far outweigh the disadvantages.

Therefore, we are making an exception in this case and allowing Samson and Delilah to merge.

I would like to announce that the Samson and Delilah Company is now negotiating at the White House with the President to buy the United States. The Justice Department will naturally study this merger to see if it violates any of our strong antitrust laws.

When Buchwald wrote that in 1966, the consumer movement still belonged to a few radicals, the word "consumerism" was openly ridiculed in the circles of corporate power, and it is probable that few of his readers reflected seriously on the fact that the country already was so dominated by corporate power, be it by two hundred corporations instead of Buchwald's fictional one, that substantial control over people's lives already had passed into corporate hands. Even further from most people's minds at that time was the understanding that the new consumer revolution then starting was inextricably connected to the irresponsible use of that corporate power.

The consumer movement, which is now acknowledged as one of the most significant social movements in this century, was deceptively modest in its origins. It began on many fronts but always concerned itself with the manifestations of corporate power which daily touched people's lives: unsafe automobiles, dangerously adulterated and filthy food, overpriced drugs, hidden credit charges, and the reckless use of pesticides. These issues, taken separately, were not generally perceived to be a concerted attack against a common opponent, the nearly limitless power of big business. Even so, it was a novel approach. The previous targets of consumer protectors had been the "bad apples in the barrel," the fly-by-nights, the few who polluted the honest business atmosphere and spoiled it for legitimate businessmen. This was a myth that business, through such organizations as the Better Business Bureau, cultivated assiduously. It was, therefore, a monumental shock to the business guardians of this myth when they were exposed as the rottenest apples of all. Consumer advocates began to document that consumers were defrauded, injured, and manipulated not by the corner gyp market but by the largest business entities in the world: the U.S. blue-chip business firms such as General Motors, Ford, Union Carbide, General Foods, and the mammoth pharmaceutical firms. It was a new concept, a new emphasis which, as business knew, could only lead to more alarming exposures and more probing ques-

tions. It was a strike at the heart of business crimi-
nality and irresponsibility; it was an unprecedented
challenge to corporate power.

It is at this stage we find ourselves today. The
consumer revolt has matured with the realization that
consumer reforms cannot be separated from corporate reforms: they are two sides of the same coin.
Consumer discontent and abuses flow from the un-
bridled power corporations have over the marketplace and the government.

The challenge to [the] corporate state must be
then, as it is with other authoritarian institutions, to
devise the economic and political machinery necessary to regain control of our individual and collective
futures.   □

PUBLIC POLICIES TOWARD MONOPOLY AND COMPETITION IN THE UNITED STATES

The eternal vigilance toward corporate abuses that
is the hallmark of consumerism will doubtless continue to play an important role in rendering American
business more responsive to public needs. However,
it is also clear that such vigilance is not enough: One
also needs systematic policies that set the basic
structure within which business activities take place.
One needs alert referees, but one also needs a clear
book of rules. This, indeed, is the point that Nader
himself makes in the latter part of the preceding
reading.

As we might expect, partly because of the complexity of the problem, partly because of the pressures
and counterpressures of the political process, public
policy toward business in this country sometimes
seems a maze of conflicting principles. There is not
one book of rules but several; not one game, but
many different games are being played.

In one part of the economy, for example, bigness
is taken as an accepted fact and government policy
is exercised via various regulatory commissions at the
state and federal levels. This is true in the general
areas of transportation, utilities, and communications.
In these sectors, the main federal agencies are the
Interstate Commerce Commission, the Civil Aeronautics Board, the Federal Power Commission, and
the Federal Communications Commission. In each
of these cases, the consumerist question (How can
we insure vigorous and effective protection for the
consumer in the face of a general tendency for regulators and regulated to see problems from a common
point of view?) is very much to the point. However,
the main premise of the regulatory approach—
namely, the acceptance of large, noncompeting
firms, whose behavior is then controlled by public
commissions—makes sense to the economist in an
area where "natural monopoly," at least in a local
sense, is characteristic.

Much less sensible from the economist's point of
view are those governmental interventions that seem
designed to restrict or eliminate competitive behavior.
In agriculture, our price-support programs are clearly
designed to modify the ordinary workings of supply
and demand. In the retail trades, the Robinson-
Patman Act of 1936 and various state "fair trade"
laws have restricted competition in retail pricing. Our
patent system is a publicly protected means of granting monopolies to individual inventors. In these and
other cases, there are specific justifications for the
programs involved—adjusting low or unstable farm
incomes, protecting small retail outlets against the
chain stores, encouraging and rewarding inventors,
and so on—but in each instance this form of state
intervention has at least some negative effect on
economic efficiency. Economists generally would
prefer other forms of intervention to those that limit
competition—say, direct subsidies to individuals or
families injured by competition—precisely because of
these efficiency considerations.

In any event, the forms of state intervention that
limit competition, like those that permit (but regulate)
natural monopolies, clearly operate from rule books
quite different from what many observers consider

the *basic* American policy. This policy roughly consists of these elements: (1) let the private sector do the job if possible; (2) keep the private sector competitive—if not purely, at least "workably"; and (3) where private forces do not produce such workably competitive results, let the state intervene to make the market more effective. After what we have said above, no one will be inclined to think that this is our only national policy (or that that policy is in any way consistent); still, the notion that private competition is desirable and that at least some minimal government intervention may be necessary to secure it runs deep in our national history and deserves special comment.

Let us now say a few words about the main form that this governmental intervention has taken—the American antitrust laws—and then take up some specific current problems to show the complications of applying these laws.

ANTITRUST LEGISLATION

The two main antitrust laws in this country are the Sherman Act of 1890 and the Clayton Act of 1914. The Sherman Act prohibits "every contract, combination in the form of trust or otherwise, or conspiracy, in restraint of trade or commerce" and prescribes punishments for "every person who shall monopolize, or attempt to monopolize, or combine or conspire with any other person or persons, to monopolize any part of trade or commerce among the several States, or with foreign nations." The Clayton Act adds to this a number of prohibited business policies, such as price discrimination against different buyers, and, in Section 7, forbids mergers that might "substantially lessen competition or tend to create a monopoly." The anti-merger provisions of Section 7 of the Clayton Act were greatly strengthened by the passage of the anti-merger Celler-Kefauver Act of 1950.

The meaning and impact of these laws has, of course, depended very much upon the vigor with which cases under them have been initiated and by the interpretations given them by the courts. The

prosecution of antitrust suits by the Justice Department has followed a somewhat erratic course since the passage of the Sherman Act in 1890. There have been periods of relative inactivity, as in the decade after the Sherman Act was passed or in the period from World War I to the depression of the 1930s, and periods of vigorous prosecution, as in the early 1900s and especially beginning in the late 1930s, under the then Assistant Attorney General Thurman Arnold.

Similarly, court interpretations of the laws have altered considerably over time. For example, in two famous cases in 1911 (Standard Oil and American Tobacco), the Supreme Court enunciated a "rule of reason" in interpreting the phrase "restraint of trade" in the Sherman Act. Firms were to be condemned not merely for size, nor merely for restraint of trade, but only when they violated the rules "unreasonably." In 1945, however, in the landmark *Alcoa* case, the Court ruled that mere size *could* constitute a violation of the antitrust laws. *How big* was big enough to constitute a monopoly was left somewhat vague, but clearly the Court felt that Alcoa's control of 90 percent of U.S. aluminum production was too big even in the absence of any unreasonable or predatory practices.

Market Performance

Underlying the shifting fortunes of antitrust activity in this country have been certain questions about the *criteria* to be used in deciding whether particular industries should be subject to legal action. In a sense, it seems that the key criterion should be *market performance.* By *market performance* we mean how a firm, industry, and ultimately the economy as a whole fulfill certain roughly agreed upon economic objectives. These would include efficiency in the use and allocation of resources, the "progressiveness" of the firms and industries in the economy, and perhaps also some approximate standard of a desired distribution of income. If these various performance goals could be achieved, we should all probably agree that public policy had been successful in this area.

The problem of using performance as a criterion for governmental intervention (in addition to the very considerable problems of actually *measuring* performance) is that it would be likely to involve the government in a constant, direct, and intimate regulation of the affairs of all the firms and industries in the economy. The key feature of a private economy is that the market bears the main responsibility for assuring satisfactory performance in the economy as a whole. If we believed that the market would fail completely in this task, we might want to go to some scheme whereby the government directly regulates profits, input combinations, output levels, prices, advertising expenditures, etc., and thus controls the performance of firms and industries by explicit directive. (To some degree, the battle against inflation and the initiation of price and wage controls in the early 1970s moved us in this direction, if only temporarily.) The more common approach in the United States, however, has been to continue central reliance on the market for assuring satisfactory performance and to limit governmental intervention to making sure that the market is given a chance to work as it should.

Market Conduct

This more limited approach, however, is still rather vague about how and when the government should intervene. In particular, two basic strands of thought have been evident in the history of antitrust policy in the United States. One strand emphasizes governmental regulation of the *market conduct* of firms. This approach tends to emphasize predatory practices, collusion between rivals, and direct agreements that have the effect of undermining competition and enhancing the monopoly powers that firms in an industry may collectively possess. Even Adam Smith, in the early days of capitalism, was well aware of such dangers. "People of the same trade," he wrote, "seldom meet together, even for merriment or diversion, but the conversation ends in a conspiracy against the public or in some contrivance to raise prices."[2] Such activities illustrate bad market con-

duct. The "rule of reason" is another example of the market conduct approach—judging firms in violation of the antitrust laws when they misbehave, possibly lowering their prices beneath costs in certain localities, to drive out potential competitors. The 1961 case against several major companies in the electrical industry is a similar illustration of legal action based on unacceptable market conduct. The companies were found guilty of holding secret meetings to fix prices and divide up the market (some executives were actually imprisoned).

Market Structure

The second strand of thought emphasizes not conduct but *market structure*. The *Alcoa* case (1945) is a good example of this approach, since the Court did not allege misconduct on Alcoa's part but simply that the firm, by virtue of its dominant size in the industry, constituted an illegal monopoly. On the structural approach, the fact that a firm had substantial monopoly power (how much is *substantial* is a difficult question) would make it subject to the antitrust laws even if its conduct were impeccable and even if its efficiency, progressiveness, and other performance attributes were wholly satisfactory.

In theory, these various concepts are not unrelated. The last chapter was largely devoted to showing how different market structures (monopoly, oligopoly, etc.) lead to different kinds of conduct (determination of prices, differentiation of products, etc.) that, in turn, lead to different kinds of performance (in terms of efficiency, and so on). In practice, however, the approaches tend to differ rather significantly. On the conduct approach, even relatively small firms will be forbidden to engage in collusive agreements that limit competition, while a much bigger firm, already in existence, may be allowed to stand even though it is capable of exercising far more monopoly power than the smaller conspirators. One of the interesting features of American antitrust policy is that it is relatively tough on mergers within an industry, though it may not touch existing corporations larger than the merged firms in the same industry.

2. Adam Smith, *Wealth of Nations* (New York: Modern Library, 1937), p. 250.

There is also an underlying philosophic difference that may separate these approaches. Some observers feel that in addition to the ordinary economic performance goals, there is an independently valuable goal of limiting the concentration of economic power in the nation. These observers are likely to be thinking of the potential political and social effects of huge agglomerations of economic wealth, a point we mentioned earlier. If such limitation of power is an important goal in itself, then the way in which that power is exercised either in terms of conduct or performance is not of the essence; a structural criterion will be preferred.

Finally, we should note that the application of either of these criteria in a consistent way is made very difficult because financial and industrial developments are constantly posing new sets of problems, many of them largely unforeseen, and some of which contradict older categories of thought. Two challenging developments of this nature that have occurred recently are (1) the conglomerate merger movement of the 1960s, and (2) the extraordinary expansion of multinational corporations from the late 1950s to the present. As a way to increase our understanding of public policy toward business in actual practice, therefore, let us comment briefly on these current phenomena.

THE CONGLOMERATE MERGER MOVEMENT

In the late 1960s, a flood of corporate mergers in the United States suggested that even the oldest and most established corporations in the country might be subject to take-overs. In 1968, some 4,400 merger proposals were made. This was 50 percent above the 1967 figure, which itself was 25 percent above the 1966 figure.[3] Although the trend has reversed somewhat in the early 1970s, this movement has had a lasting effect in that it expanded the reach of a relatively modern form of enterprise: the conglomerate.

The central feature of a conglomerate merger is that it involves firms operating in different markets. These markets may simply be geographically separated; however, the pure form of conglomerate involves firms producing quite distinct and unrelated products. One firm produces toothpaste, another textbooks: their merger would give us a pure conglomerate.

Now the significance of such mergers, from the point of view of our analysis in this and the preceding chapter, is that they tend to break the linkages we developed between firm size, market structure, market conduct, and performance—or certainly to alter these relationships. With a conglomerate merger, we may have a huge firm that has only a small share of the sales in any particular market. If we look at firm size alone, we are likely to come to a different conclusion than if we look at market structure as measured, say, by our "concentration ratios" of chapter 5.

But the link between market structure, so conceived, and conduct and performance is also likely to be affected. For surely it is not irrelevant that a firm, though small in a particular market, has tremendous overall financial assets behind it. Clearly such a firm would be capable of misconduct in that industry in a way that a firm of equal size in that industry, but without other industrial connections, would not. The latter could hardly sustain a long predatory price war; the former clearly could.

And market performance is also at stake. Are there economies of scale that occur when firms in different industries merge? What kind of economies are they and how, if at all, should they be taken into account?

One expert on antitrust matters, Professor F. M. Scherer, has concluded that four main grounds have been used for prohibiting or restricting conglomerates:[4]

1. Reduction of potential competition. The courts have applied this criterion even when neither of the firms was in the industry in question but each had

3. John J. Abele, "Take-Overs Shake Business," The New York Times, March 9, 1969.

4. F. M. Scherer, Industrial Market Structure and Economic Performance, Chicago: Rand McNally & Co., 1970, pp. 482–87.

been considering going into that industry; the conglomerate is prevented on the grounds that it reduces the number of potential entrants into the industry and, hence, the competitiveness of the industry.

2. Potential for predatory pricing. That is to say, potential market misconduct; this applies to the firm that, though small in the particular industry, has great resources behind it. Scherer finds this "one of the shakiest pillars of existing anti-merger law."

3. Reciprocal purchasing leverage. Firm A acquires Firm B and then tells Firm C that, if it doesn't buy from Firm B, it will lose its sales to Firm A; the Supreme Court rules such mergers out if Firm A is sufficiently large to be able to exert this kind of leverage on Firm C.

4. Efficiency advantages of the merged firm. A performance criterion almost in reverse. It is not clear whether this criterion will be sustained by the courts, but certain decisions by the Federal Trade Commission argue that, if smaller firms are hurt, the merger should not be allowed to stand even if the problem is the superior efficiency of the conglomerate.

Even a casual inspection of these criteria reveals how flimsy they are, depending either on *potential* actions or, in the case of the fourth criterion, on the proof of *benefits,* as opposed to harms, bestowed by the conglomerate. It is little wonder that, until the merger movement greatly accelerated in the late 1960s, the Justice Department and the Federal Trade Commission actually took contrary views on the issue: The Justice Department saw little to oppose, the FTC was trying hard to fight off the mergers.

Because the ordinary performance, conduct, and structure linkages are obscured in this type of firm, a more general criteria may be required. Scherer concludes that ultimately "one's choice may turn on a basic value judgment regarding the social and political acceptability of bigness untainted by more familiar manifestations of monopoly power." If this view is to prevail, then it may well be that new legisla-

tion will be needed to spell out precisely what our objection to bigness is, and how firms may know when they are in violation of society's standards of size. It seems safe to say that the final word is not yet in on conglomerates, and that it may not be for some time.

EXPANSION OF THE MULTINATIONAL CORPORATIONS

Multinational corporations pose equally difficult challenges to our antitrust laws, because, by definition, these corporations operate within different national jurisdictions. By their very nature, they may be exposed to quite different concepts of what is acceptable business behavior.

The rise of the multinational corporation has been a prominent economic fact during the past two decades. Figure 25–1 shows what has been happening to direct investment by business firms abroad, by country of origin. The United States is the largest investor in multinational enterprises abroad, but the rise of other countries, notably West Germany and Japan, is quite striking. On the receiving side, Canada is the recipient of the largest amount of foreign investment, and in terms of percentage, the multinational corporation looms larger in her economy than in any other. The United States, however, has also received considerable investment from abroad—a total of $13.2 billion in 1970.

From the point of view of antitrust policy, a salient fact about the situation of the multinationals is that the United States, however inconsistently, has generally tended to be tougher against monopolies and cartels than have our international trading partners. This, in turn, reflects the fact that most other nations have been concerned only with a performance criterion and have not worried too much whether market conduct or market structure are theoretically satisfactory or unsatisfactory. Raymond Vernon, a leading authority on multinationals, sums up the problem:

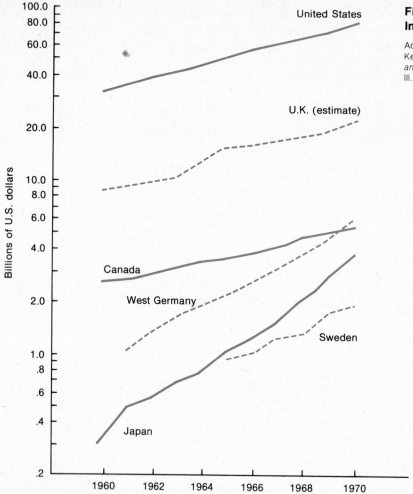

Figure 25–1. Growth Trends in International Direct Investment.

Adapted from Stefan H. Robock and Kenneth Simmonds, *International Business and Multinational Enterprises.* Homewood, Ill.: Richard D. Irwin, 1973, p. 52.

"The tolerance of other governments for restrictive practices is generally higher. And the concept of a per se violation—an act that is *ipso facto* illegal without regard to its economic consequences—is almost uniquely a U.S. idea."[5] Thus, for example, the four criteria mentioned earlier with respect to the restriction of U.S. conglomerates would have little, if any, counterpart in many countries abroad.

In view of the great growth of the multinationals, these differences of approach would appear to be in need of some reconciliation. The following reading takes up the differences and also notes some trends toward their possible harmonization over time.

5.   Raymond Vernon, "Competition Policy Toward Multinational Corporations," *American Economic Review,* Vol. LXIV, No. 2, May 1974, p. 280.

Antitrust and the Multinational Corporation

Stefan H. Robock and Kenneth Simmonds

The transnational reach of national laws regulating domestic business behavior can present vexatious problems for the international enterprise, particularly in the fields of antitrust and securities regulation. Such laws are intended to govern business behavior within the specific nation and are not directed specifically toward business transactions that cross national boundaries. But in their application they can have an extraterritorial reach when foreign-based conduct has a significant impact on the domestic scene.

In many respects, the international enterprise can adjust its global strategy and operating policies to differences in national laws. But the effects of certain business actions or policies are not coterminous with the national boundaries within which such actions are taken or policies decided upon. Certain practices may be legal in one jurisdiction, but the same action may be considered in violation of the laws in another country in which the enterprise is operating. Such a situation raises the difficult problem of extraterritoriality, because legal action in one jurisdiction can have significant effects on activities in another area where the law being applied does not have legal jurisdiction. In this way, the international enterprise can be the vehicle through which conflicts between nations arise.

ANTITRUST LAWS AND RESTRICTIVE BUSINESS PRACTICES

Restrictive business agreements are agreements among enterprises to fix prices, limit production, allocate markets, restrain the application of technology, or engage in similar schemes likely to reduce competition. Such practices have been illegal in the United States for many decades under various antitrust laws, but, until World War II, they were either permitted or positively encouraged in most countries outside of North America. The situation changed drastically after World War II when many other nations followed generally the American pattern and adopted laws designed to curb restrictive business practices. Presently, at least twenty-four countries—thirteen in Europe, four in Latin America, and seven others—have national antitrust laws. National laws in the European Economic Community countries have been supplemented with Articles 85 and 86 of the Rome Treaty, which are directed toward regulating competition in the Common Market area.

Some significant differences in national laws exist. In its domestic application, the U.S. law looks at the *act* of conspiracy, or of monopolizing, whereas the European laws look at the *effects*. The basic philosophy of antitrust laws in the United States is that competition per se is good and that any acts to restrain competition are illegal. The basic philosophy of European antimonopoly law is that some anticompetitive agreements may be beneficial and others may be harmful. It takes the position that certain types of cooperation or mergers can lead to increased productivity, economic growth, technological advance, and price reductions.

The Sherman Act of 1890 passed by the U.S. Congress at a time when few American firms had foreign subsidiaries holds in Section 1 that:

Every contract, combination in the form of trust or otherwise, or conspiracy, in restraint of trade or commerce among the several states, or with foreign nations, is hereby declared to be illegal.

The Sherman Act and subsequent legislation extends the U.S. laws to actions abroad which "substantially affect" the commerce of the United States and competition in the U.S. markets. To do otherwise, it is argued, and to make enforcement turn on nationality or physical events, would open the door to widespread evasion and abuse.

Excerpted from Stefan H. Robock and Kenneth Simmonds, *International Business and Multinational Enterprises*, Homewood, Ill.: Richard D. Irwin, 1973, pp. 347–353. © 1973 Richard D. Irwin. Used with permission.

The non-U.S. antitrust laws are relatively recent, and the applications are still limited in number. Yet indications are that they will also have a transnational reach. West Germany and Austria, for example, expressly extend their laws to include restrictive business practices abroad having ''effects'' within their territory. The Canadian Restrictive Practices Commission has similarly interpreted Canadian law.

As a practical matter, a nation must be able to assert jurisdiction over the international enterprise in order to enforce its laws. The legal test of jurisdiction by U.S. courts is whether the foreign corporation is transacting business ''of a substantial character,'' and the test governing service or process is whether the corporation is *found* in the jurisdiction. The wide reach exercised by the U.S. laws is illustrated by the Swiss Watchmakers Case. Two Swiss trade associations in the watch industry were held subject to local jurisdiction because of the activities of a jointly owned New York corporation doing advertising and promotional work and acting as a liaison agency in servicing the American market with repair parts.*

The U.S. courts found the defendants guilty of conspiracy to restrain the commerce of the United States and ordered them to stop all restraints on exports to the United States and to change industry practices developed in Switzerland with the active support and participation of the Swiss government. The decree imposed wide prohibitions on contracts made in Switzerland and on agreements made between the Swiss industry and manufacturers in Great Britain, France, and Germany. It also ordered sweeping changes in certain bylaws of the Swiss Watch Federation which were considered restrictive of U.S. commerce. After the Swiss government intervened directly with the U.S. government, important changes were made in the final judgment, including the inser-

---

*United States v. Watchmakers of Switzerland Information Center, 133 F. Supp. 40, SDNY (1955).

tion of a provision that nothing in it would limit or circumscribe the sovereign right and power of the Swiss government.

Foreign mergers and acquisitions have been challenged under U.S. antitrust laws. A suit was brought against the Gillette Company in 1968 to prevent its acquisition of Braun, A.G., a German concern, on the grounds that the acquisition would eliminate a potential competitor in the domestic shaving-instrument industry. Through the threat of court action, the U.S. Department of Justice delayed and reshaped a merger of two foreign firms: Ciba and Geigy. These two major Swiss pharmaceutical companies postponed a merger and revised their merger plans in 1970 when officially informed that the merger as planned might be in violation of U.S. law. The alleged grounds were that the combining of the U.S. operations of both companies would reduce competition in the American dyestuff market.

The transnational reach of enforcement techniques of one government can be interpreted as interference by another government with the international enterprise in the middle. For example, U.S. courts have ordered U.S. banks to turn over bank records on foreign companies held in the bank's foreign affiliates. As a result, a number of governments have passed laws prohibiting companies located in their jurisdiction from complying with the orders of foreign courts to produce documents.

Still another aspect of the transnational reach of antitrust laws has been the concern expressed by foreign firms interested in establishing operations in the United States that U.S. authorities may seek to apply U.S. laws to their activities outside of the United States.

FUTURE TRENDS

Clearly the legal environment is in a transitional stage of adaptation to new international business patterns, and the international enterprise must be sensitive to future trends in the legal framework. In traditional international trade activities, the adaptation of national legal systems has been substantial and new legal problems are likely to be minimal. In the case of securing legal protection for foreign investment and industrial property rights (such as patents, know-how, and trademarks), adaptation has been only partial despite a long history of legal concern over such matters. With regard to multinational business enterprises operating transnationally with global strategies and integrated operations, the legal response is only in a beginning stage, and the legal framework is likely to change most in the future. Furthermore, as previously independent foreign investments increasingly become part of an integrated system of multinational business operations, many long-standing issues related to legal protection of foreign investment and industrial property rights have also become more complex.

Given the highly divergent national interests in the international business field, the consensus needed to establish an international legal system for simplifying and harmonizing the legal environment for international business has not emerged and is unlikely to emerge in the near future. If, for political reasons, the nations of the world move toward a strong world government, a comprehensive system of world law would be created which could include broad coverage of international business matters. But as of the early 1970s, the political route toward an international legal framework for international business does not appear promising.

One possibility at the international level, short of a comprehensive system of world law, is the "Cosmocorp" proposal to permit multinational enterprises to become truly international or nonnational autonomous entities. This could be achieved through agreement by members of the United Nations to create an organization that could grant international incorporation. Another way might be for companies to incorporate in places like Luxembourg or Bermuda, with general recognition that such incorporation is a *de facto* declaration of independence from all significant relationships to a home country.

The Cosmocorp proposal emerged from legal circles and has attracted academic support in the investor countries. But despite the appealing logic of having an international companies law for international business enterprises, neither business firms nor nations have urgently pressed for action on the Cosmocorp proposal. The multinational enterprise apparently recognizes that having a nationality may have advantages over statelessness. In a world of nation-states, the business firm would be giving up access to national investment-guarantee and incentive programs as well as the potential support that a home government could give the business interests of the firm in international tariff negotiations and in the resolution of conflicts concerning such matters as taxes and the taking of property. Furthermore, the enterprise would still be considered as a foreign company by any nation so long as its home base is not in that specific country. The lack of interest by nations in the Cosmocorp proposal may result from the nations' greater concern for expanding rather than reducing their control over foreign business activities in their countries.

A more certain trend is toward expanded coverage of international business matters through partial international regulation. Partial international regulation may be expanded through the extension of the activities of existing international organizations such as the IMF, GATT, UNCTAD, and the OECD. When these agencies were created, the multinational enterprise was not an explicit matter of their concern. Yet the work of these organizations has facilitated the expansion of international business, and the operations of multinational enterprises are having an increasing impact on the goals and programs of the agencies. In lieu of or as a complement to a new international organization, an extension of existing organizations into international business matters appears logical and inevitable.

In the antitrust field, the trend favored by most U.S. international firms is a simple formula of having the jurisdiction of antitrust laws stop at the country's border. But the simplicity of this solution is deceptive. In its nature, international business, whether in the form of trade or multinational business operations, involves the jurisdictions of more than one country.

Any country that would adopt a self-denying policy to disregard restraint of trade conspiracies entered into outside of the country would simply be giving away the right to protect itself against foreign arrangements that it thought harmful to its national interest.

Another possible future trend would be for the many nations with antitrust legislation to adopt uniform trade regulation laws and policies. One legal authority claims that there has been some harmonization of law and policy by others moving in the direction of U.S. practices. Yet as the new laws become more systematic and as interpretations in each country harden into precedents, complete uniformity in trade regulation policies becomes increasingly difficult. Aside from some harmonization, the most likely trend appears to be an increasing use of bilateral agreements and diplomatic negotiations to handle conflict issues arising in the antitrust field. □

SUMMARY

Despite the efficiency advantages of pure competition under certain circumstances, few economists would advocate a wholesale dismemberment of large firms in the American economy. Besides the administrative problems involved, realistic policy would have to take into account possible economies of scale, the growth-advantages of large firms in some industries, and the general complications raised by the problem of *second best*. On the other hand, a do-nothing attitude to industry is unsatisfactory, too. *Consumerism* shows popular discontent with many of the practices of modern business and the need for more adequate consumer protection.

In actual fact, public policy toward business in the United States is something of a mixed bag, involving the recognition of "natural monopolies" in certain areas such as transportation, utilities, and communications; the *limitation* of competition in other areas such as agriculture, retail trade, and patents; and—what many would consider the *main* theme of U.S. policy—the encouragement of "workable" competition and the restriction of excessive monopoly through the antitrust laws.

The ultimate goal of such laws as the Sherman Act of 1890, the Clayton Act of 1914, and the Celler-Kefauver Act of 1950 has been to secure a satisfactory *market performance* by American firms and industries in terms of efficiency and other economic objectives. Rather than regulate this performance directly, however, the government has sought to make the market a more effective regulator. In doing this, two approaches have been used at various times: (1) a *market conduct* approach, stressing the prosecution of collusive and other predatory practices that undermine competition (e.g., the 1911 "rule of reason"), and (2) a *market structure* approach, stressing the size and market power of a firm even if that power is impeccably exercised (e.g., the 1945 *Alcoa* case).

One of the problems of applying any criterion consistently is that changing circumstances are continually throwing up new challenges to antitrust concepts. The *conglomerate merger* movement of the late 1960s is a case in point. When firms become large through the merger of smaller firms in unrelated industries, the traditional links between firm size, market structure, market conduct, and economic performance are likely to be broken or at least altered. Similarly, the *multinational corporations* raise issues about jurisdiction over business firms, and also about national differences in antitrust philosophy.

Governments and the courts, both here and abroad, are now struggling with these latest major developments on the antitrust scene.

IMPORTANT TERMS TO REMEMBER

Economies of Scale
Growth and Monopoly Power
"Second Best"
Consumerism
Antitrust Laws
Market Performance
Market Conduct
Market Structure
"Rule of Reason"
Conglomerate Mergers
Predatory Pricing
Multinational Corporation

QUESTIONS FOR DISCUSSION

1. It has been said of certain U.S. policies toward business that they protect not competition but *competitors.* How would you interpret such a statement? Give examples of policies that might fit this description.

2. If you were engaged in the regulation of a "natural monopoly" in the utility field, do you think that the analysis of competitive efficiency would have any effect on the policies—say, pricing policies—you might determine for this firm? Discuss.

3. "The main problem with American business is not how the game is played, but the nature of the game itself." Discuss this statement, relating it to such topics as consumerism, and the debate between market conduct and market structure in antitrust policy.

4. This chapter has emphasized efficiency as a "performance" goal, though noting that there are other equally (or more) important goals that also must be taken into account. State some of these other goals. Would taking them into account make you more, less, or sometimes-more-and-sometimes-less sympathetic to monopoly elements in the economy than when you consider efficiency alone?

5. Show how conglomerate mergers and multinational corporations complicate the traditional analysis of linkages between firm size, market structure, market conduct, and market performance.

SUGGESTED READING

Kaysen, Carl, and Turner, Donald F. *Antitrust Policy.* Cambridge, Mass.: Harvard University Press, 1959.

Scherer, F. M. *Industrial Market Structure and Economic Performance.* Chicago: Rand McNally & Co., 1970.

Sethi, S. Prakash. *Up Against the Corporate Wall.* Englewood Cliffs, N.J.: Prentice-Hall, 1971.

Vernon, Raymond. "Multinational Enterprises: Performance and Accountability," in Backman, Jules and Bloch, Ernest, eds., *Multinational Corporations, Trade and the Dollar.* New York: New York University Press, 1974.

GREAT DEBATE 3:
GALBRAITH AND THE NEW INDUSTRIAL STATE

GREAT DEBATE 3:
GALBRAITH AND THE NEW INDUSTRIAL STATE

No economics book has attracted more public attention in the last decade then John Kenneth Galbraith's The New Industrial State. It stimulated, among other discussions, a sharp debate in the pages of the journal The Public Interest, in 1967 and 1968. Galbraith's opponent in this debate was the highly respected M.I.T. economist, Robert M. Solow. Besides excerpts from this debate, we have introduced a few pages from The New Industrial State itself, bringing out some of the central issues at dispute.

In some respects, this debate concerns the validity of the kind of microeconomic analysis that we have been presenting throughout Part Three of this book. Like Milton Friedman with his monetarist doctrine in macroeconomics, Galbraith views himself as presenting a major alternative to the textbook view of microeco-

nomic realities. As he writes explicitly in a more recent book: "I've also had the emancipation of the student from the textbook very much in mind."[1] Galbraith believes that the basic way of understanding our industrial system must depart from the traditional view that focuses on markets and then adjusts the analysis depending on whether the markets are largely competitive, monopolistic, oligopolistic, and so on. He would give up the concept of a market system almost completely—at least for the large-scale corporate, manufacturing sector of the modern industrial economy. He believes that a different kind of mechanism is called for.

What kind of mechanism? If we think of the traditional approach as involving business firms that try to maximize profits in response to a market that is largely governed by con-

---

1. John Kenneth Galbraith, Economics and the Public Purpose, Houghton Mifflin Company, Boston, 1973, p. xii.

sumer preferences, Galbraith would substitute the following:

In place of firms that are subject to control by the market, he pictures firms that control their markets through planning. Not completely, perhaps, but in important ways. This control is exercised over the prices at which they buy and sell goods, the quantities of goods they buy and sell, the sources of new capital for the firm, and even basic consumer tastes.

In place of firms that try to maximize their profits, he pictures firms that seek other goals, which are determined largely by the technostructure of the firm and the society. The firm must secure a certain minimum of earnings to survive, but beyond this it is free to seek goals that its technical experts, scientists, and management value, these being especially the growth of output. In such a society, technological change is accorded a high priority.

And, finally, in place of consumers who dictate the goods that are to be produced, he pictures business firms who essentially manage consumer demand. Through advertising and other means of persuasion, the great corporations convince people that the goals of the technostructure—ever more output of automobiles, toothpastes, etc.—are valid and should be supported by purchasing the goods that the firm's planning requires that they should purchase.

How accurate is this alternative picture? The following pages do not answer that question, but they do present two very different and warmly argued points of view. They also bring the student to the frontier issues in the economic analysis of the modern corporation. It is safe to predict that these will be important issues in the field for many years to come.

The New Industrial State

John Kenneth Galbraith

The market has only one message for the business firm. That is the promise of more money. If the firm has no influence on its prices, as the Wisconsin dairy farm has no influence on the price of milk, it has no options as to the goals that it pursues. It must try to make money and, as a practical matter, it must try to make as much as possible. Others do. To fail to conform is to invite loss, failure and extrusion. Certainly a decision to subordinate interest in earnings to an interest in a more contented life for workers, cows or consumers would, in the absence of exceptional supplementary income, mean financial disaster. Given this need to maximize revenue, the firm is thus fully subject to the authority of the market.

When the firm has influence on market prices—when it has the power commonly asso-

Excerpted from John Kenneth Galbraith, *The New Industrial State* (Boston: Houghton Mifflin, 1967; London: Andre Deutsch, 1967), pp. 109–11, 115–17, 160–65, 210–15. Copyright © 1967, 1971 by John Kenneth Galbraith. Reprinted by permission of the publisher, Houghton Mifflin Company.

ciated with monopoly—it has also long been assumed that it will seek as large a profit as possible. It could settle for less than the maximum but it is assumed that it seeks monopoly power in order to be free of the limitations set by competition on its return. Why should it seek monopoly power and then settle for less than its full advantages? When demand is strong, the monopolistic firm can extract more revenue from the market; when demand slackens, it can get less. But so long as it tries to get as much as possible it will still be subject to control by the market and ultimately, as sustained by the compulsions of avarice, by the preferences of consumers, as expressed by their purchases. Were the monopolist regularly to settle for something less than a maximum return, the causes of this restraint would have to be explained by forces apart from the market. Along with the state of demand these forces would be a factor determining prices, production and profit. Belief in the market as the transcendent regulator of economic behavior requires, therefore, a parallel

John Kenneth Galbraith. Perhaps the most famous of all contemporary economists, Galbraith has sought an audience in the public at large as well as among his fellow economists. His views—whether about the structure of modern industry or the perils of "affluence"—are invariably highly stimulating.

mitments of capital and time have forced the firm to emancipate itself from the uncertainties of the market. And specialized technology has rendered the market increasingly unreliable. So the firm controls the prices at which it buys materials, components and talent and takes steps to insure the necessary supply at these prices. And it controls the prices at which it sells and takes steps to insure that the public, other producers or the state take the planned quantities at these prices. So far from being controlled by the market, the firm, to the best of its ability, has made the market subordinate to the goals of its planning. Prices, costs, production and resulting revenues are established not by the market but, within broad limits later to be examined, by the planning decisions of the firm.

The goal of these planning decisions could still be the greatest possible profit. We have already seen that a high and reliable flow of earnings is important for the success of the technostructure. But the market is no longer specifying and enforcing that goal. Accordingly profit maximization—the only goal that is consistent with the rule of the market—is no longer necessary. The competitive firm had no choice of goals. The monopoly could take less than the maximum; but this would be inconsistent with its purpose in being a monopoly. But planning is the result not of the desire to exploit market opportunity but the result, among other factors, of the unreliability of markets. Subordination to the market, and to the instruction that it conveys, has disappeared. So there is no longer, *a priori*, reason to believe that profit maximization will be the goal of the technostructure. It could be, but this must be shown. And it will be difficult to show if other things are more important than profit for the success of the technostructure. It will also be difficult to show if the technostructure does not get the profit.

belief that participating firms will always seek to maximize their earnings. If this is assumed there is, by exclusion, no need to search for other motives.

When planning replaces the market this admirably simple explanation of economic behavior collapses. Technology and the companion com-

THE APPROVED CONTRADICTION

It is agreed that the modern large corporation is, quite typically, controlled by its management. The managerial revolution as distinct from that of the technostructure is accepted. So long as earnings are above a certain minimum it would also be widely agreed that the management has little to fear from the stockholders. Yet it is for these stockholders, remote, powerless and unknown, that management seeks to maximize profits. Management does not go out ruthlessly to reward itself—a sound management is expected to exercise restraint. Already at this stage, in the accepted view of the corporation, profit maximization involves a substantial contradiction. Those in charge forgo personal reward to enhance it for others.

The contradiction becomes much sharper as one recognizes the role of the technostructure. If power is regarded as resting with a few senior officers, then their pecuniary interest could be imagined at least to be parallel to that of the owners. The higher the earnings the higher the salaries they can justify, the greater the return on any stock they may themselves hold, and the better the prospect for any stock options they may have issued to themselves. Even these contentions stand only limited examination. There are few corporations in which it would be suggested that executive salaries are at a maximum. As a not uncritical observer has recently observed, ". . . [the] average level of salaries of managers even in leading corporations is not exceptionally high."* Astronomical figures, though not exceptional, are usually confined to the very top. Stock holdings by management are small and often non-existent. Stock options, the right to buy stock at predetermined prices if it goes up in value, though common, are by no means universal and are more widely valued as a tax dodge than as an incentive. So even the case for maximization of personal return by a top management is not strong.

But with the rise of the technostructure, the notion, however tenuous, that a few managers might maximize their own return by maximizing that of the stockholders, dissolves entirely. Power passes down into the organization. Even the small stock interest of the top officers is no longer the rule. Salaries, whether modest or generous, are according to scale; they do not vary with profits. And with the power of decision goes opportunity for making money which all good employees are expected to eschew. Members of the technostructure have advance knowledge of products and processes, price changes, impending government contracts and, in the fashionable jargon of our time, technical breakthroughs. Advantage could be taken of this information. Were everyone to seek to do so—by operations in the stock of the company, or in that of suppliers, in commodity markets, by taking themselves and their knowledge into the employ of another firm for a price—the corporation would be a chaos of competitive avarice. But these are not the sort of thing that a good company man does; a remarkably effective code bans such behavior. Group decision-making insures, moreover, that almost everyone's actions and even thoughts are known to others. This acts to enforce the code and, more than incidentally, a high standard of personal honesty as well. The technostructure does not permit of the pri-

*Wilbert E. Moore, *The Conduct of the Corporation* (New York: Random House, Inc., 1962), p. 13.

vacy that misfeasance and malfeasance require.

So the technostructure, as a matter of necessity, bans personal profit-making. And, as a practical matter, what is banned for the ordinary scientist, engineer, contract negotiator or sales executive must also be banned for senior officers. Resistance to pecuniary temptation cannot be enforced at the lower levels if it is known that the opportunity to turn a personal penny remains the prerogative of the high brass.

The members of the technostructure do not get the profits that they maximize. They must eschew personal profit-making. Accordingly, if the traditional commitment to profit maximization is to be upheld, they must be willing to do for others, specifically the stockholders, what they are forbidden to do for themselves. It is on such grounds that the doctrine of maximization in the mature corporation now rests. It holds that the will to make profits is, like the will to sexual expression, a fundamental urge. But it holds that this urge operates not in the first person but the third. It is detached from self and manifested on behalf of unknown, anonymous and powerless persons who do not have the slightest notion of whether their profits are, in fact, being maximized. In further analogy to sex, one must imagine that a man of vigorous, lusty and reassuringly heterosexual inclination eschews the lovely, available and even naked women by whom he is intimately surrounded in order to maximize the opportunities of other men whose existence he knows of only by hearsay. Such are the foundations of the maximization doctrine when there is full separation of power from reward.

THE PRINCIPLE OF CONSISTENCY

The mature corporation, as we have seen, is not compelled to maximize its profits and does not do so. This allows it to pursue other goals and this accords similar alternatives to the members of the technostructure. The need for consistency, nonetheless, still holds. The goals of the corporation, though so freed, must be consistent with those of the society and consistent, in turn, with those of the individuals who comprise it. So also must be the motivations.

More specifically, the goals of the mature corporation will be a reflection of the goals of the members of the technostructure. And the goals of the society will tend to be those of the corporation. If, as we have seen to be the case, the members of the technostructure set high store by autonomy, and the assured minimum level of earnings by which this is secured, this will be a prime objective of the corporation. The need for such autonomy and the income that sustains it will be conceded or stressed by the society.

So with other goals, and so matters work also in reverse. If the society sets high store by technological virtuosity and measures its success by its capacity for rapid technical advance, this will become a goal of the corporation and therewith of those who comprise it. It may, of course, be subordinate, as a goal, to the need to maintain a minimum level of income—the fact that the goals of the mature corporation are plural rather than singular does not mean that all have the same priority. Rather, a hierarchy of goals is quite plausible. And given the requisite consistency between social, corporate and individual goals there is no *a priori* reason for assuming that the priorities will be exactly the same for any two corporations.

The same consistency characterizes motivation—the stimuli that set individuals and organizations in pursuit of goals. Pecuniary compensation is an extremely important stimulus to individual members of the technostructure up to a point. If they are not paid this acceptable and expected salary, they will not work. But once this requirement is met, the offer of more money to an engineer, scientist or executive brings little or no more effort. Other motivation takes over. Similarly, until the minimum requirements of the corporation for earnings are reached, pecuniary motivation will be strong. For it too, above a certain level, additional income brings little or no additional effort. Other goals become more important.

Consistency is equally necessary in the case of identification. The individual will identify himself with the goals of the corporation only if the corporation is identified with, as the individual sees it, some significant social goal. The corporation that is engaged in developing a line of life-preserving drugs wins loyalty and effort from the social purpose its products serve or are presumed to serve. Those engaged in the design or manufacture of a space vehicle identify themselves with the goals of their organization because it, in turn, is identified with the scientific task of exploring space or the high political purpose of outdistancing the Russians. The manufacturer of an exotic missile fuel, or a better trigger for a nuclear warhead, attracts the loyalty of its members because their organization is seen to be serving importantly the cause of freedom. It is felt no doubt that human beings, whose elimination these weapons promise, have an inherent tendency to abuse freedom.

There is no similar identification if the firm is simply engaged in making money for an entrepreneur and has no other claimed social purpose. It is noteworthy that when a corporation is having its assets looted by those in control it simultaneously suffers a very sharp reduction in executive and employee morale. All concerned recognize that the corporation is no longer serving any social purpose of any kind.

Consistency in the identification of individuals and organizations with social goals is possible because, running as a parallel thread from individual through organization to social attitudes, is the presence of adaptation as a motivating force. The individual serves organization, we have seen, because of the possibility of accommodating its goals more closely to his own. If his goals reflect a particular social attitude or vision, he will seek to have the corporation serve that attitude or vision. More important, he will normally think that the goals he seeks have social purpose. (Individuals have a well-remarked capacity to attach high social purpose to whatever—more scientific research, better zoning laws, manufacture of the lethal weapons just mentioned—serves their personal interest.) If he succeeds, the corporation in turn will advance or defend these goals as socially important. The corporation becomes, thus, an instrument for attributing social purpose to the goals of those who comprise it. Social purpose becomes by this process of adaptation what serves the goals of members of the technostructure.

This process is highly successful in our time. Much of what is believed to be socially important is, in fact, the adaptation of social attitudes to the goal system of the technostructure. What counts here is what is believed. These social goals, though in fact derived from the goals of the technostructure, are believed to have original social purpose. Accordingly, members of the corporation in general, and of the technostructure in particular, are able to identify themselves with the corporation on the assumption that it is serving social goals when, in fact, it is serving their own. Even the most acute social conscience is no inconvenience if it originates in one's own.

The process by which social goals become adapted to the goals of the corporation and ultimately the technostructure is not analytical or cerebral. Rather it reflects a triumph of unexamined but constantly reiterated assumption over exact thought. The technostructure is principally concerned with the manufacture of goods and with the companion management and development of the demand for these goods. It is obviously important that this be accorded high social purpose and that the greater the production of goods, the greater be the purpose served. This allows the largest possible number of people to identify themselves with social function.

From a detached point of view, expansion in the output of many goods is not easily accorded a social purpose. More cigarettes cause more cancer. More alcohol causes more cirrhosis. More automobiles cause more accidents, maiming and death; also more preemption of space for highways and parking; also more pollution of the air and the countryside. What is called a high standard of living consists, in considerable measure, in arrangements for avoiding muscular energy, increasing sensual pleasure and for enhancing caloric intake above any conceivable nutritional requirement. Nonetheless, the belief that increased production is a worthy social goal is very nearly absolute. It is imposed by assumption, and this assumption the ordinary individual encounters, in the ordinary course of business, a thousand times a year. Things are better because production is up. There is exceptional improvement because it is up more than ever before. That social progress is identical with a rising standard of living has the aspect of a faith. No society has ever before provided such a high standard of living as ours, hence none is as good. The occasional query, however logically grounded, is unheard.

There are other examples. Successful planning in areas of expensive and sophisticated technology requires that the state underwrite costs, including the costs of research and development, and that it insure a market for the resulting products. It is important to the technostructure, therefore, that technological change of whatever kind be accorded a high social value. This too is agreed. In consequence, the underwriting of sophisticated technology by the state has become an approved social function. Few question the merit of state intervention for such social purpose as supersonic travel or improved applications of nuclear power. Even fewer protest when these are for military purposes. Social purpose is again the result of adaptation. This is a matter of obvious importance and one to which I will return.

None of this is to suggest that all social attitudes originate with the technostructure and its needs. Society also has goals, stemming from the needs which are unassociated with its major productive mechanism, and which it imposes on the mature corporation. As elsewhere I argue only for a two-way process. The mature corporation imposes social attitudes as it also responds to social attitudes. Truth is never strengthened by exaggeration. Nor is it less the truth by being more complex than the established propositions that assert the simple eminence of pecuniary goals and pecuniary motivation.

THE REVISED SEQUENCE

In virtually all economic analysis and instruction, the initiative is assumed to lie with the consumer. In response to wants that originate within himself, or which are given to him by his environment, he buys goods and services in the market. The opportunities that result for making more or less money are the message of the market to producing firms. They respond to this message of the market and thus, ultimately, to the instruction of the consumer. The flow of instruction is in one direction—from the individual to the market to the producer. All this is affirmed, not inappropriately, by terminology that implies that all power lies with the consumer. There ''is always a presumption of consumer sovereignty in the market economy.'' The uni-directional flow of instruction from consumer to market to producer may be denoted the Accepted Sequence.

We have seen that this sequence does not hold. And we have now isolated a formidable apparatus of method and motivation causing its reversal. The mature corporation has readily at hand the means for controlling the prices at which it sells as well as those at which it buys. Similarly, it has means for managing what the consumer buys at the prices which it controls. This control and management is required by its planning. The planning proceeds from use of technology and capital, the commitment of time that these require and the diminished effectiveness of the market for specialized technical products and skills.

Supporting this changed sequence is the motivation of the technostructure. Members seek to adapt the goals of the corporation more closely to their own; by extension the corporation seeks to adapt social attitudes and goals to those of the members of its technostructure. So social belief originates at least in part with the producer. Thus the accommodation of the market behavior of the individual, as well as of social attitudes in general, to the needs of producers and the goals of the technostructure is an inherent feature of the system. It becomes increasingly important with the growth of the industrial system.

It follows that the accepted sequence is no longer a description of the reality and is becoming ever less so. Instead the producing firm reaches forward to control its markets and on beyond to manage the market behavior and shape the social attitudes of those, ostensibly, that it serves. For this we also need a name and it may appropriately be called The Revised Sequence.

The revised sequence sends to the museum of irrelevant ideas the notion of an equilibrium in consumer outlays which reflects the maximum of consumer satisfaction. According to this doctrine, beloved in economic instruction and still honored in economics textbooks, the individual or household arranges his or its purchases so there is approximately equal satisfaction from the last dollar spent for each of the several opportunities for consumption or use of goods. Were it otherwise—were it so that a dollar spent on cosmetics returned more satisfaction than a dollar spent on gasoline—then spending on cosmetics would have been increased and that on gasoline diminished. And the reverse being true of comparative satisfaction from cosmetics and gasoline, the reverse would have occurred. In other words, when the return to a small added outlay for different purposes is unequal, satisfaction can always be increased by diminishing the expenditure where the satisfaction is less, and enlarging it where the satisfaction is greater. So it follows that satisfaction is at a maximum when the return to a small increment of expenditure is the same for all objects of expenditure.

But it is also true that, since an individual's satisfaction from his various opportunities for expenditure is his own, there must be no interfering with this equalizing process. Dictation from any second person on how to distribute income, however meritorious, will not reflect the peculiar enjoyment pattern of the person in question. Presumably it will reflect the preferences of the instructor.

Such is the established doctrine. And if the individual's wants are subject to management this is interference. The distribution of his income between objects of expenditure will reflect this management. There will be a different distribution of income—a different equilibrium—in accordance with the changing effectiveness of management by different producers.* It is to the nature and purposes of this management, not simply to the effort of the individual to maximize his satisfactions, that the scholar must look if he is to have any adequate view of consumer behavior.

It is true that the consumer may still imagine that his actions respond to his own view of his satisfactions. But this is superficial and proximate, the result of illusions created in connection with the management of his wants. Only those wishing to evade the reality will be satisfied with such a simplistic explanation. All others notice that if an individual's satisfaction is less from an additional expenditure on automobiles than from one on housing, this can as well be corrected by a change in the selling strategy of General Motors as by an increased expenditure on his house. Similarly, a perfect state of equilibrium with marginal utilities everywhere equal can be upset not by a change in the individual's income or by a change in the goods available but by a change in the persuasion to which he is subject.

The problem of economics here, once again, is not one of original error but of obsolescence. The notion of the consumer so distributing his income as to maximize satisfactions that originate with himself and his environment was not inappropriate to an earlier stage of economic development. When goods were less abundant, when they served urgent physical need and their acquisition received close thought and attention, purchases were much less subject to management. And, on the other side, producers in that simpler and less technical world were not under compulsion to plan. Accordingly they did not need to persuade—to manage demand. The model of consumer behavior, devised for these conditions, was not wrong. The error was in taking it over without change into the age of the industrial system. There, not surprisingly, it did not fit.   □

---

*What the lay reader will recognize, for example, to be the ordinary and expected result of the changing effectiveness of advertising campaigns.

The New Industrial State
or Son of Affluence

Robert M. Solow

More than once in the course of his new book Professor Galbraith takes the trouble to explain to the reader why its message will not be enthusiastically received by other economists. Sloth, stupidity, and vested interest in ancient ideas all play a part, perhaps also a wish—natural even in tourist-class passengers—not to rock the boat. Professor Galbraith is too modest to mention yet another reason, a sort of jealousy, but I think it is a real factor. Galbraith is, after all, something special. His books are not only widely read, but actually enjoyed. He is a public figure of some significance; he shares with William McChesney Martin the power to shake stock prices by simply uttering nonsense. He is known and attended to all over the world. He mingles with the Beautiful People; for all I know, he may actually be a Beautiful Person himself. It is no wonder that the pedestrian economist feels for him an uneasy mixture of envy and disdain.

There is also an outside possibility that the profession will ignore *The New Industrial State* (Houghton, Mifflin) because it finds the ideas more or less unhelpful. The world can be divided into big-thinkers and little-thinkers. The difference is illustrated by the old story of the couple who had achieved an agreeable division of labor. She made the unimportant decisions: what job he should take, where they should live, how to bring up the children. He made the important decisions: what to do about Jerusalem, whether China should be admitted to the United Nations, how to deal with crime in the streets.

From Robert M. Solow, "The New Industrial State or Son of Affluence," *The Public Interest* no. 9, Fall 1967, pp. 100–108. Copyright © National Affairs, Inc., 1967. Reprinted by permission of the publisher and the author.

Economists are determined little-thinkers. They want to know what will happen to the production of houses and automobiles in 1968 if Congress votes a 10 percent surcharge on personal and corporate tax bills, and what will happen if Congress does not. They would like to be able to predict the course of the Wholesale Price Index and its components, and the total of corporate profits by industry. They are not likely to be much helped or hindered in these activities by Professor Galbraith's view of Whither We Are Trending.

Professor Galbraith makes an eloquent case for big thinking, and he has a point. Little-thinking can easily degenerate into mini-thinking or even into hardly thinking at all. Even if it does not, too single-minded a focus on how the parts of the machine work may lead to a careful failure ever to ask whether the machine itself is pointed in the right direction. On the other side, Professor Galbraith gingerly pays tribute to the little-thinkers whose work he has used, but it is evident that he has been exposed only very selectively to the relevant literature. There is no point squabbling over this: big-think and little-think are different styles, and the difference between them explains why this book will have more currency outside the economics profession than in it. It is a book for the dinner table not for the desk.

I shall try to summarize the main steps in Galbraith's argument and shall then return to discuss them, one by one.

(1) The characteristic form of organization in any modern industrial society is not the petty firm but the giant corporation, usually producing many different things, and dominating the market for most of them. Nor is this mere accident. The complicated nature of modern technology and the accompanying need for the commitment of huge sums of capital practically demand that industry be organized in large firms.

(2) With few exceptions, the giant corporation is in no sense run by its owners, the common stockholders. The important decisions are made —have to be made—by a bureaucracy, organized in a series of overlapping and interlocking committees. The board of directors is only the tip of an iceberg that extends down as far as technicians and department managers. The members of the bureaucracy are all experts in something, possibly in management itself. Galbraith calls them the "technostructure," but that awkward word is probably a loser.

(3) It is the nature of the highly-capitalized bureaucratically controlled corporation to avoid risk. The modern business firm is simply not willing to throw itself on the mercy of the market. Instead, it achieves certainty and continuity in the supply of materials by integrating backward to produce its own, in the supply of capital by financing itself out of retained earnings, in the supply of labor by bringing the unions into the act. It eliminates uncertainty on the selling side by managing the consumer, by inducing him, through advertising and more subtle methods of salesmanship, to buy what the corporation wants to sell at the price it wants to charge. The major risk of general economic fluctuations is averted by encouraging the government in programs of economic stabilization.

(4) It would be asking much too much of human nature to expect that the bureaucracy should manage the firm simply in the interests of the stockholders. There is, therefore, no presumption that the modern firm seeks the largest possible profit. Nor does it. The firm's overriding goal is its own survival and autonomy; for security it requires a certain minimum of profit and this it will try to achieve. Security thus assured, the firm's next most urgent goal is the fastest possible growth of sales. (Since firms grow by reinvesting their earnings, this goal is not independent of profits; nevertheless, once the minimum target in profits is achieved, the modern firm will expand its sales even at the expense of its profits.) There are two lesser goals: a rising dividend rate, presumably to keep the animals from getting restless, and the exercise of technological virtuosity.

(5) Modern industry produces mainly things, and it wishes to grow. Everyone will be happier if everyone believes that a growing production of things is the main object of the national life. People will be happier because that it what they in fact get, and the bureaucracy will be happier because they can feel that they serve the national purpose. This belief has been widely inculcated, but it takes effort really to believe it, because American society already has more things than it knows what to do with.

(6) The key resource in the modern industrial state is organized intelligence, especially scientific and managerial intelligence. One of the important things the government does to support the system is the extension of education to provide a supply of recruits for the bureaucracy, and the subsidization of scientific and technological research to provide something interesting for them to do. What Galbraith calls the "scientific and educational estate" therefore acquires a certain moral authority and even mundane power in the society. This is an important circumstance, because the scientific and educational estate—at least its youngest members—can see through the cult of the GNP and observe that it slights the claims of leisure, art, culture, architectural design, and even the innocent enjoyment of nature. Here is the most promising source of social change and of a rather more attractive national style of life.

There is a lot more in the book, much of it full of insight and merriment, but the main logic of the argument seems to be roughly as I have stated it.

It may be unjust and pointless to consider the degree of literal truth of each of the assertions that make up this argument. One would hardly discuss *Gulliver's Travels* by debating whether there really are any little people, or criticize the *Grande Jatte* because objects aren't made up of tiny dots. Nevertheless, it may help to judge the truth of Galbraith's big picture if one has some idea about the accuracy of the details. So, at the risk of judging big-think by the standards of little-think, I proceed.

(1) Professor Galbraith is right that modern economics has not really come to terms with the large corporation. Specialists in industrial organization do measure and describe and ponder the operations of the very large firm. Occasionally some of these specialists propound theories of their financial or investment or pricing behavior. It cannot be said that any of these theories has yet been so successful as to command widespread assent. Perhaps for that reason, much economic analysis, when it is not directly concerned with the behavior of the individual firm, proceeds as if the old model of the centralized profit-maximizing firm were a good enough approximation to the truth to serve as a description of behavior in the large. But this is not always done naively or cynically. Professor Galbraith is not the first person to have discovered General Motors. Most close students of industrial investment or pricing do make room in their statistical behavior equations for behavior that is neither perfectly competitive nor simply monopolistic (The long debate over the incidence of the corporate profits tax hardly suggests universal reliance on any simple model.)

There is, after all, a moderate amount of economic activity that is not carried on by General Motors, or by the 100 largest or 500 largest corporations. In fact, only about 55 percent of the Gross National Product originates in non-financial corporations at all. Not nearly all of that is generated by the giant corporations (of course, some financial corporations are among the giants). Nor is it entirely clear which way the wind is blowing. The giant corporation is preeminently a phenomenon of manufacturing industry and public utilities; it plays a much less important role in trade and services. If, as seems to be in the cards, the trade and service sectors grow relative to the total, the scope of the large corporation may be limited. Alternatively, big firms may come to play a larger role in industries that have so far been carried on at small scale.

Enough has been said to suggest that it is unlikely that the economic system can usefully be described either as General Motors writ larger or as the family farm writ everywhere. This offers at least a hint that it will behave like neither extreme. In any case, counting noses or assets and recounting anecdotes are not to the point. What is to the point is a "model"—a simplified description—of the economy that will yield valid predictions about behavior.

(2) The "separation of ownership from control" of the modern corporation is not a brand new idea. It is to be found in Veblen's writings and again, of course, in Berle and Means' *The Modern Corporation and Private Property*. Recent investigation shows that the process has continued; only a handful of the largest American corporations can be said to be managed by a coherent group with a major ownership interest. (The non-negligible rest of the economy is a different story.) I do not think the simple facts have ever been a matter for dispute. What is

in dispute is their implications. It is possible to argue—and many economists probably would argue—that many management-controlled firms are constrained by market forces to behave in much the same way that an owner-controlled firm would behave, and many others acquire owners who like the policy followed by the management. I think it may be a fair complaint that this proposition has not received all the research attention it deserves. It is an error to suppose it has received none at all. Such evidence as there is does not give a very clear-cut answer, but it does not suggest that the orthodox presupposition is terribly wrong. Galbraith does not present any convincing evidence the other way, as I think he is aware. The game of shifting the burden of proof that he plays at the very end of this book is a child's game. Economics is supposed to be a search for verifiable truths, not a high-school debate.

(3) The modern corporation—and not only the modern corporation—is averse to risk. Many economic institutions and practices are understandable only as devices for shifting or spreading risk. But Galbraith's story that the industrial firm has "planned" itself into complete insulation from the vagaries of the market is an exaggeration, so much an exaggeration that it smacks of the put-on.

Galbraith makes the point that the planning of industrial firms need not always be perfect, that a new product or branch plant may occasionally go sour. By itself, therefore, the Edsel is not a sufficient argument against his position. His is a valid defense—but it is not one he can afford to make very often. No doubt the Mets "plan" to win every ballgame.

Consider the supply of capital. There is a lot of internal financing of corporations; it might perhaps be better if companies were forced more often into the capital markets. But external finance is hardly trivial. In 1966 the total flow of funds to nonfarm nonfinancial corporate business was about $96 billion. Internal sources accounted for $59 billion and external sources for the remaining $37 billion. Besides, depreciation allowances amounted to $38 billion of the internal funds generated by business, and much of this sum is not a source of net finance for growth. External sources provided about one-half of net new funds. In 1966, bond issues and bank loans alone added up to about two-thirds of undistributed profits. Trade credit is another important source of external funds, but it is complicated because industrial corporations are both lenders and borrowers in this market. I don't know how the proportions of external and internal finance differ between larger and smaller corporations, but the usual complaint is that the large firm has easier access to the capital market. I do not want to make too much of this, because self-finance is, after all, an important aspect of modern industrial life. But there is, I trust, some point in getting the orders of magnitude right. There might also be some point in wondering if the favored tax treatment of capital gains has something to do with the propensity to retain earnings.

Consider the consumer. In the folklore, he (she?) is sovereign; the economic machinery holds its breath while the consumer decides, in view of market prices, how much bread to buy, and how many apples. In Galbraith's counterfable, no top-heavy modern corporation can afford to let success or failure depend on the uninstructed whim of a woman with incipient migraine. So the consumer is managed by Madison Avenue into buying what the system requires him to buy. Now I, too, don't like billboards or toothpaste advertising or lottery tickets of un-known—but probably negligible—actuarial value with my gasoline. (Though I put it to Professor Galbraith that, in his town and mine, the Nar-ragansett beer commercial may be the best thing going on TV.) But that is not the issue; the issue is whether the art of salesmanship has suc-ceeded in freeing the large corporation from the need to meet a market test, giving it "decisive influence over the revenue it receives."

That is not an easy question to answer, at least not if you insist on evidence. Professor Galbraith offers none; perhaps that is why he states his conclusion so confidently and so often. I have no great confidence in my own casual observations either. But I should think a case could be made that much advertising serves only to cancel other advertising, and is therefore merely wasteful.

If Hertz and Avis were each to reduce their advertising expenditures by half, I suppose they would continue to divide the total car rental business in roughly the same proportion that they do now. (Why do they not do so? Presum-ably because each would then have a motive to get the jump on the other with a surprise advertising campaign.) What would happen to the total car rental business? Galbraith presumably believes it would shrink. People would walk more, sweat more, and spend their money in-stead on the still-advertised deodorants. But suppose those advertising expenditures were reduced too, suppose that all advertising were reduced near the minimum necessary to inform consumers of the commodities available and their elementary objective properties? Galbraith believes that in absence of persuasion, reduced to their already satiated biological needs for guidance, consumers would be at a loss; total

consumer spending would fall and savings would simply pile up by default.

Is there anything to this? I know it is not true of me, and I do not fancy myself any cleverer than the next man in this regard. No research that I know of has detected a wrinkle in aggregate consumer spending behavior that can be traced to the beginning of television. Perhaps no one has tried. Pending some evidence, I am not inclined to take this popular doctrine very seriously. (It is perhaps worth adding that a substantial proportion of all the sales that are made in the economy are made not to con-sumers but to industrial buyers. These are often experts and presumably not long to be diverted from considerations of price and quality by the provision of animated cartoons or even real girls.)

Consider the attitude of the large corporation to the economic stabilization activities of the Federal Government. It is surely true that big business has an important stake in the main-tenance of general prosperity. How, then, to account for the hostility of big business to dis-cretionary fiscal policy, a hostility only lately ended, if indeed traces do not still persist? Here I think Professor Galbraith is carried away by his own virtuosity; he proposes to convince the reader that the hostility has not come from the big business bureaucracy but from the old-style entrepreneurial remnants of small and medium-sized firms. Their fortunes are not so dependent on general prosperity, so they can afford the old-time religion. Professor Galbraith is probably wrong about that last point; large firms are better able than small ones to withstand a recession. He is right that the more Paleolithic among the opponents of stabilization policy have come from smaller and middle-sized business.

But up until very recently, the big corporation has also been in opposition. Even in 1961 there was considerable hostility to the investment tax credit, mainly because it involved the government too directly and obviously in the management of the flow of expenditures in the economy at large. It was only after further acquaintance with the proposal excited their cupidity that representatives of the large corporation came around. More recently still, they have generally opposed the temporary suspension of the credit as a counterinflationary stabilization device, and welcomed its resumption. (This warm attachment to after-tax profits does not accord well with the Galbraith thesis.) There is a much simpler explanation for the earlier, now dwindling, hostility that would do no harm to the argument of the book: mere obtuseness.

(4) Does the modern industrial corporation maximize profits? Probably not rigorously and single-mindedly, and for much the same reason that Dr. Johnson did not become a philosopher —because cheerfulness keeps breaking in. Most large corporations are free enough from competitive pressure to afford a donation to the Community Chest or a fancy office building without a close calculation of its incremental contribution to profit. But that is not a fundamental objection to the received doctrine, which can survive if businesses merely *almost* maximize profits. The real question is whether there is some other goal that businesses pursue systematically at the expense of profits.

The notion of some minimum required yield on capital is an attractive one. It can be built into nearly any model of the behavior of the corporation. I suppose the most commonly held view among economists goes something like this (I am oversimplifying): for any given amount of invested capital, a corporation will seek the largest possible profits in some appropriately long-run sense, and with due allowance for cheerfulness. If the return on capital thus achieved exceeds the minimum required yield or target rate of return, the corporation will expand by adding to its capital, whether from internal or external sources. If the return on equity actually achieved (after corporation tax) is any guide, the target rate of return is not trivial. The main influence on profits in manufacturing is obviously the business cycle; for fairly good years one would have to name a figure like 12 percent, slightly higher in the durable-goods industries, slightly lower in nondurables. In recession years like 1954, 1958, 1961, the figure is more like 9 percent.

Alternatives to this view have been proposed. Professor Galbraith mentions William Baumol and Robin Marris as predecessors. Baumol has argued that the corporation seeks to maximize its sales revenue, provided that it earns at least a certain required rate of return on capital. This is rather different from Galbraith's proposal that corporations seek growth rather than size. These are intrinsically difficult theories to test against observation. Some attempts have been made to test the Baumol model; the results are not terribly decisive, but for what they are worth they tend to conclude against it. Marris's theory is very much like Galbraith's, only much more closely reasoned. He does propose that corporate management seeks growth, subject to a minimum requirement for profit. But Marris is more careful, and comes closer to the conventional view, because he is fully aware, as Galbraith apparently is not, of an important discipline in the capital market. The management that too freely sacrifices profit for growth will find that the stock market puts a relatively low valuation on its assets. This may offer an aggressive management elsewhere a tempting opportunity to acquire assets cheap, and the result may be a merger offer or a takeover bid, a definite threat to the autonomy of the management taken over. Naturally, the very largest corporations are not subject to this threat, but quite good-sized ones are.

Professor Galbraith offers the following argument against the conventional hypothesis. A profit-maximizing firm will have no incentive to pass along a wage increase in the form of higher prices, because it has already, so to speak, selected the profit-maximizing price. Since the modern industrial corporation transparently does pass on wage increases, it can not have been maximizing profits in the first place. But this argument is a sophomore error; the ideal textbook firm will indeed pass along a wage increase, to a calculable extent.

There is, on the other hand, a certain amount of positive evidence that supports the hypothesis of rough profit-maximization. It has been found, for instance, that industries which are difficult for outsiders to enter are more profitable than those which are easily entered and therefore, presumably, more competitive. It has been found also, that there is a detectable tendency for capital to flow where profits are highest. Serious attempts to account for industrial investment and prices find that the profit-supply-demand mechanism provides a substantial part of the explanation, though there is room for less classical factors, and for quite a lot of "noise" besides.

(5) Professor Galbraith does not have a high opinion of the private consumption of goods and services. "What is called a high standard of living consists, in considerable measure, in arrangements for avoiding muscular energy, increasing sensual pleasure and for enhancing caloric intake above any conceivable nutritional requirement. . . . No society has ever before provided such a high standard of living as ours, hence none is as good. The occasional query, however logically grounded, is unheard." One wonders if that paragraph were written in Gstaad where, we are told, Professor Galbraith occasionally entertains his muse.

It is hard to disagree without appearing boorish. Nevertheless, it is worth remembering that in 1965 the median family income in the United States was just under $7000. One of the more persistent statistical properties of the median income is that half the families must have less. It does not seem like an excessive sum to spend. No doubt one could name an excessive sum, but in any case the reduction of inequality and the alleviation of poverty play negligible roles in Galbraith's system of thought. His attitude toward ordinary consumption reminds one of the Duchess who, upon acquiring a full appreciation of sex, asked the Duke if it were not perhaps too good for the common people.

(6) I have no particular comment on Professor Galbraith's view of the role of the scientific and educational estate as an agent of social and cultural improvement. But this is perhaps a convenient place for me to state what I take to be the role of this book. Professor Galbraith is fundamentally a moralist. His aim is to criticize seriously what he believes to be flaws in American social and economic arrangements, and to make fun of the ideological myths that are erected to veil the flaws. More often than not, in such expeditions, his targets are well chosen

and he is on the side of the angels—that is to say, I am on his side. I trust that readers of his work will acquire some resistance to the notion that any interference by the government in a corporation's use of its capital is morally equivalent to interference in the citizen's use of his toothbrush. I share his belief that American society is under-provided with public services and over-provided with hair oil. I agree with him that men ought to be more free to choose their hours of work, and that this freedom is worth some loss of productivity.

But Professor Galbraith is not content to persuade people that his values ought to be their values. I don't blame him; it's slow work. He would like an elaborate theory to show that his values are, so to speak, objective, and opposition to them merely ideological. He would like to do, in a way, for the scientific and educational estate what Marx and "scientific socialism" tried to do for the proletariat. The ultimate point of the basic argument is that the economy does not efficiently serve consumer preferences—first because industrial corporations evade the discipline of the market by not seeking profit anyway, and second because the preferences are not really the consumer's own.

As theory this simply does not stand up, a few grains of truth and the occasional well-placed needle notwithstanding. There are, however, other powerful arguments against *laissez-faire:* the existence of monopoly power, inadequate information and other imperfections of the market, the presence of wide divergences between private and social benefits and costs, and a morally unattractive distribution of income. These need to be argued and documented from case to case. It is a kind of joke, but if Professor Galbraith would like to see more and better public services, he may just have to get out and sell them.   □

A Review
of a Review

John Kenneth Galbraith

Professor Robert Solow is one of the most distinguished and prestigious economists of our time. He is a calm and confident scholar with rare mastery of the technical tools of economic and quantitative analysis. To the extent that economics qualifies as a science, it is men like Professor Solow who have earned it the reputation. The rather subjective standards of the social sciences in general and of economic theory in particular allow men a certain liberty in defining their own competence. A scholar is often what he claims to be. But Professor Solow's superior mastery of his discipline is acknowledged and admired I think by all.

It is because Professor Solow is so intimately associated with the scientific claims of our profession that I find myself writing this comment. It is not to dispute his view of *The New Industrial State;* this naturally differs from mine, and did I agree with it I would hardly have been justified in publishing the book. But the book is in the public domain and to a degree surpassing my far from modest expectations. Reviews of books that are technical or otherwise obscure are of no slight importance. Others depend on them as do theatre goers to whom first night admission is denied. But human vanity what it is, the person who has seen for himself will reach his own conclusions. So it is here, and this is the principal reason, as I have often said, why I years ago determined to seek a substantial audience. One is not at the risk of those who react adversely to that with which they disagree or find otherwise distasteful.

From John Kenneth Galbraith, "A Review of a Review," *The Public Interest* no. 9, Fall 1967, pp. 109–18. Reprinted by permission of the author.

However, Professor Solow's review seems to merit a word on its own account. It exemplifies a tendency of social scientists, unconscious but not above reproach, to divest themselves of the rules of scientific discourse when they encounter something they do not like. Carelessness also no doubt plays a part. This tendency acquires its special poignancy when, as in the case of Professor Solow, the writer is, and with reason, conscious of his scientific prestige. He is held to even higher standards than the rest of us. The phenomenon is worth explicit examination, and I trust that Professor Solow will not be perturbed by my using him, in effect, as a case study. Thus this review of his review.

2

Although the rules of scientific discourse have never been fully codified, a number enjoy wide acceptance in the common law. They can all best be stated in negative form. One should avoid comment *ad hominem*—that is to say, one should not attack a position by slighting or adverse comment on the personality or behavior of the person who defends it. One should be accurate. One should avoid *obiter dicta;* that is to say, nothing should be allowed to rest on the unsupported word of the speaker, however great his prestige. Both over- and understatement should be avoided—matters where I long ago learned to confess guilt. It is possible that another rule might be added although this may be a counsel of perfection. The scientist should be aware of, and disclose, personal interest. It is this, more than incidentally, that may cause him to violate the other rules. In the review in question Professor Solow is in more or less serious violation of the first three canons. There is at least a possibility that he violates the last. Even for a scholar with no special scientific pretensions this is a poor score. Let me specify.

He begins his review with a number of *ad hominem* observations—the alleged social life of the author and his association with what he calls the Beautiful People, the power that "he shares with William McChesney Martin . . . to shake stock prices by simply uttering nonsense," and this form of comment recurs when he takes exception to my suggestion that higher living standards are not a primary measure of social excellence. "One wonders if that paragraph were written in Gstaad where, we are told, Professor Galbraith occasionally entertains the muse."

Were this all and true, one would doubtless dismiss it as harmless needling, not damaging to careful discourse. I wouldn't, in reply, comment on Professor Solow's social preoccupations or choice of recreation or residence, but these are matters on which there is room for many levels of taste. But the reader will observe, I think, that these observations are in keeping with, and in some small measure serve, the larger design of his article. They suggest a certain frivolity of purpose. (One notices the use of the word nonsense.) Clearly, the deeply serious scholar should not be detained. It would surely be better scientific method though rather more demanding work simply to argue the case. More significant, perhaps, none of it is true. I regard most social activities, fashionable or otherwise, as a bore, and since I have been an ambassador there is even documentary evidence in the archives. In March of 1955 I gave testimony before the Senate Banking and Currency Committee, carefully prepared and not before described as nonsense, on the nature of the speculative fever in 1929 and the measures that might prevent a recurrence. I had just finished a book on the subject. While I testified the market dropped very sharply. On *no other* occasion have I ever seen it suggested that a remark of mine has affected the market. As opportunity allows, I certainly do go to Switzerland (as did Alfred Marshall), but in recent years it has been because I can work there free of both interruption and a disagreeable respiratory ailment. So even Professor Solow's personal comments, it will be evident, establish a rather disconcerting pattern of unreliability. Presumably, even *ad hominem* argument should be accurate. And his reliability does not become greater when he comes to substantial matters, and we measure his essay against the scientific canon that requires accurate meaning accurately conveyed. Let me offer what can only be a partial list.

3

The *New Industrial State* draws rather extensively from the empirical work of other economists. That, presumably, is one thing such empirical work is for. Professor Solow states that the author "gingerly pays tribute to the little-thinkers [his term and assuredly not mine] whose work he has used. . . ." That most readers will take to mean that I was miserly in my credit to others. Here, that the reader may judge, is what I said:

This book has not, it will be agreed, been confined to narrow points. But I have singularly little quarrel with those who so restrict themselves. I have drawn on their work, quantitative and qualitative, at every stage; I could not have written without their prior efforts. So I have nothing but admiration and gratitude for the patient and skeptical men who get deeply into questions,

and I am available to support their application to the Ford Foundation however minute the matter to be explored. I expect them to judge sternly the way their material has been used in this book.[1]

In commenting on my contention that the large corporation is a highly important, strongly characteristic feature of the American economy Professor Solow says that "Professor Galbraith is not the first person to have discovered General Motors" and that "There is, after all, a moderate amount of activity that is not carried on by General Motors, or by the 100 largest or 500 largest corporations." Most readers would conclude from Professor Solow that I somehow claim originality as the discoverer of the great corporation and that I equate all economic activity with the large firms. There are no such suggestions in the book. I do say that the great firm has not made its way in modern economic theory. This Professor Solow concedes. I am careful to point out that the world of the large corporations, what I call the Industrial System, is not the whole of the economy. The remaining "part of the economic system is not insignificant. It is not, however, the part of the economy with which this book . . . [is] concerned."

I might add that Professor Solow then concludes this part of his discussion by saying that "enough has been said to suggest that it is unlikely that the economic system can usefully be described either as General Motors writ larger or the family farm writ everywhere." His logic here will surely seem casual. He is saying, in effect, that one cannot (as I do) describe a part of the economy, even a highly important part. One must do nothing unless he has a model

---

1. *The New Industrial State.* John Kenneth Galbraith (Boston: Houghton Mifflin Co., 1967), p. 402.

that will cover all. This, I am sure, he does not intend.

Professor Solow says that "The 'separation of ownership from control' in the modern corporation is not a brand new idea," adding that it is to be found in Veblen's writings as well as in Adolph A. Berle, Jr. and G. C. Means.[2] Again the reader will suppose that Professor Solow is correcting, perhaps mildly rebuking, a spurious claim to novelty. None was made. Veblen's great point was, in fact, a different one. The engineers and the technicians he believed to be held in check by the greater power of the controlling pecuniary interest. The owners were unduly in control. Relying on his admitted competence on these matters, rather than more meticulous scholarship, Professor Solow uses error to rebuke precision. And my acknowledgement of the work of Adolf Berle, R. A. Gordon as well as of such later writers as Edward Mason, Carl Kaysen and Robin Marris on the separation of ownership from control could hardly be more complete or heartfelt.[3] But there is no need to argue a point that can otherwise be decided. Let Professor Berle, the scholar mentioned by Professor Solow as somehow slighted, say whether or not, both here and over the years, I have done less than justice to his work.

---

2. *The Modern Corporation and Private Property* (New York: Macmillan, 1934). When this book first appeared economists and statisticians of high technical reputation, the men of the professional establishment, led in this instance by Professor W. L. Crum of Harvard, attacked it vigorously. They pointed to shortcomings in its measures of concentration and in its concept of control. These being present, it was held, in effect, that the book should be ignored.

3. One name, to my embarrassment, is missing, that of James Burnham. Scholars, perhaps put off by his subsequent extreme views on foreign policy, have not given sufficient credit to the ideas he offered in *The Managerial Revolution*. Their importance is at least suggested by the phrase he added to the language and which I do, of course, acknowledge.

The reader will see what Professor Solow, however innocently, has sought to suggest. Here speaks the superior scholar. I must warn you against something that is not quite careful. I do not protest Professor Solow's superior view of his competence; it has much to commend it, and we are all allowed the enjoyment of our vanity. He has, however, gravely underestimated his task. An author will usually be more knowledgeable about his work than any critic. Accordingly, the latter has only slight leeway for error. And it will be evident that Professor Solow, so far from being careful, has been very careless. One final small example will show what he has let himself in for. In noting the importance that I attach to growth as a goal of the corporation he observes that Mr. Robin Marris, the distinguished British economist, has reached the same general conclusion, only his effort is "much more closely reasoned." Again the warning flag. But I do not disagree. Marris' reasoning occupies an entire book as compared with a chapter in my case. And as I told in the book, and most explicitly in the Reith lectures which have also been published, I made great use of Mr. Marris' argument. I did not duplicate it. In large measure I followed it. Professor Solow is in the odd position of finding something less well done that wasn't attempted.

In arguing against growth and in favor of profit maximization as a primary goal of the corporation, Professor Solow comes out on the side of the latter. That, of course, is his privilege; it is the received view and one that is vital if the omnipotence of the market is to be assumed. But it is hardly proper that Professor Solow should ignore what, from his viewpoint, is the most difficult point. If the technostructure—the autonomous and collegial guiding authority of the corporation—maximizes profits, it maximizes them, in the first instance at least for others, for the owners. If it maximizes growth, it maximizes opportunity for, among other things, advancement, promotion and pecuniary return for itself. That people should so pursue their own interest is not implausible. Professor Solow, as he elsewhere makes clear, does not think it so.

In attacking the importance that I attach to the control by the large corporation of its own capital supply—an importance that Professor Solow also concedes—he compares for 1966 the total flow of funds from within nonfarm, nonfinancial corporation to that coming from outside. More came from outside. Professor Solow then observes: "I don't know how the proportion of external and internal finance differs between large and smaller corporations although the usual complaint is that the larger firm has easier access to the capital market." It is hard to explain this by carelessness. For Professor Solow knows that construction and trade (the latter with its need to finance inventories and sales) rely heavily on borrowed funds. Firms here tend also to be relatively small—as he agrees elsewhere in the case of trade. It is from such firms as he also knows that complaints come when money is tight. And his reference to the easier access to the capital market of the larger firm is surely disingenuous. He knows that the security that is associated with an ample flow of funds from internal sources will favor the firm so blessed when it goes into the capital markets for additional supplies. Such "ease of access" proves nothing as regards reliance on outside funds.

When there is an industrywide wage increase a normal expectation is of a compensatory price increase with, perhaps, something more. I note that if an industry is able to so increase revenues the day after a wage increase, it could have done

so the day before, always assuming that it could find some substitute for the wage increase as a signal for action. It follows that before the wage increase it was not maximizing its revenues; it had some unliquidated margin of monopoly gain. The conclusion is based, Professor Solow states, in language that many will think a trifle lofty if not otherwise unsuited to scholarly discourse, on "sophomore error." The textbook firm, already maximizing its profits, would also raise its prices "to a calculable extent." Alas, the error is again Professor Solow's—though I naturally forego any pejorative adjectives. He omitted to notice that the two responses—my full and immediate compensation for the wage increase and an unspecified response to a cost change—are not the same. The first would not generally be possible were profit already at a maximum. And he did not notice that I carefully allowed for the second.[4]

One will sense that Professor Solow's desire to attribute error has undermined his instinct to precision. This is most disturbingly evident in the last example I will cite. He suggests that I ignore the danger of a "takeover bid" for the firm that sacrifices earnings for growth and thus abnormally depresses the value of its securities thereby making them open to acquisition. Thus I am indifferent to the disciplines of the capital market. But then he concedes that the takeover is not

---

4. I fear that I, in some sense, tricked Professor Solow into this error. In an article in *The Review of Economics and Statistics* in 1957 I explored this problem in detail. I did not refer to it in *The New Industrial State*—I sought to ration footnotes beginning with those to my own work. Had Professor Solow been reminded of this earlier work he would not have fallen into the error of assuming a more simplistic rather than a more comprehensive view than his own. But it could be also argued that scholars should check the literature before reacting so strongly.

a threat to the very large firms with which I am concerned. (It arises only farther down the size scale.) And he has elsewhere himself suggested that I write of an economy in which General Motors is writ large. The reader at this point will surely have begun to wonder. I am accused of being indifferent to dangers that by his admission do not exist for the large firms with which I am excessively concerned. In point of fact I considered this problem at length. The danger of involuntary takeover is negligible in the management calculations of the large firm and diminishes with growth and dispersal of stock ownership.

The list of the points on which Professor Solow has left himself vulnerable could be extended. I have not said, as he states, that the "industrial firm has 'planned' itself into complete insulation from the vagaries of the market." To have to make a point vulnerable by exaggeration is again to suggest a determination to find error so compulsive as to allow it to be invented. On the defense of consumer sovereignty, a vital matter as I will suggest presently, there is already something approaching an agreed line. To this Professor Solow adheres. I have not shown that demand can be managed fully and for all. So the effort can be safely dismissed. (Much or most advertising Professor Solow ventures "serves only to cancel other advertising and is therefore merely wasteful." He suspects that I am influenced by a dislike for billboards and singing commercials.) I argue only for a partial management of consumer choice. But it will hardly be suggested that what is imperfect or incomplete can, as a matter of sound scientific method, be ignored. Professor Solow to the contrary, I do deal with the stabilization of markets for nonconsumer's goods, and I treat at length of the influence of producers on public procurement including, in particular, weaponry. Enough has

been said, I think, to indicate a fairly serious default in the canon of scientific discourse that requires careful attention to subject and statement. Let me now advert more briefly to the use of *obiter dicta*—to reliance not on evidence but on the undoubted scientific reputation of the speaker.

4

There are two of these which troubled me and which may well have troubled readers who have approached these matters with more care than Professor Solow. One is his concluding statement, which I confess I came upon with surprise, that "the reduction of inequality and the alleviation of poverty play negligible roles in Galbraith's system of thought." Rightly or wrongly the treatment of poverty in *The Affluent Society* has been widely cited as helping pave the way for the modern belief that, in the forms therein described, it would survive a steady increase in aggregate income. (The observations of Michael Harrington are perhaps relevant in this regard.) The same book had at least something to do with drawing attention to deficiencies in the public sector—shortcomings in education, the squalor of the cities—as sources of residual poverty and the anger we now experience in the ghettoes.[5] A paper I presented before a special group working on the problem of "pockets of poverty" in the autumn of 1963 was at least well-timed

---

5.   The very first title of this book was *Why People are Poor,* and it was under this cachet that I negotiated a small grant for research from the Carnegie Corporation of New York in the early fifties. Later titles, *The Opulent Society* and then *The Affluent Society,* reflected my more mature view of the problem. That was less why people are poor than why residual poverty persists and other problems remain unsolved under conditions of generally high and rising income. I think it possible that Professor Solow might wish to plead that he has not read *The Affluent Society.* This is a wholly legitimate defense, one that would be offered by many other intelligent people, but it does, I would judge, deny him the right to pass on my preoccupations.

in relation to the legislation establishing the Office of Economic Opportunity the following year.[6] I participated actively in drafting that legislation and served on the statutory advisory board to the Office until new legislation, plus possibly my views on Vietnam, brought my involuntary severance. I also served, though not with any great usefulness, on Mayor Lindsay's task force on this problem. None of this is final proof of a preoccupation with poverty and inequality, and in the nature of the case my own assessment is hardly to be trusted. But most fairminded readers will agree, I believe, that it is sufficient to place a certain burden of proof on Professor Solow. He could conceivably be suggesting, though the words do not imply it, that *The New Industrial State* is not directly concerned with poverty and inequality. But one does not cover all subjects in one book, and I was additionally careful to say:

There are many poor people left in the industrial countries, and notably in the United States. The fact that they are not the central theme of this treatise should not be taken as proof either of ignorance of their existence or indifference to their fate. But the poor, by any applicable tests, are outside the industrial system. They are those who have not been drawn into its service or who cannot qualify. And not only has the industrial system—its boundaries as here defined are to be kept in mind—eliminated poverty for those who have been drawn into its embrace but it has also greatly reduced the burden of manual toil. Only those who have never experienced hard and tedious labor, one imagines, can be wholly indifferent to its elimination.[7]

6. "Let Us Begin" published in Harper's Magazine in the spring of 1964.

7. *The New Industrial State, op. cit.,* p. 318.

With equal absence of proof Professor Solow suggests that I have exposed myself only "very selectively" to the vast empirical literature relevant to the facets of the system I establish. Here again one is a poor witness for himself. I am naturally impressed by the time I have spent in the last ten years in tracking down and assimilating the distressingly vast material within the ambit of this volume—the case material on the management of the corporation, monographs on organization theory and practice, on the nature of scientific and technical development, trade union development and attitudes, socialist and Soviet planning including one substantial and one lesser journey for work on the ground, literature on political change and business ideology and the newer materials on the much more limited range of matters on which I consider myself a specialist and much, much more. (I need scarcely add that to my distress I keep on encountering materials that I should have seen.) Professor Solow as a teacher and scholar and distinguished public servant has, most plausibly, covered even more completely this same range of literature. Only as a result of having done so could he claim to pass on the adequacy or inadequacy of anyone else's coverage. But again the reader can rightly ask for at least some argument on behalf of his own greater and more systematic diligence. To let it stand on his own unsupported assertion is surely to trade unduly on scholarly reputation.

5

I come now to the point of it all. And here I am on less certain ground. Professor Solow's error and his use of *obiter dicta* are objective. They are visible to all. To ascribe reasons other than the obvious one of carelessness in the case of so distinguished a scholar involves elements of subjectivity. One could easily find himself in scientific default. Moreover, I am not wholly critical of Professor Solow for failing to disclose the interest which forces him into so unappealing a posture and performance. He may not be fully aware of it.

The issue concerns the future of economics in general and of the highly prestigious work with which Professor Solow is associated in particular. That work is within a highly specific frame. Within that frame it is the best of its kind. But it is only good if the frame is reasonably intact. When the frame goes so do the scholars it sustains.

What is the frame? It is that the best society is the one that best serves the economic needs of the individual. Wants are original with the individual; the more of these that are supplied the greater the general good. Generally speaking the wants to be supplied are effectively translated by the market to firms maximizing profits therein. If firms maximize profits they respond to the market and ultimately to the sovereign choices of the consumer. Such is the frame and given its acceptance a myriad of scholarly activities can go on within. Any number of blocks can be designed and fitted together in the knowledge that they are appropriate to—that they fit somewhere in—the larger structure. There can be differences of opinion as to what best serves the purposes of the larger structure. Mathematical theorists and model builders can squabble with those who insist on empirical measurement. But this is a quarrel between friends.

Should it happen, however, that the individual ceases to be sovereign—should he become, however subtly, the instrument or vessel of those who supply him, the frame no longer serves. Even to accommodate the possibility that humans are better served by collective than by individual consumption requires the framework to be badly warped. Should the society no longer accord priority to economic goals—should it accord priority to aesthetic accomplishment or mere idleness—it would not serve. And no one quite knows the effect of such change. One can only be certain that, for a long time, economics, like the lesser social sciences, will be struggling with new scaffolding. And the work of economists will be far less precise, far less elegant, seemingly far less scientific than those who are fitting pieces into a structure the nature of which is known and approved and accepted. And if social priority lies elsewhere, it will be less prestigious.

The threat to economics is a serious one; it could become like sociology and partly a branch of political theory. And there are even more pointed aspects. Students are attracted to economics partly by the fascination of working with men of precise and well articulated mind like Professor Solow. But they must be assured, also, that their work is within a framework of sound social purpose. (There remains considerable attraction, though not sufficient attraction, in being a member of a small band of technical initiates. It is somewhat like being a member of a fraternity, a lodge or a chess club.) To enhance the well-being of the individual has, in the past, seemed a sound social purpose. To assist the individual in his subordination to General Motors will not be so regarded. The sanctity of economic purpose will also be questioned if well-being as conventionally measured continues to improve and leaves unsolved the problems associated with collective need—those of the cities and their ghettoes and the by-passed rural areas—or if this progress involves an unacceptable commitment to the technology of war. And the doubts so engendered will be especially acute if concentration on narrow economic priority appears to be a cause of other social shortcomings. The fate of the business schools is a warning of what happens when scholars lose their reputation for association with social purpose. The better students desert in droves and what is a scholar without a school?

I have been looking, however inadequately, at the frame. This, it is plain from the response, does not seem an unreasonable exercise to those outside the profession. Nor to those within who do not feel endangered—whose temperament allows them to watch and philosophically adjust. But it is a threat to those whose prestige and academic position is profoundly associated with the existing structure. It is perhaps not too surprising that it should inspire a counter-offensive. It is less agreeable that it should be compulsively negligent of the scientific mood which, given the old frame, could be so proudly avowed. □

A Rejoinder
Robert M. Solow

I have always laughed at Professor Galbraith's jokes, even when they have been directed at me or my friends. So it is naturally a little disappointing that he should come on so solemn when I tease him a little.

There are one or two places where Professor Galbraith, and therefore possibly other readers, may have misunderstood me. I mentioned that the existence of very large corporations, and the separation of ownership from control within them, had been observed before now. My intention was not at all to hint that Professor Galbraith has tried to palm these off as brand new observations of his own. He has not. My purpose was to suggest to the reader that ideas so long in circulation must have evoked some response, one way or the other, from economists. I agreed that the response had not been wholly satisfactory from an analytical point of view, but I did not think Professor Galbraith had done it justice. The facts about the size and organization of industrial firms matter to the workaday economist mainly as they affect the substance of pricing, production, and investment decisions. There is, in fact, a large body of empirical work on pricing, production and investment behavior in manufacturing industry. Much of it explains the data moderately well while staying loosely within the framework of supply-demand theory. The facts of large size and diffused stock-ownership do not seem to change that very much.

By the way, it was this range of material that I had in mind when I observed that Professor

From Robert M. Solow, "A Rejoinder," *The Public Interest* no. 9, Fall 1967, pp. 118–19. Copyright © National Affairs, Inc., 1967. Reprinted by permission of the publisher and the author.

Galbraith seemed to have missed some of the relevant literature.

I wrote that the reduction of inequality and the alleviation of poverty play negligible roles in Galbraith's system of thought. Professor Galbraith interprets me to be accusing him of indifference to the plight of the poor. But the context of my remarks was a discussion of the low valuation Professor Galbraith puts on the growth of private consumption and real output generally. My point was not that Professor Galbraith is hard-hearted, but that it is difficult to accommodate drastic reduction of the extent of poverty in a system of thought based on the unimportance of increased real output, except perhaps by sharply redistributive taxation. But the mean income is not so high as all that, and anyway Professor Galbraith does not talk much about redistribution.

Professor Galbraith is wrong to ascribe to me a belief in wants that are "original with the individual" and in "the omnipotence of the market." As to the first, it is hardly a deep thought that nearly all consumer wants beyond the most elementary physiological ones are socially or culturally determined. Indeed, that is precisely why I fear the whole issue is rather tricky. It is a very fine line between analytical statements about the creation of wants by advertising and elaborate indications that one believes one's own tastes to be superior to those of the middle classes.

As to the second, it is only to Professor Galbraith that I seem to believe in the omnipotence of the market. To people who really believe in it, I suppose I seem like Professor Galbraith. I do believe that market forces operate over a large part of the modern economy, sometimes loosely,

sometimes tightly. That does not mean that whatever the market turns up is good, or immune from tinkering on the part of the political authority. It does suggest that it will often be efficient to accomplish the social good by *using* the market.

Finally, Professor Galbraith suggests that I disbelieve his argument not because it is unconvincing or unhelpful, but because I have a personal interest to protect. His doctrine is so subversive of conventional economics that if it were to be widely accepted my sort of work would fall in the academic pecking order, my students would diminish in number and quality, and economics would take a tack uncongenial to my sort of mind. About my motives, he may of course be right. Who knows what evil lurks in the hearts of men, as Lamont Cranston used to say. As for the rest, he may equally be right. I shall try to roll gracefully with the punch, and if I cannot, well, then *Après moi, la sociologie.*   □

CHAPTER 26
LABOR AND COLLECTIVE BARGAINING

Not only product markets, but also factor markets, show significant departures from pure competition in a modern industrial economy. In this chapter, we shall consider these "imperfections" in a general sense and then develop some points about the American labor market and the important process of *collective bargaining*.

IMPERFECT COMPETITION IN THE FACTOR MARKET

In chapter 5 of Part One, we gave a first approximation view of imperfectly competitive factor markets when we discussed a labor union bargaining for, and getting, a wage above the level determined by supply and demand (Figure 5–5, p. 115). The analysis at that time was incomplete because we had not yet derived the demand curve for labor (electricians, in

that particular case); nor had we specified anything about the process that would determine how high the wage demand might be. If the wage could be set at 10 percent above the supply-and-demand determined level, why not 15 percent—or 80 percent! In short, what we did was to illustrate a departure from the competitive market result, without explaining the forces that might determine the nature and extent of the departure.

Let us now go into that explanation, analyzing first the demand side, then the supply side, and then bringing the two together. This theoretical analysis will give us a framework for seeing how the process of collective bargaining fits into the modern industrial scene.

DEMAND FOR FACTORS

In a private economy, the "demanders" of factors of production are business firms. When these firms are not purely but imperfectly competitive, this will have an effect on their demand for the several factors.

Recall first the purely competitive situation. Under pure competition, business firms will find it profitable to hire any factor to the point where its price equals the value of its marginal product ($P_F = VMP_F$). For the individual firm hiring a single variable factor in the short run, its demand curve for the factor will be the marginal product curve of that factor, multiplied at each point by the going market price of the product. In the longer run and for the industry as a whole, the demand for the factor will be influenced by the ease of substituting that factor for other factors and also by the nature of the consumer demand for the product. The demand curve for the factor will slope downward to the southeast, partly because the marginal product of the factor is falling as more units are hired but also because the price of the product will be falling as there is industry-wide expansion in its production.

Monopoly Elements in the Product Market

When business firms are no longer "pure" but "imperfect" competitors, the above analysis must be modified. One important reason is that when monopoly elements are present, each business firm will be aware that it can sell additional output only at a lower price. When it hires more of a factor and expands output, therefore, it must take into account not only the new revenue added but also *the loss in revenue on each previous unit of product sold, because of the fall in the price of the product.* The relevant concept here, as the reader may have guessed, is marginal revenue. The competitive rule for factor hirings that $P_F = VMP_F$ (where $VMP_F = P \times MP_F$) is now replaced by the rule that $P_F = MRP_F$ (where $MRP_F = MR \times MP_F$). The term MRP_F is usually called the *marginal revenue product* of the factor. Hence, where business firms have some element of monopoly power in the product market, we can state that they will hire any factor of production to the point where the price of the factor equals its *marginal revenue product.*

To make this logic clear, the reader should microscopically examine the behavior of one firm in its decision about hiring the services of one more factor—an additional acre of land. Suppose the businessman knows that the addition of this one acre of land will increase production of his product by 10 units. Suppose he also knows the shape of the demand curve for his product and estimates that when he increases his production by 10 units—from 500 units to 510 units—the price of his product will fall from $100 per unit to $99 per unit.

Now to estimate the net addition to total revenue from hiring this factor, we must subtract from the gross revenue added by the factor the loss in revenue on each preceding unit of sales. The gross additional revenue is equal to the marginal product of the factor times the new price, or 10 × $99 (= $990). The loss in revenue on preceding units of output is 500 × $1 ($1 being the estimated fall in price). Hence, the net addition to revenue, or marginal revenue product, is $990 minus $500, or $490. If the price of an acre of land is below $490, the businessman will buy it; if above, he will not. By contrast, in pure competition, where the firm assumes that the price of the product ($100) is independent of his output, the businessman would be prepared to hire land to the point where its price was $1,000 per acre ($100 × 10 units of product).

Since marginal revenue is below price in imperfect competition, this general conclusion means that, other things equal, the business firm will hire fewer units of a factor of production and pay them a lower price than under pure competition.

Monopsony Buying Power

The foregoing analysis applies when there are monopoly elements in the *product* markets of firms hiring factors of production. But there could also be monopoly *buying* power on the part of the firm when it hires its factors. This will also affect the firm's demand for the factor.

To illustrate monopoly *buying* power, we must imagine some very large firm that is the only industry in a particular locality. It is in a monopoly position with respect to the hiring of the services of labor and land in that immediate vicinity. Such monopoly buying power we have earlier called *monopsony* (meaning "single buyer"). Now the monopsonistic firm must take into account a still further element in its hirings of factors of production. When it tries to hire more laborers, for example, by offering them higher wages, it will also have to pay higher wages to all the laborers currently employed.[1] Thus, the *cost* of hiring one more laborer is not simply the wage of that laborer but also the *increase in wages going to all previously employed laborers*. The net effect of monopsony elements, where they exist, will also be to reduce hirings and wages as compared to the purely competitive case. In monopsony, moreover, the firm will not have any simple demand curve for labor, since the price of labor (or land or any other factor in the locality) will not be taken as given by the firm but will be *set* by the firm in order to maximize its profits.

SUPPLY OF FACTORS

Throughout the above analysis of demand for factors, we have assumed that there was pure competition in terms of the supply of factors. Now let us exactly reverse course and imagine that we are dealing with competitive business firms (with neither monopolistic nor monopsonistic power to any degree) but that we have monopoly elements on the part of *factor owners*. To be specific, let us imagine that we are talking about labor and that the "monopoly" elements are institutionalized through a union of workers in some particular craft.

If this union were a "pure monopolist"—that is, if the entire supply of labor hours in this particular craft were subject to a collective decision by the union—then the analysis of its effects would be closely analogous to that of the effects of a "pure monopolist" in the product market. In the case of a monopolistic firm in the product market, the businessman faces, on the revenue side, the consumer demand curve for his product. On the cost side, he has his marginal cost curve representing the costs of producing additional units of output. He will maximize profits by producing where $MR = MC$. This will be at a higher price and lower quantity of output than under pure competition.

Compare this now to the situation of our "pure monopolist" union. On the revenue side, the union faces the demand curve for *its* product—i.e., the business demand curve for hours of labor of this particular craft. Its demand curve (since the firms are assumed to be purely competitive) will be the VMP_F curve of the firms hiring this factor.

What about the "cost" side? If the union has a fixed number of craft laborers under its control, then the cost to each laborer of supplying additional hours of work is the cost of foregoing additional leisure.[2] The union leadership might find out these costs by asking its membership: How many hours would you

---

1. We are tacitly assuming here that whatever the wage, it has to be uniform for all laborers of a given quality in the market. Throughout our analysis we are ignoring the possible complications that would arise if *price discrimination* were employed—i.e., paying different wages to different laborers for the same work, or in the product market, charging different consumers different prices for the same product.

2. Of course, the assumption of a constant number of laborers in the union is a simplification. In a more realistic analysis, we would want to recognize that one of the important questions facing the union leadership would be how much or how rapidly to expand its membership. More members might strengthen the bargaining power of the union, but they might also mean loss of some income to the current membership. Also, we would want to recognize that laborers are not forever bound to any particular union or particular craft. In deciding how much of his labor to offer, the worker will consider alternative employments as well as the possibility of enjoying more or less leisure.

be willing to work at a wage of $3.00 an hour? At $3.50? At $3.62? And so on. Each worker would attempt to answer this question in such a way that the cost to him of the last hour of work supplied (the marginal cost of work in terms of leisure foregone) was equal to the wage in question, say, $3.00.

But this is not the end of the matter. In our simple case, the union is acting as a pure monopolist; hence, it does not take the wage as given—it *sets* the wage. Under what principle will it do this? As in the case of the product monopolist, the union will set the wage where *MR = MC*, where *MR* now stands for the marginal revenue (addition to total income) coming to the workers for the last hour of labor sold, and *MC* stands for the marginal cost in terms of leisure foregone for the last hour of labor supplied. To offer *more* labor than this would mean incurring *additional* costs above the *additional* revenues received or, in other words, that the added income for the workers gave them less additional satisfaction than they would have obtained from the added leisure.

The contrast between this "monopoly" equilibrium and the competitive equilibrium is shown in Figure 26–1. $F_D F_D$ is the ordinary factor demand curve for this particular kind of labor. $F_S F_S$ is the supply curve of this factor on the assumption that the laborers act individually and take the wage as independent of their individual actions—i.e., the competitive supply curve. The equilibrium wage and quantity of labor hours under pure competition are w_c and q_c, respectively.

To get the "monopoly" solution, the union must first determine the MR curve from the business demand curve. Then it must determine the marginal cost of offering additional hours of labor. But this is what the competitive supply curve $F_S F_S$ tells it. Under pure competition, each worker will offer hours of labor until the point where the wage per hour is equal to the marginal cost in terms of foregone leisure. Thus, $F_S F_S$ is the relevant marginal cost curve.

Finally, MR and MC are equated at point *a*, and the equilibrium wage and quantity of labor employed under this form of "union monopoly" are equal to w_u and q_u, respectively. As simplified as this analysis is, it does bring home the important point that mo-

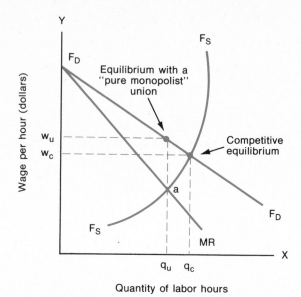

Figure 26–1. Effect of Pure Monopoly of Factor Supply.

When we have pure competition on both sides of the factor market, we get the competitive equilibrium where the factor demand and supply curves intersect. We have drawn the factor supply curve in a "backward-bending" fashion. Why? (See pp. 476–78.) If the firms continue to be purely competitive, but there is a "pure monopolist" union, then the union will equate the additional income from the sale of one more labor hour (this will be given by the *MR* curve drawn from the $F_D F_D$ curve) to the additional cost in terms of leisure foregone by selling one more labor hour (this will be given by the $F_S F_S$ curve, which is the *MC* curve of providing more labor hours). Result: higher wages and fewer hours of work than under pure competition.

nopoly elements on the factor-supply side tend to lead to a higher factor price and lower employment of the factor than would be the case under pure competition. This particular union has succeeded in raising hourly wages and lowering hours of work in this particular industry. And, of course, even in the complicated real world, these are two highly important objectives of union activity.

IMPERFECT COMPETITION ON BOTH SIDES OF THE MARKET

But the real world *is* complicated, and by looking at each side of the market separately, we run the risk of creating a misleading general impression. Although there may be a few cases where imperfect competition exists only on one side of the factor market, the characteristic situation is to have monopoly (or monopsony) elements on both sides simultaneously, and in varying degrees. We have already mentioned (p. 108) that John Kenneth Galbraith developed the concept of "countervailing powers" to explain this phenomenon. According to Galbraith, economic units in a modern industrial economy are subject to restraints not so much from competitors on the same side of the market (e.g., other firms producing the same or similar products) as from countervailing forces on the *opposite* side of the market (in this case, big business facing big labor on opposite sides of the factor market). Thus, while monopoly (or monopsony) elements on the demand side for labor would ordinarily produce a lower wage than would obtain under pure competition, monopoly elements on the supply side of labor would ordinarily produce a wage higher than the purely competitive. Where the actual wage will be will depend on the relative strengths of the countervailing forces involved.

One of the complications that arises when we have imperfect competition on both sides of the factor market is that the equilibrium factor price may be indeterminate, at least in terms of the ordinary assumptions of economic theory. This is not difficult to see if we imagine an extreme case, where we have one huge firm facing one large union in a particular labor market. The firm, making an assessment of the individual laborers' willingness to work rather than be idle (or having to move or train for a new occupation), determines that it will maximize profits at a certain wage: $3.00 an hour. The union, making its assessment of the firm's ability and willingness to pay for labor services, determines that the welfare of the union members will be maximized at a different wage: $5.30 an hour. Now either wage is a *possible* wage in the sense that if the government stepped in and fixed either wage by law (and if there were no possibility of a union strike or a business lockout), then it would be in the private interest of the firm to hire labor even at the higher wage, and it would be in the private interest of labor to work even at the lower wage. But if no outside agency steps in, where will the actual wage be?

The point is that it is impossible to say. Or rather, that it is impossible to say without specifying a host of factors that might affect the relevant bargaining strengths of the two parties. What is the state of the firm's profits? What is the anticipated state of demand for its product? Is the union treasury large enough to sustain a strike? How strong is the allegiance of union members in view of the personal costs of a strike? What is the state of unemployment in that industry or in the economy as a whole? How likely *is* it that the government may step in if a work stoppage affects the public interest? And so on.

In short, when there is strong imperfection on both sides of the factor market, we enter a new world of *bargaining,* where the private interest of one party or group may be opposed to the private interest of another,[3] and where the outcome may be significantly affected by historical and institutional circumstances, and even by the personal characteristics of the participants in the bargaining process. In particular, it is at this point that *collective bargaining* has such a significant role to play in the modern American economy.

---

3. The reader should notice that when we were discussing "efficiency," we were generally dealing with situations in which we could improve the private position of one (or all) parties without harming the position of anyone else. Thus, when production is "inefficient" we can produce more of some goods without cutting the production of others—i.e., there are more goods for everybody. But "bargaining" situations often involve the problem that one person's gain is another person's loss—the question is one of distributing income as between the parties involved. Income distribution is a large subject that we shall touch on at the end of this chapter, and in more detail in chapter 29.

COLLECTIVE BARGAINING IN THE LABOR MARKET

That collective bargaining is terribly important in the United States in the 1970s, everyone is agreed. *Defining* the process, however, is a rather different matter. Witness the comment of a seasoned observer:

I am a great believer in collective bargaining; the only trouble is that after thirty years of watching it at close range in dozens of industries, large and small, I am not sure I know what it is.[4]

The problem derives from the many different institutions, methods, and goals involved in union-management bargaining.

For one thing, firms and unions differ greatly in their structures and in their influence over their respective markets. We have already discussed the variety of market structures in industry. In the case of unions, an important distinction is between those organized on a *craft* basis (a single craft cutting across industries) and those organized on an *industrial* basis (a single industry cutting across crafts). This distinction was a matter of heated debate in the 1930s and was an important factor in causing the Congress of Industrial Organizations to splinter off from the craft-oriented American Federation of Labor. (They merged, however, in 1955, to form the combined AFL-CIO.) In practice, collective bargaining may involve management in negotiations not with one but with a whole variety of different unions.

Also, there are the legal aspects of unionization and collective bargaining. Since the 1930s, and especially since the Wagner Act of 1935, the people and government of the United States have expressed a commitment to the right of workers to organize and to engage in collective bargaining with management. However, as in the case of antitrust legislation, the interpretation of the laws is not always clear-cut, nor do the laws themselves always express a consistent position. Thus, a commitment to unions might mean a commitment to permitting a *closed shop* (only union members may be hired), a *union shop* (nonunion members may be hired but must join the union after a specified period of time), or an *open shop* (unions are permitted, but employees may or may not be union members and, if nonmembers, may remain so). Now the Taft-Hartley Act of 1947 permits the establishment of union-shop agreements, but it also provides that the states may prohibit such agreements under certain circumstances. This has caused many labor leaders to attack the law as, in effect, an encouragement to states to pass "right to work" legislation that, in their view, completely undermines the effectiveness of union activity.

Finally, there is the major complication that collective bargaining does not have just one goal—the setting of a particular money-wage for a particular group of workers—but a variety of different objectives. Indeed, one of the major defenses of collective bargaining (including the right to strike, if bargaining breaks down) is that it resolves a great many issues that arise in industrial situations that might otherwise have to be resolved by complex bureaucratic procedures.[5] The following reading by two outstanding labor experts—John Dunlop, an economist, and Derek Bok, a lawyer and now president of Harvard University—will give the reader an appreciation of the varied tasks that collective bargaining is called upon to perform in this country.

---

4. A. H. Raskin, "Two Views of Collective Bargaining," in *Challenges to Collective Bargaining*, ed. L. Ulman for the American Assembly (Englewood Cliffs, N.J.: Prentice-Hall, 1967), p. 155.

5. On the possible bureaucratic costs of alternative procedures, see the article by Thomas Kennedy, pp. 110–114.

Labor and the American Community

Derek C. Bok and John T. Dunlop

THE SOCIAL AND ECONOMIC FUNCTIONS OF COLLECTIVE BARGAINING

If society is to evaluate the institution of collective bargaining and compare it with alternative procedures, its social and economic functions must be clearly perceived. Five functions seem particularly important.

Establishing the Rules of the Workplace

Collective bargaining is a mechanism for enabling workers and their representatives to participate in establishing and administering the rules of the workplace.* Bargaining has resulted in the development of arbitration and other safeguards to protect the employee against inequitable treatment and unfair disciplinary action. More important still, the sense of participation through bargaining serves to mitigate

---

*Some writers have contended that collective bargaining is a process of joint decision making or joint management. It is true that many rules are agreed to by the parties and written into the collective agreement. But many other functions are left exclusively to management. Moreover, labor agreements typically specify areas within which management takes the initiative, with unions being left to file grievances if they feel that management has violated the contract. Although management may consider it wise to consult with the union before taking certain types of action, it is normally not obligated to seek advance consent from the union. It is misleading to equate collective bargaining with joint management by unions and employers.

Excerpted from Derek C. Bok and John T. Dunlop, *Labor and the American Community* (New York: Simon and Schuster, 1970), pp. 222–28. Copyright © 1970 by the Rockefeller Brothers Fund, Inc. Reprinted by permission of Simon and Schuster.

the fear of exploitation on the part of the workers. Whether or not wages would be lower in the absence of bargaining, many employees would doubtless feel that their interests would be compromised without the presence of a union or the power to elect a bargaining representative. In view of these sentiments, collective bargaining may well serve as a substitute for sweeping government controls over wages as a device for insuring adequate, visible safeguards to protect the interests of employees.

Choosing the Form of Compensation

Collective bargaining provides a procedure through which employees as a group may affect the distribution of compensation and the choices between money and hours of work. One of the most significant consequences of collective bargaining over the past two decades has been the growth of fringe benefits, such as pensions, paid holidays, health and welfare, and vacations with pay. If unions had not existed, it is unlikely that individual workers would have spent added income in exactly the same way; indeed, it is doubtful whether, in the absence of collective bargaining, health and pension plans at present prices would have grown widespread. Moreover, though speculations of this kind are treacherous, the history of social-insurance legislation in the United States suggests that, under a system where the government was responsible for setting wages and terms of employment, fringe benefits would not have grown to the extent they have.

These fringe benefits have had a significant impact upon the whole economy. There can be little question that collective bargaining played a major role in focusing priorities and attention upon medical care in the past decade. With the growth of health and welfare plans, information about medical care has been widely disseminated and developed; a body of experts in business and labor have arisen, and the pressures for public programs in the medical field have been accelerated. In much the same way, the extent of expansion in vacation-oriented industries—motels, resorts, transportation, boating, and leisure goods—must be partly attributed to the emphasis in collective bargaining on greater vacation benefits for employees.

Standardization of Compensation

Collective bargaining tends to establish a standard rate and standard benefits for enterprises in the same product market, be it local or national. Labor contracts in the ladies' garment industry seek to establish uniform piece rates (and labor costs) for all companies that produce the same item within the same general price brackets; all the firms in the basic steel industry confront virtually the same hourly wage schedule for all production and maintenance occupations; and all construction firms bidding on contracts in a locality confront known and uniform wage schedules.

Such uniformity is naturally sought by unions. As political institutions, they desire "equal pay for equal work" in order to avoid the sense of grievance that results when one group of members discovers that another group is performing the same job in another plant at a higher wage. Thus, unless there are strong economic reasons for maintaining wage differentials, unions will normally push hard for standardization.

From the standpoint of employers, it should be observed that uniform wage rates do not necessarily imply uniform labor costs. Firms paying the same hourly rates may have varying wage costs as a result of differences in equipment and managerial efficiency. But competition tends to remove these differences and promote more uniform labor costs among close rivals. In highly competitive industries, employers often have a keen regard for such standardization; it protects the enterprises from uncertain wage rate competition, at least among firms subject to the collective agreement.

From the standpoint of the economy as a whole, the effects of standardization are mixed. In some instances, wage uniformity may be broadened artificially beyond a product market area, as when the wage rates in a tire company are extended to apply to its rubber-shoe work. The effect is to produce a less efficient use of economic resources. The resulting premium over the wages paid in other rubber-shoe plants eventually will compel the tire companies to give up doing business in the rubber-shoe field. In a more important sense, however, the effect of uniformity has been positive in that it has favored the expansion of more profitable, more efficient firms. In a country like France, on the other hand, bargaining establishes only minimum rates, so that backward companies can often survive by paying lower wages than their competitors if they can somehow manage to retain the necessary work force.

Determining Priorities on Each Side

A major function of collective bargaining is to induce the parties to determine priorities and resolve differences within their respective organizations. In the clash and controversy between the two sides, it is easy to assume a homogeneous union struggling with a homogeneous management or association of employers. This view is erroneous and mischievous. In an important sense, collective bargaining consists of no less than three separate bargains—the agreement by different groups within the union to abandon certain claims and assign priorities to others; an analogous process of assessing priorities and trade-offs within a single company or association; and the eventual agreement that is made across the bargaining table.

A labor organization is composed of members with a conglomeration of conflicting and common interests. The skilled and the unskilled, the long-service and the junior employees, the pieceworkers and the day-rated workers, and those in expanding and contracting jobs often do not have the same preferences. A gain to one of these groups often will involve a loss to another. Thus, in George W. Taylor's words, "To an increasing extent, the union function involves a mediation between the conflicting interests of its own membership.''

Similarly, corporate officials may have differing views about the negotiations, even in a single company. The production department and the sales staff may assess differently the consequences of a strike. The financial officers may see an issue differently from the industrial-relations specialists. These divergences are compounded where an association of companies bargains with a union, for there are often vast differences among the member firms in their financial capacity, vulnerability to a strike, concern over specific issues, and philosophy toward the union.

One of the major reasons that initial demands of both parties often diverge so far from final settlements is that neither side may have yet established its own priorities or preferences, or assessed the priorities of the other side. In many cases, these relative priorities are established and articulated only during the actual bargaining process. (This view of the bargaining process helps to explain the sense of comradeship that labor and management negotiators often develop through the common task of dealing with their respective committees and constituents.)

This process of accommodation within labor and management is central to collective bargaining. It should not be disparaged as merely a matter of internal politics on either side. In working out these internal adjustments in a viable way, collective bargaining serves a social purpose of enormous significance. The effective resolution of these problems is essential to the strength of leadership and to the continued vitality of both the company and the union.

Redesigning the Machinery of Bargaining

A most significant function of collective bargaining in this country is the continuing design and redesign of the institution itself. While it is true that the national labor policy—as reflected in legislation, administrative rulings, and court decisions—has a bearing on some features of collective bargaining, the nature of the institution is chiefly shaped by the parties themselves. As previously noted, the collective-bargaining process largely determines the respective roles of individual bargaining and union-management negotiations. It defines the subjects to be settled by collective bargaining. It determines the structure of bargaining relationships. It establishes the grievance procedures and prescribes the uses of arbitration and economic power in the administration of an agreement. It decides the degree of centralization and decentralization of decision making. It influences the ratification procedures of the parties. The results are seldom fixed. The bargaining parties must reshape their bargaining arrangements from time to time in response to experience and emerging new problems. Thus, the design of collective bargaining and its adaptation to new challenges and opportunities have much to do with its capacity to fulfill its social functions effectively and without undue cost to the public.

FIVE MAJOR ISSUES

In certain respects, collective bargaining is being subjected to a closer scrutiny than in the past, because of the special circumstances in which the country now finds itself. On the one hand, it is plain that society is becoming more critical of its institutions and more demanding in the performance it expects of them. Collective bargaining must now be judged in the light of the American position in the world, which has created new demands for economic progress and monetary stability. The consequences of labor negotiations must be viewed in the light of more insistent demands for full employment. And though labor and management have grown more professional in their dealings with each other and more successful in avoiding strikes, Secretary of Labor Willard Wirtz could still observe that ''. . . neither the traditional collective-bargaining procedures nor the present labor-dispute laws are working to the public's satisfaction, at least as far as major labor controversies are concerned.''

At the same time, the climate in which collective bargaining must operate has also become more trying. In recent years, bargaining has been spreading rapidly into the field of public employment, where the parties are often inexperienced in labor relations and the problems involved are in many respects more difficult than in the private sector. Full employment has also placed new strains upon the bargaining process. With jobs so plentiful employees are less amenable to discipline and control. Their demands have grown larger, particularly in an economy where the cost of living has been creeping upward. Labor shortages have likewise created difficulties by forcing managers to hire less-experienced and less-qualified employees.

From these pressures have emerged five groups of questions that have been debated increasingly in recent years.

(1) *Economic strife and dispute settlement*. What can be done to protect the public interest when the parties to collective bargaining engage in economic warfare? Is the exertion of economic and political pressure an appropriate way to resolve bargaining disputes? Would not compulsory arbitration be a superior procedure, substituting facts and reason for power? What can the parties themselves and the government do to improve the performance of collective bargaining?

(2) *Efficiency and productivity*. What is the impact of collective bargaining upon management efficiency? How extensive and serious are restrictive work practices, and what can be done about them? Does the rule-making character of collective bargaining necessarily stifle management in its quest for reductions in labor costs? When is a rule of collective bargaining an appropriate protection of the health, safety, or convenience of a worker, and when is it an undue limitation of efficiency? How can uneconomic work practices be eliminated in the future?

(3) *Inflation*. What are the consequences of collective bargaining for inflation? The experience of many Western countries since World War II, including our own, raises the question whether free collective bargaining, continuing high employment, and price stability are compatible. What can be done to make collective bargaining less conducive to inflation or to reduce its inflationary bias at high levels of employment?

(4) *Public employees*. In recent years, the process of negotiations has been spreading rapidly to many sectors of public employment. Are the procedures of private bargaining appropriate to public employment? Is the strike a suitable means to induce agreement in the public sector? What is the proper relation between negotiations in the public sector and legislative bodies and civil service? What machinery is appropriate to resolve disputes in public employment?

(5) *New opportunities for bargaining*. What are likely to be the new subjects of collective bargaining in the private sector in the years ahead? What are the new needs and opportunities to which collective bargaining procedures can fruitfully be applied? □

DO UNIONS HAVE A FUTURE?

The above reading ended with a series of questions, some of which we have touched on before (for example, the problem of economic strife in chapter 5), and some of which we will raise in detail presently (for example, the inflation issue in chapter 27 and in Great Debate Four). Taken together, these questions really pose the more general query: What is the future of unions and the collective bargaining process in this country?

Despite the obvious values of collective bargaining in many connections, we know that total labor union membership in the United States has been relatively stagnant over the past fifteen or more years. Furthermore, we know that there are changes in the American labor force that might militate against unionization on a long-term basis. These changes include the decline in the number of blue-collar, as opposed to white-collar, workers; the increasing employment in sectors such as the government and service industries that, historically, have been nonunion sectors; and, in general, the increasing professionalization of the American economy.

These various points add special importance to question (4) at the end of the Bok-Dunlop reading. Will unions come to embrace rapidly growing sectors of the American labor force (such as public employees) and hence have an ever larger impact on the economic scene? Or will they simply decline in relative importance as changes in the character of employment in this country render historical union methods inappropriate?

Actually, there is already some evidence to suggest that the positive response is the more likely. This is especially true of public sector unionization, which has increased dramatically in the past decade. By 1968, one-half of all federal employees were union members and more than half of U.S. school teachers belonged to one or another labor association. By 1970, 38 percent of state and local government employees (outside of teaching) also belonged to employee associations. In fact, a higher proportion of labor is now organized in the public sector than in the private.[6]

There is also evidence that unionization is beginning to enter certain professions that, even a few years ago, might have scorned the collective bargaining process. Many difficulties are involved, but it is clear that the academic profession in our colleges and universities is now carrying on a serious flirtation with unionization.

The two readings that follow suggest changes in the making that may have an enduring impact on the American labor movement.

---

6.   Though, of course, not all employee associations in the public sector are unions in quite the same way as is, say, the Teamsters' Union. See Jack Stieber, *Public Employees and Unionism,* Washington, D.C.: The Brookings Institution, 1973.

Trade Unionism Goes Public

Everett M. Kassalow

THE RESPECTABILITY OF UNIONS

Large-scale unionization of government workers is a relatively new phenomenon in this country, although it has been common in almost all other democratic industrial countries of the world. That large-scale public-employee unionism was also inevitable in the United States at some time is clear. But why now? What new forces account for the current upsurge of public unionism?

The first of these forces has been the institutionalization of trade unionism in American life. Unions date back more than 150 years in the United States. But large-scale unionism dates only from the late 1930s, and it has only been in the past decade or so that collective bargaining has become widely accepted as the appropriate way to settle wages and working issues. During this decade unionists have become respectable. Union leaders have been named to innumerable presidential commissions dealing with every conceivable problem area of the country's foreign and domestic business.

It is not surprising thus that, despite the revelations in the Senate investigations of the malfeasance of Jimmy Hoffa and a few other union leaders, public opinion surveys show that union officers have registered a significant gain in occupational prestige between 1947 and 1963. This gain is clearly attributable to the widespread acceptance of the basic value of unionism in society, and this legitimacy is being transferred to public employees as well. For this reason, unionism among government workers has begun to advance rapidly, and there is every prospect it will continue to grow.

Excerpted from Everett M. Kassalow, "Trade Unionism Goes Public," *The Public Interest* 14 (Winter 1969): 118–20, 125–30. Copyright © National Affairs, Inc., 1969. Reprinted by permission of the publisher and the author.

There is a second, more specific reason for the recent growth of government unionism, and this is Executive Order 10988 issued by President John F. Kennedy in January 1962, which encouraged unionism in the federal service. In its support of public unionism, this order was as clear and unequivocal as the Wagner Act of 1936 had been in its support for unions and collective bargaining in the private sector. It declared that "the efficient administration of the government and the well-being of employees require that orderly and constructive relationships be maintained between employee organizations and management."

In New York City, earlier orders issued by Mayor Robert Wagner resulted in the "breakthrough" of unionism in 1961 among 44,000 teachers. Kennedy's order had a spillover effect in legitimating unionism in states and local public service. Further, the reapportionment of state legislatures seems to have had a generally liberalizing effect, and a flow of new legislation in a dozen states has expedited public employee bargaining.

The enormous growth in public employment has also acted to transform the status of the government worker. Between 1947 and 1967, the number of public employees increased over 110 percent. (During the same period, private nonagricultural employment increased only 42 percent.) Clearly, the day has passed when being a civil servant is a prestigious matter. At a time when unions and bargaining have become increasingly accepted elsewhere in the society, this expansion of public employment, with its consequent bureaucratization and depersonalization of relationships, has undoubtedly encouraged unionization in the public sector.

STRIKES IN THE PUBLIC SERVICE

No subject in recent years has provoked as much heat as the matter of strikes among public employees. It is probably the most difficult problem in the public employee field. Even expert arbitrators and mediators, men of hardheaded, pragmatic experience, have taken surprisingly rigid, ideological positions on this matter.

Because there are inherent difficulties in the adjustment to new bargaining public officials need to approach these difficulties with caution, rather than be obsessed with strikes and punishment for strikes. Admittedly, in today's transition period, most cities or states are not likely to concede the right to strike to public employees. However, rather than setting forth elaborate punishment systems for strikes which may occur, officials should take positive steps, wherever possible to improve relations.

The operation of the so-called Taylor Law in New York State illustrates the problem with punitive legislation. Despite provisions banning public employee strikes, with penalties such as dismissal or the withdrawal of recognition or check-off rights from the unions, etc., the law did not head off the New York City teachers' strike or the sanitation strike. If anything the withdrawal of the teachers' union check-off of dues and the eventual imprisonment of the local union's president Albert Shanker for fifteen days, in the wake of the 1967 New York City strike, seems to have kept union militancy at a high pitch long after the strike was over.

Theodore Kheel, an experienced mediator of New York City public employee disputes, has attacked the Taylor Law on the ground that "by prohibiting strikes of public employees, the law eliminates collective bargaining. . . ." It also creates a bad atmosphere for bargaining, Kheel contends, by compelling unions to exert pressure through threats to violate the law. Kheel's critique of the Taylor Law and its pat formula is quite cogent. But in his refusal to make any distinction between public and private collective bargaining, so far as the right to strike is concerned (though he does not rule out strikes by policemen and firemen

The 1968 New York City teachers' strike raised, with particular force, the issues of unionization and strike action in the public sector.

as "unthinkable") he does go too far. One should not anticipate that in all states, or in the federal government, collective bargaining must necessarily take on all the features of private bargaining including the right to strike for most employees.

It does not seem that the strike issue will be important in *federal* labor-management relationships. A liberal managerial policy, including important wage and benefit improvements in the past decade, has set a good framework. In his recent appearance before a special government committee reviewing experience to date under Federal Executive Order 10988, AFL-CIO President George Meany concluded that the order "has brought significant improvements in labor relations within the federal government." Although Meany recommended a number of changes in the workings of the new system, he did not question the legislative ban on strikes in the federal service. Nor did the AFL-CIO December 1967 convention resolution on federal employee bargaining say anything about the existing legal prohibition on strikes by federal government employees. Most of the unions which deal with federal employees have a voluntary strike ban provision in their constitutions.

At the state and local level, where organizing has met with more resistance, the strike issue remains more troublesome. Even here, in the words of AFSCME* President Wurf, whose own union jealously defends the right to strike, at least

The debate [now] seems to center around the right to strike, rather than the right to organize and bargain. . . . It seems only yesterday . . . that the right to bargain was at stake. . . . Now the right to strike is what is being discussed. . . . As painful as the situation is at times, it is an important step forward.

From what has already been suggested, bargaining in the public sector has to be viewed as an evolving

---

*[American Federation of State, County, and Municipal Employees.]

process. What might seem to be best today, is likely to be obsolete tomorrow. The first written agreement between General Motors Corporation and the United Automobile Workers Union signed some thirty years ago was a one-page memorandum. Twenty-five years later it was a printed contract running over 200 printed pages.

At present, general wage and hour conditions are not subject to negotiations in most public employee bargaining relationships. Both in the case of classified federal civil servants and a large proportion of state and local employees, these matters are reserved to the legislators. It seems difficult to believe that public employees, once their unions are established, will be content with a situation in which bargaining over the most basic issues is outside their purview. The general management attitude that, "We can talk about individual workers' problems, or the lights or noise in this room, but general wages and hours are out—left solely to the legislature," won't go down well. Here again the United States can look to the experience of other countries. The typical European nation entered the modern era with civil servants regarded as part of "His Majesty's Service." The private, let alone the public lives of these servants was subject to close and highly arbitrary scrutiny by the government. Personal oaths to king or emperor were given as a condition of employment. The Europeans have passed from these quaint and paternalistic times to a situation where full bargaining rights are now accorded to public employee unions. Their activities and rights now run to bargaining power over general wage and hour changes, holidays, vacations, and most of the economic benefits that one associates with a private sector collective agreement in the United States.

PUBLIC EMPLOYEE BARGAINING AND JOINT MANAGEMENT

The bitter struggles by management against union organization which were part of the beginnings of unionism almost everywhere in the private sector, have little counterpart in the upsurge of public unionism today. (Some Southern states and a few Northern cities where very difficult urban-racial factors severely complicate labor relations are exceptions. New York City's 1968 teachers' strike, for example, was more a product of racial tensions than a traditional labor relations problem.) From this new start a potentially far more cooperative relationship is possible.

Public employees in their capacities as citizens often feel they "own" the government service. Indeed, one of the most interesting aspects of the public employee unionism is that union officials frequently criticize public agencies as much in their capacities as citizens as union members. This has certainly been the case with hospital unions in New York City, nurses in public hospitals in many states, and, of course, unionized teachers everywhere. Public administrators, for their part, have generally been fearful of union interests and positions that go beyond wages and working conditions and raise questions about the very nature of the organizations and policies of the agencies themselves. New York City teacher union officials have bitterly remarked that the Board of Education has taken the position that all that really concerns the teachers are money and money related matters, whereas the teachers have had community problems in mind.

In the present era there is probably an unparalleled opportunity to make public employee union-management relationships something new and unique in American labor history. In the United States there has been an important scaling upward of educational attainments in the past twenty years. As a result of this and other factors, one finds, especially among many white-collar employees, a growing desire for wider participation in the decision making processes. If public managers turn their thoughts on how to *widen*, rather than limit, the scope of management-union relationships, to embrace serious consultation with their employees on policy matters and the organization of their agencies, all sorts of new possibilities may be opened. The public sector may provide a useful training ground for what in other countries has been variously termed co-determination, joint-consultation or workers' participation in management. Obviously these possibilities vary from agency to agency and from union to union, and there may be greater possibilities in state and local service than at the federal level. But the potentialities for new types of relationships based as much, and possibly more, on cooperative rather than conflicting bonds are formidable in the public service. As yet, however, the public managers have been more fearful than expansive in their reactions to the "new unionism."

The demands of many professional employees, most notably teachers and nurses, have from the very beginning gone far beyond wages and hours. Their very professionalism turns them to the substantive policy questions affecting the agencies that employ them. Curriculum content, the size of classes, the organization of the educational system—these and other matters run to the heart of a teacher's interests, and one can list similar professional areas for nurses.

In the long run, indeed, if public managers are to carry forward the process of enlarging the scope of union-management relationships, the unions might find it difficult to depend upon *traditional-union* member loyalty patterns and appeals. The increasing professionalization of society may be the beginning of a new kind of role for organized labor, not the guild socialism once proposed by G. D. H. Cole, but some new form of participation in authority. That is one of the aspects of what Daniel Bell has called the "post-industrial" society, the coming of a new society in which professionalization becomes the commonplace mark of skilled employment. A large-scale society of professionals inevitably means a reduction of that status. But it also means the upgrading of an older worker status, and this adds to the importance of the sweeping new public employee unionism in the United States.   □

All Professors Learning Relevant Economics

By Iver Peterson

Many of the country's college professors, librarians and student counselors are learning the same tough lesson absorbed by the migrant farm workers who stumbled out of the dustbowl into the San Joaquin Valley in the 1930's. When money is tight, demand low and there are too many applicants for one job, salaries stay low, working conditions deteriorate and job security does not last any longer than it takes to say "you're fired."

What some experts call "the new depression in higher education" is hitting academic professionals. College enrollments have leveled off; in many places they have even gone down, a trend that could grow. At the same time, funding for higher education has begun to be diverted to other fields. The tastes of young people have also shifted: College no longer holds its traditional monopoly over their aspirations.

The result is a scarcity of faculty jobs—just at a time when the boom crops of young Ph.D.'s, lured into academic training five or six years ago by the expectation of continuing expansion, begin to apply for their first appointments or to press for advancement in already over-staffed departments.

PROGRESS FOR UNIONS

The situation would seem right for professors to press ahead with the movement toward faculty unions as a means of achieving better job protection, especially since changes are occurring in the practice of tenure. Despite a long-standing feeling among professors that unions in general are anti-professional and a

threat to the community of interests between teachers and administrators, the unionization movement has made considerable headway in recent years and has been seen by many as the wave of the future. But just when the situation seems to demand it most, the movement, for various reasons, has slowed.

The number of college professors, librarians and student counselors organized into some form of collective bargaining arrangement grew, according to the Faculty Unionism Project, from 3,000 in 1966 to 42,800 in 1970, 67,300 in 1971, and 79,500 in 1972. But in 1973—the year the job and salary crunch began to be strongly felt—the increase was less than 3,000. The total is now 82,300 at most. The National Education Association, which is the largest of the several teachers unions, puts the total at even less. The N.E.A. estimates that the pool of potential union members includes 540,000 full-time college and university faculty members and some of the 287,000 part-time teachers.

The slowdown in the rate of unionization is even more surprising in light of a 1970 National Labor Relations Board decision extending collective bargaining rights to all full-time private college and university faculty members. Yet, since last September, half of the sixteen faculties that held representation elections chose "no agent," or voted against any form of collective bargaining.

Union officials give two reasons for the slowdown. The first is that the burst of organizing during the mid-1960s soaked up most of the campuses whose faculties were eager and ripe for unionization. The second reason, according to Robert Simpson of the N.E.A., may be that "employment insecurity among some faculties is causing them to teeter, and they're not convinced that a union can actually protect them."

A third reason might be second thoughts among many professors about swinging away from the traditional feeling of professionalism and community. James Hester, the president of New York University, played on this feeling in his efforts to keep his faculty from voting to unionize. And the prestigious American Association of University Professors offers itself, in its appeal for membership and representation status,

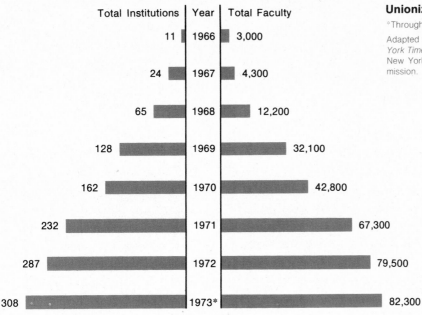

Total Institutions	Year	Total Faculty
11	1966	3,000
24	1967	4,300
65	1968	12,200
128	1969	32,100
162	1970	42,800
232	1971	67,300
287	1972	79,500
308	1973*	82,300

Unionization for Higher Education
*Through November 1973.

Adapted from Iver Peterson article, The *New York Times,* January 6, 1974. © 1974 by The New York Times Company. Used with permission.

as a more moderate, professional alternative to the big-union concept associated with the N.E.A. and the American Federation of Teachers.

One of the key factors related to the unionization question is the controversy over tenure, a practice based on the view that a career-long guarantee of job security was owed to qualified teachers as a protection of their academic freedom to teach and expound unorthodox views. During the great expansion of faculty rolls, along with the growth in enrollments, of the 1950s and 1960s, tenure became an almost automatic grant to teachers who had satisfactorily passed their probation periods of five or seven years.

The practice brought problems, however. Since a large proportion of those tenured during the expansion period were young faculty members, and since the leveling off of enrollments now is obviating faculty additions, some college departments face the prospect of having about half of their present faculties locked in until the end of this century.

During the past year, administrators on many campuses have moved to preserve their flexibility in faculty openings and a freer hand to unload the faculty slackers and academic deadwood that has always been a side effect of liberal tenure policies. Judging by the controversies that have arisen so far, tenure may be the principal campus issue during 1974, and may provide the spur toward unionization that was apparently lacking last year.

CHANGES IN TENURE

The City University of New York, for example, last fall became the first major institution to put a numerical restraint on the proportion of full-time faculty members that may be granted tenure. Under the new policy, special justifications must be offered by the college president for granting tenure once half of the tenurable faculty members in a given department have already achieved it.

In New Jersey, the state Board of Higher Education has promulgated a rule requiring state campuses to either set specific tenure quotas or get tougher on granting tenure in the future. The University of Hawaii is attempting to replace the traditional tenure system with an extended probationary period and a series of renewable five-year contracts. Virginia last year froze any further granting of tenure in all of the state's two-year community colleges. The financially ailing Bloomfield College, in Bloomfield, N.J., is also embroiled in a fight with its faculty union over a decision to do away with tenure altogether.

"Tenure is being threatened by these institutions," says Mr. Simpson of the N.E.A., "and it boils down to a loss of employment security and a possible loss of jobs. When this occurs, a faculty will start looking for guarantees, and this means a contract with provisions for fair employment rules and job protection."

NO GUARANTEE

But union membership is not in itself a guarantee of job security. In most of the examples cited above, the attacks on tenure have come at institutions with strong unions, especially in the case of the City University, whose Professional Staff Congress, affiliated with the A.F.L.-C.I.O., is one of the most powerful and politically savvy faculty unions in the country.

The patterns of faculty unionization vary widely with the type of college or university involved. The public two-year community colleges are heavily organized, as are public institutions as a whole. This is a fairly natural reflection of the political realities of public education, where the unions are in a strong position to bring pressure on the state and county governments that ultimately run public colleges and universities. Unionization is correspondingly weak in private four-year colleges, and especially so on the more prestigious campuses.

It is too soon to predict a trend, but the unions have long known that there is a big gap between a professor expressing interest in a union and actually voting for one.   □

COLLECTIVE BARGAINING AND FACTOR SHARES

We have left to the last what might seem to be one of the most important, if not *the* most important, questions about imperfect competition in factor markets: What is the effect of this imperfection on the prices (i.e., the incomes) going to the several factors of production? In the specific case of labor, what has been the effect of unions and collective bargaining on wage rates?

Unfortunately, although numerous studies of income distribution have been made in the United States,[7] we do not really have data on factor payments in any pure sense. Ideally, we should like to have separate figures for wages, rents, interest, and profits, each defined in the economist's terms. However, national income accounts are not drawn up in this precise way, a particular problem being the income of unincorporated enterprises in which interest, rents, profits, and the wages of the proprietor are effectively thrown together.

In very broad terms, however, certain estimates of relative factor shares can be made. In Table 26–1, income from unincorporated enterprises is listed as *entrepreneurial income;* interest, rent, and corporate profit are grouped together under one heading. This table reveals a perceptible growth in employee compensation (wages and salaries) over the past half century; a small relative decline in interest, rent, and corporate profit; and a sharp relative decline in entrepreneurial income. This last reflects a strong move out of self-employment into regular wage and salary employment over the past fifty-odd years.

These same general trends are shown in the more recent period discussed in the Bach-Stephenson study (p. 341). Thus, for the period 1965–71, they find that wages and salaries increased their percentage share of national income (+3.9%), unincorporated businesses lost ground (−2.1%), and so did the sum of rents, interest, and corporate profits (−3.5%).

We could, if we wished, try to separate entrepreneurial income into wages, on the one hand, and

---

7.   See chapter 29, pp. 685–86.

TABLE 26–1

U.S. NATIONAL INCOME BY PERCENTAGE "FACTOR" SHARES 1900–1963

| | DISTRIBUTIVE SHARES (percent) | | |
PERIOD	EMPLOYEE COMPENSATION	ENTREPRENEURIAL INCOME	INTEREST, RENT, AND CORPORATE PROFIT
1900–09	55.0	23.6	21.4
1905–14	55.2	22.9	21.8
1910–19	53.2	24.2	22.6
1915–24	57.2	21.0	21.8
1920–29	60.5	17.6	22.0
1925–34	63.0	15.8	21.1
1930–39	66.8	15.0	18.1
1934–43	65.1	16.5	18.4
1939–48	64.6	17.2	18.3
1944–53	65.6	16.4	18.1
1949–58	67.4	13.6	19.0
1954–63	69.9	11.8	18.3

Source: Adapted from Bernard F. Haley, "Changes in the Distribution of Income in the United States," in *The Distribution of National Income,* ed. Jean Marchal and Bernard Ducros (New York: St. Martin's Press, 1968; London: Macmillan; Basingstoke, and St. Martin's). Table 9, p. 24.

all other income on the other, and thus divide total national income into a "labor share" and a "property share." Professor Bernard F. Haley of Stanford University has drawn together various different estimates of such a division, and on each estimate he finds that the "labor share" has risen and the "property share" declined since 1900.

Such data are useful—they enable us to dispose of any oversimplified Marxian theory of "exploitation" or "immiserization" of the working classes—but they are not defined sufficiently sharply to allow us to comment much about the effect of market structure on factor shares.

Much the same must be said about the more specific question: the effect of unions on wages rates. When attempting to determine whether unions have raised wages above what they would have been in the absence of union activity, we run into two major problems. One is the effect of union activity on the wages of *non*union workers. Unions will often claim, with some justice, that when they succeed in raising wages for their members they also indirectly force employers to raise wages for nonunion members. A recent study concludes that its results "are consistent with the hypothesis of significant spill-over effects of union wages on nonunion wages, and vice versa, in *some* periods of U.S. history."[8] In other words, interaction occurs and it may vary over time.

The other problem is that the composition of the unionized and nonunionized labor force is different —unions are strong in manufacturing and among blue-collar workers, less strong in agriculture or in white-collar and professional work. Because supply and demand conditions may affect these different

8. O. C. Ashenfelter, G. E. Johnson, and J. H. Pencavel, "Trade Unions and the Rate of Change of Money Wages in U.S. Manufacturing Industry," *Review of Economic Studies,* Vol. 39, No. 1, January 1972, p. 47.

components of the labor force differently, it is difficult to single out the specific impact of unionization and collective bargaining.

Labor professor Albert Rees notes that there are some periods, as in the time of strong unionization in the mid-1930s, when unions undoubtedly contributed to a rise in real wages for union members: and other periods, as in 1939–1948, when unionized labor was actually losing ground relative to unorganized labor. Since the late 1940s, unions may have contributed to a relative rise in the real wages of organized labor in manufacturing, but Rees points out that "real wages in manufacturing were rising long before unions were important" and that much of the increase in real wages must be due to "technological progress, to the growing supply of capital per worker, and to the rising skill and education of the work force."[9] These factors, of course, would operate to raise wages even in an economy in which factor markets were operated on wholly competitive lines.

The difficulty of making generalizations about the impact of union activity on the economy *as a whole* is an important one to note, because it takes us to the borderline where microeconomic analysis must essentially merge into *macro*economics. We know from Table 26–1 that employee compensation (wages and salaries) comprises some 70 percent of national income. When we begin to talk, therefore, about *general* increases in money wages in the economy, we are talking about a change that will deeply affect consumer incomes and hence the demand curves for the products of all the business firms in the economy. These changed business demand curves will, in turn, affect the demand curves for the factors of production, including labor.

This, then, is a good point at which to conclude our analysis of microeconomic problems in isolation and to move on to Part Four, where almost all the issues under discussion will involve both microeconomic *and* macroeconomic dimensions.

9.   Albert Rees, "Patterns of Wages, Prices and Productivity," in *Wages, Prices and Productivity,* The American Assembly (New York: Columbia University Press, 1959), p. 33.

SUMMARY

In applying theories of factor incomes to the modern American economy, we are forced to recognize certain departures from the competitive model. On the *demand* side, the theory of pure competition states that firms will hire a factor according to the rule that the price of the factor equals the value of its marginal product ($P_F = VMP_F$). When the hiring firms enjoy some degree of monopoly in the product market, however, they will hire factors according to the rule that the price of the factor equals its *marginal revenue product* ($P_F = MRP_F$). Also, the firms may possess some *monopsony* buying power. When such power exists, they will take into account the increase in wages they have to pay previously employed laborers when they add additional laborers at a higher wage. Both these factors on the demand side will tend to lower the wage and reduce the amount of labor (or any other factor) employed as compared to a purely competitive situation.

On the *supply* side, there also may be monopoly elements as illustrated by our example of a purely monopolist craft union. If we assume competitive factor demand, then the intrusion of monopoly on the supply side will bring about a higher wage and a lower quantity of labor employed than would obtain under pure competition. In our simple case, the monopoly union will maximize benefits for its members by setting labor supply so that the marginal revenue of the last hour of labor supplied is equated to the marginal cost in terms of leisure foregone by offering that last hour.

Even these modifications of competitive theory are insufficient to describe real-world factor markets, however, since the characteristic industrial situation involves *imperfect competition* on *both* sides of the factor market, simultaneously. In such circumstances, actual wage determination often becomes theoretically indeterminate; or rather, it will depend upon the specific characteristics of the *bargaining* situation involved.

In the labor market in the United States, participation of unions and management in *collective bargaining* is an important method for setting wages and other conditions of work. The collective bargaining process is not easy to define, because of the variety of its objectives and methods. Legally, collective bargaining has been upheld by numerous pieces of legislation since the Wagner Act of 1935, although labor leaders claim that some postwar legislation has been unfriendly to union activities. In the future, the unionization of public employees and professional workers is likely to have an important effect on wage-setting in this country, creating important new avenues for the collective bargaining process.

As far as their effects on income distribution are concerned, it is unclear statistically whether, or how much, American labor unions have raised the real wages of their members. The difficulties are that union activity may have favorable effects on the wages of nonunion members and also that the types of labor that are unionized or nonunionized are characteristically different. Although one might assume from *micro*analysis that union activity must have produced some relative rise in real wages, the problem is complicated by the *macro*economic effects of any general round of wage increases through the economy as a whole.

IMPORTANT TERMS TO REMEMBER

Imperfect Competition in the Factor Market
Marginal Revenue Product (MRP)
$P_F = MR \times MP_F \ (= MRP_F)$
Monopsony
Countervailing Power
Bargaining
Wagner Act of 1935
Closed Shop
Union Shop
Open Shop
Public-employee Union
Unions and the Professions
Factor Shares

QUESTIONS FOR DISCUSSION

1. Suppose someone made the following argument:
"In the case of pure competition, business firms will hire factors of production to the point where $P_F = P \times MP_F$ (or the value of the marginal product). But we also know that in pure competition it will be true for the firm that $P = MR$. Therefore, we can rephrase the rule to read that in pure competition, the firm will hire the factor to the point where $P_F = MR \times MP_F$ (or the marginal revenue product). Now this is exactly the same rule that the firm with monopoly power in the product market will observe. Therefore, there is no difference as far as factor demand is concerned whether the demanders are purely competitive firms or pure monopolists in the product market."

Analyze this statement carefully, indicating precisely where you may agree or may disagree with the analysis.

2. Why do we say that a firm enjoying monopsony buying power does not have a standard demand curve for the factor it is hiring? Explain.

3. Suppose that our "monopoly union" convinced management to set the wage, w_u (Figure 26-1, p. 592) but neglected to make provision for setting the number of labor hours to be employed. Instead, the union simply allowed its members to apply for as many hours work as each wanted at the wage w_u. Can you see a possible problem here? (Hint: The supply curve $F_S F_S$ tells us how many labor hours the union members would in total be willing to work at any given wage.)

4. Do you think there should be compulsory arbitration of all labor disputes? Some? None? Describe the advantages and disadvantages of the proposal you have offered.

5. Professor Kassalow points out that collective bargaining among public employees need not have exactly the same features as collective bargaining in the private sector (p. 602). What important differences do you see between these two sectors as far as union-management issues are concerned?

6. Using the academic world as your example, describe the potential gains and losses of unionization in the professions.

7. "Since it cannot be shown that labor unions actually raise the real wages of union members, it cannot be shown that such unions are necessary—or even desirable—for the modern worker." Discuss.

SUGGESTED READING

The American Assembly. *Challenges to Collective Bargaining.* Englewood Cliffs, N.J.: Prentice-Hall, 1967.

Bowen, William G., ed. *Labor and the National Economy.* New York: W. W. Norton & Co., 1965.

Bok, Derek C., and Dunlop, John T. *Labor and the American Community.* New York: Simon & Schuster, 1970.

Taft, Philip. *Organized Labor in American History.* New York: Harper & Row, 1964.

Stieber, Jack. *Public Employee Unionism,* Washington, D.C.: The Brookings Institution, 1973.

PART 4

CONTEMPORARY ECONOMIC PROBLEMS

CHAPTER 27
SOME DILEMMAS
OF MODERN
ECONOMIC POLICY

In Parts Two and Three of this book, we focused attention on macroeconomic and microeconomic problems respectively. In this final part, we shall be delineating some further outstanding economic issues that confront modern society. These further issues characteristically involve both macro- and microeconomic dimensions and, indeed, they often involve conflicts among different worthwhile objectives. Another characteristic of these issues is that they require us to make decisions—usually collective or public decisions—about the directions in which we wish our society to go. We sometimes forget the point, but in today's world even a decision for a do-nothing, laissez-faire policy would still be a decision.[1] Finally, these issues have been chosen because they have, or seem to the author to have, considerable urgency in the 1970s.

---

1. In fact, it would be a huge decision. Just imagine the political and economic changes that would be required in our very "mixed" economy if the State were literally to institute a hands-off policy. In some ways, this would be the most radical decision of all!

DILEMMAS FACING THE POLICY MAKER

Because the problems we shall be discussing in the ensuing chapters all raise important public policy issues, it seems worthwhile to enumerate some of the difficulties that face policy makers in the actual carrying out of their work. Whether the decisions in question are being made by the president, or Congress, or the Federal Reserve Board, or any other public agency, the responsible parties face certain typical problems that make economic policy rather different from its ordinary textbook presentation. Here is a brief listing and commentary on some of these practical difficulties:

1. Different Analyses of the Problem To Be Solved.

A major difficulty for the policy maker is that there is seldom perfect agreement among the "experts" on the actual causes of any given economic problem. In some cases, the differences of opinion are extreme. This is certainly so in the case of monetarism, for example. Consider a politician who must make up his mind about how to fight inflation. One expert says: "Inflation can be generated only by the government"; the only way to control it "is to control the rate of growth in the stock of money and credit."[2] Another expert says: "The battle against inflation today is primarily an attack on inflation psychology." The only way to control it is "to create a climate where future inflation is not universally expected."[3] Still other experts might refer to labor union power, or oligopolistic industries, or shortages of particular agricultural or industrial commodities, or energy problems. Each analysis would suggest a different cure. The policy maker, sometimes without special expertise of his own in the particular area in question, must make choices on the basis of conflicting testimony. While it is not true, as the joke goes, that ten economists in a room will give you eleven different opinions, they will seldom be able to narrow things down to a single clear-cut answer either.

2. Conflicts among Objectives.

Even if there were perfect agreement about the causes of economic problems, the policy maker will normally find it very difficult to decide what his ultimate goals are. An important reason for this is that economic objectives often conflict. The issue of wage-price controls (See Great Debate Four, pp. 631–53) is an example of the difficulties of conflicting objectives. In the first place, controls were instituted because of the apparent conflict between the objectives of maintaining full employment and achieving reasonable price stability. Now the institution of wage-price controls might conceivably resolve *this* conflict—that is, if the controls could hold wages and prices down, then the government might be able to use the full arsenal of fiscal and monetary weapons to bring about full employment. However, the controls

---

2.   W. Allen Wallis, "Wage-Price Controls Won't Work," *Wall Street Journal,* December 22, 1971. Dr. Wallis is chancellor of the University of Rochester and a noted monetarist.

3.   Sidney Homer, "Phase Three: Triumph or Defeat," *New York Times,* November 14, 1971. Mr. Homer is a limited partner in the brokerage house, Salomon Brothers.

at the same time bring about a new conflict among objectives, this time between full employment with stable prices, as against such objectives as efficiency in the allocation of resources, or freedom of individuals or groups to make their own decisions. The abandoning of controls in 1974 reflected, in part, the intensity of this new conflict.

We shall return to these problems again, but for the moment we should note that the conflict of objectives will cause policy makers to seek solutions that minimize the conflict and, where this is impossible, to find some basis for determining priorities among objectives. Neither of these tasks is easy in practice.

3. Problems of Timing.

By the time the analysis of a given problem has been decided upon and the conflicts among objectives resolved—in other words, by the time the policy maker is ready to act—the problem may have changed. This question also came up in the debate over monetarism (p. 305), in terms of the issue of using discretionary monetary policy versus a fixed-increase-in-the-money-supply rule, but it is really quite a general problem. By the time a society understands what its social and economic needs are, and has geared itself up to action, the basic problems are likely to have altered substantially. It is probably true, for example, that by the time economists understood the Great Depression of the 1930s, we were out of it for other reasons (largely World War II), and our approach to the problems of an expanding economy (with inflationary tendencies) in the postwar period was to some degree distorted by this lag.

4. Problem of Factors Outside the Control of the Policy Maker.

This is the problem of what economists call *exogenous* (operating from "outside the system") forces. The previously cited problems, especially the problem of timing, are all intensified by such forces. The most notable exogenous factor in modern times has been war. Historically, weather was an extremely important exogenous factor for agrarian societies (and still is, especially in some of the less developed countries). In the sixteenth century, the Spanish discovery of gold and silver in the New World was an exogenous factor that may have had important effects on the subsequent commercialization of the Western European economy. In the twentieth century, wars, both major and minor, have had a tendency to surprise economic policy makers, making irrelevant or even counter-productive their solutions of a few months earlier.

5. Problems of the Political Process.

Societies differ greatly in their political systems, but it will seldom be the case that any economic policy maker can take a perfectly dispassionate and Olympian view of the problems to be solved. He will be subjected to other pressures that may affect his prestige, his standing with the "Central Committee," his ability to win reelection, his effectiveness with Congress, Parliament, or whatever. One of the basic contentions of the "consumerist" movement in this country is that special interests are too highly represented and the consumer's interest too little represented in the thinking of politicians. Political opportunism is not always a bad thing. Sometimes in seeking to gain reelection or curry favor with the populace, leaders adopt better policies than they would have if they had functioned in isolation. Indeed, one of the cornerstones of democratic theory is that responsiveness to such political pressures will produce better results than if (as under a dictatorship or hereditary monarchy) popular opinion could be largely ignored. But it is equally true that the sum of a group of special interests is not necessarily the public interest.

ECONOMIC POLICY IN THE SIXTIES

What is one to conclude from this list? Are economic policies merely imperfect, or are they hopeless? Before looking into the future, let us assess the record of the past. The following reading by Otto Eckstein, professor of economics at Harvard, and a former member of the Council of Economic Advisers, represents an informed account of economic policy-making in the 1960s.

The Economics of the 1960s— A Backward Look

Otto Eckstein

The 1960s are behind us. What have we learned? And what should we forget? Regretfully, there still is little study of the history of economic policy. Historians record the minutiae of foreign affairs and domestic politics, but the successes and failures of the economic policy, which affect the lives of the people more directly than the struggles of personalities for power, are still not the subject of serious study. The books by Arthur Schlesinger and Eric Goldman on the Kennedy and Johnson administrations give short shrift to economic management.

This essay cannot fill that void. It presents only the reflections of a brief participant in the economic policies of the 1960s, and a partial assessment of that decade in the area of domestic policy.

CONCERNS OF THE LATE 1950s

In 1959 the Joint Economic Committee studies on *Employment, Growth, and Price Levels* expressed concern about the slow growth of the economy in the 1950s, the rising unemployment, and the increasing frequency of recessions. All these were blamed on the restrictive policies in the management of aggregate demand, a low rate of increase in the money supply of only 1.9 percent for 1953–1959, and a destabilizing fiscal policy because of the gyrations of the defense budget. The Committee issued reports about the dimensions of poverty and the inadequacy of health care, but it implicitly argued that if the economic growth rate was increased, poverty would be reduced and the resources would be created to help solve all our problems. Economic growth, then, was the major issue as we entered the 1960s.

From Otto Eckstein, "Economics of the 1960s—A Backward Look," *The Public Interest,* Spring 1970, pp. 86–97. Copyright © 1970 by National Affairs Inc. Reprinted by permission of the publisher and the author. Footnotes have been omitted.

The critics of the 1950s maintained that the "natural" growth of the American economy was substantially higher than the performance. By "natural" growth they meant the performance that is possible, given advancing technology, the institutional arrangements (e.g., sector distributions) of the economy, and full utilization of this potential. Leon Keyserling, who made economic growth a major issue, argued that the economy was capable of growing at a full 5 percent a year. James Knowles, in his pioneer aggregate production function study for *Employment, Growth, and Price Levels*, produced a medium estimate 3.9 percent, with a half percent on either side for low or high growth policies. In reply to these voices, Edward F. Denison, in his famous study *Sources of Economic Growth*, concluded that the natural rate of growth was only 3 percent, implying that the policy of the 1950s was not in error, and that even major changes in investment in physical and human capital would accelerate the rate of growth by only a few small decimals. If 1 percent sounds like a quibble, we should realize that an additional 1 percent of economic growth during the decade is $85 billion of extra output by 1969.

NO EXTRA JOBS

Actually, the economy grew at an annual average rate of 4.6 percent during the decade 1959–1969. To obtain the natural rate of growth one must correct for the gap of 4 percent between actual and potential GNP in 1959 and for an overfull employment of 2 percent of potential in 1969. Thus, the apparent growth of potential GNP was 4 percent for the decade; James Knowles was right.

Where did Denison go wrong? The depression of the 1930s did more harm to the economy than the Denison analysis indicated. The loss in capital formation, and perhaps the lost technology and innovations as well, were not fully made up when World War II brought full employment. High employment has raised potential growth above prewar standards.

How was the high growth rate achieved in the 1960s? Economic measures enacted in 1962 stimulated the rate of growth of the economy's potential through the investment credit and more liberal depreciation allowances. The neoclassical school of investment analysts, led by Dale Jorgenson, assigns great weight to this stimulus, though other equations can probably explain the historical record as well. Without doubt, these measures helped accelerate capital goods spending by mid-1963. They led to certain abuses, including an excessive growth of leasing. But the investment credit idea has not obtained a firm place in our institutional structure and is about to disappear.

The government also launched manpower programs designed to reduce structural unemployment. These programs are generally judged to be a mixed success. Some disadvantaged workers and youth were helped, but the distribution of unemployment was little changed. The supply of highly skilled labor was not augmented significantly. Indeed, this supply, particularly in the construction trades, appears to have worsened during the decade. The bulge at the bottom of unskilled, poorly educated, and youth remains.

The government also invested heavily in health. During the 1960s, Medicare and Medicaid financed major outlays for the aged and the poor. Although desirable from a human point of view, there is little immediate impact on economic growth from such spending, though Medicaid will improve the health care of children and will ultimately help growth.

Federal outlays on education rose rapidly, though again there was little direct impact on output from these expenditures. The Elementary and Secondary Education Act is a strategic human investment that should yield handsome returns if administered properly. Government support of science and technology continued to grow in the 1960s, though mainly as a by-product of other goals; the defense and space programs paid for over half of all physical research, though toward the close of the decade the cost of the Vietnam war had begun to squeeze the vast outlays for research.

Policies to stimulate area and regional growth loomed large in the early agenda of 1960. The Area Development Act, the Appalachia programs, and their successors reflected this impulse. But it was prosperity that solved most of this problem, as the number of major labor market areas with substantial unemployment fell from twenty-five to just three (two of them in Puerto Rico). In most instances programs succumbed to politics; they provided federal public works money with above-normal generosity, but this was spread thin over too many areas. The regional development focus has now shifted to the ghettos. It remains to be seen whether the money will be spent more wisely.

In sum, the policies to stimulate growth were substantial and had some success. But the high growth performance of the decade was mainly the result of the normal, rapid technological advance which has characterized the American economy for a century (except for the depression) and the resumption of a normal rate of national investment. But all this was possible as a result of the success of the administration's "new economics" fiscal policies, which created the environment in which natural growth forces could flourish.

THE ACHIEVEMENT OF FISCAL POLICY

The central feature of economics in the 1960s was the triumph of modern fiscal policy. It was a victory slow in coming. Six years passed from the time in 1958 when many economists, Arthur Burns as well as the Keynesians, saw the need for a tax cut until the needed policy prevailed. Why did it take so long to take the common-sense step of reducing an excessive burden of taxation, so obviously in the interest of politicians and their constituencies? It is a dramatic example of the power of established prejudices over self-interest, even of ideas that were quite wrong.

First, even Keynesian economists forgot the lesson of their master, that an economy could remain at underemployment equilibrium. Public and scientific opinion had come to accept the necessity of government deficits when the economy was sliding into recession. But the classical view of the natural tendency to return to full employment remained deeply ingrained. At the bottom of the 1958 recession, the leading indicators established that the lower turning point had been reached and tax reduction was ruled out. The Samuelson task force to president-elect Kennedy concluded that the economy was in an upswing, and therefore did not endorse immediate tax reduction. Even this sophisticated group fell into the classical trap. (Or was it political realism?) Recovery proceeded, and by 1962 unemployment had fallen to 5.5 percent. But then the economy stalled. Months dragged by as a good set of figures would raise hopes of renewed advance and the next month would dash them. Only gradually was it recognized that the tax burden was excessive and that the economy was going nowhere. In this respect, the Council of Economic Advisers understood the issue long before its academic allies.

Second, the concept of the annually balanced budget and the fear of debt still held many persons in its grip. Few outside the government believed that a tax cut would pay for itself—as it did—and so it appeared that the initial impact of tax reduction would be an enlargement of the budget deficit.

Third, the structuralists, with a following both in the Federal Reserve Board and the Department of Labor, argued that the high unemployment was the outcome of an imbalance between the new, technologically advanced jobs and the supply of unskilled, disadvantaged workers. The structuralists had a legitimate point in advocating an upgrading of a portion of the labor force. But in overstating their case they were obstructionists to modern fiscal policy. When the economy finally approached full employment after 1964, the job gains of the unskilled and of the disadvantaged greatly exceeded the gains of the more skilled; we discovered the social power of a tight labor market.

Fourth, Professor Galbraith's voice, carrying from Delhi to Washington, argued that tax reduction would permanently lower the government's ability to command resources. He favored the traditional Keynesian route of stimulating the economy through expenditures. Whatever the merits of greater public spending, the simple fact was that the Congress of the early 1960s would not go that route.

Fifth, advocates of tax reform felt that tax reduction offered them the only opportunity to put together a political package which would make the Congress accept the closing of loopholes. The theory was that Congress would give the President some tax reform in exchange for the privilege of cutting taxes. Actually it was the President and his advisors who wanted tax reduction, while tax reform was a millstone around fiscal policy. Ironically, tax reform has finally been enacted by an eager Congress, forcing a mildly enthusiastic administration to accept reform in exchange for a brief extension of the tax surcharge.

Sixth, the monetary school of economists argued that tax reduction was a minor element in economic policy, and that what was really needed to stimulate the economy was a more suitable increase in the money supply. At the time of the great fiscal debate, however, the monetary school had little influence and cannot be said to have been a significant factor in the delay.

After six years the taxes were cut. By July 1965, before defense contracts began to rise, unemployment was down to 4.5 percent and falling rapidly, the economy was growing at over 5 percent a year, and wholesale prices were still stable and no higher than five years earlier. The economy had shown, at least for eighteen happy months, that it could prosper without war with sensible, modern economic management; doubts about fiscal policy were wiped out, and for a year or two economists rode high indeed.

Then came the Vietnam war and the end, for a period at least, of modern fiscal policy. The budget underestimated defense spending by $10 billion for fiscal 1967 and $5 billion for fiscal 1968. The impact on the economy was underestimated by larger amounts because of the greater jumps in defense contracts. If the economic impact of the war had been known, the excise taxes would not have been cut

in the summer of 1965. In early 1966 there should have been a broad across-the-board tax increase. But taxes were not increased because the President could not get the American people to pay for the war. In the end, the war paralyzed the political process, producing the surrealistic debate over the tax surcharge from mid-1967 to mid-1968. International financial crises followed one on another. Demand became excessive. The tax surcharge of mid-1968, which Congress voted, finally restored some fiscal order.

The impact of the federal budget on the economy in the 1960s can be measured crudely by the high employment budget surplus—an estimate of the surplus that the budget would produce if the economy were at full employment and producing revenues accordingly. The excessively restrictive policies of the 1950s had raised the full employment budget surplus to about $13 billion in 1960. Increased expenditures to fight recession, the military buildup over the Berlin crisis, and the investment credit and depreciation reform lowered the surplus to about $6.5 billion in 1962. Delay in tax reduction and a slowdown in expenditure increases raised the surplus once more, reaching an $11 billion peak at the end of 1963.

The tax cuts, and the increases in spending, caused an enormous swing in the federal budget. By the beginning of 1967, the full employment budget showed a deficit of $12 billion—a welcome stimulus during the slowdown; but its deepening to $15 billion by mid-1968 was a disaster. Once the tax surcharge was passed and expenditure restraint became effective, the swing in the opposite direction was equally massive. By the second quarter of 1969 the high employment surplus approached $10 billion again. No wonder that the economy got rather out of hand, and now faces a period of slow growth.

What judgment can be passed about discretionary policy in the light of this record?

First, while the necessary alternative model simulations have not been done, and so answers must remain qualitative at best, the record of the 1960s seems to repeat the verdict of the 1950s. Discretionary policy did harm as well as good. The policy proposed by the Committee for Economic Development in 1947, if it had been followed, would have done better. The CED recommended that the government maintain a small full employment surplus in its budget, and normally eschew the attempt to pursue a more ambitious, discretionary stabilization policy. The CED policy would have avoided the excessive full employment surpluses in the late 1950s and the early 1960s, the swings which led to the re-emergence of a very large surplus in 1963, and it would have forced the financing of the Vietnam war by current taxes. The Great Society programs still could have been financed out of the increase in full employment revenues during a period of rapid growth.

Second, it is evident that the major movements in the full employment surplus were not the result of deliberate stabilization policy. The big swings were due to exogenous events: i.e., the Vietnam war and the inability of the political process to make revenues respond to swings in expenditures. Even if the government had abandoned discretionary policy altogether, and sought to maintain a steady full employment balance of small surplus, the same political difficulties would have gotten in the way. Taxes would have had to be raised. It is likely that the political process would have failed to execute the CED policy, just as it failed to carry out a rational discretionary policy.

THE PRIVATE-PUBLIC MIX

In the 1960s, expenditures by government rose at a substantially higher rate than the gross national product. The total outlays (on national income account) of all levels of government were 27.1 percent on the GNP in 1960; by 1969, the figure rose to 31.4 percent. The outlays of states and localities rose from 9.9 percent fo 13.1 percent of GNP; federal outlays rose from 18.5 to 20.5 percent.

This increase in part represents the Vietnam war, which absorbed about 3 percent of GNP, some of it at the expense of other defense outlays. Most of the remainder was due to the growth of public activities in response to a rising population and to slow productivity growth of government service activities.

But a major reason for the rise of government spending was the Great Society programs enacted from 1964 to 1966.

It is important to understand how this change in the public-private mix came about. So long as the issue was posed in Galbraithian terms—public versus private spending—the Congress did not respond. The Great Society programs were made possible by the large spurt in the growth rate from 1964 to 1966. Public spending came out of economic growth, not out of private spending.

These are the summary figures: in 1964, before the Great Society programs, the federal government collected $113 billion and spent $119 billion, producing a $6 billion deficit. By 1968, following the substantial tax reductions, revenues were up to $154 billion, a rise of $41 billion, expenditures were up to $179 billion, a rise of $60 billion. As a result, the $6 billion budget deficit rose to $25 billion. What happened is clear enough: military spending, mainly for Vietnam, rose by $27 billion. Spending on education at the federal level rose from $2 to $7 billion; on health, from $2 to $10 billion; and the total of all other fields, including Social Security, agriculture, urban affairs, and the old-line programs, went up from $61 to $81 billion.

Thus, during the period of the Great Society legislation, there was plenty of spending for old and new programs, civilian and military. Economic growth produced the revenues, though in the end we did stumble into an enormous deficit.

MONETARY POLICY IN THE 1960s

Because human beings are fallible and policy makers all over Washington are subject to common tides of opinion and politics, the record of monetary policy has similarities to fiscal policy. Until 1965, monetary policy accommodated the gradual recovery to full employment, while interest rates remained fairly stable. One might argue that interest rates should have risen as the economy moved toward full employment, but one should also remember that interest rates were already high at the beginning of the decade because of the excessively restrictive monetary policies of 1959.

The monetary school of economists, led by Milton Friedman, claims that the recovery to full employment was really due to a good expansion of the money supply, perhaps prompted by the need to finance the budget deficits. The theoretical debate about the relative importance of fiscal and monetary policy is not likely to be settled here; but one can observe a striking contrast for the period under review. The rhythm of the economy seemed to respond to changes in fiscal policy. Unemployment stayed high so long as the budget aimed for large high employment surpluses. It fell after the tax cut of 1964. The increase in the broad money supply was fairly steady, both in the period of high level stagnation and during full recovery. If easy money alone sufficed, full employment should have come more quickly.

From 1965 on, the Federal Reserve Board no longer fully accommodated the economic growth, and interest rates began to rise. With the benefit of hindsight about the war, the federal deficit, the capital goods boom, and the inflation, it is now evident that monetary policy should have become tougher earlier. Further monetary policy was too aggressive during the 1967 slowdown, and if ever there was a case of overkill, the antirecession fiscal and monetary policies of 1967 were an example. In the summer of 1968, monetary policy eased too quickly after the passage of the tax surcharge, and the authorities have been struggling ever since to bring the banking system and inflation under control.

The monetary theorists sing a siren song which says that if money supply is expanded at a constant rate, we would free ourselves of the fallibility of human judgment about the timing of restricting or loosening the amount of money in response to the economic cycle. There is little doubt that we have overmanaged money, perhaps never more so than during the extreme restraint of 1969–70. But there are hurdles on the way to a more stable policy: if it really is the money supply that is to be regulated, there had better be agreement on the figures. The record of the money supply for the first half of 1969 has been rewritten, as it was for several other crucial

periods. Who would rest a policy on so weak a statistical reed? Further, it is difficult to define a "neutral" policy. Structural changes in the financial system give different growth trends to the various monetary magnitudes.

There has been little study of the quantitative relationships between the various monetary measures, explaining the differences in the growth of such variables as unborrowed reserves, the narrow money supply, the broad money supply, the monetary base, total bank credit, bank loans, total credit in the economy, etc. Until this work is done, adoption of any rule applicable to one concept will simply convert the present disputes into a quarrel about the selection and care of statistics.

The level of interest rates is also an indicator of monetary policy, and to me still the most unambiguous. But it is evident from experience that a stable interest rate is not a neutral policy. Interest rates should rise and fall with the business cycle. Indeed, a stable interest rate policy is probably significantly destabilizing for the economy. Thus, while interest movements are a useful gauge, they do not provide a simple rule which policy can follow.

THE GUIDEPOST EPISODE

By the end of the 1950s the need to reconcile full employment and price stability was widely recognized. The new administration, building on earlier *Economic Reports,* established "Guideposts for Wage-Price Stability." At first the guideposts only asserted some rather bland principles about price and wage behavior which a competitive economy would achieve on its own. It reminded labor that wage increases beyond productivity served mainly to raise prices; it reminded business that price increases beyond trend costs raised profits only temporarily. But until January 1966, when the guideposts were breached by the New York subway settlement, the administration had pursued an active policy of seeking to hold settlements close to the productivity rate.

The guidepost policies must be understood in the context of their day. The economy was moving toward full employment; industrial operating rates were rising. Productivity was advancing rapidly and wage demands were predicated on stable consumer prices. The longer the stable costs and prices could be preserved, the closer the economy could come to full employment without stumbling into the inflationary difficulties which had haunted us in the mid-1950s.

In their heyday, in 1964–66, the guideposts were a major element of government policy. Government spending programs, fair labor standards proposals, minerals stockpile policy, civil service pay, agricultural policy, and protective measures for specific industries both internal and at the frontier, were examined, at the President's direction, for their effect on cost-price stability. This probably was the first time in history that an administration examined its policy proposals fully from the objective of price stability.

In addition, the guideposts partially reoriented the usual government interventions in collective bargaining. Settlement of industrial conflicts was not an objective by itself but was coordinate with cost stability. For some time, at least, a Democratic government modified its traditional role of urging management to settle for large increases in order to restore industrial harmony. On the price side, presidential intervention slowed down the increases of some highly visible basic materials and a few final products.

Did these policies have any effect? Wage equations which explain other years of the postwar period fail during the guidepost years. To be sure, other explanations have been found for the extraordinarily low wage increases of 1963–66, but they are not totally convincing. Without claiming statistical proof, I would evaluate the episode as prolonging the virtuous circle of high productivity growth, stable costs, and stable price expectations by some months, and slowing the pickup of the price-wage spiral.

The guidepost policies were politically very difficult. Every time the President reduced a government program, intervened in a labor dispute, rolled back a price, let goods in from abroad, or made a release from the stockpile, he trod on sensitive toes. In due time, the affected industries sought retribution through the political process. Only a president elected

by an enormous majority and commanding firm control over the Congress could withstand the politicking of industries, which President Johnson did.

As the Vietnam war escalated and the President's popularity began to fade, the authority of the guidepost policies shrank. When the President lost his command over the Congress in the 1966 elections, the most active phase of guidepost policies drew to a close, though there were some successful interventions as late as the summer of 1968.

There has been criticism of the guideposts as violating the principles of a free market economy. These criticisms are misplaced. The markets in our economy are relatively free compared to other economies; but many industries benefit from government programs, from government purchases, government-enforced production controls, import restrictions and tariff, artificial reductions of supply through stockpile policies, and so on. Similarly, the strength of labor unions is immensely aided not only by the basic laws which redress the balance between employer and worker, but also by the Davis-Bacon Act which strengthens the grip of the construction unions, Walsh-Healey, and so on. We saw in the opening months of 1969 that the government cannot shelve all its powers to influence wage and price decisions. The absence of guidepost policies does not make the government neutral.

The guideposts were swept away in a wave of excess demand. The present administration is wise to seek to attempt to limit the growth of demand through restrictive monetary and fiscal policies. At this stage of inflation there is no other way to bring prices back under control. The present vigorous policies of anti-trust and the reorganization of human investment programs will ultimately yield rewards in price stability as well. The job of resisting textile quotas, of easing oil import quotas, and of making sure that the government promotes rather than hurts price stability in its detailed decisions, still needs doing, however. There is no point in confusing these matters with vague talk of market ideology.

The guidepost episode and the recent inflationary explosion leave a nagging question: Is the inflationary bias of the economy excessive at a 4 percent unemployment rate, and does the rate of inflation inevitably worsen at full employment? The United States has never had uninterrupted prosperity before. Now that we have unlocked the secret, are we unable to use it because we do not know how to live with full employment?

SOME LESSONS FOR THE 1970s

What should we have learned? What mistakes have we no right to repeat? And where is the new ground that should be broken? A review of the predictions made at the beginning of this decade indicates that one cannot anticipate what will be the dominant problems. In 1960 no one thought about the Vietnam war or appreciated that the inequality of economic opportunity and disparities between black and white would become the central social problem. The impact of an advancing economy on the physical environment was not totally a surprise, but was far down the agenda of the decade. Even such traditional items as the deterioration of the cities, the improvement of health and education, housing, and rural opportunity had little specificity ten years ago. So don't expect much help here in pinpointing the major problems of the 1970s even within the area of economic performance.

Nonetheless we owe it to ourselves to attempt to distill a few points from the review of the past period.

(1) The natural rate of growth of the economy for the 1970s exceeds 4 percent and we should judge economic performance accordingly. The growth of the labor force accelerated in the mid-1960s and will remain at a high rate. The advance of technology gives every sign of remaining very rapid. The current high rate of growth of the capital stock indicates the prospect of a natural rate of growth at least as great as in the 1960s.

We will begin the decade with a very slow growth year. The overfull employment of recent months will be converted into a small gap between actual and potential output in 1970. If we focus economic policy exclusively on fighting inflation, and if the fight on inflation is confined to the strictly classical medicine, we condemn ourselves to several years of slow growth and the development of a considerable gap between actual and potential output.

(2) The economy still seems unable to reconcile full employment with price stability. The need for structural changes to improve the competitiveness and flexibility of markets and to minimize the harm of government protectionist policies remains as strong as ever. Government machinery could be strengthened for these pursuits.

(3) The trend cycle in the private economy will be in an upswing phase at the beginning of the decade. While government policy may temporarily slow the conversion of fundamental strength into economic activity, rapid family formation with the resultant need for housing and durables will keep the underlying tone of the private economy strong. This is in sharp contrast to the beginnings of the 1960s.

(4) Fiscal and monetary policies should avoid the extreme swings which have characterized them in the last twenty years. Very full employment surpluses and deficits have been mistakes without exception. Periods of extreme advance or no advance in the money supply have been mistakes without exception.

(5) The informed public finally understands the question of priorities of resource use. The searching examination of our military budget and the attempt to determine the economic costs of our foreign policy commitments contain the promise of a more rational approach to resource allocation in the public sector.

(6) Economic performance is increasingly judged by its ability to meet the social and environmental goals of the society. The 1960s have shown that good macro-performance is a necessary but not a sufficient condition for adequate social progress. The realization that the resources are available may well have heightened the impatience of the black and the young with our halting ef-

forts. The systematic changes in the private and public sector necessary to assure adequate social progress and halt deterioration of the environment appear to be the main challenges to economic policy for the 1970s. But then again, the main tasks may prove to be something else: by 1980 we will know.   □

CONFLICTS OF OBJECTIVES

In the remainder of Part Four, we shall be examining some of the economic problems that are facing public policy makers with particular force in the 1970s. As Professor Eckstein recognizes in his article, these are not exactly the same problems that occupied us in the 1960s. One can go further and suggest that a special characteristic of the economic issues of the seventies is the degree to which conflicts of objectives are involved. In anticipation, let us suggest three ways in which these conflicts may appear.

1. Policies on Inflation

In a sense, we are dealing here with a carry-over from the 1960s for, as Eckstein remarks, the economy ended that decade still "unable to reconcile full employment with price stability." However, the conflict of objectives is further intensified in the 1970s by the increase of inflationary pressures in this country and abroad (See Figure 27-1). This apparent worsening of the Phillips' curves of the industrial nations means that the cost of full employment has notably risen in each of these countries. To make matters worse, most of these nations face fairly serious balance of payments problems in the 1970s, in part at least because of the increased price of oil imports. Balance of payments difficulties, as we know, require nations to increase their efforts to combat inflation. But such restrictive policies may take a still deeper toll on real national income, growth, and unemployment.

Finally, we have to note that most of these countries—the United States included—have experimented

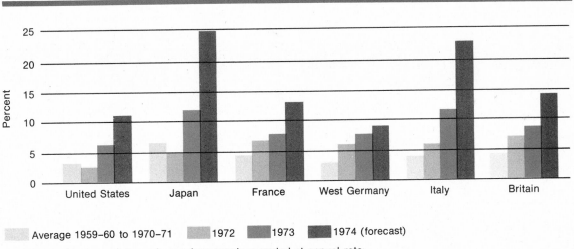

Average 1959–60 to 1970–71   1972   1973   1974 (forecast)

Consumer prices, percentage change from previous period at annual rate

Figure 27-1. Inflation in the 1960s and 1970s.

The chart indicates the increase in inflationary pressures in this decade as compared to the last. Inflation is obviously a worldwide phenomenon.

Source: Adapted from *The New York Times*, June 30, 1974 © 1974 by The New York Times Company, and used with their permission. Data from Organization for Economic Cooperation and Development.

with various forms of wage-price controls, or *incomes policies* as they are sometimes called. The experience so far has been that such policies, if loosely applied, may only postpone inflationary wage and price increases to a later day. On the other hand, if rigorously applied, they may lead to other conflicts of objectives—and, in particular, to vast losses in efficiency throughout the economy. Because these matters are taken up directly or indirectly in Great Debate Four, we need not develop them further here.

2. The New and Complicated Role of Economic Growth.

Economic growth is still an important issue in the 1970s but its role seems much more ambiguous than it did a decade ago. There is an increased awareness now of the things that growth cannot accomplish by itself. One of these—and a very important one—is a more equitable distribution of income between rich and poor in the society. Another is the removal of technological or structural unemployment. Although it is not clear that technological advance, even in the form of computer technology and automation, need reduce the number of jobs available in the economy as a whole, it *is* clear that the kinds of labor and management skills required in a growing economy need not correspond exactly to those abundant in the labor force. Rapid growth and pockets of heavy unemployment can occur simultaneously.[4]

Perhaps even more significant is the increased belief that growth actually contributes to rather than helps solve our problems. This is a clear example of the kind of conflict among economic objectives that seems increasingly characteristic of the present decade. An important illustration is concerned with the environmental and ecological costs of economic growth. It is widely believed that unfettered economic expansion at the rates common during the past cen-

tury or two in the industrial societies could lead to societies so congested, polluted, and dehumanized that they would suffocate, or perhaps revert to a state of irrational primitivism.

This conflict is further intensified in the 1970s as development efforts continue to mount in the poorer and still relatively unindustrialized areas of the world. Can the world stand growth on the North American-European-Japanese scale in India, China, Africa, Latin America? The conflicts of objectives (not to mention the possible conflicts among nations) inherent in this new view of growth are manifold.

3. Complications Caused by Energy Problems

The preceding conflicts of objectives are intensified by the energy problems whose existence was hardly noted in the 1960s but which became headline news in the 1970s. Energy shortages, as reflected especially in higher-priced oil, contribute to the full employment–price stability conflict by threatening the international-balance-of-payments positions of the oil-importing nations, including the United States. As we have said, this leaves less tolerance for inflation, and more danger of recession, unemployment, and slow growth. These same shortages also intensify the growth-versus-environment conflict. Should we, in efforts to save energy (and thus permit continued economic growth), allow increased strip-mining, the use of "dirty" fuels, and the removal of pollution devices that increase gasoline consumption? Indeed, this second conflict spills over on the first. If we decide to accept slower growth—less energy-use and less pollution—and also to fight hard against inflation, where will the jobs for our expanding labor force come from? Will we head into a period of decline such as the "stagnationists" of the late 1930s and 1940s were predicting?

And if stagnation is a possibility in the industrial nations, what about the less-developed world? Should scarce oil be used for an American motorist to drive to work, or to increase the supply of fertilizer on which the Green Revolution in India and Pakistan depends? The energy crunch intensifies the potentiality of conflict of interest among nations in much the same way

---

4.   For a good discussion of the issues involved in technological change in relationship to employment, see Robert M. Solow, "Technology and Unemployment," *The Public Interest,* Fall 1965.

that it increases the conflict among objectives within each nation.

Thus, the general conclusion seems inescapable: The current decade is witnessing conflicts among economic objectives greater than those of a few years ago. We may have to learn not merely to add and multiply but to subtract and divide as well: relatively new skills in the "affluent" society.

THE ECONOMIST AND PUBLIC POLICY

We shall be taking all these matters up in more detail in the following chapters, but we should notice here that these conflicts of economic objectives do have a bearing on the role of economic analysis in public policy making. Certain conclusions are fairly obvious. For one thing, it seems clear that, when objectives are in conflict, great attention should be given to the search for those policies that reduce, or at least do not increase, the range of conflict. Example: That full-employment policies do not hurt but assist low income groups, and thus promote a better income distribution, is a good further argument for adopting such policies. "Two (or more) birds with one stone" policies must be sought out as enthusiastically as possible.

For another thing, the great number of different and conflicting objectives should suggest skepticism about the use of single policy tools to the exclusion of all others. A range of approaches will usually be required. Decision-making theorists sometimes put this in terms of a distinction between *objectives* and *instruments*. The former concern what we are trying to achieve (full employment, stable prices, equitable income distribution, a certain rate of growth, etc.), while the latter concern the tools we may use to achieve these goals (money supply, taxes, wage-price controls, investment incentives, etc.). Under certain technically specifiable conditions, decision theory tells us that, for the model to work, the number of effective instruments used must be equal to the number of objectives. In general, the more objectives

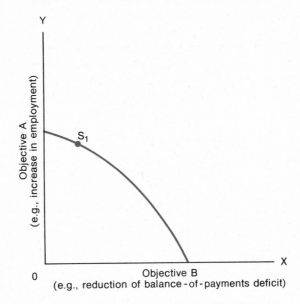

Figure 27–2. Choice among Objectives.

Society may have to choose among economic goals, just as it has to choose between food and steel.

we have, the greater the number of instruments we shall have to use.[5]

Perhaps most important of all is the fact that conflicting economic objectives involve us in what is, after all, the heartland of economics, and especially microeconomics: the theory of choice. For example, we can readily see analogies between a society's choices among competitive production possibilities (such as food or steel) and its choices among economic objectives that possibly conflict (say, higher levels of employment or reducing a balance-of-payments deficit). In Figure 27–2, a hypothetical society may choose to locate itself at S_1, giving a relatively higher preference to employment expansion

5. A pioneer in this area of work is the Nobel Prize-winning Dutch economist, Jan Tinbergen; e.g., *On the Theory of Economic Policy* (Amsterdam, 1952); and *Economic Policy: Principles and Design* (Amsterdam, 1956). We consider some of Tinbergen's thinking in another connection, pp. 774–80.

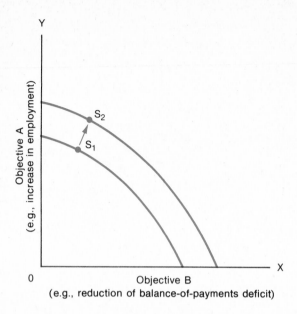

Figure 27–3. Objectives and Instruments.

By using a greater number of policy instruments (say, manpower training, as well as fiscal and monetary policy), we may be able to achieve more of both of two conflicting objectives, i.e., to move from S_1 to S_2.

than to balance-of-payments reduction. Figure 27–3 suggests that, if a wider range of policy instruments is used, this society might possibly get more of both objectives and move out to S_2.

There are dangers in trying to carry this kind of analysis too far. The basic point we wish to make here is valid, however. This is that economic analysis lends itself very naturally to the subject of choice among alternatives, even when these choices are as complex as those facing a public policy maker. In later chapters, whether the question is how to limit air pollution or how to evaluate government expenditures, we shall find that economic analysis, while seldom giving us the complete answer, usually has something interesting and useful to say in public policy decisions.

SUMMARY

This chapter was concerned with some of the problems facing public policy makers in the area of economic policy, and with the help that economic analysis might provide in the decision process.

Economic policy making in practice is hampered by a number of difficulties: (1) expert advice on the causes of economic problems is seldom completely consistent; (2) there are frequently conflicts among several economic objectives that have to be resolved; (3) by the time policies are formulated and implemented, the problems may have altered; (4) exogenous factors, like war, may upset all predictions; and (5) the political process may cause conflicts between special interests and the public interest.

A survey (by Otto Eckstein) of American economic policy in the 1960s reveals some triumphs and defeats. A key triumph was that of "modern fiscal policy." On the other hand, war, political pressures, and "extreme swings" in fiscal and monetary policies prevented the decade from being an unqualified success.

In the decade of the 1970s, evidence so far indicates the likelihood of increasing conflict among economic objectives. This can be seen when we take into account recent developments in the areas of inflation, unemployment, growth, environment, balance of payments, and energy shortages.

The existence of conflicting economic objectives suggests an important role for economic analysis. This analysis can tell us something about minimizing conflicts among objectives, about the selection of instruments to meet more than one objective, and, in general, about the theory of policy-making choice. Microeconomic analysis will thus provide a useful guide (though no simple answers) for the public policy maker.

IMPORTANT TERMS TO REMEMBER

Problems of Policy - Makers:
  Different Analyses;
  Conflicts Among Objectives;
  Timing; Exogenous Factors;
  the Political Process
"Natural" Growth of the U.S. Economy
Public-Private Mix
Great Society Programs
Wage-Price Guideposts
Incomes Policies
Policy Objectives

QUESTIONS FOR DISCUSSION

1. Sometimes economic goals are complementary—e.g., if we decrease the rate of unemployment, we will usually increase the short-run rate of economic growth—but often they are conflicting. Try to imagine circumstances in which we might have conflict between each member of the following pairs of economic objectives: (*a*) price stability/full employment; (*b*) price stability/balance-of-payments equilibrium; (*c*) full employment/balance-of-payments equilibrium; (*d*) higher rate of growth/balance-of-payments equilibrium; (*e*) higher rate of growth/ecological balance; (*f*) ecological balance/increased energy utilization; (*g*) price stability/efficiency; (*h*) efficiency/more equitable distribution of income; (*i*) more equitable distribution of income/higher rate of growth.

2. Political pressures may affect economic policy both in a democratic and in a more centralized or authoritarian political system. Discuss what some of these pressures might be under each kind of system.

3. Using Professor Eckstein's account of the 1960s as a basis, evaluate the degree to which United States economic policy during this period was influenced by rational economic analysis as opposed to other factors (e.g., exogenous forces, political pressures, etc.).

4. Explain why economic policy in the 1970s may be particularly concerned with conflicts of objectives and how economic analysis may help us sort through these conflicts.

SUGGESTED READING

Eckstein, Otto. *Public Finance.* 3rd ed. Englewood Cliffs, N.J.: Prentice-Hall, 1973.

Kirschen, E. S. and Associates. *Economic Policy in Our Time.* 3 vols. Amsterdam: North Holland Publishing Co., 1964.

Okun, Arthur M. *The Political Economy of Prosperity.* New York: W. W. Norton & Co., 1970.

Slesinger, Reuben E.; Perlman, Mark; and Isaacs, Asher, *Contemporary Economics.* 2nd ed. Boston: Allyn & Bacon. 1967, section IV.

GREAT DEBATE 4:
COMBATING INFLATION: CONTROLS OR COMPETITION?

GREAT DEBATE 4:
COMBATING INFLATION: CONTROLS OR COMPETITION?

For most industrial countries, one of the most difficult conflicts among economic objectives over the last decade has been that between full employment and price stability. This conflict, as we have noted in the previous chapter, has been intensified in the last few years by the accelerating rate of inflation throughout the world and by pressures on the international balance-of-payments positions of many nations because of higher-priced petroleum imports.

Broadly speaking, two main lines of approach have been developing among economists in the United States in recent years. One line of attack emphasizes direct controls over wages and prices in the economy, at least on a last-resort basis. The approach here is, in the words of Gardner Ackley that follow, "not a head-on attack on the basic sources of market power, but is rather a limitation on the exercise of that power where it specifically contributes

to inflation." The reasoning behind controls is fairly simple. Because inflation cannot be cured by measures affecting aggregate demand (over-all monetary and fiscal policies) except at an unacceptable cost in terms of unemployment, it is argued, why not prevent inflation by controlling wages and prices directly? This would then leave the nation free to pursue those vigorous fiscal and monetary policies necessary to the maintenance of full employment.

The other main line of approach argues that controls are not likely to be effective in holding down wages and prices and that, furthermore, they cause considerable allocational inefficiency throughout the economy. This group feels that one should attack the basic sources of market power head-on and develop what Houthakker below calls a "procompetitive strategy." The logic here is that the conflict between full employment and price stability is largely caused by too much market power, whether in concentrated industries, or in labor unions, or in both. Therefore, it is argued, the government should attempt to restore as much competition as possible in product and factor markets, being especially sure that its own actions do not lead toward restrictive rather than competitive conditions. With market power thus reduced, the government can go ahead with fiscal and/or monetary policies to promote full employment without having to worry about excessive inflation developing.

Between 1971 and 1974, American economists had a unique opportunity to put some of these contentions to the test, as this country went through a series of wage-price freezes, controls, and relaxations described briefly in chapter 14. Probably the net effect of this experience was to dim somewhat the ardor of those who were most enthusiastic for controls. Inflation

was proceeding more rapidly in 1974 than in 1971, when the whole process began (Figure A).

However, the issue has by no means been unequivocally decided. Both supporters and critics of the program admit that it may have had some impact in postponing demands for wage increases. How much this may have been due to the personal effectiveness of John Dunlop, then director of the Cost-of-Living Council, is difficult to say, but the fact is that these wage increases did slow down during the controls period (Figure B). Moreover, supporters and critics are also fairly well agreed that the program did not really give controls a fair test—the administrative effort and preparation time was very limited compared to the magnitude of the task.

Thus, at the end of the control period, in mid-1974, economists still differed fundamentally about the better approach to use. In the pages that follow, we present excerpts from a symposium on "The Future of U.S. Wage-Price Policy" that appeared in the Review of Economics and Statistics in August 1972, at a time when Phase II of the "New Economic Policy" was in full swing. This selection is followed by a question-and-answer debate that appeared in the New York Times in late April 1974, just as the whole program, including the Cost-of-Living Council, was being jettisoned.

Two of the participants favor some form of controls, at least as a last resort if "jawboning" or a "guide-post" system fails to work. These participants are both former chairmen of the President's Council of Economic Advisers under Democratic administrations: Gardner Ackley, now professor of economics at the University of Michigan, and Arthur M. Okun, currently of the Brookings Institution.

The other two participants favor a "procompetitive," "anticontrol" strategy. They are Carl H. Madden of the Chamber of Commerce of the United States, and Hendrik S. Houthakker, professor of economics at Harvard University and formerly a member of the Council of Economic Advisers under a Republican Administration.

An Incomes Policy for the 1970s

Gardner Ackley

I believe it a safe guess that wage-price policy will assume, in the 1970s, a position of coordinate importance with employment policy, both in the United States and in most other industrialized countries which rely on reasonably free markets. Committed, as they are, to the maintenance of "full employment," these economies will remain prone to a degree of intermittent and creeping inflation which, although modest by comparison with celebrated inflations of the past, will nevertheless be exceedingly visible. Even if the costs in economic terms of such inflation may be judged tolerable, I doubt that its costs in social and political terms will permit any government simply to ignore it, or to rely on policies that appear ineffective.

Today's endemic inflationary problem is obviously no simple phenomenon. Its "causes" surely relate to fairly stable "structural" aspects of labor and product markets, the effects of which depend on the degree of resource utilization—which we can assume will usually be "high." Another important element is the dynamic mechanism through which current perceptions of price and income changes are generated from past events. But in addition to these basically economic elements, the process involves major sociopsychological and political aspects.

My vision of the type of inflationary process which now concerns us sees it as essentially the by-product of a struggle over income distribution, occurring in a society in which most sellers of goods and services possess some degree of market power over their own wages or prices (in money terms). The extent of each firm's or union's power at any given time is affected by structural and market factors: the manner in which that power is used is affected by perceptions of what is happening, and by political attitudes and social norms. Market power is used both in an attempt to increase real incomes, and, defensively, in an effort to

Excerpted from Gardner Ackley, "An Incomes Policy for the 1970s," *The Review of Economics and Statistics*, Vol. 54, No. 3, August 1972, pp. 218–23. © the President and fellows of Harvard College.

protect real incomes from past and expected increases in production or purchase costs. An inflationary process can be tripped off in any of a number of ways. And, once it begins, most increases in wages and prices are basically defensive—made in an effort not to fall behind. Yet every defensive wage or price increase threatens the real incomes of other sectors, and prompts an endless chain of further defensive moves. Although some groups achieve relative gains and others experience loss of position during such a price-war spiral, the main effect is simply to raise the entire level of prices and money incomes.

In my view, this model of an inflation-generating struggle to increase or protect income shares—although here grossly oversimplified—provides a substantially meaningful description of wage and price behavior in a modern industrial economy. But what is most significant is that the problem it describes appears to have become aggravated in recent years, as the social norms regulating group behavior have for various reasons become more tolerant of—or even now encourage—an increasingly aggressive use of market power. Moreover, there is an increasing sophistication of business and union leadership, along with better and prompter measurements of relative position—i.e., the perception-generating mechanism is altering. And recent experience with inflation has substantially heightened the sensitivity of most groups to actual or potential losses of relative position. For these reasons, there is a tendency to react more quickly, more fully, and frequently preemptively. The more prompt and complete are the defensive reactions to inflation, the faster is its rate—that is, the more there is to defend against.

Few would deny, I think, that society is becoming more sensitive to the existence of "inequities" or "injustices" in the distribution of income, and is therefore more supportive—or at least more tolerant—of efforts by "underprivileged" groups to improve their relative incomes, through political or economic action or both. But when the market prices of products and productive services become weapons in a struggle over income shares, the underprivileged—who often possess little market power—are likely to lose out to the already favored groups. In the absence of new social instruments for resolving these problems, I am convinced that our society and economy remain subject to substantial inflationary pressures—particularly when at the same time we remain determined to maintain full employment—i.e., labor markets and product markets strong enough that almost every group has some considerable degree of market power.

I conclude that the inflationary consequences of a struggle over income shares can only be controlled through the institution of an "incomes policy"—a system of direct restraints (i.e., more explicit and forceful social norms) limiting efforts to advance incomes through raising wages and prices. The pattern of these direct restraints can and should be systematically integrated with tax and other measures, so as together to guide the evolution of income shares in a manner which society judges to be fair and equitable.

Belief that an incomes policy is needed of course does not mean that other methods for the control of inflation can or should be neglected. Perhaps the single most important thing we can do to improve our control of inflation is to make more vigorous and timely use of fiscal and monetary policies to combat surges of aggregate demand that occur when the economy is already at or close to full employment. But inflation will not disappear merely by avoiding future mistakes of demand-management policy, of the kind we made in 1966–1968. Moreover, some policy mistakes are nearly unavoidable, and we should have other means to assure that mistakes will not be disastrous.

There are many structural changes which could reduce the inflationary bias in our economy. Many of the most important would be improvements of manpower policy, designed to make the labor supply more easily shiftable from one employer, one industry, one occupation, one region, to another. We should also work to eliminate a host of private practices and government policies which grew up or were adopted in an effort to protect one or another private interest in an era when full employment was neither a policy nor a reality. Today these create strong downward rigidities of particular wages and prices and unnecessary bottlenecks and immobilities at high employment. Some provide artificial support for the market power of particular groups. Others directly and unnecessarily raise costs. Unfortunately, it is a slow and politically difficult job to achieve each of these many changes. It is important to get ahead with this job, whatever else we do. But it will not solve the immediate problem.

Beyond this, there are, of course, possibilities for major changes in basic labor legislation and institutions, which would effectively reduce the market power of labor unions, and for direct limits on the size and/or market shares of giant corporations. Even if, on balance, desirable, these changes are not going to occur in the near future. In any case, I believe that the more practicable approach is not a head-on attack on the basic sources of market power, but is rather a limitation on the exercise of that power where it specifically contributes to inflation—and, for that matter, where its use collides with other important social objectives.

Elsewhere, I have considered at some length the possibility of a permanent system of compulsory wage and price controls, and have concluded that it would inevitably create distortions and inefficiencies of resource use so serious as to make the system undesirable and probably unworkable.* There is not space to repeat that argument. But there are other options for the design of a system of direct restraints. One would be to return essentially to the system of wage-price "guideposts" used by the Kennedy and Johnson Administrations. As is well known, the guideposts constituted a set of definitions of patterns of wage and price behavior which, if generally followed, would be consistent with efficient resource allocation, reasonable equity, and approximate stability of the overall price level. Adherence to the guideposts was voluntary; but the government was prepared to—and frequently did—publicly criticize behavior which appeared to be inconsistent with the guideposts, and commend behavior which appeared consistent. It also propagandized generally about the importance and desirability of adherence to the

---

*See "The Future of Wage and Price Controls," *Atlanta Economic Review,* 22 (April 1972), pp. 24–33, and my "Statement" before the Joint Economic Committee, August 31, 1971, in *Hearings on the President's New Economic Program* (Part 2, pp. 242–256).

guideposts, and frequently held private discussions with firms and unions in which it urged their specific adherence.

Many critics—economists and others—asked how a system of purely voluntary standards and government appeals could cause *any* wage or price setter to accept a wage or price below that which would maximize net income. Is not the answer that, in collective bargaining and most industrial pricing, wage rates and prices are set not by impersonal market forces but rather by human (usually collective) decisions? The decision makers have room for judgment (or there would be no real decision). Over the relevant time horizon, they usually do not know even approximately what wage or price would maximize net income. They must and do settle questions by rule of thumb, comparison, or compromise; by considerations of equity, policy, or public appearance.

To the extent that the government's arguments for restraint made sense to any of the participants in a decision; to the extent that some of the participants preferred to avoid or minimize public criticism; and to the extent that they believed the government's appeals—*and their own decisions*—would affect *other* wage and price decisions, the guideposts clearly could and would have made some difference for their own decision.

To be sure, many professional mediators reported that the guideposts never appeared consciously to have entered anyone's thinking during wage bargaining which they observed in the 1960s. Interestingly, however, many unions professed to believe that the guideposts were influencing collective bargaining, and frequently and bitterly attacked the government's policy.

Moreover, 3.2 percent settlements came up much more frequently than they would have by chance alone. I believe that the guideposts did have some impact on wage decisions, primarily through influencing employers' bargaining positions, rather than by directly affecting union attitudes or aggressiveness, although I do not rule that out.

So far as prices are concerned I personally know that many significant price increases were either avoided or postponed, their size or their coverage reduced, or, in a fair number of cases that came to public attention, rolled back in full or in part. When, after 1965, the rate of unemployment fell progressively below 4 percent, it was not surprising that a voluntary system was unable to prevent an acceleration of wage and price increases. But, even then, I am convinced that it made an appreciable difference. The real question, of course, is whether the guideposts made *enough* difference. Could voluntary guideposts have survived as a viable system even if there had been a less serious mistake of fiscal policy than the one actually made in 1966–1968? Before attempting to answer this question, let me first indicate some specific and, I believe remediable, weaknesses of the guidepost system of the 1960s.

(1) It seems to me undeniable that any successful stabilization system—whether described as "compulsory" or "voluntary"—demands the consent or at least the tolerance of those whose wages and prices are to be stabilized. For this consent to be forthcoming, those regulated—and the general public as well—must see the system as one that is basically fair and equitable, or, at least, that embodies sacrifices by "our side" roughly equivalent to those imposed on the "other side." Moreover, members of each group must believe that the restrictions its members

accept on their freedom to do as they please will achieve something important—that slowing the rise in prices is a highly desirable objective, and that this system will be effective in achieving it.

In my view, this consent can only be secured through an active participation by the major groups in society—and particularly by the organizations of labor and business—in the process of recognizing the problem to which the policy is addressed, in planning the strategy to be used, and in formulating the basic standards. This was not the case for the guideposts. Rather, the guideposts were unilaterally promulgated by the government, with no serious effort to involve the leadership of labor, business, and public opinion in the process. I know that many individual business and labor leaders did recognize the problem, and had sympathy for the approach used. Their active participation, even in an advisory role, could have made them assume some responsibility for the success of the guideposts, and surely would have given the policy somewhat greater "legitimacy" in the eyes of others. Moreover, Congress was never asked to consider the matter, so that the guideposts drew no legitimacy from the legislative branch of our political system.

(2) Administration of the policy in the Council of Economic Advisers, with the occasional involvement of the White House, had advantages. The prestige of the Presidency—whether exerted directly by the President or reflected through an agent known to have the President's confidence —was an important asset in securing adherence by business and labor. But the President's support for the steps needed to make the policy work had to be affected by broader political considerations. For example, a time when labor support was vitally needed for passage of a crucial element in the President's legislative program was not a good time for him or his personal representative to be exerting pressures for wage restraint against a strong union.

(3) The government never made an adequate commitment of resources to the administration of the guidepost program. There were, at most, one to three staff members at the Council of Economic Advisers devoting some fraction of their time to guidepost activities, with occasional research assignments to others. It was thus impossible to anticipate more than the most obvious problems, or to provide the kinds of information and analysis needed to deal effectively with potential or actual cases of guidepost violation.

Moreover, the policy never had government-wide support. Although Presidents Kennedy and Johnson gave it their clear backing, the Secretaries or other high officials of the Departments of Labor, Commerce, Interior, and others were often indifferent or hostile, as were relevant independent agencies, such as the Conciliation and Mediation Service, and the regulatory commissions.

(4) One basic problem was that although everyone knew when important wage questions were coming up for decision, there was no way fully to anticipate major price increase decisions and to bring to bear the relevant information, persuasion, and considerations of the public interest which the government might wish the price setters to be exposed to at the time when it would do the most good. Clearly, it is far easier to prevent or delay or modify an inappropriate price increase before rather than after it has been publicly announced. At one point businesses

were requested to notify the Council in advance of major price changes. Some did, and were willing to discuss them before their announcement, but most did not. Indeed, some price changes which previously would have been publicly announced now began to be heard about only second hand.

Even if the foregoing weakness of the guidepost policy had been avoided (as they perhaps are in the proposals made below), and even if there had been no serious mistake of fiscal policy in 1966–1968, the question remains whether a purely voluntary policy could have succeeded during a prolonged period of high employment, or whether a chain reaction of increasingly serious violations of the policy would not ultimately have destroyed it.

I do not think that the answer is clear-cut. Yet, as I review the experience and the current problem, I conclude that it might be unwise to take a chance on a purely voluntary system. Even if the policy can enlist the support of a substantial majority of the public and of the leaders of labor, business, and other interests, will there not always be a number of smaller firms and unions, and at least a few reasonably important ones, whose publicized and flagrant noncooperation may progressively erode the adherence of others? I wonder if—rather than overfull employment—it was not the clear desire of the leadership of the airline mechanics in 1966 to prove that they could successfully defy the government—thereby encouraging other unions to do the same—that caused the wage guidepost to crumble. Indeed, the attempt to obtain adherence mainly through giving widespread publicity to

violations may be a potentially self-destructive policy. The airline mechanics' case was inherently unimportant. It was only the union's rejection of repeated highly publicized efforts by President Johnson to secure their approximate cooperation that made the case important—and its outcome so destructive of cooperation by other unions.

Doubts about the validity of a system which lacks any means of effective enforcement against the occasional flagrant noncooperator lead me to conclude that the existence of a "big stick in the back of the closet"—seldom used, and the use of which is not entirely predictable—could mightily enhance the force of public opinion in deterring clear and deliberate violations of the standards, thereby making it easier for all others to give at least approximate adherence to the standards.

I come, thus, to my suggestions for a future system of longer-run wage and price restraints for the United States. For want of a better name I will call this system the "Stabilization Agency." It would be created by legislation and responsible directly to the Congress.

1. The authority of the Stabilization Agency would be limited to the wages, fringe benefits, salaries, and executive compensation paid by employers who engage in significant collective bargaining, and to the prices of listed basic materials and of goods and services sold by the 1500–2000 largest corporations. However, all retail prices, rents, personal services, and farm prices would be excluded.

2. The agency's legitimacy would derive, first, from its creation through legislation, and, second, from some formal arrangement for labor-management-public participation in the formulation and review of its basic principles and policies. A relatively small tripartite board

would have the basic "legislative" responsibility for formulating the agency's wage and price standards and its procedures for intervention in particular cases. But a much larger body representing the principal interest groups and segments of public opinion would meet regularly to debate major policy statements and periodic reports on the agency's activities, and might participate in the selection of the nonpublic members of the board.

3. The executive functions would be performed by a full-time staff of several hundred professionals, headed by a single administrator (appointed by the President), rather than by the tripartite board. He would be authorized to intervene, formally or informally, publicly or privately, in the determination of all wages and prices subject to the restraints. The administrator would have legal authority to require that significant price and wage changes be reported in advance, to delay for limited periods the putting into effect of proposed changes while the agency studied them, and to require submission of relevant information from firms, unions, and government agencies. Based on its analysis of any case in which it chose to intervene, the agency would have the authority to recommend specific changes of wages or prices privately to the parties or publicly to the country. It could also make appropriate recommendations on related matters to federal, state, or local government agencies.

4. The agency's standards would be widely publicized, explained, and adherence to them promoted. However, the standards would not need to be so simple or numerical that they could in all cases be easily self-applied either by those making decisions or by the public

in judging the propriety of those decisions.

5. As a last resort, in particularly flagrant or crucial cases, authority would be available to prohibit specific wage or price changes substantially inconsistent with the agency's standards. The administrator could apply to a special court set up for this purpose for an injunction, running for a specific period of time, up to (say) one year, against the charging by named firms of specific listed or described prices, or against the payment by named employers of specific wage rates. The request for injunction would have to demonstrate that the specific changes in prices or wages to be enjoined were clearly inconsistent with the agency's standards for wages or prices, and that other workers or employers were, in general, voluntarily observing these standards. There would be no direct compulsory arbitration; but, in effect, the agency (and the special court) could in crucial cases determine the highest wage level it would permit to be paid.

I believe that a system set up along these general lines could be reasonably effective in exercising an appropriate restraint on wage and price increases, and, assuming adequate support from fiscal and monetary, farm, import, and manpower policies, in keeping inflation under reasonable control. Since the basic adherence would be voluntary, the system could not insure absolute price stability, nor should it attempt to. But, in part for the same reason, I believe that it offers enough flexibility to permit the relative wage and price changes that are essential for efficient resource allocation. Of course, it may be expected that, sooner or later, there would be a breakdown of consensus and hence of the system. After an appropriate interval, and with new names, faces, and slogans, it will then have to be renegotiated.

Incomes policies attempt to assure that the income claims within their purview—along with the income claims left to other determination—add up to roughly 100 percent of the total national income generated by current aggregate production, valued in current prices. But in this process, it is almost impossible to escape questions as to the *appropriate distribution* of aggregate income: as among wages, profits, farm and professional and interest incomes, and managerial compensation—and, within wage income—the appropriate differentials among various skills, occupations, industries, and regions. This distribution is only in part affected by the standards set in a wage and price policy; but it is also significantly affected by the government's tax, regulatory, tariff, agricultural, minimum wage, social security, manpower, and other policies.

Many believe that the "consent" of the great economic interest groups—which, in the long run, is the only possible basis for a successful system of inflation control—can only be secured and maintained if the system of wage-price restraints is coordinated with the other tools of government policy in order quite consciously to promote a progressive *redistribution* of income in specific directions which society approves. Indeed, to the extent that the source of existing inflationary pressure lies in a fundamental dissatisfaction with the existing income-distribution on the part of one or more powerful groups, while other groups resist any significant change in that distribution, there can probably be no real "consent" to an incomes policy unless that policy is directed not only toward the total of incomes but as well to their relative size.

Others fear that mixing up such questions with the control of inflation simply guarantees the failure of an incomes policy. An explicit policy on income shares might be avoided at the beginning of an incomes policy. But I suspect that sooner or later it cannot be escaped.   □

Controls or Competition— What's at Issue?

Carl H. Madden

The issue is stated that after Phase II the United States faces "controls or competition." Leading economists—Charls Walker, Charles Schultze, Murray Weidenbaum and others—who oppose controls in principle nevertheless caution (forecast?) against expecting an early "return" to "free markets."

CONCENTRATION AND INFLATION

Developing establishmentarian consensus calls for a permanent incomes policy in the absence of dealing with "those concentrations of private economic power which have become insulated from the influences of aggregate monetary and fiscal policy" (Weidenbaum). Incomes policy would prevent such concentrations of power from using their power to the fullest. Charles L. Schultze cites five elements in the structure of the United States economy that lead to inflation with high unemployment: (1) In concentrated industries, prices are sticky downward; therefore, price rises in expanding markets are not offset by price cuts in stable or declining markets. Also, wages rates will rise more uniformly, raising prices and costs in other industries. (2) The nature of wage-bargaining leads to the so-called "wage-wage" spiral or "follow-the-leader" union settlements. (3) The changing nature of the labor market, with increasing teen-agers and women, has worsened the trade-off between inflation and unemployment. (4) Price-fixing policies of the

Excerpted from Carl H. Madden, "Controls or Competition—What's at Issue?" from *The Review of Economics and Statistics*, Vol. 54, No. 3 (August 1972), pp. 224, 228–30. With permission of *The Review of Economics and Statistics*. © the President and Fellows of Harvard College.

federal government create inflationary bias. (5) Concentrated industries pass on wage and other cost increases through "target-rate-of-return" pricing. Schultze does not believe concentrated industries generate inflation by upping profit margins arbitrarily during recessions or recoveries when unemployment is high and markets weak, but he is concerned about sticky prices and the pass-through of wage increases.* However, if Schultze's thesis were correct, then prices in concentrated industries should have risen faster than prices in nonconcentrated industries. The facts are otherwise. From 1967 to 1971, wholesale prices rose by 17.9 percent in industries where the top four firms had less than one-quarter of industry sales compared to a lesser 10.7 percent rise in industries where the top four firms accounted for more than three-quarters of industry sales.†

Economists such as Houthakker and Meltzer, on the other hand, appear to oppose incomes policies. They emphasize, instead, the crucial importance of removing governmental restraints on competition such as: import quotas, restrictions on banking, laws regulating wages in construction, laws restricting entry to industries, laws restricting through regulation of industries their freedom to reduce prices, and the like.†† Houthakker points out that ". . . the general public interest, especially the interest of consumers, is being given less and less weight. . . . The consumer movement has rarely if ever taken a clear stand in favor of competition; on the contrary, many of its positions have implied increased

regulation and government intervention." Houthakker points out that our antitrust laws do *not* apply to such important sectors as organized labor, the regulated industries, and agricultural cooperatives. He says: "In general it is not obvious why the unions should continue to enjoy exemption from the antitrust laws, considering that some of them have far more market power than the large majority of firms and that they represent only a fraction of the total labor force."

The evidence abroad on incomes policy in Great Britain, the Netherlands, Sweden, and Canada during the 1960s reveals that it was not successful because it did not gain the cooperation of labor. The hortatory approach to anti-inflation action in the United States in the 1960s was not successful for the same reason. The recent walk-out of the AFL-CIO from the President's wage board indicates that cooperation from labor in an incomes policy after Phase II is not likely to be maintained, judging from past experience both here and abroad. The establishmentarian view of the need for incomes policy, I conclude, is inferior in its empirical support to the proven value of opening up the economy to the fresh breezes of competition. Furthermore, a permanent incomes policy involves real risks (1) that labor unions would not submit to wage discipline and (2) that the "elitism" of business-government cooperation in incomes policy weakens market forces in the economy.

CONCLUSION

Therefore, in Phase III wage-price controls should be abandoned wholly while other policies are pursued for controlling inflation. De-control should be accompanied by a positive program to avoid future direct controls. Since inflation is caused by excessive creation of money, usually stimulated by federal deficits at high employment, large deficits should be attacked by new

---

*C. L. Schultze, in testimony before Senate Subcommittee on Antitrust and Monopoly, January 1972.

†J. Fred Weston, "Appraising Price and Pay Controls," Presentation to Public Hearings of U.S. Price Commission, San Francisco, California, April 6, 1972, p. 4a, table 2.

††Statements of Hendrik S. Houthakker and Allan H. Meltzer, respectively, before the Subcommittee on Anti-trust and Monopoly of the Senate Committee on the Judiciary, January 21, 1972 and January 19, 1972.

policies: (1) evaluation of the federal budget as a whole by Congress through re-activating the Joint Committee on the Legislative Budget; (2) pilot testing, where feasible, all new spending proposals; (3) zero-based budgeting on a three-year rotating basis for all major federal budgetary programs; and (4) required five-year budgetary projections for Congressional obligational authority and actual expenditures.

Widespread improvements are needed in federal statistics purporting to measure industrial concentration, national wealth, and in other areas, if comprehensive control of government fiscal and antitrust programs are to be effective.

The federal government should advance a specific legislative proposal and institute a comprehensive program for removing federal restrictions on competition which now exist in law and regulation. The proposal and program should be accompanied by widespread public education, perhaps including a White House Conference on Enhancing Productivity.

Finally, the nation should place a much higher priority on improving and extending effective human power (manpower and womanpower) policy. Enlightened and effective private and public investment in upgrading, retraining, and continuously adapting the skills of people to the demands of markets will reduce the pressure on monetary and fiscal policy to over-expand the money supply in order to cope with unemployment. Such policy should impartially examine evidence of racial or other discrimination, based on realistic measurement and on other valid evidence that discrimination exists, both in industry, among unions, and in government and non-profit institutions alike.   □

Are Controls the Answer?

Hendrik S. Houthakker

We shall not know for many months if the introduction of direct controls over wages and prices in late 1971 was followed by a significant slowdown in the trend of price and wage increases. . . . Even if attained, the modest reduction in the inflation rate officially set as a goal provides only weak justification for this drastic departure from our generally successful economic traditions. There is some indication that the Pay Board and Price Commission will serve less as a means of curtailing inflation than as watchdogs over big business and big labor. . . .

There is indeed a case for better supervision of the labor unions. In the last few years we have come closer to the situation already reached in the United Kingdom (prior to the recent legislation), where the unions could obtain wage increases not only regardless of productivity, but also regardless of the state of the labor market. Our labor laws appear to be inadequate to deal with this problem, which has greatly complicated the preservation of full employment. The power of the unions may therefore have to be constrained in other ways. Although the Pay Board and the Construction Industry Stabilization Committee have so far demonstrated only limited effectiveness in dealing with excessive wage increases, they may learn in due course. Perhaps the introduction of an official link between unemployment and wage changes (an institutionalized Philips curve) would lead to better results.

However this may be, systematic government intervention in collective bargaining may be nec-

Excerpted from Hendrik S. Houthakker, "Are Controls the Answer?" from *The Review of Economics and Statistics*, Vol. 54, No. 3 (August 1972), pp. 231–34. © the President and Fellows of Harvard College.

essary pending a general restoration of competition in the labor markets and elsewhere. The great danger of regulatory bodies, as experience in other areas suggests, is that they will come under the control of the sector they are supposed to regulate. The departure of the labor members of the Pay Board does not necessarily remove this danger; it may indicate, on the contrary, that they were satisfied the Pay Board would be responsive to the unions even without their overt participation. Any tendency on the part of the Pay Board to favor organized over nonorganized labor will no doubt make union membership more attractive and thus make the unions even more powerful. While this result may be partly offset by employers substituting nonunion for union labor, discriminatory wage controls are not likely to improve the working of the labor market.

For somewhat different reasons much the same is true if the Price Commission concentrates on big business. The danger here is not so much that large firms will have undue influence over the commission; for one thing there are far more large firms than large unions, and their interests are more diverse. The danger is on the contrary that the Price Commission will reduce the profit margins of the more efficient firms (who are usually among the larger ones) to such an extent that marginal firms (who are often small) will be squeezed; even if the latter can avoid bankruptcy, they will then have difficulty attracting capital. In view of the increasing emphasis on profit controls, this danger is by no means theoretical. Many economists (including at least one in this symposium) believe that price controls should be confined to large firms, and recent political trends also favor this emphasis. There may well be more immediate effect on prices if firms with large profits are forced

to roll back their prices, but their less profitable competitors will, by the same token, see their market share or their profits (and probably both) vanish. Those who want to use controls as an instrument against big business will thus have gained a Pyrrhic victory at best.

Presumably not all qualified observers will agree with my assessment of the short-term results of price-wage controls as modest at best, and of the long-term results as harmful. Only time will tell. But unless my fears are groundless, continued controls do not appear to be the answer to inflation, at least from an economic point of view. Let us therefore consider alternatives.

One alternative that does not need much attention is the milder "incomes policy" practiced in the United States during the middle 1960s and also widely adopted abroad. While much less disruptive than direct controls, this milder approach has not had any lasting results.

There is considerably greater promise in what may be called a "procompetitive strategy," under which the government attempts to make the factor and product markets more responsive to overall fiscal and monetary policy. Such a strategy would involve legislative reforms in the areas of labor, antitrust, transportation, energy and agriculture, in addition to liberalization of import restrictions.

The advantages of competition for the efficient allocation of resources have, of course, long been recognized, but its benefits for economic stability are no less important. In markets where competition is restricted, prices tend to be not only too high, but also too sticky. In competitive markets prices respond more promptly to changes in supply and demand, and this is especially important for the success of anti-inflationary policies. Although aggregate demand was curtailed significantly between late 1968 and early 1970, prices and wages were not affected as much as similar experiences (most recently in the late 1950s) suggested. Wages continued to rise despite considerable unemployment, and prices followed suit, despite a fall in profits. As far as the labor markets are concerned there is admittedly little direct evidence of a change in structure which would have made them less responsive to unemployment. Nevertheless better response could have been obtained by policies aimed at racial discrimination, apprenticeship requirements, hiring halls, product boycotts and other restrictive practices. Such measures were especially needed in the construction and transportation industries, where wage increases were largest.

In several important product markets measures could have been taken to let declining demand show up in lower prices rather than in lower output. Some of these measures relate to imports, which are often the most potent source of competition in oligopolistic markets. Thus, if so-called voluntary quotas on steel exports from Japan and Europe had not been negotiated in 1968 the behavior of steel prices would have been quite different. Similarly, the adoption of the Cabinet Task Force report on oil imports would have had a major impact on petroleum prices. The substantial increase in dairy support prices in March 1971 was contrary to anti-inflationary policy. So were the readiness of the Interstate Commerce Commission to grant general freight rate increases, and the efforts of the Civil Aeronautics Board to prevent overcapacity from depressing domestic air fares; these in turn encouraged the carriers to agree to the large wage increases demanded by the unions in-

volved. Many more cases could be cited (including a few where competition was promoted and prices fell as a result, notably in international aviation), but on balance they would not change the conclusion that the government has generally been prepared to help politically powerful sectors in keeping prices up. This was one reason why the losses of output and employment implicit in the anti-inflationary policy followed up to mid-1971 were largely in vain. In fact the perverse response of these protected markets to the decline in aggregate demand may have aggravated these losses.

The principal lesson from this experience is that a procompetitive strategy is politically costly since it tends to offend powerful and well-organized interest groups. However, a strategy of controls cannot succeed either unless it hurts somewhere. As was pointed out earlier, the controls have not so far inflicted much pain, but neither have they done much to reduce inflation. The political advantage of controls is that the pain can be directed to the less vocal sectors. This is presumably why the wage boards have been willing to give preferential treatment to certain unions and why little or nothing has been done to restrain farm prices. It remains to be seen whether this selective approach will yield the desired results.

There is still another alternative: to let inflation take its course, thus avoiding the costs inherent in an effective procompetitive or controls strategy. The many studies of the effects of inflation suggest that the U.S. economy has developed fairly good adjustment mechanisms for the rather mild inflation we have experienced until now. Wages and prices go upward in tandem; long-term interest rates fully reflect the rate of change of prices; most transfer payments are adjusted periodically. For most Americans who own any property at all their main asset is a house, whose value rises at least as fast as the general price level, and their main liability is a mortgage contracted long ago and fixed in money terms; they clearly stand to gain by inflation. Of course there are flies in this ointment. The gains of homeowners are matched by the losses of thrift institutions, but expedients have been found to take care of this. More seriously, inflation through the Pigou effect leads to a rise in personal savings,* and this complicates the attainment of full employment. Moreover it is conceivable, though by no means certain, that inflation has a tendency to accelerate if left alone.

Of the three options before us—controls, competition, and benign neglect—my own preference as an economist and citizen is clearly for the second, the only one that is consistent with established economic analysis. The sudden switch to controls one year ago resulted from an unwillingness to bear the short-term political costs inherent in a more constructive approach. But in economic policy the hard choices cannot be avoided, and the consequences of controls, even if they reach their primary objective, may not be very appealing either. We must all hope that the present policy will work, but at the same time we must remain on the alert for indications that it will ultimately do more harm than good. □

---

*This is the most likely explanation of the high savings rates that have surprised so many observers of the economy. These rates are not surprising if savings are viewed as the planned accumulation of assets, and if the desired money value of assets is related to money income.

U.S. Abandons Controls with Inflation Thriving and No Extra Answers

Interview with Hendrik S. Houthakker and Arthur M. Okun by Soma Golden, *New York Times*

Question: First, I'd like each of you to take a moment to sketch out your view of wage-price controls as a policy alternative in this country. Are you in brief a pro, or con, controls man and why?

Houthakker: I have not been an enthusiast for controls. I criticized them when they were first adopted, and I must say that nothing that has happened since then has convinced me that I was wrong. I believe they have been a failure and that they were bound to be a failure. So I feel that if we want to do something about inflation we have to find something other than controls.

Okun: It's been 30 months since August 1971, and you can divide that into two halves. In the first, we had a marked deceleration of inflation. It's only the second half that has looked bad. The fact is that by late 1972 we were down to a 3 percent inflation rate. My own view is that Phase 1 and Phase 2 did make a significant contribution toward that deceleration—riding a tide that was probably moving in that direction anyway, but helping it along.

I think that what has happened since then has reflected a number of factors, one of them that we have the kind of inflation that controls cannot do that much about, in the food and fuel areas.

Soma Golden, *New York Times*, Business and Finance Section, Sunday, April 28, 1974, pp. 1, 24–25. © 1974 by The New York Times Company. Reprinted with permission.

I don't view myself as an enthusiast for controls but I think that some type of government wage-price effort of a direct sort, probably demanding mandatory powers, ought to be one of the tools that's available in trying to hold down inflation.

Q: Dr. Okun, were you an enthusiast of the first freeze?

Okun: I would never have recommended the kind of plunging in with a total freeze and drawing lines between pickles and cucumbers and professional football salaries that we had. Indeed, I think we were confronted with that partly because we operated with such an unwillingness to tiptoe into the area, to use government powers on anything. When we finally decided to do something, the only alternative was going all the way.

Houthakker: I feel that we had considerable slack in the economy in 1971, and this by itself would have taken care of a lot of inflationary pressure. When the slack disappeared, the controls suddenly didn't work any more. Now I attribute this to the fact that the price behavior was determined by the amount of slack in the economy, and not by the controls.

Okun: It is awfully hard to explain why the slack suddenly took hold in late 1971 without invoking controls as part of the answer.

Houthakker: Well, controls can have a temporary effect, but as President Lincoln might have said: "You can hold all prices down some of the time and some prices down all of the time, but you can't hold down all prices all of the time."

Okun: We can agree on that.

Q: Let's shift towards January 1973, and Phase 3. Would you say that we should have gotten out of the controls business then as the super boom developed?

Houthakker: Well, in testimony before the Joint Economic Committee in November 1972, my answer was that the controls should be phased out on an industry-by-industry basis, having regard to the state of the market in each industry.

Okun: I think we never should have gotten into areas where controls were creating genuine shortages. The crusade on lumber prices was one of the most absurd spinning of wheels in Phase 2.

Q: Can we read out of this that we got ourselves into too much of a detailed controls system—too many forms to file, too many little rules that each businessman had to keep up with?

Houthakker: No, I would put it the other way around. I think what was done during the last two-and-a-half years was to run a price controls system without adequate allocation mechanisms. When you control prices, you deeply affect the whole economy, and this I think was not fully realized.

As far as I can see, the controls effort starting in 1971 was largely a cosmetic exercise. It was an appearance of action without much substance to it.

If I had been asked in 1971, as a technician, 'What does it take to have an effective controls mechanism?' then I would have said you need a bureaucracy of a quarter of a million people, just to take a figure out of thin air. It would also mean a complete change in the nature of our economy and that is the main reason why I would have opposed it. But my feeling was that the effort that was made with 3,000 to 5,000 people really wasn't promising, as I think the results have shown.

Q: Prof. Houthakker, you left the Council of Economic Advisers one month before the 1971 controls hit. Your advice was not asked on this subject?

Houthakker: No, it was not. No. Of course there were various earlier efforts. There was something called the Inflation Alert in which I myself was much involved. I never quite understood what it was meant to do, but it was another of these cosmetic efforts.

Q: Are you saying that we got ourselves into a very detailed controls system at the same time we were reluctant to build a bureaucracy?

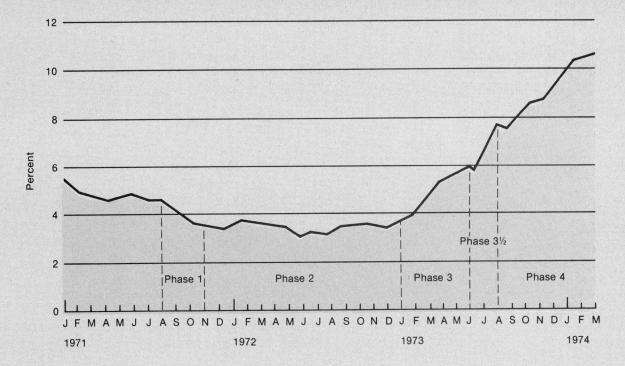

Figure A. Price Inflation. Percentage Increase in the Consumer Price Index over Same Month in Previous Year.

The controls program approached—but failed to attain —its target of cutting price inflation to 2–3 percent by the end of 1972, but failed miserably in its stated aim of lowering the rate to 2.5 percent by the end of 1973.

Source: Department of Labor

Okun: I think that is exactly it. We set up inconsistent objectives. Either you decide to do what you can do with a very small bureaucracy, which I think is to pick the rotten apples out of the barrel rather than to try to define the shape of the ideal apple, or else you move to the much more detailed set of rules and regulations such as what marked World War II and Korea and then you have the big bureaucracy. My preference would have been the first.

Q: Would the first have done much for the kind of inflation that we had with the worst inflation in the food and commodity sector? Were there many rotten apples to pick from? Was there a big company or a big union or any such visible villain in this?

Okun: No, I don't think any reasonable set of controls would have changed the story much in 1973.

Q: Let's take another tack. The Cost of Living Council, since last summer, has been trying to spread out the post-freeze price bulge, in the hope that maybe if the economy slowed, some price increases might not even go into effect. Has that strategy been helpful?

Houthakker: No, I would say the strategy has indeed caused some very serious dislocations. I think delaying price increases was one of the major reasons why the whole controls system got into discredit—trying to control prices without controlling quantities.

Okun: The economy has areas where prices can really be read as equating supply and demand and doing a pretty sensitive job of calling the signals, and others where there is just a great deal more fuzziness.

I see the opportunities for government action to alter the price of automobiles and prevent it from rising as having much more potential and much less danger of disallocation than efforts to try to fix the price of soybeans, for example.

Q: In this discussion so far we have almost ignored the wage side. Can we all agree that Cost of Living Council director John T. Dunlop is a magician on that and that the wage side has been much less of a problem than the price side?

Okun: I think the magic in 1972 was setting the standard of 5.5 percent. Basically, people believed that that was a fair wage increase, was what other people were getting and was a reasonable increase in real wages.

One of the key factors in what happened to wages in 1973 was that the biggest price increases took place in areas that don't hire a lot of labor—farms and the oil industry—and there is no way workers in other industries can benefit from those price gains. In effect, the ability of other employers to pay has not been boosted by these particular price increases.

Houthakker: I am not at all sure that we are really better off for having delayed wage acceleration in 1973, if that is what really happened. In other words, we may just have postponed these troubles to a time when they might be more difficult to solve.

Q: Where do we go from here? The controls may be over, the controls legislation may end, but inflation isn't over by any means. Don't we need some sort of anti-inflation effort that goes beyond fiscal and monetary policy?

Houthakker: Oh yes, we do. We need structural reform, which is essentially a matter of making competition more effective and increasing supply. This is something that was tried in a few areas with generally rather little success. There have been various efforts by the Council of Economic Advisors, Democrats and Republicans, to deregulate the transportation industry, to liberalize farm policy, to beef

up the antitrust laws. There are quite a number of other areas, in the energy field, for example, that have seen similar things, too.

Fiscal and monetary policy is a relatively simple thing compared to much more scattered structural policies. Also, structural policy runs into much more political opposition. By now, very few members of Congress really object to fiscal-monetary policy, but when you touch the Interstate Commerce Commission, then you are touching some raw nerves.

Q: Dr. Okun, do you also feel that we must move on structural things or is that like pledging allegiance to apple pie and motherhood? Economists have been calling for these things for 15 years at least.

Okun: Yes, and everybody has been saying we have to lick inflation and we haven't either. So it seems to me that we have got to try some things that we haven't tried before, and this is one promising approach. I'd be pretty eclectic about it, and I think it ought to be sold much more as an anti-inflation package. You might get some consumer enthusiasm to countervail the producer interests that make this such a tough political problem.

Q: Wouldn't we need somebody who is in charge of doing that? Can the Council of Economic Advisors do it, or do we need what some people call a new "watchdog agency?"

Okun: Quite apart from whether any controls authority is retained, the end of the Cost of Living Council would be very undesirable in my opinion. I think the Cost of Living Council has the mechanism of being a watchdog agency and I don't think the job ought to be put on the back of the Council of Economic Advisors.

Houthakker: I believe there is a need of some reorganization of the economic policy-making mechanism. The one thing that I regret about Congress's unwillingness to extend the controls program is that John T. Dunlop was in there with a proposal for a watchdog agency, and, in fact, the Cost of Living

Council would have become a watchdog agency which it really hasn't been until now. But that went down the drain with everything else.

There are two agencies in Washington that could do it—well, three perhaps. The Council of Economic Advisors is one, the Office of Management and the Budget is another, and to some extent the Justice Department.

Apart from that, we all know that departments like agriculture, interior, commerce—these are all client agencies. They speak for their clients. They will oppose any effort to improve these things.

Q: What kind of jobs would you see for this watchdog agency other than fighting within the government against inflation? Would it be useful for it to have public hearings, for example, if a union or a business seemed to step out of line in either way—on wages or prices?

Houthakker: I would say that the main purpose would be to stimulate competition by other means, not by appealing to the public responsibility of businessmen or labor leaders.

I am not saying you should never appeal to public responsibility, but on the whole I believe it is not a very fruitful approach. For one thing, it tends to be too concentrated in a few industries. It always boils down to metals—steel, copper, aluminum, these are the ones that get 90 percent of the attention, and maybe a little bit on rubber tires and shoes and then you've just about had it.

By that time you have accounted for maybe 4 percent of the economy. If you want to control inflation by this kind of approach, then you have to worry about the undertakers in Omaha who raise their burial fees by 20 percent without anyone ever knowing about it.

Q: Do you agree with that, Dr. Okun?

Okun: No. I think there is more hope of what I call picking the rotten apple out of the barrel. When I put the list [of key industries] together, it accounts

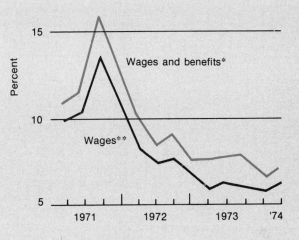

Figure B. Wage Settlements.

First-year changes in wage rates alone and in wages plus benefits. Major collective bargaining settlements, private nonfarm economy.
The controls program was fairly successful in achieving its objective of reducing wage settlements to a 5.5 percent annual increase, or 6.2 percent, including benefits.
*Wage and benefit figures cover agreements for 5,000 workers or more.
**Wage figures cover agreements for 1,000 workers or more.
Source: Department of Labor

for more like 15 percent of industrial wholesale prices than 4 percent. But I think the real impact of these prices is that a lot of them are associated with key collective bargaining settlements in industry.

On that score, I regard Congress's seeming unwillingness to extend controls legislation—even in a very weak form—as the result of a very effective lobbying effort by business and labor combined.

Q: Instead of controls, some have suggested the wide use of indexing* or escalator clauses to protect people and to induce the Government to slow things down without as much pain from unemployment. Are we naked to inflation without controls unless we follow the indexing route?

Okun: We are not quite naked to inflation, but we would be with a comprehensive indexing system. So far as I can see, a fully indexed economy means any disturbance on any price has no upper limit. If we had had complete indexing in the past 15 months, our inflation rate would be double and triple what it is today.

Houthakker: I am not much in favor of indexing either, though I believe it could overcome some equity problems. In fact, when I was a member of the council, we had a session with the labor union economists

---

[*By *indexing* is meant tying all contracts in the economy to some price index—say, the consumer price index—so that inflation has no redistributional effects, as between creditor and debtor, etc. The disadvantage, as Okun points out, is that this virtually guarantees a more rapid rate of inflation. RTG]

in late 1970 where we made some delicate remarks about the possibility of 100 percent cost of living clauses. But they evidently didn't feel they could sell it to their members.

Q: Do you remember why?

Okun: Yes. People want to believe in money, both business and labor. They don't want to have the yardstick stretched.

Q: Professor Houthakker, what was the logic behind the C.E.A.'s indexing proposal? Did you think that it would help slow inflation if you could get labor to buy it?

Houthakker: Yes, but it was primarily a way of eliminating what we saw as an emerging bias against organized labor. As far as we could see, union wages were falling behind. . . . That's why we thought it would appeal to them, but it didn't.

There was another aspect of this proposal—we did see a price deceleration ahead. We were worried about the fact that labor would try to get large recoupments of price increases that were already slowing.

Some Limited Support

Question: Why do you think that business—eager to get rid of them now—was so enthusiastic about controls in the beginning?

Okun: The drowning man grasping for a straw is the best explanation. Nothing else was working.

Houthakker: I would say there is a more specific explanation. I think business was essentially looking at controls as a way of reinforcing its hand with the unions.

Q: And what about labor?

Houthakker: Labor was much more reluctant. There were many entries and exits by George Meany [president of the American Federation of Labor–Congress of Industrial Organizations]. His various representatives withdrew from the Pay Board and labor was never very happy with the efforts, at least if you can identify labor with George Meany and, politically, I guess you can.

Q: But they never struck against the Government, which some people view as quite an achievement.

Okun: There are institutions in this country that make it awfully hard for any private group to raise a fist against the government. I think that is a good thing.

Okun: Talking about the kinds of schemes that are not politically feasible at the moment, I've got a variation on indexing that I think is better than simply letting wages rise to chase prices. If labor were willing to accept cost-of-living adjustments, I think that could better be done through tax credits than the sort of pay jumps that put direct upward pressure on employers' costs and thus on prices.

Q: Have you tried out this idea on labor?

Okun: Yes, with very unenthusiastic responses.

Q: What should happen at the end of this month to the controls legislation?

Houthakker: Abolish it, with the exception of a watchdog agency—but one without the power to roll back wages and prices. The agency might hold hearings, but not on particular wage and price decisions. In fact, it would probably serve as a watchdog over regulatory commissions, which I think is most necessary of all.

Okun: I'd like a continuation of some statutory control or authority that would permit wage or price decisions to be overturned after some due process. Still, I think we'll be out of the controls business for a while. Then, after its bad reputation wears off, we'll be back into it. This has been the history of a lot of European countries.

I'm always reminded of the P. T. Barnum story that it's easy to put a lion and a lamb in the same cage as long as you have a large reserve supply of lambs. I think that's the story with the lamb of controls and the lions of business, labor and excessive fiscal and monetary enthusiasm—you need a big supply of lambs.

Q: Then, we're stuck, as are most other industrialized countries that have tried to pursue full-employment policies. . . .

Houthakker: No, no, there's still another route which we haven't talked about and that is a somewhat tighter monetary policy. I believe that the present inflation not only in the United States but especially in other countries is due to a very large extent to unduly accommodating monetary policies caused by too much worry about interest rates.

I think we should aim for a little more slack in the economy. But slack isn't just the unemployment rate; I would say it has three main components—unemployment, capacity utilization and inventories.

Okun: Unemployment is generally a good indicator of overall utilization, but in 1973 for the first time in the postwar generation we really had very different signals from capacity and inventory on the one hand and unemployment rates on the other. I think we will be alert to those very different signals in the future.

Q: It seems as if, starting in 1973, there has been a whole bag of problems that nobody and no controller could deal with—they weren't the problems of a controller. . . .

Okun: Not a wage controller, and not a price controller, and not a money controller, or a tax and spending controller is my view. Let me replay fiscal and monetary policy with perfect hindsight over the last two years and I don't think I could save you more than a couple of points on the rate of inflation. Let me replay agricultural policy and energy policy, however, and I'll give you five points.

Houthakker: I would give fiscal and monetary policy more blame for the problem and agriculture less.

Q: In the sum then, what is your view of the success or failure of controls or incomes policy? Does it help only when you don't need it?

Okun: No, my view is that at most controls buys you a couple of points of growth before you run into the problem of excess demand, of inevitable inflation.

But if it buys you those few points, I'm willing to pay the price of having the Government's scope increased, and I think that's really what it comes back to in looking at how different people evaluate controls.

Houthakker: I don't have strong feelings on the grounds of principle on this. If I could be convinced that it did have an effect I would talk quite differently about it. But this I think is really the issue—did it make a difference or not? I'm not convinced.   □

CHAPTER 28
ECONOMIC GROWTH AMONG NATIONS

In the 1950s and early 1960s, there was little doubt about what seemed the main economic issue facing the United States. It was concern about the growth performance of this country in relation to that of the other industrialized nations—especially Russia, but also Japan and the countries of the European Common Market. In the early 1970s, our concerns altered somewhat. We became more domestically oriented, and problems of income distribution and poverty within our borders took on new urgency (chapter 29). Also, we became far more worried about pollution and the other environmental costs of growth than we were a decade before (chapter 30).

Still, "international growthmanship" has by no means disappeared as a major issue of our times. If we take more than a very short-run view, there is little in our lives that will not be affected by the pattern of growth performance in the next quarter-century. In the year 2000, will the United States still be the major producer among the nations of the world, or will it be only one among many equals, or will it (like Britain, the "workshop of the world" in the nineteenth century) have fallen to the status of a second-rank economic power? Which outcome should we prefer? What might the political and social consequences of these various outcomes be?

These questions make it clear that the problem of growth is still very much with us. In this chapter, we shall discuss economic growth in an international context, focusing especially on the recent growth experiences of the Soviet Union, Japan, and Canada.

MACROECONOMIC AND MICROECONOMIC ASPECTS OF GROWTH

First, however, let us try to single out some of the key issues in the discussion to follow. As in the case of measures to combat inflation (discussed in Great Debate Four), economic growth ultimately involves a combination of macroeconomic and microeconomic factors. Indeed, the borderline between the two fields becomes rather vague. Capital formation, for example, is clearly an important factor in growth and yet we treat it both as a macroeconomic subject (focusing on investment demand) and a microeconomic subject (discussing such topics as the marginal productivity of capital and consumer time-preference with respect to present versus future income).

Generally speaking, any improvement either in the macroeconomic or microeconomic functioning of the economy will contribute positively to a nation's rate of economic growth. Take for example the problem of reducing unemployment, a central concern of Part Two of this book. If a country is able to use effective fiscal and monetary policies to reduce its rate of unemployment over time, it may achieve as high a rate of growth as another country with higher growth potential but with increasing unemployment (Figure 28–1).[1]

The same thing can be said about making improvements in the *efficiency* of an economy—a central concept of microeconomics in Part Three. An inefficient economy can achieve some degree of growth

---

1.   The country in Figure 28–1(b) shows the kind of pattern of growth that was predicted for the United States by the *stagnationists* (See chapter 16, p. 407). These economists felt not so much that growth opportunities would be absent as that increasing unemployment would prevent our seizing these opportunities. Or, more accurately, that if we wanted to seize them we would require a much more active monetary and fiscal policy along Keynesian lines. A latter-day stagnationist could claim even today that we escaped a dismal future primarily because of the increased role of government in the past thirty years.

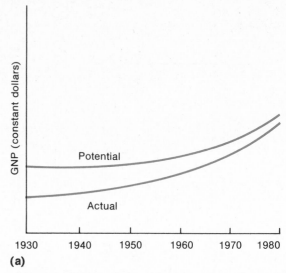

(a)

A Country with Decreasing Unemployment

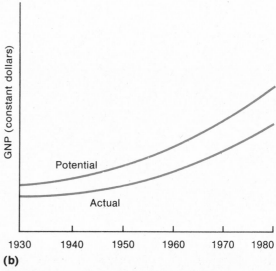

(b)

A Country with Increasing Unemployment

Figure 28–1. Effects of Unemployment.

The actual rates of growth of these hypothetical countries are identical although (b) has much greater growth potential. Reason: country (a) is doing a much better job of reducing unemployment.

by moving closer to its production-possibility curve, even though that curve may not be shifting outward very rapidly. Figure 28–2 shows examples of two different patterns of growth. Both hypothetical countries have grown by the same amount between 1930 and 1980. The country in (a) has achieved this in no small part by reallocating its resources in a more efficient way; the country in (b), by contrast, has become increasingly *in*efficient but, either through great expansion of factor inputs or technological progress, has experienced a marked outward shift of its production-possibilities. We can now understand a comment we made in chapter 3 when we noted that the Soviet economy had exhibited both numerous inefficiencies and rapid growth. Clearly, something like the pattern of Figure 28–2(b) was involved.

Indeed, we can go a step further, and notice that the effects of macro- and microeconomic factors on growth may be quite similar. Thus, Figure 28–1, which describes the effects of falling or increasing unemployment, is actually interchangeable with Figure 28–2, which shows the effects of increasing or decreasing allocative efficiency. Among other things, mass unemployment is clearly ''inefficient'' in the technical sense of that term.

What all this means is that the number of influences that conspire to affect a country's growth rate is very great indeed. In our earlier discussion of growth in chapter 16, we spoke of growth as being a result of increases in factor inputs (capital and labor force) and increases in output per unit of input (especially technological progress). Now we would want to know not only how great the increases in capital and labor force are, but also whether the capital and labor are being allocated in efficient ways, and to what degree they are being fully employed. We might get a certain rate of growth in total output because our labor force had increased, or it might come about, with a given labor force, because we had more efficiently transferred labor from low to high productivity occupations.

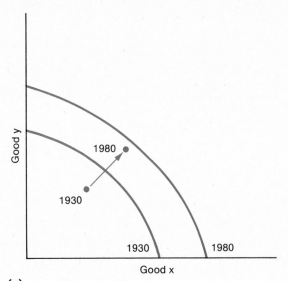

(a)
Growth with Increasing Efficiency

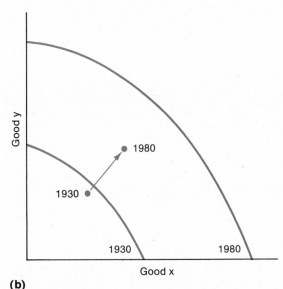

(b)
Growth Despite Increasing Inefficiency

Figure 28–2. Effects of Allocative Efficiency.

These two countries have grown identically between 1930 and 1980, but in quite different ways. Country (a) has made up in increasing efficiency what it lacks in expanded production possibilities.

The situation is similar with respect to increased output per unit of input. This might come about because of the application of new technologies, or it might come about because a reorganization of industry had permitted economies of scale to be exploited, or it might occur because à la the theory of international trade) comparative advantages among different countries had benefited all trading partners.

To complicate matters a bit further, it must be said that there is no single pattern that explains all (or even most) countries' growth experiences. Many students of growth have thus come to speak of certain patterns of growth or "models," such as the "English model," the "American model," the "Soviet model," and the "Japanese model." The notion is that different countries, in different circumstances, may combine the elements of growth in very dissimilar ways, but also that each different pattern has to have a certain internal logic of its own—otherwise there wouldn't be any growth at all. The following sections and readings in this chapter attempt to suggest some of the constituents of such "growth models" in countries other than the United States. After reading the remainder of this chapter, the reader should go back to chapter 16, where we discussed the growth record of the United States, and see what contrasts and parallels he can draw.

THE SOVIET GROWTH MODEL

When he was locating the *take-off* periods[2] for various nations emerging onto the path of modern growth, W. W. Rostow selected the years 1890–1914 for Russia. The particular years are of no special significance, but the fact that Russia's industrial revolution is often placed *before* the Communist revolution of 1917 is obviously of some importance. If, as many observers believe, getting started on the path of modern growth is the hardest part of the battle,

---

2. See p. 398.

and if Russia had succeeded in accomplishing this task before the radical transformation of her economic system, then our evaluation of the successes and failures of the Soviet command economy must be significantly affected.

Unfortunately, the matter is not quite so clear-cut as this. On certain points, almost everyone would be agreed: first, that Russia was an economically backward nation (as compared, say, to most Western European countries) during the nineteenth century. England, for example, had seen the end of serfdom for all practical purposes by the middle of the sixteenth century. In Russia, two centuries later, roughly 15 million out of the country's 19 million people were serfs. It was not until 1861, almost a century after the beginning of the British Industrial Revolution, that the Russian serfs were finally emancipated.

It would also be agreed that Russia had made serious efforts both before and during the nineteenth century to "catch up" with the more economically advanced nations. Peter the Great (1682–1725) launched such an effort with the particular purpose of strengthening the army and navy. His visits to England and Western Europe and his hiring of foreign technicians are well known, and he also used his state treasury directly to initiate the building of factories and new industries. In the late nineteenth century, the Czarist government financed extensive railroad construction, the state bank lent assistance to private enterprises, the government continued to press for the entry of technicians and technology from abroad, and government tariffs were used to protect new industries. Thus, in the period of which Rostow speaks, there was without doubt very substantial economic progress in Russia: It would have seemed, indeed, that she was moving through her industrial revolution, with somewhat more active State participation, but nevertheless in a manner roughly comparable to what had happened in Europe proper.

What makes all this difficult to evaluate, however, is the succession of cataclysmic events that followed. The toll of war and revolution in Russia was enormous. It has been estimated that between 1913 and 1921, Russian agricultural output fell by 50 percent, industrial output by 80 percent, and total national income by more than 60 percent. An interruption of this magnitude makes any projection of past trends a questionable procedure. What we can say is that, when Russia did resume her forward progress in the late 1920s, it was on the basis of a substantially altered political and economic system. State intervention had been significant in the past, but now it was totally dominant, and this domination was being exercised economically for the almost exclusive purpose of achieving the most rapid possible rate of economic growth.

We have spoken earlier of the problems of administering the Soviet system (p. 55); now we direct our attention to the growth performance in particular. The central fact here is that, despite evidences of certain inefficiencies, the Soviet Union has shown persistently high rates of growth ever since the beginning of the first Five-Year Plan in 1928.

Table 28–1 shows a comparison between U.S. and U.S.S.R. growth rates from 1913 to 1965. Comparisons of rates of growth of GNP are always extremely difficult to evaluate. In this particular case, moreover, the significance of the figures would have to be modified by our knowledge: (1) that the U.S.S.R. began at a much lower level and thus had all the advantages of coming up from behind; (2) that the periods include both World Wars I and II, when Russia suffered terrible economic and other losses; and (3) that there is evidence that in the late 1960s the Soviet rate of growth was beginning to slow down substantially. Thus, Western estimates are that Soviet growth (annual average percentage increase in real national income) fell from 6.4 percent in 1950–58 to 5.3 percent in 1958–67, to 5.0 percent in 1967–70. Soviet growth estimates show an even greater drop for the later period (though from a higher level).[3]

---

3. See Abram Bergson "Soviet Economic Perspectives: Toward a New Growth Model," *Challenge,* Vol. 17, 2 (May–June 1974), p. 24. Interestingly, Bergson feels that the Soviet Union may now be entering a new phase of its growth. Rapid growth of output combined with extraordinarily high rates of investment and capital formation may now, he believes, give way to somewhat lower output growth, but with increasing attention to consumer needs.

TABLE 28–1

COMPARATIVE GROWTH RATES OF TOTAL OUTPUT (GNP) U.S.A. AND U.S.S.R., 1913–1965

	ANNUAL AVERAGE COMPOUND GROWTH RATE	
	U.S.A.	U.S.S.R.
1913–38	2.0	2.8
1938–53	5.1	3.4
1953–65	3.3	6.1

These very rough estimates of growth show that the Soviet Union, beginning at a much lower starting level, has generally grown more rapidly than the United States during recent decades.

Source: Angus Maddison, *Economic Growth in Japan and the U.S.S.R.* (New York: W. W. Norton and Co., 1969), pp. 36, 47, 51.

Some of these points cut one way, some the other. Still, the overall conclusion is clear:

The Soviet Union has clearly achieved very rapid growth over a substantial period of time and under a very highly directed and controlled economy.

But directed and controlled in what way? *How* was this growth achieved? Or, to put it in terms of our earlier discussion, what can we say about the "Soviet model" of economic growth?

The following reading by Charles Wilber, excerpted from a longer chapter, is a systematic attempt to account for the particular aspects of Soviet growth strategy that differentiate it from our own experience, or, indeed, from that of most Western nations. Although there are always some differences of opinion, Wilber's basic points would be widely accepted by most Western experts on the Soviet economy:

The Soviet Strategy of Development

Charles K. Wilber

Strategies are ways of using resources in order to attain a given long-run objective. In the Soviet Union the overriding objective has been rapid economic development. As in market economies in wartime, all resources were mobilized and allocated to activities that furthered the attainment of the primary objective. Activities that detracted from that objective were suppressed or neglected.

The atmosphere and terminology during the 1930s was that of a wartime economy—bottlenecks, campaigns, assaults, and victories. As in wartime, mistakes were made and there was a great deal of waste. Economic criteria were often ignored and entire sectors of the economy, mainly the consumer sectors, were neglected. Yet, despite the lack of balance and other shortcomings in Soviet development, significant progress in the transformation of the Soviet economy to a modern economy was made in a very brief period of time.

The main features that distinguished Soviet industrial development strategy may be summarized as follows:

1. Industry was treated as the leading sector in the development program and investment in agriculture held to the minimum necessary to allow agriculture to provide industry with a growing marketed surplus of agricultural products and an expanding source of labor supply.

2. A very high investment (and savings) rate was maintained, because of the planners' propensity to discount the future at a low rate.

3. An unbalanced growth pattern was adopted of allocating a very large share of industrial investment to heavy industry.

Excerpted from Charles K. Wilber, "The Soviet Strategy of Development" from *The Soviet Model and Underdeveloped Countries* (Chapel Hill: University of North Carolina Press, 1969), 76–78, 83–92, 94–99, 101–4, 106–8. Reprinted by permission of the publisher.

4. In choosing among alternative productive techniques, the most advanced technology was utilized, while at the same time, the scarcest inputs—capital and skilled labor—were economized.

    (a) A mixed or dual technology was adopted. Advanced Western technology with a high capital-labor ratio was favored in the basic production processes while old-fashioned methods and techniques with a low capital-labor ratio were favored in auxiliary and subsidiary processes.

    (b) They utilized multiple shift operation and plants and equipment were typically kept in operation long after they would have been retired in the more advanced countries of the West.

    (c) Strong preference was shown for the construction of integrated, large-scale plants, specialized with respect to product and having a high fixed cost to variable cost ratio.

5. During the industrialization drive heavy emphasis was placed upon vocational and technical training to build up the stock of human capital and the factory itself was used as a major training device.

6. An import-substitution policy of international trade was adopted.

INDUSTRY AS THE LEADING SECTOR IN THE SOVIET DEVELOPMENT PROGRAM

In the Soviet Union, industry has been treated as the leading sector in the development program. Consequently, investment in agriculture has been held to the minimum necessary to allow agriculture to provide industry with food, raw materials, and labor. Gross investment in agriculture accounted for 16.1 percent of total gross investment during the period 1928–32, 12.6 percent during 1933–37, 11.4 percent during 1938–41, 12.8 percent during 1946–50, 15.5 percent during 1951–55, 17.6 percent in 1956, 16.3 percent in 1957, 15.8 percent in 1958, and 15.8 percent during the period 1959–64. In 1928, at the

AMERICAN STOCK PHOTO

Novolipetsk Iron and Metal Works. Russian industrialization from the early days on has emphasized iron and steel, capital goods, and other heavy industry.

beginning of industrialization, 49.2 percent of the net national product originated in agriculture, forestry, and fisheries. By 1958, the share of agriculture in net national product had declined to 22.1 percent. Agriculture has continuously received, therefore, a smaller share of gross investment than its share of net national product. In addition, agriculture's share in net investment has been much lower. Naum Jasny estimates that up to 1938 net investment was zero, because of the vast decline in livestock, and that half of the prewar investment in agriculture was lost during World War II.

Soviet investment in agriculture was sufficient to generate enough agricultural output to feed the growing industrial work force, to provide the required raw materials for industry, to provide for export needs, and to release the labor necessary to fill the new jobs. This enabled the modern industrial sector to be constructed. However, the Soviets probably went too far in emphasizing industry and minimizing investment in agriculture. That is, more investment in agriculture would probably have increased the growth rate of national income. At the same time, however, it should be remembered that the agricultural investment picture would look much better if the blunders of livestock collectivization and World War II had not occurred.

THE CHOICE OF AN INVESTMENT RATE

Once having made the decision to embark upon a development program, the choice of an appropriate investment rate assumes prime importance.

In the Soviet Union, the rate of gross investment increased from 12.5 percent of gross national product in 1928 to 25.9 percent in 1937 and 28.1 percent in 1955. Over fairly long periods in the past in Argentina, Canada, Germany, Norway, the United States, and the Union of South Africa, the gross investment rate exceeded 20 percent. What is distinctive about the Soviet experience is the speed at which the rate

was increased. Furthermore, in comparison with underdeveloped countries generally, investment rates over 20 percent are very high.

The reason that a high investment rate is desirable, of course, is because it rapidly increases the stock of capital in the economy. The size of the stock in any period, in turn, is a main determinant of total output in that period. If the capital-output ratio does not significantly increase, higher rates of investment will yield higher growth rates of total output.* In the Soviet Union, incremental capital-output ratios only increased, on a gross basis, from 3.53 in 1928–40 to 3.69 in 1950–58, and actually declined on a net basis from 2.76 to 2.60. No capitalist economy has combined over long periods relatively low incremental capital-output ratios with high investment rates. Kuznets has pointed out that ". . . the distinctive feature of the USSR record is that so much capital formation was possible without an increase in the capital-output ratio to uneconomically high levels."

What was the optimum rate of investment for the Soviet Union in the 1930s? There is no uniquely determinate economic solution to this question. Increasing the rate of investment today means lowering the share of consumption in gross national product (though not necessarily the absolute amount) in the present in exchange for a larger income and consumption in the future. A lower rate of investment will yield greater consumption in the present, but lower amounts in the future, than would higher rates of investment. The key to the solution, therefore, is the trade-off between present and future consumption contained in a community's social time preference function.

A central planning board cannot simply imitate the rate of investment that would emerge from individual time preferences. The social perspective of the future

---

[*We have met the concept of the capital-output ratio earlier —in the form of its reciprocal, the output-capital ratio (p. 408). If K is capital, Y is income (or output) and I is investment, the capital-output ratio is K/Y. The "incremental" (or *marginal*) capital-output ratio is $\Delta K/\Delta Y$ or $I/\Delta Y$. It was the reciprocal of this last term that we discussed in chapter 16. RTG]

and the time horizon of a community differ significantly from those of an individual. More importantly, the choice of investment rate cannot be determined independently of the choice of investment projects and technique. The decision on the investment rate is dependent on the *allocation* of investment and vice versa. In the Soviet Union particularly, the decision on allocation greatly affected the final determination of the rate of savings and investment. This problem of allocation between sectors and projects is the next aspect of the Soviet experience to be considered.

THE ALLOCATION OF INVESTMENT AND UNBALANCED GROWTH

Exponents of unbalanced growth have stressed that if a country decides to industrialize, the correct development strategy is not to seek an optimal allocation of resources at any given time nor to dissipate scarce resources by attempting to advance on all fronts simultaneously but, rather, to concentrate on a few major objectives most conducive to transforming the economy to a higher stage. Efficiency is attained in the dynamic sense of finding the most effective sequences for converting a stagnant, backward economy into one which is dynamic and modern. In other words, to be breathlessly climbing a peak in a mountain range is considered more important than standing poised on the crest of a ridge in the foothills.

There is not an infinite number of alternative investment allocation patterns. Because of complementarities and indivisibilities, each individual investment project cannot be evaluated in isolation. The construction of a steel industry requires increased coal mining and investment in steel-using industries.

". . . problems of economic planning seem to acquire a resemblance to the problems of military strategy, where in practice the choice lies between a relatively small number of plans, which have in the main to be treated and chosen between as organic wholes,

and which for a variety of reasons do not easily permit of intermediate combinations. The situation will demand a concentration of forces round a few main objectives, and not a dispersion of resources over a very wide range.''†

The Soviet Union pursued a "shock" strategy of bottlenecks successively created and resolved. Thus, Soviet planning concentrated on certain key branches in each plan to overcome particular bottlenecks. Scarce capital and managerial talent were then concentrated on these key targets. This gave Soviet planning its peculiar nature of planning by "campaigning." During the first Five-Year Plan the main target was heavy industry with particular emphasis on machine building. During the second and third Five-Year Plans the target was again heavy industry with metallurgy, machine building, fuel, energetics, and chemicals singled out for emphasis. This emphasis on key branches yielded high growth rates. The average annual rates of growth in Soviet heavy industry between 1928/29 and 1937 were 18.9 percent for machinery, 18.5 percent for iron and steel, 14.6 percent for coal, 11.7 percent for petroleum products, 22.8 percent for electric power, and 17.8 percent for all heavy industry. Sectors which did not contribute directly to further growth (consumption) were neglected while sectors which enhanced growth (capital goods) were emphasized.

Growth tempos such as these caused acute shortages and strains. The industrial bottlenecks which appeared then became the new targets. This is unbalanced growth with a vengeance. However, economic planning of the type used by the Soviet Union during the industrialization period, and by extension in less developed countries today, is a relatively crude affair. "Campaigns," with their ensuing bottlenecks, substitute for the profit motive in keeping the planning bureaucracy on its toes.

---

†Maurice Dobb, *Soviet Economic Development Since 1917* (London: Routledge & Kegan Paul, 1960), p. 6.

". . . the entire rationale of the Soviet 'campaign' approach to economic planning rests upon . . . the need to stimulate not only the executants but also the controllers . . . Campaigns are among other things, a means of goading the goaders, of mobilizing the controllers, of providing success indicators for officials at all levels.

". . . Hence the vital role of campaigns as controller mobilizers. Hence the value of bottlenecks as stimulators to effort."‡

This does not imply that the Soviets deliberately created bottlenecks or that they understood the meaning of unbalanced growth. Rather, the bottlenecks and unbalanced growth were necessary byproducts of the high growth tempos that the planners adopted.

As an economy becomes more sophisticated, "campaign" planning becomes less appropriate. The number of products multiply and "balance" becomes more important. Since structural change is slower, and firms and industries are operating closer to equilibrium, marginal calculations become more feasible. This seems to be the present situation of the economy of the Soviet Union. Failure to pull up lagging sectors, particularly agriculture, and to develop more sophisticated planning methods is causing the Soviets severe problems and slowing their growth tempo.

CHOICE OF TECHNOLOGY AND SOVIET DEVELOPMENT STRATEGY

Another feature of Soviet industrial strategy involves choice of technology in production. In Soviet literature this problem resolved into a question of whether capital should be devoted to large-scale units using

---

‡Alec Nove, *The Soviet Economy* (New York: Frederick A. Praeger, 1961), p. 292. Also, see Gregory Grossman, "Soviet Growth: Routine, Inertia and Pressure," *American Economic Review* 50 (May 1960): 62–72. Preplanned coordination of investment projects through central planning does not conflict with unbalanced growth and "campaigns." Unbalanced growth is a strategy designed to obtain a dynamic equilibrium through time, and "campaigns" are a means of implementing the plans.

advanced and expensive technology or to smaller-scale enterprises using simple tools and employing relatively more workers. It is often argued in Western economic writings that since, practically by definition, there is a shortage of capital and a surplus of labor in less developed countries, labor-intensive techniques should be used wherever possible so as to conserve on capital and provide as much employment as possible.

Dual Technology

Soviet development policy has been aware of this conflict between requirements of progress and factor endowment and has dealt with it by adopting the strategy of a "dual technology." On the one hand, in the key industries, they utilized to the maximum the advantage of borrowing the most advanced technologies developed in economies with very different factor endowments. On the other hand, they allowed for these differences by utilizing manual labor in auxiliary operations and by aiming at high performance rates per unit of capital instead of per man. In this fashion they obtained the best of two worlds and achieved the overall effect of saving capital.

In many Soviet plants it is common to find the most advanced capital equipment in the basic processes and, at the same time, the most primitive labor-intensive methods in maintenance, intra-plant transport, and materials handling. In such enterprises as the Gorky Automotive Plant, which was a direct copy of the Ford River Rouge plant, they allowed for their lower level of labor skills by redesigning job descriptions so that each worker performed fewer and simpler tasks. Thus, the Soviets obtained the advantages of advanced technology, conserved scarce capital in auxiliary operations that did not limit output, and utilized their relatively abundant unskilled labor.

Multi-Shift Operation

Another way capital was used intensively was by multi-shift operation of plants. In both the prewar and postwar periods, many Soviet industrial plants operated on a two-shift basis. Three-shift operation, although introduced in manufacturing plants in the early 1930s, has been discarded except in those industries where the technology demands it. It was soon discovered that the third shift was needed for repairs, clean up, and the production of deficit parts. Multi-shift operation reached a peak in the Soviet Union in 1932 when the shift coefficient (the ratio of total man-days worked to those in the main shift) reached 1.73. It declined slightly in the mid-1930s. When figures were next published in 1959 the coefficient for all industry had declined to 1.55. These figures may be compared with figures for United States manufacturing in 1959–60 of 1.30. In England and leading European industrial countries the ratio is even lower. It is clear that Soviet practice regarding multi-shift operation of her plants deviated from the pattern in the United States and other advanced Western countries.

The difference in multi-shift operations stems partly from the relative scarcity of capital in the Soviet Union and the concern of Soviet planners to minimize the use of capital. With labor and output measured as flows and capital as a stock, two-shift operation, for example, reduces the capital-labor ratio by one-half. If capital is also measured as a flow of services to take account of more rapid physical wear and tear under multi-shift operation the reduction would be somewhat less. As a consequence of multi-shift operation the Soviets have been able to adapt a more advanced technology with a higher capital-labor ratio than would have been possible with single shift operations. Thus, the benefits of modern technology were reaped while at the same time minimizing the demand for capital, which is the scarce factor.

The Soviets have also used another means to obtain this result. While progressively adding the newest capital equipment they have continued to operate obsolescent plants far beyond the time possible in a competitive market system. Here again, within limits, the factor endowment of the Soviet Union was taken into consideration.

Plant Scale and Design

Another consideration regarding Soviet choice of technique concerns the scale and design of fixed plants. The Soviets exhibited a strong preference for large-scale, integrated plants with high fixed-to-variable cost ratios and specialized with respect to product. This emphasis upon size has often been pointed to by Western economists as an apt illustration of the irrationality of Soviet planning. In a number of instances this was undoubtedly the case. Indeed, the Soviet leadership itself became concerned with wastes involved and roundly condemned the "gigantomania" of the early 1930s.

In addition to building large plants, the Soviets tended to build highly integrated plants. During the early stages of the Soviet industrialization drive in the late 1920s and early 1930s, the Soviet economy lacked the well-developed system of separate supplier plants necessary to support a complex, highly specialized industrial economy. The transport system was overloaded, as well, and the delivery of parts or materials from other plants could not be relied upon. Under such circumstances new plants, if they were to operate successfully, had to be constructed along highly integrated, less specialized lines than was originally intended by Soviet planners. In the automotive industry, for example, the major plants included every process from the pouring of metal to shipping the finished product. They also manufactured repair parts for machine tools and even made their own special tools and equipment in the absence of other suppliers.

THE ROLE OF VOCATIONAL AND TECHNICAL TRAINING IN THE FORMATION OF HUMAN CAPITAL

A basic feature of Soviet development strategy is the stress upon vocational and technical training and the use of the factory itself in the educational process. From the outset of the industrialization drive the Soviets have indicated a profound appreciation of the importance of human capital in the development

TABLE A

U.S.S.R., 1928–1959, AND U.S.A., 1926–1958: NUMBER OF GRADUATES OF HIGHER EDUCATIONAL ESTABLISHMENTS

FIELD	U.S.S.R.	U.S.A.	U.S.S.R. AS PERCENT OF U.S.A.
Engineers	1,117,800	620,300	180.0
Science majors	430,000	704,400	61.0
Medical doctors	420,000	181,700	231.2
Agricultural specialists	389,200	166,400	233.9
Sum of above fields	2,357,000	1,672,800	140.9
Humanities, social sciences, etc.	1,772,300	5,198,600	34.1
All fields	4,129,300	6,871,400	60.1

Source: Warren W. Eason, "Labor Force," in *Economic Trends in the Soviet Union,* eds. Abram Bergson and Simon Kuznets (Cambridge: Harvard University Press, 1963), p. 63.

process and have shown a willingness to commit substantial sums and effort to build up not only a skilled labor force but also professionals able to lead and direct the industrial effort.

Most of the training was on-the-job in character, but numerous schools known as F.Z.U. (factory and work apprentices' schools) were opened at the factories to train apprentices for skilled trades. During the first Five-Year Plan the F.Z.U. schools trained over 450 thousand skilled workers. Each year since the first Five-Year Plan about 100 thousand skilled workers have been trained through these factory apprentice schools. In addition, an annual average of 2.5 million workers and employees between 1940 and 1959 were taught new trades and specialities on the job, and an additional 5.0 million were trained to improve their skills each year. Also, many workers learned their "three R's" in factory-run evening schools.

In the Soviet Union, formal education has been devoted principally to those subjects most amenable to classroom methods of instruction and which are considered to be especially important for economic development. The natural sciences and engineering have been particularly emphasized. Night schools for adults have been extensively used to train technicians. Table A summarizes the Soviet emphasis on development oriented subjects at the higher educational level.

THE ROLE OF INTERNATIONAL TRADE

The final question that arises in a discussion of development strategy is the role of international trade in the Soviet model. Foreign trade in the Soviet Union has always been subordinated to the requirements of economic development and central planning. It is seen as a means to an end—the end being the attainment of needed imports.

Both political and economic considerations shaped Soviet trade policy. The Soviet Union undoubtedly would have preferred to increase its imports through long-term credits but in the world situation of the 1930s was unable to do so. A high degree of self-sufficiency was deliberately pursued because of fear (rightly or wrongly) of further foreign attack.

Viewed from static equilibrium analysis the Soviet strategy of import substitution—substituting higher cost domestic production for imports—led to a misallocation of resources and a reduction in real national income. However, if the Soviet policy of allocating investment to import-replacing industries instead of to export-oriented industries is viewed dynamically, it is possible that this policy increased the rate of growth enough to cover any static allocation losses. In the case of the Soviet Union, the import-replacing industries were the heavy capital-goods industries and the export-oriented industries were in nondurable consumer goods, wood products, and agriculture.

During the first Five-Year Plan the Soviet Union exported relatively large quantities of agricultural products, consumer goods, and wood products in return for capital goods that enabled them to expand their import-replacing industries. While the Soviet Union probably pushed its import-substitution policy too far, there is no reason why other countries must pursue the strategy fo the same *degree*. International trade can certainly alleviate some of the difficulties of economic development. Trade is particularly important for smaller countries because it can enable them to develop without establishing the entire range of modern industry. But, at a minimum, industrialization in those areas of *potential* comparative advantage seems necessary. Comparative advantage shifts over time with changes in relative development patterns between countries. This makes static equilibrium analysis inapplicable in the context of economic development.

It is necessary in ending this chapter on Soviet development strategy to emphasize again that the policies comprising this strategy have application mainly to a backward economy trying to achieve the one overriding goal of economic development. The methods are basically those of a war economy. As such, when the economy has reached some level of sophistication, the time for war economy methods has passed. The required economic strategy then changes from one of maximum concentration of available resources on a few main goals towards successively greater dispersion.   □

THE JAPANESE ECONOMIC "MIRACLE"

During the period after the end of the Marshall Plan in the early 1950s, it became common to discuss various economic "miracles" in Western Europe: the very rapid growth of West Germany, then of Italy, then of France. The persistent rapid growth of the Soviet Union, which we have just discussed, was also very much noted. It was actually only a bit later that economists began to notice that the real economic "miracle" hadn't taken place in Europe at all, but in Asia. From 1950 to 1960, Japan had the highest rate of growth of any major industrial nation in the world. Not only did she outmatch the Soviet Union, but her growth was substantially higher even than that of the "miracle" countries of Western Europe: twice that of France, 40 percent higher than that of Italy, and 25 percent higher than that of West Germany. Indeed, by the 1970s Japan had become the third-ranking industrial producer in the world.

This phenomenal rate of growth—often averaging around 10 percent per year in *real* GNP—clearly could not have taken place without preparation. Since the reading below focuses primarily on Japan's postwar experience, let us say just a few words about the earlier Japanese development that laid the groundwork for what followed.

The key dates in this earlier history are probably 1853 and 1868—the former representing the arrival of Commodore Perry and the opening of Japan to Western culture and influence, the latter representing the political revolution that led to the restoration of the emperor (Emperor Meiji) and to the installation of a number of vigorous samurai-bureaucrats in government who began promoting modern-style Western growth. As in the case of the British Industrial Revolution (pp. 392–96), one cannot stress discontinuities too much—there is increasing evidence of economic progress in the pre-Meiji (Tokugawa) period, nor was Japan totally closed off from Western ideas before Perry's visit. Still the last half, and especially the last quarter, of the nineteenth century, does seem a particularly decisive period in Japan's development. Something very much like a take-off seems to have occurred at this time.

Now the Japanese model necessarily shows some resemblances to the Soviet model that we have been analyzing, if only because of the similar objective of increasing the growth rate. Thus, both countries had to find some way to raise the rate of investment so as to accelerate capital formation. Both countries had to introduce new technologies and, since both countries were economically backward during the nineteenth century, they were each heavily reliant on foreign technological inventions and innovations. Furthermore, since not everything could be done at once, both countries exhibited dualistic economies —i.e., the existence of both modern capital-intensive methods and traditional labor-intensive methods side by side over long periods of time.

Still, the Japanese experience was affected by the fact that fundamental conditions were in many ways quite different from those of Russia. Japan was very densely populated even in the nineteenth century; unlike Russia, she was highly deficient in natural resources, including many resources necessary for modern industrial growth; and, finally, her political "revolution" was not so drastic as that of the Russians in 1917. These differences probably account for the following aspects of the Japanese model that differentiate it from that of the Soviet Union.

Agriculture

Although the Japanese relied, as did the Russians, for agriculture to provide support for the industrial sector, there was no vast institutional reorganization of agriculture in Japan comparable to collectivization in the late 1920s and 1930s in the Soviet Union. The Russian picture is one of a heavy reorganization of agriculture, tremendous exactions from the agricultural sector to support industrial development, and stagnant agricultural productivity until fairly recent years. Japan, by contrast, appears to have secured at least moderate increases in agricultural output throughout the key period of the last quarter of the nineteenth century. Some commentators believe that it was such progress in the traditional sectors of the Japanese economy that made possible the "initial establishment and subsequent development of the modern economy."[4] Given her heavy population density, it is doubtful whether Japan could have subjected agriculture to quite such abusive treatment as did the Russians in the late 1920s and 1930s and still achieved general economic development.

International Trade

If Japan was somewhat more dependent on the traditional sector than the Russians, she was certainly substantially more dependent on international trade. While the Russian experience in the 1930s involved increasing isolation from the rest of the world, the Japanese experience involved an "invasion" of foreign markets to secure the exports necessary to pay for the vital raw material and industrial imports without which modern growth could not take place. Even with her extraordinary export efforts, Japan's history in the nineteenth and twentieth centuries was dotted with balance-of-payments crises because of her exceptional need for foreign imports (reflecting, in part, the deficiencies in natural resource endowment mentioned earlier).[5] Initiative in seeking foreign markets for silk and textiles in the nineteenth century, and for every conceivable product in recent times, has undoubtedly been a highly significant feature of the Japanese achievement.

---

4. Kazuschi Ohkawa and Henry Rosovsky, "A Century of Japanese Economic Growth," in *The State and Economic Enterprise in Japan,* ed. William W. Lockwood (Princeton, N.J.: Princeton University Press, 1965), p. 68. It should be noted, however, that the *degree* of Japan's progress in agriculture in this period is still a subject for debate among historians.

5. A new balance-of-payments crisis was looming for Japan in 1974 as the prices of her oil imports tripled. Indeed, Japan's dependence on imported oil (99.7 percent of her consumption in 1972) is likely to have, at least, some restrictive impact on her long-run growth prospects.

LOS ANGELES TIMES PHOTO

An assembly line at Nissan Motor Co., Oppama, Japan. The ability of the Japanese to capture a significant share of world export markets has been a major factor in postwar Japanese growth.

Role of the State

Finally, we must mention the quite different political situation, affecting virtually every aspect of the development process. While the Soviet picture is one of almost total State domination of the earlier phases of industrialization, the Japanese picture is quite mixed. The Japanese state did, of course, stimulate capital formation, but there was also substantial private saving and investment, encouraged in the nineteenth century by an extremely unequal distribution of income and also by historically low consumption patterns. More generally, the relationship of the Japanese State and private business, and especially the large, oligopolistic *Zaibatsu*—huge firms like Mitsubishi, Mitsui, and Sumitomo, with interests in a great variety of financial and industrial enterprises—has been very involved and complex. In the early Japanese industrialization effort, the government would in some cases act as innovator in a particular industry, establishing new enterprises that were subsequently turned over to large private capitalistic firms. In sum, as compared to the Soviet picture of opposition between private and public institutions, the Japanese model has involved more of a cooperative or partnership arrangement.

With these background comments in mind, let us turn to Japan's exceptional achievements in the postwar period.

Japan's Economic Future

Henry Rosovsky

From the mid-1950s to the present, Japan not only developed much more rapidly than at any other time in her history but also did better than any other comparable economy. Why? No one "secret" exists, and the real factors are intertwined in necessarily complicated relationships. Nevertheless, the basic elements in Japan's so-called economic miracle can be identified.

ECONOMIC GROWTH, 1950–1970

Economists frequently use the concept of the aggregate production function, which states that the growth rate of output is related to the growth rates of the conventional inputs: labor and capital. In specific cases the relationship between inputs and output varies both in time and internationally. Two countries—or one country at different historical periods—may have identical rates of growth of inputs and very different rates of growth of aggregate output. This difference is usually called "the residual,"[*] and its existence has generally been ascribed to technological progress, to the possibilities of exploiting economies of scale, and to qualitative improvements in inputs. The point is that in postwar Japan—since the 1950s—the residual has been growing at an unprecedented rate; to put it in somewhat different words, the Japanese have succeeded in squeezing more output out of every unit of input than at any other time in their modern development. The rest of the world has not been able to match these results. Why?

[*The *residual* is roughly the same thing as our *increased output per unit of input*. Another term frequently used in this connection is *increased factor productivity*. RTG]

Excerpted from Henry Rosovsky, "Japan's Economic Future," *Challenge*, Vol. 16, No. 3 (July–August 1973) pp. 6–17. Reprinted with permission of the publisher.

Surely a key element must be the massive inflow of foreign technology, which in the 18 years between 1950 and 1968 represented about 10,000 contracts and payments in excess of $1.4 billion. These inflows permitted the modernization of old and the creation of new industries under extremely favorable conditions. Foreign technology was, in almost all instances, superior to domestic types; and until recently it was cheap. Furthermore, Japanese enterprise raised the adaptation of foreign methods to a fine art through the development of what has been called "improvement engineering." This refers to systematic attempts at improving imported technology. It is largely an activity of "carefully taking apart and putting together a little better." I have been told by Japanese businessmen that they have frequently succeeded in running a foreign process at up to 130 percent of rated capacity simply by making a set of minor—though carefully considered—improvements.

The advantages inherent in acquiring advanced technology are not a Japanese monopoly, and one has to ask why they were so successful. In part, it can be argued that the opportunities were obvious and plentiful in a semideveloped economy recently devastated by war and out of contact with more advanced countries for over ten years. But this was almost equally true for most Western European economies.

A more distinctive Japanese feature is the level and growth of investment. In this area Japan has topped all competitors. During the 1950s and 1960s, fixed capital formation has averaged well over 30 percent of GNP, with most of this going into private productive investment embodying recent technological improvements. (Residential housing accounted for only a very small share of this total.) Other countries produced far less impressive figures: for comparable periods, U.S. investment shares were 17 percent; in France they were 19 percent; and in West Germany, 24 percent.

What made it possible for such a large share of GNP to be invested in an essentially free-market economy? One factor was the high return obtainable from private investment. Capital-output ratios, especially in those industries which imported technology, tended to decline, leading to more output per unit of capital input. Giving the labor force more and better equipment also raised output per worker, but luckily for entrepreneurs this did not lead to a comparable rise in wages. During the fifties worker productivity rose more than wages; for most of the sixties productivity has kept pace with wage increases. In European countries as well as in the United States, wage increases outstripped worker productivity gains in this period.

The labor situation remained unusually favorable in Japan until the late 1960s. Real strikes—i.e., lengthy work stoppages—were almost unknown, and the national unions continued to dissipate their energies on problems of foreign policy. On the shop floor, where it counted, the employer dealt with docile and cooperative enterprise unions. Labor supply remained elastic owing to the large reservoir of able, educated workers still available in agriculture and in assorted pockets of traditional underemployment. All this kept cost pressures under control while labor productivity continued to rise at about 9 percent per year in the aggregate—another record.

Undoubtedly, the government deserves considerable credit for Japan's high growth. It taxed moderately—20 percent of GNP, as opposed to 27 percent in the United States and 35 percent in the United Kingdom—supported growth industries by controlling foreign exchange allocations and guiding the inflow of technology, and ultimately guaranteed the availability of industrial bank credit through the Bank of Japan. Business and government worked hand in hand toward the common objective of rapid economic growth; sometimes it was hard to know where one entity began and the other left off. Of course the fact that defense expenditures were less than 1 percent of GNP helped both government and business. It is perhaps worth recalling that Japanese defense was so inexpensive because of American guarantees.

The public also supported the all-out growth effort primarily by supplying the savings needed to finance the enormous investments. In the 1960s personal savings were about 20 percent of disposable income, compared with 12 percent in West Germany and 7 percent in the United States. Why and how the Japanese manage to be so frugal is a frequently debated issue among social scientists. Some of the most crucial factors may be repeated here. The individual Japanese is largely responsible for his own welfare—clearly this is related to the low level of government expenditures—and he must provide for education, retirement, and "rainy day" emergencies. Welfare is, as yet, private; and this heightens the incentive to save in order to make up for the inadequacies of Japan's social security system. It is also true that personal income has been rising rapidly during the past 20 years; and, although consumption expenditures have also risen, there has been a time lag of only one to two years. In other words, the Japanese have been rather conservative consumers, and the lag alone will assure a large and growing pool of savings.

Japan's postwar growth has also been greatly supported by an expansion of exports, running at about 15 percent per year, which is more than twice the rate of expansion of world trade. Again, I think the absorption of new technology is relevant in explaining this phenomenon. Foreign customers purchased a rising proportion of Japanese goods because these represented good buys in terms of price and quality. And indeed, while domestic consumer prices rose over 50 percent in the decade of the 1960s, export prices for many commodities declined and in the aggregate remained almost stable. The incongruity between domestic and export prices is complicated, but one reason undoubtedly is the fact that Japanese exports have increasingly concentrated on those commodities in which cost-reducing technological progress has made its largest contributions. Obviously the government has also had a lot to do with building up these strong and increasingly competitive export industries through its explicit methods of preferential credit rationing, tax exemptions, extraordinary depreciation allowances, readier

permission to import know-how and, at times, tight protection against foreign imports.

We should also keep in mind that the past 20 years created an especially congenial climate for trade expansion. Japan's largest customer, the United States, espoused free trade, and there was little difficulty in penetrating markets in South and Southeast Asia and in Latin America.

Finally, a word about the human element in Japan's recent success story. Thus far we have concentrated on relatively "pure" economic factors. Somehow account has to be taken of the tremendous burst of entrepreneurial energy in postwar Japan. The Japanese have a long history of entrepreneurial achievements; throughout this century they have been strong, imaginative, and sometimes ruthless competitors. I am convinced, however, that there was something special about the postwar era—and so are some very knowledgeable Japanese. World War II destroyed Japan's "proper order of things," and this may be the exceptional ingredient which favored entrepreneurship. One hundred years ago, the Meiji Restoration destroyed the Tokugawa system and liberated the long-pent-up energies of all classes. What happened after that is history: Japan became the only non-Western nation to achieve modern economic growth. With time, however, the new order developed rigidities, especially from the point of view of new enterprise. New ventures and ideas came to be judged not only in terms of their intrinsic merit but also in terms of who made the suggestion, what his connections were, where he had been to school, and so forth. These rigidities were wiped away when the World War II establishment was displaced. For a time, talent and ability counted more than age, university degrees from the right schools, and family or banking connections. A new and vital entrepreneurial class emerged, and it has served Japan brilliantly ever since.

THE 1970s

Next, we should consider the meaning of what took place during the last 20 years. What are the implications for the future—especially for this decade? Were these years a specific growth phase and the consequence of transitory economic opportunities, or do they represent a style of growth that will maintain itself for the next 30 years?

Let us begin with the inflow and absorption of foreign technology. There seems to be general agreement on the following points: that in the 1950s and 1960s Japan lagged behind the technological leaders (primarily the United States and, to a lesser extent, West Germany); that since the mid-1960s this technological gap has been rapidly growing smaller; and that Japanese business is now making great efforts through increased R&D expenditures and similar devices to develop its own advanced technology.

The facts have recently been thoroughly analyzed by James Abegglen in his *Business Strategies for Japan* (1970). He notes that since 1958 approximately 10 percent of total manufacturing in Japan has been carried out using foreign technology. However, if only the modern sectors are considered, the dependency on foreign technology would rise to 25 to 30 percent. Although the number of technical agreements has continued to increase constantly, "the proportion of agreements representing technology new to Japan and previously unlicensed is dropping steadily, from 70 percent in 1961 to only one-third in 1966."

It seems to me that the long-run implications of the present situation are frequently misunderstood. There are many reasons for believing that Japan will, in the coming decades, create numerous significant and profitable technological advances. No doubt Japan will also continue to avail herself of progress made elsewhere. There is, however, a fundamental difference between closing a gap (or eliminating a lag) and depending on the extension of a domestic or foreign technological frontier. In the former case one can—if other conditions are right—proceed at great speed. Gains can accrue in a relatively short time. In the latter case, one may face lengthy bottlenecks. The technological frontier is inevitably surrounded by uncertainties, hesitations, and false starts; soon an element of easy success in Japanese development may disappear.

Let us turn our attention now from technology and the productivity of capital to labor, wages, and employment. Japan's current position has frequently been described as "second and fourteenth": the second largest GNP in the capitalist world and number fourteen from the top in income per capita. Low income per capita in the aggregate is a direct consequence of low productivity in certain backward sectors, primarily agriculture, forestry, fisheries, service industries, and small and medium-sized enterprises. However, a growing body of evidence indicates that certain changes are now discernible within the long-established dual structure—the gap created by wages and productivity in the modern, or advanced, sectors rising more rapidly than in the traditional, or backward, sectors. These changes began in the first half of the 1960s. A tendency toward both narrowed wage differentials and small labor supply elasticities has been widely noted. In 1967, for the first time since World War II, the ratio of labor demand to supply (active openings/active application job seekers) exceeded 1.00. (In 1959 the ratio was 0.44.) And the Japanese government estimates that from 1970 to 1980 the working-age population will rise by only 1 percent per year. Since 1967 wage differentials have continued to narrow, though at a somewhat slower pace.

Productivity differentials, however, present a very different picture: The gap between advanced and backward sectors is still there, and it is still widening. This sharp contrast in wage and productivity gaps is a new phenomenon of the late 1960s, and its consequences must be taken into account in evaluating Japan's economic future. Two problems, in particular, require attention: wage-income-price relations, and patterns of labor shift.

The wage-income-price relations of Japan, up to the present, differ fundamentally from those of other advanced countries. In Western Europe and the United States, cost-push or inflationary wage increases have generally been recognized as one of the primary causes of rising prices. This has not been true in Japan, where the causes of inflation are structural. In the past—until the early 1960s—the dual structure meant that low-productivity sectors also paid low wages; and the prices of their goods and services remained relatively low, though as a trend they were slowly rising. Now the situation has changed. Labor shortages are reducing wage differentials without affecting productivity levels. The persistent strong demand for the output of the more backward sectors—they supply much of the food and many other daily needs—has caused their prices to rise. This is the mechanism of Japan's inflation in the 1960s and today: it is a new version of the dual structure.

The transfer of workers from less to more productive occupations has as yet been unaffected by the new dual structure. Higher wages are required to get the needed numbers, but the ever-rising productivity attainable in modern industry has kept demand strong. Net outflows of labor continue unabated, despite rising prices, wages, and incomes in agriculture and other traditional sectors.

So much for the current situation. What of the future? This is the crucial question. No easy answer is possible, but one can suggest what appears to be a distinct possibility. On the one hand, modern industry will continue to require a large number of workers. On the other hand, the labor supply will be less plentiful, and the pressure for rising wages emanating in backward sectors should be powerful. If this is combined with more limited technological opportunities in the coming decade, the appearance of cost-push sometime during the 1970s is not just conceivable: it is highly likely.

The reaction of organized labor to this possible situation should also be considered. Until now the Japanese worker has done well. His real wages have increased despite inflation, and individually and collectively he has had a somewhat superficial sweetheart relationship with his bosses—at the plant level. Yet one may have doubts about the future. Management has shown little resistance to sizable wage increases largely because these were more than matched by gains in productivity. But will management not be tempted to resist if it becomes more difficult to raise productivity levels? If this happens, if prices continue to go up, if labor shortages still exist, we can safely assume more severe and open worker-management conflict in the 1970s.

Foreign trade is another area in which changes cannot be excluded, although these are always difficult to predict. As a trend, Japan's share in world trade has more than doubled between 1955 and 1970, and plans for the future remain very ambitious.

Can this great expansion continue beyond the 1970s? Let us briefly dwell on some of the straws in the wind. Japan's export capability depends not only on her prices but also on world prices. Should cost-push develop in the 1970s, it stands to reason that export prices will not escape this pressure, and

no one can argue that this is a competitive advantage in world markets.

This is all the more dangerous because a rise in protectionist sentiment is in evidence in many parts of the world. Talk of Japanese dumping is more frequent, and various industries are seeking relief from foreign competition. If the United States adopts quotas, tariffs, and other restrictions, this will undoubtedly hurt Japan's trade account. In Asia also there is increasing nervousness about Japanese economic and political intentions, usually expressed as a fear of "domination." Perhaps the Japanese will reach 18 percent of the American and 35 percent of the Asian market, but it is also likely that the attempt will generate strong resistance.

CHANGING PRIORITIES

I have tried to suggest that some of the very favorable factors in Japanese growth may be transitory. Now I should like briefly to consider the likelihood and consequences of new socioeconomic priorities.

A recent article in the influential *Japan Economic Journal* (May 1970) stated:

The Japanese economy has passed the time when it should be satisfied only with the expansion of gross national product. It, instead, has entered the state in which it should pay closer attention to the level and distribution of stocks.

Environmental improvement based on social investments is the principal theme in this stage.

By now this has become a familiar refrain, and anyone concerned with Japan will be familiar with criticisms of "growth at any cost," *kogai* (public nuisances), and assorted horror stories concerning pollution. To understand the problem, one needs only to know that Japan has the largest per area gross national product in the world. More economic activity takes place in less space than in any other country, and the consequences in terms of noise, water, and air pollution are not hard to imagine.

Japan also suffers from a deficiency in social security. The percentage ratio of social security payments to national income was 6.2 in 1966, and it has hardly risen since then. Comparative ratios were 7.6 percent in the United States, 13.8 percent in Great Britain, 19.9 percent in West Germany, 19.2 percent in France, and 15.0 percent in Italy.

A higher ratio of public investments, badly needed at this time, has in the past been vigorously and successfully resisted by a powerful private sector. Given the fact that sources for financing capital formation are limited, intensified social investments compete with business expansion plans, and leading enterprisers have used their considerable influence within the government to minimize the impact of desirable social policies on their affairs. Thus far, obvious steps like increased interest rates or higher corporate taxation have been successfully avoided despite much lip service by business and government leaders in favor of improving the quality of life. Since the 1950s, Japan has been not only a businessman's economic paradise: It has been an economic *and* political paradise; and therein lies the problem. But we should also remember that the Japanese are good at institution building, and what is needed now is some national machinery that could reach a new consensus concerning overall investment allocations. Presumably the voices of all the citizens—labor, capital, farmers, small business, and so forth—would be heard.

There are, of course, problems of a more narrow economic character associated with the trade-off between public and private expenditures. Shifting resources from private to public capital formation may lower the output effect of these expenditures because the capital-output ratio is generally higher for social overhead investments.

Undoubtedly these trade-offs have been stated in naïve form. An improvement of the social overhead capital stock should raise the efficiency of private investment. Other types of social expenditures may favorably affect labor force quality. Offsetting possibilities, however, are not likely to change the net trade-offs: the choice of the future lies in curbing either private investment or private consumption. It is this latter alternative that is especially difficult to imagine as Japanese policy, for it would entail asking the people to make consumption sacrifices while their income per capita was still low. This is just the time when desires for more and better consumption are great—and they are growing greater. Japan is on the threshold of becoming a mass consumption society, which means a time when no politician—in or out of office—will advocate a large dose of austerity on behalf of the public good.

THE FUTURE

Toward the end of the 1970s, for reasons already presented, I foresee a slowdown in the rate of growth of Japan's national product. By the end of this decade it is likely that Japan's rate of growth of aggregate output will have fallen from its postwar rate of 10 percent to somewhere in the neighborhood of 6.5 percent. . . .

With the perspective of history, we can say that in the nineteenth century Japan experienced initial modern economic growth, and that the period 1900 to 1965 represented a much bigger step, which I would label "the leap toward a semideveloped state." These were the years of the great private investment spurts and trend acceleration (in the sense that the rate of growth of aggregate output climbed to ever higher levels). For reasons already indicated, I believe this phase to have ended at about the present time. The easy availability of both technology and labor is a less certain asset from now on. National priorities may also be redirected. For these reasons I am inclined to call Japan's next long phase of growth "the movement from semidevelopment to economic maturity."

These prognostications can in no way be considered pessimistic. Compared with that of other advanced countries, Japan's growth will still be rapid during the coming 15 or 20 years; only the gap may become somewhat smaller. . . . If the rate of growth is reduced for the right reasons, Japan may not surpass the West in aggregate income by the year 2000. It may, however, surpass it in aggregate happiness, and this might yet be the real meaning of the "Japanese Century" when it arrives.

Will it actually happen? There is some cause for optimism. For a number of reasons I think that the Japanese have a better chance of achieving an intelligent and rational industrial order than many other democratic countries. The level of consensus in the society is still impressive, central government is strong, and the nation has frequently demonstrated a social capability to make basic changes. And yet, the final outcome is not all obvious. Prime Minister Tanaka appears committed to a policy of maintaining the very high rates of growth while simultaneously raising welfare levels and improving the quality of life. This may prove to be a very difficult task that carries with it the serious danger of a greater and more pervasive inflation. Furthermore, one wonders whether the neglect of the social aspects of growth has not become a habit of the party in power: in other words, at the margin will choices inevitably favor more growth? As a student of Japan's past I hope for and would welcome a redirection of priorities toward social welfare and improved quality of life, because these new targets will bring about a more stable Japan, capable of more intelligent leadership in Asia.   □

CANADA IN A WORLD OF SHORTAGES

Professor Rosovsky's article on Japan was published in 1973, before the impact of the energy crisis was fully known. Japan, with her extraordinarily weak natural resource base, can expect shortages of energy and raw materials to have unfavorable effects on her balance of payments and rate of economic growth.[6] By the same token, shortages have created new opportunities for Canada, a nation "richer in raw materials in relation to its current requirements than any other industrialized nation."[7] Indeed, what has sometimes worried Canadians in the past—their important role as an exporter of raw materials—may now become their greatest asset.

The Canadian economy appears small compared to that of the United States, but it is actually a substantial economy by world standards and, in 1969, was the sixth largest participant in world trade. The role of trade, and especially the trade in what are called *staples,* goes far back into Canadian history. Staples are commodities with a large natural resource content that are in international demand and can bear the transport charges involved in international trade. Part of the story of Canadian economic development can be told in terms of the successive development of staples and their exploitation for the world market. In the seventeenth and eighteenth centuries, it was fish, and later the expanding fur trade, that brought Canada into world markets. In the nineteenth century, it was timber and other lumber products, and then the great expansion of foodstuff exports, especially wheat but also meat and dairy products. In the twentieth century were added a number of mineral products, whose production expanded greatly just after World War II. Before the late 1940s, it seemed that Canadian development might be limited by energy shortages, but discoveries of natural gas and oil in the prairies drastically altered this situation.[8] Canada is now a major producer not only of petroleum and natural gas but also of important industrial metals—copper, nickel, gold, and zinc.

This development of staples is, of course, only part of the story. For along with the development of her natural resources, Canada has long followed a policy of encouraging manufacturing. The expansion of the staples themselves has led to large investments in processing facilities. Thus, the mining industry not only required heavy capital investments but stimulated the growth of smelting and refining capacity, petro-chemical plants, and the like. Transportation and other service activities were required to move the commodities east and west and north and south. In total, in Canada as in all developed economies, secondary (manufacturing and construction) and tertiary (public utility, government, and service) industries far outweigh the primary industries (agriculture and mining), both in value of output and in employment.

Thus, we are dealing with a nation that has experienced all-around, balanced growth during the past two centuries, not simply development in one dimension. Still, the particular feature that marks Canada off in the mid-1970s (and especially as compared to her virtual opposite, Japan) is her rich and varied resource base. The potential consequences of this special position are suggested in the following reading.

---

6. Thus, predictions for Japan in 1974 were for a growth in real GNP falling from over 10 percent in 1973 to under 2 percent in 1974, a balance-of-payments deficit running to several billion dollars on current account, and a rate of inflation of 20 percent for the year. Interestingly, however, despite these shocks some Japanese businessmen were predicting a return to at least 7 percent real growth by 1975. In view of the great flexibility and capacity to adjust to difficult conditions the Japanese have shown historically, these optimistic views cannot be written off as mere wishful thinking.

7. William Diebold, Jr., *The United States and the Industrial World, Op. cit.,* p. 103.

---

8. See Richard E. Caves and Richard H. Holton, *The Canadian Economy: Prospect and Retrospect,* Harvard University Press, Cambridge, Mass., 1959, p. 72.

Economy of Canada Expands, Outpacing Most Other Nations

John E. Cooney and Tim Metz

Canada's first.

It is, at least, if you listen to what a lot of economists are saying. Evidence is quickly mounting that Canada, long thought simply to mirror good times and bad in the United States, will wind up in the healthiest economic position of any industrialized Western nation this year.

Barring unforeseen developments, analysts expect the Canadian boom to continue for some time to come. And because the U.S. and Canada are one another's largest trading partners, the predicted second-half rebound in the American economy following the lifting of the Arab oil embargo only promises to further brighten prospects here.

"For the first time, the Canadian economy has become the envy of most of the industrial countries of the Western world," says Kurt E. Haas, a Montreal economist.

His comments don't stem from smug jingoism. Canada has been snugly insulated from the shortages and economic shocks besetting other nations by three big assets: oil, mineral resources, and a maturing manufacturing sector.

"A GALLOPING ECONOMY"

As the only Western power exporting oil, Canada has largely avoided shortages during the energy crisis while achieving a near-perfect trade balance by taking advantage of spiraling oil-export prices. Domestic factories are expanding rapidly to satisfy growing

Excerpted from John E. Cooney and Tim Metz, "Economy of Canada Expands, Outpacing Most Other Nations," *The Wall Street Journal,* April 9, 1974, with permission of *The Wall Street Journal.*

consumer demand for durable goods. And, after years of trying to shed its image as an exporter of raw materials rather than sophisticated technology or manufactured goods, Canada now finds its reputation enhanced as industries around the world bid record prices for its nickel, copper, and zinc treasures.

"The economy here is galloping along," says a U.S. State Department economist based in Ottawa. "It's time for Canada to own up to the fact that it isn't a little country anymore, but a major nation with one of the strongest economies in the world."

With a gross national product last year of just under $118 billion, the size of the Canadian economy falls far short of that of the U.S., for example, where the GNP reached $1,289.1 billion in 1973. But Richard N. Thomson, president of Toronto-Dominion Bank, predicts that Canada's GNP in 1974 will hit $134 billion, a 14% increase over 1973.

OUT IN FRONT

How does Canada's economic outlook compare with the major industrial powers? Apparently extremely well. Top U.S. government economists—drawing on domestic figures as well as those of the Organization for Economic Cooperation and Development, an international economic research organization—say that Canada comes off better than any of the big nations surveyed.

Consider the survey's findings:

—Canada expects real economic growth of some 4.5 percent this year compared with just 1 percent in the U.S. Canada's anticipated growth rate is the best among the surveyed nations, which also include Great Britain, France, Germany and Italy. Forecasts range from 4.25 percent growth in France to a jolting 2.5 percent decline for Britain.

—Canada should have the smallest rise in unemployment this year—0.6 percent versus a high of perhaps 1 percent in the U.S., Japan and Britain. (Canada, however, has had a chronic unemployment problem and the current rate is 5.5 percent.)

—While it's difficult to pinpoint now, Canada's inflation rate this year should range between 8 percent and 10 percent, about in line with expectations for the U.S. and Germany, but less than France or Italy and only about half the rate expected in Japan.

—On the balance-of-payments front, Canada stands alone. All the surveyed nations except Canada expect. big blows to their trade accounts due to sharply higher oil prices. Anticipated imbalances range from $4.1 billion for Italy to $10 billion for the U.S.

Because no pipeline yet links Western Canada's oil reserves with markets in Eastern Canada, the nation imports 900,000 barrels of foreign oil a day, or as much as it exports to the U.S. To subsidize soaring import prices, the Canadian government charges an export tax of $6.40 a barrel. The result: virtually a zero trade balance.

THE MANUFACTURING SECTOR

Another strong point: After more than two decades of government-prompted industrial expansion, Canada's domestic manufacturing sector is rolling into high gear. This year alone, for instance, Canadian companies forecast that capital expenditures will rise more than 20 percent from last year's $16 billion. This includes starts on projects such as Steel Co. of Canada's $495 million expansion project near Toronto and Syncrude Canada Ltd.'s billion-dollar Tar Sands oil-extraction plant in Alberta.

''Canada's economy now has a full-blown manufacturing sector and a substantial, sharply expanding service sector,'' says Harvard University economist Richard Caves, who is on a research and teaching sabbatical at the University of Toronto.

Nationwide, government economists predict corporate profits will increase again this year, following last year's 37 percent gain to an aggregate record $17 billion. However, most economists are predicting this year's gains won't be as dramatic as in 1973.

Following sales that were sharply higher in January and level in February, the Canadian auto industry suffered nearly a 20 percent sales decline in March. Sales incentive contests a year ago and auto shipper strikes this year distorted the sales comparison, industry men say. Executives like William L. Hawkins, general manager of Ford's Canadian unit, still see ''a very strong spring car selling season—nearly up to last year's record levels.''

There's no shortage of foreign, especially U.S., investors seeking a stake in the Canadian economic bonanza. In the banking industry, for instance, such U.S. giants as Chase Manhattan, First National City Bank and Bankers Trust all have set up or beefed up their Canadian operations during the past year.

They're here competing with world-scale Japanese and British banks to share in providing tens of billions of financing for Canadian resource developments already under way or slated for the rest of the Seventies and into the Eighties.

And, despite growing Canadian nationalism, foreign investors are still welcome. For example, this year Quebec is spending $200,000 on promotional activities to persuade U.S. companies to establish subsidiaries in the province.

The general optimism about the economy can be measured by consumer spending, which is advancing at a healthy pace and shows no sign of sluggishness. ''Consumer confidence is decidedly higher in Canada than in the U.S.,'' says Mr. Haas, the Montreal economist. ''It should be high,'' adds Robert Dunn, associate professor of economics at George Washington University in Washington, D.C. He points out that Canadians, unlike Americans, aren't worrying about such things as the energy crisis or Watergate.

A number of other factors enhance the sunny outlook for the Canadian economy. Housing starts reached a record 268,500 last year and are expected to approach that figure again this year. Farm income in 1973 was up 30 percent over the previous year and is holding strong. And retail sales, which last year jumped 14 percent from 1972 levels, will rise another 10 percent this year, economists at the Toronto-Dominion Bank predict.

Perhaps the brightest spot of all on the Canadian landscape is its trove of mineral resources. Because mineral reserves are being depleted faster than new ones can be found, the U.S. and many other nations will produce less and less of their own metallic mineral requirements in the years ahead. Canada's production is expected to increase correspondingly, especially as rapid economic expansion in many parts of the globe pushes demand sharply upward.

Currently, for example, the U.S. produces 68 percent of its own metallic mineral demand. This is expected to drop to only 42 percent by 1985. Meanwhile, by 1980, Canada is expected to be producing 80 percent more copper, 61 percent more iron ore, 23 percent more lead, 30 percent more nickel and 55 percent more zinc than in 1970.

"It is precisely Canada's long abhorred role as a hewer of wood and drawer of water that will likely make it an increasingly important world power through the remainder of this century," says Harvard's Mr. Caves.   □

SUMMARY

The full study of economic growth involves an interweaving of macroeconomic and microeconomic elements. In general, a country's growth rate will depend upon the increases in its factor inputs, labor and capital, technological progress, and changes in the degree of employment of the factors and in the efficiency of their allocation among different employments. Different countries have combined the elements of growth in different ways, leading many economists to speak of different *models* of growth, as, for example, the "Soviet model" or the "Japanese model."

Economic growth under the Soviet Five-Year Plans followed upon earlier Russian economic progress in the late nineteenth and early twentieth centuries, but also took place after massive disruptions in the economy caused by the revolution and World War I. Soviet growth was characterized by heavy emphasis on industry above agriculture, very high investment rates, emphasis within industry on heavy industry, dualistic technology, vocational and technical training, and an import-substitution international trade policy. This model involved State domination of the economy through industrial planning and, in agriculture, forced collectivization of farming.

The Japanese model of growth involved many of the same elements as the Russian model, since Japan in the nineteenth century was also an economically "backward" nation and since she was also striving to "catch up" with the West. However, a number of differences did exist because Japan, as compared to the Soviet Union, faced a different population problem (more densely settled), a different resource situation (fewer resources), and a different political situation (the Meiji Restoration was not as violent nor as total a reconstruction of society as was the Russian revolution). In general, these differences are reflected in the fact that there was a greater increase in agricultural productivity, a much heavier reliance on international trade, and a more mixed pattern of State intervention and private initiatives in Japan during her take-off than was the case in Russia. Japanese growth since World War II has been phenomenal, exceeding even that of the Soviet Union.

Canada has emerged in the mid-1970s as a country with a very high growth potential. The export of staples has long been an important feature of Canadian growth. In the age of new material shortages, Canada's strong natural resource base (in sharp contrast to Japan) augurs well for future growth.

IMPORTANT TERMS TO REMEMBER

Unemployment and Growth
Efficiency and Growth
Increase in Factor Inputs
Increased Output per Unit of Input
Soviet Growth Model
Leading Sectors
Unbalanced Growth
Rate of Investment
Dual Technology
Japanese "Miracle"
Imported Technology
Exports and Growth
Economic Staples

QUESTIONS FOR DISCUSSION

1. In the light of this chapter's discussion of economic growth in an international context, what features of U.S. growth (see chapter 16) seem to you to be (a) fairly universal or (b) rather specific to the particular conditions of the American economy?

2. Explain why it is true that, if the capital-output ratio is constant, a high rate of investment will yield a high rate of economic growth. What factors might alter the value of an economy's capital-output ratio? From the point of view of growth, would a society prefer a high or a low capital-output ratio?

3. "When a country is 'catching up,' its growth pattern is necessarily different from that of a country like Britain or the United States, which was one of the 'early developers.' " Discuss with reference to (a) capital formation, (b) technological change, and (c) economic efficiency. How might attitudes to (a), (b), and (c) above change as the "catching up" economy became more "mature"?

4. "Although many of the world's underdeveloped nations have flirted with the 'Soviet model' of growth, the true and natural 'model' for these countries is that of Japan." Discuss, paying special attention to such problems as population, agriculture and trade.

5. Why do you believe that, in the past, Canadians might have abhorred their role as "a hewer of wood and drawer of water"? Why might this attitude change in the next quarter-century?

6. If you had the choice, would you prefer a society that took its potential growth in the form of increased goods or increased leisure? Does society have this choice? Do you personally have this choice?

SUGGESTED READING

Bergson, Abram. "Soviet Economic Perspectives: Toward a New Growth Model," *Challenge*, May–June 1974.

Campbell, Robert W. *Soviet Economic Power*, 2nd ed. Boston: Houghton Mifflin, 1966.

Caves, Richard E., and Holton, Richard H. *The Canadian Economy: Prospect and Retrospect*, Cambridge: Harvard University Press, 1959.

Lockwood, William W., ed. *The State and Economic Enterprise in Japan*. Princeton: Princeton University Press, 1965.

Rosovsky, Henry, and Ohkawa, Kazushi. *Japanese Economic Growth: Trend Acceleration in the Twentieth Century*, Stanford University Press, 1973.

Supple, Barry, ed. *The Experience of Economic Growth*. New York: Random House, 1963.

CHAPTER 29
INCOME DISTRIBUTION AND POVERTY

It was common in the 1960s—when economic growth, as discussed in the last chapter, was a prime subject of interest among statesmen and economists—to argue that growth had deprived the issue of *income distribution* of most of its bite. The problem of income distribution—who gets how much?—had, of course, been a very important one in the history of economics. Even those economists who had been most impressed by the "efficiency" of a private enterprise system had usually admitted that it might not do very well in terms of income distribution. The British classical economist David Ricardo, for example, was generally for laissez-faire in economic matters, but he was also aware that landowners under such a regime might reap increasingly large incomes over time—incomes that they had done nothing in particular to deserve. Henry George, the American economist, used Ricardian logic to argue for heavy taxes on rents in his famous "single tax" scheme. Karl Marx, who was actually very much in debt to Ricardo in terms of economic theory, made bourgeois income distribution (especially as between capitalists and the proletariat) a central objection to capitalism.

But economic growth seemed to have solved, or at least to have taken most of the sting out of, this issue. If the pie was constantly getting bigger, who cared whether one's particular share of the pie was growing or diminishing relative to someone else's? When everyone could count on getting more, how the extra income was distributed seemed a relatively minor matter.

In the 1970s, however, this view of the question of income distribution seems wholly unsatisfactory. Seldom in the history of our nation has the striving for greater equality—and not in economic matters alone—been more to the forefront than now. Why is this so? Especially why is this so after the great economic advances of the post-Depression–World War II period?

Observers will naturally differ on the explanation, but the author's view is that two main elements have been involved. The first is that there are aspects of economic growth that not only do not moderate but actually *intensify* the concern over income distribution. When the poor are very poor—like the poor, say, in an underdeveloped country where survival is often literally at stake—then economic growth, by raising living standards to some minimum level of comfort, may satisfy the primary aspirations of the lower economic classes, even though the society's income distribution is grossly unequal. As the society, including the poor, gets increasingly better off, absolute gains in income may be less important than *relative* gains. If I don't have enough to eat, my main concern is more food. If I do have enough to eat, my main concern may be my position relative to my neighbor's position. In a rich society, inequality can be more galling than in a poor society.

The other element in the picture is that in those cases where something close to "absolute poverty" exists, the situation seems particularly disgraceful when the surrounding society is so comfortable. Poverty in the affluent society is hard to forgive because it is, in principle, easily correctable.

These two considerations have done much to make the subject of income distribution one of the most frequently discussed economic topics in America in the 1970s.

INCOME DISTRIBUTION IN GENERAL

There are many different ways of analyzing a society's income distribution. In Part Three, when we were concerned with the microeconomics of the price system, we discussed income distribution in terms of factor prices and factor "shares."[1] In this kind of analysis one begins with the competitive case, in which factors of production are paid the values of their marginal products, and then takes up the deviations from such payments caused by various forms of market imperfection and by economic uncertainty and change.

From the point of view of social welfare, however, the more interesting view of income distribution has to do with the sizes of the incomes going to different groups in the society. This concern, in turn, may be about *absolute* incomes or about *relative* incomes.

---

1.   See especially chapters 21 and 26.

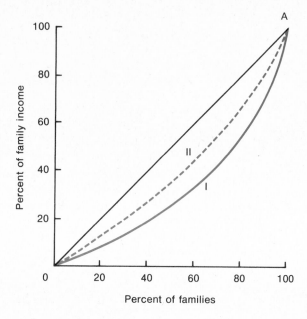

Figure 29–1. Income Distribution As Represented by Lorenz Curves.

Curves I and II each show an income distribution that departs from complete equality. Many people feel that in view of the problem of relative poverty, our society should attempt to move toward a more equal income distribution; e.g., from a distribution like that of Curve I to a distribution like that of Curve II.

In some ways, the question of the absolute levels of income seems the most important. Do the poor in a given society have enough food to eat, clothing to wear, shelter from the elements? This is obviously a basic concern for any society.

Still, as we have said, the question of relative income distribution can, in an affluent society, be felt almost as keenly. What proportion of the income of the society goes to the top 5 percent of rich families; the top 10 percent? How much is left over for the bottom quarter or half? What are the trends in this relative distribution of income over time?

The general pattern of a society's income distribution in this relative sense can be illustrated as in Figure 29–1, by what is called a Lorenz curve. If there were a perfectly equal distribution of income in the society, then income distribution could be prepresented by the straight line, *OA*. Twenty percent of the households have 20 percent of the income; 60 percent of the households have 60 percent of the income, and so on. The degree of *in*equality of the income distribution can then be measured by the extent to which the curve departs from the straight line. Curve I represents a greater, and curve II a lesser, inequality of income distribution.

There is some slight evidence to suggest that, in the very long run, economic growth tends to move a society in the direction of a somewhat greater equality of income distribution (i.e., moves the economy from curve I towards curve II)[2]. However, this process is uncertain and slow, and it also varies greatly from country to country.

INCOME DISTRIBUTION IN THE UNITED STATES

What of the income distribution in the United States? Does poverty exist in the affluent society? What trends can we observe?

In absolute terms, poverty still exists in the United States, even to the degree of producing malnutrition and other health defects. In 1972, nearly 12 percent of the population lived below an income level called the "poverty" line, which was the equivalent of $4,275 per year for a nonfarm family of four. This level is defined as about three times the amount needed to give a nutritionally adequate diet. It was, in 1972, about 38 percent of the median income of American families. This is not poverty on the scale of Ethiopia (pp. 8–10), or India or other underdeveloped countries (chapters 6 and 31), but it is a serious problem, particularly for that part of the 12 percent which falls considerably below the dividing line.

The evaluation of the above facts depends somewhat on the angle from which they are viewed. If

2. See Simon Kuznets, *Six Lectures on Economic Growth* (New York: The Free Press, 1959).

TABLE 29–1

PERSONS BELOW THE POVERTY LEVEL, U.S., 1959–1972

PERSONS BELOW POVERTY LEVEL	1959	1966	1969	1971	1972
Number (millions)	39.5	28.5	24.1	25.6	24.5
Percent (%) of population	22.4	14.7	12.1	12.5	11.9

Source: Department of Commerce, Bureau of the Census.

one looks at absolute poverty and the trend over time, then it is possible to take a relatively hopeful view about the gradual elimination of the problem. Back in the 1940s, some 45 million people, or about a third of the population, had incomes below the poverty line. By 1959, this had been reduced to 39 million people out of a larger population. From 1959 to 1972, the percentage of U.S. citizens below the poverty line (a line adjusted upward each year for inflation) had been approximately halved (Table 29–1). There seems no reason to believe that this progress will not continue in the future. To look forward to the elimination of absolute poverty in the United States is not, therefore, Utopian, but a quite reasonable expectation.

On the other hand, if we look at relative poverty and *its* trend, then our optimism may seem considerably less justified. Although there seems to have been some movement toward greater equality of the income distribution from 1929 to the end of World War II, recent years have seen very little change in relative income shares. Table 29–2 suggests that the percentage of income received by the lowest fifth of families has remained at about 5 percent throughout the postwar period. This bottom fifth still receives about a third of what the top 5 percent of families receives. The members of the top 5 percent are likely to stress that their income levels are not really all that high. In 1972, for example, an annual income of $28,000 and above put you in the top 5 percent. Many families in the $30,000 income class doubtless

TABLE 29–2

SHARES OF TOTAL INCOME (BEFORE TAXES)
RECEIVED BY FIFTHS OF FAMILIES, RANKED
BY INCOME

FAMILIES	1947	1950	1960	1966	1972
Lowest Fifth	5.1	4.5	4.8	5.6	5.4
Second Fifth	11.8	11.9	12.2	12.4	11.9
Third Fifth	16.7	17.4	17.8	17.8	17.5
Fourth Fifth	23.3	23.6	24.0	23.8	23.9
Highest Fifth	43.3	42.7	41.3	40.5	41.4
Top 5 percent	17.5	17.3	15.9	15.6	15.9

Source: Dept. of Commerce, Bureau of the Census.

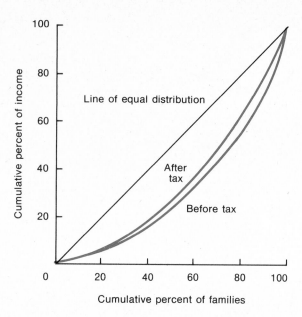

Figure 29–2. Lorenz Curves of the Distributions of U.S. Family Income Before and After Federal, State, and Local Taxes, 1966.

Taxes have some impact, but only a very small one, on relative income distribution in the United States.

Adapted from Joseph A. Pechman and Benjamin A. Okner, *Who Bears the Tax Burden?*, The Brookings Institution, 1974, p. 7. With permission of The Brookings Institution and the authors.

felt themselves very strapped at 1972 prices. Since this 5 percent had three times as much income as the bottom 20 percent, however, the seriousness of the problem of relative income inequality is clear.

These results, moreover, are not notably changed when we take taxes into account. Although we think of the federal income tax as a basically progressive tax, its progressivity is very much weakened by numerous possibilities for exemptions and deductions; furthermore, certain other taxes—as, for example, social security payroll taxes—are regressive (p. 278). The net result is that our tax system, while apparently progressive for high incomes, tends to be neutral over most of the income range, and is actually regressive at very low incomes. Joseph Pechman and Benjamin Okner in a recent study conclude that: "Because there is so little difference in effective rates over most of the income distribution, the tax system has very little effect on the relative distribution of income."[3]

Figure 29–2 displays this conclusion in diagrammatic form for 1966. The shift toward greater equality as a result of taxes exists, but it appears very small. In short, the persistence of a substantial degree of relative income inequality in the United States remains a fact, whether we consider it on a before-tax or after-tax basis.

INCOME DISTRIBUTION AND THE BLACK COMMUNITY

Our discussion so far has been largely in terms of over-all income distribution. But the fact is that poverty in the United States is unevenly distributed, with especial impact on particular groups in the society.

---

3.   Joseph A. Pechman and Benjamin A. Okner, *Who Bears The Tax Burden?* Washington, D.C.: The Brookings Institution, 1974, p. 6. The effects on the income distribution ultimately depend on the analysis of the *incidence* of various taxes, e.g., property taxes, corporate income taxes, etc. In the Lorenz curves of Figure 29–2, Pechman and Okner base the tax effects on what they call "the Most Progressive Incidence Varient." Were other assumptions about incidence used, the effect of taxation in moving the income distribution to greater equality might be even less than that shown in the diagram.

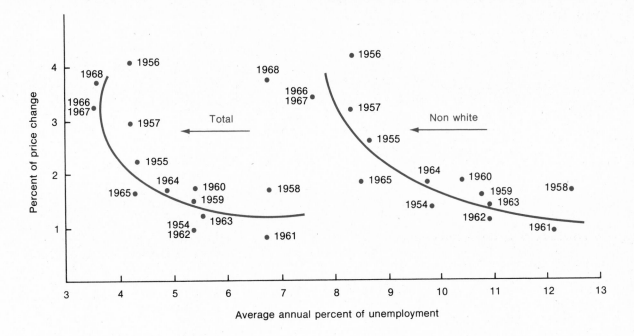

Figure 29-3. Phillips' Curves for Total and Non-White Unemployment, 1954-1968.

Source: Economic Report of the President, January 1969 (Washington, D.C.: U.S. Government Printing Office), p. 95, Chart 8 and p. 255, Table B-24. Taken from Carolyn Shaw Bell, *The Economics of the Ghetto* (New York: Pegasus, 1970), p. 106.

Take, for example, the aged: While the number of poor persons in the age group 22-to-54 averaged less than 8 percent in 1970, the number for individuals 65 or older was nearly 25 percent—more than three times as high a percentage.

Or take families headed by women: In 1970, families headed by women comprised about 37 percent of all low-income families. This was up sharply from the comparable 23 percent in 1959.

Or take lack of education: About half of the low-income families in 1970 had completed less than one year of high school. Or children: Persons under 14 comprised about one-third of the poor in 1970. Or region of residence: You had a greater chance of being poor if you lived on a farm as opposed to the city, but if you lived in a metropolitan area, you had more chance of being poor if you lived in the central city as opposed to outside it.

This uneven incidence of poverty is nowhere illustrated more forcefully than in the case of the black community in the United States. Not only are the wages of black workers lower than those of whites, but their unemployment rate is substantially higher. A dramatic way of putting this is to draw two Phillips' curves, one for total unemployment and one for non-white unemployment. Figure 29-3 suggests that if the government were to fight inflation by allowing the unemployment rate to increase, black workers would suffer far more than proportionately in consequence.

Because of the magnitude of the problem, and as an illustration of the uneven impact of economic misfortune, we present the following reading, which gives a summary of the present state of black economic conditions, and at least one encouraging sign for the future.

Economic Developments in the Black Community

Andrew F. Brimmer

Only a few of the economic and social programs launched during the 1960s were focused primarily on blacks. The most visible effort in this category, the "black capitalism" program of the Nixon Administration, came very late in the decade. However, blacks were prominent among the target populations aimed at by many of the New Frontier and Great Society programs.

The most fundamental economic goal of the early 1960s, of course, was the stimulation of an economy that had remained sluggish for nearly a decade. Consequently, any appraisal of economic changes among blacks during the period must begin with an assessment of the benefits they received from economic expansion. These benefits can be traced in the growth of black employment and the reduction in joblessness, as well as in rising black income, especially among the better educated. Unfortunately, however, this progress must be viewed against the background of a deepening schism in the black community between those enjoying expanding prosperity and those caught in a widening web of poverty.

The economic history of blacks in the United States during the last decade mirrors that of the country at large. However, blacks as a group did slightly better in the 1960s—and considerably worse in the last few years—than the nation as a whole. The principal changes in employment and income among blacks can be traced in Table A. From 1961 through 1969, the black labor force rose in line with the total civilian labor force; however, the participation rate (i.e., total labor force as a percentage of the non-institutionalized population) of blacks declined noticeably.

Excerpted from Andrew F. Brimmer, "Economic Developments in the Black Community," *The Public Interest*, no. 34 (Winter 1974), pp. 146–53. Reprinted with the permission of *The Public Interest*.

WIDE WORLD PHOTO

Andrew F. Brimmer, then a member of the Federal Reserve Board, gives interview in Washington, D.C. Brimmer is currently a professor at the Harvard Business School.

Blacks got a moderately larger share of the increase in employment during the 1960s than they had at the beginning of the decade. Within the black group, adult females got a relatively larger share of the expanded jobs than was true of black men. This general pattern paralleled that evident among whites, except that black men did slightly better than their white counterparts. On the other hand, black youths made virtually no progress toward improving their relative employment position during the decade. This was in sharp contrast to the situation among white youths, who expanded their share of the total.

Between 1960 and 1969, the total number of workers without jobs dropped by 1,021,000. Unemployment rose appreciably during the 1960–61 recession, but the subsequent growth of the economy during the decade was large enough to absorb an 11 million

TABLE A

TRENDS IN EMPLOYMENT AND INCOME IN THE BLACK COMMUNITY[1]

	1960	1965	1969	1972
Employment (thousands)	65,778	71,088	77,902	81,702
Negro and other races[2]	6,927	7,643	8,384	8,628
White	58,850	63,445	69,518	73,074
Percent of total				
Negro and other races	10.5	10.8	10.8	10.7
Unemployment (thousands)	3,852	3,366	2,831	4,840
Negro and other races	787	676	570	956
White	3,063	2,691	2,261	3,884
Percent of total				
Negro and other races	20.4	20.1	20.1	19.8
Unemployment rate (percent)				
Total	5.5	4.5	3.5	5.6
Negro and other races	10.2	8.1	6.4	10.0
White	4.9	4.1	3.1	5.0
Ratio: Black to white	2.1	2.0	2.1	2.0
Median family income (current dollars)				
Total	$5,620	$6,957	$9,433	$11,116
Negro and other races	3,233	3,994	6,191	7,106
Black	n.a.	3,886	5,999	6,864
White	5,835	7,251	9,794	11,549
Income gap				
White/Negro & other races	2,602	3,257	3,603	4,443
White/Black	n.a.	3,365	3,795	4,685
Ratio: Negro and other races to white	.55	.55	.63	.62
Black to white	n.a.	.54	.61	.59

[1] Sources: Labor force, employment and unemployment: U.S. Department of Labor, Bureau of Labor Statistics. Income: U.S. Department of Commerce, Bureau of the Census.
[2] About 90 percent of the persons in this category are black.

increase in the labor force and to take more than 1 million workers off the unemployment roles. Over the same years, the black labor force rose by 1.2 million, but unemployment among blacks still declined by 217,000. This reduction was about in line with the decrease in joblessness in the economy generally. On the other hand, the distribution of unemploy-ment within the black community changed signifi-cantly. Among black adult males and black females, the level of unemployment decreased over the dec-ade, as did unemployment among all components of the white group. But among black youths, the level of unemployment was 55,000 higher in 1969 than it was in 1960. The inability of the economy to meet the job needs of black youth was one of the main shortfalls in national economic policy during the last decade.

The 1969–70 recession had a disproportionately adverse impact on blacks, and the subsequent recovery brought them a relatively small proportion of benefits. In fact, after two and one-half years of substantial economic expansion, blacks as a group ended up with a smaller proportion of the nation's jobs than they had at the time of the recession. The relative decline in their job shares was especially noticeable in lower-skilled occupations.

INCOME TRENDS AMONG BLACKS

The extent to which blacks benefited from the long period of economic expansion during the 1960s can also be traced in income trends. In 1959, blacks' money income amounted to $19.7 billion, representing 6.2 percent of the total for the nation as a whole. By 1969, the amount for blacks had just about doubled (to $38.7 billion)—compared with a gain of 89 percent for whites—and their share had edged up to 6.4 percent. Although blacks did not participate in the recent recovery as fully as did whites, by 1972 their total income had climbed to $51.8 billion—or 6.7 percent of the total of $773 billion.

Over the decade of the 1960s, the median family income of blacks just about doubled. The figure for these families in 1969 was $5,999, compared with $9,794 for whites. In 1959, median income was $3,047 for blacks and $5,893 for whites. The ratio of black to white median income rose from .52 in 1959 to .61 in 1969. In absolute terms, however, black families in 1969 received an average of $3,795 less than their white counterparts, whereas they had received $2,846 less in 1959. By 1972, the median income of black families had climbed to $6,864 compared to $11,549 for white families, but the black/white income ratio declined to .60 in 1971 and to .59 in 1972—the level at which it had been in 1967. So the 1969–70 recession—like the recession in

1960–61—resulted in a widening of the white/black income gap, which in absolute terms amounted to $4,685 in 1972. The explanation of these shortfalls in black income is widely known: A legacy of racial discrimination and deprivation has limited blacks' ability to acquire marketable skills and barred them from better-paying jobs.

One of the dominant features of the black experience in the United States during the 1960s was the continued net migration of blacks from the South to the North and West. The explanation of this movement remains controversial. Some observers attribute it primarily to the relative attractiveness of the public welfare system in urban areas outside the South, but I attribute it principally to the pull of better employment opportunities and higher incomes in the rest of the country.

Between 1960 and 1970, the South expanded faster than any other major region in all principal types of economic activity, and blacks living in the South shared in the benefits yielded by this faster pace of economic growth. In 1960, the South had 61 percent of the nation's black population, but this had declined to 53 percent by 1970, mainly because of out-migration to the North and West. The net result was that blacks living in the South accounted for 6.04 percent of the nation's total population in 1970 vs. 6.23 percent in 1960. At the same time, their share of the country's total money income rose from 2.21 percent in 1959 to 2.74 percent in 1969. So some improvement occurred during the 1960s in per capita as well as in total income of blacks in the South.

ESCAPE FROM POVERTY

One of the central aims of national economic policy during the 1960s was the reduction of poverty. It was generally assumed that accelerated economic growth would provide the main bridge over which the poor would escape into a better life. But numerous specialized programs were also launched, among which manpower and community action schemes were particularly important. Since blacks are heavily represented among the poorest of the nation's poor, they are especially affected by the success or failure of anti-poverty efforts.

According to the federal government's poverty index, a nonfarm family of four was classed as poor in 1959 if its annual income was below $2,973. By 1968, the poverty threshold was $3,553. Measured against these criteria, there were 38.7 million poor people in the United States in 1959. Of this number, 9.9 million were black, 28.3 million were white, and the remaining .5 million were other races (mainly American Indians). By 1968, the total number of poor persons had declined to 25.4 million, of whom about 7.6 million were black, 17.4 million were white, and .4 million were other races. A closer look at these figures suggests, however, that the rate at which blacks were able to escape from poverty during the 1960s fell considerably short of that experienced by whites. The total number of persons classified as poor dropped by one-third; for whites the decline was two-fifths, but for blacks the decrease was less than one-quarter.

The much more rapid exodus from poverty by whites during this period is partly explained by the fact that in 1959 the average poor white family was not caught nearly so deeply in poverty as the average poor black family. But a more important explanation of the differential success of the two races in escaping poverty lies in the changing structure of families within the two groups. During the 1960s, male-headed families were more likely to be successful in raising their income than were families headed by females. Between 1959 and 1968, the rate of decline in poverty among individuals in male-headed families for both blacks and whites was roughly equal and also rather rapid, but for female-headed families the pattern was quite different: For the white population, the number of poor individuals in female-headed households declined by one-sixth, but the number of poor in families headed by black females *rose* by one-quarter, and the number of children in these families increased by over one-third. The 1969–70

recession checked the rate of escape from poverty by both blacks and whites. Yet by 1972, the number of poor whites had declined to 16.2 million, while among blacks the number of poor persons climbed fairly sharply and in 1972 amounted to 7.7 million.

Broken black families are among the main contributors to the expanding system of public welfare in the United States. This is especially true of the federally supported program of Aid to Families with Dependent Children (AFDC). In 1961, for example, black families constituted about two-fifths of all AFDC families, and the proportion rose to about one-half by 1970. The representation of blacks in other segments of the welfare system is far less marked than it is in AFDC. In 1971, about 25 percent of all black families received some form of public assistance, compared to 5 percent of white families. However, those black families receiving public assistance had a substantially lower median income than their white counterparts ($3,353 vs. $4,117 in 1971).

Because of the persistence of poverty and the expanding public welfare rolls—particularly the growing dependence of families on AFDC—I was a strong supporter of the Family Assistance Program (FAP) proposed by the Nixon Administration in August 1969. Even in its most restrictive form (which would have provided a basic allowance of $1,600 per year for a family of four), the FAP would have made a sizable contribution toward easing the burdens of poor families on AFDC. More important, the FAP contained the basic elements of a nationwide income maintenance program. Benefits would have been available to poor families generally—whether they worked or not. The representation of blacks would have remained substantial, but by no means as prominent as under AFDC. The FAP failed to win Congressional approval for a variety of reasons—including bipartisan opposition, lack of support by the Administration, and persistent suspicion and hostility on the part of civil rights groups. The ultimate losers were the nation's poor. The revival of FAP (or some other version of an income maintenance arrangement) remains high on the nation's agenda of unfinished business.

EDUCATION AND PROSPERITY

If the discussion stopped here, we would leave an unbalanced picture of the black economic experience in the 1960s, and an underlying trend holding significant implications for the 1970s would be missed—the role of education and its contribution to blacks' advancement. Between 1960 and 1972, the proportion of the black population 20 to 29 years old who had completed high school rose from 38 percent to 64 percent for males and from 43 percent to 66 percent for black females. For white males in the same age group, the rise was from 64 percent to 84 percent; for white females the rise was from 66 percent to 83 percent. Moreover, within the last few years the proportion of young blacks completing high school accelerated noticeably. An even sharper acceleration occurred in the case of college education. In 1960, 4.1 percent of all blacks in the 25–34 age range had completed four years or more of college, compared with 11.9 percent for all whites in the same age group. By 1972, about 7.9 percent of all blacks in the 25–34 age bracket had completed four years or more of college; among whites, the figure was 18.8 percent.

An even more crucial trend is the rising propensity for young black people to attend college. In 1972, 540,000 blacks 18 to 24 years old were enrolled in college, compared to 297,000 in 1967. The 1972 figure represented 18 percent of all blacks in that age range (vs. 13 percent in 1967). For young whites, the enrollment was 4,710,000 in 1967 and 5,624,000 in 1972—27 percent and 26 percent, respectively. By 1967, blacks represented 4.9 percent of total college enrollment, and this had climbed further to 8.8 percent in 1972.

These advances in educational attainment made a substantial difference in the degree of economic progress made by blacks during the 1960s. Just how much difference is indicated by the figures in Tables B and C. Table B shows median income in 1959 and 1969 and years of school completed by males 25

to 54 years old. The median income at each educational level is expressed as a ratio to the median for all men in the age range: $6,408 in 1959 (in 1969 dollars) and $8,465 in 1969. In Table C, median income and education in 1969 are shown for both men and women for age groups 25–34 and 35–54. In this case, the base is the median income ($9,651) for white men, aged 35–54, who had completed four years of high school.

Several features stand out in these tables. As one would expect, for both races and for both men and women median income increased progressively with both age and education. However, education clearly had the greater influence. This general pattern also held for blacks, except that the extra income yielded by extra education was slightly smaller. In 1969, the grade school/high school and high school/college differentials were about the same as in 1959 for all men in the 25–54 age group. Among black men, the grade school/high school gap was also unchanged over the decade. But the earnings for black college graduates had climbed to two and one-quarter times those of grade school drop-outs, and the margin of college over high school graduates had widened appreciably.

In recent years, young black men with better educations have advanced their incomes relative to whites much more rapidly than older blacks have. For instance, in 1969, at both the elementary and high school level, black/white earnings ratios were approximately the same for men 25 to 34 years old and men 35 to 54 years old. In contrast, education past the high school level generally raised the ratio of black-to-white earnings for young black men more than it did for older black men. (The earnings of black female workers with education beyond the high school level roughly equalled the earnings of their white counteparts in both age groups.) Despite these improvements, however, the absolute income gaps between blacks and whites—at all educational levels—remain substantial.

As shown in Table C, the average black man with a high school education was still earning in 1969 about the same amount as a white man who only went to grade school. Among black women, the situation was only slightly better. Black men with a

TABLE B

MEDIAN INCOME IN 1959 AND 1969 BY YEARS OF SCHOOL COMPLETED, MALES
25 TO 54 YEARS OLD[1]

| | 1959 (IN 1969 DOLLARS) | | | 1969 | | |
	TOTAL	BLACK	WHITE	TOTAL	BLACK	WHITE
Median Income	$6,408	$3,570	$6,637	$8,465	$5,222	$8,795
Ratio to Median Education	1.00	.56	1.04	1.00	.62	1.04
Elem: Total	.75	.47	.82	.70	.49	.75
Less than 8 years	.63	.44	.71	.61	.46	.65
8 years	.87	.58	.90	.80	.53	.83
High School: Total	1.03	.66	1.05	.98	.69	1.01
1–3 years	.98	.64	1.01	.88	.63	.92
4 years	1.06	.70	1.08	1.02	.73	1.04
College: Total	1.32	.82	1.35	1.28	.94	1.30
1–3 years	1.19	.78	1.22	1.14	.88	1.16
4 years	1.48	.88	1.50	1.44	1.02	1.46

[1]Median income at each educational level is expressed as a ratio to the median for all men
in the age range 25–45 years. Source: U.S. Department of Commerce, Bureau of the Census,
"Social and Economic Characteristics of the Population in Metropolitan and Nonmetropolitan
Areas: 1970 and 1960," Current Population Reports, Series P-23, No. 37, June 24, 1971, Table
12, p. 54.

TABLE C

MEDIAN EARNINGS AND EDUCATIONAL ATTAINMENT OF YEAR-ROUND WORKERS, 25 TO 34 AND 35 TO 54
YEARS OLD (1969)[1]

| | BLACK | | | | WHITE | | | |
| | MALE | | FEMALE | | MALE | | FEMALE | |
	25–34	35–54	25–34	35–54	25–34	35–54	25–34	35–54
Median Income	$6,346	$6,403	$4,403	$3,901	$8,839	$9,736	$5,175	$4,966
Ratio to Median ($9,651)	.66	.66	.46	.40	.92	1.01	.54	.51
Elem: 8 years or less	.49	.54	.30	.27	.69	.77	.41	.42
High School								
1–3 years	.60	.67	.38	.37	.82	.91	.44	.46
4 years	.70	.77	.48	.47	.89	1.00	.52	.53
College								
1–3 years	.80	.85	.57	.59	.95	1.19	.59	.60
4 years	.90	.97	.72	.76	1.16	1.51	.75	.76
5 years or more	1.03	1.27	.82	.94	1.22	1.74	.84	.96

[1]Median income at each educational level is expressed as a ratio to the median income ($9,651) for white men,
aged 35–54, who had completed four years of high school. Source: Bureau of the Census, "The Social and
Economic Status of the Black Population in the United States, 1972," July 1973, Tables 15 and 16, pp. 25, 26.

college degree had earnings about equal to or somewhat below those of a white high school graduate. But taken as a whole, the evidence presented here supports an encouraging conclusion: Younger blacks are making substantial progress in achieving secondary and higher education, and this increased education is yielding higher incomes both absolutely and relative to whites.   □

POLICIES TO ALTER INCOME DISTRIBUTION

Although many observers would agree that the extremes of income inequality in the United States ought to be corrected, the manner in which this is to be accomplished is subject to deep controversy. Questions of income distribution almost invariably involve some social conflict, since any redistribution of income is precisely that—taking away one person's income and giving it to another. The one who receives is likely to feel that this is only proper; the one who loses may take a different view. There are, however, some ways in which poverty can be ameliorated without incurring heavy costs to others.

In the first place, any move toward the solution to the great macroeconomic problems of full employment and price stability is likely to have at least some favorable effects on the distribution of income. To put it negatively, the burdens of unemployment and price inflation are likely to fall with particular severity on the nation's poor, and, consequently to worsen the poverty problem both in a relative and absolute sense. This is perhaps especially true of unemployment with respect to the nation's blacks, though we have also noted the harmful effects of inflation on the nation's elderly. In other words, if we succeeded in solving our great macroeconomic problems (or coming closer to solving them), then we would with one stroke (1) benefit society as a whole by providing a greater social product, and (2) benefit those groups who suffer particularly when the economy in the aggregate is unstable.

Much the same thing can be said about the great microeconomic issue of an efficient allocation of resources. Namely, there are many measures designed either to make the market work better (as in removing various forms of discrimination) or to improve the health, education, training, and skills of the underprivileged, wherein there is a net gain in social product for all to share. Insofar as poverty represents an inefficient use of society's resources, it will be possible in theory to reduce poverty and increase society's overall income at the same time. To that degree, an improved income distribution need not come at the expense of the incomes of the nation's well-to-do.

The above represents the bright side of the picture. Conflict emerges when we go a step further, however. Thus, many critics of society feel that improving the macro- and microeconomic functioning of the economy would barely scratch the surface of the distribution problem. They argue that any society in which the top 5 percent of income recipients receive far more income than the bottom 20 percent needs a thorough overhauling.

Even those who would work in more modest ways to limit the extremes of affluence and poverty are likely to run into serious social conflicts. Some economists, for example, believe that housing discrimination is an important source of poverty in the black community.[4]

Since the workings of the marketplace are unlikely to solve this problem, public intervention will almost certainly be necessary to improve matters. This intervention will be costly for the taxpayer. Public monies may have to be spent in increasing the flow of employment information to the isolated ghetto dweller, in improving mass transport from the ghetto to the suburbs, in providing rent subsidies for poorer families. Further, urban expert John Kain, suggests that the government may have to step in to provide low-income, nondiscriminatory housing, not in the cities but in the suburbs. In the early 1970s, the New York City newspapers were filled with the objections of local residents to various "scatter-site" housing proj-

---

4. See John F. Kain and Joseph J. Persky, "The Ghetto, the Metropolis and the Nation," Program on Regional and Urban Economics, Discussion Paper No. 30 (March 1968).

TABLE 29–3

SOCIAL WELFARE EXPENDITURES UNDER PUBLIC PROGRAMS
(FEDERAL, STATE, AND LOCAL)

	1960	1965	1970	1972
			(in billions of dollars)	
Total	52.3	77.2	146.0	192.7
Social insurance	19.3	28.1	54.8	75.1
Public aid	4.1	6.3	16.5	25.6
Health and medical programs	4.5	6.2	9.8	12.4
Veterans programs	5.5	6.0	9.0	11.5
Education	17.6	28.1	50.8	61.1
Housing	.2	.3	.7	1.4
Other social welfare	1.1	2.1	4.4	5.7

Source: Alfred M. Skolnik and Sophie R. Dales, "Social Welfare Expenditures,
1971–72," *Social Security Bulletin,* December 1972, Table 1.

ects within the city. Imagine the social conflict that would develop if large-scale housing projects of this nature were imposed upon the plush suburbs surrounding our major cities. Direct attacks on the roots of poverty in this country are unlikely to escape debate and disagreement. The test of the strength of our society will be whether it can encompass such disagreements and work out solutions that, though perfectly satisfactory to no one, will be at least grudgingly accepted by all.

While these long-range approaches are being developed, there is in the meantime the obvious fact that many people in our society are extremely poor and must be taken care of in one way or another. Another obvious fact is that the governmental expenditures designed to cope with the problems of the poor have been increasing substantially—skyrocketing, some would say—in recent years. Table 29–3 puts together all the various social welfare expenditures at the federal, state, and local governmental levels. In 1960, these programs came to 10.6 percent of GNP; 12 years later, in 1972, they represented 17.6 percent of GNP. By no means are all of these programs focused on the problem of poverty, and only a proportion of the payments actually go to the poor. Nevertheless, the magnitude of these programs is substantial, and the effect on the redistribution of income is considerable. And this raises a number of important issues about *welfare*—or *income-maintenance*—programs in general:

The *scale* of welfare programs. Have these programs grown out of hand and do they require important cutbacks? Or are they still insufficient to remove even the grossest forms of poverty that stain the conscience of a rich society?

The *administration* and *funding* of these programs. Whose responsibility is it to see that the incomes of the poor are maintained at a decent level? The city? county? state? federal government? This raises the issue of revenue-sharing[5] and also the question of centralizing versus decentralizing the administering of the funds, however they may have been provided.

The *form* of the program. In some ways the most difficult of the problems concern the system by which incomes are to be maintained. Should there be a

---

5. See chapter 4, pp. 83–89.

means' test and if so, how should it be administered? Should welfare recipients be required to work (say, on public projects) in order to receive welfare? What relationship in general should there be between employment opportunities and welfare payments? Do present schemes negatively affect the incentive to work? Do they tend to drive families apart (say, if the wife loses her welfare payment if the husband and father comes home to live)? Is there any agreement about the best form in general that income-maintenance programs should take?

To go into all these issues would take up far more space and time than are at our disposal here. However, we can sharpen the debate considerably by looking at one specific income-maintenance program that has attracted great attention from economists in the past few years. This is the program (which has been advanced by both ''liberal'' and ''conservative'' economists) of a *negative income tax*.

THE NEGATIVE INCOME TAX

The basic idea of the negative income tax is simple. Under the present federal personal income tax system, there is (say, for a family of four) a certain level of income at which taxes are zero. Below this level, taxes remain zero. What is proposed is that, for very low incomes, taxes become *negative*—result in payments from the government to the taxpayer—rather than remain at zero, and that these payments *to the citizen* be handled in exactly the same systematic way that taxpayers' payments *to the government* are handled for higher income levels.

Even this brief description should make it clear that we are dealing with not a single program but a family of possible programs, some of which would involve very heavy, and some relatively small, government expenditures. Decisions that would have to be made for any single plan would include these matters: (1) determining the level of incomes at which taxes would become negative: (2) determining the percentage of

income that would come back to the poor family and whether or not that percentage would increase as the family's income was lower; and (3) establishing a method for allowing for the number of children and other dependents. Generous decisions on these questions could lead to a program that would cost many times what more niggardly decisions would entail. This may help explain why neither liberals nor conservatives as a group oppose the negative income tax idea.

The advantages that supporters of this idea see are several. For one thing, such a program would place on the federal government some of the welfare responsibilities that are now burdening lower levels of government. Many people feel that welfare is simply too big a job for cities and states to handle financially, particularly when the federal government has substantially (though, of course, not completely) taken over the personal income tax as a source of revenue. Building welfare schemes into the federal tax system seems a fairly obvious response to this difficulty.

For another thing, there are many flaws in present-day welfare schemes that would be avoided by the negative income tax proposals. These flaws include everything from what many consider a degrading ''means' test'' (as compared to the negative income tax plan where the poor would do no more nor less than the rich—i.e., fill out an income tax form) to the effect on family life of welfare plans that reduce welfare payments by the amount of the husband's income and thus make it advisable for him to live away from home. More generally, as Professor James Tobin of Yale has noted, our welfare programs often involve a ''marginal tax rate'' of ''100 percent'' for poor families. This happens when welfare payments plus family income are adjusted to meet some minimum level. Suppose the level is $2500 and that if family income is zero, the state provides $2500; if family income is $1000, the state provides $1500; and so on. In effect, each dollar earned (up to $2500) is completely ''taxed'' away. The effect of such schemes on incentives to work can hardly be favorable.

Finally, many supporters like the idea that the negative income tax implies governmental support of the poor as a matter of governmental obligation and private right. They see this relationship as analogous to that of the taxpayer who is obliged to pay taxes as a matter of the government's right. The relationship is thus seen as symmetrical and fitting, not a question of charity or "the dole."

All of these arguments, of course, have responses. Thus, opponents of the negative income tax are worried by the very notion of a "right to income" that supporters of the plan usually praise. Furthermore, just as both conservatives and liberals can find reasons to support the negative income tax idea, so can both groups find reasons to oppose it. Opponents can argue that it will cost too much, *or* that it will not cost enough—i.e., that it will be used as a substitute for other important welfare programs that aid the poor directly in terms of health, housing, education, training, and so on. Thus, it might actually hurt some of the poor who are benefiting under present programs.

The pros and cons of this proposal are discussed in the readings that follow. The authors are Milton Friedman, one of the originators of the negative income tax idea, and Richard P. Nathan, a Senior Fellow at the Brookings Institution, who participated in developing President Nixon's Family Assistance Plan in 1969.

Negative Income Tax

Milton Friedman

1

The negative income tax, as Paul Samuelson remarked in one of his recent columns, is a striking example of an idea whose time has come. First suggested decades ago, it has attracted widespread interest only in the past few years as the defects of present methods of assisting the poor have become more obvious and more flagrant.

The widespread interest is remarkable. But the appearance of growing agreement—of support for a negative income tax by the right and the left, by businessmen and professors, by Republicans and Democrats—is highly misleading. In large part, it reflects the use of the same term to describe very different plans. For example, some months ago, more than 1,200 economists from 150 different colleges and universities signed a petition favoring a negative income tax. Despite my longtime advocacy of a negative income tax, I found it impossible to join in sponsoring the petition or even to sign it because I did not agree with the plan it advocated or the arguments it presented.

A SPECIFIC PLAN

The basic idea of a negative income tax is to use the mechanism by which we now collect tax revenue from people with incomes above some minimum level to provide financial assistance to people with incomes below that level.

Under present law, a family of four (husband, wife and two dependents) is entitled to personal exemptions and minimum deductions totaling $3,000 ($2,400 personal exemptions, $600 deductions).

The 1040 A Tax Form. The negative income tax could be administered in the same way that tax payments or refunds are handled today.

If such a family has an income of $3,000, its exemptions and deductions just offset its income. It has a *zero taxable* income and pays no tax.

If it has an income of $4,000, it has a *positive taxable income* of $1,000. Under current law, it is required to *pay* a tax of 15.4 percent, or $154. Hence it ends up with an income after tax of $3,846.

If it has an income of $2,000, it has a *negative taxable income of* −$1,000 ($2,000 minus exemptions and deductions of $3,000 equals −$1,000). This negative taxable income is currently disregarded. Under a negative income tax, the family would be entitled to *receive a fraction* of this sum. If the negative tax rate were 50 percent, it would be entitled to receive $500, leaving it with an income after tax of $2,500.

If such a family had no private income, it would have a negative taxable income of −$3,000, which would entitle it to receive $1,500. This is the minimum income guaranteed by this plan for a family of four.

Let me stress the difference between the *break-even income* of $3,000 at which the family neither pays taxes nor receives a subsidy and the *minimum guaranteed income* of $1,500. It is essential to retain a difference between these two in order to preserve an incentive for low-income families to earn additional income.

Let me stress also that these numbers are all for a family of four. Both the break-even income and the minimum guaranteed income would be higher for larger families and lower for smaller families. In this way, a negative income tax automatically allows for differences in need because of differences in family size—just as it does for differences in need because of differences in income.

This plan is intended to replace completely our present programs of direct relief—aid to dependent children, public assistance, and so on. For the first year or two, it might cost slightly more than these programs—because it is so much more comprehensive in coverage. But, as the incentive effects of the plan started to work, it would begin to cost far less than the present exploding direct-assistance programs that are creating a permanent class of people on welfare.

ALTERNATIVE PLANS

By varying the break-even income and the negative tax rate, by adding the negative income tax to present programs rather than substituting it for them, it is possible to go all the way from the rather modest and, I believe, eminently desirable plan just outlined to irresponsible and undesirable plans that would involve enormous redistribution of income and a drastic reduction in the incentive for people to work. That is why it is possible for persons with so wide a range of political views to support one form or another of a negative income tax.

2

The proposal to supplement the incomes of the poor by paying them a *fraction* of their unused income-tax exemptions and deductions, which I termed a *negative income tax* years ago, has many advantages over present welfare programs:

(1) It would help the poor in the most direct way possible.

(2) It would treat them as responsible individuals, not as incompetent wards of the state.

(3) It would give them an incentive to help themselves.

(4) It would cost less than present programs yet help the poor more.

(5) It would eliminate almost entirely the cumbrous welfare bureaucracy running the present programs.

(6) It could not be used as a political slush fund, as so many current programs—notably in the "war on poverty"—can be and have been used.

In the course of advocating a negative income tax like the one outlined above, I have repeatedly encountered the same objections time and again. Let me try to answer a few of them.

(1) *By removing a means test, the negative income tax establishes a new principle in the relation between citizens and the government.*

This is simply a misunderstanding. The negative income tax retains a means test—the straightforward numerical test of income rather than the present complex and demeaning test. It uses the same means test to decide who shall receive assistance from the government as the one we now use to decide who shall pay the expenses of government.

True, it guarantees a minimum income to all. But that is not a new principle. Present welfare arrangements guarantee a minimum income in practice, and in some states, even in law. The trouble is that these present welfare programs are a mess.

(2) *The minimum levels of income proposed are too low.* We are talking about a Federal program and a *nationwide* minimum. The levels of assistance are decidedly higher than current levels in most states. They are decidedly lower than current levels in states like New York, Illinois, California. It would be absurd to enact such high levels as national standards. But there is every reason to encourage the more affluent states to supplement the Federal negative income tax out of state funds—preferably by enacting a supplementary state negative income tax.

(3) *The poor need regular assistance. They cannot wait until the end of the year.* Of course. The negative income tax, like the positive income tax, would be put on an advance basis. Employed persons entitled to negative income tax would have supplements added to their paychecks, just as most of us now have positive taxes withheld. Persons without wages would file advance estimates and receive estimated amounts due to them weekly or monthly. Once a year, all would file a return that would adjust for under- or over-payments.

(4) *The negative income tax destroys incentives to work.* Under present programs, persons on welfare who obey the law generally lose a dollar in relief for every additional dollar earned. Hence, they have no incentive whatsoever to earn the dollar. Under the negative income tax plan that I propose, such a person would keep fifty cents out of every additional dollar earned. That would give him a far greater incentive than he now has.

One additional point. A welfare recipient now hesitates to take a job even if it pays more than he gets on welfare because, if he loses the job, it may take him (or her) many months to get back on relief. There is no such disincentive under a negative income tax.

(5) *The negative income tax will foster political irresponsibility.* If we adopt an open and aboveboard program for supplementing the incomes of people below some specified level, will there not be continued political pressure for higher and higher break-even incomes, for higher and higher rates on negative income? Will the demagogues not have a field day appealing to have-nots to legislate taxes on haves for transfer to them?

These dangers clearly exist. But they must be evaluated in terms of the world as it is, not in terms of a dream world in which there are no governmental welfare measures. These dangers are all present now—and have clearly been effective. The crucial question is, how do we get out of the mess into which these pressures have driven us? The negative income tax offers a gradual and responsible way to work ourselves out of this mess. No other way of doing so has as yet been suggested.   □

Tax Aid to the Poor— Reconsidered

Richard P. Nathan

A negative income tax (NIT) is the wrong social policy in 1974 for anyone sincerely interested in helping the poor. In this connection, we need to look at some history. When the Family Assistance Plan (FAP) was advanced in 1969, there was a very serious gap in the coverage of the poor under federally aided welfare programs. (The Family Assistance Plan had important characteristics that are the same as a negative income tax but was significantly less comprehensive in its proposed coverage. For example, it did not cover single persons, childless couples, or the aged. The main group which it would have added to coverage was the working poor—that is, intact families where the family head is working at a low income.)

These families headed by males where both the mother and father were present in the home received no benefits at all in some states in 1969 no matter how low their income was. In other states, they were added only if the breadwinner was out of work. Thus, most poor families with two parents were left out of the welfare picture, whereas broken families were assisted in all states under AFDC (the problem-ridden Aid for Families with Dependent Children program.)

But all of this was changed by the federal food stamp program, which provides aid to all needy families, including those headed by a working male parent. A virtual pilot program assisting around 2 million persons in a few counties five years ago, the food stamp program today assists over 13 million persons and is universally available.

The dramatic growth of the food stamp program *is the single most important welfare change in America since the passage of the Social Security Act of 1935.* Food stamps today provide more aid to working poor families than they would have received

From Richard P. Nathan, "Tax Aid to the Poor—Reconsidered," *The Wall Street Journal*, April 24, 1974. Reprinted with the permission of *The Wall Street Journal*, © Dow Jones & Co., Inc., 1974.

had President Nixon's Family Assistance Plan been enacted in 1972 when it died in the 92nd Congress. Furthermore, food stamp benefits are adjusted automatically every six months according to the price of food which typically goes up faster than the overall price level. Federal food stamp expenditures will soon be running at $5 billion annually and, according to one estimate, could go as high as $10 billion in 1976.

In sum, conditions are very different today than when President Nixon's FAP plan was put forward in August 1969. This is true for essentially two reasons: (1) Male-headed families now have coverage, although in many cases it is not adequate, and (2) total welfare-program growth in this period has been tremendous.

As regards the latter point, federal spending for all of what are called "income support" programs (this includes Social Security, Medicaid, Medicare, food stamps and housing subsidies) rose by 120 percent from 1969 to 1974, compared to a 50 percent rise from 1964 to 1969. The 1975 budget projects federal spending for all "income support" programs (about 55 percent of which is for the poor) at over $100 billion. This function alone accounts for one-half of the civilian budget of the federal government and by itself is larger than defense spending as projected for fiscal year 1975.

What's more, since Census Bureau figures do not reflect in-kind transfer (such as food stamps and Medicaid) and since welfare cash payments are generally under-counted, the contribution of these programs to the well-being of the nation's poor is not adequately reflected in available income statistics.

Taking all of these and other factors into account, there are five reasons why an NIT in 1974 is not a good idea for those concerned about meeting the needs of the poor.

—First and foremost, we don't have the *FAP gap* for male-headed families that we had five years ago, although we do need to improve benefits for many working-poor families.

—Second, in this politically difficult period, it makes no sense to raise the divisive issue of an NIT with its multi-billion-dollar price tag. In this regard, the lessons of the Family Assistance Plan are instructive. The Pandora's Box of emotional issues which it opened had a great deal to do with its ultimate defeat.

—Third, and perhaps most important of all, there is what one expert calls *"the NIT dilemma."* The disturbing, but compelling arithmetic of every NIT plan I have seen that is politically feasible in terms of its costs is such that it would *hurt* millions among the poor by cutting their benefits. This is especially true for families headed by females and the children in those families.

—Fourth, the kind of a welfare crisis needed to bring together a coalition for major reform does not exist today. In my view, the theoreticians of welfare are much more concerned about conceptual neatness and program symmetry than they should be. A lack of neatness in current welfare programs is no national crisis.

—Fifth, there *is* a better way. If our aim is to fill the remaining gaps and generally to promote greater equity and fairness in welfare programs for working age persons and their families, I believe we can achieve these goals better through a series of lesser legislative changes than with an NIT.

AN INCREMENTAL STRATEGY

For example, I am intrigued by the possibility of an *"incremental strategy"* which does such things as (1) standardize and expand unemployment insurance; (2) institute a national minimum for benefit levels for AFDC families; (3) create more jobs for unemployed family heads; (4) achieve program coordination through mandatory state (as opposed to county) administration, using common rules and definitions for all welfare programs that aid working-age persons; and (5) possibly also provide a work-bonus or housing allowance for the working poor to supplement food stamps.

This is the kind of a reform agenda which needs to be fully developed and debated as an alternative to an NIT.   □

SUMMARY

Income distribution has become one of the most heated topics of discussion in the United States in the 1970s. Income distribution may be viewed in many ways: in terms of factor prices (as in Part Three), or in terms of income size in either an absolute or a relative sense. Relative income distribution is often characterized by means of the Lorenz curve.

Income distribution in the United States shows considerable inequality. In absolute terms, the rising living standard of the nation has resulted in a steady reduction of the percentage of families with below-poverty-level incomes. In relative terms, however, although there was some movement toward greater equality from the 1930s to the end of World War II, there appears to have been little change in the degree of equality since that time. Although the federal income tax is progressive over a certain range, other taxes tend to be regressive and thus the considerable inequality of American income distribution survives the impact of taxes.

Poverty in this country is concentrated heavily in certain groups, such as the elderly, and especially the blacks and other minorities. In terms of income, unemployment, housing, and other measures, the special difficulties of the ghetto population become apparent.

Eliminating the worst extremes of high-income and (especially) low-income categories need not always involve conflicts of interest. Improving the economy in its macroeconomic performance with respect to unemployment and inflation would do much to help the poor. Similarly, eliminating discrimination and other artificial barriers may improve income distribution and efficiency simultaneously. Nevertheless, important conflicts will often arise when society attempts to redistribute income from one group to another. Although welfare programs have grown enormously over the past 10 to 15 years, there are notable divisions in American society in the 1970s about the desirable scale, administration, and structure of the programs.

One attempt to eliminate serious poverty is the plan for a *negative income tax*. Advanced by both conservative and liberal economists, this plan involves extending the federal income tax negatively (that is, in terms of payments *to* the taxpayer) for low levels of income. It has been criticized for involving too heavy (or too little) government expenditure in this area, but the plan appeals to many because of its simplicity and because it avoids many of the disincentive and other harmful effects of current welfare programs.

IMPORTANT TERMS TO REMEMBER

Income Distribution
Lorenz Curves
Equality vs. Inequality
Before- vs. After-Tax Income Distribution
Poverty Level
Absolute vs. Relative Poverty
Uneven Incidence of Poverty
Poverty in the Black Community
Income-Maintenance Programs
Means' Test
Negative Income Tax
"Incremental Strategy"

QUESTIONS FOR DISCUSSION

1. "Economic efficiency is a concept applicable to situations where all parties can benefit from reallocations of economic resources; in the case of income distribution, however, it is always a case of one person's gain against another person's loss." Discuss critically.

2. The following table represents income distribution in three hypothetical countries (A, B, and C) for the year 1975:

DISTRIBUTION OF FAMILY PERSONAL INCOME IN THREE HYPOTHETICAL COUNTRIES IN 1975

QUINTILES	PERCENT DISTRIBUTION COUNTRY		
	A	B	C
Lowest	5	5	20
Second	7	11	20
Third	9	18	20
Fourth	11	24	20
Highest	68	42	20

Show how these patterns of income distribution could be displayed in terms of Lorenz curves. Incidentally, which of these income distributions comes closest to approximating that of the United States in the 1970s?

3. If you were a citizen of one of the hypothetical countries in question 2, and if you had reason to believe that the pattern of income distribution would not affect other economic objectives (growth, efficiency, etc.), would you prefer the pattern of country C to that of the other countries? If you would permit any inequalities, on what basis would you do so?

4. The preceding question assumed no conflicts among economic objectives, but a characteristic problem is that objectives often do conflict. A highly progressive income tax, for example, may be strongly advocated on income-distribution grounds, yet may be criticized on efficiency grounds, because it involves a high *marginal* rate of taxation (you pay more on additional dollars earned) and therefore may undermine incentives to work. Similarly, high taxes on profits may be preferred on income-distribution grounds but opposed on the grounds that they may limit investment and hence the expansion of employment and production.
(a) Explain how conflicts of objectives may arise in the case of the two tax programs mentioned above.
(b) Give examples of other public programs in which you can see potential conflicts between income distribution and other economic objectives.

5. In chapter 6, we spoke of the possibility of a kind of "vicious circle of poverty" in the less developed countries of Asia, Africa, and Latin America. Might such a concept be applicable to the minority populations of our inner cities? Discuss.

6. Write an essay either for or against the negative income tax, including a consideration of the main arguments of the opposing position, and also a statement of how your particular plan might differ from that of Professor Friedman as outlined in his *Newsweek* articles (pp. 695–99).

SUGGESTED READING

Beer, Samuel H., and Barringer, Richard E., eds. *The State and the Poor.* Cambridge, Mass.: Winthrop Publishers, 1970.

Bell, Carolyn Shaw. *The Economics of the Ghetto.* New York: Pegasus, 1970.

Lampman, Robert J. "What Does It Do for the Poor—A New Test for National Policy," *The Public Interest,* 34 (Winter 1974).

Marchal, Jean, and Ducros, Bernard, eds. *The Distribution of National Income.* London: Macmillan & Co., 1968.

Meade, J. E. *Efficiency, Equality and the Ownership of Property.* Cambridge: Harvard University Press, 1965.

Pechman, Joseph A. and Okner, Benjamin A. *Who Bears the Tax Burden?* Washington, D.C., The Brookings Institution, 1974.

CHAPTER 30
EXTERNAL EFFECTS, POLLUTION, AND PUBLIC POLICY

We noted in the previous chapter that economic growth by no means automatically "solves" the problem of income distribution. In this chapter, we take up a number of problems that arise at least in part *as a consequence* of economic growth. Many of these problems, moreover, are not likely to be handled satisfactorily by the private marketplace, since they involve certain effects which are "external" to the ordinary supply-and-demand mechanism. Adam Smith's "invisible hand" fails us here, and public intervention of one sort or another is almost certain to be necessary.

THE COSTS OF ECONOMIC GROWTH

In the 1970s, citizens and scholars have raised a fundamental question: Is economic growth desirable? Or to put it only slightly less grandly: When a society has reached a stage of wealth where all the necessities of life and a high (by historical standards) degree of comfort have been assured to the overwhelming number of its citizens, does it thereby reach a stage when the costs of growth begin to exceed its benefits, when its energies should properly be turned in other directions?

This is not an altogether new question. Even in the nineteenth century, the great philosopher-economist John Stuart Mill yearned for the day when mankind would look for "better things" than a continuation of the constant "struggle for riches." Mill wrote:

I confess I am not charmed with an ideal of life held out by those who think that the normal state of human beings is that of struggling to get on; that the trampling, crushing, elbowing, and treading on each other's heels, which form the existing type of social life, are the most desirable lot of human kind, or anything but the disagreeable symptoms of one of the phases of industrial progress.

John Stuart Mill (1806–1873): Mill was a logician and political philosopher as well as an economist. Raised in the British Classical tradition, he had David Ricardo for an economics tutor.

Mill actually looked forward to the coming of a "stationary state," providing, of course, that the population problem (which had worried his predecessors, Malthus and Ricardo) could be handled and a decent standard of life could be guaranteed to the working classes.

In the United States in the eighth decade of the twentieth century, we have achieved a standard of life for the average man that far exceeds anything that Mill had hoped for. In consequence, there are those who argue that the time has now come to reconsider the pivotal role of economic growth in our social life. The argument has many variants, but it is built around two fundamental themes.

The first theme stresses the *declining benefits* of modern growth in the affluent society. Why do we want more goods, the critics ask. Certainly not out of economic necessity. Not even for added material comfort; historically, men have been content with far less abundance than we now enjoy. Essentially, they answer, we want more goods because a growing society creates the very wants that it in turn supplies. These wants may be created by other consumers in the manner of "keeping up with the Joneses": My neighbor has a new and fancy automobile and thus I, too, must have a new and fancy automobile. Or they may be created by the industrial producers through advertising and other means of public persuasion—if you do not buy such-and-such a product, your personal and social life will be jeopardized if not ruined. In either case, a kind of self-canceling process of want-creation and want-satisfaction is established. If I buy more because my neighbor buys more, and if he buys more because I buy more, then we can both keep on accumulating purchases indefinitely without either being any better off than if we had remained content with less in the beginning. Similarly, in the case of producer-induced demand, business firms advertise to convince the consumer that they need the goods that they would not have missed had the advertising and the additional production never occurred.

Few critics would claim that these are the *only* motives that make consumers wish additional goods —one may want to buy more records or books, for example, simply because one likes to listen to music or to read—but such motives clearly do enter into many of our purchases and, to this degree, the benefits that accrue from still additional economic growth are far less than they appear in the statistics. As the society becomes ever more affluent, these benefits can be expected continually to decline.

The second theme of this argument, and increasingly the more important theme, has to do with the *costs* of economic growth. Growth has always had associated costs. At the time of the English Industrial Revolution, there was the tremendous dislocation in the traditional pattern of life that the birth of the industrial system involved. Indeed, even the *measurement* of growth is made difficult by the fact that many of the products that we include in our GNP may actually be nothing but costs of an industrial-urban society. Suppose we lay tracks and set up a commuter train service from the suburbs to the city. Should we consider this act of production an addition to GNP, or should we argue that commuter services are simply a required cost of having an industrial-urban society and would have no value were our society organized differently?[1] Within the category of costs of growth, critics can point to a number of effects that amount to a catalog of the weaknesses of our industrial-urban society. Our air is becoming befouled with chemicals and smog. Our streams and rivers are being polluted with industrial wastes and detergents. We are despoiling our natural resource base. Our fields, meadows, and forests are being defaced by highways and billboards. The story is nearly endless and, in the 1970s, very familiar.

The critics of growth emphasize these and other deficiencies arising from the growth process, while at the same time pointing to the declining benefits (at least for the rich countries) that this process brings. They ask: Is it not a paradox that the affluent society should be creating not great works of art, beauty, and culture, but the megalopolis, the freeway, and the slum?

SPACESHIP EARTH

For some observers, the questions raised in the above paragraphs suggest that a total reconstruction of our social purposes and patterns is now required. Indeed, many in this group believe that the alternative to reconstruction is social and economic disaster. These dramatic issues are taken up in Great Debate Five: Ecology and Economic Growth. The reader of this debate will notice that scientists are by no means

---

1. See chapter 8, pp. 194–95, and also the appendix to chapter 8.

agreed on the degree of ecological dangers that are involved in a perpetuation of our present industrial system. It is also probably true that economists (with exceptions, of course) are slightly skeptical of the doomsayers, partly because they have heard a very similar story before (from Malthus, in particular), but mainly because they have studied the way in which societies, through technological change, have been able to adjust to developing scarcities and shortages. They see economic growth as a main source of society's increasing capacity to cope with problems of pollution, waste, and so on. If growth imposes costs, they say, it also confers the ability to mitigate or remove those costs.

Still, the sharp current interest in ecology is a major fact of our times and, even for the most cautious observer, it raises questions about the basic way in which we view our economic system. One of the more interesting of the new views of the economy has been put forward by Kenneth Boulding, a philosophically minded economist who has served as president of the American Economic Association. He suggests that what we are required to do now is to move from a *throughput economy* to the concept of *spaceship earth*. It is fundamental, Boulding writes, that:

all of economics . . . assumes that economic activity is a throughput, a linear process from the mine to the garbage dump. The ultimate physical product of economic life is garbage. The system takes ores and fossil fuels (and in a boom the unemployed) out of the earth, chews them up in the process of production, and eventually spews them out into sewers and garbage dumps. . . .

The throughput is going to come to an end. . . . Up to now, man has psychologically lived on a flat earth—a great plain, in fact a "darkling plain" where "ignorant armies clash by night," as Matthew Arnold says. Man has always had somewhere to go. . . .

The photographs of the earth by astronauts in lunar orbit symbolize the end of this era. Clearly the earth is a beautiful little spaceship, all blue and green and white, with baroque cloud patterns on it, and its destination is unknown. It is getting pretty crowded and its resources rather limited.

The problem of the present age is that of the transition from the Great Plains into the spaceship or into what Barbara Ward and I have been calling spaceship earth. We do not have any mines and we do not have any sewers in a spaceship. The water has to go through the algae to the kidneys to the algae to the kidneys, and so on, and around and around and around. If the earth is to become a spaceship, we must develop a cyclical economy within which man can maintain an agreeable state.[2]

What is new about this concept of a spaceship? After all, haven't economists long presented the workings of the economic system as cyclical via the image of the *circular flow?* The contrast between the spaceship view and the old view is suggested by Figures 30–1 and 30–2.

In Figure 30–1, we present the traditional circular flow representation of economic life, but now amended so that its character as a *throughput* system is made clear. In this economy natural resources are pumped into the system either as household-owned factors (private property) or "free" resources (air, water, sunlight, etc.); the circular flow combines these with labor and other factors to produce goods that go to consumers. In the course of this production, industrial wastes are produced and, later, the acts of household consumption create further wastes. In a throughput economy, this is the end of the process. The wastes go into dumps and sewers. The total amount of wastes accumulated tends ever to increase (suggested by the dotted line); simultaneously, the quantity of available natural resources tends ever to decrease (shown, similarly, by the dotted line in the natural resource container). In the

2.   Kenneth E. Boulding, "Fun and Games with the Gross National Product," in *The Environmental Crisis,* ed. Harold W. Helfrich, Jr. (New Haven: Yale University Press, 1970), pp. 162–63. For further discussion of the concepts of a throughput or spaceship economy, see Edwin G. Dolan, *TANSTAAFL* (*There ain't no such thing as a free lunch*) (New York: Holt, Rinehart & Winston, 1971), chapter 1.

long run, such a process cannot keep going on because natural resources will run out. This is alleged to be a major flaw in a throughput economic system.

The specific picture we have drawn in Figure 30–1 must be considered only a point of departure. In two major ways, it tends to *understate* the problem. In the first place, it does not explicitly represent the costs of *pollution.* To do this, we would have to acknowledge that, as the wastes accumulate on the right side of the diagram, there will be negative consequences on the natural resource picture on the left side. It is not only that we are using up our supplies of, say, petroleum, but that, in so doing, we are also diminishing our supplies of pure air, water, and so on.

The second major understatement in Figure 30–1 derives from the fact that the circular flow is presented as unchanging in dimension, whereas the characteristic form of modern industrial life, as we know, involves rapid economic growth. To represent the consequences of growth, we would have to show the circular flow in the top half of the diagram increasing in size over time. As it increased in size, it would make increased demands on our natural resources and would also accelerate the rate at which wastes (and hence pollution) are being accumulated.

On the other hand, the diagram can also be faulted for *overstating* certain aspects of the problem. Those who take a more optimistic view of our ecological situation might criticize the diagram on at least three grounds: (1) It ignores natural recycling. Although no one would agree with the pure classical view of land as the "original and indestructible" powers of the soil,[3] nevertheless it is clear that many resources are not "used up" in production, but can be used over and over again. If the total natural resource base is fairly large, these natural processes may protect us for a considerable time. (2) The diagram suggests the erroneous conclusion that production leads either to consumption or waste, whereas a very important product of our economic system is capital. That is to say, we translate iron ore in the ground into a much more useful shape—a hammer, a steel girder, a bridge—many of which products have considerable durability. (3) And, finally, the diagram makes no

3.   See chapter 21, p. 480.

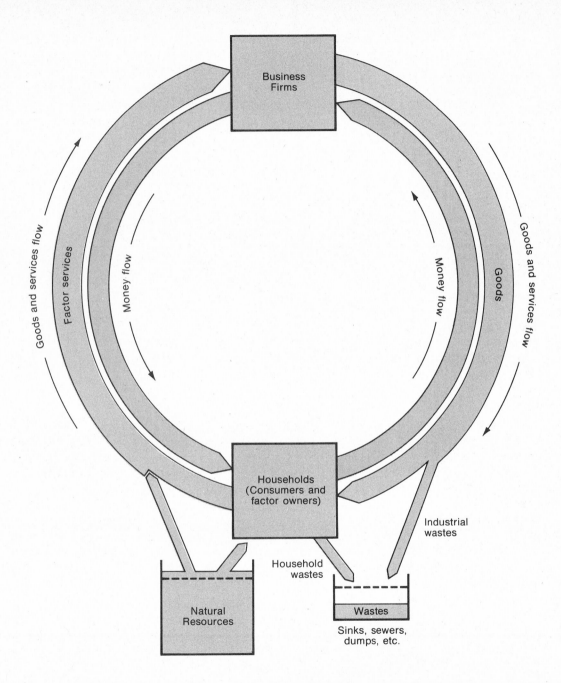

Figure 30–1. A Throughput Economy.

In this diagram, the economic flow is fueled by natural resources that come from outside the system. These resources are, in effect, converted into garbage by the system.

allowance for the fact that the economic system tends to economize on scarce resources—the scarcer they become, the more expensive they become, and the more we try to find ways to do without them. Human ingenuity will generally attempt to find ways of making use of what we have and getting along without what we no longer have (or are fast running short of). These attempts have historically been very successful, though, of course, there is no way of knowing how long that pattern of success can be maintained.

Thus, the picture is mixed. Still, the need to modify our approach to economic life in the direction of spaceship-thinking is widely acknowledged. This new approach is suggested by Figure 30–2, in which a vital link has been added between the waste container and the resource container. What this diagram suggests is that our economic survival and/or comfort in the long run may depend significantly on our ability to recycle our waste products in such a way that, far from producing negative effects on our resource base, they keep that base replenished. Whether such a cyclical economy could sustain growth over time is not clear—the advocates of Zero Growth would doubtless say no. It seems fairly certain, however, that at a minimum the creation of spaceship earth would require a different mentality from that which stimulated the Industrial Revolution of the eighteenth and nineteenth centuries. Maintenance, rather than expansion, might easily become the key word.

WHERE THE MARKET MAY FAIL

The foregoing discussion raises a very important question for the student of economics. In Part Three, we spent a considerable amount of time developing the point that a market economy produces, at least under certain circumstances, an ''efficient'' solution to society's economic problems. Now we are talking about the possibility of ecological and environmental disaster. What, we must ask, has happened to the ''invisible hand''? Has Adam Smith's metaphor turned out to be nothing but a cruel hoax?

Although this conclusion is a bit hard on the workings of a market system—environmental problems

may easily be as serious in the command economy of the Soviet Union as in our mixed market economy—nevertheless, it is true that the qualifications to the invisible hand doctrine seem to loom particularly large in an advanced industrial economy. Let us list some of the areas in which, even in pure theory, the market economy may be deemed to give an unsatisfactory social outcome; then let us show how this analysis applies in the specific case of air pollution.

First, our brief list:[4]

1. **Unacceptable consumer wants.** Consumer sovereignty is highly prized in a market-oriented society, but not invariably. Certain classes of consumers—infants, the insane, imprisoned criminals—and certain classes of goods—tanks, atom bombs, harmful drugs, or poisons—are considered to have a status in the marketplace different from ordinary consumers or ordinary goods. We shall not dwell on this point since, for the most part, we do assume that consumers are the ultimate arbiters of economic performance; however, it is notable that many currently controversial questions about government intervention in the economy touch on such matters. Examples: Should the government forbid the production and consumption of marijuana? Should it pass a gun law? Should it regulate cigarette advertising or obscene movies? Such matters are often decided by the political process rather than by any simple reliance on market supply and demand.

2. **Public goods.** It would be practically impossible to sell certain goods to individual consumers; the goods must be provided collectively or not at all. Imagine an individual homeowner living in a neigh-

---

4.   This is not an exhaustive list of all the possible defects of a market system. It does not include, for example, the fact that a market economy does not necessarily (or ordinarily) produce a socially desirable distribution of income (see chapter 29), nor the whole range of issues involved in the fiscal and monetary policies required to maintain full employment (Part Two). This list is focused primarily on those areas where the market fails to bring us ''efficiency'' and where public intervention of one sort or another will ordinarily be required. The reader should also supplement the list by recalling our discussion of market imperfections—especially in chapters 24–26.

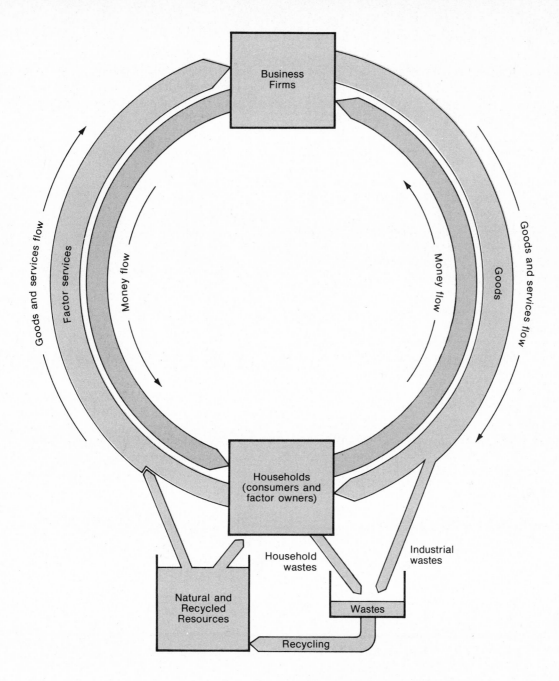

Figure 30–2. Spaceship Earth.

In this economy, wastes are recycled to keep the total
of resources constant. There is a similarity between
this kind of economy and life aboard a spaceship.

borhood near which there is a mosquito-infested swamp. There is essentially no way for him to buy mosquito protection for himself without buying it for all the other homeowners in the neighborhood. Unless there is some collective agreement to control insect life in the swamp as a whole, there may be no mosquito protection for anyone.

National defense is the classic example of a public good, and an important one, since it usually accounts for a substantial fraction of the expenditures of the U.S. federal government. Other important examples are police protection and provision for the administration of justice through the court system.

Public goods and services usually have the characteristic that if they are provided to some consumers, there is no cost in providing them to additional consumers. If a lighthouse is set up, it will service 100 or 1,000 passing ships at the same cost. Moreover, it will usually be difficult or impossible to exclude consumers from the consumption of such goods and services, even if they have not paid for any of their costs. If fifty individuals in our mosquito-ridden neighborhood decide to set up a mosquito control program, the other homeowners will also be protected, even though they have not paid for the service. (In fact, it will be in their purely *private* interest not to pay, but to accept the protection provided by the others.) In such cases, the market will generally not provide a satisfactory allocation of resources, and some kind of collective political decision will be required.

3. Decreasing-cost goods. We have already mentioned the problem of decreasing-cost industries in connection with monopoly elements in the economy (see chapter 24, p. 531). We raise it again here only to point up a special feature of the problem—namely, that simple government regulation of such industries may not be enough to bring economic efficiency. More active intervention, including subsidies or outright public ownership, may be required.

Take the case of a public utility or a mass transport system. We may have a situation in which two conditions are fulfilled: (a) it is socially desirable that this

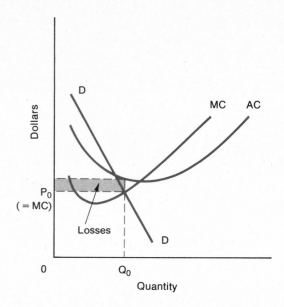

Figure 30–3. Decreasing-Cost Industry.

If the government requires a private monopolist to price his product efficiently ($P = MC$) when decreasing costs prevail, the firm will make losses (as shown by the shaded rectangle). If the industry is to continue, therefore, the government may have to subsidize it or engage in public ownership.

particular service be provided; and (b) if the government requires a private monopolist to price the service in an economically "efficient" way, the monopolist would have to go out of business. The problem is that in a decreasing-cost industry, the average cost of the firm is falling as output increases and, hence, marginal cost is below it. To secure efficiency, the government may regulate the industry so that $P = MC$. (If $P > MC$, output would be too low, since consumers could get greater satisfaction out of additional units of the service than the additional [marginal] cost to society of providing those services.) But as Figure 30–3 shows, such a price would involve the firm in perpetual losses, as indicated by the shaded rectangle.

Of course, not *all* such industries should exist at all. It is also necessary that the first condition be fulfilled—i.e., the total benefits that consumers receive from having this particular industry must exceed the total costs of providing those services.[5] However, it is not difficult to think of cases in which this holds true. We might imagine a highway that is expensive to construct, but the cost of driving additional cars on it is very low. Bridges are often cited as examples. In such cases, private ownership with government regulation may not be adequate to guarantee efficiency; public ownership, or other complicated forms of public subsidy, may be required.

4. External economies and diseconomies. In addition to *internal* economies of scale (the decreasing-cost industries just discussed), production in our economy may involve certain *external* effects. Indeed, such "externalities" may occur with respect to consumption as well as production.

An external economy *occurs when the activity of an economic unit confers a real benefit upon other producers or consumers in the economy, beyond the benefits for which the individual unit is paid. An* external diseconomy *occurs when this unit confers real costs upon other producers or consumers, for which it is not charged.*

Although the concept may seem complicated, such external effects are among the everyday experience of anyone living in a modern economy. Take the area

of education, for example. A person benefits from an education because it provides direct satisfactions and enhances his earning power. But it is also a benefit to society at large to have widespread education for political, social, and cultural purposes. *I* benefit because *you* are educated, and vice versa. My benefit is an external economy of your education, for which you are not recompensed. External *dis*economies are also easy to find, especially in modern urban life. Many of the costs of economic growth that we discussed earlier in this chapter involve external diseconomies. Pollution is a notable example, which we shall consider in a moment.

The significance of external economies and diseconomies is that they create a gap between *private* benefits and costs (measured through prices in the marketplace) and *social* benefits and costs. It may be socially undesirable to have a boiler factory in a residential neighborhood; but if the businessman is not charged for the mental anguish of the neighbors caused by the constant noise, it may be in his private interest to build the factory anyway. Consider why school education is generally publicly financed in the United States.

If education were left purely in private hands, each person would theoretically purchase it to the point where the additional private gains from one more unit (say, another year of schooling) were equal to the additional cost of that unit. But from society's point of view, this will be too little education, since the additional *social* benefit (private benefit plus external effects) is greater than the marginal cost of having this person take another year of schooling. Where such external effects are important, a strong case can be made for public intervention, ranging all the way from regulation to subsidies and taxes and, as in the case of public education, direct provision of the goods and services by the State.[6]

5.   The examination of this issue is technically complicated, involving concepts such as *consumer's surplus,* which we have not developed in this book. The basic idea can be understood, however, if we reflect that consumers generally get greater satisfactions from the consumption of the first units of a commodity than from subsequent units. Since the price of the good reflects satisfaction at the margin—i.e., of the last units purchased—consumers derive a kind of "surplus" satisfaction on all the previous units consumed. Thus, if the choice were between paying more for the good or doing without it *in total,* consumers would undoubtedly be willing to pay more than they do at the margin. Such "surpluses" have to be taken into account in deciding whether any good is worth producing in terms of total net benefits.

6.   The case for public intervention does not apply to all external effects of any kind. When more firms enter an industry, they may cause a rise in the factor prices and hence costs to other firms in the industry, but these higher factor prices *do* reflect the increased scarcity—and hence social cost—of using these factors. Such external effects, where there is no divergence between private and social benefits and costs, are sometimes called *pecuniary external economies* (or *diseconomies*).

5. Inadequate access to product and factor markets. A final category of problems that may lead the market to produce unsatisfactory social results is the differential access of various individuals *to* the markets of the economy. Generally, in our analysis of market economies, we assumed that individuals in the economy were aware of the available alternatives in purchasing goods or seeking employment and that they were able to act effectively on this knowledge. But in any society there will always be groups for which this assumption is not true. Sometimes the problem may be informational and geographical. Appalachia has sometimes been cited as a particular area of the economy where workers and their families, being poor, isolated, and little educated, lack any real knowledge of market alternatives; nor do they have the physical and cultural mobility necessary to take advantage of them if known. But access to the market can also be artificially contrived, as in the important case of racial discrimination. Racial discrimination can be thought of in economic terms as a special form of market imperfection, though it is different from other such imperfections in its historical and social roots, and it may not depend on the overt existence of monopoly power in the rest of the economy.

Where access to markets is denied either by lack of information, by cultural disadvantages, or by discrimination, the market will not give an efficient allocation of resources as indicated in purely competitive theory. Society as a whole loses when productive individuals are either unemployed, partly unemployed, or employed in lower productivity positions than their abilities warrant. In such cases, society may decide that collective action to increase information and mobility and to lower or remove artificial barriers is required.

URBAN AIR POLLUTION

The above discussion of market failure is somewhat abstract. It is easy, however, to make it quite concrete, and also to show its bearing on some of the "costs" of modern industrial society. There is probably no better nor more important example than that of urban air pollution.

This problem is by no means confined to the United States, but may be found in any industrial society with large numbers of people and machines crowded into a limited space; it affects virtually all European countries at the present time and is very intense in Japan, where people sometimes go out into the streets with gas masks because of traffic-polluted air. Nor is it a phenomenon of the last few years only.

One of the most dramatic examples of the harmful effects of urban air pollution occurred in London in 1952. Because of certain atmospheric conditions, the London fog suddenly turned black, and this black fog lasted a week. During that period, it is estimated that the normal death toll increased by 4,000. The basic cause: polluted air.[7]

The effects of air pollution are not always so dramatic as this, but they are evident in hundreds of ways in most of our major cities. Polluted air can damage eyes, lungs, crops, animals, building materials, metals. It can create an atmosphere of dirt and grime and can destroy the pleasure ordinary citizens take in breathing pure air. If pollution continues to mount, it may even be sufficient to affect the earth's weather and temperature. No one can live in a major urban area today without at times feeling depressed, if not outraged, that man seems to be systematically destroying one of the most precious, indispensable features of his natural environment.

Polluters are both consumers and producers. The automobile is the prime single offender; transportation in general accounts for about 60 percent of total air pollution in American cities. Other major sources are industry, electric power generation, space heating, and refuse incineration.

From the point of view of the economic analyst, urban air pollution is a dramatic case of the operation of external diseconomies. Pollution almost invariably represents an external cost that the individual or private business firm places upon society without charge to himself. When such externalities exist, a divergence between private and social interest will

---

7. See Roger Revelle, "Pollution and Cities," *The Metropolitan Enigma,* ed. James Q. Wilson (Washington, D.C.: Chamber of Commerce of the United States, 1967), p. 81.

arise, and some form of collective intervention will be required if the problem is to be solved.

This is shown by the need, for example, to have a legal requirement that automobiles be equipped with anti-pollution devices. The cost of such devices may not be exorbitant—let us suppose they are $50 per car on the average. However, the *private* benefit to any individual from installing such a device will be negligible, i.e., the effect of his own contribution to total pollution on himself is practically nil. Hence, unless he is required to do so, or unless he is operating in the spirit of public-mindedness rather than of private interest, he will not install such a device. In short, there is nothing in the workings of the market that will encourage either the private motorist or the automotive manufacturer to correct the situation.

If this is true of devices that can be installed on private cars, it is even more true of other solutions of a more public nature. One expert, Professor Roger Revelle, has suggested that it may be necessary to reconstruct our cities in two layers, "one for automobiles and one for people":

All vehicle traffic would be in tunnels and other enclosed spaces from which air could be rapidly pumped and treated to remove noxious substances. Alternatively one might conceive of a system for penetrating the atmospheric inversion layers and replacing the polluted air with fresh air sucked from aloft. The construction of many very high stacks equipped with enormous pumps has sometimes been discussed by engineers for the Los Angeles area, but the costs and amount of energy required, not to mention the hazards to air traffic, seem prohibitive.[8]

Such a reconstruction of our cities would clearly fall in the category of a public rather than a private project. Similarly, the provision of more effective mass transit systems—a favorite recommendation for reducing urban air pollution—would require government intervention in one form or another.

Indeed, the problems facing mass transit systems illustrate vividly how the "invisible hand" may fail us in this important area. The ideal situation for a private

individual may be to have a mass transit system that everyone else uses while *he* enjoys the convenience (particularly with the uncrowded streets that would occur) of his own automobile. Since all individuals would tend to look at the matter in the same way, the potential subversion of the socially preferable solution is easily understood.

If, then, the market fails in this area, what is to be done about the pollution problem? Clearly, public programs will have to be introduced, and these may be costly. Revelle, for example, estimates that if we wished to control *all* pollution in the United States —air, water, and land pollution—it might cost in the vicinity of 3 percent of national income over the next fifteen years. In a trillion dollar economy, this would be upwards of $30 billion per year (which works out to about $600 a year, on the average, for a family of four). The difficulty of evaluating governmental expenditures to make sure that these monies are spent wisely will be taken up in the next section.

Another possible approach—and one favored by many economists—is to try, by appropriate tax and subsidy policy, to make private and social interest coincide. Under this approach, one would try to *use* market forces so as to make them produce a better solution rather than replacing them completely with public ownership or yes-or-no controls. In the case of pollution, which involves external diseconomies, this would mean taxing the polluter—say, the private motorist—according to the amount of pollution for which he was responsible.

The logic of this approach derives from our considerations of efficiency in chapter 22. At that time we discussed the virtues of having $P = MC$ under ordinary circumstances.[9] These circumstances are not fulfilled when there are external diseconomies, since MC does not cover the true cost to society of the good in question. To discover that cost, we must also add the external pollution cost. What is proposed, then, is that a tax be added to the use of automobiles in such a way that MC *plus* the tax will reflect the true cost of the automobile to society.

In the following reading, such a proposal is briefly outlined and defended.

---

8. Ibid., p. 88.

9. See pp. 499–500.

How To Make Pollution Go Away

Edwin G. Dolan

If pollution is such an undisputably bad thing, the reader may say, not only unpleasant and aesthetically offensive but inefficient and harmful to polluter and victim alike, then let's just get rid of it! Let's get the government to ban leaded gasoline, outlaw DDT, regulate the type of fuel used by Con Ed, require secondary treatment for all sewage, impose standards on atomic power stations, insist on chemical toilets on all pleasure boats, punish people who litter the highways, and control the phosphate content of detergents! After all, isn't that what the government is for—to ban, outlaw, regulate, require, impose, insist, punish, and control?

This seems to be the instinctive reaction of a great many Americans upset about the pollution problem. The politicians whom they send to our legislatures at regularly appointed intervals are only too happy to oblige—if this new public concern will give them a chance to control something which they do not yet control, or set up a bureau or regulatory commission where one does not yet exist, what intelligent politician would pass up the opportunity?

To succumb to the urge to control pollution via the imposition of direct controls out of the belief that these are quick, expedient, or effective ways of getting the job done, would, I believe, be a grave mistake. Instead, I would like to offer some guidelines for a more efficient, equitable, and effective pollution abatement policy.

The first guideline which I propose is to make minimum use of direct controls in fighting pollution, and maximum use of market mechanisms and the price system. To illustrate how this guideline might

Excerpted from "How to Make Pollution Go Away," in TANSTAAFL* (*There Ain't No Such Thing As A Free Lunch), *The Economic Strategy for Environmental Crisis*, pp. 32–36, by Edwin G. Dolan. Copyright © Holt, Rinehart and Winston, Inc., Reprinted by permission of Holt, Rinehart and Winston, Inc.

be applied in a specific case let us take the very important example of automobile exhaust pollution. This is, incidentally, an area in which direct controls are already being used in the form of requiring certain emission control devices on all cars produced in and imported into the United States. Other direct controls are pending, including regulation of permissible types of fuels, still more effective emission control devices, and the outright banning of automobile traffic from certain urban areas.

As an alternative to such proposals, I would argue in favor of controlling auto exhaust pollution by putting a price tag on the privilege to pollute. In our Capitalist economy you can impose upon me the inconvenience of work or the inconvenience of using my lawn as a parking lot only by paying a price, and if I do not judge the price to be high enough I am free to decline your offer. Why, then, should you be able to impose upon me the inconvenience of breathing the noxious gases emitted from your exhaust pipe without paying a price, when, because of the simple physics of the situation, I don't even have the opportunity to refuse your offer to have me breathe them?

The idea of putting a price on exhaust emission at first may bring to mind the image of a little gadget like a water meter which would be clamped on the tailpipe of a car to be read once a month and a bill sent out, so much per cubic foot. If the construction of such a meter were practical, it would be an ideal method to use. As far as I know, this meter has not yet been developed, but a somewhat more primitive approach using existing institutions and technology could accomplish much the same purpose. For example, in a state like Vermont, which already requires a semiannual trip to the inspection station, the pollution charge could be combined with regular inspection. When a car was taken in, it would be rated according to an established scale of points. Starting with a basic score scaled to the engine displacement and mileage since the last inspection, so many points could be deducted for a P.C.V. system, and so many points for fuel injection, a catalytic muffler, and so

Smog Contributors. Cars on the Pomona Freeway near Los Angeles city limits add to air pollution as the sun, looking more like the moon, tries to penetrate the eye-watering smog.

on and so forth. At the end, a fee would be paid in proportion to the points remaining, which might range, let us imagine, from $100 for a massive Chrysler with no technical refinements down to $2.00 for a Volkswagen converted to run on natural gas.

Compared to the current system of direct controls, the price system would offer distinct advantages with respect to efficiency, equity, and incentives. Let us look at these advantages one by one.

The price system would be more efficient because it would observe the equimarginal principle. If you are going to use up resources in a variety of related but not identical activities, you will get the greatest yield per unit expenditure by dividing your resources among the different activities in such a way that the benefit of spending an additional penny at the margin is the same for each activity.

This principle applies also to the control of automobile exhaust. The total amount of pollution control expenditure should be divided among individual cars in such a way that the marginal yield, measured in terms, say, of cubic feet of carbon monoxide reduction per dollar spent, would be the same for all cars.

Now, direct controls clearly violate this principle. The current law requires that some fixed sum—let us say about $10.00—be spent on every car for positive crankcase ventilation. In the case of a big car which is driven a lot that $10.00 does a great deal of good. In the case of a little car, or a little used one, it does less good. Clearly, it would be more efficient to spend some of the money used on the little cars for still better control devices on big cars. Under the price system this would be done. A Buick-owning traveling salesman would probably get almost every device in the book before he got to the point where another dollar spent on technical refinements would not pay off in terms of reduced inspection tax, while the proverbial little old lady who drives her Renault once a week to church might find that even the most basic devices weren't worth putting on.

The second point of superiority of the price system lies in its equity. This has already been hinted at in our previous example—it is clearly equitable that the salesman pay more pollution tax than the little old lady. In addition to this aspect of equity, which makes people pay in proportion to the cost which they impose on others by pollution, there is another, almost reverse aspect. It is also equitable to allow people to pollute more in proportion to the benefit which they gain from pollution! Compare two car owners, one of whom views his car just as a means of getting from place to place and the other for whom his car is his principal hobby and driving his chief source of amusement. The first man will be little inconvenienced by the slight reduction in performance which is produced by the mandatory P.C.V. system. The second man, however, will be grievously annoyed when he finds that his zero to sixty acceleration time has risen from 9.6 seconds to 9.7. Would it not be more equitable to allow this second man to take his P.C.V. valve off, as long as he is willing to pay the increased inspection tax which will result and as long as that tax realistically reflects the cost which he imposes upon others by so doing?

Finally, the price system for exhaust emission control would be superior to the direct control system with respect to its incentive value. This must already be clear in general terms, but let us add a few specifics. It must be pointed out that under the current system there is no incentive whatsoever for the car owner to *maintain* pollution control devices installed by law on his car. Here we are not just worried about the hot rodder who purposely takes the thing off to get that extra edge of performance. More significantly, how many car owners even *know* that the Rochester valve of the P.C.V. system must be replaced every 10,000 miles or the system is rendered useless? And of those who do know this, how many are tempted to save the dollar or two a year involved by just letting the matter slide?

Furthermore, in the matter of incentives it is not so much the car owner as the car manufacturer who counts. The present system by insisting that every car maker, domestic and foreign, be treated exactly equal guarantees that no manufacturer can get a competitive advantage by producing a more pollution-free car. In fact, the situation is if anything the exact opposite. If the manufacturer is going to act rationally in his own self-interest to maximize his profits, it will pay him to spend millions not in the research laboratories but in the lobbies of Congress fighting pollution control legislation tooth and nail! There is much talk about a ''conspiracy'' of the big three to suppress technical developments which could reduce pollution. Maybe there is a conspiracy and maybe there isn't, but how long do you think one could last against the competition of Volkswagen, Fiat, and Toyota if the annual pollution charge paid by the owner for an American car was triple that for their foreign competitors? Let's take the profit out of pollution and put it into pollution *control*, then we'll get a real look at the capitalist economy in action.

There are a few signs on the horizon that the price system for pollution control may be gaining favor. For automobiles, President Nixon's tax on the lead additive in gasoline appears to be a small step in the right general direction. The system has been widely suggested for control of water pollution also, where the metering of wastes is more practical. A similar system is already in use in the Ruhr Valley in Germany, and pilot programs are underway in this country. The possibilities have still not been fully explored. How about, for example, a differential charge for garbage collection in the city according to whether noisy metal cans or quiet plastic ones are used? How about a differential liquor tax on beer according to whether the product is sold in indestructible aluminum cans or biodegradable plastic containers?

EVALUATING GOVERNMENT EXPENDITURES

In discussing approaches to the pollution problem, we have more or less automatically argued for an increased government intervention in the economy—whether by taxing the polluter, subsidizing a mass transit system, establishing direct controls, or whatever. Such arguments apply to virtually all the categories in the economy presented on our brief list of ''where the market may fail.''

In solving one set of issues, however, we raise another set—the question of the efficacy of governmental action. For if real-world markets may ''fail,'' so also may real-world governments. An omniscient and omnibenevolent government might solve a great many problems in our society; but, like completely ''pure'' competition, such governments have never existed. How, then, can we be sure that public intervention will not do more harm than good?

The answer is that we cannot be certain. History has shown us countless examples where governments have acted inefficiently or counter to the wishes of the consuming public. As we know, Adam Smith was aware of the antisocial propensities of some businessmen, but he also considered that the British government of his day was wasteful, extravagant, and unproductive. The Soviet government in the 1930s did not hesitate to place cruel and extraordinary hardships upon the backs of the Russian peasantry. In fact, when it comes to the problem of pollution, what are we to make of the fact that even State ownership of industry is not necessarily protective, as seen in the pollution of Lake Baikal in present-day Russia?

The fact is that governments everywhere are plagued by problems of bureaucracy and inefficient management. In our own particular form of democracy, governmental action often seems at the mercy of various groups and counter-groups who exert pressures for ends that seem more serving of self than of society as a whole. Furthermore, just as we might worry about the agglomerations of power in the hands of giant private corporations, so will many citizens be concerned about the concentration of power in the hands of the most giant of all our corporations, the federal government. The federal government, for example, has become increasingly involved in the financing of higher education in this country. There may be good and compelling reasons for a still further increase in federal involvement in our colleges and universities, but is this a desirable thing? For many, the answer will depend not simply on considerations of efficiency and the like, but also on judgments about the long-run political and cultural consequences of increasing the scope of governmental responsibility.

In short, it is not sufficient to say that the market departs from our ideal and hence that public intervention is required. We must also make a judgment as to whether, in total, the less than ideal form of public intervention we are likely to get will bring us closer to, or perhaps lead us even further away from, the desired outcome. Such judgments will generally require the skills of the political scientist and sociologist as well as the economist and, indeed, a great deal of informed intelligence and common sense.

BENEFIT-COST ANALYSIS

Even when such judgments have been made—and in some cases, as, for example, urban air pollution, it is difficult to see how public intervention can be avoided—we have the further difficult task of assuring efficiency in the operation of the public sector.

Economists in recent years have spent much time in extending their traditional techniques so that they might be helpful in evaluating governmental expenditures. Perhaps the best known example is *benefit-cost analysis*. The government may be faced with a number of possible projects, and it may wish to determine criteria for selecting some projects and rejecting others. Or with a given project, the government may wish to determine a criterion for judging

what the scale of output should be. Benefit-cost analysis provides a systematic way of approaching these public resource allocation problems.

In one sense, benefit-cost analysis is exactly analogous to the analysis of private decision-making. Suppose the government is constructing an urban transport system and wishes to determine the appropriate level of output of public transport services. Benefit-cost analysis will indicate that the government should produce at the point where the marginal cost of the project equals the marginal gains or benefits derived from it. This is very much like the private businessman determining his output where $MC = MR$. However, the governmental decision is complicated by the fact that public outputs are often not directly sold in the market (e.g., we do not buy national defense on the market, but rather collectively through public taxation). Also, even if the public services are sold to consumers (as might be the case with public transport), the market test may not cover the many externalities that the government will wish to take into account.

Hence, the relevant sense of costs and benefits is in terms of *social costs* and *social benefits*.[10] In Figure 30–4, we have drawn hypothetical curves of marginal social cost and marginal social benefit for the output of public urban transport services. By the principle of benefit-cost analysis, the government should determine its output at OQ_0 where marginal social benefit and marginal social cost are equal. At any lower output, society will be losing potential benefits, since additional dollars spent on the project will bring further net gains to society. At any higher output, additional dollars spent on the project will cost more, in terms of alternative uses of that money either in the private or the public sector, than the additional benefits accruing.

Although it is easy enough to draw hypothetical curves such as those in Figure 30–4, the matter is understandably much more complicated in reality. In measuring benefits in this social sense, for example,

10.   This, of course, is basically the same principle by which taxing polluting motorists is defended in the previous section. The tax is meant to bring private and social marginal cost in line together.

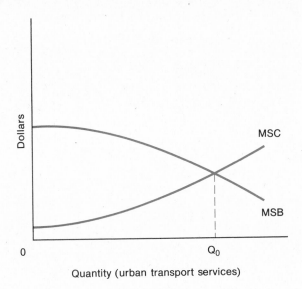

Figure 30–4. Benefit-Cost Analysis.

The government will ideally guide its expenditure decisions on the principle that *marginal social benefits* should equal *marginal social cost.* These terms are not easy to measure, however, either in theory or in practice.

the government faces the problem that external effects, even when they are theoretically measurable, will by definition not be reflected in the market in any simply observable way. Moreover, many of these external effects may be essentially intangible. How do we evaluate numerically the effect of the new urban transport system on the beauty of the city? If we are talking about education, how do we measure the political and cultural importance of having an alert, well-informed citizenry? The problem of external effects and intangibles has raised the criticism that benefit-cost analysis, in a search for false precision, may concentrate too heavily on those aspects of a problem that are measurable and hence lead to socially undesirable results.

There are other problems. One of the more difficult is the fact that most government projects will involve expenditures and benefits running over considerable periods of time. This implies that the government must use some form of interest rate to discount future costs as well as benefits. But what interest rate to choose? This raises certain practical problems, but it also may raise difficult theoretical issues, since it is not clear that collective decisions about the accumulation of capital and private decisions as reflected in market interest rates will necessarily be the same.[11]

Furthermore, the benefits accruing from any public project will often involve different objectives. One project may contribute important efficiency benefits but may do little to improve the distribution of income. One project may accelerate growth but may actually cause sacrifices in terms of efficiency or income-distribution benefits. In such cases, the government may be faced with the complicated task of trading off one kind of benefit against another.

Despite these difficulties, however, benefit-cost analysis can be an important technique for encouraging the systematic exploration of the issues that must be answered whenever the government undertakes an expenditure program. It is a clear improvement over commonly used alternative approaches

11. See, for example, Stephen A. Marglin, "The Social Rate of Discount and the Optional Rate of Investment," *Quarterly Journal of Economics* 77, no. 1 (February 1963). By "discounting" in this connection, we refer to the process by which future dollars are translated into the equivalent of present dollars. How many dollars today are $110, a year from today, worth to me? If the rate of interest is 10 percent, the answer will be $110/1.10, or $100. The general formula for deriving the "present value" of a stream of future dollars is:

$$\text{P.V. (\$)} = \$a_0 + \frac{\$a_1}{(1+i)} + \frac{\$a_2}{(1+i)^2} + \frac{\$a_3}{(1+i)^3} +$$

$$\ldots \frac{\$a_n}{(1+i)^n} + \ldots$$

where P.V. ($) is present value of the income stream, $\$a_n$ is the number of dollars received in year n, and i is the interest rate. In benefit-cost analysis, it will generally be necessary to discount both benefits *and* costs, since the expenditures on a project as well as its benefits will usually take place over long periods of time.

that do not relate benefits to costs at all, simply saying either "We must do this" (no matter what the costs) or "We can only afford that" (no matter what the benefits). Former Budget Director Charles Schultze believes that benefit-cost analysis can help to improve the public decision making process by:

Uncovering the irrelevant issues

Identifying the specific assumptions and factual bases upon which alternative recommendations rest, and,

Tracing out the knowable consequences and costs of each alternative.[12]

In this way, economic analysis has decided relevance for some of the hard practical issues of public policy in the modern American economy.

---

12.   Charles L. Schultze, "Why Benefit-Cost Analysis?" in *Program Budgeting and Benefit-Cost Analysis* (Pacific Palisades, Calif.: Goodyear Publishing Co., 1969), p. 6.

SUMMARY

Industrial societies have come under increasing criticism in the past few years because of the costs they impose on the environment. Many critics believe that the benefits of further economic growth are now outweighed by the costs in terms of pollution, tension, and the destruction of natural resources. Some, indeed, believe that the process cannot go on much longer without destroying our natural environment (see Great Debate Five: Ecology and Economic Growth).

One suggestion is that we move from a *throughput* to a *spaceship* economic system. In the former, we use up natural resources and turn them into garbage that is deposited in dumps and sewers, causing pollution that, in turn, further diminishes our natural resource base. In the spaceship concept, wastes are recycled so that the natural resource base is maintained and the accumulation of pollutants is limited.

The worries about ecological disaster raise an important question for the student of economics: Why has the "invisible hand" of the market apparently failed in this area of economic life?

The answer is that there are important problems where, even in pure theory, the invisible hand of the market will not ordinarily give us a socially desirable result. A partial list of these problems includes: (1) unacceptable consumer wants; (2) public goods; (3) decreasing-cost goods; (4) external economies and diseconomies; and (5) inadequate access to product and factor markets.

External effects are particularly important in explaining one of the most urgent of modern problems: air pollution. Pollution represents an external cost that the individual or business firm places upon society without charge to himself. This causes a gap between private and social marginal cost and is likely to require state intervention, either through direct controls, the provision of mass transit systems, or various schemes of taxation that attempt to use market forces while modifying them so as to bring private and social costs and benefits into line.

Although government intervention is to be expected in most of these areas where the market "fails," it is no panacea (witness the pollution problem in the State-run Soviet economy). Also, care must be taken that government intervention is as socially efficient as possible. Economists can help here through the techniques of *benefit-cost analysis*. These techniques apply tools used in the theory of the private economy to evaluating government expenditures in terms of marginal social costs and benefits. Although this analysis has its weaknesses, it can be used effectively to outline some of the issues involved in alternative solutions to public problems.

IMPORTANT TERMS TO REMEMBER

"Stationary State"
Spaceship Earth
Throughout Economy
Recycling Resources
Public Goods
Decreasing-Cost Industries
External Economies and Diseconomies
Private vs. Social Costs
Costs of Pollution
Benefit-Cost Analysis
MSB = MSC

QUESTIONS FOR DISCUSSION

1. "The critics who complain so loudly about the dangers of modern growth are simply rehashing old Malthusian arguments. And, in point of fact, they are just as wrong today as he was then." Discuss.

2. One of the ways in which an economy would protect itself, at least partially, against running out of natural resources would be to economize on the use of those resources that had become particularly scarce. Show how a price system in general equilibrium (see chapter 22) would react to a shortage of, say, iron ore, by altering (*a*) methods of production and (*b*) quantities of different goods produced.

3. Show that a private price system will tend to overproduce goods that have external diseconomies and to underproduce goods that enjoy external economies. Give examples of each from present-day economic life. Show the arguments for imposing taxes in some cases and giving public subsidies in others.

4. Selling hand guns on a simple supply-and-demand basis has been attacked by some as involving a serious divergence between private and social interest. It can be argued that this is an area involving unacceptable consumer wants (use of guns for robberies, etc.), public goods (the security of the community), and external effects (your possession of a gun affects my well-being). Write an essay on the economics of regulating the sale of hand guns to private individuals.

5. Do we as a society seek *no* pollution or merely *less* pollution? Discuss.

6. What is the difference between *private marginal cost* and *social marginal cost?* Between *private marginal benefit* and *social marginal benefit?* Why would we want to use the "social" concepts when evaluating a proposed public project? What difficulties could you envisage in making such evaluations for a project that, say, involved forbidding all vehicular traffic from the center of a large city and creating a large park and pedestrian mall there?

SUGGESTED READING

Dorfman, Robert, and Dorfman, Nancy, eds., *Economics of the Environment.* New York: W. W. Norton, 1972.

Freeman, A. Myrick; Haveman, Robert; and Kneese, Allen. *The Economics of Environmental Policy.* New York: John Wiley & Sons, 1973.

Hinrichs, Harley H., and Taylor, Graeme M., eds. *Program Budgeting and Benefit-Cost Analysis.* Pacific Palisades, Calif.: Goodyear Publishing Company, 1969.

North, Douglass C., and Miller, Roger LeRoy. *The Economics of Public Issues.* New York: Harper & Row, 1971.

Phelps, Edmund S., ed. *Private Wants and Public Needs.* rev. ed. New York: W. W. Norton & Co., 1965.

Turvey, R., ed. *Public Enterprise.* Baltimore, Md.: Penguin Books, 1968.

GREAT DEBATE 5:
ECOLOGY AND
ECONOMIC GROWTH

GREAT DEBATE 5:
ECOLOGY AND
ECONOMIC GROWTH

In the early 1970s, a number of documents were published purporting to show that economic growth in the industrialized world was not only of questionable benefit, but harmful, and, in the not so very distant future, would be potentially disastrous. These works included Jay Forrester's World Dynamics *(Wright-Allen Press, 1971), the Club of Rome's* Limits To Growth *(New York: Universe Books, 1972) and the British "A Blueprint for Survival," excerpts from which are included below.*

These works made front-page news in the New York Times *and countless other newspapers and have been discussed at length in articles and editorials in this country and abroad. The reader who wishes to pursue the matter further after studying the Great Debate that follows should consult the above-mentioned works directly and also some of the criticisms that have been levied at the*

methods employed and conclusions reached in those works. Such criticisms appear in the works of a Columbia University economist, Peter Passell, and a Columbia University lawyer, Leonard Ross, such as "Don't Knock the $2-Trillion Economy," in The New York Times Magazine *(March 5, 1972) and in their book,* The Retreat from Riches: The Gross National Product and Its Enemies *(New York: Viking Press, 1972).*

Since one of the contentions of those who advocate slower (or zero) growth is that continued growth is impossible with limited natural resources, there is some overlap between this debate and Great Debate Six (Energy: Restrain Demand or Stimulate Supply?) at the end of this book. However, the overlap is very small and, indeed, the authors of the following Blueprint *argue that unlimited sources of energy would only worsen the global problem. Why? Because of the enormous pollution and waste problems which unlimited energy would cause (see below, p. 732). Thus, the argu-*

ments made in the following pages would doubtless continue to be advanced even if a magic wand should remove the world's energy problems for now and for evermore.

In view of the passionate nature of the concern shown in these readings, it is unnecessary to stress that the issues involved are of monumental importance to modern man.

A Blueprint for Survival

The Ecologist*

I. INTRODUCTION: THE NEED FOR CHANGE

The principal defect of the industrial way of life with its ethos of expansion is that it is not sustainable. Its termination within the lifetime of someone born today is inevitable—unless it continues to be sustained for a while longer by an entrenched minority at the cost of imposing great suffering on the rest of mankind. We can be certain, however, that sooner or later it will end (only the precise time and circumstances are in doubt), and that it will do so in one of two ways: either against our will, in a succession of famines, epidemics, social crises and wars; or because we want it to—because we wish to create a society which will not impose hardship and cru-

*This document has been drawn up by a small team of people involved in the study of global environmental problems.

elty upon our children—in a succession of thoughtful, humane and measured changes.

Radical change is both necessary and inevitable because the present increases in human numbers and *per capita* consumption, by disrupting ecosystems and depleting resources, are undermining the very foundations of survival. At present the world population of 3,600 million is increasing by 2 percent per year (72 million), but this overall figure conceals crucially important differences between countries. The industrialised countries with one-third of the world population have annual growth rates of between 0.5 and 1.0 percent; the undeveloped countries on the other hand, with two-thirds of the world population, have annual growth rates of between 2 and 3 percent, and from 40 to 45 percent of their population is under fifteen. It is commonly overlooked that in countries with an unbalanced age structure of this kind the population will continue to increase for many years even after fertility has fallen to the replacement level. As the Population Council has pointed out: "If replacement is achieved in the developed world by 2000 and in the developing world by 2040, then the world's population will stabilise at nearly 15.5 billion (15,500 million) about a century hence, or well over four times the present size."

The *per capita* use of energy and raw materials also shows a sharp division between the developed and the undeveloped parts of the world. Both are increasing their use of these commodities, but consumption in the developed countries is so much higher that, even with their smaller share of the population, their consumption may well represent over 80 percent of the world total. For the same reason, similar percentage increases are far more significant in the developed countries; to take one example, between 1957 and 1967 *per capita* steel consumption rose by 12 percent in the U.S. and by 41 percent in India, but the actual increases (in kg per year) were from 568 to 634 and from 9.2 to 13 respectively. Nor is there any sign that an eventual end to economic growth is envisaged, and indeed industrial economies appear to break down if growth ceases or even slows, however high the absolute level of consumption. Even the U.S. still aims at an annual growth of GNP of 4 percent or more. Within this overall figure much higher growth rates occur for the use of particular resources, such as oil.

The combination of human numbers and *per capita* consumption has a considerable impact on the environment, in terms of both the resources we take from it and the pollutants we impose on it. A distinguished group of scientists, who came together for a "Study of Critical Environmental Problems" (SCEP) under the auspices of the Massachusetts Institute of Technology, state in their report the clear need for a means of measuring this impact, and have coined the term "ecological demand," which they define as "a summation of all man's demands on the environment, such as the extraction of resources and the return of wastes." Gross Domestic Product (GDP), which is population multiplied by material standard of living appears to provide the most convenient measure of ecological demand, and according to the UN *Statistical Yearbook* this is increasing annually by 5 to 6 percent, or doubling every 13.5 years. If this trend should continue, then in the time taken for world population to double (which is estimated to be by just after the year 2000), total ecological demand will have increased by a factor of six. SCEP estimate that "such demand-producing activities as agriculture, mining and industry have global annual rates of increase of 3.5 percent and 7 percent respectively. An integrated rate of increase is estimated to be between 5 and 6 percent per year, in comparison with an annual rate of population increase of only 2 percent."

It should go without saying that the world cannot accommodate this continued increase in ecological demand. *Indefinite* growth of whatever type cannot be sustained by *finite* resources. This is the nub of the environmental predicament. It is still less possible to maintain indefinite *exponential* growth—and unfortunately the growth of ecological demand is proceeding exponentially (i.e., it is increasing geometrically, by compound interest).

The implications of exponential growth are not generally appreciated and are well worth considering. As Professor Forrester explains it, ". . . pure exponential growth possesses the characteristic of behaving according to a 'doubling time.' Each fixed time interval shows a doubling of the relevant system variable. Exponential growth is treacherous and misleading. A system variable can continue through many doubling intervals without seeming to reach significant size. But then in one or two more doubling periods, still following the same law of exponential growth, it suddenly seems to become overwhelming."

Thus, supposing world petroleum reserves stood at 2,100 billion barrels, and supposing our rate of consumption was increasing by 6.9 percent per year, then as can be seen from Figure 1, demand will exceed supply by the end of the century. What is significant, however, is not the speed at which such vast reserves can be depleted, but that as late as 1975 there will appear to be reserves fully ample enough to last for

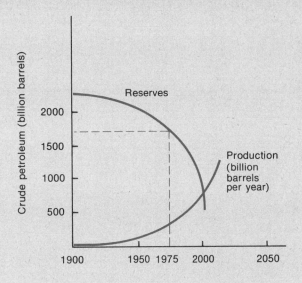

Figure 1. World Reserves of Crude Petroleum at Exponential Rate of Consumption.

Note that in 1975, with no more than fifteen years left before demand exceeds supply, the total global reserve has been depleted by only 12½ percent.

considerably longer. Such a situation can easily lull one into a false sense of security and the belief that a given growth rate can be sustained, if not indefinitely, at least for a good deal longer than is actually the case. The same basic logic applies to the availability of any resource including land, and it is largely because of this particular dynamic of exponential growth that the environmental predicament has come upon us so suddenly, and why its solution requires urgent and radical measures, many of which run counter to values which, in our industrial society we have been taught to regard as fundamental.

If we allow the present growth rate to persist, total ecological demand will increase by a factor of thirty-two over the next sixty-six years—and there can be no serious person today willing to concede the possibility, or indeed the desirability, of our accommodating the pressures arising from such growth. For this can be done only at the cost of disrupting ecosystems and exhausting resources, which must lead to the failure of food supplies and the collapse of society. It is worth briefly considering each in turn.

Disruption of Ecosystems

We depend for our survival on the predictability of ecological processes. If they were at all arbitrary, we would not know when to reap or sow, and we would be at the mercy of environmental whim. We could learn nothing about the rest of nature, advance no hypotheses, suggest no "laws." Fortunately, ecological processes *are* predictable, and although theirs is a relatively young discipline, ecologists have been able to formulate a number of important "laws," one of which in particular relates to environmental predictability: namely, that all ecosystems tend towards stability, and further that the more diverse and complex the ecosystem the more stable it is; that is, the more species there are, and the more they interrelate, the more stable is their environment. By stability is meant the ability to return to the original position after any change, instead of being forced into a totally different pattern—and hence predictability.

Unfortunately, we behave as if we knew nothing of the environment and had no conception of its predictability, treating it instead with scant and brutal regard as if it were an idiosyncratic and extremely stupid slave. We seem never to have reflected on the fact that a tropical rain forest supports innumerable insect species and yet is never devastated by them; that its rampant luxuriance is not contingent on our overflying it once a month and bombarding it with insecticides, herbicides, fungicides, and what-have-you. And yet we tremble over our wheatfields and cabbage patches with a desperate battery of synthetic chemicals, in an absurd attempt to impede the operation of the immutable "law" we have just mentioned—that all ecosystems tend towards stability, therefore diversity and complexity, therefore a growing number of different plant and animal species until a climax or optimal condition is achieved. If we were clever, we would recognise that successful long-term agriculture demands the achievement of an artificial climax, an imitation of the pre-existing ecosystem, so that the level of unwanted species could be controlled by those that did no harm to the crop-plants.

Instead we have put our money on pesticides, which although they have been effective, have been so only to a limited and now diminishing extent: according to SCEP, the 34 percent increase in world food production from 1951 to 1966 required increased investments in nitrogenous fertilisers of 146 percent and in pesticides of 300 percent. At the same time they have created a number of serious problems, notably resistance—some 250 pest species are resistant to one group of pesticides or another, while many others require increased applications to keep their populations within manageable proportions—and the promotion of formerly innocuous species to pest proportions, because the predators that formerly kept them down have been destroyed. The spread of DDT and other organochlorines in the environment has resulted in alarming population declines among wood-cock, grebes, various birds of prey and seabirds, and in a number of fish species, principally the sea trout. SCEP comments: "the oceans are an ultimate accumulation site of DDT and its resi-dues. As much as 25 percent of the DDT com-pounds produced to date may have been trans-ferred to the sea. The amount in the marine biota is estimated to be in the order of less than 0.1 percent of total production and has already pro-duced a demonstrable impact upon the marine environment. . . . The decline in productivity of marine food fish and the accumulation of levels of DDT in their tissues which are unacceptable to man can only be accelerated by DDT's con-tinued release to the environment. . . ."

There are half a million man-made chemicals in use today, yet we cannot predict the behaviour or properties of the greater part of them (either singly or in combination) once they are released into the environment. We know, however, that the combined effects of pollution and habitat destruction menace the survival of no less than 280 mammal, 350 bird, and 20,000 plant spe-cies. To those who regret these losses but greet them with the comment that the survival of *Homo sapiens* is surely more important than that of an eagle or a primrose, we repeat that *Homo sapiens* himself depends on the continued resil-ience of those ecological networks of which eagles and primroses are integral parts. We do not need to utterly destroy the ecosphere to bring catastrophe upon ourselves: all we have to do is to carry on as we are, clearing forests, "re-claiming" wetlands, and imposing sufficient quantities of pesticides, radioactive materials, plastics, sewage, and industrial wastes upon our air, water and land systems to make them inhos-

pitable to the species on which their continued stability and integrity depend. Industrial man in the world today is like a bull in a china shop, with the single difference that a bull with half the information about the properties of china as we have about those of ecosystems would prob-ably try and adapt its behaviour to its environ-ment rather than the reverse. By contrast, *Homo sapiens industrialis* is determined that the china shop should adapt to him, and has therefore set himself the goal of reducing it to rubble in the shortest possible time.

Failure of Food Supplies

Increases in food production in the undeveloped world have barely kept abreast of population growth. Such increases as there have been are due not to higher productivity but to the opening up of new land for cultivation. Unfortunately this will not be possible for much longer: all the good land in the world is now being farmed, and according to the FAO, at present rates of expan-sion none of the marginal land that is left will be unfarmed by 1985—indeed some of the land now under cultivation has been so exhausted that it will have to be returned to permanent pasture.

For this reason, FAO's programme to feed the world depends on a programme of intensifica-tion, at the heart of which are the new high-yield varieties of wheat and rice. These are highly responsive to inorganic fertilisers and quick-ma-turing, so that up to ten times present yields can be obtained from them. Unfortunately, they are highly vulnerable to disease, and therefore re-quire increased protection by pesticides, and of course they demand massive inputs of fertilisers (up to 27 times present ones). Not only will these disrupt local ecosystems, thereby jeopardising long-term productivity, but they force hard-pressed undeveloped nations to rely on the agro-chemical industries of the developed world.

Whatever their virtues and faults, the new genetic hybrids are not intended to solve the world food problem, but only to give us time to devise more permanent and realistic solutions. It is our view, however, that these hybrids are not the best means of doing this, since their use is likely to bring about a reduction in overall diversity, when the clear need is to develop an agriculture diverse enough to have long-term potential. We must beware of those "experts" who appear to advocate the transformation of the ecosphere into nothing more than a food-factory for man. The concept of a world consisting solely of man and a few favoured food plants is so ludicrously impracticable as to be seriously contemplated only by those who find solace in their own wilful ignorance of the real world of biological diversity.

We in Britain must bear in mind that we depend on imports for half our food, and that we are unlikely to improve on this situation. The 150,000 acres which are lost from agriculture each year are about 70 percent more productive than the average for all enclosed land, while we are already beginning to experience diminishing returns from the use of inorganic fertilisers. In the period 1964–69, applications of phosphates have gone up by 2 percent, potash by 7 percent, and nitrogen by 40 percent, yet yields per acre of wheat, barley, lucerne and temporary grass have levelled off and are beginning to decline, while that of permanent grass has risen only slightly and may be levelling off. As *per capita* food availability declines throughout the rest of the world, and it appears inevitable it will, we will find it progressively more difficult and expensive to meet our food requirements from abroad.

The prospect of severe food shortages within the next thirty years is not so much a fantasy as that of the continued abundance promised us by so many of our politicians.

Exhaustion of Resources

As we have seen, continued exponential growth of consumption of materials and energy is impossible. Present reserves of all but a few metals will be exhausted within fifty years, if consumption rates continue to grow as they are. Obviously there will be new discoveries and advances in mining technology, but these are likely to provide us with only a limited stay of execution. Synthetics and substitutes are likely to be of little help, since they must be made from materials which themselves are in short supply; while the hoped-for availability of unlimited energy would not be the answer, since the problem is the ratio of useful metal to waste matter (which would have to be disposed of without disrupting ecosystems), not the need for cheap power. Indeed, the availability of unlimited power holds more of a threat than a promise, since energy use is inevitably polluting, and in addition we would ultimately have to face the problem of disposing of an intractable amount of waste heat.

Collapse of Society

The developed nations consume such disproportionate amounts of protein, raw materials and fuels that unless they considerably reduce their consumption there is no hope of the undeveloped nations markedly improving their standards of living. This vast differential is a cause of much and growing discontent, made worse by our attempts at cultural uniformity on behalf of an expanding market economy. In the end, we are altering people's aspirations without providing the means for them to be satisfied. In the rush to industrialise we break up communities, so that the controls which formerly regulated behaviour are destroyed before alternatives can be provided. Urban drift is one result of this process, with a consequent rise in anti-social practices, crime, delinquency, and so on, which are so costly for society in terms both of money and of well-being.

At the same time, we are sowing the seeds of massive unemployment by increasing the ratio of capital to labour so that the provision of each job becomes ever more expensive. In a world of fast diminishing resources, we shall quickly come to the point when very great numbers of people will be thrown out of work, when the material compensations of urban life are either no longer available or prohibitively expensive, and consequently when whole sections of society will find good cause to express their considerable discontent in ways likely to be anything but pleasant for their fellows.

It is worth bearing in mind that the barriers between us and epidemics are not so strong as is commonly supposed. Not only is it increasingly difficult to control the vectors of disease, but it is more than probable that urban populations are being insidiously weakened by overall pollution levels, even when they are not high enough to be incriminated in any one illness. At the same time international mobility speeds the spread of disease. With this background, and at a time of widespread public demoralisation, the collapse of vital social services such as power and sanitation, could easily provoke a series of epidemics —and we cannot say with confidence that we would be able to cope with them.

At times of great distress and social chaos, it is more than probable that governments will fall into the hands of reckless and unscrupulous elements, who will not hesitate to threaten neighbouring governments with attack, if they feel that they can wrest from them a larger share of the world's vanishing resources. Since a growing number of countries (an estimated thirty-six by 1980) will have nuclear power stations, and therefore sources of plutonium for nuclear warheads, the likelihood of a whole series of local (if not global) nuclear engagements is greatly increased.

By now it should be clear that the main problems of the environment do not arise from temporary and accidental malfunctions of existing economic and social systems. On the contrary, they are the warning signs of a profound incompatibility between deeply rooted beliefs in continuous growth and the dawning recognition of the earth as a space ship,* limited in its resources and vulnerable to thoughtless mishandling. The nature of our response to these symptoms is crucial. If we refuse to recognise the cause of our trouble the result can only be increasing disillusion and growing strain upon the fragile institutions that maintain external peace and internal social cohesion. If, on the other hand, we can respond to this unprecedented challenge with informed and constructive action, the rewards will be as great as the penalties for failure.

Our task is to create a society which is sustainable and which will give the fullest possible satisfaction to its members. Such a society by definition would depend not on expansion but on stability. This does not mean to say that it would be stagnant—indeed it could well afford more variety than does the state of uniformity at present being imposed by the pursuit of tech-

---

*[See discussion of this concept, pp. 707–710.]

nological efficiency. We believe that the stable society, as well as removing the sword of Damocles which hangs over the heads of future generations, is much more likely than the present one to bring the peace and fulfilment which hitherto have been regarded, sadly, as utopian.

II. TOWARDS THE STABLE SOCIETY

Introduction

The principal conditions of a stable society—one that to all intents and purposes can be sustained indefinitely while giving optimum satisfaction to its members—are: (1) minimum disruption of ecological processes; (2) maximum conservation of materials and energy—or an economy of stock rather than flow; (3) a population in which recruitment equals loss; and (4) a social system in which the individual can enjoy, rather than feel restricted by, the first three conditions.

The achievement of these four conditions will require controlled and well-orchestrated change on numerous fronts and this change will probably occur through seven operations: (1) a control operation whereby environmental disruption is reduced as much as possible by technical means; (2) a freeze operation, in which present trends are halted; (3) asystemic substitution, by which the most dangerous components of these trends are replaced by technological substitutes, whose effect is less deleterious in the short-term, but over the long-term will be increasingly ineffective; (4) systemic substitution, by which these technological substitutes are replaced by "natural" or self-regulating ones, i.e., those which either replicate or employ without undue distur-

bance the normal processes of the ecosphere, and are therefore likely to be sustainable over very long periods of time; (5) the invention, promotion and application of alternative technologies which are energy and materials conservative, and which because they are designed for relatively "closed" economic communities are likely to disrupt ecological processes only minimally (e.g. intermediate technology); (6) decentralisation of polity and economy at all levels, and the formation of communities small enough to be reasonably self-regulating and self-supporting; and (7) education for such communities.

In putting forward these proposals we are aware that hasty or disordered change is highly disruptive and ultimately self-defeating; but we are also mindful of how the time-scale imposed on any proposal for a remedial course of action has been much-abbreviated by the dynamic of exponential growth (of population, resource depletion and pollution) and by the scarcely perceived scale and intensity of our disruption of the ecological processes on which we and all other life-forms depend. Within these limitations, therefore, we have taken care to devise and synchronise our programme so as to minimise both unemployment and capital outlay. We believe it possible to change from an expansionist society to a stable society without loss of jobs or an increase in real expenditure. Inevitably, however, there will be considerable changes, both of geography and function, in job availability and the requirements for capital inputs—and these may set up immense counter-productive social pressures. Yet given the careful and sensitive conception and implementation of a totally integrated programme these should be minimised, and an open style of government should inspire the trust and cooperation of the general public so essential for the success of this enterprise.

Minimizing the Disruption of Ecological Processes

Ecological processes can be disrupted by introducing into them either substances that are foreign to them or the correct ones in the wrong quantities. It follows therefore that the most common method of pollution "control," namely dispersal, is not control at all, but a more or less useful way of playing for time. Refuse disposal by dumping solves the immediate problem of the householder, but as dumping sites are used up it creates progressively less soluble problems for society at large; smokeless fuels are invaluable signs of progress for the citizens of London or Sheffield, but the air pollution from their manufacture brings misery and ill-health to the people near the plants where they are produced; in many cases the dispersal of pollutants through tall chimneys merely alters the proportion of pollution, so that instead of a few receiving much, many receive some; and lastly, in estuarine and coastal waters—crucial areas for fisheries—nutrients from sewage and agricultural run-off in modest quantities probably increase productivity, but in excess are as harmful as organochlorines and heavy metals.

Thus dispersal can be only a temporary expedient. Pollution control proper must consist of the recycling of materials, or the introduction of practices which are so akin to natural processes as not to be harmful. The long-term object of these pollution control procedures is to minimise our dependence on technology as a regulator of the ecological cycles on which we depend, and to return as much as possible to the natural mechanisms of the ecosphere, since in all but the short-term they are much more efficient and reliable.

Conversion to an Economy of Stock

The transfer from flow to stock economics can be considered under two headings: resource management and social accounting.

Resource management. It is essential that the throughput of raw materials be minimised both to conserve nonrenewable resources and to cut down pollution. Since industry must have an economic incentive to be conservative of materials and energy and to recycle as much as possible, we propose a number of fiscal measures to these ends:

(*a*) A raw materials tax. This would be proportionate to the availability of the raw material in question, and would be designed to enable our reserves to last over an arbitrary period of time, the longer the better, on the principle that during this time our dependence on this raw material would be reduced. This tax would penalise resource-intensive industries and favour employment-intensive ones. Like (*b*) below it would also penalise short-lived products.

(*b*) An amortisation tax. This would be proportionate to the estimated life of the product, e.g., it would be 100 percent for products designed to last no more than a year, and would then be progressively reduced to zero percent for those designed to last 100 + years. Obviously this would penalise short-lived products, especially disposable ones, thereby reducing resource utilisation and pollution, particularly the solid-waste problem. Plastics, for example, which are so remarkable for their durability, would be used only in products where this quality is valued, and not for single trip purposes. This tax would also encourage craftmanship and employment-intensive industry.

Social accounting. By the introduction of monetary incentives and disincentives it is possible to put a premium on durability and a penalty on disposability, thereby reducing the throughput of materials and energy so that resources are conserved and pollution reduced. But another important way of reducing pollution and enhancing amenity is by the provision of a more equitable social accounting system, reinforced by antidisamenity legislation. Social accounting procedures must be used not just to weigh up the merits of alternative development proposals, but also to determine whether or not society actually wants such development. Naturally, present procedures require improvement: for example, in calculating "revealed preference" (the values of individuals and communities as "revealed" to economists by the amount people are willing and/or can afford to pay for or against a given development), imagination, sensitivity and commonsense are required in order to avoid the imposition on poor neighbourhoods or sparsely inhabited countryside of nuclear power stations, reservoirs, motorways, airports, and the like; and in calculating the "social time preference rate" (an indication of society's regard for the future) for a given project, a very low discount should be given, since it is easier to do than undo, and we must assume that unless we botch things completely many more generations will follow us who will not thank us for exhausting resources or blighting the landscape.

The social costs of any given development should be paid by those who propose or perpetrate it—"the polluter must pay" is a principle that must guide our costing procedures. Furthermore, accounting decisions should be made in the light of stock economics: in other words, we must judge the health of our economy not by flow or throughput, since this inevitably leads to waste, resource depletion and environmental disruption, but by the distribution, quality and variety of the stock. At the moment, as Kenneth Boulding has pointed out, "the success of the economy is measured by the amount of throughput derived in part from reservoirs of raw materials, processed by 'factors of production,' and passed on in part as output to the sink of pollution reservoirs. The Gross National Product (GNP) roughly measures this throughput." Yet, both the reservoirs of raw materials and the reservoirs for pollution are limited and finite, so that ultimately the throughput from the one to the other must be detrimental to our well-being and must therefore not only be minimised but be regarded as a cost rather than a benefit. For this reason Boulding has suggested that GNP be considered a measure of gross national cost, and that we devote ourselves to its minimisation, maximising instead the quality of our stock. "When we have developed the economy of the spaceship earth," he writes, "in which man will persist in equilibrium with his environment, the notion of the GNP will simply disintegrate. We will be less concerned with income-flow concepts and more with capital-stock concepts. Then technological changes that result in the maintenance of the total stock with *less* throughput (less production and consumption) will be a clear gain." We must come to assess our standard of living not by calculating the value of all the air-conditioners we have made and sold, but by the freshness of the air; not by the value of the antibiotics, hormones, feedstuff and broiler-houses, and the cost of disposing of their wastes, all of which put so heavy a price on poultry production today, but by the flavour and nutritional quality of the chickens themselves; and so on. In other words, accepted value must reflect real value, just as accepted cost must reflect real cost.

Stabilising the Population

We have seen already that however slight the growth rate, a population cannot grow indefinitely. It follows, therefore, that at some point it must stabilise of its own volition, or else be cut down by some "natural" mechanism—famine, epidemic, war, or whatever. Since no sane society would choose the latter course, it must choose to stabilise.

Our task is to end population growth by lowering the rate of recruitment so that it equals the rate of loss. A few countries will then be able to stabilise, to maintain that ratio; most others, however, will have to slowly *reduce* their populations to a level at which it is sensible to stabilise. Stated baldly, the task seems impossible; but if we start now, and the exercise is spread over a sufficiently long period of time, then we believe that it is within our capabilities. The difficulties are enormous, but they are surmountable.

First, governments must acknowledge the problem and declare their commitment to ending population growth; this commitment should also include an end to immigration. Secondly, they must set up national population services with a fourfold brief:

(1) to publicise as widely and vigorously as possible the relationship between population, food supply, quality of life, resource depletion, etc., and the great need for couples to have no more than two children. The finest talents in advertising should be recruited for this, and the broad aim should be to inculcate a socially more responsible attitude to child-rearing. For example, the notion (derived largely from the popular women's magazines) that childless couples should be objects of pity rather than esteem should be sharply challenged; and of course there are many similar notions to be disputed.

(2) to provide at local and national levels free contraception advice and information on other services such as abortion and sterilisation;

(3) to provide a comprehensive domiciliary service, and to provide contraceptives free of charge, free sterilisation, and abortion on demand;

(4) to commission, finance, and coordinate research not only on demographic techniques and contraceptive technology, but also on the subtle cultural controls necessary for the harmonious maintenance of stability. We know so little about the dynamics of human populations that we cannot say whether the first three measures would be sufficient. It is self-evident that if couples still wanted families larger than the replacement-size no amount of free contraception would make any difference. However, because we know so little about population control, it would be difficult for us to devise any of the socio-economic restraints which on the face of it are likely to be more effective, but which many people fear might be unduly repressive. For this reason, we would be wise to rely on the first three measures for the next twenty years or so. We then may find they are enough—but if they aren't, we must hope that intensive research during this period will be rewarded with a set of socio-economic restraints that are both *effective* and *humane.* These will then constitute the third stage, and should also provide the tools for the fourth stage—that of persuading the public to have average family sizes of slightly *less* than replacement size, so that total population can be greatly reduced. If we achieve a decline rate of 0.5 percent per year, the same as Britain's rate of growth today, there should be no imbalance of population structure, as the depen-

dency ratio would be exactly the same as that of contemporary Britain. Only the make-up of dependency would be different: instead of there being more children than old people, it would be the other way round. The time-scale for such an operation is long of course.

Creating a New Social System

Possibly the most radical change we propose in the creation of a new social system is decentralisation. We do so not because we are sunk in nostalgia for a mythical little England of fetes, olde worlde pubs, and perpetual conversations over garden fences, but for four much more fundamental reasons:

(a) While there is good evidence that human societies can happily remain stable for long periods, there is no doubt that the long transitional stage that we and our children must go through will impose a heavy burden on our moral courage and will require great restraint. Legislation and the operations of police forces and the courts will be necessary to reinforce this restraint, but we believe that such external controls can never be so subtle nor so effective as internal controls. It would therefore be sensible to promote the social conditions in which public opinion and full public participation in decision-making become as far as possible the means whereby communities are ordered. The larger a community the less likely this can be: in a heterogeneous, centralised society such as ours, the restraints of the stable society if they were to be effective would appear as so much outside coercion; but in communities small enough for the general will to be worked out and expressed by individuals confident of themselves and their fellows as individuals, "us and them" situations are less likely to occur—people having learned the limits of a stable society would be free to order their own lives within them as they wished, and would therefore accept the restraints of the stable society as necessary and desirable and not as some arbitrary restriction imposed by a remote and unsympathetic government.

(b) As agriculture depends more and more on integrated control and becomes more diversified, there will no longer be any scope for prairie-type crop-growing or factory-type livestock-rearing. Small farms run by teams with specialised knowledge of ecology, entomology, botany, etc., will then be the rule, and indeed individual smallholdings could become extremely productive suppliers of eggs, fruit, and vegetables to neighbourhoods. Thus a much more diversified urban-rural mix will be not only possible, but because of the need to reduce the transportation costs of returning domestic sewage to the land, desirable. In industry, as with agriculture, it will be important to maintain a vigorous feedback between supply and demand in order to avoid waste, overproduction, or production of goods which the community does not really want, thereby eliminating the needless expense of time, energy and money in attempts to persuade it that it does. If an industry is an integral part of a community, it is much more likely to encourage product innovation because people clearly want qualitative improvements in a given field, rather than because expansion is necessary for that industry's survival or because there is otherwise insufficient work for its research and development section. Today, men, women, and children are merely consumer markets, and industries as they centralise become national rather than local and supranational rather than national, so that while entire communities may come to depend on them for the jobs they supply, they are in no sense integral parts of those communities. To a considerable extent the "jobs or beauty" dichotomy has been made possible because of this deficiency. Yet plainly people want jobs *and* beauty, they should not in a just and humane society be forced to choose between the two, and in a decentralised society of small communities where industries are small enough to be responsive to each community's needs, there will be no reason for them to do so.

(*c*) The small community is not only the organisational structure in which internal or systemic controls are most likely to operate effectively, but its dynamic is an essential source of stimulation and pleasure for the individual. Indeed it is probable that only in the small community can a man or woman be an individual. In today's large agglomerations he is merely an isolate—and it is significant that the decreasing autonomy of communities and local regions, and the increasing centralisation of decision-making and authority in the cumbersome bureaucracies of the state, have been accompanied by the rise of self-conscious individualism, an individualism which feels threatened unless it is harped upon.

(*d*) The fourth reason for decentralisation is that to deploy a population in small towns and villages is to reduce to the minimum its impact on the environment. This is because the actual urban superstructure required per inhabitant goes up radically as the size of the town increases beyond a certain point. For example, the *per capita* cost of high rise flats is much greater than that of ordinary houses; and the cost of roads and other transportation routes increases with the number of commuters carried. Similarly, the *per capita* expenditure on other facilities such as those for distributing food and removing wastes is much higher in cities than in small towns and villages. Thus, if everybody lived in villages the need for sewage treatment plants would be somewhat reduced, while in an entirely urban society they are essential, and the cost of treatment is high. Broadly speaking, it is only by decentralisation that we can increase self-sufficiency—and self-sufficiency is vital if we are to minimise the burden of social systems on the ecosystems that support them.

Although we believe that the small community should be the basic unit of society and that each community should be as self-sufficient and self-regulating as possible, we would like to stress that we are not proposing that they be inward-looking, self-obsessed or in any way closed to the rest of the world. Basic precepts of ecology, such as the interrelatedness of all things and the far-reaching effects of ecological processes and their disruption, should influence community decision-making, and therefore there must be an efficient and sensitive communications network between all communities. There must be procedures whereby community actions that affect regions can be discussed at regional level and regional actions with extra-regional effects can be discussed at global level. We have no hard and fast views on the size of the proposed communities, but for the moment we suggest neighbourhoods of 500, represented in communities of 5,000, in regions of 500,000, represented nationally, which in turn as today should be represented globally. We emphasise that our goal should be to create *community feeling* and *global awareness,* rather than that dangerous and sterile compromise which is nationalism.

III. THE GOAL

There is every reason to suppose that the stable society would provide us with satisfactions that would more than compensate for those which, with the passing of the industrial state, it will become increasingly necessary to forgo.

We have seen that man in our present society has been deprived of a satisfactory social environment. A society made up of decentralised, self-sufficient communities, in which people work near their homes, have the responsibility of governing themselves, of running their schools, hospitals, and welfare services, in fact of constituting real communities, should, we feel, be a much happier place.

Its members, in these conditions, would be likely to develop an identity of their own, which many of us have lost in the mass society we live in. They would tend, once more, to find an aim in life, develop a set of values, and take pride in their achievements as well as in those of their community.

It is the absence of just these things that is rendering our mass society ever less tolerable to us and in particular to our youth, and to which can be attributed the present rise in drug addiction, alcoholism, and delinquency, all of which are symptomatic of a social disease in which a society fails to furnish its members with their basic psychological requirements.

Real Costs

We might regard with apprehension a situation in which we shall have to make do without many of the devices such as motor-cars, and various domestic appliances, which, to an ever greater extent, are shaping our everyday lives.

These devices may indeed provide us with much leisure and satisfaction, but few have considered at what cost. For instance, how many of us take into account the dull and tedious work that has to be done to manufacture them, or for that matter to earn the money required for their acquisition? It has been calculated that the energy used by the machines that provide the average American housewife with her high standard of living is the equivalent of that provided by five hundred slaves.

In this respect, it is difficult to avoid drawing a comparison between ourselves and the Spartans, who in order to avoid the toil involved in tilling the fields and building and maintaining their homes employed a veritable army of helots. The Spartan's life, as everybody knows, was a misery. From early childhood, boys were made to live in barracks, were fed the most frugal and austere diet and spent most of their adult life in military training so as to be able to keep down a vast subject population, always ready to seize an opportunity to rise up against its masters. It never occurred to them that they would have been far better off without their slaves, fulfilling themselves the far less exacting task of tilling their own fields and building and maintaining their own homes.

In fact "economic cost," as we have seen, simply does not correspond to "real cost." Within a stable society this gap must be bridged as much as possible.

This means that we should be encouraged to buy things whose production involves the minimum environmental disruption and which will not give rise to all sorts of unexpected costs that would outweigh the benefits that their possession might provide.

Real Value

It is also true, as we have seen, that "economic value" as at present calculated does not correspond to real value any more than "economic cost" corresponds to real cost.

In a stable society, everything would be done to reduce the discrepancy between economic value and real value, and if we could repair some of the damage we have done to our physical and social environment, and live a more natural life, there would be less need for the consumer products that we spend so much money on. Instead we could spend it on things that truly enrich and embellish our lives.

In manufacturing processes, the accent would be on quality rather than quantity, which means that skill and craftsmanship, which we have for so long systematically discouraged, would once more play a part in our lives. For example, the art of cooking would come back into its own, no longer regarded as a form of drudgery, but correctly valued as an art worthy of occupying our time, energy, and imagination. Food would become more varied and interesting and its consumption would become more of a ritual and less a utilitarian function.

The arts would flourish: literature, music, painting, sculpture, and architecture would play an ever greater part in our lives, while achievements in these fields would earn both money and prestige.

A society devoted to achievements of this sort would be an infinitely more agreeable place than is our present one, geared as it is to the mass production of shoddy utilitarian consumer goods in ever greater quantities. Surprising as it may seem to one reared on today's economic doctrines, it would also be the one most likely to satisfy our basic biological requirements for food, air, and water, and even more surprisingly, provide us with the jobs that in our unstable industrial society are constantly being menaced.

There must be a fusion between our religion and the rest of our culture, since there is no valid distinction between the laws of God and Nature, and Man must live by them no less than any other creature. Such a belief must be central to the philosophy of the stable society, and must permeate all our thinking. Indeed it is the only one which is properly scientific, and science must address itself much more vigorously to the problems of co-operating with the rest of Nature, rather than seeking to control it.

This does not mean that science must in any way be discouraged. On the contrary, within a stable society, there would be considerable scope for the energies and talents of scientist and technologist.

Basic scientific research, plus a good deal of multidisciplinary synthesis, would be required to understand the complex mechanisms of our ecosphere with which we must learn to co-operate.

There would be a great demand for scientists and technologists capable of devising the technological infra-structure of a decentralised society. Indeed, with the application of a new set of criteria for judging the economic viability of technological devices, there must open a whole new field of research and development.

The recycling industry which must expand very considerably would offer innumerable opportunities, while in agriculture there would be an even greater demand for ecologists, botanists, entomologists, mycologists, etc., who would be called upon to devise ever subtler methods for ensuring the fertility of the soil and for controlling "pest" populations.

Thus in many ways, the stable society, with its diversity of physical and social environments, would provide considerable scope for human skill and ingenuity.

Indeed, if we are capable of ensuring a relatively smooth transition to it, we can be optimistic about providing our children with a way of life psychologically, intellectually and aesthetically more satisfying than the present one. And we can be confident that it will be sustainable as ours cannot be, so that the legacy of despair we are about to leave them may at the last minute be changed to one of hope.   □

A Response to the Blueprint

Nature

I. THE CASE AGAINST HYSTERIA

Britain is being assaulted by the environmentalists. This weekend, Dr. Paul Ehrlich, president of Zero Population Growth Inc., and a professor of biology at Stanford University, is to recite for the Conservation Society his now familiar dirge that the world is about to breed itself to death. Last week, a distinguished group of doctors, many of whom should have known better, published in *The Lancet* and the *British Medical Journal* a declaration that Britain is so overcrowded that there is "a direct threat to the mental and physical well-being of our patients" and a plea that doctors should unite "to combat

"A Response to the Blueprint," excerpted from editorials in *Nature*, January 14, 1972 and January 28, 1972. Reprinted by permission of the publisher.

the British disease of over-population." At the same time, the new magazine *The Ecologist* published what it called "A Blueprint for Survival" which reflects and sometimes amplifies a good many of the half-baked anxieties about what is called the environmental crisis. On this occasion, the doctrine that dog should not eat dog notwithstanding, the magazine deserves to be taken to task if only for having recruited a "statement of support" from thirty-three distinguished people, many of them scientists, at least half of whom should have known better. Nobody pretends that there are no serious problems to be worried about but the time seems fast approaching when the cry of disaster round the corner will have to be promoted to the top of the list of causes for public concern.

That professional people should lend their names to attempts like these to fan public anxiety about problems which have either been exaggerated or which are nonexistent is reprehensible. It is especially regrettable that declarations like these should myopically draw attention to the supposed difficulties of moderating population growth in Britain when there is no evidence worth speaking of to suggest that Britain is overpopulated (which is not, of course, the same thing as to say that the country is properly managed). The doctors who signed the round robin to the medical weeklies say that the problems of the developing countries "are formidable and may defy any rational solution," but that they are also "gravely concerned" at the pace of growth of the British population, which exceeds 55 million, and which is expected to increase to 66.5 million by the end of the century.

In reality, the doctors seem to have added an extra 500,000 to the latest estimates of the population of the United Kingdom in the year 2000, for the Government Actuary's latest calculation, published three months ago, gives an even 66 million for that date. It is, however, much more relevant that the forward projections of the British population have been declining steadily over the past decade, as the statisticians have been persuaded by experience that the trend of fertility in Britain, like that in much of the rest of Western Europe, is downward. The doctors also choose, by design or ignorance, to overlook the plain truth that only a quarter of such increase of the British population as there may be between now and the end of the century can be attributed to what they call "the present reproductive bonanza." The rest is simply a consequence of their own craft, which has now made it possible for people to live longer and to survive a good many of the previously fatal hazards of middle life. So is it to be expected that the same people will band together in public to wring their hands about the once and for all increase of the British population which is likely to come about when, at some time in the next two decades, ways are found of treating or even preventing some forms of cancer?

The same unreflectiveness appears to have marred *The Ecologist's* "Blueprint for Survival." Those who have compiled it say that "the relevant information available has impressed upon us the extreme gravity of the global situation today." They foresee "the collapse of society" and consider that if present trends persist, "life support systems on this planet" will be irreversibly disrupted if not by the end of the century then "within the lifetime of our children." Governments, they say, are either refusing to face facts or are "briefing their scientists in such a way that their seriousness is played down." So, the argument goes, there must be a redefinition of the philosophy of civilized life and a restructuring of society as a whole.

The errors in this simplistic view of the present stage in the history of the human race are by now familiar. Much turns on the way in which industrialized societies are at present consuming raw materials at a substantial rate, and it is true that it seems increasingly unlikely that petroleum companies will be able indefinitely to discover new reserves at such a pace that future supplies are always ensured. Oil, indeed, may be the most vulnerable of the resources at present used, just as in Europe 2000 years ago native stands of timber proved not to be inexhaustible. But does it follow from this simple-minded calculation that there will come a time when, to everybody's surprise, petroleum deposits are worked out and industry is forced to grind to a halt? Is it not much more likely, about a century from now, that prices for petroleum will be found to be so high that even the least successful nuclear power companies will find themselves able to sell reactors more easily?

In the same way, is it not likely that the apparently impending scarcity of copper (belied for the time being by the obstinately low price at which the metal is at present marketed) will encourage the use of aluminum as a conductor of electricity? To be sure, as the developing countries gather economic momentum, they will begin to make larger demands on raw materials such as these, yet it does not follow that they will have to repeat in every detail the industrial history of the countries now industrialized, and it remains a comforting truth that the raw materials on which the products of modern industry are based loom less large in economic terms than the products of the Industrial Revolution. Computers, after all, need very little copper for their manufacture. In general, the problem of raw materials is not a problem of the exploitation of a finite resource, however much it might be made to seem as such, but is a problem in economics—how best to regulate the prices of raw materials so as to balance the present demand against the probable demand in the future, how best to encourage what kinds of substitutions, how best to bring into production new reserves (not the least of which are the oceans of the world). Nobody should think that there is nothing to worry about. Good planetary housekeeping, as *The Ecologist* would no doubt describe it, should be an important objective of public policy. But it is a public disservice to describe such intricate and interesting problems in such simple and scarifying terms.

Similar fallacies attend *The Ecologist's* analysis of the supply of food. The document says that food production in the developing world has "barely kept abreast of population growth" and that such increases as there have been are a consequence of the "opening up of new land for cultivation." It goes on to say that this will not be possible for much longer, for "all the good land in the world is now being farmed." Factually, these statements are incorrect. In many parts of South-East Asia, the past few years have seen dramatic improvements in agricultural productivity, acre for acre. In any case, it remains a fact and even something about which agronomists should hang their heads that tropical regions are still comparatively unproductive of food. But the chief complaint of this declaration is that the "FAO programme to feed the world" depends on an intensification of agriculture and that the strains of wheat and rice likely to be

the work horses of Asian agriculture are more vulnerable to disease and more demanding of fertilizer.

So what? must surely be the moderate reply. In North America and Western Europe, after all, agriculture is much more intensive than most agricultural practices likely to be common in Asia in the next few years. And the benefits of intensive agriculture are not merely that a given acre of land can produce more food each year but that it can be made to do so at a lower labour cost. Indeed, it might well be calculated that until the populations of the developing world are able to feed themselves without employing more than half of their labour force on the land, they will not be free to develop either along the lines of Western industrialization or along some other route that they might prefer. The fact that intensive agriculture entails crops which are highly specialized and therefore vulnerable to epidemic diseases of one kind or another is no more relevant in Asia than in, for example, North America.

The abiding fault in these discussions is their naïvety, and nowhere is this more true than in speculations about the social consequences of the phenomena over which *The Ecologist* wrings its hands. Starting with the assertion that the developed nations have already collared the raw materials with which developing nations might seek to improve their standards of living, the journal goes on to say that "we are altering people's aspirations without providing the means for them to be satisfied. In the rush to industrialize, we break up communities, so that the controls which formerly regulated behaviour are destroyed. Urban drift is one result of this process, with a consequent rise in antisocial practices, crime, delinquency and so on. . . ." This is an echo of the distinguished doctors' declaration about the consequences of crowding, but is it fair to describe this, as *The Ecologist* does, as a portent of the collapse of society? Is it reasonable to say that in such circumstances, "it is more than probable that governments will fall into the hands of reckless and unscrupulous elements, who will not hesitate to threaten neighbouring governments with attack if they feel they can wrest from them a larger share of the world's vanishing resources"? The truth is, of course, that this is mere speculation. All the attempts which there have been in the past few years to discover correlations between such factors as population density and prosperity per head of population with the tendency to violence, either civil or international, have been fruitless. Who will say that the crowded Netherlands are more violent than the uncrowded United States? And who will say that the forces which have in the past 2000 years helped to make civilized communities more humane can now be dismissed from the calculation simply because a new generation of seers sees catastrophe in the tea leaves?

II. CATASTROPHE OR CHANGE?

Predictably, anxiety about environmental catastrophe has spread to Britain, and it is hard not to remember Professor D. J. Bogue's description of the same phenomenon in the United States as the "nonsense explosion." Many readers of *Nature* appear to have been surprised that a journal which counts Sir Julian Huxley's grandfather as one of its sponsors should have taken such a fierce line on the warnings of environmental catastrophe now commonly to be heard. The truth is that public confusion which has been created in the past few years by warnings of

catastrophe is a serious impediment to the rational conduct of society. A part of the difficulty is technical, for whether the prophets are complaining of the hazards of DDT, carbon dioxide in the environment, the threatened exhaustion of natural resources, or the growth of population, a proper understanding of what happens and is likely to happen is fraught with uncertainty, complexity and error. Understandably, people at large are puzzled to know what weight to give to warnings of catastrophe around the corner and to assurances that the problems are not nearly as alarming as they are said to be.

The question whether the years immediately ahead will bring catastrophe is not so much technical as philosophical. The document published two weeks ago by *The Ecologist* says that "the principal defect of the industrial way of life . . . is that it is not sustainable. Its termination within the lifetime of somebody born today is inevitable—unless it continues to be sustained for a while longer by an entrenched minority at the cost of imposing great suffering on the rest of mankind." The calculations supposedly implicit in statements like this are that particular resources, petroleum for example, may be seriously depleted on time scales of the order of a century, or that, after a century of unrestricted growth, the population of the world may have grown to such a point that life is intolerable or even insupportable. As yardsticks which show what kinds of problems may in future be important, pieces of arithmetic like this are no doubt of some value. The error in supposing that they constitute a proof of imminent calamity is the assumption that administrative and social mechanisms which exist already or which are in the course of being developed will do nothing to fend them off, but this is to ignore the beneficent tendencies already apparent—the rapid decline of fertility in the past decade in South-East Asia and the Caribbean and the working of the classical economic laws of scarcity, originally described by the great Victorians, to strike a balance between exploitation and conservation and the way in which governments in North America and Western Europe have succeeded in improving the quality of urban air and water by laying out money on pollution control. In short, those who prophesy disaster a century or more from now and ask for apocalyptic remedies overlook the way in which important social changes have historically been effected by the accumulation of more modest humane innovations.

In the circumstances, it is not surprising that the remedies suggested for the avoidance of catastrophe are often unpleasantly unrealistic. *The Ecologist*'s manifesto may be controversial because of its over-sharp definition of the supposed threat, but it shares with other declarations of this kind the advocacy of thoroughly pernicious changes in the structure of society. It is tempting to ask how many of those who gave their names to the document solemnly consider that industrialized societies such as Britain will be better off if they are organized in small communities in which social mobility is deliberately restricted and in which agriculture is central to everybody's life. Are these not potentially illiberal arrangements? Is there not a serious danger that to strive for them will weaken the will of civilized communities, developed and developing, to work towards humane goals—the removal of poverty and the liberty of the subject?   □

To Grow and To Die

Anthony Lewis

1

Our diverse worlds—developed, underdeveloped, East, West—have at least one article of faith in common: economic growth. For individuals, for economic enterprises and for nations, growth is happiness, the specific for ills and the foundation of hope. Next year our family will be richer, our company bigger, our country more productive.

Now the ecologists have begun to tell us that growth is self-defeating, that the planet cannot long sustain it, that it will lead inevitably to social and biological collapse. That was the central thesis of the recent "Blueprint for Survival" published in Britain, and it is a theme increasingly found in analytical studies of the earthly future.

The proposition is so shocking that the natural reaction is to wish it away. Some economists, the apostles of growth, do just that. There was an especially acute example of wishfulness in a *Newsweek* column by Henry C. Wallich, Yale professor and former U.S. economic adviser, condemning the opposition to growth as dangerous heresy.

"It is an alarming commentary on the intellectual instability of our times," Professor Wallich said, "that today mileage can be made with the proposal to stop America dead in her tracks. Don't we know which way is forward?"

As long as there is growth, he said, "everybody will be happier." By "allowing everybody to have more" and refusing to "limit resources available for consumption," we shall also have "more resources" to clean up the environment.

Excerpted from Anthony Lewis "To Grow and To Die," in *The New York Times* January 29, January 31, February 5, 1972. © 1972 by The New York Times Company. Reprinted by permission.

If Professor Wallich's opinion is representative of the American intellectual community, it is an alarming comment on our awareness of the most important facts of life today. For he is evidently in a state of ecological illiteracy.

There are no such things as endless growth and unlimited resources for everyone and everything. We live in a finite world, and we are approaching the limits. Discussion of growth as an environmental factor has to begin with some understanding of such considerations.

The crucial fact is that growth tends to be exponential. That is, it multiplies. Instead of adding a given amount every so often, say 1,000 tons or dollars a year, the factors double at fixed intervals. That tends to be true of population, of industrial production, of pollution, and of demand on natural resources—some of the main strains of planetary life.

The rate of increase determines the doubling time. If something grows 7 percent a year, it will double in ten years. Right now world population is growing 2.1 percent a year; at that rate it doubles in thirty-three years. And with each doubling, the base is of course larger for the next increase. The world had about 3.5 billion people in it in 1970. At the present rate of increase, it will have seven billion in 2003.

Exponential growth is a tricky affair. It gives us the illusion for a long time that things are going slowly; then suddenly it speeds up. Suppose the demand for some raw material is two tons this year and doubles every year. Over the next fifteen years it will rise to only 32,768 tons, but just five years later it will be 1,048,576 tons.

That phenomenon is what makes it so hard for people to understand how rapidly we may be approaching the limits of growth. For as population and per capita consumption both grow, the curves of demand suddenly zoom upward.

Consider the case of aluminum as a sample of resource demand and supply. The known reserves of aluminum are enough to supply the current demand for 100 years. But the use is increasing exponentially, and at the rate of increase the supply will be enough for only 31 years. Moreover, the multiplying demand is a much larger factor, mathematically, than any likely discovery of new sources of supply. If reserves were multiplied by five, the same growth of demand would still exhaust them in 55 years.

The example of aluminum is not especially chosen to disturb, for there are others that even more dramatically indicate the way exponential growth can run up to projected limits. One is simply arable land. At the present rate of world population growth, the supply of land necessary for food production will run out by the year 2000. If agricultural productivity were doubled, the limit would be pushed back thirty years.

2

A hundred years ago John Stuart Mill urged human society to limit its population and wealth and seek "the stationary state." He had a vision of a cramped and depleted earth. He sincerely hoped, he said, that men "will be content to be stationary long before necessity compels them to it."

Mill's was a premature vision, and for a long time hardly anyone shared it. Now, suddenly, impressive scientific evidence is being put to us that necessity compels an early end to the dominant earthly ambition of economic growth. For the exponential growth of population and production is putting strains on our environment that cannot be sustained.

To talk about limiting growth as a philosophical matter is easy enough. But when one begins to consider the specific changes of course that would be required of mankind, the difficulties are soon seen to be enormous. The economic habits of a millennium, the motivations, the very conception of a good society would be affected.

The whole question of equality as a social goal, for example, would be transformed. In most societies, East and West, there are gross inequalities of wealth today. They are made politically tolerable in good part by the notion of the whole economic pie growing constantly larger so that everyone can have a bigger slice. That is why politicians from Brezhnev to Edward Heath promise their constituents faster economic growth.

But what happens if everyone in a society knows that there can be no increase in the total volume of material goods? Is it still bearable that one man has three cars in his garage and another not enough to eat?

Similar considerations affect our traditional view of competition as a motivating economic force. Leading ecologists say we must adopt a policy of no net increase in capital investment from now on—only enough to match depreciation of capital.

But if the United States had such a policy, how could manufacturers compete in the traditional way of more productive machinery? Would it not follow that new forms of social control would have to be imposed on production, on marketing, on advertising? And how would they be squared with our ideas of freedom?

Equality is an issue not only within but between societies. If the ecologists are right, then it is foolish and dangerous for developing countries to dream of having industrial economies and a standard of material wealth like the developed world's.

But how can the rich few advise the poor many that they will be better off forsaking the old material goals? And does not that again imply a change in one's whole view of social organization, toward a less material society on the Chinese model, with enough for everyone to eat but little competition for goods or ease? Does it not follow in international as in national life that an end to growth must not be an imposition by the rich on the poor and hence requires a fresh commitment to a decent level of equality?

Merely to state such problems is to make one thing evident: the complete irrelevance of most of today's political concerns to the most important problem facing the world in the long run. And not very long at that.   □

A World without Growth?

Henry C. Wallich

Anthony Lewis, in two recent issues of *The New York Times*, warns us of the deadly consequences of growth. Running out of resources, running into total pollution, running to the point of total exhaustion and collapse—those are the ultimate rewards of growth. We must stop growth, not just of population, but of production and income.

The group of ecologists who generated this well meaning scare are members of an old club. Its founder, the Rev. Thomas Malthus, issued dire warnings of inevitable starvation in 1798. This having proved a poor bet, the emphasis today shifts to a dearth of all natural resources and mounting pollution.

It does not take an ecologist to explain that if the world's population doubles every so many years, after a while there will be Standing Room Only, at least on the surface of this planet. Likewise, it is fairly obvious that if we deplete existing resources without discovering new sources, developing methods of recycling, and inventing substitutes, we shall some day run out. But perhaps an economist can be helpful in clarifying why these problems are not top priority today.

In the first place, the economy will simply substitute things that are plentiful for things that become scarce. If we run out of aluminum, the price of aluminum will go up. That will encourage manufacturers to use something else, and will stimulate research and development to produce substitutes.

Some scientists believe that matter and energy are fundamentally interchangeable in many forms, but as a layman, I would not bet on any near-term miracles. The simple processes of economics will keep us going. If they don't, the ecologists' advice to slow down will not be worth much—it would only postpone the day of disaster without avoiding it.

In the course of centuries, more basic adjustments will probably be needed. Population may stop growing, production may stop growing. The chances are that the world will adapt to the changing environment gradually. Lack of space will cause families to shrink, if families then still exist. Great per capita income will reduce interest in producing and consuming more. We do not need to rely on "misery," as the Rev. Malthus thought, to bring about the adjustment.

The real question is at what time this transition will have to be faced. New York restaurants carry signs to the effect that occupancy by more than some maximum number is unlawful. If half a dozen persons were to gather in an otherwise empty restaurant with such a sign and discuss heatedly the urgency of keeping newcomers out, they would be in something like the position of Americans debating the zero growth notion. To stop growing now, generations before the real problems of growth arise, if ever, would be to commit suicide for fear of remote death.

The ecologists do not seem to be aware of what it would mean to freeze total income anywhere near today's level. Do they mean that the present income distribution is to be preserved, with the poor frozen into their inadequacies? Would that go for the underdeveloped countries too? Or do they have in mind an equalization of incomes? It will take pretty drastic cuts in upper income bracket standards to bring them down to the average American family income of about $10,000, to say nothing of a cut to average world income. We can and perhaps should approach this condition over generations. Trying to do it quickly would create completely needless problems.

The ecologists also do not seem to be aware of what their prescriptions, contrary to their wishes, might do to the environment. If growth came to a halt, it is obvious that every last penny of public and private income would be drawn upon to provide minimal consumer satisfactions. There would be very little left for the cleaning-up job that needs to be done. Growth is the main source from which that job must be financed.

I would like to end with a quote from my *Newsweek* column on which Mr. Lewis commented. "A world without growth, that is, without change, is as hard for us to imagine as a world of everlasting growth and change. Somewhere in the dim future, if humanity does not blow itself up, there may lie a world in which physical change will be minimal . . . hopefully a much more humane and less materialistic world. We shall not live to see it."   □

CHAPTER 31

THE UNDERDEVELOPED WORLD: A PRESENT CRISIS

Although inflation, pollution, and energy problems have created intense economic concern in the advanced industrial nations, there is no doubt where the great economic crisis of the present moment is happening: it is in the poor, less developed countries where more than half the world's population lives. Because of continuing poverty in these countries and because of their rapid rates of population growth, there are more seriously poor people in the world today than ever before in history. A rather sad commentary on the twentieth century!

We have described conditions in these countries earlier (chapter 6) and now, as we approach the end of this book, we want to consider various policies that might help promote development in these nations. Our interest now is in what has been and what can be done to help.

LESSONS FROM ECONOMICS

The first point to make is that, although political and social systems are highly important for development, no underdeveloped country can afford to ignore underlying economic phenomena, as these have been analyzed by economists and scholars over the past century.

More specifically, the policymakers in such countries must have a thorough grasp of the main topics covered in a text such as this one. They must be concerned to preserve overall macroeconomic stability (Part Two), since an economy with rampant unemployment or inflation is unlikely to be a successful developer. They must be concerned with microeconomic interdependence and efficiency (Part Three), since they are too near the edge of survival to waste resources by allocating them unwisely and without concern for their alternative uses. And, of course, they must acquaint themselves with the factors that make for economic growth (chapters 6, 16, 28, and 30), since growth is their immediate need and objective.

Nothing that we have studied is irrelevant to their needs—international trade, for example, is obviously a crucial subject for many poor countries, but so also are income distribution, economic controls, pollution, and, really, everything we have discussed. At the same time, however, we must add that nothing that we have learned can be applied to these countries without adaptation and qualification. Indeed, to fail to be aware of this latter point could be almost as costly as ignoring the former.

Let's take a specific case. We have mentioned that many poor countries are suffering from massive unemployment. Often this is covert or disguised unemployment (people appear to be working but a reorganization of production would show them to be redundant). In Taiwan, for example, in 1965 unemployment was estimated at 11.5 percent. This is about twice the rate that, in the United States, led to complaints about unemployment in the 1970s. Actually, many countries are doing far less well than Taiwan on this front; rates of 20 percent or even 30 percent effectively unemployed may not be unrealistic.

A student, fresh from mastering the theory of national income determination, might easily say: The problem is clearly one of inadequate aggregate demand. Through modern fiscal and monetary policies, we must raise $C + I + G$ to the point where full employment is achieved or, more realistically, where employment is so high that we begin running into serious inflationary problems.

But this would be dangerous advice and would be very likely to lead to high inflation without any commensurate effect on employment. The reason is that the student has failed to study sufficiently the specific causes of unemployment in an underdeveloped country. One of the major causes is likely to be the relative lack of factors of production complementary to labor—in agriculture, land; and in industry, capital. If the land is overcrowded and if industry is plagued by factor proportions inherited to some degree from the advanced industrial nations (i.e., relatively high capital-intensity), then merely demanding more products is not going to generate a demand for more laborers to produce them. The bottlenecks are elsewhere, and so also must be the solutions. The real solutions to this kind of unemployment thus would not involve Keynesian style fiscal-monetary policies as much as policies to reduce the increase in the labor supply (population policy), to develop more labor-intensive techniques of production (technology), and to increase the supply of the complementary factors (capital accumulation).

In short, we must apply what we have learned *but* we must apply it to actual, not general or hypothetical, problems. With this in mind, let us now consider approaches to some of the difficulties we have earlier singled out as being particularly acute for today's underdeveloped countries.

POPULATION POLICY

While population growth did not pose a serious obstacle to economic development in the West, it clearly does for today's underdeveloped countries, particularly those that are already heavily overpopulated.

Fundamentally, there are two ways of approaching the problem of population growth. The first is to take the rate of population growth as given and to try to cope with its effects. The other is to try to alter the rate of increase itself.

Coping with Effects

The first approach—dealing with effects only—may seem a mere palliative, but it is important not to neglect this aspect of the phenomenon. For no matter how successful attempts at population control are, there is no doubt that rates of growth will remain quite high for many years and, unless this fact is understood, much human misery could result. Perhaps the most harmful effect of population growth is the painful unemployment that will result unless countermeasures are taken. As we have said above, this unemployment arises as a consequence of the fact that the industrial capital stock is not growing rapidly enough to employ massive increases in the labor force, while the land—in the more populated underdeveloped countries—offers few further effective opportunities for employment on the required scale.

Under these circumstances, *employment-creation* becomes an independent goal of national policy. The mobilization of the rural unemployed in community development projects where village authorities cooperate with the government in undertaking public-works programs becomes a task of high priority. The country, furthermore, may attempt to emphasize high-labor/low-capital industries. Thus, a handicraft industry may be preferred to its factory equivalent, not on the grounds of efficiency, but because it provides more jobs for those who would otherwise go idle. The difficulty here, of course, is that the goals of employment-creation and economic growth do not necessarily coincide. Should a country use its scarce capital where it will provide the most jobs or where it will provide the greatest increase in output?

In the early postwar period, some economists felt that a way could be found around this dilemma by using the unemployed and/or the disguised unemployed to create capital.[1] Similar logic seems to have been applied in China during the Great Leap Forward period, when there was considerable emphasis on establishing communes that would mobilize the rural labor force to produce not only agricultural improvements but also industrial products, like the famous

"backyard blast furnaces" for increasing iron and steel production.

The theory of this approach is unassailable—a country has surplus labor and little capital: Why not use the former to increase the latter? In practice, however, the problems of organizing a largely unskilled labor force, plus the drain on the very scarce factor of production, managerial capacity, have made it doubtful that the hoped-for wonders can be achieved by this approach. Even China had to abandon many of the Great Leap Forward concepts; as someone has said, the main result of the backyard blast furnaces was to produce a lot of unusable steel at the cost of a great many melted down pots and pans. In sum, a poor country is well advised (1) to pay serious attention to its unemployment problem and (2) not to hope for miracles in this area. In the long run, control of the rate of population growth itself is indispensable.

Altering the Rate of Population Growth

We come then to the second aspect of population policy—that having to do with causes. The main cause, as we know, is the continuation of high birthrates in countries where medical and public health advances have brought sizeable reductions in the deathrates. The basic cure is to foster means that will bring the birthrates down (as they are already down in the industrialized countries) as rapidly as possible.

The major poor countries of the world are agreed on this objective. In India, for example, economic planners in the early 1960s were given a great shock when they realized, as the preliminary results of the 1961 census became available, that they had badly underestimated the nation's population growth. Expenditures on family planning programs have increased rapidly since that time and 10 million Indian men and women have undergone voluntary sterilization. China also now supports population control measures, though in the early period after the civil

---

1. This was one of the themes of the classic work of Ragnar Nurkse, *Problems of Capital Formation in Underdeveloped Areas* (New York: Oxford University Press, 1953). This seminal work in the development field is still worth reading today.

war, Chinese leaders were rather ambiguous on this point.[2] A Chinese official was quoted in the early 1970s:

Family planning is fundamental for the economic planning of the country. It involves an ideological revolution to change basic concepts and traditional ways. Furthermore, family planning represents the demands of the masses, especially of the many women who want to be free of the burden of excessive children in order to be able to contribute to the reconstruction of the country.[3]

Reports are that contraceptive devices and abortion are readily available in China and that official policy now encourages small families and later marriages.

There is also evidence that, in a few countries at least, birthrates are now beginning to fall. Taiwan is often cited as such an example. Between 1951 and 1966, the number of registered births per 1000 women (aged fifteen to forty-nine) fell from 211 to 149; during the same period the birthrate declined from 50 to 32 per thousand of population. However, the case of Taiwan brings out some of the difficulties of judging the potential success of birth control and other similar family planning programs. For the fact is that this decline was mainly accomplished before the family planning campaign in Taiwan began (1963). The population expert, Kingsley Davis, at-

tributes most of Taiwan's success to the fact that it "is sufficiently developed to be placed in the urban-industrial class of nations."[4] Already in 1950, over half of Taiwan's population was urban and her rate of economic development during the past twenty years has been among the most rapid in the underdeveloped world. This, plus the fact that she is very densely populated, undoubtedly created pressures for reducing births even in the absence of a family planning program. Undoubtedly, too, these factors created a favorable environment for such a program to be effective.

These comments about Taiwan bring out what is essentially the most difficult issue in this whole field: Will family planning programs be able to have any major effect on birthrates in the absence of the other accoutrements of development—urbanization, rising standards of living, increased levels of education, and so on? In the West, we know, birthrates did fall (and in the absence of such population control programs) as development proceeded. Can the poor countries reverse the order of this process, bringing down birthrates in order to help *produce* development?

The evidence is mixed. On the optimistic side, we have, first, the dramatic increase in awareness of the problem throughout the world. (India's expenditures on family planning, for example, rose by over tenfold just between her Second Five Year Plan [1956–61] and her Third Five Year Plan [1961–66].) We have, second, the fact that the technology of birth control has improved dramatically over the last several years and will undoubtedly show similar advances in the future. Hopes can be dashed here—the "loop," for example, has not proved to be quite the panacea that it was once proclaimed—but the efforts to improve this area of technology are now going forward rapidly. Third, and strengthening the above, economists have shown that in many cases investment in family planning programs can yield much higher economic results than similar amounts of

---

2.   The problem was at least in part ideological. Karl Marx had argued that Malthusianism was a "libel on the human race," because it suggested that natural causes were at the root of human misery, rather than flaws in the capitalistic system. We also, of course, have an ideological issue in the West, in terms of the attitude of Catholicism toward family planning. It is notable, however, that European Catholic countries have been among the lowest in rates of population increase.

3.   Quoted by Jaime Zipper, M.D., in the *New York Times*, April 30, 1972, section 12 (Supplement sponsored by the Population Crisis Committee in association with the Planned Parenthood Federation of America), p. 21.

4.   Kingsley Davis, "Population Policy: Will Current Programs Succeed?" *Science*, 158, reprinted in Garrett Hardin, ed., *Population, Evolution and Birth Control* (San Francisco: W. H. Freeman and Co., 1969), p. 352.

money invested in factories or machinery.[5] If great steel mills were the early signs of development efforts, increasingly the proffered evidence is the family planning clinic or research institute.

On the negative side, we have the extreme slowness of results so far. Thus, although India's birthrate has come down somewhat in the last few years (from 40 per thousand to 37 or 38), the decline is small, and population growth actually increased from 21.6 percent in 1951–1961 to 24.7 percent in 1961–1971. It will obviously take all of mankind's capacity for creative adaptation to respond to this new challenge.

TECHNOLOGICAL ADVANCE

One of the most important means of creative adaptation is the development of new technology. In the case of birth control for the poor countries, such new technology would ideally involve devices that are highly effective, very cheap (where average per capita income may be $100–200 per year, cost is clearly a decisive factor), easily applied under circumstances where literacy is low and knowledge of personal hygiene may be rudimentary, and acceptable to prevailing attitudes and customs. Because of the basically different economic circumstances, the technological approach best suited to a poor country might not be the same as that which would be most effective in a highly developed country.

What is true in the specific case of birth control technology is true of advanced technology in general. As we know, the great single advantage that today's poor country has over the developers of the past is the tremendous accumulation in the storehouse of Western technology. The great *dis*advantage of using that technology is that it is ill-suited to the economic and/or geographic conditions in most poor countries. The major problem in this area, therefore, is to develop a new technology that is basically an adaptation of Western scientific know-how to the specific circumstances of today's underdeveloped country.

As in the case of the population problem, there was considerable pessimism on this point in the 1950s and early 1960s. It seemed that some poor countries, in their desire to achieve "showcase" development, had overemphasized industrial development and especially the big, modern project at the expense of slow, steady, fundamental improvements, particularly in the agricultural sector. The fear was that this would lead to a worsening unemployment picture (because the big, modern projects seldom require much unskilled labor), to unbalanced growth (with a lagging agricultural sector),[6] to balance-of-payments problems (agricultural imports being required, along with Western machinery for the big industrial projects), and to *enclave* development (the relative overdevelopment of certain urban sectors of the economy while the rural hinterland is allowed to remain wholly stagnant). These fears were heightened by the fact that, in the crucial agricultural sector, Western technology had been developed for the soils and climate characteristic of the temperate zone, while most of today's poorer countries lie in whole or in part in the tropics.

Indeed, the problem of introducing new technology seemed to be virtually centered in the agricultural sector. Industry might be expected to make fairly rapid strides. But what about the dominant (often 70 or 80 percent of the population) rural sector with its remote, tradition-bound, poverty-stricken ways?

For a period during the late 1960s and early 1970s, however, there was a substantial change in outlook about the future prospects of the agricultural sectors of the less developed countries. The basis for a sudden upswing of hope was what was called the *Green Revolution*.

---

5.   See especially the work of Stephen Enke, such as "Population and Development: A General Model," *Quarterly Journal of Economics,* February 1963; or *Economics for Development* (Englewood Cliffs, N.J.: Prentice-Hall, 1963).

6.   However, it should be said that some economists feel that unbalanced growth—certain key sectors of the economy shooting ahead of other sectors—is actually a *desirable* strategy for a poor country. The main reason is that these "unbalances" create pressures on the lagging sectors to catch up, and general development may result. For a good account of the unbalanced growth arguments, see Albert O. Hirschman, *The Strategy of Economic Development* (New Haven: Yale University Press, 1965).

The Green Revolution involves the development of certain new seeds, particularly of wheat and rice, that produce very large increases in crop yields under certain circumstances. Most relevant for our purposes is the fact that these new seeds have been developed with particular reference to conditions in the less developed countries, i.e., to tropical and subtropical weather and especially to the great availability of solar energy in areas near the equator.

Figure 31–1 shows the dramatic gains in yield per acre that were made possible in the 1950s and 1960s by the new seeds, particularly in Mexico and Taiwan, where this research was originally launched.

In India, this progress continued into the early 1970s. In 1971, India produced a record grain output of 108 million tons. In 1972, there was actually talk that India would have to look for foreign markets to export an expected grain surplus. But the summer monsoon failed and India's 1972–73 crop fell to 95 million tons. The 1973–74 crop seemed likely to be well below the 1971 record—meanwhile, the population had increased by 13 million a year during the interval.

The Green Revolution is clearly controversial. The new seeds generally require changes in fertilizer and irrigation practice. There is the danger of rusts and blights developing in response to the new varieties. (This has already happened in the case of new corn in certain areas of the United States.) Without continuing agricultural research efforts, the advantages of the new seeds may be temporary and the ecological vulnerability of the less developed countries may actually grow worse. Also, if mishandled, the new technology might lead to further displacement of labor from the land, increasing both rural and urban

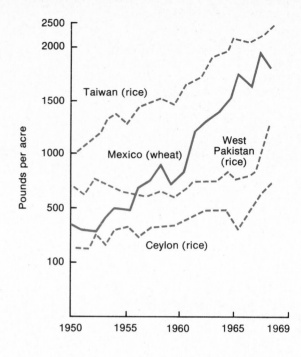

Figure 31–1. Rice and Wheat Yields per Acre in Mexico, West Pakistan, Ceylon, and Taiwan.
Source: Adapted from Lester Brown, *Seeds of Change,* New York: Praeger Publishers, 1970, pp. 37, 39. With permission of Praeger Publishers.

unemployment and unrest. Finally, the new worldwide increases of petroleum-based fertilizer prices have left many countries (like India) far short of the fertilizer requirements of the new technology.

Because of the importance of these issues, and because they so well illustrate the specific problem of adaptive technological research, the following two brief readings on the Green Revolution present some leading (and opposing) points of view.

Green Revolution: Con

Paul R. Ehrlich

All of the technological panaceas for increasing food production are either impractical, impossible, ludicrous, or worse. One that is highly touted by our Department of Agro-business in Washington is known in the trade as the "Green Revolution." I believe the "Revolution" is to be created in the bankrolls of certain businesses in the United States, because it certainly is not being created anywhere else. The reversal of stories from the U.S. Department of Agriculture is something magnificent to behold. In the 1965–66 "bad weather" time, everybody was filled with pessimism. Then, in 1967, the weather improved in India and the other key regions. All of a sudden agriculture was doing a great job; all the high-yield wheat, sorghum, and rice varieties were going to save the world. This is still the current story.

If we are going to increase food production, the most intelligent way is to get higher yields from land already in cultivation. There is nothing wrong with that idea if it is done with great care for the ecological consequences—which, of course, it is not. But there are all kinds of problems in the new high-yield grains; they are high-yield only with proper cultivation, including a great input of fertilizer, and in most of the areas where they are being planted, there are serious problems of fertilizer distribution. Raymond H. Ewell at the State University of New York (Buffalo) has been India's chief fertilizer consultant for the last dozen years; he says quite frankly that he does not think that India has a hope of producing enough. It is certainly impossible for the United States to produce enough fertilizer for India, in addition to meeting our domestic needs, to get the maximum yield out of these grains; it also seems unlikely that the world will donate enough fertilizer to India. So there is a

Excerpted from "Famine 1975: Fact or Fallacy?" by Paul R. Ehrlich in Harold W. Helfrich, Jr., ed. *The Environmental Crisis* (New Haven: Yale University Press, 1970), pp. 58–61. Reprinted by permission of the publisher.

very big fertilizer problem. You have to grow crops exactly right to get successful harvests. From what other people and I have seen personally in India, the chance of their doing things exactly right seems to be about zero. An even more serious problem arises in planting grains which have been inadequately field tested against pest and blight resistance because this project is rush-rush. Already IR-8 rices have had a lot of trouble from this problem (recently "miracle rats" have invaded "miracle rice" fields in the Philippines), but even bigger monocultures are being created. A complete switch to the new high-yield grain varieties would leave India with only about half of the possible diversity of wheat strains. This means that, instead of a Bihar or a Pakistan famine, when a virus gets in and wipes out the crops, it will cover a much larger area. These are dangers of increased monoculture.

Another problem which seems to be endemic to agriculturists is that almost all of their projections are based on optimism—that good years are normal years. When I visited Australia, that country was having a colossal drought, and the agriculturists were saying in the press: "This is once in a million years; we have got to build, we have got to get relief; everything is going to be all right when the rains come." However, Australian weather records indicate that similar droughts occur with monotonous regularity every ten years or so. It is the same story in India, the same in China. They have deforested most of their land; among other things, this helps to create unstable weather. We know very well that you cannot expect long stretches of good years. There are good years interspersed with doses of bad years. For instance, last July the Indian government—which was churning out all kinds of propaganda about how it is going to become self-sufficient in agriculture by 1971—was so pleased with the year's crops that it created a special commemorative postage stamp about the great agricultural breakthrough. If India, which now can feed adequately only 10 million out of 530 million inhabitants, is to gain self-sufficiency in food by 1971, it will mean feeding 530 million people—plus an increment of 50 to 60 million. I have yet to meet any person who has been there who thinks that India could possibly be close to self-sufficiency in food by 1971. Indeed, I am willing to predict that India will never be self-sufficient in food unless it succeeds in cutting its population far back.

The headlines of the "Green Revolution" have been seen all over India. The Indian government is afraid that we will not send them any more food if it does not make progress in agriculture, so it makes unwarranted claims. However, if you look in the *New York Times*, you will find the following pieces of information: on September 24, 1968, six of seventeen Indian states were drought-stricken, with uncertain crop outlooks; the Indian government was looking around for additional food; on October 13, a cholera epidemic hit other states of India which were flooded.

Still, agriculturists have a general feeling that somehow these new crops will solve the world's food problem. This feeling resulted primarily from a square yard of corn planted in Iowa. Five agronomists crouched over it constantly, gave it absolutely perfect everything, and got a yield from it. Then they ran inside, took out an atlas, and figured how many square yards there are in the Amazon basin. By multiplication they determined the amount of food that could be provided in the Amazon basin—and everything is going to be all right.

Unfortunately, that just is not the way the game is played. We do not know how to farm the tropics. We do know that most tropical soils are abysmal. We are not really making substantial progress with farming anywhere in the tropics, and it seems highly unlikely that we are going to. In other words, we will score some little gains with these high-yield crops, but they will be made at great ecological risk.   □

Green Revolution: Pro

James G. Horsfall

What about a Green Revolution in the hungry nations?

It has been written that in the tropics the stork has passed the plow. The question is: Can we put wings on the plow so it can fly faster than the stork? Paul Ehrlich, speaking in this series, has suggested clipping the wings of the stork. I do not quarrel with that. This is another device, and we will probably have to use both of them. As a biologist concerned with the food supply, I make it my business to put wings on the plow so that it can fly at least as fast as the stork. To do this we must engineer a Green Revolution in the tropics through education and applied science.

The hungry nations are at the crossroads where the United States stood a century ago. They have their universities as we did at that time, but the teaching of agriculture has a pretty low priority in those universities—as it had here 100 years ago. Commissioners of Agriculture throughout the tropics are not agriculturally educated. That is tantamount to having a farmer for the Surgeon-General. Who would think of putting the Ministry of Medicine in the hands of a lawyer? Yet the Ministers of Agriculture in the hungry nations are most often lawyers or nonagriculturists. Training of agricultural specialists in the universities of the tropics is almost nonexistent. Universities have traditionally served the elite; they will have to educate the common man if they hope to engineer a Green Revolution similar to ours.

Ever since World War II, the United States has been promising to raise the hungry nations out of their predicament by industrialization. We enunciated that policy in the Department of State right after the war. But that puts the cart before the horse. Nobody can industrialize a nation with 85 to 90 percent of the people on the land any more than we could have

Excerpted from James G. Horsfall, "The Green Revolution: Agriculture in the Face of the Population Explosion," in *The Environmental Crisis*, ed. Harold W. Helfrich Jr., pp. 93–98. Reprinted by permission of Yale University Press. Copyright © 1970 by Yale University.

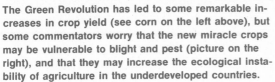

**The Green Revolution has led to some remarkable in-
creases in crop yield (see corn on the left above), but
some commentators worry that the new miracle crops
may be vulnerable to blight and pest (picture on the
right), and that they may increase the ecological instability of agriculture in the underdeveloped countries.**

done so 100 years ago. It has been a terrific waste of our strength; we poured money into industrializing India, and food production declined through the entire period.

Then we adopted a second procedure: the exportation of American knowhow. We would send retired county agents into the hungry nations. We would export our American agricultural technology. Those farmers in Iowa know how to grow good food, we said; now why don't you foreign farmers do it the same way? This operation sadly failed, too. Congress did not learn about it very fast; in fact, it recently passed another edition of the Food for Freedom business and created a section called Farmer to Farmer. It decided to send farmers to carry the know-how, since the county agents had failed. That program, too, fell by the wayside. This is what I call the know-how, show-how fallacy.

Why didn't the program work? We can send Jeeps that can negotiate the roads in underdeveloped countries. Why can't we send hybrid corn to help solve their food supply problems? Biologically, the answer is not very complicated to understand. If we put fertilizer—our classical method for increasing yields—on most of the crops of the tropics, we get less yield than if none was applied. This is not always the case, but it is true often enough. For thousands of years the plants growing in the tropics have had no appreciable applications of fertilizer. If a plant had a high-yielding gene, it almost certainly would have been lethal because it would overgrow the rest of its environment. If we come along and put fertilizer on a plant that has lost its high-yielding genes by natural selection, we will damage the plant more than help it. The result: if you tell an Indian farmer to put on fertilizer and he gets less yield than he had before, you lose your lofty position on your self-erected pedestal.

I was in India about ten years ago, when our national efforts were at their nadir. There were no agricultural universities in the sense of our land-grant colleges and, therefore, very weak training of agricultural experts in India. The country had its Oxfords and Cambridges (somebody called them "Oxbridge" schools) in which were educated the future lawyers and doctors and clergymen, but few in the practical world of agriculture. Only the Brahmans—the top caste—were educated in India in those days. The Brahmans were supposed to become educated, but not to soil their hands. They could not very well improve the agriculture because that involved working in the soil. And so India remains today a vast nation with a relatively few rich and educated people on top and the multitude of poor farmers with no means of education and a dismal food supply at the bottom. It is now in the process of establishing agricultural universities.

The Rockefeller Foundation has already engineered quite a respectable revolution by using precisely the same technique which we used in this country: education plus adaptive research. It encouraged the establishment of a sophisticated College of Agriculture in Mexico in 1943.

The Foundation's efforts began in that year when George Harrar went to Mexico. He quickly discovered the know-how, show-how fallacy. He learned that we cannot go down there and transfer American know-how directly, that we have to develop the technology on the specific site. This principle has since been called adaptive research; it involves "on location" plant breeding, genetics, soils work, and plant protection.

Of course, Harrar's staff started out by trying fertilizers, and they quickly learned that this remedy—so successful in the United States—tended to *reduce* the wheat and corn yields of Mexico. Then they imported some high-yielding varieties of corn and wheat that grow so well in Nebraska, Minnesota, and Iowa. Again, failure; these varieties achieved less yield than the Mexicans got with their own corn, and put on practically no ears at all. They later found out that the diurnal length was wrong. U.S. corn and wheat grow in long days, and the days are relatively short in Mexico's lower latitudes. Besides, the high-yield varieties wound up with all kinds of diseases that they never suffered up in Iowa.

So the Rockefeller Foundation researchers had to work with the measly corn and wheat that they found in Mexico because those varieties were adapted to the day length, the high temperatures, low rainfall, high elevation, and all the rest of the ecological factors involved. They introduced high-yielding genes from Iowa and Minnesota into the local varieties, and then selected the hybrids with both high-yielding genes and local adaptation. It was simple plant breeding, but it had to be done right there in Mexico; it could not be done in Iowa or in Connecticut.

When the genes of the local varieties were sufficiently upgraded, then fertilizer worked wonders as it does in the United States. The Connecticut Agricultural Experiment Station is proud of discovering the principle of hybrid corn, but hybrid corn which will flourish in Mexico had to be developed in Mexico. We cannot successfully transfer the Connecticut strains to Mexico.

Adaptive research is the principle discovered by the Rockefeller Foundation in its work in Mexico. Using this principle, it developed some strains that just about doubled the yield of Mexican wheat. The success in Mexico led the Foundation to decide about 1957 to set up, in cooperation with the Ford Foundation, a similar place—the International Rice Research Institute—in the Philippines.

What did the researchers do when they got to the Philippines? They tried fertilizer. Even after the work in Mexico, they tried fertilizer first. The Foundation had new researchers in the Philippines, fresh out of agricultural America. They put fertilizer on the rice, and grew less rice than they harvested without any fertilizer. They had to learn the hard way. They acquired rice with high-yielding genes from Taiwan and Japan, and crossed them with the locally adapted plants that did not have high-yielding genes. When they put fertilizer on the resultant strains they tripled the yield.

Somebody once said farmers may be ignorant but they are not stupid. All the researchers had to do was put IR-8 rice, this elegant new variety, in a Filipino's field beside the old indica rice, pile on fertilizer, and wait for results. The farmer wound up with three times as much rice from the new variety. He did not have just 10 percent more rice; you need a computer to tell the difference with such a small increase. A farmer is not interested in computers; he is interested in crops. When he gets 300 percent more yield, he does not need a college degree to see it. He is no fool; he wants that new rice as fast as he can get it. As a result, a vast black market has developed all over the tropics for IR-8 rice.

The same thing has happened with wheat. India's Punjab wheat area is at just about the same latitude as Mexico's. It too is on a higher elevation, and the daylight hours are approximately equal in both regions. Wheat can be transported across the lines of longitude because day length is the same. Thus, Mexican wheat will do as well in India as in Mexico. The yields in the Punjab went up two and three times, and the farmers started a sprawling black market in wheat. When such a black market develops, we know we have hit on something pretty good.

At last we fairly well understand the methodology for improving agriculture in the hungry countries of the world: research must be done locally.

The tropics, for all their lush beauty, desperately need a Green Revolution in agriculture. Easing the hunger of those nations will depend on a huge number of factors. A few bright spots have become visible. For the first time, the Philippines are exporting rice instead of importing it at almost unbearable cost—thanks to IR-8. The yields of wheat have doubled in Mexico, in the Punjab, and in Pakistan.

We dare not forget, however, that the population also is rapidly increasing. Food is life, but if we would bequeath to our descendants their full measure of that life, we should remember John Muir's words: "Everybody needs beauty as well as bread, places to play and pray in which nature may heal and cheer and give strength to body and soul alike."   □

CAPITAL AND FOREIGN AID

We come finally to the third main element in growth—capital accumulation. For observers from the industrial world, this third element also raises the large question of foreign aid. If capital accumulation is difficult for a poor country to sustain from its own resources, can the problem be mitigated by an inflow of resources from abroad?

That a purely domestic solution to the capital accumulation problem will involve great hardship for an underdeveloped country we have mentioned before. The difficulties derive from the intense poverty of many of these countries, from their consequent desire for rapid growth, from the capital-using bias of much Western technology, and, in the early stages, from the inability of many of these countries to produce certain types of equipment and machinery—thus requiring imports from abroad. In those poor countries that are dependent on foreign oil, these difficulties have also been vastly increased by the great 1973–74 rise in world petroleum prices.

Whether the domestic efforts of a poor country to increase its rate of saving and investment are largely private or wholly governmental in origin, the effect must be a restraining of private consumption for a substantial period of time. If capital formation is undertaken under something like Western-style business auspices, then this restraint will be reflected in a substantially unequal income distribution with low wages, high profits, and a high reinvestment of profits into business capital expansion. If the bulk of investment is undertaken under State auspices, the process will still involve low wages, but now the surplus for investment will be reflected in high tax revenues and government expenditures, or, alternatively, high "profits" to State-run enterprises.

In any given society, the choice of which method is preferable may depend in part on where the Schumpeterian "entrepreneurs" are mostly located. High profits do not guarantee capital accumulation

if the rich are interested in luxury and ostentation (or, as Adam Smith would have put it, in the employment of "unproductive labourers"); on the other hand, high taxes and government expenditures may lead to corruption, favoritism, and even greater personal aggrandizement. In one southeast Asian country, for example, the accumulated fortune of a now-deceased ruler represented a substantial fraction of the country's entire national income!

In either case, the process of capital accumulation is bound to be difficult and this brings us to our special interest in this matter as citizens of the affluent world. What about foreign aid? Can it really help?

As we all know, for the past two and a half decades, the United States has been engaged in one form of foreign aid program or another. At the start of this period, our foreign aid was heavily focused on European reconstruction through the Marshall Plan. Beginning in 1949 with President Truman's Point Four program of technical assistance and continuing on to the present time, however, the United States has been giving regular and substantial economic assistance to the less developed countries of the world. We are currently giving such assistance both unilaterally and multilaterally, as in our contributions to the World Bank. Although cold war motives and strategic considerations have played a part in these programs, simple humanitarianism has never been completely absent, either.

CONTROVERSIES OVER FOREIGN AID

Still, foreign aid is controversial, and it has become increasingly so in the early 1970s. Why?

Some of the criticism of aid derives primarily from noneconomic considerations. There is, for example, the sometimes expressed view that by aiding foreign countries we are likely to find ourselves entering into military commitments that may in turn lead us into ever more costly wars. The economist alone cannot judge this kind of criticism, since it is basically a political or foreign policy criticism. Still, one may wonder in passing whether it is foreign aid that is leading us into these further commitments or simply that these commitments provide part of the motive for the foreign aid. If the latter is the case, we should ask if there are other grounds that justify aid even if further commitments are not to be entered into.

There are, however, at least two criticisms of foreign aid that deal fairly directly with economic questions. The first has to do with the *cost* of the aid program to this country and whether or not it is sustainable over time. Foreign aid clearly does cost this country something, both directly and in terms of our balance of payments. Without belittling these costs, it is only accurate to state the following facts: (1) our economic assistance to underdeveloped countries constitutes a very small percentage of the expenditures of the federal government and a minuscule percentage (under 1/2 of 1 percent) of our gross national product;[7] (2) the percentage of our national income going into foreign aid has been declining in recent years and, indeed, is very substantially below the percentage of national income we devoted to the economic assistance of Europe under the Marshall Plan; (3) the practice of tying aid expenditures to purchases of American goods has drastically curtailed the net cost to the American balance of payments of aid expenditures. Some cost is clearly there, but it is not so heavy as the critics would suggest, and furthermore it has been declining over time.

The other central criticism from an economic point of view has to do with the effect of aid on the prospects of the recipient countries. Does aid really help? Or does it simply encourage dependence on the United States, with the consequence that the aid program may go on forever?

These questions are very difficult to answer, the main reason being that time is still too short to tell. Some Americans have been disappointed because the aid program has not brought quick results. Such expectations were encouraged perhaps by the out-

standing success of the Marshall Plan in Europe. Some of it may have been due to the overzealous advocacy of aid by its supporters in the early days. In any event, in the early 1970s it does begin to seem to many citizens that the aid program is going on forever, and they begin to wonder if it is really having any useful effect at all.

ECONOMIC ANALYSIS OF AID

Economic analysis helps put this problem in some perspective. For one thing, it makes it clear why the analogy with the Marshall Plan is virtually irrelevant. There we were dealing with countries that had already mastered the tricks of modern technology and growth; had a literate, technically skilled labor force and abundant managerial talent; and needed only a modest infusion of resources to put them on the path again. In the case of the underdeveloped countries, however, the problems they face are extremely difficult and their poverty is so acute that, even under the best of circumstances, the achievement of a decent living standard will be accomplished only by the end of the century. To demand quick results under these circumstances is simply to misconceive the nature of the problem.

Economic analysis can also help us in understanding more specifically the potential impact of aid on an underdeveloped country. Some economists have described these countries as facing two fundamental *gaps* as they try to make their way to self-sustaining growth.[8] The first is a gap between domestic savings and the rate of investment required for a desired rate of growth—the *investment gap*. The second is the gap between the country's exports and the imports required for a desired rate of growth—the *trade gap*. The investment gap arises, as we have seen, because the need for capital is so great and the ability of the poor country to provide the capital

---

7. Thus, in 1972, our total official foreign aid, both on a bilateral and multilateral basis, amounted to $4.2 billion, or about a third of 1 percent of U.S. GNP.

8. See, for example, Hollis Chenery and A. M. Strout, "Foreign Assistance and Economic Development," *American Economic Review* 56, No. 4, Part 1 (September 1966).

is so limited. The trade gap arises because the export capabilities of the poor country may be limited, and yet it may require imports to provide the capital and other industrial goods needed for growth.

Now the fundamental *economic* case for foreign aid (assuming, of course, that it is our goal to help these countries develop) rests on three propositions.

(1) If these various gaps are not filled, the countries involved will not be able to achieve modern development, or at least not in an acceptable length of time.

(2) Foreign aid is an effective means for filling these gaps.

(3) There is reason to believe that these gaps will diminish and ultimately disappear as development proceeds over time.

This third proposition is particularly relevant for those who ask whether foreign aid must go on forever. It is based on the belief that as a country develops, various forces will emerge that will reduce its dependence on foreign assistance. In the ideal case, this will happen because: (*a*) development will raise total output and output per capita, and it will be possible to channel a large fraction of these increases in output into added saving and investment; (*b*) development will provide the country with a greater export capacity and, at the same time, with a greater ability to produce domestically the capital and other industrial goods needed for further development; (*c*) development will bring improvements in the agricultural sphere and hopefully, an improved environment for solving the population problem. If such trends occur, then aid still may be required for a substantial length of time, but an eventual end will be in sight.

Now these propositions cannot guarantee us that aid will do the job. They certainly cannot guarantee us that the end of aid is near at hand. In 1974, increases in the prices of energy, grains, fertilizer, and other raw materials created sharply higher foreign aid requirements—the World Bank estimated that $9 billion more aid was needed—in the poor countries. For what it is worth, however, most economists feel that aid has been making a considerable difference. A recent study by development expert Gustav Papanek concluded that "foreign aid . . . has a more significant effect on growth than savings or the other forms of foreign resource inflows."[9]

Nothing is certain. There is no ironclad case for foreign aid. But there is *a* case for it, and the reader himself will have to decide whether it is strong enough to merit the sustainable but nevertheless real costs aid involves.

EAST MEETS WEST

Despite the numerous obstacles we have mentioned, the period since World War II has seen substantial economic advance in some of the less developed countries of the world. In the decade of the 1960s, total output in the underdeveloped countries grew at an estimated annual average rate of 5 percent and this exceeded the (rapid) rates of population growth so that output *per capita* increased at an annual average rate of 2.5 percent during this period. This rate, although slow by some expectations, is in fact higher than the historic rate of growth of the United States.

Of course, if development in the poor countries succeeds, the more intense become those global problems that the industrial countries are already beginning to face. In particular: How much growth and development can this planet earth sustain? If China or India or Pakistan in fact had anything like the standard of living of the United States or Western Europe, the potential drain on the world's resources and the potential sources of industrial pollution would, of course, be greatly magnified.

The issue thus becomes whether man can adapt creatively to this global problem, or whether the forces unleashed are simply too strong to be coped with. Is new and better technology the answer, or

9.   Gustav Papanek, "Aid, Foreign Private Investment, Savings, and Growth in Less Developed Countries," *Journal of Political Economy*, Vol. 81, No. 1, January/February, 1973, p. 129.

should we seek the simple and the primitive? Should we move forward, or should we stand still? As a matter of fact, which way *is* forward?

At the moment, these development issues tend to divide the world rather than unite it. For whatever consolation it is, however, the long-run outlook is rather different. In that more distant future, mankind, East and West, for better or for worse, is likely to share a common problem and a common destiny.

And this brings us to the question of the future of the industrial world. For, if the history of the West is the future of the East, we had better know which way that history is tending.

SUMMARY

The economic outlook for the underdeveloped countries will depend largely on how they handle the basic problems of population growth, technological change, and capital formation.

In the short run, rapid population growth requires poor countries to pay serious attention to employment-creation as well as to economic growth. In the longer run, however, the key objective must be to lower the birthrate, and the key question is, can this be done in the absence of prior urban and industrial development? Experience so far is somewhat limited (Taiwan's success in lowering the birthrate, for example, may be due more to her general economic growth than to her family planning program), and hopes must rest in the fact that most countries now give a high priority to family planning, that birth control technology is steadily developing, and that economists have shown that investments in population control can be among the most economically productive a poor country can undertake.

The advantage to an underdeveloped country from using the storehouse of Western technology is con-

siderably qualified by the fact that this technology is seldom exactly appropriate to the economic or climactic conditions prevailing in that country. That creative adaptation of Western technology can take place, and even within the relatively stagnant agricultural sector, is shown by the recent Green Revolution. However, there are dangers in this revolution—without continuing research, the new crops might actually increase the economic vulnerability of a poor country—and these have been intensified lately by the energy crisis and the shortfalls in fertilizer production.

Capital formation is likely to cause many sacrifices in a poor country (consumption must be held down whether investment is being undertaken by the State or by private capitalists), and the question arises: Can we in the West help through foreign aid? The political outlook for foreign aid is very clouded in the early 1970s, partly perhaps because of its association with military involvements abroad. Nor is it clear that *over*-dependence on foreign aid necessarily helps a poor country. Still, an economic case can be made for foreign aid as helping to fill two important development gaps—the investment and the trade gaps.

Despite obstacles, economic development in the poor countries has shown some modicum of progress in the last two decades, and aid appears to have played a fairly important role in this achievement.

IMPORTANT TERMS TO REMEMBER

Complementary Factors of Production
Employment-Creation Policies
Family Planning
Enclave Development
Green Revolution
Adaptive Technology
Reinvestment of Profits
State Investment
Foreign Aid
Investment Gap
Trade Gap

QUESTIONS FOR DISCUSSION

1. In chapter 29, we indicated that there was still considerable inequality in the income distribution within the United States. This inequality is much greater, however, if we consider disparities among nations (see Figure A). Should the United States take the same attitude toward income equality across its borders as within its borders? Make a rough calculation (see Table 6–1, pp. 120–21), of what an equalization of average income between, say, the United States and India would mean in terms of per capita income in both countries. What economic arguments would you use to support or oppose such an equalization program?

2. "Ghandi was not only not foolish in supporting handicraft industry in India, he was being very wise considering what we know about factor proportions in factory industry and about population growth." Discuss.

3. What are the possible obstacles and advantages to the poor countries of the world if the developed nations follow a policy of "trade not aid" (e.g., lowering tariff barriers to imports rather than sending gifts of foreign resources through an aid program)?

4. "The full economic development of the poor countries of the world will be the greatest economic (blessing) (disaster) planet earth has ever seen." Choose and discuss.

SUGGESTED READING

Brown, Lester B. *Seeds of Change*. New York: Frederick A. Praeger, 1970.

Goulet, Denis. *The Cruel Choice: A New Concept in the Theory of Development*. New York: Atheneum, 1971.

Higgins, Benjamin. *Economic Development*. Rev. ed. New York: W. W. Norton & Co., 1968.

Lewis, W. Arthur. *Development Planning*. New York: Harper & Row, 1966.

Maddison, Angus. *Economic Progress and Policy in Developing Countries*. New York: W. W. Norton & Co., 1970.

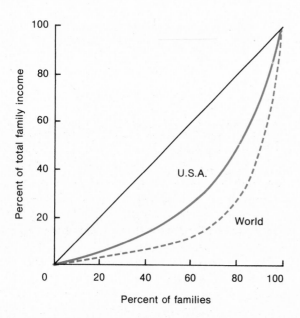

Figure A. Income Distribution in the U.S. and the World (Approximate).

CHAPTER 32
THE INDUSTRIAL SOCIETY: AN UNCERTAIN FUTURE

Ever since the day in October 1929 when Professor Irving Fisher of Yale (a distinguished economic theorist) said that the stock market had reached a permanently high plateau, economists have been cautious about predicting the future. The Eternal Optimists have often been wrong, but so have the Eternal Pessimists. If we look at the actual predictions made by Malthus, Marx, the "stagnationists" of the Great Depression period, and other prophets of doom, we will find that they have not done much better on the average. In the intellectual world, one tends to get a certain number of academic credits for being grim about future prospects—but this does not necessarily mean that one has a better percentage as a prognosticator.

Despite the dangers of looking into the future, the task seems peculiarly necessary as the industrial nations of the world march towards the last quarter of the twentieth century. The reason lies basically in the vast technological revolution that gained strength in the eighteenth and nineteenth centuries and that continues at the present time. Besides creating the possibilities of global destruction and ecological disaster, this continuing revolution also holds out the promise of extraordinary abundance. Indeed, it may be that our central problem is precisely the enormous range of these possible outcomes. In olden times, the future seemed to grow out of the present, as the present had grown out of the past almost automatically—sometimes with changes barely perceptible. Now change is evident everywhere. And this creates an obligation upon us, not always a pleasant one either, to mold our future, to choose among these outcomes. The following pages contain not so much predictions as the discussion of a few interesting possibilities.

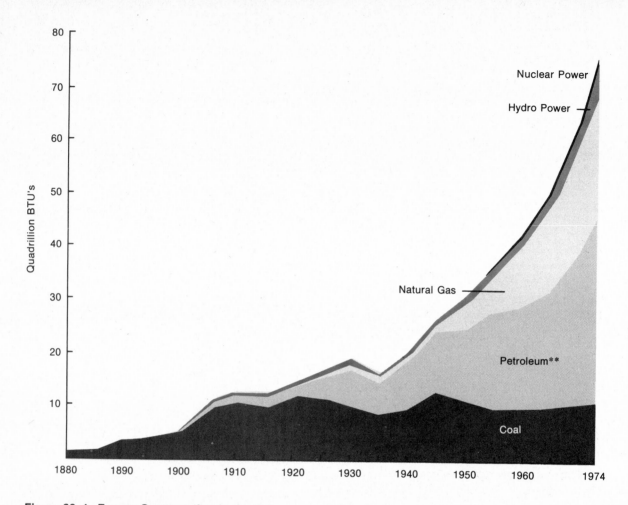

Figure 32–1. Energy Consumption in the U.S. by Sources* Selected Years 1880–1973.

Source: U.S. Bureau of Mines; *Exploring Energy Choices,* Energy Policy Project of the Ford Foundation, 1974, p. 89.

*Includes fossil fuels and primary electricity; excludes wood.

**Includes natural gas liquids.

POSSIBLE CONSEQUENCES OF THE ENERGY CRISIS

One rather dramatic possibility is that the whole process of industrialization, urbanization, and growth that began with the Industrial Revolution may suddenly grind to a halt because we have exhausted our supplies of energy. This was an unthinkable idea in 1972. By 1974, it was commonplace, at least among economic pessimists. The only question remaining for them was how many decades it would take before, literally, we ran out of gas.

A Few Facts. The basic problem can be suggested by a few numbers and diagrams. In the United States, the consumption of energy has been growing rapidly since the late nineteenth century and, in recent years, that rate has been accelerating. Figure 32–1 shows the enormous increase in our energy consumption during this period, and also the change in the sources of that energy. As late as 1920, coal accounted for 78 percent of our total energy use. By 1973, coal was the source of only 18 percent; the great difference being accounted for by an enormous growth in our use of petroleum and natural gas. By 1973, petroleum accounted for nearly half (46 percent) of our total energy sources and natural gas nearly a third (31 percent).

On the production side, domestic sources have not been able to keep pace with this enormous growth of energy consumption. In the postwar period, the United States changed from a net exporter to a net importer of energy. In the last few years, petroleum production in the United States actually began to decline, as did natural gas production in 1972–73. As a consequence, the United States in the early 1970s was importing roughly a third of its oil from abroad. In this respect, the United States was actually in a far stronger position than was the rest of the non-Communist industrialized world. Figure 32–2 shows the extraordinary dependence of Western Europe and Japan on oil imports. Furthermore, energy consumption in these countries was growing at a more rapid rate than in the United States, as their great economic development surges of the 1950s and 1960s proceeded apace.[1]

Where did this oil come from? From both non-Arab and Arab sources. However, the pivotal position of the Middle East is suggested by Figure 32–3. Indeed, if the Middle East and Africa are added together, we have included nearly three-quarters of the entire world's proved oil resources. One country alone— Saudi Arabia—contains about a quarter of the world's proved reserves.

The above facts alone would not produce an oil "crisis." What did produce the crisis was the joining together of the (mainly Arab) oil-producing nations in the Organization of Petroleum Exporting Countries

1. U.S. energy consumption is still very large by world standards, but it has been declining sharply in percentage terms: from 47 percent of world energy consumption in 1925 to 33 percent in 1968.

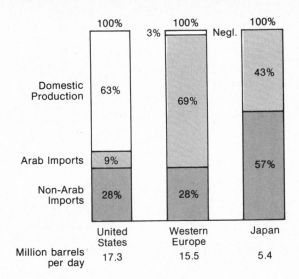

Figure 32–2. Petroleum Sources, 1973.
Source: International Economic Report of the President, 1974, p. 47.

(OPEC), a temporary embargo on oil exports to the United States in 1973, and then the approximate quadrupling of the price of oil over the year 1973–74. Indeed, the price of light Arabian oil that had been running at $1.80 a barrel in 1970 was up to nearly $12 a barrel in mid-1974. The estimate was that the oil import bill for the United States, Europe, and Japan might be $50 billion more in 1974 than in 1973. A transfer of wealth, perhaps unprecedented in human history, was in the making.

Long-Run Supply and Demand. Even given the enormous oil-producing potential of the Middle East, it is apparent that the oil reserves of the world would not be sufficient to sustain endless increases in energy consumption of the kind experienced in the industrial world during the past few decades. Optimist and pessimist both agree on this point.

The central dividing issue, as far as the long-run future is concerned, is how much of the adjustment must come on the demand side and how much on the supply side. There are many adjustments on the demand side that will tend to come about almost

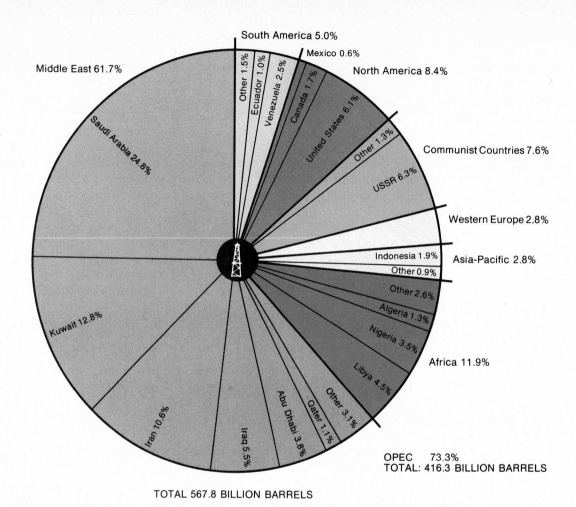

**Figure 32–3. World Proved Oil Reserves—
Year-end 1973.**

Source: International Economic Report of the President, 1974, p. 48.

automatically as a consequence of the higher prices firms and individuals now have to pay for energy. Thus, in earlier examples (see Part Three, pp. 417–18 and 487–90), we have suggested how higher-priced energy might lead to the expansion of certain industries (which used relatively little energy) as opposed to other industries (that used relatively more). Consumers may strive to substitute low-gas-consumption cars for high-gas-consumption cars if the price of gasoline is high. The government, furthermore, could stimulate the process of energy conservation in any number of ways. The lowering of national speed limits in 1973 is one of innumerable possible examples of such public action.

On the supply side, similarly, there could be both market-directed and government-stimulated adjustments. As oil goes up in price, business firms will have incentives to try to produce more oil, and also to develop new technologies to meet energy needs. Certain techniques in coal production or the production of synthetic oil from shale become economic when the price of oil and natural gas rise high, even though they were prohibitively expensive before. Similarly, the federal government may get involved in schemes to provide incentives for private production of energy and in the basic research needed to develop new energy sources. Nuclear fission appears likely to become an increasingly important source of energy over the coming decades. Nuclear fusion offers a tantalizing prospect of almost unlimited future energy. The possibilities of geothermal and solar energy are now being explored. In each case, there are safety, environmental, technological and other problems to be solved. And, in each case, both the marketplace and the government are likely to be involved in promoting the needed developments.

But will it work? Will the long-run supply of energy be able to increase in such a fashion that the customary increase in living standards may continue to take place in the industrial world (and in the poor countries, too)? Or have we entered an era when our basic life-styles must be modified—our growth in demand for energy curtailed, perhaps reduced to zero growth? No one knows for sure, but for alternative possibilities and some of their implications, the reader should turn to Great Debate Six (pp. 791–817).

The "Recycling" Problem. Even apart from these long-range considerations, there is an intermediate-run problem arising from the energy crisis of such magnitude that it might seriously affect the future of the industrial world. This has to do with the economic consequences of the vast sums of money—billions and billions of dollars—that are likely to be transferred to the OPEC countries. This is sometimes called the "recycling" problem, the question being how this money gets back to the countries from which it originates and what the consequences of different patterns of recycling might be.

Economic analysis, and especially our macroeconomic analysis of Part II, enables us to understand the basics of this problem. We start with two countries, one an oil-exporter, the other an oil-importer.

The price of oil is raised sharply. What then happens?

In the easiest case, the oil-exporter increases her imports from the oil-importing country in such a manner that the balance of trade remains more or less unchanged. The *terms of trade* (the prices of a country's exports relative to the prices of its imports) will have altered in favor of the oil-exporting country. This means that the oil-importing country will have to give up more of her commodities to get the needed oil than in the past. Hence, there is a transfer of real income from the oil-importer to the oil-exporter, but no basic balance of payments or employment effects.

This simple case is, however, quite unrealistic for the immediate future. The reason is that the sums of money involved in the massive oil price increases are so huge in relation to the capacity of the OPEC countries to absorb imports from the industrial world. Let us, therefore, go to the other extreme and assume that there is no (or is a negligible) increase in imports by the oil-exporting country. Let us suppose, further, that there is no additional flow of funds in any form from the oil-exporter to this particular oil-importing nation. The price of oil jumps very high. The country—Italy would be a good example in 1974—suddenly begins running a massive balance of payments deficit.

In this case, we do begin to get employment effects. Aggregate demand, we know, is determined by $C + I + G + (X - M)$. In our supposed case, the value of M has shot up because of the higher-priced oil. Consumers in Italy are spending more of their incomes on foreign goods than before, leaving them with less to spend on domestic goods. The total $C + I + G + (X - M)$ schedule will fall and, in the absence of compensatory action of some sort, there would be a fall in equilibrium national income and employment. Worst of all, the higher-priced oil would probably also stimulate further inflation in Italy. A balance of payments crisis, increased unemployment, and increased inflation simultaneously could result: not a very happy picture.

And this situation is a real possibility, although, for the oil-importers as a whole, a further factor has to be considered. This is that the surplus earnings of the OPEC countries essentially have to be invested back in the oil-importing countries. If the export of oil is maintained at a reasonably high level but at much higher prices than in the past, and if the OPEC countries are too small to absorb the massive increase in funds in the form of increased imports, and if, finally, they are unwilling to devote any major part of these funds to foreign aid for the oil-poor underdeveloped countries (like India), then they really have no alternative but to invest their funds back in the countries that bought oil from them. Thus, in contrast to the Italian case just imagined, we could suppose a much more comforting picture. The OPEC countries take their surplus and invest it back in the oil-importing countries, so that the balance-of-payments deficit on merchandise account is offset by foreign investment coming in from abroad. This financial investment from abroad could stimulate real investment in the receiving countries, so that the negative impact of increased imports (M) could be offset by increased I. There might still be an inflation problem, because of the higher priced energy, but, on the whole, the situation would be quite manageable, certainly nowhere near as threatening as it originally seemed.

Too pretty a picture? Definitely. And for a number of reasons:

(1) There is no reason to believe that the funds flowing back to the oil-importing countries will in any way be proportionate to their balance-of-payments needs—the not-so-hypothetical Italian case above *can* happen.

(2) There are dangers in the possibility of massive shifts of funds from one market to another and from one country to another—creating enormous potentialities for world monetary disturbances.

(3) How will the receiving countries react politically to very heavy investment by OPEC nations in their domestic economies—Arab ownership of General Motors? Of great tracts of American real estate? Is this conceivable?

(4) There is no reason for believing that financial investment by the OPEC countries in the industrial nations will lead directly to increased real I to counterbalance the decreased consumption demand in these countries.

On this last point, it is worth noting that the transfer of wealth from the industrial nations to the oil-importing nations can be thought of as a tendency for world savings to rise. The cuts in domestic consumption in the industrial nations are not counterbalanced by increased consumption (through sufficiently higher imports) in the OPEC nations. Of course, if real investment in the industrial nations did not increase to fill the gap, the governments of these countries could engage in expansionary fiscal and monetary policy to increase domestic I or C in the proportions needed. However, the oil-importing nations might be reluctant to do this, in that they would all be showing large balance-of-trade deficits with the OPEC countries and also would probably be experiencing inflation simultaneously.[2]

Thus, the road ahead seems quite rocky. In the long run, these recycling problems need not be insoluble for the industrial nations—although they could prove a major disaster for certain underdeveloped countries like India—but they could be sticky in the extreme. Economic dislocation may be preventable only at the price of much closer cooperation among the oil-importing nations than in the past. If each nation decides to go it alone—making self-protecting bilateral deals—the net result might be near-disaster for all. Hopefully, a recognition of this mutual interest, combined with an understanding among the OPEC nations that the well-being of the West is to their own ultimate economic advantage, will prove sufficient to meet the challenge.

CAPITALISM, COMMUNISM, OR CONVERGENCE?

Speaking of international challenges, what of that other great international challenge: capitalism versus communism? Looking into the future, what can we say about the prospects for the great rival economic systems of East and West?

---

2. For an analysis of this point, see Gerald A. Pollack, ''The Economic Consequences of the Energy Crisis,'' *Foreign Affairs*, April, 1974, pp. 466–7.

Some years ago, Joseph Schumpeter posed the question, Can capitalism survive? Schumpeter was himself a rather conservative economist, but he answered the question in the negative, indicating that this was his prediction but not necessarily his preference.

Schumpeter's prediction was based on his own particular analysis of capitalism, which we have touched on before (p. 215). He saw the central feature of capitalism as growth and the central initiator of growth in the figure of the innovator or *entrepreneur*. According to Schumpeter, capitalism ultimately destroys itself by its own success. As growth becomes routinized, there is no longer any need for the robber-baron entrepreneur of an earlier era—a bureaucracy (whether of American Telephone and Telegraph or of a socialist state planning commission) will do just as well. Also, capitalism by its achievements spawns a large educated class; the intellectuals become very critical of the flaws of capitalism, and also of the business entrepreneurs who are increasingly on the defensive as time goes on. In due course, and largely because of its historic triumphs, capitalism becomes weaker and weaker, and socialism is the "heir apparent."[3]

On the other hand, a fair-minded observer might also come up with a negative answer to the question, Can communism survive? Our discussion of the stirrings within Eastern European countries and even within the Soviet Union herself (chapter 3) suggested that a move toward greater decentralization of decision-making was evident throughout the Communist world. Also, it seems at least probable that this decentralization might take the form of a greater use of a price system and even of such concepts as "profits." One could go further and argue that communism will very probably be undone by *its* success. Thus, one could say that a key goal of the Communist system has been to forge the rapid industrialization of relatively backward countries by ensuring an emphasis on investment above consumption, industry above agriculture, heavy industry above light industry, and so on. This goal has been largely achieved in countries like the Soviet Union. Now—the argument would go—communism is likely to become eroded for two reasons: (1) there is no longer a need for a command economy to produce forced-draft industrialization; and (2) in the more mature stage of society, the task of getting the consumers the goods they want in a reasonably efficient way is much better handled by decentralization.

But if we seem to be a step or two on the road to socialism and if they are a step or two on the road to capitalism, may we not, in fact, meet? And here we come upon one of the more interesting speculations of the postwar period—the doctrine of *convergence*. This doctrine, in its broadest form, derives from the view that there are basic similarities in the running of all modern industrial systems (that is, once the initial hurdles of getting on the path have been overcome). Thus, we should expect that the common problems in ours and the Soviet experience would prove in the long run more significant than our different starting-points. In due course, the systems should converge in some kind of "mixed economy," not very far apart in practice—though, of course, the rhetoric of the two systems might still be quite different.

This doctrine is a rather tricky one, for it is by no means demonstrable that the converging of the two rival economic systems would diminish that rivalry in a political sense. Sometimes, one's deepest quarrels are with those who are closest to one in spirit. Nevertheless, the convergence hypothesis is highly interesting in its own right. It is explored in the following reading by the Nobel Prize-winning economist from the Netherlands, Jan Tinbergen.

---

3. Schumpeter's fascinating analysis is contained in his *Capitalism, Socialism and Democracy*, 3d ed. (New York: Harper & Row, 1950), part II.

Do Communist and Free Economies Show a Converging Pattern?

Jan Tinbergen

(1) We are witnessing today the coexistence of two radically different economic systems, the "communist" and the "free" economies (according to Western terminology) or the "socialist" and "capitalist" systems (according to the Eastern vocabulary). The various names given to them are far from precise. Perhaps the most imprecise thing about them is the suggestion that each of these systems represents something well-defined and hence invariant. Reality shows both to be in permanent change. Analysis of the nature of this change can prove quite fascinating. This essay proposes to show that the changes are in many respects converging movements. As will be seen, our essay is a very brief sketch only, trying to indicate a few main tendencies and not going into any detail, or, for that matter, into differences between the Communist countries.

The main forces behind the changes may be brought under two broad headings. On the one hand each system is learning from experience and trying to overcome some of its own weaknesses. On the other hand the systems begin to influence each other more and more. While in the beginning the Communist system was not taken seriously by the free system this has changed to a considerable extent. The Communist system has been interested in some "capitalist" achievements from its very start. Now it is not so much imitating some of the western methods as learning economics from its own experience.

From Jan Tinbergen, "Do Communist and Free Economies Show a Converging Pattern?" in *Soviet Studies* 12, no. 4 (April 1961): 331–41. Reprinted by permission of Basil Blackwell & Mott Ltd. and the author.

WIDE WORLD PHOTOS

Jan Tinbergen. An outstanding Dutch economist, Tinbergen is noted for his work in econometrics (mathematical economics applied to real-world quantitative data) and the theory and practice of economic planning.

(2) Some of the major changes which have occurred in the Communist system since the Russian revolution will very briefly be summarized in this section:

(i) For a short while it was thought that specialized management was superfluous and that "the workers" could take care of this activity. It was soon learned that specialization is more efficient with regard to management. In fact, the traditional principle of resistance to specialization in all forms is becoming increasingly less prevalent.

(ii) For a short while an attempt was made to equalize incomes in a drastic way. The well-known consequences of such equalization by decree forced the regime to introduce a wage system which makes wages largely dependent on productivity. Strangely enough, this was then labelled "socialist wage policy."

(iii) For some time planning was done in terms of physical quantities and not in terms of money values. Gradually the use of money as a common denominator penetrated into the planning system and the significance of prices and costs was more and more recognized.

(iv) For a long time interest was considered an unnecessary concept as a consequence of the elimination of private ownership of capital goods. Gradually it was discovered that the elimination of interest as a form of private income does not mean that it should also be disregarded as a cost element.

(v) Rationing was abolished a few years after the Second World War and free consumer choice accepted as a proper institution. Gradually some more emphasis was given to consumption as the purpose of production.

(vi) Mathematical methods of planning, considered as "capitalist" for a long period, were recently recognized to be objective and helpful and are now widely discussed and applied.

(vii) A profound change is under way in the concepts of international trade, not only between Communist countries but also between Communist and free economies. The idea that each country should have its own heavy industry is no longer adhered to.

(3) The so-called free economies have also undergone thorough changes, which will now be summed up.

(i) The public sector nowadays is considerably larger than it was in the nineteenth century. Especially in western Europe public utilities are publicly owned; railways and tramways, coal mines, steel works, insurance companies and banks are often in the public sector.

(ii) The amount of taxes levied in western economies, often in the neighborhood of one quarter of national income, means that taxes are among the important regulators of economic activity. In addition a considerable portion of the nation's savings is made in the public sector.

(iii) Free competition has been limited in many ways as a natural consequence of some technical forces (high fixed costs of production). It has also been voluntarily restricted by such movements as the drive for standardization.

(iv) Partly as a consequence of (iii), governments have limited the freedom of entrepreneurs by anti-trust laws.

(v) Access to education has been given gradually to an increasing portion of the population, often by providing education without charge. Moreover, education has been made compulsory up to a certain age.

(vi) Market forces have been eliminated or modified in some particularly unstable markets, especially in agriculture, and in some cases even international commodity agreements have been concluded.

(vii) Planning has gradually been given an increasingly important role, both in big private enterprises and in the design of national economic policy.

(viii) Deliberate development policies have been in existence for a long time. In the nineteenth century, already transportation facilities were often created with public help. At present a whole range of measures, from tax facilities to government investments in infrastructure as well as in manufacturing industry proper, are applied to further the development of remote areas or poor regions.

(ix) Some forms of price and wage control as a direct means to prevent inflation have been used recently in a few "free" economies.

(4) Several of the changes recorded above are in fact bringing the Communist and the free economies closer together. This cannot be said, however, to mean that the differences are already small. There are very large differences still. But the process has not stopped. Both types of economies are facing many problems. They will have to move further. In this section we try to give a picture of the most striking differences still in existence and in the subsequent sections of the most important problems to be solved in both types of economies.

(i) The most striking difference is, of course, the size of the public sector. It should not be forgotten, however, that the power of the private sector in western countries is not commensurate with its formal size. In many indirect ways Western societies have reduced this power. For example, taxes take away almost half of the profits. Of the remainder, a large part is invested and only a small part paid out as dividends. Western as well as Communist economies are to a large extent dominated by managers. In the West, shareholders are no longer powerful. Social legislation in many respects also restricts the freedom of action of private entrepreneurs. So do a number of regulations with regard to quality control, pollution of water and air, building activity, town and country planning, and so on.

(ii) Another important difference is the degree of freedom in production decisions. Factory managers in the West have much more freedom in this respect than managers in Communist countries, where a still very large number of items is planned centrally.

(iii) Accordingly, there is a considerable difference in the degree of detail in which the future course of the economy is planned in Communist countries and in "free" economies. This refers to production as well as, e.g., to foreign trade.

(iv) Prices are controlled centrally in the Communist countries to a much higher degree than in Western countries, where, as a rule, only a few agricultural prices are under direct contol. Here again, however, Western countries use more indirect means of influencing prices. Among these, competition is the main institutional means, but import duties and monetary policies and (in Holland) wage control and price control of some other items are supplementary instruments.

(v) Industrial democracy is very different in the two types of countries. In the West, only some beginnings have been made with co-determination of workers or their organizations in some social issues. In the Communist world, workers are given opportunities to participate in the discussions about the economic plans of the enterprise and about the use of a portion of the enterprise surplus.

(vi) Education constitutes another subject in which there is still considerable difference. In the "free" countries a certain portion of the potential students of secondary and university training cannot receive the education they need for lack of financial means. The portion is declining, however, as a consequence of several types of financial help, which in some countries enable as much as half of the student body to carry on their studies.

(vii) The differences in the level of savings are recently less striking, between such countries as the continental European countries and the Communist countries, than they were before. Savings of about 20 percent of national income are now no exception in these Western countries; Japan is saving nearly 30 percent. The United States and the United Kingdom, however, save considerably less.

(viii) Regarding the principles of the international division of labour and priorities of investment projects, the differences between East and West are rapidly disappearing.

(5) Corresponding to these problems, the Communist countries may have to face the following issues:

(i) A major problem seems to be the question of whether or not a gain in efficiency will result from making a large number of small enterprises in essence "private" enterprises by some sort of lease or concession system. If one tries to imagine the volume of administration now usual, say, in shops, it must be a burden on general efficiency.

(ii) A second major problem seems to be whether or not more freedom in production decisions can be given to managers. With rising real incomes citizens of the Communist countries will require a finer pattern of qualities and assortment, which it is hardly possible to plan centrally. Those closest to the market can probably best judge the needs. There does not seem to be any danger of the central authorities losing control over general economic development as a consequence of granting this type of freedom for the individual manager.

(iii) One also wonders whether or not the number of items planned centrally should be diminished, in order to relieve the central planning agencies of a heavy burden which appears to have relatively unimportant qualifications in terms of increments in national well-being produced. The same may well apply to international trade planning.

(iv) The next question Communist countries might put to themselves relates to price fixing. What harm is there in permitting prices to move as a consequence of relative shortages or abundances and letting them contribute to restore equilibrium? Is not such a method in fact quicker than a mere adaptation in production programs or stocks? Prices will have to move anyhow as a consequence of technical progress and changes in crops. It remains an open question whether the changes should be permitted to individual sellers or only to central authorities. In other words, there seems to be a choice here where the answer is not so clear beforehand and where there is an element of discretion.

(v) A very fundamental question, going far beyond economic institutions, is of course the one about a possible widening of democracy in our sense. It is not within the scope of this essay to make any speculations on this important subject.

(6) Certainly the "free" economies also have to face questions.

(i) Has the public sector the correct size? In the United States important commentators have made the point that it is too small in that country and that recently some public tasks have been neglected.

Even if in European countries the question does not seem to be a controversial issue, the related question of how further to restrict the privileges of some forms of private income or capital still is one under discussion. There is an interesting argument about the possibility of restricting consumption financed out of capital gains, introduced by Nicholas Kaldor's book on "An Expenditure Tax." Possible restrictions on the income paid to directors are discussed and the case for higher inheritance taxes has not been decided upon. The impression of a certain stagnation in the reforms in this field is due not so much to general satisfaction about the present state of affairs as it is to the fact that progressive political parties are re-thinking their programs.

(ii) There is not much debate in Western countries about restricting the freedom of decisions of managers about their production programs. Rather there is an increasing interest on the side of management for general economic forecasts and market analysis to help them in their decisions.

(iii) Accordingly, the case for some more planning is a living issue in the West. One government after the other feels it has to do something in this field. The most recent example is Belgium, with a possibility for Germany to follow. In Asian countries planning is generally accepted; only the methods differ. The borderline European and Asian country, Turkey, has

just established a planning agency. Latin American countries are one after the other engaging in some planning. There is a wide variation in the degree of detail planned, and the time has come to discuss in a more precise way which degree of detail is the most appropriate. The outcome of such a discussion may also have its value for the Communist countries.

(iv) Price formation is an issue of discussion in the West mainly when the general price level is at stake: Should not governments have more instruments to counteract inflationary price rises, especially of the cost-push type? The existing situation is unsatisfactory. The use of only monetary and financial means contains the danger of creating unemployment before the price level goes down. Wage control as an indirect means of controlling prices is not accepted. International integration, in order to strengthen competition may give some help in small countries, but does not solve the problem for larger countries. It may therefore be that after all some new form of price setting is necessary.

(v) There is a continued pressure in Western countries to facilitate the access to education for larger groups of the population. Some of the proposals are going into the direction of the Communist solution, namely to pay a wage to the student. Other proposals are more traditional.

(vi) Industrial democracy is an unsolved question, too. The attempts so far made in Western Europe differ from country to country. None is very satisfactory.

(7) The picture given shows that Communist as well as "free" countries have to solve some problems and that there may be further tendencies to a converging movement. This is true particularly for the main question about the degree of decentralization in production decisions and planning. It is to some extent also true for the process of price formation. It is less clear with regard to the formal side of property, but a distinction between formal property and the real situation must be made. As already observed, both the income from property and the freedom of decision with regard to its use have been strongly reduced in the West and the process may continue.

It is interesting to add a more theoretical analysis to the factual description already attempted. What does economic science have to tell us about the probability of a further convergency of the organization patterns? It is evident that economic science can only tell us something about the subject insofar as economic forces will determine the movements. Clearly, in the past other-than-economic forces have been at work. Nevertheless, would it be denied that economic considerations are important both to Communists and, let us say, to Americans?

The chapter of economic science we may first consult is welfare economics. In principle, it tells us about the conditions which the optimum pattern of organization of society has to fulfill. Its contents have long been considered a defense of the free enterprise system, but wrongly so. It is true that welfare economics show that uniform prices (i.e., absence of price discrimination) are among the conditions for maximum welfare. But these can be established just as well by a system of government-controlled pricing as by competitive markets.

Another proposition of welfare economics is that prices should be equal to marginal costs. This statement implies that for the activities characterized by high fixed costs and technical surplus, capacity private enterprise cannot be the system leading to maximum welfare.* Socialization may be the best solution, therefore, for all the activities concerned.

Similar remarks are valid with regard to activities showing external effects. It can be shown, at the basis of welfare economics, that activities of this kind should be carried out by integrated units; integrated, that is, with the producers or consumers whose well-being is affected by the external effects. Socialization may again be a solution.

---

*[This is a reference to what we called falling (average) cost industries, pp. 464. RTG]

In concrete terms, the most important activities falling under these two categories are about the same as those already socialized in Western European countries, namely public utilities, rail and air transportation, highway construction, and education. Possibly also steel and coal should be added and perhaps other types of transportation.

A further subject relevant to welfare economics is taxes. Two principles are important: first, that there must be some form of income redistribution and second, that income tax is not the optimal way of doing so. The redistribution taxes should approach as much as possible the lump-sum type, i.e., the type not taxing marginal income. Wealth taxes are perhaps the nearest example we know today.

All this points to the desirability of some sort of a mixed system, as far as property is concerned, and to a tax system which may hit personal wealth more than it now does in the West. It also points in the direction of admitting more decentralization with regard to the activities showing constant or increasing costs, i.e., generally for industries where small units are justified, as the Communist countries may discover in the future.

(8) Reference to another chapter (or chapters) of economics may be needed, in order to answer the following questions. What element of truth is there in the contention sometimes made that there is no optimum in the middle, but rather a tendency for optima to be at the extremes?

This opinion is sometimes illustrated by the argument that "once you start to deviate from market-price formation you have to regulate more and more until the whole economy is regulated." Is this illustration relevant to our subject and would it, in a general way, disprove the assumption of an optimum somewhere halfway? The alleged tendency to divergency rather than convergency can no doubt be observed in some cases of war economy regulations. If you start rationing and price control in some markets, you will soon find it necessary to regulate other markets, too. The argument does not necessarily apply to other types of intervention, however. An interesting example to the contrary can be found in business cycle policy. Here it is generally accepted that if you regulate the total flow of demand by appropriate instruments—e.g., financial and monetary policy—you may then leave most markets to themselves. You can, in addition, select a few markets showing characteristics of instability, which may be controlled without the necessity for controlling other markets. Those to be controlled are the ones showing long production lags or a long life of the products.

In the same manner the ownership of the means of production is not characterized, as such, by a tendency to spread. In Western Europe there exists a public sector of a certain size which has maintained itself for years without making it necessary to expand it rapidly in order to preserve some equilibrium. If in the USSR private business has virtually vanished, it is because it was discriminated against on ideological grounds and, in the initial period, for reasons of political power.

In the case of planning a similar position can be maintained. Planning the main elements of the economy does not necessarily imply the need for detailed planning.

It cannot be argued, therefore, that there is an inherent tendency for economic regimes to move to the extremes. Our theoretical reconnaissance, therefore, seems to support rather than to undermine the views derived from observation. No doubt the optimum organization of the economy will differ from country to country and from period to period. It is also hardly conceivable that we will soon be able to indicate precisely where the optimum lies, or even to say whether "East and West" will actually "meet" in their attempts to find the "welfare summit."

(9) This essay may be concluded with a few remarks about the "noncommitted" countries, that is noncommitted to one of the two economic systems at the extremes. Being underdeveloped countries at the same time, they still have a significant number of feudal elements. They are less subject to preconceived ideas about the economic system. If the state

sector plays an important role in some of them it is because the necessary initiative was first taken in this rather than in the private sector (Turkey, India).

This group of countries is now facing some very urgent economic needs, partly as a consequence of increasing contacts with the outside world, partly because they have only recently become independent states. The most pressing need is the one for a higher level of production. Another need is to live under a system of stabler prices. Several secondary aims of policy can be derived from these primary ones, such as the full use of resources, an increase in investment levels, and a diversification of their production pattern.

Because of the presence, in today's world, of the two major systems, the underdeveloped countries are looking to both in order to learn from them. They are above all interested in rapid growth and less in such issues as parliamentary democracy, since they have hardly ever had it. The Communist example impresses them greatly. Planning is in high esteem. State initiative does take up part of the tasks neglected by private initiative. The willingness to interfere with price formation is understandable since they are often depending on typically unstable markets. Conditions seem favorable in these countries to try to combine the best elements from communism and free enterprise. These countries therefore may become the experimental ground for economic regimes.

They may, as they sometimes do in technical matters, skip one phase in their development and at once aim at the best solution. They should try to. And we may follow with particular interest the pattern of society that is emerging. □

THE POSSIBILITIES OF AFFLUENCE

The doctrine of convergence concerns economic systems. But what of future economic *conditions*? Many feel (presuming, of course, that we pay sufficient attention to the problems of energy, pollution, and ecology) that that future holds out the promise of unparalleled affluence.

The Affluent Society is, of course, the title of Professor Galbraith's famous book. The argument of that book does not ignore the economic deficiencies of our society—income distribution, poverty, pollution, the need for more public services, etc.—but it does suggest that fundamentally we have reached a new state of affairs, where abundance rather than scarcity has become the major problem. Galbraith writes:

The greatest prospect that we face—indeed what must now be counted one of the central economic goals of our society—is to eliminate toil as a required economic institution. This is not a utopian vision. We are already well on the way. Only an extraordinarily elaborate exercise in social camouflage has kept us from seeing what has been happening.[4]

In this stage of society, the central social goal (apart from securing peaceful survival) is to expand what Galbraith calls the "New Class." This New Class is that group of individuals in modern life whose work is interesting and rewarding in itself. He divides work into two major categories (with all kinds of possible overlapping): (1) work whose only reward is the pay, and (2) work that is basically an end in itself. Members of the New Class may not in the least object to high pay, but they would be offended by the notion that pay was what really motivated them. The key thing is to find work that is personally satisfying, and members of the New Class also pass on this attitude to their children.

Historically speaking, there has always been a leisure class (whose members, incidentally, may have worked very hard at their hobbies, whether archeology, social intrigue, or simply "putting on the dog"), and also there have been artists and members of the various professions who have taken it for granted that their work would be interesting and valuable even in the absence of monetary recognition. However, the great mass of mankind has faced work as a necessary but disagreeable, monotonous, and toilsome duty, required by the basic fact of scarcity. The novel feature of the age to come is that it may prove possible to expand the New Class so that it includes not simply a handful, but the great majority, of citizens.

4. John Kenneth Galbraith, *The Affluent Society* (Boston: Houghton Mifflin Company, 1958), p. 340.

The reader will recognize in the above an anticipation and somewhat more formal statement of the arguments, current in the 1960s and early 1970s, that everyone should "do his own thing." We should look not for jobs but for self-fulfillment and self-realization. Some would argue that this slogan, and Galbraith's case, are a bit premature, but it is interesting that somewhat similar ideas were put forward by John Maynard Keynes more than forty years ago. What is even more remarkable is that, when Keynes was writing about the prospects of leisure and abundance, there was a massive worldwide depression going on.

Both as an indication of Keynes' extraordinary sense of perspective and as a still highly relevant statement about the possibilities (and problems) of affluence, we reproduce his brief essay in its entirety.

Economic Possibilities for Our Grandchildren

John Maynard Keynes

1

We are suffering just now from a bad attack of economic pessimism. It is common to hear people say that the epoch of enormous economic progress which characterised the nineteenth century is over; that the rapid improvement in the standard of life is now going to slow down—at any rate in Great Britain; that a decline in prosperity is more likely than an improvement in the decade which lies ahead of us.

I believe that this is a wildly mistaken interpretation of what is happening to us. We are suffering, not from the rheumatics of old age, but from the growing-pains of over-rapid changes, from the painfulness of readjustment between one economic period and another. The increase of technical efficiency has been taking place faster than we can deal with the problem of labour absorption; the improvement in the standard of life has been a little too quick, the banking and monetary system of the world has been preventing the rate of interest from falling as fast as equilibrium requires. And even so, the waste and confusion which ensue relate to not more than 7½ percent of the national income; we are muddling away one and sixpence in the £, and have only 18s. 6d., when we might, if we were more sensible, have £1; yet, nevertheless, the 18s. 6d. mounts up to as much as the £1 would have been five or six years ago. We forget that in 1929 the physical output of the industry of Great Britain was greater than ever before, and that the net surplus of our foreign balance available for new foreign investment, after paying for all our imports, was greater last year than that of any other country, being indeed 50 percent greater than the corresponding surplus of the United States. Or again—if it is to be a matter of comparisons—suppose that we were to reduce our wages by a half, repudiate four-fifths of the national debt, and hoard our surplus wealth in barren gold instead of lending it at 6 percent or more, we should resemble the now much-envied France. But would it be an improvement?

The prevailing world depression, the enormous anomaly of unemployment in a world full of wants, the disastrous mistakes we have made, blind us to what is going on under the surface—to the true interpretation of the trend of things. For I predict that both of the two opposed errors of pessimism which now make so much noise in the world will be proved wrong in our own time—the pessimism of the revolutionaries who think that things are so bad that nothing can save us but violent change, and the pessimism of the reactionaries who consider the balance of our economic and social life so precarious that we must risk no experiments.

My purpose in this essay, however, is not to examine the present or the near future, but to disembarrass myself of short views and take wings into the future. What can we reasonably expect the level of our economic life to be a hundred years hence? What

From John Maynard Keynes, *Essays on Persuasion*, pp. 358–73. Included in the *Collected Writings of John Maynard Keynes*, vol. 9, *Essays in Persuasion* published by Macmillan London and Basingstoke and St. Martin's Press, Inc. New York. Reprinted by permission of the publisher.

are the economic possibilities for our grandchildren?

From the earliest times of which we have record—back, say, to two thousand years before Christ—down to the beginning of the eighteenth century, there was no very great change in the standard of life of the average man living in the civilised centres of the earth. Ups and downs certainly. Visitations of plague, famine, and war. Golden intervals. But no progressive, violent change. Some periods perhaps 50 percent better than others—at the utmost 100 percent better—in the four thousand years which ended (say) in A.D. 1700.

This slow rate of progress, or lack of progress, was due to two reasons—to the remarkable absence of important technical improvements and to the failure of capital to accumulate.

The absence of important technical inventions between the prehistoric age and comparatively modern times is truly remarkable. Almost everything which really matters and which the world possessed at the commencement of the modern age was already known to man at the dawn of history. Language, fire, the same domestic animals which we have today, wheat, barley, the vine and the olive, the plough, the wheel, the oar, the sail, leather, linen and cloth, bricks and pots, gold and silver, copper, tin, and lead—and iron was added to the list before 1000 B.C.—banking, statecraft, mathematics, astronomy, and religion. There is no record of when we first possessed these things.

At some epoch before the dawn of history—perhaps even in one of the comfortable intervals before the last ice age—there must have been an era of progress and invention comparable to that in which we live to-day. But through the greater part of recorded history there was nothing of the kind.

The modern age opened, I think, with the accumulation of capital which began in the sixteenth century. I believe—for reasons with which I must not encumber the present argument—that this was initially due to the rise of prices, and the profits to which that led, which resulted from the treasure of gold and silver which Spain brought from the New World into the Old. From that time until to-day the power of accumulation by compound interest, which seems to have been sleeping for many generations, was reborn and renewed its strength. And the power of compound interest over two hundred years is such as to stagger the imagination.

Let me give in illustration of this a sum which I have worked out. The value of Great Britain's foreign investments to-day is estimated at about £4,000,000,000. This yields us an income at the rate of about 6½ percent. Half of this we bring home and enjoy; the other half, namely, 3¼ percent, we leave to accumulate abroad at compound interest. Something of this sort has now been going on for about 250 years.

For I trace the beginnings of British foreign investment to the treasure which Drake stole from Spain in 1580. In that year he returned to England bringing with him the prodigious spoils of the *Golden Hind*. Queen Elizabeth was a considerable shareholder in the syndicate which had financed the expedition. Out of her share she paid off the whole of England's foreign debt, balanced her Budget, and found herself with about £40,000 in hand. This she invested in the Levant company—which prospered. Out of the profits of the Levant Company, the East India Company was founded; and the profits of this great enterprise were the foundation of England's subsequent foreign investment. Now it happens that £40,000 accumulating at 3¼ percent compound interest approximately corresponds to the actual volume of England's foreign investments at various dates, and would actually amount to-day to the total of £4,000,000,000 which I have already quoted as being what our foreign investments now are. Thus, every £1 which Drake brought home in 1580 has now become £100,000. Such is the power of compound interest!

From the sixteenth century, with a cumulative cre-scendo after the eighteenth, the great age of science and technical inventions began, which since the be-ginning of the nineteenth century has been in full flood—coal, steam, electricity, petrol, steel, rubber, cotton, the chemical industries, automatic machinery and the methods of mass production, wireless, print-ing, Newton, Darwin, and Einstein, and thousands of other things and men too famous and familiar to catalogue.

What is the result? In spite of an enormous growth in the population of the world, which it has been necessary to equip with houses and machines, the average standard of life in Europe and the United States has been raised, I think, about fourfold. The growth of capital has been on a scale which is far beyond a hundredfold of what any previous age had known. And from now on we need not expect so great an increase of population.

If capital increases, say, 2 percent per annum, the capital equipment of the world will have increased by a half in twenty years, and seven and a half times in a hundred years. Think of this in terms of material things—houses, transport, and the like.

At the same time technical improvements in manu-facture and transport have been proceeding at a greater rate in the last ten years than ever before in history. In the United States factory output per head was 40 percent greater in 1925 than in 1919. In Europe we are held back by temporary obstacles, but even so it is safe to say that technical efficiency is increasing by more than 1 percent per annum compound. There is evidence that the revolutionary technical changes, which have so far chiefly affected industry, may soon be attacking agriculture. We may be on the eve of improvements in the efficiency of food production as great as those which have already taken place in mining, manufacture, and transport. In quite a few years—in our own lifetimes I mean—we may be able to perform all the operations of agricul-ture, mining, and manufacture with a quarter of the human effort to which we have been accustomed.

For the moment the very rapidity of these changes is hurting us and bringing difficult problems to solve. Those countries are suffering relatively which are not in the vanguard of progress. We are being afflicted with a new disease of which some readers may not yet have heard the name, but of which they will hear a great deal in the years to come—namely, *techno-logical unemployment*. This means unemployment due to our discovery of means of economising the use of labour outrunning the pace at which we can find new uses for labour.

But this is only a temporary phase of maladjust-ment. All this means in the long run *that mankind is solving its economic problem*. I would predict that the standard of life in progressive countries one hundred years hence will be between four and eight times as high as it is to-day. There would be nothing surprising in this even in the light of our present knowledge. It would not be foolish to contemplate the possibility of a far greater progress still.

2

Let us, for the sake of argument, suppose that a hundred years hence we are all of us, on the average, eight times better off in the economic sense than we are to-day. Assuredly there need be nothing here to surprise us.

Now it is true that the needs of human beings may seem to be insatiable. But they fall into two class-es—those needs which are absolute in the sense that we feel them whatever the situation of our fellow human beings may be, and those which are relative in the sense that we feel them only if their satisfaction lifts us above, makes us feel superior to, our fellows. Needs of the second class, those which satisfy the desire for superiority, may indeed be insatiable; for the higher the general level, the higher still are they. But this is not so true of the absolute needs—a point may soon be reached, much sooner perhaps than we are all of us aware of, when these needs are satisfied in the sense that we prefer to devote our further energies to non-economic purposes.

Now, for my conclusion, which you will find, I think, to become more and more startling to the imagination the longer you think about it.

I draw the conclusion that, assuming no important wars and no important increase in population, the *economic problem* may be solved, or be at least within sight of solution, within a hundred years. This means that the economic problem is not—if we look into the future—*the permanent problem of the human race.*

Why, you may ask, is this so startling? It is startling because—if, instead of looking into the future, we look into the past—we find that the economic problem, the struggle for subsistence, always has been hitherto the primary, most pressing problem of the human race—not only of the human race, but of the whole of the biological kingdom from the beginnings of life in its most primitive forms.

Thus we have been expressly evolved by nature—with all our impulses and deepest instincts—for the purpose of solving the economic problem. If the economic problem is solved, mankind will be deprived of its traditional purpose.

Will this be a benefit? If one believes at all in the real values of life, the prospect at least opens up the possibility of benefit. Yet I think with dread of the readjustment of the habits and instincts of the ordinary man, bred into him for countless generations, which he may be asked to discard within a few decades.

To use the language of to-day—must we not expect a general ''nervous breakdown''? We already have a little experience of what I mean—a nervous breakdown of the sort which is already common enough in England and the United States amongst the wives of the well-to-do classes, unfortunate women, many of them, who have been deprived by their wealth of their traditional tasks and occupations—who cannot find it sufficiently amusing, when deprived of the spur of economic necessity, to cook and clean and mend, yet are quite unable to find anything more amusing.

To those who sweat for their daily bread leisure is a longed-for sweet—until they get it.

There is the traditional epitaph written for herself by the old charwoman:

Don't mourn for me, friends, don't weep for me never,
For I'm going to do nothing for ever and ever.

This was her heaven. Like others who look forward to leisure, she conceived how nice it would be to spend her time listening-in—for there was another couplet which occurred in her poem:

With psalms and sweet music the heavens'll be
  ringing,
But I shall have nothing to do with the singing.

Yet it will only be for those who have to do with the singing that life will be tolerable—and how few of us can sing!

Thus for the first time since his creation man will be faced with his real, his permanent problem—how to use his freedom from pressing economic cares, how to occupy the leisure, which science and compound interest will have won for him, to live wisely and agreeably and well.

The strenuous purposeful money-makers may carry all of us along with them into the lap of economic abundance. But it will be those peoples, who can keep alive, and cultivate into a fuller perfection, the art of life itself and do not sell themselves for the means of life, who will be able to enjoy the abundance when it comes.

Yet there is no country and no people, I think, who can look forward to the age of leisure and of abundance without a dread. For we have been trained too long to strive and not to enjoy. It is a fearful problem for the ordinary person, with no special talents, to occupy himself, especially if he no longer has roots in the soil or in custom or in the beloved conventions of a traditional society. To judge from the behaviour and the achievements of the wealthy classes to-day in any quarter of the world, the outlook is very depressing! For these are, so to speak, our advance guard—those who are spying out the promised land for the rest of us and pitching their camp there. For they have most of them failed disastrously, so it seems to me—those who have an independent income but no associations or duties or ties—to solve the problem which has been set them.

I feel sure that with a little more experience we shall use the new-found bounty of nature quite differently from the way in which the rich use it to-day, and will map out for ourselves a plan of life quite otherwise than theirs.

For many ages to come the old Adam will be so strong in us that everybody will need to do *some* work if he is to be contented. We shall do more things for ourselves than is usual with the rich to-day, only too glad to have small duties and tasks and routines. But beyond this, we shall endeavour to spread the bread thin on the butter—to make what work there is still to be done to be as widely shared as possible. Three-hour shifts or a fifteen-hour week may put off the problem for a great while. Three hours a day is quite enough to satisfy the old Adam in most of us!

There are changes in other spheres, too, which we must expect to come. When the accumulation of wealth is no longer of high social importance, there will be great changes in the code of morals. We shall be able to rid ourselves of many of the pseudo-moral principles which have hag-ridden us for 200 years, by which we have exalted some of the most distasteful of human qualities into the position of the highest virtues. We shall be able to afford to dare to assess the money-motive at its true value. The love of money as a possession—as distinguished from the love of money as a means to the enjoyments and realities of life—will be recognised for what it is, a somewhat disgusting morbidity, one of those semi-criminal, semi-pathological propensities which one hands over with a shudder to the specialists in mental disease. All kinds of social customs and economic practices, affecting the distribution of wealth and of economic

rewards and penalties, which we now maintain at all costs, however distasteful and unjust they may be in themselves, because they are tremendously useful in promoting the accumulation of capital, we shall then be free, at last, to discard.

Of course there will still be many people with intense, unsatisfied purposiveness who will blindly pursue wealth—unless they can find some plausible substitute. But the rest of us will no longer be under any obligation to applaud and encourage them. For we shall inquire more curiously than is safe to-day into the true character of this "purposiveness" with which in varying degrees Nature has endowed almost all of us. For purposiveness means that we are more concerned with the remote future results of our actions than with their own quality or their immediate effects on our own environment. The "purposive" man is always trying to secure a spurious and delusive immortality for his acts by pushing his interest in them forward into time. He does not love his cat, but his cat's kittens; nor, in truth, the kittens, but only the kittens' kittens, and so on forward for ever to the end of cat-dom. For him jam is not jam unless it is a case of jam to-morrow and never jam to-day. Thus by pushing his jam always forward into the future, he strives to secure for his act of boiling it an immortality.

Let me remind you of the Professor in *Sylvie and Bruno:*

"Only the tailor, sir, with your little bill," said a meek voice outside the door.

"Ah, well, I can soon settle his business," the Professor said to the children, *"if you'll just wait a minute. How much is it, this year, my man?"* The tailor had come in while he was speaking.

"Well, it's been a-doubling so many years, you see," the tailor replied, a little gruffly, *"and I think I'd like the money now. It's two thousand pound, it is!"*

"Oh, that's nothing!" the Professor carelessly remarked, feeling in his pocket, as if he always carried at least that amount about with him. *"But wouldn't you like to wait just another year and make it four*

thousand? Just think how rich you'd be! Why, you might be a king, if you liked!''

''I don't know as I'd care about being a king,'' the man said thoughtfully. ''But it dew sound a powerful sight o' money! Well, I think I'll wait—''

''Of course you will!'' said the Professor. ''There's good sense in you, I see. Good-day to you, my man!''

''Will you ever have to pay him that four thousand pounds?'' Sylvie asked as the door closed on the departing creditor.

''Never, my child!'' the Professor replied emphatically. ''He'll go on doubling it till he dies. You see, it's always worth while waiting another year to get twice as much money!''

Perhaps it is not an accident that the race which did most to bring the promise of immortality into the heart and essence of our religions has also done most for the principle of compound interest and particularly loves this most purposive of human institutions.

I see us free, therefore, to return to some of the most sure and certain principles of religion and traditional virtue—that avarice is a vice, that the exaction of usury is a misdemeanour, and the love of money is detestable, that those walk most truly in the paths of virtue and sane wisdom who take least thought for the morrow. We shall once more value ends above means and prefer the good to the useful. We shall honour those who can teach us how to pluck the hour and the day virtuously and well, the delightful people who are capable of taking direct enjoyment in things, the lilies of the field who toil not, neither do they spin.

But beware! The time for all this is not yet. For at least another hundred years we must pretend to ourselves and to every one that fair is foul and foul is fair; for foul is useful and fair is not. Avarice and usury and precaution must be our gods for a little longer still. For only they can lead us out of the tunnel of economic necessity into daylight.

I look forward, therefore, in days not so very remote, to the greatest change which has ever occurred in the material environment of life for human beings in the aggregate. But, of course, it will all happen gradually, not as a catastrophe. Indeed, it has already begun. The course of affairs will simply be that there will be ever larger and larger classes and groups of people from whom problems of economic necessity have been practically removed. The critical difference will be realised when this condition has become so general that the nature of one's duty to one's neighbour is changed. For it will remain reasonable to be economically purposive for others after it has ceased to be reasonable for oneself.

The *pace* at which we can reach our destination of economic bliss will be governed by four things—our power to control population, our determination to avoid wars and civil dissensions, our willingness to entrust to science the direction of those matters which are properly the concern of science, and the rate of accumulation as fixed by the margin between our production and our consumption; of which the last will easily look after itself, given the first three.

Meanwhile there will be no harm in making mild preparations for our destiny, in encouraging, and experimenting in, the arts of life as well as the activities of purpose.

But, chiefly, do not let us overestimate the importance of the economic problem, or sacrifice to its supposed necessities other matters of greater and more permanent significance. It should be a matter for specialists—like dentistry. If economists could manage to get themselves thought of as humble, competent people, on a level with dentists, that would be splendid!   □

WHAT ARE OUR GOALS?

In the title of this chapter, we included the phrase, "an uncertain future." Considering that observers have seen as a logical projection of the trends of our industrial society either (1) everybody on the average being "eight times better off" (Keynes), or (2) "a succession of famines, epidemics, social crises and wars" (Great Debate Five, p. 727), it is clear that "uncertain" is a rather mild adjective for what we face.

Interestingly enough, however, even in these rather widely separated views we can find a certain common theme. This theme may be said to involve the erosion of the *idea of progress.* In terms of the future-abundance school of thought, the necessity for further material advance will decline as we become richer and richer. What we must look forward to is a society in which, far from building for the tomorrow, we must develop the capacities for enjoying today. Yesterday's virtues—saving, thrift, abstinence—will have no relevance in a society ripe with riches.

But a similar basic theme is also present in the ecological-cataclysm school. The outlook is pessimistic—they would say that what we have called economic "progress" has been deeply delusive—but their conclusion is much the same. We must move from an expanding, spreading, aggressive society to a much more stable, non-exploitive society. This may be Boulding's spaceship earth, or John Stuart Mill's "stationary state." In any event, instead of always moving forward, we must learn to become content with a society whose basic dimensions remain unchanged over time.

Now this decline in the notion of progress is a development of extraordinary importance, the full consequences of which have not yet been analyzed. In the 1930s, in an introduction to J. B. Bury's classic work *The Idea of Progress,* the historian Charles Beard wrote: "Now among the ideas which have held sway in public and private affairs for the last two hundred years, none is more significant or likely to exert more influence in the future than the concept of progress."[5] J. B. Bury himself argued that, by the end of the nineteenth century, the idea of progress was becoming a "general article of faith." In many ways, it was a this-worldly equivalent to the concept of immortality and an afterlife of the great religions that had so dominated thought in earlier periods. Through progress, the individual could find redemption for himself, not in the thought of heavenly rewards, but in the imagination of the better world that would come in the future. Mankind was seen as moving forward and upward—whether inevitably or as a result of one's hard efforts was never fully resolved—but the movement was definitely in a positive direction, and this provided both a discipline and a sense of purpose in life.

The idea of progress is clearly not an economic phenomenon only. It was rooted in the philosophic thought of the Enlightenment of the eighteenth century (before the Industrial Revolution had struck with full force); it was given practical reality and much wider appeal by the great strides in science, technology, and material standards of living from the late eighteenth century on; and it was also given an enormous boost by the mid-nineteenth century development of the theory of evolution. Man was not only progressing in historic time, but also in biological time. The French philosopher, Henri Bergson, expressed this in his notion of "creative evolution." It is not too much to say that Western man—the peoples living in the economically advanced, industrial world—entered the twentieth century with the concept of progress in economics, science, art, biology, democracy, and all phases of human life writ large on the banners of his beliefs.

It is this idea—basically a religious idea—that is coming under fire. It raises the embarrassingly direct but extremely difficult question: If we are not living

---

5. Charles A. Beard, "Introduction," in *The Idea of Progress,* J. B. Bury (New York: Dover Publications, Inc., 1955), p. xi. Beard's introduction was written in 1931; Bury's original book was published in 1920.

for the good of posterity, exactly what are we living for?

Now in the economic sphere in particular this painful question may be avoided for a time, perhaps for a very long time. The essential reason is that economic inequalities of major dimension exist in the modern world—within the affluent societies, but even more as contrasted with the poor societies of the world. It may be possible that the new interest in equality (see chapter 29) is, in part, an attempt to avoid the still deeper question of long-run purposes. There is something close to a contradiction in arguing (1) that the rich are corrupted by their wealth and (2) that we should all have the same as they have.

Perform the mental experiment: We all have equal goods and enough. The energy problem has been solved by new technology. We are recycling our wastes as a matter of course. The future will be no worse than today, but also no better. We will not achieve salvation through our children, nor they through theirs. We will live securely, painlessly, without toil, for today.

In such a world, the phrase from Keynes' essay might haunt us bitterly. How few of us can sing!

Still, this world is not yet. And economics, born in the Enlightenment, nourished by the Industrial Revolution and the advance of material well-being, fresh from the conquest of Great (if not smaller) Depressions, is not yet ready to close its books. If the 1970s have taught us anything, it is that we had best hold on to the idea of scarcity—for a little longer, at least.

SUMMARY

In this chapter, we have discussed a few of the many possibilities that may lie ahead for the industrialized world in the future.

One such possibility is that the future development of the West may be seriously compromised by shortages of energy. This difficulty could occur either because of the failure of long-run supplies to keep pace with the growth of long-run demand or because of the "recycling" problem. Enormous wealth is being transferred to the OPEC countries as a consequence of the higher prices of petroleum. This transfer could lead to world monetary problems and to national problems of unemployment and inflation. (For various future possibilities, see Great Debate Six.)

Another question for the future is, what will happen to the great rival economic systems of East and West? A case can be made that neither capitalism nor communism can survive. Indeed in both cases, following Schumpeter's example, it can be argued that both will be undone by their own respective "successes." But if both systems seem to be on their way to modification, what is the possibility that they may converge? The doctrine of *convergence* is discussed in the reading by Jan Tinbergen, who considers a move in this direction a reasonable possibility.

Another question, frequently discussed in recent years, concerns the implications of growing affluence in the industrial world. An affluent future is not certain because of the dangers of global war, energy shortages, and ecological disaster, but it is a possibility that, in view of our past history, cannot be overlooked. Galbraith has seen in affluence a challenge to rid ourselves of "toil" and to expand the New Class of those whose work is rewarding and self-satisfying in its own terms. Lord Keynes, in an early essay, considers some of the opportunities but also problems that living for today may bring to mankind.

There is a common bond between the affluence-school and the ecological-disaster school—namely, a downgrading of the *idea of progress* which, in the nineteenth century, at least, was one of the most important guiding concepts of Western man.

Since this idea was basically a spiritual idea (though nourished, of course, by material advancement), its erosion poses the very deepest kind of problem in terms of the psychological goals and purposes of modern society.

IMPORTANT TERMS TO REMEMBER

Long Run Supply and Demand for Energy
OPEC Countries
''Recycling'' Problem
Capitalist vs. Communist Bureaucracy
Doctrine of Convergence
Affluent Society
The ''New Class''
The ''Power of Compound Interest''
Fear of Abundance
Idea of Progress

QUESTIONS FOR DISCUSSION

1. Explain the automatic adjustments by which a market economy might try to *solve* the energy crisis. Why might this solution be seriously complicated by (*a*) external effects and (*b*) international aspects?

2. Schumpeter considered that society's intellectuals, whose education and elevation were essentially a product of the capitalistic system, would be in the forefront in undermining that system. Do you consider this analysis accurate? If it were accurate, would there be anything improper in intellectuals behaving in this way?

3. ''The convergence of economic systems has nothing to do with world peace. The greatest wars in modern history have been fought between nations with closely parallel economic systems.'' Beginning with the Napoleonic Wars, discuss this statement with reference to the major wars of the nineteenth and twentieth centuries.

4. In the discussion of affluent societies, the distinction between work that is satisfying in itself and work that is done merely for the pay is often made. Consider the difficulties involved in making such a distinction with respect to the academic work a student does in college. Sometimes people do similar work but for very different motives—the farmer plants vegetables to sell, the retired businessman plants a garden for his own pleasure. Is the real distinction not in the kind of work but in the fact that one has chosen it oneself? If expanded choice is involved, do you feel that it is the case that people in the 1970s want more choices? Or are they anxious and bewildered because of the array of choices they already face? Do you yourself feel that you have too few or too many choices to make in shaping your future life?

5. What are the implications of Keynes' statement that in an ideal future society economists would be in the same category as dentists? (Hint: the correct answer is *not* that economists would then get better pay.)

6. ''Living in a society without progress would be like living in a room with walls and no windows. Only a spiritual monk could accomplish it.'' Discuss.

SUGGESTED READING

Boulding, Kenneth E. ''Is Scarcity Dead?'' In *Is Economics Relevant?* ed. Robert L. Heilbroner and Arthur M. Ford. Pacific Palisades, Calif.: Goodyear Publishing Company, 1971, pp. 177–91.

Bury, J. B. *The Idea of Progress.* New York: Dover Publications, 1955.

Galbraith, John Kenneth. *The Affluent Society.* Boston: Houghton Mifflin Co., 1958.

Pollack, Gerald A. ''The Economic Consequences of the Energy Crisis,'' *Foreign Affairs,* Vol. 52, No. 3, April 1974.

Schumpeter, Joseph A. *Capitalism, Socialism and Democracy.* New York: Harper & Row, 1950.

Toffler, Alvin. *Future Shock.* New York: Bantam Books, 1971.

GREAT DEBATE 6:
ENERGY: RESTRAIN DEMAND OR STIMULATE SUPPLY?

GREAT DEBATE 6:
ENERGY: RESTRAIN DEMAND OR STIMULATE SUPPLY?

We end this book with a Great Debate on one of the most widely discussed economic developments of the early 1970s: the energy crisis. As we know from earlier chapters, this crisis has many dimensions. The effect of higher-priced oil and oil-based fertilizers may be a near disaster for certain of the oil-poor under-developed countries (India being a notable example). The problem of "recycling" oil revenues in the hands of OPEC countries to the oil-consuming nations poses potentially enormous problems for particular nations (e.g., Italy), and could be a major threat to the world's monetary system.

Beneath these specific problems lies the deeper long-run issue: Is the world running out of energy resources? Is the shortage that was dramatized by the Arab oil boycott of 1973 and the quadrupling of oil prices in 1973–74 simply a prelude to the ultimate exhaustion of energy resources, with potentially cataclysmic effects on future generations? Or are there plenty of energy resources, really, if we will only go out and exploit them?

One's views on this question are likely to produce quite different opinions about how we should adjust to our energy situation. One broad line of thought suggests primary emphasis on conservation. We should, in every way possible, restrain the growth of our demand for energy. The focus should be on doing without, where possible, and, where energy resources must be used, contriving the most energy-efficient method of utilizing those resources. The emphasis here is on smaller cars, mass transit, better building insulation, and shifting from more- to less-energy-intensive industries and from a product-oriented to a service-oriented economy.

An alternative line of thought is to argue that, for practical purposes, the growth of demand can only be limited in relatively minor ways, or at great cost to our accepted way of life; in consequence, primary emphasis must be placed on stimulating supply. The focus of research should be on the increased exploration and exploitation of energy resources, and especially the improvement of new technologies applicable to shale oil, nuclear fission (and ultimately fusion), geothermal, and solar energy sources.

These two views are not mutually exclusive—a reasonable man might say, "Why, of course, do both!" Yet there is an important underlying issue. It relates to the socially desirable rate at which nonrenewable natural resources should be exploited.[1] Are we using up these resources too fast: in effect, making an inadequate provision for the needs of future generations? Or have we been going too slow, losing important opportunities to develop new resources because of needless worries about the environment, pollution, and the like?

These quite different emphases are brought out in the following readings. First, there is a selection from Exploring Energy Choices, a preliminary report of the Ford Foundation's Energy Policy Project; its publication in 1974 attracted much public attention. This is followed by two dissenting statements and then by excerpts from a Public Television Debate ("The Open Mind," hosted by Richard Heffner) between one of these dissenters, W. P. Tavoulareas, president of Mobil Oil Corporation, and the Ford Project director, S. David Freeman.

---

1. For an interesting discussion of this question from an economic theorist's point of view, see Robert M. Solow's Richard T. Ely lecture before to the American Economic Association, "The Economics of Resources or the Resources of Economics," American Economic Review, Vol. LXIV, No. 2, May 1974. Solow suggests that, in a market economy, resources may be used up too rapidly because individuals apply too high a discount to future needs and because not enough people take a truly long-view of the problem. To make things come out right, "someone—it could be the Department of the Interior, or the mining companies, or their major customers, or speculators—must always be taking the long view." To help promote the long view, he suggests that the government should be engaged "in a continuous program of information-gathering and dissemination covering trends in technology, reserves and demand."

Three Energy Growth Scenarios

Ford Foundation Energy Policy Project

We believe that the future, though full of surprises, is in some measure within our control. Choices we make now will shape that future. In order to illuminate the range of choices the Project has developed a method of analyzing the long-term implications of present energy decisions. We have constructed three plausible but very different energy futures for the period through the year 2000, as shown in Figures A and B.

The alternative futures, or scenarios, are based on different assumptions we have made about the energy growth patterns our society might adopt for the years ahead, and the policies and consequences that each would entail. Of course, an infinite number of futures is possible; and it is most unlikely that the real energy future of the United States will conform closely to any of the three scenarios we have chosen to describe. They are not predictions, but a tool for rigorous

Excerpted from Ford Foundation's Energy Policy Project (Preliminary Report), *Exploring Energy Choices*, 1974, pp. 39–53. Graphs shown here were adapted from those in the Report.

thinking. We do not advocate one option over the others but present each for comparative analysis by the reader.

Our first scenario, which we call *historical growth,* assumes that the use of energy will continue to grow much as it has in the past. It assumes that the nation will not deliberately impose any policies that might affect our ingrained habits of energy use, but will make a strong effort to develop supplies at a rapid pace to match rising demand.

Early results suggest that this energy future is indeed possible, even with domestic resources alone, through the year 2000. It would require very aggressive development of all our possible supplies—oil and gas onshore and offshore, coal, shale, nuclear power. If it proved feasible to increase oil imports on a large scale, then the pressure on domestic resources would relax somewhat. Still, the political, economic, and environmental problems of getting that much energy out of the earth would be formidable.

Our *technical fix* scenario shares with *historical growth* a similar level and mix of goods and

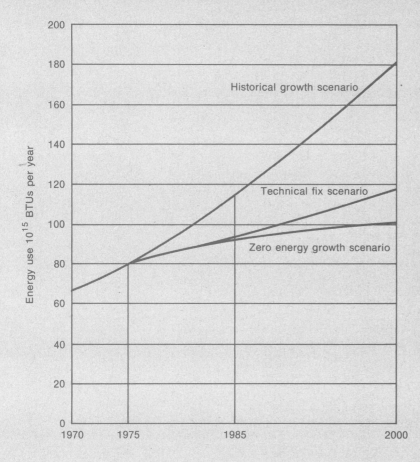

Figure A. Scenarios at a Glance

services. But it reflects a determined, conscious national effort to reduce demand for energy through the application of energy-saving technologies. Our work so far has revealed that the slower rate of energy growth in *technical fix*—about half as high as *historical growth's*—permits more flexibility of energy supply, but still provides a quality of life at home, travel convenience, and economic growth that, to our minds at least, differs little from the historical growth scenario.

Only one of the major domestic sources of energy—Rocky Mountain coal or shale, or nu-clear power, or oil and gas—would have to be pushed hard to meet the energy growth rates of this scenario.

Zero energy growth is different. It represents a real break with our accustomed ways of doing things. Yet it does not represent austerity. It would give everyone in the United States more energy benefits in the year 2000 than he enjoys today, even enough to allow the less privileged to catch up to the comforts of the American Way of Life. It does not preclude economic growth.

It might come about if society became concerned enough about the social and environmental costs of energy growth, and if technology

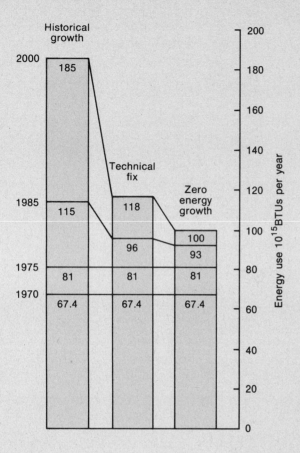

Figure B.

RESUMING HISTORICAL GROWTH IN ENERGY CONSUMPTION

The nation has the option of resuming its consumption growth over the next 25 years at a rate approximating the average for 1950–1972—3.4 percent per year. Energy consumption could grow from 75 quadrillion BTU's in 1973 to about 95 in 1980, 115 in 1985, and 185 quadrillion BTU's in 2000.

The primary emphasis of this scenario is in developing and producing sufficient energy supplies to meet the growth in consumption. Preliminary results from a study by Resources for the Future indicate that enough energy could be produced to meet historical growth demand between now and 2000 providing that institutional constraints did not prevent it. Decisions, especially those involving the environmental impacts and foreign policy problems of one energy source relative to another, could shift the supply mix heavily in favor of either domestic fossil fuels, nuclear power or imported oil. Relative prices will also play a key role. At the same time, it is clear that significant increases in output from all major domestic sources would be required if energy consumption were to resume the historic growth rate. The RFF conclusions are based primarily on an econometric analysis of past production in response to price rather than a detailed technical projection of future production rates. The production was, however, compared to a variety of resource estimates.

Figure C depicts the likely consumption patterns of energy consumption in the *historical growth* scenario and is the base from which savings in the other scenarios are estimated.

The achievement of . . . the scenario as a whole requires that environmental and safety concerns be met with modest increases in cost and that major expansions of any energy source not be effectively blocked through moratoriums

seemed unable to solve these problems. It might also reflect broader social concerns, like uneasiness about the dehumanizing aspects of big centralized institutions. *Zero energy growth* would emphasize durability, not disposability of goods. It would substitute for the idea that "more is better," the ethic that "enough is best."

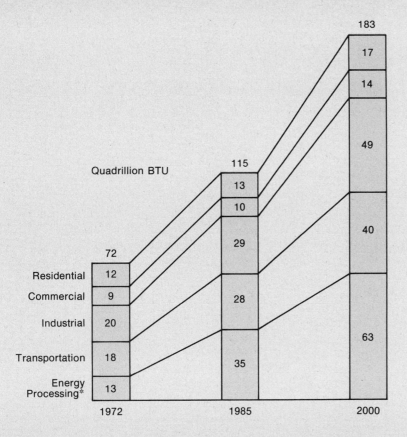

Figure C. Energy Consumption Pattern in Historical Growth Scenario.

*Energy processing—electric generation and transmission losses, oil refining, gas processing, uranium enrichment.

on new construction or by outright prohibitions. In addition, the scenario requires either that the government permit basic fuel prices to rise to the levels needed to bring forth the supplies indicated, that sufficient subsidies be provided to the industry to accomplish the same ends, or that the federal government itself explore and develop the energy resources.

This *historical growth* scenario would require a few basic policy decisions in the near future which would then be followed by some detailed implementation plans.

(1) The government would have to emphasize expanded energy supplies in its actions rather than stressing active measures to promote conservation. Continued subsidies to limit increases in the price of energy may be needed. Demand would also be stimulated by a continuation of economic growth along current patterns. Policies generally favoring energy-intensive private automobiles, detached housing, and energy-intensive industries might be needed while government funding for mass transit or new housing construction to save energy would receive a lower priority.

(2) The nation would have to develop *all* the major sources of energy growth—oil imports, OCS [Outer Continental Shelf] oil and gas, Rocky Mountain shale and coal and nuclear power—in the near and medium term. Even so, it is possible to forego vigorous development of one of the options over the longer term if the others are pushed more aggressively. For example, under this scenario a reduction in imports leading to self-sufficiency in the late 1980s is possible. Or, development of *one* of the following could be slowed but not eliminated: oil and gas development on the Atlantic and Pacific OCS, Rocky Mountain fossil fuel production or nuclear power. To do so would require pushing the other three options very hard.

(3) Exploration and development of oil and gas would have to be encouraged by favorable government price, tax, and federal leasing policies. To get the large quantities required in the domestic oil and gas supply case, it would be essential to develop the Atlantic and Pacific Outer Continental Shelves (OCS), Alaska, the Gulf of Mexico, and the Alaskan OCS rapidly. Development of Western oil shale would have to be pushed as well. This raises the federal leasing problems and the environmental and regional development problems. Greater reliance on imported oil could ease some of these pressures, but it would require the construction of super-ports and would subject the coastal waters to oil spills and coastal industrialization similar to that which would accompany OCS production.

(4) Increased coal use requires resolution of the strip mining and air pollution problems as well as the labor and economic problems. With the anticipated prices for oil and gas, coal should have no problem competing with them on an economic basis but the environmental question would have to be resolved.

(5) Significant growth in nuclear power is required in this scenario no matter which supply case is selected. A twelve to fifteen times increase in on-line nuclear capacity between now and 1985 is projected, based on the large number of plants now on order or under construction. It would be followed by an additional three- to four-fold increase by the year 2000, depending on the degree to which transportation is switched to electric power and the extent to which coal could be used to fuel electric power growth. Thus, questions of nuclear power safety, safeguarding nuclear materials, and handling of radioactive wastes would have to be resolved. To achieve the necessary rate of energy supply growth would require that design, siting, and federal licensing procedures for individual power plants be streamlined and standardized and that other elements in the nuclear power fuel cycle such as enrichment, reprocessing, and waste handling proceed apace.

(6) All of the supply options for this scenario require extremely large investments in refineries, power plants, pipelines, transmission lines, and other large facilities. The capital requirements are large in comparison with other investments made by the economy, and may need to grow. Serious siting, technical manpower, and construction labor problems also arise in addition to the capital problem. Unless speedy solutions are found to this broad class of problems, the scenario would not be achieved.

(7) Research and development programs which concentrate on enhancing energy supply and conversion technology and on environmental clean-up are crucial to the *historical growth* scenario. The effort would emphasize medium-term technologies rather than fundamentally new, long-term technologies.

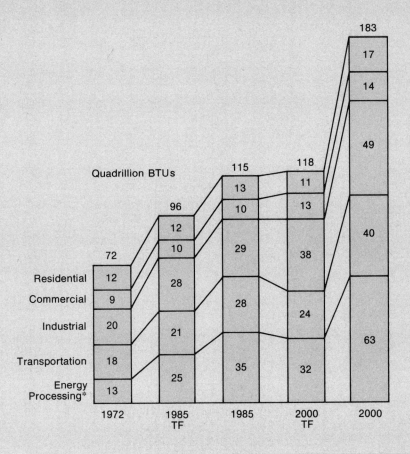

Figure D. Energy Consumption Patterns: Technical Fix vs. Historical Growth.

*Energy processing—electric generation and transmission losses, oil refining, gas processing, uranium enrichment.

TECHNICAL FIX SCENARIO

A second model of the future offers the option of reducing energy demand substantially below historical growth rates. This is accomplished by making consumption efficiency, rather than increased supply, the focal point of energy policy.

The scenario under discussion was developed by applying economically feasible energy-saving "technical fixes" to the end uses of energy in the *historical growth* scenario. As a result, energy demand grows at half the 3.4 percent rate in the *historical growth* scenario, but without reducing the standard of living or significantly changing life-styles.

Figure D shows the magnitude of the energy savings in the major categories of use by 1985 and 2000 if the conservation efforts are begun in the near future. The total possible energy savings by 2000 in the *technical fix* scenario are about 65 quadrillion BTU's per year—one-third of the energy consumed in the *historical growth* scenario and almost as much as our total energy consumption today.

TECHNICAL OPPORTUNITIES
FOR SAVINGS

Although there are a large number of ways in which to cut energy consumption without reducing our standard of living or the benefits we receive from energy, the greatest savings come from a relatively few—space heating and cooling, industrial process heat production, and automobiles.

Reducing the energy required to heat and cool homes and commercial buildings involves three different but complementary approaches: improved building design and construction so that less heating and cooling are required, more efficient systems for heating and cooling, and the use of renewable sources such as the sun. In the first instance, more widespread use of insulation and double glazing can be combined with construction of "tighter" buildings so that outside air does not leak in. These relatively simple approaches already pass the test of technical and economic feasibility.

The heat pump is the best example of a more efficient heating system. Heat pumps are electric or heat operated refrigerators or air conditioners operating in reverse. They warm the house by cooling the out-of-doors. They use mechanical energy, generally from electric motors, to bring in the "free" but low temperature energy in the natural environment and pump it up to useful temperatures. For every BTU a heat pump consumes in electricity, it produces two or three in heating for a house. This compares with the one BTU of energy provided by electric resistance heaters for every BTU they consume. The use of the heat pump for space heating, and cooling when they are reversed, has to date been economically feasible only in the South, but now

higher energy prices make it economical in most regions of the nation.

Solar heating and cooling systems exploit a neglected resource. Solar heating has already caught the public's eye through widespread publicity of the relatively few solar homes built around the country. The sun's energy is gathered in rooftop collectors to provide most of the energy for heating. Additional research and development is expected to produce air conditioning systems which use this solar heat, further expanding the usefulness and benefits of this approach. Because of the difficulties and higher costs associated with installing solar heating and cooling in existing homes, the Project estimates that this technology will achieve widespread use in new homes only after 1985.

Industrial heat production accounted for 28 percent of total energy consumption in 1968 and it offers a major opportunity for conservation. Improvements involve both existing and new technology. Heat recovery systems which use the heat from the exhaust gases of a furnace or other processes to warm incoming air have been around for years, but with cheap energy it was not often economically attractive to install them. The economics are now more favorable.

A similar approach combines process steam generation (60 percent of industrial heat production) with electric production. Whenever fossil or nuclear fuels are used to generate electric power, about two-thirds of the heat is released into the environment. Sometimes this waste heat can be used to generate process steam or heat. When this concept is used in residential or commercial applications, it is called "total energy." It is also used in industrial applications where high temperature energy is used to generate electric power before it is used as process steam. The hardware—whether it be diesel engines, gas turbines, or steam turbines—exists and is becoming a better investment as energy prices rise. Institutional and technical problems associated with operating these systems as part of a larger electric power system need to be solved before they will achieve more widespread use.

The heat pump principle may also be used to produce process steam. Residential heat pumps can frequently use the outdoor air as a source of low grade energy. However, the surrounding air may not contain enough heat for producing industrial steam. Industrial or power plant waste heat, low-temperature, solar flat-plate collectors or ground water could fill this need. This approach is still in the research stage, but looks promising.

The use of energy in automobiles is also a significant fraction of the nation's energy budget and offers technical options for conservation. Overall vehicle weight and fuel consumption are closely related. . . . The current trend toward smaller vehicles will produce energy savings. Technical developments—for example, the use of radial tires, better streamlining, and improved matching of the engine, transmission, and differential—could improve gasoline mileage without reducing the size or versatility of the automobile. Such improvements would result from design changes using existing technology. More fundamental changes, such as the use of the diesel engine or electric propulsion systems to replace the internal combustion engine, could also reduce the energy required for automobile transportation but would take longer to implement.

The major uncertainties in this scenario are political, institutional and economic questions rather than physical or technical limitations. A few of the technical fixes such as solar heating and cooling, the use of heat pumps to produce industrial steam, and alternatives to the internal combustion engine require some more R&D, but most of them are available commercially today. A fundamental assumption in this scenario is that individual and corporate consumers of energy would in fact respond to higher prices and direct federal action, and use these more efficient technologies.

POLICIES TO IMPLEMENT CONSERVATION MEASURES

The basic tool for achieving the energy savings in the *technical fix* scenario is a marketplace in which energy is priced to reflect its full costs to society. At this point in our study, it is not clear just what the price level of energy would be with all existing subsidies removed, and the total social or environmental costs included in the price. Nor has the impact of higher prices on the level of demand been established with any degree of certainty. It appears, however, that market prices alone will not bring about all of the energy savings possible. Government policy changes are needed in order to eliminate institutional obstacles so that the marketplace can function more effectively. Other changes may be necessary to encourage market decisions in favor of conservation rather than consumption. Finally, in those instances in which market solutions are not feasible, direct regulation may be required. Any tax or regulation measures, of course, run the risk of distorting rather than correcting the market, and the social and economic consequences of government action should be weighed against the benefits.

Improving the operation of the market system requires that consumers have better information about the energy performance of the items they buy in terms of BTU's and dollars. The most immediate need appears to be for a "Truth in Energy Law" to require labeling for automobiles, appliances, and even homes which clearly spells out average energy use and operating costs. The object is to give a purchaser the opportunity of making an informed decision on the basis of both the initial cost and the fuel costs for running the item over time. Today the consumer often lacks the information to take energy operating costs into account.

Information is useful only when the purchaser has a real choice of products and access to the credit needed to finance capital investments. Many government and private actions are needed to overcome this problem. One exemplary approach to financing additional insulation in private homes has already been initiated by a few utilities. The company provides homeowners with low-interest loans, repayable through their utility bills, to meet insulating costs. The gas costs are, of course, reduced due to the lowered fuel heating requirements. This reduction is usually more than enough to offset the cost of insulation within a year, providing a vivid example of the benefits of life cycle costing.

In many instances, however, it will take more than better information to correct existing imbalances in the market or to shift the balance in favor of conservation. Taxes and subsidies are the basic tools for dealing with this. Metals recycling is a case in point. Depletion allowances on raw materials and regulated freight rates currently favor the use of new metals. Unless there are significant technical breakthroughs which would make processing waste metals much cheaper than at present, specific government action will be needed to encourage recycling. Removal of the subsidies on new metals, or the provision of comparable ones for scrap, as well as federally-funded demonstration of recycling metals from urban wastes, might be required.

In the transportation sector, a similar strategy of removing subsidies for less energy-efficient modes of transportation, and of supporting urban mass transportation and intercity railroads with new federal funding, would be necessary to achieve the savings projected in this scenario. Highway and air transportation now receive most of the government support in the transportation sector.

Federal research and development (R&D) funding is a common method for subsidizing civilian activities. It is being used extensively for developing energy consumption technology. Basic R&D on energy conservation in building construction, equipment design, and industrial processing could provide significant benefits to the public, but it may not be possible for an individual firm to profit from them and justify a corporate effort. Joint government-industry demonstration projects could pay large dividends if they were designed to encourage widespread implementation of the technology rather than simple technical development.

Some areas of the economy, particularly the industrial sector, are too varied and complex to address with specific taxes and subsidies. Here the use of a broadly based excise tax which reflects the social costs of using energy may be an effective tool. Such a tax could produce moderately higher prices sufficient to stimulate the use of less energy-intensive industrial processes.

Other areas of the economy such as the residential and transportation sectors may not be as amenable to market-oriented solutions. Where additional information is not enough to stimulate the changes, and taxes or subsidies cause undesirable equity problems or do not work, regulatory measures may be used. Energy performance standards which specify the energy efficiency of buildings, appliances, and automobiles have been suggested. To preserve the most design flexibility and room for innovation, it is preferable to regulate performance—the maximum permissible heat loss from a building or minimum fuel economy for an automobile—rather than to specify the technology for accomplishing it. These regulations can be made rigid, permitting no deviations, or more flexible through a steeply graduated tax. This mixed approach might be used for automobiles: no tax for efficient cars meeting a certain minimum standard coupled with high taxes for less efficient cars.

IMPACT OF CONSERVATION ON SUPPLY

The substantial reduction in energy consumption in the *technical fix* scenario gives us greater flexibility to select those energy supply options with minimum environmental, social, economic, and foreign policy costs. Because less energy would be required, less expensive sources may be developed, less land would need to be devoted to energy production, and less pollution would result from its consumption. Another important difference between the scenarios involves capital investment. Greater investments in energy consumption systems such as mass transit would be required in the *technical fix* scenario, but there would be less investment in new energy supply facilities.

Numerous supply mixes for the *technical fix* scenario are possible and three have been examined by the Project. All of the cases move rapidly toward self-sufficiency. The "base case" achieves it first by developing all of the domestic sources. A domestic fossil fuel (or low nuclear) case requires oil, gas, and coal production approaching the *historical growth* scenario. A high nuclear case permits domestic oil, gas and coal production to level off after 1980.

Under the *technical fix* scenario, it would be necessary to increase at least *one* major source of energy significantly above current production levels. More oil, whether it is imported oil, traditional domestic petroleum, or synthetic oil, is required in all but the high nuclear case. More natural gas and coal are included in all of the supply cases. Even nuclear power increases in all of the cases, although it is kept to a minimum in the low nuclear case. The size of these increases varies widely depending on the option selected. For coal the increases range from 30 percent to 300 percent and for nuclear the range is even larger. Due to their large current production, the percentage increases in petroleum liquids and gas are not so large, except in terms of specific sources such as shale oil, coal liquids, and oil from the Atlantic and Pacific Outer Continental Shelves.

In the *historical growth* scenario, this flexibility in supply is *not* possible. Major sources like nuclear power or strip-mined coal cannot be eliminated, only developed at a slower rate.

Finally, since reduced growth in energy use gives a lower total energy use, new sources of energy such as solar or geothermal that may be environmentally or otherwise superior could contribute a greater fraction of the energy supply in a shorter period. The economy is also less dependent on short term payoffs from its energy research and development programs. A greater proportion of the federal R&D could be focused on long term energy sources such as solar energy, wind energy, and controlled thermonuclear fusion than would be possible with more rapid energy growth.

A ZERO ENERGY GROWTH SCENARIO

The concept of zero growth, first for population, later for resource use, and now for energy in particular, has caught the attention of many citizens. This stems in part from a growing concern that we are rapidly approaching the limits to growth on our planet. Besides the concern over physical limits, there is growing dissatisfaction with the automatic acceptance of "progress," as well as a feeling of "dehumanization" that stems from disillusionment with ever-growing consumption of material goods, and with the huge bureaucracies which produce, dispense, regulate, and otherwise service those goods.

One of the Project's scenarios for the future is designed to work out the implications of zero growth in energy. It is not our aim to explore the notion of zero economic growth. On the contrary, our preliminary work suggests that some sectors of the economy must grow vigorously for the nation to reach zero energy growth in a satisfactory way.

The transition to zero energy growth might come about naturally in response to ever-rising prices for energy and other commodities which result from scarcity or environmental limitations. It might also be one feature of the transition to a "post-industrial society," with an emphasis on services rather than goods production.

There are many reasons for seriously considering a *zero energy growth (ZEG)* option.

First, it is important to note that there is a fundamental difference between zero and slow growth. The slow growth of the *technical fix* scenario serves, in effect, to buy time before the problems associated with high consumption become acute. If the pace and mix of economic growth remains unchanged, energy consumption in the *technical fix* scenario would resume at a higher rate of growth, beyond the year 2000, as new opportunities for cutting out waste become harder to find. Even if the *technical fix* growth rate stays at 1.7 percent per year extended into the next century, a level of 180 quadrillion BTU's would be reached by 2025 and 275 quadrillion BTU's per year by 2050.

Providing the energy supplies to meet such demand levels would strain existing technology and known resources to the utmost. New technologies like nuclear fusion may be developed in time to support increasing energy growth early in the twenty-first century. But they are by no means certain to come to the rescue. They could prove to be less feasible or more polluting than they now appear.

Second, even if new technologies are developed, the earth has a finite capacity for absorbing environmental insults. What these finite limits are is uncertain. Recent scientific calculations indicate that the world may be rapidly approaching certain of those limits. Continued rapid growth in the burning of fossil fuels for the next 30 years means an accompanying atmospheric buildup of carbon dioxide and particle matter. Analysis increasingly suggests that this could trigger substantial global climatic change. A "point of no return" may be reached as soon as 30 years from now or as many as 100 or more years into the future. One prudent response to this uncertainty would be to plan now for reaching a manageable level of energy use as soon as possible.

A third reason for zero energy growth in the United States is simply that the rich nations of the world may limit their energy consumption either by choice or necessity so that the poor nations have a better opportunity, especially when it comes to using nonrenewable resources, of achieving a decent standard of living. Because of its influence in world affairs, America could take the lead in restraining its consumption of resources.

A fourth motivating factor for the *zero energy growth* scenario is the concern by some people that rapidly growing technology is dominating their lives and is beyond their control. There is a growing unwillingness among many citizens to leave to experts in remote bureaucracies the task of determining what technologies are or are not socially acceptable.

Both the *historical growth* and *technical fix* energy futures assume that there will be long-term growth in the large industrial complexes which supply, process, and use energy. Effective public participation in the decisions about the desirability of these large technologies has been virtually impossible. Events move too fast, technical knowledge is too specialized, and the future becomes the present before we know it. For example, the social acceptability of nuclear power is only now being publicly debated, many decades and many billions of dollars later. With zero energy growth, the pace of development

and innovation would be more amenable to public involvement. Gradual decentralization of technology could be an important element in the economic and institutional reorganization necessary to achieve a *ZEG* scenario.

The *zero energy growth* scenario we are developing closely parallels the *technical fix* scenario until the mid-1980s, and then reaches zero or even negative growth in the period thereafter. The nature of the economy in a zero energy growth society would certainly be very different from that of the other scenarios. But economic activity would not stagnate. Present-day society is geared to a relatively heedless use of plentiful, relatively low-cost energy. To develop a society that husbands its resources, including energy, would require a different kind of economic emphasis.

Redesign of cities and transportation systems would be a must. Growth in energy-intensive industries, like making plastics from petrochemicals, would be deemphasized. Instead there would be more vigorous growth in the service sector of the economy (education, medicine, government, etc.) and in industries, which use less energy. The trend toward a service economy in the United States is already well under way; the service sector share of the labor force having increased from 50 to 60 percent during the last two decades. In the *ZEG* Scenario, the shift would accelerate.

The idea of *zero energy growth* sometimes evokes the image of Spartan austerity. The *ZEG* ture we envision does not match this image. An energy consumption level of 100 quadrillion BTU's per year in 2000 would provide 10 percent more energy per person than the United States uses today. And the energy would be used more efficiently, thus providing more benefits to society. There is nothing inherent in the *ZEG* scenario which would preclude national redistribution of the "energy income." Those who do not have an adequate standard of living need not be stopped from achieving one because of lack of energy. Nor is there any inherent reason why those in the middle to high energy income brackets would have to give up any of the things they enjoy today.

It would, however, mean an end to the "more is better" philosophy, replacing it with one saying "enough is best." There would be a saturation point where no further increases in annual energy consumption would be needed. Further, because of its greater efficiency in using energy, the ZEG scenario would include many more energy benefits than the nation now enjoys. All of the householder's basic energy needs could be met. Appliances like air conditioners and dishwashers, often classed as luxuries today, could be in such wide use as to be considered "basic." Use of electronic devices such as stereo high fidelity sound systems would be quite compatible with the scenario, since they use little electricity.

ACHIEVING ZEG

This discussion has described some general features of our ZEG scenario as it is evolving in our thinking. Our analysis so far indicates that the implications of zero energy growth for our economic and political systems might be significant. Yet managing a transition to zero energy growth appears to be possible if the change takes place gradually over ten to twenty years as part of long-term planning and a growing social consensus as to its desirability.

In order to achieve a smooth transition, policies which allow gradual increases in energy prices through energy excise taxes in addition to removal of existing subsidies would be needed. Government fiscal and monetary policies to maintain economic growth and full employment during this period would be crucial. Many of the policy tools now used to achieve this objective serve to increase energy-intensive capital investment. In a ZEG scenario full employment would require a different economic game plan. Special programs would be required to provide displaced workers with new jobs during the transition.

Some of these changes, such as zero population growth, are already beginning to take place without government action. There is no clear indication that more government coercion would be needed to achieve this scenario than the others.

Statement by D. C. Burnham,

*Chairman,
Westinghouse Electric Corporation**

I am concerned that this preliminary report makes it sound too easy to solve our energy problems and that it makes it seem that life styles would not change significantly with lower energy usage.

It is my belief that the following are major basic deficiencies in the report:

1. *Future Energy Demand Is Underestimated.* The "Technical Fix Scenario" seriously underestimates the magnitude of future energy demand required to maintain a healthy economic situation in the United States. The very substantial energy reductions postulated in that scenario result from inadequately supported and unrealistic assumptions regarding projected efficiency improvements and acceptable life-style changes.

2. *Future Oil-Gas Production Is Overestimated.* The report assumes that future U.S. petroleum

---

*Excerpted from *Exploring Energy Choices, op. cit.,* p. 56.

and natural gas production can be greatly increased above current levels, thereby relieving the pressure for other energy sources for the remainder of the century. That assumption regarding increased oil and gas production is in direct opposition to studies by most government agencies and petroleum industry experts, who have concluded that the peak in U.S. oil and gas production has already passed, and that new areas such as Alaska and offshore Atlantic sites will merely retard the decline.

As a result of items No. 1 and No. 2, the report seriously understates the magnitude of the energy gap which must be closed by energy sources other than petroleum and natural gas. This understatement and overoptimism can mislead the nation to believe that we have adequate time and numerous options which in fact do not exist.

3. *The Finite Nature of Oil-Gas Resources Is Ignored.* The report almost entirely overlooks the finite nature of petroleum and natural gas resources, and the fact that both U.S. and world resources will be virtually exhausted in a few decades.

By so doing, the report encourages continued and increased reliance on oil and gas, our smallest and most rapidly depleting energy resources. In no instance is an analysis made nor even a warning given of the potentially catastrophic consequence of following a policy of continued heavy reliance on petroleum and natural gas for the nation's future energy base.

Comments
by W. P. Tavoulareas,
President,
Mobil Oil Corporation **

The Energy Policy Project was established by the Ford Foundation in May 1972, with the purpose expressed at that time as that of "shedding light on the total energy problem . . . to help prepare an informed and reasoned base for a national energy policy."

It seems to me that the clear implication of the report is that we should delay the development of additional energy supplies on the assumption that they will not be needed because we can reduce our use of energy. The alternative is, of course, to accelerate the development of supplies while we examine the various possibilities for reducing consumption to see whether such reductions are consistent with the way of life we want and with expectations for improving the way of life of many poorer members of our society.

Recognizing the uncertainties that always exist in attempts to understand the future, especially in a subject that reaches into so many aspects of society, the Project has constructed three alternative energy consumption case studies (scenarios). It is important to understand the implications of the rather complex data which formed the basis for the three scenarios. Although the report avoids making specific recommendations, it is clear that there is little enthusiasm for the "historical growth" scenario. The scenario involving lower levels of growth is called the "technical fix." The report makes the point that the technical fix scenario "still provides a

---

**Excerpted from *Exploring Energy Choices, op. cit.*, pp. 57–61.

quality of life . . . that, to our minds, at least, differs little from the historical growth scenario." It is virtually impossible for the reader to reach a judgment as to whether or not this is true, based on information given in the report. It is therefore important to see what is meant by the "historical growth" scenario, in relation to present living conditions in the United States, and then to see how "technical fix" involves further changes.

"Historical growth" is described simply as continuation of the rate of growth that prevailed in the period 1950 through 1972—3.4 percent per year. Elsewhere in the report it is acknowledged that energy consumption has in fact accelerated in the last half of the period just mentioned. Unfortunately, the only history from which consumption in the 1980s can be judged is the pattern which has been more recently established in the latter half of the sixties and thus far in the seventies. Indeed, forecasts of energy consumption which were prepared by others before the current crisis generally reflected higher consumption levels. As the report indicates, the current consumption growth rates are running a full percentage point higher than in the fifties and early sixties. While such a difference sounds small, the continuation of the current trends through 1985 would produce a very much higher consumption level than contemplated in the "historical growth" scenario. The differences are significant.

If we look at the year 1985 we see that the "historical growth" scenario has a 5.4 quadrillion BTU's lower level of residential and commercial energy consumption than results from extending current trends. This is equivalent to the current space heating requirements of the 25 million households in the states of the East coast, together with that of their related shopping and business areas. In industrial and raw materials usage, the variance by which the historical growth case falls below current trends is equivalent to the combined usage of the paper, printing, and furniture industries, which together employ more than 2 million workers. In transportation, the difference is equivalent to more than the fuel requirements of 10 million vehicles. Thus, the so-called historical growth scenario is in no sense a reflection of current trends, but in fact involves a sharp reduction from recent historical growth.

Further reductions associated with the technical fix scenario are also of a very major nature. These reductions amount to a further 19 quadrillion BTU's. To give some perspective to the size of that number, it should be noted that if the reduction in U.S. imports resulting from the oil embargo is taken at about 2 million barrels per day, that reduction is equivalent to 4.2 quadrillion BTU's. Consequently, the technical fix scenario reduces demand by the amount we have just discussed for the "historical growth" scenario, *plus* a further amount equivalent to more than *four* Arab embargoes. (Quite apart from the life-style implications of the substantial reductions in both scenarios, the report also implies that energy not used in one sector can be readily applied to another. In the relatively short period of time we are dealing with, this assumption is, at best, questionable.) It is therefore little wonder that the report notes that consumer education alone may not be sufficient to reduce consumption levels to the point contemplated in the technical fix scenario, that is, direct governmental controls would be required.

The report is not explicit in terms of all of the governmental controls that would be necessary to achieve such a major reduction in consumption, but some are implied. A few examples are the following:

- Utility rates should not be based upon the cost of service but instead should increase according to the size of the customer's requirements. The idea, of course, is to "discourage" industry from using energy (on the apparent assumption that the cost of the energy in industrial products is not passed on to customers).
- Taxes are mentioned at various points as a means of reducing usage of energy below the level determined by the forces of the marketplace.
- There is reference to "performance standards," which apparently means that a customer should not be permitted to purchase an energy-consuming appliance if the government feels it does not meet "performance standards."
- There is reference to the possibility of "encouraging" multi-family housing rather than single-family housing.
- The use of automobiles and airplanes would be "discouraged."

Implicit in the report is the assumption that we will deal with the problems of the poor in a way that will not increase their energy consumption. Because of the wide disparity in standard of living in the United States, bringing the lower one-third of the population up to the average will require very large additional consumption of energy in the form of energy-using appliances and products. The only alternative method for improving standards of living for this sector is through some sort of redistribution among the population. Indeed, such a redistribution may be implied in the report. If automobiles, airplanes, and single-family housing are to be restricted by the government, we will ultimately be allocating these "luxuries" across the population on some basis that is not made clear.

Even beyond the suggestion for a multiplicity of controls, the report also stresses alternatives which require detailed government planning. While there is a legitimate role for government in many aspects of our social and economic system, we must question whether making the government the operator of a commercial activity will produce an efficient result. The experience of the last few months with price controls and various allocation schemes points up the weakness of such a government role. We continue to believe that the marketplace under a freely competitive system is the most efficient means of allocating resources. A businessman with a profit motive has the incentive to reduce costs. The oil industry has a record it need not be ashamed of in providing energy at low cost. For example, in the period 1967–1973 the price of gasoline increased less than 19 percent, while all consumer prices increased more than 33 percent. Thus, in terms of buying power of the 1967 dollar, the price of gasoline actually declined. It was only when the government regulation—much of it well intentioned—began to impact on the industry that it had difficulty in making available the necessary supplies.

No one today would seriously suggest a return to laissez-faire. Indeed, the oil industry was already subject to a network of controls, even before the current crisis. But during the last several years increased controls have progressively worsened the energy supply situation.

- In 1959 the mandatory import program was installed; modifications up through 1972 progressively discouraged the growth of U.S. refining capacity.

- The pipeline from the North Slope of Alaska was treated as a political football for more than five years while the industry marked time waiting for approval. (There are still hundreds of permits to be issued on the line.) This delay has also brought exploration in Alaska to a virtual standstill.

- The virtual government moratorium on federal offshore leasing from 1969 through 1972 sharply reduced the amount of acreage available for exploration in the United States.

- The suspension of operations on the leases in the Santa Barbara Channel prevented exploration of leases that had already been purchased, and prevented the full development of discoveries already made. Some of the known reserves in that area are still not on production.

- The regulation of natural gas at a price lower than its heating value created enormous demand for the use of this fuel, while at the same time reducing the incentive to search for new gas supplies.

- The telescoping of the timetable for achieving low automotive emission levels effectively required the manufacture of automobiles with low efficiency, rather than permitting the orderly development of technology which would retain efficiency and meet the emission requirements at the same time.

Without these governmental restrictions there would have been no U.S. supply shortage in 1974.

The energy resources of the earth are virtually unlimited if one includes geothermal, nuclear, solar, wind and tidal energy, etc. As for oil, the potential there is also still very large. For example, we have not really begun to explore the continental margins. In just one such area, the North Sea, it is evident that Norway and the United Kingdom—both substantial importers of energy—will become self-sufficient within a few years. The same possibility exists for a number of other nations, with obvious implications for the world oil supply. Decisions to limit our future use of energy must therefore involve considerations other than ultimate supply.

We firmly believe the safest course for the U.S. will be to encourage the development of additional energy supplies while continuing the national dialogue with respect to the desirable level of consumption—whether it be "historical growth" or otherwise. In all likelihood the correct answer will not be as simple as any of the scenarios suggested; a mixed strategy will most likely be called for. We would like to suggest some elements of such a strategy.

- First, we should have the objective to eliminate government controls which interfere with the development of additional supplies.

- Secondly, we should go forward with the orderly development of supplies, even to the point of creating an energy surplus again. If it appears desirable the entire development scheme can later be modified at any stage in its implementation. We should recognize that all the decisions will not be taken at one time. Coal mines will be opened one at a time. Oil wells offshore will be drilled one at a time. Refineries will be built one at a time.

- Thirdly, the timetable on environmental objectives should be carefully reviewed in relation to the energy needs. Here we particularly emphasize we are referring to the *timetable* and not to the *objectives* themselves. We continue to believe that the advance of technology and the development of clean energy sources will permit us to realize our environmental objectives. We only ask that the two programs be viewed as part of a single problem, allowing for the trade-offs between them.

- Fourthly, we must encourage energy research so that the problems that we have experienced in the seventies will not again become problems in the eighties and nineties. Energy resources are abundant; and if we have the technology to utilize them in an optimal fashion, we need have no concern for future energy growth.

- Finally, we must deal with the social costs of higher-priced energy. The appearance of higher energy costs in the economy will create dislocations. The extent of these dislocations is at present unclear. However, to the extent that there is an adverse impact on the lower income segments of the economy, we must deal with that problem and not turn our backs on it. To deal directly with (e.g., by subsidy) rather than through a general distortion of price levels in the economy, will in the end be the most effective and least expensive solution. Arbitrary controls which delay the development of additional supplies only aggravate the problem of the poor.

This solution to the energy problem would involve less controls than the report implies, would involve a return to a surplus of energy as a means of keeping prices down, would involve reasonable preservation of our environmental objectives, and would involve explicit attention to the problems of the poor.

In summary:

- The "historical growth" scenario reduces energy growth substantially below current levels; the "technical fix" scenario involves further very drastic reductions. The statement that the technical fix scenario involves no significant change in life-style is a conclusion, not a factual statement; it is not based upon detailed examination of the energy consumption changes which would be required.

- While no one denies the need for government planning and intervention in business affairs, the pervasive regulatory framework implicit in the report would involve government even more deeply than today in areas where it has been a notable failure: in directing the search for new energy supplies at reasonable cost to the consumer.

There are essentially two alternatives in dealing with the energy problem. The first would delay the development of new supplies *on the assumption* that energy usage can easily be reduced enough to bring supply and demand into balance. This is the case which the report implicitly adopts. The second alternative, not covered in the report, would increase supplies, eliminate waste usage, and examine all implications of further energy reductions which may have an impact on life-styles. We should ask ourselves which course carries the greater risk. If the assumptions behind the low growth cases are wrong the result will be energy scarcity, high energy prices, unemployment, and other economic and social dislocations. On the other hand, if the assumptions supporting the case for increased supplies are wrong we will have energy surplus and low prices. It seems clear to us that this latter risk is the more tolerable one. □

Discussion from "The Open Mind"

Heffner: I know that Mr. Tavoulareas issued a dissenting report [see above]. And I wonder, Mr. Tavoulareas, if you would indicate what your concerns are about what's stated in this report.

Tavoulareas: I'm very pleased to.

When you are trying to predict energy use in the future there are two sides to the equation. One side is demand, the other side is supply. I have a fundamental objection to the report. Almost the entire emphasis has been on restricting demand, with almost no emphasis—as a matter of fact, with a negative inference—on the building of supplies.

Now, let's for a moment examine our supply base. The report commissioned a couple of studies, and one of them states quite clearly that there are sufficient energy resources in the world to meet our demands, even if we follow the historical road. The only constraints, says the report, and it's in this book, are the ones which we self impose. We will, of course, have to decide how much we'd like to depend on foreign resources, how much we will depend on domestic resources, and, among those domestic resources, which resources are to be developed. But there is no shortage of resources. The only shortage we have is the shortage of developed resources at the present time.

Unless we understand that, we can't understand why I object to this part of the study. If you want to put restrictions of use on the American people, you've got to explain to them why you are being restrictive. So, again, I say that restrictions cannot be justified on a basis of resource base.

Now, let me for the moment move to the other side, the supply and the demand side. We have the chart [see Figure A, p. 795]. Now, this chart is the

Excerpted from the television program "The Open Mind," televised June 9, 1974 by WPIX-TV. Used with permission from WPIX-TV, New York, New York.

fundamental chart in the whole book. It describes the three growths: the historical, which we spoke about, that is really a projection of use over the years, beginning in 1950. On the opposite side is what we call zero growth. The book describes zero growth as a fundamental change in our life-styles. And now we have the technical fix, which the report seems to say we ought to be moving toward—either technical fix or zero growth. As a matter of fact, one of my objections to the report is that they don't really tell you what they recommend.

Look at the difference between those two lines, those two low-growth lines. It's less than six-tenths of 1 percent a year. I've been in the oil business 27 years. I've made all kinds of predictions. You can't find the difference, in a six-tenths-of-1-percent-a-year difference. So let's examine the report for what it is. It is saying let's go zero or low growth, because it discards historical growth completely.

It says, "The government has more effective policy tools than the marketplace." It's quite an outstanding statement. It says, "We would need imaginative and generous forms of multi-lateral assistance to the poor countries of the world and perhaps be in a position to export some of our energy. We will have to have mandatory allocation and rationing. There will be a vigorous growth in the service sector of the economy. Remember that government is the fastest-growing service sector already. We must design new communities so people can get around by foot and bicycles. Windmills could play a more significant role. We will limit the number of single-family houses. Special programs will be required to provide more jobs for displaced workers. Income redistribution would be required."

It may be that some of the things enumerated have some social significance and should be studied by the American people. I think Mr. Freeman's study, however, has been used to suggest a new social governmental order, all under the assertion that the development of any energy source might have such an adverse effect on the environment that we must rearrange our entire society.

I'd rather think of the problem in much more simple terms. Let's reduce waste. There's no problem on conservation. We shouldn't spend much time on that; we all can agree. The marketplace has already taken care of that with increased price.

Let's start massive research. Let's maximize development of those energy supplies that entail the minimum adverse effect on the environment, and let's start now. It's already too late.

Heffner: Okay, fair statement, a good statement of criticism. Mr. Freeman,* we don't want to make this a debate; we do want to make it a discussion. So I think it's proper now if you want to address yourself . . .

Freeman: Yes, I'd like to say that Tav is very generous in his inference that our report recommends all sorts of almost revolutionary type changes. I must say that I don't believe that's a fair characterization of the facts that are contained therein.

In the first place, we are talking about precisely the last item on his list, the elimination of waste. The heart of our report, the heart of the backup in the high and the lower growth scenarios are calculations that support the proposition that the same services that we get today can be produced with far less energy.

In the technical-fix scenario, which if it were implemented would result in a savings of roughly one-third of the total energy requirements in the year 2000, we were talking about savings in the next twenty or thirty years that would be almost as large as all the energy we are using today. One of the things that has been very misleading in all of this discussion about energy is to talk about a 2.5 percent growth and a 3 percent growth. We are talking about 3 percent of very, very big numbers, and the difference between 3.5 percent and 1.7 percent growth is projected over a number of years, as on the chart [Figure A]. If you look at the year 2000, you see that the technical-fix line gives us an energy consumption of about 115 quadrillion BTU's. Now, no one can visualize a billion BTU's, but it's a tremendous amount of energy. As compared to 200, this is roughly a one-third reduction.

*[S. David Freeman, Project Director, Ford Foundation's Energy Policy Project]

Now, how do we achieve that reduction? It's not through the kind of vague things that Tav was referring to. It's through some very understandable measures. It's insulating buildings so they don't leak so much energy—better insulation is one major thing. Building automobiles with mileages that steadily increase, so that in the 1980s we have on the road cars doing on the average upward of 20 miles per gallon. That is not going to revolutionize your lifestyle, if the engine in your car happens to be less of a gas-guzzler than the one that's in there now.

The third major aspect in reduction is all of these major energy-intensive industries, the ones that make aluminum and steel and paper; the work in our project done with the conference board and industrial managers suggests that there are savings of 20 percent if they can make them.

So my point is that the conservation opportunities are large. They are enormous. We are finding this out, and people in industry tell me over and over again they are red-faced to find that they could have been making these savings in the past. But my major point is that we are talking about simply squeezing out the enormous waste and making some investments in energy conservation technology, rather than putting that extra million dollars into excavating Colorado or drilling off Long Island.

Heffner: May I ask this? My understanding is that you gentlemen agree on the need for conservation.

Tavoulareas: Yes, I don't think we should even discuss conservation.

Heffner: What about the level of conservation? Is that a matter of difference between the two? You said, Mr. Freeman, you were not talking about vague statements of conservation, and then you talked about insulation, about homes, about automobile mileage increase. Are these things that you would agree with, Mr. Tavoulareas?

Tavoulareas: Why, of course. I think, really, that spending time and needing tremendous amounts of government controls in order to have people do what is economic is really illustrative of the fact that we don't understand how the marketplace operates.

For example, the price of oil was increased, unfortunately, four times in the last part of last year through certain actions of certain foreign governments. Now, we have substantial reductions in demand. We, in our own business, have always worked—as business has always worked—on savings. And if you raise the price, business will work on more savings, and more savings. All I am talking about is what this report is talking about. It talks about designing new cities, new communities. People will live near their work. I love that.

Freeman: We certainly talk about building new communities as part of what might be done in the zero-energy growth. But we do not rely on those savings in the scenario shown on the chart, which indicates that we could save one-third of the energy consumption in the year 2000.

Let me just make the point again. The savings that we are talking about are savings that will be made in the energy used by people living in their homes and in the cities today. You have picked out some of the possible actions that would supplement the essential conservation actions that are the background of our report. Now we can debate, if you like, about the need for new communities to house the citizens who will be coming of age, the 30, 40, 50 million Americans who will be needing housing. And I think it will make quite a bit of difference whether they live in just wider and wider doughnut-shaped circles surrounding existing communities, sentenced to an hour and a half a day of transportation back and forth to their jobs. It seems to me that the marketplace is not going to automatically provide housing for them, decent housing that they can afford in places that they would probably prefer, close to their jobs.

But that's not the heart of the savings that are in back of our scenarios. Those savings are made up

from the things that I enumerated: buildings that just don't leak so much heat, cars that have better mileage, and the energy-intensive industries taking advantage of the savings that they can.

The marketplace is not going to build this nation the transportation system that it needs. And I think we both agree on that.

Heffner: What is your response to that, Mr. Tavoulareas?

Tavoulareas: Well, Mobil is on record for the last five years: We favor mass transit. I mean no problem at all.

And I'll tell you one thing about mass transit. You take a car and come from Long Island to the city, with three people in it, and it will beat mass transit any day. Where in the book does it say that? Because obviously, with mass transit you are moving a tremendous piece of equipment. What is transportation but moving weight? Now, you move that railroad car in the middle of the day and have 10 percent occupancy, and the saving you had during the commuting hour is all finished.

So if you want to make savings in mass transit, you have to change the hours fantastically. I mean we can't have cars deadheading back and forth. So all I can say is I'm for mass transit. We've always been for mass transit. But I think it is fair to point out that if you put three people in a car and bring them from Long Island to New York, it would be less energy than to put them on mass transit.

Freeman: The problem is that the average occupancy of cars is much closer to one than three, and is apt to stay that way.

Heffner: It seems to me, as I read and as I listen, that you, Mr. Tavoulareas, are putting your emphasis on production and, in a supplementary fashion, on conservation. And it seems to me, Mr. Freeman, that you are putting your emphasis just the other way, essentially on conservation; but I doubt that you would urge us not to produce more, or perhaps I read you wrong.

Freeman: No, we obviously have to produce enough energy to meet the needs expressed on that chart. And the report states so. What we have found is that if we continue to try to chase the kind of growth curve that we have experienced in the last year, we are going to continue to have the shortages, the pollutions, the high prices, and the foreign-policy problems that exist.

Now, our report lays out this scenario. It is one that is technically feasible. As Tav says, there are the resources in the ground. The question is whether the country wants to pay the price in terms of damage to the environment and in terms of the foreign-policy problems involved in meeting much of that growth with imports, which seem to be the most available source of supply. Because what has happened, since the embargo has been lifted, is that we have resumed rather extensive imports of oil from the Middle East. And I think that most thinking is that the growth in the seventies, if it continues at this high rate, will be met primarily from imports of oil. So we feel that the country needs these other options.

Up to now, the whole energy-policy debate has been supply-oriented. We have laid before the country the opportunity of putting our money and some of our technical talent into machines that will use energy more efficiently. And our findings are that we can buy five, ten, fifteen years to develop these new sources if we pursue these conservation options. We need that time.

Heffner: But how do you respond, then, to the criticism that your low-growth estimates are unrealistic and that even at the lowest growth you posit, we are going to be consuming much more than you assume?

Freeman: Well, my answer is that we will need less energy at the lower-growth options than at the higher-growth options. That's just a matter of arithmetic.

Heffner: Yes, but there is another side to that. If the arithmetic is wrong and you're not producing more at the same time, we can end up being losers again.

Freeman: Yes. And the other side of *that* is that if we continue as we have in the past, there is a seven- or eight-year lead-time; and if we take the energy companies' projections on how much we need and they go ahead and build for that kind of growth, you can be sure that they will sell us that much energy. In the meantime, Colorado will have been excavated, the Atlantic will be drilled, and the environmental damage will be done. And the consumers are going to pay for all of that investment, whether it's used or not, just as the electric consumers of New York City are paying for all of Con Ed's investments.

Tavoulareas: I think Dave has made about twenty points. I'd like to just respond to two or three of them.

I think he really showed his hand in one point, in a nice way, when he said, "The reason I don't want to develop supplies [which really would bring down the price, not raise the price, as he said] is because maybe then we'll be so weak we want to use that supply." In other words, "Let me be sure you don't create the supply."

Then he talks about dependence on foreign governments. Personally, I worry about dependence on foreign governments, because I don't think you can expect a country like Saudi Arabia to ever increase its production merely to satisfy our needs. They have no need for the currency.

So I say: Have an additional supply, before the time you need it. You're eventually going to get whatever harm he says exists. I don't think the harm is anything like he says it is, but you're going to produce it another time. I'm saying have it in reserve at all times. I know then that I've got the protection I need. I know then the worst that can happen is I have low price. If you try to guess this thing and you don't guess right, you have all kinds of government controls.

Now, what Dave's report says is: Let's get tight. Let's not get the supplies, and we'll really keep the people back. Let's talk about the problem and talk about the problem and talk about the problem. Yet, on the other hand, he says it needs tremendous lead-time to produce a coal-mine, or anything you think about. How are we going to get from here to there? We're just going straight toward chaos, unless the American people accept this new type of life-style. If they don't, we have chaos, we have social revolution.

This report puts the emphasis, all the emphasis, on conservation. I agree with conservation, so let's not even talk about it. The report de-emphasizes supplies, as he keeps on saying and I agree. And I think that's wrong for the United States, to de-emphasize supplies. And furthermore, the energy project has been used as a basis for a new social, governmental order of things. And I still like the free market price in our system.

Heffner: Mr. Freeman, what about that?

Freeman: Well, I think we all like the free market price in our system. And our report suggests that we make use of it and make use of a very basic notion of efficiency. But up to now we have, in effect, had a low-price promotional policy for energy. We have had tax incentives for the oil industry, to make it easier for them to produce more. We have had incentives for the automobile highway program. We have had all sorts of incentives. We have public power agencies that don't pay any taxes at all. The price of energy does not include all the costs to society of producing it. What we are suggesting is that we now move to a policy of conservation, where we attempt to make Tav's job easier by consuming less energy to do the things that need to be done for America. And then he is going to be able to meet the demands without the shortages, without being under the pressure of the producing nations quite

as much, without quite the environmental damage. But it will be easier to reduce the air pollution standards, because if we burn less fuel the controls on the cars won't need to be as stringent.

This policy will help us in all of the crucial problems of energy, including the foremost one, and that is the pocketbook problem of being able to have enough money to pay for it. But if you talk about having enough money to pay for the fertilizer, I think a lot of people are worried about having enough money to pay their gasoline and electric power and food bills. And it seems to us—I agree with Tav in part, in a great number of respects—that "save energy, save money" is something that will come about naturally through the marketplace. But it's going to require a few governmental actions, such as building a transportation system, doing something about the housing codes, and making sure that the automobile industry moves to better-mileage cars. I think that with those three things—and with some revisions of the regulation of electric power so that these industries can have power plants located next to them and use the waste heat, and some research-and-development money going into the conservation side instead of all of it going on the supply side—we can buy the time to develop these renewable sources of energy that will sustain a high-energy civilization forever.

We've got to buy the time to learn how to expand nuclear energy safely, to learn how to take the oil out of the shale without excavating Colorado in the process, and to develop fusion power, solar energy, and geothermal energy. These are all going to take a lot of time. And the thrust of the options that we are presenting to the American people is to flag, in a very important way, the opportunities for making those savings and buying that time and making the job easier.

Heffner: Mr. Tavoulareas.

Tavoulareas: I think we ought to try to get down to some basic facts. Dave has spent a lifetime in energy. He's had the benefit of $4 million spent by the Ford Foundation to educate him. He keeps on worrying about the environment; I'm worried about the environment, too. I think that's like motherhood. But let's ask a very simple question. You've had a lot of experience now, Dave, and we've got four basic energies resources: oil, shale, coal, and nuclear. Which is the least detrimental to the environment?

Freeman: There are very serious environmental problems with each source of supply, as you inferred. But they are of a different kind, and in a sense it's a question of whether or not you're a gambler. If you're a gambler you would say that nuclear power is our best source of supply, because it is relatively clean, and it produces no air pollution; but it has this one-in-a-question-mark chance of causing a catastrophic accident. Whereas the fossil fuels, as they are burned, produce air pollution that scientists tell us is affecting human health, and the extent to which we can cut down the burning cuts down the pollution. For that reason, there is a direct relationship between the conservation of energy and protecting human health.

Tavoulareas: Well, that's what I say: We haven't got an answer. If you don't get an answer from an expert who has studied the field with $4 million, how are we ever going to get started? That's why I want to get started on some course of building supplies.

Heffner: What's your answer to your question?

Tavoulareas: Well, I would experiment in all four fields. I'm so convinced this country needs increased energy. We will experiment in each one of the four fields, find out which is the least detrimental from an economic and environmental point of view, and move ahead more aggressively. I would have to say we should do this all right now, but I am sure people would say I am prejudiced. I would also go ahead on nuclear energy. I think someone has to give direction. And out of this long report, we don't have anybody telling us which way we should point ourselves. □

GLOSSARY OF IMPORTANT ECONOMIC TERMS

This Glossary includes definitions of the economic terms used most frequently in this book. These are also terms that the reader will confront often in his further readings and studies in economics. Where alternative terms are used to express related ideas, cross references have been provided to simplify the use of the Glossary.

A.F. of L.: American Federation of Labor, a union founded in 1886 on a craft union basis, merged with the C.I.O. in 1955.

Absolute Advantage: In international trade, a country's productive advantage is said to be absolute when it uses fewer factors of production (say, less labor) to produce a given commodity than another country. Usually distinguished from *comparative advantage*.

Absolutely Diminishing Returns: The stage of production where the addition of one more unit of a variable factor, to a given stock of fixed factors, does not add to, but actually decreases, total output. E.g., the addition of more labor to an already heavily overcrowded piece of land might lead to laborers ''getting in each other's way,'' trampling the crops, etc. *See* Law of Diminishing Returns.

Acceleration Principle: On the assumption that businessmen wish to keep their capital stock in some fairly constant relationship to the output they are producing, business investment will be related to the rate of increase of national output. At a high, but constant, level of national output, investment will be zero. A simple slowing down of the rate of increase of national output will, by the accelerator, lead to an actual decline in investment. *See* Output-Capital Ratio.

Acreage Restrictions: *See* Agricultural Programs.

Affluent Society: Term used by Galbraith and others to suggest that the advanced industrial societies have reached a new stage of development where general poverty is no longer the dominant problem, and where work is no longer a required institution, but can be pursued for its own interest.

Aggregate Demand: Total value of output that consumers, investors, and the government are willing to purchase at any given time.

Aggregate Supply: Total value of output offered for sale in the economy at any given time.

Aggregative Economics: *See* Macroeconomics.

Agricultural Programs: The United States government has been involved in various programs to support farm income since the 1930s. These programs have involved direct price supports (the government buys the surplus of the farm commodity that cannot be sold to the public at the support price); direct-income payments (the farmer sells to the public at the market-determined price but the government supplements the farmer's income with direct payments); and crop and acreage restrictions (the farmer produces less, but gets more because of inelastic demand).

Agriculture and Consumer Protection Act of 1973: Provides a complicated system of assistance for U.S. agriculture, relying on price supports, direct-income payments and acreage restrictions in the event of the production of surpluses of certain farm commodities.

Allocation of Resources: The way in which an economy distributes and combines its factors of production to produce the goods that society wants. The effectiveness of a society's allocational system is a central question for microeconomic analysis.

Antitrust Laws: Laws that attempt to limit the degree of monopoly in the economy and promote competition. In the U.S., the passage, interpretation and enforcement of antitrust laws have involved varying degrees of emphasis on: (a) *market performance*—how efficient firms in the industry are, how progressive, etc.; (b) *market conduct*—whether firms compete with each other or misbehave by predatory pricing or collusive agreements; and (c) *market structure*—whether the industry structure involves large numbers of small firms or is dominated by one or a few giants. *See* Sherman Act, Clayton Act, Rule of Reason.

Assets: Items of value owned by a business firm, bank, individual, or society.

Automatic Stabilizers: Those aspects of the economic system, both private and public, which tend, without conscious alteration, to correct recessionary or inflationary tendencies. For example, higher federal tax rates on inflated money incomes will tend to curb excessive aggregate demand in inflationary conditions. Another example: the tendency of people to maintain a once-achieved level of consumption will put a brake on recessionary declines in aggregate demand.

Backward-Bending Supply Curve: In the case of labor, the supply curve may bend backward at very high wages. The reason is that the income effect (at higher wages, workers will want to buy more of the good, "leisure") may outweigh the substitution effect (a high wage means that the cost of an hour of leisure has increased, thus leading to the substitution of work for leisure).

Balanced Budget: In public finance, where governmental expenditures are matched by equivalent taxes.

Balanced Budget Multiplier: The number of dollars by which national income is increased when government expenditures and taxes are both increased by $1. Under certain circumstances, the balanced budget multiplier will equal one (1).

Balance of Payments: Statement of the international financial transactions of a nation over a period of time, say a year. In a formal accounting sense, *credit* items and *debit* items must balance since each good that a country buys or sells must be paid for in one way or another.

Balance of Trade: That part of a nation's balance of payments covering merchandise imports and exports. When exports exceed imports, the balance of trade is said to be *favorable;* when imports exceed exports, it is said to be *unfavorable.*

"Basic" Balance of Payments: That part of a nation's balance of payments covering the balance on current account (merchandise, services, and unilateral transfers) and long-term capital flows. It excludes often volatile short-term capital movements and is thus sometimes considered a good indicator of a nation's fundamental balance of payments' position.

Balance Sheet: Financial statement of a business firm or bank at a particular moment in time. The assets of the firm (what it owns) are balanced by its liabilities (what it owes) and a residual item (its net worth).

Beggar-My-Neighbor Policies: In international trade, policies which attempt to secure an advantage (usually temporary) for one nation at the expense of another, thus often inviting retaliation.

Benefit-Cost Analysis: A systematic way of evaluating government projects in terms of marginal benefits and marginal costs, using these concepts in their social as opposed to private sense. *See* Social Cost.

Business Cycle: Recurrent ups and downs of business activity, shown in a host of business indicators. Expansion and contraction phases are both thought to have certain cumulative features; they may also contain the seeds of the turning-points at the "peak" and "trough." Although there is some regularity in business cycles, the rhythm is fairly uneven, partly because there may be overlapping cycles of different lengths, e.g., inventory cycle, major cycle, construction cycle, etc.

C.I.O.: Congress of Industrial Organizations, union founded in 1935 on an industrial union basis, merged with the A.F. of L. in 1955.

Capital: A factor of production, along with labor and land. The stock of a society's produced means of production, including factories, buildings, machines, tools and inventories of goods in stock. Distinguished in this *real* sense, from *financial capital.*

Capital Accumulation: *See* Investment

Capital goods: Goods produced for use in further production, as in the case of machines, factory buildings, etc. Distinguished from *consumer goods.*

Capitalism: An economic system in which the basic resources and capital goods of the society are privately owned. Decision making is usually done by individual units which may be relatively small (as in purely competitive markets) or quite large (as in the imperfect competition of large corporations). Profitability in the case of businesses, and economic self-interest in the case of individuals, help guide the economic directions of capitalistic society.

Ceteris paribus: "Other things equal"; an economist's way of holding certain quantities fixed while he examines changes in other variables.

Circular Flow: A representation of economic life as: (1) a goods-and-services flow in which the services of labor and other factors of production are purchased by business firms and transformed into products which are then sold back to the factor owners; and (2) a money-and-spending-flow in which the factor owners receive money from the business firms which they then pay back to buy the consumer goods the firms have produced. The circular flow representation can be modified to include a state sector, saving and investment decisions, and other complications of economic life.

Class Conflict: In the Marxian view, the history of economic societies is basically one of class conflict. In the particular case of capitalism, the conflict is between the owners of capital (bourgeoisie) and labor (the proletariat). According to Marx, this conflict will end with the triumph of the proletariat and the ultimate establishment of communism.

Classical Economics: Usually refers to the doctrines of the British Classical School of the late 18th and early 19th centuries, especially Adam Smith and his followers. They emphasized competition, free trade, and minimal state intervention in the economy.

Clayton Act: A major U.S. antitrust law passed in 1914. Ruled out various forms of price discrimination, interlocking directorates and other business practices that might tend to lessen competition. Its antimerger provisions in Section 7 were later strengthened by the Celler-Kefauver Act of 1950.

Closed shop: A firm agrees that only union members may be hired, and that, after hiring, all employees must remain union members. In the U.S., made illegal by the Taft-Hartley Act of 1947.

Collective Bargaining: A system for settling labor disputes in which workers bargain as groups, through unions or other labor associations, with management. Is widely used in the United States for setting wages, hours, conditions of work, and other aspects of labor-management relations.

Command Economy: An economy in which the basic directions are determined by central planning boards or state commissions and not by private producers or individual consumers.

Commodity Inflation: Inflation caused primarily by specific shortages of basic commodities, e.g., oil, beef, sugar, etc. The resulting sharp rises in the prices of these commodities are not offset by declines in the prices of other goods and services.

Communism: A form of socialism, usually associated with Marxian doctrine, and with the view that capitalism can be overthrown only by revolutionary, as opposed to evolutionary, methods. As practiced in Russia, the closest thing we have to a command economy.

Comparative Advantage: In international trade, a country's productive advantage with respect to commodity A is said to be comparative when it must give up fewer other commodities to produce a unit of A than another country. It is this relative cost of production that is most significant in determining mutually beneficial patterns of trade among nations. Usually distinguished from *absolute advantage*.

Compound Interest: Computing interest on a principal sum and also on the accrued interest earned by that principal sum.

Compulsory Arbitration: A system for settling labor disputes where, if other means fail, unions and management are forced to go to an arbitrator or arbitration panel whose decision will be binding on both groups.

Concentration Ratio: A measure of the degree of dominance in particular industries or industry groups of very large firms. Usually consists of the ratio of the value of sales (shipments) of the four largest firms in the industry to the total value of the industry's sales.

Conglomerate Merger: A merger involving firms producing different products and/or operating in different markets.

Constant Prices: To measure national income or its various components in two different periods, the prices of one period are used throughout. This is to enable a distinction to be made between real and simply inflationary changes in the numerical value of national income.

Consumer Goods: Goods produced for consumption immediately or within a relatively short period of time. Distinguished from *capital goods*.

Consumer Sovereignty: Obtains where consumers, by their purchases in the marketplace, are able to guide the productive decisions of the economy in the direction of their economic preferences.

Consumerism: Widespread movement in the U.S., greatly stimulated by the work of Ralph Nader, that attempts by investigation, publicity and legal action, to correct business abuses that harm consumers. Also involves scrutiny of those regulatory agencies that are supposed to monitor business activities, but in some cases may not do so effectively.

Consumption: Expenditures by households and individuals on consumer goods.

Consumption Function: Curve showing how much consumers will want to spend on consumer goods and services at various levels of national income. Consumption is seen as a function of national income.

Convergence: The doctrine that, because of the fundamental similarities of the economic problems facing advanced industrial nations, there will be a gradual lessening of the differences between the economic systems of capitalism and communism. Such economic convergence, if it occurred, would not necessarily mean political convergence, or, indeed, any reduction of the Cold War rivalry between East and West.

Corporation: Form of business organization in which the firm is a "legal person" that can own property, sell stocks, and enter into contracts. Owned by stockholders who are protected by limited liability. In the case of large corporations, operations are usually characterized by a divorce of ownership and control.

Cost: The expenses incurred in producing commodities or services. Costs may be divided into *fixed* costs, those which are incurred even at zero output, sometimes called "overhead costs," and *variable* costs, those which vary with the level of output. Costs may also be divided into the following categories:
1. *Total Cost (TC):* The sum of fixed and variable costs at any given level of output.
2. *Average Cost (AC):* TC, at any given level of output, Q, divided by Q.
3. *Total Variable Cost (TVC),* TC at any given level of output minus fixed costs.
4. *Average Variable Cost (AVC):* TVC at output Q divided by Q.
5. *Marginal Cost (MC):* At any given level of output, the added cost of producing one more unit of output.

Cost-Push Inflation: Inflation where the primary sources derive from imperfect competition on the supply side: the ability of unions to gain wage-increases in excess of productivity increases; the ability of oligopolistic industry to pass such wage-increases on to consumers; etc. May occur even when there is substantial unemployment and excess capacity in the economy as a whole. Distinguished from *demand-pull* and *commodity inflation.*

Countervailing Power: Concept associated with John Kenneth Galbraith: power on one side of the market (e.g., big businesses) tends to stimulate countervailing on the opposite side of the market (e.g., large labor unions).

Craft Union: *See* Union.

Crawling Peg: A compromise between a fixed exchange rate and a completely flexible exchange rate, where the exchange value of a currency is allowed to alter over time but only by some agreed upon percentage per year.

Credit Item: In international trade, a transaction that creates a demand for your country's currency.

Debit Item: In international trade, a transaction that creates a supply of your currency seeking to purchase other currencies.

Decreasing-Cost Industry: An industry in which the average cost curve of a typical firm tends to fall with expansion of output. *See* Returns to Scale, Natural Monopoly.

Deficit Spending: In public finance, where government expenditures exceed its revenues; it involves increasing the size of the national debt.

Demand Curve: A hypothetical construction that tells us how many units of a particular commodity consumers would be willing to buy over a period of time at all possible prices, assuming that the prices of other commodities and the money incomes of the consumers are unchanged.

Demand Deposits: Checking accounts in commercial banks; these deposits can be turned into currency "on demand"; i.e., by writing a check. Demand deposits are the main form of money (M_1) in the United States.

Demand-Pull Inflation: Inflation where the primary cause is an excess of aggregate demand above aggregate supply, especially at or very near the full employment level of national income. Distinguished from *cost-push inflation* and *commodity inflation.*

Deposit Creation: *See* Multiple Credit Creation.

Depreciation: 1. Fall in the value of a capital asset due to use, age, wear and tear, or obsolescence. 2. In international trade, fall in the value of a currency with respect to other currencies.

Depression: A prolonged slowing down of economic activity exemplified by mass unemployment and a level of national income well below its potential level. More severe and long-lasting than a recession. Sometimes used to refer to the particular economic breakdown of the industrialized world in the 1930s, the "Great Depression."

Derived Demand: The demand for factors of production will ultimately reflect (is "derived" from) consumer demands for the products those factors produce. Hence the elasticity of demand for consumer products will affect the elasticity of demand for the factors that produce those products.

Devaluation: Official lowering of the value of a currency in terms of gold or other currencies.

Diminishing Returns: *See* Law of Diminishing Returns, Absolutely Diminishing Returns.

Direct-Income Payments: *See* Agricultural Programs.

Direct Taxes: Taxes that fall directly on persons (as, for example, the individual income tax.) *See* Indirect Taxes.

Discount Rate: Interest rate charged on loans from the Federal Reserve Bank to its member banks. An instrument of Federal Reserve monetary policy.

Discretionary Policy: This term may be applied to fiscal policy, monetary policy or any other governmental policy which is consciously altered to produce some desired economic effect. Is in contrast with policies which operate either automatically or according to fixed rules with no deliberate intervention to meet changed circumstances. For contrast, *see* Automatic Stabilizers, Monetarism.

Disguised Unemployment: *See* Underemployment.

Disinvestment: Negative investment. For example, when businesses reduce their stock of inventories, or allow their capital goods to depreciate without replacement.

Disposable Personal Income: Equals Personal Income *minus* personal taxes.

Dissaving: Negative saving; i.e., consuming more than one's income, by borrowing, living off one's "capital," etc.

Distribution of Income: The division of the total product of a society among its members. The distribution is sometimes described by a classification according to income size (e.g., the top x percent of income recipients receive y percent of total income) or by a classification according to the kind of factor payment (wages, rents, interests, profits, etc.). *See* Lorenz Curve.

Division of Labor: The subdivision of a productive process into its component parts which are then handled by specially skilled or trained laborers. Adam Smith believed it was a major source of increased productivity over time.

Divorce of Ownership and Control: In large corporations, there are so many stockholder owners, each holding such a small fraction of the company's stock, that effective control of corporate decisions may pass to management, even though the managers may actually own very little stock themselves.

Double-Counting: A danger, to be avoided, in measuring national income is that one will count intermediate goods as well as final goods and thus, in effect, count some goods more than once. Sometimes avoided by using *value-added* method of national income measurement.

Double-digit Inflation: Inflation at an annual rate of 10 percent or above.

Ecological Demand: A summation of all men's demands on the environment, such as the extraction of resources and the return of wastes.

Economic Choice: Because of the phenomenon of scarcity, choice is central to economics. Characteristically, a society must choose from among varying combinations of commodities, alternative methods of production, and different patterns of income distribution.

Economic Growth: A general expansion of an economy, usually measured by the rate of increase of its GNP or, sometimes, of its GNP per capita.

Economies of Scale: *See* Returns to Scale; External Effects.

Efficiency: A technical term indicating a situation in which it is impossible to make any individual better off without making some other individual worse off. Where *in*efficiency exists, changes can be made that are *mutually* beneficial (e.g., more of all goods can be produced) and nobody gets hurt. Subject to a number of important qualifications (economies of scale, external effects, etc.), pure competition provides a model of an efficient economic system.

Elasticity: In general, it is a measure of the percentage change in the quantity of a commodity in response to a change in price or income. In the specific case of *price elasticity of demand*, it is measured by the percentage change in the quantity of a commodity demanded by consumers divided by the percentage change in the price of that commodity. If the percentage change in quantity is the greater, demand is said to be relatively *elastic;* if the percentage change in price is the greater, demand is said to be relatively *inelastic.* A *perfectly* (or *infinitely*) *elastic* demand curve would be a horizontal straight line. A *perfectly* (or *infinitely) inelastic* demand or supply curve would be a vertical straight line.

Enclave Development: The tendency, in many less-developed countries, to achieve development in one particular geographic (often urban) area of the nation while the surrounding hinterlands remain undeveloped and poverty-stricken.

Endogenous: In economics, forces operating on the economic system that can be explained by features of that system: e.g., an expansion of demand for their products will cause businessmen to want to invest more, etc.

Energy Crisis: The shortage of easily accessible energy sources, particularly petroleum, in relation to the ever-growing demand for energy throughout the world. Sometimes used to refer to the specific shortages that occurred during the Arab oil embargo of 1973.

Entrepreneur: 1. Any businessman. 2. In the Schumpeterian sense, specifically a businessman who introduces *innovations.*

Equilibrium: A condition in which there is no inherent tendency for a change, as, for example, where quantity supplied and quantity demanded are equal.

Equimarginal Principle: A consumer will be maximizing his satisfactions when a dollar spent on any commodity (tea, shoes, paperback books, etc.) brings him the same marginal utility. It can be phrased as:

$$\frac{P_1}{\cdot MU1_1} = \frac{P_2}{MU_2} = \frac{P_3}{MU_3} = \cdots = \frac{P_n}{MU_n} \cdots$$

where P_n is the price of any commodity n, and MU_n is the marginal utility of commodity n for this consumer. Alternatively, the principle can be rewritten.

$$\frac{P_1}{P_2} = \frac{MU_1}{MU_2} \; ; \quad \frac{P_2}{P_3} = \frac{MU_2}{MU_3} \; ; \text{ etc.}$$

Or, where there is no cardinally measurable marginal utility, the principle can be phrased in terms of the marginal rate of substitution in consumption (MRS) as:

$$\frac{P_n-1}{P_n} = MRS_{(n-1 \text{ for } n)}$$

Excess Capacity: Where output is below that at which average cost is at a minimum. In ideal pure competition, firms in the long run will produce at minimum average cost and hence there will be no excess capacity. In monopolistic competition, even when there are zero pure profits, excess capacity may persist over time.

Excess Reserves: Instead of remaining "fully loaned up," banks may sometimes accumulate reserves in excess of those legally required; usually, this occurs in periods of great economic uncertainty.

Exchange Rates: In international trade, the prices of one currency in terms of other currencies.

Exogenous: In economics, forces operating on the economic system from outside the system: e.g., political factors, weather, etc.

External Contraints: In general, the limitations that foreign trade and balance-of-payments problems place on a country's ability to achieve important domestic objectives. Often used to refer to the international trade problems facing underdeveloped countries seeking faster economic growth. *See* Trade Gap.

External Economies and Diseconomies: An external economy occurs when the activity of an economic unit confers a real benefit upon other producers or consumers in the economy, beyond the benefits for which the individual unit is paid. An external diseconomy occurs when that unit confers real costs upon other consumers or producers, for which it is not charged. To be distinguished from *economies* (or *diseconomies*) *of scale,* where, say, a business firm finds its *own* costs falling as it expands its level of output. Economies of scale (sometimes called *internal* economies of scale), if they persist over large ranges of output, are incompatible with pure competition and lead to natural monopoly. External economies are compatible with pure competition; i.e., with the persistence of small firms. However, where external economies (or diseconomies) exist, they undermine the theory that pure competition is *efficient.* They do so by creating a gap between *private* and *social* benefits and costs.

Factor Demand Curve: Represents the quantities of a factor of production (say, labor) that business firms will want to hire at various hypothetical prices per unit of the factor (in the case of labor, wage-rates).

Factor Market: A market in which the services of the factors of production—labor, land, and capital—are bought and sold. In a private economy, the main sellers are private laborers and owners of land and capital, and the main buyers are private business firms. Distinguished from Product Market.

Factor Supply Curve: Represents the quantities of a factor of production (say, labor) that factor-owners (wage-earners) will be willing to sell to business firms at various hypothetical prices per unit of the factor (wage-rates).

Factors of Production: Any implement or agent whose services are used in the production of economic goods and services.

Federal Reserve System: Established in the U.S. in 1913 to supervise the commercial banking system and to promote macroeconomic stability in the economy. Federal Reserve banks are banker's banks and the deposits of commercial banks in the Federal Reserve Banks form the reserves of the member banks. The "Fed" is instrumental in determining monetary policy, for which its main weapons are: (1) altering reserve requirements; (2) changing the discount rate at which member banks may borrow from the Federal Reserve Banks and (3) open-market purchases and sales of government securities.

Financial Capital: A society's or individual's stock of money, bonds, stocks or other securities. Distinguished from *real capital.*

Financial Investment: An addition to an individual's holdings of bonds, stocks, or other securities in some given period. Distinguished from *real investment.*

Fiscal Policy: Governmental policy concerned with the tax and expenditure activities of the federal government, including the size of public spending, and the balancing or unbalancing of the federal budget; designed to promote certain macroeconomic objectives, usually full employment, stable prices, economic growth, and balance of payments' equilibrium. Sometimes contrasted to *monetary policy.*

Flexible Exchange Rates: Currency exchange rates alter freely in response to the forces of international supply and demand.

Flow: *See* Stock.

Foreign Aid: Economic assistance from one nation or group of nations to another nation or group of nations. Aid may take the form of capital assistance, through grants or low-interest loans, or technical assistance, as in President Truman's original Point Four Program (1950). Aid may be given on a nation to nation basis or on a multilateral basis, as in the case of the *World Bank.* In the United States, foreign aid funds are administered by the Agency for International Development (A.I.D.)

Fractional Reserve Banking: System where commercial banks are not required (either by law or economic pressure) to maintain reserves equal to their demand or other deposits. *See* Multiple Credit Creation.

Full Employment: A condition where those who wish to work at the prevailing wage are able to find work. *See* Unemployment.

Full Employment Balanced Budget: Budgeting a level of government expenditures that are equal to what government tax revenues would be at full employment. If the economy does *not* attain full employment, then a full employment balanced budget will usually entail actual budget deficits.

Gold Standard: In international trade, a system in which the values of individual currencies are set at a fixed rate in terms of gold, and in which gold can be used to settle payment accounts between nations.

Green Revolution: The development of high-yielding new seeds, especially for wheat and rice, with special applicability to the weather and soil conditions in tropical and subtropical underdeveloped countries. The efficacy of the "revolution" often depends upon improved irrigation, fertilizer application, and better general farming practices in the countries involved. Without these, the ecological vulnerability of the agricultural sector may be increased.

Gross Investment: Total investment in a given period (say, a year), without deducting any allowance for the depreciation of the economy's capital stock during that period.

Gross National Product (GNP): Total output of final goods and services produced in an economy in a given period of time (say, a year), including gross investment.

Guideposts: *See* Wage-Price Guideposts.

Historical Growth Scenario: An alternative described by the Ford Foundation's Energy Policy Project. It involves a continuing increase in energy utilization at the historic growth rate. In the case of the United States, this scenario is considered feasible, even from domestic resources alone, but it would require very aggressive development of all possible energy sources: oil and gas onshore and offshore, coal, shale, nuclear power. *See* Technical Fix Scenario, Zero Energy Growth Scenario.

Imperfect Competition: A general category of market structures which involve greater or lesser deviations from pure competition. *See* Monopoly, Oligopoly, Monopolistic Competition, Monopsony.

Incidence of Taxation: Where the final, as opposed to the initial or apparent, burden of a tax rests. For example, a tax on corporate profits may be ultimately paid by the stockholders of the corporation, the employees of the corporation, and the consumers of the products of the corporation; a sales tax may be partly paid by business, partly by the public, etc.

Income-Consumption Relation: *See* Consumption Function.

Income Effect: In consumer-demand theory, a fall in the price of a commodity will generally cause the consumer to purchase more of that commodity because, among other reasons, that fall in price has increased his "real" income. With more income, he will usually want to buy more of all commodities, including this one.

Income-Maintenance Programs: Programs designed by the government to raise the incomes of poor families and individuals when they fall below certain levels.

Incomes Policies: Governmental policies designed to limit inflation by various direct and indirect controls over prices, wages, profits and other incomes.

Income Velocity of Money: The number of times an average unit of money (currency or demand deposits) circulates through the economy during a given period in exchange for final output. Equivalently, it is money national income $(P \times Q)$ divided by the stock of money (M).

Indexing: A means of coping with inflation by tying all contracts in the economy to some price index, e.g., the consumer price index, so that inflation has little redistributional effect on income or wealth.

Index-Number Problem: When the prices and quantities of goods produced change not only absolutely but relatively to each other over time, then changes in over-all real national income cannot be unambiguously measured. "Growth" of national income will have different values depending upon what particular "constant prices" are used.

Indirect Taxes: Taxes that fall directly on goods and services, but only indirectly on persons (as, for example, sales and excise taxes). *See* Direct Taxes.

Industrial Revolution: 1. In Britain, the period in the late 18th and early 19th centuries that saw the transformation of a largely agrarian society into one characterized by industrial growth, factories, capital accumulation, technological and social change. 2. Generally, the transition process of any country moving from a traditional economy to one demonstrating modern economic growth.

Industrial Union: *See* Union.

Inelastic Demand or Supply: *See* Elasticity.

Infant Industries: Industries which have recently been established in a country and have not yet had time to exploit possible economies of scale and other efficiencies. Such industries provide one of the traditional arguments for tariff protection.

Inflation: A general rise in the average level of all prices in an economy, as defined by some index (e.g., in the U.S., the Consumer Price Index, the Wholesale Price Index, or the GNP Price Deflator).

Innovations: Introduction of new products or methods of production. Schumpeter distinguished "inventions" (the thinking up of new ideas) from "innovations" (their actual carrying out into business practice).

Interdependence: 1. Important principle showing the interlocking nature of economic causes and effects. In an economy in overall or general equilibrium, interdependence is evidenced by the mutual influence of supply and demand in both product and factor markets. 2. *See* Oligopoly.

Interest rate: 1. The price of borrowing money; i.e., of credit 2. The rate of return to the owners of capital goods. The interest rate is the amount of interest expressed as a percentage of a principal sum.

Internal Finance: In business, financing investment out of retained earnings, as opposed to external bond or security markets.

International Monetary Fund (IMF): Founded in 1944 by the United Nations with the goal of encouraging trade by establishing an orderly procedure for stabilizing foreign exchange-rates and for altering those rates in the case of fundamental balance of 'payments' disequilibria. Is involved in expanding international liquidity through the issue of *Special Drawing Rights (SDRs)*.

Inventory: Stocks of goods kept on hand to meet orders from other producers or consumers.

Investment: An addition to a firm's or society's stock of capital (machines, buildings, inventories, etc.) in a certain period of time, say, a year. Distinguished in this *real* sense from *financial investment.*

Investment Demand Curve: Real investment expressed as a function of the interest rate. The lower the interest rate, the more businessmen will want to investment. Some investment (e.g., construction) may be fairly sensitive to interest rate changes; other investment may be interest-inelastic.

Investment Gap: In the case of a less developed country, the gap between the investment needed to sustain a desired rate of growth and the domestic savings capacity of the country. The existence of such a gap provides an important argument for foreign aid. *See* Trade Gap.

"Invisible Hand": Adam Smith's term: it suggests that individuals who are motivated only by private (not social) interest will nevertheless be guided invisibly by the market to actions and decisions that will promote the welfare of society.

Keynesian Economics: The theory of John Maynard Keynes (1883–1946) and his many followers. The theory is characterized by its emphasis on macroeconomic problems, the special role accorded aggregate demand in determining the level of national income, its stress on the possibility of unemployment equilibrium, its attempt to synthesize real and monetary analysis, and, finally, its argument for a greater government intervention in the economy than traditional economics had prescribed. The basics of Keynesian thought are now widely accepted, although some critics (notably the monetarists) offer a different analysis of macroeconomic problems, and all economists recognize that Keynesian theories and policies are not fully adequate for a world in which inflation and unemployment coexist simultaneously.

Kinked Demand Curve: A demand curve that may be characteristic of firms in certain oligopolistic industries. It will occur if a firm judges that if it cuts its price, other firms will cut theirs too, but that if it raises its price, other firms may be content to leave theirs unchanged—thus depriving the original firm of some of its share of the market. Thus, the demand curve will be relatively elastic *above* the going price, and relatively inelastic *below* the going price.

Labor Theory of Value: Theory, held in somewhat differing forms by David Ricardo and Karl Marx, that the value of a commodity is proportional to the labor embodied in its production.

Labor Union: *See* Union.

Laissez Faire: The doctrine that the State should largely leave the economy to its own devices; a "hands off" policy. This doctrine is associated with Adam Smith and British Classical Economics.

Land: In economics, a factor of production that includes all natural resources as well as "land" in the narrower sense.

Lange-Type Socialism: *See* Market Socialism.

Law of Diminishing Marginal Rate of Substitution in Consumption: As a consumer consumes more of one commodity relative to another commodity, the MRS of the first commodity in terms of the second will tend to decline.

Law of Diminishing Marginal Utility: As a consumer increases his rate of consumption of a particular commodity, its marginal utility for him will diminish.

Law of Diminishing Returns: In the production of any commodity, as we add more units of a variable factor of production to a fixed quantity of other factors of production, the addition to total product (the marginal product) of each added unit of the variable factor will eventually begin to diminish. Sometimes called the *Law of Diminishing Marginal Productivity*.

LDCs: Less Developed Countries. *See* Underdevelopment.

Legal Reserve Requirement: Legally required ratio of reserves to bank deposits; varies with type of deposit and size of commercial bank. One of the Federal Reserve System's main instruments for influencing the money supply and interest rate in the economy as a whole.

Liabilities: Financial obligations of a business firm, bank, or individual; what is "owed" as distinguished from what is "owned."

Limited Liability: The stockholders of a corporation are not liable for the debts of that corporation beyond their original investment therein. Not true of the partnership form of business organization.

Liquidity: Command over goods in general, or, equivalently, the ease with which an asset can be translated into money.

Liquidity Demand for Money: Demand for money to hold as a store of value as opposed to less liquid assets such as bonds or securities; other things equal, the liquidity demand for money will vary inversely with the rate of interest.

Liquidity Trap: The possibility that, at some low level of interest rates, the liquidity demand for money may become perfectly elastic; i.e., a horizontal curve. If such a "trap" exists, further efforts to increase the quantity of money by the monetary authority will yield no further decreases in interest rates, and hence no expansionary effect on investment, employment and national income. Hence, this could be an important limitation on monetary policy in a period of depression.

Long Run: *See* Short Run.

Lorenz Curve: In measuring the income distribution of a society, a curve showing what percent of families get what percent of the society's family income; thus, a curve demonstrating the degree of inequality in the society's income distribution.

M_1, M_2, M_3: *See* Money.

MR = MC: *See* Profit Maximization.

Macroeconomics: Deals with large economic aggregates such as GNP, total employment, the overall price level, and how these aggregates are determined. Usually contrasted with *micro-economics*.

Malthusian Theory of Population: Theory of Thomas Robert Malthus (1766–1834) that population has a tendency to grow at a geometric ratio while food supplies can, at best, grow at an arithmetic ratio. Hence, unless *preventive checks* (such as moral restraint) keep population down, its further growth will be halted by *positive checks*. These positive checks include extreme poverty, famine, plague and war. Because of population pressures, Malthus did not expect the wages of the mass of mankind ever to rise much above a bare *subsistence* level.

Marginal: In economics, a small change in a total of some quantity.

Marginal Cost: *See* Cost.

Marginal Cost Pricing: Under certain circumstances (absence of "external effects," etc.), an economy will find it efficient to have $P = MC$ hold throughout the economy. This condition tells us that the relative evaluation of commodities by consumers and their relative costs of production have been equated at the margin.

Marginal Product: The marginal product of a factor of production is the addition to total product resulting from the addition of one more unit of that factor, the employment of all other factors being held constant.

Marginal Propensity to Consume (MPC): The fraction of an additional $1 of income consumers want to spend on consumption.

Marginal Propensity to Save (MPS): The fraction of an additional $1 of income consumers wish to devote to saving. In relation to consumption:
$$MPS = 1 - MPC.$$

Marginal Rate of Substitution in Consumption (MRS): The marginal rate of substitution in consumption of commodity A for commodity B is the amount of commodity B the consumer will give up for one unit of commodity A while still remaining equally well off.

Marginal Rate of Substitution in Production: The marginal rate of substitution in production of factor A for factor B is the amount of factor B that the producer can give up for one unit of factor A while still leaving total output unchanged. It is equal to the ratio of the marginal product of factor A to the marginal product of factor B.

Marginal Revenue: *See* Revenue.

Marginal Revenue Product: The marginal product of a factor of production times the marginal revenue of the product, or: MP $\times$ MR.

Marginal Utility: *See* Utility.

Market Conduct, Performance, Structure: *See* Antitrust Laws.

Market Economy: A decentralized economy in which fundamental economic decisions are made by private individuals and business firms who offer their goods or services for sale in response to relatively impersonal market forces. Often used to refer to economies in which purely competitive market structures are dominant.

Market Socialism: A form of socialism in which some economic decisions (e.g., the determination of income subsidies, the rate of capital formation) are made centrally while other economic decisions (e.g., what consumer goods to produce, what laborers to hire) are made through supply and demand in the marketplace. Sometimes called Lange-type socialism after the Polish economist, Oskar Lange.

Mercantilism: A characteristic European economic doctrine in the 16th and 17th centuries, emphasizing the role of money and trade in economic life, and the desirability of active State intervention in the economy.

Microeconomics: Deals with the interrelationships of the individual business firms, industries, consumers, laborers and other factors of production that make up the economy. Usually contrasted with *macroeconomics*.

Military/Industrial Complex: Term originally coined by former President Eisenhower, but later also employed by radicals, to describe the complicated relationships between the U.S. defense establishment and the private business firms who are its suppliers. Because of the special nature of the buyer, these firms, though officially private, often take on the character of submanagement units in the public sector. Some have feared that these firms might also wield undue influence on the policies of government.

Mixed Economy: An economy in which there are substantial public and private sectors, where private enterprise and the market are significant determining factors, but where the State also takes on certain basic economic responsibilities, e.g., to assure reasonably full employment, to provide for those in poverty, to regulate certain activities of business

and labor, etc. Is in some ways more characteristic of modern industrial economies than either the pure Market Economy or the pure Command Economy.

Modern Economic Growth: A sustained, relatively regular and rapid increase in a nation's GNP, and especially its GNP per capita. A form of economic growth known only since the English Industrial Revolution, spreading thence to the Continent, the U.S., Russia, Japan, and a few other selected nations.

Monetarism: A doctrine, especially associated with the theories of Milton Friedman, that places special emphasis on the role of money in the economy. Monetarists believe that the supply of money largely determines money national income in an economy, that fiscal policy is of little effect in promoting economic stability, and that monetary policy should be governed by relatively unchanging rules, e.g. a fixed percentage increase in the money supply each year.

Monetary Policy: Governmental policy concerned with the supply of money and credit in the economy and the rate of interest; designed to promote certain macroeconomic objectives, usually full employment, stable prices, economic growth, and balance of payments' equilibrium. Sometimes contrasted with *Fiscal Policy*.

Money: A generally accepted asset that can be used as (1) a measure of value, (2) a medium of exchange, and (3) a store of value. In practice and in theory, it can be any kind of commodity or piece of paper (cattle, beads, gold, currency, etc.) that is accepted by the society for these functions. In the United States, under any definition of money, coins and currency are a relatively small part of the money supply as compared to various forms of credit, such as demand deposits in commercial banks. Common definitions of money include: M_1 = currency plus demand deposits; $M_2 = M_1$ plus certain time deposits at commercial banks; and $M_3 = M_2$ plus deposits at mutual savings banks and savings and loan associations.

Monopolistic Competition: A market structure in which each firm is relatively small but where each firm has a monopoly on its particular version of the product in question. There is "competition" among these "monopolists," often taking the form of advertising, further product differentiation, and other types of nonprice competition.

Monopsony: A market structure in which there is a single buyer of a product or service.

Monopoly: A market structure in which there is a single seller of a commodity or service which has no very close substitutes.

Multiple Credit Creation: The ability of the banking system to "create" demand deposits in multiples of their reserves. If there is no leakage of cash and currency, and the legal reserve requirement *(LR)* represents the fraction of a bank's demand deposits it must hold in the form of reserves, then the credit creation multiplier will be:

$$mc = \frac{1}{LR}$$

Thus if the legal reserve requirement is .20, then the banking system will be able to create $5 of demand deposits for each added dollar of reserves.

Multinational Corporation: A corporation which operates within different national jurisdictions.

Multiplier: The number of dollars by which a $1 increase in spending *(C, I, or G)* will raise the equilibrium level of national income. Its relation to the *marginal propensity to consume* is:

$$m = \frac{1}{1-MPC}$$

Its relation to the *marginal propensity to save* is:

$$m = \frac{1}{MPS}$$

National Debt: Debt owed by the federal government; sometimes refers to debt owed by all three levels of government, federal, state and local. The federal debt is financed by the issuing of government bonds, which may be sold to the public, the commercial banks, or the Federal Reserve Banks.

National Income: Sometimes used as a generic name for the various different measures of the total output of an economy. In the U.S., also specifically used to equal Net National Product (NNP) *minus* indirect business taxes.

Natural Monopoly: An industry in which there are persistent economies of scale for the firms involved and where, consequently, natural forces would lead to the establishment of single large firm to supply the whole market.

Near-Money: Assets, like government bonds, that are very nearly as liquid as currency, demand deposits, and other forms of money proper.

Negative Income Tax: A program under which incomes below a certain level are taxed negatively, i.e., payments are made by the government to the individuals involved. NIT covers a variety of possible programs depending on what base level of income is chosen, what the percentage of negative tax is, what allowance is made for dependents, etc.

Net Investment: Gross Investment minus depreciation (or capital consumption) allowances.

Net National Product (NNP): Total output of final goods and services produced in an economy in a given period of time (say, a year), including net rather than gross investment. NNP = GNP — Depreciation.

"New Economic Policy": 1. Policy introduced by the Nixon administration in 1971 involving a freeze on wages and prices, followed by various "phases" of wage-price controls, and a number of international measures, such as a 10-percent surtax on imports and the complete severing of the dollar from gold, leading up to the Smithsonian Agreement of December 18, 1971. 2. Lenin's Policy *(NEP)* after World War I of temporarily restoring markets and capitalistic incentives in certain sectors of the Soviet economy to stimulate its more rapid reconstruction.

"New Economics": *See* Keynesian Economics.

Nominal: Sometimes used to refer to the mere money value, as opposed to the *real* value, of an economic quantity.

OPEC: The Organization of Petroleum Exporting Countries. Organization of Arab and a few non-Arab oil producing nations for the purpose of controlling the production, export and price of petroleum. In 1974, OPEC members were responsible for 66 percent of the world's oil production and held 76 percent of the non-Communist world's petroleum reserves.

Oligopoly: A market structure in which there are a few large firms which dominate the industry. Some of these industries produce an undifferentiated product, others a differentiated product. In either case, a special feature of oligopoly is that the firms recognize their mutual *interdependence,* i.e., firm A knows that firms B, C, etc. are likely to react to its decisions, and firms B, C, etc. know the same thing about firm A.

Open-Market Operations: Federal Reserve purchases and sales of government securities on the open market. Perhaps the most important instrument of monetary policy. Federal Reserve sales of government securities tend to reduce the money supply, while its purchases of government securities tend to increase the money supply.

Open Shop: A firm may hire employees who either are or are not members of the union, and, if nonmembers, they may remain so indefinitely.

Opportunity Cost: The cost of an economic good can be measured in terms of the alternative goods (opportunities) one must forego to secure that good.

Output-Capital Ratio: The ratio of national output (or income) for a given period (say, a year) to the capital stock of the economy. Or: $\frac{Y}{K}$. Often used in its marginal form to measure the ratio of the addition to national income in a certain period (ΔY) to the addition to the capital stock in that period (real investment = I), or:

$$\frac{\Delta Y}{I}$$

The acceleration principle is based on the assumed constancy of this ratio.

P = MC: *See* Profit Maximization; Marginal-Cost Pricing.

Paradox of Value: How is it that diamonds, which are of relatively little use, are expensive, when water, which is of great use, is cheap? This paradox kept many economists from drawing a connection between the utility of a commodity and its value. The difficulty was largely removed with the development of the concept of marginal utility.

Partnership: Form of business organization in which a group of people pool their capital and share the profits and financial obligations of an enterprise. Each partner is liable to the full for the debts of other partners.

Personal Income: Equals National income *minus* retained profits, corporate profit taxes and contribution for social insurance *plus* transfer payments.

Phillips Curve: Curve showing the relationship between the amount of unemployment in an economy and its rate of inflation: the lower the level of unemployment, the greater the rate of inflation.

Pigou Effect: When the overall price level goes down (or up), the real value of the money assets we hold will go up (or down). This increase (or decrease) in our real assets will, according to the British economist A. C. Pigou, have an effect on our spending for goods and services.

Planning: 1. Decisions by the state to control or indicate (as in "indicative planning") the future direction of certain sectors of the economy, or of the economy at large. In the Five-Year Plans in the Soviet Union beginning in 1928, certain key industries (e.g., iron and steel) were given special emphasis in the government's decisions. 2. In Galbraith's theory, the attempt by large corporations to subordinate the market to the corporation's own decisions about prices, production, capital supply, technology.

Positive Checks: *See* Malthusian Theory of Population.

Poverty Level: In the United States, a level of income below which an individual or family is said officially to be "poor." This level depends on family size and other variables and is also adjusted over time to take inflation into account. In 1972, as an example, the poverty level for a nonfarm family of four was an annual income of $4,275.

Preventive Checks: *See* Malthusian Theory of Population.

Price Leadership: Historical pattern established in certain oligopolistic industries where one firm, always a big firm but not necessarily the largest in the industry, takes the initiative in making pricing decisions and where, in most instances, the other firms in the industry follow with similar decisions.

Price-Specie-Flow Mechanism: Under the classical gold standard, the mechanism by which balance of payments' disequilibria are corrected. If country A is importing more than it exports, it will have to pay for the extra imports with gold; this flow of gold will reduce country A's money supply and increase the money supply of its creditors; the changes in money supplies will lower country A's price-level and raise the price-levels of its creditors; these price changes will tend to correct the initial disequilibrium by making it cheaper to buy from country A and more expensive to buy from its creditors. The working of this mechanism depends on many assumptions, including the assumed validity of the *quantity theory of money*.

Price-Setter: Refers to a firm or individual in imperfect or monopolistic competition, where there is some leeway for altering the price of one's product or service, rather than simply accepting a market-determined result. Distinguished from Price-Taker.

Price-Supports: *See* Agricultural Programs.

Price-Taker: Refers to a firm or individual in pure competition, where the price of a product or service is "taken" as given by the market rather than set by the firm or individual. Distinguished from Price-Setter.

Product Differentiation: Characteristic of monopolistic competition and certain oligopolistic industries. It involves competition by means of changes in the style, gadgetry, appearance and/or effectiveness of a given product, with the specific purpose of differentiating that product from other close substitutes in the minds of consumers.

Product Market: A market in which commodities and services are bought and sold. In a private economy, the main sellers are private business firms and the main buyers are private consumers or households. Distinguished from Factor Market.

Production-Possibility Curve: A curve showing the maximum level of production of one commodity (say, steel) that an economy can sustain for each possible level of production of another commodity (say, food). It will generally have a "bowed-out" shape, meaning that it gets progressively harder to produce additional units of one commodity the more of that commodity the economy is producing.

Productivity Increase: An increase in output per unit of factor input. A major element in modern economic growth.

Profit Maximization: Producing at that output where *TR* minus *TC* is at a maximum. The general condition for profit maximization is that $MR = MC$. In the specific case of pure competition, it will also be the case that $P = MC$. Furthermore, in the long run in pure competition, profit maximization will occur where $MC = $ minimum AC.

Profits: Excess of revenues above costs. *Normal profits* are included in the concept of costs. They represent the "wages of management," or, roughly, what the management of the business firm could have earned in some similar, alternative employment. *Pure profits* represent the excess of revenues above costs when these costs include normal profits so defined. In pure competition, in the long run, pure profits are zero. In other forms of market structure, and in pure competition in the *short* run, pure profits may be positive or negative.

Public Goods: Goods which must be provided collectively to consumers or not at all. If these goods are provided for some consumers, there is usually no cost in providing them to additional consumers: e.g., a lighthouse which, if it serves any ship that passes, serves all ships that pass. It is usually characteristic of such goods that it is difficult to exclude consumers from the consumption of these goods even if they have not paid for them.

Pure Competition: Market structure where firms and individuals are price-takers rather than price-setters. Business firms in pure competition have little control over the prices at which they are able to sell their products. Technically, they face a perfectly (or infinitely) elastic demand curve for their products. Pure competition requires large numbers of firms producing a homogeneous product, with free exit from and entry into the industry in question.

Quantity Theory of Money: Theory that the quantity of money in the economy largely determines the level of prices. Usually stated in terms of the equation:
$$M \times V = P \times Q$$
where M is the quantity of money in the economy, V is the income velocity of money, P is the price-level and Q is real national income. The theory postulates that V is largely determined by institutional factors and Q is determined by factor supplies and technology. Hence, changes in M will be reflected in proportionate changes in P. This theory was one of the points of departure for modern *monetarism*.

Real: In economics, refers to the goods-and-services, as opposed to money value, equivalent of the entity in question. E.g., *real wages* mean wages as measured by their actual purchasing power, not by their level in simple dollars and cents.

Real Capital: *See* Capital.

Real Investment: *See* Investment.

Recession: A slowing down of economic activity, resulting in an increase in unemployment and in excess industrial capacity. Less severe than a depression. In the U.S., sometimes defined in terms of a decline in GNP in two or more successive quarters of a year.

Recycling: 1. Using the waste products of industrial society and turning them into factor inputs for further production. 2. In specific reference to the "recycling problem": the question of how Arab oil revenues can be returned to the oil-consumer nations from which they originally derive. The problem arises because the oil revenues are potentially so huge that the Arab states cannot effectively spend them on increased imports from the oil consumers.

Reinvestment of Profits: An important source of economic growth in a privately oriented economy is the reinvestment of profits by business firms in expansion of their capital stock. Such internal financing accounts for a high proportion of business investment in the U.S.

Rent: 1. Payment for the services of the factor of production, land. 2. Payment for the services of any factor of production that is in inelastic supply; i.e., a surplus payment above that required to bring forth the supply of the factor in question. In this second sense, sometimes called *economic rent*.

Returns to Scale: A measure of the responsiveness of the output of a commodity when all factor inputs are increased or decreased in a given proportion. The three possible cases are:

1. **Constant Returns to Scale:** A given increase in factor inputs leads to a proportionate increase in output.
2. **Increasing Returns to Scale** (also called, **economies of scale**): A given increase in factor inputs leads to a more than proportionate increase in output.
3. **Decreasing Returns to Scale** (also called, **diseconomies of scale**): A given increase in factor inputs leads to a less than proportionate increase in output.

Notice that decreasing returns to scale must be distinguished from *diminishing returns* as used in the *law of diminishing returns*. In the former case, we are varying all factor inputs; in the latter, we are altering one "variable" input only while holding all other inputs constant.

Revenues: The income to a firm from the sales of its commodities or services. *Total revenue (TR)* includes all this income at any given level of output, Q. *Average Revenue (AR)* at output Q, is equal to TR divided by Q. *Marginal Revenue (MR)* at output Q is the addition to revenue that would result from the sale of one more unit of output. In pure competition, $AR = MR$, but in other market structures, MR is below AR.

Revenue-Sharing: A policy whereby the federal government shares the revenue it receives from federal taxation with state and local governments, with relatively few strings attached.

Rule of Reason: Interpretation by the courts of the Sherman Act in Standard Oil and American Tobacco (1911) that put most emphasis not on the size of the dominant firms in an industry but whether they behaved "unreasonably," i.e., by predatory price competition, etc. This rule was considerably modified in the Alcoa case (1945).

Say's Law: The doctrine (after J. B. Say, 1767–1832) that "supply creates its own demand." In an economy in which the "veil" of money has been removed, the production of one good, while creating an addition to aggregate supply, also creates an addition to aggregate demand, i.e., because one will use this added production to offer in exchange for other goods. In this nonmonetary Say's world, depressions and mass unemployment are not possible.

Saving: That part of income which is not consumed.

Scarcity: The relative limitation of resources for satisfying mankind's economic wants as compared to the range and scope of those wants. Scarcity makes economic choice inevitable and careful "economizing" desirable.

Second Best: A problem arising where monopoly elements pervade many areas of the economy. Perfect efficiency may be impossible to achieve and moving to pure competition in one isolated sector of the economy may be less efficient than a "second best" solution that permits some monopoly elements to remain in this sector, as in the rest of the economy.

Short-run: Over a fairly short period, usually a year or less. In the analysis of business competition, it sometimes refers to a period too short for (a) a firm to alter its plant capacity and other fixed costs, and (b) other firms to enter or leave this particular industry. By contrast, in the *long run* all costs are variable costs and exit from or entry into the given industry has time to take place.

Sherman Act: A major U.S. antitrust Law passed in 1890. It prohibits "every contract, combination in the form of trust or otherwise, or conspiracy, in restraint of trade or commerce" and prescribes penalties for "every person who shall monopolize, or attempt to monopolize, or combine or conspire with any other person or persons, to monopolize any part of trade or commerce among the several states, or with foreign nations." *See* Rule of Reason.

Single Proprietorship: Form of business organization in which the individual businessman puts up his own financial capital, and runs his own firm.

Social Benefit: The benefit to society at large of a particular act. In economic terms, it includes the private benefits of the act, as measured by the revenues it produces in the marketplace, but also the external economies that are attendant upon the act. *See* Social Cost.

Social Cost: The cost to society at large of a particular act. In economic terms, it includes the private cost of the act as measured in the market place, but also the external diseconomies that are attendant upon that act. Thus, the social cost of producing a good may include not only the costs measured in a firm's costs curves, but also the monetary costs caused to other producers and consumers in the area through the pollution caused by this firm's factory, and, in addition, the intangible costs caused, say, by the factory's effect on the "beauty" of the neighborhood. Because these further effects are not captured by the measuring-stick of the market, social costs are not measurable in any simple agreed-upon way. The same analysis applies to *social benefits*.

Socialism: An economic system in which there is public ownership of the basic resources and capital goods of the society. Often associated in theory with a more egalitarian distribution of income than under capitalism.

Social Security Program: In the United States, a system of social insurance developed on the basis of the Social Security Act of 1935. Involves old age, survivors, disability and health insurance, and also various provisions for welfare services and unemployment payments. Payroll taxes to finance social security and unemployment compensation are the second largest source of federal tax revenues.

Spaceship Earth: A view of the earth's economic system as one in which, as in a manmade spaceship, resources must be recycled rather than converted into wastes which are thrown away. The emphasis is on a self-contained system which exhibits relatively little expansion over time.

Special Drawing Rights (SDRs): Agreed-upon international means of payment ("paper gold") created by the International Monetary Fund in proportion to each country's original contribution to the IMF. Designed to increase international liquidity.

Stagflation: Term coined in the 1970s for the combination of unemployment (stagnation) and inflation afflicting the U.S. and other industrial countries.

Stagnationist Theory: Theory, prominent in the 1940s, that the U.S. faced a future of increasing unemployment unless the government took a more active role in sustaining the economy, especially through a vigorous fiscal policy. It was based on a view that the slowing of population growth, the vanishing of the frontier, etc. had lowered investment opportunities while savings propensities might be expected to remain high.

Staples: Commodities with a large natural resource content that are in international demand and can bear the transport charges involved in international trade. Expanded trade in various staples (e.g., furs, wheat, timber, minerals, etc.) is considered a major part of the development history of Canada.

Stationary State: 1. In classical economics, especially Ricardian and Malthusian theories, the final destiny of society after population growth has destroyed the possibility of further economic expansion. 2. The goal of many ecology minded modern economists: a society which maintains a certain level of population and income per head, but does not increase these levels over time.

Stock: 1. Shares of ownership in a corporation, such as common stock or preferred stock. 2. A quantity measured at a particular moment of time. In contrast to a *flow* which is a quantity measured over a period of time. The money supply and the quantity of real capital in the economy are stocks. GNP and real investment are flows. 3. *Economy of stock:* Phrase used by ecologically-minded economists to suggest a society in which flows (yearly production and consumption) are reduced and an attempt is made (by recycling and conservation) to maintain and enlarge our total stock of goods.

Strikes: Work stoppages initiated by labor, usually through union decisions. Are sometimes classified as: (1) *political,* where the hope is to influence governmental decisions (uncommon in the U.S.); (2) *organizational,* where the union is trying to force the employer to recognize it as the employees' representative; (3) *jurisdictional,* where unions are fighting each other over whose members should do a particular job; (4) *grievance,* where the union objects to management's way of carrying out a prior agreement; and (5) *contract,* where labor and management cannot find mutually agreeable terms for writing a new labor contract (over 90 percent of strikes in the U.S. are of the contract variety.) Where splinter groups cause a work stoppage in the absence of, or in opposition to, the decision of the parent union, we have a *wildcat strike.*

Subsistence Wages: *See* Malthusian Theory of Population.

Substitution Effect: In consumer-demand theory, a fall in the price of a commodity will usually cause the consumer to purchase more of that commodity because, among other reasons, that fall in price has made this commodity less expensive compared to other similar commodities. Therefore, he will tend to substitute this now cheaper commodity for those other commodities.

"Supply Creates Its Own Demand": *See* Say's Law.

Supply Curve: A hypothetical construction that tells us how many units of a particular commodity business firms would be willing to sell over a period of time at all possible prices. The supply curve assumes that business firms are basically "price-takers."

Technical Fix Scenario: An alternative described by the Ford Foundation's Energy Policy Project. It involves increasing energy utilization in the future, but at less than the historic growth rate. It makes consumption efficiency, rather than increased supply, the main goal of energy policy. *See* Historical Growth Scenario, Technical Fix Scenario.

Technological Change: Development of new and more economic methods of production and products; involves an upward shift in production curves (total product curve, marginal product curve, etc.) of the particular commodity involved. Is a major factor in Modern Economic Growth.

Technostructure: In Galbraith's theory, the bureaucracy of scientific, economic, and management experts who effectively run the modern corporation, in contrast to its stockholder owners.

Terms of Trade: The prices of a country's exports in relation to its imports. An improvement in a country's terms of trade means a relative increase in its export prices, while a deterioration in its terms of trade means a relative increase in its import prices.

Throughput Economy: An economy in which resources are regularly used up without replacement or recycling; the basic processes of the economy convert useful resources into garbage, waste, trash, etc. The contrast is with Spaceship Earth.

Time Preference: The relative evaluation of present versus future goods; usually, the preference given a present as opposed to a future good of the same nature.

Trade Gap: In the case of a less developed country, the gap between the imports required by the country's development effort and its current capacity to export to the outside world. The existence of such a gap provides an important argument for foreign aid. *See* Investment Gap.

Trade Union: *See* Union.

Transactions Demand for Money: Demand for money to be held for carrying out ordinary purchases of goods and services; will vary with the size of money national income.

Transfer Payments: A transfer of purchasing power from one unit to another, where there is no good delivered or service rendered in exchange. In the case of governmental transfer payments, an example would be the transfer of money from a taxpayer to a recipient of a welfare check.

Transformation Curve: *See* Production-Possibility Curve.

Underdevelopment: A condition where an economy has not achieved the levels of national production and living standards that are technologically possible. Often used as a synonym for a condition of poverty, as in the case of the poor countries of Africa, Latin America, and Asia.

Underemployment: Condition where workers are apparently employed but are either working only part-time or are working inefficiently and could be displaced with little effect on total production. *Disguised unemployment* is a term often used to describe the widespread underemployment of labor in many less developed countries; many economists believe that substantial labor could be removed from many production processes without lowering output in these countries.

Unemployment: A condition where workers who are ordinarily part of the labor force are unable to find work at prevailing wages. Even at "full" employment, there will usually be some degree of frictional unemployment, perhaps 2–4 percent of the labor force, as workers move from one job to another.

Union: A labor organization representing workers in their varied negotiations with management. May be organized on a *craft* union basis (joining together particular kinds of workers, e.g., electricians, orchestral musicians, etc.) or on an *industrial* union basis (joining together workers of different crafts in a given industry, e.g., steel-workers, automotive workers, etc.). In the U.S., in the early 1970s, over 20 million workers were labor union members.

Union Shop: A firm is permitted to hire nonunion employees with the understanding they must join the union within a specified period of time.

Utility: The satisfaction that a good has for a consumer, or for society. Can be used in the sense of *cardinal* utility—goods can be assigned a numerically measurable utility, e.g., 6.7 "utils"; or in the sense of *ordinal* utility—consumers can order combinations of goods according to their preferences, e.g., first, second, third, etc. The cardinal utility of a good may be either its total utility for the consumer in question, or its *marginal utility*. By marginal utility is meant the addition to the total utility of the consumer from having one more unit of the commodity.

Value: The worth of a commodity or service. Usually used in a relative sense to indicate the price of a good in terms of other goods or money.

Value-Added: The value of the sales of a firm or industry minus its purchases of products from other industries. The sum of values added in the economy as a whole will be equal to the value of final products produced in the economy, thus eliminating double-counting in the measurement of national income.

Value of the Marginal Product: The marginal product of a factor of production times the price of the product. In pure competition, the price or wage of a factor will equal its VMP.

Vicious Circles of Poverty: Theory that the poor remain poor because they are poor. Often applied to underdeveloped countries, e.g., these countries may not accumulate much capital because their output per capita is so low; but their output per capita will remain low because they have so little capital to work with.

Wage-Price Controls: Mandatory regulation of wages and prices by the government. In the U.S., were applied to certain segments of the economy, with varying force (Phases I through IV), from 1971 to 1974.

Wage-Price Guideposts: Policy of the 1960s to curb inflation in the U.S.; the President's Council of Economic Advisers set wage-price standards for labor and industry based on the principle that wage increases should be no greater than productivity increases and that prices should, on the average, be stable. In contrast to *wage-price controls*, the guideposts were not mandatory.

Wagner Act (National Labor Relations Act): Landmark legislation in the labor movement, passed in 1935, which guaranteed employees the right to organize, to form labor unions, and to bargain collectively with management.

Welfare: 1. In a broad sense, the objective against which economic systems and policies are measured; there is imperfect agreement in society about the nature of this objective and how it is related to specific goals, e.g., raising GNP, reducing income inequality, etc. 2. Refers to certain specific programs designed to help the needy, including income-maintenance programs, unemployment compensation, medicaid, etc.

Workers' Council: In Yugoslavia, the mechanism by which workers in an enterprise take part in the management of that enterprise. The councils are elected by the workers through direct and secret ballot.

World Bank: Officially, the International Bank for Reconstruction and Development (IBRD). Established after World War II by the United Nations to promote postwar reconstruction and the development of the less developed countries. It assists poor countries through loans, or by insuring private loans, in the financing of development projects.

Zaibatsu: Large Japanese oligopolistic firms with interlocking interests in banking, industry, shipping, etc., such as Mitsubishi and Mitsui. Very important to the Japanese economy historically, and again today.

Zero Energy Growth Scenario: One alternative described by the Ford Foundation's Energy Policy Project. It would involve redesign of cities and transportation systems, the deemphasis of energy-intensive industries like plastics, and a more vigorous growth of the service sector of the economy. *See* Historical Growth Scenario, Technical Fix Scenario.

Zero Population Growth: The objective of a number of economists, demographers and interested citizens, who feel that only with a stable population can modern society survive over the long run.

INDEX

LIST OF READINGS